MANAGEMENT SCIENCE
BUILDING AND USING MODELS

The Irwin Series in Quantitative Analysis for Business
Consulting Editor: Robert B. Fetter, *Yale University*

MANAGEMENT SCIENCE
BUILDING AND USING MODELS

Thomas W. Knowles
Stuart School of Business Administration
Illinois Institute of Technology

1989

Homewood, Illinois 60430

To
Julie Bailey Knowles

Sponsoring editor: *Richard T. Hercher, Jr.*
Project editor: *Joan A. Hopkins*
Production manager: *Carma W. Fazio*
Designer: *Maureen McCutcheon*
Artist: *Benoit Design*
Compositor: *Better Graphics, Inc.*
Typeface: *10/12 Times Roman*
Printer: *R. R. Donnelley & Sons Company*

Library of Congress Cataloging-in-Publication Data

Knowles, Thomas W.
    Management science.

    Includes index.
    1. Management science. 2. Management science—Case studies. I. Title.
T56.K615 1989   658.4′034   88–13269
ISBN 0-256-05682-X

Printed in the United States of America
1 2 3 4 5 6 7 8 9 0 DO 5 4 3 2 1 0 9 8

Preface

This is an exciting time for management science (MS). Since its beginning in the 1940s, management science has been dominated by mathematicians. Originally, the lack of quantitative analysis tools for decision making made it necessary to develop them for each particular management science study. Developing the analysis tools required a good knowledge of mathematics. If computers had not developed, management science tools would be less widely used today because many of these required large amounts of arithmetic calculations. Even so, early computers and management science software had limited capabilities, and because of this management science was difficult to use and remained in the province of the mathematician and the specialist.

Today, software and computer capabilities allow nonmathematicians to use management science effectively. High-quality management science software is available for microcomputers, and most managers will have such computer capabilities at their fingertips. Easy-to-use and relatively inexpensive software tools are important decision-making aids for the modern manager, and justifying your decisions with quantitative analysis is often necessary.

In this book, we emphasize how management science is *used* in decision making. Models of decision problems, which play a central role in the book, are formulated and then solved. We emphasize *model formulation,* in which models of the decision problems are developed. Most often, solving such a model means inputting it to an appropriate management science software package. We don't emphasize how the software package solves the model; but focus instead on how to *interpret the software output* and how to use that output in decision making. We also emphasize the important roles of *sensitivity analysis and model manipulation* in providing decision-making information.

This book is intended for the business students who will be the final users of management science information. These students need to know when management science can be used and how to use it effectively in decision making. The course may be offered at either the undergraduate level (junior or senior year) or the graduate level, and either of two instructional approaches may be used. In the first approach, instructors *survey* many topics and the goal is breadth, as opposed to depth. In the second approach, instructors select a small number of topics and cover them in more depth. The book is amenable to either approach, but it was written in the hope that it would be well-suited for the second. Consequently, the text includes more material than can be covered in a one-quarter or one-semester course. Thus, the instructor will be able to choose the topics and the depth of coverage. The text is also appropriate for many multiterm courses.

For instructors who prefer more depth on a small number of topics, there is extensive coverage of the two most used management science tools—linear programming and computer simulation. The treatment of LP sensitivity analysis and model manipulation is exceptionally complete. In Chapter 7, having discussed output interpretation and sensitivity analysis in earlier chapters, we consider "more" linear programming applications. Thus, we "close the loop" between solving models and using the results for decision making. In Chapter 16, the discussion of statistical analysis and the design of probabilistic simulations is thorough and relatively advanced for an introductory book.

Advanced topics are illustrated by examples and developed so that you understand why. Emphasizing the usefulness of such topics makes it more likely that you will utilize them after graduation. For completeness, Theory sections containing advanced information appear at the end of chapters where appropriate. For example, the simplex algorithm and dynamic programming are treated in such sections. However, the book is completely understandable if these sections are skipped.

The book requires a minimal mathematical background. You must understand algebra, because many of the management science models require algebraic manipulation. An understanding of calculus may provide additional insights in a few places, but you don't need to know calculus to use management science. We assume that you have had prior exposure to probability and statistics. Beginning in Chapter 10, we study decision problems with uncertain outcomes and review the concepts of expected values and variance when necessary. Similarly, we quickly introduce standard probability distributions such as the normal, exponential, Poisson, and Student-t when they are needed, but not with the same detail that a statistics text would provide.

Because we emphasize the usefulness of management science, each chapter begins with an "application opener" that describes a successful implementation of the chapter's concepts. Many of these openers are based on articles from *Interfaces*. Within many chapters, additional applications are also described.

Each chapter summary includes applications, cautions, and information regarding the limitations of the material. The cautions warn you about common misunderstandings and mistakes. In discussing the limitations, we point out that not every decision problem fits a particular management science tool.

Following the text of each chapter, there are problems for you to solve in three sections. The Questions section reviews basic concepts and follows up on issues raised in the chapter. The Exercises section contains problems that require relatively straightforward application of the basic material in the chapter. We believe that students improve their model building skills and learn to appreciate model assumptions in small building steps. Thus, many of the formulations in the exercises section are modifications of formulations that were developed earlier. The More Challenging Exercises section contains two types of problems. First, it poses more difficult or challenging formulation problems than those posed by the Exercises section. Second, it explores advanced or subtle aspects of the chapter material. In the latter case, the instructors can decide whether technical subtleties and additional advanced topics are introduced and covered by the problems selections.

Many of the chapters conclude with one or more small cases, and the appropriate method of analysis is the subject of the given chapter. These minicases are the next step in developing analysis abilities. Several more complex cases appear at the end of the book, and for these you must choose the method of analysis. This is the culminating step in recognizing and analyzing realistic situations.

The book ends with the answers to the odd-numbered chapter Exercises. Generally, consecutive odd-numbered and even-numbered Exercises are similar. Because the answers are available for the odd-numbered Exercises, students should find it easier to take the small learning steps afforded by the Exercises.

You will develop greater confidence in your ability to use management science if you use software to solve the models that you formulate. In this book, we show output from the LINDO package for linear and integer programming models. LINDO is available on microcomputers through mainframe computers and is frequently used in management science education. However, you can use any available software without any loss of understanding. For example, you can use Gordon H. Dash, Jr., and Nina M. Kajiji, *Operations Research Software* (Homewood, Ill.: Richard D. Irwin, 1988).

We wish to thank the following reviewers, who provided, at various stages of the completion of the manuscript, tough criticism, warm compliments, and most important, insightful suggestions:

Peter Ellis, Utah State University

Saul Gass, University of Maryland

Chang-tsek Hsieh, Tennessee Technological University

Ram Mohan R. Kasuganti, Youngstown State University

David Olson, Texas A&M University

Jeffrey Ringuest, Boston College

Paul Rubin, Michigan State University

Ramesh Sharda, Oklahoma State University

Wei Shih, Bowling Green State University
Francis Tuggle, Rice University
F. C. Weston, Jr., Colorado State University
Li D. Xu, University of Wisconsin

The most important acknowledgment goes to my wife, Fay, and my daughter, Jenny, for their support and encouragement of this project. I also want to acknowledge the suggestions of faculty colleagues on some of the chapters—particularly Spencer Smith, Nick Thomopoulos, and Marty Bariff. The comments of students at Illinois Institute of Technology, where I tested this book in the classroom, were very helpful. My teaching assistants, Alex Tan, Mariska Absil, and Terry Niego, made valuable contributions. Finally, I want to thank Dick Hercher and Kate Wickham of Richard D. Irwin for their encouragement and suggestions. At all times, I have kept my attention on what is useful to know about management science. I hope that you will feel the excitement of management science and use it to good advantage in your career.

Thomas W. Knowles

Contents

MANAGEMENT SCIENCE

BUILDING AND USING MODELS

1

Introduction to Management Science

The Decision-Making Environment
Deterministic versus Probabilistic / Static versus Dynamic
Environments / The Unpredictability of Nature versus
Competitors' Decisions Uncertainty

What Is a Model?
Decision Models: Optimization versus Simulation

Models, Methods, and Computers: History of Management Science

Sensitivity Analysis, Model Manipulation, and Decision Making

AIR PRODUCTS AND CHEMICALS, INC.

Air Products and Chemicals, Inc. distributes industrial gases from 23 depots to 3,500 customers in the United States. It uses insulated tank trucks to service its customers. Its sales exceeded $1.5 billion in 1982, when it introduced a computerized system that integrated inventory management at customer locations with vehicle scheduling and dispatching. A team made up of company personnel and management science consultants developed the system. Many of the management science methods discussed in this book were used.

Air Products had to decide which depot should be responsible for each customer. The team used linear programming (Chapters 3–7) to assign customers to depots so as to minimize total production and distribution costs. The depots operate independently after customers are assigned to them.

When a tank truck reaches a customer, it can fill up the customer's storage tank. If the tank truck arrives too early, it can deliver only a small amount because the customer's tank is close to full. On the other hand, if the tank truck arrives too late, the customer's tank is already empty. Estimates of customer's usage rates are important for the timing of deliveries. The system forecasts each customer's usage rate using exponential smoothing (Chapter 12). Inventory management at the customer locations includes determining safety stocks (Chapter 13), so that the customer's tank is unlikely to be empty before the tank truck arrives.

A tank truck makes deliveries to several customers before returning to the depot to be refilled. There are millions of possible tank truck trips depending on the customers visited and the visit sequence. An integer linear programming model (Chapter 9) is used for truck routing and dispatching on an hour-by-hour basis. For each tank truck trip, the model gives the starting time, the scheduled vehicle, and the amount and delivery time for each of the customers on the route. The model has as many as 200,000 constraints and 800,000 variables. The model is run daily and has a time horizon of two to five days. (In this chapter, we discuss multiple-period models and rolling time horizons.)

There may be several possible routes from a depot to a customer. The cost of a possible route depends on distance traveled, travel time, and tolls. An input to the truck routing and dispatching model is estimates of travel times, distances, and tolls. A shortest-route model (Chapter 8) is solved to find the best route from a depot to each customer and between pairs of customers.

The system is used successfully by schedulers who don't understand the highly sophisticated management science models and methods on which it is based. Attention was paid to training the schedulers who use the system and to developing easily understood graphical interfaces. The schedulers learned that the system was a tool that helped them make good decisions. The scheduler must be able to rapidly evaluate the impact of changes in customer usage and trucks available on truck routing and dispatching. For example, if a customer's usage rate increases and a delivery needs to be expedited, the system allows the scheduler to specify the necessary schedule changes. The system then checks the scheduler's changes for feasibility, resequences the truck's customer stops, and calculates the cost change. Based on this information, the scheduler can make those schedule changes or try others.

The estimated savings from the computerized system are 6–10 percent of the operating costs. Those savings couldn't have been achieved without management science.

W. Bell, L. Dalberto, M. Fisher, A. Greenfield, R. Jaikumar, P. Kedia, R. Mack, and P. Prutzman, "Improving the Distribution of Industrial Gases with an On-line Computerized Routing and Scheduling Optimizer," *Interfaces* 13, no. 6 (December 1983), pp. 4–23.

The objective of management science is to aid managers in decision making. As a manager, you must make decisions and justify them. If you want to be a successful manager, management science is important to you.

Intuitive decision making

One approach to decision making uses intuition to choose the decision that "feels right." In this approach, the decision maker considers the impact of different decisions qualitatively and on that basis makes a seat-of-the-pants decision. However, justifying decisions with, "It feels right," isn't acceptable for modern managers because as organizations become larger and more complex, it becomes harder to consider all the ramifications of decisions. For example, Air Products distributes industrial gases from 23 depots to 3,500 customers. Typically, a depot has several hundred customers and about 20 trucks. Thus, there are millions of possible truck trips for each depot. The complexity of the distribution system and the interrelationships caused by deliveries to several customers on a single trip make it difficult to develop a good truck routing and dispatching schedule intuitively. By using management science techniques for this purpose, Air Products has saved millions of dollars.

Quantitative decision making

Management science is characterized by the application of the scientific method to decision making; it bases decisions on rational, systematic analysis. The analytical tools developed to help you in such analysis are quantitative, not qualitative. You estimate the impacts of decisions quantitatively, not qualitatively. For example, it's not adequate to just say that sales will decrease. You must estimate that a $1 price increase will decrease annual sales by 15,000 units.

In many large organizations, decisions in one part of the organization affect other parts. A price increase affects the entire organization—marketing, manufacturing, finance, human resources, and so on. As a manager, you must be able to "do the numbers" to justify your decisions. This does not mean that using management science eliminates intuition and qualitative factors from decision making. The quantitative analysis of management science provides information that you use along with intuition and qualitative factors.

Management science is sometimes viewed as a collection of tools that assist the decision maker. However, it is more than that; it is the appropriate use of those tools and the analysis of the results they produce. The *process* of conducting a management science study can be more important than the tools themselves.

Henri Fayol described five areas of managerial activity—planning, organizing, commanding, coordinating, and controlling. Management science tools are designed to help the manager in planning, organizing, and coordinating. The tools that can be embedded in a managerial system, however, may help in commanding and controlling as well.

Decisions can be forced on you or grasped as an opportunity. As a decision maker, you may be confronted by a situation in which you are forced to make a decision. For example, if you are responsible for managing a manufacturing facility, you may have to decide what is produced next Monday. This decision is forced on you, the decision maker, and it is likely that you have had to make similar decisions in the past (e.g., last Monday). Alternatively, you might perceive the situation, not as a forced decision, but as an opportunity to change the framework in which decisions are made. This requires that you choose to change the framework. For example, if you are responsible for managing a manufacturing facility, you might consider making an additional product at that facility and thus improving its overall operation. An example of this is adding snowblowers to the product line of a company that manufactures lawn mowers. Sales of lawn mowers peak in the spring. If the company produces at the rate of next month's anticipated sales, the number of lawn mowers produced changes from month to month. Because the peak sales periods for lawn mowers and snowblowers fall at different times of the year, the combined sales of lawn mowers and snowblowers are more constant throughout the year than the sales of lawn mowers alone. Also, because the production process for the two products is similar, both products are made on the same equipment. Introducing snowblowers therefore evens out the volume of production over the course of the year.

In one case a decision is viewed as thrust on the decision maker, and in another it is grasped as an opportunity for improvement. Thus, manage-

A forced decision

A decision opportunity

ment science is more than the application of tools to improve status quo decision making. It also includes questioning and changing the framework within which decisions are made. Because management science requires that the decision problem be specified in detail, it discloses opportunities for changing the framework to the alert decision maker.

THE DECISION-MAKING ENVIRONMENT

Whether a decision is thrust on the decision maker or grasped as an opportunity for improvement, decision making is seldom successful unless the environment in which it is done is clearly understood. In discussing decision-making environments, it is helpful to classify such environments by several criteria.

Deterministic versus Probabilistic

First, decision-making environments are classified as *deterministic* or *probabilistic*. A **deterministic environment** is one in which the uncertainty about the outcome of any particular decision is so small that it can be ignored. A **probabilistic environment** is one in which the uncertainty about the outcome of a particular decision is great enough to require explicit consideration. In fact, the treatment of that uncertainty may be the heart of the decision problem.

A deterministic decision environment example

The planning of next week's production for a manufacturing company with a two-month backlog of orders is a deterministic decision-making environment. In this case, the outcome of a particular production plan is to have a particular number of each of the products available at a certain date. There may be some uncertainty (e.g., a machine breakdown), but the decision maker judges this as negligible and does not have to consider it explicitly. This is not to say that the uncertainty is ignored. Rather, it is regarded as a qualitative factor along with any quantitative information obtained as the decision environment is studied.

If a manufacturing company does not have a backlog of orders and demand is uncertain, the actual sales that will result from a production plan are uncertain. If demand is more than the finished goods on hand, not all customer orders can be filled right away and some customers are unhappy. If demand is less than the finished goods on hand, all customer orders can be filled right away and some goods are left over. There is uncertainty about the outcome of a production plan in this probabilistic decision environment.

Air Products faced a probabilistic decision environment when it chose safety stock levels for a customer. The uncertainty in customer usage rates was considered in choosing the safety stock levels.

A probabilistic decision
environment example

Another probabilistic decision environment is the design of the pump configuration for a new gasoline station. That is, how many islands should there be, and how many pumps of each variety of motor fuel should there be per island? In this case, there is uncertainty about the amount of demand for each motor fuel and about when customers will arrive. Customers do not arrive at a gas station in the same way as they arrive at a dentist's office (e.g., every 30 minutes). Customers arrive at a gas station intermittently, and their arrival rate varies based on the time of the day and the day of the week. This means that even if a single pump can pump 50,000 gallons per month of unleaded regular gasoline and you expect to sell only 10,000 gallons per month, you cannot assume that a customer who wants unleaded regular gasoline will never have to wait for service. Uncertainty, or inability to predict the exact outcome of a particular decision, is at the heart of this decision problem. And ignoring that uncertainty is likely to end in an unsatisfactory decision.

Static versus Dynamic Environments

Static versus dynamic

Second, decision environments are classified as *static* or *dynamic*. The length of time considered in making decisions is called the **time horizon.** If the time horizon chosen is one year, it can be visualized as 1 time period of one year, or 12 time periods of one month each, or 365 time periods of one day each. A *static* **decision-making environment** is one in which there is a single time period and that time period is considered independently of future time periods. A *dynamic* **decision-making environment** is one in which there is more than one time period, and the impact on other time periods of a decision made in one time period is explicitly considered. The number of time periods is determined when the time horizon and the length of each time period have been specified. If the time horizon is one year and each time period is one month, then there are 12 time periods over the time horizon. Some management science tools specify what things should be done during a time period but do not specify at what points during the time period those things should be done. Subdividing the time horizon into multiple, dynamic time periods provides information on such timing. Subdividing a one-year time horizon into 12 one-month time periods provides information on the month-by-month decisions that have to be made.

Considerations in
choosing the time
horizon

What time horizon is appropriate and whether that time horizon should consist of one static time period or a sequence of interrelated time periods depends on the decision-making environment. For example, in the deterministic decision-making environment of the manufacturing company mentioned above, should you consider next week's production plan independent of its impact on the plans of future weeks? If the product being manufactured were a Boeing 767 with a manufacturing time of many months, would you plan each week independent of other weeks? If the product were processed fresh pineapple, would you plan a week at a time? The decision problem can be complicated if the raw materials needed are available only during certain times of the year. It can be further complicated if the demand for the product is seasonal in nature (e.g., snowblowers).

Sometimes, you choose a finite time horizon for the analysis even though the actual impact of the contemplated decision might continue forever. If you do, you must carefully examine the terminal state of the decision environment at the end of the time horizon. The terminal state summarizes conditions at the beginning of the period after the end of the horizon.

The end of the time horizon

Consider the common situation in which decisions are made repeatedly as time passes, for example, a situation in which next week's production schedule is planned every Friday of the preceding week. Scheduling one week at a time to satisfy the following week's demand is not practical if the demand in any week is more than the weekly production capacity. Because of the variation in demand and limited capacities, you may choose an eight-week time horizon for planning the production schedule and subdivide that time horizon into eight interrelated one-week periods. On Friday of this week, you create the production schedule for next week, considering the impact of that schedule on the schedules of the next seven weeks. In fact, during the planning process, you create production schedules for each of the eight weeks. However, the first week's production schedule is the only one you actually use. On Friday of the following week, there is additional information on the actual production achieved compared to the production planned and on actual sales and shipments compared to orders received or forecast. Based on this additional information, you should change the second week's previously planned production schedule. Although it is possible to analyze the new decision environment as one with a seven-week time horizon, it is preferable to consider a new eight-week time horizon. This is done by dropping the previous week from the decision environment and including the ninth week. In this way, the time horizon stays at eight weeks but is "rolled" one week into the future. A **rolling time horizon** is one in which the periods in the time horizon are periodically changed by deleting the past period and adding the next period in time. A rolling time horizon is preferable in decision-making environments that require periodic repetitions of the decision-making process.

The time horizon for repeated decisions

Air Products' truck routing and dispatching model used a time horizon of two to five days, divided into one-hour time periods. The model was run daily, and the first day's schedule from each daily run was used. The following day, the data was updated and a new schedule was formulated. Air Products used a rolling time horizon for its dynamic decision environment.

The Unpredictability of Nature versus Competitors' Decisions Uncertainty

Sources of uncertainty

Third, decision-making environments are classified based on the source of the uncertainty that makes it difficult to predict the outcome of particular decisions. There are two possible sources of such uncertainty. One source is the **unpredictability of nature.** For example, the yield of corn in bushels per acre is influenced by weather conditions and therefore uncertain. The other source is the **decisions of competitors.** If a competitor markets a product that has a degree of substitutability for your product, the sales that result from your pricing policy are influenced by that competitor's pricing policy. The competitor is a thinking opponent whose pricing policy is being chosen at the same time that you are choosing yours. If natural variations over time affect sales, the uncertainty of sales also results from the unpredictability of nature.

Classifying decision environments

Many classes of decision-making environments are defined by classifying such environments on all three criteria—deterministic versus probabilistic, static versus dynamic, and the uncertainty of outcome resulting from the unpredictability of nature versus the decisions of competitors. Figure 1.1 illustrates these classes. Different management science meth-

FIGURE 1.1 Classification of Decision Environments

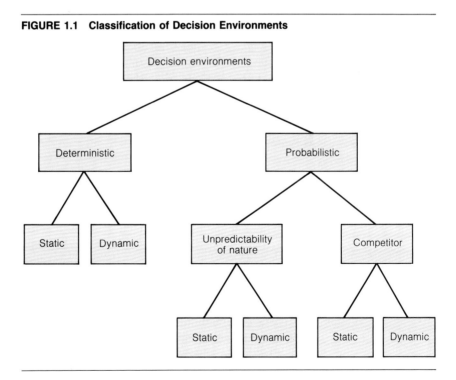

ods are appropriate for different classes of decision-making environments.

Choosing the correct classification of a decision environment may be a difficult task. In fact, such choices may involve a degree of subjectivity. Different classifications may be correct for the same decision environment but different sets of decisions. Chapter 2 provides two examples of decision environments in which the issues of choosing a time horizon, deterministic versus probabilistic, static versus dynamic, and the unpredictability of nature versus a competitors' decisions uncertainty are discussed.

In the next section, we discuss the role of models in decision making. Keep in mind the classifications of decision environments. You may decide to treat a decision environment in a simple way for convenience in model building, but if you do, you must weigh the benefits of simplification against the loss of reality. For example, although you believe that a competitor's pricing decisions have an impact on your sales, you may decide to treat the uncertainty of those decisions as due to the unpredictability of nature rather than explicitly incorporating competitor actions into your analysis. Note that the term *nature* as used here refers to the general unpredictability of the world and is not limited to weather. Government actions are uncertain and are therefore included in the unpredictability of nature, because except in unusual situations involving litigation, the government is not a competitor. Whether a competitor's decisions and your decisions impact on both of you, and whether the interaction is included in the analysis, determines if the uncertainty is treated as the unpredictability of nature or the actions of a competitor.

WHAT IS A MODEL?

Models play a central role in management science. After studying the decision environment, you construct a model of it to assess the impact of decision alternatives. A management science **decision model** is a mathematical representation of the decision environment that has been chosen for use in evaluating the available decision alternatives. You must provide a rational basis for choosing one of those alternatives.

The term *model* may bring to mind a model airplane. If such a model is designed to represent the actual airplane, the model is "better" if it is a more accurate representation. However, the interior layout of a model airplane used in a wind tunnel to determine airflow characteristics does not have to be accurate. More accuracy of this kind is not necessarily an improvement for a wind tunnel evaluation.

Decision models

The model builder decides what parts of the environment and what level of detail should be incorporated into the model. It is not easy to determine what factors in the decision-making environment should be chosen for this purpose. Ask yourself whether additional factors should be included in any decision model you develop or use. Chapter 2 discusses some important issues in building decision models.

A model is intended to aid you in analyzing the decision environment and in choosing a decision alternative. The model does not replace you as the decision maker; it gives you additional information to aid you in making decisions. Not all models are effective aids in decision making. The model builder may have misunderstood the decision environment or neglected to include important considerations.

Decision Models: Optimization versus Simulation

Decision models are widely used in management science to provide decision makers with additional information. Such models can be classified as either *optimization models* or *simulation models*.

Optimization models

An **optimization model** chooses the best decision from among those consistent with the model representation. For example, a model that minimizes the total production cost within limits imposed by capacities, outstanding orders, and due dates would be an optimization model because it is used to choose the best (vis-à-vis cost) plan.

Air Products used optimization models to assign customers to depots so that production and distribution costs were minimized. It also used optimization models to find the best route from a depot to each customer and between pairs of customers and to route and dispatch trucks.

Simulation models

A **simulation model** is sometimes called a **"What if?" model.** A "What if?" model is designed to answer the question "What will be the result if I make a particular decision?" An input to such a model is a particular decision alternative, and the output includes the outcome of that alternative. A simulation model only tells what the outcome of a particular decision alternative will be. It does not find the best alternative. However, trying different decision alternatives gives you useful information.

If the decision environment represented by the decision model is probabilistic, there is more than one possible outcome of a particular decision. In this case, the simulation model provides one of those outcomes, which is called a scenario. Repeated application of the simulation model is used to explore different scenarios for a particular decision and to assess their likelihoods. Simulation models are useful when methods of analysis for optimizing the model are not available.

The methods (or tools) of analysis for models depend on the mathematical structure of the models. In the next section, we describe the relationships among models, methods, and computers.

MODELS, METHODS, AND COMPUTERS: HISTORY OF MANAGEMENT SCIENCE

Models have been used as an aid in decision making for a long time. The use of mathematical models provides great insight in such diverse fields as economics, physics, chemistry, the biological sciences, engineering, and architecture. Mathematical models have been used to analyze supply and demand price-quantity relationships in economics, relationships between the location of a falling body and its initial location and velocity in physics, and double-entry bookkeeping relationships in accounting.

A model is a representation of the actual environment or system that is being studied. The representation includes the factors that the model builder has chosen. An economist developed the price-quantity relationship for the demand for a particular commodity as illustrated in Figure 1.2. This economist knows that factors other than price have an effect on the quantity of a commodity demanded. Quality is one such factor; the prices and available quantities of competing commodities are others. The model builder must judge what factors are important for his purpose. The model is a good one if it represents the environment or system in a way accurate enough to yield important information and insights. There is an art as well as a science to model building. As you study a model, you discover modifications and extensions that give additional insight.

Mathematical models include factors that can be quantified. A number can be associated with the value of each factor. Thus, the price of a commodity can be quantified in number of dollars; the quantity demanded of the commodity can be quantified in number of units (e.g., pounds). The demand, price-quantity relationship illustrated in Figure 1.2 is a graphical model. An equivalent mathematical model equates the quantity de-

A graphical model

FIGURE 1.2   Demand: Price-Quantity Relationship

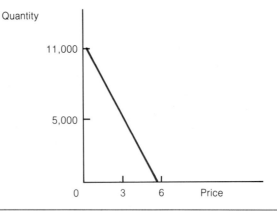

A mathematical model

manded to 11,000 units minus 2,000 times the price. Symbolically representing quantity demanded by Q and price by P makes the mathematical model

$$Q = 11,000 - 2,000 \times P$$

Mathematics provides the tools required to analyze this model. If the model is an appropriate representation of the environment, the analysis of the model will provide an understanding of the environment.

Analytical methods for mathematical models

The methods of analysis of mathematical models vary depending on the mathematical structure of the model. Calculus provides a powerful tool for the analysis of "smooth" relationships between factors and of the effect of incremental changes in the amounts of factors. The mathematical model from physics that relates the position of a falling body after t seconds (s_t) to its initial position (s_0) and its initial velocity (v_0) is

$$s_t = s_0 + v_0 t + \frac{1}{2} 32 t^2$$

Intuitively, the body is assumed to fall smoothly (unless it hits some object). Calculus is used to determine the velocity and acceleration of the body after t seconds.

The analysis of the supply and demand of a commodity requires a different tool. Figure 1.3 represents the relationship between the quantity supplied and the price. The mathematical model is

$$Q = 2,000 + 1,000 \times P$$

The price at which supply equals demand is called the **market-clearing price.** In Figure 1.4, the market-clearing price is the point at which the supply and demand lines intersect.

FIGURE 1.3   Supply: Price-Quantity Relationship

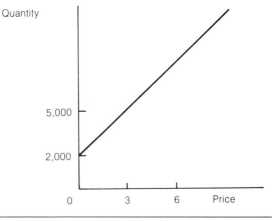

FIGURE 1.4   Graph of the Market Clearing Price

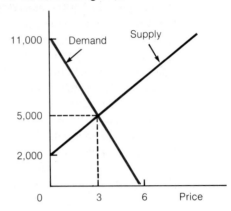

Solving for the market-clearing price requires that the models representing the supply quantity and the demand quantity both be satisfied. In this case, therefore, determining the market-clearing price requires solving the two simultaneous equations

$$Q = 11,000 - 2,000P$$
$$Q = 2,000 + 1,000P$$

The market-clearing price is $3, and the quantity is 5,000 units.

A solution of a mathematical model

A mathematical model specifies the relationships among various factors—called **variables** by mathematicians. A **solution** of a mathematical model is a value of those variables that satisfies the model. For the falling body model, if the original position is at 0 feet above sea level and the initial velocity is 0 (i.e., at rest), then the "solution" for t equals 5 seconds is $s_5 = 400$. That is, after five seconds have passed, the body will have fallen 400 feet. The "solution" of the economic market-clearing model is $P = 3$ and $Q = 5,000$.

A decision model is designed to allow the analysis of the decision environment for different possible decisions. The methods of analysis for decision models depend on the mathematical structure of the models. Quantitative decision models (or mathematical decision models as they are sometimes called) use calculus, simultaneous equations, and other methods of analysis.

Many new mathematical tools for analyzing decision models have been developed since the 1940s.[1] These tools are sometimes regarded as man-

---

[1] See Hugh J. Miser, "The History, Nature, and Use of Operations Research," in the *Operations Research Handbook,* ed. J. J. Moder and S. E. Elmaghraby (New York: Van Nostrand Reinhold, 1978) for a fascinating account of the history of operations research/management science.

agement science. However, management science has been defined as "the application of the methods of science to complex problems arising in the direction and management of large systems of men, machines, materials, and money in industry, business, government, and defence. The distinctive approach is to develop a scientific model of the system, incorporating measurements of factors such as chance and risk, with which to predict and compare the outcomes of alternative decisions, strategies, or controls. The purpose is to help management determine its policy and actions scientifically."[2] This definition includes the application of such mathematical methods as calculus and the solution of simultaneous equations, as well as more recently developed tools of mathematical analysis. Thus, management science is the application of mathematical models to the analysis of decision environments.

Computer developments

The use of early mathematical models was hampered by the lack of available tools of mathematical analysis. The development of new tools of mathematical analysis has paralleled the development of the modern digital computer. Because of increases in the speed of computers, procedures requiring many mathematical computations became practical. As computer storage capabilities expanded, procedures that required storing large amounts of data also became practical. The surge in the development of management science methods to analyze management science models would not have occurred if it had not been paralleled by developments in digital computers.

Early military applications

The history of management science or operations research dates from 1935. Management science originated in the effort of interdisciplinary teams of British scientists, military officials, and technicians to prepare an adequate response to the increased threat of German air power. That effort resulted in the development and testing of new tactics involving a new technology—radar. The success of that effort resulted in the establishment of similar teams to analyze military decision problems in the United States and Canada. Among the problems analyzed were tactics for antisubmarine warfare. The interdisciplinary teams included mathematicians, physicists, chemists, engineers, and social scientists. Today, such teams also include computer scientists and management scientists.

Another class of military decision problems analyzed by interdisciplinary teams was the allocation of scarce resources, such as men and equipment, between competing areas of need. The efforts to resolve allocation problems resulted in the development of linear programming. The simplex algorithm for linear programming was developed by George Dantzig in the middle of the 1940s. This development is regarded by historians of management science as a major focal point for the future thrusts of management science. Still another class of military decision

---

[2] D. Hicks, "Education for Operational Research," *Omega* 1, no. 1 (1973), p. 109. The quote is from a British publication, which explains the spelling "defence."

problems that interdisciplinary teams analyzed was the logistics planning required to move men and equipment to competing areas of need. This class of decision problems also involves the allocation of scarce resources, but it focuses, not on what resources should be at each area of need, but on how to transport those resources.

After World War II, the scientists who had been instrumental in the development and use of planning models for the war effort returned to private industry and to nonmilitary governmental agencies. Many of the decision problems that these scientists had studied in the military were also relevant to decision problems in their new environments. (The allocation of scarce resources, for example, is necessary in private industry and in nonmilitary governmental agencies.) These scientists brought the practice of management science from the military sphere to the nonmilitary sphere. Since World War II, there has been a great and continuing expansion in the range of problems, models, and methodologies dealt with by management science. The developments in management science have been adopted in the study of functional areas of business such as production, marketing, and finance. The central focus of management science, however, continues to be its use as an aid in decision making.

SENSITIVITY ANALYSIS, MODEL MANIPULATION, AND DECISION MAKING

Models don't replace decision makers

A model provides information that helps the decision maker; it does not replace the decision maker. The reason for this is that a model does not incorporate every conceivable factor. If a model incorporated every conceivable factor, it would be as unwieldy and complex as the complete decision environment. A model includes only those quantifiable factors that the model builder considers important. It excludes factors that are difficult to quantify or that the model builder considers of secondary importance. You, as a decision maker, must consider such factors even though they do not appear in the model. The model does not make the decisions; you do.

Models provide information

Thus, the construction and solution of a model are not the end result but the point at which the model *begins* to provide useful information to the decision maker. (The decision maker may have discovered useful information in the process of studying the decision environment before constructing the model.) Additional information about the decision environment is obtained by sensitivity analysis and model manipulation.

Sensitivity analysis provides information

Sensitivity analysis is the result of determining the impact of changes in parameters on the solution of the model. **Parameters** are numerical inputs to the model. For example, the unit sales of a product next week might be an input to a model that is constructed to analyze a production-planning decision environment. Sensitivity analysis includes studying how the production plan changes for a specified change in product sales. Both the amount of the change and the manner of the change are interesting information to the decision maker. It is also interesting to know whether there is a range of changes in the parameter that doesn't cause the model solution to change at all.

The impact of changes in parameters is important because some parameter values are difficult to estimate. This difficulty arises either from incomplete data or from the natural variability of the parameters. Sometimes, a parameter is somewhat controllable by the decision maker. For example, sales next week can be influenced by additional advertising or price discounts. Thus, sensitivity analysis is very helpful in decision making.

There is generally a solution method for a management science model (or class of models). Because the number of computations required for many of the methods is large, a computer is often used to solve management science models. **Brute force sensitivity analysis** is the process of explicitly changing the value of a parameter in a model and applying the solution method again. In this manner, information on the sensitivity of the solution to the model is obtained. Often, a lot of computer resources are used to solve one version of a model. If so, considerable computer resources are necessary to get sensitivity analysis information using brute force.

Management science methods have been studied to provide as much information for sensitivity analysis as possible. **Simple-sensitivity analysis** provides sensitivity analysis information without actually re-solving the model after parameter changes. It is not possible to obtain all of the sensitivity analysis information that is useful to the decision maker by simple-sensitivity analysis. However, it is best to make complete use of the information yielded by simple-sensitivity analysis before resorting to brute force sensitivity analysis. Simple-sensitivity analysis has been done by studying the mathematical methods, and many computer systems automatically provide simple-sensitivity analysis information.

Sensitivity analysis plays a central role as the decision maker uses a model to get information about the decision environment. Solving the original model is only the beginning of its use. The Air Products truck routing and dispatching model did not replace the scheduler. Instead, the scheduler used the model as a tool to help make decisions. The scheduler could use the model to evaluate changes from the schedule that the model proposed. For example, the scheduler could call a customer and ask whether it was OK to make an early delivery if this improved the truck routing. Then, the scheduler made the change and used the model to evaluate the change.

Model manipulation refers to studying the impact of changes in the original model that are more complex than changes in parameters. For

Margin note: Brute force and simple-sensitivity analysis

Manipulating the model

example, what is the impact on the model and its solution if a static model is converted into a dynamic model or if the length of the time horizon is changed? After a model has been constructed and solved but before its results have been used by the decision maker, the decision maker considers the impact of changes in the decision environment and in the model that represents it. You might decide that the additional information you get from actually making the structural changes in the model and re-solving it isn't worth the additional effort. However, you should consider possible structural changes. Some of those changes should have been considered when the decision environment was first studied and the original model constructed. But after all of the data has been gathered and the model has been constructed, the underlying assumptions and design decisions are reconsidered. Gathering the data often yields new insights about the decision environment.

In model manipulation, the decision maker should be as creative as possible in considering changes in the decision environment and the resulting model. It is the decision maker who provides the creative ideas. Recall the example of the decision maker who perceived an opportunity to change the framework within which decisions had been made in the past. The creative individual who added snowblowers to the product line of the lawn mower manufacturer could use a model to analyze the impact of that decision. But the model would not include the possibility of snowblowers unless the creative individual had thought of it.

Model manipulation and sensitivity analysis are activities that are central to management science. This holds true for both optimization models and simulation models. Simple-sensitivity analysis is developed most completely for optimization models. However, sensitivity analysis is important for any type of model as the model is used to get more information about the decision environment.

SUMMARY

As a manager, you are responsible for making and justifying decisions. Because the objective of management science is to help managers in decision making, management science is important to you. Since management science provides a quantitative, rational basis for decision making, it enables you to justify your decisions. Furthermore, in this complex and interrelated world, it's hard to make decisions intuitively. Management science enables you to build a model of a decision environment that represents its complexity and interrelationships.

We described a framework for the analysis of decision environments. Decision environments are either deterministic or probabilistic, depending on the uncertainty of the outcomes of decisions. The time horizon is the period of time considered as a result of decisions. If the time horizon is a single time period, the decision environment is static. If the time horizon is subdivided into multiple interrelated time periods, the decision environment is dynamic. Subdividing the time horizon provides information on the timing of decisions during the time horizon. A rolling time horizon is often used for multiple-period decisions that are repeated over time. We explained that the uncertainty of the outcomes of decisions can be caused either by the unpredictability of nature or by the decisions of competitors.

You use decision models to analyze decision environments for different possible decisions. Decision models are either optimization models or simulation models. Optimization models find the best decision. Simulation models answer the question "What will be the result if I make a particular decision?"

The solution of a mathematical decision model is the value of the variables that satisfies the model. The tools of analysis for solving a decision model depend on the mathematical structure of the model. The methods developed for solving decision models often require many arithmetic calculations and large databases. If computer developments had not paralleled the development of decision models and methods, much of management science would not be practical.

The model does not make the decision. The model gives you information that helps *you* make the decision. Sensitivity analysis and model manipulation provide information to you, the decision maker. Sensitivity analysis studies the impact of changes of input parameters on the model solution. Simple-sensitivity analysis does not require re-solving the model. Brute force sensitivity analysis requires changing the parameters and re-solving the model. You should make full use of simple-sensitivity analysis before you begin brute force sensitivity analysis. In model manipulation, you consider possible changes in the decision environment. This is your opportunity to change the framework within which your decisions are made.

QUESTIONS

1. What is a decision model?
2. Discuss whether a decision model ever makes decisions.
3. What is the objective of management science?
4. What is the difference between a deterministic and a probabilistic decision environment?
5. Give an example of a deterministic decision environment in finance. Give an example of a probabilistic decision environment in finance.

6. Give an example of a deterministic decision environment in marketing. Give an example of a probabilistic decision environment in marketing.

7. Give an example of a deterministic decision environment in production/operations. Give an example of a probabilistic decision environment in production/operations.

8. What is the time horizon for a decision environment?

9. Describe a decision environment in finance that should have a long time horizon and another that should have a short time horizon.

10. Describe a decision environment in marketing that should have a long time horizon and another that should have a short time horizon.

11. Describe a decision environment in production/operations that should have a long time horizon and another that should have a short time horizon.

12. What is an advantage of dividing the time horizon into smaller time periods?

13. Can you envision a decision environment in which the actions of a competitor would not affect your decision? Should all models include the actions of competitors?

14. Time-dependent refers to items that change over time, such as sales of snow blowers. Could a static model be useful in a time-dependent environment? Give an example.

15. What is sensitivity analysis?

16. What is the difference between simple-sensitivity analysis and brute force sensitivity analysis?

17. What is a rolling time horizon, and when should you use one?

18. Give a finance example of uncertainty from the unpredictability of nature.

19. Give a marketing example of uncertainty from the unpredictability of nature.

20. Give a production/operations example of uncertainty from the unpredictability of nature.

21. What is an optimization model?

22. What is a simulation model?

23. What is the significance of the terminal state at the end of a time horizon?

24. For the supply and demand model, say that the demand equation becomes $Q = 11,500 - 2,000 \times P$.
    a. Find the new market-clearing price and quantity.
    b. In Part a, you probably determined the impact of a change in the Q intercept of the demand equation by brute force sensitivity analysis. Find the impact by simple-sensitivity analysis by replacing the 11,000 by $(11,000 + A)$, where A is an unspecified amount, and then solving for the market-clearing price.

2

Issues in Model Building

The Three Steps of the Model Builder

Example 1: A Potato Processing Example
The Linear Programming Model / Graphical Solution of the
Model / The Role of Sensitivity Analysis

Example 2: A Hair Dryer Example
The Decision Tree Model / Solving the Decision Tree
Model / The Role of Sensitivity Analysis

Considerations in Model Building
Reliance on Data / Aggregation versus Disaggregation of
Data / Model Detail versus Model Tractability / A Hierarchy of
Models and the Length of the Time Horizon

The Impact of Model Structure on Sensitivity Analysis

OWENS-CORNING FIBERGLAS

Owens-Corning Fiberglas manufactures fiberglass mat that is sold to boat manufacturers for hulls. The mat is also used as the reinforcement in pipelines and bathroom fixtures. The entire product line consists of over 200 items. Twenty-eight of the items (representing over 80 percent of volume) are treated as standard products. The rest are special order products.

The Anderson, South Carolina, plant has two manufacturing lines that have different costs and capabilities. The demand for fiberglass mat is very seasonal. Owens-Corning can change the type and volume of production by changing the number of shifts on each line or by using overtime. Changing the number of shifts and using overtime increase costs. Furthermore, the cost of shutting down a line to change from one product to another is high. The changeover time depends on the sequence of the products made on the line. The downtime cost was estimated to be $275 per hour on one line.

Scheduling production for Owens-Corning's Anderson plant is complicated because of seasonal demands, shift change costs, overtime, and changeover costs. The decisions to be made include: the number of shifts for each line, month by month; the amount of overtime for each line, month by month; the amount of each product in each production run; and the sequence in which regular and special products are made.

Owens-Corning developed management science models to schedule production at the Anderson plant. It used three models with different time horizons and different levels of detail to do the scheduling. The first model planned the month-by-month number of shifts, the amount of overtime on each line, and the aggregate inventory levels. The model aggregated demand for all products and had a 3- to 12-month time horizon. This model didn't schedule at the product level, but gave aggregate inventory levels to the second model.

The second model generated lot sizes, line assignments, and inventory levels for each product, month by month. Inputs included the aggregate monthly inventory levels from the first model and monthly demand by product. The time horizon for this model is the same as that for the first model, but it has detail at the product level and it takes the number of shifts, overtime, and aggregate inventory levels from the first model. The model is a linear programming model with 10,000 variables and 10,000 constraints. This model assigned the production runs to the lines, but it didn't specify the sequence during a month or when each production run started.

The third model specified the sequence during a month and when each production run started. It used the product lot sizes and line assignments from the second model and scheduled the standard jobs and special orders so that changeover-related costs were minimized. The time horizon for this model is one or two weeks.

By using a hierarchy of models that address different levels of decisions, Owens-Corning Fiberglas saved over $100,000 during the first two years of operation at Anderson.

In this chapter, we illustrate the steps in building a decision model, using two examples. We also discuss issues in model building, including choosing the level of detail and using hierarchies of models for decision making.

M. Oliff and E. Burch, "Multiproduct Production Scheduling at Owens-Corning Fiberglas," *Interfaces* 15, no. 5 (September 1985), pp. 25–34.

Building a model is a relatively small part of conducting a management science study. Agin[1] includes these steps:

Steps in a management science study

1. Definition of objectives
2. Development of the project plan
3. Formulation of the problem
4. Development of the model
5. Development of a computational approach
6. Development of program specifications, programming, and debugging
7. Collection of data
8. Validation of the model
9. Implementation of the model

Steps 3 and 4 are crucial for ensuring that the model does not solve the wrong problem. The model must represent the decision environment selected. Steps 5 and 6 can use computational approaches and computer programs created by others. An increasing number of easy-to-use computer programs are available that solve different classes of management science models. If such a computer program is available for the model developed, the focus of the model builder is on problem formulation, model development, and validation, not on computational strategies. However, many types of decision problems require creating unique models and computational strategies. Don't assume that software exists for every decision problem you encounter.

---

[1] N. I. Agin, "The Conduct of Operations Research Studies," in *Handbook of Operations Research*, ed. J. J. Moder and S. E. Elmaghraby (New York: Van Nostrand Reinhold, 1978).

The steps are not necessarily done in the order listed above. Information is often obtained in a later step that causes the result of an earlier step to be reexamined. For example, the definition of the objectives and problem formulation often change as you study the decision environment. Data collection requires close interaction with the decision environment, and additional insights can change the problem formulation or the model. Remember, the process of a management science study often gives increased understanding of the decision environment. Because the model must represent the decision environment, understanding the decision environment is a necessary prerequisite.

Before the model provides useful information to you, the decision maker, it must be validated. You must verify that the model's results are reasonable. If the model's results are inconsistent with your ideas, be a skeptic. Insist on being convinced that the model provides useful information! Sensitivity analysis plays an important role in model validation. Examine the impact of model changes on the model's results. If the model provides results you do not understand, either the model is incorrect or you need additional insight into the decision environment. Repeated application of the decision model provides insight and aids in model validation. Future chapters provide concrete examples.

Remember, decisions can be forced on you or used as an opportunity to change the framework of the decision environment. Model manipulation provides an opportunity to change the framework of the decision environment. For decisions that are repeated many times, the decision model can be implemented or embedded into a managerial system.

In this book, we stress the role that management science methods and models have in decision making. We focus on the issues of problem definition, model development, sensitivity analysis, and model manipulation for the most frequently applied management science methods.

THE THREE STEPS OF THE MODEL BUILDER

It is important to keep model building in perspective when conducting a management science study. Assuming that computer software is available for the model developed, the model builder is concerned with problem definition, model development, and model validation. Figure 2.1 shows the model builder's three steps.

The model builder's three steps

In Step 1, the problem is defined. The boundaries of the environment that the model represents must be defined. In Step 2, the decision model is constructed. In Step 3, the model is solved, sensitivity analysis is performed, and the model is manipulated. This step helps validate the model and provides information for decision making. Note that the flowchart shows loops backward to previous steps. As you get more

FIGURE 2.1   The Model Builder's Three Steps

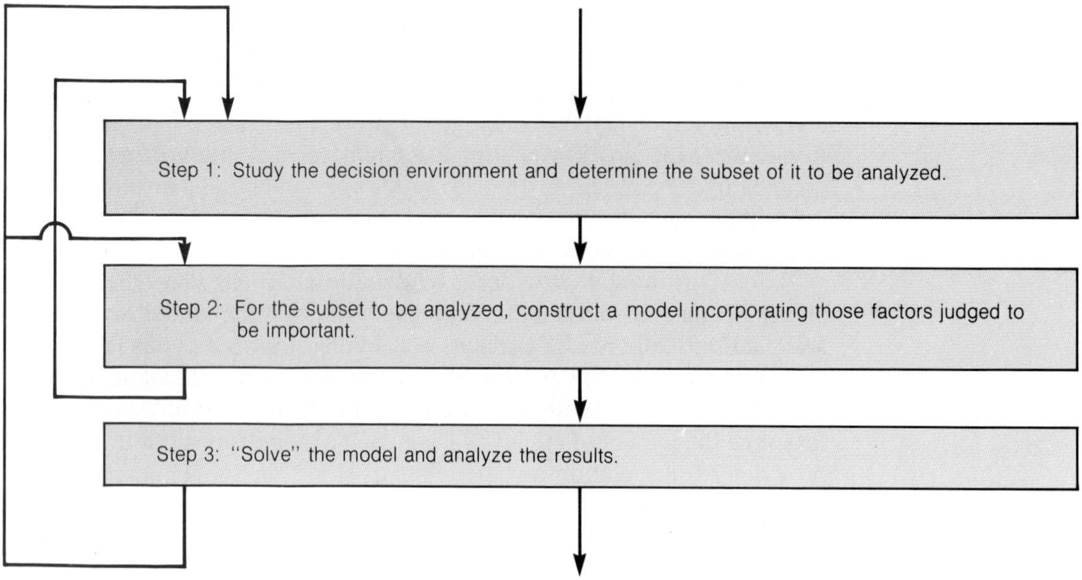

Step 1: Study the decision environment and determine the subset of it to be analyzed.

Step 2: For the subset to be analyzed, construct a model incorporating those factors judged to be important.

Step 3: "Solve" the model and analyze the results.

information about the decision environment, you might revise the subset to be analyzed or the decision model.

At this point, the three steps of model building and the concept of a model can still be difficult to grasp. The distinction between deterministic and probabilistic decision environments has been only generally illustrated. The length of the time horizon to be considered and the issue of static versus dynamic environments are perhaps only abstract concepts. Let's discuss two examples to illustrate these issues. In each example, the decision maker contemplates the environment, chooses the issues to be addressed (Step 1), and constructs a model that represents the chosen decision problem (Step 2). Finally, the model is solved and the role of sensitivity analysis is shown (Step 3). Future chapters expand on these models and methods.

EXAMPLE 1: A POTATO PROCESSING EXAMPLE

A potato processing plant located in Blue Island, Illinois (a suburb of Chicago), purchases Idaho potatoes from a local supplier. The supplier has recently become a broker for potatoes from Michigan and has inquired whether the potato processing plant would be interested in pur-

TABLE 2.1   Percentages of Products, by Weight

	Idaho Potatoes	Michigan Potatoes
French fries	30%	20%
Hash browns	10	20
Flakes	30	30
Waste	30	30
	100%	100%

chasing potatoes from Michigan because they cost less to buy and to ship. What are the important considerations for the decision maker? It is clear that more information is needed to make a rational decision, but *what* information? Your thought process as the decision maker might be as follows:

One thing that concerns me about making this change is the differences in quality between the two types of potatoes. A test on the Michigan potatoes indicated that the average size of the Michigan potato was smaller, producing a lower yield of french fries on a weight basis. Table 2.1 shows the relative percentages of products for the Michigan and Idaho potatoes. However, while the *yields* are different, the resulting products are indistinguishable—the crunchiness of the french fries is the same when either Michigan or Idaho potatoes are processed. The implication is that I could use products made from Michigan potatoes as a substitute for those made from Idaho potatoes and keep the same selling prices.

My selling price for french fries has been higher than the selling prices of other products. I wonder whether the reduced proportion of french fries from the Michigan potatoes would be offset by the savings on the purchasing and shipping costs. The cost per pound of Michigan potatoes delivered at my receiving dock in Blue Island is estimated to be $0.20. However, the delivered cost per pound of Idaho potatoes has been $0.225. The selling prices per pound of my products have been $0.90 for french fries, $0.75 for hash browns, and $0.50 for flakes. Waste results from scrubbing the skin off the outside of the potato and is sold as animal feed for $0.10 per pound.

I estimate, based on a test of the Michigan potatoes, that the cost of processing and packaging a pound of the potatoes is the same for the Michigan and Idaho potatoes, about $0.16 a pound. That is reassuring. I was concerned that the smaller Michigan potatoes would be more difficult to process.

I could then calculate the profit margin based on each of the two sources of potatoes. If I buy 1 pound of potatoes from Idaho and

sell the resulting products, the revenue I receive is $0.525, (0.3 ×
$0.90) + (0.1 × $0.75) + (0.3 × $0.50) + (0.3 × $0.10). The first
term reflects receiving 0.3 of a pound of french fries from each
pound of Idaho potatoes processed. The total cost per pound of the
delivered potatoes and the processing is $0.385 ($0.225 + $0.16). So
my profit margin on a pound of Idaho potatoes is $0.14 ($0.525 −
$0.385).

For a pound of Michigan potatoes, the resulting revenue is $0.51,
(0.2 × $0.90) + (0.2 × $0.75) + (0.3 × $0.50) + (0.3 × $0.10). My
profit margin on a pound of Michigan potatoes is $0.15 ($0.51 −
$0.20 − $0.16).

It appears that Michigan potatoes have a higher profit margin than
Idaho potatoes, assuming that I can sell *all of the products* produced
at current selling prices. That concerns me because Michigan potatoes give equal proportions of french fries and hash browns, and at
current selling prices the market for french fries is 50 percent larger
than the market for hash browns. Therefore, I can sell more french
fries than hash browns. When I purchased Idaho potatoes in the
past, I determined that the market for french fries was the limiting
factor in the total amount of potatoes processed. I do not want to
accumulate french fries in frozen storage, because it's too expensive. I've been able to sell all of the hash browns produced from
Idaho potatoes because the french fries have been the limiting factor.

Perhaps I should consider buying one month's potatoes from
Michigan. I anticipate that the maximum I could sell at current
prices next month would be 18,000 pounds of french fries, 15,000
pounds of hash browns, and 30,000 pounds of flakes. I can sell a virtually unlimited amount of waste as animal feed.

If I buy the potatoes from Idaho, the limiting factor, french fries,
would cause me to buy 60,000 pounds. This results in 18,000 pounds
of french fries, 6,000 pounds of hash browns, and 18,000 pounds of
flakes. I anticipate that I could sell those amounts of products with a
profit margin of $0.14 per pound of Idaho potatoes processed, for a
total monthly profit of $8,400 (60,000 × 0.14).

If I buy the potatoes from Michigan, the limiting factor is the potential sales of hash browns, so I order 75,000 pounds of potatoes.
This results in 15,000 pounds of french fries, 15,000 pounds of hash
browns, and 22,500 pounds of flakes. The hash browns are the limiting factor since the number of pounds of flakes produced is less than
the 30,000 pounds I believe I could sell at the current price. I could
maintain the profit margin per pound of Michigan potatoes processed
for a monthly profit of $11,250 (75,000 × 0.15).

It certainly appears that buying Michigan potatoes is a smart thing
to do. Not only is the profit margin higher, but I can also buy more

potatoes to process and be able to sell the resulting products. I wonder whether buying a combination of potatoes from Idaho and Michigan would be even better? What are the possible combinations that I should try? It seems that there are too many possible combinations of Idaho and Michigan potatoes to consider each one. Well, at least I know the Michigan potatoes are worth trying. But what is the best plan?

As a decision maker, you must first define the decision problem. Your thought process is the first step: *Study the decision environment and determine the subset of the decision environment that is to be analyzed.* Let's analyze the decision environment using the framework introduced in Chapter 1. Is the decision environment deterministic or probabilistic? The profit calculations assumed that the yields, amounts sold, and profit resulting from a purchasing plan were certain. The decision environment is *deterministic*. Any uncertainty is not treated explicitly but is considered by sensitivity analysis. What is the length of the time horizon? One month was selected as the time horizon. If it is necessary to sign a long-term contract for Michigan potatoes, a different time horizon is needed. And if potatoes are ordered more frequently than once a month, a different time horizon is appropriate. Is the time horizon a single time period (static) or multiple time periods (dynamic)? The impact of the purchasing decision on a one-month period provides the basis for the analysis. The timing of activities within the month was not considered. Therefore, the decision environment chosen is *static*. The following month, you confront a similar decision problem, but you do not explicitly consider the impact of this month's decision on next month's decision. If extra production this month is frozen for sale in the following month, this month's decision has an effect on next month's decision and a multiple-period model is appropriate.

Having chosen the subset of the decision environment to be analyzed, you *construct a model incorporating those factors judged to be important.*

A deterministic decision environment

One-month time horizon

Static

The Linear Programming Model

You have determined the scope of the decision problem to be considered, and your goal is to order the best amounts of potatoes from Michigan and Idaho, amounts that maximize the total profit *without making more of any product than can be sold at the current prices.* A model can be formulated that symbolically represents the decision problem.

Let M represent the number of pounds of Michigan potatoes to be purchased, and let I represent the number of pounds of Idaho potatoes to be purchased. Then, the profit contribution from Michigan potatoes is $0.15M$ and the profit contribution from Idaho potatoes is $0.14I$. The goal

FIGURE 2.2 Potato Processing—French Fries Limitation

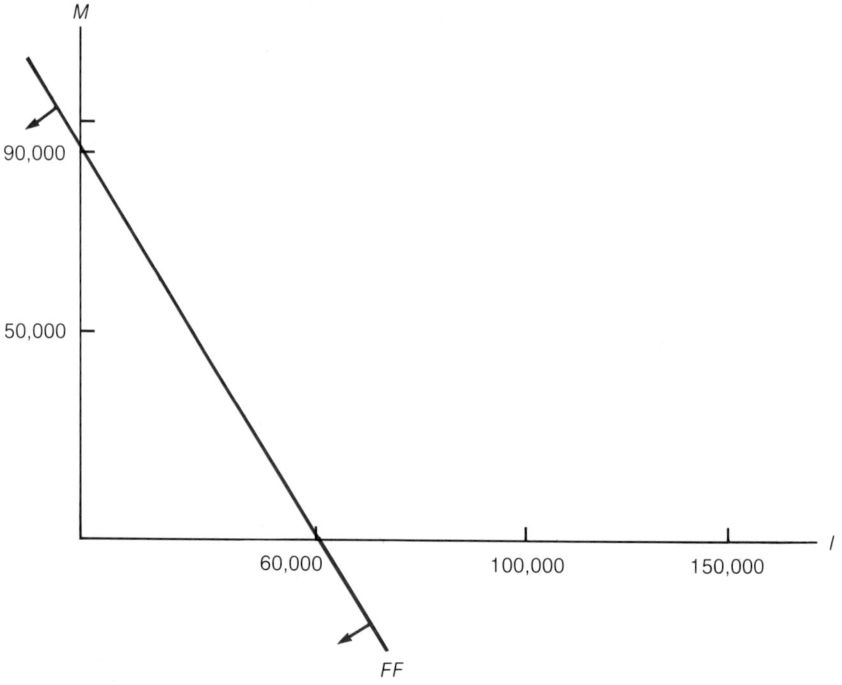

is to determine values for M and I that maximize $0.14I + 0.15M$. However, a combination of values of M and I is possible only if it meets the restrictions on possible sales. If M pounds of potatoes from Michigan are processed, $0.2M$ pounds of french fries will be produced. If I pounds of potatoes from Idaho are processed, $0.3I$ pounds of french fries will be produced. The total number of pounds of french fries produced is $0.3I + 0.2M$, and that total must be less than or equal to the 18,000 pounds that can be sold at current prices. Mathematicians represent the less than or equal to relationship by the symbol $\leq$. Symbolically, the restriction on french fry production is

$$0.3I + 0.2M \leq 18000$$

(*Note:* A comma will not be used to separate thousands in symbolic illustrations. The reason is that most software does not allow for the use of commas to denote thousands in the input. The commas are excluded so that the reader will not be tempted to include them in the input.) Combined with the similar restrictions on hash browns and flakes, the symbolic representation (model) is

The symbolic model

FIGURE 2.3   French Fries and Hash Brown Limitations

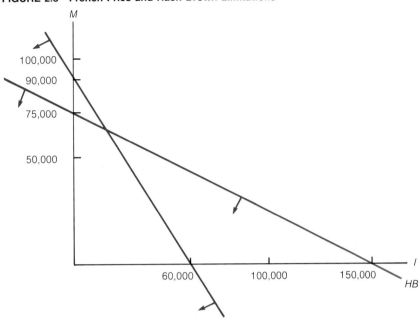

maximize $0.14I + 0.15M$
subject to $0.3I + 0.2M \leq 18000$
                     $0.1I + 0.2M \leq 15000$
                     $0.3I + 0.3M \leq 30000$
                 $I, M \geq 0$

The last line ($I, M \geq 0$) indicates that only values of 0 or positive amounts are considered for the values of I and M.

This model, called a **linear programming model** or a **constrained optimization model,** meets the requirement that a model must represent the decision problem selected. Linear programming models and constrained optimization models are discussed further in Chapter 3.

Having constructed a model of the decision environment, you *solve the model and analyze the results.*

Graphical Solution of the Model

A solution to this model is determined by finding the set of values of M and I that satisfies all of the limitations and by then calculating the profit for each of the possible plans. Rather than list all of these possibilities, we

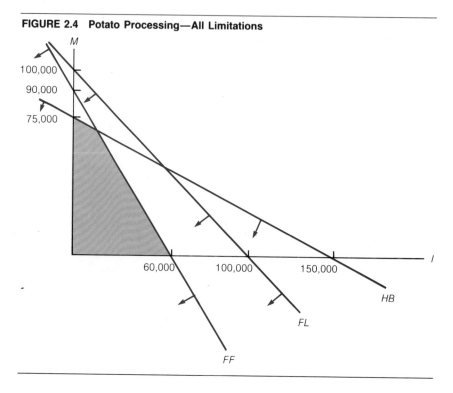

FIGURE 2.4 Potato Processing—All Limitations

can define them by using a graph. (In Chapter 4, we discuss graphical solutions in greater detail.) This discussion introduces the concept of a solution to linear programming models and the role of models and sensitivity analysis in making decisions.

The line labeled *FF* in Figure 2.2 shows the combinations of *M* and *I* that result in 18,000 pounds of french fries. All of the points on or below the line satisfy the french fry limitation. Similarly, the hash brown limitation can also be included as line *HB* in the graph in Figure 2.3. Which points satisfy both of the limitations? Remember, you want to satisfy all of the limitations.

Figure 2.4 superimposes the flakes limitation line, *FL*, and has shaded the points that satisfy all three limitations. The flakes limitation line lies just above the set of points that satisfies both the french fry line and the hash brown line. It does not affect the points that satisfy all three limitations, but it should not be ignored. Although the flakes limitation is not needed when the limitation is 30,000 pounds, it might be critical for a different limitation value. Novice model builders often try to eliminate considerations that they consider extraneous, whereas experienced model builders avoid this.

The graphical solution

Among all of the shaded points, which one would result in the most profit? Are there any shaded points with a profit of $15,000? In Figure 2.5, the dashed line is the set of points that has a profit of $15,000; there are no

FIGURE 2.5 Potato Processing—Profit of $15,000 and $12,225

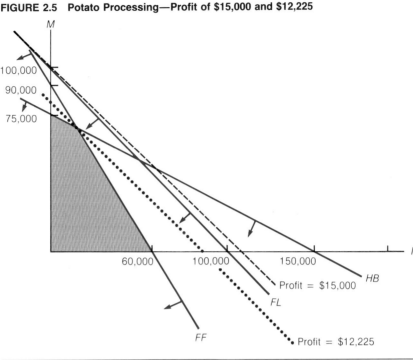

shaded points with a profit of $15,000. The dotted line is the set of all points with a profit of $12,225. This is the largest profit for which there is a shaded point that satisfies all of the limitations. The only point that has this profit and satisfies all of the limitations is $I = 15,000$ and $M = 67,500$. This is at the intersection of the french fry limitation and the hash brown limitation. The exact values can be obtained by solving those two equations in two unknowns,

Finding the exact variable values.

$$0.3I + 0.2M = 18000$$
$$0.1I + 0.2M = 15000$$

The Role of Sensitivity Analysis

Sensitivity analysis and model manipulation are necessary to validate the model and provide information for decision making. Let's develop questions useful for decision making.

Sensitivity analysis questions

The developed model has numerical values or parameters that may be uncertain or that can vary from month to month. Sensitivity analysis studies the impact of changes in parameters on the solution. For example, what is the impact if the selling price of french fries is renegotiated to $0.91 per pound? What is the impact if the market for french fries increases to 20,000 pounds?

You believed that the important limitations were on french fries and hash browns and that the "best" plan satisfied the flakes limitation. If the flakes limitation had been 24,000 pounds, would the "best" plan still satisfy the flakes limitation? No, it would not! The number of flakes produced would be 24,750 pounds, $(0.3 \times 15,000) + (0.3 \times 67,500)$, which is 750 pounds more than the revised flakes limit. Although you believed that the flakes limitation was unimportant, *the limitation should be included because the assessment may be wrong or the parameter values may change.*

What is the impact if using the Michigan potatoes resulted in 21 percent french fries and 19 percent hash browns? Would you then purchase potatoes only from Michigan? What would the yield proportions have to be so that it is better to purchase only Idaho potatoes?

Model manipulation

You should consider the impact of changes in structure as well as the impact of changes in parameters. For example, if extra french fry production could be processed into hash browns at an extra cost of $0.02 per pound, what would you do? Alternatively, could you sell extra french fries as animal feed and make even greater profit? This is another approach that circumvents the limitation of the french fry sales potential. For either of these modifications, the resulting model has more than two decision variables and can't be solved graphically.

Is the sales pattern of french fries different depending on the season? Should you freeze extra french fries during periods of low sales and sell them during periods of high sales? If so, you should develop a dynamic, multiple-period model that considers the interrelationships between different months. The model provides useful information, but it does not solve the decision problem. It is a representation of a selectively created decision environment, and its underlying assumptions must be questioned.

EXAMPLE 2: A HAIR DRYER EXAMPLE

A small manufacturer of hair dryers is concerned about the expiration of its current labor union contract. The manufacturer's profit margin has been squeezed due to price competition, and it appears that the price cannot be increased, even if costs increase, because the purchasers are very price conscious. If the price is increased, sales will decrease dramatically. The current selling price is $25, and the current manufacturing cost is $19, of which $10 is labor.

The manufacturer's stance in this year's labor negotiations is critical in the long run as well as the short run. But there is a further complication. For years, the manufacturer has been trying to bid on a contract with

Montgomery Ward & Co. Under the contract, rather than putting its own label on the hair dryer, the manufacturer would attach the Ward's label. This contract would enable the manufacturer to utilize excess manufacturing capacity. The manufacturer's capacity is 3,000 units per month, but its current sales are only 2,000 units per month. The Ward's contract would be for 1,200 units per month. So, if the manufacturer received the Ward's contract, it would sell 1,800 units per month of the private label hair dryers through existing marketing channels. The complication is that in the event of a strike, the opportunity to bid on the Ward's contract would be withdrawn. Unfortunately, even if there is a good labor offer and no strike, the bid on the Ward's contract may not be accepted. In that case, the manufacturer's profit margin would still be squeezed and its sales would continue to be under capacity.

As the decision maker, your thought process might be as follows:

> I am confident that I can get the union to settle for close to what I offer. There is relatively high unemployment in the area around my plant. However, I might have to take a strike to get a settlement for a low wage offer. Let's think about two extreme offers—no raise and a 10 percent raise. If I offer no raise, my costs will stay at $19, but I believe I will have a strike that could last as long as two months. If I offer a 10 percent raise, my costs will increase to $20 due to the increase in labor costs. In this case, I think there is a 0.1 probability of a strike, but it will probably only be for one month. I am considering a raise as high as 10 percent because I think there is a pretty good chance that my bid on the Ward's contract will be accepted. Even while the plant is shut down by a strike, I will still have ongoing operating expenses of $5,000 each month of the strike.
>
> The Ward's contract is for 12 months, and the likelihood of obtaining it will be affected by the price I bid. If I bid $18, I am sure I will get the contract, but I will lose money on it. Realistically, I think a bid between $20 and $22 is still in the ballpark. I estimate that at $20, the bid has a 60 percent chance of being accepted. I estimate the likelihood of acceptance to be 40 percent at $21 and 20 percent at $22.
>
> It's too bad I can't postpone the labor negotiations until after I receive the information concerning the Ward's bid. However, the deadline for the Ward's bid is such that I have to submit the bid before the deadline for the labor contract and I won't be notified whether I am the successful bidder until after a strike has been announced. If a strike is called, then I will have to withdraw the Ward's bid. Even if I offered a 10 percent raise and a strike were called, I would be unable to reduce the labor offer because that would not be "bargaining in good faith." I could continue to adhere to a 10 percent offer, but I couldn't decrease the offer.

The labor contract we will be negotiating will have a one-year duration, the same length as the Ward's contract. Over what time
period should I consider the impact of these decisions? The labor
contract negotiations will have an impact on costs as well as on labor relations after this year. Also, if I get the Ward's contract this
year, I may have a better chance of getting the Ward's contract in
subsequent years. Of course, I believe Ward's is a very price-com-
petitive purchaser, so I really do not think that will have much
impact.

Let's consider the impact of the decisions on profits over the next
year so I will have a basis for evaluating the alternatives. To compare the various alternatives, I will calculate the *expected profit*[2] for
each and choose the alternative with the largest expected profit. I
can incorporate other subjective concerns, such as longer-term considerations in addition to the one-year analysis, when I make my
decision. Another consideration to check is the likelihood of each of
the possible profits as well as that of the expected profit.

I wish I'd had the foresight to build up inventories before the
deadline for the labor negotiations. If I had, I could sell the hair
dryers from inventory even if there were a strike. It's too bad customers aren't loyal to my brand of hair dryers, but that's why the
market is so competitive.

As a decision maker, you must first define the decision problem. Your
thought process is the first model-building step: *Study the decision environment and determine the subset of the decision environment that is to
be analyzed.* Let's analyze the decision environment using the framework
introduced in Chapter 1. Is the decision environment deterministic or
probabilistic? In this case, uncertainty is at the heart of the decision
environment. Will there be a strike? Will the Ward's bid be accepted?

*A probabilistic decision
environment*

Any appropriate analysis of the decision environment must explicitly
incorporate the uncertainty, which means that the decision environment
is *probabilistic*.

One-year time horizon

We use a one-year time horizon and a single time period. The impact of
this year's decisions on future years is not explicitly considered. However, you know that this year's decisions have impacts on future years.
For example, if you offer a 10 percent raise this year, this affects your
future labor costs. We don't include those future costs in our model, but
we do consider future impacts and other qualitative factors when we
make our decisions. If the labor contract or the Ward's contract were of a
different length, a different time horizon would be appropriate. Say that

---

[2] The expected profit is calculated by multiplying each possible profit by its probability
and then summing the products.

the labor contract is for two years and the Ward's contract is awarded annually. The uncertainty of obtaining the Ward's contract in the second year results in a time horizon of two years, and the model would thus have two one-year periods.

What is the source of the uncertainty of the outcomes? Let's say that it is the unpredictability of nature. Obviously, competitors' bids influence whether you obtain the Ward's contract. However, competitors' actions have been included in the assessment of the success probabilities for different bids and are not considered in any other way.

Having chosen the subset of the decision environment to be analyzed, you *construct a model incorporating those factors judged to be important.*

The Decision Tree Model

You have determined the scope of the decision problem to be analyzed. Your profit for the year must be calculated for each of the possible scenarios. For example, if you offer no raise, then 10 months' production of 2,000 units will be sold at the current price, for a total profit of $10 \times 2,000 \times (25 - 19)$ minus the $10,000 two-month cost of the strike, or $110,000. If the labor offer is 10 percent and there is a one-month strike, our profit will be $11 \times 2,000 \times (25 - 20)$ minus $5,000, or $105,000.

Figure 2.6 shows each of the possible scenarios, with the time sequence from left to right. This representation is called a **decision tree** or a **decision tree model,** and it satisfies the requirement that a model represent the decision problem chosen. For example, the bottommost branch of the tree is this scenario: You offer a 10 percent raise, there is no strike, and then you bid $22 to Ward's, but you don't get the contract. The profit for this is $12 \times 2,000 \times (25 - 20)$, or $120,000. That is, your costs increase to $20 per unit, and since there is no strike, you produce for 12 months and sell the private label to your current customers. If the scenario is a labor offer of 10 percent, no strike, and a successful bid of $20, then the total profit from selling 1,200 units to Ward's at $20 $[12 \times 1,200 \times (20 - 20)]$ plus 1,800 units to your regular customers at $25 $[12 \times 1,800 \times (25 - 20)]$ would be $108,000.

The squares represent decision points in the decision tree. The first decision point is the labor offer. If there is no strike, another decision point is the bid price. The circles represent uncertain future events, each weighted by its probability. One uncertain event is whether a strike will occur. Another is whether the Ward's bid will be successful. Thus, given an offer of a 10 percent raise with no strike and a $20 bid to Ward's, the uncertain outcome of getting the contract has a probability of 0.6 and the uncertain outcome of not getting the contract has a probability of 0.4.

The best decisions are calculated at the decision points by comparing the expected value of the decision alternatives, assuming that you reach

The decision tree model

FIGURE 2.6   Decision Tree—Hair Dryer Company

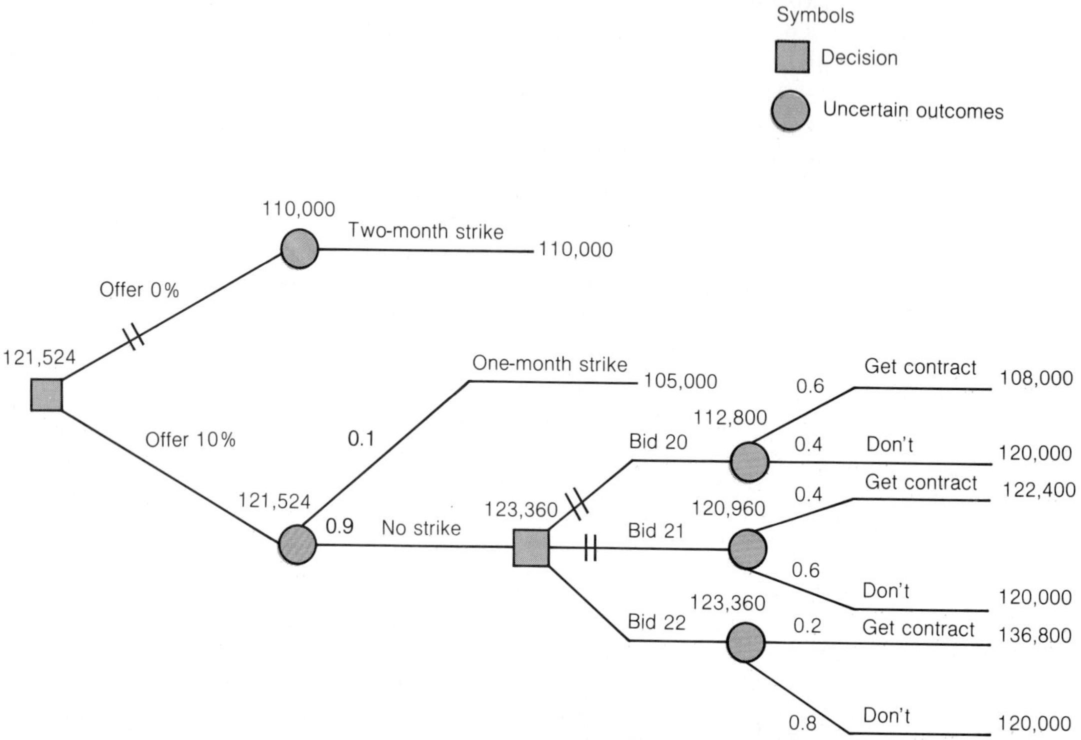

this point in the scenario. Therefore, if you have an opportunity to bid on the Ward's contract, you should pick the bid price with the largest expected value.[3]

Having constructed a model of the decision environment, you *solve the model and analyze the results.*

Solving the Decision Tree Model

If the bid is $20, the expected profit is (0.6 × Profit if you get the contract) + (0.4 × Profit if you don't get the contract), or (0.6 × 108,000) + (0.4 × 120,000) = $112,800. The expected profit is $120,960 from a bid of $21 and $123,360 from a bid of $22. So, if there is an opportunity to bid on the Ward's contract, a bid of $22 gives the largest expected profit. The resulting profit is written over the decision tree box for the bid decision

---

[3] This assumes that you are indifferent to risk and that you use expected profit as the criterion for evaluating decision alternatives. In Chapter 10, we discuss attitudes toward risk and criteria for decision making in probabilistic decision environments.

point. We drew double lines through the decisions that give smaller expected profits.

If you offer a 10 percent raise, what is the expected profit? With a probability of 0.1, there will be a one-month strike and a yearly profit of $105,000. With a probability of 0.9, there will not be a strike and the expected profit if you bid $22 is $123,360. The expected profit for a 10 percent raise is $121,524. (Try to verify this value.) The expected profit for a 10 percent raise is larger than the $110,000 expected profit for the no-raise alternative. We drew double lines through the no-raise decision because it has a smaller expected profit than does a 10 percent raise. Based on these considerations, the best decision is to offer a 10 percent raise. What should you bid to Ward's? If you *don't* have a strike and you *do* have an opportunity to bid, you should bid $22.

The Role of Sensitivity Analysis

Sensitivity analysis and model manipulation are necessary to validate the model and provide information helpful for decision making. Let's develop questions useful for decision making.

Sensitivity analysis
questions

Parameters including the probabilities, selling prices, strike length and operating costs, and manufacturing costs were estimated for the analysis. If the probability of a one-month strike with a 10 percent offer were larger, it might be best to offer no raise. How large would the probability have to be? It is useful to know whether the decision is sensitive to changes in the probability. If sales of our label decreased to 1,900 units per month, how would that affect the decision? What is the impact of an increase in the market price to $25.50?

Model manipulation

An appropriate analysis evaluates the sensitivity of the decisions to changes in the parameters and to other structural changes. Why not consider a 5 percent raise? What happens if the strike, after an offer of no raise, is three months long and is settled for a 5 percent raise? Other alternatives can be evaluated by including additional branches on the decision tree.

The decision tree represents decisions and events for next year. Could a two-year contract with Ward's change the bidding strategy? How could you incorporate a second year into the analysis? These and other possibilities can be considered as the model is used to explore the decision environment.

CONSIDERATIONS IN MODEL BUILDING

Building decision models is an art as well as a science. Model builders rely on data to estimate model parameters. The data can be aggregated or disaggregated. More detail makes solving a model more difficult. Models with different levels of detail and different time horizon lengths are appropriate for different types of decisions. In the following sections, we discuss these considerations in model building.

Reliance on Data

The ability to construct mathematical models for decision making depends on numerical information, called data. Among the sources of data are historical records, accounting records, and government documents. Your assessment of such parameters as the processing cost and the yield of french fries is based on data. Assessing such parameters without numerical information is more difficult. Perhaps an experiment can be done, such as "trying" a bag of Michigan potatoes to estimate yields. Issues regarding estimation are generally studied in an introductory statistics course and are not repeated in this book. However, we stress that even though numerical data is available, there is likely to be some uncertainty on the estimates of parameters. Furthermore, there may be natural variation, such as variation in the size (and proportionate product yields) of Michigan potatoes in a sack. For these reasons, *sensitivity analysis is very important in decision making*.

Expert opinion is another possible source of information. An engineer can estimate the yields of potato products if information on potato size is provided. Or an engineer may be familiar with the results of a similar situation—say the use of a similar machine on Wisconsin potatoes. But, again, the parameter values are only estimates and sensitivity analysis is crucial. If the model's solution is sensitive to possible changes in parameter values, then you can get additional information to reduce the uncertainty of the estimates.

Aggregation versus Disaggregation of Data

The Potato Processing example required estimating potential sales of french fries. The underlying data for this assessment is the marketing records for orders in the past or the accounting records for billings for orders filled. The market potential, not how much was shipped, is the information desired. The amount that was shipped can be less than the market potential because we did not make as much product as we could have accepted orders for. Also, there might be a delay between when orders are placed and when orders are filled. This delay is likely to be short for frozen french fries but long for machine tools or airplanes. Data may be useful or worthless, depending on its source and on how it was compiled. Lack of *appropriate* data is a common problem for model builders.

The marketing records have data on each order—customer name and address, date order placed, date order shipped, quantity, and price. To assess the monthly potential for french fries, that data is more easily evaluated if it is aggregated. That is, by adding the quantities of all the orders placed in a month and using the totals for several months, the potential for the upcoming month can be estimated. This determination, called **forecasting,** is discussed in Chapter 12.

The important point is that *models rely on data,* and data can be **aggregated** or **disaggregated.** Disaggregated data provides more information but makes it more difficult to "see the forest for the trees." Aggregated data is easier to understand. The appropriate level of aggregation of data depends on its use. For the Potato Processing example, aggregation to the monthly level is appropriate. However, if the company were considering the possible expansion of the loading dock because of the large number of orders being placed, data at the individual transaction level would be appropriate.

Owens-Corning aggregated product demand for all products in its first model, which determined the number of shifts, overtime, and the aggregate inventory level. The other two models used demand disaggregated to individual products. The level of data aggregation depends on the decisions you are considering.

Model Detail versus Model Tractability

What makes a model harder to solve or analyze? In the Potato Processing example, the model is more complex if there are more than two sources of potatoes. In fact, if Wisconsin potatoes are a third possibility, solution by the graphical method is much more difficult. Furthermore, if there are limits on the quantities of potatoes processed or minimum requirements of a particular product or other products, such as crinkle-cut french fries, additional complexities are added.

Many management science models require a computer program for their solution. Additional complexity is a major consideration if it converts a model to a form that can't be solved. Additional complexity is either a major or a minor consideration, depending on how much computer time and computer storage it requires. **Model tractability** refers to the ease with which a model can be solved. If a model has more detail, it's less tractable.

The detail of a model is related to aggregation or disaggregation of the data. All of the important factors should be considered in the model. For example, failure to consider the possibility of Wisconsin potatoes is an error. By ignoring that possibility, you might miss a good opportunity. And by ignoring a limitation on potato processing capacity, you might purchase more potatoes than you can process. *All of the appropriate considerations must be included in the model.* The difficulty lies in determining what amount of detail is appropriate. This depends on the purpose of the model. For example, the model could be at the level of detail that shows the processing of individual orders for potato products or hair dryers. In this case, the same basic considerations are incorporated, but there is a much greater level of detail. The additional level of detail could give better decision-making information. The ultimate issue is, "Does the benefit of the additional detail outweigh its cost?" Furthermore, is there data available that is accurate enough at the detail level to support a more detailed model? Before the model is developed, the model builder should clearly define its purpose, so that model tractability and the appropriate level of detail can be determined. This is still a judgment, but if the purpose is not well understood, a rational judgment cannot be made.

A Hierarchy of Models and the Length of the Time Horizon

The appropriate time horizon and the level of detail of the model are both related to the purpose of the model. Since there are many types of decisions, there is a hierarchy of decision models for different purposes.

Let's consider the decision environment of a major oil company. The decisions made range from the board of directors level to the level of the refinery engineer. The decisions can be categorized as **long term, intermediate term,** and **short term.** The number of categories is arbitrary, but it is useful as a framework for discussion.

A decision on whether to build a new oil refinery in Louisiana is a long-term decision because the useful life of an oil refinery is many years and the construction cost is high. Many years are required to do the detailed engineering design and the construction. What time horizon is appropriate? Certainly, it is 5 to 10 years, or more. This decision is made at the highest level of the oil company. Important inputs for the decision include estimates of future sales quantities and prices of finished products, crude oil availabilities and costs, and the characteristics of the new refinery as well as existing refineries. Because of the uncertainty of the inputs for future years, it is inappropriate (or unreasonable) to be concerned with day-to-day sales of unleaded gasoline at a particular gas station five years from now. That level of detail is not needed. This is not to say that the construction of the oil refinery will not affect that gas station. It might result in a complete realignment of which refineries furnish unleaded gasoline to which gas stations. However, it is not necessary to include that level of detail in deciding whether to build a new refinery. For long-term decisions, the model has a time horizon of several years and does not contain a great deal of detail.

Deciding how to accumulate heating oil in storage during warm months so that enough is available to satisfy needs during cold months is an intermediate-term decision. In this case, the length of the time horizon should be at least past the next winter's heating season, 12 to 15 months. The inputs include monthly or quarterly estimates of sales of heating oil and other petroleum products. (*Note:* It is possible to change the relative amounts of the different products by altering the operating conditions of the refinery processing units.) Other inputs are operating characteristics and storage capacities. The decisions require a monthly or quarterly level of detail to determine the accumulation of heating oil during the 12- to 15-month time horizon. More detail on the operating characteristics of the refineries is needed for the intermediate-term decision than for the long-term decision.

Deciding how to operate the refinery over the next week and how to blend the results into finished products is a short-term decision. In this case, the requirements of each product are an input. The problem is to produce what is required at the lowest cost. The amount of each blending stock on hand and detailed information on the operating characteristics of the refinery are required.

Short-term models have more detail

In general, the shorter the time horizon, the more detailed the model. The detailed week-to-week operating plan for a particular refinery is not crucial when what is being considered is whether to build a new oil refinery. Additional detail of this kind would add little insight, yet make the model less tractable and obscure the more important considerations.

Owens-Corning used three models to schedule fiberglass mat production at its Anderson plant. The first model was for intermediate-term decisions, such as number of shifts, amount of overtime, and aggregate inventory level, month by month. This model had the least detail and used a time horizon of 3 to 12 months. The second model used the aggregate inventory levels from the first model to determine production lot sizes, line assignments, and inventory levels at the product level, month by month. This model had more detail than the first model because it scheduled at the product level. The third model, for short-term decisions, used the second model's results as an input. It specified starting times for each product on a production line during a month. This model had the most detail and the shortest time horizon—one month. Owens-Corning used a hierarchy of models with different time horizons and different levels of detail for different parts of the same decision problem: "How should we schedule our production?" Different models focused on different parts of the decision problem.

THE IMPACT OF MODEL STRUCTURE ON SENSITIVITY ANALYSIS

If there is a methodology for solving a decision model with one set of parameters, then the model can be solved again with a different set of parameters. The changes in the solution can then be evaluated based on the parameter changes. This is sensitivity analysis by brute force.

In certain cases, rather than using trial and error to adjust the parameters, you may be able to analytically calculate the amount that a parameter must change before a decision changes. Look at the hair dryer manufacturer. Before the labor decision is changed to no raise at all, what must be the probability of a one-month strike in response to a 10 percent raise? You could check by trying a large number of different probabilities, or you could see from Figure 2.6 that only one factor would change in the decision tree. Rather than change the factor by trial and error, ask what the value of the probability would have to be to provide the same expected profit for both labor offers. That is, for what value of p would the expected value of the 10 percent offer equal the profit from an offer of no raise?

$$[p \times 105,000] + [(1 - p) \times 123,360] = 110,000$$

Solving for p, we find that $p = 0.728$. The probability must be more than 0.728 before the preferred labor offer would be no raise. This is useful information. Remember, your assessment of the probability of a strike is 0.1. Even though you are uncertain as to how accurate your assessment of the probability is, you may feel confident that it is nowhere close to 0.728. In this case, the optimal decision is not very sensitive to changes in that parameter.

Model structure affects ease of sensitivity analysis

In general, determining the sensitivity of the optimal solution to changes is easiest analytically when only one parameter changes at a time. This influences the way you formulate the model. In the Potato Processing example, an increase in the cost per pound of Michigan potatoes changes only the profit margin on M. However, an increase in the selling price of french fries changes the profit margins on both I and M. This is more difficult to evaluate analytically. *The ease and manner of performing sensitivity analysis are influenced by the model structure chosen by the model builder.* Because there can be more than one correct model, the model builder should consider the types of sensitivity analysis that are of interest before the model has been finalized.

SUMMARY

We discussed the steps in conducting a management science study proposed by Agin. Existing software can be used for some, but not all, decision problems. Problem definition, model development, model validation, and the use of decision models are stressed in this book. These issues and the categorizing of the decision environment were illustrated by two examples. The Potato Processing example illustrated a deterministic decision environment; the hair dryer example illustrated a probabilistic decision environment. The time horizon for the Potato Processing example was one month; the time horizon for the hair dryer example was one year. A linear programming model represented the Potato Processing example. A decision tree model represented the hair dryer example. The decision model representing each example consisted of a single period (static). The source of the uncertainty of the hair dryer example was treated as the unpredictability of nature. For both examples, a decision model was constructed and solved. Questions on the impact of changes in parameters and assumptions were proposed. The importance of sensitivity analysis and the role of the model in decision making was illustrated.

Although decision models and their solution play a central role in management science, model building is an art as well as a science. We discussed many issues in model building. First, models depend on data. Unfortunately, adequate or sufficiently accurate data is sometimes not available. For this reason, the study of the sensitivity of the model's solution to changes in parameters is very important. Data can be aggregated or disaggregated. Aggregated data contains less information than disaggregated data, but it is easier to study.

Model tractability is the ease with which a model can be solved. The level of detail of a model affects its tractability. More model detail makes a model more difficult to solve and analyze. The level of model detail must be consistent with the decision to be made. Ask whether the benefit of additional detail outweighs its cost.

Long term, intermediate term, and short term are categories of decisions. Long-term decisions require longer time horizons and less detail but have more uncertainty for the inputs. Short-term decisions require shorter time horizons and more detail but have less uncertainty for the inputs. Intermediate-term decisions have time horizons of about one year and are between long-term and short-term decisions in amount of detail and in uncertainty for the inputs. Long-term decisions are generally strategic decisions; short-term decisions are operational or tactical decisions.

Finally, sensitivity analysis was done on the probability of a strike in the hair dryer example. Because of the structure of the model, the necessary probability to change the decision to offer no raise was found by algebra. In general, sensitivity analysis is easier if only one parameter changes at a time. The types of sensitivity analysis desired influence the model structure chosen by the model builder.

In future chapters, we discuss many management science models and methods. In reading those chapters, it is important to bear in mind the lessons of this chapter. Models aren't useful if they don't accurately represent the decision environment *you choose* to analyze. For that reason, we showed how we chose the factors considered in the Potato Processing and hair dryer examples. We decided whether the decision environment was deterministic, what the length of the time horizon should be, and what level of detail should be used. Remember, as a management science user, you make the choices. Question the choices and the underlying assumptions. If you do, you'll use management science to its full potential.

QUESTIONS

1. In the Potato Processing example, the greatest profit was obtained if potatoes from both sources were purchased. Give the revised model if the percentage of french fries were 21 and the percentage of hash browns were 19 for the Michigan potatoes. Solving the revised model is not required. Do you think this change is enough to result in potatoes being purchased only from Michigan?

2. In the Potato Processing example, could the cost per pound of Idaho potatoes be cheap enough so that the most profitable alternative would be to buy only Idaho potatoes? Solving the revised model is not required. Do you think a one cent per pound reduction is enough? Solving the revised model is not required. (This is useful information, and in later chapters we show how to obtain it easily.)

3. A machine has been developed that processes french fries into hash browns without creating additional flakes or waste. This allows french fry production that is greater than the limitation to be converted into hash browns. Each pound of excess french fries is converted into 1 pound of hash browns. If only Idaho potatoes are purchased and the amount purchased is 75,000 pounds, how many pounds of excess french fries are converted into hash browns? If the operating cost of the new machine is $0.18 per pound of french fries processed, what is the profit from the purchase of 75,000 pounds of Idaho potatoes?

4. Say that a 2 percent discount is received on the purchase price of potatoes in excess of 50,000 pounds from a single supplier (i.e., Michigan or Idaho). This discount is applicable only to the amount above 50,000 pounds. If 60,000 pounds of Idaho potatoes are purchased and processed, what is the profit? If potatoes are purchased only from Michigan, what is the profit? If the optimal plan from the chapter ($M = 15,000$ and $I = 67,500$) is used, what is the profit? Do you think the discount changes the optimal plan? Solving the revised model is not required.

5. In the hair dryer example, verify that the expected profit from a $21 bid to Ward's is $120,960 and that the expected profit from a $22 bid is $123,360.

6. Verify that the expected profit for a 10 percent raise is $121,524.

7. If the private label sales of hair dryers dropped to 1,900 per month, would the decision still be the same? What would be the expected profit?

8. Construct the decision tree model that also includes the following possibility: Offer a 5 percent raise with a probability of 0.3 for a one-month strike. Do not solve the model.

9. For the optimal decision based on the decision tree analysis, list every possible scenario and its probability. (*Hint:* Three scenarios are possible.)

10. Construct the decision tree needed if the Ward's contract is for two years and the labor union contract is also for two years. Assume that if the 10 percent is given at the beginning of the first year, no raise is given for the remainder of the labor union contract. Do not solve the decision tree, but determine the economic results of every scenario.

11. Can you suggest a creative offer to the union based on the success of the bid to Ward's? Can you construct the decision tree needed to analyze that creative offer?

12. It has been suggested that a price increase of $0.25 on the private label hair dryers might be appropriate if the Ward's contract were received. The expectation is that private label sales would decrease to 1,800 units per month because of the price increase. What changes are required in the decision tree model because of this price increase? Is the optimal decision the same?

13. It has been suggested that if the Ward's bid were successful, the excess requirements could be produced by working overtime. Because labor is paid time and a half for overtime, this increases the labor cost per unit by 50 percent. What do you think of this suggestion?

14. What are the three steps of the model builder?

15. What considerations affect the level of detail chosen for a decision model?

16. What is a "hierarchy of models"?

17. Why is sensitivity analysis important?

3

An Introduction to Linear Programming Models

Formulating Linear Programming Models

The Product Mix Model
Verbal Model / Decision Variables / Symbolic Model

The Machine Assignment Model
Verbal Model / Decision Variables / Symbolic Model

Blending Models
Standard Unit Blending Model / Operational Blending Model /
The Impact of Linear Programming Model Formulation on
Sensitivity Analysis

Case: American Steel Company

Appendix: Use of LINDO
Model Development

CENTRAL CAROLINA BANK AND TRUST COMPANY

Central Carolina Bank and Trust Company (CCBT) had assets of approximately $360 million when a Financial Planning Committee (FPC) was established to coordinate the bank's activities. A linear programming model was developed by the FPC to "optimize" the bank's balance sheet. Because the FPC consisted of CCBT's senior officers and they participated in formulating the model, the model was well accepted.

In initial meetings, the FPC discussed the length of the planning horizon, the number of decision points within the planning horizon, and the amount of detail in the balance sheet. A one-year, single-period model was chosen. The decision variables were dollar quantities in different asset and liability categories. Examples of asset categories were cash, Treasury securities, consumer loans, commercial loans, and real estate loans. Examples of liability categories were demand deposits, savings accounts, money market certificates, certificates of deposit (CDs), and repurchase agreements. The yields and costs for different categories were estimated by the FPC. Adjusting the dollar quantities in the categories changes the bank's profit.

The objective was maximizing the one-year profit subject to five classes of restrictions on balance sheet composition. One restriction class was maximum activity levels for some variables. Maximums were imposed either for policy reasons or based on forecasts of demand for categories of bank services. Because of limitations on the turnover of some categories, lower limits were set for these categories. For example, only part of the five-year CDs mature in any year. As they mature, the bank can make decisions that influence additional five-year CD investments, but the dollar quantity on the balance sheet can't be decreased to zero within a year. Another restriction class was policy constraints based on operating and financial ratios. For example, management placed limits on the average maturity of its Treasury securities. Legal and regulatory constraints were another class. The final restriction class assured adequate liquidity through funds flow constraints.

Each month, senior officers estimated input parameters (e.g., yields on consumer loans) and the model was run before the FPC meeting. At the meeting, the current balance sheet was compared with the one generated by the model. The model's results also generated sensitivity analysis information that was used to rank the profitability of bank services. The model's information formed the basis for decisions on which services to promote. The FPC viewed the model's balance sheet as a strategic plan to which tactical modifications and subjective judgment were applied.

S. D. Balbirer and D. Shaw, "An Application of Linear Programming to Bank Financial Planning," *Interfaces* 11, no. 5 (October 1981), pp. 77–83. An interesting follow-up is S. D. Balbirer and D. Shaw, "The Evolution of Financial Planning Models at a Commercial Bank," *Interfaces* 14, no. 6 (November–December 1984), pp. 67–69.

Surveys of management science users show that linear programming models are used more than most other types of quantitative methods. Only computer simulation, statistical analysis (Chapters 15 and 16), and project management (Chapter 8) are used more.[1] Linear programming models have many applications. In Chapter 1's opening, we discussed how Air Products used linear programming to assign customers to depots so that the total production and distribution costs were minimized. In Chapter 2's opening, we said that Owens-Corning used a linear programming model to choose lot sizes, line assignments, and inventory levels on a product basis, month by month. Linear programming has many applications like these in operations planning, but it also has applications in other functions of business. Central Carolina Bank and Trust Company (CCBT) used linear programming to plan changes in its balance sheet so that annual profit was maximized. In this chapter, we introduce linear programming. We describe the mathematical form of linear programming models and discuss the three-step model formulation process. We formulate three classes of linear programming problems and show how to formulate the models. In Chapters 4 to 7, we show how to solve linear programming models, how to interpret the computer output, and how linear programming is used in decision making.

The Potato Processing example in Chapter 2 is a linear programming model. The decision variables are I and M, representing the number of pounds of potatoes purchased from Idaho and Michigan, respectively. Because of anticipated sales potential, limitations are imposed on the number of pounds of french fries, hash browns, and flakes produced. The profit maximization symbolic model is

$$
\begin{aligned}
\text{maximize} \quad & 0.14I + 0.15M \\
\text{subject to} \quad & 0.3I + 0.2M \le 18000 \\
& 0.1I + 0.2M \le 15000 \\
& 0.3I + 0.3M \le 30000 \\
& I, M \ge 0
\end{aligned}
$$

[1] G. A. Forgionne, "Corporate Management Science Activities: An Update," *Interfaces* 13, no. 3 (June 1983), pp. 20–23.

As we discussed in Chapter 1, we use *decision variables* in quantitative decision models. For optimization decision models, we chose the "best" value of the decision variables for a particular **objective.** For a profit-making organization, the objective might be to maximize profit or to minimize cost. For a governmental agency or a not-for-profit organization, the objective might be to minimize the cost of services provided or to maximize the ratio of benefits to costs. If the objective is clearly defined, it should be possible to list every possible decision and calculate the value of the objective associated with it. Then, choosing the largest (or smallest) objective value is simple. The **optimal decision** is the one with the best objective value.

The objective in the Potato Processing example is to maximize the profit during the next month. The formula (or function) that calculates the objective for particular values of the decision variables is called the **objective function.** The objective function for the Potato Processing example is $0.14I + 0.15M$. Given the values of I and M, you calculate the value of the profit using the objective function. For a linear programming model, the objective function can be either maximized or minimized. Let's assume that the decision environment has one objective.

Because the sales limitation is 18,000 pounds, a decision producing more than 18,000 pounds of french fries cannot be considered, which indirectly limits the amount of potatoes purchased. Limitations imposed by algebraic equations and inequalities are called **constraints.** The french fry limitation is imposed by the constraint $0.3I + 0.2M \leq 18000$. The set of constraints is introduced by the "subject to" in the symbolic model. A **constrained optimization model,** sometimes called a **mathematical programming model,** consists of an objective function to be optimized and one or more constraints. Linear programming models are a subset of all constrained optimization models.

An objective function and constraint(s)

CCBT's balance sheet planning model was a constrained optimization model. Its objective function was to maximize the annual profit. Constraints were imposed for legal and regulatory requirements, adequate liquidity, and maximum and minimum activity levels.

"Programming," whether linear or mathematical, conjures up visions of computer programming but is unrelated to it. In decision making, programming refers to planning. A program is a plan, and determining the values of the decision variables gives a plan. A mathematical programming model is a mathematical decision model for planning (programming) decisions that optimize an objective function and satisfy limitations imposed by mathematical constraints.

Programming means planning

In general, a constrained optimization model consists of decision variables, an objective function, and constraints. A general symbolic model is

General symbolic form
for a constrained op-
timization model

$$\text{maximize or minimize} \quad f(x_1, x_2, \ldots, x_n)$$
$$\text{subject to} \quad g_1(x_1, x_2, \ldots, x_n) \{\leq, \geq, =\} b_1$$
$$g_2(x_1, x_2, \ldots, x_n) \{\leq, \geq, =\} b_2$$
$$\cdots \qquad \cdots \qquad \cdots$$
$$g_m(x_1, x_2, \ldots, x_n) \{\leq, \geq, =\} b_m$$

There are n decision variables in the above, named $x_1, x_2, \ldots, x_n$, and m constraints, numbered $1, 2, \ldots, m$. The names of the variables and the numbering scheme for the constraints are intended to be general. The number of variables, n, and the number of constraints, m, could be any positive integers. Mathematicians often represent "unknowns" by the symbol X. The subscripts on the decision variables indicate a list of unknowns (e.g., x_2 is the second unknown).

Three parts of a con-
straint

For each constraint, only one of the relationships—$\leq$ or $\geq$ or $=$—is used. Each constraint consists of (1) a constraint function, (2) a relationship, and (3) a constant on the right-hand side (RHS) of the relationship. For Constraint 1, the constraint function is represented by $g_1(x_1, x_2, \ldots, x_n)$ and the RHS constant by b_1. The constraint function appears on the left-hand side (LHS) of the relationship.

A less than or equal to relationship, $\leq$, says that the only variable values considered are those such that the LHS is less than or equal to the RHS. A greater than or equal to relationship, $\geq$, says that the only variable values considered are those such that the LHS is greater than or equal to the RHS. For an $=$ relationship, the LHS must equal the RHS. A constraint of a mathematical programming model includes exactly one of the three relationships—$\leq$ or $\geq$ or $=$. Strict inequalities are not permitted

$<$ and $>$ not allowed

for relationships. The $<$ strict inequality says that the LHS must be less than the RHS; they may not be equal. The $>$ strict inequality says that the LHS must be greater than the RHS; they may not be equal. Neither $>$ nor $<$ is permitted as a constraint relationship. A theoretical (as well as computational) problem results from the difficulty of determining whether a strict inequality is satisfied. If a strict inequality is desired, change the RHS constant by a small amount and use the appropriate inequality, $\leq$ or $\geq$. For example, change $x + y < 4$ to $x + y \leq 3.999999$. The amount that the RHS constant is changed depends on the numerical accuracy of the computer software. Most of the software for solving constrained optimization models use real [2] arithmetic and are accurate to six or seven significant digits.

An example of a constrained optimization model is

$$\text{maximize} \quad 4x_1 + 3x_2$$
$$\text{subject to} \quad x_1{}^2 + x_2{}^2 \leq 10$$
$$2x_1 + x_2 \geq 5$$
$$x_1 - x_2 = 1$$

---

[2] Computers represent numbers either as integers or as real numbers.

In this case, m, the number of constraints, is 3 and n, the number of decision variables, is 2. The first constraint function is $g_1(x_1, x_2) = x_1^2 + x_2^2$, the relationship is $\leq$, and the RHS constant, b_1, is 10. The second constraint function is $2x_1 + x_2$, the relationship is $\geq$, and the RHS constant is 5.

A function is said to be a linear function if it is written in the form of a constant times the first variable, plus another constant times the second variable, plus . . . , plus another constant times the nth variable. Symbolically, the function $f(x_1, x_2, \ldots, x_n)$ is a **linear function** if it is written as $f(x_1, x_2, \ldots, x_n) = c_1x_1 + c_2x_2 + \ldots + c_nx_n$, where $c_1, c_2, \ldots, c_n$ are constants. The objective function for the Potato Processing example is $0.14I + 0.15M$, a linear function. The three constraint functions of the Potato Processing model are also linear functions.

A decision variable is **continuous** if it can have fractional values as well as integer values. If the objective function and all of the constraint functions are linear functions and the variables are continuous, a constrained optimization model is called a **linear programming model**. Because the objective function and the three constraint functions are linear, the Potato Processing model is a linear programming model.

A linear programming model

A function that is not a linear function is called a **nonlinear function.** Because $x_1^2 + x_2^2$, the first constraint of the above constrained optimization model example, is a nonlinear function, the model is not a linear programming model. Functions that include the products or quotients of decision variables are also nonlinear (e.g., x_1x_2 or $x_1/x_2 - 1$).

The general symbolic form of a linear programming model can be written as

General symbolic form for a linear programming model

$$\begin{array}{ll}
\max \text{ (or min)} & c_1x_1 + c_2x_2 + \ldots + c_nx_n \\
\text{st} & a_{11}x_1 + a_{12}x_2 + \ldots + a_{1n}x_n \quad \{\leq, \geq, =\}\, b_1 \\
& a_{21}x_1 + a_{22}x_2 + \ldots + a_{2n}x_n \quad \{\leq, \geq, =\}\, b_2 \\
& \quad \cdots \qquad\qquad\qquad\qquad\qquad\quad \cdots \quad \cdots \\
& a_{m1}x_1 + a_{m2}x_2 + \ldots + a_{mn}x_n \quad \{\leq, \geq, =\}\, b_m \\
& x_j \geq 0 \quad j = 1, \ldots, n
\end{array}$$

Parameters are numerical values for a particular model. The objective function coefficient represented above by c_1 is the objective function coefficient of the first variable, x_1. In the Potato Processing example, c_1 represents the parameter 0.14, the objective function coefficient for the first decision variable, I. The parameter a_{ij} represents the coefficient in constraint i of variable j. In the Potato Processing example, a_{21} represents the coefficient in the second constraint (the hash brown limitation) for the first decision variable (I); its numerical value is 0.1. Only one of the relationships, $\leq$, $\geq$, or $=$, is used in each constraint.

The objective function of a linear programming model is either maximized or minimized. Note that the abbreviation "max" is used for maximize, "min" is used for minimize, and "st" is used for subject to. We use these abbreviations in this book for linear programming symbolic models. In the appendix of this chapter, we describe the use of LINDO, a linear programming software package often used for instruction in management science. This package uses these abbreviations, so you type the model in a form almost identical to the symbolic model. Commas denoting thousands are not allowed as inputs. Thus, commas do not appear in any linear programming symbolic model.

Nonnegative variables in linear programming

The restrictions, $x_j \geq 0$ for $j = 1, \ldots, n$, say that the decision variables may take on only **nonnegative** values. This means that a value of 0 or a positive value is acceptable, but a negative value is not. Because the variables are continuous, they can have fractional values as well as integer values. Any nonnegative value is possible if it satisfies all of the constraints.

Let's consider the major difference between the linear programming symbolic model and LINDO input. Because we assume that all of the variables are nonnegative, the nonnegativities are not part of the model input. For the potato processing example, the model input is

max $0.14I + 0.15M$
st $0.3I + 0.2M \leq 18000$
       $0.1I + 0.2M \leq 15000$
       $0.3I + 0.3M \leq 30000$

The LINDO model input is identical to the linear programming symbolic models in this book, except that the nonnegativities are not entered. If a variable is not restricted to nonnegative values in a model, the model is reformulated so that all of the variables must be nonnegative. In Chapter 4's appendix, we discuss these reformulations. We list the nonnegativities of decision variables in the symbolic model to stress the possibility of reformulation.

Model input properties

Table 3.1 summarizes additional properties of the input form for linear programming models. Because it violates the first property, $0.3I + 0.2M - 18000 \leq 0$ is not correct input. You must transpose the -18000 constant to the right of the relationship. Because it violates the second property, $0.3I \leq -0.2M + 18000$ is not correct input. All variables must appear to the left of the relationship. Because it violates the third property, $5x - 2x + y$ is an incorrect objective function. You should combine terms and rewrite the objective function as $3x + y$.

The values of the decision variables may not be restricted by strict inequalities. Remember, a number is **positive** if it is greater than 0 (> 0).

TABLE 3.1   Properties of Linear Programming Model Input

1. No constant term can appear to the left of a constraint relationship.
2. No variable can appear to the right of a constraint relationship.
3. No variable can appear more than once in any function—objective or constraint.

Zero is not a positive number. A variable cannot be restricted to only positive values for the same reason that strict inequality relationships are not permitted.

In Chapters 3 through 7, we discuss the use and interpretation of linear programming models. The methodology for solving these models is well developed, and computer software is readily available. Models with thousands of constraints and tens of thousands of variables are often solved. In Chapter 2, we described how Owens-Corning used a linear programming model with 10,000 variables and 10,000 constraints to schedule production at its Anderson, South Carolina plant. Linear programming is the most commonly used method of analysis for deterministic decision environments. All parameters, including those in the objective function (c_j), RHS constants (b_i), and constraint coefficients (a_{ij}), are assumed to be known. Any uncertainty, which must be minimal and not the major driving force in the decision environment, must be considered by using sensitivity analysis.

Nonlinear functions

Integer variables

If possible, reformulate to eliminate non-linearities

If any of the functions (objective or constraint) is not linear, the result is a **nonlinear programming model.** If any of the decision variables is restricted to only integer values and the functions are all linear, the result is an **integer (linear) programming model.** In Chapter 9, we discuss nonlinear and integer linear programming models. For both nonlinear and integer linear programming models, the solution methodologies are well developed. Although computer software is available for linear programming models, it is less common for integer linear programming models and often not available to students for nonlinear programming models. The trend in computer software for constrained optimization models is toward powerful, easy-to-use microcomputer software. Even so, more computer time is required to solve nonlinear programming models and integer linear programming models than linear programming models. If possible, you should reformulate nonlinear programming models to linear programming models to make solution and analysis easier. Chapter 7 describes one such reformulation to a linear programming model, and Chapter 9 describes reformulations of nonlinear programming models to integer linear programming models. Remember, the model is constructed to help you analyze the decision environment. If the model is too difficult or unwieldy to create, solve, and maintain, it is not useful.

FORMULATING LINEAR PROGRAMMING MODELS

Formulating models is (at least in part) an art. A model that solves the wrong problem may be worse than no model at all. A skilled model builder cannot build a good model unless the decision environment is well understood. Even with a complete understanding of the decision environment, model building is difficult.

In Chapter 2, we described the concerns of the model builder as problem definition, model development, and validation. Model formulation is the second step, model development. For the subset of the decision environment to be analyzed, we formulate a model incorporating those factors that we judge to be important.

Our goal in the following discussion of model building is twofold—to introduce classical applications that have proved useful in practice and to improve your ability to formulate a model in a nonclassical application by developing model-building skills.

Perhaps the most common error in building models is trying to write the symbolic representation of the model before preliminary definitions have been formalized. We recommend that three distinct steps be used to get the model's symbolic representation.

The three steps for formulating linear programming models

First, construct a verbal model. If you cannot put your objective or constraints into words, you certainly cannot do it symbolically.

Second, list each decision you need to make and associate a symbol with that decision. Each decision is a number measured in explicit units (e.g., pounds, hours). Thus, M, representing Michigan potatoes, is inadequately defined. However, M, representing the number of pounds of Michigan potatoes to be purchased next month, is adequately defined.

Third, write the symbolic representation of the model. The objective function is often the most difficult to express symbolically, and you may need to introduce more variables and constraints in order to do this. You may want to construct the objective function after you have developed the constraints.

Figure 3.1 contains a flowchart summarizing the three-step model

---

FIGURE 3.1 Flowchart of the Linear Programming Model Formulation Process

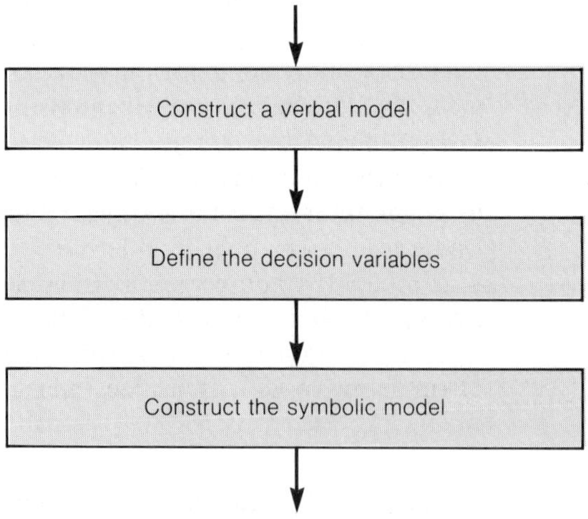

formulation process. You should use the three-step process to formulate linear programming models.

Let's expand on the proper form of the verbal model. Each constraint of the verbal model must be in the form.

Proper form for a ver-
bal constraint

{a verbal description of the LHS} {a relationship} {an RHS constant}

The units of the LHS verbal description must be the same as the units of the RHS constant. For example, if the units of the RHS constant are pounds of french fries, the verbal description must begin with "the number of pounds of french fries." If you express the constraints in the proper verbal form, expressing them symbolically is easier. The relationships and the RHS constants are identical for the verbal model and the symbolic model. The symbolic representation of the constraint is completed when you determine how to express the LHS symbolically.

In the remaining sections of this chapter, we will use this three-step procedure in formulating a number of classical applications. But you should constantly question why a certain part of the decision environment was chosen for modeling. Are there other important considerations that were not included? Why was this time horizon chosen? And if the model is for a single-period model, should it be made into a multiple-period model?

THE PRODUCT MIX MODEL

A company is concerned with the amounts of its products that it should make. Each of those products consumes resources that are in short supply. These resources may include time on various machines or raw materials. In the past, certain resources have been bottlenecks. The company has attempted to cope with this problem by altering the mix of products so as to schedule fewer products that are large consumers of the bottleneck resources and more products that are smaller consumers of those resources.

How the company should alter the mix of products so that optimal decisions are made is the **product mix** problem. Many companies face this problem. For example, Ponderosa International[3] uses a linear programming model to choose the mix of plywood products that it should make, given its potential sales and limited manufacturing capacity.

As an example, let's consider the Sound-Design Company, which makes three types of portable radios—AM, AM/FM, and AM/FM/CB.

---

[3] Asim Roy, E. E. De Falomir, and Leon Lasdon, "An Optimization-Based Decision Support System for a Product Mix Problem," *Interfaces* 12, no. 2 (April 1982), pp. 26–33.

TABLE 3.2 Minutes Required per Radio

| | Radio | | |
Operation	AM	AM/FM	AM/FM/CB
Component assembly	11	12	15
Final assembly	15	15	16
Inspection and packaging	4	6	9

Each radio requires time in two work areas—component assembly and final assembly. Also, an inspector gives each radio a final inspection and then boxes it. The time required for one radio is shown in Table 3.2.

The current plan is to operate the component assembly work area for two shifts, for a total of 80 hours each week. The final assembly work area is also available for 80 hours each week. The inspection and packaging operation is available for only 40 hours each week. Let's convert the hours available per week to minutes. The number of minutes per week available for the component assembly operation, the final assembly operation, and the inspection and packaging operation are 4,800, 4,800, and 2,400, respectively. We will discuss the reason for the conversion to minutes later.

The restrictions imposed by the limited times available are apparent (conceptually, if not mathematically). However, what is the objective? For profit-making organizations, the most common primary objective is economic—profit maximization or cost minimization. Along with eco-
Economic objectives
nomic objectives, other objectives may be of concern. For example, using most of the available hours in the two work areas and in the inspection and packaging operation may be desirable. Remember, linear programming models have only one objective function. Because the model is used to analyze the decision environment, secondary objectives as well as qualitative factors should be considered by you, the decision maker, after the model has been developed and solved.

In general, the preferred economic objective is profit maximization. Are profit maximization and cost minimization equivalent? Profits are revenues minus costs. *If revenues are fixed, then the objectives of max-*
Fixed revenues: cost minimization equivalent to profit maximization
imizing profits and minimizing costs are equivalent. In this example, since we are deciding what amounts of the various radios to produce, the total revenues are not fixed and profit maximization and cost minimization are *not* equivalent. The profit margins for AM, AM/FM, and AM/FM/CB radios are $10, $12, and $15, respectively. The objective function chosen is profit maximization. Do you see the result of selecting cost

minimization? With the lowest-cost plan, nothing is produced. This does not provide the decision maker with any useful information on the best product mix.

We will use the three-step approach to formulate the linear programming model. First, the verbal model is required.

Verbal Model

maximize total profit per week

subject to number of minutes used in component assembly per week ≤4800

number of minutes used in final assembly per week ≤4800

number of minutes used in inspection and packaging per week ≤2400

Keep the units the same

Note that the unit of time, minutes, was specified in the verbal LHS description of the constraints. Minutes is the unit of the RHS constant, so minutes must be compared to it.

Decision Variables

One possible decision is to stop making the AM radio. However, even if we knew that dropping the AM radio was best, we still would not know the amounts of the other two radios. The decision must specify the number of each of the radios made. If the best number of AM radios made is 0, we should consider dropping the AM radio from the product line.

Symbolically, the decisions are represented as

A—number of AM radios made per week

F—number of AM/FM radios made per week

C—number of AM/FM/CB radios made per week

Symbolic Model

If there are A AM radios made, the profit is $10A$ dollars. Adding the profit for the three types of radios, the total profit would be $10A + 12F + 15C$. If there are A AM radios made, $11A$ *minutes* of component assembly time are required. Since all three varieties of radios share the 4,800 minutes of component assembly time, the resulting constraint is

$$11A + 12F + 15C \leq 4800$$

The complete symbolic model is

max $10A + 12F + 15C$
st $11A + 12F + 15C \leq 4800$
       $15A + 15F + 16C \leq 4800$
       $4A + 6F + 9C \leq 2400$
       $A, F, C \geq 0$

This is a linear programming model. The last line of the symbolic model indicates that the three decision variables must be 0 or greater. A negative number of AM radios cannot be made; thus, nonnegativity is imposed on the decision variable A. These are restrictions on the variables, not constraints. The method for finding the optimal solution for linear programming models makes this distinction and treats nonnegative variable restrictions differently from the constraints. This is not true of all the solution methods for other types of constrained optimization models.

Changing the time units

Let's return to the issue of time units, minutes or hours. How would the model have changed if the RHS constant of the component assembly time constraint had been 80 hours instead of 4,800 minutes? If A AM radios are made, 11A minutes or $^{11}\!/_{60}A$ hours are required. The component assembly constraint would have been written as

$$\frac{11}{60}A + \frac{12}{60}F + \frac{15}{60}C \leq 80$$

Minutes are compared to minutes, and hours are compared to hours. Do not mix the units!

Input rounding considerations

Most linear programming software does not allow ratios as inputs. Therefore, each ratio must be divided to yield a decimal number. For example, $^{15}\!/_{60} = 0.25$. Unfortunately, some of the ratios do not divide evenly. For example, $^{11}\!/_{60} = 0.18333\ldots$. The 3 repeats forever, but we must stop or truncate the repeating value and round so that we can input the model to the linear programming software. Truncating at four decimal places, the symbolic model is

max $10A + 12F + 15C$
st $0.1833A + 0.2F + 0.25C \leq 80$
       $0.25A + 0.25F + 0.2667C \leq 80$
       $0.0667A + 0.1F + 0.15C \leq 40$
       $A, F, C \geq 0$

Because accuracy is lost in truncating the repeating decimals, we prefer the symbolic model using minutes. That is why the RHS constants were converted to minutes.

Does the model capture the important considerations of the decision environment? If the optimal solution indicated that AM/FM/CB radios should be made, what do you do with a value that is not an integer? You might insist that the optimal solution be restricted to integer values.[4] Remember, an integer linear programming model is a linear programming model in which at least one variable is restricted to integer values. The solution methods and computer software for linear programming models are different from those for integer linear programming models. In general, integer-restricted models are more difficult to solve than models with continuous variables. Since the model is designed only to aid the decision maker, obtaining a noninteger solution may not be a major problem. For the linear programming model, the solution obtained by rounding the number of AM/FM/CB radios from 184.67 down to 184 is not likely to be far from the optimal solution to the integer-restricted problem. Rounding the values of noninteger variables is often a reasonable approach. However, you must use caution when rounding variable values. If the number of AM/FM/CB radios is rounded up, you may exceed the time available for one of the operations.

Should a variable be restricted to integer values? In Chapter 9, we discuss integer-restricted variables and illustrate that rounding is not always reasonable. For example, a decision model can be formulated to decide whether to build a plant. Let $Y = 1$ correspond to building the plant, and let $Y = 0$ correspond to not building the plant. If Y is not restricted to integer values and $Y = 0.43$ is obtained from the linear programming model, should the plant be built? Rounding up corresponds to building the plant, and rounding down corresponds to not building the plant. In this case, rounding isn't reasonable. Building a plant is too important to be decided by rounding. Ultimately, you must decide whether to restrict the variables to integer values, based on the availability of computer software and resources and on the usefulness of the model results without the integer restrictions.

THE MACHINE ASSIGNMENT MODEL

Consider a company that makes several products on different facilities at its only manufacturing plant. These facilities have a variety of operating costs and manufacturing rates based on their design characteristics and their ages, and they could be machines, groups of machines, open-hearth furnaces for steelmaking, or any other types of facilities. How should the products be assigned to the facilities? Intuitively, each product should be

---

[4] Actually, you can consider a fractional value for the product mix model as work in process that is completed the following week.

TABLE 3.3   Cups Produced per Hour

Machine	Cup		
	A	B	C
1	25	18	22
2	26	19	23
3	23	20	20

assigned to the facility that is most effective for it. However, if there is not enough capacity in every facility for the resulting assignments, adjustments must be made.

Machine assignment models are an important class of models that are used to help solve decision problems of this type. Many companies face such decision problems. For example, S. C. Bhatnagar[5] shows how a linear programming model is used to assign different fabrics to textile looms. The model has 280 constraints and 1,200 variables.

The Drillem Company makes three styles, A, B, and C, of specialized metal cups. These cups can be made on three machines. After examining the numbers of cups on hand and the outstanding orders for cups, we have determined that next week's production requirements for Cups A, B, and C are 1,000, 950, and 600, respectively. The current plans are to have each machine available for 40 hours next week. The number of cups produced by each machine per hour of operation is given in Table 3.3.

Table 3.4 gives the operating cost for each hour that each machine is assigned to a particular cup. Note that Table 3.4's operating costs are small. The operating cost should not include any fixed costs. Fixed costs are "costs that remain the same in total regardless of changes in the activity level."[6] Depreciation of a factory building is an example of a fixed cost that shouldn't be included. *Be wary of accounting cost data because it might include fixed costs.*

Don't include fixed costs

Verbal Model

Fixed revenue

It is necessary to produce the exact number required of each cup. This means that the total revenue is fixed and that maximizing profit and

[5] S. C. Bhatnagar, "Implementing Linear Programming in a Textile Unit: Some Problems and a Solution," *Interfaces* 11, no. 2 (April 1981), pp. 87–91.

[6] J. J. Weygandt, D. E. Kieso, and W. G. Kell, *Accounting Principles* (New York: John Wiley & Sons, 1987), p. B5.

TABLE 3.4 Operating Cost ($ per hour)

Machine	Cup		
	A	B	C
1	0.32	0.29	0.32
2	0.35	0.25	0.34
3	0.36	0.34	0.36

minimizing cost are equivalent. Let's arbitrarily select cost minimization as the objective function. We assume that it is reasonable to divide a product's manufacturing requirement between more than one machine.

minimize   total operating cost for next week
subject to   hours used on Machine 1 next week $\leq$ 40
hours used on Machine 2 next week $\leq$ 40
hours used on Machine 3 next week $\leq$ 40
number of units produced next week of Cup A $=$ 1000
number of units produced next week of Cup B $=$ 950
number of units produced next week of Cup C $=$ 600

Decision Variables

The important issue is the association of cups with machines. What is the definition for the units of the decision variables? One possibility is the number of *hours* a particular machine is assigned to a particular product. Let A_1 represent the number of hours Cup A is made on Machine 1. The variables for Cup A are defined as follows:

A_1—number of hours Cup A is made on Machine 1
A_2—number of hours Cup A is made on Machine 2
A_3—number of hours Cup A is made on Machine 3.

Similarly, the other six decision variables could be represented as B_1, B_2, B_3, C_1, C_2, and C_3.

An example of another possible definition of the decision variables is the number of Cup A produced on Machine 1, represented by a_1. In this case, if a_1 equals 400, then $^{400}\!/_{25}$ or 16 hours would be required to produce those cups.

Different variable units give different models

We will adopt the first definition of the decision variables. The development of the symbolic model for the second definition is left to the exercises.

Symbolic Model

Because \$0.32 is the operating cost per hour that Machine 1 is assigned to Cup A, the cost for that assignment would be $0.32A_1$. How would this have changed if the second possible definition of the decision variables had been adopted?

The requirements for Cup A can be made on any of the three machines. The number of A cups produced in A_1 hours on Machine 1 is $25A_1$. The total number of A cups made on all three machines is $25A_1 + 26A_2 + 23A_3$. The 40 hours available on each machine can be shared among the products.

The complete symbolic model is

$$
\begin{aligned}
\text{min} \quad & 0.32A_1 + 0.35A_2 + 0.36A_3 + 0.29B_1 + 0.25B_2 + 0.34B_3 \\
& + 0.32C_1 + 0.34C_2 + 0.36C_3 \\
\text{st} \quad & A_1 + B_1 + C_1 \leq 40 \\
& A_2 + B_2 + C_2 \leq 40 \\
& A_3 + B_3 + C_3 \leq 40 \\
& 25A_1 + 26A_2 + 23A_3 = 1000 \\
& 18B_1 + 19B_2 + 20B_3 = 950 \\
& 22C_1 + 23C_2 + 20C_3 = 600 \\
& A_1, A_2, A_3, B_1, B_2, B_3, C_1, C_2, C_3 \geq 0
\end{aligned}
$$

If the production rate information had been in minutes required for each unit produced rather than units produced per hour, how would the model change? The operating costs are sometimes on a per unit basis rather than the per hour basis shown in Table 3.4. How would this change the symbolic model?

BLENDING MODELS

Historically, blending models were among the first models solved by linear programming methods, and they continue to be an important class of linear programming models. For example, feed grains are blended to meet dietary requirements and chemicals are blended to obtain specific chemical and physical properties. In this section, we discuss blending a single finished product.

Two blending environ-
ments

Two blending environments are possible—one at a strategic level and the other at an operational level. At the strategic level, the issue is choosing the best proportion of various blending stocks for a standard unit. For example, what is the best way to mix feed grains for a 100-pound sack that satisfies minimal nutritional specifications? Generally, in the strategic-level blending model, the available amounts of each blending stock are limitless.

The goal at the operational level is to determine the blending plan for an order of the finished product from the limited amounts of the available blending stocks. A feed mix example would determine how to blend 1,000 100-pound sacks of feed from the amounts of the feed grains currently on hand.

First, we illustrate the **standard unit blending formulation,** or the strategic formulation, by blending feed grain. Second, we illustrate the **operational blending formulation** by blending gasoline.

Standard Unit Blending Model

Chicken feed is sold in 100-pound sacks that contain a mixture of corn, wheat, and oats. However, the relative proportions of these grains are influenced by the specification that each 100-pound sack include at least 30 percent protein by weight (or 30 pounds of protein), a maximum of 10 percent water, and a 15 percent minimum for carbohydrates. What amounts of each grain should be in the 100-pound sack, given the current cost of each?

The relative percentages of interest for each grain are given in Table 3.5. The percentages given for corn total 57 percent, not 100 percent. This is because corn contains other components that are not of interest in the quality specifications. The costs per pound are $0.085, $0.08, and $0.09 for corn, wheat, and oats, respectively.

Verbal model. The selling price of the standard unit, a 100-pound sack, is unaffected by the decisions being modeled. Since the revenue is fixed, cost minimization is a reasonable objective.

Fixed revenues

TABLE 3.5 Percentages of Nutritional Components by Weight

Nutritional Component	Grain		
	Corn	Wheat	Oats
Water	7	9	12
Protein	32	27	39
Carbohydrate	18	7	18

minimize   cost of a 100-pound sack
subject to   pounds of water in sack $\leq$ 10
                pounds of protein in sack $\geq$ 30
                pounds of carbohydrate in sack $\geq$ 15
                weight of sack in pounds = 100

We have calculated the RHS constants as pounds, so the units of the LHS must also be pounds. Remember, pounds must be compared to pounds!

Decision variables. The decisions include the amounts of each grain in the chicken feed mixture. The logical definition of the variables is the number of pounds of each grain (in the standard 100-pound sack). This results in variables defined and represented symbolically as

C—number of pounds of corn in the mixture

W—number of pounds of wheat in the mixture

O—number of pounds of oats in the mixture

What units other than pounds could be used? An alternative is discussed after the symbolic model has been developed.

Symbolic model. If C is the number of pounds of corn in the mixture, then $0.085C$ is the cost of the corn in the mixture. The total cost of the mixture is $0.085C + 0.08W + 0.09O$. Because corn is 7 percent water, the weight of water from corn is $0.07C$. The total weight of water in the mixture is $0.07C + 0.09W + 0.12O$.

The complete symbolic model is

min $0.085C + 0.08W + 0.09O$
st $0.07C + 0.09W + 0.12O \leq 10$
          $0.032C + 0.27W + 0.39O \geq 30$
          $0.18C + 0.07W + 0.18O \geq 15$
          $C + W + O = 100$
          $C, W, O \geq 0$

The last constraint is needed so that the weight of the sack is 100 pounds. If the constraint were not included, then the Department of Weights and Measures (or some other agency) would question the chicken feed supplier. The chicken feed supplier may be able to add filler so that the weight of the sack totals 100 pounds. Then, you must define a variable representing the amount of filler and include its cost in the objective function and any contributions of water, protein, and carbohydrate in the constraints. *The omission of the standard unit amount constraint is a common error in this type of blending model.*

Why was the objective function cost minimization? Would it be better to maximize the profit? Since the standard unit must weigh 100 pounds,

Don't omit the standard unit amount constraint

the revenue is fixed and the two objectives are equivalent. If you use profit maximization, you get the same decisions. The objective function coefficients for the grain variables should include the cost of transporting the grains to the bagging operation. No cost has been included for the bagging operation or the bag. We have assumed that these costs are independent of the relative proportions of the grains. If not, the objective function should include these costs, as well as the delivered cost of the grains. Any costs influenced by the decisions should be included in the decision model. Cost accountants refer to these costs as the **relevant costs.**

Consider relevant costs

Another model results from defining the decision variables as fractions of the 100-pound sack. A correct formulation of the example with the redefined variables, *c, w,* and *o,* where each symbol represents a fraction of a 100-pound sack, is left to the chapter exercises.

A different variable definition

Usually, blending models are used for mixing blending components into a finished product so that quality specifications are satisfied. However, such models have other applications. For example, Chandy and Kharabe[7] use a linear programming model to optimize Treasury security portfolios. The decision variables are the proportion of each security in the portfolio, and the objective is to maximize the portfolio yield. Each security has constraints for its minimum and maximum proportion. Chandy and Kharabe estimate the risk for each security, and the "quality" constraint imposes a limit on the portfolio risk.

Operational Blending Model

An operational formulation for a specific order is illustrated by an example of an oil company that wants to blend regular gasoline from the blending stocks contained in storage tanks. The three blending stocks are called butane, naphtha, and reformate, and 22,000, 10,000, and 14,000 barrels of each, respectively, are on hand. The two major quality specifications are octane number and vapor pressure. For regular gasoline, the minimum octane number is 87 and the maximum vapor pressure is 6.5 pounds per square inch (psi). The quality characteristics of the tanks' contents are shown in Table 3.6.

A cut-rate gasoline supplier has offered to purchase as much as 30,000 barrels of regular gasoline for $1.20 per gallon. How much should you sell to the supplier, and how would you blend the order to meet the desired quality specifications? What other information do you require to make a decision? You also need to know that the costs per barrel of butane, naphtha, and reformate are $36, $48, and $51, respectively.

---

[7] P. R. Chandy and Prakash Kharabe, "Pricing in the Government Bond Market," *Interfaces* 16, no. 5 (September–October 1986), pp. 65–71.

TABLE 3.6   Data for Gasoline Blending Example

	Butane	Naphtha	Reformate
	Tank Contents		
Barrels	22,000	10,000	14,000
Octane number	85.0	89.0	92.0
Vapor pressure	3.0	8.7	11.0
Cost, $/barrel	36.00	48.00	51.00
Regular gasoline requested			
Barrels (up to)	30,000		
Octane number	87.0		
Vapor pressure	6.5		
Price, $/gallon	1.20		

Verbal model. If you decide to provide the maximum order size of 30,000 barrels, then the revenue is fixed and minimizing cost is equivalent to maximizing profit. However, if the amount you decide to provide is less than the maximum, then the revenue is not fixed and the objective is to maximize profit. Because you must decide how much to blend, maximizing profit is the correct objective function.

The resulting verbal model is

maximize   profit on the order
subject to number of barrels of butane used $\leq$ 22000
            number of barrels of naphtha used $\leq$ 10000
            number of barrels of reformate used $\leq$ 14000
            total barrels blended $\leq$ 30000
            octane number of the blend $\geq$ 87
            vapor pressure of the blend $\leq$ 6.5

Other blending problems have similar constraints

Since the classes of constraints are associated with the availability of the blending stocks, the total amounts blended, and quality specifications, these classes of constraints are also appropriate for blending animal feed, steel scrap, or chemicals.

Decision variables. The required decisions are the amounts to be used in the regular gasoline blend of each of the three blending stocks. The decision variables could be defined as either barrels or gallons. Note that both units were used in the problem description. We arbitrarily choose barrels for the units, resulting in the following definitions:

B—number of barrels of butane blended into regular gasoline

N—number of barrels of naphtha blended into regular gasoline

R—number of barrels of reformate blended into regular gasoline

This set of decision variables is sufficient. Are there any other variables to be defined? After we develop the symbolic model based on these variables, we'll revisit this question.

Symbolic model. The profit is revenue minus cost. The revenues are $1.20 per *gallon* of regular gasoline. The costs of the blending stocks are per *barrel*. It is required that the conversion factor between gallons and barrels be known. In the petroleum industry, one barrel is 42 gallons. Therefore, the revenue per barrel of regular gasoline is $1.20 $\times$ 42 = $50.40.

For previous models, you have accepted without question that like items add linearly. For example, hours on Machine 1 making Cup A added linearly with hours on Machine 1 making Cup B. That seems obvious. But if you mix one barrel of butane with one barrel of naphtha, do you obtain two barrels? This seems probable, but before assuming that it is true, you should question it. What would be the octane number of the resulting mixture of butane and naphtha? Again, this requires investigation.

After consulting your chemical engineer, you are told that in *this* blending problem the qualities of interest—volume, octane number, and vapor pressure—interact proportionally. The result of blending one barrel of butane with an octane number of 85 and one barrel of naphtha with an octane number of 89 is two barrels with an octane number of 87. Because there are equal amounts of butane and naphtha, the octane number is the average. The octane number and the vapor pressure vary linearly with the proportions of the blending stocks.

The total volume in barrels is $B + N + R$ and the revenue is 50.40 $\times$ $(B + N + R)$. The costs of the blending stocks are $36B + 48N + 51R$. The profit is $50.40B + 50.40N + 50.40R - (36B + 48N + 51R)$. After we perform the algebraic manipulation so that each variable is multiplied by only one constant, the objective function is $14.40B + 2.40N - 0.60R$. The constraints imposed by the limited tank contents of the blending stocks are apparent (e.g., $B \leq 22000$). The RHS constant is barrels for the constraint on the total volume of the blend for the order, so the LHS should also be barrels. Because the volumes add linearly, the constraint becomes

$$B + N + R \leq 30000$$

The octane number and vapor pressure quality constraints are not obvious. If one barrel of butane and one barrel of naphtha result in two barrels with an octane number of 87, the octane number is the average. The octane number is calculated as a weighted average based on the proportion of each of the blending stocks. For example, the weight for the octane number of butane (85) is

$$\frac{B}{B + N + R}$$

(margin note:) Check the linearity

which is the volume fraction of the blend composed of butane. The octane number constraint is

$$\frac{85B + 89N + 92R}{B + N + R} \geq 87$$

The octane number constraint is a bona fide constraint, but it is not in the form of a linear constraint. Note that $B + N + R$ must be nonnegative because each variable value must be nonnegative. Therefore, the constraint can be multiplied by $(B + N + R)$ (as long as $B + N + R > 0$) without affecting the direction of the inequality. The constraint can then be rewritten as

$$85B + 89N + 92R \geq 87(B + N + R)$$

Since there are still variables to the right of the relationship, they must be transposed to the left of the relationship and combined, yielding the following linear constraint:

$$-2B + 2N + 5R \geq 0$$

The coefficient of the B variable is the octane number of butane relative to the quality specification; its octane number is 2 *less* than the specification. A similar manipulation is required to express the vapor pressure constraint as a linear constraint.

The complete linear programming symbolic model is

max $14.40B + 2.40N - 0.60R$
st $B \leq 22000$
         $N \leq 10000$
         $R \leq 14000$
         $B + N + R \leq 30000$
         $-2B + 2N + 5R \geq 0$
         $-3.5B + 2.2N + 4.5R \leq 0$
         $B, N, R \geq 0$

Because the objective function and all constraint functions are linear, this is a linear programming model.

The Impact of Linear Programming Model Formulation on Sensitivity Analysis

In Chapter 5, we discuss the interpretation of computer output for linear programming models. One point made is the *ease of analysis if only one constant of the model changes at a time*. If the cut-rate supplier suggests increasing the order size to 31,000 barrels, only one parameter changes— the RHS constant 30,000 becomes 31,000. You might be able to determine the impact of that change without re-solving the changed problem!

If the price the cut-rate supplier offers is $1.21 per gallon rather than $1.20 per gallon, what constant or constants change in the symbolic model? The constraints are not affected, but the objective function is. The profit margin per barrel of butane blended into regular gasoline increases to $1.21(42) − $36, or $14.82. That is an increase of $0.42. At the same time, the profit margins of naphtha and reformate also increase by $0.42. When only the price changes, three constants in the symbolic model change. This is more difficult to analyze.

Reconsider the specified decision variables. Along with B, N, and R, define G as the number of barrels of regular gasoline blended. G is an example of an **intermediate variable,** one that is not required in the model but is added for convenience. Since an intermediate variable often defines the value of an intermediate result, it is sometimes called a **definitional variable.** The variable G defines the amount of regular gasoline blended. Say that you did not define G and you obtained the optimal solution to the linear programming model. To calculate the total amount blended, you would have to add the optimal values of B, N, and R. If G is defined, the total amount blended appears in the solution output. Let's consider the impact of including G in the objective function. The symbolic representation could then be rewritten as $50.40G - 36B - 48N - 51R$.

The complete symbolic model becomes

$$
\begin{aligned}
\max \quad & 50.40G - 36B - 48N - 51R \\
\text{st} \quad & B \leq 22000 \\
& N \leq 10000 \\
& R \leq 14000 \\
& B + N + R - G = 0 \\
& G \leq 30000 \\
& -2B + 2N + 5R \geq 0 \\
& -3.5B + 2.2N + 4.5R \leq 0 \\
& G, B, N, R \geq 0
\end{aligned}
$$

If the price per gallon increases to $1.21, then the coefficient of G

Model structure affects ease of sensitivity analysis

becomes 50.82. Only one constant changes for this formulation. *When the model is formulated, you should consider the types of sensitivity analysis to be done.* The particular model formulation chosen by the model builder will have its own characteristics for the ease of sensitivity analysis.

A **definitional constraint** is required to define any intermediate variable introduced. The fourth constraint—a definitional constraint defining the relationship between the barrels of the blending stocks used and the resulting barrels of regular gasoline—is required. Note that the gasoline variable was transposed to the left of the relationship. *A common for-*

Don't omit the definitional constraint

mulation error is the omission of definitional constraints. If the definitional constraint were omitted, what would be the optimal solution to the above symbolic model? (*Hint:* Do the other constraints imply that you have to blend anything for *G* to be positive?) If the definitional constraint were omitted, the optimal decision would blend 30,000 barrels of regular gasoline, so that the revenue would be obtained without using any of the costly blending stocks. Check to see that values of 0 for *B, N,* and *R* and a value of 30,000 for *G* satisfy all of the constraints. This is not a realistic plan since you cannot have regular gasoline unless the blending stocks are used. The reason for this unrealistic solution is that the definitional constraint has been eliminated. The definitional constraint must be included for a realistic solution!

SUMMARY

A constrained optimization model has a single objective function to be maximized or minimized, subject to algebraic constraints. If the objective function and the constraint functions are all linear and the variables are continuous, the model is a linear programming model. Nonlinear programming models and integer linear programming models are other types of constrained optimization models.

The three-step model formulation process was described and used for three types of linear programming models—product mix, machine assignment, and blending. Given limited resources, the product mix problem determines what amounts of products should be made so as to maximize profit. The machine assignment problem determines the amounts of products made on different facilities to satisfy requirements at minimum cost.

Two types of blending problems were formulated—the standard unit formulation and the operational blending formulation. The first formulation type assumes that unlimited blending stocks are available and blends them into a standard unit that satisfies quality specifications at minimum cost. The operational blending formulation determines how *much* and how *to* blend from limited blending stocks to maximize the profit on the order.

The three types of linear programming models developed are examples of useful applications. We've discussed how Air Products, Owens-Corning, and CCBT use linear programming. In this chapter, we also referred to actual applications of product mix, machine assignment, and blending models. After graphical solutions and computer solutions are described in Chapters 4 and 5, additional examples are developed in Chapter 7. In that chapter, the discussion of model formulation, computer solution, model validation, and the role of models and sensitivity analysis in decision making will "close the loop" and provide additional understanding.

The reformulation of the gasoline blending example to include the variable *G* illustrated that the formulation *you choose* affects the ease of sensitivity analysis for linear programming models. Often, introducing definitional variables makes the model output more useful and results in simple-sensitivity analysis.

You should keep in mind some cautions introduced in this chapter. First, before you choose cost minimization rather than profit maximization as the objective function, check whether the revenue is fixed. Second, the units of a constraint's LHS must be the same as the units of its RHS. Also, remember to specify the units on the decision variables before you try the symbolic model. Two possible variable definitions were given for both the machine assignment example and the standard unit blending example. Lastly, two common formulation errors are failure to include the standard unit amount constraint for blending models and failure to include definitional constraints when definitional variables are introduced.

Because of software availability and efficiency, it is more convenient to work with linear programming models than with other mathematical programming models. Nonlinear programming models and integer linear programming models are more difficult to solve and analyze. The algebraic manipulations of the octane number constraint for the gasoline blending example changed a nonlinear constraint to a linear constraint. If a model you formulate has a nonlinear function, try to manipulate it algebraically to eliminate the nonlinearity.

Linear programming models assume that the functions are all linear and that the variables are continuous. These are restrictive assumptions. A linear programming model is preferred, but it must not misrepresent the decision environment. You must check whether the functions are all linear. For example, it was necessary to check whether the blending stocks of the gasoline example interact linearly. You should also check whether any of the variables should be restricted to integer values. It is probably reasonable to treat the decision variables for the product mix example as if they are continuous and then to round the variable values to integers. However, for the plant location variable ($Y = 1$: build the plant; $Y = 0$: do not build the plant), treating the variable as continuous and rounding is not reasonable.

QUESTIONS

1. Which of the following are linear functions? (Each letter represents a decision variable.)

    a. $2A + 3B - 6C$

    b. $2AB - C$

    c. $A + B$

    d. $(\frac{1}{3})A + 6B$

    e. $\log(2x) + 4y$

    f. $4x^2 - 3y$

2. Which of the following are linear objective functions?
   a. maximize $A + B$
   b. minimize $3.25A + 3.10B$
   c. maximize $(A + 2)/(B + 1)$
   d. max $\{\min[(2A + B), (3A + 4B)]\}$
   e. max $(\frac{1}{3})X + (\frac{2}{3})Y$
   f. min $x^2 + y^2$

3. What is the RHS constant of each of these constraints?
   a. $XY \leq 10$
   b. $2X + 3Y \geq -5$
   c. $4X + 2Y = I - 100$
   d. $4X - 3Y - 10 = 0$
   e. $x(1/y) + 4 \leq 17$

4. Give the contraint functions of each of the constraints of Question 3.

5. Which of the constraint functions of Question 3 are linear constraints?

6. What are the similarities and differences between a linear programming model and an integer linear programming model?

7. What are the similarities and differences between a linear programming model and a nonlinear programming model?

8. Explain why the operating costs for the machine assignment example could be so small. What costs might be included? What costs might be excluded?

9. What is a relevant cost? What is a fixed cost?

10. What is an objective function?

11. What is a continuous variable?

12. What is the difference between LINDO input and the linear programming symbolic model?

13. Give three properties of linear programming model input.

14. What is a constrained optimization model?

15. What is an intermediate variable?

16. Discuss whether there can be more than one correct way to formulate a linear programming model.

17. Why should you consider the types of sensitivity analysis you want to do before you finalize your model?

EXERCISES

For each model formulation exercise, the three-step process must be used.

1. *Product Mix Example.* The component assembly limitation of 80 hours was based on a union contract that prevented transferring workers between the component assembly line and the final assembly line. It was planned to have two groups of workers on each of the two assembly lines. Assume now that there is no other reason for the two separate constraints on available component assembly time and final assembly time and that there is enough capacity

at the assembly stations on the lines for as many as four groups of workers at a time. If the workers can be transferred between the two assembly lines at no additional cost and if the total labor-hours available for assembly operations stays at 160, give the new model formulation. Assume that transfer of workers between inspection/packaging and assembly is not allowed.

2. *Product Mix Example.* Give the new model formulation if the right-hand sides are all measured in eight-hour days.

3. *Product Mix Example.* Consider adding a new radio to the product line of the example. This new model will also play cassettes. The profit margin anticipated is $20. The component assembly time will be ½ hour per radio. The inspection/packaging time and the final assembly time will be 20 minutes and 15 minutes per radio, respectively. Give the revised model formulation.

4. *Product Mix Example.* Because of a contract with a major customer, at least 10 AM radios and 15 AM/FM radios must be produced. Give the revised model formulation.

5. *Product Mix Example.* The contract of Exercise 4 has been revised so that the minimum number of AM radios and AM/FM radios provided must be at least 25 in total. Give the revised model formulation.

6. *Product Mix Example.* All three of the radios in the example are built on the same chassis. It has been discovered that only 180 chassis will be available next week. Give the revised model formulation.

7. *Machine Assignment Example.* Give the alternative formulation of the machine assignment example if the decision variables are defined as the number of each type of cup produced on each machine.

8. *Machine Assignment Example.* How would the model formulation be affected if the maximum number of Cup A that could be produced and sold were 1,000? Remember that it was previously required that 1,000 be produced; now, up to 1,000 may be produced, but it is possible to produce fewer. Be careful of your answer.

9. *Machine Assignment Example.* A minimum of 100 Type A cups must be made on Machine 1. Give the revised model.

10. *Standard Unit Blending Example.* Give the alternative formulation of the Standard Unit Blending example if the decision variables are defined as fractions of the 100-pound sack.

11. *Standard Unit Blending Example.* If water in a sample of corn is actually 7.5 percent by weight, give the revised model.

12. *Standard Unit Blending Example.* If there is an additional limitation of at least 8.5 percent by weight of water in the 100-pound sack, give the revised model.

13. *Standard Unit Blending Example.* Consider packaging 50-pound sacks of chicken feed in the example. These sacks are easier to handle. Give a new model for the determination of the most economical blend of 50-pound sacks if all costs and quality specifications remain the same.

14. *Standard Unit Blending Example.* Your brother-in-law raises corn and would appreciate it if you would use at least 25 pounds of corn in each 100-pound sack. He is willing to meet the market price for corn of $0.085 per pound. How would the model have to be revised to reflect this request?

15. *Standard Unit Blending Example.* Virtually unlimited amounts of corn and oats are available for purchase at the indicated prices. Only 120,000 pounds of wheat is available for the next month's operation of the chicken feed blending company. There is a contract to provide 10,000 of the 100-pound sacks next month. Give the revised model.

16. *Operational Blending Example.* Give the alternative formulation of the operational blending example if the decision variables are defined as the number of gallons of each of the blending stocks blended into regular gasoline.

17. *Operational Blending Example.* Give the revised model if the selling price of regular gasoline increases to $1.25 per gallon.

18. *Operational Blending Example.* Give the revised model if the minimum octane number increases from 87 to 87.5.

19. *Operational Blending Example.* Give the revised model if exactly 30,000 barrels of regular gasoline must be blended from existing tank inventories.

20. *Operational Blending Example.* For Exercise 19, could the model be reformulated as a cost minimization model? Is there any advantage to such a reformulation? Give the revised model.

21. *Operational Blending Example.* For Exercise 19, the equality relationship $B + N + R = 30,000$ could be used to eliminate the denominator in the quality specification constraints before they are manipulated. This would eliminate the necessity for the manipulation, because the model would already be a linear programming model. Give this revised model. Can you see any advantages or disadvantages to this approach?

22. *Operational Blending Example.* If the cost of butane in the tank were $38 per barrel, what would be the revised model?

23. *Operational Blending Example.* Consider the formulation that explicitly defined the variable G, the number of barrels of regular gasoline blended. If the cost of butane in the tank were $38 per barrel, what would be the revised model?

24. *Operational Blending Example.* Consider the formulation that explicitly defined the variable G, the number of barrels of regular gasoline blended. If the selling price of regular gasoline increased to $1.25 per gallon, what would be the revised model?

MORE CHALLENGING EXERCISES

For each model formulation exercise, the three-step process must be used.

1. A company makes wooden tables in several varieties. One of these varieties is a round kitchen table. This table is also offered with two leaves, which makes it appropriate for dining rooms. Sales of both of these tables have been excellent. In fact, there is more demand for both of them than can be met with the existing manufacturing capacity. There is a higher profit margin on the table with leaves, but this table requires more time on the planer machine,

which has been used to its capacity. It is desired to determine whether the higher profit margin is enough to justify the current manufacturing strategy of making the table with leaves almost exclusively. The profit margins are $43 for the round table and $49 for the round table with leaves. The manufacturing operations require time on a lathe to make the legs, time on the planer to make the top and leaves, and some hand-finishing time. The times required in hours per table are

| | Machine | | Hand |
Table	Lathe	Planer	Finishing
Round	0.15	0.13	0.25
Round with leaves	0.15	0.18	0.30

The shop works 7 days a week and 24 hours a day. There are 2 people who work each shift to do the hand finishing. Formulate a linear programming model to determine the best product mix.

2. A foundry makes four basic products. Each of these requires that a mold be formed and molten metal poured into it. The amount of metal in each of the four basic molds is 1 ton. The foundry's capacity is enough to melt 15 tons during each work week. After each mold has been formed and poured, the casting is removed. As the casting is removed, the mold is destroyed. Because of different complexities of the four basic products, the time required to form the different types of molds varies significantly. The four basic products are $L1$, $L2$, $L3$, and $L4$. The number of molds of each type that can be formed per hour are 0.5, $\frac{1}{3}$, 0.8, and 0.4, respectively. The cleanup and pouring require about 10 hours per week. The company works one shift, an 8-hour day. Because of a contractual obligation, it is necessary to produce a total of at least 10 of $L1$ and $L2$. The profit margins are $1,000, $1,950, $1,225, and $2,450 for $L1$, $L2$, $L3$, and $L4$, respectively.

   a. One possibility is that the cleanup and pouring time decreases the amount of time available for mold formation. Formulate a linear programming model to determine the best product mix for this possibility.

   b. Another possibility is that the cleanup and pouring are done in such a manner that the time available for mold formation is not affected. Formulate a linear programming model to determine the best product mix for this possibility.

3. Ray's Cherry Hut produces its own private label cherry jelly when the cherries are harvested. Some of the cherries were damaged in a recent hailstorm. Cherries that were damaged are Grade C. The highest-quality cherries are Grade A. Grade B cherries are somewhat more tart than Grade A and Grade C cherries. The two main quality considerations are tartness and clarity. The hail-damaged cherries are much cheaper than the Grade A and Grade B cherries, but because of the bruises, these result in cloudy jelly. The costs per pail of the cherries are $0.50, $0.40, and $0.18 for Grades A, B, and C, respectively. The tartness and clarity ratings are as follows:

Grade	Tartness	Clarity
A	11.0	1.0
B	8.9	1.5
C	10.5	3.7

The jelly must have a tartness rating between 10.0 and 10.5. The maximum clarity rating is 1.9. The yield of jelly is one 8-ounce jar for each pail. An 8-ounce jar sells for $1.59. Assume that more than enough of each grade of cherries is available for purchase.

    a. Formulate a model to detemine the best way to blend a standard 8-ounce jar of jelly. Did you assume that tartness and clarity blend linearly?

    b. Assume that it is desired to produce 8,500 8-ounce jars of jelly. Formulate a model that will determine the number of pails of each grade of cherries to buy and the amount of profit. The processing costs are $0.21 per jar.

4. Ray's Cherry Hut (MCE 3) has discovered that a mistake was made in the solution to Part *a*. There is a yield of two 8-ounce jars per pail of cherries. Give the revised formulation. How do you expect the optimal solution to change because of this error?

5. A salesman has a choice of products to push when he calls on a client. He believes that he has, at most, ½ hour for the sales call. He believes that the commission he receives on each product will be proportional to the amount of time he spends describing the product. He has five new products that he could introduce. His boss will be upset if he doesn't spend at least 5 minutes on her new product. The potential commission based on the entire 30 minutes spent on a single product is estimated as follows:

Product	Commission Potential
A1	$125
A2	110
A3	130
A4	140
A5 (boss's)	128

    a. Construct a model to determine the amount of time given to each product that will maximize the commission received.

    b. Do you think that this is a deterministic decision environment?

    c. Can you determine the best plan by inspecting the information given?

6. A chemical company desires to blend ethylene glycol and distilled water to obtain antifreeze for automobiles. This antifreeze will be marketed as premixed for 25 degrees below 0. It is expected that consumers will prefer a premixed product over attempting to measure the pure ethylene glycol and mix it themselves. The freezing point of ethylene glycol is 67 degrees below 0. The freezing point of water is 32 degrees above 0. Also, 6 ounces of a rust-

preventive additive is required; it has a freezing point of 10 degrees above 0. The selling price will be $3.50 per gallon. Ethylene glycol costs $1.05 per gallon. The additive cost is $0.07 per ounce. The distilled water costs $0.00001 per gallon. A gallon contains 128 ounces.

a. Formulate a linear programming model to blend a gallon with a maximum freezing point of 25 degrees below 0. Assume that the freezing point of the blend is the weighted average of the freezing points of the components.

b. Discuss whether the objective function could be cost minimization as well as profit maximization.

c. How would the cost of the additive be included in the objective function?

d. The packaging and distribution cost is estimated as $1.34. How would this affect the objective function of your model? How would this affect the profit margin per gallon?

7. An investor wants to determine the best portfolio of gold, savings account, IBM common stock, and Commonwealth Edison common stock. She has $20,000 to invest. She does not wish to have more than 10 percent in gold or less than 20 percent in savings. The total in common stock is to be no more than 60 percent. This investor estimates that the rate of return for the investments will be as follows for the next year:

Gold	9.0%
Savings account	5.25
IBM	8.5
Commonwealth Edison	10.0

a. Formulate a linear programming model to maximize the portfolio's annual rate of return.

b. Do you think that this is a deterministic decision environment?

c. Discuss whether transaction costs should be included in the analysis.

d. What time horizon did you use for your formulation? What are the appropriate considerations in this investor's choice of a time horizon?

e. Is your model static or dynamic? Do you believe that a dynamic model is preferred? Why or why not?

8. The investor of MCE 7 is concerned about the potential risk of certain investments. The savings account is insured by the Federal Deposit Insurance Corporation, and she is certain of the 5.25 percent return. However, the return on the common stocks is dependent on changes in the value of the shares. She believes that a decrease in the share price of Commonwealth Edison, a utility stock, is less likely than a decrease in the share price of IBM. She has developed a risk point system to protect herself against this uncertainty. She assesses risk points per $5,000 invested in each of the investments as follows: 25 for gold, 0 for a savings account, 35 for IBM common stock, and 12 for Commonwealth Edison common stock. She wants a portfolio whose risk point total is no greater than 80.

a. Revise the formulation of MCE 7 to show this consideration. Assume that risk points add linearly.

b. Formulate a new model to minimize the total number of risk points if the minimum return is $1,200.

9. A company slits rolls of 20-inch steel into 6-inch, 8-inch, and 10-inch rolls. Its sales prices for the finished rolls are $240, $360, and $440 for 6-inch, 8-inch, and 10-inch rolls, respectively. The company has on hand 100 of the 20-inch rolls and none of the finished rolls. The 20-inch rolls cost $590 each. The company needs to produce finished rolls from the available 20-inch rolls. It has developed several slitting patterns. The results of these patterns are given below:

| Pattern | Number of Rolls | | | Inches of Waste |
	6-inch	8-inch	10-inch	
1	3	0	0	2
2	2	1	0	0
3	1	0	1	4
4	0	1	1	2
5	0	0	2	0
6	0	2	0	4

a. Formulate a linear programming model to maximize the number of finished rolls that can be produced from the available 20-inch rolls.

b. Formulate a linear programming model to maximize the revenue obtained from the available 20-inch rolls.

c. Formulate a linear programming model to maximize the profit obtained from the available 20-inch rolls. Should the cost of the 20-inch rolls be considered in calculating the profit margins? What would be the relationship between an optimal solution to the model of Part *b* and an optimal solution to this model?

d. If the 20-inch rolls had cost $1,000 each, would your answers to the questions of Part *c* be different?

10. The company described in MCE 9 wants to produce finished rolls from the 100 available 20-inch rolls. The required numbers of the finished rolls are 156, 80, and 40 of the 6-inch, 8-inch, and 10-inch rolls, respectively.

a. Formulate a linear programming model to minimize the number of 20-inch rolls needed to satisfy the requirements. Consider carefully whether the constraints should be equations or inequalities.

b. Formulate a linear programming model to maximize the profit consistent with producing exactly the required number of finished rolls. How would the optimal solution to Part *a* be related to the optimal solution of this part?

c. Formulate a linear programming model to minimize the waste consistent with producing exactly the required number of finished rolls. How would the optimal solution to Part *a* be related to the optimal solution of this part?

    d. Say that more finished rolls than the required numbers can also be sold. Formulate a model to maximize the total revenue.

11. The Bailey Steel Company has two open-hearth furnaces and one basic oxygen furnace. These furnaces are used to make four types of steel. The furnaces have different operating characteristics that give different production rates and operating costs. These are summarized as

Furance	Production Rates (tons/day)			
	Stainless	Armor	Carbon	Alloy
Open Hearth A	60	105	115	—
Open Hearth B	70	115	120	—
Basic oxygen	90	90	100	95

Furnace	Operating Costs ($/day)			
	Stainless	Armor	Carbon	Alloy
Open Hearth A	1,000	1,050	1,050	—
Open Hearth B	1,100	1,100	1,100	—
Basic oxygen	900	900	900	900

Alloy steel cannot be produced on either open hearth. The required tons to be produced next month are 1,030, 1,800, 1,500, and 1,000 for stainless, armor, carbon, and alloy steels. There are 30 operating days next month for all three furnaces.

    a. Formulate a linear programming model to minimize the total operating costs.

    b. Discuss whether the objective should be to maximize the total profit.

    c. Discuss whether one month is an appropriate time horizon.

12. A company is trying to determine the production plan for next week. Next week, 80 hours will be available on the drill press and 40 hours will be available on the lathe. Each of the four products requires one piece of bar stock, and there are only 250 pieces on hand.

Product	Time Required (hours/unit)		Profit Margin
	Drill Press	Lathe	
A	0.4	0.1	$16
B	0.2	0.08	11
C	0.15	0.09	16
D	0.3	0.15	15

A commitment has been made to produce at least 5 of Product B next week.

a. Formulate a linear programming model to maximize the total profit.

b. Modify your model of Part *a* with the additional restriction that a maximum of 150 of Product A should be produced.

13. The little old winemaker is attempting to blend three California reds into a cheap table wine. The emphasis is on cheap; he wants the blend that costs the least. He wants no more than ⅓ to be California Sour. The blend must be at least 10 percent of California Ruby. He has 2,000 gallons of California Sour and 1,000 gallons of California Ruby. The other blend is California Bland, (2,500 gallons). The costs per gallon are $1.25, $1.60, and $2.35 for California Sour, California Bland, and California Ruby, respectively. The selling price of the cheap table wine is $3.99 per gallon.

a. Formulate a linear programming model to maximize the profit from the available blending stocks.

b. Formulate a linear programming model to maximize the total number of gallons of cheap table wine blended. What relationship, if any, do you expect between the optimal blending plan of Part *a* and that of Part *b*?

c. Discuss whether the costs of the wines used in the blend should be considered in calculating the profit margins. Would this have an impact on the relationship between the optimal blending plans of Parts *a* and *b*?

14. A company produces a single product. This product requires two distinct operations. Two machines are available to do the first operation; these are called Machines 1 and 2. Another three machines are available to do the second operation; these are called Machines 3, 4, and 5. The machines have different operating costs and production rates. The first operation is referred to as Operation A; the second is referred to as Operation B. The operating costs and production rates are given below.

Operation A

	Machine	
	1	2
Production rate, units/hour	18	19
Operating cost, $/hour	305	400

Operation B

	Machine		
	3	4	5
Production rate, units/hour	14	12	10
Operating cost, $/hour	255	241	200

Next week, a total of 1,315 units of the product should be produced. Machine 3 will be available for 32 hours. The other machines will be available for 40 hours. Formulate a linear programming model to determine the production plan with the least operating cost. Use the following as an example of the definition of the decision variables:

a1—number of hours that Operation A must be done on Machine 1.

15. The company of MCE 14 is considering another linear programming model for the same decision problem. Use the following as an example of the definition of the decision variables:

A1—number of units for which Operation A must be done on Machine 1.

a. Formulate the model to determine the production plan with the least operating cost with this definition of the decision variables.
b. If four machines were available to do a third required operation, C, what would be the total number of constraints and the total number of decision variables?
c. If *m* machines are available to do Operation A and *n* machines are available to do Operation B, what is the total number of constraints and the total number of decision variables?

16. The company of MCE 14 is considering another approach for defining the decision variables for the same decision problem. Use the following as an example of the definition of the decision variables:

A1B3—number of units for which Operation A must be done on Machine 1 and Operation B must be done on Machine 3.

a. Formulate the model to determine the production plan with the least operating cost with this definition of the decision variables.
b. If four machines were available to do a third required operation, C, what would be the total number of constraints and decision variables?
c. If *m* machines are available to do Operation A and *n* machines are available to do Operation B, what is the total number of constraints and the total number of decision variables?

17. A steel company has three iron-ore mines, located in Minnesota, Wyoming, and West Virginia. A total of 50,000 tons of iron ore per week is required from the mines. The weekly mine capacities and the costs per ton delivered to the processing plant are

Mine	Capacity (tons/week)	Cost ($/ton)
Minnesota	35,000	87
Wyoming	42,000	93
West Virginia	32,000	69

The ore at the processing plant must contain at least 45 percent iron and no more than 1.0 percent sulfur. The percentages of iron and sulfur at the three mines are

Mine	Percent Iron	Percent Sulfur
Minnesota	43.0	1.1
Wyoming	53.0	0.5
West Virginia	67.0	1.4

    a. Formulate a linear programming model to determine the amount of iron ore from each mine per week for cost minimization.

    b. Discuss whether the objective should be profit maximization.

    c. Discuss whether one week is an appropriate time horizon.

CASE

American Steel Company

For over a decade now, major U.S. oil companies have been prospecting for difficult to find domestic oil reserves in remote locations and offshore tracts and the oil shale deposits on the western slopes of Colorado. Although a successful pilot plant for beneficiation of oil shale has been operating in that state since the mid-1960s, the projected danger to the environment has blocked appropriate legislation which would have freed state lands for such development. Consequently, the search for more domestic oil moved to remote and offshore areas of the United States in addition to the traditional oil-producing areas.

In February 1968, the Atlantic Richfield Company (ARCO) reported that while drilling for gas, it had found oil deposits in a sandstone formation on Alaska's North Slope. This was the first oil found in this region in 20 years, and ARCO was understandably cautious in calling this well a discovery.

ARCO's discovery was confirmed with a test hole drilled seven miles from the site of the original wildcat well. By June 1968, other companies were also beginning exploration in the Prudhoe Bay area. In July, ARCO stated that "Alaska's new North Slope oil field was potentially one of the world's largest, containing 5–10 billion barrels of recoverable oil."[1]

Needless to say, these findings shifted the emphasis from oil shale reserves to the larger, potentially cheaper Alaskan oil. One of the first questions that needed to be resolved was how the oil could be shipped to market. Because of the severe climate, the Prudhoe Bay area is open to shipping only a few months each year. The only economically feasible way to move the crude oil was to ship it via pipeline to a warmwater port. Four ports were available, but the nearest pipeline was 900 miles south. Humble Oil Company and ARCO contracted Bechtel Corporation's Pipeline Technologists, Inc. of Houston, Texas, to determine the feasibility of and location for a pipeline. This company was reported gathering information for a bid prospectus on a

Raj Aggrawal and Inder Khera, *Management Science: Cases and Applications,* © 1979, pp. 56–61. Reprinted by permission of Holden-Day, Inc.

---

[1] *Oil and Gas Journal,* July 22, 1968, p. 34.

EXHIBIT 1 The Trans-Alaska Pipeline

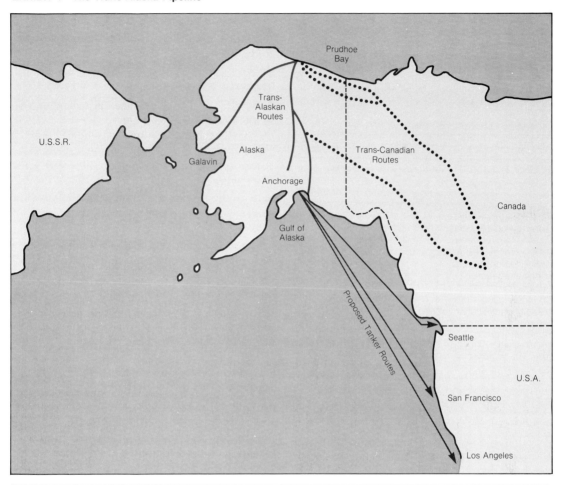

pipeline from the slope to the tidewater either at Seward or Whittier, California.

In February 1969, Humble, ARCO, and British Petroleum made a tentative commitment to spend $900 million to build a 48-inch diameter pipeline across Alaska's rugged terrain from the North Slope, to a tanker terminal on the Gulf of Alaska to transport the crude. (See Exhibits 1 and 2). Construction survey crews were to fly into remote areas of Alaska

to make soil tests and conduct other studies which would lead to the selection of a route for the line.

A U.S. Department of Interior task force was created in April 1969 to formulate guidelines for the development of Alaska's North Slope. The department stated, "If private interests are free to locate roads, airstrips, and pipelines wherever they desire, the North Country will be ruined. Such facilities must be

EXHIBIT 2   Who Will Own the Pipeline

Atlantic Richfield	28.08%
British Petroleum	28.08
Humble Oil	25.52
(Standard Oil of New Jersey)	
Mobil Oil	8.68
Phillips Petroleum	3.32
Union Oil	3.32
Amerada Hess	3.00

SOURCE: *Business Week*, March 25, 1972.

EXHIBIT 3   Land Use Requirements (in acres)

	Permanent	Temporary
Pipeline right-of-way	5,176	
Pipeline working area		3,590
Pipeline cleared area		5,315
Pump stations and related		
construction camps	703	1,270
Terminal at Valdez	910	
Access road	1,500	1,270
Communication sites		
Telecommunication systems	90	
Remotely controlled valves	23	
Interim sites		4
Construction camps		980
Temporary airstrips		240
Permanent airstrips	150	
Material storage sites		40
Totals	8,552	12,709

SOURCE: "Final Environmental Impact Statement," *Proposed Trans-Alaskan Pipeline* (Washington, D.C.: U.S. Government Printing Office, 1972).

planned with care. Their location should be fixed and their numbers limited."[2] (Also see Exhibit 3.) By October, Department of Interior Secretary Walter Hickel had approved environmental stipulations that the pipeline companies would have to meet in building and operating the line. Next, Hickel had to obtain approval of the Senate and House Interior Committees of his intentions to lift portions of the land freeze imposed by the former secretary in 1967. The committees gave their approval to Hickel's action in December.

After the committees' approval, the project still had to await the results of the permafrost study. Permafrost is a loose, permanently frozen combination of gravel, sand, and ice topped by a thin cover of grass and vegetation. It was feared that heated oil running through an underground pipe would adversely affect the Arctic permafrost areas. Humble Pipeline Company and the U.S. government were concurrently studying this as a possible problem. They were also seeking to determine the effects of the arctic environment on the pipeline itself.

While the permafrost problem was being resolved, another problem developed. A U.S. district judge issued a preliminary injunction blocking the pipeline project for environmental reasons. The conservationists argued that the pipeline violated the Mineral Leasing Act of 1920 and the National Environmental Policy Act of 1969. The Mineral Leasing Act restricts pipeline right-of-way on public lands to 25 feet on either side of the pipe. The trans-Alaskan pipeline system had asked for an additional 44 feet along the pipeline plus a 200-foot easement for the hauling road.

From an ecological point of view, the conservationists argued that oil leaks may occur from earthquakes, glacier surges, slope and bank erosions, and the oil pressure from within the line itself. Since the pipeline was to be buried in the permafrost, the oil, being pumped at 150°–160°F., would warm the pipe and cause widespread thawing. A final argument was that heavy construction equipment would destroy the vegetation, leading to the eventual thawing of the permafrost.

In April 1970, Secretary Hickel announced that expert research findings had established that the pipeline could be built with complete safety. He was expected to approve the construction as soon as legal and technical difficulties were met. However, Hickel was

---

[2] *Oil and Gas Journal*, April 21, 1969, p. 59.

unexpectedly removed from his position on November 25, 1970. Roger C. B. Morton was appointed the new secretary of the interior and reopened hearings on the pipeline and ordered his own studies. Finally, on May 4, 1972, Secretary Morton announced that a permit for the pipeline construction would be issued as soon as it could be done without violating a court order.

After Morton's announcement, bidding was immediately begun for the various aspects of the pipeline construction. The American Steel Company, seeing a large market opening up for its products, bid on several material supply contracts. Many of the large steel companies throughout the world were also bidding for these contracts, and American Steel Company felt somewhat lucky when notified that it had been awarded the contract for supplying the monthly requirements of 13,000 tons of steel pipe.

From the extensive testing and research done to determine the Arctic environment's effect on the pipe, only four grades of steel were deemed metallurgically acceptable for the construction of the pipeline. American Steel Company estimated its production costs and monthly tonnage limits of the four grades of steel to be shown in Exhibit 4.

In addition, the company's sales department had determined that either Grade 1 *or* Grade 4 could be used, but not both.

In order to clarify the above cost and volume figures, the quality control department proposed that quality data be considered prior to making the decision regarding the quantities of the different steel grades that would be allocated to the pipeline project. According to its data, rejections for reasons of quality (pipe uniformity, chemical segregation, low mechanical properties, etc.) vary between the four grades. Next, the management estab-

EXHIBIT 4 American Steel Company Production Data on Steel Grades 1–4

Steel Grade	Cost ($/ton)	Monthly Tonnage Available
1	$58	6,000
2	60	2,000
3*	51	5,000
4*	53	6,000

* The machinery and other production requirements are such that there is practically a costless switch possible between production of Grades 3 and 4 without any changes in costs/ton. Further, for economic levels of production runs and because of containerized shipping, at least 1,000 tons of each kind of steel must be shipped for the arctic pipeline.

EXHIBIT 5 Quality and Profit Data for Steel Grades 1–4

Steel Grade	Profit ($/ton)*	Relative Quality Factor	Adjusted Profit ($/ton)*
1	$22	0.95	$20.90
2	20	1.00	20.00
3	29	0.93	26.97
4	27	0.90	24.30

* Losses for on-site rejections due to quality are estimated to be 5 percent, 0 percent, 7 percent, and 10 percent, respectively, for the steel grades 1–4.

lished a minimum *average* profit per ton standard of $23 on this type of product. Based on a sales price of $80/ton, Exhibit 5 indicates the differences of quality and profits for the four steel grades. The management has also overruled the sales department's decision to make only Grade 1 *or* Grade 4 steel. Instead, a compromise to make a little less than twice as much Grade 1 as Grade 4 has now been reached. In view of all of these various foregoing factors, including the need for a highly reliable pipeline, Mrs. Weekly, vice president of operations, must make a decision on the amounts of each grade of steel to be produced.

Use of LINDO

Often, LINDO is the linear programming software used for instruction in management science. This brief description of the use of LINDO and its commands is provided for students using LINDO. Access to LINDO is not necessary for the study of linear programming, but this appendix provides a brief overview for those who have access to it. LINDO is available on MS/DOS personal computers and Apple Computer's Macintosh as well as most minicomputers.

One advantage of LINDO for instruction is its interactive nature. If the student desires to solve the model

```
max   2A + 3B
st    A + 2B < 10
      2A + 3B < 15
```

the model is entered exactly that way. Note that most keyboards do not contain a $\leq$ key, so LINDO accepts either $<$ or $<\,=$; either is interpreted as $\leq$. The $\geq$ relationship is treated similarly. Also, note that the non-negativities on the variables are not entered. LINDO assumes that all variables are greater than or equal to 0.

Personal computer software is either menu driven or command driven. LOTUS 1-2-3, a popular package, is an example of menu-driven software. The menu is "pulled down" by the / key. Then, the user chooses from the menu.

LINDO is command driven. The user specifies the command by typing it, not by choosing it from a menu. Interactive computers use different characters to **prompt** the user. When LINDO is waiting for a command, the prompt : appears. Therefore, if you receive the prompt : , you are at the LINDO command level.

To start LINDO on a personal computer, insert the LINDO/PC diskette in Drive A and type

```
a:
```

followed by

```
lindo
```

Figure 3.A1 illustrates the use of LINDO/PC to solve the Potato Processing example. For illustrative purposes, lowercase was used for all input at the keyboard. LINDO/PC prints its responses in uppercase. Notice that after you typed lindo, the prompt : appeared on the screen. Typing the command

```
help
```

FIGURE 3.A1   Potato Processing Example, LINDO Session

```
: max .14i+.15m
? st .3i+.2m<18000
? .1i+.2m<15000
? .3i+.3m<30000
? end

: look all

MAX      0.14 I + 0.15 M
SUBJECT TO
      2)    0.3 I + 0.2 M <=   18000
      3)    0.1 I + 0.2 M <=   15000
      4)    0.3 I + 0.3 M <=   30000
END

: go

LP OPTIMUM FOUND AT STEP      2

        OBJECTIVE FUNCTION VALUE

      1)     12225.0000

   VARIABLE        VALUE          REDUCED COST
        I     15000.000000           .000000
        M     67500.000000           .000000


      ROW   SLACK OR SURPLUS     DUAL PRICES
      2)          .000000           .325000
      3)          .000000           .425000
      4)        5250.000000         .000000

NO. ITERATIONS=        2
DO RANGE(SENSITIVITY) ANALYSIS?
? y

RANGES IN WHICH THE BASIS IS UNCHANGED:

                          OBJ COEFFICIENT RANGES
VARIABLE          CURRENT        ALLOWABLE        ALLOWABLE
                  COEF           INCREASE         DECREASE
      I           .140000        .085000          .065000
      M           .150000        .130000          .056667

                          RIGHTHAND SIDE RANGES
      ROW         CURRENT        ALLOWABLE        ALLOWABLE
                  RHS            INCREASE         DECREASE
      2       18000.000000    7000.000000      3000.000000
      3       15000.000000    3000.000000      9000.000000
      4       30000.000000      INFINITY       5250.000000



: save
FILE NAME:
b:potato.mod
: dive
FILE NAME:
b:potato.out
: look all
: go
LP OPTIMUM FOUND AT STEP      2
        OBJECTIVE FUNCTION VALUE
      1)     12225.0000

DO RANGE(SENSITIVITY) ANALYSIS?
? y
: rvrt
: quit
```

FIGURE 3.A2 List of LINDO Commands Generated by the Com Command

```
: com

LINDO COMMANDS BY CATEGORY.    FOR INFORMATION
ON A SPECIFIC COMMAND,   TYPE ''HELP'' FOLLOWED
BY THE COMMAND NAME.

 1) INFORMATION
      HELP     COM      LOCAL         CAT
 2) INPUT
      MAX      MIN      RETR          RMPS      TAKE      LEAV      RDBC
 3) DISPLAY
      PIC      TABL     LOOK          NONZ      SHOC      SOLU      RANGE
      BPIC     CPRI     RPRI
 4) FILE OUTPUT
      SAVE     DIVE     RVRT          SMPS      SDBC
 5) SOLUTION
      GO       PIV
 6) PROBLEM EDITING
      ALT      EXT      DEL           SUB       APPC      SLB
 7) QUIT
      QUIT
 8) INTEGER, QUADRATIC, AND PARAMETRIC PROGRAMS
      INT      QCP      PARA          POSD      TITAN     BIP       GIN
      IPTOL
 9) CONVERSATIONAL PARAMETERS
      WIDTH    TERS     VERB          BAT       PAGE      PAUS
10) USER SUPPLIED ROUTINES
      USER
11) MISCELLANEOUS
      INV      STAT     BUG
```

---

from the command level provides overall information on your version of LINDO, including the size limits for the model. After each command, hit the return key to send the command to LINDO. Obtain a list of all LINDO commands by typing the

    com

command. (*Note:* com is an abbreviation for command.) The commands have abbreviations to minimize the typing necessary to specify them. Figure 3.A2 gives the result of the com command for LINDO/PC. Additional help on any command is obtained by typing help, a space, and then the abbreviation for the command. For example, help on the command go is obtained by typing

    help go

from the LINDO command level.

Useful commands for the first session include

max	Starts input for a maximization model.
min	Starts input for a minimization model.
end	Ends input and returns to command level.
look	Printed selected portions of the current formulation.
go	Solves the current formulation and prints the solution report.

Examination of Figure 3.A1 shows that ? is another LINDO prompt. The ? prompt indicates that the input for a particular command is not complete. A return after the objective function for the Potato Processing example has been typed results in a ? prompt. The ? prompt indicates that the model input is incomplete. After all the constraints have been entered, an end command indicates that the model input is complete and the command prompt : appears. (Some minicomputer versions of LINDO use the > prompt instead of the ? prompt.) The look all command causes the entire model to appear on the screen. It is at this point that typing errors are often discovered.

The go command solves the current model and prints the solution report. After the solution appears, a prompt will ask you whether you want range (sensitivity) analysis. Enter y if you want it; enter n if you do not.

Entering models with a long objective function and/or long constraints requires that these be broken up into several lines. After entering part of the long objective function or constraint, just hit the return key and continue on the next line. LINDO allows only 80 characters as input on a line. Break up the line at a convenient point, but not in the middle of a variable name.

If LINDO encounters a typing error in your input line, you will be prompted for the necessary information to complete that line. Comply with the prompting message. You can fix errors after you have completed the entire model. Do what you are told by LINDO!

Two useful commands for modifying the model or fixing it after observing typing mistakes are alt and ext. The alt command allows the formulation to be altered. Only one alteration is done each time the command is used. The alt command allows changing between max and min, changing an objective function coefficient, changing a constraint function coefficient, changing an RHS constant, and changing the relationship for a constraint. For the most common alterations, the alt command prompts you for row information, variable information, and a numerical value.

To change between max and min, respond 1 to the row query and dir to the variable query. Then, you will be prompted for the new direction; type max or min, as desired.

To change the value of an objective function coefficient or a constraint function coefficient, give the row number and the variable name. Then, you will be prompted for the new coefficient value; type the new number.

To change an RHS constant, give the row number and give rhs as the variable name. Then, when you are prompted for the new coefficient value, enter the new number.

To change the direction of a constraint, give the row number and give dir as the variable name. Then, when you are prompted for the new direction, respond <, >, or =, as desired.

Sometimes, it is necessary to add missing constraints. Use the ext command to extend the current model. After you have entered the missing constraints, use the end command to specify the end of the new constraints.

Model Development

After becoming familiar with the use of LINDO, you might want to develop more complex models. Because the input of the model is tedious and fraught with possible typing mistakes, save the model after you have developed it. Then you can retrieve, modify, and manipulate the same model in the future. You must choose a name for the file that contains your model. We strongly recommend that you add the extension mod to your file name. For example, if you desire to name the file potato, you would specify the file name as

    potato.mod

Adding the extension reminds you that the file contains a model created by LINDO. To save the model, type

    save

from the LINDO command prompt. When you are prompted for the file name, type in the desired name, including the extension. For example,

    potato.mod

To retrieve the model that has been previously saved, you can type

    retr potato.mod

from the LINDO command prompt. If you are not sure of the file name, just type

    retr

and the names of files on the default drive will appear on the screen. (Minicomputer versions of LINDO do not have this useful feature.) Use the arrow keys to move the highlight to the file you wish to retrieve, and press the return key to choose that file. (*Note:* If you modify a previously saved file and save it again with the same file name, the old version is overwritten. If you want to save both versions, use a different file name.)

   LINDO output appears on the screen by default. You can divert parts of the output into a file for printing or editing. Type

    dive

from the LINDO command prompt to divert output into a file. When you are prompted for the file name, we recommend that you add the extension out. For example, to specify the file name of potato with the extension of out, respond

    potato.out

Using the same file name with the extension of mod for a model file and the extension of out for an output file explains the relationship between the two and the source of each. After the divert command, any output that

LINDO commands would print on the screen by default is written into that file. At a minimum, we recommend that the look all and go commands be given. This writes the symbolic model and its solution into the file. Do not be concerned because very little output appears on the screen after the divert command. The output is being diverted into the file. Use the command

    rvrt

to redirect the output to the screen.

New versions of LINDO/PC accept full DOS 2.x pathnames of the form

    DRIVE:/PATH/FILE.EXT

Also, as part of an input file name, the DOS wildcard characters * and ? are supported. The input commands that support them include retr, previously discussed, and take, rmps, and rdbc. You can get information on the latter commands by using the help system.

4

Graphical Solutions of Linear Programming Models and Algebraic Manipulations

Solution of Linear Programming Models by the Graphical Method

The Four Outcomes of Linear Programming Models
Unique Optimal Solution / Alternate Optimal Solutions / No
Feasible Solution / Unbounded Optimal Solution

Algebraic Manipulation of Linear Programming Models
The Standard Algebraic Form—Simplex Algorithm / Conversion
between Minimization and Maximization / Conversion of a ≤
Constraint to an = Constraint / Conversion of a ≥ Constraint to
an = Constraint / Summary of Algebraic Manipulations of Linear
Programming Models and an Example / Conversion of a
Constraint with a Negative RHS

**Slack and Surplus Variables, Graphical Solutions, and Degenerate
Solutions**

Case: Sherman Motor Company

Appendix: More Algebraic Manipulations
Conversion of a Model with Unrestricted Variables to a Model with
All Variables ≥ 0 / Conversion of a Model with Nonpositive
Variables (≤ 0) to a Model with All Variables ≥ 0 / Conversion of
an = Constraint to Two Inequality Constraints

NATIONAL AIRLINES

In 1973, the Mideast war and the rise of the Organization of Petroleum Exporting Countries (OPEC) caused petroleum shortages and rapid increases in prices. Fuel costs were 18 percent of National Airlines' costs in 1974, and the percentage was increasing. National Airlines purchased fuel from different vendors at many cities, but the fuel crisis was causing shortages at some cities. National Airlines had to cancel some flights and pay "exorbitant" prices at some cities.

National Airlines developed a linear programming model that actually decreased the average fuel cost per gallon by 11 percent in the first month of operation, even though fuel prices were generally rising. Let's consider an example strategy to understand the savings opportunity. Say that fuel is relatively cheap and readily available at an airport served by National Airlines. When a flight arrives at that airport, the plane's tanks are filled. The fuel in the full tanks is sufficient for several additional flight segments. By careful planning, the plane's tanks are close to empty when a flight takes it to an airport with a favorable fuel supply, so the plane doesn't have to add fuel at airports with an unfavorable fuel supply.

National Airlines used rotations to schedule its flights. A rotation is a sequence of flight segments that return to the starting city. For a rotation, the decisions are where to purchase the fuel for each flight segment. You can purchase the fuel at the departure city or at one of the previous cities on the rotation. The model considered fuel costs and the additional fuel required to "tanker" fuel from one city to another when it wasn't needed for that flight segment.

The system started with National Airlines' complete flight schedule. The objective function was minimization of the fuel costs plus the additional operating costs caused by tankering. The constraints included fuel availabilities at the airports. Other considerations included minimum reserve fuel for each plane, maximum amount of fuel each plane could carry, distances for flight segments, fuel consumption for each type of plane as a function of weight, and fuel remaining on board at the end of each leg of a flight.

The model, for 350 flight segments, 50 airport/vendor combinations, and several aircraft types, had approximately 800 constraints and 2,400 variables. In its first year of operation, the estimated savings were $3 million. A follow-up report showed that National Airlines' average fuel cost in 1978 was the second lowest among 11 domestic airlines.

D. W. Darnell and C. Loflin, "National Airlines Fuel Management and Allocation Model," *Interfaces* 7, no. 2 (February 1977), pp. 1–16. A follow-up evaluation appears in D. W. Darnell and C. Loflin, "Fuel Management and Allocation Model," *Interfaces* 9, no. 2 (February 1979), pp. 64–65.

National Airlines used linear programming to choose how much fuel to add to airplane tanks at different airports on its flight segments. The linear programming model, for 350 flight segments, 50 airport/vendor combinations, and several aircraft types, had about 800 constraints and 2,400 variables. Complex models, such as that of National Airlines, must be solved on a computer and can seldom be solved graphically. The linear programming model for Chapter 2's Potato Processing example provides a good example of a model that can be solved graphically. In that example, a graph of combinations of Idaho and Michigan potatoes was constructed by labeling the two axes *I* and *M*. If Wisconsin potatoes as well as Idaho potatoes and Michigan potatoes had been a possibility, labeling the three axes would have required a three-dimensional representation. Although it is difficult to solve complex problems graphically, it is easier to illustrate concepts graphically than algebraically. In this chapter, we introduce and graphically illustrate important concepts and definitions from the field of linear programming.

In the next section, we provide details on how to graphically solve a linear programming model. Then, we discuss the four possible solution outcomes of linear programming models and illustrate them with examples of graphical solutions. A section describing the algebraic manipulations necessary for conversion to the standard form required for computer solution is followed by a section relating graphical solutions to algebraic standard form solutions. The final section also introduces the concept of a degenerate solution and its implication for sensitivity analysis.

SOLUTION OF LINEAR PROGRAMMING MODELS BY THE GRAPHICAL METHOD

Functions are an important building block of mathematical models. A linear programming model uses functions for both the objective function and the constraint functions. A **function** is a procedure that assigns a number to a set of numbers. Symbolically, $f(A)$ indicates that given a numerical value of A, another numerical value, $f(A)$, can be calculated.

Graphing a function of one variable

For example, $f(A) = 5A + 3$ calculates the function value by multiplying the numerical value of A by 5 and adding 3 to the result. Figure 4.1 graphically illustrates this function. Verify that $f(0) = 3$, $f(1) = 8$, and $f(2) = 13$ by substituting the numerical value for A. The horizontal axis is labeled A, and the vertical axis is labeled $f(A)$.

Most linear programming models have several variables, so functions with several variables appear in both the objective function and the constraint functions. Since one dimension is required for the function value and one dimension is required for each variable, a function of one variable can be graphed in two dimensions. A function of more than one

FIGURE 4.1   The Function 5A + 3

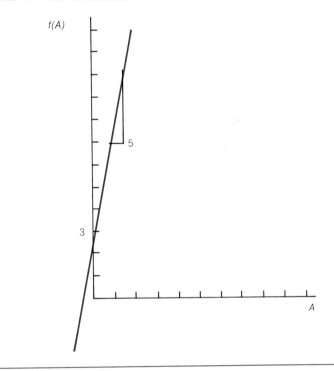

variable can't be graphed in two dimensions. Thus, $f(A, B) = 3A + 2B$ can't be graphed in two dimensions.

We graphically solve linear programming models that have two variables. Let's show how to graph the points that satisfy equations and inequalities that have two variables. In Figure 4.2, the solid line represents the values of A and B that satisfy the equation $3A + 5B = 15$. *If the function is linear, the graph is a straight line.* You determine the straight line by finding two points on it. For example, if $B = 0$, then $3A + (5 \times 0) = 15$ and $A = {}^{15}/_3 = 5$. This is the intersection of the line with the horizontal axis. Similarly, if $A = 0$, then $B = 3$. This is the intersection of the line with the vertical axis. Then, you draw a straight line between the two points $(A, B) = (5, 0)$ and $(0, 3)$. The points that satisfy the equation are those on the line.

Finding the points that satisfy a linear inequality is similar to finding the points that satisfy a linear equation. For example, let's find the points that satisfy the inequality $3A + 5B \leq 15$. First, you graph the equation $3A + 5B = 15$. The result is a straight line identical to that in Figure 4.2. The points that satisfy the strict inequality $3A + 5B < 15$ are on one side of the equation's line. The side that is included is found by substituting the

Graphing a linear equation with two variables

Graphing a linear inequality with two variables

FIGURE 4.2   The Equation 3A + 5B = 15

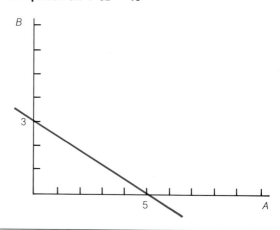

Check a point not on
the line

variable values for any point *not on the line* and determining whether the relationship is satisfied at that point. For example, let's check whether the relationship is satisfied at the **origin,** (0, 0). At (0, 0), $3A + 5B = 0$. Because 0 is ≤ 15, the point (0, 0) satisfies the constraint and the side that includes (0, 0) comprises those points that satisfy the strict inequality. The points that satisfy the inequality are those on the line and on the left side of the line, as indicated by the arrows in Figure 4.3.

Feasible set

A **feasible solution** or **feasible point** satisfies all of the constraints and any restrictions on the variable values (e.g., nonnegativities). The **feasible set** is the set of *all* feasible solutions. Assuming that A and B are non-negative, the feasible set has been shaded in Figure 4.3.

An **optimal solution** to a linear programming model is the feasible solution that yields the best value of the objective function. Let's show how to graphically find an optimal solution for a linear programming model with two variables. Because the model has two variables, you can't graph the objective function in two dimensions. The function value requires one axis, and the two variables require two more. You need three dimensions to plot the objective function. However, we graphically found the optimal solution to the Potato Processing example. How was this done? We plotted several equal value contours of the objective function to find the optimal solution.

An **equal value contour** is the combinations of variable values for a specific value of the objective function. For example, the 24-contour is the set of variable values that have an objective function value of 24. Say that the objective function is $3A + 2B$. The 24-contour is the values of A and B that satisfy

$$3A + 2B = 24$$

FIGURE 4.3 The Inequality **3A + 5B ≤ 15**

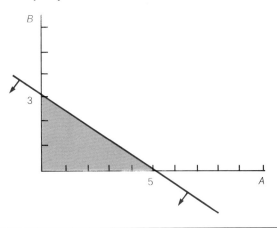

Equal value contours
of a linear function are
straight lines

Because the objective function is linear, the equal value contours are linear equations. This set of points is a straight line, and the points at which it intersects the axes are calculated. For example, if $B = 0$, then $A = 8$, and if $A = 0$, then $B = 12$.

There is a different contour for each value of the objective function. For $3A + 2B$, the 24-contour and the 6-contour are illustrated in Figure 4.4a. In Figure 4.4b, the contours are superimposed on the feasible set from Figure 4.3. Are there points in the feasible set that gain an objective function value as large as 24? No points on the 24-contour lie in the shaded region, but many points on the 6-contour are in the feasible set.

Let's find the optimal solution to the linear programming model

max $3A + 2B$
st $3A + 5B \leq 15$
       $A, B \geq 0$

The solution is associated with the contour that has the largest value for which there is a combination of values of A and B in the feasible set.

You could find the solution to this linear programming model by trial and error. You pick a value for the contour and then check whether any points on the contour satisfy the constraint and the nonnegativities. If you try the 24-contour first, no point in the feasible set gains that value, so you try a smaller value for the contour. If you try the 6-contour next, many points in the feasible set have that value, so a value of 6 is possible. Next, you might try a value between 6 and 24. Using trial and error, you try different contour values until if the contour value is increased any more, no point in the feasible set lies on the contour.

This is not a very efficient method for determining the optimal solution. Note that the 24-contour and the 6-contour have the same slope but

FIGURE 4.4a   6-Contour and 24-Contour of 3A + 2B

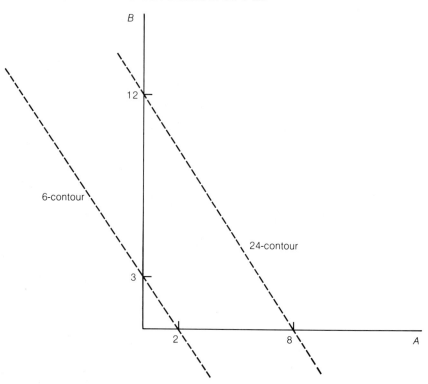

different *B*-axis intercepts. *The equal value contours of a linear program-ming model are always parallel lines.* By plotting the two contours, you discover the slope of the equal value contour lines and you find that the line moves to the right when the contour value increases. Just slide the 6-contour line to the right until if you moved it any farther, no points in the shaded, feasible set would lie on it. The optimal solution, which is at the point where the equal value contour of the objective function barely touches the feasible set, is the 15-contour, with $A = 5$ and $B = 0$. **The optimal value of the objective function** is called Z^*. For this example, $Z^* = 15$.

Graphically solving a minimization model requires sliding the equal value contour in the direction that decreases the objective function value until if you moved it any farther, no points on it would be in the feasible set. Suppose the objective function is minimize $3A + 2B$. Because the objective function decreases as the equal value contour slides to the left, the optimal solution to the minimization model is the origin, $A = 0$ and $B = 0$, with $Z^* = 0$.

FIGURE 4.4b 6-Contour and 24-Contour of 3A + 2B with Constraint 3A + 5B ≤ 15

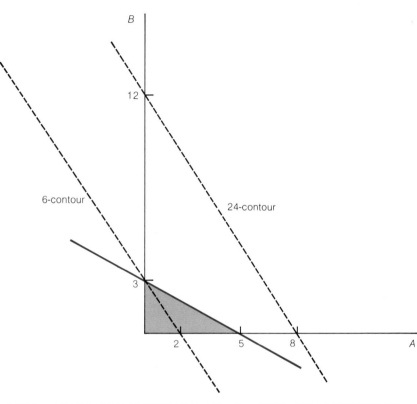

As a preview of sensitivity analysis, observe the impact of changing an RHS constant of a linear programming model. The constraint line moves parallel, just as equal value contours move.

Changing an RHS constant

The above example has only one constraint. Remember, if there are multiple constraints, all of the constraints must be satisfied. In the next section, we show more examples of graphical solution of linear programming models.

Let's summarize the steps in the graphical solution of a linear programming model.

1. Graph each constraint as an equation.

Steps for graphical solution

2. For each inequality constraint, determine which side of the equation's line is included in the feasible set by substituting a point not on the line.

3. Shade the set of points that satisfy all of the constraints and the nonnegativities.

4. Plot an arbitrarily selected equal value contour of the objective function.
5. Determine the direction in which to move the equal value contour line so that the objective function improves.
6. Slide the equal value contour line as far as possible in the improving direction, so that the contour includes at least one point in the feasible set.

Note that in Steps 5 and 6 we refer to the objective function value as improving, not as increasing. Maximization and minimization models are solved graphically in the same way. The only difference is that improving is *larger* for a maximization model and *smaller* for a minimization model.

A good arbitrary choice for the objective function equal value contour is one that passes through or close to the feasible set and that both of the objective function coefficients divide evenly. If the objective function is $3x + 2y$, a good choice is 6 or 12 or 18 or . . . Choose from among those values so that the contour passes through or close to the feasible set.

THE FOUR OUTCOMES OF LINEAR PROGRAMMING MODELS

In this section, we graphically solve several linear programming models. By doing so, we illustrate the four possible solution outcomes for linear programming models: a unique optimal solution, alternate optimal solutions, no feasible solution, and an unbounded optimal solution. Repeating graphical solution of these examples improves your ability to graphically solve other linear programming models.

Unique Optimal Solution

Let's graphically find the optimal solution for the linear programming model

$$
\begin{aligned}
\max \quad & 5A + 3B \\
\text{st} \quad & 3A + 5B \le 15 \\
& -3A + 6B \ge 12 \\
& A, B \ge 0
\end{aligned}
$$

The first constraint is identical to that illustrated in Figure 4.3. Figure 4.5 shows both constraints and has the feasible set shaded. The circled numbers by the lines indicate the constraint numbers. Let's graph the second inequality. First, we consider the equation $-3A + 6B = 12$. If $B = 0$, $-3A + (4 \times 0) = 12$ and $A = 12/_{-3} = -4$. Next, if $A = 0$, then $B = 12/_6 = 2$. These two points, $(-4, 0)$ and $(0, 2)$, determine the straight line of the equation. Now, let's check the origin by substituting $(0, 0)$ into

FIGURE 4.5 Feasible Set Example

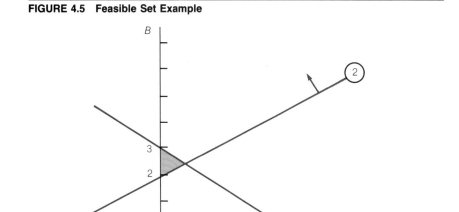

the inequality, giving $0 \geq 12$. This is not a true statement. Therefore, $(0, 0)$ is not included in the feasible set and the points on and to the left of the second constraint line satisfy the second constraint. Note that the points that satisfy each equation or inequality are determined independently but that the shaded feasible set contains the points that satisfy every constraint and the variable nonnegativities.

In Step 4, we plot an equal value contour of the objective function. Because the objective function coefficients are 5 and 3, 15 is a good choice for the equal value contour. It can be divided evenly by both 5 and 3, and the 15-contour is close to the feasible set. Figure 4.6 is obtained by superimposing the 15-contour of the objective function on the feasible set of Figure 4.5. There is no feasible point with an objective function value of 15. If the contour value is increased, the equal value contour line slides to the right and there is still no point in the feasible set with such a value. The contour value must therefore be decreased, sliding the equal value contour line parallel to the left. The point at the intersection of the two constraint lines is the optimal solution. Remember that constraint lines were determined by first graphing the equations. Both inequalities are satisfied as equations at this optimal point. The exact values of A and B are obtained by solving the two equations

$$3A + 5B = 15$$
$$-3A + 6B = 12$$

FIGURE 4.6 Feasible Set Example with 15-Contour

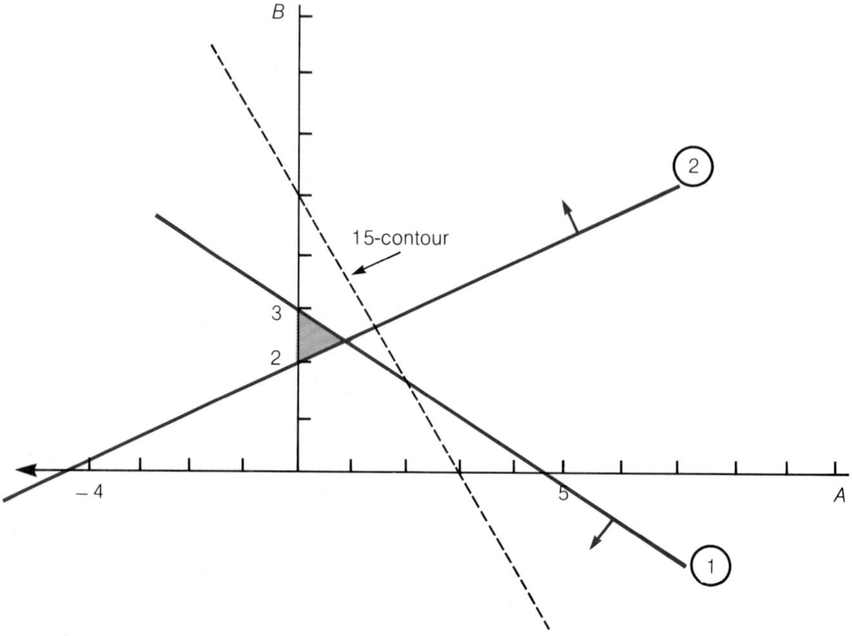

The optimal solution is $A = {}^{10}/_{11}$ and $B = {}^{27}/_{11}$, with the objective function value, Z^*, equal to $^{131}/_{11}$. No other point in the feasible set lies on the $^{131}/_{11}$-contour. A linear programming model has a **unique optimal solution** if only one point in the feasible set has the best objective function value. This linear programming model has a unique optimal solution.

Only one optimal point

A common misconception is that the optimal solution is *always* at the intersection of the constraint lines. This is not the case. For the objective function $5A + 3B$, the slope of the equal value contour line is between the slopes of the two constraints. Changing the objective function changes the slope of the equal value contours. If the objective function is changed enough, a different solution is optimal. For example, if the objective function is to maximize $A + 3B$, the optimal solution is $A = 0$ and $B = 3$—not the intersection of the two constraints.

Changing an objective function coefficient

Alternate Optimal Solutions

It is always true that there is only one optimal value of the objective function. However, several points in the feasible set may attain that optimal value. When more than one point in the feasible set attains the optimal value of the objective function, there are **alternate optimal solutions.** You use qualitative factors and/or a secondary objective function to choose among such solutions.

Alternate optimal solutions exist because of the relative values of the coefficients in a linear programming model. For example, consider the linear programming model

$$\max \quad 3x_1 + 2x_2$$
$$\text{st} \quad -x_1 + 2x_2 \leq 0$$
$$6x_1 + 4x_2 \leq 12$$
$$x_1, x_2 \geq 0$$

Let's find the optimal solution graphically. *First,* you graph each constraint as an equation. Let's graph the first constraint equation. If you set $x_2 = 0$, the equation $-x_1 + (2 \times 0) = 0$ gives $x_1 = 0$. Thus, the point $(0, 0)$ is on the line. If you set $x_1 = 0$, the equation yields the same point, $(0, 0)$. You need two distinct points to determine the line. You let x_2 be some value other than 0 to get a distinct point. For example, if $x_2 = 1$, then $-x_1 + (2 \times 1) = 0$ and $x_1 = 2$. The two points $(0, 0)$ and $(2, 1)$ determine the straight line of the equation $-x_1 + 2x_2 = 0$. *Second,* you determine which side of the line satisfies the inequality. You cannot use the origin to check because point $(0, 0)$ is on the line. However, any point not on the line can be used to determine the side of the line that satisfies the inequality. For example, $x_1 = 1$ and $x_2 = 0$, represented as $(1, 0)$, can be used. Since $(-1 \times 1) + (2 \times 0) = -1$ is less than 0, the point $(1, 0)$ is included in the set of points that satisfy the inequality. *Third,* you shade the feasible set. Figure 4.7 shows the feasible set of this linear programming model including both constraints.

You need two different points to graph the line

Check a point not on the line

FIGURE 4.7 Feasible Set

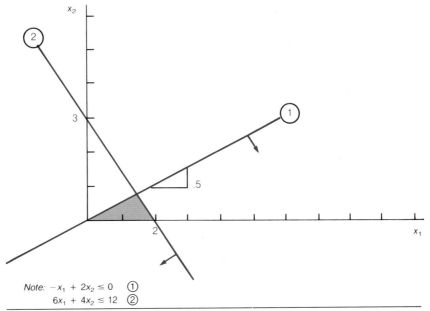

Note: $-x_1 + 2x_2 \leq 0$ ①
$6x_1 + 4x_2 \leq 12$ ②

Fourth, you plot an equal value contour of the objective function. The objective function coefficients are 3 and 2, so choosing the 6- or 12-contour makes it easier to graph the contour. Say that we choose the 12-contour to graph. Are there any points in the feasible set that attain the objective function value of 12? The 12-contour is superimposed on Figure 4.7 to create Figure 4.8. There is no point in the feasible set that has an objective function value of 12. After the first contour has been graphed, it is not necessary to plot any other contour; it is only necessary to determine the direction in which the parallel lines move when the objective function value changes. As the objective function increases, the equal value contour slides to the right. For this objective function, you must slide the contour to the left to reach the feasible set. If the objective function value for the contour is smaller, the line of the contour is to the left of that for the 12-contour. Because the objective function is to be maximized, the contour for the optimal solution would be the line that is moved to the left as little as possible so that it touches the feasible set— the 6-contour.

The 6-contour line has been superimposed on Figure 4.8. For any larger objective function value, the contour moves to the right and there is no longer a feasible point on the contour. Since the objective function was to be maximized, the optimal objective function value is 6. What point or points in the feasible set attain the value of 6? The 6-contour line lies directly on the second constraint. The point (2, 0) is an optimal solution because it is feasible and because it has a value of 6 for the objective function. The point at the intersection of the two lines is also a feasible point and has a value of 6 for the objective function. All of the points on the line segment between (2, 0) and the intersection of the two lines are optimal. The variable values at the intersection are $x_1 = \frac{3}{2}$ and $x_2 = \frac{3}{4}$. Verify that the value of the objective function is 6 for the point ($\frac{3}{2}$, $\frac{3}{4}$). The points (2, 0) and ($\frac{3}{2}$, $\frac{3}{4}$) are called **corner points of the feasible set** or

Points on the line segment are also optimal

corner points. *If two corner points are optimal, then all of the points on the line segment connecting them are also optimal.*

The constraint set for *virtually* every linear programming model has alternate optimal solutions for *some* objective function. For example, look at Figure 4.6, which illustrated a unique optimal solution. There would have been alternate optimal solutions if the objective function had been to maximize $\frac{9}{5}x_1 + 3x_2$. (Try to verify this statement.) For a given feasible set, different optimal solutions may result for different objective functions. This is reasonable. If costs or profit margins change enough, the best decision is almost certain to change.

Is there an optimal corner point?

Note that for all the examples of optimal solutions for linear programming models, there has been an optimal solution at a corner point. In the case of alternate optimal solutions, there are also optimal solutions that are not corner points. *If there is a finite optimal solution for a linear programming model, an optimal solution will be at a corner point.* This

FIGURE 4.8   Feasible Set of Figure 4.7 with 12-Contour and 6-Contour

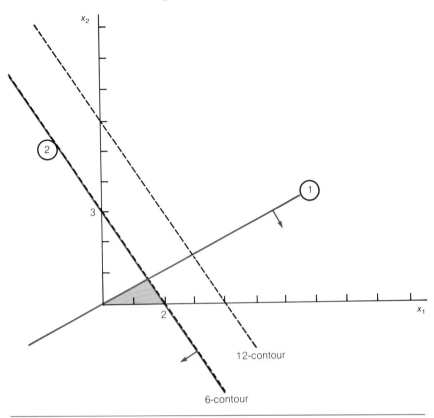

observation motivates the development of the simplex algorithm for linear programming, which is discussed at length in Chapter 6.

No Feasible Solution

Note the qualifier "finite optimal solution" in the statement about the existence of a corner point that is an optimal solution. The qualifier is necessary because there may not be even one optimal solution. In the real world, this is a rare event. Models are created to aid in analyzing the decision environment and are expected to produce results useful for exploring the decision environment. If there is not even one optimal solution to a model, the model should be reexamined for accuracy and modified to provide information useful to the decision maker.

A linear programming model is **ill-behaved** if it does not have a finite optimal solution. This section develops the possibility that there are no points in the feasible set, described as **no feasible solution.** The next section develops the possibility that the feasible set contains points with a

value for the objective function as favorable as desired, called an **unbounded optimal solution.** An ill-behaved linear programming model has
either no feasible solution or an unbounded optimal solution. If you
determine that a model is ill-behaved, you need to reexamine the model's
underlying assumptions and goals, as well as the possibility of an input
error.

Consider the linear programming model

$$\begin{array}{ll}
\max & 4x_1 + 2x_2 \\
\text{st} & 3x_1 + x_2 \geq 5 \\
& x_1 - x_2 = 3 \\
& 2x_1 + x_2 \leq 3 \\
& x_1, x_2 \geq 0
\end{array}$$

Figure 4.9 shows the three constraints. How can you shade the feasible
set—the points that satisfy all three constraints? There is no point in the
feasible set; it is empty. This situation is called **no feasible solution.**

Mistakenly linking no feasible solution to the relationship between the
number of constraints and the number of variables in the model can cause
confusion. In the preceding example, there were three constraints and
only two variables, x_1 and x_2. However, if any one of the three constraints
is dropped, there is still no feasible solution even though the number of
constraints is now equal to the number of variables. In fact, the following
example has no feasible solution although it has only one constraint:

$$\begin{array}{ll}
\max & 3x_1 + 2x_2 \\
\text{st} & -x_1 - x_2 \geq 4 \\
& x_1, x_2 \geq 0
\end{array}$$

One possible reason for no feasible solution is an error in transcribing
the data or inputting the model. For example, perhaps the RHS value of 4
in the model should have been -4. A type of error that is harder to
determine is the inclusion of reasonable constraints, but with no possibility of satisfying them all. For example, there may not be enough
available manufacturing capacity to satisfy all of the requirements. If that
is the case, the model could be modfied to provide additional useful
information, such as the additional capacity needed to satisfy the requirements.

Unbounded Optimal Solution

Before this section, all of our examples of feasible sets were bounded. A
bounded feasible set is one in which a finite number may be specified so
that any variable value, at any point in the feasible set, is less than or
equal to that number. You can see that the feasible set of Figure 4.6 is
bounded by specifying the bound number as 5 (or 6 or 7 or . . .).

FIGURE 4.9 Example of No Feasible Solution

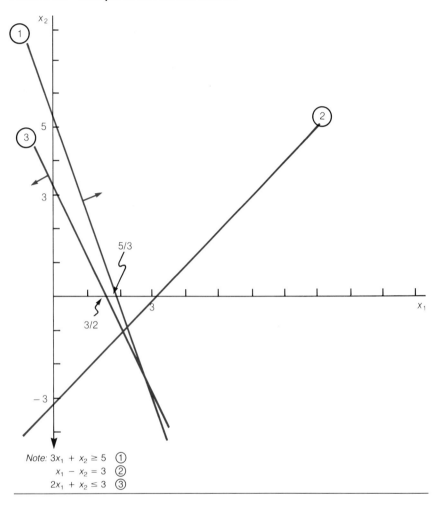

Note: $3x_1 + x_2 \geq 5$ ①
       $x_1 - x_2 = 3$ ②
       $2x_1 + x_2 \leq 3$ ③

Unbounded feasible set

An **unbounded feasible set** is a feasible set that is not bounded. For example, Figure 4.10 represents the set of constraints

$$-x_1 + 2x_2 \geq 2$$
$$3x_1 - x_2 \geq -3$$
$$x_1, x_2 \geq 0$$

In this example, there is an unbounded feasible set. Both x_1 and x_2 can be made large without limit and still be in the feasible set. Only one variable has to be limitless for a feasible set to be unbounded. For example, Figure 4.11 has no limit on x_1, though there is a limit on x_2. Is it an unbounded

FIGURE 4.10   Example of an Unbounded Feasible Set

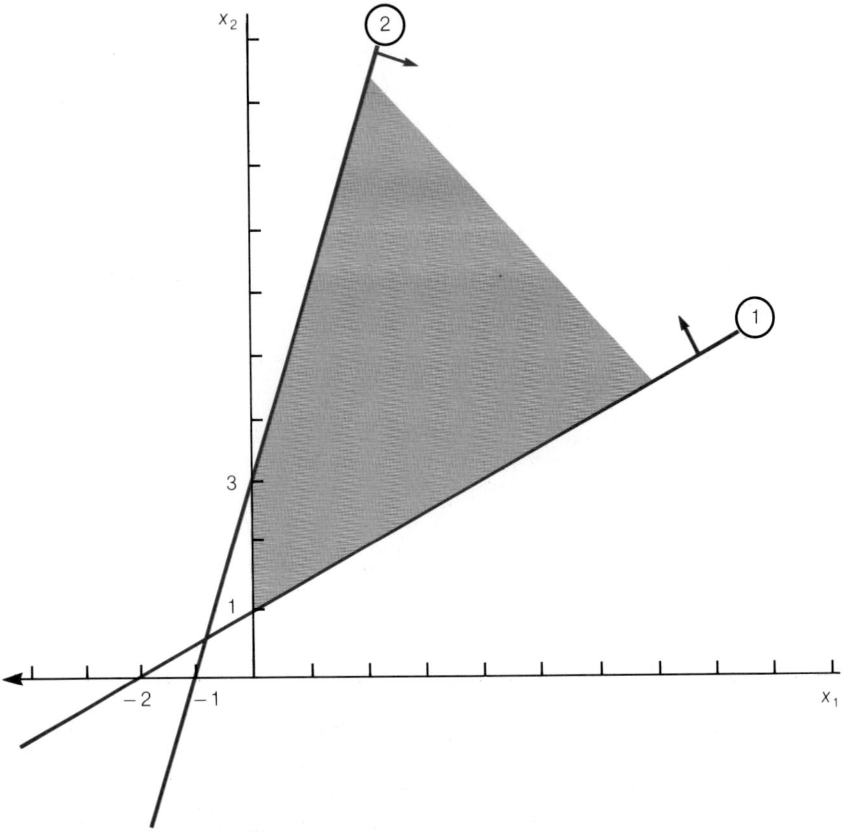

Note: $-x_1 + 2x_2 \geq 2$ ①
$3x_1 - x_2 \geq -3$ ②

feasible set? Yes. The algebraic constraints that correspond to the graphical region in Figure 4.11 are

$$x_1 - x_2 \geq -1$$
$$x_2 \leq 3$$
$$x_1, x_2 \geq 0$$

Consider the feasible set of Figure 4.11 with the objective function maximize $x_1 + x_2$. The 5-contour has been superimposed on Figure 4.11. As the objective value increases, the contour slides upward and to the right. The objective function value can be as large as desired because a feasible point exists that attains that value. If feasible points exist with the objective function value as favorable as desired, a model is said to have an

FIGURE 4.11   Example of an Unbounded Feasible Set

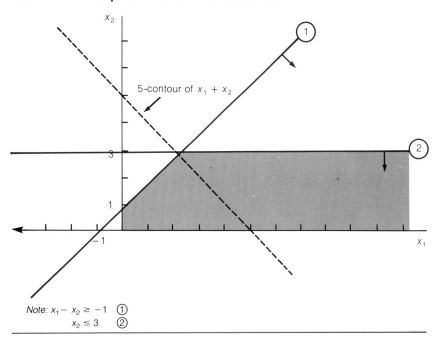

Note: $x_1 - x_2 \geq -1$ ①
      $x_2 \leq 3$ ②

Unbounded optimal solution

unbounded optimal solution. An unbounded optimal solution can occur for either a maximization or a minimization model. The definition of an unbounded optimal solution refers to "the objective function value as *favorable* as desired." For a maximization model, favorable is large; for a minimization model, favorable is small. For an unbounded optimal solution to a maximization model, the objective function value goes to plus infinity ($+\infty$). And for an unbounded optimal solution to a minimization model, the objective function value goes to minus infinity ($-\infty$).

Note that there is a difference between an unbounded feasible *set* and an unbounded optimal *solution*. An unbounded optimal solution implies an unbounded feasible set. However, an unbounded feasible set does not have to result in an unbounded optimal solution. For example, although Figure 4.11 illustrates an unbounded feasible set, if the objective function is maximize $-x_1 + 2x_2$, then the optimal solution is $x_1 = 2$ and $x_2 = 3$, with an objective function value of 4. *This is a problem that has an unbounded feasible set but does not have an unbounded optimal solution.*

Not all unbounded feasible sets have unbounded optimal solutions

Correct models are not ill-behaved. Input errors or model formulation errors can make a model ill-behaved. In this section, we graphically illustrated ill-behaved models. In Chapter 6, we discuss how to use the computer output to find the reason that the model is ill-behaved.

ALGEBRAIC MANIPULATION OF LINEAR PROGRAMMING MODELS

There are many forms of linear programming models. The objective function may be to maximize or minimize, and the constraints can be $\leq$, $\geq$, or $=$. The variables can also have sign restrictions. Remember, a variable is **positive** if its value is greater than 0. Variables are often restricted to **nonnegative** values (i.e., ≥ 0). Variables may also be restricted to **nonpositive** values (i.e., ≤ 0) or may be **unrestricted in sign.** Remember, strict inequalities are not allowed for constraints or variable values. Linear programming models can have a variety of algebraic forms depending on the objective function, the constraint relationships, and the variable sign restrictions.

Algorithm　　　The procedure used to solve linear programming models is the simplex algorithm, which is described in the Theory section of Chapter 6. An **algorithm** is a step-by-step procedure in which each step is clearly described. A simple-minded solution procedure for linear programming models is to "examine the objective function value at each corner point." An algorithm for this procedure must describe step-by-step how to generate each corner point. The simplex algorithm is similar to this simple-minded procedure, but it does not explicitly examine all corner points.

Initialization　　　An algorithm must specify how to start its step-by-step procedure. This is called the **initialization of the algorithm.** To initialize the simple-minded procedure, you must specify the starting corner point. The description of the algorithm can be simplified if there is only one form for initialization. Most linear programming software packages use the same initialization form. The linear programming model must be converted to the standard form by algebraic manipulation before the simplex algorithm starts. In this section, we discuss the algebraic manipulation of linear programming models to the standard initialization form for the simplex algorithm. Some software may automatically do some or all of the algebraic manipulations necessary to convert the linear programming model to the standard form. For example, LINDO automatically does all of the algebraic manipulations we discuss in this section. However, because of different software capabilities for *automatic* manipulations, we discuss the necessary manipulations. The algebraic manipulations also provide insight into the interpretation of computer-generated solutions, discussed in Chapter 5. Remember, LINDO assumes that all of the variables are nonnegative. Algebraic manipulations for nonpositive variables and for variables unrestricted in sign are discussed in the appendix of this chapter; LINDO does not automatically do these manipulations.

The Standard Algebraic Form—Simplex Algorithm

The standard initialization form is to maximize the objective function, subject to all of the constraints being equalities and all of the variables being nonnegative:

The standard initialization form

$$\text{max} \quad c_1x_1 + c_2x_2 + \ldots + c_nx_n$$
$$\text{st} \quad a_{11}x_1 + a_{12}x_2 + \ldots + a_{1n}x_n = b_1$$
$$a_{21}x_1 + a_{22}x_2 + \ldots + a_{2n}x_n = b_2$$
$$\cdots$$
$$a_{m1}x_1 + a_{m2}x_2 + \ldots + a_{mn}x_n = b_m.$$
$$x_j \geq 0 \quad j = 1, \ldots, n$$

The c_j, a_{ij}, and b_i are known values. The goal of the algebraic manipulation is to transform a problem that is not in standard form into standard form. The manipulation must give an equivalent model. A pair of models are **equivalent** if (1) any solution feasible to either is also feasible to the other and (2) the objective function values for the two models give the same values *relative to each other for all solutions.*

Conversion between Minimization and Maximization

The linear programming models of Chapter 3 include examples of both maximization and minimization objective functions. For the product mix model, the objective function is maximize profit, and for the machine assignment example, the objective function is to minimize cost. Say that you want to solve the machine assignment model, but your software solves only maximization models. Then, convert the minimization model to an equivalent maximization model. If the objective function is

$$\text{minimize } c_1x_1 + c_2x_2 + \ldots + c_nx_n$$

convert it to

$$\text{maximize } -c_1x_1 - c_2x_2 - \ldots - c_nx_n$$

That is, multiply the objective function by -1. The constraints are not changed, so Requirement 1 is satisfied.

Multiply the objective function by -1

For example,

$$\text{minimize } 3x_1 + 0x_2 - 2x_3$$

is converted to

$$\text{maximize } -3x_1 + 0x_2 + 2x_3$$

For a particular solution, such as $x_1 = 1$, $x_2 = 2$, and $x_3 = 0$, the value of the objective function changes from $+3$ to -3 if the minimization model is changed to the maximization model. For a solution (e.g., $x_1 = 2$, $x_2 = 2$, and $x_3 = 0$) with a smaller minimization model objective function (-6), the maximization model objective function is larger ($+6$). Thus, any solution that is "better" for the minimization model is also "better" for the maximization model. The objective function values for the two models relative to each other are the same for all solutions. *The optimal value of the objective function for the minimization model is the negative of the optimal value of the objective function for the maximization model; a set*

Change $Z*$'s sign

of values of the variables that is optimal for one model is also optimal for the other model.

Conversion of a ≤ Constraint to an = Constraint

Converting $3x_1 + 2x_2 \leq 5$ to $3x_1 + 2x_2 = 5$ does *not* yield an equivalent model because there are solutions satisfying the inequality that do not satisfy the equation. For example, the solution $x_1 = 1$ and $x_2 = 0$ satisfies the inequality yielding an LHS value of 3. However, that solution does not satisfy the equation $3x_1 + 2x_2 = 5$.

A new variable is introduced to allow the LHS of the converted constraint to be equal to the RHS. That is,

$$3x_1 + 2x_2 + s = 5$$

The variable s is called a **slack variable.** Are the two constraints equivalent? The objective function is unchanged, so Requirement 2 is satisfied. The values $x_1 = 2, x_2 = 3, s = -7$ satisfy the converted constraint but do not satisfy the original constraint. The constraints are equivalent if, in addition, all slack variables are required to be nonnegative (i.e., ≥ 0). The nonnegativity of the slack variables presents no difficulty since this is the standard form requirement.

Slack variables are nonnegative

The value of the slack variable is the amount that the LHS of the original constraint is less than the RHS constant. *A different slack variable must be introduced for each ≤ inequality.*

Conversion of a ≥ Constraint to an = Constraint

The approach for a ≥ constraint is similar, but not identical, to the approach for a ≤ constraint. In a ≥ constraint, the LHS can be larger than the RHS for a particular solution. The amount by which it is larger is called the value of the **surplus variable.** Consider the ≥ constraint

$$5x_1 + 3x_2 \geq 17$$

This is algebraically manipulated to

$$5x_1 + 3x_2 - s = 17$$

Surplus variables are nonnegative

where $s \geq 0$ ensures that the LHS of the original constraint cannot be smaller than the RHS constant. The nonnegativity of the surplus variables also presents no difficulty since this is the standard form requirement. Observe that surplus variables are subtracted from the LHS, whereas slack variables are added.

Objective function coefficient is 0

The objective function is the same as that of the original model. That is, the objective function coefficient for surplus and slack variables is always 0.

Summary of Algebraic Manipulations of Linear Programming Models and an Example

Conversion to standard form is summarized in the following three steps:

1. Convert the model to a maximization model if it is a minimization model.
2. Convert each $\leq$ constraint to an equation by adding a nonnegative slack variable.
3. Convert each $\geq$ constraint to an equation by subtracting a nonnegative surplus variable.

The steps are summarized in the flowchart in Figure 4.12.
Let's convert the model below to the standard form:

FIGURE 4.12   Flowchart for Conversion to the Standard Form

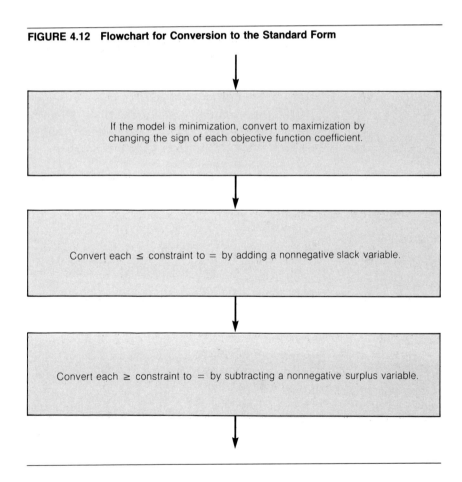

$$\begin{aligned}
\min \quad & -3x_1 + 2x_2 - x_3 \\
\text{st} \quad & x_1 - x_2 + 3x_3 \geq -4 \\
& 2x_1 + x_2 + 4x_3 \leq 12 \\
& 2x_1 - x_2 - x_3 = -2 \\
& x_1, x_2, x_3 \geq 0
\end{aligned}$$

First, the objective function is changed to maximize $3x_1 - 2x_2 + x_3$. Using a surplus variable in the first constraint and a slack variable in the second constraint results in the standard form:

$$\begin{aligned}
\max \quad & 3x_1 - 2x_2 + x_3 \\
\text{st} \quad & x_1 - x_2 + 3x_3 - s_1 = -4 \\
& 2x_1 + x_2 + 4x_3 + s_2 = 12 \\
& 2x_1 - x_2 - x_3 = -2 \\
& x_1, x_2, x_3, s_1, s_2 \geq 0
\end{aligned}$$

Conversion of a Constraint with a Negative RHS

Some linear programming systems also convert the model to an initialization form that requires nonnegative RHS constants. Whether this is necessary depends on the software's implementation of the simplex algorithm. The Theory section of Chapter 6 discusses this further. Because an RHS constant may be negative for your formulation, it may be necessary to manipulate a constraint so that the RHS constant becomes positive. If the relationship is an equation, this is done by multiplying each constraint coefficient, including the RHS constant, by -1. For example,

$$4x_1 - 2x_2 + 3x_3 = -5$$

is converted to

$$-4x_1 + 2x_2 - 3x_3 = 5$$

Algebraically, the constraints are equivalent and the objective function is unchanged.

However, if the constraint is an inequality, multiplying by -1 to change the sign of the RHS constant is *not* equivalent to multiplying each coefficient by -1. *Multiplying an inequality by a negative number reverses the direction of the inequality.* For example, 5 is greater than or equal to 3 (represented as $5 \geq 3$), and -5 is less than or equal to -3 (represented as $-5 \leq -3$). The direction of the inequality is reversed for both $\leq$ and $\geq$ inequalities when the inequality is multiplied by -1.

Multiplying by -1 changes an inequality direction

For example, the constraint

$$3x_1 + 4x_2 - x_3 \geq -1$$

is converted to

$$-3x_1 - 4x_2 + x_3 \leq 1$$

You can verify that the constraints are equivalent by checking that any variable values satisfying one constraint also satisfy the other. The objective function, other constraints, and variable nonnegativities are unchanged. Thus, this manipulation gives an equivalent model.

SLACK AND SURPLUS VARIABLES, GRAPHICAL SOLUTIONS, AND DEGENERATE SOLUTIONS

All of our graphical solution examples contained two variables, and each axis was labeled with the name of one of the variables. We indicated a $\leq$ (or $\geq$) constraint by an arrow showing the side of the line satisfying it. The simplex algorithm, used by linear programming software, converts every $\leq$ ($\geq$) inequality to an equation by adding a slack (surplus) variable. Because the software reports information concerning slack/surplus variables, you should understand the relationship between slack/surplus variables and graphical solutions. In this section, we discuss that relationship.

Structural variables

The variables you introduce to formulate the linear programming model are called **structural variables.** Consider the following model:

$$\begin{aligned}
\max \quad & 2x_1 + 3x_2 \\
\text{st} \quad & 2x_1 + x_2 \leq 6 \\
& x_1 - x_2 \geq -2 \\
& x_1 + 2x_2 \leq 8 \\
& x_1, x_2 \geq 0
\end{aligned}$$

Figure 4.13 illustrates the feasible set for this model. The structural variables are x_1 and x_2. To convert the inequalities to equations, slack variables are added to the first and third equations and a surplus variable is added to the second equation, yielding

$$\begin{aligned}
\max \quad & 2x_1 + 3x_2 \\
\text{st} \quad & 2x_1 + x_2 + s_1 = 6 \\
& x_1 - x_2 - s_2 = -2 \\
& x_1 + 2x_2 + s_3 = 8 \\
& x_1, x_2, s_1, s_2, s_3 \geq 0
\end{aligned}$$

After conversion to the standard form, the model has five variables—two structural variables and three slack/surplus variables. Consider the origin, labeled Point C, in Figure 4.13. At that point, both x_1 and x_2 are 0. The values of the slack/surplus variables are $s_1 = 6$, $s_2 = 2$, and $s_3 = 8$. Structural variables differ from the slack-and-surplus variables that are used to convert all inequalities into equations. Slack-and-surplus variables allow points to be reached that are not on the inequality equation lines. Remember that a positive variable has a value greater than 0. If the

FIGURE 4.13   Example with Corner Point A Degenerate

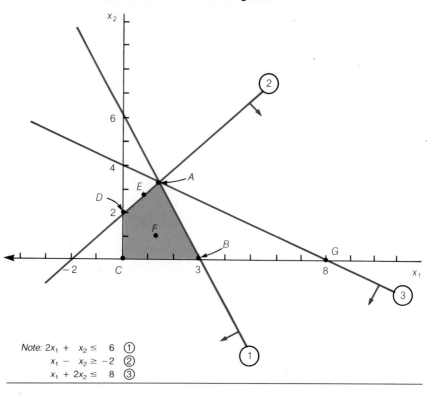

Note: $2x_1 + x_2 \leq 6$ ①
$x_1 - x_2 \geq -2$ ②
$x_1 + 2x_2 \leq 8$ ③

point is not on the line for a constraint and the inequality is satisfied, the slack or surplus variable is positive. At Point C, the slack-and-surplus variables are all positive, so the inequalities are all satisfied. The nonnegativity of slack-and-surplus variables ensures that the inequality is satisfied.

If the point is not on the line for a constraint and the inequality is not satisfied, the slack or surplus variable is negative. Consider the point labeled G in Figure 4.13. At that point, $x_1 = 8$ and $x_2 = 0$. Substituting those values into the equations with the slack-and-surplus variables, we get $s_1 = -10$, $s_2 = 10$, and $s_3 = 0$. Because s_1 is negative, the first inequality is not satisfied and the point isn't in the feasible set.

At Point B, x_1 is positive and x_2 is 0. From Figure 4.13, can you tell which slack/surplus variables are positive at Point B? Point B lies on the line of Constraint 1, so the slack variable for Constraint 1 is 0. Point B does not lie on the lines of Constraints 2 and 3, so the surplus variable for Constraint 2 and the slack variable for Constraint 3 are both positive.

A **degenerate solution** is a solution in which the number of positive variables *after adding all of the required slack and/or surplus variables for inequality constraints* is less than the number of constraints. Figure 4.13's model has three constraints. Both Points C and B have three positive variables and are not degenerate solutions.

At this time, it is not apparent that it is worthwhile to introduce the concept of a degenerate solution. However, the interpretation of computer-generated sensitivity analysis information is different for degenerate and nondegenerate optimal solutions. Chapter 5 discusses the differences. Also, the existence of degenerate solutions presents a theoretical problem for linear programming models that are solved by the simplex algorithm. Although mathematicians are interested in the theoretical complication, degenerate solutions pose no serious practical complication. In Chapter 6, we discuss the theoretical complication.

Is Corner Point D a degenerate solution? No! At Corner Point D, $x_1 = 0$ and x_2 is positive. Because Point D is on the line of the second constraint, the surplus variable for the second constraint is 0. The slack variables for both the first and third constraints are positive because Point D does not lie on either line. Because three variables are positive at Point D, the solution is not a degenerate solution.

The unique optimal solution for the linear programming model is Point A, $x_1 = \frac{4}{3}$ and $x_2 = \frac{10}{3}$, with $Z^* = \frac{38}{3}$. At Point A, both x_1 and x_2 are positive. All three lines intersect at Point A. Because Point A is on the three lines, the slack/surplus variables for all three constraints are 0. Because only two variables are positive and there are three constraints, Corner Point A is a degenerate solution. Because Point A is a degenerate optimal solution, its sensitivity analysis is different from that of a nondegenerate optimal solution.

Points A, B, C, and D are corner points of the feasible set. Corner Point C is the intersection of the lines $x_1 = 0$ and $x_2 = 0$. Corner Point B is the intersection of the lines $x_2 = 0$ and $2x_1 + x_2 = 6$. Corner Point C is the intersection of the lines $x_1 = 0$ and $x_1 - x_2 = -2$. Each nondegenerate corner point is at the intersection of only two lines. Point A is at the intersection of the lines $2x_1 + x_2 = 6$, $x_1 - x_2 = -2$, and $x_1 + 2x_2 = 8$. The degenerate corner point is at the intersection of three lines. Observe that removing the third constraint does not change the feasible set or the optimal solution. Point A, the optimal solution, is a degenerate solution. Graphically, if more than two lines (including the nonnegativities) intersect at the same point, the point is a degenerate solution.

Point A is the *only* degenerate solution in Figure 4.13. Verify that at Point E, four variables are positive. At Point F, there are five positive variables—x_1, x_2, and all three slack/surplus variables.

You shouldn't think that the relative numbers of constraints and variables cause degeneracy. Let's examine a linear programming model that has two constraints and two structural variables. Consider the model.

$$\begin{aligned}
\max \quad & 4x_1 + 3x_2 \\
\text{st} \quad & x_1 + x_2 = 2 \\
& x_1 + 3x_2 \le 3 \\
& x_1, x_2 \ge 0
\end{aligned}$$

You add a slack variable to Constraint 2 to convert it to an equation. After this has been done, the model has two constraints and three variables, including the slack variable. A degenerate solution has fewer than two positive variables. Figure 4.14 illustrates the feasible set for this model. The feasible set consists of the points on the line segment from Point A to Point B. At Point A, there are two positive variables, x_1 and x_2. At Point B, x_1 is positive and the slack variable for the second constraint is positive. Again, there are two positive variables. Since the model has only two constraints, neither Point A nor Point B is a degenerate solution. At Point C, there are three positive variables—x_1, x_2, and the slack for the second constraint.

Figure 4.15 illustrates the feasible set of the problem

$$\begin{aligned}
\max \quad & 4x_1 + 3x_2 \\
\text{st} \quad & x_1 + x_2 = 1 \\
& x_1 + 3x_2 \le 3 \\
& x_1, x_2 \ge 0
\end{aligned}$$

This is the same model as the previous one except that the RHS for the first constraint has been changed from 2 to 1. Again, there are three

---

FIGURE 4.14   Example with *No* Degenerate Corner Points

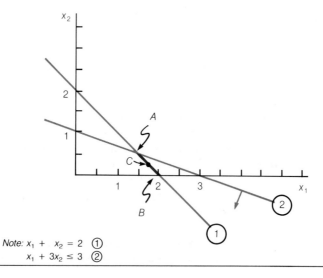

Note: $x_1 + x_2 = 2$ ①
$x_1 + 3x_2 \le 3$ ②

FIGURE 4.15   Example with Corner Point A Degenerate

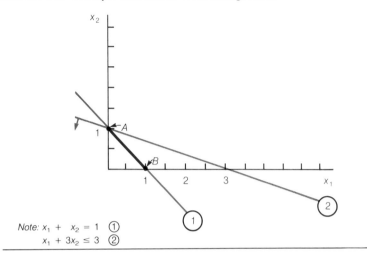

Note: $x_1 + x_2 = 1$ ①
$x_1 + 3x_2 \leq 3$ ②

---

variables, including the slack variable. At Point A, the only positive variable is x_2. Since the number of positive variables (one) is less than the number of constraints (two), Point A is a degenerate solution. Graphically, the lines of the two constraints and the $x_1 = 0$ line intersect at Point A. The relative values of the constraint coefficients and the RHS constants caused the point to be a degenerate solution. The relative numbers of the constraints and the structural variables did not.

SUMMARY

We began this chapter with a discussion of graphically solving linear programming models. Graphical solution is useful for introducing concepts, but it is not practical for the solution of realistically complex problems. For example, the National Airlines model has about 2,400 variables. Because you need to label an axis for each variable, you can't solve the model graphically.

You solve a linear programming model graphically by graphing the feasible set. Then, you plot an equal value contour of the objective function and slide it as far as possible in the improving direction until if you move it any farther, no points in the feasible set will be on it. The point(s) in the feasible set on that best equal value contour is (are) the optimal solution(s).

Two of the possible outcomes for linear programming solutions are a *unique optimal solution* and *alternate optimal solutions*. If only one point in the feasible set has the best objective function value, the optimal solution is unique. If more than one point in the feasible set has the best objective function value, alternate optimal solutions exist. If a linear programming model has alternate optimal solutions, the best equal value contour lies on one of the lines. If a linear programming model has a finite optimal solution, one or more corner points are optimal.

If a linear programming model is ill-behaved, there is no optimal corner point. Two ill-behaved outcomes for linear programming solutions are *no feasible solution* and an *unbounded optimal solution*. No feasible solution means that it is impossible to satisfy all of the constraints and the variable nonnegativities at the same time. The feasible set is empty. An un-bounded optimal solution means that there are points in the feasible set for which the objective function is as favorable as desired. This can occur only if the feasible set is unbounded. If your linear programming model is ill-behaved, you should check the model input and the model formulation. Useful linear programming models aren't ill-behaved.

After discussing graphical solutions, we discussed the concept of an algorithm and its initialization. We presented the initialization standard form for the simplex algorithm for linear programming. We described the algebraic manipulations required to convert any linear programming model to the standard form. These manipulations include converting minimization models to maximization models by changing the sign of each objective function coefficient (i.e., multiplying by -1). You add non-negative slack variables to the LHS of $\le$ inequalities to convert them to equations. You subtract nonnegative surplus variables from the LHS of $\ge$ inequalities to convert them to equations.

The final section relates graphical solutions and the values of slack-and-surplus variables. If a point is on the constraint line of an inequality, the value of the slack/surplus variable is 0. If a point is not on the constraint line of an inequality, the value of the slack/surplus variable is not 0. If the point satisfies the inequality, its value is positive. If the point does not satisfy the inequality, its value is negative and the point is not in the feasible set.

Finally, we introduced the concept of a degenerate solution, one for which the number of positive variables, including the slack-and-surplus variables, is less than the number of constraints. The interpretation of sensitivity analysis computer output is different for degenerate and non-degenerate optimal solutions. Chapter 5 discusses the differences.

Let's observe some limitations of this chapter's information. First, all of our graphical solutions were for *linear* programming models. If a constraint function is linear, the graph is a straight line. If a constraint function is nonlinear, the graph is not a straight line and the graph is harder to draw. Similarly, if the objective function is linear, an equal value contour is a straight line and all equal value contours are parallel. If the objective function is not linear, an equal value contour isn't a straight line and all equal value contours aren't parallel lines. It's harder to graphically find the optimal solution of a nonlinear programming model than the optimal solution of a linear programming model. Second, if a model has more than two structural variables, graphing the feasible set is more difficult. If there are three variables, you try to visualize the feasible set in three dimensions. If there are more than three variables, it's impossible to visualize. All of our graphical solution examples had two variables.

Let's observe some cautions. First, you need two distinct points to determine the straight line for a linear equation. Second, you must check a point *not* on the line to determine which side of the line satisfies an inequality. Third, a feasible solution satisfies all of the constraints and all of the variable nonnegativities. You graph the constraints independently. Fourth, remember to check the direction in which the equal value contour slides when you change the objective function value. Fifth, remember that favorable means larger for a maximization objective and smaller for a minimization objective. Sixth, if two points are alternate optimal solutions, all of the points on the line segment between them are also optimal. Seventh, it's possible for a model to have a finite optimal solution even though the feasible set is unbounded. But if there is an unbounded optimal solution, the feasible set must be unbounded. Eighth, for a nonlinear programming model, even if a finite optimal solution exists, it may be in the interior of the feasible set or along an edge. Graphical solution of nonlinear programming problems is possible, but it is more difficult than graphical solution of linear programming problems. Ninth, you must add different slack/surplus variables to each inequality. Tenth, when a minimization model is converted to a maximization model, the optimal objective function value changes sign. Intelligent software changes the sign again before the solution is reported. Eleventh, remember that when an inequality is multiplied by -1, the direction of the inequality is reversed.

QUESTIONS

1. What is the feasible set of a linear programming model?
2. Do two alternate optimal solutions have the same objective function values?
3. Do two alternate optimal solutions have the same decision variable values?
4. What is the origin?
5. What is meant by the expression "no feasible solution"?
6. Give two potential reasons why there may be no feasible solution to a constrained optimization model.
7. What is an unbounded feasible set? Give a graphical example of an unbounded feasible set.
8. What is an unbounded optimal solution?
9. Do all models with unbounded feasible sets have unbounded optimal solutions?

10. Give the two possible outcomes of ill-behaved models.

11. Is there a unique optimal solution for Chapter 2's Potato Processing example?

12. What is a degenerate solution? Draw a feasible set with a degenerate solution and indicate the degenerate solution.

13. How do you determine which side of a constraint line satisfies an inequality?

14. Draw a feasible set and indicate its corner points.

15. Under what condition(s) does a linear programming model have an optimal solution at a corner point?

16. If you change an RHS constant, what happens to the graph of the constraint?

17. If you change an objective function coefficient, what happens to the equal value contours?

18. Do all linear programming models with unbounded optimal solutions have unbounded feasible sets?

19. What is the standard initialization form for the simplex algorithm?

20. If you multiply the objective function by -1, what happens to the optimal objective function value?

21. What is the objective function coefficient for all slack and surplus variables?

22. When do you add a slack variable?

23. When do you add a surplus variable?

24. What is $Z*$?

25. If you multiply an inequality by -1, what happens to the direction of the inequality?

26. If a linear programming model has two $\leq$ inequalities, how many slack variables are added?

27. If a slack variable is 0 at a point, where is the point relative to the constraint line?

28. If a slack variable is positive at a point, where is the point relative to the constraint line?

29. If a slack variable is negative at a point, where is the point relative to the constraint line?

30. Why is the concept of a degenerate solution important?

31. What is a structural variable?

32. What is an algorithm?

EXERCISES

For each exercise in which a graph is required, label both of the axes. For the exercises 19 to 22 and 27 to 34, give the exact values of the decision variables and the objective function. If there are alternate optimal solutions, indicate them.

1. Graph each of the following functions:
   a. $f(A) = 5 + 2A$
   b. $G(z) = -3 + z$
   c. $F(x) = -3x$
   d. $L(a) = 4 - 2a$
   e. $f(A) = -3$

2. Graph each of the following functions:
   a. $G(x) = -5 - 4x$
   b. $f(x) = 7 - (\frac{1}{3})x$
   c. $f(a) = -4 + 2a$
   d. $f(b) = 2b - 8$
   e. $g(x) = (\frac{1}{b})$
   f. $g(x) = (\frac{1}{b}) + 3$

3. Graph each of the following equations:
   a. $3A + 4B = 12$
   b. $3A + 4B = 6$
   c. $3A + 4B = -6$
   d. $2A - 3B = 6$
   e. $2A - 3B = 12$
   f. $2A = 6$
   g. $3B = 6$
   h. $2A + 3B = 0$
   i. $2A - 3B = 0$

4. Graph each of the following inequalities:
   a. $3X + 2Y \le 12$
   b. $3X + 2Y \ge 12$
   c. $-X + 2Y \le 6$
   d. $2Y - 2X \ge 6$
   e. $-Y - 7X \le -3$
   f. $4X + 2Y \ge -8$
   g. $4X - 3Y \ge 0$
   h. $-X - 2Y \le 0$

5. Convert each of the following inequalities to an equivalent equation:
   a. $3A + 4B \ge 12$
   b. $3a - 7b + 4c \le -6$
   c. $-X + 3Y - Z \ge 7$
   d. $2X + 4Y \le 12$

6. Convert each of these inequalities to an equality for which the RHS constant is nonnegative:
   a. $3B - 4C \ge -7$
   b. $2X - 4Y \le 0$
   c. $4A + 2C \le -15$

7. Graph and shade the feasible set for the following constraints:

$$2X + Y \le 8$$
$$4X + 7Y \le 28$$
$$X, Y \ge 0$$

8. Graph and shade the feasible set for the following constraints:

$$2X + 4Y \leq 16$$
$$4X + 3Y \leq 24$$
$$X, Y \geq 0$$

9. Graph and shade the feasible set for the following constraints:

$$4X + 3Y \leq 24$$
$$2X + 3Y \geq 15$$
$$3X - 2Y \leq 0$$
$$X, Y \geq 0$$

10. Graph and shade the feasible set for the following constraints:

$$-4X + 4Y \geq 12$$
$$2X + 3Y \leq 18$$
$$3X + 3Y \leq 21$$
$$X, Y \geq 0$$

11. Graph and shade the feasible set for the following constraints:

$$2X + 4Y \leq 12$$
$$2X - 3Y \leq 8$$
$$X - Y = 5$$
$$X, Y \geq 0$$

12. Graph and shade the feasible set for the following constraints:

$$-X + 2Y = 2$$
$$2X - 3Y \leq 8$$
$$2X + 2Y = 0$$
$$X, Y \geq 0$$

13. For each of the following objective functions, plot the 1-contour and the 10-contour on the same graph:
    a. $2A + 3B$
    b. $-A + 2B$
    c. $-A - 2B$

14. For each of the following objective functions, plot the (-1)-contour and the 10-contour on the same graph:
    a. $-2A - 2B$
    b. $-0.5A + 0.5B$
    c. $2A + 2B$

15. Convert the following linear programming model to the standard form:

    max $3X + 2Y + 2.5Z$
    st $2X + 7Y - Z \leq 12$
          $3X + Z \geq 4$
          $X, Y, Z \geq 0$

16. Convert the following linear programming model to the standard form:

    max $2X + 6Y + 3Z$
    st $7X + 6Y + 2Z \geq 12$
          $3X - 6Y + 3Z \geq -8$
          $2X + 3Y = 18$
          $X, Y, Z \geq 0$

17. Convert the following linear programming model to the standard form, in which all RHS constants are nonnegative:

    max $\quad -3X + 4Y - 5Z$
    st $\qquad 3X + 6Y + 2Z \leq -12$
    $\qquad 23X + 2Y \geq 7$
    $\qquad X, Y, Z \geq 0$

18. Convert the following linear programming model to the standard form, in which all RHS constants are nonnegative:

    min $\quad 4X - 3Y$
    st $\qquad -3X + 4Y + Z \leq -2$
    $\qquad 12X - 2Y - Z \geq -7$
    $\qquad 2X - 3Y - 2Z = -10$
    $\qquad X, Y, Z \geq 0$

19. Graphically find the optimal solution to Exercise 7 with the following objective functions:
    a. max $2X + 2Y$
    b. max $3X + Y$
    c. max $X + 2Y$
    d. max $2X + Y$

20. Graphically find the optimal solution to Exercise 8 with the following objective functions:
    a. max $2X + 2Y$
    b. max $3X + Y$
    c. min $X + 2Y$
    d. min $2X - 2Y$
    e. max $X + 2Y$

21. Graphically find the optimal solution to Exercise 9 with the following objective functions:
    a. max $2X + 2Y$
    b. max $3X + Y$
    c. max $X + 2Y$

22. Graphically find the optimal solution to Exercise 10 with the following objective functions:
    a. max $X + 2Y$
    b. max $3X + Y$
    c. min $X + 2Y$

23. Determine the number of corner points in the feasible set for Exercise 7.

24. Determine the number of corner points in the feasible set for Exercise 8.

25. Determine the number of corner points in the feasible set for Exercise 9.

26. Determine the number of corner points in the feasible set for Exercise 10.

27. Consider the following linear programming model:

    max $\quad 2X + 2Y$
    st $\qquad 3X + 2Y \leq 3$
    $\qquad 2X + 3Y \leq 2$
    $\qquad -X + Y \leq 0$
    $\qquad X, Y \geq 0$

    a. Graphically find the optimal solution. Give the variable values and the optimal value of the objective function.

    b. What is the number of corner points in the feasible set? Label the corner points.

    c. How many variables, including slack-and-surplus variables, are positive at each corner point?

    d. Are any of the corner points degenerate corner points?

28. Consider the following linear programming model:

$$
\begin{aligned}
\max \quad & 3X + 3Y \\
\text{st} \quad & 3X + 2Y \le 2 \\
& 2X + 3Y \le 2 \\
& -X + Y \ge 0 \\
& X,\ Y \ge 0
\end{aligned}
$$

    a. Graphically find the optimal solution. Give the variable values and the optimal value of the objective function.

    b. What is the number of corner points in the feasible set? Label the corner points.

    c. How many variables, including slack-and-surplus variables, are positive at each corner point?

    d. Are any of the corner points degenerate corner points?

    e. Is the optimal solution unique?

29. Consider the following linear programming model:

$$
\begin{aligned}
\max \quad & 6X + 4Y \\
\text{st} \quad & 3X + 2Y \le 3 \\
& 2X + 3Y \le 2 \\
& X,\ Y \ge 0
\end{aligned}
$$

    a. Graphically find the optimal solution. Give the variable values and the optimal value of the objective function.

    b. What is the number of corner points in the feasible set? Label the corner points.

    c. How many variables, including slack-and-surplus variables, are positive at each corner point?

    d. Are any of the corner points degenerate corner points?

    e. Is the optimal solution unique?

30. Consider the following linear programming model:

$$
\begin{aligned}
\max \quad & X + 3Y \\
\text{st} \quad & 4X + 2Y \le 12 \\
& 5X + 3Y \le 15 \\
& -X + Y \le 0 \\
& X,\ Y \ge 0
\end{aligned}
$$

    a. Graphically find the optimal solution. Give the variable values and the optimal value of the objective function.

    b. What is the number of corner points in the feasible set? Label the corner points.

    c. How many variables, including slack-and-surplus variables, are positive at each corner point?

    d. Are any of the corner points degenerate corner points?

    e. Is the optimal solution unique?

31. Graphically find the optimal solution to the linear programming model

$$
\begin{aligned}
\max \quad & 2X + 3Y \\
\text{st} \quad & 4X + 2Y = 8 \\
& 3X + 3Y \geq 15 \\
& -X + Y \leq 0 \\
& X,\ Y \geq 0
\end{aligned}
$$

32. Graphically find the optimal solution to the linear programming model

$$
\begin{aligned}
\max \quad & 2X + 3Y \\
\text{st} \quad & 4X - 2Y \leq 8 \\
& -3X + 3Y \geq 15 \\
& -X + Y \leq 0 \\
& X,\ Y \geq 0
\end{aligned}
$$

33. Graphically find the optimal solution to the linear programming model

$$
\begin{aligned}
\max \quad & 3X + 3Y \\
\text{st} \quad & 4X + 2Y \geq 8 \\
& X + Y \geq 1 \\
& X,\ Y \geq 0
\end{aligned}
$$

34. Graphically find the optimal solution to the linear programming model

$$
\begin{aligned}
\max \quad & 3X + 3Y \\
\text{st} \quad & -4X + 2Y \geq -8 \\
& X - Y \leq 1 \\
& X,\ Y \geq 0
\end{aligned}
$$

35. *Appendix.* Convert the model below to an equivalent model with all non-negative variables:

$$
\begin{aligned}
\max \quad & 2X + 4Y - 2Z \\
\text{st} \quad & 2X - 4Y + 3Z = 6 \\
& -3X + 2Y - 2Z = 4 \\
& X + Y + Z = 3 \\
& X \text{ unrestricted in sign} \\
& Y \leq 0 \\
& Z \geq 0
\end{aligned}
$$

36. *Appendix.* Convert the model below to an equivalent model with all non-negative variables:

$$
\begin{aligned}
\max \quad & 3X - 2Y - 7Z \\
\text{st} \quad & -X + 4Y + 2Z = 11 \\
& 2X - 5Y + Z = 8 \\
& X + Y + Z = 1 \\
& X \text{ unrestricted in sign} \\
& Y \leq 0 \\
& Z \geq 0
\end{aligned}
$$

37. *Appendix.* Convert the model below to an equivalent model with only $\leq$ inequalities:

max $\quad 2X + 4Y - 2Z$
st $\quad\;\; 2X - 4Y + 3Z \geq 6$
$\quad\quad\; -3X + 2Y - 2Z = 4$
$\quad\quad\;\; X + Y + Z \leq 3$
$\quad\quad\;\; X,\, Y,\, Z \geq 0$

38. *Appendix.* Convert the model below to an equivalent model with only $\leq$ inequalities:

max $\quad -3X + 4Y + Z$
st $\quad\;\; -2X + 2Y + 2Z \geq -3$
$\quad\quad\;\; 3X + 3Y + 2Z \leq 4$
$\quad\quad\; -2X + 3Y + 4Z = -1$
$\quad\quad\;\; X,\, Y,\, Z \geq 0$

MORE CHALLENGING EXERCISES

For each model where the optimal solution is to be found graphically, give the variable values as well as the optimal value of the objective function.

1. Construct a linear programming model with one constraint that has an unbounded feasible set.

2. Construct a linear programming model with three constraints that has an unbounded feasible set.

3. A company makes wooden tables in several varieties. One of these varieties is a round kitchen table. This table is also offered with two leaves, which makes it appropriate for dining rooms. Sales of both of these tables have been excellent. In fact, there is more demand for both of them than can be met with the existing manufacturing capacity. There is a higher profit margin on the table with leaves, but this table requires more time on the planer machine, which has been used to its capacity. It is desired to determine whether the higher profit margin is enough to justify the current manufacturing strategy of making the table with leaves almost exclusively. The profit margins are $43 for the round table and $49 for the round table with leaves. The manufacturing operations require time on a lathe to make the legs, time on the planer to make the top and leaves, and some hand-finishing time. The times required in hours per table are

	Machine		Hand Finishing
Table	Lathe	Planer	
Round	0.15	0.13	0.25
Round with leaves	0.15	0.18	0.30

The shop works 7 days a week and 24 hours a day. There are 2 people who work each shift to do the hand finishing. Formulate a linear programming model to determine the best product mix. Graph the feasible set and find the optimal solution to the model.

4. For MCE 3, do the following:
   a. Find the optimal solution to the model if the profit margin on the round table is $40.
   b. Find the optimal solution to the model if the profit margin on the round table is $45.

5. If the flakes limitation is 33,000 pounds for the Potato Processing example of Chapter 2, find the optimal solution.

6. If the flakes limitation is 24,750 pounds for the Potato Processing example of Chapter 2, find the optimal solution.

7. If the flakes limitation is 20,000 pounds for the Potato Processing example of Chapter 2, find the optimal solution.

8. Find the amount that the profit margin on Idaho potatoes would have to increase before the optimal solution would be a different potato purchasing plan. What would be the profit at that new optimal solution? What would be the new purchasing plan?

9. Find the amount that the profit margin on Idaho potatoes would have to decrease before the optimal solution would be a different potato purchasing plan. What would be the profit at that new optimal solution? What would be the new purchasing plan?

10. Construct a linear programming model with one inequality constraint (in addition to the nonnegativity requirements) for which there is no feasible solution. Repeat with one equality constraint.

11. Construct a linear programming model with two inequality constraints (in addition to the nonnegativity requirements) for which there is no feasible solution. Repeat with two equality constraints.

12. Construct a linear programming model with three inequality constraints (in addition to the nonnegativity requirements) for which there is no feasible solution. Repeat with two inequality constraints and one equality constraint.

13. Consider the feasible set

    st $4A + 3B \leq 12$
        $A + 2B \leq 10$
        $A, B \geq 0$

    a. Find the optimal solution with the objective function max $0A + 2B$.
    b. Find the optimal solution as the objective function coefficient of A increases from 0 to 20. Give the objective function value each time the optimal solution point changes.
    c. Graph Z^*, the optimal value of the objective function, versus the objective function coefficient value of A between 0 and 20.

14. Consider the feasible set

    st $4A + 3B \leq 12$
        $2A + 2B \geq 5$
        $A, B \geq 0$

   a. Find the optimal solution with the objective function max $0A + 3B$.

   b. Find the optimal solution as the objective function coefficient of A increases from 0 to 20. Give the objective function value each time the optimal solution point changes.

   c. Graph Z^*, the optimal value of the objective function, versus the objective function coefficient value of A between 0 and 20.

15. Consider the feasible set

$$\text{max} \quad 2A + 3B$$
$$\text{st} \quad 4A + 3B \leq 12$$
$$A + 2B \leq 10$$
$$A, B \geq 0$$

   a. Find the optimal solution with the RHS constant of the first constraint equal to 0.

   b. Find the optimal solution as the RHS constant increases from 0 to 20. Give the objective function value and the variable values each time the optimal corner point changes.

   c. Graph Z^*, the optimal value of the objective function, versus the RHS constant of the first constraint for values from 0 to 20.

16. Consider the feasible set

$$\text{max} \quad 2A + 3B$$
$$\text{st} \quad 4A + 3B \leq 12$$
$$2A + 2B \geq 5$$
$$A, B \geq 0$$

   a. Find the optimal solution with the RHS constant of the first constraint equal to 0.

   b. Find the optimal solution as the RHS constant increases from 0 to 20. Give the objective function value and the variable values each time the optimal corner point changes.

   c. Graph Z^*, the optimal value of the objective function, versus the RHS constant for the first constraint for values between 0 and 20.

17. Ray's Cherry Hut produces its own private label cherry jelly when the cherries are harvested. Some of the cherries were damaged in a recent hailstorm. Cherries that were damaged are Grade C. The highest-quality cherries are Grade A. The two main quality considerations are tartness and clarity. The hail-damaged cherries are much cheaper, but because of the bruises, these result in cloudy jelly. The costs per pail of the cherries are $0.50 and $0.18 for Grades A and C, respectively. The tartness and clarity ratings are as follows:

Grade	Tartness	Clarity
A	11.0	1.0
C	9.0	3.0

The jelly must have a tartness rating between 10.0 and 10.5. The maximum clarity rating is 1.9. The yield of jelly is one 8-ounce jar for each pail. An 8-ounce jar sells for $1.59. Assume that more than enough of each grade of cherries is available for purchase.

a. Formulate a model to determine the best way to blend a standard 8-ounce jar of jelly.

b. Graph the feasible set and find the optimal solution graphically.

18. A chemical company desires to blend ethylene glycol and distilled water to obtain antifreeze for automobiles. This antifreeze will be marketed as pre-mixed for 25 degrees below 0. It is expected that consumers will prefer a premixed product over attempting to measure the pure ethylene glycol and mix it themselves. The freezing point of ethylene glycol is 67 degrees below 0. The freezing point of water is 32 degrees above 0. Ethylene glycol costs $1 per gallon. The distilled water costs $0.10 per gallon.

a. Formulate a linear programming model to blend a gallon with a maximum freezing point of 25 degrees below 0. Assume that the freezing point of the blend is the weighted average of the freezing points of the components.

b. Graph the feasible set and graphically find the mixture with the minimum cost.

19. A steel company has two iron-ore mines, located in Minnesota and West Virginia. A total of 50,000 tons of iron ore per week is required from the mines. The weekly mine capacities and the costs per ton delivered to the processing plant are

Mine	Capacity (tons/week)	Cost ($/ton)
Minnesota	35,000	87
West Virginia	32,000	69

The ore at the processing plant must contain at least 45 percent iron and no more than 1.3 percent sulfur. The percentages of iron ore and sulfur at the two mines are

Mine	Percent Iron	Percent Sulfur
Minnesota	43.0	1.1
West Virginia	67.0	1.4

a. Formulate a linear programming model to determine the amount of iron ore from each mine per week for cost minimization.

b. Graph the feasible set and find the optimal solution graphically.

CASE

Sherman Motor Company

The Sherman Motor Company manufactured two specialized models of trucks in a single plant. Manufacturing operations were grouped into four departments: metal stamping, engine assembly, Model 101 assembly, and Model 102 assembly. Monthly production capacity in each department was limited as follows, assuming that each department devoted full time to the model in question:

Department	Monthly Capacity	
	Model 101	Model 102
Metal stamping	2,500	3,500
Engine assembly	3,333	1,667
Model 101 assembly	2,250	—
Model 102 assembly	—	1,500

That is, the capacity of the metal stamping department was sufficient to produce stampings for either 2,500 Model 101 trucks or 3,500 Model 102 trucks per month if it devoted full time to either model. It could also produce stampings for both models, with a corresponding reduction in the potential output of each. Since each Model 102 truck required five sevenths as much of the capacity of the department as one Model 101 truck, for every seven Model 102 trucks produced, it would be necessary to subtract five from the capacity remaining for Model 101. If, for example, 1,400 Model 102 trucks were produced, there would be sufficient stamping capacity available for $2,500 - (5/7 \times 1,400) = 1,500$ Model 101 trucks. Thus, the capacity restrictions in the four departments could be represented by the straight lines shown in Exhibit 1. Any production combination within the area bounded by the heavy portion of the lines was feasible from a capacity standpoint.

EXHIBIT 1   Diagram Showing Production Possibilities

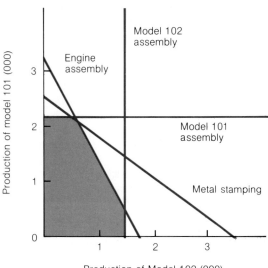

The prices to dealers of the two models, FOB the Sherman plant, were $2,100 for Model 101 and $2,000 for Model 102. Sherman followed the price leadership of one of the larger manufacturers in the industry.

As a result of a seller's market in 1953, Sherman was able to sell as many trucks as it could produce. The production schedules it had followed during the first six months of the

This case was prepared by Charles J. Christenson as the basis for class discussion rather than to illustrate either effective or ineffective handling of an administrative situation. Reprinted by permission of the Harvard Business School.

Harvard Business School
Case 107–010.

EXHIBIT 2   Standard Costs of Two Truck Models

	Model 101		Model 102	
Direct materials		$1,200		$1,000
Direct labor				
Metal stamping	$ 40		$ 30	
Engine assembly	60		120	
Final assembly	100	200	75	225
Overhead*				
Metal stamping	$216		$169	
Engine assembly	130		251	
Final assembly	445	791	175	595
Total		$2,191		$1,820

* See Exhibit 3.

EXHIBIT 3   Overhead Budget for 1953

Department	Total Overhead per Month*	Fixed Overhead per Month†	Variable Overhead/Unit	
			Model 101	Model 102
Metal stamping	$ 325,000	$135,000	$120	$100
Engine assembly	420,000	85,000	105	200
Model 101 assembly	148,000	90,000	175	—
Model 102 assembly	262,000	75,000	—	125
	$1,155,000	$385,000	$400	$425

* Based on planned 1953 production rate of 333 Model 101 trucks and 1,500 Model 102 trucks per month.

† Fixed overhead was distributed to models in proportion to degree of capacity utilization.

year resulted in a monthly output of 333 Model 101 trucks and 1,500 Model 102 trucks. At this level of production, both the Model 102 assembly and the engine assembly departments were operating at capacity, but the metal stamping department was operating at only 56.2 percent of capacity and the Model 101 assembly department was at only 14.8 percent. Standard costs at this level of production are given in Exhibit 2, and further details on overhead costs are given in Exhibit 3.

At a monthly planning session of the company's executives in July 1953, dissatisfaction was expressed with the company's profit performance as reported in the six-month income statement just prepared (see Exhibit 4). The sales manager pointed out that it was impossible to sell the Model 101 truck to yield a profit and suggested that it be dropped from the line in order to improve overall profitability.

The controller objected to this suggestion. "The real trouble, Dick, is that we are trying to absorb the entire fixed overhead of the Model 101 assembly department with only a small number of units production. Actually these units are making a contribution to overhead, even though it's not adequate to cover fixed costs, and we'd be worse off without them. In fact, it seems to me quite possible that we'd be better off by *increasing* production of Model 101 trucks, cutting back if necessary on Model 102 production.''

The production manager pointed out that there was another way in which output of Model 101 trucks could be stepped up, which would not require a cutback in Model 102 production. This would be through purchase of engines from an outside supplier, thus relieving the present capacity problem in the engine assembly department. If this course of action were followed, Sherman would probably furnish the necessary materials but would reimburse the supplier for labor and overhead.

At this point, the president entered the discussion. He asked the controller, the sales manager, and the production manager to get together to consider the two questions raised by their comments and to report their recommendations to him the next day. The two questions were: (1) Assuming no change in present capacity and demand, what would be the most profitable product mix? (2) What was the maximum labor and overhead charge that Sherman could afford to pay for engines if it purchased them from an outside supplier?

EXHIBIT 4 Income Statement for Six Months Ending June 30, 1953 ($000s)

Net sales	$21,950
Cost of goods sold	20,683
Gross margin	$ 1,267
Selling, administrative, and general expense	1,051
Net income before taxes	$ 216
Taxes on income	115
Net income after taxes	$ 101

More Algebraic Manipulations

In this chapter, we discussed several algebraic manipulations that are used to change linear programming models to the standard initialization form. We showed how to convert a model with a minimization objective function to a model with a maximization objective function. We showed how to convert a $\leq$ inequality constraint to an equality constraint by adding a slack variable and how to convert a $\geq$ inequality constraint to an equality constraint by subtracting a surplus variable.

In this appendix, we show additional algebraic manipulations. In the standard initialization form, all of the variables are nonnegative. Usually, only nonnegative values of decision variables make sense. For example, you can't buy a negative number of trucks. In some circumstances, however, a variable may be nonpositive (i.e., ≤ 0) or unrestricted in sign. In this appendix, we show how to convert a model with a ≤ 0 variable or a variable unrestricted in sign to a model with only nonnegative variables. We also show how to convert a model with an equality constraint to a model with inequality constraints.

Conversion of a Model with Unrestricted Variables to a Model with All Variables ≥ 0

Sometimes, a variable can be negative as well as positive or 0, and we call this type of variable **unrestricted in sign.** Remember, in the standard initialization form for the simplex algorithm, all of the variables are nonnegative. Also, linear programming software such as LINDO assumes that all of the variables are nonnegative, and you don't even indicate that this is so. Consequently, if you enter a model with a variable unrestricted in sign, all of the variables are assumed to be nonnegative and negative variable values aren't considered. Therefore, to use LINDO to solve a model with unrestricted variables, you must convert the model to an *equivalent* model in which all of the variable values must be ≥ 0.

Say that variable x_j is unrestricted in sign. You introduce two nonnegative variables, x_j^+ and x_j^-, and define the relationship

$$x_j = x_j^+ - x_j^-$$

You modify the model by substituting $x_j^+ - x_j^-$ for x_j. The new model doesn't contain the variable x_j. Even though x_j^+ and x_j^- are ≥ 0, x_j is unrestricted in sign. For example, if $x_j^+ = 5$ and $x_j^- = 0$, then $x_j = 5 - 0 = 5$. But if $x_j^+ = 0$ and $x_j^- = 5$, then $x_j = 0 - 5 = -5$. x_j can be positive, negative, or 0. Let's explain the notations x_j^+ and x_j^-. If x_j is positive, then the variable x_j^+ takes on the *positive* value of x_j. If x_j is negative, then the variable x_j^- takes on the *negative* of the value of x_j. That is, if $x_j = -100$, then $x_j^- = 100$.

Let's do this algebraic manipulation on an example. Consider the following model with x_1 unrestricted in sign:

$$\begin{aligned}
\text{max} \quad & 3x_1 - 2x_2 + x_3 \\
\text{st} \quad & -x_1 + x_2 - 3x_3 + s_1 = 4 \\
& 2x_1 + x_2 + 4x_3 - s_2 = 12 \\
& -2x_1 + x_2 + x_3 = 2 \\
& x_2, x_3, s_1, s_2 \geq 0 \\
& x_1 \text{ unrestricted in sign}
\end{aligned}$$

You substitute $x_1^+ - x_1^-$ for x_1, giving

$$\begin{aligned}
\text{max} \quad & 3x_1^+ - 3x_1^- - 2x_2 + x_3 \\
\text{st} \quad & -x_1^+ + x_1^- + x_2 - 3x_3 + s_1 = 4 \\
& 2x_1^+ - 2x_1^- + x_2 + 4x_3 - s_2 = 12 \\
& -2x_1^+ + 2x_1^- + x_2 + x_3 = 2 \\
& x_1^+, x_1^-, x_2, x_3, s_1, s_2 \geq 0
\end{aligned}$$

Note that the coefficients of x_1^+ and x_1^- are exactly opposite in sign and that the variable x_1 doesn't appear in the model. You solve the model involving x_1^+ and x_1^- and calculate the optimal value of x_1 using $x_1 = x_1^+ - x_1^-$.

Conversion of a Model with Nonpositive Variables (≤ 0) to a Model with All Variables ≥ 0

A **nonpositive variable** can be negative or zero; it can't be positive. Because LINDO assumes that all variables are nonnegative, you must convert a model that contains a nonpositive variable to an equivalent model with only nonnegative variables. You introduce the nonnegative variable x_j^- and define the relationship

$$x_j = -x_j^-$$

You modify the model by substituting $-x_j^-$ for x_j in the model. The new model doesn't contain the x_j variable. When x_j^- is ≥ 0, the value of x_j is ≤ 0. For example, if $x_j^- = 100$, then $x_j = -x_j^- = -100$. Because $x_j^- \geq 0$, the value of x_j must be ≤ 0.

Say that $x_1 \leq 0$ in the previous example. Let's convert it to the standard form with all nonnegative variables. You substitute $-x_1^-$ for x_1, giving

$$\begin{aligned}
\text{max} \quad & -3x_1^- - 2x_2 + x_3 \\
\text{st} \quad & x_1^- + x_2 - 3x_3 + s_1 = 4 \\
& -2x_1^- + x_2 + 4x_3 - s_2 = 12 \\
& 2x_1^- + x_2 + x_3 = 2 \\
& x_1^-, x_2, x_3, s_1, s_2 \geq 0
\end{aligned}$$

After you have obtained the optimal solution to the model of the standard form, you calculate the optimal value of x_1 using $x_1 = -x_1^-$.

If a linear programming model has variables that are nonpositive or unrestricted in sign, you add the following step to the three steps we used to convert a general model to the standard form:

4. By using the appropriate substitutions, convert any variables unrestricted in sign or ≤ 0 so that all variables are nonnegative.

Conversion of an = Constraint to Two Inequality Constraints

In the Theory section of Chapter 5, we discuss the dual problem of linear programming. The standard form for creating the dual problem has a maximization objective function, all $\leq$-type constraints, and all ≥ 0 variables. We've shown how to convert models with nonpositive variables and variables unrestricted in sign to models with all variables ≥ 0. We've also shown how to convert an objective function from minimization to maximization. You multiply a $\geq$-type constraint by -1 to reverse the inequality.

The only conversion we haven't discussed is the conversion of an equality constraint to an equivalent model with only inequality constraints. You replace each equality constraint by *two* inequality constraints. Let's consider the equation $3x_1 + 2x_2 - x_3 = 5$. You replace this equation by the pair of constraints

$$3x_1 + 2x_2 - x_3 \leq 5$$
$$3x_1 + 2x_2 - x_3 \geq 5$$

Any solution that satisfies this pair of inequalities must have $3x_1 + 2x_2 - x_3 = 5$. If all constraints must be $\leq$, then the second inequality is multiplied by -1. The pair of constraints is then

$$3x_1 + 2x_2 - x_3 \leq 5$$
$$-3x_1 - 2x_2 + x_3 \leq -5$$

Note that the coefficients, including the RHS constants, are opposite in sign.

5

Interpretation of Computer-Generated Solutions and Sensitivity Analysis

NEW ENGLAND MERCHANTS LEASING CORPORATION

New England Merchants Leasing Corporation, a subsidiary of New England Merchants Bank's holding company, is the 16th largest bank lessor in the United States. Leases account for approximately 20 percent of all capital goods in the United States. Leveraged leases are commonly used to finance commercial aircraft, supertankers, and other capital equipment and often have a length of 15 to 25 years. The financing arrangements for such leases are very complex and often include several banks as debt and equity participants. Leases may generate tax shelters because of depreciation and large interest payments for financing. The tax losses that a lease generates are greatest early in the lease because of accelerated depreciation and loan amortization.

New England Merchants participates in many different types of leases. Its corporate goal is to balance "the aggregate portfolio among these various (lease) markets and to structure individual transactions in a manner consistent with the aggregate strategic goals." Tax shelters have benefits if there are profits from other operations that can be offset by the losses. Lease decisions are constrained by available capital and anticipated profits from other activities.

Considering leases individually misses the interactions among them for capital requirements and tax benefits. The structuring of individual leases should be considered in the context of their impact on the entire lease portfolio.

New England Merchants Leasing developed a computer-based lease portfolio planning model. The objective function is maximization of the net present value (NPV) of cash flows. Tax shelter constraints are based on the holding company's forecast of future taxable income and profit projections from current leases. Other constraints result from limitations on total new financing in a period and on overall net cash flows. Still other constraints represent managerial policies. For example, a minimum annual return on assets may be required.

An aggregate planning model selects the mix of lease types that maximizes the NPV of cash flows. A major use of the model is evaluation of different strategies. By forcing variable values, particular portfolios can be evaluated. In fact, the model is used more in this simulation mode than in the optimization mode. An extensive set of financial reports is generated by the system. Strategies for structuring leases in different market segments are evaluated by sensitivity analysis.

The negotiation of a multimillion-dollar lease often takes several months. There are many factors that can be changed during the negotiation of the lease. New England Merchants uses the aggregate model to evaluate how different contemplated lease structures fit into its portfolio of existing leases.

Another approach that New England Merchants uses in evaluating a lease proposal is to estimate the values of tax shelters generated by means of the aggregate model's dual prices (discussed in this chapter) in future years. The aggregate model is solved quarterly to estimate these values and to evaluate the mix of the lease portfolio.

Long-range corporate planning at New England Merchants Leasing is based on the aggregate model. During a two-year period, the lease portfolio almost doubled, to $230 million. Current lease income and future earnings increased by 160 percent and 157 percent ($51 million) during this period. Company management stated that the model was essential to this aggressive growth.

In this chapter, we study the sensitivity of optimal solutions to model changes and the useful managerial information obtained by computer solution.

B. D. Smith, "A Lease Portfolio Planning Model," *Interfaces* 12, no. 6 (December 1982), pp. 53–65.

New England Merchants Leasing's linear programming models are too complex to solve graphically. In Chapter 4, we graphically solved models with two decision variables on a two-dimensional sheet of paper. New England Merchants Leasing's linear programming models have many more than two variables. Most realistically complex models can't be solved graphically, but graphically introducing linear programming concepts makes it easier to understand them.

New England Merchants Leasing used linear programming computer programs, sometimes called software packages, to solve its linear programming models. Linear programming software packages are available for most computers. These software packages use an algebraic solution method called the *simplex algorithm,* developed by George Dantzig in 1947.[1] Linear programming software packages differ in their implementation details, but all are based on the simplex algorithm. The implementation details reduce the required computer storage space, minimize numerical difficulties (caused by the accumulation of rounding errors), and accelerate the solution method. Linear programming models can be used effectively without an understanding of the simplex algorithm and its implementation details. However, a basic understanding of the algorithm is provided in Chapter 6.

---

[1] Abraham Charnes and W. W. Cooper independently developed the theory of linear programming at about the same time.

New England Merchants Leasing used linear programming models to analyze its decision environment. Knowing the optimal solution is only part of such an analysis. You also need to study how the solution changes when the model's parameters change. Remember, brute force sensitivity analysis is changing the model and re-solving it. Simple-sensitivity analysis is obtaining information about the impact of parameter changes without re-solving the model. The availability of simple-sensitivity analysis from linear programming software packages makes linear programming models very useful. In this chapter, we discuss how to use the computer output to find the optimal solution and do sensitivity analysis. Linear programming software packages obtain simple-sensitivity analysis information from simplex algorithm calculations, but, believing that a picture is worth a thousand words (or algebraic calculations), we illustrate that information by the graphical method.

Recently, N. Karmarkar developed a new algorithm for linear programming models that may prove superior to the simplex algorithm. If so, his algorithm may become the basis for the next generation of linear programming software packages. Even if this should happen, however, the usefulness of simple-sensitivity analysis is such that the output of the new software will have to include the sensitivity analysis information that is available from existing software. The solution method may change, but interpreting the computer-generated results will remain important in decision making. The impact of model changes on the optimal solution is independent of the solution method used to find it.

First, this chapter discusses the input forms of linear programming models. After you've inputted the model, you must interpret the computer-generated results and analyze how parameter changes affect the solution. We will discuss the output-report information of several models and illustrate its meaning with graphical solutions. We also discuss the impacts of changing RHS constants, objective function coefficients, and constraint coefficients and of adding variables and constraints.

DATA INPUT FORMS

The input forms for linear programming computer systems are not all the same. As linear programming software became standardized for batch-oriented mainframe computers, the **MPS input form** became the standard. Table 5.1 illustrates the MPS input for Chapter 2's Potato Processing example.

MPS input form   In MPS form, the NAME card (record) specifies the model name. Because LINDO generated Table 5.1, the model name specifies this. The ROWS section specifies the type of each row. Row 1 is the objective

TABLE 5.1　Potato Processing Example Input in MPS Format

```
NAME      LINDO GENERATED MPS FILE( MAX)
ROWS
 N  1
 L  2
 L  3
 L  4
COLUMNS
    I          1              .14000000
    I          2              .30000000
    I          3              .10000000
    I          4              .30000000
    M          1              .15000000
    M          2              .20000000
    M          3              .20000000
    M          4              .30000000
RHS
    RHS        2             18000.
    RHS        3             15000.
    RHS        4             30000.
ENDATA
```

function and is not a constraint. The other rows are specified as L ($\leq$), G ($\geq$), or E ($=$). Because the linear programming model for the Potato Processing example has three $\leq$ constraints, Rows 2, 3, and 4 are specified as L. The COLUMNS section includes the objective function and constraint coefficients by column; that is, all of the first variable's *nonzero* coefficients are inputted before those of any other variable. Each nonzero coefficient is specified by giving the variable name and the row number. The RHS section includes the *nonzero* RHS constants. For example, Row 2's RHS constant is 18,000, the french fry limitation. By not inputting zero-valued coefficients, you eliminate performing multiplications by 0. Mainframe systems such as IBM's MPSX use MPS input. MPS input is the standard for batch-oriented mainframe linear programming systems.

There is no standard input form for interactive computer systems. However, the model is inputted by row for most interactive computer systems. That is, the objective function is inputted first and is followed by the first constraint, the second constraint, and so on. The model is inputted in the same form that it is typed on a typewriter. The linear programming computer output illustrated in this and later chapters was created by the Linear Interactive aNd Discrete Optimizer (LINDO) system. If you use another interactive software package, the format of the data input and solution output are unlikely to vary significantly.

LINDO allows input either by row or in MPS form. We input linear programming models by row because this is more intuitive. You enter the model in the same way as you write it on a piece of paper. Remember,

TABLE 5.2 Potato Processing Example: LINDO LOOK ALL Output

```
: look all

MAX      0.14 I + 0.15 M
SUBJECT TO
        2)   0.3 I + 0.2 M <=   18000
        3)   0.1 I + 0.2 M <=   15000
        4)   0.3 I + 0.3 M <=   30000
END
```

LINDO assumes that all variables are nonnegative and you don't have to enter them as constraints. In Chapter 3, we discussed LINDO's input form. Figure 3.A1 shows a sample LINDO session for the Potato Processing example. LINDO's LOOK ALL command lists the model by row, the preferred input form. Table 5.2 contains the result of the LOOK ALL command for the model of the Potato Processing example. The objective function was entered first and is called Row 1. As we discussed in Chapter 2, the constraints were imposed by the limitations on french fries, hash browns, and flakes, *in that order*. The french fry limitation, the first constraint, is called Row 2. The hash brown and flakes limitations are Rows 3 and 4, respectively. Because the nonnegativities weren't entered, they don't appear in Table 5.2.

Variable Names

Because it makes interpreting the output easier, you should choose variable names that have apparent meanings. The Potato Processing example named as M the variable representing the number of pounds of potatoes purchased from Michigan. It could have been named x_1 or Sue. However, if you name it x_1, you must refer to a "dictionary" that contains the definition of x_1. By naming it M, you avoid the need to find out from a dictionary what the variable represents.

Different computer systems have different rules for variable names. Generally, a variable name can have a maximum of eight characters, and the first character *must* be a letter. Characters other than the first can be letters or numerals. The special characters (e.g., *) allowed in a variable name depend on the system. In general, you can't use blanks within a variable name and no subscripts or superscripts are allowed. Thus, M_1 is not an acceptable name, but $M1$ is. Some computer systems allow you to name constraints. If your system allows row naming, choose descriptive names. For example, naming Row 2 *FF* tells you that it is the french fry limitation.

THE POTATO PROCESSING EXAMPLE—A MAXIMIZATION MODEL WITH A NONDEGENERATE OPTIMAL SOLUTION

Table 5.3 contains the result of the GO command of LINDO. The GO command uses the simplex algorithm to find the optimal solution. If there is no feasible solution or if there is an unbounded optimal solution, that information is given. In Table 5.3, the model isn't ill-behaved, so the model's optimal solution is printed. The optimal solution information contains a standard section and an optional section that contains additional sensitivity analysis information. Now, we will discuss the optimal solution information in detail for the Potato Processing example. By using a model with two variables, we can illustrate graphically the impact of model coefficient changes.

The Objective Function Value and Structural Variable Values

The optimal value of the objective function, Z^*, shown in Table 5.3 is 12225.0000, the maximum profit. In Chapter 2, we graphically solved the linear programming model and found that the maximum profit was

---

TABLE 5.3   Potato Processing Example: LINDO GO Output

```
 : go

LP OPTIMUM FOUND AT STEP        2

        OBJECTIVE FUNCTION VALUE

     1)    12225.0000

  VARIABLE         VALUE          REDUCED COST
        I     15000.000000           .000000
        M     67500.000000           .000000


     ROW    SLACK OR SURPLUS     DUAL PRICES
      2)          .000000          .325000
      3)          .000000          .425000
      4)      5250.000000          .000000

NO. ITERATIONS=        2

DO RANGE(SENSITIVITY) ANALYSIS?
? y

RANGES IN WHICH THE BASIS IS UNCHANGED:

                        OBJ COEFFICIENT RANGES
  VARIABLE         CURRENT       ALLOWABLE      ALLOWABLE
                    COEF         INCREASE       DECREASE
        I         .140000        .085000        .065000
        M         .150000        .130000        .056667

                        RIGHTHAND SIDE RANGES
     ROW         CURRENT        ALLOWABLE      ALLOWABLE
                   RHS          INCREASE       DECREASE
       2      18000.000000     7000.000000    3000.000000
       3      15000.000000     3000.000000    9000.000000
       4      30000.000000       INFINITY     5250.000000
```

$12,225. In Table 5.3, the value of Z^* is exactly the same as the value of the graphical solution. But in other cases, there can be small differences due to computer rounding errors. You can expect the computer solution to be accurate to six or seven digits.

The objective function sign

In Chapter 4, we showed how to algebraically convert between maximization and minimization objective functions by multiplying by -1. Remember, if the objective function is multiplied by -1, the optimal objective function value changes sign. Most linear programming software packages, including LINDO, allow inputting either maximization or minimization objective functions. These software packages convert the model automatically to its standard initialization form. If necessary, LINDO converts the objective function to its standard form and then changes the sign of the optimal objective function value before printing the solution. Therefore, the sign of the objective function value is correct.

Structural variable values

Remember, a *structural variable* is one defined by you, the model builder, whereas slack and surplus variables are automatically provided by most computer programs to convert inequalities to equations. The only structural variables of the Potato Processing example are I and M. For each structural variable, two numerical values are provided. The first column, headed VARIABLE, contains the variable names. The second column, headed VALUE, contains the variables' optimal values. The number 15000.000000 is the optimal number of pounds of Idaho potatoes to be purchased. From Table 5.3, the optimal value of M is 67,500. For this model and computer installation, there are no rounding errors on these values. However, another computer system may obtain slightly different values. The third column, headed REDUCED COST, is the first item of sensitivity analysis information. If the optimal variable value is 0,

Reduced cost

the **reduced cost** is the amount that the variable's objective function coefficient must *improve* before it is worthwhile for that variable to become positive. In this example, both I and M have positive values, so this interpretation is not applicable. We will discuss the interpretation of reduced costs in later examples in this chapter.

In New England Merchants Leasing's model, the objective is maximizing the net present value (NPV) of future cash flows from leases. The structural (decision) variables include the dollar volume of each market for each year in the planning horizon. The objective function value and decision variable values are obtained from the output of the linear programming system.

Slack and Surplus Variable Values

Slack and surplus variable values

For each constraint, two numerical values are provided. The column headed ROW provides the row numbers of the constraints. Because the objective function is Row 1, the constraints start with Row 2. In this example, there are three constraints, numbered 2, 3, and 4. The column headed SLACK OR SURPLUS provides the optimal value of the slack and/or surplus variables for each constraint. Note that there are not separate columns for slack and surplus variables. This doesn't cause any confusion because each constraint has either a slack variable ($\leq$ constraint), a surplus variable ($\geq$ constraint), or neither ($=$ constraint). A constraint can't have both a slack and a surplus variable.

In this example, all three constraints are of the less than or equal to ($\leq$) type. Consequently, a *slack variable* is introduced for each constraint. The slack variable's optimal value for the first constraint is .000000. This constraint refers to the french fry limitation, Row 2. Because the optimal solution has a slack variable value of 0 for Row 2, the LHS is equal to the RHS constant. The number of pounds of french fries produced is exactly 18,000. This is verified by substituting the optimal values of I and M into the constraint for the french fry limitation. The number of pounds of french fries produced is $(0.3 \times 15,000) + (0.2 \times 67,500) = 18,000$, the french fry limitation. The slack variable value for the hash brown limitation is also 0. The slack variable value for the flakes limitation is 5250.000000. The flakes production is 5,250 pounds less than the limitation of 30,000, giving 24,750 pounds of flakes. (Try to verify this by substituting the optimal values of I and M into the LHS of the constraint.)

This solution is not degenerate

If the number of positive variables, including slack and surplus variables, is less than the number of constraints, the solution is called degenerate. The model has three constraints and three positive variables—I, M, and the slack variable for Row 4. Thus, the optimal solution is not degenerate. It is important to check whether the optimal solution is degenerate. We will discuss the complications of output interpretation for degenerate optimal solutions in a later section of this chapter.

Changes in an RHS Constant—Binding Constraints

A constraint is **binding** at a point if the LHS equals the RHS constant. Because Row 2's slack variable value is 0, the french fry limitation constraint is binding. Let's consider the impact of an increase in the french fry limitation from 18,000 to 20,000. First, we illustrate the impact using the graphical method. Then, we show how Table 5.3 (for 18,000) can be used to get information for other RHS constant values.

Increasing the RHS constant

Figure 5.1 illustrates that the feasible set is larger with a 20,000 limitation than with an 18,000 limitation. Changing the RHS constant of a constraint moves the equation line *parallel*. If the RHS constant of a binding $\leq$ inequality increases, the feasible set is larger and the optimal solution changes.

The new optimal solution is at the intersection of the changed french fry limitation and the hash brown limitation. The new values of the decision variables are determined by solving for I and M in the following two equations:

$$0.3I + 0.2M = 20000$$
$$0.1I + 0.2M = 15000$$

FIGURE 5.1 Potato Processing Example with 18,000-Pound and 20,000-Pound French Fry Limitations

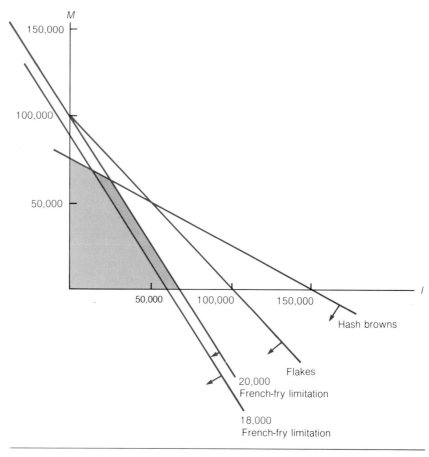

The values of I and M are 25,000 and 62,500, respectively. This gives an objective function value of $Z^* = (0.14 \times 25,000) + (0.15 \times 62,500)$, or \$12,875. The objective function improved by \$650 when the RHS constant increased by 2,000. The improvement per unit increase of the RHS constant is $^{(12,875 \ - \ 12,225)}/_{2,000} = \$0.325$.

The output's dual price information is useful for sensitivity analysis on RHS constants. In Table 5.3, observe that .325000 is the value in the column headed DUAL PRICES for Row 2. The **dual price** for a constraint is Z^*'s rate of *improvement* per unit change in its RHS constant, *given that the set of positive variables does not change*. If a dual price is positive, Z^* improves when the RHS constant increases and gets worse when the RHS constant decreases. If a dual price is negative, Z^* gets worse when the RHS constant increases and improves when the RHS

If the set of positive variables does not change

constant decreases. In this case, the set of positive variables does not change when you increase the RHS constant by 2,000, so Z^*'s improvement is calculated as

$$\text{Improvement in } Z^* = (\text{RHS}_{new} - \text{RHS}_{old}) \times \text{Dual price}$$

Because Row 2's dual price is .325000, if the french fry limitation increases by 2,000, to 20,000, Z^* improves by $(20,000 - 18,000) \times 0.325 = 2,000 \times 0.325 = \$650$. Note that we used *improvement* in the definition of the dual price. An improvement for a maximization model is an *increase* in Z^*, and an improvement for a minimization model is a *decrease* in Z^*.

Improvement: increase for maximization, decrease for minimization

If the french fry limitation increases to 20,000, Z^* increases (improves) by 650, to $12,875. You can determine the impact on Z^* from Table 5.3 without changing the RHS constant to 20,000 and re-solving.

Table 5.4 contains the Potato Processing example's solution after the french fry limitation changes to 20,000. Observe that Z^*'s value is 12,875, the value predicted from the dual price information. Although you can predict Z^*'s new value from the original output in Table 5.3, you must re-solve the changed model to determine the new variable values. Table 5.4 shows that the new values of the structural variables I and M are 25,000 and 62,500, respectively. We found the same variable values using the graphical method. Also, observe that Row 4's slack variable, the flakes limitation, is 3,750. Note that the same three variables are positive in Tables 5.3 and 5.4. If the same three variables weren't positive, the true value of Z^* might not equal the predicted value.

Re-solve to get the new variable values

TABLE 5.4   LOOK ALL and GO Output for Potato Processing Example with French Fry Limitation Increased by 2,000, to 20,000

```
MAX       0.14 I + 0.15 M
SUBJECT TO
      2)    0.3 I + 0.2 M <=    20000
      3)    0.1 I + 0.2 M <=    15000
      4)    0.3 I + 0.3 M <=    30000
END

          OBJECTIVE FUNCTION VALUE

      1)      12875.0000

   VARIABLE        VALUE           REDUCED COST
        I       25000.000000          .000000
        M       62500.000000          .000000

      ROW     SLACK OR SURPLUS      DUAL PRICES
      2)            .000000           .325000
      3)            .000000           .425000
      4)         3750.000000           .000000
```

Variable values change linearly

The model's linear functions cause Z^*'s constant improvement rate. As the RHS constant changes, the binding constraint moves parallel and the structural variable values change linearly. From Tables 5.3 and 5.4, we see that an increase of 2,000 in the RHS constant causes I to increase by 10,000 (25,000 − 15,000). For each 1-pound increase in the french fry limitation, an additional $^{10,000}/_{2,000} = 5$ pounds are purchased from Idaho. For each 1-pound increase in the french fry limitation, the change in Michigan potatoes purchased is $^{(62,500\ -\ 67,500)}/_{2,000} = 2.5$ pounds less. You can check these results by solving for I and M in the following two equations:

$$0.3I + 0.2M = 18001$$
$$0.1I + 0.2M = 15000$$

If the french fry limitation is 18,001, the optimal values of I and M are 15,005 and 67,497.5, respectively.

Continuous variables

The dual prices assume that the decision variables are *continuous*. If I and M must be integers and the solution after re-solving the model contains fractional values, the new solution is not realistic. For example, if the french fry limitation is 18,001, the optimal value of M is 67,497.5 pounds. If you must buy an integer number of pounds of Michigan potatoes, the solution isn't realistic. Even in this case, however, the dual price information is useful as a guideline for the economic consequence of a change in the RHS constant.

Decreasing the RHS constant

Now, say that the original french fry limitation decreases by 1, to 17,999. Then, Z^* improves by $(17,999 - 18,000) \times 0.325 = -1 \times 0.325 = -0.325$. The profit decreases by $0.325, to $12,224.675. Because the optimal variable values change linearly, you calculate the optimal values of I and M as $15,000 - 5 = 14,995$ and $67,500 + 2.5 = 67,502.5$, respectively.

Figure 5.1 shows that for sufficiently small changes in the RHS constant for the french fry limitation, the optimal solution is at the intersection of the french fry constraint and the hash brown constraint. A 1-pound increase in the french fry limitation causes the purchase of 5 additional pounds from Idaho and 2.5 fewer pounds from Michigan, and the profit change is $(0.14 \times 5) + (0.15 \times -2.5) = 0.325$, the dual price. Row 2's dual price is .325000 in Tables 5.3 and 5.4. However, if the RHS constant for the french fry limitation changes enough, the optimal solution is no longer at the intersection of the french fry constraint line and the hash brown constraint line, and the set of positive variables changes.

Graphically finding the maximum increase

Let's graphically determine the maximum that Row 2's RHS constant can increase, so that the optimal solution remains at the intersection of the french fry constraint line and the hash brown constraint line. As Row 2's RHS constant increases, the optimal solution slides down the hash

---

FIGURE 5.2   Potato Processing Example with 25,000-Pound French Fry Limitation

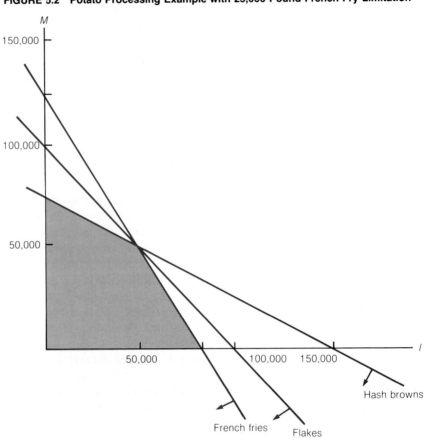

brown constraint line. The maximum limitation occurs when the optimal solution slides down the hash brown constraint line to the intersection of the hash brown constraint line and the flakes constraint line. Figure 5.2 illustrates the feasible set where the french fry constraint line passes through the intersection of the hash brown constraint line and the flakes constraint line.

You can calculate the values of *I* and *M* at the intersection of the hash brown constraint line and the flakes constraint line by solving

$$0.1I + 0.2M = 15000$$
$$0.3I + 0.3M = 30000$$

At that point *I* = 50,000 and *M* = 50,000, yielding a profit of $14,500. You calculate the RHS constant for the french fry limitation so that the line passes through that point by substituting those variable values into the french fry constraint function, $0.3 \times 50,000 + 0.2 \times 50,000 = 25,000$. Compared to the original RHS constant, 18,000, the maximum allowable increase is $25,000 - 18,000 = 7,000$.

For a linear programming model with more than two variables, you can't use the graphical method to determine the maximum allowable increase of an RHS constant. However, the optional sensitivity analysis information gives this information. The optional RANGE (SENSITIV-ITY) ANALYSIS information contains two sections. The first pertains to objective function coefficient changes, the second to RHS constant changes.

In Table 5.3, Row 2's maximum allowable increase is 7,000.[2] The dual price is 0.325 for RHS constant increases as large as 7,000. If the french fry limitation increases to 25,000, the profit improves by $7,000 \times 0.325$, or $2,275. If the RHS constant increases by more than 7,000, the profit improves by at least $2,275. However, you need to re-solve the model with the changed RHS constant to determine the exact amount that Z^* changes. Simple-sensitivity analysis is possible only *within* the range of values indicated by the range output. For changes greater than the allow-able ranges, brute force sensitivity analysis is required—you change the coefficient and re-solve the model.

Re-solve if the RHS constant changes more than the limit

Table 5.5 contains the optimal solution after the RHS constant in-creases by 7,000, the maximum allowable. Observe that the solution in Table 5.5 is degenerate. *I* and *M* are the only positive variables, and the model has three constraints. When you change the RHS constant to 25,000, all three constraint lines pass through the optimal solution, so all three slack variables are 0. If you change an RHS by the maximum allowable amount, the new optimal solution is *degenerate*. Examine the heading RANGES IN WHICH THE BASIS IS UNCHANGED. To the mathematician, this is a more precise version of the assertion that the set of positive variables remains the same.[3]

Degenerate solution at the limit

In Table 5.5, Row 2's maximum allowable increase is 0. For any additional increase in Row 2's RHS constant, a different set of variables

---

[2] LINDO reports the amount of the change. Some linear programming systems report the end points of the ranges.

[3] For a degenerate solution, the number of positive variables is less than the number of constraints. This possibility introduces the need for more precision. Chapter 6 shows that the optimal solution corresponds to a partition of the variables. At least one basic variable equals 0 in a partition for a degenerate solution. A change in basis corresponds to a changed partition, even though the variable values may be the same.

TABLE 5.5   LOOK ALL and GO Output for Potato Processing Example with French Fry Limitation Increased to 25,000: Degenerate Optimal Solution

```
MAX      0.14 I + 0.15 M
SUBJECT TO
        2)   0.3 I + 0.2 M <=    25000
        3)   0.1 I + 0.2 M <=    15000
        4)   0.3 I + 0.3 M <=    30000
END

        OBJECTIVE FUNCTION VALUE

    1)     14500.0000

   VARIABLE          VALUE            REDUCED COST
        I        50000.000000            .000000
        M        50000.000000            .000000

     ROW     SLACK OR SURPLUS       DUAL PRICES
      2)           .000000            .325000
      3)           .000000            .425000
      4)           .000000            .000000

RANGES IN WHICH THE BASIS IS UNCHANGED:

                          OBJ COEFFICIENT RANGES
   VARIABLE        CURRENT         ALLOWABLE        ALLOWABLE
                    COEF           INCREASE         DECREASE
        I          .140000          .085000          .065000
        M          .150000          .130000          .056667

                         RIGHTHAND SIDE RANGES
     ROW          CURRENT          ALLOWABLE        ALLOWABLE
                    RHS            INCREASE         DECREASE
      2        25000.000000         .000000      10000.000000
      3        15000.000000         .000000       6666.666667
      4        30000.000000        INFINITY          .000000
```

are positive and the dual price changes. Table 5.6 shows the optimal solution after changing the RHS constant to 26,000. Row 2's dual price changed to 0. The set of positive variables changed to *I, M,* and the french fry limitation slack variable. Figure 5.3 shows that the french fry limitation is not binding at the optimal solution for a 26,000 french fry limitation. Thus, you can increase the french fry RHS constant without limit and the optimal solution never changes. In Table 5.6, Row 2's maximum allowable increase is infinity.

Figure 5.4 shows the value of Z^* as Row 2's RHS constant changes. In Table 5.3, Row 2's maximum allowable decrease is 3,000, so no information is available concerning Z^*'s value for an RHS constant smaller than 15,000. Between 15,000 and 25,000, the slope of the line equals 0.325. For RHS constants greater than 25,000, the slope equals the new dual price, 0.

If the RHS constant is 25,000, the solution is degenerate and the dual price is not uniquely determined. The dual price can be either 0.325 or 0.

TABLE 5.6 LOOK ALL and GO Output for Potato Processing Example with French Fry Limitation Increased to 26,000

```
MAX      0.14 I + 0.15 M
SUBJECT TO
       2)    0.3 I + 0.2 M <=    26000
       3)    0.1 I + 0.2 M <=    15000
       4)    0.3 I + 0.3 M <=    30000
END

       OBJECTIVE FUNCTION VALUE

     1)     14500.0000

   VARIABLE          VALUE          REDUCED COST
       I        50000.000000            .000000
       M        50000.000000            .000000

     ROW     SLACK OR SURPLUS      DUAL PRICES
      2)        1000.000000            .000000
      3)            .000000            .100000
      4)            .000000            .433333

RANGES IN WHICH THE BASIS IS UNCHANGED:

                          OBJ COEFFICIENT RANGES
   VARIABLE          CURRENT        ALLOWABLE        ALLOWABLE
                       COEF          INCREASE         DECREASE
       I             .140000          .010000          .065000
       M             .150000          .130000          .010000

                          RIGHTHAND SIDE RANGES
     ROW            CURRENT         ALLOWABLE        ALLOWABLE
                      RHS            INCREASE         DECREASE
       2         26000.000000       INFINITY      1000.000000
       3         15000.000000     5000.000000     1000.000000
       4         30000.000000      750.000000     7500.000000
```

Table 5.7 illustrates the optimal solution after the RHS constant has been changed from 26,000 to 25,000 and re-solved. The values of I, M, the slack variables, and Z^* are the same as in Table 5.5, but the dual price of Row 2 is 0. Degenerate corner points introduce *ambiguity* in output interpretation.

Changing Row 3's RHS constant

Consider the effect of changing the hash brown limitation on the original model shown in Table 5.3. The dual price is 0.425, so an increase in the limitation of 1 pound results in profit improvement of $0.425. The maximum allowable increase is 3,000, and the maximum allowable decrease is 9,000. Within a range from 6,000 (15,000 − 9,000) to 18,000 (15,000 + 3,000), the dual price is 0.425. If the hash brown limitation decreases from 15,000 to 6,000, the profit decreases by 9,000 × 0.425 = $3,825, and the new optimal solution is degenerate. The structural variable values change, but you cannot tell how from Table 5.3. To determine the new variable values, you must re-solve the changed model. If Row 3's

FIGURE 5.3 Potato Processing Example with 26,000-Pound French Fry Limitation

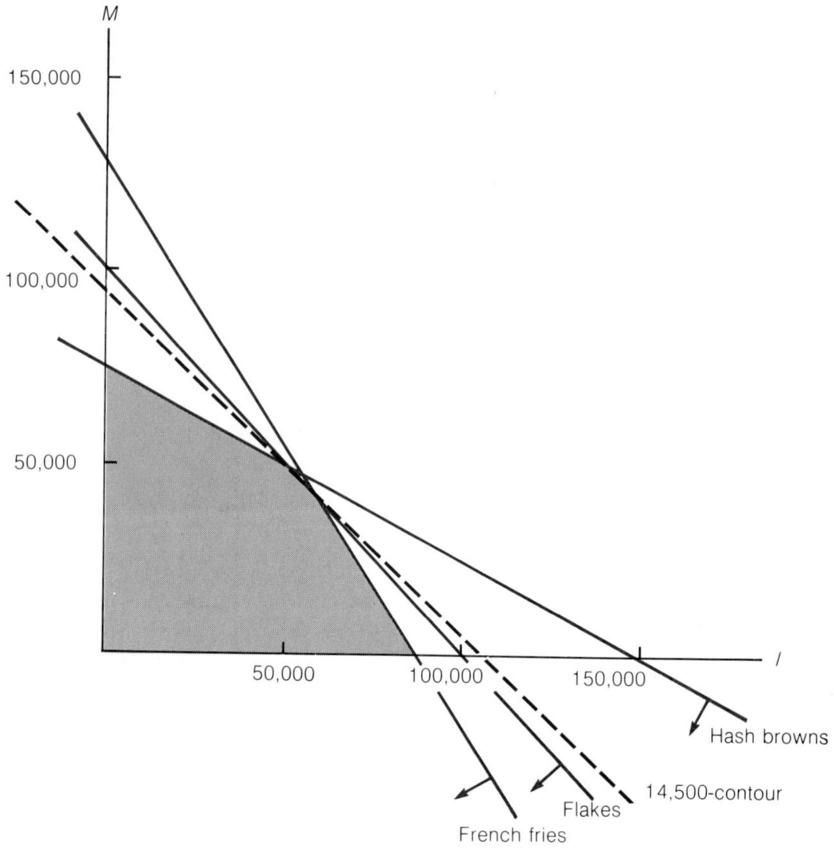

RHS constant decreases more than 9,000, there is a new set of positive variables and a new dual price.

Summary for non-degenerate solution

Table 5.8 summarizes the impact of changing the RHS constant for a binding constraint if the optimal solution is *not degenerate*. Within the allowable range, the dual price is the rate of improvement of Z^*, the values of some structural variables change, and the set of positive variables is unchanged. At the limit, the optimal solution is degenerate. For an RHS constant change greater than the limit, the set of positive variables and the dual price change.

New England Merchants Leasing uses the dual prices to study its decision problem. For example, one set of constraints establishes a maximum and minimum for the dollar volume of each market in each year of the planning horizon. These limits are chosen based on the size and experience of the marketing staff, market conditions, and management

FIGURE 5.4 Graph of Z* versus the French Fry Limitation

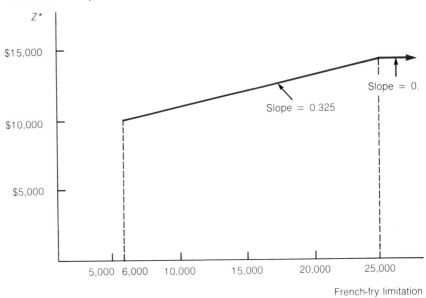

TABLE 5.7 LOOK ALL and GO Output for Potato Processing Example with French Fry Limitation Increased to 25,000: Degenerate Optimal Solution

```
MAX     0.14 I + 0.15 M
SUBJECT TO
    2)    0.3 I + 0.2 M <=    25000
    3)    0.1 I + 0.2 M <=    15000
    4)    0.3 I + 0.3 M <=    30000
END

        OBJECTIVE FUNCTION VALUE

    1)      14500.0000

    VARIABLE        VALUE          REDUCED COST
        I        50000.000000         .000000
        M        50000.000000         .000000

    ROW     SLACK OR SURPLUS     DUAL PRICES
    2)            .000000           .000000
    3)            .000000           .100000
    4)            .000000           .433333

RANGES IN WHICH THE BASIS IS UNCHANGED:

                        OBJ COEFFICIENT RANGES
    VARIABLE        CURRENT        ALLOWABLE        ALLOWABLE
                     COEF          INCREASE         DECREASE
        I           .140000        .010000          .065000
        M           .150000        .130000          .010000

                        RIGHTHAND SIDE RANGES
    ROW             CURRENT        ALLOWABLE        ALLOWABLE
                     RHS           INCREASE         DECREASE
    2           25000.000000       INFINITY          .000000
    3           15000.000000      5000.000000        .000000
    4           30000.000000        .000000        7500.000000
```

TABLE 5.8 Summary of the Impacts of Changing an RHS Constant for a Binding Constraint—Nondegenerate Optimal Solution

Within the allowable range:

1. The values of some structural variables change.
2. The set of positive variables is unchanged.
3. The dual price is the rate of improvement of $Z*$.
   a. An improvement for a maximization model is an increase in $Z*$.
   b. An improvement for a minimization model is a decrease in $Z*$.

At the allowable limit:

1. The solution is degenerate.
2. The dual price is not uniquely determined.

For a change greater than the limit:

1. The dual price changes.
2. The set of positive variables changes.

policy. Say that you examine the dual price for the maximum of one market in a particular year. The dual price value is the rate of increase in the portfolio NPV if you increase the maximum. You can use the dual prices to evaluate which maximums and minimums have the greatest impact on the portfolio NPV. Then, you can consider the changes in marketing staff or policies that have the greatest impact.

Changes in an RHS Constant—Nonbinding Constraints

In Table 5.3, Row 4's slack variable value is 5,250. Thus, the flakes limitation is not binding for the optimal solution to the Potato Processing example. You can graphically see that it's not binding in Figure 5.1, because the optimal solution does not lie on the flakes limitation line. The dual price value is 0 on Row 4. This means as the flakes limitation changes that the per unit improvement in $Z*$ is 0. When the flakes limitation RHS constant increases from 30,000 to 30,001, $Z*$ is unchanged. Does this make sense? When the RHS constant is 30,000, the slack variable is positive (5,250). If you increase the RHS constant by 1, there is more slack and the slack variable increases to 5,251. All of the structural variable values, the other slack variables values, and $Z*$ remain the same. How much can the RHS constant increase above 30,000 without changing the set of positive variables and the dual price? Infinitely! The slack becomes larger and larger. In Table 5.3, note that Row 4's allowable increase is infinity, or limitless.

If Row 4's RHS constant decreases, $Z*$'s value remains the same (up to a point). If the RHS constant of the flakes limitation decreases by 1, then the slack for the flakes limitation also decreases by 1, to 5,249 pounds. You can decrease the RHS constant until there is no slack. The allowable decrease is the value of the slack variable, 5,250. Table 5.3's sensitivity

Nonbinding constraint

Increasing the RHS constant for a nonbinding $\leq$ constraint

Decreasing the RHS constant for a nonbinding ≤ constraint

analysis shows that the maximum allowable decrease for Row 4 is 5,250. Say that the RHS constant is decreased to 24,750. Then, the flakes limitation slack variable is 0 and the solution is degenerate. The new flakes limitation line passes through the point $I = 15,000$ and $M = 67,500$. When the flakes limitation is smaller than 24,750, determining Z^* requires re-solving the model with the changed parameter.

Asking whether it makes sense for the flakes limitation dual price to equal 0 is more than just a rhetorical question. Unfortunately, some model builders allow the model to dominate their common sense. If it is not possible to reconcile the two, reexamine the model; it may be incorrect.

Dual price ≥ 0 for ≤ constraint

The dual price sign doesn't depend on the objective function type

We use sign conventions for dual prices and reduced costs that are consistent with LINDO output. Some software packages have different sign conventions. By using common sense, you can eliminate any possible confusion. For example, say that you increase the RHS constant for a ≤ constraint. All of the points that used to satisfy the constraint still do, and so do some additional points. If you relax a ≤ constraint by increasing the RHS constant, the objective function value should not become worse, so the dual price must be ≥ 0. If you relax a ≤ constraint in a minimization model, does Z^* improve or get worse? It should improve! Using our definition of the dual price, *the dual price sign doesn't depend on whether the objective function is to be maximized or minimized.* Whether the objective function increases or decreases, however, does depend on whether the objective function is to be maximized or minimized. For a minimization model, the dual price can't be negative and Z^* should decrease (or stay the same). Relaxing a constraint for a minimization model should not cause Z^* to become larger.

Dual price ≤ 0 for ≥ constraint

If you increase the RHS constant for a ≥ inequality, the constraint is harder to satisfy. Some points that used to satisfy the constraint violate it when the RHS constant increases. If you tighten a ≥ constraint by increasing the RHS constant, Z^* should not improve, so the dual price must be ≤ 0.

Equality (=) constraint

For an equality (=) constraint, increasing the RHS constant moves the points on the line parallel. All of the points in the feasible set change, and the sign of the dual price for an equality constraint can't be determined by common sense—it can be positive, negative, or zero.

Summary for non-degenerate solution

Table 5.9 summarizes the impact of changing an RHS constant for a nonbinding constraint. Within the allowable increase and decrease, the dual price is 0, all of the variable values except the slack or surplus variable for the changed constraint remain the same, and the set of positive variables remains the same. For a ≤ constraint, the maximum allowable increase is infinity and the maximum allowable decrease equals the slack variable's value. For a ≥ constraint, the maximum allowable decrease is infinity and the maximum allowable increase equals the surplus variable's value. At the limit, the slack or surplus variable value is 0

TABLE 5.9　Summary of the Impacts of Changing an RHS Constant for a Nonbinding Constraint—Nondegenerate Optimal Solution

Within the allowable range:

1. Only the slack or surplus variable of the changed constraint changes value. In particular, the structural variable values do not change.
2. The set of positive variables is unchanged.
3. The dual price is 0.

At the allowable limit:

1. The solution is degenerate.
2. The dual price is not uniquely determined.

For a change greater than the limit:

1. The dual price changes.
2. The set of positive variables changes.

The limits are:

1. For a ≤ constraint, the maximum allowable increase is infinity and the maximum allowable decrease is the slack variable value.
2. For a ≥ constraint, the maximum allowable increase is the surplus variable value and the maximum allowable decrease is infinity.

---

and the solution is degenerate. For an RHS constant change greater than the limit, the set of positive variables and the dual price change.

Changes in an Objective Function Coefficient— Positive-Valued Variables

Increasing the objective function coefficient

In the last two sections, we discussed the impact of an RHS constant change on the optimal solution. In this section, we discuss the impact of changing the objective function coefficient of a positive-valued variable. Both I and M have positive values in Table 5.3. Let's consider the impact of increasing the profit margin of Idaho potatoes from \$0.14 to \$0.15. Figure 5.5 illustrates the equal value 12,225-contours for the old and new objective functions.

The dashed line in Figure 5.5 is the original objective function with a 0.14 coefficient for I, and the dotted line is the new objective function with a 0.15 coefficient for I. Note that the change in the objective function coefficient rotates the equal value contour clockwise but does not affect the feasible set. The optimal point does not lie on the 12,225-contour of the new objective function. You find the optimal solution by sliding the

Same point optimal; Z^* increases

new contour to the right. For the new objective function, the *same point is optimal*, $I = 15,000$ and $M = 67,500$, but the objective function's value is different. The new value of Z^* is $[(0.14 + 0.01) \times 15,000] + [0.15 \times 67,500] = 12,225 + (0.01 \times 15,000) = \$12,375$. Z^* increases by the amount of the change in the objective function coefficient times the

FIGURE 5.5 12,225-Contours for Potato Processing Example

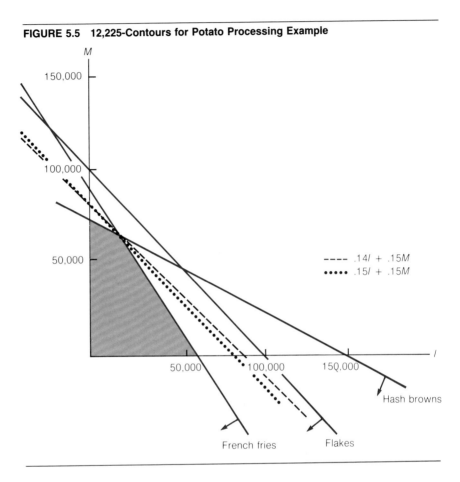

variable's optimal value. Table 5.10 contains the solution for the objective function, $0.15I + 0.15M$, and confirms the graphical solution.

Figure 5.5 shows that when I's objective function coefficient changes to 0.15, the slope of the new equal value contour is between the slope of the french fry limitation and the slope of the hash brown limitation. The intersection of the two limitation lines is still optimal. If the objective function coefficient of I decreases to 0.12, the equal value contour line rotates in the other direction. However, the slope of the equal value contour is still between the slopes of the two limitations and the optimal point remains $I = 15,000$ and $M = 67,500$. Z^* decreases by $0.02 \times 15,000$, or $300.

As I's objective function coefficient changes, the slope of the equal value contour lines changes. If I's objective function coefficient decreases

Decreasing the objective function coefficient

TABLE 5.10 LOOK ALL and GO Output for Potato Processing Example with Profit Margin on Idaho Potatoes Increased to 0.15

```
MAX      0.15 I + 0.15 M
SUBJECT TO
       2)   0.3 I + 0.2 M <=   18000
       3)   0.1 I + 0.2 M <=   15000
       4)   0.3 I + 0.3 M <=   30000
END

          OBJECTIVE FUNCTION VALUE

    1)      12375.0000

    VARIABLE          VALUE          REDUCED COST
         I       15000.000000            .000000
         M       67500.000000            .000000

       ROW    SLACK OR SURPLUS     DUAL PRICES
       2)            .000000          .375000
       3)            .000000          .375000
       4)         5250.000000          .000000

RANGES IN WHICH THE BASIS IS UNCHANGED:

                           OBJ COEFFICIENT RANGES
    VARIABLE         CURRENT       ALLOWABLE      ALLOWABLE
                       COEF        INCREASE       DECREASE
         I           .150000       .075000        .075000
         M           .150000       .150000        .050000

                           RIGHTHAND SIDE RANGES
       ROW          CURRENT       ALLOWABLE      ALLOWABLE
                      RHS         INCREASE       DECREASE
        2       18000.000000    7000.000000    3000.000000
        3       15000.000000    3000.000000    9000.000000
        4       30000.000000     INFINITY      5250.000000
```

or increases enough, the optimal point changes. If I's objective function coefficient increases by 0.085, to a new value of 0.225, the slope of the equal value contour is exactly the same as the slope of the french fry limitation. Figure 5.6 illustrates the optimal equal value contour for the objective function, $0.225I + 0.15M$.

Any further increase in I's objective function coefficient changes the optimal point. In Table 5.3, the maximum allowable increase for I's objective function coefficient is 0.085. Table 5.11 contains the solution for the objective function, $0.225I + 0.15M$. The variable values are unchanged, and $Z^* = 13,500$.

When an RHS constant changes the limit amount, the optimal solution is degenerate. For a nondegenerate optimal solution, when an objective function coefficient changes the limit amount, an alternate optimal solution exists. You can see that in Figure 5.6, because there many points on the 13,500-contour that are in the feasible set. For example, $I = 60,000$ and $M = 0$ is also an optimal solution.

Alternate optimal solution at the limit

The change limits for the structural variable objective function coeffi-

FIGURE 5.6 Optimal Contour for Potato Processing Example for Objective 0.225*I* + 0.15*M*

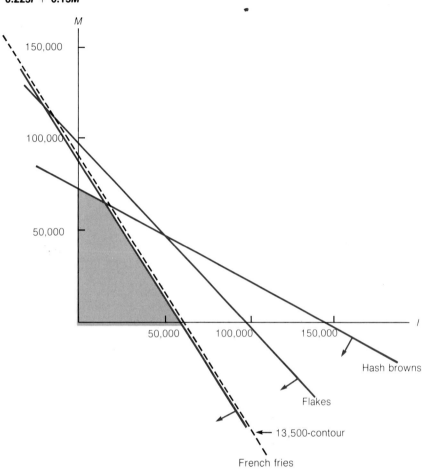

cients are given in the first section of the optional range or sensitivity analysis output. For variable *I*, the maximum allowable increase is 0.085. If the *profit margin* on *I* increases by no more than 0.085, the current optimal point remains optimal. If the profit margin on *I* becomes $0.20 per pound, what is the optimal solution? Since $0.20 - 0.14 = 0.06$ is within the allowable increase, the values of *I* and *M* are unchanged at 15,000 and 67,500, respectively; the profit increases by $0.06 \times 15{,}000$, to $13,125.

If the change exceeds the limit, a different point is optimal and the set of positive variables changes. If the profit margin on *I* increases by 0.09, the optimal point changes and a different set of variables is positive.

TABLE 5.11 LOOK ALL and GO Output for Potato Processing Example with Profit Margin on Idaho Potatoes Increased to 0.225

```
MAX      0.225 I + 0.15 M
SUBJECT TO
       2)   0.3 I + 0.2 M <=    18000
       3)   0.1 I + 0.2 M <=    15000
       4)   0.3 I + 0.3 M <=    30000
END

       OBJECTIVE FUNCTION VALUE

       1)      13500.0000

    VARIABLE          VALUE          REDUCED COST
       I         15000.000000          .000000
       M         67500.000000          .000000

       ROW    SLACK OR SURPLUS     DUAL PRICES
       2)            .000000          .750000
       3)            .000000          .000000
       4)         5250.000000         .000000

RANGES IN WHICH THE BASIS IS UNCHANGED:

                            OBJ COEFFICIENT RANGES
    VARIABLE         CURRENT        ALLOWABLE        ALLOWABLE
                      COEF          INCREASE         DECREASE
       I            .225000         .000000          .150000
       M            .150000         .300000          .000000

                            RIGHTHAND SIDE RANGES
       ROW          CURRENT        ALLOWABLE        ALLOWABLE
                      RHS           INCREASE         DECREASE
       2         18000.000000    7000.000000     3000.000000
       3         15000.000000    3000.000000     9000.000000
       4         30000.000000      INFINITY      5250.000000
```

Re-solve if the change exceeds the limit

Because the profit margin on Idaho potatoes increases, you purchase more Idaho potatoes. You must re-solve the changed model to determine the new purchasing plan and $Z*$. However, it is correct to state that $Z*$ increases by at least $0.09 \times 15,000 = \$1,350$ (to $13,575). Table 5.12 contains the solution for the objective function, $0.23I + 0.15M$. The changed solution purchases 60,000 pounds of Idaho potatoes and no Michigan potatoes. The profit is $13,800.

Figure 5.7 shows $Z*$ as I's profit margin changes. In Table 5.3, I's maximum allowable decrease is 0.065. You must re-solve the model to determine $Z*$ if the profit margin is less than 0.085 (0.15 − 0.065). Between 0.065 and 0.225, the slope of the line is equal to I's value, 15,000. The slope for profit margins greater than 0.225 is 60,000. Because Table 5.12's maximum allowable increase for I's objective function coefficient is infinity, the solution remains the same—to purchase 60,000 pounds from Idaho and none from Michigan.

Now, say that the profit margin for Idaho potatoes remains $0.14 and

TABLE 5.12 LOOK ALL and GO Output for Potato Processing Example with Profit Margin on Idaho Potatoes Increased to 0.23

```
MAX      0.23 I + 0.15 M
SUBJECT TO
       2)   0.3 I + 0.2 M <=   18000
       3)   0.1 I + 0.2 M <=   15000
       4)   0.3 I + 0.3 M <=   30000
END

       OBJECTIVE FUNCTION VALUE

   1)      13800.0000

  VARIABLE          VALUE           REDUCED COST
     I          60000.000000          .000000
     M              .000000          .003333

     ROW     SLACK OR SURPLUS      DUAL PRICES
     2)          .000000            .766667
     3)        9000.000000          .000000
     4)       12000.000000          .000000

RANGES IN WHICH THE BASIS IS UNCHANGED:

                         OBJ COEFFICIENT RANGES
  VARIABLE          CURRENT        ALLOWABLE       ALLOWABLE
                     COEF          INCREASE        DECREASE
     I              .230000        INFINITY         .005000
     M              .150000         .003333        INFINITY

                         RIGHTHAND SIDE RANGES
     ROW           CURRENT        ALLOWABLE       ALLOWABLE
                     RHS          INCREASE        DECREASE
     2          18000.000000    12000.000000    18000.000000
     3          15000.000000      INFINITY       9000.000000
     4          30000.000000      INFINITY      12000.000000
```

that the profit margin for Michigan potatoes changes. If the profit margin for Michigan potatoes decreases by $0.02 per pound, to $0.13, what is the impact on the optimal solution? In Table 5.3, the allowable decrease is 0.056667 for M's objective function coefficient. Since the decrease of 0.02 is within the allowable decrease of 0.056667, the same point is optimal. The set of positive variables and their values is unchanged. *Z* decreases* by 0.02 × 67,500, or $1,350, and the new profit is $10,875 (12,225 − 1,350).

A decrease of 0.06 for M's profit margin is more than the allowable decrease of 0.056667. To obtain the exact solution, you must re-solve the changed model. Without re-solving, you know that decreasing the profit margin for Michigan potatoes does not result in purchasing more Michigan potatoes. The profit decreases by at least 0.056667 × 67,500, or $3,825.0225. From the output, you cannot determine M's new optimal value without re-solving the model. If the new optimal value is 0, decreasing the objective function coefficient the additional amount from 0.056667

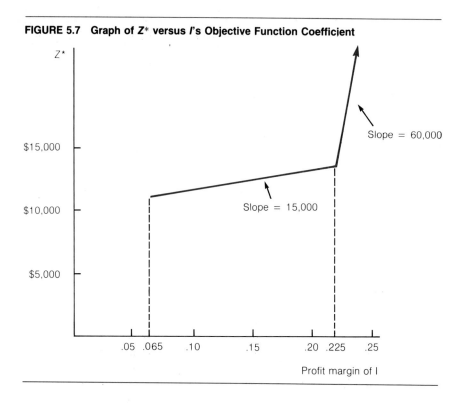

FIGURE 5.7   Graph of Z* versus I's Objective Function Coefficient

to 0.06 does not decrease Z^* further. If the new optimal value is greater than 0, decreasing the objective function coefficient decreases Z^* more than 3,825.0225. From Figure 5.1, you can see that the new optimal value of M is 0, so $Z^* = 12,225 - 3,825.0225 = \$8,399.9775$. From Table 5.3's output, however, you can only say that the profit is \$8,399.9775 or less.

Table 5.13 summarizes the impacts of changing the objective function coefficient of a positive-valued variable for a nondegenerate solution. Within the allowable range, all of the variables have the same values and Z^* changes linearly with the variable's value. If the objective function coefficient increases more than the maximum allowable, the variable's value increases for a maximization model and decreases for a minimization model. If the objective function coefficient decreases more than the maximum allowable, the variable's value decreases for a maximization model and increases for a minimization model. If the objective function coefficient changes the limit amount, an alternate optimal solution exists.

Summary for non-degenerate solution

Alternate Optimal Solutions

Knowing that alternate optimal solutions exist is useful information. Some linear programming software packages report the existence of alternate optimal solutions. For example, IBM's MPSX system prints "AO"

TABLE 5.13 Summary of the Impacts of Changing an Objective Function Coefficient for a Positive-Valued Variable—Nondegenerate Optimal Solution

Within the allowable range:

1. All variable values are unchanged.
2. The set of positive variables is unchanged.
3. $Z*$ changes linearly with the variable's value.

At the allowable limit:

1. There is an alternate optimal solution.

For an increase greater than the maximum allowable increase:

1. The set of positive variables changes.
2. For a maximization model, the variable value increases.
3. For a minimization model, the variable value decreases.

For a decrease greater than the maximum allowable decrease:

1. The set of positive variables changes.
2. For a maximization model, the variable value decreases.
3. For a minimization model, the variable value increases.

in the solution report next to a variable whose current value is 0 if there may be an alternate optimal solution when that variable is positive. LINDO does not have such a feature in the solution report. For LINDO, the indication of a possible alternate optimal solution is the existence of a maximum allowable increase or decrease of 0 for an objective function coefficient.

In Table 5.3, I's maximum allowable increase is 0.085 (to a value of 0.225). In Table 5.10, after I's objective function coefficient has been increased by 0.01, its maximum allowable increase is 0.075 (to a value of 0.225). In Table 5.11, after I's objective function coefficient has been increased to 0.225, its maximum allowable increase is 0. Figure 5.6 shows that alternate optimal solutions exist when the objective function is $0.225I + 0.15M$. When a nondegenerate optimal solution has a maximum allowable objective function coefficient increase or decrease equal to 0, an *alternate optimal solution* exists. In Table 5.11, noting that the maximum allowable increase for I equals 0 or that the maximum allowable decrease for M equals 0 is enough to conclude that an alternate optimal solution exists.

| Indication of alternate optimal solution

Table 5.14 shows the optimal solution after I's profit margin has been changed from 0.23 to 0.225 and re-solved. $Z*$ has the same value in Tables 5.11 and 5.14. Because the variable values are different, the solutions are alternate optimal solutions. Your computer system might yield either solution.

| Indication of unique optimal solution

If no objective function's maximum allowable increase or decrease is 0, no alternate optimal solution exists even if the optimal solution is degenerate. A later section of this chapter discusses the complication in identifying alternate optimal solutions caused by a degenerate optimal solution. For a degenerate solution, the optimal solution can be unique

TABLE 5.14   LOOK ALL and GO Output for Alternate Optimal Solution to Potato Processing Example with Profit Margin on Idaho Potatoes of 0.225

```
MAX      0.225 I + 0.15 M
SUBJECT TO
       2)    0.3 I + 0.2 M <=   18000
       3)    0.1 I + 0.2 M <=   15000
       4)    0.3 I + 0.3 M <=   30000
END

            OBJECTIVE FUNCTION VALUE

       1)    13500.0000

   VARIABLE         VALUE           REDUCED COST
          I      60000.000000          .000000
          M            .000000         .000000

       ROW    SLACK OR SURPLUS       DUAL PRICES
       2)            .000000          .750000
       3)        9000.000000          .000000
       4)       12000.000000          .000000

RANGES IN WHICH THE BASIS IS UNCHANGED:

                        OBJ COEFFICIENT RANGES
   VARIABLE          CURRENT        ALLOWABLE        ALLOWABLE
                       COEF         INCREASE         DECREASE
          I          .225000        INFINITY          .000000
          M          .150000         .000000         INFINITY

                        RIGHTHAND SIDE RANGES
       ROW           CURRENT        ALLOWABLE        ALLOWABLE
                       RHS          INCREASE         DECREASE
        2         18000.000000    12000.000000     18000.000000
        3         15000.000000      INFINITY        9000.000000
        4         30000.000000      INFINITY       12000.000000
```

even if there is a 0 value for a maximum allowable increase or decrease.

Let's review checking for an alternate optimal solution. Is the optimal solution in Table 5.3 unique? Because no objective function coefficient's maximum allowable increase or decrease is 0, you conclude that the optimal solution is unique. Is the optimal solution in Table 5.11 unique? In Table 5.11, because the solution is not degenerate and 0 limits exist, you conclude that an alternate optimal solution exists.

TABLE 5.15   Summary of Identification of Existence of Alternate Optimal Solutions

1. If no objective function coefficient has a maximum allowable increase or decrease of 0, the solution is unique.
2. If at least one objective function coefficient has a maximum allowable increase or decrease of 0.
   a. If the solution is not degenerate, an alternate optimal solution exists.
   b. If the solution is degenerate, the optimal solution can be unique or an alternate optimal solution can exist. You can't tell.

Alternate optimal solution summary

Table 5.15 summarizes the ways to identify the existence of alternate optimal solutions. If no objective function coefficient's maximum allowable increase or decrease is 0, the optimal solution is unique. For a nondegenerate optimal solution, the existence of a 0 value for an objective function coefficient's maximum allowable increase or decrease signals the existence of an alternate optimal solution. For a degenerate optimal solution, however, such an indication does not guarantee the existence of an alternate optimal solution.

MODEL STRUCTURE AND SENSITIVITY ANALYSIS

One at a time

We must stress that the maximum allowable ranges for RHS constants and objective function coefficients are appropriate only when *one* parameter changes at a time. The formulation of the model affects the types of questions that can be answered from the output without re-solving the model. This point was emphasized in Chapters 2 and 3. Can you answer the following questions from the Potato Processing example output in Table 5.3?

1. How much must the cost per pound of Michigan potatoes increase before the optimal purchase plan changes?

Increasing the cost per pound of Michigan potatoes decreases the profit margin per pound of Michigan potatoes. The maximum allowable decrease in the objective function coefficient of M is 0.056667. Therefore, the cost has to increase by at least $0.056667 per pound.

2. How much must the selling price of french fries increase before the optimal purchase plan changes?

Let p represent the amount of the increase in the selling price per pound of french fries. The profit margin per pound of Idaho potatoes processed and sold is

$$[0.3 \times (0.90 + p)] + [0.1 \times 0.75] + [0.3 \times 0.50] + [0.3 \times 0.10] - 0.225 - 0.16$$

or $0.14 + 0.3p$. The maximum allowable increase in the objective function coefficient of I is 0.085. A selling price increase greater than $^{0.085}/_{0.3} = 0.283333$ need not change the solution, because the objective function coefficient of M is changing at the same time, to $0.15 + 0.2p$. Therefore, the sensitivity analysis information does not answer the question, because the single change in the french fry selling price changes two objective function coefficients.

Now, we introduce a second formulation that gives the same optimal solution but answers the question. In this formulation, the revenue terms are treated separately from the cost terms.

In addition to M and I, define

FF—number of pounds of french fries produced and sold

HB—number of pounds of hash browns produced and sold

FL—number of pounds of flakes produced and sold

WT—number of pounds of waste produced and sold

The reformulated model is

max $0.90FF + 0.75HB + 0.50FL + 0.10WT - 0.385I - 0.36M$
st $0.3I + 0.2M - FF = 0$
      $0.1I + 0.2M - HB = 0$
      $0.3I + 0.3M - FL = 0$
      $0.3I + 0.3M - WT = 0$
      $FF \leq 18000$
      $HB \leq 15000$
      $FL \leq 30000$
      $FF, HB, FL, WT, I, M \geq 0$

The first four constraints are required to define the FF, HB, FL, and WT variables.

Table 5.16 contains the LOOK ALL and the solution for the reformulated model. The resulting profit and purchasing plan are unchanged. In this formulation, however, only the objective function coefficient of FF changes when the selling price of french fries changes. With this formulation, the second question is easily answered without changing model parameters and re-solving. In this case, FF's maximum allowable increase is infinity. Thus, the optimal variable values do not change no matter how much the price per pound of french fries increases.

Model formulation affects ease of sensitivity analysis

This example illustrates that the way in which the model builder formulates the model influences the ease of sensitivity analysis. Ask yourself, "What types of sensitivity analysis interest me?"*before* you finalize the formulation.

THE CHICKEN FEED BLENDING EXAMPLE—A MINIMIZATION MODEL WITH A NONDEGENERATE OPTIMAL SOLUTION

In Chapter 3, we formulated a linear programming model to blend corn, wheat, and oats into a 100-pound sack of chicken feed at minimum cost. Because the model's three variables make graphical visualization difficult, we must rely on the output to understand the optimal solution. In

TABLE 5.16 LOOK ALL and GO Output for Alternative Formulation of Potato Processing Example

```
MAX      0.9 FF + 0.75 HB + 0.5 FL + 0.1 WT − 0.385 I − 0.36 M
SUBJECT TO
       2) − FF + 0.3 I + 0.2 M =     0
       3) − HB + 0.1 I + 0.2 M =     0
       4) − FL + 0.3 I + 0.3 M =     0
       5) − WT + 0.3 I + 0.3 M =     0
       6)   FF <=   18000
       7)   HB <=   15000
       8)   FL <=   30000
END

       OBJECTIVE FUNCTION VALUE

    1)     12225.0000

VARIABLE          VALUE        REDUCED COST
      FF      18000.000000         .000000
      HB      15000.000000         .000000
      FL      24750.000000         .000000
      WT      24750.000000         .000000
       I      15000.000000         .000000
       M      67500.000000         .000000

    ROW   SLACK OR SURPLUS      DUAL PRICES
    2)            .000000        −.575000
    3)            .000000        −.325000
    4)            .000000        −.500000
    5)            .000000        −.100000
    6)            .000000         .325000
    7)            .000000         .425000
    8)         5250.000000         .000000

RANGES IN WHICH THE BASIS IS UNCHANGED:

                         OBJ COEFFICIENT RANGES
VARIABLE        CURRENT       ALLOWABLE      ALLOWABLE
                COEF          INCREASE       DECREASE
      FF         .900000      INFINITY        .325000
      HB         .750000      INFINITY        .425000
      FL         .500000      INFINITY        .433334
      WT         .100000      INFINITY        .433334
       I        −.385000       .085000        .065000
       M        −.360000       .130000        .056667

                         RIGHTHAND SIDE RANGES
    ROW         CURRENT       ALLOWABLE      ALLOWABLE
                RHS           INCREASE       DECREASE
     2          .000000     7000.000000    3000.000000
     3          .000000     3000.000000    9000.000000
     4          .000000    24750.000000    5250.000000
     5          .000000    24750.000000     INFINITY
     6      18000.000000    7000.000000    3000.000000
     7      15000.000000    3000.000000    9000.000000
     8      30000.000000     INFINITY     5250.000000
```

this example, we study a minimization objective and the importance of the word *improvement* in the dual price and reduced cost definitions. Because this example has a zero-valued structural variable, illustrating the interpretation of a reduced cost is possible.

Table 5.17 contains the LOOK ALL output for this model. The first constraint requires that the water weight not be more than 10 percent; the second constraint imposes a minimum of 30 percent protein; the third

TABLE 5.17   LOOK ALL for Chicken Feed Blending Model

```
: look all
MIN      0.085 C + 0.08 W + 0.09 0
SUBJECT TO
       2)    0.07 C + 0.09 W + 0.12 0 <=    10
       3)    0.32 C + 0.27 W + 0.39 0 >=    30
       4)    0.18 C + 0.07 W + 0.18 0 >=    15
       5)    C + W + 0 = 100
END
```

constraint ensures that there is at least 15 percent carbohydrate; and the fourth constraint guarantees that the contents of the sack weigh 100 pounds. The decision variables are the number of pounds of each grain blended.

The solution output and the sensitivity analysis output are shown in Table 5.18. The output indicates that the least cost plan includes 72.727 pounds of corn, 27.273 pounds of wheat, and no oats.[4] The minimum cost for the 100-pound sack is approximately $8.36. The output is easy to read because the symbolic names are easily associated with the decision variables (e.g., C represents the number of pounds of corn in the blend). Note that the decision variables did not attain integer values in the optimal solution. In blending feed grains, it is possible to include a fraction of a pound of grains.

Slack and Surplus Variable Values and Changes in RHS Constants

The optimal solution is *not degenerate*. There are four constraints and four positive variables—C, W, Row 2's slack variable, and Row 3's surplus variable.

What water weight is included in this "best" sack? Because the constraint relationship was of the $\leq$ type, a slack variable is added. The value of Row 2's slack variable is 2.455. The actual water content is 2.455 pounds less than the limit of 10, or 7.545 pounds. Because Row 2's dual price is 0, as the water limitation increases from 10 to 11, the objective function (cost) does not improve (decrease). This is reasonable because the present solution contains less water than the current 10-pound limit. Increasing the RHS constant only increases the slack variable value. In

---

[4] The numerical values are rounded for discussion purposes, except if rounding obscures calculation results.

TABLE 5.18   GO Output for Chicken Feed Blending Model

```
         OBJECTIVE FUNCTION VALUE

     1)      8.36363600

   VARIABLE          VALUE          REDUCED COST
        C          72.727260          .000000
        W          27.272730          .000000
        O            .000000          .005000

      ROW     SLACK OR SURPLUS      DUAL PRICES
      2)          2.454545           .000000
      3)           .636363           .000000
      4)           .000000          -.045455
      5)           .000000          -.076818

RANGES IN WHICH THE BASIS IS UNCHANGED:

                           OBJ COEFFICIENT RANGES
   VARIABLE          CURRENT        ALLOWABLE        ALLOWABLE
                      COEF          INCREASE         DECREASE
        C            .085000         .005000          .005000
        W            .080000         .005000         INFINITY
        O            .090000        INFINITY          .005000

                           RIGHTHAND SIDE RANGES
      ROW           CURRENT        ALLOWABLE        ALLOWABLE
                      RHS           INCREASE         DECREASE
       2          10.000000        INFINITY         2.454545
       3          30.000000          .636363        INFINITY
       4          15.000000         3.000001         1.399999
       5         100.000000        23.893800         2.671753
```

Table 5.18, the maximum allowable increase for Row 2's RHS constant is infinity. If the water limit is tightened to 9 pounds, the cost and the associated blending plan don't change. In that case, the slack variable value decreases to 1.455 pounds. The sensitivity output for Row 2 indicates that the dual price of 0 is appropriate for a maximum decrease of 2.455. At the maximum allowable decrease, the water constraint slack variable is 0 and the solution is degenerate.

Review Table 5.9's summary of the impacts of changing an RHS constant for a nonbinding constraint. Because the water limitation constraint is nonbinding, Table 5.9 applies. The summary applies to any nondegenerate optimal solution, not just the Potato Processing example.

What protein weight is included in the optimal solution? Because the protein limitation is a minimum, a surplus variable is added to convert it to an equation. Row 4's entry in the SLACK OR SURPLUS column of Table 5.18 is approximately 0.636. Therefore, the protein total is 30 + 0.636, or 30.636 pounds. In a $\geq$ type constraint, the value in the SLACK OR SURPLUS column is added to the RHS constant to obtain the actual value of the left-hand side (LHS). Because there is a surplus of protein, its dual price is 0. Using Table 5.9, because the constraint is a $\geq$ type, the maximum allowable increase is 0.636, the value of the surplus variable, and the maximum allowable decrease is infinity. Why is the maximum allowable increase equal to 0.636? When the RHS constant becomes 30.636, there is no surplus protein for the current solution. Why is the maximum allowable decrease equal to infinity? If the RHS is decreased from 30 to 29, the current solution still has 30.636 pounds of protein; the limit is now exceeded by 1.636 pounds (the new value of the surplus variable). Consequently, the RHS constant can decrease by any amount without affecting the optimal solution.

Let's consider changing the RHS constant for a binding constraint. The entries for Rows 4 and 5 under the SLACK OR SURPLUS column are both 0. In Row 4, this indicates that the carbohydrate minimum of 15 percent is satisfied and that there is no surplus. Because Row 5, the sack weight limitation, is an equation, there is no slack or surplus variable. The original constraint was

$$C + W + O = 100$$

The value in the SLACK OR SURPLUS column is always 0 for an equality-type constraint.

The dual price for Row 4 is -0.045455. This is Z^*'s rate of *improvement* per unit change in its RHS constant, *if* the same set of variables remains positive. Since the dual price is negative, Z^* gets worse as the RHS constant increases. The constraint is a $\geq$ type, so if you increase the RHS constant, the constraint is harder to satisfy. Because the constraint is currently binding in the optimal solution, an increase in its RHS constant worsens the optimal objective function value. Because the objective function is cost minimization, a "worse value" of the objective function is an increase in the cost. If the RHS constant increases to 16, the cost increases by 0.045455, to \$8.409091. Before saying that this is Z^*'s change, you must check whether the dual price value is appropriate for an increase of 1 in the RHS constant. In Table 5.18, Row 4's maximum allowable increase is 3. Thus, the minimum carbohydrate percentage can increase by as much as 3 (to a value of 18), which increases the cost by 0.045455 per percentage point.

If the carbohydrate limit decreases by 1 pound and the set of variables with positive values remains the same, the minimum cost of a 100-pound sack decreases by \$0.045455. The maximum allowable decrease is 1.4 pounds. If the RHS constant decreases to 13.6, the cost decreases by 1.4 $\times$ 0.045455, or \$0.063637, to about \$8.30. As the RHS constant decreases over this range, the set of positive-valued variables remains the same, but their numerical values change. You must re-solve the changed model to find the new variable values. What results from decreasing the carbohydrate limitation more than its maximum allowable decrease? There is a change in the dual price and the set of variables that attain positive values in the optimal solution. You need to re-solve the model

Re-solve to get the variable values

with the changed parameters to determine Z^*, the new dual price, and the new variable values.

What is the interpretation of Row 5's dual price? If the RHS constant of the last constraint increases from 100 to 101, the value of the objective function worsens by 0.076818. That is, if the weight equation increases by 1 pound, the cost increases by $0.076818, *if* all other parameters remain the same. You can't infer that an extra pound can be blended that satisfies all of the quality restrictions at a cost of $0.076818. Remember that the RHS of the water constraint was 10 percent of 100 pounds, or 10 pounds. If the percentage restriction remains 10 percent, when the last constraint's RHS constant increases to 101, the RHS constant of the water constraint changes to 10.1. Similarly, the RHS constants for the protein and carbohydrate constraints change. Thus, changing the weight of the sack contents changes four RHS constants. It is not possible to use the dual price on Row 5 to determine the cost of a 101-pound sack. However, the solution to the original model also yields the proportions with the minimum cost per pound. That is, you use 0.727 pounds of corn and 0.273 pounds of wheat. The cost of an additional pound that satisfies the current percentage quality restrictions is $^{8.363636}/_{100}$ = $0.08363636.

Changes in an Objective Function Coefficient— Zero-Valued Variables

Remember that both structural variables were positive in the optimal solution of the Potato Processing example. We couldn't use that example to illustrate the effect of changing a zero-valued variable's objective function coefficient. In this section, we use the chicken feed model to discuss this type of model change.

Nondegenerate
solution

In Table 5.18, no oats are used in the least cost mixture. The reduced cost of variable O is 0.005000. Because O is zero-valued, the reduced cost is "the amount that its objective function coefficient must improve before it is worthwhile for the variable to become positive." In this case, the cost per pound of oats must improve by 0.005, which is a decrease of 0.005, to a new cost per pound of $0.085. Another interpretation of the reduced cost is the amount that Z^* worsens if the costs don't change and O's value is forced to equal 1. The reduced cost has two interpretations. In this section, we use the first interpretation. When we discuss whether adding a new variable to a model changes the optimal solution, we use the second interpretation.

Table 5.19 contains the LOOK ALL and GO output when the objective function is $0.085 C + 0.08W + 0.085O$. Z^* and all of the variable values are the same, but O's reduced cost is now 0. Note that C's objective function coefficient maximum increase and O's objective function coefficient maximum decrease are 0. If O's objective function coefficient improves by the reduced cost, an alternate optimal solution exists with O positive!

TABLE 5.19   LOOK ALL and GO Output for Chicken Feed Blending Model with Oats Cost Changed to 0.085—Alternate Optimal Solutions Exist

```
MIN     0.085 C + 0.08 W + 0.085 O
SUBJECT TO
       2)    0.07 C + 0.09 W + 0.12 O <=    10
       3)    0.32 C + 0.27 W + 0.39 O >=    30
       4)    0.18 C + 0.07 W + 0.18 O >=    15
       5)    C + W + O =    100
END

       OBJECTIVE FUNCTION VALUE

       1)    8.36363600

VARIABLE         VALUE          REDUCED COST
       C       72.727260          .000000
       W       27.272730          .000000
       O         .000000          .000000

     ROW    SLACK OR SURPLUS    DUAL PRICES
      2)        2.454545          .000000
      3)         .636363          .000000
      4)         .000000         -.045455
      5)         .000000         -.076818

RANGES IN WHICH THE BASIS IS UNCHANGED:

                         OBJ COEFFICIENT RANGES
VARIABLE        CURRENT          ALLOWABLE        ALLOWABLE
                 COEF            INCREASE         DECREASE
       C        .085000          .000000          .005000
       W        .080000          .005000          INFINITY
       O        .085000          INFINITY         .000000

                         RIGHTHAND SIDE RANGES
     ROW        CURRENT          ALLOWABLE        ALLOWABLE
                 RHS             INCREASE         DECREASE
       2      10.000000          INFINITY         2.454545
       3      30.000000           .636363         INFINITY
       4      15.000000          3.000001         1.399999
       5     100.000000         23.893800         2.671753
```

Because the optimal solution is not degenerate, it is correct to conclude that if the cost decreases by more than 0.005, the optimal solution changes and the oats variable is positive in the new optimal solution. Table 5.20 contains the optimal solution after the cost per pound of oats decreases by 0.006, to 0.084. Table 5.20's set of positive variables is different from that of Table 5.19. In Table 5.20, the *O* variable is positive.

Note that the reduced costs for all positive-valued variables in Tables 5.19 and 5.20 are 0. This is always true. What if a zero-valued variable's reduced cost is 0? If the solution is not degenerate, an alternate optimal solution exists and improving the objective function coefficient causes the variable to become positive. If the solution is *degenerate,* you can't be sure. If the optimal solution is *degenerate,* do *not* assume that an improvement greater than the reduced cost results in the variable becoming positive in the new optimal solution. It may become positive, or it may remain at 0. An example later in this chapter illustrates this ambiguity caused by a degenerate optimal solution.

Degenerate solution

TABLE 5.20   LOOK ALL and GO Output for Chicken Feed Blending Example with Oats Cost Changed to 0.084

```
MIN      0.085 C + 0.08 W + 0.084 O
SUBJECT TO·
        2)    0.07 C + 0.09 W + 0.12 O <=    10
        3)    0.32 C + 0.27 W + 0.39 O >=    30
        4)    0.18 C + 0.07 W + 0.18 O >=    15
        5)    C + W + O =     100
END

        OBJECTIVE FUNCTION VALUE

        1)     8.31454600

    VARIABLE          VALUE        REDUCED COST
        C          23.636360          .000000
        W          27.272730          .000000
        O          49.090910          .000000

        ROW    SLACK OR SURPLUS      DUAL PRICES
        2)            .000000          .020000
        3)           4.072726          .000000
        4)            .000000         -.041818
        5)            .000000         -.078873

    RANGES IN WHICH THE BASIS IS UNCHANGED:

                          OBJ COEFFICIENT RANGES
    VARIABLE         CURRENT        ALLOWABLE        ALLOWABLE
                       COEF         INCREASE         DECREASE
        C           .085000        INFINITY          .001000
        W           .080000         .004600         INFINITY
        O           .084000         .001000          .011500

                        RIGHTHAND SIDE RANGES
        ROW          CURRENT        ALLOWABLE        ALLOWABLE
                       RHS          INCREASE         DECREASE
         2         10.000000        1.181818         2.454545
         3         30.000000        4.072726         INFINITY
         4         15.000000        3.000001         4.333334
         5        100.000000       23.893800        16.666660
```

Reduced costs and ranges

The information concerning the reduced cost for oats is also available in the sensitivity analysis section of Table 5.18. The maximum allowable decrease for the oats variable's objective function coefficient is 0.005. This also indicates that if the cost coefficient of the oats variable decreases by more than 0.005, the optimal solution changes. Note that the maximum allowable increase of the objective function coefficient of O is infinity. That is reasonable because if oats are not used at the current price of 0.090, they won't be used if they become more expensive.

Summary for non-degenerate solution

Table 5.21 summarizes the impacts of changing an objective function coefficient for a zero-valued variable if the solution is not degenerate. For a maximization model, the maximum allowable increase equals the reduced cost and the maximum allowable decrease is infinity. For a minimization model, the maximum allowable increase is infinity and the maximum allowable decrease equals the reduced cost. Within the allowable range, Z^* and all of the variable values are unchanged. At the allowable limit, an alternate optimal solution exists with the zero-valued variable

---

TABLE 5.21   Summary of the Impacts of Changing an Objective Function Coefficient for a Zero-Valued Variable—Nondegenerate Optimal Solution

For a maximization model:
1. The maximum allowable increase equals the reduced cost.
2. The maximum allowable decrease is infinity.

For a minimization model:
1. The maximum allowable increase is infinity.
2. The maximum allowable decrease equals the reduced cost.

Within the allowable range:
1. All variable values are unchanged.
2. The set of positive variables is unchanged.
3. Z^* is unchanged.

At the allowable limit:
1. An alternative optimal solution exists with the variable positive.

For a change greater than the limit:
1. The variable becomes positive.
2. The set of positive variables changes.

Reduced cost summary

positive. For a change greater than the allowable limit, the optimal solution changes and the zero-valued variable becomes positive.

Table 5.22 summarizes reduced cost information for nondegenerate and degenerate solutions. If the variable's value is forced to equal 1, Z^* worsens by the reduced cost. For a nondegenerate solution, if the variable's objective function coefficient improves by the reduced cost, an alternative optimal solution exists with that variable positive. For a nondegenerate solution, if the variable's objective function coefficient improves by more than the reduced cost, the optimal solution changes and that variable's value is positive in the new optimal solution. For a degenerate solution, you can't be sure.

Changes in an Objective Function Coefficient— Positive-Valued Variables

In Table 5.18, the maximum allowable increase of W's objective function coefficient is 0.005. Because this current optimal solution is not degenerate, any increase of more than 0.005 results in a change in the set of positive variables (a change in the basis, as mathematicians describe it). In this example, it seems probable that increasing the cost of wheat more than 0.005 results in decreasing the amount of wheat used and purchasing oats. However, the only way to be sure is to change W's objective function coefficient and re-solve the model.

Consider an increase of $0.001 in the cost of wheat. Because the increase is within the allowable increase, the optimal values of the variables do not change. Because the variable values do not change, the set of positive variables also remains the same. The value of the objective

---

TABLE 5.22 Summary of Reduced Costs for a Zero-Valued Variable

For a nondegenerate optimal solution:
1. If the variable's value is forced to equal 1, Z^* worsens by the reduced cost.
2. If the variable's objective function coefficient improves by the reduced cost, an alternate optimal solution exists with the variable positive.
3. If the variable's objective function coefficient improves by an amount greater than the reduced cost, the current solution is no longer optimal and the variable's value is positive in the new optimal solution.

For a degenerate optimal solution:
1. If the variable's value is forced to equal 1, Z^* worsens by the reduced cost.
2. If the variable's objective function coefficient improves by the reduced cost, the optimal solution may be unique or an alternate optimal solution may exist with the variable positive.
3. If the variable's objective function coefficient improves by an amount greater than the reduced cost, the current solution *may* remain optimal.

---

function increases by \$0.027272709. You obtain this by multiplying the optimal value of the wheat variable, 27.272709, by the amount of the change in the objective function coefficient of the variable, 0.001. After rounding to the nearest penny, the cost per 100-pound sack is \$8.39.

INTERPRETATION OF DEGENERATE OPTIMAL SOLUTION OUTPUT

A degenerate optimal solution's output has many interpretations that are identical to those for nondegenerate solutions. In this section, we discuss only the differences in interpretation. Knowing these differences makes you better able to predict the impact of coefficient changes on the optimal solution.

First, the dual prices are not uniquely determined. Tables 5.5 and 5.7 contain two degenerate solutions to the Potato Processing example when the french fry limitation is 25,000 pounds. In both cases, you purchase

Dual prices not unique

50,000 pounds from Idaho and Michigan. The variable values are the same, so they aren't alternate optimal solutions. However, the french fry limitation's dual price is 0.325 in Table 5.5 and 0 in Table 5.7. You can see from Figure 5.3 that if Row 2's RHS constant increases further, the solution doesn't change, so the dual price is actually 0. If Row 2's RHS constant decreases, the dual price is actually 0.325. Figure 5.4 confirms this.

Second, an objective function change greater than the allowable limit does not always result in a different solution point. In Table 5.7, I's maximum increase is 0.01; in Table 5.5, its maximum increase is 0.085. Figure 5.8 illustrates the reason for the difference. When I's objective function coefficient increases by 0.01, the equal value contour line has the

An objective function coefficient greater than the limit may not change the solution

FIGURE 5.8 Potato Processing Example with 25,000-Pound French Fry Limitation

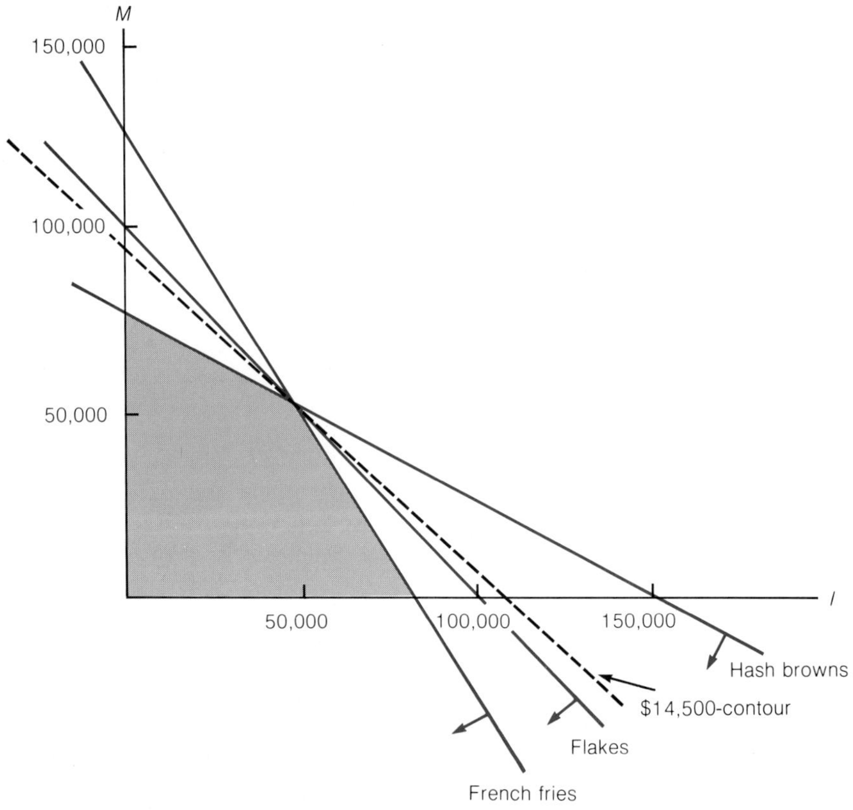

same slope as that of the flakes limitation.[5] When I's objective function coefficient increases by 0.085, the equal value contour line has the same slope as that of the french fry limitation. The larger increase, 0.085, results in alternate optimal solutions, and a greater increase changes the optimal solution to purchasing 60,000 pounds of Idaho potatoes and none from Michigan. An objective function change greater than the allowable limit may or may not result in a different solution.

Third, if the maximum allowable increase or decrease of an objective function coefficient is equal to 0, this does not always mean that an

---

[5] More than one partition corresponds to a degenerate optimal solution. The difference is caused by this. The maximum allowable limits are imposed by a change in partition (basis). Chapter 6 discusses this further.

TABLE 5.23 LOOK ALL and GO Output for Potato Processing Example with Idaho Profit Margin Changed to 0.15 and French Fry Limitation Changed to 25,000

```
MAX      0.15 I + 0.15 M
SUBJECT TO
        2)    0.3 I + 0.2 M <=    25000
        3)    0.1 I + 0.2 M <=    15000
        4)    0.3 I + 0.3 M <=    30000
END

        OBJECTIVE FUNCTION VALUE

    1)        15000.0000

    VARIABLE           VALUE          REDUCED COST
        I        50000.000000           .000000
        M        50000.000000           .000000

        ROW    SLACK OR SURPLUS    DUAL PRICES
        2)           .000000          .000000
        3)           .000000          .000000
        4)           .000000          .500000

RANGES IN WHICH THE BASIS IS UNCHANGED:

                          OBJ COEFFICIENT RANGES
    VARIABLE           CURRENT        ALLOWABLE        ALLOWABLE
                        COEF          INCREASE         DECREASE
        I              .150000         .000000          .075000
        M              .150000         .150000          .000000

                          RIGHTHAND SIDE RANGES
        ROW            CURRENT        ALLOWABLE        ALLOWABLE
                        RHS           INCREASE         DECREASE
         2          25000.000000      INFINITY          .000000
         3          15000.000000     5000.000000        .000000
         4          30000.000000       .000000       7500.000000
```

Alternate optimal indication inconclusive

alternate optimal solution exists. Table 5.23 contains the Potato Processing example's solution when I's profit margin is 0.15 and the french fry limitation is 25,000. I's maximum increase and M's maximum decrease are 0, but examination of Figure 5.9 shows that the optimal solution is unique. Ambiguity exists because the slope of the equal value contour line equals the slope of the flakes line. If the maximum allowable increase or decrease of an objective function coefficient equals 0, there may or may not be an alternate optimal solution.

Reduced cost interpretation questionable

Fourth, if a zero-valued variable's objective function improves more than the reduced cost, there may or may not be a changed solution with the value of the variable positive. If you modify the Potato Processing example so that you purchase only one type of potatoes in the optimal solution, you can construct an example of this.

Degenerate solution summary

Table 5.24 summarizes the ambiguities introduced if the optimal solution is degenerate. All other interpretations are not affected by the degeneracy.

FIGURE 5.9 Potato Processing Example with 25,000-Pound French Fry Limitation—Max 0.15*I* + 0.15*M*

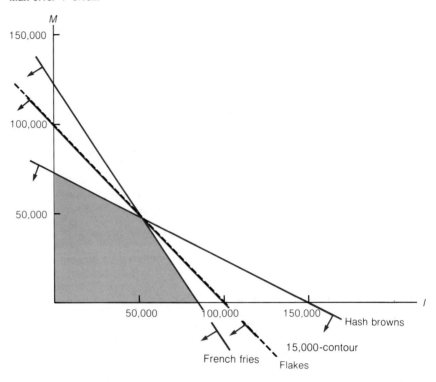

TABLE 5.24 Ambiguities Introduced by a Degenerate Optimal Solution

1. Dual prices are not uniquely determined.
2. If a zero-valued variable's objective function coefficient improves by the reduced cost, there may or may not be an alternate optimal solution.
3. If a zero-valued variable's objective function coefficient improves by more than the reduced cost, the solution may or may not change.
4. If a variable's objective function coefficient changes to its limit, there may or may not be an alternate optimal solution.
5. If a variable's objective function coefficient changes more than its limit, the solution may or may not change.
6. If the maximum increase or decrease in a variable's objective function coefficient equals 0, there may or may not be an alternate optimal solution.

SIMULTANEOUS CHANGES—THE 100 PERCENT RULE

Our discussions of changing RHS constants and objective function coefficients have assumed only one change at a time. Now, we discuss the impact on Z^* of many changes at the same time. For each change, calculate the fraction of the maximum allowable change. If the total of the fractions is not greater than 1, the **100 Percent Rule** is satisfied and the individual changes to Z^* are added. Otherwise, you must re-solve the changed model to determine the new Z^*.

An example changing two RHS constants

Say that the french fry limitation increases by 2,000, to 20,000 pounds, and that the hash brown limitation decreases by 1,000, to 14,000 pounds. In Table 5.3, the maximum increase in the french fry limitation is 7,000 and the maximum decrease in the hash brown limitation is 9,000. Row 2's fraction is $2,000/7,000 = 0.286$. Row 3's fraction is $1,000/9,000 = 0.111$. The sum of the fractions, $0.286 + 0.111 = 0.397$, does not exceed 1, so the individual changes to Z^* are added. The improvement in Z^* from Row 2 is $(20,000 - 18,000) \times 0.325 = \$650$. The improvement in Z^* from Row 3 is $(14,000 - 15,000) \times 0.425 = -\$425$. Z^*'s total improvement is $650 + (-425) = \$225$. The profit increases by \$225, to \$12,250. You must re-solve the changed model to determine the new variable values.

An example changing two objective function coefficients

Now, let's consider simultaneously changing objective function coefficients in the Potato Processing example. Say that the selling price of french fries increases by \$0.10 per pound. Because the french fry yield of Idaho potatoes is 30 percent, I's profit margin increases by \$0.03. Because the french fry yield of Michigan potatoes is 20 percent, M's profit margin increases by \$0.02. From Table 5.3, the maximum allowable increases of the objective function coefficients of I and M are 0.085 and 0.13, respectively. The fraction for I is $0.03/0.085 = 0.353$. The fraction for M is $0.02/0.13 = 0.154$. The total fraction is $0.353 + 0.154 = 0.507$. Because the total fraction is not more than 1, you add the individual Z^* changes. Z^* increases by $0.03 \times 15,000 = 450$ and $0.02 \times 67,500 = 1,300$ for the I and M changes, respectively. The new Z^* is \$13,975. The optimal point and the variable values are the same.

If the french fry selling price increases by \$0.20, the total fraction is 1.14 and the 100 Percent Rule is not satisfied; you must re-solve the changed model. Remember, we solved an alternative Potato Processing formulation that included intermediate variables (e.g., FF representing french fries produced) in an earlier section of this chapter. For that formulation (Table 5.16), the maximum allowable increase for the french fry selling price is infinity. Using the alternative formulation, you can tell the impact of a \$0.20 french fry selling price increase. The variable values do not change and Z^* increases by \$3,600. From Table 5.3's formulation, you cannot tell the impact. The 100 Percent Rule guarantees that if the total fraction is *not* more than 1, you can add the individual Z^* changes. In this case, even though the total fraction is more than 1, Z^* changes by the sum of the individual Z^* changes. However, you must re-solve the changed model to discover that fact. You can't be sure of the impact. *Do not rely on the 100 Percent Rule as an alternative to a formulation that makes simple-sensitivity analysis easier.*

A good formulation is better than the 100 Percent Rule

ADDING A CONSTRAINT

After you develop and solve a model, you may become aware of other factors that should have been incorporated into the model. For example, an unforeseen limitation might cause another constraint. Before you re-solve the model with the additional constraint, you should check whether including that constraint affects the old optimal solution. Adding a constraint *never* makes the feasible set *larger*. It either makes the feasible set smaller or leaves the feasible set unchanged. If the current optimal solution satisfies the additional constraint, the current optimal solution remains optimal when you add the constraint. If the current optimal solution violates the additional constraint, adding the constraint changes the optimal solution.

Check whether the old optimal solution satisfies the added constraint

For example, say that the Potato Processing plant can process only 85,000 pounds of potatoes per month. The additional constraint is

$$I + M \leq 85000$$

The original optimal solution was $I = 15{,}000$ and $M = 67{,}500$. Substituting the variables' values into the additional constraint, we find that the total pounds processed is $15{,}000 + 67{,}500 = 82{,}500$. Because this satisfies the processing limitation, the optimal solution is unchanged. However, if the processing limitation were less than 82,500 pounds, the optimal solution would change.

ADDING A VARIABLE

After you have developed and solved a model, you may discover a variable that you didn't consider in the model. For example, you may want to consider purchasing Wisconsin potatoes. It is not necessary to re-solve the model with the additional variable to determine whether the variable is worthwhile. Because the variable wasn't included in the model, its value is 0. You calculate the reduced cost for the additional variable using the dual prices from the current solution. Remember the second interpretation of the reduced cost: the amount that Z^* worsens if a zero-valued variable is forced to a value of 1. If the reduced cost is

If the reduced cost is negative, re-solve the changed model
negative, Z^* improves when the variable becomes positive. Thus, the variable is worthwhile and you should re-solve the changed model. If the reduced cost is positive, introducing the variable hurts Z^* and the current solution remains optimal. If the reduced cost is 0, Z^* is unchanged and the current solution remains optimal.

Say that Wisconsin potatoes produce 22 percent french fries, 18 percent hash browns, 30 percent flakes, and 30 percent waste, with a profit margin of $0.145 per pound. Let us determine whether Wisconsin potatoes are worth purchasing.

Say that W is forced to a value of 1. That affects the RHS amounts available for I and M. Because 0.22 pounds of french fries are produced, the french fry limitation is reduced by 0.22. Similarly, the hash brown and flakes limitations decrease by 0.18 and 0.3, respectively. The french fry limitation's dual price is 0.325. A decrease of 1 for the RHS constant worsens Z^* by 0.325; a decrease of 0.22 worsens Z^* by $0.22 \times 0.325 = 0.0715$. Similarly, Z^* worsens by $0.18 \times 0.425 = 0.0765$ and $0.3 \times 0 = 0$ for the hash brown and flakes limitations, respectively. Z^* worsens a total of $0.0715 + 0.0765 + 0 = 0.148$. This is partially offset by the $0.145 additional profit on 1 pound of Wisconsin potatoes. In total, however, Z^* worsens by $0.003 ($0.0148 - 0.145$). Thus, Wisconsin potatoes are not worth purchasing.

Now that you understand the logic, let's consider how to calculate reduced costs for a general model. Let DP_i represent the dual price of the ith constraint, a_i represent the ith constraint coefficient for the added variable, and c the objective function coefficient of the added variable. Say that the model has m constraints. Then, for a *maximization* model, calculate the reduced cost of the added variable by

Maximization model

$$\text{Reduced cost} = \sum_{i=1}^{m} DP_i a_i - c$$

Minimization model

For a *minimization* model, calculate the reduced cost of the added variable by

$$\text{Reduced cost} = \sum_{i=1}^{m} DP_i a_i + c$$

The summation term is the amount that Z^* worsens when the effective RHS constants are changed by forcing the variable to equal 1. In a maximization model, this amount is reduced by the additional profit. In a minimization model, it is increased by the additional cost.

For Wisconsin potatoes, the a_i coefficients are 0.22, 0.18, and 0.3 for the french fry, hash brown, and flakes limitations, respectively. Multiplying by the respective dual prices and subtracting the profit margin, the reduced cost is calculated as

$$\text{Reduced cost} = (0.22 \times 0.325) + (0.18 \times 0.425)$$
$$+ (0.3 \times 0) - 0.145 = 0.003$$

Because the reduced cost is positive, Wisconsin potatoes are not worth purchasing. If the profit margin of Wisconsin potatoes were more than $0.148, the reduced cost would be negative and Wisconsin potatoes would be worth purchasing. You must then re-solve the changed model to find the new solution.

For New England Merchants Leasing, the negotiation of financing and lease terms often took many months. You can treat a particular lease proposal as a new decision variable. Then, you can evaluate how the lease proposal affects the portfolio NPV by calculating its reduced cost. If the reduced cost is negative, the lease proposal improves the portfolio NPV. You can use the dual prices to evaluate a proposal and to develop a more favorable counter proposal. You prefer that the lease proposal have more impact on constraints with large dual prices and less impact on constraints with small dual prices.

SUMMARY

This chapter revisited the Potato Processing example model in Chapter 2 and the chicken feed blending model in Chapter 3. However, the concepts in this chapter apply to all linear programming models. In Chapter 7, we use these concepts in the solution analysis and model manipulation phase for many more linear programming applications. Solution analysis, sensitivity analysis, and model manipulation play a central role in the use of models for decision making. New England Merchants Leasing didn't solve its linear programming model just once. It solved the model again and again to study how lease proposals, market conditions, and policy constraints affected its portfolio NPV. Sometimes simple-sensitivity analysis was possible, and sometimes brute force sensitivity analysis was necessary.

In Chapter 4, we introduced the graphical solution method for linear programming models. This chapter graphically illustrates the impact of changes in an RHS constant or an objective function on the optimal solution. If you understand the graphical impact, the interpretation of the solution output is easier.

The solution output contains Z^*, the structural values, and the values of slack or surplus variables. Besides this information, much information on the sensitivity of the optimal solution is available. A constraint's dual price is the rate of improvement of Z^* as the RHS constant changes, if the set of positive variables does not change. For a nondegenerate solution, the objective function coefficient for a zero-valued variable must improve by at least the amount of that variable's reduced cost before it is worthwhile for the variable to become positive.

The model's formulation affects the ease of answering some sensitivity analysis questions. Introducing definitional and intermediate variables often aids in the analysis of the model, even if the model's size increases.

Determining whether adding a constraint or a variable changes the solution is possible without re-solving the model. If the optimal solution satisfies the added constraint, the optimal solution is unchanged. For an added variable, you calculate the reduced cost. If the reduced cost is nonnegative, the optimal solution is unchanged. If the reduced cost is negative, the optimal solution changes. If the optimal solution changes, you must re-solve the changed model.

Note the following cautions concerning output interpretation. First, when the RHS constant of a binding constraint changes within the allowable range limits, the optimal values of some structural variables change. You must then re-solve the model to discover the new optimal variable values. When the RHS constant of a nonbinding constraint changes within the allowable range limits, only the value of the constraint's slack or surplus variable changes. Second, when an objective function coefficient for a positive-valued variable changes within its allowable range limits, all of the variable values remain the same and Z^*'s rate of increase is equal to the value of the variable whose coefficient changes. When an objective function coefficient for a zero-valued variable changes within its allowable range limits, Z^* and the variable values do not change. Third, a degenerate optimal solution causes ambiguity in the output's interpretation. A maximum allowable increase or decrease of 0 for an objective function coefficient does not guarantee the existence of an alternate optimal solution. A change in an objective function coefficient greater than the maximum allowable does not guarantee a change in the optimal solution. Further, the dual prices are not unique. Fourth, the maximum range limits assume that only one RHS constant or objective function coefficient changes at a time. If the changes satisfy the 100 Percent Rule, the individual Z^* impacts are added. But the 100 Percent Rule is not a substitute for a formulation that eases sensitivity analysis.

This chapter's information is limited to *linear* programming models. If the objective function or a constraint function is not linear, the interpretations of the dual prices, reduced costs, and allowable ranges change. The assumption that all variable values are *continuous* also limits the interpretations. If the model has an integer-restricted variable, the interpretations do not apply. However, for some integer linear programming models, you can use the information as approximate results.

QUESTIONS

1. What are the two interpretations of a reduced cost?
2. Discuss the following: "The ease of sensitivity analysis is influenced by the model structure selected by the model builder."
3. What is a dual price?
4. If the RHS constant of a less than or equal to ($\le$) inequality is increased, could the feasible set become larger? Could the optimal value of the objective

function improve? Become worse? From your response, give a range of possible values of the dual price of that type of constraint.

5. If the RHS constant of a less than or equal to (≤) inequality is decreased, could the feasible set become larger? Could the optimal value of the objective function improve? Become worse? From your response, give a range of possible values of the dual price of that type of constraint.

6. If the RHS constant of a greater than or equal to (≥) inequality is increased, could the feasible set become larger? Could the optimal value of the objective function improve? Become worse? From your response, give a range of possible values of the dual price of that type of constraint.

7. If the RHS constant of a greater than or equal to (≥) inequality is decreased, could the feasible set become larger? Could the optimal value of the objective function improve? Become worse? From your response, give a range of possible values of the dual price of that type of constraint.

8. If the RHS constant of a less than or equal to (≤) inequality is increased and the objective function is to be maximized, could the optimal value of the objective function increase? Decrease?

9. If the RHS constant of a less than or equal to (≤) inequality is increased and the objective function is to be minimized, could the optimal value of the objective function increase? Decrease?

10. If the RHS constant of a greater than or equal to (≥) inequality is increased and the objective function is to be maximized, could the optimal value of the objective function increase? Decrease?

11. If the RHS constant of a greater than or equal to (≥) inequality is increased and the objective function is to be minimized, could the optimal value of the objective function increase? Decrease?

12. How do you determine whether the optimal solution to a linear programming model is degenerate?

13. If there are 5 constraints and 10 variables after adding the slack and surplus variables, must the optimal solution be degenerate?

14. If there are 10 constraints and 5 variables after adding the slack and surplus variables, must the optimal solution be degenerate?

15. How can the existence of an alternate optimal solution be detected from the optimality ranges of the objective function coefficients? What is the additional complication of a degenerate optimal solution?

16. If the RHS constant of an equality constraint (=) increases, can the feasible set become larger? Smaller? Give an example of each.

17. How can you tell from the output that the optimal solution is unique?

18. What is the 100 Percent Rule?

19. How do you check whether adding a constraint changes the optimal solution?

20. How do you calculate the reduced cost for a maximization model?

21. How do you calculate the reduced cost for a minimization model?

22. Give the value of the reduced cost for any positive variable.

23. If an objective function coefficient changes within the allowable limits,
    a. Does Z* change?
    b. Does the set of positive variables change?
    c. Do any variable values change?

24. If an RHS constant changes within the allowable limits,
    a. Does Z* change?
    b. Does the set of positive variables change?
    c. Do any variable values change?

25. What happens if an objective function coefficient changes the maximum allowable amount?

26. What happens if an RHS constant changes the maximum allowable amount?

27. *Theory.* If a linear programming model has five constraints and seven variables, what are the dimensions of its dual problem?

28. *Theory.* Explain the interpretation difference between dual variable values and dual prices.

29. *Theory.* What is the relationship between the optimal objective function values of the primal and dual problems?

EXERCISES

The following exercises require the interpretation of computer output. Answer each part based on the output presented. If it is impossible to answer a question from the output presented, indicate what new model must be solved. If a question or part of a question asks for the impact of a model change, no other change is assumed.

1. The following output was generated for the Potato Processing example when the flakes limitation decreased to a value of 24,900.

```
MAX     0.14 I + 0.15 M
SUBJECT TO
       2)    0.3 I + 0.2 M <=    18000
       3)    0.1 I + 0.2 M <=    15000
       4)    0.3 I + 0.3 M <=    24900
END

LP OPTIMUM FOUND  AT STEP     2

            OBJECTIVE FUNCTION VALUE

       1)      12225.0000

VARIABLE          VALUE          REDUCED COST
       I       15000.000000        .000000
       M       67500.000000        .000000

   ROW       SLACK OR SURPLUS      DUAL PRICES
      2)            .000000          .325000
      3)            .000000          .425000
      4)         150.000000          .000000
```

RANGES IN WHICH THE BASIS IS UNCHANGED

VARIABLE	CURRENT COEF	OBJ COEFFICIENT RANGES ALLOWABLE INCREASE	ALLOWABLE DECREASE
I	.140000	.085000	.065000
M	.150000	.130000	.056667

ROW	CURRENT RHS	RIGHTHAND SIDE RANGES ALLOWABLE INCREASE	ALLOWABLE DECREASE
2	18000.000000	200.000000	3000.000000
3	15000.000000	200.000000	9000.000000
4	24900.000000	INFINITY	150.000000

a. What is Z^*?

b. How many pounds of Idaho and Michigan potatoes are purchased?

c. How many pounds of french fries are produced? Hash browns? Flakes?

d. Is this optimal solution a degenerate solution? Explain.

e. Is the optimal solution unique? Explain.

f. If the french fry limitation increases to 18,100,

   (1) What is Z^*?

   (2) Do you still purchase potatoes from Idaho and Michigan?

   (3) How many pounds of potatoes from Idaho and Michigan are purchased?

g. If the hash brown limitation increases to 16,000,

   (1) What is Z^*?

   (2) Do you still purchase potatoes from Idaho and Michigan?

   (3) Do you still purchase the same number of pounds of potatoes from Idaho and Michigan?

h. If the flakes limitation increases to 35,000,

   (1) What is Z^*?

   (2) Do you still purchase potatoes from Idaho and Michigan?

   (3) Do you still purchase the same number of pounds of potatoes from Idaho and Michigan?

2. The following output was generated for the Potato Processing example when the flakes limitation decreased by the ALLOWABLE DECREASE, 5,250.

```
MAX     0.14 I + 0.15 M
SUBJECT TO
        2)    0.3 I + 0.2 M <=    18000
        3)    0.1 I + 0.2 M <=    15000
        4)    0.3 I + 0.3 M <=    24750
END

LP OPTIMUM FOUND  AT STEP    2

            OBJECTIVE FUNCTION VALUE

        1)      12225.0000
```

VARIABLE	VALUE	REDUCED COST
I	15000.000000	.000000
M	67500.000000	.000000

ROW	SLACK OR SURPLUS	DUAL PRICES
2)	.000000	.325000
3)	.000000	.425000
4)	.000000	.000000

RANGES IN WHICH THE BASIS IS UNCHANGED

		OBJ COEFFICIENT RANGES	
VARIABLE	CURRENT COEF	ALLOWABLE INCREASE	ALLOWABLE DECREASE
I	.140000	.085000	.065000
M	.150000	.130000	.056667

		RIGHTHAND SIDE RANGES	
ROW	CURRENT RHS	ALLOWABLE INCREASE	ALLOWABLE DECREASE
2	18000.000000	.000000	3000.000000
3	15000.000000	.000000	9000.000000
4	24750.000000	INFINITY	.000000

a. What is Z^*?

b. How many pounds of Idaho and Michigan potatoes are purchased?

c. How many pounds of french fries are produced? Hash browns? Flakes?

d. Is this optimal solution a degenerate solution? Explain.

e. Is the optimal solution unique? Explain.

f. If the french fry limitation increases to 18,100,
  (1) What is Z^*?
  (2) Do you still purchase potatoes from Idaho and Michigan?
  (3) How many pounds of potatoes from Idaho and Michigan are purchased?

g. If the hash brown limitation decreases to 14,000,
  (1) What is Z^*?
  (2) Do you still purchase potatoes from Idaho and Michigan?
  (3) Do you still purchase the same number of pounds of potatoes from Idaho and Michigan?

h. If the flakes limitation increases to 25,100,
  (1) What is Z^*?
  (2) Do you still purchase potatoes from Idaho and Michigan?
  (3) Do you still purchase the same number of pounds of potatoes from Idaho and Michigan?

3. The following output was generated for the Potato Processing example when the flakes limitation decreased to a value of 24,500.

```
MAX     0.14 I + 0.15 M
SUBJECT TO
     2)    0.3 I + 0.2 M <=    18000
     3)    0.1 I + 0.2 M <=    15000
     4)    0.3 I + 0.3 M <=    24500
END

LP OPTIMUM FOUND   AT STEP     2

          OBJECTIVE FUNCTION VALUE

     1)     12116.6700
```

VARIABLE	VALUE	REDUCED COST
I	13333.330000	.000000
M	68333.340000	.000000

ROW	SLACK OR SURPLUS	DUAL PRICES
2)	333.334100	.000000
3)	.000000	.100000
4)	.000000	.433333

RANGES IN WHICH THE BASIS IS UNCHANGED

OBJ COEFFICIENT RANGES

VARIABLE	CURRENT COEF	ALLOWABLE INCREASE	ALLOWABLE DECREASE
I	.140000	.010000	.065000
M	.150000	.130000	.010000

RIGHTHAND SIDE RANGES

ROW	CURRENT RHS	ALLOWABLE INCREASE	ALLOWABLE DECREASE
2	18000.000000	INFINITY	333.334100
3	15000.000000	1333.333000	333.334100
4	24500.000000	250.000600	2000.000000

a. What is Z^*?

b. How many pounds of Idaho and Michigan potatoes are purchased?

c. How many pounds of french fries are produced? Hash browns? Flakes?

d. Is this optimal solution a degenerate solution? Explain.

e. Is the optimal solution unique? Explain.

f. If the french fry limitation increases to 18,100,

    (1) What is Z^*?

    (2) Do you still purchase potatoes from Idaho and Michigan?

    (3) How many pounds of potatoes from Idaho and Michigan are purchased?

g. If the hash brown limitation increases to 17,000,

    (1) What is Z^*?

    (2) Do you still purchase potatoes from Idaho and Michigan?

    (3) Do you still purchase the same number of pounds of potatoes from Idaho and Michigan?

h. If the flakes limitation increases to 20,000,

    (1) What is Z^*?

    (2) Do you still purchase potatoes from Idaho and Michigan?

    (3) Do you still purchase the same number of pounds of potatoes from Idaho and Michigan?

i. What is the interpretation of the dual price on Row 2, the french fry limitation?

4. From the computer output in Exercises 1, 2, and 3, graph Z^* versus the flakes limitation RHS constant. The graph should contain only the portion for which Z^* is known.

5. Answer the following questions from the computer output in Exercise 1.

    a. If the profit margin per pound of Idaho potatoes increases by $0.01, to a new value of $0.15,

        (1) What is the optimal profit?

        (2) Do you still purchase potatoes from Idaho and Michigan?

        (3) Do you still purchase the same number of pounds of potatoes from Idaho and Michigan?

    b. If the profit margin per pound of Idaho potatoes decreases by $0.05, to a new value of $0.09,

        (1) What is the optimal profit?

        (2) Do you still purchase the same number of pounds of potatoes from Idaho and Michigan?

    c. If the profit margin per pound of Michigan potatoes increases to $0.16,

        (1) What is the optimal profit?

        (2) Do you still purchase the same number of pounds of potatoes from Idaho and Michigan?

        (3) Is the new optimal solution unique?

    d. If the profit margin per pound of Michigan potatoes increases to $0.28,

        (1) What is the optimal profit?

        (2) Do you still purchase the same number of pounds of potatoes from Idaho and Michigan?

        (3) Is the new optimal solution unique?

    e. If the profit margin per pound of Michigan potatoes increases to $0.29,

        (1) What is the optimal profit?

        (2) Do you still purchase the same number of pounds of potatoes from Idaho and Michigan?

6. Answer the following questions from the computer output in Exercise 3.

    a. If the profit margin per pound of Idaho potatoes increases by $0.01, to a new value of $0.15,

        (1) What is the optimal profit?

        (2) Do you still purchase potatoes from Idaho and Michigan?

        (3) Do you still purchase the same number of pounds of potatoes from Idaho and Michigan?

    b. If the profit margin per pound of Idaho potatoes decreases by $0.05, to a new value of $0.09,

        (1) What is the optimal profit?

        (2) Do you still purchase the same number of pounds of potatoes from Idaho and Michigan?

    c. If the profit margin per pound of Michigan potatoes increases to $0.16,

        (1) What is the optimal profit?

        (2) Do you still purchase the same number of pounds of potatoes from Idaho and Michigan?

        (3) Is the new optimal solution unique?

    d. If the profit margin per pound of Michigan potatoes increases to $0.28,

        (1) What is the optimal profit?

        (2) Do you still purchase the same number of pounds of potatoes from Idaho and Michigan?

        (3) Is the new optimal solution unique?

    e. If the profit margin per pound of Michigan potatoes increases to $0.29,

        (1) What is the optimal profit?

        (2) Do you still purchase the same number of pounds of potatoes from Idaho and Michigan?

7. Answer the following questions from the computer output in Exercise 2.

    a. If the profit margin per pound of Michigan potatoes increases to $0.16,

(1) What is the optimal profit?

(2) Do you still purchase the same number of pounds of potatoes from Idaho and Michigan?

(3) Is the new optimal solution unique?

b. If the profit margin per pound of Michigan potatoes increases to $0.28,

(1) What is the optimal profit?

(2) Do you still purchase the same number of pounds of potatoes from Idaho and Michigan?

(3) Is the new optimal solution unique?

c. If the profit margin per pound of Michigan potatoes increases to $0.29,

(1) What is the optimal profit?

(2) Do you still purchase the same number of pounds of potatoes from Idaho and Michigan?

8. The optimal solution to the model, after the profit margin per pound of Michigan potatoes has been changed to $0.29, is given below:

```
MAX      0.14 I + 0.29 M

SUBJECT TO
        2)   0.3 I + 0.2 M <=   18000
        3)   0.1 I + 0.2 M <=   15000
        4)   0.3 I + 0.3 M <=   30000
END

LP OPTIMUM FOUND   AT STEP      1

        OBJECTIVE FUNCTION VALUE

    1)     21750.0000

    VARIABLE          VALUE        REDUCED COST
        I            .000000          .005000
        M       75000.000000          .000000

        ROW    SLACK OR SURPLUS      DUAL PRICES
        2)        3000.000000          .000000
        3)           .000000         1.450000
        4)        7500.000000          .000000

RANGES IN WHICH THE BASIS IS UNCHANGED
```

	OBJ COEFFICIENT RANGES		
VARIABLE	CURRENT COEF	ALLOWABLE INCREASE	ALLOWABLE DECREASE
I	.140000	.005000	INFINITY
M	.290000	INFINITY	.010000

	RIGHTHAND SIDE RANGES		
ROW	CURRENT RHS	ALLOWABLE INCREASE	ALLOWABLE DECREASE
2	18000.000000	INFINITY	3000.000000
3	15000.000000	3000.000000	15000.000000
4	30000.000000	INFINITY	7500.000000

---

a. What is the interpretation of *I*'s reduced cost?

    b. If the profit margin per pound of Idaho potatoes increases by $0.01, to a new value of $0.15,

        (1) What is the optimal profit?

        (2) Would you still purchase the same number of pounds of potatoes from Idaho and Michigan?

        (3) Would you purchase potatoes from Idaho?

    c. If the profit margin per pound of Michigan potatoes increases to $0.31,

        (1) What is the optimal profit?

        (2) Would you still purchase the same number of pounds of potatoes from Idaho and Michigan?

    d. Say that the profit margin per pound of Idaho potatoes decreases by $0.01, to a new value of $0.13,

        (1) What is the optimal profit?

        (2) Would you still purchase the same number of pounds of potatoes from Idaho and Michigan?

    e. If the profit margin per pound of Michigan potatoes decreases by $0.02,

        (1) What is the optimal profit?

        (2) Would you still purchase the same number of pounds of potatoes from Idaho and Michigan?

    f. How much must the profit margin per pound of Idaho potatoes increase before the purchase plan changes?

    g. Is the optimal solution unique?

9. From the computer output for the Potato Processing example in the chapter and in Exercise 8, graph Z^* versus the objective function coefficient for M. The graph should contain only the portion for which the optimal value of the objective function is known.

10. The following computer output is for the Potato Processing example, with the profit margin per pound of Michigan potatoes equal to $0.28.

```
MAX     0.14 I + 0.28 M

SUBJECT TO
        2)    0.3 I + 0.2 M <=    18000
        3)    0.1 I + 0.2 M <=    15000
        4)    0.3 I + 0.3 M <=    30000
END

        OBJECTIVE FUNCTION VALUE

    1)    21000.0000
```

VARIABLE	VALUE	REDUCED COST
I	15000.000000	.000000
M	67500.000000	.000000

ROW	SLACK OR SURPLUS	DUAL PRICES
2)	.000000	.000000
3)	.000000	1.400000
4)	5250.000000	.000000

```
NO. ITERATIONS =     1

RANGES IN WHICH THE BASIS IS UNCHANGED:
```

VARIABLE	OBJ COEFFICIENT RANGES		
	CURRENT COEF	ALLOWABLE INCREASE	ALLOWABLE DECREASE
I	.140000	.280000	.000000
M	.280000	.000000	.186667

ROW	RIGHTHAND SIDE RANGES		
	CURRENT RHS	ALLOWABLE INCREASE	ALLOWABLE DECREASE
2	18000.000000	7000.000000	3000.000000
3	15000.000000	3000.000000	9000.000000
4	30000.000000	INFINITY	5250.000000

a. Is this optimal solution a degenerate solution?

b. Is the optimal solution unique?

c. If the profit margin per pound of Michigan potatoes increases by $0.01,
   (1) What is the optimal profit?
   (2) Would you still purchase potatoes from Idaho and Michigan?
   (3) Would you still purchase the same number of pounds of potatoes from Idaho and Michigan?

d. How much must the profit margin per pound of Idaho potatoes increase before the purchase plan changes?

11. A marketing consultant has recommended a plan that she guarantees will increase french fry sales by 200 pounds. The implementation of the plan costs $50. Should this plan be undertaken? What is the optimal profit?

12. A marketing consultant has recommended a plan that she guarantees will increase french fry sales by 200 pounds. The implementation of the plan costs $75. Should this plan be undertaken? What is the optimal profit?

13. A marketing consultant has recommended a plan that she guarantees will increase french fry sales by 1,000 pounds. The implementation of the plan costs $50. Should this plan be undertaken? What is the optimal profit?

14. A marketing consultant has recommended a plan that she guarantees will increase french fry sales by 1,000 pounds. The implementation of the plan will cost $250. Should this plan be undertaken? What is the optimal profit?

15. If the processing cost for the Potato Processing example increases by $0.01 per pound,
    a. What is Z^*?
    b. What is the potato purchasing plan?

16. If the processing cost for the Potato Processing example increases by $0.02 per pound of Michigan potatoes and $0.01 per pound of Idaho potatoes,
    a. What is Z^*?
    b. What is the potato purchasing plan?

17. If the french fry limitation and the hash brown limitation both increase by 4,000 pounds,
    a. What is Z^*?
    b. What is the potato purchasing plan?

18. If the french fry limitation increases by 3,000 pounds and the flakes limitation decreases by 4,000 pounds,
    a. What is Z^*?
    b. What is the potato purchasing plan?

19. The computer output for the machine assignment model of Chapter 3 is shown below.

```
MIN     0.32 A1 + 0.35 A2 + 0.36 A3 + 0.29 B1 + 0.25 B2
      + 0.34 B3 + 0.32 C1 + 0.34 C2 + 0.36 C3
SUBJECT TO
      2)    A1 + B1 + C1 <=    40
      3)    A2 + B2 + C2 <=    40
      4)    A3 + B3 + C3 <=    40
      5)    25 A1 + 26 A2 + 23 A3 =    1000
      6)    18 B1 + 19 B2 + 20 B3 =    950
      7)    22 C1 + 23 C2 + 20 C3 =    600
END

LP OPTIMUM FOUND  AT STEP      5

            OBJECTIVE FUNCTION VALUE

      1)      36.7019300
```

VARIABLE	VALUE	REDUCED COST
A1	12.727270	.000000
A2	.000000	.016043
A3	29.644270	.000000
B1	.000000	.055304
B2	40.000000	.000000
B3	9.500000	.000000
C1	27.272730	.000000
C2	.000000	.003909
C3	.000000	.004269

ROW	SLACK OR SURPLUS	DUAL PRICES
2)	.000000	.071304
3)	.000000	.073000
4)	.855731	.000000
5)	.000000	−.015652
6)	.000000	−.017000
7)	.000000	−.017787

RANGES IN WHICH THE BASIS IS UNCHANGED

		OBJ COEFFICIENT RANGES	
VARIABLE	CURRENT COEF	ALLOWABLE INCREASE	ALLOWABLE DECREASE
A1	.320000	.055304	.003739
A2	.350000	INFINITY	.016043
A3	.360000	.003440	.050880
B1	.290000	INFINITY	.055304
B2	.250000	.003909	INFINITY
B3	.340000	.061449	.004115
C1	.320000	.003739	INFINITY
C2	.340000	INFINITY	.003909
C3	.360000	INFINITY	.004269

		RIGHTHAND SIDE RANGES	
ROW	CURRENT RHS	ALLOWABLE INCREASE	ALLOWABLE DECREASE
2	40.000000	27.272730	.787273
3	40.000000	10.000000	.900770
4	40.000000	INFINITY	.855731
5	1000.000000	19.681820	681.818200
6	950.000000	17.114630	190.000000
7	600.000000	17.320010	600.000000

---

a. How many hours is Machine 2 used to produce Cup B? How many units of Cup B are produced by Machine 2?

b. How many hours are used on each of the 3 machines?

c. Is the optimal solution degenerate?

d. Is there an alternate optimal solution?

e. A total of 1,000 units of Cup A are required. How many units are produced on each machine?

f. What is the economic interpretation of the dual price on Row 2?

g. What is the economic interpretation of the dual price on Row 4?

h. What is the economic interpretation of the dual price on Row 5?

i. If 1 additional unit of Cup A had to be produced,
   (1) What would be the optimal cost?
   (2) Would the production plan change?

j. Calculate the reduced cost of A2 using the dual prices.

20. The optimal solution to the machine assignment model from Chapter 3 is shown in Exercise 19.

a. How many hours is Machine 3 used to produce Cup B? How many units of Cup B are produced by Machine 3?

b. Is there an alternate optimal solution?

c. A total of 950 units of Cup B are required. How many units are produced on each machine?

d. How many hours are unused on each machine?

e. What is the economic interpretation of the dual price on Row 3?

f. What is the economic interpretation of the dual price on Row 6?

g. If 1 additional unit of Cup C had to be produced,
   (1) What would be the optimal cost?
   (2) Would the production plan change?

h. There has been an offer for additional units of Cup A. What would be the additional cost of producing an extra 10 units?

i. There has been an offer for additional units of Cup A. What would be the additional cost of producing an extra 100 units?

j. If Machine 1 were operated on Saturday, an additional 8 hours would be available. Ignoring the additional cost of operating on Saturday, what would be the impact on the optimal cost?

k. If Machine 3 were operated on Saturday, an additional 8 hours would be available. Ignoring the additional cost of operating on Saturday, what would be the impact on the optimal cost?

21. The optimal solution to the machine assignment model from Chapter 3 is shown in Exercise 19.

a. Is the optimal solution degenerate?

b. What is the interpretation of the reduced cost on A2?

c. If the cost per hour that Machine 1 makes Cup A increases by $0.03,
   (1) What is Z^*?
   (2) What is the production plan?

d. If the cost per hour that Machine 1 makes Cup A decreases by $0.02,
   (1) What is Z^*?
   (2) What is the production plan?

  e. How much must the production rate associated with $A2$ increase before it is worthwhile for $A2$ to become positive?

  f. If an additional 8 hours are available on Machines 1, 2, and 3,

   (1) What is Z^*?

   (2) What is the production plan?

22. The optimal solution to the machine assignment model from Chapter 3 is shown in Exercise 19.

  a. Is the optimal solution degenerate?

  b. What is the interpretation of the reduced cost on $B1$?

  c. If the cost per hour that Machine 2 makes Cup A decreases by $0.01,

   (1) What is Z^*?

   (2) What is the production plan?

  d. If the cost per hour that Machine 2 makes Cup A decreases by $0.02,

   (1) What is Z^*?

   (2) What is the production plan?

  e. How much must the production rate associated with $C2$ increase before it is worthwhile for $C2$ to become positive?

  f. If the cost per hour increases by $0.01 for all three products,

   (1) What is Z^*?

   (2) What is the production plan?

  g. Calculate the reduced cost for $B1$ using the dual prices.

23. The output for the radio product mix example, Chapter 3, with time in minutes, is:

```
MAX     10 A + 12 F + 15 C
SUBJECT TO
     2)    11 A + 12 F + 15 C <=    4800
     3)    15 A + 15 F + 16 C <=    4800
     4)     4 A +  6 F +  9 C <=   2400
END

     OBJECTIVE FUNCTION VALUE

     1)      4246.15400

VARIABLE            VALUE        REDUCED COST
     A             .000000          .307692
     F          123.076900          .000000
     C          184.615400          .000000

   ROW      SLACK OR SURPLUS      DUAL PRICES
     2)          553.846100          .000000
     3)            .000000          .461538
     4)            .000000          .846154

RANGES IN WHICH THE BASIS IS UNCHANGED
```

		OBJ COEFFICIENT RANGES	
VARIABLE	CURRENT COEF	ALLOWABLE INCREASE	ALLOWABLE DECREASE
A	10.000000	.307692	INFINITY
F	12.000000	2.062500	.169014
C	15.000000	.400000	2.200000

		RIGHTHAND SIDE RANGES	
ROW	CURRENT RHS	ALLOWABLE INCREASE	ALLOWABLE DECREASE
2	4800.000000	INFINITY	553.846100
3	4800.000000	1200.000000	533.333200
4	2400.000000	299.999900	480.000000

a. What is the maximum weekly profit?

b. How many radios of each type are produced?

c. Is the optimal solution unique? Explain.

d. Is the optimal solution degenerate? Explain.

e. How much must the profit margin on AM radios increase so that it is worthwhile to produce them?

f. How many *hours* are used in each work area?

g. How much would you be willing to pay for an additional hour of component assembly time?

h. Say that an additional 8 hours/week could be obtained by working overtime in the final assembly work area. Ignoring the additional overtime cost,

   (1) What would be the optimal profit?

   (2) Would you produce the same numbers of each type of radio?

i. Repeat Part *h* for the inspection and packaging work area.

j. If the profit margin on AM/FM radios increased by $1,

   (1) What would be the optimal profit?

   (2) Would you produce the same numbers of each type of radio?

k. If the profit margin on AM/FM/CB radios decreased by $3,

   (1) What would be the optimal profit?

   (2) Would you produce the same numbers of each type of radio?

l. How much must the number of final assembly minutes per AM radio decrease before you make them?

24. The output for the radio product mix example, Chapter 3, after the inspection and packaging time increases by 5 hours, to 2,700 minutes, is:

```
MAX     10 A + 12 F + 15 C
SUBJECT TO
        2)    11 A + 12 F + 15 C <=    4800
        3)    15 A + 15 F + 16 C <=    4800
        4)     4 A +  6 F +  9 C <=    2700
END
                            0
        OBJECTIVE FUNCTION VALUE

        1)    4500.00000

VARIABLE            VALUE        REDUCED COST
       A          .000000            .307693
       F          .000000            .000000
       C       300.000000            .000000

      ROW     SLACK OR SURPLUS     DUAL PRICES
       2)       300.000000            .000000
       3)          .000000            .461538
       4)          .000000            .846154
```

```
NO. ITERATIONS =    0

RANGES IN WHICH THE BASIS IS UNCHANGED:

                               OBJ COEFFICIENT RANGES
VARIABLE            CURRENT         ALLOWABLE        ALLOWABLE
                     COEF           INCREASE         DECREASE
   A              10.000000          .307693         INFINITY
   F              12.000000         2.062500          .169014
   C              15.000000          .400000         2.200000

                               RIGHTHAND SIDE RANGES
  ROW               CURRENT         ALLOWABLE        ALLOWABLE
                     RHS            INCREASE         DECREASE
   2             4800.000000        INFINITY        300.000000
   3             4800.000000       650.000000         .000000
   4             2700.000000         .000000        780.000000
```

Answer the questions below considering only this output.

a. What is the maximum weekly profit?

b. How many radios of each type are produced?

c. Is the optimal solution unique? Explain.

d. Is the optimal solution degenerate? Explain.

e. What is the interpretation of the reduced cost of *A*?

f. How much would you be willing to pay for an additional hour of final assembly time?

g. Say that an additional 8 hours/week could be obtained by working overtime in the component assembly work area. Ignoring the additional overtime cost,
   (1) What would be the optimal profit?
   (2) Would you produce the same numbers of each type of radio?

h. If the profit margin on AM/FM radios increased by $1,
   (1) What would be the optimal profit?
   (2) Would you produce the same numbers of each type of radio?

i. If the required component assembly minutes per AM radio increased by 1,
   (1) What would be the optimal profit?
   (2) Would you produce the same numbers of each type of radio?

j. How much must the number of final assembly minutes per AM radio decrease before you make them?

k. Calculate the reduced cost of *A* using the dual prices.

25. Answer the following questions from this output for MCE 3-10(b).

```
MAX     720 P1 + 840 P2 + 680 P3 + 800 P4 + 880 P5 + 720 P6
SUBJECT TO
     2)    3 P1 + 2 P2 + P3 =    156
     3)    P2 + P4 + 2 P6 =     80
     4)    P3 + P4 + 2 P5 =     40
     5)    P1 + P2 + P3 + P4 + P5 + P6 <= 100
END
     OBJECTIVE FUNCTION VALUE

     1)    83840.0000
```

VARIABLE	VALUE	REDUCED COST
P1	4.000000	.000000
P2	72.000000	.000000
P3	.000000	.000000
P4	.000000	.000000
P5	20.000000	.000000
P6	4.000000	.000000

ROW	SLACK OR SURPLUS	DUAL PRICES
2)	.000000	240.000000
3)	.000000	360.000000
4)	.000000	440.000000
5)	.000000	.000000

RANGES IN WHICH THE BASIS IS UNCHANGED:

OBJ COEFFICIENT RANGES

VARIABLE	CURRENT COEF	ALLOWABLE INCREASE	ALLOWABLE DECREASE
P1	720.000000	INFINITY	.000000
P2	840.000000	.000000	INFINITY
P3	680.000000	.000000	INFINITY
P4	800.000000	.000000	INFINITY
P5	880.000000	INFINITY	.000000
P6	720.000000	INFINITY	.000000

RIGHTHAND SIDE RANGES

ROW	CURRENT RHS	ALLOWABLE INCREASE	ALLOWABLE DECREASE
2	156.000000	4.000000	36.000000
3	80.000000	2.000000	24.000000
4	40.000000	2.000000	24.000000
5	100.000000	12.000000	1.000000

a. What is the total revenue?

b. How many 20-inch rolls are slit in each pattern?

c. How many inches of waste are created?

d. Is the optimal solution degenerate? Explain.

e. Is the optimal solution unique? Explain.

f. If 4 more 6-inch rolls are required,
   (1) How does the objective function value change?
   (2) Does the slitting plan change?

g. If the revenue for 6-inch rolls increases by $50,
   (1) How does the objective function value change?
   (2) Does the slitting plan change?

26. Answer the following questions from this output for MCE 3-3(a).

```
MIN     0.5 A + 0.4 B + 0.18 C
SUBJECT TO
   2)   A + B + C =  1
   3)   11 A + 8.9 B + 10.5 C >=  10
   4)   11 A + 8.9 B + 10.5 C <=  10.5
   5)   A + 1.5 B + 3.7 C <=  1.9
END
        OBJECTIVE FUNCTION VALUE
```

1)   .376420700

VARIABLE	VALUE	REDUCED COST
A	.328413	.000000
B	.415129	.000000
C	.256458	.000000

ROW	SLACK OR SURPLUS	DUAL PRICES
2)	.000000	− .391513
3)	.000000	− .020295
4)	.500000	.000000
5)	.000000	.114760

RANGES IN WHICH THE BASIS IS UNCHANGED:

		OBJ COEFFICIENT RANGES	
VARIABLE	CURRENT COEF	ALLOWABLE INCREASE	ALLOWABLE DECREASE
A	.500000	INFINITY	.050000
B	.400000	.040741	1.244000
C	.180000	.296191	.220000

		RIGHTHAND SIDE RANGES	
ROW	CURRENT RHS	ALLOWABLE INCREASE	ALLOWABLE DECREASE
2	1.000000	.103609	.074503
3	10.000000	.500000	.809091
4	10.500000	INFINITY	.500000
5	1.900000	1.112500	.661905

a. What is the minimum cost?

b. How many pails of each grade are used?

c. Is the optimal solution degenerate? Explain.

d. Is the optimal solution unique? Explain.

e. What is the tartness?

f. If the tartness maximum increases to 11,
   (1) How does the minimum cost change?
   (2) Are all grades of cherries used?

g. If the clarity maximum increases to 2.3,
   (1) How does the minimum cost change?
   (2) Are all grades of cherries used?

h. If the clarity maximum increases to 3.1,
   (1) How does the minimum cost change?
   (2) Are all grades of cherries used?

See Theory: The Dual Problem at the end of this chapter for questions 25–28.

27. *Theory.* Give the dual problem of the machine assignment model.

28. *Theory.* Give the dual problem of the radio product mix model.

29. *Theory.* From the output in Exercise 19, give the optimal dual variable values. Evaluate the dual problem objective function for those values.

30. *Theory.* From the output in Exercise 23, give the optimal dual variable values. Evaluate the dual problem objective function for those values.

MORE CHALLENGING EXERCISES

The following exercises require the interpretation of computer output that the student must provide. Answer each part based on the output to the original formulation. If it is impossible to answer a question from the output generated, indicate what new model would have to be solved.

1. Solve the first formulation of the gasoline blending model of Chapter 3.
   a. What is the optimal profit?
   b. How much butane, naphtha, and reformate are used in the blend?
   c. What is the total number of gallons of regular gasoline blended?
   d. What is the profit associated with selling an additional barrel of regular gasoline?
   e. What is the profit associated with selling an additional 1,500 barrels of regular gasoline?
   f. If the cost of butane increased by $1 per barrel,
      (1) What would be the optimal profit?
      (2) Would the blending plan still be the same?
   g. If the cost of naphtha decreased by $10 per barrel,
      (1) What would be the optimal profit?
      (2) Would the blending plan still be the same?
   h. If additional butane were available, what is the highest price you would be willing to pay? How much would you be willing to buy?
   i. If additional reformate were available, what is the highest price you would be willing to pay? How much would you be willing to buy?
   j. If the selling price of regular gasoline were decreased by $0.20 per gallon,
      (1) What would be the optimal profit?
      (2) Would the blending plan still be the same?
   k. Is the optimal solution unique?

2. Solve the revised formulation of the gasoline blending model of Chapter 3. Answer the same questions as in MCE 1 above.

3. Formulate and solve MCE 1 of Chapter 3.
   a. What is the optimal profit?
   b. How many round tables and how many round tables with leaves are made?
   c. Is any time unused for any of the three operations?
   d. If the selling price on round tables were increased by $5,
      (1) What would be the optimal profit?
      (2) Would the production plan still be the same?
   e. If the selling price on round tables were decreased by $7,
      (1) What would be the optimal profit?
      (2) Would the production plan still be the same?
   f. An additional skilled hand finisher has been located who is willing to work on Saturday for $12 per hour. Is this worthwhile?
   g. Subcontracting some of the lathe work is being considered. The cost will be $45 per hour, but the subcontractor has assured the same rates of production as those of the company's employees.
      (1) How many hours would you be willing to subcontract?

(2) If you subcontracted that number of hours, what would be the additional profit?

(3) If you subcontracted that number of hours, would the production plan be the same?

h. A long-term contract has been signed guaranteeing the delivery of 500 round tables each week at the same selling price. How will this affect the optimal profit and the optimal production plan?

i. Suppose the long-term contract of Part *h* guarantees the delivery of 800 round tables each week at the same selling price. How will this affect the optimal profit and the optimal production plan?

j. Is the optimal solution unique?

4. Formulate and solve the Product Mix model for the foundry of Part *a* for MCE 2 in Chapter 3.

a. What is the maximum profit?

b. How many of each type of mold should be made?

c. If an additional ton of molten metal could be obtained, what would be the maximum profit?

d. How much would the profit margin have to increase before it would be worthwhile to make any of each mold for which the current best decision is to make none?

e. If an additional 8 hours were available for mold formation,

(1) What would be the additional profit?

(2) What would be the optimal plan for mold formation?

f. Is the optimal solution unique?

5. Formulate and solve the Roll Slitting model of Part *b* for MCE 9 of Chapter 3.

a. What is the maximum revenue?

b. How many 6-inch, 8-inch, and 10-inch rolls should be made?

c. If the selling price of 8-inch rolls increased to $385,

(1) What would be the additional revenue?

(2) How may rolls of each size would be made?

d. What is the profit contribution associated with your optimal solution?

e. The cost of slitting the 20-inch rolls has not been included. The cost is $25 for each cut. Therefore, the cost of cutting a roll into three 6-inch rolls is $75. If this cost is included,

(1) How does the model change?

(2) What is the profit associated with the slitting plan you obtained?

(3) Is the optimal solution that includes this cost different from your original optimal solution?

f. Is the optimal solution unique?

6. Formulate and solve the Basic Steel Company model for MCE 11 of Chapter 3.

a. What is the minimum cost?

b. How are the required 1,030 tons of stainless steel produced?

c. If the basic oxygen furnace had to be shut down for one day of preventive maintenance,

(1) How would the minimum cost change?

(2) Would the assignment of types of steel to each furnace change?

d. If an additional 100 tons of stainless steel were required, what would be the minimum cost?

      e. If the production rate for stainless steel on Open Hearth A were increased to 65 tons/day, how would the minimum cost change?

      f. Is the optimal solution unique?

7. Formulate and solve MCE 14 of Chapter 3.

      a. What is the minimum cost?

      b. How many of the 1,315 units are processed on Machines 1 and 2?

      c. How many of the 1,315 units are processed on Machines 3, 4, and 5?

      d. If 8 additional hours are available on Machine 1,

         (1) How does the minimum cost change?

         (2) Does the manufacturing plan change?

      e. If an additional 10 units must be made,

         (1) How does the minimum cost change?

         (2) Does the manufacturing plan change?

      f. If an additional 100 units must be made,

         (1) How does the minimum cost change?

         (2) Does the manufacturing plan change?

      g. If the hourly processing cost for Machine 1 increases by $2.00,

         (1) How does the minimum cost change?

         (2) Does the manufacturing plan change?

      h. If the hourly processing cost for Machine 5 increases by $2.00,

         (1) How does the minimum cost change?

         (2) Does the manufacturing plan change?

CASE
Bailey Oil Company

Frank Smith, manager of Bailey Oil Company's refinery in Bay City, Louisiana, was excited as he went to work on Monday. He was meeting with Julie Townsend, a management science professor, who was going to make a proposal for a new refinery scheduling system. She said that all large oil companies used linear programming for refinery scheduling, and that there wasn't any reason why a small company, such as Bailey, couldn't use it too.

When Julie arrived, Frank discovered that she didn't know much about refinery operations. Fortunately, he had prepared Exhibit 1, which summarizes the material flows through the refinery.

Bailey Oil Company markets three products—regular gasoline, premium gasoline, and distillate. Bailey uses three basic refinery units—a distillation column, a catalytic cracking unit, and an ultraformer. Frank explained that four cuts were produced when crude oil was processed in the distillation column. The relative amounts of the four cuts depend on the type of crude oil processed. Gas oil, one of the cuts, can be blended into distillate or used as the feedstock for the catalytic cracking unit. Another cut is the feedstock for the ultraformer. The other two cuts are blended directly into gasoline and distillate.

The gas oil processed in the catalytic cracking unit gives a 55 percent cut and a 45 percent cut that are blended into gasoline and distillate, respectively. The ultraformer gives high-octane gasoline that can be blended into either regular gasoline or premium gasoline. The operating costs per barrel are $0.55, $0.50, and $0.63 for the distillation column, the catalytic cracking unit, and the ultraformer, respectively.

Bailey has contracts to supply 10,000, 6,500, and 18,000 barrels per week of regular gasoline, premium gasoline, and distillate, respectively. It can sell extra regular, premium, and distillate production for $37.80, $49.70, and $33 per barrel, respectively. The minimum octane numbers for regular and premium gasoline are 87 and 91, respectively. Distillate has a maximum contamination number of 56.

The quality of each of the cuts from the refinery units are:

Blended to Gasoline

Source	Octane Number
Distillation column	85
Catalytic cracker	90
Ultraformer	92

Blended to Distillate

Source	Contamination Number
Gas oil	54
Distillation column	50
Catalytic cracker	64

Julie said, "Well, I think I understand the refinery processes now. You have some flexibility in choosing the amount of gas oil processed by the catalytic cracking unit, and you can change the cut proportions from the distillation column by choosing different crude oils." She asked, "What are the prices and availabilities of the different crude oils?"

"We have three different crude oils available," replied Frank. "Here's the information on their costs."

Crude Oil	Cost/ Barrel	Maximum Barrels Available
S1	$19.40	10,000
S2	19.46	17,000
S3	19.48	15,000

"We can buy up to the maximum amount of each crude oil, but the distillation column can't process more than 39,500 barrels a week. Here are the fractions of the four cuts for each crude oil."

	S1	S2	S3
Gas oil	0.49	0.51	0.48
Ultraformer feed	0.20	0.17	0.19
Distillate blend	0.16	0.10	0.16
Gasoline blend	0.15	0.22	0.17

"Let me take this information with me and try to develop a linear programming model for you," Julie said. "When I have some preliminary results, I'll show them to you."

Two days later, Julie brought some computer output to a meeting with Frank. She proudly explained, "This is the linear programming model of your refinery." (See Exhibit 2)

After looking at the output, Frank said, "I don't understand this at all. I thought this would help me schedule my refinery, but how does it do that?"

"That model only describes the problem," Julie replied. "Here is the solution that tells you what to do." (See Exhibit 3)

"I don't understand this gobbledygook!" Frank exclaimed. "If I don't understand it, I'm sure not going to use it. Can't you explain it so that I understand it? I've got other things to do, rather than fool around with something I don't understand."

EXHIBIT 1   Product Flows for Bailey Oil Company Refinery

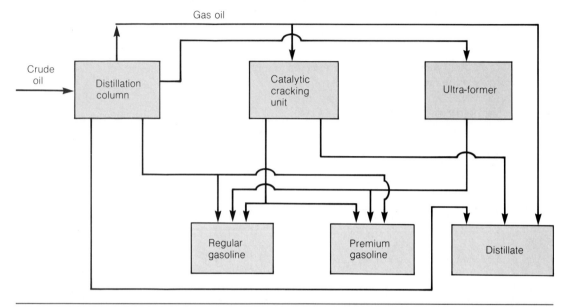

EXHIBIT 2

```
: look all

MAX    - 19.95 S1 - 20.01 S2 - 20.03 S3 - 0.5 GOCC - 0.63 UF
       + 37.8 GASEXTRA + 33 DISEXTRA + 49.7 PRMEXTRA

SUBJECT TO
      2)    0.49 S1 + 0.51 S2 + 0.48 S3 - GO =     0
      3)    0.2 S1 + 0.17 S2 + 0.19 S3 - UF =     0
      4)    0.16 S1 + 0.1 S2 + 0.16 S3 - DIDC =     0
      5)    0.15 S1 + 0.22 S2 + 0.17 S3 - GASDC =     0
      6) - GOCC + GO - DIGO =     0
      7)    0.55 GOCC - GASCC =     0
      8)    0.45 GOCC - DICC =     0
      9)    UF - GASUF =     0
     10)    GASDC - GASDCR - GASDCP =     0
     11)    GASCC - GASCCR - GASCCP =     0
     12)    GASUF - GASUFR - GASUFP =     0
     13) - GASEXTRA + GASDCR + GASCCR + GASUFR =     10000
     14) - 2 GASDCR + 3 GASCCR + 5 GASUFR >=     0
     15) - PRMEXTRA + GASDCP + GASCCP + GASUFP =     6500
     16) - 6 GASDCP - GASCCP + GASUFP >=     0
     17) - DISEXTRA + DIDC + DIGO + DICC =     18000
     18) - 6 DIDC - 2 DIGO + 8 DICC <=     0
     19)    S1 + S2 + S3 <=     39500
     20)    S1 <=     10000
     21)    S2 <=     17000
     22)    S3 <=     15000
END
```

EXHIBIT 3

```
: go

LP OPTIMUM FOUND AT STEP      25

        OBJECTIVE FUNCTION VALUE

   1)    -561650.400

VARIABLE         VALUE        REDUCED COST
     S1     10000.000000        .000000
     S2     14500.000000        .000000
     S3     15000.000000        .000000
   GOCC     12627.270000        .000000
     UF      7315.000000        .000000
GASEXTRA      767.500100        .000000
DISEXTRA        .000000       12.815910
PRMEXTRA     4232.500000        .000000
     GO     19495.000000        .000000
   DIDC      5450.000000        .000000
  GASDC      7240.000000        .000000
   DIGO      6867.728000        .000000
  GASCC      6945.000000        .000000
   DICC      5682.272000        .000000
  GASUF      7315.000000        .000000
 GASDCR      6460.500000        .000000
 GASDCP       779.500100        .000000
 GASCCR      4307.000000        .000000
 GASCCP      2638.000000        .000000
 GASUFR        .000000         .000002
 GASUFP      7315.000000        .000000

    ROW    SLACK OR SURPLUS    DUAL PRICES
     2)         .000000       -45.815910
     3)         .000000       -52.045000
     4)         .000000       -45.815910
     5)         .000000       -31.850000
     6)         .000000       -45.815910
     7)         .000000       -46.725000
     8)         .000000       -45.815910
     9)         .000000       -52.675000
    10)         .000000       -31.850000
    11)         .000000       -46.725000
    12)         .000000       -52.675000
    13)         .000000       -37.800000
    14)         .000000        -2.975000
    15)         .000000       -49.700000
    16)         .000000        -2.975000
    17)         .000000       -45.815910
    18)      977.277400         .000000
    19)         .000000        23.792350
    20)         .000000         1.224487
    21)     2500.000000         .000000
    22)         .000000         .802876

DO RANGE(SENSITIVITY) ANALYSIS?
? y
```

EXHIBIT 3 continued

```
RANGES IN WHICH THE BASIS IS UNCHANGED:

                        OBJ COEFFICIENT RANGES
VARIABLE          CURRENT        ALLOWABLE        ALLOWABLE
                   COEF          INCREASE         DECREASE
      S1        -19.950000       INFINITY          1.224487
      S2        -20.010000        .802876         23.792350
      S3        -20.030000       INFINITY           .802876
    GOCC          -.500000       INFINITY          7.048749
      UF          -.630000       INFINITY         40.143780
 GASEXTRA         37.800000      11.074150         51.263630
 DIXEXTRA         33.000000      12.815910         INFINITY
 PRMEXTRA         49.700000      INFINITY          11.074150
      GO           .000000       26.762520         46.651670
    DIDC           .000000       INFINITY          13.381260
   GASDC           .000000       16.057510        108.147100
    DIGO           .000000        7.048749         INFINITY
   GASCC           .000000       INFINITY          12.815910
    DICC           .000000       INFINITY          15.663890
   GASUF           .000000       INFINITY          40.143780
  GASDCR           .000000        .000005          59.500000
  GASDCP           .000000       59.500000          .000005
  GASCCR           .000000        9.916668          .000001
  GASCCP           .000000        .000001          9.916668
  GASUFR           .000000        .000002          INFINITY
  GASUFP           .000000       INFINITY           .000002

                        RIGHTHAND SIDE RANGES
   ROW            CURRENT        ALLOWABLE        ALLOWABLE
                   RHS           INCREASE         DECREASE
       2           .000000      2931.111000        119.445000
       3           .000000      3386.000000       3070.000000
       4           .000000      2931.111000        233.696800
       5           .000000       511.666700       4396.666000
       6           .000000      2931.111000        119.445000
       7           .000000      2931.111000       5196.667000
       8           .000000      2931.111000         53.750260
       9           .000000      3386.000000       3070.000000
      10           .000000       511.666700       4396.666000
      11           .000000      2931.111000       5196.667000
      12           .000000      3386.000000       3070.000000
      13      10000.000000       767.500100        INFINITY
      14           .000000      8793.332000       3070.000000
      15       6500.000000      4232.500000        INFINITY
      16           .000000      5196.667000       3070.000000
      17      18000.000000      2931.111000         95.982600
      18           .000000       INFINITY          977.277400
      19      39500.000000       212.872300       1744.318000
      20      10000.000000      7487.807000       2500.000000
      21      17000.000000       INFINITY         2500.000000
      22      15000.000000     10586.210000       2500.000000
```

The Dual Problem

In this Theory section, we define a dual problem for any linear programming model. The original linear programming model is called the **primal.** The dual problem is also a linear programming model. We also explain the economic significance of the dual problem and show how to obtain its optimal solution from the optimal solution to the primal. Finally, we conclude with a discussion of the computational significance of solving the dual problem.

A maximization model with all $\le$ constraints and all nonnegative variables is in **canonical form.** The Potato Processing example is in canonical form and has the following dual problem:

$$
\begin{array}{ll}
\min & 18000u_1 + 15000u_2 + 30000u_3 \\
\text{st} & 0.3u_1 + 0.1u_2 + 0.3u_3 \ge 0.14 \\
& 0.2u_1 + 0.2u_2 + 0.3u_3 \ge 0.15 \\
& u_1, u_2, u_3 \ge 0
\end{array}
$$

The variables u_1, u_2, and u_3 are called the **dual variables.** Note that the dual problem is a linear programming model.

The following general rules apply for constructing the **dual problem** for a maximization model in canonical form:

1. The objective of the dual is minimization.
2. The primal's RHS constants become the dual problem's objective function coefficients.
3. The primal's objective function coefficients become the dual problem's RHS constants.
4. When the primal has n variables, the dual has n constraints. The constraint coefficients of the jth dual constraint are the constraint coefficients of the jth primal variable.
5. When the primal has m constraints, the dual has m variables. The ith dual variable is associated with the ith primal constraint.
6. All dual constraints are $\ge$ type.
7. All dual variables are nonnegative.

After discussing the economic significance of the dual problem, we discuss constructing dual problems for primal problems that are not in canonical form.

Economic Significance of the Dual Problem

Although the primal and dual problems use the same numerical values, the relationship between the two is not obvious. If one model is ill-behaved, then so is the other. More significantly, if one model has a finite optimal solution, then so does the other and the optimal objective function values are *equal*. Table 5.T1 contains the optimal solution found using LINDO for the Potato Processing example's dual problem. The dual objective function value is 12,225, the same value as that of the Potato Processing example's solution.

Note that the dual variables in Table 5.T1 are named *FF, HB,* and *FL* for the french fry, hash brown, and flake limitations, respectively. Say that you are a competitor of the potato processing company and that you wish to offer an economic package to capture its share of market. For example, you wish to offer a price per pound for the french fry sales potential of 18,000 pounds. Let *FF* represent the offering price for french

---

TABLE 5.T1 LOOK ALL and GO Output for the Dual of the Potato Processing Example

```
MIN      18000 FF + 15000 HB + 30000 FL
SUBJECT TO
       2)    0.3 FF + 0.1 HB + 0.3 FL >=   0.14
       3)    0.2 FF + 0.2 HB + 0.3 FL >=   0.15
END

         OBJECTIVE FUNCTION VALUE

      1)     12225.0000

   VARIABLE        VALUE        REDUCED COST
         FF        .325000          .000000
         HB        .425000          .000000
         FL        .000000      5250.000000

      ROW   SLACK OR SURPLUS    DUAL PRICES
      2)          .000000    -15000.000000
      3)          .000000    -67500.000000

RANGES IN WHICH THE BASIS IS UNCHANGED:

                      OBJ COEFFICIENT RANGES
   VARIABLE        CURRENT        ALLOWABLE        ALLOWABLE
                      COEF         INCREASE         DECREASE
         FF   18000.000000     7000.000000     3000.000000
         HB   15000.000000     3000.000000     9000.001000
         FL   30000.000000         INFINITY     5250.000000

                      RIGHTHAND SIDE RANGES
      ROW         CURRENT        ALLOWABLE        ALLOWABLE
                      RHS         INCREASE         DECREASE
        2          .140000          .085000          .065000
        3          .150000          .130000          .056667
```

---

fries; *HB*, the offering price for hash browns; and *FL*, the offering price for flakes. The total offering cost is

$$18000FF + 15000HB + 30000FL$$

The offering prices must be high enough so that processing each type of potatoes has a smaller profit margin than the revenue from the offer. For Idaho potatoes, the offer per pound translates into $0.3FF + 0.1HB + 0.3FL$. To forgo purchasing and processing Idaho potatoes, the offering prices must be such that

$$0.3FF + 0.1HB + 0.3FL \geq 0.14$$

Similarly, for Michigan potatoes

$$0.2FF + 0.2HB + 0.3FL \geq 0.15$$

The offering prices must be nonnegative. The problem facing the competitor is to minimize the total offering cost:

$$
\begin{array}{ll}
\text{min} & 18000FF + 15000HB + 30000FL \\
\text{st} & 0.3FF + 0.1HB + 0.3FL \geq 0.14 \\
& 0.2FF + 0.2HB + 0.3FL \geq 0.15 \\
& FF, HB, FL \geq 0
\end{array}
$$

This is the dual problem.

The dual variable's value is the rate of *change* of Z^* as the RHS constant changes, *given that the same set of variables is positive in the optimal solution.* If the potato processor expands french fry sales potential by 1 pound, the cost to the competitor increases by $0.325 and the profit to the potato processor increases by the same amount.

The terms *dual price* and *dual variable* are related. For a *maximization model,* the values of the dual variables equal the dual prices. In Table 5.T1, the variable values of the dual problem equal the dual prices of the Potato Processing example. For a *minimization model,* the dual variables's values equal the *negative* of the dual prices. Notice that the dual variable's economic interpretation refers to Z^* rate of change, not to its rate of improvement. For a maximization model, an improvement is an increase in Z^*. For a minimization model, an improvement is a decrease in Z^*. That is why you must change the sign of the dual price to get the dual variable's value.

Forming General Dual Problems

Table 5.T2 contains the relationships used for forming a general dual problem. The constraint types of one model affect the variables' sign restrictions of its dual. The variables' sign restrictions of one model affect the constraint types of its dual.

TABLE 5.T2   Rules for Constructing Dual Problems

Maximization Model	Minimization Model
i^{th} constraint $\leq$	i^{th} variable ≥ 0
i^{th} constraint $\geq$	i^{th} variable ≤ 0
i^{th} constraint $=$	i^{th} variable unrestricted
j^{th} variable ≥ 0	j^{th} constraint $\geq$
j^{th} variable ≤ 0	j^{th} constraint $\leq$
j^{th} variable unrestricted	j^{th} constraint $=$

Let's use Table 5.T2 to find the dual of the following model:

$$
\begin{array}{llrl}
\min & 3u_1 + 4u_2 + 5u_3 & & \\
\text{st} & 2u_1 + 3u_2 + 4u_3 & \leq & 10 \\
& -3u_1 + 2u_2 & \geq & 5 \\
& 5u_1 + 3u_2 - u_3 & = & 3 \\
& u_1, u_2, u_3 \geq 0 & &
\end{array}
$$

This is a minimization model, so we use Table 5.T2's right-hand column to form the dual. We introduce a dual variable for each constraint. Let x_1, x_2, and x_3 correspond to Constraints 1, 2, and 3, respectively. (These names are arbitrary.) The dual problem's objective function is max $10x_1 + 5x_2 + 3x_3$. The variable nonnegativities of the minimization model result in its dual problem having all $\leq$-type constraints. The first dual constraint uses the constraint coefficients of variable u_1, resulting in

$$2x_1 - 3x_2 + 5x_3 \leq 3$$

The two constraints for u_2 and u_3 are similarly constructed. Because the first constraint is $\leq$ type, the associated dual variable, x_1, must be ≤ 0. Because the second constraint is $\geq$ type, the associated dual variable, x_2, must be ≥ 0. Because the third constraint is $=$ type, the associated dual variable, x_3, is unrestricted in sign.

The complete dual problem is

$$
\begin{array}{llrl}
\max & 10x_1 + 5x_2 + 3x_3 & & \\
\text{st} & 2x_1 - 3x_2 + 5x_3 & \leq & 10 \\
& 3x_1 + 2x_2 + 3x_3 & \geq & 5 \\
& 4x_1 - x_3 & = & 3 \\
& x_1 \leq 0, x_2 \geq 0, x_3 \text{ unrestricted in sign} & &
\end{array}
$$

Computational Significance of the Dual Problem

If the original model has m constraints and n variables, its dual has m variables and n constraints. If the number of constraints is much greater than the number of variables, solving the dual problem is easier. Say that $m = 100$ and $n = 5$. Then, the dual has only 5 constraints and 100 variables. Because the computational complexity increases approximately proportionally to m^2n, reducing the number of constraints decreases the complexity from $100^2 \times 5 = 50,000$ to $5^2 \times 100 = 2,500$.

An important fact is that *the dual of the dual is the original model*. The values of the dual variables of the dual problem are the optimal values of the original model's variables. In Table 5.T1, the dual variables' optimal values are 15,000 and 67,500. Remember that because Table 5.T1 is a minimization model, you must change the signs of the dual prices to find its dual variable values. Tables 5.3 and 5.T1 show that the reduced costs of one model are associated with its dual problem's slack or surplus variable values. Also, the ranges of the primal's RHS constants (objective function coefficients) are the same as the dual's objective function coefficients (RHS constants).

Unless the computational savings are very important, you should solve the model that interests you, not its dual. Sensitivity analysis and model modification are easier on the original model.

6

Algebraic Solution Methods for Linear Programming

KARMARKAR ALGORITHM PROVES ITS WORTH

THE WALL STREET JOURNAL—Less than two years after discovery of a mathematical procedure that Bell Labs said could solve a broad range of complex business problems 50 to 100 times faster than current methods, AT&T is filing for patents covering its use. The Karmarkar algorithm, which drew headlines when discovered by researcher Narendra Karmarkar, will be applied first to AT&T's long-distance network.

Thus far, Bell Labs has verified the procedure's capabilities in developing plans for new fiber-optic transmission and satellite capacity linking 20 countries bordering the Pacific Ocean. That jointly owned network will be built during the next 10 years. Planning requires a tremendous number of "what if" scenarios involving 43,000 variables describing transmission capacity, location, and construction schedules, all juggled amid political considerations of each connected country.

The Karmarkar algorithm was able to solve the Pacific Basin problem in 4 minutes, against 80 minutes by the method previously used, says Neil Dinn, head of Bell Labs' international transmission planning department. The speedier solutions will enable international committees to agree on network designs at one meeting instead of many meetings stretched out over months.

AT&T now is using the Karmarkar procedure to plan construction for its domestic network, a problem involving 800,000 variables. In addition, the procedure may be written into software controlling routing of domestic phone calls, boosting the capacity of AT&T's current network.

From *The Wall Street Journal*, July 18, 1986.

In this chapter, we discuss algebraic methods for solving linear programming models. Most of our discussion is based on the *simplex algorithm*, which has been the basis for linear programming software since its discovery in 1947. First, we discuss how the characteristics of a linear programming model affect its solvability. Then, we geometrically describe the simplex algorithm's path from one feasible point to another until the optimal solution has been reached. We illustrate possible paths for the Potato Processing example, which has two variables and no degenerate corner points. Then, we algebraically characterize the sequence of points on the solution path. Each point on the solution path is a corner point of the feasible set, which is characterized by partitioning the variables into a basic variable set and a nonbasic variable set. This algebraic characterization is the basis for the simplex algorithm, which is described in detail in the first Theory section of the chapter. A degenerate corner point corresponds to more than one partition, causing the sensitivity analysis ambiguities examined in Chapter 5. We discuss this later in the chapter.

We also discuss how to identify the causes of an unbounded optimal solution or no feasible solution from the computer output. The examples used in this discussion are also used in the Theory section describing the simplex algorithm to explain how the simplex algorithm concludes that there is an unbounded optimal solution or no feasible solution. Finally, a second Theory section describes a new algorithm for linear programming models that has been developed by N. Karmarkar. Bell Labs reported that it solved its Pacific Basin problem in 4 minutes using the Karmarkar algorithm, compared to 80 minutes using the simplex algorithm. More development and testing of Karmarkar's method is needed before concluding that it is superior to the simplex algorithm. If it is superior, the next generation of linear programming software may be based on Karmarkar's method, which follows a path to the optimal solution different from that of the simplex algorithm.

CONSIDERATIONS IN SOLVING LINEAR PROGRAMMING MODELS

Computer resources required

Solving a linear programming model by a computer requires two main computer resources—computer storage and computer time. If the computer system does not have adequate storage, it is impossible to solve the model. If the computer time is excessive, the results may be available only after the decision has been made. Developing and using computer models is time consuming and expensive. In this section, we discuss computer storage, computer time, and whether a computer model is practical.

Computer Storage

Available storage varies for different computer systems. Say that a linear programming model has m constraints and n variables. Visualize a rectangle (matrix) storing all of the input data. Including the objective function and the RHS constants, the matrix has $(m + 1)$ rows, $(n + 1)$ columns, and $(m + 1) \times (n + 1)$ elements. Often, large models have many zero-valued parameters.

Density is the model's fraction of nonzero coefficients.[1] For the Potato Processing example, $m = 3$ and $n = 2$; the matrix storing all of the input data has four rows and three columns and contains $4 \times 3 = 12$ elements. For the objective function, constraints, and RHS constants, the model has two, six, and three nonzero values, respectively. Because 11 of the 12 elements are nonzero, the density is $^{11}/_{12} = 0.917$. Many linear programming computer systems have commands that report statistics about models. The STATS command for LINDO reports statistics about linear programming models. Table 6.1 shows the statistics generated by LINDO for the Potato Processing example.

Linear programming models with a density of a few percent are called **sparse.** Most large models are sparse, many having densities smaller than 1 percent.

The input storage requirements depend on the number of constraints, the number of variables, and the density of the model. Remember, you input only the nonzero coefficients for a linear programming model, thereby reducing the storage required for the input data. Storage requirements for the solution method depend on the implementation details of the solution method.

The largest version of LINDO/PC accepts models with up to 2,000 constraints, 4,000 variables, and 32,000 nonzeros, for a microcomputer with 640K of memory. A mainframe computer system can solve problems

TABLE 6.1 LOOK ALL and STATS LINDO Commands for the Potato Processing Example

```
: look all

MAX      0.14 I + 0.15 M
SUBJECT TO
        2)    0.3 I + 0.2 M <=    18000
        3)    0.1 I + 0.2 M <=    15000
        4)    0.3 I + 0.3 M <=    30000
END

: stats

ROWS=      4 VARS=       2 NO. INTEGER VARS=       0
NONZEROES=      11 CONSTRAINT NONZ=     6(     0 ARE +- 1) DENSITY= .91
SMALLEST AND LARGEST ELEMENTS IN ABSOLUTE VALUE=    .1000000    300000.C
NO.  < :  3 NO. =:    0 NO. > :    0, OBJ=MAX, GUBS <=    1
```

---

[1] We describe LINDO's method of calculating density. The method differs for other linear programming software.

with thousands of constraints and a virtually unlimited number of variables.

Once you determine that the computer system can handle the model's size, you must consider how much computer time is needed to find the optimal solution.

Computer Time

The simplex algorithm forms the basis for most linear programming software. The simplex algorithm generates a sequence of points as it finds the optimal solution. The **solution path** is the sequence of points. Each time a new point is generated, an **iteration** occurs. As a general rule of thumb, the number of iterations averages 2 to 3 times the number of constraints. Before the problem has been solved, the actual number of required iterations is unknown. However, you can use this general rule to evaluate model structure changes that you are considering. Fortunately, the simplex algorithm is **robust;** changes in the model's coefficients usually have little impact on the number of points on the solution path.

The number of iterations

Generally, as the number of constraints increases, more iterations and computer time are required to find the optimal solution. The computer time required depends on the number of constraints and variables and on the model's density, as well as the solution path. Do not expect the amount of computer time to increase linearly as the number of constraints increases. The time required per iteration also increases. As a general rule of thumb, the computer time is proportional to m^2n. Increasing the number of variables has little impact on the required time for the computer solution, while increasing the number of constraints has a significant impact. Doubling the number of variables doubles the computer time. Doubling the number of constraints increases the computer time by a factor of 4.

The computer time

Chapters 2, 3, and 5 illustrated how the selected model's structure affects the ease of sensitivity analysis. Including definitional constraints and variables can make some sensitivity analyses easier, but this also increases the size of the model. If a model has 100 constraints and 1,000 variables, adding a definitional constraint and variable results in a model with 101 constraints and 1,001 variables. The required computer time increases a small fraction.

Is Computer Solution Practical?

Whether it is practical to solve a large model is a subjective judgment. Ask yourself, "How will I make the decision without a computer model?" If the benefits of the improved decisions that result from a model outweigh the cost of the model, then the model is practical.

We must stress that *the effort involved with the computer is a small part of the project effort.* Much more time is involved in defining the problem and in gathering and inputting data. Also, because large models are likely to include either input or conceptual errors, you must solve various versions of the model to validate it. After the model has been validated, it starts to provide information on the decision environment. During the sensitivity analysis and model manipulation phases of using the model, many more models are solved to explore the decision environment.

THE GEOMETRY OF THE SIMPLEX ALGORITHM'S SOLUTION PATH—NO DEGENERATE CORNER POINTS

In this section, we describe the simplex algorithm's solution path to the optimal solution. We illustrate the paths geometrically for the Potato Processing example, which has no degenerate corner points. A later section in this chapter describes the impact of a degenerate corner point.

Figure 6.1 illustrates the feasible set for the Potato Processing exam-

FIGURE 6.1 Feasible Set for Potato Processing Example

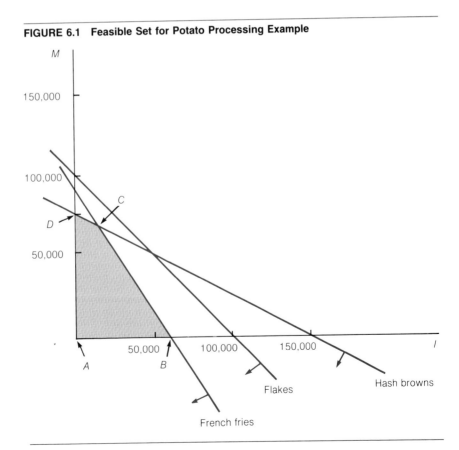

The starting point

ple. One possible solution path is from Point *A* to Point *B* to Point *C*. The simplex algorithm starts at the *origin* and generates a sequence of points that has the following characteristics: (1) Each point is within the feasible set; and (2) the objective function value of each point in the sequence improves relative to that of the previous point. For a maximization model, the objective function *increases* from point to point. For a minimization model, the objective function *decreases* from point to point. For the path *A* to *B* to *C*, Point *A* is the origin, the initial point; Point *B* is the next point generated; and the third point generated is Point *C*, the optimal solution. Each point is within the feasible set. The objective function values at Points *A*, *B*, and *C* are 0, 8,400, and 12,225, respectively. The objective function value increases at successive points.

Each point generated by the simplex algorithm for the *A* to *B* to *C* path is a **corner point** of the feasible set. A corner point is easily visualized in a two-dimensional space (Figure 6.1) or in a three-dimensional space. If there are more than three decision variables, it is difficult or impossible to visualize the feasible set and its corner points. However, the solution method generates only corner points of the feasible set.

Geometrically, **adjacent corner points** lie on the same line segment representing an edge of the feasible set. Thus, *B* and *A* are adjacent corner points because they lie on the *I* axis. The *I* axis is the line representing *M*'s nonnegativity restriction. *D* and *A* are adjacent corner points because they lie on the *M* axis, but *C* is not adjacent to *A*. Visualizing adjacent corner points is difficult for more than three variables. In the next section, we algebraically clarify the concept of corner points and adjacent corner points. Figure 6.1 shows that the successive corner points on the solution path are adjacent corner points. Corner Point *B* is adjacent to Corner Point *A*, and Corner Point *C* is adjacent to Corner Point *B*.

We redefine the **characteristics of the simplex algorithm's solution path** as

Solution path
characteristics

1. Each successive point is an adjacent corner point,
2. The successive values of the objective function improve.

More than one
solution path

There is another path that also satisfies the two characteristics. For *A* to *D* to *C*, the successive values of the objective function are 0, 11,250, and 12,225, respectively. The *A* to *D* to *C* path may also be obtained, depending on the implementation of the simplex algorithm. All computer systems terminate (or stop) when an optimal solution has been reached. Although the paths to an optimal point may differ for different computer systems, their Z^* values are the same except for rounding errors. If there are alternate optimal solutions, different computer systems may terminate at different optimal solutions with the *same, best value* of the objective function.

PARTITIONS, BASIC FEASIBLE SOLUTIONS, AND CORNER POINTS

You can graphically visualize the solution path for the Potato Processing example because it has only two variables. You can visualize corner points and adjacent corner points. If the model has more variables, you can't visualize them. In this section, we algebraically characterize the concept of a corner point of the feasible set. We also algebraically characterize the concept of adjacent corner points. The algebraic characterizations are the basis of the simplex algorithm, which is described in the Theory section.

After the three slack variables needed to convert the model of the Potato Processing example to the standard equality form have been added, the model is

Convert to the standard equality form

$$\text{max} \quad 0.14I + 0.15M$$
$$\text{st} \quad 0.3I + 0.2M + s_1 = 18000$$
$$0.1I + 0.2M + s_2 = 15000$$
$$0.3I + 0.3M + s_3 = 30000$$
$$I, M, s_1, s_2, s_3 \geq 0$$

The system of constraints has three equations and five variables. Remember that in Chapter 4 we learned that the number of positive variables at a corner point is $\leq$ the number of constraints.

Let's arbitrarily **partition** the variables into two sets. In the first set, three variables are included (i.e, the number of constraints). In the second set, the remaining variables are included. For example, the first set might be $\{s_1, s_2, s_3\}$, and the second set, $\{I, M\}$. The first set is called the set of **basic variables,** and the second set is called the set of **nonbasic variables.**

We calculate the variable values for a partition in *two steps:*

Calculating the variable values for a partition

1. The values of the nonbasic variables are set to 0.
2. The values of the basic variables are determined by solving the resulting equations.

For this partition, after setting I and M to 0, the resulting three equations in three variables are

$$s_1 = 18000$$
$$s_2 = 15000$$
$$s_3 = 30000$$

This resulting system of equations appears in solved form. The numerical value of the first slack variable, s_1, is 18,000. The numerical values of s_2 and s_3 are 15,000 and 30,000, respectively. Graphically, this corresponds to Point *A*, a *corner point*, in Figure 6.1.

Another partition

Let's calculate the variable values for the partition where the set of basic variables is $\{s_1, M, s_3\}$ and the nonbasic variables are $\{I, s_2\}$.[2] Setting I and s_2 to 0, the three equations in three variables become

$$
\begin{aligned}
0.2M + s_1 &= 18000 \\
0.2M &= 15000 \\
0.3M + s_3 &= 30000
\end{aligned}
$$

Dividing the second equation by 0.2, the set of equations is tranformed into

$$
\begin{aligned}
0.2M + s_1 &= 18000 \\
1M &= 75000 \\
0.3M + s_3 &= 30000
\end{aligned}
$$

Now, the top constraint is transformed: you subtract 0.2 times the new second constraint from the top constraint, yielding

$$
\begin{aligned}
0M + s_1 &= 3000 \\
1M &= 75000 \\
0.3M + s_3 &= 30000
\end{aligned}
$$

The bottom constraint is transformed: you subtract 0.3 times the new second constraint from the bottom constraint, yielding

$$
\begin{aligned}
0M + s_1 &= 3000 \\
1M &= 75000 \\
0M + s_3 &= 7500
\end{aligned}
$$

Now, the basic variable values are $s_1 = 3,000$, $M = 75,000$, and $s_3 = 7,500$. This corresponds to Corner Point *D* in Figure 6.1.

Solving for the basic variables

How would you characterize having "solved for the numerical values of the basic variables"? Each variable "solved for" has a coefficient of $+1$ in one row and 0 in all other rows. Thus, s_1 was solved for in the top row, and its numerical value was equal to the constant to the right of the "$=$" sign in the first equation. Similarly, M was solved for in the second equation, and its value was 75,000. The other basic variable, s_3, was solved for in the bottom equation, and its value was 7,500.

Table 6.2 contains all 10 possible partitions of the five variables. The variable order within the partition does not form a different partition. The set $\{s_1, M, s_3\}$ and the set $\{M, s_1, s_3\}$ are identical. However, use care when reporting numerical values for the basic variables. The numerical values of the basic variables in Table 6.2 are in the same order as the

---

[2] This procedure is called **Gaussian elimination** or the **Gauss-Jordan method** for solving simultaneous equations.

TABLE 6.2 The Partitions for the Potato Processing Example

Partition	Basic Variables	Values of Basic Variables	Nonbasic Variables	Values of Nonbasic Variables
1	$\{s_1, s_2, s_3\}$	(18000, 15000, 30000)	$\{I, M\}$	(0, 0)
2	$\{s_1, M, s_3\}$	(3000, 75000, 7500)	$\{I, s_2\}$	(0, 0)
3	$\{I, s_2, s_3\}$	(60000, 9000, 12000)	$\{M, s_1\}$	(0, 0)
4	$\{I, M, s_3\}$	(15000, 67500, 5250)	$\{s_1, s_2\}$	(0, 0)
5	$\{s_1, s_2, I\}$	(−12000, 5000, 100000)	$\{M, s_3\}$	(0, 0)
6	$\{s_1, s_2, M\}$	(−2000, −5000, 100000)	$\{I, s_3\}$	(0, 0)
7	$\{I, s_2, M\}$	(−20000, −7000, 120000)	$\{s_1, s_3\}$	(0, 0)
8	$\{M, s_2, s_3\}$	(90000, −3000, 3000)	$\{I, s_1\}$	(0, 0)
9	$\{s_1, I, s_3\}$	(−27000, 150000, −15000)	$\{M, s_2\}$	(0, 0)
10	$\{s_1, I, M\}$	(−7000, 50000, 50000)	$\{s_2, s_3\}$	(0, 0)

listing in the set of basic variables. For example, the third partition in Table 6.2 shows that $I = 60{,}000$, $s_2 = 9{,}000$, and $s_3 = 12{,}000$.

The first partition corresponds to Corner Point *A* in Figure 6.1, and the third partition corresponds to Corner Point B. Corner Points A and B are adjacent corner points. Do you notice any relationship between the partitions? As an adjacent corner point is generated, one *basic* variable is replaced by one *nonbasic* variable. Partition 3, which corresponds to an adjacent corner point of Partition 1, replaces the basic variable s_1 by the nonbasic variable I. Partitions 1 and 3 have two basic variables in common, s_2 and s_3.

Adjacent corner points

Partitions 1 and 2 correspond to the adjacent corner points *A* and *D*. In Partition 2, the basic variable s_2 is replaced by the nonbasic variable M. Partitions 1 and 2 have in common all of the other basic variables—s_1 and s_3. Partitions 2 and 3 are *not* adjacent corner points; the only basic variable that Partitions 2 and 3 have in common is s_3.

Adjacent partitions are two partitions that have the same sets of basic variables, except for one. Note that Corner Point *C* in Figure 6.1 is adjacent to Corner Point *B* and that the associated partitions, 4 and 3, respectively, are adjacent partitions. They share the basic variables I and s_3.

Adjacent corner points result from adjacent partitions that correspond to distinct corner points of the feasible set. In Chapter 5, we said that a degenerate optimal solution causes some ambiguity in sensitivity analysis. For example, the dual price for a constraint may not be unique. If a corner point is a degenerate corner point, some adjacent partitions correspond to the same corner point. Later in this chapter, we discuss how this causes ambiguity.

The algebraic solution path

Algebraically, the simplex algorithm moves from one partition to an adjacent partition by selecting a nonbasic variable that increases the objective function value if that variable becomes positive and introducing

TABLE 6.3 LOOK ALL and PIV Output for Potato Processing Example

```
: look all

MAX      0.14 I + 0.15 M
SUBJECT TO
       2)    0.3 I + 0.2 M <=    18000
       3)    0.1 I + 0.2 M <=    15000
       4)    0.3 I + 0.3 M <=    30000
END

: piv
       M ENTERS AT VALUE    75000.    IN ROW    3 OBJ. VALUE=  11250.

: piv
       I ENTERS AT VALUE    15000.    IN ROW    2 OBJ. VALUE=  12225.

: piv

LP OPTIMUM FOUND AT STEP      2

          OBJECTIVE FUNCTION VALUE

      1)    12225.0000

   VARIABLE         VALUE       REDUCED COST
       I      15000.000000         .000000
       M      67500.000000         .000000


       ROW    SLACK OR SURPLUS    DUAL PRICES
       2)           .000000         .325000
       3)           .000000         .425000
       4)       5250.000000         .000000

 NO. ITERATIONS=           2
```

the nonbasic variable into the basic variable set. Table 6.3 shows the output generated by LINDO's PIV command. By using this command, you can discover the nonbasic variable that becomes basic in each iteration as LINDO finds the optimal solution. The initial point is the origin. First, *M* becomes a basic variable. Next, *I* becomes a basic variable. Finally, after it has been determined that there is no nonbasic variable worth introducing into the basic variable set, the optimal solution is reported. LINDO's solution path is *A* to *D* to *C*.

In the first Theory section of this chapter, we describe how the simplex algorithm determines whether it is worthwhile to introduce a nonbasic variable. If the current corner point is not degenerate, the adjacent partition results in a (different) adjacent corner point and the objective function value always improves. If the current corner point is degenerate, the adjacent partition may correspond to the same corner point and if so, the objective function value doesn't change. We discuss this further in the section Degenerate Corner Points and Partitions.

Adjacent corner points have been algebraically characterized before corner points themselves. *Every corner point of the feasible set corres-*

Not all partitions
correspond to corner
points

ponds to a partition, but not every partition necessarily corresponds to a corner point. Consider Partition 5, where the basic variables are $\{I, s_1, s_2\}$ and the nonbasic variables are $\{M, s_3\}$. Setting the nonbasic variables to 0, the resulting set of three equations in three variables is

$$\begin{aligned}
0.3I + s_1 &= 18000 \\
0.1I + s_2 &= 15000 \\
0.3I &= 30000
\end{aligned}$$

To begin solving, the third equation is divided by 0.3 to obtain the set of equations

$$\begin{aligned}
0.3I + s_1 &= 18000 \\
0.1I + s_2 &= 15000 \\
1I &= 100000
\end{aligned}$$

After the appropriate multiple (0.3) of the *new* third equation is subtracted from the top equation, the following set is obtained:

$$\begin{aligned}
s_1 &= -12000 \\
0.1I + s_2 &= 15000 \\
1I &= 100000
\end{aligned}$$

After a similar operation on the second equation, the following solution is obtained:

$$\begin{aligned}
s_1 &= -12000 \\
s_2 &= 5000 \\
1I &= 100000
\end{aligned}$$

This is *not* a corner point of the feasible set. Because $s_1 = -12,000$, it is not even a member of the feasible set; s_1 must be ≥ 0 to be feasible.

Figure 6.2 associates the geometric points with the 10 partitions. Partitions 1–4 correspond to corner points of the feasible set. Partitions 5–10 do not correspond to corner points of the feasible set because for each of those partitions, at least one basic variable value is negative. This violates the nonnegativity restrictions on all of the variables. Each partition corresponds to the point of intersection of the constraints and/or the coordinate axes. The coordinate axes represent the edges for the non-negativity restrictions.

It is possible to solve for the basic variable values for all 10 partitions of the Potato Processing example. In some cases, it is not possible to "solve for" the basic variable values for a particular partition. Consider the constraint set specified by

$$\begin{aligned}
3x_1 + 1x_2 + s_1 &= 3 \\
6x_1 + 2x_2 + s_2 &= 8 \\
x_1, x_2, s_1, s_2 &\geq 0
\end{aligned}$$

FIGURE 6.2   Graphical Representation of 10 Partitions of the Potato Processing Example

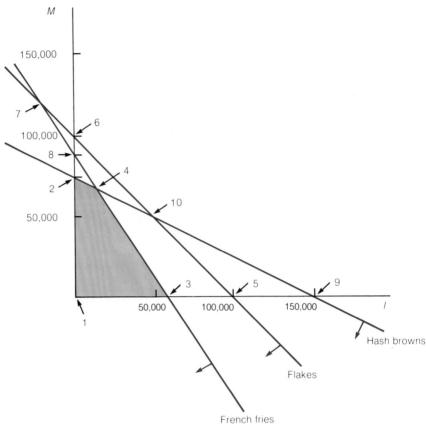

In this case, the nonnegativities of all the variables are explicitly stated, but there are really only two constraints. In a partition, there are two basic variables and two nonbasic variables. Partition the variables so that $\{x_1, x_2\}$ are the basic variables and $\{s_1, s_2\}$ are the nonbasic variables. Setting the nonbasic variables to 0, the resulting two equations in two variables are

$$3x_1 + 1x_2 = 3$$
$$6x_1 + 2x_2 = 8$$

After dividing the top equation by 3, the new set of equations becomes

$$1x_1 + \frac{1}{3}x_2 = 1$$
$$6x_1 + 2x_2 = 8$$

After multiplying the new top equation by 6 and subtracting the result from the bottom equation, the two equations are

$$1x_1 + \frac{1}{3}x_2 = 1$$
$$0x_1 + 0x_2 = 2$$

There are no values of x_1 and x_2 that satisfy the second equation. It is impossible to solve for the basic variable values corresponding to that partition!

Partitions, corner points, and basic feasible solutions

When it is possible to solve for the basic variable values corresponding to a partition and the resulting variable values are all nonnegative, a **corner point** of the feasible set is obtained. Mathematicians call this a **basic feasible solution.** A **feasible solution** satisfies the constraints and variable nonnegativities. A *basic* feasible solution is a feasible solution that corresponds to a partition. Note that Partitions 1, 2, 3, and 4 satisfy the definition of corner points and correspond, respectively, to Corner Points *A, D, B,* and *C* of Figure 6.1. Partitions 1, 2, 3, and 4 correspond to basic feasible solutions.

Remember from Chapter 4 that if a linear programming model has a finite optimal solution, a corner point of the feasible set is optimal. Let's describe a method that you could use to find the optimal solution to a model with a finite optimal solution. First, you list all of the partitions. For each partition, you calculate the variable values by solving a system of simultaneous equations. Then, for each partition that corresponds to a corner point (i.e., all variable values nonnegative), you calculate the objective function value. Finally, you select the feasible corner point that has the largest objective function value (for a maximization model).

Listing all of the partitions is difficult for large models. Say that the model has *m* constraints and *n* variables, including the slack and surplus variables. The number of partitions is the number of combinations of "*n* things taken *m* at a time."[3] For *m* = 10 and *n* = 20, the number of partitions is 3,628,800. *Listing all of the partitions is impractical for large values of m and n.*

The simplex algorithm is selective

Also, listing all of the partitions gives little guidance in identifying ill-behaved models or determining why they are ill-behaved. The simplex algorithm is amazingly selective in the number of partitions it examines. Remember, the number of points generated is usually between 2 and 3 times the number of constraints. The simplex algorithm selectively examines partitions and either reports the optimal solution or reports that the model is ill-behaved.

---

[3] This is represented symbolically a $\binom{n}{m}$ and is calculated as $\dfrac{n}{m!(n-m)!}$. You calculate n factorial as $n! = n \times (n-1) \times (n-2) \times \ldots \times 2 \times 1$.

In the first Theory section of this chapter, we discuss how the initial point is chosen, how the sequence of points is algebraically generated, and how ill-behaved models are identified by the simplex algorithm. In the following section, we discuss how a degenerate solution introduces ambiguity into the step-by-step improvement of the objective function and into sensitivity analysis.

DEGENERATE CORNER POINTS AND PARTITIONS

Consider the constraint set

$$2x_1 + 1x_2 + s_1 = 4$$
$$2x_1 + 2x_2 + s_2 = 8$$
$$x_1, x_2, s_1, s_2 \geq 0$$

Figure 6.3 illustrates the feasible set graphically. Because Point A lies on both constraint lines, the two slack variable values are 0. Because there are two constraints and only x_2 is positive, Corner Point A is degenerate.

Table 6.4 lists the six partitions. Partitions 1, 2, 3, 4, and 5 have nonnegative basic variable values; they correspond to corner points and are basic feasible solutions. However, Partitions 3, 4, and 5 have identical variable values. All three of these partitions have $x_2 = 4$ and all other variables equal to 0. All three of these partitions correspond to the same corner point, A.

Remember, the simplex algorithm moves from one partition to an adjacent partition by selecting a nonbasic variable that increases the objective function value if that variable becomes positive and by introducing the nonbasic variable into the basic variable set. If the corner point is degenerate, however, the two adjacent partitions may correspond to the same corner point. Even though the objective value would improve if the nonbasic variable becomes positive, the nonbasic variable may have a zero value when it becomes basic. This can happen only if a corner point is degenerate. If the adjacent partitions correspond to the same corner point, the objective function value doesn't change even though the set of basic variables changes.

Convergence of the simplex algorithm

Let's consider how the simplex algorithm converges to the optimal solution. Say that there aren't any degenerate corner points. When a simplex algorithm iteration is done, the objective function value always improves if the corner point isn't degenerate. Thus, it's impossible for the simplex algorithm to revisit a partition, because the objective function value of a revisited partition is worse than that of any subsequent parti-

FIGURE 6.3   Feasible Set for the Degenerate Corner Point Example

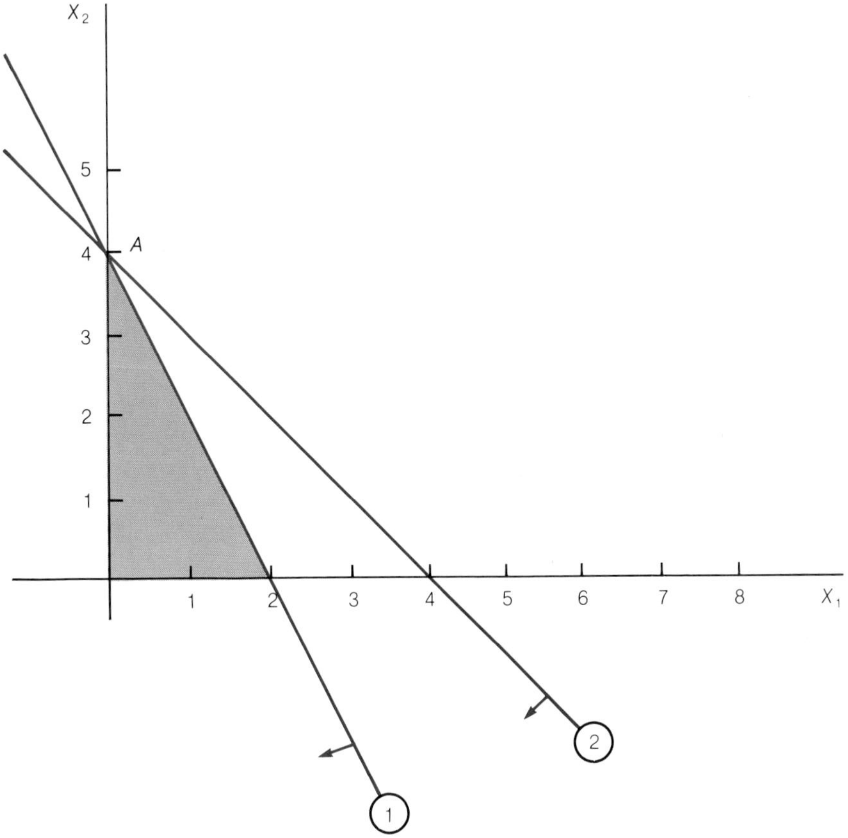

TABLE 6.4   Partitions for the Degenerate Corner Point Example

Partition	Basic Variables	Values of Basic Variables	Nonbasic Variables	Values of Nonbasic Variables
1	$\{s_1, s_2\}$	(4, 8)	$\{x_1, x_2\}$	(0, 0)
2	$\{x_1, s_2\}$	(2, 4)	$\{x_2, s_1\}$	(0, 0)
3	$\{x_2, s_2\}$	(4, 0)	$\{x_1, s_1\}$	(0, 0)
4	$\{x_2, s_1\}$	(4, 0)	$\{x_1, s_2\}$	(0, 0)
5	$\{x_1, x_2\}$	(0, 4)	$\{s_1, s_2\}$	(0, 0)
6	$\{s_1, x_1\}$	(−4, 4)	$\{x_2, s_2\}$	(0, 0)

tion. Because there are a finite number of partitions, the simplex algorithm must converge after visiting a finite number of partitions.

Now, say that there are degenerate corner points. Then, the objective function value of adjacent partitions can be the same if the adjacent partitions correspond to the same corner point. This poses a theoretical problem for the convergence of the simplex algorithm. It is possible to generate a sequence of adjacent partitions, all corresponding to the same degenerate corner point, that **cycles** back to a partition already examined. Thus, the value of the objective function could stay at the same value forever. Cycling is only of theoretical interest, however; examples of linear programming models that cycle are extremely rare. As a user, you need not worry about this issue.

A degenerate corner point corresponding to more than one partition causes the sensitivity analysis ambiguity that we discussed in Chapter 5. Say that the objective function coefficient of a nonbasic variable changes enough to cause a change to an adjacent partition. In the simplex algorithm, the objective function value increases if the nonbasic variable becomes *positive*. If the adjacent partition corresponds to the same corner point, the nonbasic variable becomes a basic variable with a value of 0; the objective function value is unchanged. This possibility causes ambiguities in sensitivity analysis.

ANALYSIS OF ILL-BEHAVED MODELS

If the model is ill-behaved, the simplex algorithm starts at the origin and generates a sequence of points until it reaches a point at which it receives an indication that the problem is ill-behaved. At this point, it indicates that the model has either an *unbounded optimal solution* or *no feasible solution*. The model builder has to examine the output and determine why the model is ill-behaved. For such cases, most computer systems provide additional information that aids the model builder in determining the cause or causes.

No Feasible Solution

No points in the feasible set

If a model indicates no feasible solution, the model is overconstrained. The model has so many constraints and they are so restrictive that there is no combination of nonnegative variable values that satisfies all of the constraints and variable nonnegativities. In this case, the simplex algorithm can't generate a sequence of points that are adjacent corner points of the feasible set because there are *no points* in the feasible set.

Most computer systems try to solve linear programming models by the **Two-Phase Method.** This is necessary when the origin is not a feasible point. The first phase starts at the origin and tries to find a feasible point by minimizing the sum of the infeasibilities. The **infeasibility** of a constraint is the amount that the constraint is unsatisfied. The second phase begins at the feasible point found in Phase 1 and optimizes the original objective function. If the sum of the infeasibilities at the end of Phase 1 is greater than 0, it was impossible to eliminate all of the infeasibilities and the model has no feasible solution. You must examine the model and discover why there is no feasible solution. You may have made an input error or a conceptual error in the model formulation. Most computer systems report the *constraints that are unsatisfied at the end of Phase 1.* You should check these constraints first, because they may be incorrect.

First, check the constraints unsatisfied at the end of Phase 1

Table 6.5 contains the LINDO output for a model with no feasible solution. With LINDO, you examine the constraints whose values under the SLACK OR SURPLUS column are negative for inequality constraints or nonzero for equality constraints. These constraints have not been satisfied at the end of Phase 1. For this example, Row 2 has a positive value in the SLACK OR SURPLUS column, but the constraint is

$$-X + Y = 3$$

TABLE 6.5   No Feasible Solution Example

```
: look all

MAX      X + 4 Y
SUBJECT TO
        2)  - X + Y =     3
        3)  - 2 X - Y >= - 2
END

: go

NO FEASIBLE SOLUTION AT STEP      1
SUM OF INFEASIBILITIES=  1.00000

VIOLATED ROWS HAVE NEGATIVE SLACK,
OR (EQUALITY ROWS) NONZERO SLACKS.
ROWS CONTRIBUTING TO INFEASIBILITY
HAVE NONZERO DUAL PRICE.

        OBJECTIVE FUNCTION VALUE

      1)     8.00000000

    VARIABLE         VALUE          REDUCED COST
           X          .000000           3.000000
           Y         2.000000            .000000


        ROW    SLACK OR SURPLUS      DUAL PRICES
        2)         1.000000          -1.000000
        3)          .000000          -1.000000

NO. ITERATIONS=         1
```

Because this is an equality-type constraint, the SLACK OR SURPLUS entry must be 0 if the solution satisfies the constraint. You can verify that Table 6.5's solution does not satisfy the first constraint by substituting $X = 0$ and $Y = 2$. The LHS is 2 and the RHS is 3. Because the LHS and RHS must be equal, the infeasibility is 1. Thus, the constraint is violated by 1.

Secondary checking for LINDO

You examine Row 2 first because the solution violates it. Perhaps a coefficient was incorrectly entered. In this case, it's possible for you to satisfy Row 2, but you can't satisfy Rows 2 and 3 at the same time with nonnegative variable values. If Row 2 is correct, you must check a secondary set of rows. For LINDO, you check the other rows with nonzero dual prices. In this example, both Rows 2 and 3 have nonzero dual prices.

Figure 6.4 illustrates the constraints for this example. Either of the

FIGURE 6.4 No Feasible Solution Example

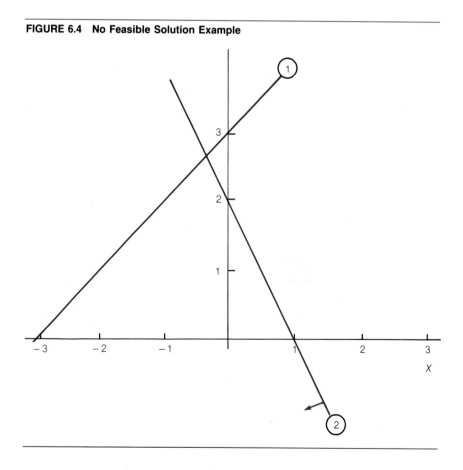

constraints can be satisfied, but not both. The two constraints together cause no feasible solution.

Another secondary checking method

Some linear programming systems do not give the dual prices at the end of Phase 1. They report only the constraints that have not been satisfied at the end of Phase 1. Let's discuss identifying the secondary rows to check for such a system. For a row that indicates no feasible solution (NFS), check all of the other rows that have *nonzero entries in the same columns*. For the example of Table 6.5, both X and Y have nonzero entries in both constraints, so Row 3 is checked second.

Figure 6.5 illustrates the *second-order checking* for a more complex model. Row 4 is the one that indicates no feasible solution, so you check it first. Next, you check Row 2. Rows 2 and 4 both have nonzero coefficients for x_2. Row 3 does not share any nonzero coefficient variables with Row 4.

Another method

Another method of finding out why there is no feasible solution is for you to identify a solution that you believe is possible. Because you understand the decision environment, this is not difficult. Then, add constraints forcing the variables equal to that solution. Re-solve the model and identify the constraints that have been violated. Reexamine the violated constraints.

Both input errors and model formulation errors can cause no feasible solution. In a model formulation error, the model builder's perception of the decision environment may be in error. It is also possible that the model builder has included the constraints desired, but "you can't have your cake and eat it." Reexamine the constraints. Are some of them goals rather than constraints?

Unbounded Optimal Solution

If a model has an unbounded optimal solution, the model is under-constrained. An unbounded optimal solution implies that there is an *unbounded feasible set*. This means that at least one variable can take a limitless value and still satisfy the constraints. Most computer systems

---

FIGURE 6.5 Example of Secondary Checking for No Feasible Solution

```
        Row 2        + 2 X2 +    X3                    =  5
        Row 3                    + 4 X3 + 3 X4         =  7
 NFS    Row 4  3 X1 + 4 X2 +               + 2 X5      = 10
          .
          .                                               .
          .                                               .
          .                                               .
```

provide a list of the variables that indicate an unbounded optimal solution. You now ask, ''What limits those variables from attaining extremely large values?'' Perhaps certain considerations (and associated constraints) were not included in the representation of the decision environment.

Check the unbounded
variables

Alternatively, there may be an error in the model input. Are the nonzero constraint coefficients correct for those variables? Many computer systems have utilities that display the nonzero coefficients for a particular variable. For LINDO, the SHOC (SHOw Column) command does this.

Table 6.6 presents the LINDO output for a model that has an unbounded optimal solution. This output indicates that the slack variables for Row 3, X, and Y are unbounded variables. Figure 6.6 shows the feasible set for this example. Note that X and Y are both limitless.

Generally, it is easier to determine the cause of an unbounded optimal solution than the cause of no feasible solution. The software is sometimes useful in searching for the cause of an unbounded optimal solution. For example, additional restrictions may be added and the model solved again. Do these restrictions change the model from one with an unbounded optimal solution to one with a finite optimal solution? Re-

TABLE 6.6   Unbounded Optimal Solution Example

```
: look all

MAX      2 X + 3 Y
SUBJECT TO
        2)  - X + Y <=    3
        3)  - 2 X + Y <=    2
END

: go

UNBOUNDED SOLUTION AT STEP       2
   UNBOUNDED VARIABLES ARE:
  SLK     3
          Y
          X

        OBJECTIVE FUNCTION VALUE

     1)    14.0000000

   VARIABLE          VALUE           REDUCED COST
          X         1.000000            .000000
          Y         4.000000            .000000


        ROW    SLACK OR SURPLUS      DUAL PRICES
        2)          .000000           8.000000
        3)          .000000          -5.000000

NO.  ITERATIONS=       2
```

FIGURE 6.6   Feasible Set of Unbounded Optimal Solution Example

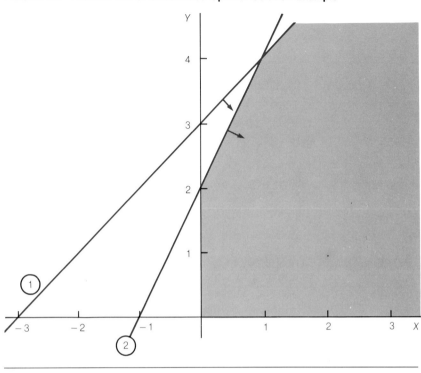

strictions should not be arbitrarily added to the model. They should be added only to study the model in an effort to discover what is incorrect and/or missing.

SUMMARY

This chapter discussed algebraic methods that linear programming software uses to find the optimal solution. These methods generate a sequence of points that eventually reaches the optimal solution. A basic understanding of the solution method gives insight into computer requirements and into the means for diagnosing why a model is ill-behaved.

We considered the factors that affect the computer solvability of a linear programming model. Computer storage and computer time are limited. The required amount of these resources depends on the number of constraints, the number of variables, and the density of the model. To determine whether computer solution of a linear programming model is practical, you must compare the benefits of the improved decisions you obtain in this way with the cost of obtaining them.

We geometrically described the simplex algorithm's path to the optimal solution. Successive path points are adjacent corner points of the feasible set and improve the value of the objective function.

Partitioning the variables into a basic set and a nonbasic set aids algebraic characterization of path points. The simplex algorithm moves from one partition to an adjacent partition. Each corner point of the feasible set corresponds to at least one partition. Adjacent corner points correspond to adjacent partitions. If a corner point is degenerate, more than one partition corresponds to it. We showed an example of this and described how it causes sensitivity analysis ambiguities.

We discussed identifying the cause of a model having an unbounded optimal solution or no feasible solution, from the computer output. We also discussed how you can solve modified versions of ill-behaved models to aid you in identifying why these models are ill-behaved.

In the first Theory section, we describe the details of the simplex algorithm, which is the basis for linear programming software. In the second Theory section, we outline a new method, developed by N. Karmarkar, that shows promise of being more effective than the simplex algorithm.

You can use algebraic methods for any linear programming application. However, these methods are limited by the assumptions of all linear programming models. All of the functions must be linear, and all of the variables must be continuous. Corner points of the feasible set can have fractional variable values. If a variable is restricted to integer values, a corner point can violate that restriction. You use algorithms other than the simplex algorithm for constrained optimization models that are not linear programming models.

Note the following cautions about this chapter. (1) The time involved with the computer is a small portion of the effort required to develop and use a linear programming model. Problem definition, model formulation, gathering input data, and model validation often dominate that effort. (2) Solution paths vary for different computer systems, depending on the implementation of the simplex algorithm. However, all computer systems should give optimal solutions with the same objective function value. (3) For a partition, the number of variables in the basic variable set is always equal to the number of constraints. The nonbasic variable values are always 0. (4) Not all partitions correspond to corner points of the feasible set. However, all corner points correspond to partitions. (5) If a corner point on the solution path is degenerate, the objective function value may remain the same when the simplex algorithm does an iteration. This occurs if adjacent partitions correspond to the same corner point.

QUESTIONS

1. What is the density of the standard unit blending model of Chapter 3?

2. What is the density of the operational blending model of Chapter 3?

3. Discuss the following: "The amount of numerical effort involved in solving a linear programming model is influenced by the model structure that the model builder selects."

4. What is an iteration of the simplex algorithm?

5. What is a corner point of the feasible set? Describe with a graphical example.

6. Under what circumstances is a corner point adjacent to another corner point of the feasible set? Illustrate with a graphical example.

7. What is the Two-Phase Method?

8. If Phase 1 of the simplex algorithm terminates unsuccessfully, what do you conclude about the optimal solution?

9. What is a partition of the variables?

10. If a linear programming model has 5 constraints and a total of 10 variables, including the slack and/or surplus variables, how many partitions exist?

11. If a linear programming model has 5 constraints and a total of 100 variables, including the slack and/or surplus variables, how many partitions exist?

12. If a linear programming model has 10 constraints and a total of 15 variables, including the slack and/or surplus variables, how many partitions exist?

13. If a linear programming model has 10 constraints and a total of 150 variables, including the slack and/or surplus variables, how many partitions exist?

14. Under what circumstances are two partitions adjacent?

15. Is it possible for a linear programming model to have more partitions than corner points?

16. Is it possible for a linear programming model to have more corner points than partitions?

17. Is it true that all partitions are corner points of the feasible set?

18. Is it true that all corner points of the feasible set are partitions?

19. If you generated all of the partitions, could you determine that there is an unbounded optimal solution?

20. If you generated all of the partitions, could you determine that there is no feasible solution?

21. Under what circumstance can a corner point of the feasible set correspond to more than one partition?

22. Give the two characteristics of the simplex algorithm's solution path.

23. For LINDO, which constraints should you check if there is no feasible solution?

24. Will two different linear programming software packages always find the same optimal solution?

See Theory: The Simplex Algorithm at the end of this chapter for questions 25–37.

25. *Theory.* What are the substitution coefficients for a nonbasic variable?
26. *Theory.* What is the profit forgone rate for a nonbasic variable?
27. *Theory.* What is the profit improvement rate for a nonbasic variable?
28. *Theory.* What is a pivot element?
29. *Theory.* How does the simplex algorithm indicate that there is an alternate optimal solution?
30. *Theory.* How does the simplex algorithm indicate that there is an unbounded optimal solution?
31. *Theory.* How does the simplex algorithm indicate that there is no feasible solution?
32. *Theory.* What is the Big M Method?
33. *Theory.* When is it necessary to add an artificial variable to a constraint?
34. *Theory.* When do you stop doing simplex algorithm iterations?
35. *Theory.* What is the easy form?
36. *Theory.* What are the values of the nonbasic variables?
37. *Theory.* How do you choose the nonbasic variable that becomes a basic variable?

EXERCISES

1. Calculate the values of the basic variables corresponding to Partition 2 of the Potato Processing model as specified in Table 6.2.
2. Calculate the values of the basic variables corresponding to Partition 4 of the Potato Processing model as specified in Table 6.2.
3. Calculate the values of the basic variables corresponding to Partition 6 of the Potato Processing model as specified in Table 6.2.
4. Calculate the values of the basic variables corresponding to Partition 7 of the Potato Processing model as specified in Table 6.2.
5. Consider the following linear programming model:

$$\max \quad 3x + 2y$$
$$\text{st} \quad x + y \le 5$$
$$x - y \le 2$$
$$x, y \ge 0$$

   a. Give all six possible partitions of the model.
   b. Find the values of all four variables for each of the partitions.
   c. Calculate the objective function value for each of the partitions.
   d. List the partitions that correspond to corner points of the feasible set.
   e. Graph the feasible set and determine the optimal solution. Indicate the partition or partitions that correspond to each corner point.

    f. Starting at the origin, give all of the possible simplex paths to the optimal solution.

6. Consider the following linear programming model:

max $3x + 2y$
st $2x + 3y \leq 5$
          $x + y \leq 2$
          $x, y \geq 0$

    a. Give all six possible partitions of the model.
    b. Find the values of all four variables for each of the partitions.
    c. Calculate the objective function value for each of the partitions.
    d. List the partitions that correspond to corner points of the feasible set.
    e. Graph the feasible set and determine the optimal solution. Indicate the partition or partitions that correspond to each corner point.
    f. Starting at the origin, give all of the possible simplex paths to the optimal solution.

7. Answer the following as a continuation of Exercise 5.
    a. The origin is a corner point of the feasible set. Give all the adjacent partitions of the partition corresponding to the origin.
    b. Which of the adjacent partitions correspond to adjacent corner points of the origin?

8. Answer the following as a continuation of Exercise 6.
    a. The origin is a corner point of the feasible set. Give all the adjacent partitions of the partition corresponding to the origin.
    b. Which of the adjacent partitions correspond to adjacent corner points of the origin?

9. Consider the following linear programming model:

max $8R + 9L$
st $R + 2L \leq 9$
          $2R + L \leq 9$
          $R + L \leq 5$
          $R, L \geq 0$

    a. Give all 10 partitions of the model.
    b. Find the values of all five variables for each of the partitions.
    c. Which partitions correspond to feasible points of the feasible set?
    d. For each corner point of the feasible set, calculate the objective function value.
    e. Give all the solution paths of the simplex algorithm, starting at the origin.

10. Consider the following linear programming model:

max $5R + 4L$
st $1R + 1L \leq 10$
          $1R + 2L \leq 15$
          $3R + 2L \leq 20$
          $R, L, \geq 0$

    a. Give all 10 partitions of the model.

    b. Find the values of all five variables for each of the partitions.

    c. Which partitions correspond to feasible points of the feasible set?

    d. For each corner point of the feasible set, calculate the objective function value.

    e. Give all the solution paths of the simplex algorithm, starting at the origin.

11. Consider the following linear programming model:

$$\max \quad A + B$$
$$\text{st} \quad A + 2B \le 4$$
$$2A + 2B \le 6$$
$$-A + B \le 1$$
$$A, B \ge 0$$

    a. Give all 10 partitions of the model.

    b. Find the values of all five variables for each of the partitions.

    c. Calculate the objective function value for each of the partitions.

    d. List the partitions that correspond to corner points of the feasible set.

    e. Graph the feasible set and determine the optimal solution. Indicate the partition or partitions that correspond to each corner point.

    f. Starting at the origin, give all of the possible simplex paths to the optimal solution.

12. Consider the following linear programming model:

$$\max \quad 4A + 6B$$
$$\text{st} \quad 2A + 3B \le 5$$
$$2A + B \ge 3$$
$$A + 2B \le 4$$
$$A, B \ge 0$$

    a. Give all 10 partitions of the model.

    b. Find the values of all five variables for each of the partitions.

    c. Calculate the objective function value for each of the partitions.

    d. List the partitions that correspond to corner points of the feasible set.

    e. Graph the feasible set and determine the optimal solution. Indicate the partition or partitions that correspond to each corner point.

    f. Starting at the origin, give all of the possible simplex paths to the optimal solution.

See Theory: The Simplex Algorithm at the end of this chapter for questions 13–20.

13. *Theory.* Complete the following simplex tableau:

c_j	Basic Variables	Basic Variable Values	3	2	0	0
			A	B	S_1	S_2
3	A	2	1	-1	2	0
0	S_2	3	0	2	1	1
	z_j	?	?	?	?	?
	$c_j - z_j$		?	?	?	?

14. *Theory.* Complete the following simplex tableau:

C_j	Basic Variables	Basic Variable Values	3	2	0	0
			A	B	S_1	S_2
?	B	5	2	1	-2	?
0	S_2	4	-3	0	1	?
	Z_j	?	?	?	?	?
	$C_j - Z_j$		?	?	?	?

15. *Theory.* Consider the following simplex tableau:

C_j	Basic Variables	Basic Variable Values	4	6	0	0
			A	B	S_1	S_2
4	A	5	1	1	2	0
0	S_2	3	0	2	1	1
	Z_j	20	4	4	8	0
	$C_j - Z_j$		0	2	-8	0

a. Circle the pivot element.
b. Do one pivot and give the updated tableau.
c. What is the new value of the objective function after the pivot?
d. Is the new tableau optimal? If so, give the optimal values of all four variables.

16. *Theory.* Consider the following simplex tableau:

C_j	Basic Variables	Basic Variable Values	5	6	0	0
			A	B	S_1	S_2
5	A	4	1	1	1	0
0	S_2	3	0	1	1	1
	Z_j	20	5	5	5	0
	$C_j - Z_j$		0	1	-5	0

a. Circle the pivot element.
b. Do one pivot and give the updated tableau.
c. What is the new value of the objective function after the pivot?
d. Is the new tableau optimal? If so, give the optimal values of all four variables.

17. *Theory.* Consider the following simplex tableau:

C_j	Basic Variables	Basic Variable Values	-2	6	0	0
			A	B	S_1	S_2
-2	A	1	1	-2	2	0
0	S_2	3	0	-2	1	1
	Z_j	-2	-2	-4	-4	0
	$C_j - Z_j$		0	10	4	0

    a. Circle the pivot element.
    b. What is the optimal solution?

18. *Theory.* Consider the following simplex tableau:

C_j	Basic Variables	Basic Variable Values	5	6	0	0
			A	B	S_1	S_2
5	A	4	1	-1	1	0
0	S_2	3	0	-2	1	1
	Z_j	20	5	-5	5	0
	$C_j - Z_j$		0	11	-5	0

    a. Circle the pivot element.
    b. What is the optimal solution?

19. *Theory.* Set up the following model for solution by the simplex algorithm. Construct the initial simplex tableau and determine the first pivot element. Do not do the pivot.

    max $2A + 4B$
    st $-A + 2B = 4$
           $2A + B \geq 3$
           $A, B \geq 0$

20. *Theory.* Set up the following model for solution by the simplex algorithm. Construct the initial simplex tableau and determine the first pivot element. Do not do the pivot.

    max $2A + 4B$
    st $-A + 2B \leq -4$
           $2A + B \geq 3$
           $A, B, \geq 0$

MORE CHALLENGING EXERCISES

MCEs 1 to 8 focus on the relationships among degenerate corner points, partitions, and the solution path.

1. Consider the following linear programming model:

$$\begin{aligned}
\max \quad & 3x + 2y \\
\text{st} \quad & x + y \le 5 \\
& x - y \le 0 \\
& x, y, \ge 0
\end{aligned}$$

   a. Give all six possible partitions of the model.
   b. Find the values of all four variables for each of the partitions.
   c. Calculate the objective function value for each of the partitions.
   d. List the partitions that correspond to corner points of the feasible set.
   e. Graph the feasible set and determine the optimal solution. Indicate the partition or partitions that correspond to each corner point.
   f. Starting at the origin, give all of the possible simplex paths to the optimal solution.

2. Answer the following as a continuation of MCE 1.
   a. The origin is a corner point of the feasible set. Give all of the partitions corresponding to the origin.
   b. Starting at the origin, give all the possible sequences of adjacent partitions that cause the value of the objective function to increase or to remain the same.
   c. Is it possible to find a sequence of adjacent partitions that cycles forever without improving the value of the objective function?

3. Consider the following linear programming model:

$$\begin{aligned}
\max \quad & 3x + 2y \\
\text{st} \quad & x + y \le 3 \\
& 2x + y \le 6 \\
& x, y \ge 0
\end{aligned}$$

   a. Give all six possible partitions of the model.
   b. Find the values of all four variables for each of the partitions.
   c. Calculate the objective function value for each of the partitions.
   d. List the partitions that correspond to corner points of the feasible set.
   e. Graph the feasible set and determine the optimal solution. Indicate the partition or partitions that correspond to each corner point.
   f. Starting at the origin, give all of the possible simplex paths to the optimal solution.

4. Answer the following as a continuation of MCE 3.
   a. The point $x = 3$ and $y = 0$, denoted $(3, 0)$, is a corner point of the feasible set. Give all the partitions corresponding to that point.

    b. Starting at the origin, give all the possible sequences of adjacent partitions that cause the value of the objective function to increase or to remain the same.

    c. Is it possible to find a sequence of adjacent partitions that cycles forever without improving the value of the objective function?

5. Consider the following linear programming model:

$$
\begin{aligned}
\text{max} \quad & 3A + B \\
\text{st} \quad & 3A + 2B \le 12 \\
& 2A + 3B \le 21 \\
& -A + B \le 6 \\
& A, B, \ge 0
\end{aligned}
$$

    a. Give all 10 partitions of the model.

    b. Find the values of all five variables for each of the partitions.

    c. Calculate the objective function value for each of the partitions.

    d. List the partitions that correspond to corner points of the feasible set.

    e. Graph the feasible set and determine the optimal solution. Indicate the partition or partitions that correspond to each corner point.

    f. Starting at the origin, give all of the possible simplex paths to the optimal solution.

6. Answer the following as a continuation of MCE 5.

    a. The point $A = 0$ and $B = 6$, denoted $(0, 6)$ is a corner point of the feasible set. Give all the adjacent partitions of the partition corresponding to $(0, 6)$.

    b. Which of the adjacent partitions correspond to adjacent corner points of the origin?

    c. Starting at the origin, give all the possible sequences of adjacent partitions that cause the value of the objective function to increase or to remain the same.

    d. Is it possible to find a sequence of adjacent partitions that cycles forever without improving the value of the objective function?

7. Consider the following linear programming model:

$$
\begin{aligned}
\text{max} \quad & A + B \\
\text{st} \quad & A + 2B \le 4 \\
& 2A + 2B \le 6 \\
& -A + B \ge 0 \\
& A, B, \ge 0
\end{aligned}
$$

    a. Give all 10 partitions of the model.

    b. Find the values of all five variables for each of the partitions.

    c. Calculate the objective function value for each of the partitions.

    d. List the partitions that correspond to corner points of the feasible set.

    e. Graph the feasible set and determine the optimal solution. Indicate the partition or partitions that correspond to each corner point.

    f. Starting at the origin, give all of the possible simplex paths to the optimal solution.

8. Answer the following as a continuation of MCE 7.

    a. The origin is a corner point of the feasible set. Give all the adjacent partitions of the partition corresponding to the origin.

    b. Which of the adjacent partitions correspond to adjacent corner points of the origin?

    c. Starting at the origin, give all the possible sequences of adjacent partitions that cause the value of the objective function to increase or to remain the same.

    d. Is it possible to find a sequence of adjacent partitions that cycles forever without improving the value of the objective function?

See Theory: The Simplex Algorithm at the end of this chapter for questions 9–17.

9. *Theory.* Consider the following model:

$$
\begin{aligned}
\max \quad & 3x + 2y \\
\text{st} \quad & x + y \le 4 \\
& 2x + y \le 6 \\
& x, y, \ge 0
\end{aligned}
$$

    a. Solve the model by the simplex algorithm.

    b. Graph the feasible set and label the successive points generated by the simplex algorithm.

    c. From the final tableau, give the values of the objective function and all of the variables, including any slack, surplus, or artificial variables.

    d. Is your set of variable values in Part *c* an optimal solution?

    e. Are there any alternate optimal solutions?

10. *Theory.* Consider the following model:

$$
\begin{aligned}
\max \quad & x + 2y \\
\text{st} \quad & x + 3y \le 4 \\
& 2x + y \le 6 \\
& x, y, \ge 0
\end{aligned}
$$

    a. Solve the model by the simplex algorithm.

    b. Graph the feasible set and label the successive points generated by the simplex algorithm.

    c. From the final tableau, give the values of the objective function and all of the variables, including any slack, surplus, or artificial variables.

    d. Is your set of variable values in Part *c* an optimal solution?

    e. Are there any alternate optimal solutions?

11. *Theory.* Consider the following model:

$$
\begin{aligned}
\max \quad & 3x_1 + 2x_2 \\
\text{st} \quad & -x_1 + 2x_2 \le 0 \\
& 6x_1 + 4x_2 \le 12 \\
& x_1, x_2 \ge 0
\end{aligned}
$$

    a. Solve the model by the simplex algorithm.

    b. Graph the feasible set and label the successive points generated by the simplex algorithm.

    c. From the final tableau, give the values of the objective function and all of the variables, including any slack, surplus, or artificial variables.

    d. Is your set of variable values in Part *c* an optimal solution?

    e. Are there any alternate optimal solutions?

12. *Theory.* Consider the following model:

$$\max \quad 2A + 4B$$
$$\text{st} \quad -A + 2B = 4$$
$$2A + B \le 3$$
$$A, B \ge 0$$

  a. Solve the model by the simplex algorithm.
  b. Graph the feasible set and label the successive points generated by the simplex algorithm.
  c. From the final tableau, give the values of the objective function and all of the variables, including any slack, surplus, or artificial variables.
  d. Is your set of variable values in Part c an optimal solution?
  e. Are there any alternate optimal solutions?

13. *Theory.* Consider the following model:

$$\max \quad 2A + 4B$$
$$\text{st} \quad -A + 2B \le -4$$
$$2A + B \ge 3$$
$$A, B \ge 0$$

  a. Solve the model by the simplex algorithm.
  b. Graph the feasible set and label the successive points generated by the simplex algorithm.
  c. From the final tableau, give the values of the objective function and all of the variables, including any slack, surplus, or artificial variables.
  d. Is your set of variable values in Part c an optimal solution?
  e. Are there any alternate optimal solutions?

14. *Theory.* Consider the following model:

$$\max \quad 2A + 4B$$
$$\text{st} \quad A + 2B \le 4$$
$$2A + B \ge 3$$
$$A, B \ge 0$$

  a. Solve the model by the simplex algorithm.
  b. Graph the feasible set and label the successive points generated by the simplex algorithm.
  c. From the final tableau, give the values of the objective function and all of the variables, including any slack, surplus, or artificial variables.
  d. Is your set of variable values in Part c an optimal solution?
  e. Are there any alternate optimal solutions?

15. *Theory.* Consider the following model:

$$\max \quad 3A + 3B$$
$$\text{st} \quad 4A + 2B \ge -8$$
$$A - B \le 1$$
$$A, B \ge 0$$

  a. Solve the model by the simplex algorithm.
  b. Graph the feasible set and label the successive points generated by the simplex algorithm.

    c. From the final tableau, give the values of the objective function and all of the variables, including any slack, surplus, or artificial variables.

    d. Is your set of variable values in Part *c* an optimal solution?

    e. Are there any alternate optimal solutions?

16. *Theory.* Consider the following model:

$$
\begin{aligned}
\max \quad & 3A + B \\
\text{st} \quad & 4A + 2B = -8 \\
& A - B \le 1 \\
& A, B \ge 0
\end{aligned}
$$

    a. Solve the model by the simplex algorithm.

    b. Graph the feasible set and label the successive points generated by the simplex algorithm.

    c. From the final tableau, give the values of the objective function and all of the variables, including any slack, surplus, or artificial variables.

    d. Is your set of variable values in Part *c* an optimal solution?

    e. Are there any alternate optimal solutions?

17. *Theory.* Consider the following model:

$$
\begin{aligned}
\max \quad & 2A + B \\
\text{st} \quad & 4A + 2B = 8 \\
& A - B \le 1 \\
& A, B \ge 0
\end{aligned}
$$

    a. Solve the model by the simplex algorithm.

    b. Graph the feasible set and label the successive points generated by the simplex algorithm.

    c. From the final tableau, give the values of the objective function and all of the variables, including any slack, surplus, or artificial variables.

    d. Is your set of variable values in Part *c* an optimal solution?

    e. Are there any alternate optimal solutions?

18. Solve MCE 10 by the computer software that is available to you. If the software allows the pivot-by-pivot solution, determine the sequence of points generated by the simplex algorithm and plot them on the graph of the feasible set.

19. Solve MCE 12 by the computer software that is available to you. If the software allows the pivot-by-pivot solution, determine the sequence of points generated by the simplex algorithm and plot them on the graph of the feasible set.

20. Solve MCE 14 by the computer software that is available to you. If the software allows the pivot-by-pivot solution, determine the sequence of points generated by the simplex algorithm and plot them on the graph of the feasible set.

21. Solve MCE 16 by the computer software that is available to you. If the software allows the pivot-by-pivot solution, determine the sequence of points generated by the simplex algorithm and plot them on the graph of the feasible set.

Chippewa County Economic Development Authority

Chippewa County Economic Development Authority (CCEDA) is an economic development organization that has been created by Chippewa County to attract industry and jobs. CCEDA has ambitious plans to develop an industrial park. Improvements to the industrial park will be financed by tax-exempt bonds. CCEDA hopes to use proceeds from the sale of land in the industrial park to pay off the bonds. Otherwise, property taxes must be increased to pay them off.

Years to Maturity	Yield
1	5.10%
2	5.20
3	5.30
4	5.40
5	5.50
6	5.60
7	5.75
8	5.85
9	5.95
10	6.10

CCEDA has sent information to several potential underwriters for the bonds. Each bond will have a face value of $1,000, and 100 will be issued to mature at the end of each of the next 10 years. The total face amount of the bonds is $1 million. CCEDA specifies that no bond can be priced at less than $1,000 and that no coupon rate can exceed 7 percent. CCEDA will allow the successful underwriter a "spread" of $12 per bond, for a total of $12,000.

CCEDA will choose the underwriter that submits the proposal with the smallest net interest cost (NIC). (There is additional information on bond underwriting at the end of the case.)

Frank Johnson, a new employee at First National Bank, has been given the responsibility for preparing the proposal for CCEDA's bond issue. He must determine the coupon rate for the bonds of each maturity. All bonds of the same maturity must have the same coupon rate. By examining current yields in the bond market, Frank has estimated the market yields to maturity shown in the next column. What coupon rates should he propose so that the NIC is minimized?

BOND UNDERWRITING
Bond underwriters must give CCEDA the face value of the bonds at the issuing time. Because CCEDA plans to issue 1,000 bonds, First Na-

tional must pay CCEDA $1 million at the issuing time. CCEDA must pay $1,000 for each bond at maturity. It must also pay annual interest at the coupon rate of the bonds.

For a one-year bond, say that the coupon rate is 6.0 percent. The interest payment is $0.06 \times \$1,000 = \$60$, which is paid at the end of Year 1. The $1,000 face value must also be paid at the end of Year 1. The bond must be priced at the present value of the future cash flows, using the market yield as the discount rate. Because the market yield for a one-year maturity is 5.1 percent, the offering price is

$$\text{Price} = \frac{0.06 \times 1,000}{(1 + 0.051)} + \frac{1,000}{(1 + 0.051)}$$
$$= \$1,008.56$$

For a two-year bond, say that the coupon rate is 6.0 percent. The interest payment is $0.06 \times \$1,000 = \$60$, which is paid at the end of Years 1 and 2. Because the market yield for a two-year bond is 5.2 percent, the offering price is

$$\text{Price} = \frac{0.06 \times 1,000}{(1 + 0.052)} + \frac{0.06 \times 1,000}{(1 + 0.052)^2}$$
$$+ \frac{1,000}{(1 + 0.052)^2} = \$1,014.83$$

Say that an n-year bond is issued at the coupon rate of c and that the market yield is r.

At the end of each of the n years, an interest payment of $c \times \$1,000$ is made. At the end of the n years, the \$1,000 face value is paid. The bond is priced at

$$\text{Price} = \sum_{t=1}^{n}\left[1,000c \times \frac{1}{(1+r)^t}\right] + \frac{1,000}{(1+r)^n}$$

Let $A = 1/(1+r)$. Using infinite sums, the price can be calculated as

$$\text{Price} = 1,000c \times \frac{(A - A^{n+1})}{(1 - A)} + 1,000A^n$$

Exhibit 1 shows one possible coupon schedule and illustrates how the NIC is calculated. In Exhibit 1, the coupon rate is 6 percent for all maturities. The offering price depends on the coupon rate, market yield, and maturity. The offering prices for one- and two-year bonds were calculated in our examples above. Because 100 bonds will be offered for each maturity, the offering proceeds are the offering price times 100. For all maturities, the total offering proceeds to the underwriter are

\$1,012,423.00. You calculate the adjustment by subtracting from the total offering proceeds the face value of the bonds and the spread allowed.

The interest paid on each bond is \$60 per year. For the 10-year bonds, 10 payments of \$60 are made for each bond. Because there are 100 10-year bonds, the interest paid on them is \$60,000. The gross interest cost (GIC) is the total interest paid, \$330,000. The NIC is the GIC minus the adjustment. If the adjustment is greater than 0, the underwriter must give CCEDA \$1 million plus the adustment. The underwriter can keep only the \$12,000 spread from the offering proceeds.

Remember, CCEDA placed two limitations on the proposals. Exhibit 1 satisfies CCEDA's requirement that no coupon rate can be more than 7 percent. However, Exhibit 1 violates CCEDA's requirement that no bonds can be priced at less than \$1,000. The 10-year bond in Exhibit 1 violates this, so Exhibit 1 is not an acceptable proposal.

EXHIBIT 1 An Example of NIC Calculation

Years to Maturity	Number of Bonds	Yield to Maturity	Coupon Rate	Offering Price	Offering Proceeds	Interest Paid
1	100	5.10%	6.00%	\$1,008.56	\$ 100,856.00	\$ 6,000.00
2	100	5.20	6.00	1,014.83	101,483.00	12,000.00
3	100	5.30	6.00	1,018.96	101,896.00	18,000.00
4	100	5.40	6.00	1,021.08	102,108.00	24,000.00
5	100	5.50	6.00	1,021.35	102,135.00	30,000.00
6	100	5.60	6.00	1,019.92	101,992.00	36,000.00
7	100	5.75	6.00	1,014.08	101,408.00	42,000.00
8	100	5.85	6.00	1,009.37	100,937.00	48,000.00
9	100	5.95	6.00	1,003.41	100,341.00	54,000.00
10	100	6.10	6.00	992.67	99,267.00	60,000.00
				Total	\$1,012,423.00	\$330,000.00
				Par Value	(1,000,000.00)	(423.00)
				Spread	(\$12,000.00)	329,577.00 NIC
				Adjustment	423.00	

The Simplex Algorithm

The Simplex Algorithm for the Easy Form

The easy form

The simplex method is easier to explain if the model is of the easy form. The **easy form** has (1) all constraints of the ≤ type, (2) all RHS constants nonnegative, and (3) all variables restricted to nonnegative values. (This is similar, but not identical, to the standard form of Chapter 4.) Furthermore, in this entire Theory section we assume that the objective function is to be *maximized*. If the objective function is to be minimized, the objective function is converted to maximization, as we discussed in Chapter 4.

The starting point

The easy form assures that the origin is a feasible solution, and we use it as the starting point. Partition the variables so that all of the slack variables are in the set of basic variables and the set of nonbasic variables includes all of the structural variables. There is one slack variable for each constraint, and slack variable values are equal to the RHS constants. Because we assumed that the RHS constants are nonnegative, the values of the basic variables are nonnegative. The Potato Processing model has the easy form. After adding the slack variables, the model is

$$\begin{aligned}
\max \quad & 0.14I + 0.15M \\
\text{st} \quad & 0.3I + 0.2M + s_1 = 18000 \\
& 0.1I + 0.2M + s_2 = 15000 \\
& 0.3I + 0.3M + s_3 = 30000 \\
& I, M, s_1, s_2, s_3 \geq 0
\end{aligned}$$

The initial set of basic variables is $\{s_1, s_2, s_3\}$, with values of 18,000, 15,000, and 30,000, respectively. An advantage of using the slack variables for the initial set of basic variables is that the variables have already been "solved for." The variable s_1 has been solved for in the top row; it has a coefficient of 1 in the top constraint and an entry of 0 in all other constraints. Variables s_2 and s_3 have been solved for in Constraints 2 and 3, respectively. This corner point (and basic feasible solution) has $I = M = 0$, $s_1 = 18,000$, $s_2 = 15,000$, and $s_3 = 30,000$. Note that all of the variable values are nonnegative and that there are three positive variables.

Now, consider increasing Variable I's value away from its current value of 0, while keeping $M = 0$. If this is done, the values of s_1, s_2, and s_3 must be adjusted or the constraints are not satisfied. In fact, the coefficients of Variable I indicate how they are adjusted. Such coefficients are called the **substitution coefficients** of a variable. If the value of I is increased to 1, the value of s_1 decreases by 0.3. Similarly, for each unit that I is increased, the value of s_2 decreases by 0.1. If I is increased to 10, what is the adjusted value of s_3? The value of s_3 decreases by 0.3×10, or 3, and s_3 attains a new value of 29,997.

Profit forgone rate

Since the objective function coefficients of the three slack variables are all 0, when the values of the slack variables are adjusted as I's value increases, no profit is forgone. There is no profit for the slack variable values. The **profit forgone rate** is the sum of the objective function coefficients of the basic variable times the substitution coefficients. Let Z_j represent the profit forgone rate of the variable in the jth position.

For Variable I,

$$Z_1 = (0 \times 0.3) + (0 \times 0.1) + (0 \times 0.3) = 0$$

For Variable M,

$$Z_2 = (0 \times 0.2) + (0 \times 0.2) + (0 \times 0.3) = 0$$

For Variable s_1,

$$Z_3 = (0 \times 1) + (0 \times 0) + (0 \times 0) = 0$$

Similarly, the profit forgone rates are $Z_4 = 0$ and $Z_5 = 0$ for Variables s_2 and s_3, respectively.

Profit improvement rate

The **profit improvement rate** for Variable I is the objective function coefficient minus the profit forgone rate. Let C_j represent the objective function coefficient of the variable in the jth position. The profit improvement rate is $C_j - Z_j$. We must stress that this is the rate *per unit* that the nonbasic variable is increased.

It is convenient to organize these calculations in tableau format, as shown in Table 6.T1. The numerical values in each column under the variables are the original coefficients of the variables in the constraints. The order in which the basic variables are listed corresponds to the constraints they were "solved for." Thus, Variable s_1 has a coefficient of 1 in the first constraint and is listed first. The objective function coefficients listed above the variables are the original objective function coefficients. The coefficients listed to the left of the basic variables are the objective function coefficients of those variables.

Tableau format

The tableau of Table 6.T1 is associated with the origin. What are the values of all *five* variables, including the slack variables? From the tableau, we note that $s_1 = 18,000$, $s_2 = 15,000$, and $s_3 = 30,000$. What are the values of I and M? They are both 0 because they are nonbasic variables! For this reason, the value of the objective function is the sum of each objective function coefficient of a basic variable times the value of

TABLE 6.T1   First Simplex Tableau—Potato Processing Example

C_j		Basic	0.14	0.15	0	0	0
	Basic	Variable					
	Variables	Values	I	M	s_1	s_2	s_3
0	s_1	18000	0.3	0.2	1	0	0
0	s_2	15000	0.1	(0.2)	0	1	0
0	s_3	30000	0.3	0.3	0	0	1
	Z_j	0	0	0	0	0	0
	$C_j - Z_j$		0.14	0.15	0	0	0

the basic variables. Let Z represent the objective function value. For this tableau, the result is

$$Z = (18000 \times 0) + (15000 \times 0) + (30000 \times 0) = 0$$

Remember, we use Z^* for the optimal objective function value. The $*$ means optimal. This terminology was inspired by the tabular representation. The objective function value, 0, is entered in the Z_j row under the Basic Variable Values column. The objective function value is determined in the same manner as the Z_j values.

The profit improvement rate for I is 0.14. This means that for each unit that I is increased above 0, the objective function value increases by $0.14. The $C_j - Z_j$ for M is 0.15. This means that for each unit that M is increased above 0, the objective function value increases by $0.15. Is the current corner point optimal? No! There are better solutions if either M or I takes on a positive value. To move to an adjacent corner point, only one of the two variables, M or I, is increased from its current value of 0. *We generally prefer to increase the value of the nonbasic variable with the largest positive profit improvement rate.* In this situation, M is preferred. (If we chose I instead of M, the method follows a different path to the optimal solution.)

At the origin, the objective function value is 0. M's profit improvement rate is 0.15, so if M increases from 0 to 1, the objective function value increases by 0.15. If M increases from 0 to 100,000, the objective function value increased by $0.15 \times 100,000 = 15,000$. You want to increase M as much as possible so that the objective function value increases as much as possible. However, as the value of M increases, the values of the basic variables must be adjusted so that the constraints are satisfied. The coefficients under M in Table 6.T1 are its substitution coefficients. If M increases to 100,000, the value of s_1 decreases by $0.2 \times 100,000 = 20,000$.

Choose the nonbasic variable with the largest positive $C_j - Z_j$

However, since the current value of s_1 is 18,000, its adjusted value is $18,000 - 20,000 = -2,000$. Because this results in a negative variable value, M cannot increase by 100,000. M should increase until the adjusted value of one of the basic variables is about to become negative. The limit imposed by the first constraint is $18,000/0.2 = 90,000$; the limit imposed by the second constraint is $15,000/0.2 = 75,000$; and the limit imposed by the third constraint is $30,000/0.3 = 100,000$. Because all variable values must be nonnegative, the smallest of the limit values is the overall limit. The limit is the minimum of (90,000, 75,000, 100,000), which is 75,000. If M increases to 75,000, the adjusted value of s_1 is $18,000 - (0.2 \times 75,000) = 3,000$, the adjusted value of s_2 is $15,000 - (0.2 \times 75,000) = 0$, and the adjusted value of s_3 is $30,000 - (0.3 \times 75,000) = 7,500$. When M increases to the limit (75,000), the value of the variable s_2 becomes 0 and M replaces s_2 as a basic variable in the partition.

Table 6.T2 contains the initial information for the set of basic variables $\{s_1, M, s_3\}$. The basic variables remaining in the partition, s_1 and s_3, are in the same positions in the basic variables list in Table 6.T1. The only change is that M has replaced s_2. The new partition corresponds to an adjacent corner point. To examine the new corner point, you must solve for the new set of basic variables.

Table 6.T1 must be changed as follows: (1) the coefficient of M in the second constraint must become 1; and (2) the coefficients of M in all of the other constraints must become 0. The circled number in Table 6.T1 is called the **pivot element**. The pivot element is the coefficient that must be converted to 1.

The tableau changes

The tableau changes require two steps:

1. The row of the pivot element is divided by the pivot element.
2. "The coefficient in its row and the pivot column" times "the new pivot row" is subtracted from the other rows.

TABLE 6.T2 Initial Second Simplex Tableau—Potato Processing Example

C_j	Basic Variables	Basic Variable Values	0.14	0.15	0	0	0
			I	M	s_1	s_2	s_3
0	s_1						
0.15	M						
0	s_3						
	Z_j						
	$C_j - Z_j$						

TABLE 6.T3   Partial Second Simplex Tableau—Potato Processing Example

C_j	Basic Variables	Basic Variable Values	0.14 I	0.15 M	0 s_1	0 s_2	0 s_3
0	s_1						
0.15	M	75000	0.5	1	0	5	0
0	s_3						
	Z_j						
	$C_j - Z_j$						

Table 6.T3 shows the result of the first step.

Let's update the top row in the next step. In Table 6.T1, the coefficient in the top row and the pivot column is 0.2. The new pivot row appears in Table 6.T3. The top row values are changed as follows:

$(18000, 0.3, 0.2, 1, 0, 0) - 0.2(75000, 0.5, 1, 0, 5, 0)$

$$= (3000, 0.2, 0, 1, -1, 0)$$

The new top row values appear in Table 6.T4.

The new values for the third row are

$(30000, 0.3, 0.3, 0, 0, 1) - 0.3(75000, 0.5, 1, 0, 5, 0)$

$$= (7500, 0.15, 0, 0, -1.5, 1)$$

These new values are entered in Table 6.T4.

TABLE 6.T4   Completed Second Simplex Tableau

C_j	Basic Variables	Basic Variable Values	0.14 I	0.15 M	0 s_1	0 s_2	0 s_3
0	s_1	3000	⓪.2	0	1	-1	0
0.15	M	75000	0.5	1	0	5	0
0	s_3	7500	.15	0	0	-1.5	1
	Z_j	11250	0.075	0.15	0	0.75	0
	$C_j - Z_j$		0.065	0	0	-0.75	0

Doing the calculations in this order preserves the structure associated with solving for s_1 in the top constraint and s_3 in the bottom constraint. The new objective function value is $(0 \times 3,000) + (0.15 \times 75,000) + (0 \times 7,500) = 11,250$. Before this change in the basic variables, the objective function value was 0. Because M's profit improvement rate is 0.15, the objective function value should increase by 0.15 times the amount that M is increased above 0. The limit on M's increase was calculated as 75,000. Thus, the objective function value should increase by $0.15 \times 75000 = 11,250$. That is *exactly* the amount of the increase in the objective function value. It increased from 0 to 11,250. Also, the basic variable values in Table 6.T4 are the same as the values we calculated above when we substituted $M = 75,000$.

The objective function value change

A change in the set of basic variables corresponds to an **iteration** or **step** of the simplex method. This change is also sometimes called a **pivot.**

Now, we must calculate the Z_j and $C_j - Z_j$ rows for Table 6.T4. The C_j values of the basic variables are changed, reflecting the change in the set of basic variables. The new profit forgone rate for I is

$$Z_1 = (0 \times 0.2) + (0.15 \times .5) + (0 \times 0.15) = .075$$

The profit forgone rate is the sum of the results of multiplying the objective function coefficients of the basic variables by the substitution coefficients.

The profit improvement rate for I is

$$C_1 - Z_1 = 0.14 - 0.075 = 0.065$$

Profit improvement rate for basic variables

The results of the calculation of the Z_j and the $C_j - Z_j$ for the other variables appear in Table 6.T4. The profit improvement rate is *always 0* for all of the basic variables in any tableau. The profit improvement rate for I is positive, so the optimal solution has not been found. Since I has the most positive (and in this case, the only positive) profit improvement rate, I's value is increased from its current value of 0. *Whenever a positive profit improvement rate exists for a nonbasic variable, you must do at least one more iteration.*

The new substitution coefficients for I in Table 6.T4 are 0.2, 0.5, and 0.15. The limit on the increase of I is the minimum of $(^{3,000}/_{0.2}, {}^{75,000}/_{0.5}, {}^{7,500}/_{0.15}) = (15,000, 150,000, 50,000)$, or 15,000. The pivot element, 0.2, is circled in Table 6.T4. The first basic variable, s_1, is replaced by the variable I in the partition.

The new tableau appears in Table 6.T5. First, the pivot row was divided by the pivot element. Then, all of the other rows were updated so that the entries in the column of the new basic variable, I, are 0. The new objective function value is $(0.14 \times 15,000) + (0.15 \times 67,500) + (0 \times 5,250) = 12,225$. The objective function value increases from 11,250

TABLE 6.T5   Third and Optimal Simplex Tableau

C_j	Basic Variables	Basic Variable Values	0.14 I	0.15 M	0 s_1	0 s_2	0 s_3
0.14	I	15000	1	0	5	−5	0
0.15	M	67500	0	1	−2.5	7.5	0
0	s_3	5250	0	0	−0.75	−0.75	1
	Z_j	12225	0.14	0.15	0.325	0.425	0
	$C_j - Z_j$		0	0	−0.325	−0.425	0

to 12,225 in this iteration. This increase of 975 is exactly the amount anticipated, $0.065 \times 15{,}000$, where 0.065 is the profit improvement rate for the entering variable and 15,000 is its new value. After calculating all of the Z_j and $C_j - Z_j$ values and entering them in Table 6.T5, all of the profit improvement rates are negative or 0. There is no nonbasic variable that increases the objective function value if the variable value increases above 0.

The optimal solution

The optimal solution has been found. *If there are no positive $C_j - Z_j$ values, the optimal solution has been found.* From Table 6.T5, the optimal value of the objective function is 12,225. The optimal values of the basic variables are $I = 15{,}000$, $M = 67{,}500$, and $s_3 = 5{,}250$. Because s_1 and s_2 are nonbasic variables, these values are 0.

The solution path corresponds to the corner point sequence of A to D to C in Figure 6.1. In Table 6.T1, both I and M had positive profit improvement rates. If I rather than M had become a basic variable in the first iteration, the optimal path would correspond to A to B to C. The same optimal solution would be obtained, but the path would be different. The solution path depends on the way the simplex method is implemented.

Reexamine the computer output for the Potato Processing example found in Table 5.3. The entries in the $C_j - Z_j$ row for the I and M variables are the same as the reduced costs. Also, the entries in the Z_j row for the slack variables are the same as the dual prices for the constraints. Different linear programming software implementations of the simplex algorithm and the treatment of models not in the standard form can cause some confusion, particularly about sign differences between the tableau values and the computer output values. However, the values in the Z_j row and the $C_j - Z_j$ row are the source of the dual price and reduced cost information, respectively. For LINDO, the $C_j - Z_j$ entries for the structural variables are the negatives of the reduced costs.

For a nonbasic variable, (1) if the profit improvement rate is positive, increasing the nonbasic variable's value increases the objective function value, (2) if the profit improvement rate is negative, increasing the nonbasic variable's value decreases the objective function value, and (3) if the profit improvement rate is 0, increasing the variable's value does not change the objective function value.

The existence of an *alternate optimal solution* is indicated if a nonbasic variable has a $C_j - Z_j$ equal to 0 in the final tableau. IBM's MPSX uses this test to identify variables that indicate an alternate optimal solution. But remember, if the optimal solution is degenerate, there may not be an alternate optimal solution even if a nonbasic variable has a $C_j - Z_j = 0$. When that nonbasic variable becomes a basic variable, the adjacent partition may correspond to the same corner point. If the optimal solution is not degenerate, however, the nonbasic variable becomes positive when it becomes a basic variable and an alternate optimal solution exists.

Alternate optimal solution indication

Unbounded Optimal Solution

We use the easy form of the model for the simplex method to illustrate an unbounded optimal solution. We discuss applying the simplex method to models that are not of the easy form in the next section. You identify an unbounded optimal solution in the same way for a model that is not of the easy form.

Consider applying the simplex method to the following model:

$$
\begin{aligned}
\max \quad & 2X + 3Y \\
\text{st} \quad & -X + Y \le 3 \\
& -2X + Y \le 2 \\
& X,\ Y \ge 0
\end{aligned}
$$

First, convert the model to equality form by adding slack variables to each of the inequalities. The two slack variables, s_1 and s_2, are the initial basic variables. Table 6.T6 is the initial simplex table. The profit improve-

TABLE 6.T6 Initial Simplex Tableau—Unbounded Example

C_j	Basic Variables	Basic Variable Values	2	3	0	0
			X	Y	s_1	s_2
0	s_1	3	-1	1	1	0
0	s_2	2	-2	①	0	1
	Z_j	0	0	0	0	0
	$C_j - Z_j$		2	3	0	0

ment rate is 2 for Variable X and 3 for Variable Y. Because the two profit improvement rates are positive, the optimal solution has not been found. Variable Y, the nonbasic variable with the largest profit improvement rate, is selected to become a basic variable. The limit on the increase of Variable Y from the first constraint is $\frac{3}{1} = 3$. The limit on the increase of Variable Y from the second constraint is $\frac{2}{1} = 2$. The smaller of the limits is 2, and the pivot element is the 1 circled in Table 6.T6.

The new pivot row is obtained by dividing the second row in Table 6.T6 by the pivot element, 1. Table 6.T7 shows this new simplex table. The new values for the first row are changed as follows:

$$(3, -1, 1, 1, 0) - 1.0(2, -2, 1, 0, 1) = (1, 1, 0, 1, -1)$$

The two basic variables are s_1 and Y, with objective function coefficients 0 and 3, respectively. The objective function value for the new corner point is 6. In Table 6.T7, only Variable X has a positive profit improvement rate, so it becomes a basic variable. The substitution coefficient for s_1 is 1. For each unit that X is increased, s_1 must decrease by 1. This sets a limit of $\frac{1}{1} = 1$. Because the substitution coefficient for Y is -2, for each unit that X is increased, the value of Y *increases* by 2. The second row imposes no limit on the increase of X. *A limit on the amount of the increase of a nonbasic variable is imposed by a row only if the substitution coefficient is positive.* There is only one limit, 1, and it is the pivot element circled in Table 6.T7.

After the pivot has been completed, the simplex tableau in Table 6.T8 is obtained. The objective function value is now 14. Is the new tableau optimal? No, s_2 has a positive profit improvement rate. In the two rows of Table 6.T8, the substitution coefficients of s_2 are both -1. For the first row, if the value of s_2 is increased by one unit, the value of X must increase by 1. Similarly, for the second row, if the value of s_2 is increased by one unit, the value of Y must increase by 1. Neither of the rows imposes a limit on the increase of s_2. If s_2 increases by 1 unit, the

Limits are imposed only by *positive* substitution coefficients

TABLE 6.T7   Second Simplex Tableau—Unbounded Example

C_j	Basic Variables	Basic Variable Values	2	3	0	0
			X	Y	s_1	s_2
0	s_1	1	①	0	1	-1
3	Y	2	-2	1	0	1
	Z_j	6	-6	3	0	3
	$C_j - Z_j$		8	0	0	-3

TABLE 6.T8 Final Simplex Tableau—Unbounded Example

C_j	Basic Variables	Basic Variable Values	2	3	0	0
			X	Y	s_1	s_2
2	X	1	1	0	1	-1
3	Y	4	0	1	2	-1
	Z_j	14	2	3	8	-5
	$C_j - Z_j$		0	0	-8	5

objective function value increases by 5, the profit improvement rate; if s_2 increases by 10 units, the objective function value increases by 50. Because there is no limit on the increase of Variable s_2, the objective function value can be made as large as desired. The model has an unbounded optimal solution.

Indication of unbounded optimal solution

If a nonbasic variable has a positive profit improvement rate and no positive substitution coefficients, the model has an *unbounded optimal solution*. Reexamine Table 6.T6, the initial simplex tableau for the unbounded example. Variable X has a positive profit improvement rate and no positive substitution coefficients. It is correct to stop at that indication and conclude that the model has an unbounded optimal solution.

Figure 6.T1 illustrates the feasible set for the unbounded example. The initial basic solution corresponds to the corner point labeled A. Increasing Y resulted in a movement up the Y axis to the corner point labeled B. Verify that the variable values correspond to those in Table 6.T7. Increasing X in the next simplex step resulted in movement from Corner Point B to Corner Point C (Table 6.T8); a movement along the line segment of the second constraint. Finally, increasing the value of s_2 from Corner Point C results in moving upward to the right along the first constraint. There is no limit on how much s_2 can be increased, because another constraint is not encountered.

At the first iteration, if Variable X rather than Variable Y had been increased, movement would have been along the X axis. In that case, you would have determined immediately that the model had an unbounded optimal solution. Because there are no positive substitution coefficients, there is no limit on how much X can be increased; another constraint is not encountered. Note that the absence of a positive substitution coefficient does not solely determine that the model has an unbounded optimal solution; the profit improvement rate of the nonbasic variable without positive substitution coefficients also must be positive.

FIGURE 6.T1   Solution Path for Unbounded Optimal Solution Example

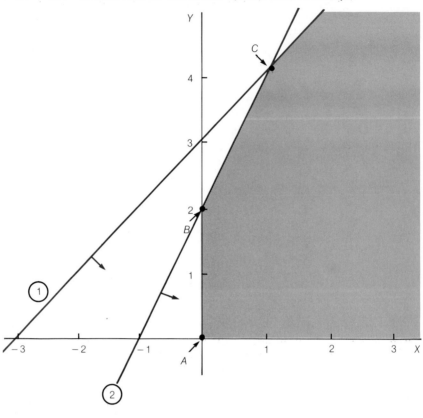

Computer systems provide various information after determining that a model has an unbounded optimal solution. At a minimum, they report the variable that indicates an unbounded optimal solution. Many systems also report the basic variables for the tableau that gives the indication of such a solution. Some systems give only the basic variables with nonzero substitution coefficients.

Models Not of the Easy Form and No Feasible Solution

The previous examples in this Theory section are all of the easy form. The constraints are all of the ≤ type, and all of the RHS constants are nonnegative. This ensures that the origin is a feasible point, that there is a slack variable for each constraint, and that the slack variables can be used as the initial set of basic variables. If the initial set of basic variables is all the slack variables, they are already "solved for" in the initial tableau. Each slack variable has a coefficient of +1 in one row and 0 in all other rows. We start at the origin, even though it's unlikely to be optimal, because this is easier than starting at another point. If you choose some other initial set of basic variables, then you must first solve for those variables, and this may be impossible or some value may be negative. If you aren't successful, you must try another initial set of basic variables. We prefer to start at the origin, rather than find a starting point by trial and error.

If the model is not of the easy form, the origin is not a feasible point. Thus, you can't start at the origin and have only nonnegative variable values. If the model is not of the easy form, we *derive* another model that has the same optimal solution, but for which the origin is feasible.

Figure 6.T2 has a flowchart of the five steps used to develop the derived model. The first two steps use algebraic manipulations from Chapter 4. *First,* if the model has a minimization objective function, convert the model to an equivalent maximization model by multiplying it by −1. Although it is possible to modify the simplex algorithm so that a minimization model can be solved directly, it is less confusing to convert the minimization model to a maximization model. *Second,* convert the model constraints so that all of the RHS constants are nonnegative. If the RHS constant is negative, multiply the constraint by −1. *Third,* convert

Five steps for the derived model

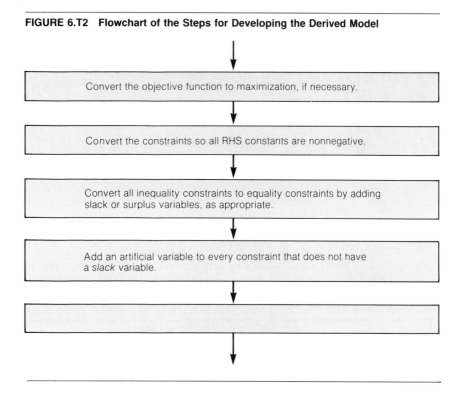

FIGURE 6.T2   Flowchart of the Steps for Developing the Derived Model

all of the inequality constraints to equations by adding appropriate slack or surplus variables. *Fourth,* add an artifical variable to every constraint that does not have a *slack* variable. Even if there is a surplus variable, an artificial variable must be added. *Fifth,* give each artificial variable an objective function coefficient of $-M$, where M represents a very large number.

The origin is a feasible solution for the derived model. By construction, each constraint contains either a slack variable or an artificial variable and all of the RHS constants are nonnegative. The initial set of basic variables includes either the slack or the artifical variable for each constraint, whichever the model contains. Then, you use the simplex algorithm on the derived problem, starting at the origin. Because the objective function is to be maximized and artificial variables have objective function coefficients that are large negative numbers, the simplex algorithm tries to make all of the artificial variable values equal to 0.

Consider the example

$$
\begin{aligned}
\max \quad & 2X + 3Y \\
\text{st} \quad & -X + Y = 3 \\
& -2X - Y \geq -2 \\
& X,\ Y \geq 0
\end{aligned}
$$

The objective function is to maximize, so the first step is not necessary. The RHS constant for the first constraint is not negative, but the RHS constant for the second constraint is negative. Multiplying the second constraint by -1, the second constraint becomes

$$2X + Y \leq 2$$

Because the second constraint is now $\leq$, the third step requires adding a slack variable. The constraints are now

$$
\begin{aligned}
\text{st} \quad & -X + Y = 3 \\
& 2X + Y + s_1 = 2
\end{aligned}
$$

Because there is a slack variable for the second constraint, an artificial variable is not added to it. Because there is no slack variable for the first constraint, an artificial variable must be added to it. Say that we call the artificial variable A_1. The derived model is

$$
\begin{aligned}
\max \quad & 2X + 3Y - MA_1 \\
\text{st} \quad & -X + Y + A_1 = 3 \\
& 2X + Y + s_1 = 2 \\
& X,\ Y,\ s_1,\ A_1 \geq 0
\end{aligned}
$$

The objective function of A_1 is $-M$. M is not a variable; it is the penalty paid because A_1 is positive. Think of it as a very large number, such as 1 million. Whenever A_1 is positive, its contribution to the objective function value is negative. As the objective function is maximized, the simplex

Artificial variable
values and feasible
solutions

algorithm tries to eliminate Variable A_1 from the set of basic variables so that its value becomes 0. *If an artificial variable has a positive value in a solution, the solution is not a feasible solution to the original model.* If all of the artificial variables have zero values for a solution, the solution is feasible for the original model. Also, *if an optimal solution to the derived problem has all artificial variables equal to 0, the solution is optimal for the original model.*

Table 6.T9 contains the initial tableau with the basic variables A_1 and s_1. The initial values of A_1 and s_1 are 3 and 2, respectively. The substitution coefficients are identical to the coefficients of the derived model. The objective function value corresponding to the initial solution is $-3M$. Because M is a very large number, the objective function value is very negative. Hopefully, this is not the maximum objective function value. The initial solution to the derived model is not feasible for the original model. Calculating the profit forgone rate for Variable X yields M. The profit improvement rate of X is its $C_j - Z_j$ or $(2 - M)$. If M is a very large number, the profit improvement rate of X is negative. The profit improvement rate for Variable Y is $(3 + M)$. Because M is a very large number, Y's profit improvement rate is positive. In fact, because Y is the only variable with a positive profit improvement rate, its current value of 0 is increased and it becomes a basic variable. The first row of Table 6.T9 imposes a limit of $3/1 = 3$; the second row imposes a limit of $2/1 = 2$. The smallest limit is 2. The pivot element is the 1 circled in Table 6.T9.

After the pivot has been completed, Table 6.T10 is obtained. The basic variables are now A_1 and Y. The value of the artificial variable is only 1. The basic solution of Table 6.T10 is closer to being feasible than the basic solution of Table 6.T9. This can be seen from the objective function value. The value in Table 6.T9 is $-3M$; the constraints are unsatisfied by the amount of the M term, 3. The value in Table 6.T10 is $6 - M$; the constraints are unsatisfied by the amount of the M term, 1. The profit improvement rates appear in Table 6.T10. Because none of these rates are

---

TABLE 6.T9   Initial Simplex Tableau—Artificial Variable Example

C_j	Basic Variables	Basic Variable Values	2	3	$-M$	0
			X	Y	A_1	s_1
$-M$	A_1	3	-1	1	1	0
0	s_1	2	2	①	0	1
	Z_j	$-3M$	M	$-M$	$-M$	0
	$C_j - Z_j$		$2 - M$	$3 + M$	0	0

TABLE 6.T10   Final Simplex Tableau—Artificial Variable Example: No Feasible Solution

C_j Basic Variables	Basic Variable Values	2 X	3 Y	$-M$ A_1	0 s_1
$-M$ A_1	1	-3	0	1	-1
3 Y	2	2	1	0	1
Z_j	$6 - M$	$6 + 3M$	3	$-M$	$3 + M$
$C_j - Z_j$		$-4 - 3M$	0	0	$-3 - M$

positive, the simplex algorithm stops. The basic variables in the final tableau are A_1 and Y with values of 1 and 2, respectively. The values of X and s_1 are 0 because X and s_1 are nonbasic.

If the final tableau of the derived model for the simplex method has at least one artificial variable as a basic variable with a positive value, the original model has no feasible solution. Substituting $X = 0$ and $Y = 2$ into the original model shows that the first constraint is not satisfied. The optimal solution to the derived model is not feasible for the original model. The original model has "no feasible solution."

Figure 6.T3 shows the simplex algorithm's path. Note that it is impossible to satisfy all of the constraints and variable nonnegativities. The initial point is the origin, labeled A. The next point (Table 6.T10) is labeled B. B is closer to satisfying all of the constraints than A. The simplex algorithm stops at B. There is no point closer to satisfying all of the constraints; that is, B has the minimum sum of the infeasibilities.

There is no feasible solution for our derived model example. For correctly formulated models, however, there are feasible solutions. Then, the simplex method eliminates the artificial variables from the basic variable set during the iterations and terminates with the optimal solution to the original model.

The above treatment of artificial variables is called the **Big M Method.** This method is convenient for solving models "by hand." M is an unspecified number that is big enough to enable the M term to always dominate in the $C_j - Z_j$ row. For computer implementation, a numerical value of M must be assigned. But no matter what value is assigned to M, it is possible to construct an example in which the value of M is not big enough to enable the M term to dominate the entries in the $C_j - Z_j$ row. This difficulty provides the motivation for the **Two-Phase Method.** In Phase 1,

No feasible solution indication

Big M Method

Two-Phase Method

FIGURE 6.T3 Solution Path for No Feasible Solution Example

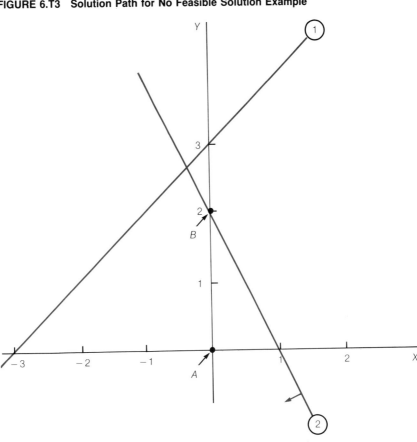

the objective is to minimize the sum of the artificial variable values. That sum is the sum of the infeasibilities. If at the end of Phase 1 the sum of the artificial variable values is 0, a feasible solution to the original model has been obtained. Then, in Phase 2, the solution obtained at the end of Phase 1 is the initial solution. The objective function is reset to the original objective function, and the simplex method is applied again. If the sum of the infeasibilities at the end of Phase 1 is greater than 0, there is no feasible solution to the original model and Phase 2 is not done.

Different implementations of the simplex method provide various information after a model has been determined to have no feasible solution. One possibility is to report the rows corresponding to artificial variables that were basic variables in the final tableau. For the Two-Phase Method,

---

TABLE 6.T11   Summary of the Simplex Algorithm

1. Construct the initial tableau.
    a. Convert the objective to maximization, if necessary.
    b. Make all RHS constants nonnegative, by multiplying constraints by -1, if necessary.
    c. Add slack and surplus variables as needed to convert all inequalities to equations.
    d. Add an artificial variable to each constraint that does not have a *slack* variable.
    e. Give each artificial variable an objective function coefficient of $-M$, where M is a very large number.
    f. The initial set of basic variables is the slack and artificial variables.

2. Perform simplex algorithm iterations.
    a. Complete the table calculations. Find the most positive $C_j - Z_j$; this variable becomes a basic variable. If no $C_j - Z_j$ is positive, go to Step 3.
    b. For the variable selected in Step 2a, calculate row-by-row, the ratio of the basic variable value to the substitution coefficient. Ignoring all ratios with a substitution coefficient that is negative or 0, find the smallest ratio. This specifies the pivot element and the basic variable that leaves the basic set and becomes nonbasic. If there are no positive substitution coefficients, stop; the model has an unbounded optimal solution.
    c. Update the tableau by converting the pivot element to $+1$ and all other coefficients for the new basic variable to 0. Return to Step 2a.

3. Analyze the solutions.
    a. If an artificial variable is a basic variable and has a positive value, stop; the original model has no feasible solution. Otherwise, the optimal solution has been found.
    b. The indication of an alternate optimal solution is a $C_j - Z_j = 0$ for a nonbasic variable. You find that solution by selecting the nonbasic variable to become a basic variable and repeating Steps 2b and 2c.

---

another possibility is to report the constraints that change the sum of the infeasibilities if their RHS constants change. These constraints are the ones with nonzero dual prices at the end of Phase 1.

Table 6.T11 summarizes the steps of the simplex algorithm. The steps fall into three overall stages: constructing the initial tableau, performing the iterations, and analyzing the solution after the iterations stop.

Simplex algorithm summary

Karmarkar's Method

The two steps of an
iteration

In 1984, N. Karmarkar reported a new method for finding optimal solutions to linear programming models.[1] Preliminary testing indicates that this method on *some* linear programming models requires less computer time than the simplex algorithm. In this section, we present an overview of the method.

The simplex algorithm's solution path is from corner point to adjacent corner point. The sequence of points is on the exterior edges of the feasible set. Karmarkar's method follows a path on the interior of the feasible set.

The new method is initialized by deriving another linear programming model. You introduce one artificial variable so that a solution with all variable values (including the artificial variable) equal to 1 is feasible. We represent this feasible point of the derived problem by P_0.

Two steps are performed for each iteration. *First,* a new point (called P_1) is generated that (1) improves the objective function value, (2) is feasible, and (3) is close to the edge of the feasible set. *Second,* the problem is transformed. The transformation redefines the variables so that at Point P_1 they are all equal to 1. The transformed Point P_1 lies in the interior of the feasible set for the transformed problem.

Each iteration generates a new point and transforms the problem. When successive points are close to each other, the iterations stop. After the positive-valued variables of the original model have been identified, an associated partition is found and the standard output report is generated.

Karmarkar's method is a polynomial time algorithm. That is, you can show that the time required to solve a linear programming model with n variables is *at most an^b,* for some constants a and b. The simplex algorithm is an exponential time algorithm. That is, you can show that the

---

[1] N. Karmarkar, "A New Polynomial Time Algorithm for Linear Programming," *Combinatorica* 4, no. 4 (1984), pp. 373–95.

time required to solve a linear programming model with n variables is *at most $c2^n$,* for some constant c. For a large n, the maximum time grows slower for Karmarkar's method than for the simplex algorithm. Fortunately, the actual time required by the simplex algorithm is much smaller than the maximum time. Remember, the number of points on the solution path is usually between 2 and 3 times the number of constraints.

Additional testing and development of Karmarkar's method must be done before we can conclude that it is better than the simplex algorithm. Preliminary results show great promise, particularly for models with special mathematical structures. The next generation of linear programming software may use Karmarkar's method. If it does, the solution path would be different, but the output reports and their analysis would be unchanged.[2]

---

[2] See J. N. Hooker, "Karmarkar's Linear Programming Algorithm," *Interfaces* 16, no. 4, (July–August 1986), pp. 75–90, for more information on Karmarkar's method.

7

More Linear Programming Models

A Multiple-Product Blending Model
Model Formulation / Model Solution Analysis / Model
Manipulations and Extensions

Multiple-Period Models
Model Formulation / Model Solution Analysis / Model
Manipulations and Extensions

Transportation Model
Model Formulation / Model Solution Analysis / Model
Manipulations and Extensions

Generalization of the Machine Assignment Model to Several Plants
Model Formulation / Model Solution Analysis / Model
Manipulations and Extensions

Piecewise Linear Costs
Model Formulation for the Machine Assignment Model / Model
Solution Analysis / Model Manipulations and Extensions

Personnel Scheduling Model
Model Formulation / Model Solution Analysis / Model
Manipulations and Extensions

Multiple Objectives, Goal Programming, and Deviational Variables
A Cost Minimization Model Formulation for Media
Selection / The Cost Minimization Model's Solution
Analysis / Reformulation as a Goal Programming Model / The
Goal Programming Model's Solution Analysis / Priority Goal
Programming

Case: Racy's Department Store

Case: Technicon Corporation

NORTH AMERICAN VAN LINES, INC.

North American Van Lines, Inc. has over 3,300 tractors in its independent owner-operator fleet. The owner-operators purchase their tractor equipment and provide lease service of that equipment to North American Van Lines. The Fleet Administration Division of North American Van Lines has the primary responsibility for recruiting and training contract truckers, selling tractors to those truckers, purchasing new tractors from manufacturers, and trading in used tractors to manufacturers. The division's primary objective is to minimize the cost of maintaining and carrying the tractors. Among the factors that the division considers are economic returns from the sale and trade-ins of tractors, training capacities for new operators, forecasts of required shipments, availability of new and used tractors, manufacturers' contractual requirements, and financing arrangements.

Previously, Fleet Administration manually developed a plan based on forecasts of required shipments. Then, it used a manual system to evaluate the financial impact of the plan. The manual system only evaluated a given plan; it didn't find the best plan. Because, using this system, it took three weeks to do the necessary financial calculations, Fleet Administration could not try enough plans to be sure it had found the best one.

Later, Fleet Administration developed a linear programming model that finds the best plan. The linear programming model plans one year into the future. Because the required shipments vary seasonally, it was necessary to get information on the timing of shipments within the year. The one-year time horizon of the model was divided into 13 four-week time periods to get information on the timing. For each four-week time period, the model recommends the number of new operators to train, the number of each model of tractor to purchase, and the number of tractors to trade in. The computerized system included modules for maintaining input parameters, generating the linear programming model, and creating fleet development reports, tractor sales and warranty reports, and used truck allowance reports.

Through the computerized system, which cost $100,000 to develop, the average inventory of tractors was decreased by $3 million, resulting in a savings of $600,000 annually. The computerized system also provided more timely information for decision making since it can develop as many as three new plans in a single day. For example, Fleet Administration can adjust the requirements forecasts and then determine how such adjustments affect the best plan.

D. Avramovich, T. Cook, G. Langston, and F. Sutherland, "A Decision Support System for Fleet Management: A Linear Programming Approach," *Interfaces* 12, no. 3 (June 1982), pp. 1–19.

Linear programming models have many applications in decision making. At the opening of this and previous chapters, we described a few of the successful applications. Let's review some of them. At the opening of this chapter, we described how North American Van Lines used linear programming for fleet planning. In previous chapters, we described some linear programming applications in finance. Central Carolina Bank and Trust used linear programming to "optimize" its balance sheet. New England Leasing used linear programming to plan its lease portfolio.

There are many linear programming applications in production and operations planning. Air Products and Chemicals used linear programming to assign customers to depots. Owens-Corning Fiberglas used it to plan production at its Anderson, South Carolina, plant. National Airlines used it to plan fuel purchases on its flight segments.

Linear programming also has applications in personnel planning, marketing, and other business areas. In this chapter, we discuss such additional applications of linear programming models. By studying examples provided, you will learn these applications and improve your model formulation skills. These examples also provide you with opportunities for analyzing model output. We discuss the manipulations and extensions of all the models shown.

The examples also teach us the following important lessons about linear programming models:

1. The mathematical structure of such models is important.
2. Definitional variables make output interpretation and sensitivity analysis easier.
3. Static, single-period models are linked into dynamic, multiple-period models.
4. Using a secondary objective, such models can be employed to choose from among alternate optimal solutions.
5. There are several approaches for decision problems with multiple objectives.

A MULTIPLE-PRODUCT BLENDING MODEL

In Chapter 3, we described two types of blending models. The strategic blending application determines the least cost for a standard unit without limits on the availability of the blending stocks. The operational blending application determines how to blend limited amounts of blending stocks to maximize profit for an order.

Say that the same blending stocks are used to blend multiple products. For the strategic blending application without limits on the availability of the blending stocks, you treat the products independently. That is, you construct and solve a separate model for each product.

You can't plan the products independently

However, if limited amounts of the blending stocks are available, you can't treat the products independently. By using some amounts of the blending stocks for one product, you affect the amounts available for the other products. The products must share the available blending stocks. You must build a model that includes all of the products. You can't construct and solve a separate model for each product.

In Chapter 3, the operational blending model mixes three blending stocks—butane, naphtha, and reformate—into regular gasoline. Say that you can also blend butane, naphtha, and reformate into premium gasoline. Recall that for regular gasoline the minimum octane number is 87 and that the maximum vapor pressure is 6.5 pounds per square inch (psi). For premium gasoline the minimum octane number is 91 and the maximum vapor pressure is 6.9 psi. A cut-rate supplier has offered to buy up to 30,000 barrels of regular gasoline at $1.20 per gallon and up to 5,000 barrels of premium gasoline at $1.27 per gallon. Table 7.1 summarizes the information on the tank contents and the cut-rate supplier's offers.

The price offered for premium gasoline is higher than that offered for regular gasoline, but premium gasoline requires a greater proportion of reformate. If more reformate is blended into premium gasoline, less is available for blending into regular gasoline. Because the high octane number of reformate offsets the low octane number of butane, if less reformate is available for regular gasoline, then less butane can be

TABLE 7.1 Data for Two-Product Blending Example

	Tank Contents		
	Butane	Naphtha	Reformate
Barrels	22,000	10,000	14,000
Octane number	85.0	89.0	92.0
Vapor pressure	3.0	8.7	11.0
Cost, $/barrel	36.00	48.00	51.00

Regular Gasoline Requested

Barrels (up to)	30,000
Octane number	87.0
Vapor pressure	6.5
Price, $/gallon	1.20

Premium Gasoline Requested

Barrels (up to)	5,000
Octane number	91.0
Vapor pressure	6.9
Price, $/gallon	1.27

blended into regular gasoline. Note also that butane costs less than reformate. To find the best blending plan, we must formulate a model that includes both regular and premium gasoline.

Model Formulation

Let's use Chapter 3's three-step method to formulate the symbolic model. First, we give the verbal model. Second, we define the variables. Third, we construct the symbolic model.

Verbal model. The verbal model is an extension of Chapter 3's verbal model for regular gasoline.

maximize total profit from regular gasoline and premium gasoline
subject to number of barrels of butane used $\leq$ 22000
number of barrels of naphtha used $\leq$ 10000
number of barrels of reformate used $\leq$ 14000
number of barrels of regular gasoline blended $\leq$ 30000
octane number of regular gasoline blended $\geq$ 87
vapor pressure of regular gasoline blended $\leq$ 6.5
number of barrels of premium gasoline blended $\leq$ 5000
octane number of premium gasoline blended $\geq$ 91
vapor pressure of premium gasoline blended $\leq$ 6.9

Decision variables. It is necessary to distinguish between butane blended into regular gasoline and butane blended into premium gasoline. The decision variables are as follows:

BR—number of barrels of butane blended into regular gasoline
BP—number of barrels of butane blended into premium gasoline
NR—number of barrels of naphtha blended into regular gasoline
NP—number of barrels of naphtha blended into premium gasoline
RR—number of barrels of reformate blended into regular gasoline
RP—number of barrels of reformate blended into premium gasoline

We develop the model using these variables. If the variables for the number of barrels of regular gasoline blended and of premium gasoline blended are also defined, sensitivity analysis is easier. By omitting these variables in our formulation at this time, we illustrate their advantage. See the gasoline blending example in Chapter 3 for an example of the use of this type of variable.

Symbolic model. The symbolic model using the six variables listed above is

max $14.4BR + 2.4NR - 0.6RR + 17.34BP + 5.34NP + 2.34RP$
st $BR + BP \leq 22000$
$NR + NP \leq 10000$

$$RR + RP \le 14000$$
$$BR + NR + RR \le 30000$$
$$-2BR + 2NR + 5RR \ge 0$$
$$-3.5BR + 2.2NR + 4.5RR \le 0$$
$$BP + NP + RP \le 5000$$
$$-6BP - 2NP + 1RP \ge 0$$
$$-3.9BP + 1.8NP + 4.1RP \le 0$$
$$BR,\ NR,\ RR,\ BP,\ NP,\ RP \ge 0$$

Algebraic manipulations are required so that the quality constraints contain linear constraint functions. Chapter 3 details the manipulations for the octane number constraint for regular gasoline. The coefficients of the quality constraints are the deviations from the quality specifications. For example, the maximum vapor pressure of butane is 3.0. The -3.9 coefficient in the last constraint shows that this is 3.9 psi less than the limit for premium gasoline, 6.9.

Model Solution Analysis

Next, we analyze the output for the optimal solution shown in Table 7.2. The maximum profit is \$303,428.60. The barrels of butane, naphtha, and reformate that are blended into regular gasoline are 21,428.57, 0, and 8,571.429, respectively. How many barrels of regular gasoline are

Using slack/surplus variable values to simplify calculations

blended? This amount can be calculated as $BR + NR + RR = 21,428.57 + 8,571.429 + 0 = 30,000$ barrels.[1] Alternatively, because the slack for Row 5, the regular gasoline blending limitation, is 0, the amount blended is $30,000 - 0 = 30,000$ barrels.

The octane number of the regular gasoline blended is calculated as

$$85\left(\frac{21,428.57}{30,000}\right) + 89\left(\frac{0}{30,000}\right) + 92\left(\frac{8571.43}{30,000}\right) = 87.0$$

An easier method of determining the octane number of the regular gasoline blended is to note that the value of the surplus variable for Row 6, the regular gasoline octane number constraint, is 0; this means that the octane number is at the limit, 87. For the regular gasoline vapor pressure limitation, Row 7's slack variable is 36,428.57, so the blend's vapor pressure is $36,428.57/30,000 = 1.2142$ less than the 6.5 limitation. The vapor pressure of the regular gasoline blended is $6.5 - 1.214 = 5.286$.

How much premium gasoline is blended? Because the slack variable of Row 8 is 5,000, you calculate the amount of premium gasoline blended as $5,000 - 5,000 = 0$. From the output in Table 7.2, it is difficult to

---

[1] Computer rounding errors cause the difference between the sum and 30,000. Numerical values are rounded in the discussion of the output.

TABLE 7.2 LOOK ALL and GO Output for Two-Product Blending Example

```
MAX      14.4 BR + 2.4 NR - 0.6 RR + 17.34 BP + 5.34 NP + 2.34 RP
SUBJECT TO
        2)    BR + BP <=    22000
        3)    NR + NP <=    10000
        4)    RR + RP <=    14000
        5)    BR + NR + RR <=    30000
        6) - 2 BR + 2 NR + 5 RR >=   0
        7) - 3.5 BR + 2.2 NR + 4.5 RR <=    0
        8)    BP + NP + RP <=    5000
        9) - 6 BP - 2 NP + RP >=   0
       10) - 3.9 BP + 1.8 NP + 4.1 RP <=    0
END
               OBJECTIVE FUNCTION VALUE

   1)        303428.600

VARIABLE          VALUE          REDUCED COST
       BR      21428.570000          .000000
       NR           .000000         3.428571
       RR       8571.429000          .000000
       BP           .000000          .000000
       NP           .000000         5.139421
       RP           .000000          .000000

     ROW    SLACK OR SURPLUS      DUAL PRICES
        2)      571.428200          .000000
        3)    10000.000000          .000000
        4)     5428.571000          .000000
        5)          .000000        10.114290
        6)          .000000        -2.142857
        7)    36428.570000          .000000
        8)     5000.000000          .000000
        9)          .000000        -3.875362
       10)          .000000         1.515942



     RANGES IN WHICH THE BASIS IS UNCHANGED

                        OBJ COEFFICIENT RANGES
VARIABLE         CURRENT        ALLOWABLE        ALLOWABLE
                  COEF          INCREASE         DECREASE
       BR      14.400000        INFINITY         8.000000
       NR       2.400000        3.428571         INFINITY
       RR       -.600000       15.000000         6.000000
       BP      17.340000        INFINITY        10.638600
       NP       5.340000        5.139421         INFINITY
       RP       2.340000        INFINITY         5.230000

                        RIGHTHAND SIDE RANGES
     ROW         CURRENT        ALLOWABLE        ALLOWABLE
                  RHS           INCREASE         DECREASE
        2     22000.000000      INFINITY          571.428200
        3     10000.000000      INFINITY        10000.000000
        4     14000.000000      INFINITY         5428.571000
        5     30000.000000       799.999500     30000.000000
        6          .000000     31875.000000      3999.997000
        7          .000000      INFINITY        36428.570000
        8      5000.000000      INFINITY         5000.000000
        9          .000000          .000000      2885.016000
       10          .000000     11828.560000          .000000
```

determine why no premium gasoline is blended. The SLACK OR SUR-PLUS column shows that 571.43, 10,000, and 5,428.57 barrels of butane, naphtha, and reformate, respectively, are not blended. Since a barrel contains 42 gallons, the revenue per barrel of premium gasoline is $1.27 × 42 = $53.34. Possibly, premium gasoline would be blended if the price offered by the cut-rate supplier were higher. If the definitional variable P, the number of barrels of premium gasoline blended, had been included in the formulation, you could examine the maximum allowable increase of its objective function coefficient. Without that definitional variable, if the price offer increases, the coefficients on BP, NP, and RP increase at the same time. The 100 Percent Rule does not answer the question. If the 100 Percent Rule is satisfied, the solution does not change. However, if the 100 Percent Rule is not satisfied, the solution need not change. In this case, the maximum allowable increase for NP's objective function coefficient is 5.139. Even if the coefficient increases by more than that, the solution may not change, because BP and RP's coefficients also change. In this case, the reason for not blending premium gasoline is that the quality specifications cannot be satisfied from the blending stocks available. You can check this by adding the constraint $BP + NP + RP \geq 1$, which forces the blending of at least 1 barrel of premium gasoline, and observing that there is no feasible solution.

Why isn't premium gasoline blended?

Increasing the regular gasoline order size

If the cut-rate supplier increases the potential order size of regular gasoline to 35,000 barrels, should you blend 35,000 barrels? The dual price of Row 5, the order size limitation, is $10.11429. The profit improves (increases) by $10.11429 for each additional barrel of the regular gasoline sales limitation *if the increase is within the allowable range*. Because the maximum allowable increase of Row 5's RHS constant is 800 barrels, an increase of 5,000 barrels is outside the allowable range. You can be confident that you can profitably provide 30,800 barrels of regular gasoline, resulting in a profit of $311,520.03 (303,428.60 + 10.11429 × 800). The model must be re-solved with 35,000 as the RHS constant of Row 5 to determine whether blending the entire order is worthwhile.

Unique optimal solution

Is the optimal solution unique? Because no objective function coefficient has a maximum allowable increase or decrease equal to 0, the optimal solution is unique. Also, note that because the optimal solution has seven positive variables and nine constraints, the optimal solution is degenerate.

Cost and price changes

In Chapter 3, we showed that introducing a variable for regular gasoline makes simple sensitivity analysis easier. When you change the selling price of the gasoline, only that variable's objective function coefficient changes. Without that variable, three coefficients change. In Chapter 3, you could determine the impact of a blending stock cost change even without the additional variable. How does the multiple-product model change if the cost of butane changes? Two objective function coefficients change—BR and BP. Simple sensitivity analysis is possible if you introduce an additional variable for each blending stock—*B, N,* and *R.* Adding these variables also makes it easier to understand what is happening at a glance. For example, how much butane is used in Table 7.2? You can calculate this as $BR + BP = 21,428.57 + 0 = 21,428.57.$ If you had used the *B* variable in the model, the output would have answered the question without the addition. *Models that include definitional variables are easier to analyze.*

Model Manipulations and Extensions

By grouping the related variables and constraints, it is possible to see the underlying structure of the multiple-product blending problem. **The structure** of a linear programming model is the pattern of nonzero coefficients and the placement of $+1$ and -1 coefficients. If you understand a model's structure, it's easier to generalize the model. Many computer systems have commands that produce a compact picture of the model. Such a picture helps you examine the underlying structure of the model and is useful for model verification. The picture generally represents nonzero coefficients of the model by a single character and a sign. The LINDO command PIC produces the compact picture, and Figure 7.1 contains that output for the multiple-product blending model. LINDO represents an integer coefficient between 1 and 9 by the integer. Otherwise, the single character representing a coefficient's value is represented by a letter that corresponds to a range of numerical values. (Typing HELP PIC provides these correspondences.) A blank represents a value of 0. The many " ' " marks on the LINDO output draw "lines" on the picture, so that the row and column of the nonzero coefficients can be identified for a large sparse model.

The picture of a given model often provides insight into the generalization of the model. Examination of Figure 7.1 indicates that Rows 5, 6, and

Model structure

Generalizing the model

FIGURE 7.1   Picture of Two-Product Blending Example—LINDO PIC Command

```
 : pic


        B N R B N R
        R R R P P P

   1: B A-T B A A MAX
   2: 1       1     < E
   3: ' 1'    ' 1'  < D
   4:     1 '    1 < E
   5: 1 1 1 '       < E
   6:-2 2'5 '  '  '  >
   7:-A A A '      <
   8:        1 1 1 < D
   9: '  '  -6-2'1 >
  10:      -A A A <
```

7 correspond to regular gasoline and that rows 8, 9, and 10 correspond to premium gasoline. The first three columns of the figure, *BR, NR,* and *RR,* correspond to the decision variables for blending regular gasoline. The next three columns correspond to the decision variables for blending premium gasoline. Suppose that we want to modify the model for a third product. How can we generalize the structure for a third product? This generalization and others are explored in the exercises at the end of the chapter.

Say that another blending stock is available for the multiple-product blending problem. Columns *BR* and *BP* of Figure 7.1 correspond to decision variables for the butane blending stock. If there were a fourth blending stock, how would the structure change?

Rows 6 and 7 correspond to quality specifications for regular gasoline, and Rows 9 and 10 correspond to quality specifications for premium gasoline. If there were an additional quality specification for the two products, how would the model structure change?

MULTIPLE-PERIOD MODELS

North American Van Lines used a one-year time horizon for its linear programming model. If the model contained only one time period, the decision variables would tell what to do during the year but not when to do it within the year. For example, a decision variable would be the number of tractors to buy during the *entire* year. By dividing the year into four-week periods, North American Van Lines got information on the timing within the year. For example, one decision variable was the number of tractors to buy during the first four weeks of the year.

All of the models we've developed so far have been single-period models. The decisions are what to do during a specified period of time, not the timing within the period. You get more information on timing by subdividing the time horizon and building a multiple-period model. Because the required shipments of North American Van Lines vary depending on the season, it was important to use a multiple-period model with shorter time periods.

In Chapter 3, we developed a one-period machine assignment model that found the number of hours each machine should make each type of cup next week. The presumption of this model is that the machines are available every week, and you solve the model every week with updated values for cup requirements, hours of machine availability, operating costs, and production rates. Plans for each week are considered independently. In weeks of low cup requirements, some machine capacity is unused, and in weeks of high cup requirements, extra machine time is needed.

A multiple-period model explicitly includes the interdependencies of successive weeks' decisions. For example, extra cups produced in a week of low requirements can be stored for sale in a future week of high requirements. Thus, the amounts in inventory link the weekly models. We use a multiple-period production planning model to show how to build multiple-period models.

Because the amounts in inventory link the periods, the inventory storage costs are considered. Some companies lease warehouse space, others use their own warehouses, and still others do both. There are costs

Types of storage costs

for storage, but it is important not to include fixed costs. If warehouse space is leased, the cost is often based on the space used and on the length of time in storage. For both types of storage, include a charge for the capital cost of the items in inventory. For warehouse space owned by the company, the material handling cost is a *variable operating cost*. This is likely to be a onetime cost that is independent of the length of time in storage. Storage space leasing costs and capital costs depend on the length of time in storage. Usually, the inventory cost is assessed based on the number of items in inventory at the end of each period. This implies that the storage cost is linear in the amount of time that the items are stored. *This is reasonable only if material handling costs are small relative to the costs that vary with the time in storage.*

Assume inventory costs linear in time stored

First, we illustrate linking time periods with inventory variables, based on the assumption that *inventory costs are linear in the amount of time stored*. In the Model Manipulations and Extensions section, we modify the model if inventory costs are not linear in time stored.

A simple model is used, so that converting a static model into a dynamic model is not obscured by other details. The approach is also applicable for linking complex static models.

Model Formulation

A company is planning its production of Cutesy dolls for the next four months. The requirements for the next four months are 1,000, 1,050, 800, and 900, respectively. At the end of the current month, 100 units are in inventory and are available to help satisfy the next four months' requirements. The capacities for the next four months are 1,000, 1,000, 1,000, and 750, respectively. The capacity is less in the last month because of a one-week vacation shutdown. The manufacturing cost per unit is now $12, but it will rise to $12.60 per unit for Months 3 and 4. Say that the annual inventory carrying cost is assessed at 20 percent of the manufacturing cost. The annual holding cost per unit for Months 1 and 2 is ($12 × 0.2), or $2.40 per unit. The monthly holding cost per unit in inventory at the end of Months 1 and 2 is $\$2.40/12 = \$0.20$. In Months 3 and 4, this is $(\$12.60 \times 0.2)/12$, or $0.21.

The preferred model

Formulate the *preferred* model by the three-step method. Other model formulations exist with the same solution but are less convenient to use.

Verbal model. If it is necessary (and possible) to satisfy the requirements in each month, then the total revenue received is a constant. In that case, maximizing profits and minimizing costs are equivalent. We choose as the objective function minimizing the total of the production costs and the inventory costs during the next four months. Constraints result from the monthly capacity limits and the monthly requirements. The verbal model is

minimize   total of production costs and inventory costs during the next four months

subject to   number of units produced in Month 1 ≤ 1000
number of units produced in Month 2 ≤ 1000
number of units produced in Month 3 ≤ 1000
number of units produced in Month 4 ≤ 750
number of units furnished for the requirement of Month 1 = 1000
number of units furnished for the requirement of Month 2 = 1050
number of units furnished for the requirement of Month 3 = 800
number of units furnished for the requirement of Month 4 = 900

Decision variables. Some of the decisions are obvious. You must decide how many units to manufacture in each of the next four months. Define x_j as the number of units manufactured in Month $j, j = 1, \ldots, 4$.

As soon as you specify the x_j variable values, the amount in inventory at the end of each month is determined. For example, say that $x_1 = 975$ and $x_2 = 1,000$. Because the initial inventory is 100 units and the Month 1 requirement is 1,000 units, if 975 units are made in Month 1, then $100 + 975 - 1,000 = 75$ units are on hand at the end of Month 1. Then, if 1,000 units are made during Month 2, the inventory on hand at the end of Month 2 is $75 + 1,000 - 1,050 = 25$.

Explicitly define the linking variables

Even though the x_j values are enough to determine the plan, let's *explicitly* define the inventory variables. Let I_j represent the number of units in inventory at the end of Month j. The initial inventory, 100, is I_0. Defining the inventory variables makes it easier to formulate the symbolic model.

Only include relevant costs

Symbolic model. The cost of manufacturing x_1 units is $12x_1$, and the inventory cost for items in inventory at the end of Month 1 is $0.2I_1$. The symbolic representation of the four-month total of manufacturing and inventory costs is $12x_1 + 12x_2 + 12.60x_3 + 12.60x_4 + 0.20I_0 + 0.20I_1 + 0.20I_2 + 0.21I_3 + 0.21I_4$. The term $0.20I_0$ is the storage cost of items in inventory at the beginning of the four months. Because this cost has already been assessed and isn't affected by future decisions, it shouldn't be included in the objective function.

The limited manufacturing capacity constraint for Month 1 is

$$x_1 \leq 1000$$

If the inventory variables are not used, mistakes are often made for the requirements constraints. *The symbolic representation is based on the method we used to calculate the inventory at the end of Month 1:*

$$I_0 + x_1 - 1000 = I_1$$

That is, the number of units in inventory at the beginning of a month plus $(+)$ the number of units made during the month minus $(-)$ the number of units required for the month equals $(=)$ the number of units in inventory at the end of the month. In the above equation, a variable is to the right of the relationship and a constant is to the left of the relationship. After transposing, the constraint is

$$I_0 + x_1 - I_1 = 1000$$

Using similar constraints for the other three months, the complete symbolic model is

The complete model

$$
\begin{aligned}
\min \quad & 12x_1 + 12x_2 + 12.60x_3 + 12.60x_4 + 0.20I_1 + 0.20I_2 + 0.21I_3 \\
& + 0.21I_4 \\
\text{st} \quad & x_1 \leq 1000 \\
& x_2 \leq 1000 \\
& x_3 \leq 1000 \\
& x_4 \leq 750 \\
& I_0 + x_1 - I_1 = 1000 \\
& I_1 + x_2 - I_2 = 1050 \\
& I_2 + x_3 - I_3 = 800 \\
& I_3 + x_4 - I_4 = 900 \\
& I_0 = 100 \\
& x_1, x_2, x_3, x_4, I_0, I_1, I_2, I_3, I_4 \geq 0
\end{aligned}
$$

The constraint $I_0 = 100$ is necessary to specify the initial inventory. Another approach is to substitute 100 for I_0 in the model and eliminate that variable completely. The symbolic model without I_0 is

Another model

$$
\begin{aligned}
\min \quad & 12x_1 + 12x_2 + 12.60x_3 + 12.60x_4 + 0.20I_1 + 0.20I_2 + 0.21I_3 \\
& + 0.21I_4 \\
\text{st} \quad & x_1 \leq 1000 \\
& x_2 \leq 1000 \\
& x_3 \leq 1000 \\
& x_4 \leq 750 \\
& x_1 - I_1 = 900 \\
& I_1 + x_2 - I_2 = 1050 \\
& I_2 + x_3 - I_3 = 800 \\
& I_3 + x_4 - I_4 = 900 \\
& x_1, x_2, x_3, x_4, I_1, I_2, I_3, I_4 \geq 0
\end{aligned}
$$

The fifth constraint's RHS constant, 900, is the net requirement in Month 1 after the initial inventory has been subtracted. Let us examine the linear programming solution to this model.

Model Solution Analysis

Table 7.3 contains the LOOK ALL and GO output for the multiple-period example. The minimum total cost for the next four months is $44,851.50. Net of the initial inventory, the total requirement for the next four months is 3,650. The total capacity for the next four months is 3,750. The available monthly capacity is completely used in Months 1, 2, and 4. Only 900 units are produced in Month 3, although the capacity is 1,000 units. The SLACK OR SURPLUS variable value is 0.0 for Rows 2, 3, and 5, but it is 100 for Row 4, Month 3's manufacturing capacity constraint. Table 7.3 shows a value of 1,000 for x_1, so the production in Month 1 is 1,000 units. The inventory at the end of Month 1 is calculated as the initial inventory plus Month 1's production minus Month 1's requirement, $100 + 1,000 - 1,000 = 100$ units. This is the same value that appears in Table 7.3 for

Check that the output satisfies the logical relationships

variable I_1. A careful model builder always verifies that the values in the output satisfy the logical relationships. The inventory at the end of Month 2 is $100 + 1,000 - 1,050 = 50$, which agrees with the output. Verify that the inventories at the end of Months 3 and 4 are 150 and 0 units, respectively.

Changing Month 1's capacity

Let's discuss the dual prices. Since dollars are the units of the objective function, Row 2's dual price is $0.20. If the RHS constant of Row 2 increases by 1, the optimal value of the objective function improves by $0.20. That is, the total cost for the four months *decreases* by $0.20. Say that the manufacturing capacity for Month 1 increases from 1,000 to 1,250. After checking that an increase of 250 is within the allowable range for Row 2, you calculate that the minimum cost decreases by $250 \times \$0.20 = \$50$, to a new value of $44,801.50. Compare the cost of increasing the capacity with the savings to determine whether it's worthwhile to increase the capacity.

Other capacity changes

Say that a breakdown in the manufacturing system decreases the capacity in Month 2 to 900 units. Row 3's dual price is $0.40, so a decrease in the RHS constant results in the minimum cost increasing by $0.40 per unit decrease. Unfortunately, a decrease of 100 is more than the maximum allowable decrease shown in Table 7.3, which is 50. You must re-solve the linear programming model with the new RHS constant of 900. You can tell that the cost increases at least $100 \times \$0.40 = \$40$. Because 100 units of Month 3's manufacturing capacity are unused, the dual price is 0 for Row 4. Its maximum allowable decrease is 100, the amount of capacity currently unused. The maximum allowable increase is infinity. The dual price is $0.41 for Month 4's manufacturing capacity.

The dual prices for Rows 6, 7, 8, and 9 are all negative, indicating that an increase in their RHS constants results in a *negative* improvement in

TABLE 7.3 LOOK ALL and GO Output for Multiple-Period Example

```
MIN     12 X1 + 12 X2 + 12.6 X3 + 12.6 X4 + 0.2 I1 + 0.2 I2
      + 0.21 I3 + 0.21 I4
SUBJECT TO
       2)   X1 <=   1000
       3)   X2 <=   1000
       4)   X3 <=   1000
       5)   X4 <=    750
       6)   X1 - I1 =     900
       7)   X2 + I1 - I2 =    1050
       8)   X3 + I2 - I3 =     800
       9)   X4 + I3 - I4 =     900
END
```

OBJECTIVE FUNCTION VALUE

1)   44851.5000

VARIABLE	VALUE	REDUCED COST
X1	1000.000000	.000000
X2	1000.000000	.000000
X3	900.000000	.000000
X4	750.000000	.000000
I1	100.000000	.000000
I2	50.000000	.000000
I3	150.000000	.000000
I4	.000000	13.020000

ROW	SLACK OR SURPLUS	DUAL PRICES
2)	.000000	.200001
3)	.000000	.400001
4)	100.000000	.000000
5)	.000000	.210000
6)	.000000	-12.200000
7)	.000000	-12.400000
8)	.000000	-12.600000
9)	.000000	-12.810000

RANGES IN WHICH THE BASIS IS UNCHANGED

		OBJ COEFFICIENT RANGES	
VARIABLE	CURRENT COEF	ALLOWABLE INCREASE	ALLOWABLE DECREASE
X1	12.000000	.200001	INFINITY
X2	12.000000	.400001	INFINITY
X3	12.600000	INFINITY	.200001
X4	12.600000	.210000	INFINITY
I1	.200000	.200001	INFINITY
I2	.200000	.200001	INFINITY
I3	.210000	INFINITY	.210000
I4	.210000	INFINITY	13.020000

		RIGHTHAND SIDE RANGES	
ROW	CURRENT RHS	ALLOWABLE INCREASE	ALLOWABLE DECREASE
2	1000.000000	900.000000	50.000000
3	1000.000000	900.000000	50.000000
4	1000.000000	INFINITY	100.000000
5	750.000000	150.000000	100.000000
6	900.000000	50.000000	900.000000
7	1050.000000	50.000000	900.000000
8	800.000000	100.000000	900.000000
9	900.000000	100.000000	150.000000

Increasing Month 4's
requirement

the cost. If the requirement for Month 4, Row 9, increases by one unit, the minimum cost *increases* by $12.81. If Month 4's requirement increases from 900 to 950, the minimum cost increases by $50 \times \$12.81 = \$640.50$. Remember, you must compare the increase of 50 with the maximum allowable increase.

Say that Month 4's manufacturing cost increases by $0.20 per unit. Because the maximum allowable increase of x_4's objective function coefficient is 0.21, the optimal production plan doesn't change and the optimal cost increases to $45,001.50 ($750 \times \$0.20 + \$44{,}851.50$). Do any other coefficients of the linear programming model change when Month 4's manufacturing cost changes? The inventory holding cost is 20 percent of the manufacturing cost, so I_4's objective function coefficient increases to $^{(12.60 \ + \ 0.20)} \times {^{0.2}/_{12}} = 0.21333$. Because I_4's allowable increase is infinity, the 100 Percent Rule is satisfied and the production plan is unchanged. Because I_4 equals 0 in Table 7.3, Z^* is not affected by the change in its objective function coefficient. The optimal cost is $45,001.50.

Increasing a
manufacturing cost

Table 7.3 shows that the inventory on hand at the end of Months 1, 2, 3, and 4 is 100, 50, 150, and 0, respectively. If the actual requirements in Months 1, 2, and 3 are more than the model's requirements, some planned month-end inventory is available to help satisfy those requirements. Because $I_4 = 0$, if the actual requirement for Month 4 is more than 900, no extra units are available and capacity is already at the limit. The extra cost of forcing I_4 to be 1 is its reduced cost, $13.02. The four-month minimum cost increases by $13.02 for each unit of forced month-end inventory for Month 4. The maximum number of units of forced month-end inventory that corresponds to a cost increase of $13.02 cannot be easily determined from Table 7.3.

Model Manipulations and Extensions

Using the model to
understand the
dual prices

Do not blindly accept numerical values in the computer-generated solution. We use the linear programming model to gain insight into the dual price for Row 3, Month 2's manufacturing capacity constraint. If the capacity increases by one unit, why does the minimum cost decrease by $0.40? Table 7.4 contains the LOOK ALL and GO output for the model after Row 3's RHS constant increases to 1,001.

Note that the same eight variables are positive in Tables 7.3 and 7.4. Since Table 7.3's maximum allowable increase for Row 3's RHS constant is 900, that is expected. In Table 7.4, the value of x_2 increases to 1,001, the value of I_2 increases to 51, and the value of x_3 decreases to 899. Because of Month 2's extra unit of capacity, one more unit is made in Month 2 and one less unit is made in Month 3. The saving in the manufacturing cost is $12.60 - \$12.00 = \$0.60$. However, the manufacturing saving is offset by $0.20, the cost of storing an additional unit at the end of Month 2. The net cost reduction is $0.60 - \$0.20 = \$0.40$, the dual price of Row 3. Note

TABLE 7.4   LOOK ALL and GO Output for Multiple-Period Example—Capacity in Month 2 Increased by 1, to 1001

```
MIN     12 X1 + 12 X2 + 12.6 X3 + 12.6 X4 + 0.2 I1 + 0.2 I2
   + 0.21 I3 + 0.21 I4
SUBJECT TO
        2)   X1 <=   1000
        3)   X2 <=   1001
        4)   X3 <=   1000
        5)   X4 <=   750
        6)   X1 - I1 =        900
        7)   X2 + I1 - I2 =        1050
        8)   X3 + I2 - I3 =        800
        9)   X4 + I3 - I4 =        900
END
```

OBJECTIVE FUNCTION VALUE

1)   44851.1000

VARIABLE	VALUE	REDUCED COST
X1	1000.000000	.000000
X2	1001.000000	.000000
X3	899.000000	.000000
X4	750.000000	.000000
I1	100.000000	.000000
I2	51.000000	.000000
I3	150.000000	.000000
I4	.000000	13.020000

ROW	SLACK OR SURPLUS	DUAL PRICES
2)	.000000	.200001
3)	.000000	.400001
4)	101.000000	.000000
5)	.000000	.210000
6)	.000000	-12.200000
7)	.000000	-12.400000
8)	.000000	-12.600000
9)	.000000	-12.810000

RANGES IN WHICH THE BASIS IS UNCHANGED

		OBJ COEFFICIENT RANGES	
VARIABLE	CURRENT COEF	ALLOWABLE INCREASE	ALLOWABLE DECREASE
X1	12.000000	.200001	INFINITY
X2	12.000000	.400001	INFINITY
X3	12.600000	INFINITY	.200001
X4	12.600000	.210000	INFINITY
I1	.200000	.200001	INFINITY
I2	.200000	.200001	INFINITY
I3	.210000	INFINITY	.210000
I4	.210000	INFINITY	13.020000

		RIGHTHAND SIDE RANGES	
ROW	CURRENT RHS	ALLOWABLE INCREASE	ALLOWABLE DECREASE
2	1000.000000	899.000000	51.000000
3	1001.000000	899.000000	51.000000
4	1000.000000	INFINITY	101.000000
5	750.000000	150.000000	101.000000
6	900.000000	51.000000	899.000000
7	1050.000000	51.000000	899.000000
8	800.000000	101.000000	899.000000
9	900.000000	101.000000	150.000000

that Row 3's RHS constant maximum allowable increase in Table 7.4 is 899, a decrease of 1 from the Table 7.3 value.

Let's consider why the dual price of Row 9, Month 4's requirement constraint, is $12.81. Because Table 7.3 shows that Month 3 has the only unused capacity, if the requirement increases by 1 in Month 4, the extra unit must be made in Month 3. Thus, the extra unit is in storage at the end of Month 3. The additional cost, $12.60 for manufacturing plus $0.21 for storage, totals $12.81. Table 7.5, containing the revised LINDO solution, confirms this.

Changing model parameters and re-solving the model aids your verification of the correctness of the model and your understanding of the decision environment. If you do not understand the value of a dual price, reduced cost, RHS constant range, or objective function coefficient range, be skeptical. Use the model to analyze the impact of changes by brute force.

Let's consider inventory storage costs that are *not linear in the amount of time stored.* Say that the storage cost is subdivided into a capital

---

TABLE 7.5 LOOK ALL and GO Output for Multiple-Period Example—Requirement for Month 4 Increased by 1, to 901

```
MIN      12 X1 + 12 X2 + 12.6 X3 + 12.6 X4 + 0.2 I1 + 0.2 I2 + 0.21 I3
       + 0.21 I4
SUBJECT TO       .
       2)   X1 <=    1000
       3)   X2 <=    1000
       4)   X3 <=    1000
       5)   X4 <=     750
       6)   X1 - I1 =       900
       7)   X2 + I1 - I2 =      1050
       8)   X3 + I2 - I3 =       800
       9)   X4 + I3 - I4 =       901
END

            OBJECTIVE FUNCTION VALUE

   1)        44864.3100

VARIABLE          VALUE        REDUCED COST
       X1     1000.000000          .000000
       X2     1000.000000          .000000
       X3      901.000000          .000000
       X4      750.000000          .000000
       I1      100.000000          .000000
       I2       50.000000          .000000
       I3      151.000000          .000000
       I4         .000000        13.020000

    ROW     SLACK OR SURPLUS     DUAL PRICES
       2)          .000000          .200001
       3)          .000000          .400001
       4)        99.000000          .000000
       5)          .000000          .210000
       6)          .000000       -12.200000
       7)          .000000       -12.400000
       8)          .000000       -12.600000
       9)          .000000       -12.810000
```

A model for significant
material handling costs

carrying cost, $0.15 per month per unit, and a material handling cost, $0.05 per unit. If a unit is put in storage at the end of Month 1 and removed during Month 2, the storage cost is $0.20. If a unit is put in storage at the end of Month 1 and remains in storage until Month 3, the storage cost is 2 × $0.15 for a capital carrying cost and $0.05 for the material handling cost, totaling $0.35. The material handling cost is incurred only once. Consider the model of Table 7.3. A unit put in storage at the end of Month 1 is included in I_1. If it remains in storage during Month 2, it is included in I_2. The two-month storage cost of the unit is $0.20 each month, for a total of $0.40. The model of Table 7.3 is appropriate if the storage cost is linear in the amount of time stored. If the material handling cost (or another onetime cost) is significant, the model of Table 7.3 is inappropriate.

Month 1 only

Let's modify the model of Table 7.3 by assuming that the only storage costs not linear in the amount of time in storage are those put in storage at the end of Month 1. This is unrealistic, but our intent is to focus on the model changes required by this modification. Similar modifications for other months are also required, but these are left to the exercises.

The new inventory variable definitions are

i_{12}—number of units in inventory at the end of Month 1 *that are withdrawn from storage during Month 2*

i_{13}—number of units in inventory at the end of Month 1 *that are withdrawn from storage during Month 3*

i_{14}—number of units in inventory at the end of Month 1 *that are withdrawn from storage during Month 4*

Note that the cost of putting an item in storage at the end of Month 1 and removing it during Month 4 is 3 × $0.15 + $0.05 = $0.50.

The model is

$$\min \quad 12x_1 + 12x_2 + 12.60x_3 + 12.60x_4 + 0.20i_{12} + 0.35i_{13} + 0.50i_{14}$$
$$+ 0.20I_2 + 0.21I_3 + 0.21I_4$$

$$\text{st} \quad x_1 \le 1000$$
$$x_2 \le 1000$$
$$x_3 \le 1000$$
$$x_4 \le 750$$
$$x_1 - i_{12} - i_{13} - i_{14} = 900$$
$$i_{12} + x_2 - I_2 = 1050$$
$$i_{13} + I_2 + x_3 - I_3 = 800$$
$$i_{14} + I_3 + x_4 - I_4 = 900$$
$$x_1, x_2, x_3, x_4, i_{12}, i_{13}, i_{14}, I_2, I_3, I_4 \ge 0$$

The requirement constraint for Month 1 allows units to be put in storage at the end of Month 1 and removed during Month 2 (i_{12}) or Month 3 (i_{13}) or Month 4 (i_{14}). The requirement constraint for Month 3 shows that units put in storage at the end of Month 1 and removed during Month 3, (i_{13}), and units put in storage at the end of Month 2, (I_2), are *both available to satisfy Month 3's requirement*.[2]

Different types of storage

If there are different types of storage (e.g., leased warehouse space versus storage in the company's warehouse), you introduce different inventory variables. For example, I_j could represent the number of items in the company's warehouse and IL_j could represent the number of items in leased storage.

Limited storage space

Say that there is limited storage space available. Then, we must calculate the maximum number of units that can be stored and impose limits on the variables representing the number of units in inventory at the end of a month. For example, if the limit is 300 units, add the constraints

$$I_j \leq 300 \quad j = 1, \ldots, 4$$

This type of restriction might also result from a policy decision designed to conserve working capital. Note that the number of units in inventory *during* a month can be more than the storage capacity, even though the month-end inventory is not. Remember, a linear programming model tells what to do within a time period, not when to do it within the time period. Subdividing the time period gives additional control over the timing. Subdividing the one-month periods into weeks or even days makes exceeding the storage capacity during the month less likely.

Formulation without the linking variables

Formulating the multiple-period model without the inventory variables is possible, but it is less useful. For the formulation above, the I_j variables are intermediate or definitional variables. If they are not used, including the inventory cost in the objective is more difficult. This is left to the exercises.

The previous example was easy because its single-period models are simple. The linking of more complex single-period models is also easy. How could you convert the machine assignment model into a multiple-period model? You just introduce an ending inventory variable for each type of cup and each time period (week). Say that there are T time periods. The model has $3T$ machine capacity constraints, $3T$ requirement constraints, $9T$ production decision variables, and $3T$ inventory variables.

Long time horizons and the time value of money

You choose the length of each time period and the number of time periods based on the decision environment, the decision problem analyzed, the availability of data, and many other factors. If the time horizon

---

[2] The validity of the model is subtle. Nothing forces units to be withdrawn only if they are needed to satisfy the month's requirement. In the example, it is cheaper to leave a unit in inventory unless it is needed. If you withdraw it from inventory next month and then replace it at the end of that month, the cost is higher ($0.40) than if you leave it in inventory for two months ($0.35). The optimal solution withdraws units only if they are needed to satisfy the month's requirement.

is long, the model should consider the *time value of money*. A dollar today and a dollar 10 years from now are not the same. You *discount* future dollars, and the objective is to minimize the total of *discounted* production and inventory costs. After the objective function coefficients have been multiplied by the appropriate discount factor, the result is a linear programming model. Be wary of incorporating the time value of money *twice* by including it in both the inventory storage cost and the discount rate.

TRANSPORTATION MODEL

Two reasons

The transportation model is an important model (1) because it is useful for studying shipping decisions and (2) because its special mathematical structure can be exploited to solve large models rapidly. In this section, we discuss the model. Chapter 8 discusses the special structure and its exploitation.

Suppose that the decision environment consists of several regional warehouses that supply customers throughout the continental United States. Which warehouse should be used to supply each customer? Intuitively, you should ship to each customer from the warehouse with the lowest shipping cost. However, when that policy is followed, a particular warehouse may not have enough units available to meet the demands. To meet demands that exceed the available units, you must change some customers' shipments to other warehouses with low shipping costs and adequate supplies.

Model Formulation

As an example, assume that there are three regional warehouses, designated Warehouses 1, 2, and 3, and that these warehouses have 500, 400, and 325 units, respectively, in stock. Assume further that customers have been aggregated into four marketing regions, 1, 2, 3, and 4, and that the requirements for these regions are 300, 115, 275, and 190 units, respectively. Table 7.6 lists the shipping cost per unit from each warehouse to each marketing region.

TABLE 7.6 Shipping Costs from Warehouses to Marketing Regions ($ per unit)

From Warehouse	To Marketing Region			
	1	2	3	4
1	1.20	0.65	0.25	0.60
2	1.10	0.90	1.05	0.75
3	0.80	0.75	0.87	0.65

Given the existing stock on hand at the warehouses, we use the three-step model formulation process to determine the least expensive shipping plan that satisfies the requirements.

Fixed revenues

Verbal model. If the amount shipped is equal to the requirements and if the amount of revenue received from a marketing region is independent of the warehouse that supplies it, then the total revenue is fixed. Cost minimization and profit maximization are equivalent objectives. We assume that the inventory holding costs are equal at all three warehouses. Then, the objective function includes only the transportation cost.

minimize total transportation cost
subject to total number of units shipped from Warehouse 1 $\leq$ 500
total number of units shipped from Warehouse 2 $\leq$ 400
total number of units shipped from Warehouse 3 $\leq$ 325
total number of units shipped to Marketing Region 1 = 300
total number of units shipped to Marketing Region 2 = 115
total number of units shipped to Marketing Region 3 = 275
total number of units shipped to Marketing Region 4 = 190

The total number of units available at warehouses is 1,225. The total number of units required at marketing regions is 880. Since more units are available than are required, warehouse constraints are of the $\leq$ type.

Assume that the shipping costs are linear

Decision variables. Assigning marketing regions to warehouses is necessary. The reasonableness of splitting a marketing region between two warehouses depends on the nature of the shipping costs. If the shipping costs are linear in the number of units shipped, splitting a marketing region between two warehouses might reduce those costs. However, if a marketing region's requirement can be delivered by a truck with a large enough capacity, splitting the requirement might increase the shipping costs. Let's assume that the shipping costs are linear and that splitting is reasonable. Then, we define

x_{ij}–number of units shipped from Warehouse i to Marketing region j

where $i = 1, 2, 3; j = 1, 2, 3, 4$.

Symbolic model. The complete symbolic model is

$$\min \quad 1.20x_{11} + 0.65x_{12} + 0.25x_{13} + 0.60x_{14} + 1.10x_{21} + 0.90x_{22}$$
$$+ 1.05x_{23} + 0.75x_{24} + 0.80x_{31} + 0.75x_{32} + 0.87x_{33} + 0.65x_{34}$$

$$\text{st} \quad x_{11} + x_{12} + x_{13} + x_{14} \leq 500$$
$$x_{21} + x_{22} + x_{23} + x_{24} \leq 400$$
$$x_{31} + x_{32} + x_{33} + x_{34} \leq 325$$
$$x_{11} + x_{21} + x_{31} = 300$$
$$x_{12} + x_{22} + x_{32} = 115$$
$$x_{13} + x_{23} + x_{33} = 275$$
$$x_{14} + x_{24} + x_{34} = 190$$
$$x_{ij} \geq 0, \ i = 1, 2, 3; j = 1, 2, 3, 4$$

Model Solution Analysis

Table 7.7 contains the LOOK ALL and GO output for the transportation model example. The minimum shipping cost is $507. From Warehouse 1, the numbers of units shipped to Marketing Regions 1, 2, 3, and 4 are 0, 115, 275, and 110, respectively. Because a total of 500 units are shipped and 500 are available, the value of the slack variable for Row 2, Warehouse 1's limitation, is 0. The only shipment from Warehouse 2 is 55 units to Marketing Region 4, and the slack variable for Row 3 is 345. All of the available units are shipped from Warehouses 3 and 4.

The 300 units required for Marketing Region 1 are shipped from Warehouse 3. The 190 units required for Marketing Region 4 are satisfied by 110 from Warehouse 1, 55 from Warehouse 2, and 25 from Warehouse 3. If splitting a marketing region among the warehouses violates company policy, Table 7.7's solution is unacceptable.

Unique, nondegenerate optimal solution

Because no objective function coefficient has a maximum allowable increase or decrease of 0, the optimal solution is unique. Because seven variable values are positive and the model has seven constraints, the optimal solution is not degenerate.

Row 3's dual price is 0. Because 345 units are not shipped, having additional units at Warehouse 2 cannot decrease the shipping costs. Because the dual price of Row 2 is 0.15, if the number of units available at Warehouse 1 increases by 1, the minimum cost improves (decreases) by $0.15. Let's explore how this saving is obtained. First, note that Marketing Region 1 receives its entire requirement from Warehouse 3, the one with the smallest shipping cost. Marketing Regions 2 and 3 also receive their entire requirement from the warehouse with the smallest shipping cost—Warehouse 1. However, although Warehouse 1 is the least expensive source for Marketing Region 4, only part of its requirement is satisfied from Warehouse 1. Warehouse 1 is the cheapest source for Marketing Regions 2, 3, and 4, with a total requirement of 580. But Warehouse 1 has only 500 units available. For that reason, Marketing Region 4's requirement is split. If one more unit were available at Warehouse 1, the additional unit would be shipped to Marketing Region 4, reducing the number shipped from Warehouse 2. The difference in cost would be $0.75 − $0.60 = $0.15, the dual price value for Row 2.

Changing warehouse availabilities

Changing Marketing Region 3's requirement

The dual price for Row 7, Marketing Region 3's requirement, is −0.40. If the RHS constant increases by 1, the minimum cost improves by −$0.40, so the total shipping cost increases by $0.40. The reason for this cost increase is not obvious. Table 7.8 contains the LOOK ALL and GO output after the requirement for Marketing Region 3 has increased by 1, to 276. The additional required unit is shipped from Warehouse 1. However, that decreases the amount available for shipment to the other marketing regions. Warehouse 1 ships one less unit to Marketing Region 4. Market-

TABLE 7.7   LOOK ALL and GO Output for Transportation Model

```
MIN     1.2 X11 + 0.65 X12 + 0.25 X13 + 0.6 X14 + 1.1 X21 + 0.9 X22
     + 1.05 X23 + 0.75 X24 + 0.8 X31 + 0.75 X32 + 0.87 X33 + 0.65 X34
SUBJECT TO
        2)   X11 + X12 + X13 + X14 <=   500
        3)   X21 + X22 + X23 + X24 <=   400
        4)   X31 + X32 + X33 + X34 <=   325
        5)   X11 + X21 + X31 =    300
        6)   X12 + X22 + X32 =    115
        7)   X13 + X23 + X33 =    275
        8)   X14 + X24 + X34 =    190
END

             OBJECTIVE FUNCTION VALUE

 1)        507.000000

VARIABLE          VALUE          REDUCED COST
     X11         .000000            .450000
     X12      115.000000            .000000
     X13      275.000000            .000000
     X14      110.000000            .000000
     X21         .000000            .200000
     X22         .000000            .100000
     X23         .000000            .650000
     X24       55.000000            .000000
     X31      300.000000            .000000
     X32         .000000            .050000
     X33         .000000            .570000
     X34       25.000000            .000000

   ROW      SLACK OR SURPLUS    DUAL PRICES
     2)         .000000            .150000
     3)      345.000000            .000000
     4)         .000000            .100000
     5)         .000000           -.900000
     6)         .000000           -.800000
     7)         .000000           -.400000
     8)         .000000           -.750000


   RANGES IN WHICH THE BASIS IS UNCHANGED

                      OBJ COEFFICIENT RANGES
VARIABLE          CURRENT      ALLOWABLE      ALLOWABLE
                   COEF        INCREASE       DECREASE
     X11        1.200000       INFINITY        .450000
     X12         .650000        .050000       INFINITY
     X13         .250000        .570000       INFINITY
     X14         .600000        .150000        .050000
     X21        1.100000       INFINITY        .200000
     X22         .900000       INFINITY        .100000
     X23        1.050000       INFINITY        .650000
     X24         .750000        .100000        .100000
     X31         .800000        .200000       INFINITY
     X32         .750000       INFINITY        .050000
     X33         .870000       INFINITY        .570000
     X34         .650000        .050000        .200000

                      RIGHTHAND SIDE RANGES
   ROW           CURRENT      ALLOWABLE      ALLOWABLE
                   RHS        INCREASE       DECREASE
     2         500.000000      55.000000     110.000000
     3         400.000000      INFINITY      345.000000
     4         325.000000      55.000000      25.000000
     5         300.000000      25.000000      55.000000
     6         115.000000     110.000000      55.000000
     7         275.000000     110.000000      55.000000
     8         190.000000     345.000000      55.000000
```

TABLE 7.8   LOOK ALL and GO Output for Transportation Model—Requirement for Marketing Region 3 Increased to 276

```
MIN     1.2 X11 + 0.65 X12 + 0.25 X13 + 0.6 X14 + 1.1 X21 + 0.9 X22
      + 1.05 X23 + 0.75 X24 + 0.8 X31 + 0.75 X32 + 0.87 X33 + 0.65 X34
SUBJECT TO
      2)    X11 + X12 + X13 + X14 <=    500
      3)    X21 + X22 + X23 + X24 <=    400
      4)    X31 + X32 + X33 + X34 <=    325
      5)    X11 + X21 + X31 =    300
      6)    X12 + X22 + X32 =    115
      7)    X13 + X23 + X33 =    276
      8)    X14 + X24 + X34 =    190
END
            OBJECTIVE FUNCTION VALUE

   1)        507.400000

VARIABLE            VALUE          REDUCED COST
      X11          .000000          .450000
      X12       115.000000          .000000
      X13       276.000000          .000000
      X14       109.000000          .000000
      X21          .000000          .200000
      X22          .000000          .100000
      X23          .000000          .650000
      X24        56.000000          .000000
      X31       300.000000          .000000
      X32          .000000          .050000
      X33          .000000          .570000
      X34        25.000000          .000000

   ROW      SLACK OR SURPLUS      DUAL PRICES
      2)          .000000          .150000
      3)       344.000000          .000000
      4)          .000000          .100000
      5)          .000000         -.900000
      6)          .000000         -.800000
      7)          .000000         -.400000
      8)          .000000         -.750000


   RANGES IN WHICH THE BASIS IS UNCHANGED

                      OBJ COEFFICIENT RANGES
VARIABLE         CURRENT        ALLOWABLE        ALLOWABLE
                 COEF           INCREASE         DECREASE
      X11       1.200000        INFINITY          .450000
      X12        .650000         .050000         INFINITY
      X13        .250000         .570000         INFINITY
      X14        .600000         .150000          .050000
      X21       1.100000        INFINITY          .200000
      X22        .900000        INFINITY          .100000
      X23       1.050000        INFINITY          .650000
      X24        .750000         .100000          .100000
      X31        .800000         .200000         INFINITY
      X32        .750000        INFINITY          .050000
      X33        .870000        INFINITY          .570000
      X34        .650000         .050000          .200000

                      RIGHTHAND SIDE RANGES
   ROW           CURRENT        ALLOWABLE        ALLOWABLE
                 RHS            INCREASE         DECREASE
      2         500.000000       56.000000       109.000000
      3         400.000000      INFINITY         344.000000
      4         325.000000       56.000000        25.000000
      5         300.000000       25.000000        56.000000
      6         115.000000      109.000000        56.000000
      7         276.000000      109.000000        56.000000
      8         190.000000      344.000000        56.000000
```

ing Region 4's requirement is satisfied by shipping one more unit from Warehouse 2. The net impact is $0.25 - $0.60 + $0.75 = $0.40, an increase of $0.40.

Maximum increase of row 7's RHS constant

Table 7.7 shows that the maximum allowable increase for Row 7's RHS constant is 110. If you understand the adjustments in Table 7.8 that were caused by increasing the RHS constant by 1, the maximum increase is clear. First, note that the same set of variables is positive in Tables 7.7 and 7.8 and that x_{13}, x_{14}, x_{24}, and the slack for Row 3 are the only variable values that changed; x_{13} and x_{24} increased by 1, and x_{14} and the slack decreased by 1. Because the model is linear, the variable values change linearly *until the limit*. That is, if the requirement increases by 2, x_{13} and x_{24} increase by 2 and x_{14} and the slack decrease by 2. In Table 7.7, x_{14} = 110 and the slack is 345. The variables change linearly until one of the decreasing variables reaches a value of 0. In Table 7.7, x_{14} has a smaller value than the slack for Row 2, so the value of x_{14} reaches 0 before the slack does. Thus, the maximum allowable increase is 110, x_{14}'s value in Table 7.7. Note that in Table 7.8 the maximum allowable increase of Row 7's RHS constant is 109. After increasing the RHS constant by 1, the amount of the additional increase is 109. Changes greater than the allowable increase result in a different set of positive variables, which means that the model must be re-solved.

Changing an unused route's cost

Table 7.7 shows that Warehouse 1 doesn't ship to Marketing Region 1. How much must the shipping cost from Warehouse 1 to Marketing Region 1 decrease for that route to be used? Recall that the optimal solution is not degenerate. Thus, the reduced cost for an unused shipping route is the amount that the objective function coefficient must improve (decrease) before you consider using the route. Since x_{11}'s reduced cost is 0.45, if the shipping cost per unit decreases by $0.45, there is an alternate optimal solution that uses Route x_{11}. If the shipping cost per unit decreases by more than $0.45, the shipping plan changes and Route x_{11} is used. You must then re-solve the model to find the new shipping plan. Note that the maximum allowable decrease for the objective function coefficient of x_{11} is also 0.45 and that the maximum allowable increase for this coefficient is infinity. Increasing the cost makes an unattractive shipping route even less attractive.

Changing the cost of a route that is used

If the shipping cost per unit from Warehouse 1 to Marketing Region 3 increases by $0.10, what is the minimum cost? Because the maximum allowable increase is 0.15, the shipping plan is unchanged. Since 275 units are shipped on the route from Warehouse 1 to Marketing Region 3, the cost increases by 275 × $0.10 = $27.50. However, if the shipping cost increases by $0.20, which is more than the maximum allowable increase, you must re-solve the model to find the new shipping plan. The optimal cost increases by at least 275 × $0.15 = $41.25, but the exact increase must be determined by re-solving.

Model Manipulations and Extensions

Transportation model structure

Figure 7.2 shows the picture of the transportation model example. All of the constraint coefficients are +1 or 0. Because of the mathematical structure of the model, the values of the optimal linear programming solution are always integers if the availabilities and requirements are integer-valued. Tables 7.7 and 7.8 confirm this observation. Also, the special structure of the transportation model can be exploited by a specialized simplex algorithm. Software based on this algorithm requires less computer time and computer storage than standard linear programming software. In Chapter 8, we discuss the transportation model further.

Let's consider some possible changes in the transportation model. If the constraints of the marketing region requirements are $\geq$ instead of $=$, does the optimal solution change? Certainly, there are solutions satisfying the $\geq$ constraints that do not satisfy the $=$ constraints. Assuming that it always costs more to ship extra units, the minimum cost solution never ships extra units. An optimal solution to the model with $\geq$ constraints is an optimal solution to the model with $=$ constraints.

A warning

If the requirement constraints were $\leq$, the optimal solution would be uninteresting. The least expensive shipping plan is not to ship anything. *Beware of cost minimization models with $\leq$ requirement constraints.* The optimal solution to such a model is usually to do nothing. Reexamine the purpose of the model, the decision-making environment, and the verbal model.

At the beginning of Chapter 1, we described a system used by Air Products and Chemicals for scheduling the delivery of industrial gases to its 3,500 customers from its 23 plant/depots. A linear programming model was used to assign customers to depots. A transportation model can be used for this problem. The 23 depots correspond to the warehouses in our example. The depot capacities correspond to the supply amounts at the

FIGURE 7.2   Picture of Transportation Model—LINDO PIC Command

```
: pic

            X X X X X X X X X X X X
            1 1 1 1 2 2 2 2 3 3 3 3
            1 2 3 4 1 2 3 4 1 2 3 4

        1:  A T T T A T A T T T T T MIN
        2:  1 1 1 1         '       '       < C
        3:  '   '   ' 1'1 1 1'   '   '       < C
        4:          '       '   1 1 1 1      < C
        5:  1       ' 1     '   1 '          = C
        6:  ' 1'    ' '1 '   '   1 '         = C
        7:      1 '       1       ' 1        = C
        8:          1     ' 1     '   1      = C
```

warehouses. The 3,500 customers correspond to the marketing regions. The cost objective coefficient for a variable that corresponds to a depot shipping to a customer includes the gas manufacturing cost at the plant and the transportation cost. Thus, the Air Products and Chemicals problem is a transportation model.

GENERALIZATION OF THE MACHINE ASSIGNMENT MODEL TO SEVERAL PLANTS

Many companies have manufacturing facilities that are located in different geographic regions. Say that a company has two manufacturing plants. Because of shipping cost considerations, such a company often assigns customers to the closest plant and independently plans production for the two plants. Using this approach, you construct and solve a single-plant machine assignment model (Chapter 3) for Plant 1. Then, you construct and solve another machine assignment model for Plant 2. The single-plant machine assignment models minimize production costs to satisfy product requirements within the available capacity. The requirement constraints are of the = type. If either model has no feasible solution, the plant doesn't have enough capacity. If a plant has insufficient capacity, you can't satisfy all of the product requirements and you must modify the model. One modification approach is to change the model to a profit maximization model and to convert the requirement

Approaches if capacity isn't adequate

constraints to constraints of the ≤ type. Although this approach maximizes the profit for each plant within the limited capacity, it leaves some customer demand unsatisfied. Another approach uses a multiple-period model that accumulates products in inventory during periods of low requirements so that peak requirements can be satisfied. Still another approach is to manufacture extra units at one plant and to ship those units to the plant with inadequate capacity. Interplant transfers are reasonable only if the extra units can be delivered in time to satisfy the customers' requirements.

A possible shortcoming of assigning customers to the closest plant is that differences in manufacturing efficiencies can offset savings in shipping costs. If the shipping costs are low and significant differences in manufacturing efficiency exist between the two plants, interplant transfers can be beneficial even if the plants have sufficient capacities when operated independently.

Allow interplant transfers

Let's generalize the single-period machine assignment models for two plants to allow interplant transfers. First, we assume that the requirements occur at the plants themselves. In the Model Manipulations and Extensions section, we consider assigning customers to plants.

Model Formulation

The machine assignment model developed in Chapter 3 assigned three products to three machines located at a single manufacturing facility. Now, consider a company that has two plants. To reduce model complexity, say that each plant produces two products and has only two machines. The generalization to more plants, more products, and more machines is straightforward. The products, designated 1 and 2, can be made on any machine. Plant 1's machines are designated A and B, while Plant 2's machines are designated C and D. Only one machine is required to make either product, but the machines have different efficiencies. The manufacturing rates and the hourly operating costs are shown in Table 7.9.

Consider a one-week time horizon. During the week, units can be manufactured at one plant for shipment to the other plant. We assume that the shipping time is short enough for timely arrival of the units shipped. We also assume that the setup or changeover time from one product to another on a machine is minimal and that making more than one product on a particular machine within a week is reasonable. Chapter 9 considers models with setup costs.

At Plant 1, the requirements are 1,400 and 1,500 units of Products 1 and 2, respectively. At Plant 2, the requirements are 1,600 and 2,000 units of Products 1 and 2, respectively. Exactly 40 hours are available next week

TABLE 7.9 Manufacturing Rates and Operating Costs for Generalization of Machine Assignment Model to Multiple-Plants Example

Units Produced per Hour

		Product	
Plant	Machine	1	2
1	A	30	41
1	B	40	36
2	C	51	41
2	D	62	29

Operating Cost ($ per hour)

		Product	
Plant	Machine	1	2
1	A	350	325
1	B	420	415
2	C	360	390
2	D	410	420

on each machine at both plants. Say that the shipping cost (regardless of product) is $3 per unit shipped between the two plants. Let's formulate the model using the three-step process.

Verbal model. Say that a policy decision has been made that the requirements must be satisfied. Because the plants have enough capacity to satisfy the requirements, the total revenue is fixed and maximizing profit and minimizing cost are equivalent. We'll use cost minimization as the objective.

minimize   total of operating costs for both plants and interplant shipping costs

subject to   number of hours used on Machine A at Plant 1 $\leq$ 40
number of hours used on Machine B at Plant 1 $\leq$ 40
number of Product 1 units furnished at Plant 1 $=$ 1400
number of Product 2 units furnished at Plant 1 $=$ 1500
number of hours used on Machine C at Plant 2 $\leq$ 40
number of hours used on Machine D at Plant 2 $\leq$ 40
number of Product 1 units furnished at Plant 2 $=$ 1600
number of Product 2 units furnished at Plant 2 $=$ 2000

Decision variables. As in Chapter 3's machine assignment model, the decision variables can be either hours or units produced. We choose hours. On this basis, define *P1A2* as the number of hours at Plant 1 that Machine A makes Product 2. The first number of the variable name is the plant, and the second is the product. The entire set of machine assignment variables is

P1A1—number of hours at Plant 1 that Machine A makes Product 1

P1A2—number of hours at Plant 1 that Machine A makes Product 2

P1B1—number of hours at Plant 1 that Machine B makes Product 1

P1B2—number of hours at Plant 1 that Machine B makes Product 2

P2C1—number of hours at Plant 2 that Machine C makes Product 1

P2C2—number of hours at Plant 2 that Machine C makes Product 2

P2D1—number of hours at Plant 2 that Machine D makes Product 1

P2D2—number of hours at Plant 2 that Machine D makes Product 2

Assume that the shipping cost for a product does not depend on the machine that made it. Let *Pij* represent the number of units shipped from Plant *i* of Product *j*, (implicitly shipped to the other plant).

Because the shipping cost per unit is $3, the objective function contribution for *P11* is 3*P11*. Note that a negative value for *P11* does not correspond to a shipment from Plant 2 of Product 1. There is *not* a rebate of $3 for each unit shipped from Plant 2 to Plant 1. *Different* variables must be defined for shipments from Plant 2 to Plant 1.

The entire set of shipping variables is

P11—number of units made at Plant 1 of Product 1 shipped to Plant 2

P12—number of units made at Plant 1 of Product 2 shipped to Plant 2

P21—number of units made at Plant 2 of Product 1 shipped to Plant 1

P22—number of units made at Plant 2 of Product 2 shipped to Plant 1

Symbolic model. If you keep the units consistent, the development of the objective function and the limited machine time constraints is easy. They are similar to those of Chapter 3's single-plant machine assignment model.

Sources = Uses

The constraints for the number of units of a product furnished at a particular plant are potentially tricky. The constraint is a **balance constraint**—*the sources equal the uses.* For example, the sources at Plant 1 include the units made at Plant 1 and the units shipped from Plant 2. The uses include satisfying the requirement at Plant 1 and shipments from Plant 1 to Plant 2. For Product 1 at Plant 1, the constraint is

$$30P1A1 + 40P1B1 + P21 = 1400 + P11$$

The LHS includes the units made on both Machines A and B. All of the variables must be transposed to the left of the relationship.

The complete symbolic model is

$$
\begin{aligned}
\min \quad & 350P1A1 + 325P1A2 + 420P1B1 + 415P1B2 + 360P2C1 \\
& + 390P2C2 + 410P2D1 + 420P2D2 + 3P11 + 3P12 \\
& + 3P21 + 3P22 \\
\text{st} \quad & P1A1 + P1A2 \le 40 \\
& P1B1 + P1B2 \le 40 \\
& 30P1A1 + 40P1B1 + P21 - P11 = 1400 \\
& 41P1A2 + 36P1B2 + P22 - P12 = 1500 \\
& P2C1 + P2C2 \le 40 \\
& P2D1 + P2D2 \le 40 \\
& 51P2C1 + 62P2D1 + P11 - P21 = 1600 \\
& 41P2C2 + 29P2D2 + P12 - P22 = 2000 \\
& P1A1, P1B1, P1A2, P1B2, P2C1, P2D1, P2C2, P2D2, P11, P12, \\
& P21, P22 \ge 0
\end{aligned}
$$

Model Solution Analysis

Table 7.10 contains the LOOK ALL and GO output for the linear programming model. The minimum cost is $56,716.11. All of the available machine time is used, except for 20.89 hours at Plant 1 on Machine B. Let's examine the decisions on Product 1. At plant 1, 520 (13 × 40) units

TABLE 7.10 LOOK ALL and GO Output for Example of the Two-Plant Generalization of the Machine Assignment Model

```
MIN     350 P1A1 + 325 P1A2 + 420 P1B1 + 415 P1B2 + 3 P11 + 3 P21
    + 3 P12 + 3 P22 + 360 P2C1 + 390 P2C2 + 410 P2D1 + 420 P2D2
SUBJECT TO
        2)   P1A1 + P1A2 <=   40
        3)   P1B1 + P1B2 <=   40
        4)   30 P1A1 + 40 P1B1 - P11 + P21 =      1400
        5)   41 P1A2 + 36 P1B2 - P12 + P22 =      1500
        6)   P2C1 + P2C2 <=   40
        7)   P2D1 + P2D2 <=   40
        8)   P11 - P21 + 51 P2C1 + 62 P2D1 =      1600
        9)   P12 - P22 + 41 P2C2 + 29 P2D2 =      2000
END

            OBJECTIVE FUNCTION VALUE

   1)         56716.1100

VARIABLE          VALUE            REDUCED COST
   P1A1           .000000          182.638900
   P1A2         40.000000            .000000
   P1B1         13.000000            .000000
   P1B2          6.111111            .000000
   P11            .000000           6.000000
   P21         880.000000            .000000
   P12         360.000000            .000000
   P22            .000000           6.000000
   P2C1           .000000          183.138900
   P2C2         40.000000            .000000
   P2D1         40.000000            .000000
   P2D2           .000000          53.694460

   ROW       SLACK OR SURPLUS     DUAL PRICES
    2)           .000000          147.638900
    3)         20.888890            .000000
    4)           .000000          -10.500000
    5)           .000000          -11.527780
    6)           .000000          205.638900
    7)           .000000           55.000000
    8)           .000000           -7.500000
    9)           .000000          -14.527780


   RANGES IN WHICH THE BASIS IS UNCHANGED

                      OBJ COEFFICIENT RANGES
VARIABLE         CURRENT       ALLOWABLE       ALLOWABLE
                 COEF          INCREASE        DECREASE
   P1A1        350.000000      INFINITY        182.638900
   P1A2        325.000000      147.638900      INFINITY
   P1B1        420.000000      143.638300       34.641580
   P1B2        415.000000       66.655190      129.634100
   P11           3.000000      INFINITY          6.000000
   P21           3.000000        .866040         3.590958
   P12           3.000000       1.851533         4.466801
   P22           3.000000      INFINITY          6.000000
   P2C1        360.000000      INFINITY        183.138900
   P2C2        390.000000      183.138900      INFINITY
   P2D1        410.000000       53.694460      INFINITY
   P2D2        420.000000      INFINITY         53.694460

                      RIGHTHAND SIDE RANGES
   ROW          CURRENT        ALLOWABLE       ALLOWABLE
                RHS            INCREASE        DECREASE
    2          40.000000        5.365854       18.341460
    3          40.000000      INFINITY         20.888890
    4        1400.000000      835.555500      520.000000
    5        1500.000000      752.000000      220.000000
    6          40.000000        5.365854       18.341460
    7          40.000000        8.387097       13.476700
    8        1600.000000      835.555500      520.000000
    9        2000.000000      752.000000      220.000000
```

are produced. At Plant 2, 2,480 (62 × 40) units are produced, but 880 are shipped to Plant 1. The net amount, 1,600, equals the requirement at Plant 2. The sources of Product 1 at Plant 1 total 520 + 880 = 1,400. Even though Plant 1 has unused capacity, additional Product 1 units are made at Plant 2 and shipped to Plant 1. The additional shipping cost, $3, is more than offset by the savings in manufacturing cost. Observing that the maximum allowable increase of the objective function coefficient of *P21* is 0.866, you can tell that even if the shipping cost per unit increases to $3.866, the interplant shipment is worthwhile.

Table 7.10 shows that Plant 1 ships 360 extra units of Product 2 to Plant 2. Plant 2 has enough capacity to satisfy its requirements, but the cost of manufacturing at Plant 1 and shipping to Plant 2 is less than the cost of producing at Plant 2.

Say that you consider working an extra four hours on Saturday on one of the machines. Which machine results in the greatest cost savings? The largest of the dual prices for Rows 2, 3, 6, and 7 is 205.64, Row 6. One overtime hour reduces the minimum cost by $205.64. Note that the maximum allowable increase is 5.37 hours. Four hours of overtime reduces the total cost by $822.56. You evaluate the wisdom of the overtime by comparing its cost to the savings. Evaluating the savings for eight hours of overtime requires re-solving the model.

Should overtime be used?

Additional regional sales promotion increases demand at a plant. For Product 1, would additional sales promotion be wiser in the region for Plant 1 or the region for Plant 2? The dual prices of Rows 4 and 8 are −10.50 and −7.50, respectively. An increase in the requirement for Product 1 increases the cost by $10.50 at Plant 1, but by $7.50 at Plant 2. If the promotional costs and the profit margins are the same for the two plant-regions, additional promotion for Plant 2 increases the total cost less and is better.

Increasing requirements

Model Manipulations and Extensions

The symbolic picture of the linear programming model shown in Figure 7.3 illustrates the linking of the single-plant machine assignment models by the interplant shipping variables. The upper-left box contains the machine assignment model for Plant 1, and the lower-right box contains the machine assignment model for Plant 2. The interplant shipping variables in the middle link the plant models. Examine the constraint coefficients of *P11* in Figure 7.3. The −1 in Row 4 shows that *P11* removes units from Plant 1's Product 1 requirement constraint. The +1 in Row 8 shows that *P11* adds units to Plant 2's Product 1 requirement constraint. Variable *P21* does the opposite. Variables *P12* and *P22* transfer Product 2 between the requirement constraints for Plants 1 and 2. Inventory variables in multiple-period models have the same structure. A −1 coefficient removes items from satisfying one period's requirement, and a +1 coefficient furnishes items for satisfying another period's requirements.

Linking the plant models

FIGURE 7.3   Picture of the Example for the Two-Plant Generalization of the Machine Assignment Problem—LINDO PIC command

```
    P P P P         P P P P
    1 1 1 1 P P P P 2 2 2 2
    A A B B 1 2 1 2 C C D D
    1 2 1 2 1 1 2 2 1 2 1 2
 1: C C C C 3 3 3 3 C C C C MIN
 2: 1 1     '     '     '     < B
 3: '  '1 1 '  '  '  '  '     < B
 4: B    B '-1 1  '     '   = D
 5:   B  B    -1 1   '       = D
 6: '  '  '  '   '1 1  '     < B
 7:           '        1 1   < B
 8:       ' 1-1 '   B ' B    = D
 9: '  '  '  '  1-1'  B 'B   = D
```

Now, consider the allocation of customers to plants. Table 7.11 shows demands for the two products by marketing regions. The previous model assigned Marketing Regions 1 and 2 to Plant 1 and Marketing Regions 3 and 4 to Plant 2. Adding the marketing region requirements by plant assigned confirms this. For example, the total requirement at Plant 1 for Product 1 is $860 + 540 = 1,400$. **Production-distribution models** are another class of models. These are created by including production decisions at multiple plants *and* the customer shipping decisions. Define the shipping variable, *pijk,* as the number of units made at Plant *i* of Product *j* that are shipped to Marketing Region *k*. For example, *p214* represents the number of units produced at Plant 2 of Product 1 shipped to Marketing Region 4. The limited machine time constraints are unchanged. The balance constraint for Product 1 at Plant 1 is

$$30P1A1 + 40P1B1 - p111 - p112 - p113 - p114 = 0$$

Because Customer 1's requirement for Product 1 is 860, the associated constraint is

$$p111 + p211 = 860$$

Allocating customers to plants

TABLE 7.11   Marketing Region Demand Requirements for the Production-Distribution Problem

Marketing Region	Demand Requirements	
	Product 1	Product 2
1	860	925
2	540	575
3	900	1,250
4	700	750
Total	3,000	3,500

Assuming that shipping product through another plant on the way to a customer is more expensive than shipping it directly, the interplant shipping variables are deleted. The total number of constraints is $8 + 2J$, where J is the number of customers. Construction of the complete model is left to the exercises.

Two possible generalizations of the static (single-period) single-plant machine assignment problem are including multiple time periods and including multiple manufacturing plants. We have discussed both of these generalizations. Models often evolve from a static, single-plant model and "grow" by being generalized. The ultimate generalization is a multiple-period, dynamic model with multiple manufacturing plants. The inventory variables and product distribution variables link the single-period, single-plant submodels.

Generalizing single-plant, single-period models

PIECEWISE LINEAR COSTS

Often, an objective function coefficient is not quite constant. For example, the constant may take on one value over one range of variable values and another value over another range. Figure 7.4 illustrates that the cost per unit is \$0.32 if A_1 is between 0 and 20 and \$0.33 for units above 20. This cost is linear over "pieces" of the range of A_1.

A **piecewise linear function** is made up of linear line segments that *coincide* at the end points of the line segments. The variable values where the slope changes are called **breakpoints.** Among the reasons for piecewise linear functions are (1) the need to go to another supplier, (2) discounts received for large-quantity purchases, (3) the need to use over-

Reasons for piecewise linear functions

FIGURE 7.4 Piecewise Linear Function

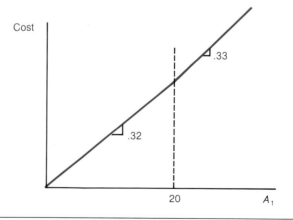

FIGURE 7.5 Not Piecewise Linear Function

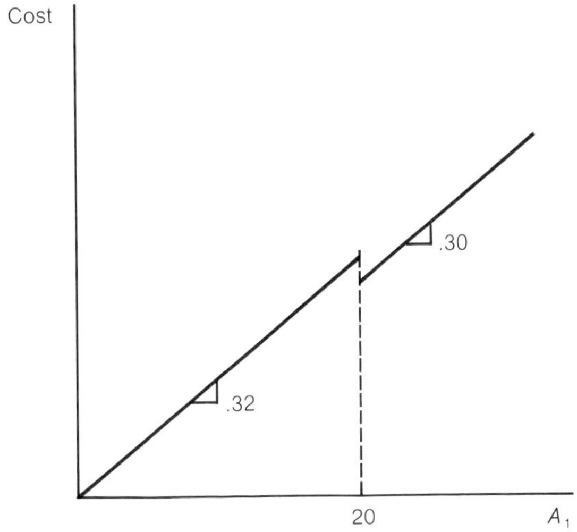

time to produce large quantities, and (4) discounts given to customers for large-quantity purchases.

Note that the definition of piecewise linear functions does not include functions such as the one in Figure 7.5. In Figure 7.5, the end points of the two line segments do not coincide. Consider the **all-units quantity discount** case in which up to 20 units each unit costs \$0.32, but if the quantity is more than 20, the cost of every unit is \$0.30. Then, 20 units cost more than 21—\$6.40 versus \$6.30. Figure 7.5 illustrates this function, which is not a piecewise linear function.

The **incremental quantity discount** case applies the discount to the units above the breakpoint. For example, the first 20 units cost \$0.32 each and each of the units above 20 costs an additional \$0.30. If 21 units are purchased, the first 20 units cost \$0.32 each and the 21st unit costs \$0.30, for a total of \$6.70. Figure 7.6 illustrates this piecewise linear function. Incremental quantity discounts result in piecewise linear functions. However, all-units quantity discounts don't result in piecewise linear functions.

Unfortunately, a piecewise linear function is a nonlinear function. However, *some* constrained optimization models with linear constraints and a piecewise linear objective function can be reformulated as linear programming models that can be solved with linear programming software packages. In this section, we discuss an example that can be reformulated as a linear programming model. Note that if a large quantity incurs additional per unit costs, the slope of the cost function increases (e.g., Figure 7.4). This is called **diseconomies of scale.** If a large quantity

Some piecewise linear objective functions can be reformulated as linear programming models

FIGURE 7.6 Piecewise Linear Function

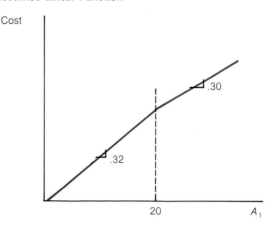

decreases the per unit cost (called **economies of scale**), the slope of the cost function decreases (e.g., Figure 7.6). This *very important distinction* is discussed in the Model Manipulations and Extensions section. Reformulation as a linear programming model is not always possible.

Model Formulation for the Machine Assignment Model

Let's use Chapter 3's machine assignment model to illustrate reformulation of a piecewise linear cost as a linear programming model. Remember, the decision variables of the machine assignment model are the number of hours that Machines 1, 2, and 3 make Cups A, B, and C. For example, A_1 is defined as the number of hours that Cup A is made on Machine 1.

The machine assignment symbolic model is

$$\min \quad 0.32A_1 + 0.35A_2 + 0.36A_3 + 0.29B_1 + 0.25B_2 + 0.34B_3 + 0.32C_1$$
$$+ 0.34C_2 + 0.36C_3$$
$$\text{st} \quad A_1 + B_1 + C_1 \le 40$$
$$A_2 + B_2 + C_2 \le 40$$
$$A_3 + B_3 + C_3 \le 40$$
$$25A_1 + 26A_2 + 23A_3 = 1000$$
$$18B_1 + 19B_2 + 20B_3 = 950$$
$$22C_1 + 23C_2 + 20C_3 = 600$$
$$A_1, A_2, A_3, B_1, B_2, B_3, C_1, C_2, C_3, \ge 0$$

The first three constraints impose limits on the total number of hours that each machine is used (during the next week). The last three constraints ensure that the total made of each cup satisfies its requirement.

The piecewise linear cost

A_1's objective function coefficient, 0.32, is the operating cost per hour that Cup A is made on Machine 1. Say that the operating cost per hour is

$0.32 for each hour up to 20 but increases to $0.33 for each hour above 20. This is the piecewise linear function shown in Figure 7.4. For simplicity, assume that only A_1 has a piecewise linear objective function term. After the development for A_1, you should be able to provide similar modifications for other variables.

Let's introduce two new variables, A_{11} and A_{12}, for the two line segments for A_1. Define A_1 equal to $A_{11} + A_{12}$. Note that A_{12} is the amount that A_1 exceeds 20. If $A_1 = 25$, then $A_{11} = 20$ and $A_{12} = 5$. Replacing $0.32A_1$ by $0.32A_{11} + 0.33A_{12}$ calculates the objective function value correctly. *Constraints must be imposed on the model to cause it to behave as desired.* Add the constraint

$$A_{11} \leq 20$$

in addition to changing the objective function. Also, add the definitional equation

$$A_1 - A_{11} - A_{12} = 0$$

The equivalent linear programming symbolic model is

$$
\begin{aligned}
\min \quad & 0.32A_{11} + 0.33A_{12} + 0.35A_2 + 0.36A_3 + 0.29B_1 + 0.25B_2 \\
& + 0.34B_3 + 0.32C_1 + 0.34C_2 + 0.36C_3 \\
\text{st} \quad & A_1 + B_1 + C_1 \leq 40 \\
& A_2 + B_2 + C_2 \leq 40 \\
& A_3 + B_3 + C_3 \leq 40 \\
& 25A_1 + 26A_2 + 23A_3 = 1000 \\
& 18B_1 + 19B_2 + 20B_3 = 950 \\
& 22C_1 + 23C_2 + 20C_3 = 600 \\
& A_{11} \leq 20 \\
& A_1 - A_{11} - A_{12} = 0 \\
& A_{11}, A_{12}, A_1, A_2, A_3, B_1, B_2, B_3, C_1, C_2, C_3, \geq 0
\end{aligned}
$$

The last constraint is a definitional constraint and must be included.

Model Solution Analysis

Table 7.12 contains the LOOK ALL and GO output for the reformulated linear programming model. The output is similar to that for Chapter 3's linear programming model, except that Variables A_{11} and A_{12} appear. The minimum cost is $36.70194. All 40 hours are used on Machine 1—12.73 for Cup A and 27.27 for Cup C. $A_1 = 12.73$, $A_{11} = 12.73$, and $A_{12} = 0$. The contribution of the A_1 hours to the objective function is correctly calculated as $(0.32 \times 12.73) + (0.33 \times 0)$.

Let's discuss the maximum allowable increases and decreases for the objective function coefficients of A_{11} and A_{12}. Why is the maximum allowable increase for A_{11} equal to 0.01? If the objective function coefficient of A_{11} increases more than 0.01, A_{12} is cheaper than A_{11}. Similarly, if the objective function coefficient of A_{12} decreases more than 0.01, A_{12}

TABLE 7.12 LOOK ALL and GO Output of the Linear Programming Model for the Machine Assignment Piecewise Linear Objection Function

```
MIN     0.35 A2 + 0.36 A3 + 0.29 B1 + 0.25 B2 + 0.34 B3 + 0.32 C1
    + 0.34 C2 + 0.36 C3 + 0.32 A11 + 0.33 A12
SUBJECT TO
    2)    A1 + B1 + C1 <=    40
    3)    A2 + B2 + C2 <=    40
    4)    A3 + B3 + C3 <=    40
    5)    26 A2 + 23 A3 + 25 A1 =    1000
    6)    18 B1 + 19 B2 + 20 B3 =     950
    7)    22 C1 + 23 C2 + 20 C3 =     600
    8)    A11 <=    20
    9)    A1 - A11 - A12 =     0
END

    OBJECTIVE FUNCTION VALUE

    1)    36.7019400

    VARIABLE          VALUE          REDUCED COST
        A1         12.727270           .000000
        A2           .000000           .016043
        A3         29.644270           .000000
        B1           .000000           .055304
        B2         40.000000           .000000
        B3          9.500000           .000000
        C1         27.272730           .000000
        C2           .000000           .003909
        C3           .000000           .004269
       A11         12.727270           .000000
       A12           .000000           .010000


    ROW    SLACK OR SURPLUS      DUAL PRICES
    2)           .000000           .071304
    3)           .000000           .073000
    4)           .855731           .000000
    5)           .000000          -.015652
    6)           .000000          -.017000
    7)           .000000          -.017787
    8)          7.272727           .000000
    9)           .000000           .320000


RANGES IN WHICH THE BASIS IS UNCHANGED:

                           OBJ COEFFICIENT RANGES
    VARIABLE        CURRENT        ALLOWABLE        ALLOWABLE
                      COEF         INCREASE         DECREASE
        A1          .000000         .055304          .003739
        A2          .350000        INFINITY          .016043
        A3          .360000         .003440          .050880
        B1          .290000        INFINITY          .055304
        B2          .250000         .003909         INFINITY
        B3          .340000         .061449          .004115
        C1          .320000         .003739         INFINITY
        C2          .340000        INFINITY          .003909
        C3          .360000        INFINITY          .004269
       A11          .320000         .010000          .003739
       A12          .330000        INFINITY          .010000

                           RIGHTHAND SIDE RANGES
    ROW             CURRENT        ALLOWABLE        ALLOWABLE
                      RHS          INCREASE         DECREASE
     2           40.000000         7.272727          .787273
     3           40.000000        10.000000          .900770
     4           40.000000        INFINITY           .855731
     5         1000.000000        19.681820       681.818200
     6          950.000000        17.114620       190.000000
     7          600.000000        17.320000       160.000000
     8           20.000000        INFINITY          7.272727
     9            .000000         12.727270         7.272727
```

is cheaper than A_{11}. Any decrease that is more than A_{11}'s maximum allowable decrease, 0.003739, results in a changed solution that produces more of Cup A on Machine 1. Because $A_{12} = 0$ in Table 7.12, any increase in its objective function coefficient makes it even less attractive; its maximum allowable increase is infinity.

Model Manipulations and Extensions

Often, a function that is not linear may be approximated by a piecewise linear function. From microeconomic theory, as price increases, the demand quantity decreases. If you intend to produce a small quantity, you can raise the price. Then, the total revenue is not a linear function of quantity. The solid line in Figure 7.7 might represent total revenues. This function is not linear, yet you can approximate it by a piecewise linear function, such as the one represented by the dashed line. By using a very large number of line segments, you can approximate the nonlinear function as closely as you desire.

Although you can reformulate *some* piecewise linear objective functions as linear programming models, other piecewise linear objective functions *cannot* be reformulated as linear programming models. The piecewise linear objective function shown in Figure 7.4 can be reformulated in this way; the one shown in Figure 7.6 cannot be.

In Table 7.12, $A_1 = 12.73$. Could $A_{11} = 0$ and $A_{12} = 12.73$? Those values of A_{11} and A_{12} satisfy all of the constraints, but the value of the objective function would be incorrectly calculated as $(0.32 \times 0) + (0.33 \times 12.73)$. The reason the linear programming model is correct is that if $A_1 = 12.73$, cost minimization ensures that $A_{11} = 12.73$ and $A_{12} = 0$. If A_1 is positive, it is cheapest for A_{11} to increase until it reaches its limit, before A_{12} becomes positive. Table 7.12 illustrates that *if the piecewise linear slope increases for a minimization model, the reformulated linear programming model yields the correct solution.* We call this the **OK**

The OK minimization case

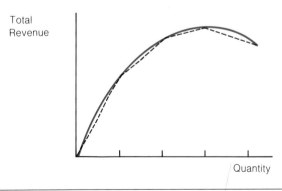

FIGURE 7.7 Piecewise Linear Approximation

minimization case. Reexamine Figure 7.6, which has a larger slope for the first segment than for the second. In this case, $A_{11} = 0$ and $A_{12} = 12.73$ makes a smaller contribution to the objective function than does $A_{11} = 12.73$ and $A_{12} = 0$. The linear programming model obtained by changing the objective function coefficient of A_{12} to 0.30 is incorrect. A_{11} is always 0, even when A_{12} is positive. Table 7.13 contains the LOOK ALL and GO output for the incorrect linear programming reformulation. Note that $A_1 = 40, A_{11} = 0$, and $A_{12} = 40$. The cost contribution of A_1 is incorrectly assessed; the solution is meaningless. In a **troublesome minimization case,** the piecewise linear objective function has the slope of the first segment greater than the slope of the second segment. Decreasing slopes are troublesome for minimization. Increasing slopes can be reformulated as equivalent linear programming models.

The troublesome mini-
mization case

Say that a model has a maximization objective function. Again, there is

---

TABLE 7.13   LOOK ALL and SOLUTION of the Linear Programming Model for the *Troublesome* Machine Assignment Piecewise Linear Objective Function

```
MIN      0.35 A2 + 0.36 A3 + 0.29 B1 + 0.25 B2 + 0.34 B3
       + 0.32 C1 + 0.34 C2 + 0.36 C3 + 0.32 A11 + 0.31 A12
SUBJECT TO
       2)    A1 + B1 + C1 <=    40
       3)    A2 + B2 + C2 <=    40
       4)    A3 + B3 + C3 <=    40
       5)   25 A1 + 26 A2 + 23 A3 =    1000
       6)   18 B1 + 19 B2 + 20 B3 =     950
       7)   22 C1 + 23 C2 + 20 C3 =     600
       8)   A11 <=    20
       9)   A1 - A11 - A12 =     0
END

            OBJECTIVE FUNCTION VALUE

   1)         36.4039078

   VARIABLE          VALUE        REDUCED COST
        A1         40.000000         0.000000
        A2          0.000000         0.022555
        A3          0.000000         0.005760
        B1          0.000000         0.059043
        B2         13.913042         0.000000
        B3         34.282608         0.000000
        C1          0.000000         0.000000
        C2         26.086956         0.000000
        C3          0.000000         0.000870
       A11          0.000000         0.010000
       A12         40.000000         0.000000

      ROW      SLACK OR SURPLUS     DUAL PRICES
       2)          0.000000         0.075043
       3)          0.000000         0.073000
       4)          5.717391         0.000000
       5)          0.000000        -0.015402
       6)          0.000000        -0.017000
       7)          0.000000        -0.017957
       8)         20.000000         0.000000
       9)          0.000000         0.310000
```

an OK case and a troublesome case. *For a maximization objective, decreasing piecewise linear slopes can be reformulated as an equivalent linear programming model.* This is the **OK maximization** case. For example, if the objective function is to be maximized, the reformulated linear programming model for Figure 7.6 is correct. If A_1 is positive, a larger objective function contribution results if A_{11} is positive up to its limit, before A_{12} becomes positive; the linear programming model gives the correct solution. In a **troublesome maximization case,** the piecewise linear objective function has the slope of the first segment smaller than the slope of the second segment. Increasing slopes are troublesome for maximization. If the objective function is to be maximized, then Figure 7.4 is troublesome.

Chapter 9 discusses the reformulation of the *troublesome cases* (maximization—increasing slopes, minimization—decreasing slopes) as integer linear programming models. Until that has been discussed, we classify any troublesome piecewise linear objective function as a nonlinear programming model, not solvable by linear programming.

PERSONNEL SCHEDULING MODEL

Governmental agencies, profit-making organizations, and not-for-profit organizations provide services to their customers. If the number of service-providers is increased, customers receive prompter service. Often, the frequency of customer requests for a service varies according to the time of the day or the day of the week. Thus, the number of individuals assigned to provide the service should also vary. For example, the frequency of police calls (and the associated number of police officers required) varies by the time of day and the day of the week. More crime is committed on weekends and during early evening hours than at other times. As another example, the number of Directory Assistance calls is highest during morning business hours, particularly on Mondays.

Adjusting days off mitigates the day-to-day variation in staffing requirements. If more police are needed on weekends, then there should be fewer assignments with Saturday and Sunday as nonwork days. Similarly, staggering employee starting times and adjusting the pattern of lunch and other breaks help compensate for time-of-day variation.

When there is some flexibility in the scheduling of days off, starting times, lunch breaks, and coffee breaks, linear programming models for personnel scheduling are useful. If there is no flexibility, you must balance the cost of having too many personnel at some times and too few at other times.

For example, Krajewski, Ritzman, and McKenzie describe how Banc-Ohio uses a linear programming model for scheduling employees to encode checks.[3] The check volume depends on the time of day and the day of the week. The model considers the number of employees assigned to each shift and overtime shifts.

Let's formulate a personnel scheduling model based on time-of-day variation. Formulating a personnel scheduling model for day-of-week variation is left to the exercises. A simple time-of-day model is discussed so that we can study its mathematical structure.

Model Formulation

You must develop the Directory Assistance operator work schedules for a small telephone company. Table 7.14 shows the minimum number of operators necessary to provide acceptable service in six four-hour blocks. Notice that the clock times are on a 24-hour basis. Clock Time 00 and Clock Time 24 both refer to midnight. Each operator works eight consecutive hours.

Verbal model. The total requirements are 86 four-hour sessions, which is equivalent to 43 operators working eight hours. But is it possible to use only 43 operators and satisfy the minimum requirements? Or is it necessary to have more than 43 operators? The minimum requirements are larger during normal business hours than during other periods. Let's develop a linear programming model to determine the minimum number of operators required to meet the established minimums for each four-hour period.

minimize   total number of operators
subject to   number of operators working during 00–04 $\geq$ 6
number of operators working during 04–08 $\geq$ 7
number of operators working during 08–12 $\geq$ 24
number of operators working during 12–16 $\geq$ 22
number of operators working during 16–20 $\geq$ 17
number of operators working during 20–24 $\geq$ 10

Decision variables. Assume that the possible starting times are 00, 04, 08, 12, 16, and 20 hours. The decision variables are the number of operators scheduled to start work at each of the starting times. Let the decision variables be

x_1—number of operators starting at Time 00
x_2—number of operators starting at Time 04
x_3—number of operators starting at Time 08
x_4—number of operators starting at Time 12

---

[3] L. J. Krajewski, L. P. Ritzman, and P. McKenzie, "Shift Scheduling in Banking Operations: A Case Application," *Interfaces* 10, no. 2 (April 1980), pp. 1–8.

TABLE 7.14 Minimum Number of Operators Required

Time Interval	Minimum Number
00–04	6
04–08	7
08–12	24
12–16	22
16–20	17
20–24	10

x_5—number of operators starting at Time 16

x_6—number of operators starting at Time 20

Symbolic model. The total number of operators is $x_1 + x_2 + x_3 + x_4 + x_5 + x_6$. If $x_1 = 10$, then 10 operators start at 00 and are available during the periods 00–04 and 04–08. Because they work eight consecutive hours, they leave work at 8 A.M. Figure 7.8 shows the sessions worked for each starting time.

An operator can be working during the period 00–04 by starting either at 00 or on the previous day at 20. An operator starting at 20 works during the 20–24 period and the 00–04 period. Symbolically, $x_1 + x_6$ is the number of operators working during 00–04.

FIGURE 7.8 Working Perious for the Personnel Scheduling Example Starting Times

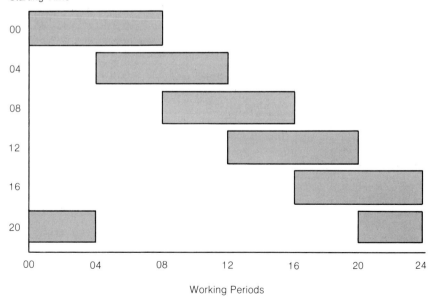

Starting Time

Working Periods

The complete symbolic model is

$$
\begin{aligned}
\min \quad & x_1 + x_2 + x_3 + x_4 + x_5 + x_6 \\
\text{st} \quad & x_1 + x_6 \geq 6 \\
& x_1 + x_2 \geq 7 \\
& x_2 + x_3 \geq 24 \\
& x_3 + x_4 \geq 22 \\
& x_4 + x_5 \geq 17 \\
& x_5 + x_6 \geq 10 \\
& x_1, x_2, x_3, x_4, x_5, x_6 \geq 0
\end{aligned}
$$

Note that the model specifies, not the starting times for particular individuals, but the number of individuals who are to begin at each possible starting time.

Model Solution Analysis

Table 7.15 contains the LOOK ALL and GO output for the linear programming personnel scheduling model. The minimum number of operators is 47, which exceeds the minimum number, 43, by 4. The surplus variable value for Row 3 is 8. Although the minimum requirement during 04–08 is 7, 15 operators are scheduled—6 starting at midnight and 9 starting at 4 A.M. Table 7.15's schedule provides exactly the minimum requirement for the other five four-hour intervals; the surplus variable values are 0 for the other constraints.

Alternate optimal solutions exist

Because six variables are positive and the model has six constraints, Table 7.15's solution is not a degenerate corner point. If the maximum allowable increase or decrease for any variable's objective function coefficient is 0, alternate optimal solutions exist. Table 7.15 shows many zero values. Thus, many alternate optimal solutions exist.

Exploring the alternate optimal solutions

Because you know that other schedules with 47 operators exist, you select from the alternate optimal solutions on a secondary criterion. A schedule with "extra" staffing allocated among time intervals besides 04–08 provides better service in more intervals. Let's search for an alternate optimal solution that uses 47 operators but allocates the extra operators to more time periods.

The dual price for Row 2, Time Period 00–04's minimum constraint, is -1. If the minimum number required during the 00–04 period increases by 1, the optimal objective function value improves by -1. That is, an additional operator is necessary and the minimum increases to 48. Similarly, the dual prices of Rows 4 and 6 indicate that any increase in the minimum requirements for 08–12 or 16–20 requires additional operators. Because the dual prices for Rows 3, 5, and 7 are 0, service above the minimum does not result in additional operators. Allocation of some of the eight extra four-hour working periods from Row 3 to Rows 5 and 7 is possible without increasing the total number of operators.

TABLE 7.15   LOOK ALL and GO Output for Directory Assistance Operator Scheduling Model

```
MIN      X1 + X2 + X3 + X4 + X5 + X6
SUBJECT TO
       2)    X1 + X6 >=    6
       3)    X1 + X2 >=    7
       4)    X2 + X3 >=   24
       5)    X3 + X4 >=   22
       6)    X4 + X5 >=   17
       7)    X5 + X6 >=   10
END

             OBJECTIVE FUNCTION VALUE

   1)        47.0000000

VARIABLE          VALUE         REDUCED COST
       X1        6.000000          .000000
       X2        9.000000          .000000
       X3       15.000000          .000000
       X4        7.000000          .000000
       X5       10.000000          .000000
       X6         .000000          .000000

   ROW      SLACK OR SURPLUS     DUAL PRICES
       2)          .000000        -1.000000
       3)         8.000000          .000000
       4)          .000000        -1.000000
       5)          .000000          .000000
       6)          .000000        -1.000000
       7)          .000000          .000000

    RANGES IN WHICH THE BASIS IS UNCHANGED

                         OBJ COEFFICIENT RANGES
VARIABLE       CURRENT      ALLOWABLE      ALLOWABLE
                COEF        INCREASE       DECREASE
       X1      1.000000       .000000      1.000000
       X2      1.000000       .000000       .000000
       X3      1.000000       .000000       .000000
       X4      1.000000       .000000       .000000
       X5      1.000000       .000000       .000000
       X6      1.000000     INFINITY        .000000

                       RIGHTHAND SIDE RANGES
   ROW        CURRENT      ALLOWABLE      ALLOWABLE
                RHS        INCREASE       DECREASE
       2      6.000000     INFINITY       6.000000
       3      7.000000     8.000000       INFINITY
       4     24.000000     INFINITY       8.000000
       5     22.000000     8.000000      15.000000
       6     17.000000    15.000000       7.000000
       7     10.000000     7.000000      10.000000
```

Table 7.16 shows the LOOK ALL and GO output for a modification to the basic personnel scheduling model. Adding Row 8, $x_1 + x_2 \leq 10$, ensures that the amount above the minimum requirement during 04–08 cannot be more than $10 - 7 = 3$. Rows 9 and 10 ensure that the amount above the minimum requirements for 12–16 and 20–24 cannot be more than 3. Table 7.16 shows that 47 operators are scheduled, but the extra eight four-hour staffings are allocated to 04–08, 12–16, and 20–24.

A fractional variable value does not make sense when you are schedul-

TABLE 7.16   LOOK ALL and GO Output for Directory Assistance Operator Scheduling Model—Additional Constraints

```
MIN      X1 + X2 + X3 + X4 + X5 + X6
SUBJECT TO
        2)    X1 + X6 >=    6
        3)    X1 + X2 >=    7
        4)    X2 + X3 >=   24
        5)    X3 + X4 >=   22
        6)    X4 + X5 >=   17
        7)    X5 + X6 >=   10
        8)    X1 + X2 <=   10
        9)    X3 + X4 <=   25
       10)    X5 + X6 <=   13
END

            OBJECTIVE FUNCTION VALUE

    1)          47.0000000

   VARIABLE           VALUE          REDUCED COST
       X1           6.000000           .000000
       X2           4.000000           .000000
       X3          20.000000           .000000
       X4           5.000000           .000000
       X5          12.000000           .000000
       X6            .000000           .000000

    ROW       SLACK OR SURPLUS        DUAL PRICES
        2)            .000000          -1.000000
        3)           3.000000            .000000
        4)            .000000          -1.000000
        5)           3.000000            .000000
        6)            .000000          -1.000000
        7)           2.000000            .000000
        8)            .000000            .000000
        9)            .000000            .000000
       10)           1.000000            .000000
```

Fractional variable values

ing personnel. Four tenths of a person cannot start at midnight! Fortunately, the optimal solutions shown in Tables 7.15 and 7.16 have integer variable values. Generalizations and extensions of the personnel scheduling linear programming model may result in noninteger variable values. If the optimal values of some of the variables are noninteger, they can be rounded to integer values. The rounded solution is not guaranteed to be the optimal integer solution, but it's likely to be close. Be careful to round noninteger variable values correctly. Because the constraints are all $\geq$, if the variables are all rounded down, the resulting values will not satisfy all of the constraints. Solving the model as an integer linear programming model is another possibility. In Chapter 9, we discuss integer linear programming. Remember, solving an integer linear programming model is significantly more difficult than solving a linear programming model.

Model Manipulations and Extensions

Figure 7.9 contains the LINDO picture for the directory assistance operator scheduling model. Understanding the model's structure makes it

FIGURE 7.9 Picture of Personnel Scheduling Example Model—LINDO PIC Command

```
: pic

            X X X X X X
            1 2 3 4 5 6

      1: 1 1 1 1 1 1 MIN
      2: 1         1 > 6
      3: 1 1'  '   '   > 7
      4:   1 1 '     > B
      5:     1 1     > B
      6: '   '  1 1'  > B
      7:        ' 1 1 > A
```

easier to generalize the model to other personnel scheduling problems. If a constraint coefficient for a work schedule is 1, a person on that schedule is available during that constraint's time period. A constraint coefficient of 0 corresponds to not being available. The variable x_1 corresponds to a work schedule for a person beginning at midnight. That person is available during the time segments 00–04 and 04–08 but not during the other time segments.

There are many possible modifications and generalizations of the personnel scheduling model. Using four-hour blocks, Tables 7.15 and 7.16 schedule eight four-hour periods more than the minimum requirements. This is an extra four operators. Perhaps, if the time periods were smaller, fewer operators would be required. For example, the actual hour-by-hour requirements between 4 P.M. and 8 P.M. vary greatly. Additional detail is incorporated by dividing the time intervals into *hours*. Then, the linear programming model has 24 constraints (one for each hour's minimum requirement) and 24 decision variables (one for each possible hourly starting time). Say that an operator begins at 00, works 00–04, has one hour for lunch, and finishes by working 05–09. The constraint coefficients are 1, 1, 1, 1, 0, 1, 1, 1, 1, 0, 0, . . . , 0, where the 1's represent hours working and the 0's represent hours not working.

In addition, say that the lunch break can be scheduled after three, four, or five hours of work. Three decision variables are defined for each starting hour. In this case, the model has 72 decision variables. By using 15-minute intervals, the model can also incorporate different patterns of coffee breaks and lunch breaks.

The above model schedules only one day. Generalization to more than one day requires a different constraint for each time period and day-of-week combination. If each day had six four-hour time periods, a weekly model would have $6 \times 7 = 42$ constraints. You define a different variable for each possible work schedule.

A more aggregated version might be useful for studying vacation

Generalizing to shorter time periods

Longer time horizons

schedules. In this case, the appropriate time interval is probably a week, not four hours. *Remember, different levels of detail and aggregation are appropriate for studying different types of decisions.*

Another extension of the above model is the payment of "shift differential." It is common in manufacturing to pay a differential for schedules other than 8 A.M. to 4 P.M. If wage rates differ for different work schedules, minimizing the total cost of the operators is preferred to minimizing the number of operators. Say that c_j is the wage rate for an individual who starts at the jth starting time. For example, c_1 is the cost per operator starting at Time 00. Minimization of the total cost of the operators results in the objective function

$$c_1 x_1 + c_2 x_2 + c_3 x_3 + c_4 x_4 + c_5 x_5 + c_6 x_6$$

MULTIPLE OBJECTIVES, GOAL PROGRAMMING, AND DEVIATIONAL VARIABLES

All of the constrained optimization models that we have developed had a single objective. Thus, the objective was represented in the objective function that was to be either maximized or minimized. For example, the radio product mix model in Chapter 3 had profit maximization as the objective, and the objective function was maximize profit. Secondary objectives and qualitative factors as well as the model's results are considered when *you* make the decision.

Sometimes, the model can be used to explore secondary objectives. For example, we used the Directory Assistance operator scheduling model to explore alternate optimal solutions to allocate extra employee shifts. The secondary objective is providing better service. Allocating the extra employee shifts to several time periods improved the service in those time periods. The original optimal solution allocated all of the extra employee shifts to one time period, which improved service in only that time period. Allocating the extra employee shifts to several time periods improved the overall service level.

One approach to multiple objectives
One approach to multiple objectives is to include some objectives as model constraints. At the beginning of Chapter 5, we described how New England Leasing used a linear programming model to choose its mix of leases. The objective function was maximizing the net present value (NPV) of the leases during the time horizon. The lease mix that maximizes NPV during the time horizon might yield a small return on assets during a particular year. Maximizing the return on assets each year was a secondary objective. New England Leasing included constraints to ensure that the return on assets each year achieved a minimum value.

In this section, we describe a media selection problem. The media buyer wants to reach as many people as possible and also wants the cost to be small. These goals conflict, so we begin with a linear programming

Two more approaches
for multiple objectives

model that has a single objective and treats the other goals as constraints. After discovering that the model has no feasible solution, we reevaluate the decision problem and introduce two objectives. We describe two approaches to a problem with multiple objectives—goal programming and priority goal programming.

You are the media buyer for an advertising agency. One of your clients has allocated $60,000 for media purchases. You have four possible media to recommend—two television shows, a radio station, and a magazine with an exclusive readership. Your client asks you to recommend a media purchase plan. She wants the media cost to be minimized.

Table 7.17 provides information on each media type. For example, a 60-second commercial on the first television program costs $10,000. Table 7.17 also provides information on the number of exposures for each media type. Advertisers use thousands as the unit of exposure. Table 7.17 shows that a 60-second commercial on the first program has 18,000 total exposures (i.e., 18 million people). This program has the lowest cost per exposure, $10,000/18,000 = \$0.555$ per thousand viewers. *Total* exposures include everyone who is exposed to the advertisement. The last column lists the number of high-income exposures. Your client believes that high-income exposures are more likely to result in sales. The exclusive magazine has the lowest cost per high-income exposure.

Your client's minimum acceptable total and high-income exposures are 110,000 and 7,500, respectively. She has previously committed herself to a minimum of four radio ads.

A Cost Minimization Model Formulation for Media Selection

We use the three-step method to formulate the linear programming model that minimizes the cost of satisfying the minimum exposure requirements and the radio commitment.

Verbal model. The verbal model is

minimize   total cost of advertising program
subject to   number of dollars spent ≤ 60000
number of total exposures ≥ 110000
number of high-income exposures ≥ 7500
number of radio ads ≥ 4

TABLE 7.17 Data for Media Selection Example

Media	Cost/Ad	Total Exposures	High-Income Exposures
TV 1	$10,000	18,000	1,000
TV 2	9,000	15,000	1,100
Radio	1,500	1,800	120
Magazine	2,500	1,900	500

Decision variables. We define the decision variables as follows:

TV1—number of ads on Television Program 1

TV2—number of ads on Television Program 2

RADIO—number of radio ads

MAG—number of ads in exclusive magazine

For example, if $TV1 = 1$, its cost is \$10,000 and the number of total exposures is 18,000.

Symbolic model. The complete symbolic model is

min $10000TV1 + 9000TV2 + 1500RADIO + 2500MAG$

st $10000TV1 + 9000TV2 + 1500RADIO + 2500MAG \leq 60000$

$18000TV1 + 15000TV2 + 1800RADIO + 1900MAG \geq 110000$

$1000TV1 + 1100TV2 + 120RADIO + 500MAG \geq 7500$

$RADIO \geq 4$

$TV1, TV2, RADIO, MAG \geq 0$

If you keep the units consistent, the constraints are not difficult.

The Cost Minimization Model's Solution Analysis

No feasible solution

Table 7.18 contains the LOOK ALL and GO output for the linear programming model and shows that no feasible solution exists. Within the budget limit, the minimum exposure requirements cannot be satisfied. When you tell your client this, she says that the budget cannot be increased and that the exposure numbers were only goals. She asks you to come as close as possible to these goals and still stay within the budget.

Reformulation as a Goal Programming Model

Let's reformulate the model. First, define new variables for the amount that the actual exposures exceed or fall short of the goals.

U1—number of exposures under the total exposure goal

O1—number of exposures over the total exposure goal

U2—number of exposures under the high-income exposure goal

O2—number of exposures over the high-income exposure goal

The new variables are **deviational variables,** which are the amount that the actual LHS value deviates from the RHS constant. Your client has two objectives: Come as close as possible to the total exposure goal and to the high-income exposure goal. For the total exposure goal, we introduce the **goal constraint**

$$18000TV1 + 15000TV2 + 1800RADIO + 1900MAG$$
$$- O1 + U1 = 110000$$

TABLE 7.18   LOOK ALL and GO Output for Media Selection Example—No Feasible Solution

```
MIN     10000 TV1 + 9000 TV2 + 1500 RADIO + 2500 MAG
SUBJECT TO
      2)    10000 TV1 + 9000 TV2 + 1500 RADIO + 2500 MAG <=    60000
      3)    18000 TV1 + 15000 TV2 + 1800 RADIO + 1900 MAG >=   110000
      4)    1000 TV1 + 1100 TV2 + 120 RADIO + 500 MAG >=    7500
      5)    RADIO >=    4
END

:go

NO FEASIBLE SOLUTION AT STEP     1
SUM OF INFEASIBILITIES= 3504.00

VIOLATED ROWS HAVE NEGATIVE SLACK,
OR (EQUALITY ROWS) NONZERO SLACKS.
ROWS CONTRIBUTING TO INFEASIBILITY
HAVE NONZERO DUAL PRICE.

        OBJECTIVE FUNCTION VALUE

      1)      60000.0000

      VARIABLE        VALUE          REDUCED COST'
        TV1         6.000000            .000000
        TV2          .000000         1000.000000
        RADIO        .000000          929.000000
        MAG          .000000         2350.000000


        ROW     SLACK OR SURPLUS      DUAL PRICES
        2)           .000000           1.900000
        3)        -2000.000000        -1.000000
        4)        -1500.000000        -1.000000
        5)           -4.000000        -1.000000
```

If the LHS is greater than the 110,000 goal, *O1* is the amount greater than the goal. If the LHS is less than the goal, *U1* is the amount less than the goal.

A **goal programming model** converts each goal to an equation by adding deviational variables and minimizes an objective that includes the deviational variables. Your client tells you that the high-income exposure goal is 7 times as important as the total exposure goal, because research indicates that a high-income exposure is 7 times as likely as a total exposure to result in a sale. You weight the unsatisfied high-income exposures by 7 and the unsatisfied total exposures by 1. The objective is to minimize *U1* + 7*U2*, the weighted unsatisfied exposures. Because your client has not expressed any favorable opinion about exceeding the exposure goals, the objective function coefficients of *O1* and *O2* are 0.

The goal programming model is

min   *U1* + 7*U2*
st $10000TV1 + 9000TV2 + 1500RADIO + 2500MAG \le 60000$

<table>
<tr><td>A linear programming
model</td><td>

$18000TV1 + 15000TV2 + 1800RADIO + 1900MAG - O1 + U1$
$= 110000$
$1000TV1 + 1100TV2 + 120RADIO + 500MAG - O2 + U2$
$= 7500$
$RADIO \geq 4$
$U1, O1, U2, O2, TV1, TV2, RADIO, MAG \geq 0$

</td></tr>
</table>

This goal programming model is a linear programming model.

The Goal Programming Model's Solution Analysis

Table 7.19 contains the LOOK ALL and GO output for the goal (linear) programming model. The minimum weighted unsatisfied exposures is 15,740. The best plan is four ads on the second television program and four radio ads. The values of $U1$ and $U2$ are 12,800 and 420, respectively. This media plan is under the total exposure goal by 12,800 and under the high-income exposure goal by 420. Because the slack of Row 2 is 0, the entire budget of $60,000 is spent.

The interpretation of Row 5's dual price is interesting. What is the impact if the radio ads aren't used? After observing that the maximum allowable decrease is 4, you conclude that if you don't purchase any radio ads, the minimum weighted unsatisfied exposures decreases by $1,143.33 \times 4 = 4,573.32$. Then, the weighted unsatisfied exposures decreases to 11,166.68 (15,740 − 4,573.32).

(margin note: Dropping the radio ads)

The dual price of Row 3 indicates that if the goal for total exposures increases by 1, the weighted unsatisfied exposures increases by 1. Because the objective function weight of high-income exposures is 7, if the goal for high-income exposures (Row 4) increases by 1, then the weighted unsatisfied exposures increases by 7.

In the model, the weights for total exposures and high-income exposures are 1 and 7, respectively. Because there is uncertainty about the relative values of these weights, you should examine the model's sensitivity to changes in their values. The maximum allowable decrease for $U2$'s objective function coefficient is 1. If $U2$'s weight is less than 6, the media plan changes and you must re-solve the model.

(margin note: The goal weights)

Priority Goal Programming

The goal programming formulation assigned weights to the amounts that goals were undersatisfied, a common approach to multiple objectives. This approach can be used for as many objectives as desired. For each objective, you introduce a goal constraint with two deviational variables—undersatisfying and oversatisfying. Then, you assign weights to the deviational variables.

Another approach to multiple objectives is **priorities.** Rather than assigning weights to the deviational variables, you establish a hierarchy of goal priorities. Using **priority goal programming,** you optimize the first

(margin note: Another approach to multiple objectives)

TABLE 7.19 LOOK ALL and GO Output for Goal Programming Formulation of the Media Selection Example

```
MIN     U1 + 7 U2
SUBJECT TO
    2)    10000 TV1 + 9000 TV2 + 1500 RADIO + 2500 MAG <=    60000
    3)    18000 TV1 + 15000 TV2 + 1800 RADIO + 1900 MAG - O1 + U1
  =    110000
    4)    1000 TV1 + 1100 TV2 + 120 RADIO + 500 MAG - O2 + U2 =  7500
    5)    RADIO >=    4
END

        OBJECTIVE FUNCTION VALUE

    1)      15740.0000

    VARIABLE          VALUE          REDUCED COST
       TV1           .000000          222.222700
       TV2          6.000000             .000000
     RADIO          4.000000             .000000
       MAG           .000000          905.555700
        O1           .000000            1.000000
        U1     12800.000000             .000000
        O2           .000000            7.000000
        U2       420.000000             .000000

       ROW    SLACK OR SURPLUS      DUAL PRICES
        2)           .000000          2.522222
        3)           .000000         -1.000000
        4)           .000000         -7.000000
        5)           .000000      -1143.333000

RANGES IN WHICH THE BASIS IS UNCHANGED:

                             OBJ COEFFICIENT RANGES
    VARIABLE          CURRENT         ALLOWABLE         ALLOWABLE
                       COEF           INCREASE          DECREASE
       TV1           .000000         INFINITY         222.222700
       TV2           .000000       200.000400           INFINITY
     RADIO           .000000         INFINITY        1143.333000
       MAG           .000000         INFINITY         905.555700
        O1           .000000         INFINITY           1.000000
        U1          1.000000          .166667            .399510
        O2           .000000         INFINITY           7.000000
        U2          7.000000         4.657143           1.000002

                             RIGHTHAND SIDE RANGES
       ROW          CURRENT          ALLOWABLE         ALLOWABLE
                      RHS            INCREASE          DECREASE
        2       60000.000000       3436.364000      54000.000000
        3      110000.000000         INFINITY       12800.000000
        4        7500.000000         INFINITY         420.000000
        5           4.000000        36.000000           4.000000
```

goal and then, using the second goal, you choose from among the solutions that optimize the first goal. Let's say that high-income exposures are the first goal and that total exposures are the second goal. First, you minimize the number of unsatisfied high-income exposures. Then, from among the media plans that have the smallest number of unsatisfied high-income exposures, you choose the one that has the smallest number of unsatisfied total exposures. Because the goals conflict, you must either solve the problem in two stages using linear programming or use priority goal programming software.

TABLE 7.20 LOOK ALL and GO Output for First Stage of Priority Programming Example

```
MIN      U2
SUBJECT TO
       2)    10000 TV1 + 9000 TV2 + 1500 RADIO + 2500 MAG <=   60000
       3)    18000 TV1 + 15000 TV2 + 1800 RADIO + 1900 MAG - O1 + U1
       =     110000
       4)    1000 TV1 + 1100 TV2 + 120 RADIO + 500 MAG - O2 + U2 = 7500
       5)    RADIO >=    4
END

        OBJECTIVE FUNCTION VALUE

     1)        .000000000

    VARIABLE         VALUE           REDUCED COST
        TV1         .000000            .000000
        TV2         .000000            .000000
      RADIO        4.000000            .000000
        MAG       14.040000            .000000
        O1          .000000            .000000
        U1       76124.000000          .000000
        O2          .000000            .000000
        U2          .000000           1.000000

      ROW     SLACK OR SURPLUS      DUAL PRICES
       2)      18900.000000          .000000
       3)          .000000           .000000
       4)          .000000           .000000
       5)          .000000           .000000

RANGES IN WHICH THE BASIS IS UNCHANGED:

                        OBJ COEFFICIENT RANGES
    VARIABLE         CURRENT        ALLOWABLE      ALLOWABLE
                      COEF          INCREASE       DECREASE
        TV1         .000000         INFINITY        .000000
        TV2         .000000         INFINITY        .000000
      RADIO         .000000         INFINITY        .000000
        MAG         .000000          .000000        .000000
        O1          .000000         INFINITY        .000000
        U1          .000000          .000000        .000000
        O2          .000000         INFINITY        .000000
        U2         1.000000         INFINITY       1.000000

                        RIGHTHAND SIDE RANGES
      ROW          CURRENT         ALLOWABLE      ALLOWABLE
                     RHS           INCREASE       DECREASE
        2        60000.000000      INFINITY      18900.000000
        3       110000.000000      INFINITY      76124.000000
        4         7500.000000     3780.000000     7020.000000
        5            4.000000       21.000000        4.000000
```

The first-stage linear programming model

Let's solve the problem in two stages using linear programming. The first stage minimizes the unsatisfied high-income exposures. Table 7.20 contains the LOOK ALL and GO output for this stage. In Table 7.20, the optimal objective function value is 0. Thus, it is possible to satisfy the high-income exposure goal, 7,500, if you ignore the total exposure goal. Note that the total exposure goal is unsatisfied by 76,124 exposures. The media plan includes radio and the exclusive magazine. Also, there is $18,900 unspent from the budget. Because the model has four positive variables and four constraints, the solution is not degenerate. And because the solution is not degenerate, the existence of the zero-valued limits for objective function coefficients means that the high-income exposure goal can be met by other media plans.

In the second stage, the high-income exposure value obtained in the first stage (7,500) becomes a constraint:

$$1000TV1 + 1100TV2 + 120RADIO + 500MAG = 7500$$

The second-stage linear programming model

If satisfying the high-income exposure goal had been impossible, the RHS constant would be the maximum number of high-income exposures obtained in the first-stage solution. In the second stage, the objective is minimize U_1, the unsatisfied deviational variable of the total exposure goal. Table 7.21 shows the LOOK ALL and GO output for the second stage. Among the media plans that satisfy the high-income exposure goal, the media plan closest to the total exposure goal misses by 17,696 exposures. Table 7.21's media plan is 5.4 ads on the second television program, 4 radio ads, and 2.16 ads in the exclusive magazine. This media plan spends the entire $60,000 budget.

Which approach should you use?

The media plans obtained by using goal programming (Table 7.19) and priority goal programming (Table 7.21) are not the same. The media plan obtained by using priority goal programming satisfies the first-priority goal, high-income exposures, but misses satisfying the second-priority goal, total exposures, by 17,696. The media plan obtained by using goal

---

TABLE 7.21   LOOK ALL and GO for Second Stage of Priority Programming Example

```
MIN     U1
SUBJECT TO
     2)    10000 TV1 + 9000 TV2 + 1500 RADIO + 2500 MAG <=   60000
     3)    18000 TV1 + 15000 TV2 + 1800 RADIO + 1900 MAG - O1 + U1
     =    110000
     4)    1000 TV1 + 1100 TV2 + 120 RADIO + 500 MAG =    7500
     5)    RADIO >=    4
END

     OBJECTIVE FUNCTION VALUE

     1)    17696.0000

VARIABLE          VALUE          REDUCED COST
    TV1           .000000         1257.143000
    TV2          5.400000           .000000
    RADIO        4.000000           .000000
    MAG          2.160000           .000000
    O1            .000000          1.000000
    U1        17696.000000          .000000

     ROW     SLACK OR SURPLUS      DUAL PRICES
     2)            .000000         3.091429
     3)            .000000        -1.000000
     4)            .000000       -11.657140
     5)            .000000      -1438.286000
```

programming undersatisfies both goals—high-income exposures by 420 and total exposures by 12,800. You can use either approach to multiple objectives. However, the approaches give solutions with different characteristics. You must consider how you view the conflicting goals. Is one goal so important that you want to reach it regardless of the other goals? If so, use priority goal programming. Are all of the goals important, but with different weights? If so, use goal programming.

The media plan in Table 7.21 contains fractional variable values. One possible response to such values is to use integer linear programming (see Chapter 9). However, if the client spends $60,000 every month, you can adjust the month-to-month frequencies to achieve the fractional values. For example, *TV2* is 5.4, so three fifths of the months you order five ads and two fifths of the months you order six.

SUMMARY

In this chapter, we discussed many applications of linear programming models. For each linear programming application, we formulated a model and discussed the computer output. We also manipulated the model and discussed extensions of the model.

The applications discussed represent a small proportion of the possible practical applications of linear programming. Oil, chemical, steel, and forest product companies use multiple-product blending models. Multiple-period models have wide applicability. Although the example used in this chapter was a production planning formulation, virtually all of the static, single-period linear programming models from Chapters 3–7 can be generalized into dynamic, multiple-period models. The variables that link the time periods are the key to the generalization.

The transportation model discussed in this chapter has many applications. Also discussed was production planning for companies with several manufacturing plants. In the production-distribution model, we generalized the production planning model to consider shipping decisions.

A generalization of the machine assignment problem provided the basis for a discussion of piecewise linear objective functions. For any model with a piecewise linear objective function, you break up the piecewise variable into different variables for each of its linear segments. The personnel scheduling problem selected the numbers of Directory Assistance operators who would start work at staggered starting times during a 24-hour period. If you consider longer time horizons, you use the same approach to determine days off and vacation schedules.

In the last section, we used a media selection problem to discuss three approaches to problems with multiple objectives. You can include all of the objectives except one in the constraints. In the goal programming approach, goal constraints are introduced and the solution with the smallest total weighted deviations is found. Another approach, priority goal programming, establishes priorities for the consideration of objectives. You obtain the priority goal programming solution by proceeding in several stages, each being a linear programming model, or by using special software.

The models discussed in this chapter were selected because they are practical applications and because they illustrate some lessons about building and using models. First, understanding the mathematical structure of a model aids in model verification and generalization. For example, if you understand the structure of the multiple-product blending model, it's easier to generalize it by adding more blending stocks, quality specifications, or finished products. Also, -1 and $+1$ coefficients have a special role in many models. For example, the -1 and $+1$ constraint coefficients for the inventory variables in the multiple-period model correspond to removing units from one period's requirement constraint and adding them to the requirement constraint of another period. The -1 and $+1$ coefficients for the interplant shipping variables play a similar role with regard to plant requirements. The variables with these coefficients link submodels.

Second, you can use the model itself to develop insight into the solution output. For example, we studied the dual prices and reduced costs of the multiple-period model by changing capacities and requirements and re-solving the model. If you don't understand a numerical value in the output, be skeptical. The model may be incorrect. Re-solve versions of the model to validate its results or obtain insight into the decision environment.

Third, identifying the existence of alternate optimal solutions allows you to explore them through the use of a secondary criterion (e.g., reallocating personnel shifts above the minimum in the personnel scheduling example). The section discussing priority goal programming also illustrated this point.

You must understand the limitations of linear programming models. First, for linear programming models, all decision variables are continuous and all functions are linear. Second, linear programming models tell what to do in a time period but not when to do it during the period. By subdividing the time period and creating a dynamic, multiple-period model, you obtain information on timing. Third, the reformulation of piecewise linear objective functions as linear programming models has two limitations: (1) The line segments must touch at the end points. (2) You cannot reformulate troublesome piecewise linear objective functions as linear programming models.

Observe several cautions in constructing and using linear programming models. First, define the inventory (or linking) variables for multiple-period models and include the constraints defining the linking relationships. A related caution is to include balance equations (e.g., Sources = Uses) whenever necessary. Also, when you introduce additional variables to reformulate a piecewise linear objective function, either include a constraint defining their relationship with the piecewise linear variable or eliminate the piecewise linear variable from the new formulation. If you aren't sure whether a constraint is needed, include it. Including a redundant constraint is preferable to omitting a needed constraint.

Second, beware of cost minimization models with ≤ requirement constraints. The minimum cost often corresponds to doing nothing.

Third, be careful of the approach you use for multiple objectives. Goal programming assumes that the contribution of each deviational variable is linear. But if a goal is missed by 10 times as much, you may not be 10 times as unhappy. Using priority goal programming, your solution may be only slightly better than another alternative on the top-priority objective but far worse than another alternative on a secondary objective.

Fourth, if the objective function is piecewise linear, check whether it's troublesome. If it's OK, you can solve the reformulated linear programming model. If it's troublesome, you can't solve the reformulated linear programming model. In Chapter 9, we show the reformulation of troublesome piecewise linear objective functions as integer linear programming models.

QUESTIONS

1. What is the structure of a linear programming model?
2. Give two reasons for examining the structure of a linear programming model.
3. What is a balance constraint?
4. What is a troublesome piecewise linear objective function?
5. Sketch an example of the OK piecewise linear objective function for a minimization model.
6. Sketch an example of the troublesome piecewise linear objective function for a minimization model.
7. Sketch an example of the OK piecewise linear objective function for a maximization model.
8. Sketch an example of the troublesome piecewise linear objective function for a maximization model.
9. Why is the all-units quantity discount not amenable to reformulation as a linear programming model?
10. If the objective function is cost minimization, can an incremental quantity discount be reformulated as a linear programming model?
11. How can you use a model to understand the economic value of a dual price?

12. Give three approaches to models with multiple objectives.

13. What is a deviational variable?

14. What is a goal programming model?

15. What is a priority goal programming model?

16. If a model has three objectives, how many stages are required to solve the priority goal programming model by linear programming?

EXERCISES

These exercises are extensions of the chapter's examples. In each exercise, you are asked to modify the models developed in the chapter. Doing so will heighten your understanding of the models and their manipulations.

1. Reformulate the two-product gasoline blending model with additional variables R and P, representing barrels blended of regular and premium gasoline, respectively. Now, give the picture of the model structure. Leave all zero-valued coefficients blank. Represent nonzero coefficients, except for $+1$ and -1, by an x.

2. Reformulate the two-product gasoline blending model with a third product that has a minimum octane number of 89 and a maximum vapor pressure of 6.7. The selling price is $1.25 per gallon, and up to 30,000 *gallons* can be sold at that price. Now, give the picture of the model structure. Leave all zero-valued coefficients blank. Represent nonzero coefficients, except for $+1$ and -1, by an x.

3. Reformulate the two-product gasoline blending model by adding minimum vapor pressures of 6.3 and 6.5 for regular and premium gasoline, respectively.

4. Say that the two-product gasoline blending model has a fourth blending stock, denoted Y. Give the picture of the model structure. Leave all zero-valued coefficients blank. Represent nonzero coefficients, except for $+1$ and -1, by an x.

5. Assuming that the number of units available at the beginning of Month 1 is 150, reformulate the multiple-period example, using the model formulation that lacks the variable I_0.

6. Assuming that the number of units available at the beginning of Month 1 is 150, reformulate the multiple-period example, using the model formulation that includes the variable I_0.

7. Assuming that the manufacturing cost in Month 3 is $12.30, reformulate the multiple-period example, using the model formulation that includes the variable I_0.

8. Give a correct model of the multiple-period example without the inventory variables.

9. Assuming that the inventory cost in Month 3 is $0.20, revise the multiple-period example model without inventory variables.

10. Assuming that the requirements for the first month are 1,100, not 1,000, revise the multiple-period example model without inventory variables.

11. Revise the multiple-period example model by adding a fifth month with a requirement of 1,075 units, a variable manufacturing cost of $12.60 per unit, and a capacity of 1,000 units.

12. Revise the multiple-period example model with significant material handling costs by treating items placed in inventory at the end of Month 2 similarly to the example for Month 1.

13. Say that the storage cost for the multiple-period model includes $0.10 per unit material handling cost plus a $0.15 per period carrying cost. Reformulate the multiple-period model to include appropriate inventory costs for all storage.

14. Reformulate the multiple-period model by defining i_t as the number of units in inventory at the beginning of Month t. Use inventory costs of $0.20 at the beginning of Months 1, 2, and 3 and of $0.21 at the beginning of Months 4 and 5.

15. Reformulate the multiple-period model in which the inventory costs are based on the average number of units in inventory during a month. Assume that the inventory cost is $0.20 per unit in every month. Define only the inventory variables at the end of each month.

16. Under what circumstances should the objective function be profit maximization, not cost minimization, for a transportation problem?

17. Marketing Region 1 has been subdivided into two new marketing regions, called 1A and 1B, with requirements of 175 units and 125 units, respectively. The transportation costs to 1A are $1.15, $1.05, and $0.85 from Warehouses 1, 2, and 3, respectively. The transportation costs to 1B are $1.05, $1.10, and $0.75 from Warehouses 1, 2, and 3, respectively. Reformulate the transportation example model for this change. How many constraints and variables does your model have? If each of the other marketing regions is also subdivided into two regions, what are the new numbers of constraints and variables?

18. Assuming that no more than 250 units can be shipped from a warehouse to a marketing region, make the necessary modifications in the transportation example model.

19. Add a material handling cost to the transportation example model. The material handling cost is $0.05 per unit at Warehouse 1 and $0.03 per unit at the other two warehouses. Reformulate the transportation model to include these additional costs.

20. Define the intermediate variables x_i, the number of units shipped from Warehouse i, $i = 1, 2, 3$. Reformulate the transportation model to include these variables.

21. Use the formulation that includes the intermediate variables x_i (see Exercise 20) to reformulate the transportation model that includes the material handling cost introduced in Exercise 19.

22. Revise the multiple-plant machine assignment example model to include an additional $0.04 for shipping Product 1.

23. Under what circumstances should profit maximization, rather than cost minimization, be the objective function of the multiple-plant machine assignment example?

24. The shipping costs per unit of the production-distribution model extension of the multiple-plant machine assignment model are

From Plant	To Customer			
	1	2	3	4
1	0.02	0.01	0.04	0.03
2	0.05	0.04	0.02	0.02

The shipping costs are the same for both products. Give the complete model.

25. Reformulate the piecewise linear formulation of the machine assignment model with an additional change in the cost of making Product A on Machine 1. For hours above 35, the cost per hour is $0.34. For hours between 20 and 35, the cost per hour is $0.33.

26. Is it possible to reformulate the piecewise linear formulation of the machine assignment model with the following additional change in the cost of making Product A on Machine 1? For hours above 35, the cost per hour is $0.30. For hours between 20 and 35, the cost per hour is $0.33.

27. Say that each of the costs for a product on a particular machine is piecewise linear for the machine assignment model. The cost per hour increases by $0.05 above 20 hours for each of the nine product-machine combinations. How many constraints and variables does the resulting linear programming model have? Are these troublesome cost functions?

28. Modify the directory assistance operator scheduling model to reflect a shift differential of $15 per day for operators who begin between midnight and 6 A.M. and $10 per day for operators who begin between 6 P.M. and 11 P.M. The basic wage cost is $75 per day. Reformulate the model to minimize the total wage cost.

29. The solution of the directory assistance operator scheduling model requires more than 43 operators, the minimum number. Thus, you are considering having the starting times be every two hours rather than every four hours. How many constraints and how many variables would the new model have?

30. Reformulate the media selection example model to maximize the number of high-income exposures. Reformulate the media selection example model to maximize the number of total exposures.

31. Reformulate the media selection example to minimize the total weighted cost and unsatisfied high-income exposures. The weight for unsatisfied high-income exposures is 100, and the weight for cost is 1.

32. For the media selection example, the number of DINK-exposures (dual income—no kids) is 300, 250, 40, and 120 for *TV1, TV2, RADIO,* and *MAG* ads, respectively. The DINK-exposure goal is 12,000. DINK-exposures have half the effectiveness of high-income exposures. Give the goal programming formulation.

33. Say that the highest-priority goal for the media selection example is total exposures. What is the first-stage linear programming model? What is the second-stage linear programming model?

MORE CHALLENGING EXERCISES

Some of the following MCEs require interpretation of computer output. Answer each part based on the output you create. If it is impossible to answer a question from that output, indicate what new model would have to be solved.

1. A company makes two products on the same production line. The production line is available 40 hours per week. A time horizon of three weeks is to be used to plan production. The two products made are regular (R) and super (S). It requires 0.4 hours to make a unit of Product R. It requires 0.6 hours to make a unit of Product S. The processing costs will be increasing during the next three weeks. The per unit processing costs will be as follows:

	Product ($/unit)	
Week	R	S
1	35	54
2	37	58
3	37	58

The inventory carrying costs are $3 per week for each kind of product. The requirements for the next three weeks are

	Product (units)	
Week	R	S
1	40	30
2	50	33
3	60	35

Currently on hand are 5 of the regular and 0 of the super.

a. Formulate the linear programming model using the three-step approach.

  b. Solve the model.
  c. Submit a short report to your manager recommending a production plan for the next three weeks. Explain your reasoning to her as if she doesn't understand linear programming.

2. A company must schedule production during the next six weeks to minimize total cost. The requirements for those weeks are

Week	Requirement (units)
1	100
2	125
3	130
4	100
5	110
6	120

The manufacturing cost is \$120/unit during Weeks 1–4 and \$125/unit during Weeks 5–6. The inventory holding cost is \$0.75/unit held at the end of every week. The capacity on regular time is 100 units/week. If necessary, up to 20 additional units can be produced on overtime at an additional cost of \$8/unit. At the beginning, 25 units are in inventory.
  a. Formulate the linear programming model using the three-step approach.
  b. Solve the model.
  c. Graph the total manufacturing cost for Week 1 versus the number of units made during Week 1. Is this piecewise linear objective function troublesome?

3. Formulate MCE 2 as a transportation problem. Let the weekly production capabilities correspond to the warehouses and the weekly requirements correspond to the customers. An example of a decision variable is the number of units made on regular time in Period 2 to satisfy the requirement in Period 4. Represent that variable as *R24*. The units must be produced before they are required.

4. The managing partner of a small accounting firm must assign four accountants to audit four clients. One accountant must be assigned to each client. The estimated hours required for each of the potential assignments are

Accountant	Client 1	2	3	4
Anderson	125	175	215	340
Brown	215	300	310	400
Jones	180	250	300	350
Smith	210	310	340	410

The variation is based on the experience of the accountant and the complexity of the audit.

a. Formulate the linear programming model to minimize the total audit time.
b. Solve the model. Who is assigned to each client?
c. Is the optimal solution degenerate?

5. Formulate a model to determine the least expensive work schedules that will meet a community's staffing requirements for emergency medical technicians during the 8 A.M. to 4 P.M. shift. The minimum number on duty are

Day	Minimum Number
Sunday	10
Monday	12
Tuesday	13
Wednesday	12
Thursday	12
Friday	15
Saturday	16

Each employee works five days per week and has two consecutive days off. The wage cost of each employee is $75 per day during the week and $85 per day on weekends.

6. A feed supplier uses the same grains in its two products, Gro-Strong and Fast-Gro. The nutritional requirements are

Product	Protein	*Minimum Percent* Carbohydrate	Fat
Gro-Strong	20	32	15
Fast-Gro	15	37	18

Limited amounts of three feed grains are available:

Feed Grain	Percent Protein	Percent Carbohydrate	Percent Fat	Cost ($/lb.)	Pounds Available
1	15	35	16	0.16	30,000
2	25	27	17	0.19	25,000
3	12	40	19	0.12	18,000

The selling prices per pound are $0.35 and $0.32 for Gro-Strong and Fast-Gro, respectively. At most, 44,000 pounds of Gro-Strong can be sold. Any amount of Fast-Gro can be sold.

a. Formulate the linear programming model.
b. Solve the model and discuss the results.

7. As treasurer of a major corporation, you are responsible for cash management. The monthly sources and needs for funds are

Month	Internally Generated Funds ($000s)
January	300
February	400
March	− 150
April	− 50
May	250
June	300
July	− 500

Thus, for example, $300,000 will be available for investment in January, but $500,000 will be needed for expansion in July. Assume that internally generated (or used) funds are at the beginning of the month. Currently, $500,000 is in a money market account yielding 6 percent per year. At the beginning of each quarter (January and April) longer-term investments are available. A three-month certificate of deposit (CD) earns 7 percent per year, and a six-month CD earns 8 percent per year. All interest is compounded monthly. All the funds must be in the money market account at the end of July.

a. Formulate the linear programming model to maximize the total funds at the end of July.

b. Explain the relationship between the CD investment variables and the inventory variables that are introduced when inventory cost is not linear in time stored.

8. Modify the Potato Processing example in Chapter 2 by allowing storage of excess production of any product at a cost of $0.01 per pound. Selling prices, costs, and yields are the same for the next two periods. The maximum demands are

Product	Period (maximum sales, lbs.)	
	1	2
French fries	18,000	20,000
Hash browns	15,000	14,000
Flakes	30,000	25,000
Waste	Unlimited	Unlimited

No inventory is on hand at the beginning of the two periods.

a. Formulate a two-period model.

b. Solve the model and discuss the results.

c. From your output, explain the use of storage.

9. A local government received a $93,000 Federal Community Development Block Grant. Two possible projects are summer programs for youths and summer programs for senior citizens. Each unit of these programs creates

jobs and provides citizen contacts. The cost, jobs created, and citizen contacts for one unit of each of these types of programs is

Programs	Cost	Jobs	Citizen Contacts
Youth	$3,000	2	300
Senior citizen	$4,500	3	250

Under the conditions of the grant, at least 5 units of Youth programs and 4 units of Senior Citizen programs are required. The goals that have been established for the programs are 8,200 citizen contacts and 70 jobs.
a. Formulate the linear programming model to maximize the total number of jobs and citizen contacts.
b. Formulate a goal programming model to minimize the underachievement of the citizen contact goal.
c. Formulate a goal programming model to minimize the total underachievement of both goals.
d. Use priority goal programming with the citizen contact goal as the highest priority.
   (1) Formulate and solve the first-stage linear programming model.
   (2) Formulate and solve the second-stage linear programming model.

10. A manufacturing company has three plants, designated A, B, and C. The capacities and manufacturing costs of these plants are

Plant	Capacity (units)	Manufacturing Cost ($/unit)
A	2,500	25.50
B	1,750	24.90
C	3,000	25.30

The requirements in four marketing regions are:

Marketing Region	Requirement (units)
1	1,500
2	2,100
3	900
4	2,100

The shipping costs per unit from the plants to the marketing regions are:

From Plant	To Marketing Region			
	1	2	3	4
A	$1.50	$2.10	$4.20	$3.75
B	2.35	3.55	2.10	2.85
C	4.20	3.10	0.90	1.70

    a. Formulate a model to minimize the cost of satisfying the requirements.
    b. Give the manufacturing and shipping plan.
    c. What is the additional cost if the requirement for Marketing Region 3 is 1,000 units?
    d. What is the minimum cost if Plant B has a capacity of 2,400 units?

11. Repeated use of an advertising vehicle reaches fewer new exposures. Say that the number of new exposures decreases by 25 percent if an ad is repeated more than five times. Potential ads include

Vehicle	Cost per Ad	New Exposures
TV1	$2,000	3,000
TV2	2,500	3,800
TV3	2,700	4,500
TV4	1,900	2,900

No more than 10 ads can be placed on any of these vehicles. The total budget is $56,300. How many ads should be placed on each television show?

12. A manufacturing company has three plants. The capacities and manufacturing costs are

Plant	Capacity (units)	Manufacturing Cost ($/unit)
A	5,000	$15.00
B	4,000	$16.00
C	5,000	$14.50

The company has five marketing regions. Each of these regions has a minimum and maximum requirement. At least the minimum must be satisfied, but any amount up to the maximum can be sold. The marketing region information is

Marketing Region	Requirement (units)		Selling Price ($/unit)
	Minimum	Maximum	
1	2,000	3,000	40.00
2	1,500	3,000	40.50
3	3,000	5,000	40.25
4	2,000	3,000	40.40
5	4,500	6,000	40.30

The shipping costs are

From Plant	To Marketing Region				
	1	2	3	4	5
A	$2.50	$2.30	$3.20	$3.65	$2.85
B	3.35	2.55	3.10	4.85	3.10
C	1.90	2.10	1.30	2.70	2.90

a. Formulate and solve the linear programming model.

b. If you increase the capacity of a plant, which plant is the best?

13. A temporary help service has added microcomputer word processing to its services. The cost of training a new operator is $500 per month, and it takes the service one month to train a new operator. It costs the service $800 per month to use one of its trained operators. The service can also use trained individuals under contract for $1,000 per month. There are 10 trained operators now, and no one is in the training program. The requirements for the next 12 months are estimated to be

Month	Requirement
1	10
2	12
3	13
4	15
5	14
6	13
7	13
8	15
9	14
10	17
11	15
12	15

a. Formulate a linear programming model to find out how many operators to train and how many trained individuals to use under contract each month.

b. Comment on how many individuals should be trained during Month 12.

14. A problem from statistics is the estimation of parameters to identify the relationship between an independent variable, X, and a dependent variable, Y. For example, a company desires to find the relationship between shipping cost and miles shipped. The farther the distance shipped, the greater the shipping cost. The shipping cost includes a constant for loading and unloading the truck. The form of the shipping cost relationship is

$$Y = a + bX$$

where X is miles shipped and Y is the shipping cost. A sample of shipping records yields the following data:

Y	X
$ 25.00	300
45.00	400
57.50	500
89.00	750
75.25	650
110.00	900
64.00	600

The most common procedure used to estimate a and b is the method of least squares, which selects a and b to minimize the sum of the squares of the differences between the actual values of Y and the estimated values of Y. Another procedure minimizes the sum of the absolute values of the differences beween the actual values of Y and the estimated values of Y. Formulate the latter as a linear programming model. (*Hint:* Create a goal constraint for each data point.) Does your model force nonnegative values of a and b?

15. The objective function max{min{$(2A + B)$, $(3A + 4B)$}} is nonlinear. Say that the constraints are

st $3A + 2B \leq 40$
      $2A + 2B \geq 25$
      $A, B \geq 0$

Formulate the nonlinear objective function as a linear programming model. (*Hint:* Introduce a variable called M that must be less than or equal to both of the two objective function values—e.g., $M \leq 2A + B$.)

16. The objective function min{max{$(2A + B)$, $(3A + 4B)$}} is nonlinear. Say the constraints are

st $3A + 2B \leq 40$
      $2A + 2B \geq 25$
      $A, B \geq 0$

Formulate the nonlinear objective function as a linear programming model. (See MCE 15.)

17. The objective function $\max\{\max\{(2A + B), (3A + 4B)\}\}$ is nonlinear but cannot be successfully reformulated as a linear programming model by the device used in MCE 15 and 16. Explain this. Can $\min\{\min\{(2A + B), (3A + 4B)\}\}$ be reformulated as a linear programming model? Is your answer influenced by the assumption that A and B must be nonnegative?

18. The following model is not a linear programming model:

$$\max \quad e^{A + B}$$
$$\text{st} \quad A - B \geq 1$$
$$2A + B \leq 6$$
$$A, B \geq 0$$

The constraints are linear, but the objective function is nonlinear. Note that the function e^x is always increasing as x increases. Give a linear programming formulation that finds the optimal solution to the nonlinear programming model.

CASE
Racy's Department Store

The treasurer of Racy's Department Store is performing his financial planning for the next six months, September through February. Because of the Christmas season, Racy's has need for large amounts of cash, particularly in the months of November and December, and a large cash inflow occurs in January and February when customers pay their Christmas bills. These requirements are summarized in Exhibit 1.

The treasurer has three sources of short-term funds to meet Racy's needs. These are

1. *Pledge accounts receivable*. A local bank will lend Racy's funds on a month-by-month basis against a pledge on the accounts receivable balance at the beginning of a given month. The maximum loan is 75 percent of the receivables in a given month. The cost of this loan is 1.5 percent per month of the amount borrowed.

2. *Stretch payment of purchases*. Payment of purchases can be delayed one month. Thus, for example, the $100,000 planned for payments for November could be delayed until December, and Racy's could use the funds to meet November needs. When purchase payments are thus stretched, Racy's loses the 3 percent discount it normally receives for prompt payment.

3. *Use short-term loan*. A bank is willing to lend Racy's any amount from $40,000 to $100,000 on a six-month basis. The loan would be taken out in full at the beginning of September for a fixed amount and paid back in full at the end of February. It would not be possible to add to the loan or to pay off part of the loan during the period. The cost of the loan would be 1 percent per month, payable each month.

In any period, if the firm has excess funds, they can be invested in short-term government securities that return 0.5 percent per month.

The objective of the treasurer is to minimize the net interest cost to Racy's while meeting the firm's cash needs.

SOURCE: Reprinted with permission from *Quantitative Analysis for Business Decisions,* 7th ed. Bierman, Bonini, and Hausman (Homewood, Ill.: Richard D. Irwin, Inc.), p. 323.

EXHIBIT 1 Racy's Cash Requirements (in $ thousands)

	Sept.	Oct.	Nov.	Dec.	Jan.	Feb.
Accounts receivable balance (at beginning of month)	$70	$50	$ 70	$120	$100	$ 50
Planned payments of purchases (on assumption that discount is taken)	80	90	100	60	40	50
Cash needs for operations	—	30	60	90	—	—
Cash surplus from operations	20	—	—	—	30	150

CASE

Technicon Corporation

Technicon was incorporated in Delaware on July 27, 1950, as the successor to the business of Technology Products Corporation of Oklahoma and Consolidated Oil Company of California. Its purpose is to furnish technical services required in drilling oil wells, identify and evaluate producing zones within a well, and stimulate and improve the flow from oil and gas reservoirs. In June 1966, the company formed a subsidiary, Formfab, Inc., to fabricate the large metal forms used in offshore oil drilling rigs. In 1968, it acquired Lakeside Terminals, Inc., Chicago, Illinois, a petrochemical storage facility and warehouse, and canner of antifreeze, for $1,500,000 cash and $1,250,000 5 percent subordinate convertible debentures due December 31, 1980. In addition, the company performs offshore contract-drilling operations and owns five semisubmersible drilling vessels and six jack-up drilling rigs, all operating in the Gulf of Mexico, North Sea, Persian Gulf, and the Arabian Gulf.

The 1978 net sales were $124,769,000, resulting in a net income after taxes of $9,460,000. The company's long-term debt consists of $16,495,000 7¼ percent notes due $1 million annually to 1988. The loan agreements contain, among other covenants, a restriction on payment of cash dividends until the loan obligation has been reduced to $3 million.

Because of the rather volatile nature of cash requirements in the oil industry, the company must keep substantial amounts of cash on hand. Instead of keeping idle cash, Victor Bitar, treasurer, usually puts any spare cash into short-term, high-quality marketable securities. On one such occasion, Victor had to decide upon the investment of $5 million in such market instruments. He was considering several types of securities with short maturity periods and varying yield (Exhibit 1).

Since two of the company's offshore rigs were due to complete contracted work in the North Sea within the next 14 weeks, Victor wanted to invest at least $2 million in securities with no more than a three-month maturity. He took this precautionary measure just in case an unexpectedly high labor turnover at the end of a contract period might result in large severance pay expenses. However, several other vessels owned by the company had reasonably long periods left in their contracts. Therefore, Victor felt pretty safe in investing some of the $5 million in securities with longer than a seven-month maturity. However, he estimated that his investment in such securities should be less than $2 million.

SOURCE: Raj Aggarwal and Inder Khera, *Management Science Cases and Applications,* Oakland, Calif: Holden-Day, Inc., 1979, pp. 190–91.

Victor also had to consider that two of the company's directors were active in managing marketable security investments during the stock market crash of the late 1920s and early 1930s. They had become firm believers in the safety of government securities and wanted to make sure that at least a part of the company's marketable security investments should be in the form of government securities. Victor prudently decided to invest at least $1,500,000 in government securities to keep the two direc-

tors satisfied, and to limit his investment in corporate securities to a maximum of $2,500,000. Since Technicon generally dealt with large banks, it had little choice but to abide by the minimum value of $500,000 to be paid for banker's acceptances. Also, the minimum order for commercial paper had to be $0.5 million. Because of the higher yield, Victor decided that the investment in corporate bonds would be at least twice that of an investment in commercial paper.

EXHIBIT 1 Acceptable Securities and Average Yields

Security	Average Maturity	Average Yield
Treasury bills	3 months	5%
Treasury notes	9 months	6
High-grade commercial paper	3 months	7
Banker's acceptances	6 months	6
High-grade short-term corporate bonds	9 months	9

8

Networks and Special Structures

CITGO PETROLEUM CORPORATION

Citgo Petroleum Corporation (Citgo) had 1984 sales in excess of $4.5 billion. The company purchases petroleum, refines it, and markets petroleum products. During the 1970s and early 1980s, escalating petroleum cost and high interest rates caused Citgo to study its operations with a view to reducing the working capital requirements of its refining and marketing inventories. Citgo "recently realized a reduction in petroleum products inventory of $116 million (based on historical inventory-to-sales ratios), resulting in annual interest savings of $14 million, as well as improvements in coordination, pricing, and purchasing decisions estimated at $2.5 million annually."

In September 1983, a team of Citgo executives and management science consultants began development of a Supply, Distribution, and Marketing Modeling System. A network optimization model was the basis for the system they developed. The system considers product sources, distribution timing, the trading of products with other companies, and pricing decisions.

Five products, which represent 85 percent of sales, are modeled independently. The distribution network uses pipelines, tankers, and barges that link 5 distribution centers/refineries, 27 product storage terminals, 9 leased terminals, and over 350 terminals where Citgo products are distributed to gasoline stations and exchanged for products of other petroleum marketers.

The model's time horizon is 11 weeks, which is subdivided into six one-week time periods and one five-week time period. The distribution network is repeated for each time period. Long transit times require links between time periods. For example, a one-week barge trip begun in one time period delays the shipment of products to a distribution center until the following time period. Product flows have upper limits corresponding to pipeline, barge, tanker, and storage limits and lower limits representing contractual commitments and policy decisions.

For each of the independently modeled products, the network model contains about 3,000 nodes (constraints) and 15,000 arcs (variables). Using a network optimization algorithm on a medium-sized computer, the times required for model generation, solution, and report creation are two minutes, one-half minute, and seven minutes, respectively.

The network model is used by schedulers for operational decisions. But its greatest benefit is in helping top management with its weekly decisions concerning refinery operations, sources of product purchases and sales, and prices paid and charged, the amount and mode of shipping, and the timing of exchange/purchasing arrangements with other marketers. Because of the extensive management reports that the modeling system creates, it is used by product managers, traders, pricing managers, product schedulers, and budget managers.

D. Klingman, N. Phillips, D. Steiger, R. Wirth, and W. Young, "The Challenges and Success Factors in Implementing an Integrated Products Planning System for Citgo," *Interfaces* 16, no. 3 (May–June 1986), pp. 1–19.

Citgo's decision problem is represented by a linear programming model for each of its products. Product schedulers use the model to make daily decisions, and executives use it to make strategic decisions. By modifying and re-solving the model, executives get information about the impact of strategic decisions. If alternatives can be evaluated quickly, managers can try more alternatives and thus improve their decisions. Remember, models are used to provide information for decision making. You, the manager, must make the decisions.

Although the decision problem is formulated as a linear programming model, Citgo uses network software, not standard linear programming software, to solve the model. Citgo's linear programming models are large and using a program such as LINDO would lengthen the solution times. A typical Citgo model has about 3,000 constraints and 15,000 variables. With network software, it takes less than 10 minutes to generate and solve a model and create the solution reports. Citgo managers can therefore evaluate decision alternatives very rapidly. Citgo traders must make fast decisions, and the model provides them with fast information. By means of the model, for example, they can rapidly evaluate the economics of another marketer's offer to purchase regular gasoline at the Atlanta terminal.

In this chapter, we describe network problems. Network problems have many applications for managers. For example, networks may represent physical distribution systems, communication systems, pipeline systems, airline flight systems, street systems, equipment replacements, personnel assignments, and multiple-period production plans. You need to be able to recognize and formulate network problems. Special software is available that solves network problems more effectively than general linear programming software. To use such software, you need to be able to recognize the special network structures.

In the next section, we discuss the role of special mathematical structures. Then, we introduce some special structures that are exploited by *standard* linear programming software. Finally, we describe general network problems and some special network problems and consider both their applications and their special structures.

THE ROLE OF SPECIAL STRUCTURES

In Chapter 7, we defined the **mathematical structure** of a linear programming model as the pattern of nonzero coefficients and the placement of $+1$ and -1 coefficients. We explained how LINDO's PIC (picture) command shows a model's structure. One reason for understanding the mathematical structure of a model is that this makes it easier to generalize the model. For example, if you understand the structure of a two-product blending model, it is easier for you to add a third product to the model. Understanding a model's structure also enables you to diagnose input errors. Say that your knowledge of a model's structure tells you that a constraint coefficient should be zero. If the constraint coefficient is nonzero in the picture, you should check the model input. Similarly, if a constraint coefficient should be nonzero and the picture shows that it's zero, you should check the model input.

The existence of more efficient optimization methods is yet another reason for understanding the mathematical structure of a linear programming model. The network software used by Citgo is an example. In this chapter, we discuss several types of mathematical structures that have more efficient solution procedures than the standard simplex algorithm. We do not describe the special algorithms. However, we do describe the special structures so that you can recognize them and understand that special software is available to deal with them. The network models that we discuss have many business applications, including operations management, marketing, finance, and accounting. The models share the same mathematical structures, but their applications are different.

The simplex method does not assume any particular mathematical structure for a linear programming model. All of the constraint functions and the objective function are linear functions. However, any constraint coefficient can be zero or nonzero and a nonzero coefficient can have any value.

In the linear programming models presented in previous chapters, certain models had a particular mathematical structure. For example, all of the blending models had a constraint relating the total of the individual components blended and the desired volume. In the gasoline blending model of Chapter 3, the constraint is

$$B + N + R \le 30000$$

This constraint states that the total of butane, naphtha, and reformate must be $\le$ the maximum order size of 30,000 barrels. All of the nonzero variable coefficients in that constraint are $+1$. Chapter 3's chicken feed mixing model has a similar constraint. In fact, this type of quantity constraint has coefficient values of $+1$ in any blending model.

The multiple-period model in Chapter 7 links the time periods with inventory variables. The inventory variables have a coefficient of -1 when items are put into inventory and $+1$ when they are removed from inventory. The $+1$ and -1 coefficients of linking variables have a special role in multiple-period models.

Certain types of mathematical structures called **special structures** lead to special computational properties or strategies that improve the standard simplex method. If a special structure is used to "customize" the simplex algorithm, the special structure is said to be **exploited.** Exploiting the special structure includes

Motivations for exploiting special structures

1. Reducing the amount of required computer storage.
2. Reducing the amount of required computer time.

The special structures of network models have been effectively exploited. Citgo used network software because it solved the model faster than standard linear programming software. By exploiting special structures, you can solve models more quickly and re-solve them more often. This gives you more information. Also, the amount of memory available limits the maximum model size for optimization software. Network software requires less computer storage than standard linear programming software, thus enabling you to solve larger models.

The full set of sensitivity analysis information for a linear programming solution includes dual prices, reduced costs, and optimality ranges for objective function coefficients and RHS constants. For a large model, determining the ranges of the objective function coefficients and the RHS constants may take considerable time. Exploiting the special structure of the model reduces this time. However, some special-purpose software does not provide the full set of information that is given by most linear programming software. This is particularly true of instructional software. Commercial software provides the full set of sensitivity analysis information.

Integer variable values at corner points

Remember, there is a corner point of the feasible set that is an optimal solution for linear programming models, and the simplex method finds an optimal corner point solution. A *special property of network models* with integer RHS constants is that every corner point has integer variable values. Therefore, the optimal solution to network models has integer variable values. Because fractional variable values may not be realistic, this is an attractive property of network models.

Before we discuss network problems, let's consider two special structures—simple bounds and generalized upper bounds. These special structures appear in many general linear programming models, and general linear programming software often exploits them. Our discussion illustrates the advantages of exploiting special structures.

SIMPLE UPPER BOUNDS AND SIMPLE LOWER BOUNDS

The simplest type of constraint is a limitation on a single variable value. A **simple upper bound** (SUB) is an upper limit on a single variable value. For example, if the value of Variable A can be no larger than 7, the constraint is

$$A \leq 7$$

In this constraint, only Variable A has a nonzero coefficient, and its coefficient is $+1$. If this SUB is treated explicitly, we input the constraint as $A \leq 7$. By doing so, we increase the number of constraints and thus add a row to the simplex table. (See the Theory section of Chapter 6.)

Some linear programming software treats SUB constraints implicitly. We won't describe the detailed procedure for doing this. Generally, the simplex rules are slightly modified so that the SUB is not violated, thus avoiding the addition of an extra row to the simplex table. This is an example of exploiting the special structure of a linear programming model. LINDO is one of the systems that treat SUBs implicitly. The SUB is not entered as a constraint. Instead, it is entered after all of the constraints have been entered. In LINDO, SUBs are entered as illustrated in Table 8.1.

Consider a gas supply planning model for a natural gas company located in a metropolitan area. Each day, gas can be purchased from two different pipeline companies or withdrawn from storage. A 365-day planning model minimizes the annual cost of satisfying the daily requirements for natural gas. The model has 365 storage withdrawal variables and 365 variables for purchases from each of the pipeline companies. This means that there are $3 \times 365 = 1,095$ variables. The model has one constraint ensuring that the total amount withdrawn from storage during the year isn't more than the amount in storage. Monthly contractual agreements with the two pipeline companies create 24 more constraints. Because of physical limitations, there is a daily maximum withdrawal from storage, so the 365 storage withdrawal variables have SUBs. The daily pipeline purchases also have maximums. Thus, the model has 1,095 variables (each with an SUB) and 25 other constraints. If the bounds are treated explicitly, the model has 1,120 constraints and 1,095 variables. Alternatively, with implicit treatment of SUBs, the model has only 25 constraints and 1,095 variables. If your software has a maximum of 100 constraints, you can solve the model by treating the SUBs implicitly. If you treat the SUBs explicitly, you can't solve the model.

Remember, the computational effort increases with the *square* of the number of constraints. The model with 1,120 constraints is far harder to

An example of the advantage of treating SUBs implicitly

TABLE 8.1 Adding SUBs and SLBs—LINDO

```
: look all

  MAX      4 A + 2 B
  SUBJECT TO
        2)    2 A + B <=    18
        3)    3 A - B =     15
  END

: sub A
BND=7
: slb A
BND=3
: look all

  MAX      4 A + 2 B
  SUBJECT TO
        2)    2 A + B <=    18
        3)    3 A - B =     15
  END
  SLB        A        3.00
  SUB        A        7.00

: go
     LP OPTIMUM FOUND  AT STEP     2

            OBJECTIVE FUNCTION VALUE
     1)          36.0000000

  VARIABLE          VALUE          REDUCED COST
        A          6.599999         0.000000
        B          4.800000         0.000000

     ROW      SLACK OR SURPLUS    DUAL PRICES
        2)         0.000000        2.000000
        3)         0.000000        0.000000
```

solve than the one with 25 constraints. Treating the SUBs implicitly requires some additional computational effort, but reducing the number of constraints is worth that effort. If your software allows it, you should treat SUBs implicitly.

A **simple lower bound** (SLB) imposes a minimum on a single variable's value. Table 8.1 shows how to specify an SLB with LINDO. In Table 8.1, the smallest possible value of A is 3. You can explicitly add the constraint

$$A \geq 3$$

or you can treat it implicitly. Explicit treatment adds one constraint to the model and one row to the simplex table. Remember, the standard form for the simplex method assumes that all of the variable values are non-negative (i.e., ≥ 0). If the lower bound is 3, the variable value must also be ≥ 0.

Conceptually, treating an SLB is quite easy. If the software available to you does not have SLB capabilities, you can use the approach we describe to explicitly modify your model so that an SLB does not add a constraint. Say that A has an SLB of 3. Redefine the decision variables so

Explicitly modifying the
model for an SLB

that *APLUS* is the amount that Variable *A* is above the lower-bound value of 3. That is, let $A = 3 + APLUS$. Because the standard form ensures that *APLUS* must be ≥ 0, the feasible values of *A* are those ≥ 3. Everywhere the Variable *A* appears in the model, substitute the value $(3 + APLUS)$. Collect terms and transpose any constants from the left of the relationship. Then, solve the modified model involving the Variable *APLUS*. Table 8.2 contains the result when this approach is applied to the model of Table 8.1.

The optimal value of *B* is 4.8 (except for rounding) in both Tables 8.1 and 8.2. In Table 8.2, the optimal value of *APLUS* is 3.6, so the optimal value of *A* is $3 + 3.6 = 6.6$. This is the same value as that in Table 8.1. Observe that the upper bound on Variable *A* is represented explicitly in Table 8.2 by the SUB constraint $APLUS \leq 4$. When $(3 + APLUS)$ is substituted in the upper-bound constraint, we get $(3 + APLUS) \leq 7$. Transposing the 3 constant from the left of the relationship gives $APLUS \leq 4$. Because of transposing constants, the RHS constants in Table 8.2 are different from those in Table 8.1. The objective function has the same coefficients in Tables 8.1 and 8.2. But when $(3 + APLUS)$ is substituted for *A* in the objective function, the constant $4 \times 3 = 12$ is not included. You can't include a constant in the objective function of a linear programming model. The objective function value in Table 8.2 must have 12 added to its optimal value after the modified model has been optimized. This gives an objective function value of $12 + 24 = 36$, the same value as that in Table 8.1.

If there are many variables with SLBs or SUBs, using software with the capability of implicitly treating SLBs and SUBs reduces considerably the required computer time and storage. If there are few variables with simple bounds, the difference in computer time and storage is small.

TABLE 8.2 Explicitly Modified Model for Simple Lower Bound

```
MAX      4 APLUS + 2 B
SUBJECT TO
       2)    2 APLUS + B <=    12
       3)    3 APLUS - B =     6
       4)    APLUS <=    4
END


          OBJECTIVE FUNCTION VALUE
   1)         24.0000000

VARIABLE          VALUE          REDUCED COST
    APLUS         3.600000          0.000000
      B           4.799999          0.000000

   ROW       SLACK OR SURPLUS      DUAL PRICES
     2)          0.000000          2.000000
     3)          0.000000          0.000000
     4)          0.400000          0.000000
```

GENERALIZED UPPER BOUNDS

A **generalized upper bound** (GUB) is an upper bound shared by several variables. This type of structure is common. In the gasoline blending model of Chapter 3, the constraint

$$B + N + R \leq 30000$$

is a GUB constraint. The variables B, N, and R share the upper bound of 30,000. The mathematical structure of an SUB has a coefficient of $+1$ for the variable with the bound and coefficients of 0 for all other variables. The mathematical structure of a GUB has a coefficient of $+1$ for variables sharing the bound and coefficients of 0 for all other variables. The coefficients of B, N, and R are all $+1$; a GUB is associated with the set of variables B, N, and R.

The machine assignment model of Chapter 3 has three GUB constraints. The time limitation constraint for Machine 1 is

$$A_1 + B_1 + C_1 \leq 40$$

Variables A_1, B_1, and C_1 share an upper bound of 40 hours.

We considered transportation models in Chapter 7, and we discuss them further in this chapter. In the transportation model of Chapter 7, the coefficients of every variable for each constraint are either $+1$ or 0. For example, a supply constraint is

$$x_{11} + x_{12} + x_{13} + x_{14} \leq 500$$

A demand constraint is

$$x_{11} + x_{21} + x_{31} = 300$$

A variable can appear in only one GUB constraint

Note that Variable x_{11} appears in both constraints. However, *for a constraint to be treated as a GUB constraint, none of its variables (with a coefficient of $+1$) can appear in any other constraint treated as a GUB constraint.* You can treat either $x_{11} + x_{12} + x_{13} + x_{14} \leq 500$ or $x_{11} + x_{21} + x_{31} = 300$ as a GUB constraint, *but not both.* Because the model has three supply constraints and four demand constraints, we prefer to treat the demand constraints as GUB constraints. (Note that GUB constraints allow equality relationships as well as inequalities.)

Some linear programming software treats GUBs implicitly. The advantage of treating GUB constraints implicitly is that this avoids increasing the number of constraints or adding rows to the simplex table. However, the simplex method has to be modified to ensure that the GUBs are satisfied. Because the additional logic for implicit treatment of GUBs is more complicated than that required for SUBs and SLBs, most microcomputer linear programming software does not have GUB capability. LINDO does not have GUB capability, but linear programming software for mainframe computers usually does (e.g., MPSX and MPS III for IBM mainframe computers).

THE TERMINOLOGY OF NETWORK MODELS

Network models have mathematical structures that are effectively exploited. We discuss the general mathematical structure of network models in this section. In later sections, we discuss special network problems.

Planning the distribution of products is a common application for network models. The Citgo model optimized the distribution of petroleum products from refineries to customers. Let's think of network models for physical distribution as we describe network models in general. Then the Citgo problem will be used to illustrate the terminology of network models.

A network model consists of **nodes** connected by **arcs.** Think of nodes as cities and arcs as roads and of a network as consisting of cities connected by roads. A **directed arc** has a direction associated with it. For example, traffic goes in only one direction on a one-way road. Figure 8.1

FIGURE 8.1   Example of Network

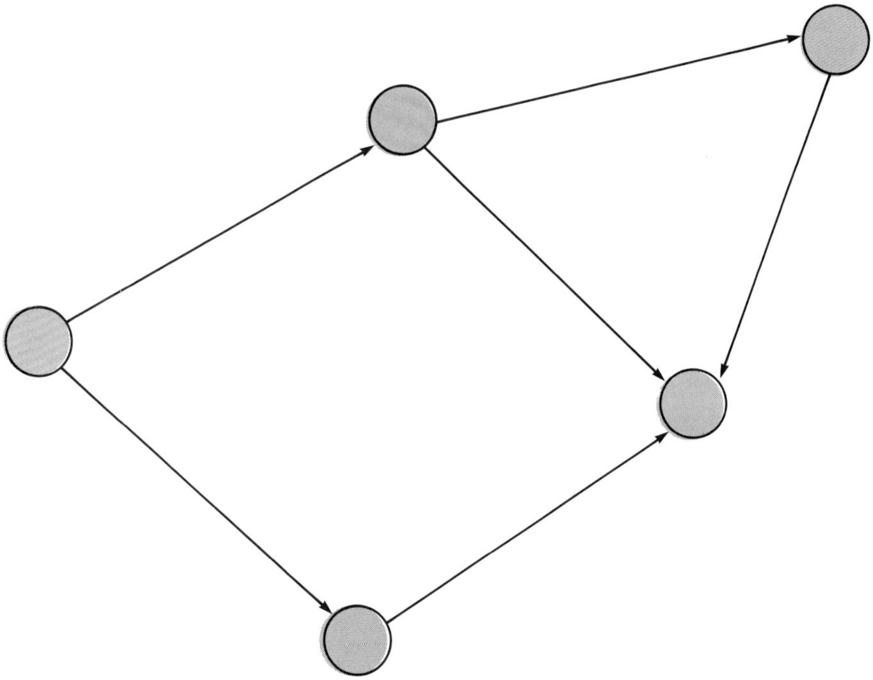

illustrates an example with five nodes and six directed arcs. The arc directions are indicated by the arrows. For each road, a cost for use and a maximum capacity limit can be imposed.

Node numbers and
arcs

Although each node (city) has a name, number the nodes so that you can easily refer to them. If there are n nodes, number them 1 through n. Then, each arc connecting a particular pair of nodes can be specified by giving its two node numbers. Figure 8.2 has the network of Figure 8.1 with the nodes numbered 1 through 5. In this example, the arc connecting Node 3 to Node 4 is called Arc (3,4). The first number is assigned to the node at the beginning of the arc, and the second number is assigned to the node at the end of the arc (arrow). Doing this specifies the direction of the arc. The cost per unit shipped from Node i to Node j is c_{ij}, and the maximum capacity from Node i to Node j is M_{ij}. Think of a network problem as the reallocation of units among the cities by shipping quantities over the roads. The decision variable for Arc (i, j) is represented as x_{ij}, the number of units shipped from Node i to Node j.

Each node has a **net stock position** showing the excess or shortage of product at that node. For Figure 8.2, Node 2 has a net stock position of

---

FIGURE 8.2   Example of Network with Nodes Numbered

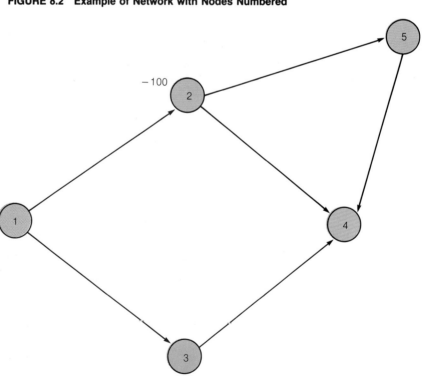

−100, which we write at the node. You need to ship 100 units to Node 2 to satisfy the requirement at that city. There is a **conservation of flow** constraint for each node. That is, the total amount remaining at a node plus the amount shipped out of it equals the amount initially at the node plus the amount shipped into it. Because the net stock position of Node 2 is −100, you need to leave 100 units there by reallocating units from nodes that have an excess.

As an example, let's write the conservation of flow constraint for Node 2. For Figure 8.2, Node 2 is connected to Node 1 by an incoming arc and to Nodes 4 and 5 by outgoing arcs. If there are no units initially at Node 2 but we desire to drop off 100 units, the conservation of flow constraint is

A conservation of flow
constraint

$$x_{2,4} + x_{2,5} + 100 = x_{1,2}$$

The constraint says that the total of the outgoing material plus the 100 units that must be dropped off has to equal the total of the incoming material. When written in the standard form, the constraint is

$$x_{2,4} + x_{2,5} - x_{1,2} = 100$$

The arc capacity constraints are

$$x_{ij} \le M_{ij}$$

Sometimes, an arc has a minimum amount that is greater than 0. For example, you might make a policy decision to ship at least some minimal amount between two cities to maintain good relations with a transportation service. Or you might have a contract specifying a minimum shipment. If the minimum is greater than 0, let m_{ij} represent it for Variable x_{ij}. The minimum constraint is

$$x_{ij} \ge m_{ij}$$

Let's relate the above terminology to the Citgo situation. The Citgo model is a multiple-period network model. Let's consider a single period to explain the terminology. The nodes are distribution centers/refineries, leased terminals, and company terminals. The arcs are transportation links connecting the nodes. Some of the nodes are connected by pipelines, some by tankers, and some by barges. The arcs have costs for shipping Citgo's petroleum products. The pipelines, tankers, and barges have capacity limits. Refined petroleum products are reallocated from the distribution centers/refineries to company terminals that serve gasoline stations. The net stock position is negative at terminals that require gasoline. The net stock position is positive at distribution centers/refineries and other terminals that have excess product (or processing capacity) available. The Citgo network model maximizes the profit for refining and distributing the petroleum products. Profit maximization is the objective because the model is also used for pricing decisions. The total revenue is not fixed in the Citgo model. A price change affects the demand for the petroleum products.

The network model

A **network model** is defined by specifying the nodes and their net stock positions, and the arcs and their costs, minimums, and maximum capacities. We call a pictorial representation such as Figure 8.2 the network model. Such a picture helps us understand the network.

There are many special network problems. We discuss such problems in the rest of this chapter. These problems are special cases of the general network model. Some of them have additional restrictions on how nodes are connected. Some don't have capacity limits. Some have different asssumptions on the initial amounts on hand or the amounts to be dropped off at nodes.

Integer variable values

Before we discuss special network problems, let's state an important property of optimal, corner point solutions for general network problems. *For each of the network models discussed, if the net stock positions, minimums, and capacities are integer values, all corner point solutions result in every variable value being integer.* Because the simplex method gives an optimal corner point solution, this method and its variants achieve optimal solutions with integer variable values.

We discuss each special network problem in a separate section. For each, we describe applications, give the linear programming model, and discuss the mathematical structure. We begin with the transportation problem.

THE TRANSPORTATION PROBLEM

The transportation problem was introduced in Chapter 7. Say that we have three regional warehouses, located at Chicago, Boston, and Cleveland. These warehouses contain 500, 400, and 325 units, respectively. We have orders for 300, 115, 275, and 190 units from customers in Baton Rouge, Toronto, Milwaukee, and Lexington, Kentucky, respectively. Table 8.3 shows the transportation costs from the warehouses to the customers.

TABLE 8.3   Transportation Costs per Unit for Unbalanced Transportation Problem

From Supply Point		To Demand Points			
Point	Location	1 Baton Rouge	2 Toronto	3 Milwaukee	4 Lexington
1	Chicago	$1.20	$0.65	$0.25	$0.60
2	Boston	1.10	0.90	1.05	0.75
3	Cleveland	0.80	0.75	0.87	0.65

FIGURE 8.3   Network Representation for Unbalanced Transportation Problem

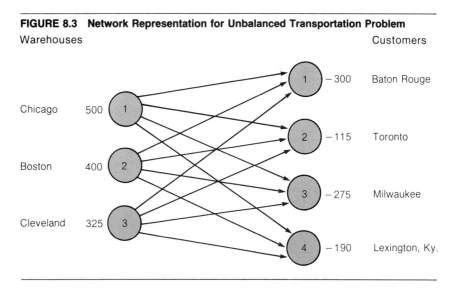

Each warehouse and each customer is represented by a node. The arc from each warehouse to each customer represents a transportation mode used for shipping. Figure 8.3 is the network model for this distribution system.

To make referring to them easier, we have numbered the warehouses 1, 2, and 3 and the customers 1, 2, 3, and 4. By doing this, we have assigned the number 1 to two nodes. In the transportation problem, it is only possible to ship out of the warehouse nodes and into the customer nodes. Thus, Arc (1,1) clearly describes shipping from Warehouse 1 to Customer 1. For network problems that allow shipping into and out of the same node, the node numbers should be unique so that the arcs are clearly defined by their node numbers. The only exceptions to the use of unique node numbers are the transportation problem and the assignment problem. All other network problems have unique numbers for each node.

Must node numbers be unique?

Figure 8.3 shows that the net stock positions are positive at the warehouses and negative at the customers. Chicago (Warehouse 1) has 500 units available for shipping. Toronto (Customer 2) needs 115 units. One alternative is to ship from Chicago to Toronto over Arc (1,2). We define the decision variable x_{12} equal to the number of units shipped from Chicago to Toronto. If a node number is greater than 9, separate the numbers by a comma to avoid confusion—for example, $x_{1,21}$. You need to ship units from the warehouses to the customers so that the customer requirements are satisfied. The objective is minimizing the total transportation cost.

Algebraic Representation

The algebraic representation of the transportation model was developed in Chapter 7. We repeat it here so that you can easily refer to it.

$$\min \quad 1.20x_{11} + 0.65x_{12} + 0.25x_{13} + 0.60x_{14} + 1.10x_{21} + 0.90x_{22}$$
$$+ 1.05x_{23} + 0.75x_{24} + 0.80x_{31} + 0.75x_{32} + 0.87x_{33} + 0.65x_{34}$$

$$\text{st} \quad x_{11} + x_{12} + x_{13} + x_{14} \leq 500$$
$$x_{21} + x_{22} + x_{23} + x_{24} \leq 400$$
$$x_{31} + x_{32} + x_{33} + x_{34} \leq 325$$
$$x_{11} + x_{21} + x_{31} = 300$$
$$x_{12} + x_{22} + x_{32} = 115$$
$$x_{13} + x_{23} + x_{33} = 275$$
$$x_{14} + x_{24} + x_{34} = 190$$
$$x_{ij} \geq 0,\ i = 1, 2, 3;\ j = 1, 2, 3, 4$$

The first constraint states the no more than the 500 available units can be shipped from Chicago. The last constraint states that enough units must be shipped from the three warehouses to satisfy the Louisville, Kentucky, order for 190 units. There is one constraint for each node (i.e., three warehouses and four customers). The symbolic model is a linear programming model and its LINDO solution appears in Table 8.4. In Chapter 7, we analyzed the LINDO solution.

Let's discuss the general transportation problem. Then, we will show how to set it up for solution by special transportation software.

The General Transporation Problem, Ill-Behaved Solutions, and the Standard Form

In the general transportation model, there are m supply points and n demand points. We number the supply nodes 1 through m and the demand nodes 1 through n. Let S_i be the number of units available at Supply Node i. The required units at Demand Node j is D_j. Let c_{ij} be the transportation cost per unit shipped from Supply Point i to Demand Point j.

The symbolic model for the general transportation problem is

$$\min \quad \sum_{i=1}^{m} \sum_{j=1}^{n} c_{ij} x_{ij}$$

$$\text{st} \quad \sum_{j=1}^{n} x_{ij} \leq S_i \quad i = 1, \ldots, m$$
$$\sum_{i=1}^{m} x_{ij} = D_j \quad j = 1, \ldots, n;$$
$$x_{ij} \geq 0,\ i = 1, \ldots, m;\ j = 1, \ldots, n$$

Read $\sum_{j=1}^{n}$ as the sum from $j = 1$ to $j = n$ of x_{ij} (i.e., $x_{i1} + x_{i2} +$ $\cdots + x_{in}$). When $i = 1$, the first constraint states that the total amount shipped from Supply Point 1 can't exceed the S_1 available units. The first

TABLE 8.4   LOOK ALL and GO Output for Unbalanced Transportation Problem

```
MIN      1.2 X11 + 0.65 X12 + 0.25 X13 + 0.6 X14 + 1.1 X21 + 0.9 X22
       + 1.05 X23 + 0.75 X24 + 0.8 X31 + 0.75 X32 + 0.87 X33 + 0.65 X34
SUBJECT TO
        2)    X11 + X12 + X13 + X14 <=    500
        3)    X21 + X22 + X23 + X24 <=    400
        4)    X31 + X32 + X33 + X34 <=    325
        5)    X11 + X21 + X31  =     300
        6)    X12 + X22 + X32  =     115
        7)    X13 + X23 + X33  =     275
        8)    X14 + X24 + X34  =     190
END

            OBJECTIVE FUNCTION VALUE

    1)        507.000000

    VARIABLE         VALUE          REDUCED COST
        X11          .000000          .450000
        X12       115.000000          .000000
        X13       275.000000          .000000
        X14       110.000000          .000000
        X21          .000000          .200000
        X22          .000000          .100000
        X23          .000000          .650000
        X24        55.000000          .000000
        X31       300.000000          .000000
        X32          .000000          .050000
        X33          .000000          .570000
        X34        25.000000          .000000

     ROW      SLACK OR SURPLUS     DUAL PRICES
        2)          .000000          .150000
        3)       345.000000          .000000
        4)          .000000          .100000
        5)          .000000         -.900000
        6)          .000000         -.800000
        7)          .000000         -.400000
        8)          .000000         -.750000
```

m constraints state that the total amount shipped from a supply point can't exceed the available units. The last *n* constraints state that the total amount shipped to a demand point must equal the required units. Using Σ notation allows easier representation of the symbolic model. Most linear programming software systems don't allow summation notation in the input.

Ill-behaved models

In Chapters 4 and 5, we discussed the ways in which a general linear programming model could be *ill-behaved*. The two ways are *no feasible solution* and an *unbounded optimal solution*. Let's show how the special structure of the transportation problem makes diagnosing ill-behaved models easier. It enables you to tell whether a problem is ill-behaved without trying to solve it. For a general linear programming problem, on the other hand, you try to solve the problem and the computer then tells you whether the problem is ill-behaved.

No feasible solution. If there is no feasible solution, there is no combination of variable values that satisfies all of the constraints and the variable nonnegativities at the same time. This may have been caused by conceptual error in formulating the model or by an error in inputting the model.

In a transportation problem, you can easily determine whether the model has no feasible solution. Determine the **total availability of supply** as $S = \sum_{i=1}^{m} S_i$; determine the **total of the requirements** as $D = \sum_{j=1}^{n} D_j$. If

No feasible solution

$S \geq D$, then there is a feasible solution. If the total availability (S) is less than the total requirements (D), it is impossible to satisfy all of the requirements and *no feasible solution exists*. For the transportation problem example of Figure 8.3, $S = 1{,}225$ and $D = 880$. Because S is greater than D in this example, there is a feasible solution. If $S = D$, the

Balanced transportation problem

transportation problem is said to be **balanced**. Figure 8.3's transportation problem isn't balanced.

Unbounded optimal solution. If you can continue to satisfy the constraints and variable nonnegativities as the objective function value becomes more and more favorable without limit, an unbounded optimal solution exists. Since the objective function is minimized for the transportation model, an unbounded optimal solution results in the objective function value becoming smaller and smaller until it approaches negative infinity. The objective function of the transportation model is the sum of the objective function coefficients (costs) times the variable values x_{ij}.

Nonnegative transportation costs

The variables must be nonnegative and the transportation costs are ≥ 0. Thus, the objective function value consists of a sum of values that can't be negative. The objective function value for any feasible solution to a transportation model can't be less than 0. Even if some costs are negative, the objective function value can't approach negative infinity, because the feasible set is bounded by the supply point inequalities. Thus, *a transportation model cannot have an unbounded optimal solution.*

The standard form for the balanced transportation problem. The standard algebraic form for the transportation problem has equalities for the requirements. Transportation costs are always smaller if you don't ship more than the requirements. In a balanced transportation problem, the total supply is equal to the total requirement, so every unit available at the supply locations must be shipped. Therefore, you can replace the $\leq$ inequalities for the supply locations by equalities. *For a balanced transportation problem, the standard algebraic form is*

$$\min \ \sum_{i=1}^{m} \sum_{j=1}^{n} c_{ij} x_{ij}$$

A balanced transportation problem

$$\text{st} \quad \sum_{j=1}^{n} x_{ij} = S_i \quad i = 1, \dots, m$$

$$\sum_{i=1}^{m} x_{ij} = D_j \quad j = 1, \dots, n;$$

$$x_{ij} \geq 0, \ i = 1, \dots, m; j = 1, \dots, n$$

TABLE 8.5 Supply Availabilities and Demand Requirements at a Later Time—Balanced Transportation Problem

From Supply Point	Location	Units Available
1	Chicago	300
2	Boston	250
3	Cleveland	300
Total		850

To Demand Point	Location	Units Required
1	Baton Rouge	200
2	Toronto	150
3	Milwaukee	175
4	Lexington	325
Total		850

Because the supply constraints are equalities, you don't need to add slack variables to convert them to the standard equality form.

Figure 8.3 is not a balanced transportation problem. Let's consider the distribution problem at a later time. The warehouses availabilities and customer requirements are shown in Table 8.5. The transportation costs are the same as in Table 8.3. The units available at the Chicago, Boston, and Cleveland warehouses are 300, 250, and 300, respectively. The requirements for Baton Rouge, Toronto, Milwaukee, and Lexington, Kentucky, customers are 200, 150, 175, and 325, respectively.

Now, $S = 850$ and $D = 850$. The transportation problem is balanced, so you can replace the inequalities by equalities:

$$\min \quad 1.20x_{11} + 0.65x_{12} + 0.25x_{13} + 0.60x_{14} + 1.10x_{21} + 0.90x_{22}$$
$$+ 1.05x_{23} + 0.75x_{24} + 0.80x_{31} + 0.75x_{32} + 0.87x_{33} + 0.65x_{34}$$

$$\text{st} \quad x_{11} + x_{12} + x_{13} + x_{14} = 300$$
$$x_{21} + x_{22} + x_{23} + x_{24} = 250$$
$$x_{31} + x_{32} + x_{33} + x_{34} = 300$$
$$x_{11} + x_{21} + x_{31} = 200$$
$$x_{12} + x_{22} + x_{32} = 150$$
$$x_{13} + x_{23} + x_{33} = 175$$
$$x_{14} + x_{24} + x_{34} = 325$$
$$x_{ij} \geq 0, \ i = 1, 2, 3; j = 1, 2, 3, 4$$

The optimal solution is degenerate for a balanced transportation problem

Table 8.6 has the optimal solution to the balanced transportaton example using LINDO. Because there are six positive variables and seven constraints, the optimal solution is degenerate. In Chapter 5, we discussed the ambiguities for a degenerate optimal solution. For any *balanced transportation problem,* the optimal solution is *degenerate.*

TABLE 8.6   Balanced Transportation Model

```
MIN      1.2 X11 + 0.65 X12 + 0.25 X13 + 0.6 X14 + 1.1 X21 + 0.9 X22
      + 1.05 X23 + 0.75 X24 + 0.8 X31 + 0.75 X32 + 0.87 X33 + 0.65 X34
SUBJECT TO
       2)    X11 + X12 + X13 + X14 =     300
       3)    X21 + X22 + X23 + X24 =     250
       4)    X31 + X32 + X33 + X34 =     300
       5)    X11 + X21 + X31 =     200
       6)    X12 + X22 + X32 =     150
       7)    X13 + X23 + X33 =     175
       8)    X14 + X24 + X34 =     325
END

       OBJECTIVE FUNCTION VALUE

       1)     540.000000

   VARIABLE         VALUE        REDUCED COST
       X11          .000000          .500000
       X12       125.000000          .000000
       X13       175.000000          .000000
       X14          .000000          .050000
       X21          .000000          .200000
       X22          .000000          .050000
       X23          .000000          .600000
       X24       250.000000          .000000
       X31       200.000000          .000000
       X32        25.000000          .000000
       X33          .000000          .520000
       X34        75.000000          .000000

     ROW    SLACK OR SURPLUS     DUAL PRICES
       2)          .000000        -.700000
       3)          .000000        -.900000
       4)          .000000        -.800000
       5)          .000000          .000000
       6)          .000000          .050000
       7)          .000000          .450000
       8)          .000000          .150000
```

For a general linear programming model, you must introduce an artificial variable for any constraint that doesn't have a slack variable. You do this to transform the model into one that has the origin as a feasible starting point. (See the first Theory section in Chapter 6.) For the transportation problem, however, you can easily construct a feasible starting point. Also, doing a simplex pivot by choosing a nonbasic variable to enter the basic variable set and updating the table has been simplified for the transportation problem. The simplex method has been "customized" for the special structure of the problem. We don't show the customization, but we do show the customized tableau format for the balanced transportation problem. You don't need to understand the details of the customized simplex method for transportation problems to use the special software. You only need to recognize the problem structure and give the inputs.

The transportation table

Figure 8.4 shows a **compact representation of the balanced transportation model,** sometimes called the **transportation table.** Each cell in the grid

FIGURE 8.4 Compact Representation for Balanced Transportation Problem

Customers

Warehouses		1	2	3	4	
	1	$1.20	$0.65	$0.25	$0.60	
			125	175		300
	2	$1.10	$0.90	$1.05	$0.75	
					250	250
	3	$0.80	$0.75	$0.87	$0.65	
		200	25		75	300
						850
		200	150	175	325	850

represents a shipping path from a supply point to a demand point. The cell (2,3) is the shipping path from Supply Point 2 to Demand Point 3. Each cell has two numbers: a cost and a variable value. The shipping cost of c_{23} is placed in the upper-left corner of that cell. The variable value for the amount shipped over that path is written in the lower-right corner. Figure 8.4's variable values are the optimal values shown in Table 8.6.

The customized tableau format is a compact representation of the balanced transportation model. The constraints for the availability of supply are represented implicitly by requiring that the total amount to be shipped from a supply point must equal the amount available at the supply point. For example, the variable values for the top row must total 300. The constraints for the requirements at a demand point are represented implicitly by requiring that the total amount shipped to a demand point must equal the amount required at the demand point. For example, the total of the variable values for the left-hand column must equal 200. For the balanced transportation table, the variable values must add down in the columns to the requirement amounts and across the rows to the supply amounts.

Model input is simplified

Using special transportation problem software simplifies model input. You only need to specify the number of supply points, m; the number of demand points, n; the supply amounts, S_i; the demand amounts D_j; and the costs, c_{ij}. The balanced transportation table illustrated in Figure 8.4 contains exactly that information. You don't need to provide the constraints because they are all implied by specifying the problem as a balanced transportation problem.

Converting unbalanced transportation problems to balanced problems. The special version of the simplex algorithm for the transportation model requires that total supply equal total requirement (i.e., that supply and demand be balanced). Many computer systems allow you to input a model that is not balanced. Then, such a computer system converts the model to a balanced transportation model before starting the customized simplex algorithm. This is similar to the automatic insertion of appropriate slack-and-surplus variables by simplex algorithm software. However, not all implementations of the transportation algorithm automatically make the appropriate transformation.

S > D: Add a dummy demand point

Let's see how an unbalanced transportation problem with $S > D$ can be converted to a balanced transportation problem. If you have a software package without the automatic conversion feature, you can convert an unbalanced model yourself so that you can use the software. Consider the unbalanced transportation example represented by Figure 8.3. The total number of units required by the four customers is 880. The total number of units available at the three warehouses is 1,225. The excess supply is 1,225 − 880 = 345. You don't have to ship 345 units. You create a **dummy** demand point with a requirement of 345 units. Because this really means not shipping the 345 units, the cost for shipping to the dummy warehouse is 0. The converted model still has three supply points, but it now has five demand points, including the dummy. The total of the requirements for the *five* demand points is 1,225, the same as the total supply. The converted transportation problem is balanced. Figure 8.5 shows the balanced transportation table.

S < D: Add a dummy supply point

Let's now see how an unbalanced transportation problem with $S < D$ can be converted to a balanced transportation problem. If the total supply is less than the total requirements, you can't satisfy all of the requirements. The unsatisfied requirement is $D − S$. You must allocate the

FIGURE 8.5   Example of Creating Balanced Transportation Table when S > D

		Customers					Supply amounts
		1	2	3	4	5	
	1	$1.20	$0.65	$0.25	$0.60	0	500
			115	275	110		
Warehouses	2	$1.10	$0.90	$1.05	$0.75	0	400
					55	345	
	3	$0.80	$0.75	$0.87	$0.65	0	325
		300			25		
Demand amounts		300	115	275	190	345	1,225 / 1,225

available units to your customers. For example, say that the Chicago warehouse has 275 units and that the other availabilities are the same as those shown in Figure 8.4. Then, $S = 825$ and $D = 850$. The unsatisfied requirement is $850 - 825 = 25$.

One approach for the unsatisfied requirement is minimizing the shipping cost of the available units. You introduce a dummy supply point whose availability is $D - S$. Because you don't actually ship from the dummy supply point, you assign transportation costs of 0 from it. Figure 8.6 shows the balanced transportation table for this approach.

Minimize the shipping cost

Another approach is maximizing the profit for the available units. If you sell the product to all customers for the same price, the revenue is fixed and cost minimization and profit maximization give the same shipping plan. However, if there are different prices, you prefer profit maximization. Let r_j represent the selling price to Customer j. If you ship from Warehouse i, the profit margin is $r_j - c_{ij}$. You introduce a dummy supply point with availability $D - S$ and assign costs of 0 from it. To convert the maximization objective function to minimization, you reverse the sign of the objective function coefficients. Figure 8.7 shows the balanced transportation table for this approach.

Maximize the profit

Other Transportation Problem Applications

The transportation problem has many applications. We just showed how it could be used to convert a profit maximization objective to the standard form—cost minimization. The U.S. Government used a transportation

---

FIGURE 8.6 Cost Minimization Example of Creating Balanced Transportation Table when $S < D$

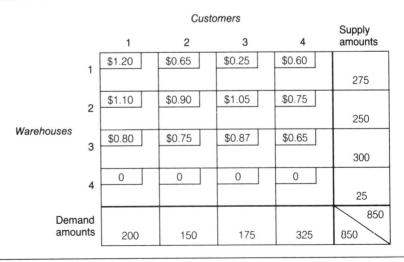

Warehouses	Customers 1	2	3	4	Supply amounts
1	$1.20	$0.65	$0.25	$0.60	275
2	$1.10	$0.90	$1.05	$0.75	250
3	$0.80	$0.75	$0.87	$0.65	300
4	0	0	0	0	25
Demand amounts	200	150	175	325	850 / 850

FIGURE 8.7   Profit Maximization Example of Creating Balanced Transportation Table when $S < D$

Customers

Warehouses	1	2	3	4	Supply amounts
1	$-r_1 +$ 1.20	$-r_2 +$ 0.65	$-r_3 +$ 0.25	$-r_4 +$ 0.60	275
2	$-r_1 +$ 1.10	$-r_2 +$ 0.90	$-r_3 +$ 1.05	$-r_4 +$ 0.75	250
3	$-r_1 +$ 0.80	$-r_2 +$ 0.75	$-r_3 +$ 0.87	$-r_4 +$ 0.65	300
4	0	0	0	0	25
Demand amounts	200	150	175	325	850 / 850

model to maximize the revenues it received for oil leases on federal land.[1]

We used warehouses and customers to describe the transportation problem. However, what is important is the structure, not the terminology. Let's illustrate this by two examples. First, we consider an example in which manufacturing facilities are the supply nodes. Second, we represent a multiple-period production planning problem as a transportation problem.

Other manufacturing and distribution problems.   Let's treat manufacturing facilities as the supply nodes. Say that the requirements are to be satisfied from units already produced at a manufacturing facility. Then, the manufacturing costs aren't affected by the decisions, so they aren't considered. (See Chapter 3.) And S_i is the number of units on hand at Facility i.

Manufacturing decisions

Now, say that you must satisfy the requirements by producing units at the manufacturing facilities. Then, the manufacturing cost is affected by the decisions. The cost, c_{ij}, includes the variable cost of manufacturing at Facility i and the transportation cost from Facility i to Demand Point j.

---

[1] Bruce L. Jackson and John Michael Brown, "Using LP for Crude Oil Sales at Elk Hills: A Case Study," *Interfaces* 10, no. 3 (June 1980), pp. 65–70.

Define the variable manufacturing cost as p_i and the transportation cost as t_{ij}. Then, $c_{ij} = p_i + t_{ij}$, and S_i is the manufacturing capacity of Facility i.

A transportation problem ships from one set of nodes (called the supply nodes) to another (called the demand nodes). If the supply nodes are manufacturing facilities, then the demand nodes can be warehouses, customers, or a combination of both. You might ship directly to major customers and fill smaller orders from regional warehouses. The D_j for a direct shipment customer is its requirements. The D_j for a regional warehouse is the number of units required for the warehouse.

The transportation problem also has applications in the service sector. Say that a bank has several branches. Checks presented for payment at the branches are sent to either of two check processing facilities. Which checks are sent to which check processing facility? The supply nodes correspond to the branches, and the number of checks at Branch i is S_i. The demand nodes are the check processing facilities, whose capacities are D_j. The "transportation" costs include the cost of delivering checks from the branches to the check processing facilities and the check processing cost. They also include any difference in the "float" cost. The float cost is the cost of delays in processing checks after the checks have been cashed. If there is excess check processing capacity, $S < D$ and the transportation problem is unbalanced. Because there are unused check processing capacities, the costs from the dummy supply point are 0.

A check processing example

A multiple-period production planning problem. The second example is a multiple-period production planning problem. Let C_i be the capacity in Period i and D_j be the demand in Period j. Let the manufacturing cost in Period i be p_i and the inventory holding cost per period be h. For this problem, Table 8.7 shows the capacities, demands, and manufacturing costs for six months. The holding cost per period is $2. If you produce and sell a unit in Month 1, the cost is $40 (i.e., p_1). You can satisfy the demand in Period j either by producing in Period j or by producing in an earlier period and storing until then. If you produce and sell a unit in Month 2, the cost is $40 (i.e., p_2). If you produce in Month 1 and sell in Month 2, the

TABLE 8.7 Data for Production Planning Example

Month (i)	Manufacturing Cost (p_i)	Capacity (C_i)	Requirement (D_j)
1	$40	400	300
2	40	400	425
3	42	500	500
4	42	500	475
5	42	500	400
6	43	400	300
Total		2,700	2,400

cost is $40 + $2 = $42 (i.e., $p_1 + h$) because the unit is stored for one period. If you produce in Month 1 and sell in Month 3, the cost is $40 + (2 \times $2) = $44—that is, $p_1 + (2 \times h)$—periods.

Let's represent this problem by a balanced transportation table. Let the supply points be the monthly production decisions, and let the demand points be the monthly requirements. We assume that there is no inventory on hand at the beginning of the six-month period. The capacity in Month 1 is 400, so $S_1 = 400$; the demand in Month 1 is 300, so $D_1 = 300$. Figure 8.8 shows the balanced transportation table. Note that Cell (1,1) corresponds to producing and selling in Month 1, so its cost is $40 per unit. Cell (1,2) represents producing in Month 1 and selling in Month 2, so its cost is $42. Cell (2,1) corresponds to producing in month 2 and selling in month 1. Cell (2,1) is not possible, so its cost is M, a big number, such as $1 million. The cost is M for all impossible cells.

The total capacity, S, is 2,700, and the total requirement, D, is 2,400. Because $S > D$, the transportation problem is unbalanced. You add a dummy demand point, 7, with a requirement of $2,700 - 2,400 = 300$. Because Column 7's cells represent unused capacity, the costs are 0.

The balanced transportation table

FIGURE 8.8 Representation of Production Planning Example as Balanced Transportation Table

Month required

Month produced		1	2	3	4	5	6	7 (dummy)	Capacity
	1	40	42	44	46	48	50	0	
		300	25					75	400
	2	M	40	42	44	46	48	0	
			400						400
	3	M	M	42	44	46	48	0	
				500					500
	4	M	M	M	42	44	46	0	
					475			25	500
	5	M	M	M	M	42	44	0	
						400		100	500
	6	M	M	M	M	M	43	0	
							300	100	400
Units required		300	425	500	475	400	300	300	2,700 / 2,700

THE TRANSSHIPMENT PROBLEM

The **transshipment problem** is similar to the transportation problem except that in the transshipment problem it is possible to both ship into and out of the same node. For the *transportation* problem, you can ship only from supply points to demand points. For the *transshipment problem,* you can ship from one supply point to another or from one demand point to another. Actually, designating nodes as supply points or demand points becomes confusing when you can ship both into and out of a node. You can make the designations clearer if you classify nodes by their net stock position—excess (+), shortage (−), or 0.

In this section, we discuss the reason for giving nodes unique numbers when you can ship into and out of some nodes. We also discuss how to solve transshipment problems using transportation software.

One reason to consider transshipping is that units can sometimes be shipped into one city at a very low cost and then transshipped to other cities. In some situations, this can be less expensive than direct shipment.

Let's consider the balanced transportation problem as an example. Figure 8.9*a* shows the net stock positions for the three warehouses and four customers. Say that it's possible to transship through Milwaukee to both Toronto and Lexington. The transportation cost from Milwaukee to Toronto is $0.35 per unit, so it costs less to ship from Chicago to Toronto

FIGURE 8.9*a* Transshipment Example Network Model—Node Numbers Not Unique

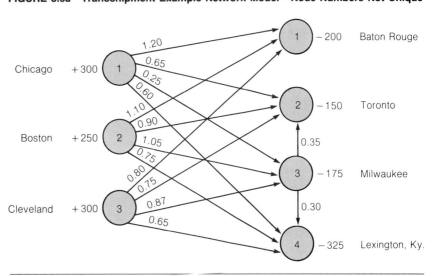

by going through Milwaukee. The direct cost is $0.65, and the transshipping cost is $0.25 + 0.35 = $0.60. Because the transportation cost is $0.30 from Milwaukee to Lexington, the cost of transshipping from Chicago through Milwaukee to Lexington is $0.55 per unit. It is cheaper to transship from Chicago through Milwaukee than to ship directly from Chicago to Lexington.

In Figure 8.9a, the node numbers are the same as in Figure 8.3. The warehouses are numbered 1, 2, and 3, and the customers are numbered 1, 2, 3, and 4. Note the confusion caused by allowing shipping into and out of Milwaukee. What transportation route is Arc (3,2)? It could represent either the Cleveland warehouse to the Toronto customer or transshipping from Milwaukee to Toronto. Cleveland and Milwaukee are both numbered Node 3. Figure 8.9b shows the network model with unique numbers for the nodes. The customers are numbered 4, 5, 6, and 7.

You can use LINDO to solve a linear programming model of the transshipment problem, or convert the transshipment problem into a transportation model and solve by transportation software. There are two possible conversions to a transportation model. In the first conversion, make each excess node a supply point and each shortage node a demand point. Then, find the cheapest method of shipping from surplus nodes to shortage nodes considering all transshipment possibilities.

The first conversion to a transportation table

Let's perform the first conversion for the Figure 8.9 example. Because Chicago, Boston, and Cleveland have excesses, they are the supply

---

FIGURE 8.9b Transshipment Example Network Model—Unique Node Numbers

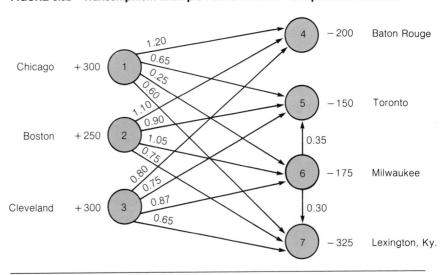

FIGURE 8.10 Balanced Transportation Table for the Transshipment Example—First Conversion

		Baton Rouge	Toronto	Milwaukee	Lexington	Excess units
		Shortages				
	Chicago	$1.20	$0.60	$0.25	$0.55	300
Excesses	Boston	$1.10	$0.90	$1.05	$0.75	250
	Cleveland	$0.80	$0.75	$0.87	$0.65	300
		200	150	175	325	850 / 850

points. Because Baton Rouge, Toronto, Milwaukee, and Lexington have shortages, they are the demand points. The cheapest cost from Chicago to Toronto is $0.60, transshipping through Milwaukee. The cheapest cost from Chicago to Lexington is $0.55, transshipping through Milwaukee. The cheapest cost from all other supply points to demand points is obtained through direct shipment. Figure 8.10 shows the balanced transportation table for Figure 8.9's transshipment problem.

For a simple network, finding all of the cheapest routes from excess nodes to shortage nodes is easy. You can list all of the possible routes and select the cheapest. However, for a network with many nodes and arcs, listing all of the possible routes is difficult.

The second conversion to a transportation table

The second conversion of a transshipment problem to a transportation model doesn't require finding all of the cheapest routes from excess nodes to shortage nodes. See Hillier and Lieberman for this conversion.[2] The second conversion requires more supply and demand nodes than the first conversion.

We prefer to solve transshipment problems using software for the general minimum cost objective network (GMCON) problem that we discuss later in this chapter. We use GMCON software because it's easier to set up and is more general than either of the two conversions to a transportation model.

---

[2] F. Hillier and G. Lieberman, *Introduction to Operations Research,* 4th ed. (Oakland, Calif.: Holden-Day, 1986).

THE ASSIGNMENT PROBLEM

Another network problem is the **assignment problem.** You can use this problem to assign tasks to people or jobs to machines. You can also use it to award contracts to bidders. Let's describe the assignment problem as assigning *n* tasks to *n* people. Each person must do one and only one task, and each task must be done by only one person. You represent each person and each task by a node. Number the people 1 to *n*, and number the tasks 1 to *n*.

For example, say that five mechanics must be assigned to five cost reduction projects. Because the mechanics have different skill levels, the total cost reduction depends on the assignments. Table 8.8 shows the cost reduction for each assignment of a mechanic to a cost reduction project.

Figure 8.11 is a network model of this problem. There are two nodes numbered 1 because both the mechanics and the cost reduction projects are numbered 1 through 5. However, this doesn't cause any confusion because the nodes on the left are mechanics and the nodes on the right are cost reduction projects. The arc from Mechanic *i* to Cost Reduction Project *j* corresponds to that assignment.

Algebraic Representation

Let's develop the linear programming model using the three-step approach. Say that the general assignment problem has *n* people and *n* tasks. Let E_{ij} represent the effectiveness if Person *i* is assigned to Task *j*. For the general assignment model, the objective is maximizing the total effectiveness of the assignments.

Verbal model. The verbal model for the assignment problem is

maximize   total effectiveness of the assignments
subject to   number of tasks Person *i* is assigned $= 1$ $(i = 1, \ldots, n)$
number of persons assigned to Task *j* $= 1$ $(j = 1, \ldots, n)$

TABLE 8.8   Cost Reductions for the Assignment Problem

Mechanic	Cost Reduction Project				
	1	2	3	4	5
1	$1,050	$850	$ 750	$1,300	$570
2	930	990	570	1,270	830
3	960	900	470	680	760
4	930	980	860	760	520
5	510	650	1,030	980	510

FIGURE 8.11 **Network Model for Assignment Problem**

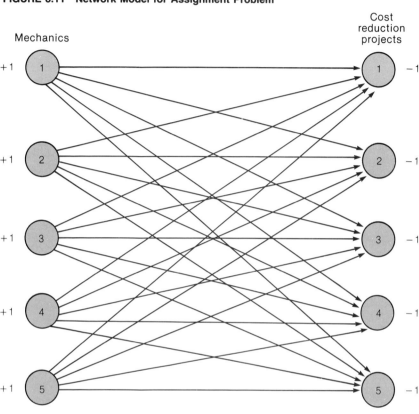

A **balanced assignment problem** has the same number of people and tasks. For a balanced assignment problem, the relationships are all equal (=). Each person must do a task. For an unbalanced assignment problem with more people than tasks, some people don't have to do a task and the first class of constraints is of the ≤ type.

Decision variables. Because there are *n* persons and *n* tasks, there are $n \times n$ E_{ij} values. Define x_{ij} to be 1 if Person *i* is asssigned to Task *j*, and define it to be 0 if the assignment is not made. In general, the simplex method does not guarantee that the optimal values of the decision variables are integers. Fortunately, *for the assignment model, all of the corner point solutions have integer values for all of the variables.* Therefore, when the simplex method determines the optimal corner point, all of the variable values are integers and the constraints require that the integers be either 1 or 0.

Integer variable values

Symbolic model. The symbolic model for the assignment problem is

$$\max \quad \sum_{i=1}^{n} \sum_{j=1}^{n} E_{ij} x_{ij}$$

$$\text{st} \quad \sum_{j=1}^{n} x_{ij} = 1 \quad i = 1, \ldots, m$$

$$\sum_{i=1}^{n} x_{ij} = 1 \quad j = 1, \ldots, n;$$

$$x_{ij} \geq 0, \, i = 1, \ldots, n; \, j = 1, \ldots, n$$

Assignment problem solutions are degenerate

Table 8.9 shows the LINDO model and solution for the mechanic assignment problem. The maximum cost reduction is $5,100. All of the variable values are either 1 or 0. You assign Mechanics 1, 2, 3, 4, and 5 to Cost Reduction Projects 4, 5, 1, 2, and 3, respectively. The optimal solution to assignment problems is always degenerate. For this example, only 5 of the variables are positive and the model has 10 constraints.

Conversion to a Balanced Transportation Table

It's not surprising that the variable values for corner point solutions to the assignment model are integers. The assignment model is a *special case* of the transportation problem, and the transportation problem has integer variable values for every corner point.

For the assignment model, the number of supply and demand points are both *n*. The supply points correspond to each person, and the demand points correspond to each task. Furthermore, every supply amount is 1 and every demand amount is 1. There is one of each person and one of each task. Figure 8.12 represents the mechanic assignment problem in the *balanced transportation table* format. For the mechanic assignment problem, you maximize the total cost reduction. Because the transportation problem objective function is minimized, you change the sign of the cost reductions in the transportation table. Because $S = 5$ and $D = 5$, the transportation problem is balanced. You can use transportation software to find the optimal solution for an assignment problem.

The important feature of network models such as the transportation and assignment models is the structure. Thinking of the transportation problem as shipping items between cities is helpful, but it's the mathematical structure that is important. The assignment problem has the same mathematical structure as the transportation problem, even though it has nothing to do with shipping units. Often, even though the application doesn't fit the textbook description of the model setting, the model has a special structure that can be exploited.

Assignment Problem Software

There are more efficient algorithms to solve the assignment problem than the transportation algorithm. One such algorithm is called the **Hungarian Method.** The inputs for this algorithm are *n* and the set of efficiency

TABLE 8.9 Mechanic Assignment Problem LOOK ALL and SOLUTION

```
MAX     1050 X11 + 850 X12 + 750 X13 + 1300 X14 + 570 X15 + 930 X21
        + 990 X22 + 570 X23 + 1270 X24 + 830 X25 + 960 X31 + 900 X32 +
        470 X33 + 680 X34 + 760 X35 + 930 X41 + 980 X42 + 860 X43 + 760
        X44 + 520 X45 + 510 X51 + 650 X52 + 1030 X53 + 980 X54 + 510 X55
SUBJECT TO
        2)   X11 + X12 + X13 + X14 + X15 =     1
        3)   X21 + X22 + X23 + X24 + X25 =     1
        4)   X31 + X32 + X33 + X34 + X35 =     1
        5)   X41 + X42 + X43 + X44 + X45 =     1
        6)   X51 + X52 + X53 + X54 + X55 =     1
        7)   X11 + X21 + X31 + X41 + X51 =     1
        8)   X12 + X22 + X32 + X42 + X52 =     1
        9)   X13 + X23 + X33 + X43 + X53 =     1
       10)   X14 + X24 + X34 + X44 + X54 =     1
       11)   X15 + X25 + X35 + X45 + X55 =     1
END

        OBJECTIVE FUNCTION VALUE

        1)     5100.00000

VARIABLE          VALUE           REDUCED COST
    X11          .000000            .000000
    X12          .000000          250.000000
    X13          .000000          600.000000
    X14         1.000000            .000000
    X15          .000000          280.000000
    X21          .000000          100.000000
    X22          .000000           90.000000
    X23          .000000          760.000000
    X24          .000000           10.000000
    X25         1.000000            .000000
    X31         1.000000            .000000
    X32          .000000          110.000000
    X33          .000000          790.000000
    X34          .000000          530.000000
    X35          .000000            .000000
    X41          .000000            .000000
    X42         1.000000            .000000
    X43          .000000          370.000000
    X44          .000000          420.000000
    X45          .000000          210.000000
    X51          .000000          220.000000
    X52          .000000          130.000000
    X53         1.000000            .000000
    X54          .000000            .000000
    X55          .000000           20.000000

    ROW     SLACK OR SURPLUS      DUAL PRICES
    2)           .000000          850.000000
    3)           .000000          830.000000
    4)           .000000          760.000000
    5)           .000000          730.000000
    6)           .000000          530.000000
    7)           .000000          200.000000
    8)           .000000          250.000000
    9)           .000000          500.000000
   10)           .000000          450.000000
   11)           .000000            .000000
```

measures. Software for the Hungarian Method is less available than that for the transportation algorithm. This is not an inconvenience since assignment problems are usually small and are effectively solved by software for the transportation problem or general purpose linear programming software such as LINDO. However, using assignment problem software to solve very large assignment problems may be worthwhile.

FIGURE 8.12 Mechanic Assignment Problem as a Balanced Transportation Table

Cost Reduction Projects

		1	2	3	4	5	
Mechanics	1	−1,050	−850	−750	−1,300 1	−570	1
	2	−930	−990	−570	−1,270 1	−830 1	1
	3	−960 1	−900	−470	−680	−760	1
	4	−930	−980 1	−860	−760	−520	1
	5	−510	−650	−1,030 1	−980	−510	1
		1	1	1	1	1	5 / 5

THE GENERAL MINIMUM COST OBJECTIVE NETWORK PROBLEM

We introduced the general minimum cost objective network (GMCON) problem in the section The Terminology of Network Models. The Citgo model is a GMCON model. The transportation and assignment problems are special cases of the GMCON problem. Those two problems are unusual because in them the nodes can be partitioned into two distinct sets and numbered within each set, beginning at 1, without introducing arc ambiguity. The transshipment problem is also a special case of the GMCON problem, but the nodes must be given distinct numbers to avoid confusion in referring to an arc. The GMCON problem requires unique node numbers. To use GMCON software for the assignment problem, number the persons $1, 2, \ldots, n$ and the tasks $n + 1, n + 2, \ldots, 2n$, so that each node has a unique number. For the transportation problem, number the supply points $1, 2, \ldots, m$ and the demand points $m + 1, m + 2, \ldots, m + n$. By assigning unique node numbers, the transportation and assignment problems can be solved using software for the GMCON problem.

Unique node numbers

The GMCON model includes nodes, arcs, and net stock positions. Each arc has a cost per unit shipped over it and a maximum capacity; some software also allows minimum arc flows greater than 0. For the arc from i to j, let the maximum arc capacity be M_{ij} and let the minimum arc flow be m_{ij}. The cost for Arc (i,j) is c_{ij}. The **net stock position** at Node i, denoted P_i, is the desired change in the number of items on hand at that node.

Let's consider a GMCON example. A major chain of appliance stores has six stores in Washington, D.C., and its suburbs. The chain needs to reallocate refrigerators among its stores before a special sale begins. At some stores, too few refrigerators are on hand and at others more refrigerators are on hand than the chain expects to sell during the sale. Figure 8.13 shows the distribution network among the six stores. Stores 1 and 2 have excesses of three and four refrigerators, respectively. Stores 3, 4, and 6 need two, three, and six additional refrigerators, respectively. The net stock positions are written by the nodes. Store 5 has the correct number of refrigerators. The costs of shipping between the stores are written on the arcs. For example, the cost of shipping a refrigerator from Store 1 to Store 3 is $18. The chain wants to reallocate the refrigerators at minimum cost.

Before you try to solve a GMCON model, sum all of the net stock positions. There are three possible cases, depending on the value of $\Sigma_i P_i$. First, if $\Sigma_i P_i = 0$, the GMCON is **balanced.** That is, the total excesses equal the total shortages and all of the excesses must be reallocated. Second, if $\Sigma_i P_i > 0$, the total excesses are larger than the total shortages and you don't need to reallocate all of the excesses. Third, if $\Sigma_i P_i < 0$, the total excesses are smaller than the total shortages and you can't satisfy all of the shortages. In the last case, the model has no feasible solution. Note that even though the total of the net stock positions is positive, no feasible solution may exist. Maximum arc capacities or the absence of certain arcs may preclude a feasible solution. For example, if the net stock position is -1 at Node 1 in Figure 8.13, the shortage cannot be satisfied because no arcs go into Node 1.

Is there a feasible solution?

The three cases are summarized in Table 8.10 and are treated similarly to the three cases for the transportation model. For example, say that a

FIGURE 8.13 **Balanced GMCON Model for Refrigerator Reallocation Example**

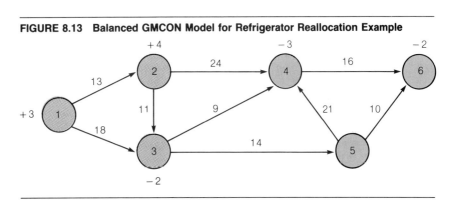

TABLE 8.10   Three Cases for General Minimum Cost Objective Network Problems

$\Sigma_i P_i$	Significance
0	Balanced. All excess units must be shipped to satisfy the shortages.
<0	Unbalanced. Not all shortages can be satisfied.
>0	Unbalanced. Not all excess units have to be shipped.

GMCON model is not balanced. For the algebraic model, you must replace some equations with inequalities. For the network model, you must add a dummy node to convert the model to a balanced GMCON model. Figure 8.13 represents a balanced GMCON problem, and we discuss it in the next section. Then, we consider an unbalanced problem.

A Balanced GMCON Problem

Figure 8.13 shows the network model for a balanced GMCON problem. Node 1 has an excess of three units, and Node 2 has an excess of four units. The shortages at Nodes 3, 4, and 6 are two, three, and two units, respectively. The sum of the net stock positions is $3 + 4 - 2 - 3 + 0 - 2 = 0$, so this is a balanced model. For a balanced model, all excess units are reallocated to the other nodes. In Figure 8.13, there are no maximum capacities and the minimum arc flows are 0.

Algebraic representation. It is not difficult to develop the algebraic model once the source of the constraints has been discovered. The decision variables are the amounts shipped on each arc. For example, $x_{1,2}$ is the amount shipped on Arc (1,2). The nine arcs result in nine decision variables. The objective function is minimizing the total of all the costs associated with the arcs. What is the source of the constraints?

The constraints are material balances for each node. *For a balanced model,* the total of the amounts going out of a node minus the total of the amounts going into a node equals the net stock position. In the case of Node 1, the constraint is

$$x_{1,2} + x_{1,3} = 3$$

For Node 4, the constraint is

$$x_{4,6} - x_{2,4} - x_{3,4} - x_{5,4} = -3$$

The RHS constants of those two constraints are the net stock positions for Node 1 and Node 4, respectively. The entire symbolic model for the example is

$$\min \quad 13x_{1,2} + 18x_{1,3} + 11x_{2,3} + 24x_{2,4} + 9x_{3,4} + 14x_{3,5} + 16x_{4,6} + 21x_{5,4} + 10x_{5,6}$$

The algebraic balanced
GMCON model

st $x_{1,2} + x_{1,3} = 3$

$-x_{1,2} + x_{2,3} + x_{2,4} = 4$

$-x_{1,3} - x_{2,3} + x_{3,4} + x_{3,5} = -2$

$-x_{2,4} - x_{3,4} - x_{5,4} + x_{4,6} = -3$

$-x_{3,5} + x_{5,4} + x_{5,6} = 0$

$-x_{4,6} - x_{5,6} = -2$

$x_{1,2}, x_{1,3}, x_{2,3}, x_{2,4}, x_{3,4}, x_{3,5}, x_{4,6}, x_{5,4}, x_{5,6} \geq 0$

Table 8.11 contains the LINDO solution. The minimum cost for the reallocation of the refrigerators is $713. The seven excess refrigerators at Stores 1 and 2 are shipped to Store 3. Store 3 needs two refrigerators. Of the other five refrigerators, three from Store 3 are shipped to Store 4 and two to Store 5. Store 5 doesn't need any additional refrigerators, so the two are shipped to Store 6. The reallocation satisfies the shortages at minimum cost.

Let's develop the symbolic model for a general *balanced* GMCON model. Say that the model has n nodes. Consider Node i. Define A_i as the set of all the nodes you can reach from Node i by using a single arc. That is, there is an arc from Node i to every node in A_i. Think of A_i as the set of nodes immediately *after* Node i. Then $\Sigma_{j \in A_i} x_{ij}$ is the amount shipped from

TABLE 8.11   LOOK ALL and GO Output for Balanced GMCON Example

```
MIN      13 X12 + 18 X13 + 11 X23 + 24 X24 + 9 X34 + 14 X35 + 16 X46
       + 21 X54 + 10 X56
SUBJECT TO
      2)    X12 + X13 =      3
      3) -  X12 + X23 + X24 =      4
      4) -  X13 - X23 + X34 + X35 =   - 2
      5) -  X24 - X34 + X46 - X54 =   - 3
      6) -  X35 + X54 + X56 =      0
      7) -  X46 - X56 =   - 2
END

           OBJECTIVE FUNCTION VALUE

      1)     173.000000

   VARIABLE           VALUE          REDUCED COST
      X12             .000000          6.000000
      X13            3.000000           .000000
      X23            4.000000           .000000
      X24             .000000          4.000000
      X34            3.000000           .000000
      X35            2.000000           .000000
      X46             .000000          1.000000
      X54             .000000         26.000000
      X56            2.000000           .000000

      ROW     SLACK OR SURPLUS      DUAL PRICES
      2)             .000000        -42.000000
      3)             .000000        -35.000000
      4)             .000000        -24.000000
      5)             .000000        -15.000000
      6)             .000000        -10.000000
      7)             .000000           .000000
```

Node i.[3] Define B_i as the set of all the nodes that reach Node i by a single arc. Think of B_i as the set of nodes immediately *before* Node i. Then $\Sigma_{k \in B_i} x_{ki}$ is the amount shipped into Node i. For the balanced GMCON model, the constraint for Node i states that the total of all its outflows minus the total of all its inflows equals the net stock position,

$$\sum_{j \in A_i} x_{ij} - \sum_{k \in B_i} x_{ki} = P_i$$

Let's illustrate the notation by examining Node 3 of Figure 8.13. Nodes 4 and 5 are immediately after Node 3, so $A_3 = \{4,5\}$. Nodes 1 and 2 are immediately before Node 3, so $B_3 = \{1,2\}$. Node 3's net stock position is -2. The constraint for Node 3 is

$$x_{3,4} + x_{3,5} - x_{1,3} - x_{2,3} = -2$$

The first two terms of the LHS are $\Sigma_{j \in A_3} x_{3j}$, and the second two terms are $-\Sigma_{k \in B_3} x_{k3}$. The RHS constant is the net stock position.

The general symbolic model for a *balanced* GMCON with n nodes is

$$\min \quad \sum_{i=1}^{n} \sum_{j \in A_i} c_{ij} x_{ij}$$

$$\text{st} \quad \sum_{j \in A_i} x_{ij} - \sum_{k \in B_i} x_{ki} = P_i \quad i = 1, \ldots, n$$

$$m_{ij} \le x_{ij} \le M_{ij} \quad i = 1, \ldots, n; j \in A_i$$

The objective function minimizes the total cost summed over all the arcs. There is a constraint for each node, and each arc can have a minimum and maximum flow.

An Example of GMCON with $\Sigma_i P_i > 0$

If the total of the net stock positions is positive, some of the excess units don't need to be reallocated. The symbolic model must be modified by changing the relationships for some of the constraints from equalities to inequalities. If the standard form for your GMCON software is a balanced model, you must transform the unbalanced model into a balanced one. In this section, we show both modifications.

Let's consider the network model shown in Figure 8.14. The network model is the same as that of Figure 8.13 except that the net stock position at Node 1 is $+7$ rather than $+3$. Now, $\sum_{i=1}^{6} P_i = +4$, so the model is un-unbalanced.

Nodes for which the net stock position is ≤ 0 remain as equalities.

---

[3] The expression $\Sigma_{j \in A_i}$ means the sum for all the nodes in A_i. The j is only a counter. We could have used k or some other letter and meant the same sum.

FIGURE 8.14 **Unbalanced GMCON Model**

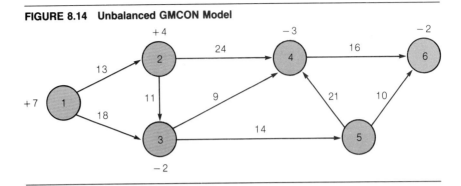

≤ constraints for
nodes with positive net
stock positions

Nodes with net stock positions > 0 are modified so that the total amount going out of a node minus the total amount going into a node is ≤ the net stock position. Then, for nodes with *positive net stock positions,* you can ship out less than the total amount available.

The symbolic model for Figure 8.14 is

$$\min \quad 13x_{1,2} + 18x_{1,3} + 11x_{2,3} + 24x_{2,4} + 9x_{3,4} + 14x_{3,5} + 16x_{4,6}$$
$$+ 21x_{5,4} + 10x_{5,6}$$

$$\text{st} \quad x_{1,2} + x_{1,3} \leq 7$$
$$-x_{1,2} + x_{2,3} + x_{2,4} \leq 4$$
$$-x_{1,3} - x_{2,3} + x_{3,4} + x_{3,5} = -2$$
$$-x_{2,4} - x_{3,4} - x_{5,4} + x_{4,6} = -3$$
$$-x_{3,5} + x_{5,4} + x_{5,6} = 0$$
$$-x_{4,6} - x_{5,6} = -2$$
$$x_{1,2}, x_{1,3}, x_{2,3}, x_{2,4}, x_{3,4}, x_{3,5}, x_{4,6}, x_{5,4}, x_{5,6} \geq 0$$

The first two constraints correspond to Nodes 1 and 2, which have positive net stock positions. The first two constraints are ≤ inequalities, and all the other constraints are equations.

Remember, the standard form for transportation problems is a balanced problem. For GMCON problems, the standard form is also balanced. If you input an unbalanced GMCON model, some GMCON software automatically transforms it into a balanced GMCON model. Let's transform the unbalanced example of Figure 8.14 into a balanced one. You don't have to transform the model yourself if your software does it automatically. But understanding how to transform the model allows you to use software without the automatic transformation feature.

Transforming an unbal-
anced GMCON into a
balanced GMCON

To *transform an unbalanced GMCON* with $\Sigma_i P_i > 0$, (1) introduce a dummy node with its net stock position equal to the negative of $\Sigma_i P_i$ and (2) introduce an arc from any node that has an excess to the dummy node. In this way, the transformed network has the total of all net stock positions equal to 0. Because the arcs to the dummy node correspond to not shipping, the costs on the dummy arcs are 0. This transformation is similar to the one we use for unbalanced transportation problems, where we create a dummy customer with a requirement equal to the excess supply.

In Figure 8.14, $\sum_{i=1}^{6} P_i = +4$. Introduce a dummy node, Node 7, with a net stock position of -4. Because Nodes 1 and 2 have excesses, you add arcs from them to Node 7. The transformed network is shown in Figure 8.15.

Some GMCON software includes information for the dummy node in the solution report. By understanding the transformation into a balanced model, you can understand this information.

Two approaches if $\Sigma_i P_i < 0$

If $\Sigma_i P_i < 0$, you can't satisfy all of the shortages. There are two approaches in this case. One approach is to minimize the cost of the units shipped to satisfy shortages. The other approach is to maximize the profit of the units shipped. In both approaches, you add a dummy node that has a net stock position equal to $-\Sigma_i P_i$. You introduce zero-cost arcs from the dummy node to nodes with a shortage. The two approaches are similar to those for unbalanced transportation problems with $S < D$.

Other GMCON Applications

There are many applications of GMCON models. Let's consider a single-period problem with manufacturing plants, warehouses, and customers. This is a common application of GMCON software. Figure 8.16 shows

---

FIGURE 8.15 Transformation of Unbalanced GMCON Model into Balanced GMCON Model

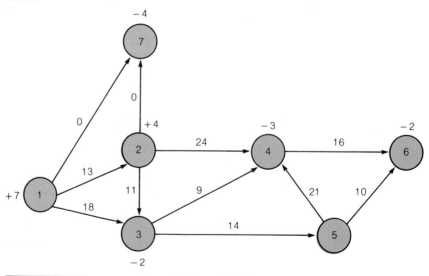

FIGURE 8.16 Product Manufacturing and Distribution System with Manufacturing Plants, Regional Warehouses, and Marketing Regions

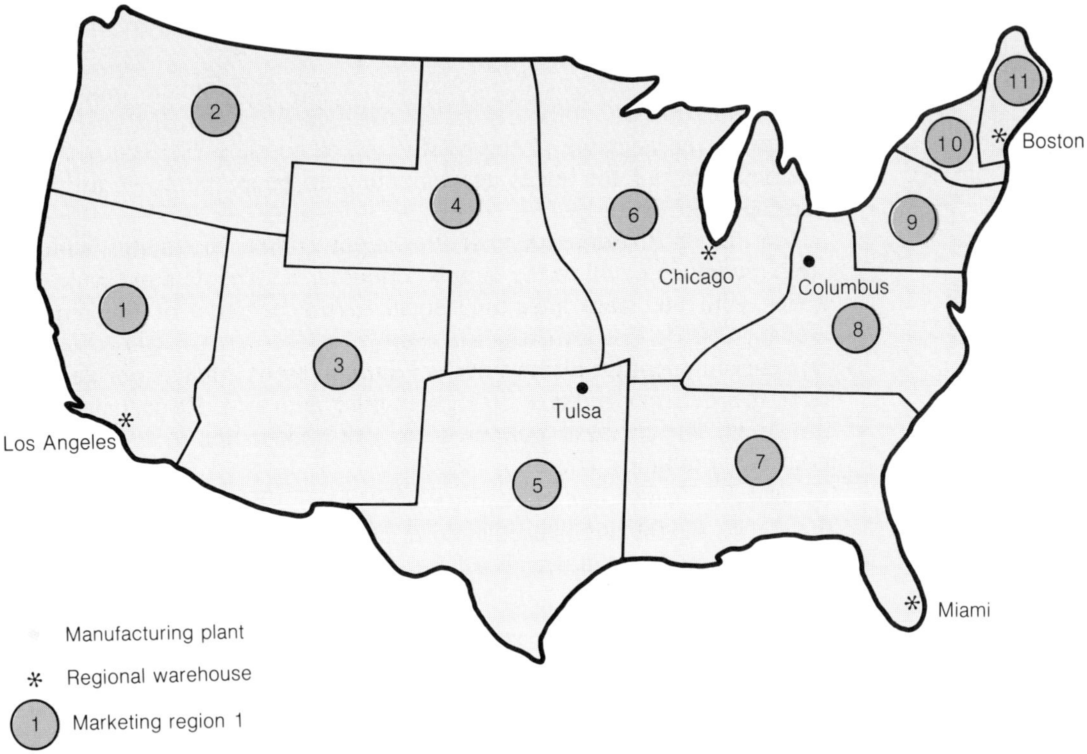

such a system. There are manufacturing plants at Tulsa, Oklahoma, and Columbus, Ohio. Warehouses are located at Los Angeles, Boston, Chicago, and Miami. The United States has been divided into 11 marketing regions. Customers in Marketing Region 5 receive goods directly from the Tulsa plant. Customers in Marketing Region 8 receive goods directly from the Columbus plant. The other marketing regions are served from the warehouses. The net stock position at the plants are the manufacturing capacities. The net stock positions at the marketing regions are the negative of the orders. The net stock positions at the warehouses are the units on hand. The arc costs from the manufacturing plants include the manufacturing cost and the transportation cost. The arc costs from the warehouses are the transportation costs. By using GMCON software, you determine the least expensive way to satisfy the customer demands. The decisions include the amount produced at each plant, the amount shipped to each warehouse, and the amount shipped to each marketing region from each warehouse.

The Citgo model is a multiple-period model. Each node is a location at

Many network prob-
lems are GMCONs

a point in time. For example, a node might be Birmingham, Alabama, in the first week. If it takes one week by pipeline from Birmingham to Atlanta, an arc connects the node for Birmingham in Week 1 to Atlanta in Week 2. The arc capacity is the pipeline capacity, and the arc cost is the shipping cost per unit.

As we discussed, you can solve assignment and transportation problems with GMCON software. In the assignment model, the cost coefficients are the negative of the relative efficiencies, $-E_{ij}$. The net stock positions are $+1$ for nodes corresponding to people and -1 for nodes corresponding to tasks.

For transportation problems, the supply points are nodes with net stock positions equal to the supply amounts, S_i. The demand points are nodes with net stock positions equal to the negative of the required amounts, $-D_j$. The arc costs are the c_{ij}.

Transshipment problems such as Figure 8.9 are GMCON problems. In fact, the network models in Figures 8.13 and 8.14 are transshipment problems. The shortest-route problem also satisfies the requirements for GMCON problems.

Again, we must emphasize that the important feature is the structure of the model, not the words used to describe it. Network models are used for equipment replacement analysis, project management, and many other applications unrelated to the physical relocation of items.

THE MAXIMUM FLOW PROBLEM

One input node and
one output node

Let's consider a network that has one input node and one output node. The **maximum flow** problem finds the maximum flow from the input node to the output node. The arcs have flow capacities. In one application of this problem, a natural gas company analyzes a pipeline system used to transport gas from fields in Texas to its market in Detroit. The capacity of a pipeline segment depends on the pipe diameter and the pumping stations. The company wants to determine the maximum flow of the pipeline system in order to plan for peak consumption during cold periods. In another application, a long-distance telephone company uses the maximum flow problem to determine the maximum number of simultaneous calls that can be made between New York and Los Angeles. Phone calls can be routed in many ways between New York and Los Angeles. Lines between pairs of cities along the routes have different capacities.

A traffic flow example

Let's consider a traffic planning problem. The repair of I-94, a major interstate highway in Milwaukee, must begin next summer. The highway contractor has recommended completely closing a section during the repair. The state of Wisconsin opposes this because the highway is a major north-south access route for tourists. When the section is closed, several detour routes are available. Let's develop a maximum flow problem to determine the maximum flow that the detour routes can handle.

The detour routes are illustrated in Figure 8.17. The arcs are roads between different points in Milwaukee. Nodes 1 and 7 are points on I-94. Node 1 is south of the planned section closing, and Node 7 is north of it.

The numbers on each arc are the number of thousands of vehicles per hour that the road can accommodate. The 4 on Arc (2,3) indicates that 4,000 vehicles is the maximum flow on the road from Node 2 to Node 3. The 6 on Arc (3,2) indicates that 6,000 is the maximum flow on the road from Node 3 to Node 2. The flows between the nodes are only in one direction except between Node 2 and Node 3. Let's find the maximum flow from Node 1 to Node 7. If the maximum flow is large enough, the state of Wisconsin will not oppose the section closing. First, let's develop the linear programming symbolic model.

Algebraic Representation

The maximum flow problem and the GMCON problem have many similarities. The decision variables are defined as x_{ij}, the number of units of flow on arc (i,j). The road capacity limits are maximum arc flows, M_{ij}. The model has conservation of flow constraints. For Node 5, the number of cars leaving the node is equal to the number entering the node:

$$x_{5,6} + x_{5,7} = x_{2,5} + x_{3,5}$$

FIGURE 8.17 Network for Milwaukee Traffic Planning—A Maximum Flow Problem

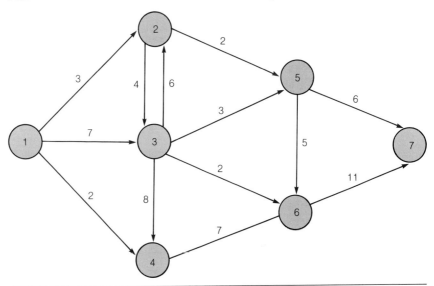

After transposing all variables to the left of the = relationship, the result is

$$x_{5,6} + x_{5,7} - x_{2,5} - x_{3,5} = 0$$

The maximum flow problem and the GMCON problem have different objective functions. Also, the maximum flow problem has no specified net stock position for any node. However, the goal is to maximize the flow from Node 1 to Node 7. Let the net stock position at Node 1 be $+F$, and let the net stock position at Node 7 be $-F$. The amount F is a decision variable, and you define it as the maximum flow amount. In the maximum flow problem, the decision variables are F and the flows for each arc. In the GMCON problem, the decision variables are the flows for each arc.

The constraint for Node 1 is

$$x_{1,2} + x_{1,3} + x_{1,4} = F$$

The maximum flow amount is a decision variable, so you transpose it to the left of the = relation, giving

$$x_{1,2} + x_{1,3} + x_{1,4} - F = 0$$

The entire symbolic model is

$$
\begin{aligned}
\max \quad & F \\
\text{st} \quad & x_{1,2} + x_{1,3} + x_{1,4} - F = 0 \\
& x_{2,3} + x_{2,5} - x_{1,2} - x_{3,2} = 0 \\
& x_{3,2} + x_{3,4} + x_{3,5} + x_{3,6} - x_{1,3} - x_{2,3} = 0 \\
& x_{4,6} - x_{1,4} - x_{3,4} = 0 \\
& x_{5,6} + x_{5,7} - x_{2,5} - x_{3,5} = 0 \\
& x_{6,7} - x_{3,6} - x_{4,6} - x_{5,6} = 0 \\
& -x_{5,7} - x_{6,7} + F = 0 \\
& x_{1,2} \le 3 \\
& x_{1,3} \le 7 \\
& x_{1,4} \le 2 \\
& x_{2,3} \le 4 \\
& x_{2,5} \le 2 \\
& x_{3,2} \le 6 \\
& x_{3,4} \le 8 \\
& x_{3,5} \le 3 \\
& x_{3,6} \le 2 \\
& x_{4,6} \le 7 \\
& x_{5,6} \le 5 \\
& x_{5,7} \le 6 \\
& x_{6,7} \le 11 \\
& \text{all } x_{ij}, \ F \ge 0
\end{aligned}
$$

TABLE 8.12 LINDO Output for Traffic Planning Maximum Flow Example

```
MAX       F
SUBJECT TO
      2)  - F + X12 + X13 + X14 =     0
      3)  - X12 + X23 + X25 - X32 =     0
      4)  - X13 - X23 + X32 + X34 + X35 + X36 =     0
      5)  - X14 - X34 + X46 =     0
      6)  - X25 - X35 + X56 + X57 =     0
      7)  - X36 - X46 - X56 + X67 =     0
      8)    F - X57 - X67 =     0
END
SUB      X12       3.00
SUB      X13       7.00
SUB      X14       2.00
SUB      X23       4.00
SUB      X25       2.00
SUB      X32       6.00
SUB      X34       8.00
SUB      X35       3.00
SUB      X36       2.00
SUB      X46       7.00
SUB      X56       5.00
SUB      X57       6.00
SUB      X67      11.00

         OBJECTIVE FUNCTION VALUE

      1)     12.0000000

      VARIABLE         VALUE        REDUCED COST
            F       12.000000          .000000
          X12        3.000000        -1.000000
          X13        7.000000        -1.000000
          X14        2.000000        -1.000000
          X23        1.000000          .000000
          X25        2.000000          .000000
          X32         .000000          .000000
          X34        3.000000          .000000
          X35        3.000000          .000000
          X36        2.000000          .000000
          X46        5.000000          .000000
          X56         .000000          .000000
          X57        5.000000          .000000
          X67        7.000000          .000000
```

Table 8.12 contains the LINDO solution. The maximum flow is 12, or 12,000 vehicles per hour. The solution shows the amount of traffic per hour for each road in the detour system. For example, 3,000 vehicles per hour use the road from Node 1 to Node 2.

Other Solution Methods

The maximum flow problem has a *special algorithm* for determining its optimal solution. Although this algorithm is well known, software for the algorithm is not widely available. The reason for this is that most maximum flow problems don't have enough nodes and arcs for substantial savings in computer storage and time.

Let's discuss using GMCON software. Some GMCON software has the additional flexibility of allowing a variable value for net stock positions. Then, you specify the net stock positions at Nodes 1 and 7 as variables. The net stock positions at the other nodes are 0.

Even if your GMCON software doesn't allow variable net stock positions, you can use it to solve maximum flow problems. First, you introduce a dummy arc from the input node to the output node. Second, you select an upper limit for the maximum flow amount; let the net stock position at the input node equal it, and let the net stock position at the output node be its negative. The other net stock positions are 0. Third, let the arc costs be -1 for all arcs leaving the input node except the dummy arc, and let the other arc costs be 0.

Let's calculate an upper limit for the maximum flow amount. Because there is a single input node, any flow must leave it. The total of the arc capacities leaving the input node is an upper limit on the maximum flow amount. For Figure 8.17, Arcs (1,2), (1,3), and (1,4) have a total capacity $3 + 7 + 2 = 12$ (12,000 vehicles). You use 12 as the net stock position at Node 1 and -12 as the net stock position at Node 7. Figure 8.18 shows the GMCON. For each arc, the first number is the capacity and the second is the cost.

FIGURE 8.18 GMCON for Milwaukee Traffic Planning—A Maximum Flow Problem

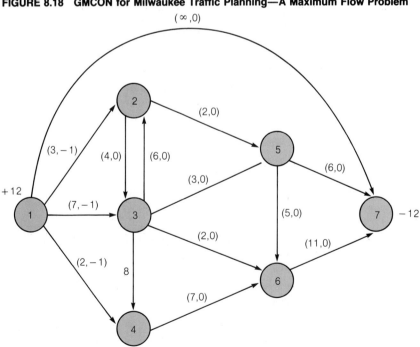

FIGURE 8.19 Maximum Flow Example with Two Starting Nodes

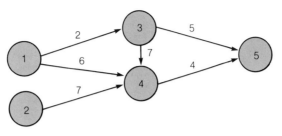

More than One Input or Output Node

Example with two input nodes

We discussed the maximum flow problem with only one input node and only one output node. Let's consider an example with two input nodes. In Figure 8.19, the output node is Node 5, but Nodes 1 and 2 are both input nodes. We want to find the total maximum flow from Nodes 1 and 2 to Node 5.

First, we construct the symbolic model. F represents the maximum flow amount, so the net stock position at Node 5 is $-F$. Define the net stock positions at Nodes 1 and 2 as F_1 and F_2, respectively. The objective function is to *maximize F*. The conservation of flow constraints imply that $F_1 + F_2 = F$, so you don't need to state this explicitly. The symbolic model is

$$
\begin{aligned}
\max \quad & F \\
\text{st} \quad & x_{1,3} + x_{1,4} - F_1 = 0 \\
& x_{2,4} - F_2 = 0 \\
& x_{3,4} + x_{3,5} - x_{1,3} = 0 \\
& x_{4,5} - x_{1,4} - x_{2,4} - x_{3,4} = 0 \\
& -x_{3,5} - x_{4,5} + F = 0 \\
& x_{1,3} \le 2 \\
& x_{1,4} \le 6 \\
& x_{2,4} \le 7 \\
& x_{3,4} \le 7 \\
& x_{3,5} \le 5 \\
& x_{4,5} \le 4 \\
& \text{all } x_{ij}, F, F_1, F_2 \ge 0
\end{aligned}
$$

Now, let's modify the network model so that it has only one input node. Some software for the maximum flow problem allows only one input node and one output node. We introduce a dummy node as we did for the unbalanced transportation and GMCON problems. Let's call this dummy node 0. You introduce arcs from Node 0 to all of the input nodes. In this example, you introduce arcs to Nodes 1 and 2 as illustrated in Figure 8.20. The capacities on Arcs (0,1) and (0,2) are infinite. This transformation allows solving a maximum flow problem with two sources

FIGURE 8.20 Dummy Starting Node Added to Figure 8.19 Example

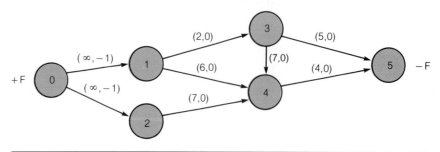

by maximum flow software that requires only one input node and one output node. The net stock positions are 0 for all nodes except Nodes 0 and 7.

If there is more than one output node, use a similar modification by creating a dummy node that follows all of the possible output nodes. Introduce an infinite capacity arc from each of the output nodes to the dummy output node.

More than one output node

We make capacities infinite for arcs connected to dummy nodes. Most software requires the specification of a finite number for each capacity. You can select a value "large enough" by adding the capacities on all of the arcs leaving the input node.

THE SHORTEST-ROUTE PROBLEM

The shortest-route problem is a network problem with many applications. As an example, say that you are planning to drive to Disney World for a vacation. You examine a road map to select the route. The road map shows cites (nodes) connected by roads (arcs) and the distances on each road connecting a pair of cities. The total distance for a route is obtained by adding all of the distances on that route. Your objective is to find the route to Orlando, Florida, with the smallest total distance. Thus, your problem is a shortest-route problem.

For a shortest-route problem, each arc has a numerical value. You want to pick the route that minimizes the sum of the numbers on the arcs. Those numbers do not have to signify distances. As another example, say that you are flying to Los Angeles. The nodes are airports, and the arcs are flights between airports. Each flight has a cost, and your objective is to minimize the cost of reaching Los Angeles. This is also a shortest-route problem. The structure, not the terminology, makes it such a problem. The numerical values on the arcs can be costs, distances, or times. At the end of this section, we show how to model an equipment replacement problem as a shortest-route problem.

At the beginning of Chapter 1, we described a system used by Air Products and Chemicals to schedule tank truck deliveries to its customers. One part of the system solves shortest-route problems. A database was developed containing information on the road system in the United States. For each road segment, the database contains the distance, average speed, and any tolls. Using that information, the total cost for each road segment, including driver, truck, and toll costs, is calculated. The driver cost depends on the travel time, which is calculated from the distance and average speed. The truck cost depends on the distance. A shortest-route problem is solved to find the cheapest route from one customer to the next on the truck's route.

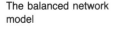

Air Products and Chemicals' shortest-route problems

Air Products and Chemicals must solve thousands of shortest-route problems as part of its system. Specialized software solves these problems very rapidly. Many algorithms are available for shortest-route problems. Also, you can solve such problems by linear programming or GMCON software. Let's show the network model for a shortest-route problem.

The balanced network model

Figure 8.21 shows possible flight segments from Atlanta to Los Angeles. The costs of each flight are on the arcs. You want to minimize the total flight cost from Atlanta to Los Angeles. The nodes are the airports, and the arcs are the flights. You define the net stock position as +1 at Atlanta and −1 at Los Angeles. The net stock positions at other nodes (airports) are 0. This is a balanced GMCON problem.

We leave developing the linear programming symbolic to the end-of-

---

FIGURE 8.21   Costs of Major Air Flights—Atlanta to Los Angeles

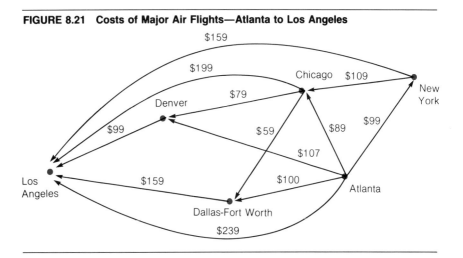

chapter questions. The model has a decision variable, x_{ij}, for each arc. Because the net stock positions are $+1, 0$, and -1, the x_{ij} must be ≤ 1. As with many network models, the optimal corner point solution has integer variable values. Thus, the x_{ij} are all 0 or 1. If $x_{ij} = 1$, the arc is included in the shortest route; if $x_{ij} = 0$, the arc is not included.

You can find the least expensive route from Atlanta to Los Angeles by careful examination of the network. List all of the possible routes and total the flight costs on each route. Then, pick the cheapest route. However, for shortest-route problems with many nodes and arcs, you need a computer. Air Products and Chemicals needs the cheapest route between many pairs of customers through a complex network.

If you must solve many shortest-route problems through a complex network, you can use shortest-route software that is more efficient than LINDO or GMCON software. But except for networks with a very large number of nodes and arcs, it is generally not necessary to search for software that uses the most efficient algorithm for your shortest-route

Two factors in short-
est-route software

problem. If you have complex shortest-route problems, you should understand *two important factors* in selecting software—the *variety* of the problem and the *network structure*.

Variety

The **variety** is the set of nodes for which you need the shortest route. For example, do you just want the shortest route between one pair of nodes—Atlanta and Los Angeles? Or do you want the shortest route from one node to all other nodes? What is the cheapest you can travel from Atlanta to all other cities? Or do you want the shortest route between all pairs of nodes? Air Products and Chemicals wanted to solve the last variety of shortest-route problem. It is possible to use an algorithm for the first variety of problem to solve all of the other varieties. You do this by repeating the algorithm for each desired pair of nodes. However, because this procedure repeats many calculations, it is inefficient. There are more efficient algorithms for the second and third variety of shortest-route problems.

Network structure

The other factor is the **network structure.** You should understand the distinction between cyclic and acyclic networks. If your network is acyclic, software using an acyclic network algorithm is more efficient than software using a cyclic network algorithm. For an **acyclic network,** it is possible to number the nodes so that if arc (i,j) exists, then $i < j$. For a **cyclic network,** it is impossible to number the nodes in that manner. Visually, *acyclic networks do not have "loops."* A **loop** or **cycle** is a path that returns to a node previously left.

Figure 8.22 is an acyclic network. Note that the nodes have been numbered so that if arc (i,j) exists, $i < j$. The network has no loops. Figure 8.23 is a cyclic network. It has a loop corresponding to the arcs from Node 2 to Node 3 to Node 5 and back to Node 2. It is impossible to number the nodes so that if arc (i,j) exists, then $i < j$. Try to renumber the nodes so that this property is satisfied. Acyclic networks are much easier

FIGURE 8.22 Acyclic Network Example

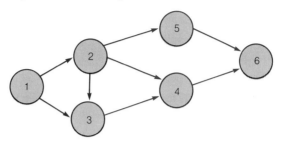

to analyze than cyclic networks. Thus, algorithms for acyclic networks are much more efficient than algorithms for cyclic networks.

If the arcs correspond to activities that have a time sequence, the network is naturally acyclic. For example, project management networks are acyclic. Next, we show an equipment replacement problem to illustrate this. Even though the numbers on the arcs are not distances, the problem has the shortest route structure.

An Equipment Replacement Problem

A company wants to determine the timing of replacements for a piece of equipment. The company is about to purchase the equipment, and it requires the same type of equipment for the next five years, but not after that. A new model of the equipment is released each year. Assume that the new models tend to have only modest changes in capabilities and that the main incentive for trading in the old equipment for the new model is reducing operating costs. As the equipment becomes older, the operating

FIGURE 8.23 Cyclic Network Example

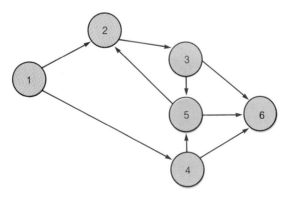

costs increase. At some point, the savings in operating costs are great enough to justify acquiring a new piece of equipment. What is the equipment replacement plan that minimizes the total of operating costs and equipment acquisition costs during the next five years?

This does not seem to be a shortest-route problem, but it has the shortest-route structure. Define p_t as the purchase cost of a new piece of equipment at the beginning of Year t. Define c_i as the operating cost during a year if a piece of equipment is i years old at the beginning of the year. Let t_i be the trade-in value of a piece of equipment that is i years old. Finally, let s_i be the salvage value of a piece of equipment that is i years old at the end of the fifth year. Table 8.13 contains the cost information.

A shortest-route problem

Node 1 is the beginning of Year 1. Five other nodes, numbered 2 through 6, are the beginnings of Years 2 through 6. Node 6 corresponds to the beginning of Year 6, which is also the end of Year 5. Figure 8.24 illustrates the network.

The arc from Node i to Node j corresponds to buying a new piece of equipment at the beginning of Year i and keeping it until the beginning of Year j, when it is replaced (or junked). Thus, the arc from Node 1 to Node 2 corresponds to buying a new piece of equipment at the beginning of Year 1 and operating that piece of equipment until the beginning of Year 2, at which time a new piece of equipment is bought. The "distance" for an arc is the cost of those activities. The cost for Arc (1,2) is the cost of acquiring a new piece of equipment in Year 1 (without a trade-in), operating it during Year 1 (as a 0-year-old piece of equipment), and trading it at the beginning of Year 2. That is, $p_1 + c_0 - t_1 = 1,000 + 200 - 900 = \$300$ is the cost for Arc (1,2). The cost for Arc (1,3) is $p_1 + c_0 + c_1 - t_2$. You buy the equipment at the beginning of Year 1, operate it for two years, and trade it in when it is two years old. You treat arcs terminating at Node 6 differently. For example, Arc (5, 6) corresponds to acquiring a new piece of equipment at the beginning of Year 5 and operating it during Year 5 until it is "salvaged" as a one-year-old piece of equipment. The cost on Arc (5, 6) is $p_5 + c_0 - s_1 = 1,000 + 200 - 850 = \$350$. Because the salvage value is usually less than the trade-in value, a distinction is

TABLE 8.13   Equipment Replacement Example Costs

i	Operating Cost c_i	Trade Value t_i	Salvage Value s_i	Purchase Cost p_i
0	200	—	—	—
1	250	900	850	1,000
2	300	800	750	1,000
3	370	750	700	1,000
4	440	700	650	1,000
5	530	660	610	1,000

FIGURE 8.24 Acyclic Network Representation of Five-Period Equipment Replacement Example

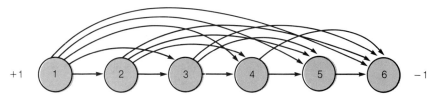

made between trade-in value and salvage value. Table 8.14 shows the result of calculating all the arc costs.

The network representation in Figure 8.24 is "naturally" acyclic because of the time sequence of the activities that the arcs represent. You can't have arcs in the other direction. Such arcs would represent buying the same piece of equipment after you trade it in. That is why Table 8.14 doesn't have arcs like (2,1). You can't trade in the same piece of equipment in Year 1 and buy it in Year 2. The arcs emanating from Node 1 represent all the possibilities for the operation of a machine that was bought at the beginning of Year 1. For Arc (1,2), it is traded in for a new piece of equipment at the beginning of the second year. For Arc (1,6), it is operated without replacement until the beginning of Year 6, when it is salvaged.

At Node 1, the net stock position is $+1$. The final node, Node 6, has a net stock position of -1. The net stock position of the other nodes is 0. The shortest route gives the minimum cost replacement policy for the five years.

COMPUTER SOFTWARE FOR NETWORK PROBLEMS

Let's discuss what software is best for solving a network problem. For example, you can solve the assignment problem using assignment software, transportation software, GMCON software, or linear programming

TABLE 8.14 Arc Costs for Equipment Replacement Example

	To j				
From i	2	3	4	5	6
1	300	650	1,000	1,420	1,950
2	—	300	650	1,000	1,470
3	—	—	300	650	1,050
4	—	—	—	300	700
5	—	—	—	—	350

software (e.g., LINDO). We emphasize that the *effort with the computer is a small part of the overall project effort.* While mathematicians are concerned with the most efficient computer solution procedure, users are concerned with the success of the project. You can solve the assignment problem with many types of software, and you need not be concerned with computer efficiency. However, you should realize that for very complex network problems, such as the Citgo model, you must get the solution fast for the decision model to be useful. Also, the linear programming formulation for your network model may need more storage capacity than your computer has. Then, you can use special network software.

For a network problem, a solution method is more efficient if it "exploits" more of the "specialness" of the model's mathematical structure. An assignment problem can be solved by many methods. Because an assignment problem is a special case of a transportation problem, assignment software solves an assignment problem more efficiently than does transportation software. Because the transportation problem is a special case of the GMCON problem, transportation software solves an assignment problem more efficiently than does GMCON software. Because the GMCON problem is a special case of linear programming, GMCON software solves an assignment problem more efficiently than does linear programming software. For an assignment problem, the software we prefer using is assignment, transportation, GMCON, and linear programming software, in that order. If a transportation problem must be solved and software for both the transportation problem and the GMCON problem is available, we prefer the transportation software. Transportation software exploits more of the "specialness" of the model.

Our preferences are based on the relative efficiencies of the solution methods. It is possible that software implementations of the solution methods are not of equal skill. Well-developed GMCON software is superior to crudely developed assignment or transportation software.

Some GMCON software has the ability to ignore arcs that don't exist. Consider an assignment problem in which Person 3 is not qualified to do Task 2. In most assignment model software, you set such an arc's efficiency measure to a prohibitive value, say $E_{32} = -1$ million. In some GMCON software, you just don't define the arc. The difference in the treatment of nonexistent arcs is unimportant unless the network is large and also sparse. In a sparse network, a relatively small number of arcs are defined compared to the complete connection of all pairs of arcs. For such a network, the reduced effort in data input makes software that ignores nonexistent arcs attractive. To the user, decreased effort in data input can be more important than reducing computer time and storage requirements.

Sparseness

If you use linear programming software for a transportation problem, you don't need to enter data for excluded shipping routes, but you do need to enter the constraints. For example, say that a transportation problem has 25 warehouses and 100 customers. The linear programming problem has $25 + 100 = 125$ constraints and $25 \times 100 = 2,500$ variables. You therefore need 2,500 shipping costs. However, there may not be a good shipping mode from some warehouses to some customers, so the cheapest shipping plan won't include those shipping routes. Usually, you can eliminate expensive shipping routes from consideration. One approach is to select a group of the closest warehouses for each customer and determine their transportation costs. For example, you might select the five closest warehouses for each customer. This reduces the data you require to construct the model. Using linear programming software, you do not define the variables from the other warehouses. Now, say that you use transportation software. If your transportation software requires that you input a transportation cost from every supply point to every demand point, you can assign a very large transportation cost to every arc that you don't want to consider. However, if your transportation software doesn't require that all arcs exist, you don't define those that you don't want. The input is easier in the latter situation.

Sparseness for transportation problems

THE CRITICAL PATH FOR PROJECT MANAGEMENT

You can use management science for planning, scheduling, and controlling complex projects consisting of many separate activities. For a simple project, you can plan, schedule, and control the activities without a computer. But if a project is very complex, using your mind to keep track of the plan and monitor the progress is difficult. To plan, schedule, and control such projects, you can use the Project Evaluation and Review Technique (PERT) and the Critical Path Method (CPM).

Common applications of PERT and CPM include:

PERT/CPM applications

1. Major construction projects
2. Research and development projects
3. Maintenance of complex equipment

You can use PERT and CPM both for onetime projects, such as the first two types named above, and for projects that are repeated, such as the third type.

There are many successful applications of PERT and CPM in project management. The U.S. Defense Department requires that bidders for weapons system contracts use PERT/CPM. The contractors must specify milestones during the contract and use the extensive reporting systems available to monitor progress and control costs. Because of the reporting capabilities of project management software, it has been used for selling X-ray equipment[4], planning investment over time, and tracking the time that accountants spend with clients.[5]

To complete projects such as these on time, you must schedule various activities. The interdependencies of the activities makes the coordination complicated. Some activities must be completed before others begin, and some activities require the same resources, so you must allocate the resources among them.

As the project manager, you want to know the answers to four questions:

1. When will the project be done?

Project management questions

2. What activities are critical? That is, which activities must be completed on time so that completion of the project is not delayed?
3. When should each activity start, and when will it be completed?
4. How long can you delay the activities that are not critical without delaying the completion of the entire project?

You can use PERT and CPM to answer these questions.

PERT was developed to manage the Polaris missile project in the 1950s. Because the time for completing activities was uncertain, PERT included probabilistic activity times. CPM was developed for major preventive maintenance projects at Du Pont. Because cost was a major consideration in these programs, CPM included costs. The differences between PERT and CPM have blurred since their development. We use either PERT or CPM to describe project management.

In recent years, user-friendly project management software has become widely available for personal computers. Prominent software packages include Microsoft PROJECT, Harvard Total Project Manager, and TIMELINE. After discussing the network representation of projects and the methods of analysis, we describe some of the advanced software features.

The Network Model

To analyze a project, you must list the activities required to complete the project. For each activity, you list its immediate predecessors and its estimated time. (Later, we discuss probabilistic activity times.) A **prece-**

---

[4] T. Hogan et al., "Project Planning Programs Put to the Test," *Business Software* 3, no. 3, (March 1985), pp. 21–56.

[5] D. Needle, "Managing Time and Resources," *Popular Computing* 9, no. 5, (May 1985), pp. 85–93.

dence requirement specifies that an activity must be completed before another is begun. For example, you must pour the foundation for a building before you erect the walls.

You can use a network to describe a project. A network consists of nodes and arcs connecting them. There are two approaches to representing a project by a network. The activities on arcs (AOA) approach represents an activity as an arc, and the activities on nodes (AON) approach represents an activity as a node. We use the *AOA approach* in this section.

Table 8.15 lists the activities and their immediate predecessors for a project. Activities A and B have no predecessors, so they can begin immediately. However, Activity E can't start until both Activity C and Activity D have been completed.

Let's construct the AOA network for the project in Table 8.15. We use the arrows on the arcs to show precedence relationships. You can't start an activity leaving a node until *all* of the activities entering that node have been finished.

Figure 8.25 shows part of a network model for Table 8.15. Each node represents an event, the starting or finishing of an activity. Node 1 is the project starting event. Node 2 is the event at which Activity A is finished. Numbering the nodes makes referring to an activity easier. Activity A is Arc (1,2). Because the arc for Activity C begins at Node 2, Activity A must be finished before Activity C starts.

There are two arcs connecting Nodes 2 and 4, corresponding to Activities C and D. You can't tell which activity Arc (2,4) represents. *You can't have two arcs connecting a pair of nodes,* so we introduce a dummy node to eliminate the confusion. Figure 8.26 shows the network after adding a dummy node, numbered Node 5. The dotted line from Node 5 to Node 4 represents a dummy activity that takes no time. The dummy activity's time, 0, appears on the arc. We introduced the dummy activity to eliminate ambiguity. The new network still requires finishing A before starting C, finishing A before starting D, and finishing both C and D before starting E.

Why can't Activity B be represented by an arc from Node 1 to Node 6?

Activities on arcs

Only one arc between nodes

TABLE 8.15 Example Activity List with Precedence Relationships

Activity	Predecessors
A	—
B	—
C	A
D	A
E	C, D
F	B, E
G	B
H	G

FIGURE 8.25 Partial Project Network for Table 8.15

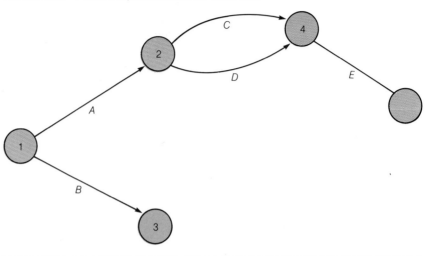

If it were, when Activity G's arc left Node 6, the network would require that both E and B be finished. But the precedence list requires finishing only B before starting G. Again, we introduce a dummy arc to give the correct precedence relationships. Figure 8.27 shows the complete AOA network model.

Figure 8.27's network model represents the precedence requirements for the activities in Table 8.15. We introduced two dummy arcs and a dummy node. Many times, you don't have to use dummy arcs or nodes.

FIGURE 8.26 Second Partial Project Network for Table 8.15

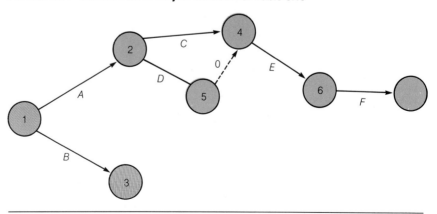

FIGURE 8.27 Complete Project Network for Table 8.15

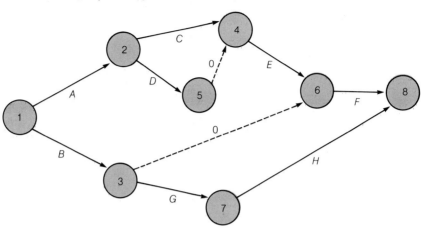

Fortunately, when using project management software, you only input the list information (e.g., Table 8.15) and the software creates the network model.

Finding the Critical Path

Say that you're responsible for opening a new sales office in San Bernardino, California. Because real estate leasing is expensive in California, you recommend constructing a new office building. Your manager wants to have the office completed as soon as possible, and she wants to know the expected completion time for the construction.

Table 8.16 shows the required tasks for constructing the office building. For convenience, a letter represents each task. For example, A represents pouring the foundation. The precedence requirements show

TABLE 8.16 Activity List for Office Building Project

Activity	Predecessors	Activity Time (Days)
A Pour foundation	---	4
B Erect walls	A	6
C Install floor	A	5
D Close in walls	B	6
E Add roof	B	4
F Finish interior	C,D	12
G Finish exterior	E	8

FIGURE 8.28   Project Network for Office Building Project

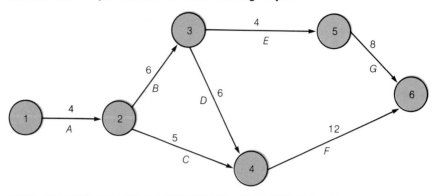

that the foundation must be poured before the exterior walls are erected. Sometimes, it's possible to work on more than one activity at a time. For example, you can close in the exterior walls and work on the roof at the same time.

Figure 8.28 shows the AOA network model. The activity times are above the arcs. Nodes 1 and 6 represent starting and finishing the project, respectively. For this simple network, we can find the completion time by inspection. There are three paths from Node 1 to Node 6. The path A–B–E–G totals 4 + 6 + 4 + 8 = 22 days. Path A–B–D–F takes 28 days, and Path A–C–F takes 21 days. Because you need to do all of the activities to complete the project, the longest path through the network is the project completion time. Twenty-eight days are required to complete the project.

The critical path is the longest path through the network. For Figure 8.28, the critical path is A–B–D–F with a duration of 28 days. The critical activities are on the critical path. Delaying the completion of a critical activity delays completion of the project. The critical activities are A, B, D and F. For example, if Activity A takes 5 days rather than 4, the project completion time increases to 29 days.

You can find the critical path by solving a longest-route problem. We discussed solving the shortest-route problem by linear programming and GMCON software. You give the starting node a net stock position of +1 and the finishing node a net stock position of −1. For minimization software, let the arc costs be the *negative* of the activity times. You can also use special, shortest-route software.

Let's discuss two methods of finding the critical path through a network. First, we describe the method used by most software. Then, we give a linear programming formulation that is different from the one we used for shortest-route type problems.

The forward and backward pass calculations for finding the critical path. For the office building project, we've answered two of the four questions. The project can be completed in 28 days, and Activities A, B, D, and F are critical. If the network is simple, you can answer the first two questions by listing all of the possible paths and finding the longest. But for complex networks, this is very cumbersome and time consuming. Also, we still need to answer the other two questions: What are the starting and finishing times for each activity, and how long can noncritical activities be delayed without delaying project completion? We show how to answer all four questions by the forward and backward pass calculations.

Table 8.17 shows the steps of the procedure for finding the critical path. We have completed Steps 1 through 3.

Before we do the forward pass calculations, note that the network is *acyclic*. Every project management network is acyclic, and this simplifies finding the longest (or shortest) path. The forward pass calculations show this simplification.

The earliest start time is the earliest an activity can start, and the earliest finish time is the earliest it can finish. In Step 4, you compute the earliest start time (*ES*) and the earliest finish time (*EF*) for each activity by forward pass calculations. You set the time for the starting node to 0 and calculate the *ES* and *EF* times moving forward through the network.

For convenience, the nodes are numbered. Node 1 is the starting node, and Node 6 is the project completion node. Remember, the nodes are events. We refer to an activity by its two node numbers. For example, Activity A is Arc (1,2). Define

E_i—earliest time of Event i

$ES_{(i,j)}$—earliest start time of Activity (i,j)

$EF_{(i,j)}$—earliest finish time of Activity (i,j)

$t_{(i,j)}$—activity time for (i,j)

TABLE 8.17   The Procedure for Finding the Critical Path

Step 1.   List the activities and the precedence relationships.
Step 2.   Construct the project network.
Step 3.   Estimate each activity time.
Step 4.   Find the earliest start time and the earliest finish time for each activity (forward pass calculations).
Step 5.   Find the latest start time and the latest finish time for each activity (backward pass calculations).
Step 6.   Calculate the total slack for each activity.
Step 7.   All of the critical activities have a total slack equal to 0.
Step 8.   A critical path from the starting node to the finishing node uses only critical activities.

TABLE 8.18   The Forward Pass Calculations

Step 1.   Set $E_1 = 0$, where the starting node is 1.
Step 2.   Moving forward through the network, let $ES_{(i,j)} = E_i$ for any j so that an arc exists leaving Node i.
Step 3.   Calculate $EF_{(i,j)} = ES_{(i,j)} + t_{(i,j)}$ for each arc leaving Node i.
Step 4.   Calculate $E_j = $ maximum $\{EF_{(i,j)}\}$, where the maximum is over i such that Arc (i,j) exists.
Step 5.   If calculations are not complete, return to Step 2. Otherwise, stop.

Table 8.18 summarizes the forward pass procedure. First, set $E_1 = 0$. Because Activity A has no predecessors, it starts at Time 0.

$$ES_{(1,2)} = E_1 = 0$$

If Activity A starts at 0 and takes 4 days, its earliest finish time is 4 days.

$$EF_{(1,2)} = ES_{(1,2)} + t_{(1,2)} = 0 + 4 = 4$$

The only activity before Node 2 is (1,2), so $E_2 = EF_{(1,2)} = 4$. Activities B and C can start only after Event 2, so their earliest start times are 4:

The forward pass calculations

$$ES_{(2,3)} = ES_{(2,4)} = E_2 = 4$$

Because it takes 6 days, B's earliest finish time is 10 days:

$$EF_{(2,3)} = ES_{(2,3)} + t_{(2,3)} = 4 + 6 = 10$$

The earliest finish time for Activity C is its earliest start time plus its activity time:

$$EF_{(2,4)} = ES_{(2,4)} + t_{(2,4)} = 4 + 5 = 9$$

Only Arc (2,3) goes into Node 3, so $E_3 = EF_{(2,3)} = 10$. The earliest start time for Activity D is $ES_{(3,4)} = E_3 = 10$ days. Activity D's earliest finish time is its earliest start time plus its activity time:

$$EF_{(3,4)} = ES_{(3,4)} + t_{(3,4)} = 10 + 6 = 16$$

Event 4 has both C and D as predecessors, so

$$E_4 = \text{maximum}(EF_{(3,4)}, EF_{(2,4)}) = \text{maximum}(16,9) = 16$$

For Activity F, $ES_{(4,6)} = E_4 = 16$, and its earliest finish time is $EF_{(4,6)} = ES_{(4,6)} + t_{(4,6)} = 16 + 12 = 28$ days. For Activity E, $ES_{(3,5)} = E_3 = 10$ and $EF_{(3,5)} = ES_{(3,5)} + t_{(3,5)} = 10 + 4 = 14$. For Event 5, $E_5 = EF_{(3,5)} = 14$. For Activity G, $ES_{(5,6)} = E_5 = 14$ and $EF_{(5,6)} = ES_{(5,6)} + t_{(5,6)} = 14 + 8 = 22$.

Because you must finish both G, Arc (5,6), and F, Arc (4,6), to complete the project,

$$E_6 = \text{maximum}(EF_{(5,6)}, EF_{(4,6)}) = \text{maximum}(20,28) = 28$$

FIGURE 8.29 Gantt Chart Showing Schedule for Earliest Start Times of Office Building Project

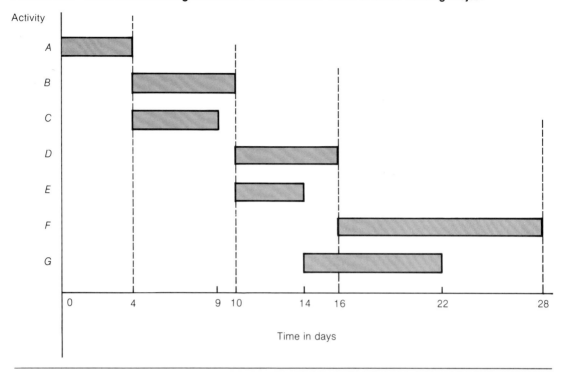

We've completed the forward pass calculations. The length of the critical path is 28 days.

Figure 8.29 shows a Gantt chart representing the schedule using the earliest start times for the activities. For example, Activity A starts at Time 0 and finishes at Time 4. The project is completed in 28 days, when Activity F is finished.

Next, we do Step 5 of Table 8.17, the backward pass calculations. The **latest start time** is the latest an activity can start and the **latest finish time** is the latest it can finish without delaying the project completion. In Step 5, you compute the latest start time (LS) and the latest finish time (LF) for each activity by **backward pass** calculations. You set the time for the finishing node to the project completion time, and you calculate the *LS* and *LF* times moving backward through the network.

Define

L_i—latest time of Event i

$LS_{(i,j)}$—latest start time of Activity (i,j)

$LF_{(i,j)}$—latest finish time of Activity (i,j)

Table 8.19 summarizes the backward pass procedure.

TABLE 8.19 The Backward Pass Calculations

Step 1. Set $L_n = 0$, where the finishing node is n.
Step 2. Moving backward through the network, let $LF_{(i,j)} = L_j$ for any i so that an arc
exists reaching Node j.
Step 3. Calculate $LS_{(i,j)} = LF_{(i,j)} - t_{(i,j)}$ for each arc reaching Node j.
Step 4. Calculate $L_i = \text{minimum}\{LS_{(i,j)}\}$, where the minimum is over j such that Arc (i,j)
exists.
Step 5. If calculations are not complete, return to Step 2. Otherwise, stop.

First, you set $L_6 = 28$. The latest time that Activities F and G can
finish is 28 days:

$$LF_{(4,6)} = LF_{(5,6)} = L_6 = 28$$

The backward pass
calculations

The latest that Activity F can start without delaying the project is its latest
finish time minus its activity time:

$$LS_{(4,6)} = LF_{(4,6)} - t_{(4,6)} = 28 - 12 = 16$$

The latest start time for Activity G is $LS_{(5,6)} = LF_{(5,6)} - t_{(5,6)} =$
$28 - 8 = 20$.

Because Node 5's only successor activity is G,

$$L_5 = LS_{(5,6)} = 20$$

Therefore, $LF_{(3,5)} = L_5 = 20$ and $LS_{(3,5)} = LF_{(3,5)} - t_{(3,5)} = 20 - 4 =$
16. Similarly, $L_4 = LS_{(4,6)} = 16$ days, so $LF_{(2,4)} = LF_{(3,4)} = L_4 = 16$.
The latest starting time for Activity D, Arc (3,4), is

$$LS_{(3,4)} = LF_{(3,4)} - t_{(3,4)} = 16 - 6 = 10$$

The latest start time for Activity C is $LS_{(2,4)} = LF_{(2,4)} - t_{(2,4)} =$
$16 - 5 = 11$.

The latest start time for Node 3 without delaying the project is the
minimum of the latest start times of its successor activities:

$$L_3 = \text{minimum}(LS_{(3,4)}, LS_{(3,5)}) = \text{minimum}(10,20) = 10$$

The latest finish time of Activity B is $LF_{(2,3)} = L_3 = 10$, and its latest start
time is $LS_{(2,3)} = LF_{(2,3)} - t_{(2,3)} = 10 - 6 = 4$.

Because Node 2 has two successors,

$$L_2 = \text{minimum}(LS_{(2,3)}, LS_{(2,4)}) = \text{minimum}(4,10) = 4$$

Therefore, $LF_{(1,2)} = L_2 = 4$ and $LS_{(1,2)} = LF_{(1,2)} - t_{(1,2)} = 4 - 4 = 0$.
Finally, $L_1 = 0$. This completes the backward pass calculations.

In Step 6 of Table 8.17, you calculate the total slack of Activity (i,j) as

Total slack

$$TS_{(i,j)} = LS_{(i,j)} - ES_{(i,j)}$$

or

$$TS_{(i,j)} = LF_{(i,j)} - EF_{(i,j)}$$

TABLE 8.20   Earliest Start Times, Latest Start Times, and Total Slack for Office Building Project

Activity	Arc	Earliest Start	Latest Start	Total Slack
A	(1,2)	0	0	0
B	(2,3)	4	4	0
C	(2,4)	4	11	7
D	(3,4)	10	10	0
E	(3,5)	10	16	6
F	(4,6)	16	16	0
G	(5,6)	14	20	6

Remember, an activity's finish and start times differ by the activity time, so both formulas give the same total slack. Table 8.20 contains the latest start times, earliest start times, and total slack for the office construction project. *Critical activities* have total slack equal to 0. The critical activities are A, B, D, and F. Activity E has a total slack of six days. Its earliest start time is 10 days, and you can delay its start time 6 days without delaying the project's completion. Its latest start time is 16 days. You can use this information in planning when activities should begin.

Total slack is 0 for critical activities.

Figure 8.30 contains a Gantt chart that shows the office building activities. Examine Activity C. The earliest time that it can begin is after four days, and the earliest time that it can finish is nine days. The latest that Activity C can finish without delaying the project is 16 days. The shaded region is the total slack, seven days.

A linear programming formulation for finding the critical path. Let's formulate a linear programming model for the office building project. We formulated a linear programming model for a shortest-route problem with decision variables—$x_{(ij)}$—equal to 1 if Activity (i, j) is on the shortest route and equal to 0 if it isn't. For PERT/CPM, we use different decision variables and a different formulation. The sensitivity analysis report for this formulation gives more useful information.

Define

S_k—start time for Activity k

F—finish time for the project

The objective is minimizing the finish time for the project. The start time of an activity must be $\geq$ the start time plus the activity time for all of its predecessors. For example, because Activity A takes four days and must be completed before Activity B begins,

$$S_B \geq S_A + 4$$

FIGURE 8.30   Gantt Chart Showing Earliest Start Times and Latest Finish Times for Office Building Project

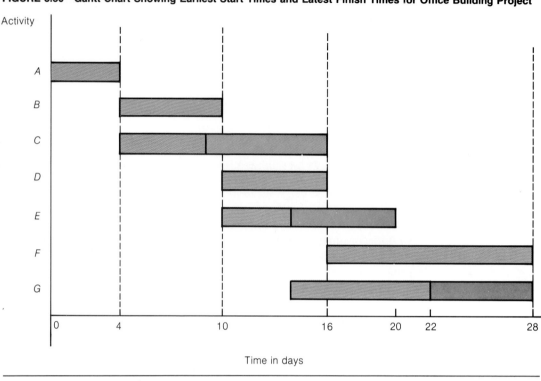

Time in days

The symbolic model is

min F
st $S_A = 0$
       $S_B \geq S_A + 4$
       $S_C \geq S_A + 4$
       $S_D \geq S_B + 6$
       $S_E \geq S_B + 6$
       $S_F \geq S_C + 5$
       $S_F \geq S_D + 6$
       $S_G \geq S_E + 4$
       $F \geq S_F + 12$
       $F \geq S_G + 8$
       $S_A, S_B, S_C, S_D, S_E, S_F, S_G, F, \geq 0$

The first constraint sets the start time of the project equal to 0. There is a constraint for each predecessor of each activity. The last two constraints show that the project finish time must be $\geq$ the finish times of both Activity F and Activity G.

Table 8.21 contains the LINDO solution. The minimum number of

TABLE 8.21   LINDO Solution for Office Bulding Project Planning Model

```
MIN     F
SUBJECT TO
        2)    SA =    0
        3)  - SA + SB >=    4
        4)  - SA + SC >=    4
        5)  - SB + SD >=    6
        6)  - SB + SE >=    6
        7)  - SC + SF >=    5
        8)  - SD + SF >=    6
        9)  - SE + SG >=    4
       10)    F - SF >=   12
       11)    F - SG >=    8
END
        OBJECTIVE FUNCTION VALUE

        1)     28.0000000

    VARIABLE          VALUE          REDUCED COST
        F          28.000000           .000000
        SA           .000000          1.000000
        SB          4.000000           .000000
        SC         11.000000           .000000
        SD         10.000000           .000000
        SE         10.000000           .000000
        SF         16.000000           .000000
        SG         14.000000           .000000

       ROW    SLACK OR SURPLUS     DUAL PRICES
        2)           .000000           .000000
        3)           .000000         -1.000000
        4)          7.000000           .000000
        5)           .000000         -1.000000
        6)           .000000           .000000
        7)           .000000           .000000
        8)           .000000         -1.000000
        9)           .000000           .000000
       10)           .000000         -1.000000
       11)          6.000000           .000000


RANGES IN WHICH THE BASIS IS UNCHANGED:

                          OBJ COEFFICIENT RANGES
    VARIABLE          CURRENT         ALLOWABLE        ALLOWABLE
                       COEF           INCREASE         DECREASE
        F           1.000000          INFINITY         1.000000
        SA           .000000          INFINITY         1.000000
        SB           .000000          INFINITY         1.000000
        SC           .000000           .000000         1.000000
        SD           .000000          INFINITY         1.000000
        SE           .000000          INFINITY          .000000
        SF           .000000          INFINITY         1.000000
        SG           .000000          INFINITY          .000000

                          RIGHTHAND SIDE RANGES
       ROW            CURRENT         ALLOWABLE        ALLOWABLE
                       RHS            INCREASE         DECREASE
        2             .000000          .000000          .000000
        3            4.000000          INFINITY         4.000000
        4            4.000000          7.000000         INFINITY
        5            6.000000          INFINITY         6.000000
        6            6.000000          6.000000        10.000000
        7            5.000000          7.000000         INFINITY
        8            6.000000          INFINITY         6.000000
        9            4.000000          6.000000        14.000000
       10           12.000000          INFINITY         6.000000
       11            8.000000          6.000000         INFINITY
```

Sensitivity analysis

days required to complete the project is 28. This formulation gives a start time for each activity. For example, you can start Activities B and C after 4 and 11 days, respectively. Examine Table 8.21. Because there are zero-valued objective function coefficient range limits, alternate optimal solutions exist. For example, you can start Activity C earlier than after 11 days and still complete the project in 28 days. The slack for Row 4 is 7. You can verify that Activity C can begin at $11 - 7 = 4$ days by examining Table 8.20. The *slack variable values do not have to equal the total slack values.* The total slack for Activity E is 6, but Row 9's slack variable is 0. The forward and backward pass calculations give the total slack, which is more useful. Compare the schedule of Table 8.21 with the Gantt chart in Figure 8.30. The noncritical activities are C, E, and G. In Table 8.21, Activity C starts at its latest start time and Activities E and G start at their earliest. The existence of alternate optimal solutions causes the ambiguity.

However, the RHS constants are activity times, and you can use sensitivity analysis to study the impact of changes in activity times. For example, say that the time for Activity D increases from six days to seven days, so that Row 8's RHS constant increases. The maximum allowable increase of Row 8's RHS constant is INFINITY, so the (-1) dual price is appropriate for an increase of 1. If the RHS constant increases by one day, the finish time *improves* by -1. That is, the finish time increases by one day. Activities that have dual prices of -1 are critical activities.

Cost Considerations

Say that your boss wants the office building constructed in less than 28 days. You can decrease the completion time by decreasing an activity time on the critical path. For example, by using more carpenters to erect the office walls, you can decrease the number of days required for Activity B. However, if you use more carpenters, the activity cost increases.

Crashing an activity is allocating more resources to decrease the activity time. Let's consider which activity you should crash to decrease the completion time to 27 days.

Crash only critical activities

Table 8.22 shows the additional cost if each activity time decreases by one day. Only consider crashing activities on the *critical path*. Decreasing the time of a noncritical activity doesn't decrease the project completion time. Crash the activity on the critical path with the smallest crashing cost per day. You should crash Activity B—erect the walls. The project cost increases $450 if you crash that activity one day, and the office building is completed in 27 days.

If an activity time decreases enough, the critical path can change. For example, if Activity F decreases to 6 days, there are two 22-day critical paths—A–B–E–G and A–B–D–F. If Activity F decreases further, the length of the critical path remains 22 days.

TABLE 8.22 Activity Crashing Cost for Office Building Project

Activity	Arc	Additional Cost per Day That Activity Time Is Reduced
A	(1,2)	$500
B	(2,3)	450
C	(2,4)	350
D	(3,4)	550
E	(3,5)	500
F	(4,6)	525
G	(5,6)	500

Sometimes, reallocating resources from a noncritical to a critical activity can decrease the completion time without increasing the cost. Carpenters are required to erect the walls, Activity B, and install the floor, Activity C. Table 8.20 shows that the total slack for Activity C is seven days. You can reallocate carpenters from installing the floor to erecting the walls without increasing the total carpenter cost.

You can modify the linear programming formulation shown in Table 8.21 to select activities to crash. First, you add a constraint that specifies the desired finish time. For example,

$$F = 27$$

Then, you introduce decision variables representing the number of days that crashing decreases an activity time. The objective is minimizing the total crash cost. We leave the formulation to the More Challenging Exercises.

Probabilistic Activity Times

For projects that are repeated, activity times can be estimated accurately. However, accurately estimating activity times for onetime projects is difficult. Let's consider uncertain activity times.

We need three estimates for each activity time:

Optimistic (a)—activity time if everything goes as well as possible
Most likely (m)—most likely activity time
Pessimistic (b)—activity time if everything goes wrong

Table 8.23 shows the three estimates for the office building project. Pouring the foundation will take between two and six days, with four days the most likely time. We calculate the **expected time of an activity** as

$$t = \frac{a + 4m + b}{6}$$

TABLE 8.23   Three Time Estimates for Each Activity of the Office Building Project

Activity	Arc	Optimistic Estimate *(a)*	Most Likely Estimate *(m)*	Pessimistic Estimate *(b)*
A	(1,2)	2	4	6
B	(2,3)	3	5	13
C	(2,4)	2	4	8
D	(3,4)	4	6	8
E	(3,5)	2	4	6
F	(4,6)	5	13	15
G	(5,6)	4	8	12

For Activity A, the expected time is

$$t_A = \frac{2 + (4 \times 4) + 6}{6} = 4$$

The **variance of an activity time** is calculated as

$$\sigma^2 = \left(\frac{b - a}{6}\right)^2$$

For Activity A, the variance of the activity time is

$$\sigma_A^2 = \left(\frac{6 - 2}{6}\right)^2 = \left(\frac{4}{6}\right)^2 = \frac{16}{36}$$

Table 8.24 contains the expected times and variances of the activity times for the office building project. Note that the expected times are the same as Table 8.16's activity times.

You estimate the project completion time by (1) calculating the expected activity times and (2) performing a forward pass. Because the activity times in Tables 8.16 and 8.24 are the same, you don't have to repeat the forward pass calculations. The expected project completion time is 28 days.

TABLE 8.24   Expected Times and Variances for Activities of the Office Building Project

Activity	Arc	Expected Time	Variance
A	(1,2)	4	$^{16}/_{36}$
B	(2,3)	6	$^{100}/_{36}$
C	(2,4)	5	$^{36}/_{36}$
D	(3,4)	6	$^{16}/_{36}$
E	(3,5)	4	$^{16}/_{36}$
F	(4,6)	12	$^{100}/_{36}$
G	(5,6)	8	$^{64}/_{36}$

You calculate the **variance of the project completion time** by adding the variances of the activities *on the critical path*. Because activities A, B, D and F are critical activities,

$$\sigma^2 = \sigma_A{}^2 + \sigma_B{}^2 + \sigma_D{}^2 + \sigma_F{}^2 = \frac{16}{36} + \frac{100}{36} + \frac{16}{36} + \frac{100}{36} = \frac{232}{36}$$

The **standard deviation of the project completion time** is

$$\sigma = \sqrt{\sigma^2} = \sqrt{\frac{232}{36}} = 2.539$$

Figure 8.31 shows the probability distribution for the project completion time. The expected time is 28 days. Use the normal distribution to calculate the probability that the project will be completed by a particular time. For example, let's calculate the probability that the project will be completed in 30 days or less. You calculate

$$Z = \frac{(30 - 28)}{2.539} = 0.79$$

From the cumulative normal distribution table, the probability is 0.7852. The probability that the completion time will be 30 days or less is 0.7852.

Let's consider some *assumptions* in probabilistic analysis. First, adding the variances on the activity times to calculate σ^2 assumes that the activity times are independent. The closer to independent they are, the better is the approximation of the true variance. Second, using the normal distribution is based on the Central Limit Theorem of probability. When the number of activities on the critical path is larger, the normal distribution is more appropriate.

Let's consider some *biases* in probabilistic analysis. First, if the actual activity times for activities on the calculated critical path are small

Assumptions for probabilistic analysis

FIGURE 8.31   Probability Distribution of Completion Time for Office Building Project

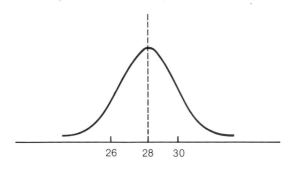

Completion time, days

enough, the critical path changes. Therefore, the true expected project completion time is greater than the sum of the expected times on the calculated critical path. Second, because the critical path changes for small actual times, the true variance is less than the sum of the variances of the critical path activities.

Project Management Software

Project management software packages are available for computers ranging from mainframe to micro. Features vary among these packages. Mainframe project management software was designed for project management specialists and is used for complex projects. See Gido for a listing of mainframe project management software.[6] Mainframe computer project management software handles more activities (as many as 10,000) than microcomputer project management software. But for most managers, microcomputer software has sufficient capabilities and is easy to use. Let's discuss the features that make project management software useful.

First, such software has built-in calendars that translate day numbers into dates. You specify the beginning of the project by giving a date. Starting a project on June 18 means more than starting it on Day 0. The calendars also allow you to specify work days. For example, you can specify that Saturday and Sunday are nonwork days and that July 4 is a holiday.

A major factor in evaluating project management software is the treatment of resources and costs. Most of this software allows you to specify the resources required and their costs for each activity. Some of this software allows you to specify an earliest starting date or a deadline for each activity. A useful feature is "lags." For example, you specify a lag of three days between pouring the concrete foundation and starting the floor. If the concrete is poured on Friday, you can start the floor on Tuesday. If Saturday and Sunday are nonwork days, pouring on Friday allows using those days for the concrete to set and delays starting the floor only one workday, whereas pouring on Monday results in a delay of three workdays.

Project management software packages usually provide both a Gantt chart and an activity report to show the schedule. The activity report shows the scheduled start and finish times for each activity, as well as other information depending on the package. Some packages give reports of project duration, total cost, and resources used. Some packages can prepare custom reports and reports for groups of activities.

Progress reporting features make PERT/CPM useful for controlling as well as planning and scheduling. For example, you input the actual start and finish times, the percentage completed, and the activity time remaining for each activity. Then, the software updates the schedule to show

---

[6] J. Gido, *Project Management Software Directory,* (New York: Industrial Press, 1985).

actual progress versus the project plan. By inputting actual costs, you can examine actual costs versus the cost budget.

Let's consider managing the resources available for the project. Say that Activity B requires three carpenters and that Activity C requires two carpenters. If you have only four carpenters, doing both activities at the same time exceeds the available supply of carpenters. Some software reports the amount of resources used by a project schedule and identifies the times when resource availabilities are exceeded. Then, you can adjust the schedule so that you don't exceed the resource limits. Most microcomputer project management software can't do "resource leveling" automatically, but some mainframe software does.

Some microcomputer project management software doesn't have some of the features we've discussed. For example, probabilistic activity times are often not allowed. Usually, automatic crashing isn't available. Instead, you examine the schedule plan and change activity times (and resources allocated) to adjust the schedule. Also, most microcomputer software doesn't allow scheduling different projects that use the same resources.

Project management software has become a general management tool. You can use its reporting capabilities to monitor project progress, allocate resources, and control costs. Assad and Wasil give an excellent survey of microcomputer project management software.[7]

SUMMARY

In this chapter, we discussed network problems, which consist of nodes and arcs. Network problems have many applications. We discussed transportation, transshipment, assignment, general minimum cost objective network (GMCON), maximum flow, and shortest-route problems.

You can model the distribution of goods to customers from warehouses as a transportation problem. You can also model manufacturing plants as supply points and warehouses (or customers) as demand points. If you can ship into and out of one or more nodes or between supply or demand points, you have a transshipment problem. A three-level system is also a transshipment problem. The three levels might be manufacturing plants, warehouses, and customers. There are two ways of converting transshipment problems into transportation problems.

Applications of the assignment problem include assigning tasks to people, assigning jobs to machines, and awarding bids to bidders. Assignment problems can be formulated as transportation problems.

GMCON problems include transportation, transshipment, assignment,

---

[7] A. Assad and E. Wasil, "Project Management Using a Microcomputer," *Computers and Operations Research* 13, nos. 2/3, (1986), pp. 231–60.

maximum flow, and shortest-route problems, as well as more general network problems. Citgo's problem is a GMCON problem.

Applications of maximum flow problems include analysis of vehicle traffic systems, communication networks, pipeline systems, and electricity transmission networks. Given the capacities of the segments, you find the maximum flow from one or more input nodes to one or more output nodes.

The shortest-route problem finds the path with the smallest sum of arc values from the starting point to the finishing point. The values on the arcs can be distances, times, or costs. Air Products and Chemicals solves shortest-route problems to find the cheapest route from one customer to the next. We find the shortest route for a driving trip by using distances on the arcs.

The structure of a problem, not the textbook description, makes it a network problem. We modeled an equipment replacement decision problem as a shortest-route problem and a multiple-period production planning problem as a transportation problem.

Network problems are important not only because of their many applications but also because there are special solution methods (and software) that exploit their special structure. You exploit special structures to decrease computer time and storage.

You can use network models for managing projects. PERT and CPM are useful for planning, scheduling, and controlling complex projects. You use the arrows on arcs to represent the precedence relationships between activities. The critical path is the longest path through the network. The forward and backward pass calculations are examples of the ways in which the structure of a network model can be exploited.

Special structures exploited by some general linear programming software are simple upper bounds (SUB), simple lower bounds (SLB), and generalized upper bounds (GUB). Again, this is done to decrease computer time and storage.

We developed linear programming models for special network problems. You can find the optimal solution to those models with general linear programming software. For simple problems, you don't need special software. To reduce computer time and storage, however, you can use special software for complex problems. This can make an application possible (and successful) for such a problem.

You should be aware of some limitations. First, for network problems, we assume that the costs are linear. Sometimes, the transportation cost per unit depends on the amount shipped. If you ship more, the cost per unit decreases. Also, if you ship in your own truck, there is a fixed charge cost for using the truck. In Chapter 9, we discuss modeling with fixed charge costs and cost economies.

Second, we assume conservation of flows. In some problems, this assumption may be incorrect. If an arc represents a "leaky" pipeline, the amount leaving one end is less than the amount entering the other.

Third, you can't have a variable that you treat as a GUB appear in more than one GUB constraint. Even though all transportation problem constraints have the GUB structure, you can't treat all of them as GUBs.

Note the following cautions. First, network problems have an integer-valued optimal solution when the net stock positions, maximum capacities, and minimums are integers. If some RHS constants are nonintegers, you can get fractional variable values. Second, check whether a network problem is balanced. If it's balanced, all of the constraints are equalities. If it's not, the constraints for the excess nodes are inequalities. You convert an unbalanced network model to a balanced one by adding a dummy node and dummy arcs. Third, if the requirements exceed the supply, you can't satisfy them. For this case, there are two approaches—cost minimization and profit maximization.

Fourth, you must number the nodes so that an arc is uniquely described by giving its node numbers. For transportation and assignment problems, the node numbers don't have to be unqiue. For all other network problems, use unique node numbers. Fifth, you can have only one arc connecting two nodes. That is why we introduced a dummy node and arc in the first example for project planning. Sixth, in project planning network models, you must make sure that the arcs give the necessary precedence relationships. For this reason, we introduced a second dummy arc for the first project planning network model.

Seventh, the forward and backward pass methods for finding the critical path of a project planning network give more information than the linear programming method. The optimal linear programming solution has alternate optimal solutions, and the slack variable values of the linear programming model are not necessarily equal to the total slack. Eighth, the optimal solution to balanced network problems is always degenerate. Remember that this causes ambiguity in sensitivity analysis. (Review Chapter 5 for the impact of degeneracy on sensitivity analysis.)

Finally, the analysis of probabilistic activity times for project planning introduces biases and assumptions. If the activity times are not independent or if several paths have lengths close to that of the critical path, the biases are significant. If the number of activities on the critical path is small, use the normal distribution cautiously.

QUESTIONS

1. What is the structure of a linear programming model?
2. What are the motivations for exploiting the special structure of a linear programming model?
3. What is a simple lower bound (SLB)?
4. What is a simple upper bound (SUB)?

5. What is a generalized upper bound (GUB)?

6. Give the general symbolic model if a transportation problem with m supply points and n demand points is balanced. Give the symbolic model if it's unbalanced.

7. What are the nodes of a transportation problem?

8. What are the arcs of a transportation problem?

9. What is the difference between a transshipment problem and a transportation problem?

10. What is an acyclic network?

11. Draw a cyclic network.

12. What is the purpose of a dummy warehouse for a transportation problem?

13. What type of network problem does the Hungarian Method solve?

14. Consider the linear programming model

max $3A + 4B + 2C$
st $2A + 3B + 1C \leq 40$
      $A + 2B + C \leq 20$
      $A \geq 5$
      $A, B, C \geq 0$

Reformulate the model so that the simple lower bound is not treated as an explicit constraint.

15. Under what conditions does the simplex method give an integer-valued solution for transportation problems?

16. Give the linear programming symbolic model to find the cheapest route from Atlanta to Los Angeles in Figure 8.21.

17. Give the linear programming symbolic model for the general balanced GMCON problem.

18. Can a transportation model have no feasible solution?

19. Can a transportation model have an unbounded optimal solution?

20. What is a maximum flow problem?

21. Why might you introduce a dummy node into a GMCON model?

22. Give two reasons for understanding the structure of a linear programming model.

23. Describe the two approaches for transportation problems with $S < D$.

24. What does a positive net stock position represent?

25. What does a negative net stock position represent?

26. What is the critical path of a project?

27. What is a critical activity?

28. What are forward pass calculations?

29. What is the total slack of an activity?

30. Give two assumptions in probabilistic analysis of project networks.

31. Give two biases in probabilistic analysis of the project networks.

32. What is crashing, and when is it done?

EXERCISES

1. The Traffic Department of a manufacturing firm is responsible for planning the shipment of goods from the firm's warehouses to its customers. Currently, the firm's warehouses are located in Chicago, Atlanta, and Los Angeles. The amounts available at the warehouses are 200, 150, and 330 units, respectively. Customers that have requested shipments are located in St. Louis, Phoenix, Milwaukee, and Bangor, Maine. The orders of these customers are for 100, 125, 240, and 170 units, respectively. The shipping costs per unit are summarized below:

	To			
From	St. Louis	Phoenix	Milwaukee	Bangor
Chicago	$ 55	$ 87	$ 45	$105
Atlanta	83	123	67	66
Los Angeles	105	56	111	145

   a. Give the linear programming symbolic model for the transportation problem.
   b. Is there a feasible solution to the linear programming model? How do you know?
   c. Does the model have an unbounded optimal solution? How do you know?
   d. Is the transportation model balanced or unbalanced?

2. A wholesaler ships to customers from its warehouses, which are located in Miami, Green Bay, and Dallas. The amounts available at the warehouses are 400, 150, and 330 units, respectively. Customers that have requested shipments are located in Denver, Seattle, Chicago, and New York City. Outstanding orders from these customers are for 200, 108, 320, and 175 units, respectively. The shipping costs per unit are summarized below:

	To			
From	Denver	Seattle	Chicago	New York
Miami	$95	$107	$64	$ 65
Green Bay	77	108	43	85
Dallas	42	96	82	101

   a. Give the linear programming symbolic model for the transportation problem.
   b. Is there a feasible solution to the linear programming model? How do you know?
   c. Does the model have an unbounded optimal solution? How do you know?
   d. Is the transportation model balanced or unbalanced?

3. Give the balanced transportation table for Exercise 1.

4. Give the balanced transportation table for Exercise 2.

5. In the network model below, the numbers next to the nodes are the net stock positions.

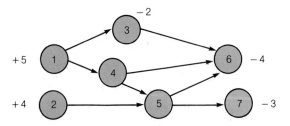

   a. Is the network model balanced?
   b. Give the constraints of the symbolic model to reallocate the excesses to the shortages.

6. In the network model below, the numbers next to the nodes are the net stock positions.

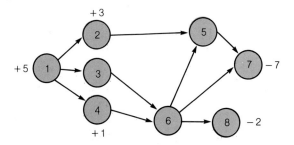

   a. Is the network model balanced?
   b. Give the constraints of the symbolic model to reallocate the excesses to the shortages.

7. The following network model is unbalanced.

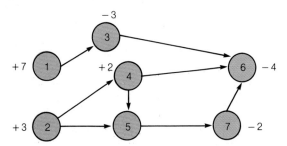

   a. Is there a feasible reallocation to satisfy the shortages?
   b. Introduce a dummy node to balance the network model. What costs are assigned to the arcs connected to the dummy node?

    c. Give the constraints of the symbolic model to reallocate the excesses to the shortages without the dummy node.

    d. Give the constraints of the symbolic model to reallocate the excesses to the shortages with the dummy node.

8. The following network model is unbalanced.

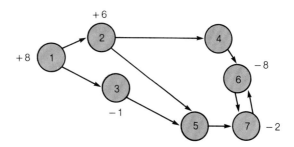

    a. Is there a feasible reallocation to satisfy the shortages?

    b. Introduce a dummy node to balance the network model. What costs are assigned to the arcs connected to the dummy node?

    c. Give the constraints of the symbolic model to reallocate the excesses to the shortages without the dummy node.

    d. Give the constraints of the symbolic model to reallocate the excesses to the shortages with the dummy node.

9. Five jobs are to be assigned to five machines with the objective of minimizing the total of the processing times of the five jobs. The five jobs cannot be done on all five machines. The total set of possibilities is given in the table of processing times below:

	Machine				
Job	1	2	3	4	5
1	5	1	7	9	6
2	6	—	3	2	7
3	8	6	—	—	5
4	3	—	6	3	—
5	—	12	8	—	—

Each machine can do only one job.

    a. Give the linear programming symbolic model to find the best assignment.

    b. Give the balanced transportation table.

    c. Give the network model for the assignment problem.

10. A homework assignment consists of four parts. Four students are working as a team on the assignment, and the team receives points depending on which student does each part. Each student must do a separate part, and the students have different abilities. The likely points received have been estimated as follows:

	Homework Part			
Student	1	2	3	4
1	25	21	17	19
2	19	—	14	8
3	—	14	9	8
4	9	4	12	—

Note that some students are unable to do some parts.

a. Give the linear programming symbolic model to find the assignment that maximizes the total number of points that the student team receives.

b. Give the balanced transportation table.

c. Give the network model for the assignment problem.

11. A manufacturing company has three plants and four marketing regions. The monthly capacities and requirements of these plants and regions are as follows:

Plant	Capacity	Marketing Region	Requirement
1	100	1	80
2	150	2	185
3	135	3	35
		4	85

The marginal production costs at Plants 1, 2, and 3 are $800, $750, and $575, respectively. A policy decision has been made that a marketing region must be satisfied from the two closest plants. The shipping costs per unit show that only the two closest plants can be used for each marketing region:

	Marketing Region			
Plant	1	2	3	4
1	30	20	—	—
2	45	—	25	45
3	—	50	40	15

a. Is this a balanced problem?

b. Give the network model that minimizes the total of production and shipping costs.

c. Convert the network model to a balanced one by adding a dummy marketing region.

d. Give the balanced transportation table.

e. Give the symbolic model.

12. A water distribution system must be analyzed to determine the maximum flow between Points A and F. The capacities on the pipelines are

Arc	Capacity (million gallons/day)
AB	100
AC	140
CB	30
BE	125
CD	80
DE	40
DF	60
EF	200

a. Give the network model.

b. Give the linear programming symbolic model.

c. Calculate an upper limit on the maximum flow.

d. Based on your answer to Part c, what are the net stock positions of the nodes?

13. Consider the problem of finding the shortest route from Node 1 to Node 7. The numbers on the arcs are the distances between the nodes.

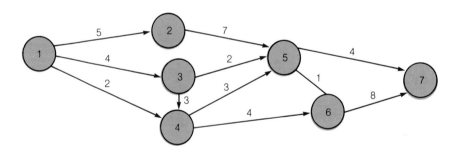

a. What are the net stock positions for the GMCON problem?

b. Give the linear programming model.

14. A company desires to establish a policy for replacing a machine during the next five years. The cost of a new machine is $10,000. The annual operating cost (c_i) increases with the age of the machine at the beginning of the year (i). The trade-in value (t_i) depends on the age of the machine at the time of the trade. Machines are replaced at the beginning of the year. The salvage value (s_i) at the end of the five-year time horizon depends on the age of the machine at that time. The costs are summarized on the following page:

i	c_i	t_i	s_i
0	2,500	—	—
1	2,950	9,000	8,500
2	3,300	8,750	7,750
3	3,600	8,000	7,000
4	3,900	7,500	6,500
5	4,300	6,900	6,000

The company is about to purchase the new machine.

a. Give the network model to find the replacement policy that minimizes the total cost of the machine during the five years.

b. Give the linear programming symbolic model.

c. Is the network model acyclic?

15. Because total supply < total demand, the following transportation problem is unbalanced.

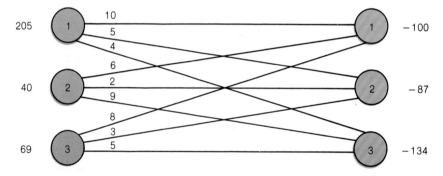

a. What is the supply amount for the dummy supply point?

b. Give the balanced transportation table to minimize the shipping cost.

c. Give the balanced transportation table to maximize profit. The selling prices are $33, $34, and $33.50 for Customers 1, 2, and 3, respectively.

16. In the following transportation problem, the total supply is less than the total requirements.

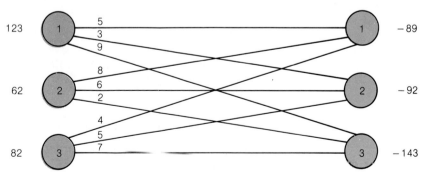

a. What is the supply amount for the dummy supply point?

b. Give the balanced transportation table to minimize the shipping cost.

    c. Give the balanced transportation table to maximize profit. The selling prices are \$51, \$52, and \$51.50 for Customers 1, 2, and 3, respectively.

17. A project consists of the following activities, activity times, and precedence relationships:

Activity	Immediate Predecessor(s)	Time (days)
A	—	5
B	—	8
C	A, B	4
D	C	5
E	B	12
F	D, E	9

    a. Construct the network model that represents the precedence relationships.

    b. Give the linear programming symbolic model to determine the critical path based on the shortest-route network model.

    c. Give the linear programming symbolic model to determine the critical path using activity start times as decision variables.

18. A project consists of the following activities, activity times, and precedence relationships:

Activity	Immediate Predecessor(s)	Time (days)
A	—	3
B	A	6
C	A	9
D	C	10
E	B	8
F	D, E	13

    a. Construct the network model that represents the precedence relationships.

    b. Give the linear programming symbolic model to determine the critical path based on the shortest-route network model.

    c. Give the linear programming symbolic model to determine the critical path using activity start times as decision variables.

19. For Exercise 17,

    a. Calculate the earliest start and the earliest finish times for the activities.

    b. What is the project completion time?

    c. Calculate the latest start and finish times for the activities.

    d. Calculate the total slack of each activity.

    e. What are the critical activities?

    f. What is the critical path?

20. For Exercise 18,
    a. Calculate the earliest start and finish times for the activities.
    b. What is the project completion time?
    c. Calculate the latest start and finish times for the activities.
    d. Calculate the total slack of each activity.
    e. What are the critical activities?
    f. What is the critical path?

21. The office building project must be completed in 26 days. The cost per day that the activity times are reduced and the maximum reductions for the activity times are

Activity	Cost/Day That Time Is Reduced	Maximum Reduction
A	$500	2 days
B	450	1
C	350	2
D	550	2
E	500	1
F	525	3
G	500	2

    a. How much should each activity be crashed?
    b. What is the additional crashing cost?
    c. What is the critical path with crashing?

22. A project consists of the following activities and precedence relationships:

Activity	Immediate Predecessor(s)
A	—
B	A
C	A
D	B
E	B
F	C
G	E, F
H	D, G

The probabilistic estimates of the activity times in days are

Activity	a	m	b
A	1	2	3
B	3	4	5
C	4	6	8
D	1	2	6
E	5	6	7
F	7	8	9
G	4	6	8
H	1	2	3

  a. Give the AOA network.
  b. Calculate the expected times and variances for the activities.
  c. Calculate the earliest start and finish times for the activities.
  d. Calculate the latest start and finish times for the activities.
  e. What are the critical activities?
  f. What is the expected project duration?
  g. What is the variance of the project duration?
  h. What is the probability that the project will be completed in 25 days or less?

23. A project consists of the following activities and precedence relationships:

Activity	Immediate Predecessor(s)
A	—
B	—
C	A
D	B
E	C, D

The probabilistic estimates of the activity times in days are

Activity	a	m	b
A	2	3	4
B	3	4	5
C	4	6	8
D	3	4	5
E	4	6	8

  a. Give the AOA network.
  b. Calculate the expected times and variances for the activities.
  c. Calculate the earliest start and finish times for the activities.
  d. Calculate the latest start and finish times for the activities.
  e. What are the critical activities?
  f. What is the expected project duration?
  g. What is the variance of the project duration?
  h. What is the probability that the project will be completed in 15 days or less?

MORE CHALLENGING EXERCISES

Some of the MCEs require that appropriate software be available.

1. Formulate a linear programming model to determine which activities of the office building project to crash. The project must be completed in 26 days. The cost per day that the activity times are reduced and the maximum reductions for the activity times are

Activity	Cost/Day That Time Is Reduced	Maximum Reduction
A	$500	2 days
B	450	1
C	350	2
D	550	2
E	500	1
F	525	3
G	500	2

2. A textbook publisher has four manuscripts, each in a different subject area, to assign to four copy editors. Two of the copy editors aren't qualified in all of the subjects covered. The estimated copy editing costs are

Copy Editor	Manuscript			
	Math	Biology	History	Computers
Alice	$5,000	$6,500	$6,000	$7,000
Mark	5,600	7,000	7,500	—
Ruth	4,500	—	6,400	7,100
Frank	5,200	6,300	7,100	6,900

  a. Give the balanced transportation table to minimize the copy editing costs.
  b. Give the GMCON to minimize the copy editing costs.

3. You have four service technicians to assign to five service calls. Because the technicians have different skill levels, the time for the service calls depends on the assignments. The service times are

Service Call	Smith	Jones	Brown	Johnson
1	95	85	105	145
2	150	190	165	205
3	85	100	95	185
4	110	125	160	195
5	95	90	85	160

One service technician must handle two calls.
  a. Give the balanced transportation table to minimize the total service time.
  b. Give the GMCON to minimize the total service time.

4. A city is planning to repair a section of sewer pipe. A major industrial company needs 50,000 gallons per hour. While the section is repaired, the city plans to use other pipelines to provide the water. The alternative pipeline system is

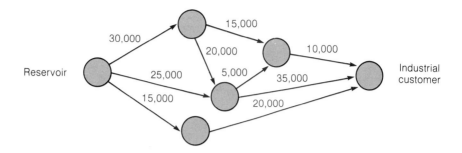

The numbers on the arcs are pipeline capacities in gallons per hour. Formulate a model to determine whether 50,000 gallons per hour can be supplied.

5. A manufacturing company has three plants that can produce its three products. Each plant has a total capacity of 5,000 units. The manufacturing costs per unit are

Plant	Products		
	Regular	Improved	Super
Chicago	$50	$52	$49
Indianapolis	51	47	53
St. Louis	61	63	62

The product requirements are 4,500, 5,200, and 4,800 units for Regular, Improved, and Super, respectively. Give the balanced transportation table to minimize the total manufacturing cost.

6. The marketing manager must settle a dispute among salespeople. The sales force has potential orders that exceed the total manufacturing capacity next month. The potential orders are

Company	Price	Product	Quantity
Abex	$1.20	Regular	10,000
Bitran	2.20	Improved	5,000
Citan	1.30	Regular	4,000
Diogenes	2.15	Improved	7,000

The manufacturing cost is $0.85 for Regular and $1.85 for Improved. The two products are very similar. The plant can make no more than 12,000 and 11,000 units of Regular and Improved, respectively. Assume that a customer will accept a partial order. Give the plan that maximizes profit.

7. A company has inventory in its factory warehouses that needs to be shipped to customers. Because most of its customers are located in the southern

United States, shipping through the Atlanta warehouse has been standard procedure. The shipping cost to Atlanta is low because the quantity shipped is large. However, the Atlanta warehouse doesn't have enough capacity to handle all of the company's orders. The Atlanta warehouse can handle only 15,000 units per week, but the company's orders total 18,000. At the New York plant 10,000 units are available, and at the St. Louis plant 9,000 units are available. You can ship directly to the customers, but the cost of doing that is greater than the cost of shipping through Atlanta. The outstanding orders are

Customer Location	Quantity
Atlanta	3,000
Orlando	8,000
Memphis	6,000
Louisville	1,000

The shipping costs are as follows:

	To			
From	Atlanta	Orlando	Memphis	Louisville
New York	$9.00	$15.00	$17.50	$16.50
St. Louis	7.50	13.50	12.00	11.00
Atlanta	—	5.00	4.00	5.00

Find the shipping plan to minimize the transportation cost.

8. A company must schedule production during the next six weeks to minimize total cost. The requirements for the next six weeks are

Week	Requirement
1	100
2	125
3	130
4	100
5	110
6	120

The manufacturing cost is $120/unit during Weeks 1 to 4 and $125/unit during Weeks 5 and 6. The inventory holding cost is $0.75/unit held at the end of every week. The regular time capacity is 100 units/week. If necessary, up to 20 additional units can be produced on overtime at an additional cost of $8/unit. At the beginning, 25 units are in inventory.

a. Give the balanced transportation table to minimize the total cost.

b. Why doesn't the solution use overtime in a week unless all of the regular time capacity has been used?

9. The managing partner of a small accounting firm must assign four accountants to audit four clients. One accountant must be assigned to each client. The estimated hours required for the potential assignments are

	Client			
Accountant	1	2	3	4
Anderson	125	175	215	340
Brown	215	300	310	400
Jones	180	250	300	350
Smith	210	310	340	410

The variation is based on the experience of the accountant and the complexity of the audit. The objective is to minimize the total audit time. Which accountant is assigned to each of the clients? What is the total audit time?

10. Your bank has two check processing facilities, called A and B, with daily processing capabilities of 5,500 and 4,500 checks, respectively. The checks are sent to the check processing facilities from five branches. The number of checks requiring processing varies from day to day, but the averages are

Branch	Average Number of Checks
1	3,000
2	2,200
3	1,300
4	2,000
5	1,300

Because Facility A is more automated than Facility B, its cost per check processed, $0.02, is less than that of Facility B, which is $0.03. The estimated delivery costs are

From Branch	To	
	A	B
1	$0.017	$0.021
2	0.005	0.013
3	0.011	0.008
4	0.019	0.016
5	0.018	0.005

The float costs are the same for the two facilities.

a. Find the number of checks sent from each bank to each check processing facility that minimizes the cost.

b. What is the minimum cost?

11. The Air Force awards bids for jet fuel on a competitive basis. Bids have been received from three companies to supply two airfields as follows:

Bidder	Location	Price ($/gal.)
A	Wright-Patterson	$0.85
A	Mitchell	0.81
B	Wright-Patterson	0.79
B	Mitchell	0.80
C	Wright-Patterson	0.82
C	Mitchell	0.86

The requirements are 180,000 and 190,000 gallons at Wright-Patterson and Mitchell, respectively. Each bidder can be awarded the contract at only one location. How should the bids be awarded to minimize the total cost?

12. Use the linear programming software available to you to solve the model of Exercise 1. Answer the following questions from the output:

a. What is the minimum total shipping cost?

b. How many units remain at each warehouse after the required units have been shipped?

c. Do any customers receive units from more than one warehouse? If so, specify the customers and the associated warehouses.

d. How much must the shipping cost from Chicago to St. Louis decrease before the shipping plan changes?

e. If the number of units available at Chicago increased by 10, how would the minimum cost change?

f. Is there an alternate optimal solution?

g. How many pivots are required to find the optimal solution?

13. Use the transportation problem software available to you to solve the model of Exercise 1. Answer as many of the questions of MCE 12 from the output as possible. Does your transportation software provide the same information concerning dual prices, reduced costs, and optimality ranges as the LP software?

14. A manufacturing company produces a product at its plants in Columbus, Ohio, and Waterloo, Iowa. The weekly capacities of the Columbus and Waterloo plants are 2,000 units and 1,200 units, respectively. Production is shipped from plants to a warehouse in either Chicago or Indianapolis. The warehousing costs per unit in the Chicago and Indianapolis warehouses are $12 and $15, respectively. The major customers are in Detroit, Lexington, Kentucky, and St. Louis, with weekly requirements of 800, 900, and 1,500 units, respectively. The shipping costs per unit are given on the next page:

From	To				
	Chicago	Indianapolis	Detroit	Lexington	St. Louis
Columbus	$32	$23			
Waterloo	26	44			
Chicago			$32	$18	$11
Indianapolis			26	13	32

The manufacturing costs per unit are $125 and $134 at Columbus and Waterloo, respectively. The objective is to minimize the total of manufacturing, warehousing, and shipping costs.
   a. Give the network model.
   b. Give the linear programming symbolic model.
   c. Solve the problem by the software available to you.

15. Solve Exercise 9, an assignment problem, by
   a. Linear programming software.
   b. Assignment model software.
   c. General minimum cost objective network model software.

16. Solve Exercise 11, a transportation problem, by
   a. Linear programming software.
   b. Transportation model software.
   c. General minimum cost objective network model software.

17. Solve Exercise 12, a maximum flow problem, by
   a. Linear programming software.
   b. Maximum flow software.
   c. General minimum cost objective network model software.

18. Find the minimum cost replacement policy for Exercise 14 by
   a. Linear programming software.
   b. Shortest-route software.
   c. General minimum cost objective network model software.

19. For the project management problem of Exercise 17, find the critical path and the total slack time of each activity by
   a. Linear programming software.
   b. Project management software.

20. In Exercise 9, assume that it is possible to assign as many as two jobs to any machine. The objective is to minimize the total processing time of the five jobs.
   a. Give the network model representation of this assignment problem. Is the network model balanced?
   b. Give the linear programming symbolic model.

21. In Exercise 16, the total supply is less than the total requirement. Say that the first customer must receive all 89 units. Modify the balanced transportation table for this assumption.

CASE

American Brands, Inc.

Brad Holgate's early interest in soap began when he discovered that he could make small amounts of it with his chemistry set. After graduating from college, Brad could not find a suitable job and decided it was time to go back to making soap. Brad's uncle, Mr. Wilfred, who was running a drugstore in his hometown, agreed to put on his store shelves any soap that Brad might manufacture, provided he was satisfied with the quality and only after informal trials had been carried out.

Soap manufacture in small quantities does not require an elaborate setup—a few vats, ladles, a hearth, and the ability to judge when the soap is just right. Brad started with an initial investment of $350 to buy the necessary equipment and chemicals. After a few spoiled batches, Brad came out with a batch of bath soap satisfactory to him and he distributed it as free samples. The response was quite gratifying. The next batch was again distributed as free samples, and the comments confirmed the results of the first trial. Two weeks later, in July 1964, "Bradbar" soap made its appearance at the corner drugstore. As Brad was his favorite nephew, Mr. Wilfred made special efforts to induce trial by his customers, particularly by those whose business he was confident of not losing even if the soap proved unsatisfactory. Things moved slowly for the first three weeks and Brad's soap looked like another "also ran," when suddenly, in the next three days, not only the same customers started coming back for a repeat purchase but also their friends to whom it had been recommended. The shelves were swept clean within the week and Brad had to make a rush repeat order. Business began to grow until five years later Mr. Bradley Holgate, president, Holgate & Co., was selling bath soaps in five different brand names. Holgate & Co. could now boast of 23 employees, including one salesman and one salesman-cum-accountant. A large number of drugstores in northeastern Delaware now carried Holgate products. However, Brad found the going tougher than ever before. Though he firmly believed in, as he called it, the intrinsic worth of his product, he felt that the growth of his company was limited. He realized that he needed better organization and a stronger financial base. He would also be entering a market where much larger and established companies were operating. Sandy, an old school friend and a successful businessman, was visiting him on a summer evening and, on listening to Brad's problem, he hinted that it might be worthwhile to investigate possible relations with some other company that might be in a similar situation. He knew of just such a company in the southern part of the state and offered to discuss the matter with it. In spite of Brad's earlier misgivings, Holgate and Lashley merged in 1968 to form American Brands, Inc., with a 65–35 partnership between Brad and Mr. Lashley. Mr. Lashley was getting on in years and was content with being the minority partner.

From 1969 onward the sales of American Brands grew rapidly and so did its problems. (See Exhibit 1.) Although it had become larger, with gross sales of $8.2 million, and had a full-time marketing manager, production

EXHIBIT 1 American Brands, Inc. Gross Sales*

1969	1970	1971	1972	1973	1974	1975
1.6	2.7	3.5	4.9	6.1	7.2	8.2

* Millions of dollars.

SOURCE: Raj Aggareval and Inder Khera, *Management Science Cases and Applications,* Oakland, Calif.: Holden-Day, Inc., 1979, pp. 88–92.

EXHIBIT 2   American Brands, Inc. Organization Chart

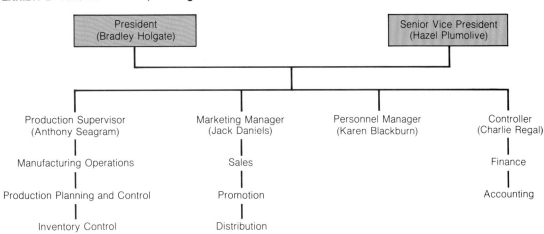

supervisor, and controller, it was finding it difficult to meet the seasonal demands for its bath soaps. (See Exhibit 2.) The consumption of bath soaps became particularly heavy during the summer months and rose considerably above winter month requirements. This heavy imbalance placed a severe strain on the production facilities in the one month preceding summer and caused production to slack off abruptly with the onset of winter. The problem was further complicated by the fact that American Brands had been marketing two product lines, regular and luxury. While the regular line had four product items, the luxury line had three. The projected demand for 1979 for the two product lines is given in Exhibit 3.

Anthony Seagram, the production supervisor, frequently complained about losses incurred from the switching in production between the luxury and the regular lines of soap because of the seemingly capricious demands made by the marketing manager, Jack Daniels. No sooner did Anthony settle down to the production of one line than Jack would come out with a change of priorities. Not only did this result in frequent stockouts of raw

materials (as proper inventory planning was not possible), but it also caused a loss in production capacity. Each time the product line had to be changed from regular to luxury, some additional equipment had to be put in place, temperature control devices installed, and molds changed. It was Anthony's estimate that the changeover from regular to luxury meant a loss of two hours 45 minutes and

EXHIBIT 3   American Brands, Inc. 1979 Sales Forecasts*

Month	Regular	Luxury	Total
January	40	24	64
February	61	27	88
March	64	61	125
April	83	109	192
May	88	126	214
June	106	137	243
July	124	165	289
August	135	161	296
September	97	147	244
October	84	114	198
November	76	62	138
December	51	46	97
Total	1,009	1,179	2,188

* Sales given in thousands of cases.

that the change from luxury to regular caused a one-hour loss. Additional time lost in trial runs when the product line was changed was, on the average, one hour for the luxury line and one-half hour for the regular line. Frequent trial runs also resulted in a rise in the percentage of waste. Jack put the blame on Anthony and his production department who "were never able to produce enough and on time." He felt he had no control over demand and simply conveyed what the market demanded. He felt it was up to Anthony to figure out the ways and means to meet that demand. As it was, he complained, sales could easily be pushed up by at least 7 percent if only Anthony could produce orders on time, particularly those for the luxury items. Jack felt that the sales of luxury soaps could be increased by at least 5 percent starting immediately. He felt that not only were opportunities being missed but also that sales were getting hurt by another 5 percent due to the ill will generated by delayed shipments. Charlie Regal, the controller, was opposed to the idea of increasing production without an accurate estimate of expected sales. He regarded Jack's attitude as being unrealistic and wanted some additional long-term orders before he would OK any proposals for increased production. He contended that if Jack could forecast the demand better, loss in capacity could be reduced. Anthony tended to agree and said that he could produce, given proper batch runs, up to 180,000 cases per month and that with overtime he could produce another 30,000 cases. Charlie, however, would not agree to overtime as this meant an additional cost per hour of $1.20. This increased cost would push up the costs per case by 80 cents for regular items and $1 for luxury items. With storage charges at 10 cents per case per month, and the deterioration that might take place in storage, he felt the total cost may have become too high. An-

thony, however, pointed out that bath soaps have a reasonably long shelf life (though the humidity in the warehouse would have to be increased slightly at a negligible cost) and consequently no deterioration was likely to occur. Jack was also opposed to overtime, as he feared that the increased manufacturing costs would necessitate higher prices, which would, in turn, make his task even more difficult. If any overtime had to be resorted to, he did not want it during production of luxury items. It was his belief that any increase in their price in the present market would make them practically unsalable. Anthony pointed out that it would not be possible for him to change to regular line production at the end of each day just so luxury soap would not be produced during overtime. The luxury brands would have to take their share of the overtime premium. However, he would try to avoid it as best as he could. Anthony, on the other hand, believed that the luxury line should be dropped altogether as the per case productivity for the regular line was 10 percent higher. Jack felt that it would be suicidal to drop the luxury items as this would have repercussions on the sales of the regular product. Many of the stores would find it more convenient to drop both if one were discontinued, and their main competitor in the region was looking for just such an opportunity. It was therefore decided not to drop the luxury line.

American Brands' profits had increased by only 3 percent in 1978, whereas sales for the same year had increased by 14 percent. Anthony Seagram had to develop a production schedule that would indicate the number of cases of the regular and the luxury lines that should be produced each month during 1979. The objective was to have available enough soap of each grade to meet each month's forecast demand while minimizing capacity loss, overtime production, and storage charges.

CASE

Shale Oil Company

The Shale Oil Company contains several operating units that comprise its Aston, Ohio, manufacturing complex. These units process the crude oil that is pumped through and transform it into a multitude of hydrocarbon products. The units run 24 hours a day, seven days a week, and must be shut down for maintenance on a predetermined schedule. One such unit is Distillation Unit No. 5, or DU5. Studies have shown that DU5 can operate only 3½ years without major equipment breakdowns and excessive loss of efficiency. Therefore,

DU5 is shut down every 3½ years for cleaning, inspection, and repairs.

DU5 is the only distillation unit for crude oil in the Aston complex, and its shutdown severely affects all other operating units. Some of the production can be compensated by Shale refineries in other locations, but the rest must be processed before the shutdown

SOURCE: Barry Render and Ralph M. Stair, Jr., *Cases and Readings in Quantitative Analysis for Management*, Boston: Allyn and Bacon, Inc., 1982, pp. 94–95.

EXHIBIT 1   Preventive Maintenance of DU5

Arc	Activities	Time Estimates (in days)		
		Optimistic	Most Likely	Pessimistic
1–2	Circulate wash water throughout unit	1	2	2.5
2–3	Install blinds	1.5	2	2.5
3–4	Open and clean vessels and columns	2	3	4
3–5	Open and clean heat exchangers, remove tube bundles	1	2	3
3–6	Open and clean furnaces	1	2	4
3–7	Open and clean mechanical equipment	2	2.5	3
3–8	Inspect instrumentation	2	4	5
4–9	Inspect vessels and columns	1	2	3
5–10	Inspect heat exchanger shells	1	1.5	2
5–11	Inspect tube bundles	1	1.5	2
6–12	Inspect furnaces	2	2.5	3
6–17	Retube furnaces	15	20	30
7–13	Inspect mechanical equipment	1	1.5	2
7–18	Install new pump mechanical seals	3	5	8
8–19	Repair instrumentation	3	8	15
9–14	Repair vessels and columns	14	21	28
10–16	Repair heat exchanger shells	1	5	10
11–15	Repair tube bundles, retube	2	5	10
12–17	Repair furnaces	5	10	20
13–18	Repair mechanical equipment	10	15	25
14–20	Test and close vessels and columns	4	5	8
15–16	Install tube bundles into heat exchanger shells	1	2	3
16–20	Test and close heat exchangers	1	2	2.5
17–20	Test and close furnaces	1	2	3
18–20	Test and close mechanical equipment	1	2	3
19–20	Test instrumentation	2	4	6
20–21	Pull blinds	1.5	2	2.5
21–22	Purge all equipment with steam	1	3	5
22–23	Start up unit	3	5	10

and stored. Without proper planning, a nation-wide shortage of Shale gasoline could occur. The timing of DU5's shutdown is critical, and the length of time the unit is down must be kept to a minimum to limit production loss. Shale uses PERT as a planning and controlling tool to minimize shutdown time.

The first phase of a shutdown is to open and clean the equipment. Inspectors can then enter the unit and examine the damage. Once damages are determined, the needed repairs can be carried out. Repair times can vary considerably depending on what damage the inspection reveals. Based on previous inspection records, some repair work is known ahead of time. Thorough cleaning of the equipment is also necessary to improve the unit's operating efficiency. Exhibit 1 lists the many maintenance activities and their estimated times.

9

Integer Linear Programming and Nonlinearities

Types of Integer Linear Programming Models
Binary Integer Variables and General Integer Variables / Pure and
Mixed Integer Linear Programming Models

Piecewise Linear Objective Functions
Linear Programming Reformulation for the OK Case / Integer
Linear Programming Reformulation for the Troublesome
Case / Integer Linear Programming Reformulation for More than
One Breakpoint

Fixed Charge Costs
The Machine Assignment Model / A Plant Location Model

Other Binary Integer Variable Formulations
Capital Budgeting / Either-Or Constraints / Minimum Batch
Size / The Monsanto Model

Introduction to Combinatorial Optimization Problems

Integer Variables—"Lucky" Models

An Approach to Discrete Alternatives—A Set of Case Studies
A Set of Case Studies for the Troublesome Machine Assignment
Problem

Integer Linear Programming Models and Sensitivity Analysis

Piecewise Linear Approximation and Separable Programming
Piecewise Linear Approximation / Linear Programming
Reformulation for a Nonlinear Constraint—OK Case / Integer
Linear Programming Reformulation for a Nonlinear Constraint
—Troublesome Case / Separable Programming Mode

Case: Alcan (X)

MONSANTO CHEMICAL COMPANY

Monsanto Chemical Company makes hundreds of chemical products. One of them, maleic anhydride, is used in many products, ranging from boat hulls to agricultural chemicals. Monsanto's annual maleic anhydride production capacity represents 45 percent of total U.S. annual capacity—359 million pounds. A savings of a fraction of a cent per pound in producing maleic anhydride translates into large annual savings.

Monsanto produces maleic anhydride in two plants. The newer and larger plant is located in Pensacola, Florida, and the other plant is located in St. Louis. Maleic anhydride is produced by catalytic oxidation of butane or benzene in a reactor. Both the Pensacola plant and the St. Louis plant have many reactors. Before the construction of the Pensacola plant, Monsanto could sell all of the maleic anhydride it produced. After the construction of the Pensacola plant, it had extra maleic anhydride capacity.

Monsanto recognized that the trade-off between the production and yield of maleic anhydride provided an opportunity for substantial cost savings. Yield is the pounds of maleic anhydride per pound of raw material. Both the production rate and the yield are functions of reactor velocity, raw material feed rate, and reactor pressure. Maximizing production decreases the yield. Maximizing the yield decreases the production rate. Because of the company's extra maleic anhydride capacity, a management science study was conducted to assign production to each plant and to adjust reactor operating conditions to minimize cost for the target quantities.

Three models were developed. A global model considered both of the plants and all of the reactors. The global model assigned production to the two plants to meet an overall production goal at minimum costs. A separate model for each plant enabled plant management to make adjustments based on minor production disruptions, such as an unexpected reactor shutdown. For major problems, the global model was used to adust the plant plans.

The relationship of yield to raw material feed rate, reactor velocity, and reactor pressure is not linear. An integer linear programming model was used to approximate the yield of each reactor under different operating conditions. A binary variable was introduced for several sets of operating conditions for each reactor. An overall constraint ensured that the desired amount was produced at each plant.

The older plant has several methods of providing the oxygen required for the manufacturing process. A separate optimization model determines the most economical method of providing the oxygen needed by the St. Louis plant.

Monsanto developed a computer system that processes the output from the optimization models and creates reports in a form that is meaningful to its users. Production engineers use the separate plant models to fine-tune the manufacturing process. Because of the interactive computer system, the models can be run several times in a half-hour period.

The system generates direct cost savings estimated at $1–3 million per year. The system is also used to evaluate changes in the configuration of facilities at the plants.

Indirect benefits of the management science study included a greater understanding of the cost and operation of compressors used in the manufacturing process. Consequently, the operating efficiency of some of this equipment was improved by adjustments.

The approximation of nonlinear functions and their representation as integer linear programming models are among the topics of this chapter.

R. F. Boykin, "Optimizing Chemical Production at Monsanto," *Interfaces* 15, no. 1 (January–February 1985), pp. 88–95.

In Chapters 3 through 8, we discussed linear programming models, a type of decision model that has many applications. However, not all decision models are linear programming models. One reason for this is that decision environments can have uncertain outcomes. If the uncertainty in a decision environment is important, the model must incorporate that uncertainty into the analysis. In Chapter 10, we begin discussing decision making for probabilistic decision environments and probabilistic decision models.

Another reason is that some constrained optimization models violate the assumptions of a linear programming model. Two such violations are (1) introducing a nonlinear function and (2) restricting the values of some or all variables to integer values. In this chapter, we discuss constrained optimization models that violate these assumptions. The Monsanto models, for example, violate the linearity assumption. In those models, the relationship of the yield and the production rate to operating conditions is not linear. Also, remember the personnel scheduling model developed in Chapter 7, which determines the number of employees who begin at each starting time. All of the variables are continuous for a linear programming model, but a fractional variable value doesn't make sense in personnel scheduling. You can't have 3.7 people start at midnight. For many decision problems, some of the variables must be restricted to integer values. Constrained optimization models can violate either the linearity assumption or the continuous variable assumption.

An **integer linear programming model** is a linear programming model in which some of the decision variables are restricted to integer values. Of course, you can always solve a linear programming model by the simplex method and hope that the variables have integer values in the optimal solution. In most of the solutions for the linear programming examples in previous chapters, some of the variable values were nonintegers. It is true that all of the variable values in the optimal solution to Chapter 7's personnel scheduling model were integers. In that case, we were lucky. But most of the time this doesn't happen.

A **nonlinear programming model** has at least one nonlinear function—either a constraint function or the objective function—and continuous variables. You can't even try to solve a nonlinear programming model by linear programming software. The software assumes that all of the functions are linear and will not accept any other input. Also, the simplex algorithm for linear programming does not solve nonlinear programming models. You must use different algorithms and software to solve such models.

Reformulating non-linear programming models

In general, software based on nonlinear programming algorithms is less widely available than software for linear programming models and integer linear programming models. This chapter focuses on nonlinear programming models that can be *reformulated* as linear programming or integer linear programming models. We introduce new variables and new constraints to represent the nonlinear programming model as a linear programming model or an integer linear programming model. Monsanto used this approach to solve its nonlinear programming problem.

In addition to permitting the use of more readily available software, reformulation permits the solution of larger models. Software for nonlinear programming solves much smaller models (both in the number of decision variables and constraints) than software for linear programming and integer linear programming.

Nonlinear programming models are common in engineering design. For example, the volume of a cylinder increases with the square of its diameter—that is, $V = \pi\left(\frac{D^2 h}{4}\right)$. Most managers are not concerned with engineering design problems. However, they are concerned with costs.

Let's consider the costs for a manufacturing plant. Costs are generally classified as either fixed or variable. The fixed cost includes rent, insurance, and salaried employee costs. The fixed cost is incurred regardless of the amount produced at the plant. Raw materials, energy, and direct labor are components of the variable cost. Commonly, the total cost is the fixed cost plus a constant variable cost. The cost function for break-even analysis is

$$\text{Cost} = F + (c \times x)$$

where F is the fixed cost, c is the variable cost rate, and x is the number of units produced.

A common application of integer linear programming is choosing between discrete alternatives. For example, should we close the manufacturing plant? If we close it, we don't have to pay the fixed cost anymore and the cost is 0. If we don't close it, we pay the fixed cost plus the variable cost. The total cost is nonlinear.

For the break-even analysis cost model, you assume that the variable cost rate is the same regardless of the value of x. Sometimes, economies or diseconomies of scale cause another nonlinear cost that managers must consider. In Chapter 7, we discussed several reasons for economies or diseconomies of scale. For example, if the amount produced is large enough, you need overtime, which increases the labor cost. The variable cost rate is higher when you need overtime. On the other hand, if a raw material supplier gives a discount for large-volume purchases, increasing production at the plant decreases the raw material cost per unit produced.

Nonlinear costs

Managers often encounter nonlinearities caused by fixed costs and by variable cost rates that change with volume. In this chapter, we reformulate models involving these practical nonlinearities as either linear or integer linear programming models.

Some integer linear programming applications

Let's consider some other applications of integer linear programming models. Maryland National Bank uses an integer linear programming model to make decisions on check clearing methods.[1] If an out-of-town check is received for deposit, the recipient bank obtains its money for the check when the check is presented for payment at the out-of-town bank. The check clears when payment is made by the out-of-town bank. A float cost arises because the recipient bank credits the deposit before receiving the money for the check. The shorter the clearing time, the smaller the float cost. Checks can be cleared by using the Federal Reserve System, a local bank that acts as a clearinghouse, or messenger. Each of these alternatives has different costs and clearing times. Maryland National Bank achieved a yearly savings of $100,000 through its use of an integer linear programming model to choose from among the check clearing alternatives for checks from different out-of-town banks.

After oil prices increased dramatically, Exxon embarked on an ambitious program of energy conservation at its oil refineries. It identified many potential projects, each with different capital costs and savings in future years. It used an integer linear programming model to choose which of these projects to undertake.[2] The company reported incremental savings of $100 million from choosing the projects in this way at the Baton Rouge refinery.

---

[1] R. E. Markland and R. M. Nauss, "Improving Check Clearing Operations at Maryland National Bank," *Interfaces* 13, no. 1 (February 1983), pp. 1–9.

[2] W. L. McMahan and P. A. Roach, "Site Energy Optimization: A Math Programming Approach," *Interfaces* 12, no. 6 (December 1982), pp. 66–82.

The Variable Annuity Life Insurance Company (VALIC) studied the number and boundaries of its sales regions. Adding a sales region requires additional cost for a regional office (a fixed cost) but locates salespeople closer to some potential customers. VALIC developed a model that considered increased sales efficiency because of decreased travel time and the additional fixed costs of regional sales offices.[3] The model is similar to the plant location model that we discuss later in this chapter.

In Chapter 1, we described a system developed by Air Products and Chemicals to plan the distribution of industrial gases to its customers. One part of the system is an integer linear programming model that determines delivery routes to its customers for each truck. That model has as many as 200,000 constraints and 800,000 variables. See Yano et al.[4] and Brown et al.[5] for other routing applications of integer linear programming models.

In the above applications, integer linear programming models are used to choose alternatives from a set of discrete alternatives. You either use the Federal Reserve System for checks written on the Bank of America, or you don't. You either select an energy conservation project, or you don't. You either open a regional sales office in Washington, D.C., or you don't. Choosing from among a set of alternatives is a frequent use of integer linear programming models.

Chapter preview

In this chapter, we develop models for piecewise linear objective functions, which are associated with increasing or decreasing returns to scale, and we show how to model fixed costs. Fixed costs have a major impact on deciding whether to open a new facility or to close an existing one. We describe some useful "tricks" in integer variable formulation, and we introduce combinatorial optimization problems. We show how you can solve an integer linear programming model by solving a set of case studies, each of which is a linear programming model, and we explain why simple sensitivity analysis is impossible for integer linear programming models.

In the last section of the chapter, we introduce separable functions and describe how to approximate them with piecewise linear functions. If a nonlinear constraint function is separable, you can find the optimal solution for the approximation model by solving either a linear programming model or an integer linear programming model, depending on conditions

[3] B. D. Gelb and B. M. Khumawala, "Reconfiguration of an Insurance Company's Sales Regions," *Interfaces* 14, no. 6 (December 1984), pp. 87–94.

[4] C. A. Yano, T. J. Chan, L. K. Richter, T. Cutler, K. G. Murty, and D. McGettigan, "Vehicle Routing at Quality Stores," *Interfaces* 17, no. 2 (March–April 1987), pp. 52–63.

[5] G. G. Brown, G. W. Graves, and D. Ronen, "Scheduling Ocean Transportation of Crude Oil," *Management Science* 33, no. 3 (March 1987), pp. 333–46.

that we describe. We conclude by describing the separable programming mode for mainframe mathematical programming systems. By using a piecewise linear approximation for a separable nonlinear function, you can use this mode to solve such models. If you don't have access to separable programming software, you can skip this information. However, you are more likely to have separable programming software (e.g., IBM's MPSX) than general nonlinear programming software.

But first, let's describe the various types of integer linear programming models and software. Knowing these will help you understand the models that we develop later. You should check the capabilities of the software you can use against the types described in the next section.

TYPES OF INTEGER LINEAR PROGRAMMING MODELS

Common mistakes in formulating integer linear programming models

There are formulation "tricks" that define integer variables to have desired characteristics. One common mistake in applying these tricks is to believe that defining a variable to have a desired characteristic makes this true. You must add constraints and modify the objective function so that the variable has the characteristic. Also, remember that the constraint functions and the objective function must be linear for an integer linear programming model. Another common mistake is to introduce nonlinear functions by multiplying variables by variables. If A and B are variables, any function containing their product, AB, is not linear. We will warn you about these two mistakes again when we formulate integer linear programming models.

Two classifications

The range of variable values for an integer-restricted variable is one classification for integer linear programming models. Another classification is one in which some or all of the variables are restricted to integer values. Let's describe both of these classifications.

Binary Integer Variables and General Integer Variables

A **general integer variable (GIN)** can attain any nonnegative integer value. If a decision variable represents the number of employees who start working at midnight, the decision variable is a general integer variable. Only integer values make sense, but only the constraints impose a limit on the value of the variable. A **binary integer variable,** often called a **0–1 variable,** can attain only integer values of 0 and 1. In many of the formulation tricks, a binary integer variable is introduced. The variable is defined so that a value of 1 corresponds to something happening and a value of 0 corresponds to its not happening. For example, you introduce a binary integer variable for Washington, D.C., and define it to be 1 if you locate a regional sales office there and to be 0 if you don't.

TABLE 9.1 Specification of Binary Integer and General Integer Variables—LINDO

```
: max 2x1 + 3x2 + 4x3
> st 2x1+x2+x3<7
> -2x1 + x2 + 2x3<5
> end

: look all

  MAX      2 X1 + 3 X2 + 4 X3
  SUBJECT TO
       2)    2 X1 + X2 + X3 <=   7
       3) -  2 X1 + X2 + 2 X3 <=    5
  END

: integer x2
: gin x3
: look all

  MAX      3 X2 + 4 X3 + 2 X1
  SUBJECT TO
       2)    X2 + X3 + 2 X1 <=   7
       3)    X2 + 2 X3 - 2 X1 <=    5
  END
  GIN      2
  SUB      X2        1.00
```

Often, linear programming software has integer linear programming capabilities. LINDO can use both binary integer variables and general integer variables. You input the underlying linear programming model in the standard way. Then, you specify the integer variables. For the LINDO system, you specify binary integer variables by the INTEGER command and general integer variables by the GIN command. Table 9.1 illustrates how you specify Variable $X2$ as a binary integer variable and Variable $X3$ as a general integer variable. The LOOK ALL in Table 9.1 shows that LINDO allows specifying a variable as a binary integer variable but treats the binary integer variable as a general integer variable with an upper bound of 1. Both $X2$ and $X3$ are GIN variables, but $X2$ has an upper bound of 1.

Table 9.2 shows Table 9.1's model in MPS format. MPS format is the standard for mainframe linear and integer programming systems. Two 'MARKER' statements designate the beginning and ending of the set of integer variables. The simple upper bound (SUB) of 1 on Variable $X2$ is imposed in a separate BOUNDS section. LINDO can also read and write model files in MPS format.

Although LINDO allows specification of both binary integer variables and general integer variables, some systems allow only one of the two types. Let's consider how to construct models for a system that doesn't have both types of integer variables.

Using GIN software for binary integer variables

Say that your software does not have binary integer variable capabilities but that your model has binary integer variables. For this type of software, you specify a binary variable as a general integer variable with a

TABLE 9.2 The Integer Linear Programming Model of Table 9.1 in MPS Format—
X2 **Binary Integer Variable and** *X3* **General Integer Variable**

```
NAME       LINDO GENERATED MPS FILE( MAX)
ROWS
 N  1
 L  2
 L  3
COLUMNS
    INTEGER1  'MARKER'                      'INTORG'
    X2        1              3.00000000
    X2        2              1.00000000
    X2        3              1.00000000
    X3        1              4.00000000
    X3        2              1.00000000
    X3        3              2.00000000
    INTEGER2  'MARKER'                      'INTEND'
    X1        1              2.00000000
    X1        2              2.00000000
    X1        3             -2.00000000
RHS
    RHS       2              7.000000
    RHS       3              5.000000
BOUNDS
 UP LINDOBND  X2             1.00
ENDATA
```

maximum value of 1. That is, you add $X2 \leq 1$ to the formulation. By doing this, you can use software that allows only general integer variables to solve formulations with binary integer variables. (If the software has simple upper bound capabilities, the constraint $X2 \leq 1$ is treated implicitly. LINDO has such capabilities. See the section Simple Upper Bounds and Simple Lower Bounds in Chapter 8.)

Some software packages allow only binary integer variables. Although you can use software that allows GIN variables for models with binary variables, you can't directly use software that allows only binary integer variables for models with GIN variables. This is because the software assumes that the variables specified as integer are only 0 or 1. Therefore, you must transform the general integer variables to construct an equivalent model including only binary integer variables. You need to replace each general integer variable by its **binary representation.** Let's illustrate this on the model in Table 9.1, for which $X3$ is a general integer variable. Because all of the coefficients in the constraint $2X1 + X2 + X3 \leq 7$ are nonnegative, the value of $X3$ cannot be more than 7 regardless of the other variable values. Replace $X3$ by the expression

$$1X31 + 2X32 + 4X33$$

where $X31$, $X32$, and $X33$ are all binary integer variables. If $X31$, $X32$, and $X33$ all equal 0, the value of the expression is 0. If they all equal 1, the value of the expression is 7. All integer values between 0 and 7 are obtained by some combination of the binary variable values. The model in Table 9.3 shows that $X3$ has been eliminated by the substitution. You find the optimal value of $X3$ by evaluating $X3 = X31 + 2X32 + 4X33$.

Using binary integer software for GIN variables

TABLE 9.3 Transformed Model for Formulation of Table 9.1's Model with Only Binary Integer Variables

```
: max 2x1 + 3x2 + 4x31 + 8x32 + 16x33
> st 2x1 + x2 + x31 + 2x32 + 4x33 < 7
> -2x1 + x2 + 2x31 + 4x32 + 8x33 < 5
> end

: integer x2
: integer x31
: integer x32
: integer x33
: look all

  MAX    3 X2 + 4 X31 + 8 X32 + 16 X33 + 2 X1
  SUBJECT TO
      2)   X2 + X31 + 2 X32 +4 X33 + 2 X1 <=   7
      3)   X2 + 2 X31 + 4 X32 + 8 X33 - 2 X1 < =    5
  END
  INTE X2
  INTE X31
  INTE X32
  INTE X33
```

This transformation is useful in solving a model with a general integer variable with software that allows only binary integer variables. While the transformation is correct, it replaces one general integer variable with three binary integer variables, thus resulting in a problem that is more difficult to solve. For this reason, if a model has GIN variables, we prefer software using GIN variables to software with only binary integer variable capabilities.

Finding the required number of binary integer variables

If the largest possible value of a general integer variable is large, a single general integer variable is replaced by a large number of binary integer variables. Let K represent the largest index for the binary representation. For Table 9.1, $K = 3$; three binary integer variables are required. In general, the GIN variable is represented by the expression

$$1X31 + 2X32 + 4X33 + 8X34 + \ldots + 2^{K-1}X3K$$

where K must be determined.

Let's consider determining the number of binary variables required to represent a general integer variable. We find an upper limit on the value of the GIN variables by examining the model constraints. In Table 9.1, a limit of 7 for $X3$ is imposed by the first constraint. Say that the largest possible variable value is 32,767. The largest possible value for the expression occurs if all of the binary variables are 1. Thus, the maximum value is

$$1 + 2 + 4 + 8 + 16 + \ldots + 2^{K-1} = 2^K - 1$$

The value of K is selected as the smallest integer such that $2^K - 1 \geq$ 32,767. In this case, because $2^{15} = 32,768$, the value of K is 15. You need *fifteen* binary integer variables to represent a general integer variable with a maximum value of 32,767.

Pure and Mixed Integer Linear Programming Models

If all of the structural variables must have integer values, the model is called a **pure integer linear programming model.** If some of the variables must have integer values, the model is called a **mixed integer linear programming model.**

Most pure integer linear programming software allows only binary integer variables. If your model has general integer variables, you replace them by their binary representation. You can solve pure integer linear programming models by mixed integer linear programming software, but you can't solve mixed integer linear programming models by pure integer linear programming software. If you use pure integer programming software on a mixed integer model, the variables that are supposed to be continuous are restricted to integer values. This might cause you to miss the best solution.

Two of the most common nonlinearities are piecewise linear objective functions and fixed charge costs. In the next two sections, we discuss formulating these problems as linear programming models or integer linear programming models.

PIECEWISE LINEAR OBJECTIVE FUNCTIONS

The first nonlinear programming models that we reformulate are those with piecewise linear objective functions. Say that the model has linear constraints but that the contribution of one variable's objective function is like the functions shown in the Figure 9.1 graphs. These functions are nonlinear. However, they are linear over "pieces."

A **piecewise linear function** consists of straight line segments that are connected at the end points. The **breakpoints** are the variable values where the slope of the line segments changes. The slope of the objective function is called the **objective function rate.** Let's use the **profit rate** for a maximization objective and the **cost rate** for a minimization objective. Objective functions other than profit and cost are often correct. However, using the profit rate and the cost rate tells whether the objective function is to be maximized or minimized without having to say so. A profit rate implies that the objective function is to be maximized; a cost rate implies that the objective function is to be minimized.

Quantity discounts from your suppliers, regular time capacity limitations, use of a second supplier, and quantity discounts to your customers cause piecewise linear objective functions. Examine Figure 9.1a. The

FIGURE 9.1 Examples of Piecewise Linear Objective Functions

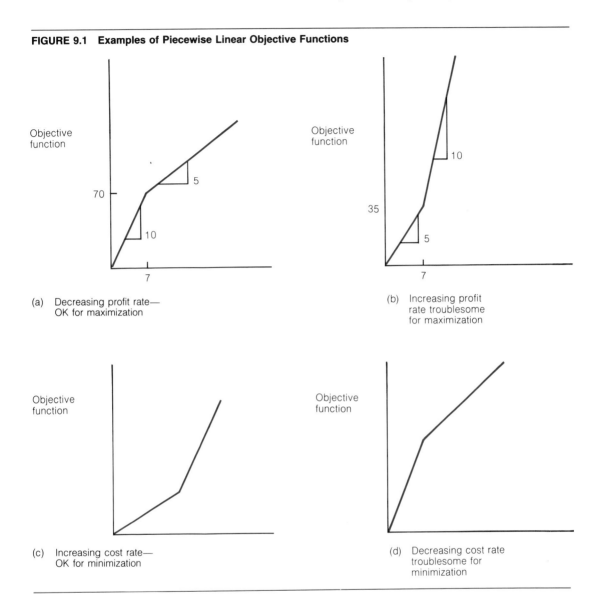

(a) Decreasing profit rate— OK for maximization

(b) Increasing profit rate troublesome for maximization

(c) Increasing cost rate— OK for minimization

(d) Decreasing cost rate troublesome for minimization

profit rate is 10 for variable values between 0 and 7, and it decreases to 5 for variable values greater than 7. The breakpoint is 7, the variable value where the slope changes. One reason for a profit function with this type of shape is capacity limitations. Say that the maximum you can produce without overtime is 7 units. Producing more than 7 units requires overtime labor and decreases the profit margin.

Examine Figure 9.1*b*. The profit rate is 5 for variable values between 0 and 7, and it increases to 10 for variable values above 7. Quantity discounts can cause profit to have this shape. If you produce large amounts of finished goods and buy raw materials in large amounts, your supplier may give you a discount. A discount for the raw material cost increases the profit margin.

We discussed piecewise linear objective functions in Chapter 7. We stated that *for a maximization problem, if the profit rate decreases as the variable value increases, you obtain an optimal solution by solving a reformulated linear programming model.* We call this the **OK** case. Note that this refers to changes in the profit *rate,* not the profit. Figure 9.1*a* illustrates an objective function with a profit rate of 10 on the first segment and 5 on the second segment. The profit rate of Figure 9.1*a* is decreasing, and reformulation to a linear programming model is correct.

The OK maximization case

For a maximization problem, if the profit rate increases as the variable value increases, you cannot obtain an optimal solution by solving a reformulated linear programming model. This is called the **troublesome** case. In this case, *the problem is reformulated as an integer linear programming model.* Figure 9.1*b* illustrates a maximization objective function with an increasing profit rate. The linear programming reformulation is incorrect.

The troublesome maximization case

In Chapter 7, we stated that *for a minimization model, if the cost rate increases as the variable value increases, you obtain an optimal solution by solving a reformulated linear programming model.* This is the **OK** case. However, *if the cost rate decreases for a minimization model, you can't obtain an optimal solution by solving a reformulated linear programming model.* This is the **troublesome** case. In this case, *the problem is reformulated as an integer linear programming model.* In Figure 9.1*c,* the cost rate increases and the linear programming reformulation is OK. Figure 9.1*d* is the troublesome case and requires reformulation as an integer linear programming model.

The OK minimization case

The troublesome minimization case

Examining the objective functions in Figure 9.1 shows why some objective functions are troublesome. For the troublesome cases, 9.1*b* and 9.1*d,* there is an economic incentive to select the right-hand line segment rather than the left-hand line segment either because the profit rate is greater or because the cost rate is smaller. Because of the economic incentives, the objective function is evaluated incorrectly by a linear programming model.

We presented the linear programming reformulation for the OK case in Chapter 7 and repeat it in the next section. In the *troublesome* cases for maximization and minimization models, the trick is introducing a binary integer variable and modifying the constraints to counteract the economic forces. After discussing the linear programming reformulation, we discuss the integer linear programming formulation.

Linear Programming Reformulation for the OK Case

As an example, let's consider the machine assignment problem discussed in Chapters 3 and 7. The problem is to assign three products to three machines within the available time on the machines so that cost is minimized.

In Chapter 3, the machine operating costs were very small, so we could discuss what cost components to include in the objective function. A very simple product, a cup, had very small raw material and operating costs. Say that the product is more complex so that the operating costs are greater. Table 9.4 contains the operating costs and production rates per hour.

The model is

$$\min \quad 32A_1 + 35A_2 + 36A_3 + 29B_1 + 25B_2 + 34B_3 + 32C_1 + 34C_2 + 36C_3$$

$$\begin{aligned} \text{st} \quad & A_1 + B_1 + C_1 \le 40 \\ & A_2 + B_2 + C_2 \le 40 \\ & A_3 + B_3 + C_3 \le 40 \\ & 25A_1 + 26A_2 + 23A_3 = 1000 \\ & 18B_1 + 19B_2 + 20B_3 = 950 \\ & 22C_1 + 23C_2 + 20C_3 = 600 \\ & A_1, A_2, A_3, B_1, B_2, B_3, C_1, C_2, C_3, \ge 0 \end{aligned}$$

Variable A_i represents the number of hours that Cup A is produced on Machine i. The first constraint is the limit of 40 hours available on Machine 1 for Cups A, B, and C. The second and third constraints are the limit of 40 hours on Machines 2 and 3, respectively. The fourth constraint

TABLE 9.4   Data for Machine Assignment Problem

	Operating Cost ($ per hour)		
	Machine		
Product	1	2	3
A	32	35	36
B	29	25	34
C	32	34	36

	Production Rates (units per hour)		
	Machine		
Product	1	2	3
A	25	26	23
B	18	19	20
C	22	23	20

is the requirement that a total of 1,000 units of Cup A be produced on the three machines. Machine 1 produces 25 units of Cup A per hour, so it produces $25A_1$ in A_1 hours. The cost per hour that Product A is produced on Machine 1 is \$32. If Cup A is produced on Machine 1 for 10 hours, the operating cost is \$320.

Say that making Cup A on Machine 1 requires a raw material that is in short supply. Your cheapest supplier can provide only 500 units per week. Because the manufacturing rate is 25 units per hour, this is a 20-hour supply. If you produce more than 500 units per week, you must get the raw material from a more expensive supplier and the operating cost per hour increases to \$33.

A_1's cost is piecewise linear

The cost per hour is \$32 for the first 20 hours and \$33 for any hours above 20, as illustrated in Figure 9.2. The cost rate increases for this minimization problem. In this case, the optimal solution for the reformulated *linear* programming model gives the correct solution. The reformulated linear programming model is

$$\min \quad 32A_{11} + 33A_{12} + 35A_2 + 36A_3 + 29B_1 + 25B_2 + 34B_3 + 32C_1$$
$$+ 34C_2 + 36C_3$$
$$\text{st} \quad A_1 + B_1 + C_1 \le 40$$
$$A_2 + B_2 + C_2 \le 40$$
$$A_3 + B_3 + C_3 \le 40$$
$$25A_1 + 26A_2 + 23A_3 = 1000$$
$$18B_1 + 19B_2 + 20B_3 = 950$$
$$22C_1 + 23C_2 + 20C_3 = 600$$

$$A_{11} \le 20$$
$$A_1 - A_{11} - A_{12} = 0$$

$$A_{11}, A_{12}, A_1, A_2, A_3, B_1, B_2, B_3, C_1, C_2, C_3 \ge 0$$

FIGURE 9.2   Piecewise Linear Function

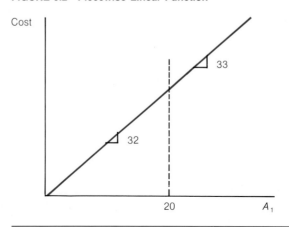

TABLE 9.5   LOOK ALL and SOLUTION for the OK Machine Assignment Piecewise Linear Model—Linear Programming Model

```
MIN      35 A2 + 36 A3 + 29 B1 + 25 B2 + 34 B3 + 32 C1 + 34 C2 + 36 C3
        + 32 A11 + 33 A12
SUBJECT TO
        2)    B1 + C1 + A1 <=    40
        3)    A2 + B2 + C2 <=    40
        4)    A3 + B3 + C3 <=    40
        5)    26 A2 + 23 A3 + 25 A1 =    1000
        6)    18 B1 + 19 B2 + 20 B3 =     950
        7)    22 C1 + 23 C2 + 20 C3 =     600
        8)    A11 <=    20
        9) -  A11 - A12 + A1 =      0
END

        OBJECTIVE FUNCTION VALUE

        1)       3670.19400

    VARIABLE           VALUE          REDUCED COST
        A2            .000000            1.604347
        A3          29.644270             .000000
        B1            .000000            5.530436
        B2          40.000000             .000000
        B3           9.500000             .000000
        C1          27.272730             .000000
        C2            .000000             .390907
        C3            .000000             .426876
        A11         12.727270             .000000
        A12           .000000            1.000000
        A1          12.727270             .000000

    ROW     SLACK OR SURPLUS      DUAL PRICES
        2)            .000000            7.130436
        3)            .000000            7.299999
        4)            .855731             .000000
        5)            .000000           -1.565217
        6)            .000000           -1.700000
        7)            .000000           -1.778656
        8)           7.272727             .000000
        9)            .000000           32.000000
```

The decision variable A_1 is "broken" into two pieces, A_{11} and A_{12}. Variable A_{11} corresponds to the first line segment, and Variable A_{12} corresponds to the second line segment. The first added constraint ensures that A_{11} does not exceed 20. The second added constraint defines the relationship between A_1, A_{11}, and A_{12}. The objective function coefficients of A_{11} and A_{12} are \$32 and \$33, respectively. In this case, the cost rate increases as the variable value increases and the resulting linear programming model is correct. Table 9.5 contains the LINDO solution for the linear programming model.

Integer Linear Programming Reformulation for the Troublesome Case

Now, say that making Cup A on Machine 1 requires a raw material that is eligible for a quantity discount. The supplier will give you a discount on any units above 500, a 20-hour supply. Say that because of this discount, the operating cost per hour above 20 decreases to \$31.

TABLE 9.6 LOOK ALL and SOLUTION for the Troublesome Piecewise Linear Machine Assignment Model—Linear Programming Model

```
MIN      35 A2 + 36 A3 + 29 B1 + 25 B2 + 34 B3 + 32 C1 + 34 C2 + 36 C3
       + 32 A11 + 31 A12
SUBJECT TO
       2)     B1 + C1 + A1 <=     40
       3)     A2 + B2 + C2 <=     40
       4)     A3 + B3 + C3 <=     40
       5)    26 A2 + 23 A3 + 25 A1 =    1000
       6)    18 B1 + 19 B2 + 20 B3 =     950
       7)    22 C1 + 23 C2 + 20 C3 =     600
       8)    A11 <=     20
       9) -  A11 - A12 + A1 =      0
END

       OBJECTIVE FUNCTION VALUE

       1)     3640.39100

   VARIABLE          VALUE          REDUCED COST
        A2          .000000           2.255474
        A3          .000000            .575996
        B1          .000000           5.904348
        B2        13.913040            .000000
        B3        34.282610            .000000
        C1          .000000            .000000
        C2        26.086960            .000000
        C3          .000000            .086956
       A11          .000000           1.000000
       A12        40.000000            .000000
        A1        40.000000            .000000

    ROW    SLACK OR SURPLUS        DUAL PRICES
       2)          .000000           7.504349
       3)          .000000           7.299999
       4)         5.717391            .000000
       5)          .000000          -1.540174
       6)          .000000          -1.700000
       7)          .000000          -1.795652
       8)        20.000000            .000000
       9)          .000000          31.000000
```

Troublesome linear programming solution

The reformulated linear programming model is incorrect. The cost rate decreases as the variable value increases. This is the troublesome case. A linear programming model like that of Table 9.5, with an objective function coefficient of \$31 for A_{12}, does not yield the correct solution. Table 9.6 contains the output for this *incorrect* linear programming model. In Table 9.6, the "optimal" value of A_1 is 40, with $A_{11} = 0$ and $A_{12} = 40$. However, this is not possible. If $A_1 = 40$, then A_{11} should be 20 and A_{12} should be 20. It is cheaper for A_{12} to be positive than it is for A_{11}, and this causes the trouble.

The integer linear programming reformulation

In the troublesome case, we introduce a binary integer variable to counteract the economic forces that cause unrealistic solutions. Let's call this variable *Y1* and define its value as 1 if A_{11} is 20 and as 0 if A_{11} is less than 20. You want the variable to have those characteristics, but *you must impose one or more linear constraints so that it has them*. Wishing does not make this happen! Because the number of available hours on Machine 1 is 40, the largest possible value for A_1 is 40. This also implies that A_{12} cannot be more than 40. (Later, we show that A_{12} cannot be as large as 40.

However, a value of 40 is "large enough" and is used.) The reformulated integer linear programming model is:

$$\min \quad 32A_{11} + 31A_{12} + 35A_2 + 36A_3 + 29B_1 + 25B_2 + 34B_3 + 32C_1$$
$$+ 34C_2 + 36C_3$$

$$\begin{aligned}
\text{st} \quad & A_1 + B_1 + C_1 \le 40 \\
& A_2 + B_2 + C_2 \le 40 \\
& A_3 + B_3 + C_3 \le 40 \\
& 25A_1 + 26A_2 + 23A_3 = 1000 \\
& 18B_1 + 19B_2 + 20B_3 = 950 \\
& 22C_1 + 23C_2 + 20C_3 = 600 \\
& A_{11} \le 20 \\
& A_1 - A_{11} - A_{12} = 0 \\
& Y1 \le 0.05A_{11} \\
& A_{12} \le 40Y1 \\
& Y1 \quad 0 \text{ or } 1 \\
& A_{11}, A_{12}, A_1, A_2, A_3, B_1, B_2, B_3, C_1, C_2, C_3, \ge 0
\end{aligned}$$

The first added constraint is

$$Y1 \le 0.05A_{11}$$

This, along with the integrality of $Y1$, ensures that $Y1$ is 1 only if $A_{11} = 20$. The coefficient of A_{11} is obtained as $\frac{1}{20}$, where 20 is the upper limit on A_{11}. If A_{11} is less than 20, $Y1$ must be 0. If $Y1$ is 0, the second added constraint,

$$A_{12} \le 40Y1$$

ensures that A_{12} must be 0. However, if $A_{11} = 20$, then $Y1$ can be 1 and the second added constraint allows A_{12} to be as large as 40. You must *transpose* the variables to the left of the $\le$ relationships. For example, the first added constraint becomes

$$Y1 - 0.05A_{11} \le 0$$

Table 9.7 contains the LOOK ALL for this model after the variables have been transposed. First, we entered the linear programming model. Then, we specified the Variable $Y1$ as a binary integer variable by using the INTEGER command.

There is an alternative form for Row 10. Originally, the constraint was

$$Y1 \le \frac{1}{20} A_{11}$$

An alternative form

We derived Row 10 by calculating $\frac{1}{20} = 0.05$. Alternatively, we can multiply by 20 to get

$$20Y1 \le A_{11}$$

Say that the upper limit was 3, not 20. In the first form, the coefficient is $\frac{1}{3} = 0.3333 \dots$ Because you can't use a fraction as an input, you must

TABLE 9.7   LOOK ALL for Integer Linear Programming Model for the Troublesome Machine Assignment Problem

```
MIN      35 A2 + 36 A3 + 29 B1 + 25 B2 + 34 B3 + 32 C1 + 34 C2 + 36 C3
      + 32 A11 + 31 A12
SUBJECT TO
       2)    B1 + C1 + A1 <=     40
       3)    A2 + B2 + C2 <=     40
       4)    A3 + B3 + C3 <=     40
       5)   26 A2 + 23 A3 + 25 A1 =     1000
       6)   18 B1 + 19 B2 + 20 B3 =      950
       7)   22 C1 + 23 C2 + 20 C3 =      600
       8)   A11 <=     20
       9) - A11 - A12 + A1 =      0
      10)   Y1 - 0.05 A11 <=      0
      11) - 40 Y1 + A12 <=      0
END
INTE        Y1
```

stop the repeating coefficients, which loses accuracy. The second alternative is more accurate.

A_{12}'s upper limit

Now, reconsider the upper limit on the value of A_{12}. If A_{11} is limited to 20 and A_1 is limited to 40, then A_{12} can't be larger than 20. For the second added constraint, Row 11, the constant multiplied by $Y1$ can be any number ≥ 20. Because a feasible solution satisfies the other constraints too, a value larger than 20 does not add any feasible values to those of A_1 and A_{12}. However, using a number smaller than 20 restricts the value of A_{12}. For example, if the constant multiplied by $Y1$ in the second added constraint is 7, A_{12} can't exceed 7 and the value of A_1 is limited to 27. If the optimal solution has A_1 greater than 27, a limit of 7 for A_{12} excludes the true optimal solution from consideration. Generally, it is easy to determine a value that is "big enough" not to arbitrarily restrict the value. We use the value of 40 for the upper limit for A_{12} in further discussions on this example.

Use a value "big enough"

The integer linear programming solution

Table 9.8 contains the optimal solution obtained by LINDO for the above integer linear programming model. The optimal solution gives $A_1 = 40$, $A_{11} = 20$, and $A_{12} = 20$. Table 9.6 contains the linear programming model solution showing $A_1 = 40$, $A_{11} = 0$, and $A_{12} = 40$. The objective function value in Table 9.6 doesn't represent the true cost. The linear programming solution violates the requirement that A_{11} attain the value of 20 before A_{12} becomes positive. This is the troublesome case, because it is cheaper to operate at \$31 per hour than at \$32.

Integer Linear Programming Reformulation for More than One Breakpoint

If a variable has more than two cost rates, you introduce a binary integer variable for each change of the cost rate. For the machine assignment model, say that the cost per hour is \$30 for every hour over 36. Now the

TABLE 9.8   SOLUTION for Integer Linear Programming Model for the Troublesome Machine Assignment Problem

```
        OBJECTIVE FUNCTION VALUE

    1)      3660.39100

  VARIABLE          VALUE           REDUCED COST
      Y1          1.000000           20.000000
      A2           .000000            2.255474
      A3           .000000            .575996
      B1           .000000            5.904348
      B2         13.913040            .000000
      B3         34.282610            .000000
      C1           .000000            .000000
      C2         26.086960            .000000
      C3           .000000            .086956
     A11         20.000000            .000000
     A12         20.000000            .000000
      A1         40.000000            .000000

    ROW      SLACK OR SURPLUS      DUAL PRICES
    2)            .000000           7.504349
    3)            .000000           7.299999
    4)           5.717391            .000000
    5)            .000000          -1.540174
    6)            .000000          -1.700000
    7)            .000000          -1.795652
    8)            .000000            .000000
    9)            .000000          31.000000
   10)            .000000          20.000000
   11)          20.000000            .000000
```

limits on A_{11}, A_{12}, and A_{13} are 20, 16, and 4, respectively. You associate *Y1* with the change of cost rate from \$32 to \$31 and *Y2* with the change from \$31 to \$30. The integer linear programming model is

$$\text{min} \quad 32A_{11} + 31A_{12} + 30A_{13} + 35A_2 + 36A_3 + 29B_1 + 25B_2 + 34B_3$$
$$+ 32C_1 + 34C_2 + 36C_3$$

st
$$A_1 + B_1 + C_1 \leq 40$$
$$A_2 + B_2 + C_2 \leq 40$$
$$A_3 + B_3 + C_3 \leq 40$$
$$25A_1 + 26A_2 + 23A_3 = 1000$$
$$18B_1 + 19B_2 + 20B_3 = 950$$
$$22C_1 + 23C_2 + 20C_3 = 600$$
$$A_{11} \leq 20$$
$$A_1 - A_{11} - A_{12} - A_{13} = 0$$
$$Y1 - 0.05A_{11} \leq 0$$
$$A_{12} - 16Y1 \leq 0$$
$$Y2 - 0.0625A_{12} \leq 0$$
$$A_{13} - 4Y2 \leq 0$$

$$A_{11}, A_{12}, A_{13}, A_1, A_2, A_3, B_1, B_2, B_3, C_1, C_2, C_3, \geq 0$$
$$Y1, Y2 \quad 0 \text{ or } 1$$

The coefficient in the constraint, $Y2 - 0.0625A_{12} \leq 0$ is $^1/_{16}$. The alter-

Add a binary variable
for each slope change

native form of the constraint is $16Y2 - A_{12} \le 0$. The coefficient of variable $Y2$ in the last constraint can be any value ≥ 4, but the coefficient of $Y1$ in the $A_{12} - 16Y1 \le 0$ constraint must be 16. For each additional change in the cost rate, you add one continuous variable, one binary variable, and two constraints to the formulation. If there are 10 cost rates for A_1, 9 binary integer variables are required.

Don't use integer linear
programming for the
OK case

If the objective function is not the troublesome case, the integer linear programming model is still correct. However, *you don't need to use the integer linear programming model for piecewise linear objective functions that are not troublesome; for such functions, you use the linear programming model.*

FIXED CHARGE COSTS

Besides piecewise linear objective functions, the other common non-linearity faced by managers is a fixed charge. A linear programming model assumes that the objective function consists of the sum of many terms, each a constant times a variable. This implies that the additional contribution to the objective function of any unit is identical to that of the first. Although this is often true, sometimes there is an additional cost for the first unit, called a **fixed charge** or a **setup cost.** If the variable value is 0, the fixed charge or setup cost is not incurred. However, if the variable value is greater than 0, the fixed charge or setup cost is incurred—but only once. For example, if a product is made on a particular machine, a modification or an adjustment is sometimes required before any units are produced. If the product is not made on that machine, there is no fixed charge or setup cost; but if some units of the product are made on that machine, then there is a fixed charge or setup cost.

A fixed charge cost plays an important role in models that are used to select from among discrete alternatives. Remember, VALIC developed a model to design marketing regions and locate regional offices. It had a fixed charge for opening any regional sales office. If the office wasn't opened, the fixed charge wasn't incurred.

We discuss two examples of using fixed charges. The first example considers a setup cost for the machine assignment problem. The second example is a plant location problem. We want to choose from several potential plant sites. The plant location problem is similar to the choosing of regional sales office locations.

The Machine Assignment Model

For the machine assignment problem, say that Machines 1 and 2 are automatically programmed and require no setup. However, when Machine 3 makes Cup A, a mechanic comes in early to set up and adjust the machine. It costs $105 for the mechanic's overtime. Because the me-

A_3 has a setup cost

chanic completes the setup before the plant's 8 A.M. starting time, Machine 3 is still available for 40 hours each week. The cost to produce Cup A on Machine 3 is now $32 per hour plus a fixed charge of $105. If no units of Cup A are produced on Machine 3, the mechanic's overtime isn't necessary and the cost is 0.

The mechanic's setup cost makes the objective function nonlinear. The cost for A_3 is represented symbolically as

$$\begin{cases} 105 + 32A_3, & \text{if } A_3 > 0; \\ 0, & \text{if } A_3 = 0 \end{cases}$$

With the exception of A_3's objective function contribution, the model is a linear programming model. It is tempting to increase A_3's objective function coefficient by allocating the setup cost. For example, if A_3 is 10, the objective function coefficient can be increased by $^{105}/_{10} = \$10.50$. Because the model is used to decide A_3's value, we don't know the correct denominator.

We prefer to reformulate the model into an integer linear programming model by introducing a binary integer variable, called Z. If Machine 3 is used to make Cup A, define Z equal to 1. If Machine 3 is not used to make Cup A, define Z equal to 0. Symbolically, define Z as

The binary variable definition

$$Z = 1, \text{ if } A_3 > 0$$
$$Z = 0, \text{ if } A_3 = 0$$

Remember, a common mistake is to believe that defining a variable to have a characteristic makes this true. Let us illustrate this mistake by giving an *incorrect* formulation:

An *incorrect* formulation

min $\quad 105Z + 32A_1 + 35A_2 + 36A_3 + 29B_1 + 25B_2 + 34B_3 + 32C_1$
$\qquad + 34C_2 + 36C_3$

st $\quad A_1 + B_1 + C_1 \le 40$
$\qquad A_2 + B_2 + C_2 \le 40$
$\qquad A_3 + B_3 + C_3 \le 40$
$\qquad 25A_1 + 26A_2 + 23A_3 = 1000$
$\qquad 18B_1 + 19B_2 + 20B_3 = 950$
$\qquad 22C_1 + 23C_2 + 20C_3 = 600$
$\qquad A_1, A_2, A_3, B_1, B_2, B_3, C_1, C_2, C_3 \ge 0$
$\qquad Z \quad 0 \text{ or } 1$

Why is this model incorrect? If $Z = 1$, the fixed charge is paid; if $Z = 0$, the fixed charge is not paid. We must add linear constraints and modify the objective function so that the binary variable has the desired characteristic. Examine the incorrect formulation. Even if the solution has A_3 greater than 0, $Z = 0$ satisfies the constraints. It is cheaper not to pay the fixed charge even if A_3 is positive. You must add a constraint so that if A_3 is positive, you must pay the setup cost. There is nothing in the incorrect model to cause that.

The binary variable definition is used by the model builder as a concep-

Add a constraint so that the definition is satisfied

tual tool. *You need to modify the constraints so that the definition's characteristic is satisfied.* You can obtain an upper limit on A_3 easily. Because only 40 hours are available on Machine 3, A_3 must be ≤ 40. Add the constraint

$$A_3 \leq 40Z$$

to the model. If $Z = 0$, the fixed charge is not paid and the added constraint requires that $A_3 = 0$. If $Z = 1$, the fixed charge is paid and the added constraint requires that $A_3 \leq 40$. This imposes no additional limit, because 40 is "large enough."

The *correct* integer linear programming model is

A correct formulation

$$
\begin{aligned}
\min \quad & 105Z + 32A_1 + 35A_2 + 36A_3 + 29B_1 + 25B_2 + 34B_3 + 32C_1 + \\
& 34C_2 + 36C_3 \\
\text{st} \quad & A_1 + B_1 + C_1 \leq 40 \\
& A_2 + B_2 + C_2 \leq 40 \\
& A_3 + B_3 + C_3 \leq 40 \\
& 25A_1 + 26A_2 + 23A_3 = 1000 \\
& 18B_1 + 19B_2 + 20B_3 = 950 \\
& 22C_1 + 23C_2 + 20C_3 = 600 \\
& A_3 - 40Z \leq 0 \\
& A_1, A_2, A_3, B_1, B_2, B_3, C_1, C_2, C_3 \geq 0 \\
& Z \quad 0 \text{ or } 1
\end{aligned}
$$

Note that the variable terms are all to the left of the relationship in the added constraint. Table 9.9 contains the solution of this fixed charge model solved by integer linear programming. The best decision is that you shouldn't produce Cup A on Machine 3.

Another common mistake

Let's observe another common modeling mistake for fixed charge costs. All of the functions must be linear in the reformulated integer *linear* programming model. Do not multiply the binary variable by any other variable. *Do not use $Z(105 + 32A_3)$ in the objective function.* That function is nonlinear because the variables Z and A_3 are multiplied.

In general, you introduce a binary variable for each variable that has a setup cost. Find an upper limit on the value of each setup cost variable by examining the other constraints. Say that the upper limit on Variable X_j is denoted by U_j. Introduce a 0–1 variable, Z_j, and add the constraint

$$X_j - U_j Z_j \leq 0$$

The optimal solution for the integer linear programming model is the optimal solution for the underlying nonlinear programming model.

A Plant Location Model

Planning the location and capacity of manufacturing and warehouse facilities is a common application of integer linear programming. There is a fixed charge cost for each facility. If a facility is used, its fixed charge as

TABLE 9.9 Integer Linear Programming Model for the Machine Assignment Problem with a Fixed Charge

```
MIN      105 Z + 32 A1 + 35 A2 + 36 A3 + 29 B1 + 25 B2 + 34 B3 + 32 C1
       + 34 C2 + 36 C3
SUBJECT TO
       2)    A1 + B1 + C1 <=    40
       3)    A2 + B2 + C2 <=    40
       4)    A3 + B3 + C3 <=    40
       5)    25 A1 + 26 A2 + 23 A3 =    1000
       6)    18 B1 + 19 B2 + 20 B3 =     950
       7)    22 C1 + 23 C2 + 20 C3 =     600
       8)  - 40 Z + A3 <=     0
END
INTE     1

         OBJECTIVE FUNCTION VALUE

       1)     3680.39100

      VARIABLE        VALUE          REDUCED COST
          Z           .000000         91.239930
          A1        40.000000           .000000
          A2          .000000          1.215477
          A3          .000000           .000000
          B1          .000000          5.904348
          B2        13.913040           .000000
          B3        34.282610           .000000
          C1          .000000           .000000
          C2        26.086960           .000000
          C3          .000000           .086956
```

well as a linear operating cost is incurred. If the facility is not used, the fixed charge is not incurred.

Let's consider choosing plant locations from among m potential sites, denoted $1, 2, \ldots, m$. Say that the design capacity for Plant Location i is C_i and that the incremental manufacturing cost is p_i. The fixed charge is F_i for Plant Location i. If no units are produced at Plant Location i, the cost is 0. If 10 units are produced at Plant Location i, the manufacturing cost is $F_i + (10 \times p_i)$.

Say that there are n customers, denoted $1, 2, \ldots, n$. The requirement for Customer j is D_j. Let the transportation cost from Plant Location i to customer j be t_{ij}.

Define x_{ij} as the number of units produced at Plant Location i and shipped to Customer j. The total transportation cost is the transportation cost per unit times the number of units shipped, summed over all i (plants) and all j (customers). We can represent this summation as $\sum_{i=1}^{m} \sum_{j=1}^{n} t_{ij} x_{ij}$.

Most linear programming and integer linear programming systems don't allow using Σ for inputting the model; the individual terms must be entered. However, we use summation notation to simplify representing the model.

The number of units produced at Plant Location i is calculated as $\sum_{j=1}^{n} x_{ij}$. Excluding the fixed charge cost, the total manufacturing cost is calculated as $\sum_{i=1}^{m} p_i \left(\sum_{j=1}^{n} x_{ij} \right)$. You introduce a 0–1 variable, Y_i, with a value of 0 if $\sum_{j=1}^{n} x_{ij} = 0$ and a value of 1 if $\sum_{j=1}^{n} x_{ij} > 0$. The integer linear programming model is

A plant location model

$$\min \quad \sum_{i=1}^{m} \sum_{j=1}^{n} (p_i + t_{ij}) x_{ij} + \sum_{i=1}^{m} F_i Y_i$$

$$\text{st} \quad \sum_{j=1}^{n} x_{ij} \leq C_i Y_i \quad i = 1, \ldots, m$$

$$\sum_{i=1}^{m} x_{ij} = D_j \quad j = 1, \ldots, n$$

$$x_{ij} \geq 0, \quad i = 1, \ldots, m; j = 1, \ldots, n$$

$$Y_i \quad 0 \text{ or } 1; i = 1, \ldots, m$$

If $Y_i = 0$, the fixed cost is not incurred and the first class of constraints ensures that $x_{ij} = 0$ for all j. If $Y_i = 1$, the fixed cost is incurred and the total shipped from Plant Location i cannot exceed the capacity, C_i.

Let's consider an example. A company is considering three potential plant locations, denoted A, B, and C. Table 9.10 gives the capacity, the variable manufacturing cost per unit, and the fixed charge of each plant location. If the company does not use a plant location, the fixed charge cost is not incurred. Plant Location A has a smaller fixed charge than

---

TABLE 9.10 Data for Plant Location Example

Plant Location	Capacity	Manufacturing Cost/Unit	Fixed Charge
A	100	$125	$1,000
B	85	120	1,200
C	105	105	1,150

Customer Group	Requirement
1	20
2	25
3	50
4	75

Transportation Cost ($/unit)

From Plant	To Customer Group			
	1	2	3	4
A	12	18	2	15
B	3	7	21	11
C	7	10	16	21

Plant Location C, but it has a higher manufacturing cost. The company has many customers, but for planning purposes they have been aggregated into four groups, designated 1, 2, 3, and 4. The total of the four requirements is 170. Examining the capacities of the plant locations indicates that only two sites are needed. Which two should you select? Table 9.10 also contains the transportation cost per unit from each plant location to each customer group.

Table 9.11 contains the LOOK ALL for an integer linear programming formulation of the plant location problem. The model differs from the general plant location problem above in two ways. First, the variable *A* is explicitly included and represents the number of units produced at Plant

The first difference

Location A. Variable *A1* represents the number of units shipped from Plant Location A to Customer Group 1. Variables *A2, A3,* and *A4* are for shipments from Plant Location A to Customer Groups 2, 3, and 4, respectively. An advantage of defining the variable *A* explicitly is that this makes it easier to interpret the output. If you include Variable *A* in the formulation, you don't need to add *A1* plus *A2* plus *A3* plus *A4* to determine the amount produced at Plant A. Also, if the manufacturing cost changes at Plant Location A, only the objective function coefficient of *A* must be changed. If you don't include Variable *A* in the formulation and the manufacturing cost changes, the coefficients of *A1, A2, A3,* and *A4* all change. The variables for Plant Locations B and C are similarly defined.

TABLE 9.11   LOOK ALL for the Plant Location Example

```
MIN      1000 YA + 1200 YB + 1150 YC + 125 A + 120 B + 105 C
       + 12 A1 + 18 A2 + 2 A3 + 15 A4 + 3 B1 + 7 B2 + 21 B3 + 11 B4
       + 7 C1 + 10 C2 + 16 C3 + 21 C4
SUBJECT TO
      2) -  100 YA + A <=     0
      3) -   20 YA + A1 <=    0
      4) -   25 YA + A2 <=    0
      5) -   50 YA + A3 <=    0
      6) -   75 YA + A4 <=    0
      7) -   85 YB + B <=   0
      8) -   20 YB + B1 <=   0
      9) -   25 YB + B2 <=   0
     10) -   50 YB + B3 <=   0
     11) -   75 YB + B4 <=   0
     12) -  105 YC + C <=   0
     13) -   20 YC + C1 <=   0
     14) -   25 YC + C2 <=   0
     15) -   50 YC + C3 <=   0
     16) -   75 YC + C4 <=   0
     17)    A - A1 - A2 - A3 - A4 =     0
     18)    B - B1 - B2 - B3 - B4 =     0
     19)    C - C1 - C2 - C3 - C4 =     0
     20)    A1 + B1 + C1 =     20
     21)    A2 + B2 + C2 =     25
     22)    A3 + B3 + C3 =     50
     23)    A4 + B4 + C4 =     75
END
INTE      3
```

You introduce three binary variables, *YA, YB,* and *YC.* For example, *YA* = 1 if Plant Location A is selected and *YA* = 0 if Plant Location A is not selected. The first constraint (Row 2 in Table 9.11) ensures that the total amount produced at Plant Location A is no greater than the capacity of 100 *if the site is selected* and that it is 0 if the site is not selected.

Rows 17, 18, and 19 define the relationships between the amounts produced at a plant location and the total amount shipped from that plant location. For example, Row 17 states that the number of units produced at Plant Location A (represented by the decision variable *A*) is equal to *A1 + A2 + A3 + A4,* the total amount shipped from Plant Location A. Rows 20, 21, 22, and 23 ensure that the amounts shipped to Customer Groups 1, 2, 3, and 4 equal the requirements.

The second difference: "tightening" constraints

The second difference from the general plant location model above is constraints such as Row 3. These constraints "tighten" the formulation. An integer linear programming model is **tighter** if the model's optimal *linear programming* solution has more variables that are supposed to be integers attaining integer values. Rows 3, 4, 5, and 6 tighten the model for the binary plant location variable *YA.* Note that Row 3's constraint is

$$A1 \le 20YA$$

where 20 is the requirement for Customer Group 1. Any solution that satisfies Row 20's constraint also satisfies Row 3's constraint. By adding the constraint, however, you get a tighter formulation, and tighter integer linear programming formulations require *less computer time.*

Tighter integer linear programming models use less computer time

Let's see how Row 3 increases the chance that *YA* will have an integer value when the model is solved ignoring the integer restrictions. Often, a customer receives all of its requirement from a single plant. Row 3 ensures that *YA* must be 1 if Customer Group 1 receives all of its requirement (20) from Plant Location A. Rows 3 to 6, 8 to 11, and 13 to 16 tighten the model in Table 9.11.

Table 9.12 contains the LINDO SOLUTION for the integer linear programming model of Table 9.11. Plant Locations A and C are selected. Customer Groups 1 and 2 receive all of their requirements from Plant Location C, and Customer Group 3 receives all of its requirement from Plant Location A. The tightening is based on this observation, but does not force it. Customer Group 4 receives shipments from both Plant Location A and Plant Location C.

OTHER BINARY INTEGER VARIABLE FORMULATIONS

In this section, we describe a variety of useful tricks with binary integer variables. However, the ability to model a decision problem as an integer linear programming model does not always result in a successful application. The computer time required for the optimization may be so long that

TABLE 9.12 SOLUTION of the Plant Location Model—Table 9.11

```
            OBJECTIVE FUNCTION VALUE

  1)        23275.0000

      VARIABLE         VALUE        REDUCED COST
           YA        1.000000        600.000000
           YB        0.000000        435.000000
           YC        1.000000       -320.000000
            A       65.000000          0.000000
            B        0.000000          0.000000
            C      105.000000          0.000000
           A1        0.000000         11.000000
           A2        0.000000         14.000000
           A3       50.000000          0.000000
           A4       15.000000          0.000000
           B1        0.000000          6.000000
           B2        0.000000          7.000000
           B3        0.000000         15.000000
           B4        0.000000          0.000000
           C1       20.000000          0.000000
           C2       25.000000          0.000000
           C3        0.000000          0.000000
           C4       60.000000          0.000000
```

the model is unable to provide enough timely information to the decision maker.

Remember, we said that linear programming models are *robust*. The number of steps required to solve a linear programming model by the simplex algorithm is usually between 2 and 3 *times* the number of constraints. A bad linear programming formulation requires about the same computer time as a good formulation. *Integer linear programming models are not robust.* Solving a bad integer linear programming formulation can take *much longer* than solving a good formulation. Tightening tricks such as the one for the plant location problem can significantly decrease computer time. Consult a model builder with skill in formulating integer linear programming models before you finalize your model. We show typical formulation tricks, but knowing the tricks does not guarantee a good integer linear programming formulation.

> Bad integer linear programming formulations can take much longer to solve

Capital Budgeting

Earlier in this chapter, we described an integer linear programming application by Exxon. Exxon identified a large number of possible energy conservation projects at its Baton Rouge refinery. It had to decide which projects to do and when they should be done. Some of the projects required capital outlays of millions of dollars. Because of the large capital outlays required, the company could not do all of them at once. It used an integer linear programming model as an aid in project selection. The savings it made from the projects chosen totaled more than $100 million.

Using management science models to solve capital budgeting problems

TABLE 9.13   Project Alternatives for the Potato Processing Company

Alternative	NPV	Capital Requirements in Year		
		1	2	3
1 Build Baltimore plant	$130,000	$40,000	$40,000	$30,000
2 Expand Blue Island plant	52,000	5,000	25,000	20,000
3 Expand Blue Island warehouse	40,000	5,000	10,000	10,000
4 Build Baltimore warehouse	145,000	40,000	40,000	40,000

A capital budgeting example

improves project selection and increases profitability for many companies. Table 9.13 contains information on four expansion projects available to the potato processing company discussed in Chapter 2. For example, consider expanding the plant in Blue Island. The net present value (NPV) of increased profits is $52,000. The capital requirements during the three-year construction period are $5,000, $25,000, and $20,000. An examination of anticipated cash flows and bank loans indicates that a limit of $75,000, $50,000, and $60,000, respectively, will be available for each of the next three years. The objective is to maximize the NPV of the projects within the available capital.

You define $Y1$ as equal to 1 if Project 1 is undertaken and as equal to 0 if Project 1 is rejected. You similarly define $Y2$, $Y3$, and $Y4$. The integer linear programming model is

$$\begin{aligned}
\max \quad & 130\,Y1 + 52\,Y2 + 40\,Y3 + 145\,Y4 \\
\text{st} \quad & 40\,Y1 + 5\,Y2 + 5\,Y3 + 40\,Y4 \le 75 \\
& 40\,Y1 + 25\,Y2 + 10\,Y3 + 40\,Y4 \le 50 \\
& 30\,Y1 + 20\,Y2 + 10\,Y3 + 40\,Y4 \le 60 \\
& Y1,\ Y2,\ Y3,\ Y4 \quad 0 \text{ or } 1
\end{aligned}$$

The thousands have been dropped to simplify inputting the model. The optimal solution to the integer linear programming model is $Y1 = Y2 = 0$ and $Y3 = Y4 = 1$. You should undertake Projects 3 and 4. The optimal NPV is $185,000.

The capital budgeting model of the potato processing company is simple, but we use it to show how you can model logical relationships among projects.

Multiple-choice constraints. Often, only one alternative of many must be selected. Say that you must either expand the Blue Island plant or build the new plant in Baltimore. You add the constraint

$$Y1 + Y2 = 1$$

This ensures that one and only one of the binary integer variables equals 1. The alternative selected is the one with a value of 1.

If *at least* one of the four alternatives must be selected, add the constraint

$$Y1 + Y2 + Y3 + Y4 \geq 1$$

If either Project 3 or 4 can be selected, but not both, add the constraint

$$Y3 + Y4 \leq 1$$

If, at most, K alternatives can be selected, add the constraint

$$Y1 + Y2 + Y3 + Y4 \leq K$$

If exactly *K* alternatives must be selected, replace the $\leq$ with $=$ in this constraint.

Logical relationships. Logical relationships among alternatives are specified by adding constraints. For example, it only makes sense to build the Baltimore warehouse if you build the Baltimore plant. You add the constraint

$$Y4 \leq Y1$$

The binary integer variable $Y4$ can be 1 only if $Y1 = 1$. Because of the inequality of the constraint, even if $Y1 = 1$, the value of $Y4$ can be either 0 or 1.

Say that Alternative 3 can be selected only if either Alternative 1 or Alternative 4 is selected, but that only one of Alternative 1 or Alternative 4 can be selected. Add the two constraints

$$Y1 + Y4 \leq 1$$
$$Y3 \leq Y1 + Y4$$

The first constraint ensures that at most, one of Alternatives 1 and 4 will be selected. The second constraint requires that either Alternative 1 or Alternative 4 be selected so that $Y3$ can be 1.

Either-Or Constraints

Sometimes *either* of a pair of constraints must be satisfied, but not both. For example, either of the two following constraints must be satisfied:

$$x_1 + 2x_2 + x_3 \leq 10$$
$$2x_1 - 3x_2 + x_3 \leq 8$$

You introduce y, a binary integer variable defined so that it is 1 if the first constraint is enforced and 0 if the second constraint is enforced. Let *M* represent a very large positive number. Instead of the two constraints above, add the constraints

$$x_1 + 2x_2 + x_3 \leq 10 + M(1 - y)$$
$$2x_1 - 3x_2 + x_3 \leq 8 + My$$

If $y = 1$, the RHS of the first new constraint is 10 and the original first constraint must be satisfied; the RHS of the second added constraint is a very large number, so the original second constraint can be violated. If $y = 0$, the original first constraint is not enforced, but the original second constraint must be satisfied.

Minimum Batch Size

In production planning, you sometimes want at least a minimum batch size if a product is produced. Otherwise, no units are produced. Say that the minimum batch size for the variable X is 100 units. Let U represent a number larger than any possible batch size for X. You define a binary integer variable, Y, such that $Y = 1$ if the batch size is ≥ 100 and $Y = 0$ if the batch size is 0. Add the pair of constraints

$$X \leq UY$$
$$X \geq 100Y$$

If $Y = 0$, the two constraints force $X = 0$. If $Y = 1$, the second constraint forces $X \geq 100$. Because you picked U larger than any possible batch size, the first constraint doesn't affect the value of X.

The Monsanto Model

The Monsanto application discussed at the beginning of the chapter used binary integer variables and multiple-choice constraints to select the operating conditions for reactors producing maleic anhydride. Let i represent the ith reactor, and let j represent the jth set of operating conditions. For each reactor, Monsanto determined the operating cost and the production at many different sets of operating conditions. Let C_{ij} and P_{ij} represent the operating cost and production, respectively, of Reactor i at Setting j. The binary variables R_{ij} are defined as equal to 1 if Reactor i operates at Setting j and as equal to 0 if it doesn't. T represents the production target. The integer linear programming model is

$$
\begin{aligned}
\min \quad & \Sigma_i \Sigma_j C_{ij} R_{ij} \\
\text{st} \quad & \Sigma_i \Sigma_j P_{ij} R_{ij} \geq T \\
& \Sigma_j R_{ij} \leq 1 \quad \text{all } i \\
& R_{ij} \quad 0 \text{ or } 1
\end{aligned}
$$

The first constraint causes the production target to be satisfied. The other constraints are multiple-choice constraints. Reactor i can only be operated at one operating condition. The $\leq$ inequality allows the reactor to be unused.

INTRODUCTION TO COMBINATORIAL OPTIMIZATION PROBLEMS

Some of the decision problems that involve selecting from among discrete alternatives are hard because there are so many alternatives. In this section, we describe such problems, called combinatorial optimization problems. Problems of this kind have many applications, but it is difficult to find their optimal solution.

The two properties of a **combinatorial optimization problem** are

1. The number of feasible solutions rapidly increases as the size increases.

2. It is easy to construct a feasible solution.

Many combinatorial optimization problems can be formulated as integer linear programming models using binary integer variables. For problems of significant size, however, the computer time required to find the optimal solution for the integer linear programming model is excessive. A "near-optimal" solution to many of these problems can be found using heuristics. A **heuristic** is a method that doesn't guarantee an optimal solution but is fast and finds a *good* solution.

Heuristics and combinatorial optimization problems

Table 9.14 lists several combinatorial optimization problems. Each is described briefly in this section.

The **traveling salesman problem** (TSP) requires selecting the order in which N cities are visited. The travel time between each of the pairs of cities is known, and the objective is to minimize the total travel time required to visit all of the cities. Like many combinatorial optimization problems, the TSP is easy to describe and difficult to solve. Say that the salesman starts at City 1 and must visit all of the other cities, 2 through N, before returning to City 1. The salesman has a choice of $(N - 1)$ possible cities to visit next. After the second city to visit has been selected, $(N - 2)$ cities are possible for the next choice. The total number of possible selections is $(N - 1)(N - 2)(N - 3) \ldots (2)(1)$, represented as $(N - 1)!$.

TABLE 9.14 Combinatorial Optimization Problems

Traveling salesman problem
Sequencing of jobs through a single machine
Sequencing of jobs through multiple machines
Routing of trucks
Postman problem
M-postman problem
Critical path problem with limited resources

If the total number of cities is $N = 5$, the number of possible orders is $4 \times 3 \times 2 \times 1 = 24$. If the total number of cities is $N = 13$, the number of possible orders is 479,001,600. As the number of cities increases, the number of possible orders increases very rapidly. Constructing a feasible order is easy. For example, the salesman might visit the cities in the order 1, 2, 3, 4, . . . , N and then return to 1. But if N is large, explicitly evaluating all of the possible orders or examining a significant proportion of them is impractical.

A TSP application

Although we describe the TSP in terms of travel between cities, it has many other applications. Metelco S.A., located in Greece, manufactures printed circuit boards. Programmable drilling machines drill holes in the circuit boards so that electronic components can be attached. Because the drilling machines were the "bottleneck" in the manufacturing process, Metelco limited its product line to simple printed circuit boards. The company recognized that the order in which the drilling machines drilled the holes in a printed circuit board was a TSP. The travel times were the times required to move between each pair of required holes. The objective was to minimize the total travel time for a circuit board. A heuristic procedure solving the TSP was introduced to control the programmable drilling machines. This decreased the drilling time, improved production, and allowed the company to expand its product line to more complex circuit boards.[6]

The problem of sequencing "N jobs through a single machine" is another combinatorial optimization problem. For some objectives, a simple rule provides the best order. If the objective is to minimize the total time that the jobs are late, no simple rule exists. How many orders are possible for the N jobs? Any of the N jobs could be first. Any of the remaining jobs ($N - 1$) could be second. The total number of possible sequences is $N!$ If there are 12 jobs, the number of possible sequences is 479,001,600. Finding a sequence is easy; finding the best sequence is difficult.

Sequencing N jobs through many machines is even more difficult than sequencing them through a single machine. The sequences at machines after the first can be different from the sequences at the first machine.

Routing trucks to customers is another combinatorial optimization problem. Say that three trucks have to deliver to 25 customers. The order in which each truck delivers to its set of customers must be determined; this is similar to a traveling salesman problem. Also, customers must be assigned to each of the three trucks. The number of possible assignments of customers and delivery orders to trucks is huge. Again, constructing a feasible solution is easy, but finding the optimal solution is difficult.

---

[6] V. Magirou, "The Efficient Drilling of Printed Circuit Boards," *Interfaces* 16, no. 4 (July–August 1986), pp. 13–23.

The **postman problem** requires delivering mail to houses on a collection of streets. What route should the postman use to visit the houses? Constructing a route for the postman is not difficult, but constructing a route to minimize the distance traveled is. An *M*-**postman problem** requires assigning streets to each of *M* postmen as well as constructing the route for each postman. This is even more difficult than the single-postman problem.

In Chapter 8, we described the critical path problem for a project with a number of activities. Some of the activities must be completed before others are started. Completing the project requires completing all of the activities. The critical path is the longest path through the network representing the project. If some of the activities require resources that are in limited supply, a combinatorial optimization problem results. For example, say that only one crane is available but that three activities require the crane. There are many possible ways in which the different activities can utilize the crane.

INTEGER VARIABLES—"LUCKY" MODELS

Figure 9.3 illustrates the feasible set for the linear programming model

$$
\begin{aligned}
\max \quad & 2x_1 + 3x_2 \\
\text{st} \quad & 2x_1 + 1x_2 \le 5 \\
& 1x_1 + 2x_2 \le 5 \\
& x_1, x_2 \ge 0
\end{aligned}
$$

The optimal solution for the linear programming model is $x_1 = 5/3, x_2 = 5/3$, and the objective function value is $25/3 = 8\frac{1}{3}$. Say that Variables x_1 and x_2 are general integer variables. Rounding the variable values from the linear programming solution to the nearest integer yields $x_1 = 2$ and $x_2 = 2$. The rounded solution violates both constraints. *Rounding the variable values from the linear programming solution does not guarantee the optimal solution for the integer linear programming model. The rounded solution can even be infeasible.*

Figure 9.4 illustrates the feasible points for the integer linear programming model. The constraints appear, but only the integer-valued points designated by the dots are feasible. Remember that a feasible solution *must satisfy all of the constraints, including any integrality requirements.* The optimal solution for the integer linear programming model is $x_1 = 1$, $x_2 = 2$, and the objective function value is 8.

Sometimes, the optimal solution for the linear programming model satisfies the integrality requirements. In this case, the optimal solution for the *linear programming* model is also the optimal solution for the *integer linear programming* model. The only difference between the integer lin-

Rounding may not give an optimal solution

FIGURE 9.3 Feasible Set for Example—Linear Programming Model

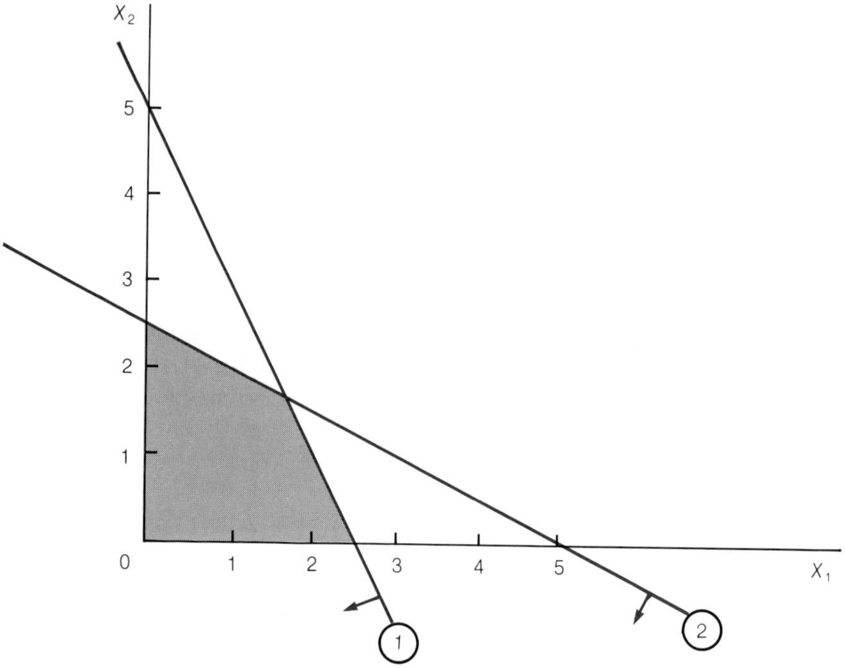

Network models are
"lucky"

ear programming model and the linear programming model is the addition of integrality requirements. If the additional integrality requirements of the integer linear programming model are satisfied by the solution for the linear programming model, then the optimal solution for the integer linear programming model has been obtained.

A **"lucky"** integer linear programming model is one whose integrality requirements are satisfied by the linear programming optimal solution. Unfortunately, not all integer linear programming models are lucky. *Because of the special structure of some linear programming models, the optimal linear programming solution always satisfies the integrality requirements.* In Chapter 8, we described network models that are always lucky. These lucky network models include the transportation problem, the assignment problem, the maximum flow problem, and the general minimum cost network problem. If all of the requirements, capacities, and net stock positions of a model are *integer-valued,* the simplex algorithm always finds an optimal solution with integer variable values.

If you examine the constraint coefficients of the network models, you see that all of them are integers. However, *the fact that the linear programming model constraints contain only integer coefficients does not guarantee a model to be lucky.* The linear programming model of

FIGURE 9.4   Feasible Set for Example—Integer Linear Programming Example

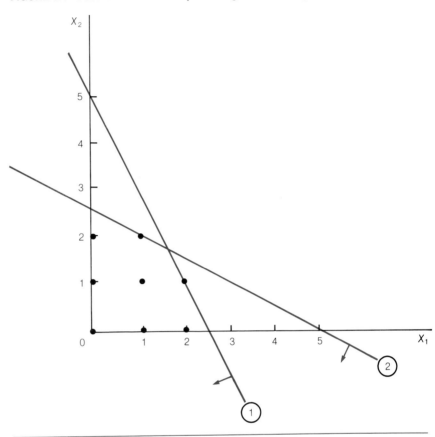

Figures 9.3 and 9.4 illustrates this. Even though all of the constraint coefficients and the RHS constants have integer values, the optimal variable values for the linear programming model include fractions.

In the network models of Chapter 8, all of the constraint coefficients are $+1$, -1, or 0. However, *the fact that all of the constraint coefficients are $+1$, -1, or 0 does not guarantee a model to be lucky.* For example, the simple model

$$\text{max} \quad x_1 + 3x_2$$
$$\text{st} \quad \ x_1 + x_2 \leq 3$$
$$x_1 - x_2 \geq 0$$
$$x_1, x_2 \geq 0$$

has the optimal linear programming solution $x_1 = \frac{3}{2}$ and $x_2 = \frac{3}{2}$.

Even though a model is not guaranteed to have a lucky solution, *if you don't have access to software for finding the optimal solution as an integer linear programming model, try solving the model as a linear programming model.* You might be lucky.

AN APPROACH TO DISCRETE ALTERNATIVES— A SET OF CASE STUDIES

If a decision variable represents the number of trucks to buy, a fractional value does not make sense. If the "optimal" variable value for the linear programming solution is a large value (but not an integer), sometimes an acceptable solution is obtained by rounding. In formulations using binary integer variables, however, rounding to a good solution is not easy. Say that in the plant location problem, the value of a binary integer variable is 0.45. Do you round it to 0 or to 1? If you round to 0, you don't build the plant and there may be no feasible solution. If you round to 1, you build the plant and there is a feasible solution, but it may not be optimal. *You must decide which variables you can round and which variables you have to restrict to integer values.* Generally, you must treat any binary integer variable as restricted integer values.

After you identify the variables that must be restricted to integer values, you solve the integer linear programming model. If integer linear programming software is available, you solve the model as an integer linear programming model. Using LINDO, you give the INTEGER or GIN command to specify the integer variables after the underlying linear programming model has been entered. Then, the GO command uses an algorithm, *not the simplex algorithm,* to find the optimal solution for the integer linear programming model. Table 9.8 contains the LINDO integer linear programming model's solution for the troublesome piecewise linear cost function of the machine assignment problem. After the linear programming model shown in Table 9.7 was entered, *Y1* was designated as a binary integer variable, and the GO command then gave the optimal solution.

If you don't have integer linear programming software, you can find the optimal solution by solving a set of case studies. In the next section, we show how to do this.

A Set of Case Studies for the Troublesome Machine Assignment Problem

For example, let's consider the troublesome piecewise linear cost function for the machine assignment problem. We reformulated the nonlinear objective function as an integer linear programming model, shown in Table 9.7. Ignoring the integrality restriction on the binary integer variable, *Y1,* you obtain the following linear programming model:

min $\quad 32A_{11} + 31A_{12} + 35A_2 + 36A_3 + 29B_1 + 25B_2 + 34B_3 + 32C_1$
$\quad\quad + 34C_2 + 36C_3$

st $\quad A_1 + B_1 + C_1 \le 40$
$\quad\quad A_2 + B_2 + C_2 \le 40$
$\quad\quad A_3 + B_3 + C_3 \le 40$
$\quad\quad 25A_1 + 26A_2 + 23A_3 = 1000$
$\quad\quad 18B_1 + 19B_2 + 20B_3 = 950$
$\quad\quad 22C_1 + 23C_2 + 20C_3 = 600$
$\quad\quad A_{11} \le 20$
$\quad\quad A_1 - A_{11} - A_{12} = 0$
$\quad\quad Y1 - 0.05A_{11} \le 0$
$\quad\quad A_{12} - 40Y1 \le 0$
$\quad\quad Y1 \le 1$
$\quad\quad Y1, A_{11}, A_{12}, A_1, A_2, A_3, B_1, B_2, B_3, C_1, C_2, C_3 \ge 0$

The model is not lucky

The variable $Y1$ can have any value between 0 and 1. Table 9.15 shows the optimal solution to the linear programming model. The value of $Y1$ is

TABLE 9.15 Linear Programming Solution of the Integer Linear Programming Model for the Troublesome Piecewise Linear Machine Assignment Problem, *Ignoring* the Integrality Restriction

```
    MIN       35 A2 +  36 A3 +  29 B1 +  25 B2 +  34 B3 +  32 C1 +  34 C2 +  36 C3
           +  32 A11 + 31 A12
    SUBJECT TO
          2)    B1 + C1 + A1 <=     40
          3)    A2 + B2 + C2 <=     40
          4)    A3 + B3 + C3 <=     40
          5)    26 A2 + 23 A3 + 25 A1 =    1000
          6)    18 B1 + 19 B2 + 20 B3 =     950
          7)    22 C1 + 23 C2 + 20 C3 =     600
          8)    A11 <=    20
          9) -  A11 - A12 + A1 =      0
         10)    Y1 - 0.05 A11 <=     0
         11) - 40 Y1 + A12 <=      0
    END
    SUB       Y1        1.00

          OBJECTIVE FUNCTION VALUE

          1)       3653.72500

       VARIABLE          VALUE          REDUCED COST
          Y1              .666667           .000000
          A2              .000000          1.908810
          A3              .000000           .269333
          B1              .000000          5.904348
          B2            13.913040           .000000
          B3            34.282610           .000000
          C1              .000000           .000000
          C2            26.086960           .000000
          C3              .000000           .086956
          A11           13.333330           .000000
          A12           26.666670           .000000
          A1            40.000000           .000000
```

0.666667. This integer linear programming model is not lucky. Also, $A_1 = 40$, $A_{11} = 13.333330$, and $A_{12} = 26.666670$ is not a valid solution. If $A_1 = 40$, then $A_{11} = 20$ and $A_{12} = 20$. Do you round $Y1$ to 0 or 1? The optimal value of $Y1$ is not obvious.

You can find the optimal solution for an integer linear programming model by solving a set of linear programming models. A **case study** is a linear programming model that represents one of the alternatives for an integer linear programming model. For this example, the two cases are $Y1 = 0$ and $Y1 = 1$. In the first case, add the restriction $Y1 = 0$; in the second case, add the restriction $Y1 = 1$. Table 9.16 contains the solution to the first linear programming model (i.e., $Y1 = 0$); the minimum cost is $3,670.19. Note that a simple upper bound (SUB) of 0 on Variable $Y1$ forces $Y1$ to equal 0, in turn forcing A_{12} to equal 0, but allows A_{11} to be as large as 20.

Case Study 1

Case Study 2

Table 9.17 contains the solution for the second linear programming model (i.e., $Y1 = 1$); the minimum cost is $3,660.39. In Table 9.17, a simple lower bound (SLB) of 1 and an SUB of 1 force $Y1$ to equal 1, in turn forcing A_{11} to equal 20 and allowing positive values for A_{12}.

TABLE 9.16   Case 1: $Y1$ = 0; Linear Programming SOLUTION of the Troublesome Piecewise Linear Machine Assignment Model

```
MIN      35 A2 + 36 A3 + 29 B1 + 25 B2 + 34 B3 + 32 C1 + 34 C2 + 36 C3
         + 32 A11 + 31 A12
SUBJECT TO
        2)    B1 + C1 + A1 <=    40
        3)    A2 + B2 + C2 <=    40
        4)    A3 + B3 + C3 <=    40
        5)    26 A2 + 23 A3 + 25 A1 =     1000
        6)    18 B1 + 19 B2 + 20 B3 =     950
        7)    22 C1 + 23 C2 + 20 C3 =     600
        8)    A11 <=    20
        9)  - A11 - A12 + A1 =     0
       10)    Y1 - 0.05 A11 <=    0
       11)  - 40 Y1 + A12 <=    0
END
SUB        Y1            .00

           OBJECTIVE FUNCTION VALUE

        1)      3670.19400

   VARIABLE         VALUE          REDUCED COST
      Y1            .000000        -40.000000
      A2            .000000          1.604347
      A3          29.644270          .000000
      B1            .000000          5.530436
      B2          40.000000          .000000
      B3           9.500000          .000000
      C1          27.272730          .000000
      C2            .000000          .390907
      C3            .000000          .426876
      A11         12.727270          .000000
      A12           .000000          .000000
      A1          12.727270          .000000
```

TABLE 9.17 Case 2: Y1 = 1; Linear Programming SOLUTION of the Troublesome Piecewise Linear Machine Assignment Model

```
    MIN     35 A2 + 36 A3 + 29 B1 + 25 B2 + 34 B3 + 32 C1 + 34 C2 + 36 C3
          + 32 A11 + 31 A12
    SUBJECT TO
            2)    B1 + C1 + A1 <=    40
            3)    A2 + B2 + C2 <=    40
            4)    A3 + B3 + C3 <=    40
            5)    26 A2 + 23 A3 + 25 A1 =    1000
            6)    18 B1 + 19 B2 + 20 B3 =     950
            7)    22 C1 + 23 C2 + 20 C3 =     600
            8)    A11 <=    20
            9)  - A11 - A12 + A1 =     0
           10)    Y1 - 0.05 A11 <=    0
           11)  - 40 Y1 + A12 <=    0
    END
    SLB        Y1        1.00
    SUB        Y1        1.00

         OBJECTIVE FUNCTION VALUE

         1)      3660.39100

       VARIABLE          VALUE            REDUCED COST
          Y1          1.000000             20.000000
          A2           .000000              2.255474
          A3           .000000               .575996
          B1           .000000              5.904348
          B2         13.913040               .000000
          B3         34.282610               .000000
          C1           .000000               .000000
          C2         26.086960               .000000
          C3           .000000               .086956
          A11        20.000000               .000000
          A12        20.000000               .000000
          A1         40.000000               .000000
```

The best case study is optimal.

The optimal solution for the integer linear programming model is the best solution of the two linear programming models. Because its minimum cost is smaller, Table 9.17 represents the optimal solution for the integer linear programming model. This is the same solution as that obtained by LINDO for the integer linear programming model, shown in Table 9.8.

Is a set of case studies a realistic approach?

A set of case studies is a realistic approach only if the number of integer variables and their possible values are small. In the machine assignment model, one binary integer variable results in two linear programming models. If two piecewise linear cost functions are troublesome, you introduce two binary integer variables. This results in $2^2 = 4$ possible sets of integer values and four linear programming models. Let $Y2$ denote the other binary integer variable. The four possible values for $(Y1, Y2)$ are $\{(0, 0), (0, 1), (1, 0), (1, 1)\}$. You solve four linear programming models for the four case studies. The integer linear programming optimal solution is the best of the four linear programming solutions. But if all of the nine decision variables have troublesome cost functions, $2^9 = 512$ possible sets of integer values, which results in 512 linear programming models. It is not practical to find the optimal solution to the integer linear programming model by solving 512 linear programming models. By carefully examining the integer linear programming model, you can eliminate many of the 512 cases from consideration. But sometimes poor intuition results in eliminating the best case. Remember, the model is only a representation of the real problem, and you might find an acceptable solution for the purpose intended by considering a small number of case studies from among the 512 possibilities.

A large range of values for a GIN variable also causes a large number of case studies. If there are only two integer variables, but each can attain values from 0 to 9, there are $10 \times 10 = 100$ possible cases. If there are many case studies, finding the optimal solution to an integer linear programming model by solving them all is impractical.

Branch and bound

Most integer linear programming software uses the **branch-and-bound algorithm.** Say that a model has a binary integer variable, Y. If Y is a branch variable, two linear programming problems are created—one with $Y = 0$ and one with $Y = 1$. This is similar to examining two cases. Note that when the integer variable values are forced to be integers, the feasible set is smaller and the objective function can't improve. Thus, the linear programming solution gives a bound on the objective function value when the integrality requirement is enforced. In the branch-and-bound algorithm, the bounds are used to prune off linear programming models that can't contain the overall optimal solution. Because it is necessary to branch on a variable only if it has a fractional value in the linear programming solution, tight formulations have fewer branches. A well-formulated integer linear programming model requires solving fewer linear programming branch models using the branch-and-bound algorithm.

INTEGER LINEAR PROGRAMMING MODELS AND SENSITIVITY ANALYSIS

Simple sensitivity analysis is impossible for integer linear programming models. For linear programming models, simple sensitivity analysis is possible for objective function coefficients and RHS constants. Without re-solving the linear programming model, information is available concerning the impact of model changes on the optimal solution. However, simple sensitivity analysis for linear programming models is based on variable values changing *continuously* as a parameter, such as an RHS constant, changes. For an integer linear programming model, the optimal solution variable values do not change continuously. Instead, the integer variable remains at an integer value until it "jumps" to another integer value for the optimal solution. Thus, sensitivity analysis based on the variable values changing continuously is not appropriate for integer linear programming models.

Be wary of simple sensitivity analysis for integer linear programming models. LINDO does not report the ranges for objective function coefficients or RHS constants for the optimal solutions of integer linear programming. Because you can misinterpret this information, LINDO doesn't report it.

Brute force sensitivity analysis is possible. Say that you want to determine the impact of an increase in a manufacturing cost on the optimal solution of the plant location model. You change the objective function coefficient and re-solve the integer linear programming model. However, brute force sensitivity analysis often requires solving many integer linear programming models to provide the desired information.

PIECEWISE LINEAR APPROXIMATION AND SEPARABLE PROGRAMMING

A function that can be expressed as the sum of the functions of a single variable is called a **separable function.** For example, if a function of two variables A and B is equal to

$$f(A, B) = f_A(A) + f_B(B)$$

the function is separable. All linear functions are separable. Consider the function $2A + 3B$. The function of the single variable A is $f_A(A) = 2A$, and the function of the single variable B is $f_B(B) = 3B$. The total function is $f_A(A) + f_B(B) = 2A + 3B$. The function $f(A, B) = A^2 + 3B$ is also separable; $f_A(A)$ is A^2, and $f_B(B)$ is $3B$. This is a nonlinear separable function. The piecewise linear objective function for the machine assignment problem is also a nonlinear separable function. The function $f(A, B) = 2A + AB + 3B$ is not separable. You can't write it as the sum of a function involving just A and another function involving just B.

For a **separable programming problem,** the objective function and all of the constraint functions are separable. This section discusses solving nonlinear separable programming problems. In such problems, at least one of the functions is not linear. If a nonlinear function is piecewise linear, you reformulate the model as either a linear programming model or an integer linear programming model. If a nonlinear function is not piecewise linear, you approximate it by a piecewise linear function. We describe two methods for solving the piecewise linear approximation model. One approach is reformulation as either a linear programming model or an integer linear programming model. Another approach is the use of the separable programming mode that is available in many mainframe linear programming systems.

Piecewise Linear Approximation

In the piecewise linear machine assignment problem, the nonlinearity appeared in the objective function for the variable A_1. Nonlinear functions can also appear in the constraints. Consider the constraint

$$3x_1 + 2x_2^2 \leq 8$$

The constraint function is $3x_1 + 2x_2^2$. This function can be rewritten as $f_1(x_1) + f_2(x_2)$, where $f_1(x_1) = 3x_1$ and $f_2(x_2) = 2x_2^2$. The function is separable. The contribution of the x_1 variable to the constraint function, $f_1(x_1)$, is a linear function, $3x_1$. The contribution of the variable x_2 to the constraint function is not linear; note that $2x_2^2$ is a nonlinear function. You don't need to approximate $f_1(x_1)$ by a piecewise linear function, because $3x_1$ is linear. The function $f_2(x_2)$, illustrated in Figure 9.5, is obviously not linear.

Let's approximate the nonlinear function $2x_2^2$ by a piecewise linear approximation. The set of values at which this function is evaluated is called the **grid.** An **integer grid** evaluates the function at integer variable values. You must examine the constraints to find an upper and lower limit on the variable's value.

Because x_2 must be nonnegative, its lower bound is 0. What is an upper bound on the value of x_2? In this example, no value of x_2 larger than 2 satisfies the constraint. If the model has other constraints, they may impose an even smaller upper bound on x_2. Even if this is the case, using 2 as the upper limit on x_2 doesn't cause an error; the other constraints

Use an upper bound that is big enough

FIGURE 9.5   The Function $f_2(x_2) = 2(x_2)^2$

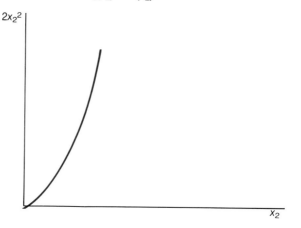

restrict x_2 from attaining too large a value. It's better to select an upper limit that is too large rather than one that is too small and eliminates potentially better solutions from consideration.

Is the optimal variable value equal to the arbitrary upper bound?

Sometimes, determining a valid upper bound *from the constraints* is difficult or the variable is limitless. In this case, arbitrarily select an upper bound. *If the variable value in the resulting optimal solution is equal to the arbitrarily imposed upper bound, increase the upper bound and solve the piecewise linear approximation again.*

The graphical piecewise linear approximation

Using a grid size of 0.5, we obtain the approximation illustrated in Figure 9.6. The function values at 0.0, 0.5, 1.0, 1.5, and 2.0 are connected by linear segments. Although Figure 9.6 represents the approximation graphically, an algebraic approximation is required to solve the model. You can't graphically solve complex models. You must use a computer. Table 9.18 contains the values of the function $f_2(x_2)$ at the five values of x_2.

A piecewise linear approximation can be OK or troublesome

In the piecewise linear objective function of the machine assignment problem, the actual function is piecewise linear. For the function of Figure 9.6, the *approximation* is piecewise linear. You represent the resulting piecewise linear (approximation) function algebraically, similarly to the piecewise linear objective function of the machine assignment model. The appearance of the nonlinearity in the constraint function does not invalidate the approach, but it does require additional caution on your part. Remember, a piecewise linear objective function can be OK or troublesome. *A piecewise linear constraint function can also be OK or troublesome.*

You introduce decision variables for each of the piecewise linear segments of Figure 9.6. For example, introduce a variable called x_{2a} for values of x_2 in the range between 0 and 0.5. Similarly, introduce the

---

FIGURE 9.6   Piecewise Linear Approximation of $2(x_2)^2$

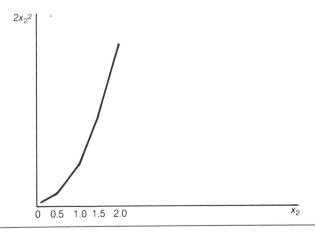

TABLE 9.18   Values of $f_2(x_2) = 2x_2^2$

x_2	$f_2(x_2)$	Change	Slope
0.0	0.0	—	—
0.5	0.5	0.5	1.0
1.0	2.0	1.5	3.0
1.5	4.5	2.5	5.0
2.0	8.0	3.5	7.0

variables x_{2b}, x_{2c}, and x_{2d} for the ranges 0.5 to 1, 1 to 1.5, and 1.5 to 2, respectively. The value of x_2 is

$$x_2 = x_{2a} + x_{2b} + x_{2c} + x_{2d}$$

The constraint function is rewritten as

$$3x_1 + 1x_{2a} + 3x_{2b} + 5x_{2c} + 7x_{2d} \leq 8$$

The coefficients are the line segment slopes

The value of the coefficient for the variable x_{2a} is the slope of the line segment joining the function values at $x_2 = 0$ and $x_2 = 0.5$. The function value at $x_2 = 0$ is 0; the function value at $x_2 = 0.5$ is 0.5. The slope of the line segment is $(0.5-0)/(0.5-0) = 1$. How can you determine the coefficient of the variable x_{2b}? The coefficient is the slope of the piecewise linear function over that range, $(2-0.5)/(1.0-0.5) = 3$. Each of these approximation variables can be no larger than 0.5. If all four of the redefined variables have a value of 0.5, then $x_2 = 2$ and the constraint function value for x_2 is

$$1 \times 0.5 + 3 \times 0.5 + 5 \times 0.5 + 7 \times 0.5 = 8$$

This is the value of $2x_2^2$ when $x_2 = 2$.

Linear Programming Reformulation for a Nonlinear Constraint—OK Case

Say that the nonlinear separable constraint we discussed above is included in the following model:

$$
\begin{aligned}
\max \quad & 2x_1 + 3x_2 \\
\text{st} \quad & 3x_1 + 2x_2^2 \leq 8 \\
& -x_1 + x_2 \geq 1 \\
& x_1, x_2 \geq 0
\end{aligned}
$$

All of the functions are separable. Only the first constraint contains a nonlinear function. You need to approximate x_2's function only in the first constraint.

The resulting model with the redefined variables is

$$
\begin{aligned}
\max \quad & 2x_1 + 3x_{2a} + 3x_{2b} + 3x_{2c} + 3x_{2d} \\
\text{st} \quad & 3x_1 + 1x_{2a} + 3x_{2b} + 5x_{2c} + 7x_{2d} \leq 8 \\
& -x_1 + x_{2a} + x_{2b} + x_{2c} + x_{2d} \geq 1 \\
& x_{2a} \leq 0.5 \\
& x_{2b} \leq 0.5 \\
& x_{2c} \leq 0.5 \\
& x_{2d} \leq 0.5 \\
& x_1, x_{2a}, x_{2b}, x_{2c}, x_{2d}, \geq 0
\end{aligned}
$$

The first linear programming formulation

Everywhere the variable x_2 appeared in a linear function for the original problem, $x_{2a} + x_{2b} + x_{2c} + x_{2d}$ was substituted for it. The resulting model is a linear programming model, and if it is solved by the simplex algorithm, the optimal solution to the piecewise linear approximation model results. You calculate the optimal value of x_2 as

$$
x_2 = x_{2a} + x_{2b} + x_{2c} + x_{2d}
$$

A second formulation of the model is

$$
\begin{aligned}
\max \quad & 2x_1 + 3x_2 \\
\text{st} \quad & 3x_1 + 1x_{2a} + 3x_{2b} + 5x_{2c} + 7x_{2d} \leq 8 \\
& -x_1 + x_2 \geq 1 \\
& -x_2 + x_{2a} + x_{2b} + x_{2c} + x_{2d} = 0 \\
& x_{2a} \leq 0.5 \\
& x_{2b} \leq 0.5 \\
& x_{2c} \leq 0.5 \\
& x_{2d} \leq 0.5 \\
& x_1, x_2, x_{2a}, x_{2b}, x_{2c}, x_{2d}, \geq 0
\end{aligned}
$$

The second linear programming formulation

This formulation contains one additional variable, x_2, and one additional constraint, the definitional constraint for x_2. For this formulation, the model calculates the optimal value of the variable x_2. Inputting the model is simplified by eliminating the need to substitute $x_{2a} + x_{2b} + x_{2c} + x_{2d}$ for x_2 where x_2 appears in linear functions in the model. In general, we prefer to include the variable and the definitional constraint. The increase in the size of the model is minimal compared to the benefits obtained in this way. *Either approach for piecewise functions is correct.*

Table 9.19 contains the LOOK ALL and SOLUTION for the second linear programming formulation. The limits on the values of the piecewise linear variables have been treated as SUBs, not as explicit constraints. The value of $x_1 = 0.7$, and the objective function value is 6.5. The value of $x_2 = 1.7$, with $x_{2a} = x_{2b} = x_{2c} = 0.5$ and $x_{2d} = 0.2$. The value of the SLACK for the nonlinear constraint (Row 2) is 0. You can calculate the true value of the LHS of the nonlinear constraint by substituting $x_1 = 0.7$ and $x_2 = 1.7$:

$$
3 \times 0.7 + 2(1.7)^2 = 7.88
$$

TABLE 9.19 Linear Programming SOLUTION of Piecewise Linear Approximation of Nonlinear Constraint—OK

```
MAX       2 X1 + 3 X2
SUBJECT TO
        2)    3 X1 + X2A + 3 X2B + 5 X2C + 7 X2D <=    8
        3)  - X1 + X2 >=    1
        4)  - X2 + X2A + X2B + X2C + X2D =     0
END
SUB      X2A        0.50
SUB      X2B        0.50
SUB      X2C        0.50
SUB      X2D        0.50

          OBJECTIVE FUNCTION VALUE

   1)          6.49999905

VARIABLE           VALUE          REDUCED COST
      X1          0.700000          0.000000
      X2          1.700000          0.000000
      X2A         0.500000         -3.000000
      X2B         0.500000         -2.000000
      X2C         0.500000         -1.000000
      X2D         0.200000          0.000000

   ROW       SLACK OR SURPLUS      DUAL PRICES
      2)         0.000000          0.500000
      3)         0.000000         -0.500000
      4)         0.000000         -3.500000
```

For the approximation (Row 2), the LHS is

$$3 \times 0.7 + 1 \times 0.5 + 3 \times 0.5 + 5 \times 0.5 + 7 \times 0.2 = 8.0$$

The approximation is better with a finer grid

The slack for the approximation is 0, but the true slack is 0.12. If you use a finer grid on x_2, then the approximated slack value is closer to the true value.

Remember, a troublesome case for the piecewise linear machine assignment problem requires a binary integer variable. A troublesome case is also possible for a piecewise linear approximation. If the piecewise linear approximation is in the objective function, the OK case and the troublesome case are the same as they would be if the function were actually piecewise linear. We discussed this earlier in the chapter.

Let's consider why this piecewise linear constraint approximation is the OK case. If it were troublesome, you would have to introduce binary integer variables to counteract the economic forces.

Why does x_{2a} attain a value of 0.5 before the variable x_{2b} takes on a positive value? Say that the constraint is binding for the optimal solution. This means that the slack is 0 and that the solution would have been even better if the RHS constant were greater. The easiest way to satisfy the constraint is for x_{2a} to be positive before any other approximation variable. If $x_{2a} = 0.5$, the approximation adds 0.5 to the LHS of the constraint, and if $x_{2b} = 0.5$, the approximation adds 1.5. The solution is better when x_{2a} takes on its 0.5 limit before x_{2b} attains a positive value. If the constraint is binding for the optimal solution, the linear programming model for this problem gives the correct approximation. A **troublesome approximation** violates the **adjacent approximation variable requirement**— that each piecewise linear approximation variable attain its maximum value *before* the next piecewise linear approximation variable (to the right) becomes positive. If the linear programming model is troublesome, you use binary integer variables.

For the troublesome case, solving a binary integer linear programming model results in the optimal solution to the linear approximation problem. In the OK case, solving a linear programming model results in an optimal solution to the linear approximation model. The above model is an example of the OK case.

Whether a constraint approximation is OK or troublesome depends on the inequality type and on the shape of the nonlinear function. The next example illustrates the troublesome case and the integer linear programming model. After we examine this example, we classify models with nonlinear constraints as OK or troublesome.

Integer Linear Programming Reformulation for a Nonlinear Constraint—Troublesome Case

The following nonlinear model illustrates the troublesome case:

$$\max \quad 4x_1 + 3x_2$$
$$\text{st} \quad 3x_1 + 2(x_2 - 1)^3 \le 2$$
$$x_1 + x_2 \le 2$$
$$x_1, x_2 \ge 0$$

From the second constraint, 2 is an upper limit on x_2. The first constraint also imposes an upper limit of 2. Figure 9.7 illustrates this function.

FIGURE 9.7 The Function $f_2(x_2) = 2(x_2 - 1)^3$

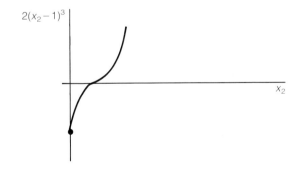

FIGURE 9.8 Piecewise Linear Approximation of $2(x_2 - 1)^3$

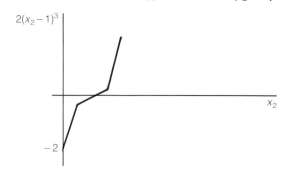

Figure 9.8 graphically illustrates the piecewise linear approximation with the grid 0.0, 0.5, 1.0, 1.5, and 2.0.

Table 9.20 shows the function values using a grid of 0.0, 0.5, 1.0, 1.5, and 2.0. The successive slopes of the four segments are 3.5, 0.5, 0.5, and 3.5. The slope of the first segment is larger than the slope of the second segment, and this is enough to make the nonlinear constraint function troublesome. The approximation of the function of x_2 is

$$-2 + 3.5x_{2a} + 0.5x_{2b} + 0.5x_{2c} + 3.5x_{2d}$$

The constant, -2, corresponds to the value of $2(x_2 - 1)^3$ when $x_2 = 0$. After transposing the constant, -2, to the RHS of the $\leq$, the first constraint becomes

$$3x_1 + 3.5x_{2a} + 0.5x_{2b} + 0.5x_{2c} + 3.5x_{2d} \leq 4$$

The complete linear programming model is

$$
\begin{aligned}
\max \quad & 4x_1 + 3x_2 \\
\text{st} \quad & 3x_1 + 3.5x_2a + 0.5x_{2b} + 0.5x_{2c} + 3.5x_{2d} \leq 4 \\
& x_1 + x_2 \leq 2 \\
& -x_2 + x_{2a} + x_{2b} + x_{2c} + x_{2d} = 0 \\
& x_{2a} \leq 0.5 \\
& x_{2b} \leq 0.5 \\
& x_{2c} \leq 0.5 \\
& x_{2d} \leq 0.5 \\
& x_1, x_2, x_{2a}, x_{2b}, x_{2c}, x_{2d} \geq 0
\end{aligned}
$$

The linear programming model

The optimal solution to the above linear programming model is shown in Table 9.21. Although $x_2 = 0.8$ in the optimal linear programming solution, it is achieved with $x_{2a} = 0$, $x_{2b} = 0.3$, $x_{2c} = 0.5$, and $x_{2d} = 0$. This violates the adjacent approximation variable requirement, according to which Variable x_{2a} must be at its limit before Variable x_{2b} is positive. This

The adjacent approximation variable requirement is violated

TABLE 9.20   Values of $f_2(x_2) = 2(x_2 - 1)^3$

x_2	$f_2(x_2)$	Change	Slope
0	−2.0	—	—
0.5	−0.25	1.75	3.50
1.0	0	0.25	0.50
1.5	0.25	0.25	0.50
2.0	2.0	1.75	3.50

is a troublesome approximation, and the constraint function is not evaluated correctly in the solution. When x_2 equals 0.8, $f_2(0.8) = -0.016$. When $x_1 = 1.2$ and $x_2 = 0.8$, the original first constraint is violated.

When $x_2 = 0.8$, it is easier to satisfy the approximation constraint with $x_{2b} = 0.3$ and $x_{2c} = 0.5$ than with $x_{2a} = 0.5$ and $x_{2b} = 0.3$. The slope of the second line segment is smaller than the slope of the first. Choosing the incorrect approximation makes possible a larger value of x_1. Therefore, the linear programming model is incorrect.

Let's summarize the OK and troublesome cases for a ≤ constraint. If the piecewise linear approximation of a nonlinear function in a ≤ constraint has slopes that are *successively increasing* as the variable increases, the approximation is OK. If the piecewise linear approximation

TABLE 9.21   Linear Programming SOLUTION of Piecewise Linear Approximation of Nonlinear Constraint—Troublesome

```
MAX      4 X1 + 3 X2
SUBJECT TO
      2)   3 X1 + 3.5 X2A + 0.5 X2B + 0.5 X2C + 3.5 X2D <=   4
      3)    X1 + X2 <=   2
      4) -  X2 + X2A + X2B + X2C + X2D =    0
END
SUB     X2A       0.50
SUB     X2B       0.50
SUB     X2C       0.50
SUB     X2D       0.50

        OBJECTIVE FUNCTION VALUE

   1)        7.19999981

   VARIABLE          VALUE           REDUCED COST
        X1         1.200000           0.000000
        X2         0.800000           0.000000
        X2A        0.000000           1.200000
        X2B        0.300000           0.000000
        X2C        0.500000           0.000000
        X2D        0.000000           1.200000

      ROW      SLACK OR SURPLUS      DUAL PRICES
        2)        0.000000            0.400000
        3)        0.000000            2.800000
        4)        0.000000           -0.200000
```

The OK and troublesome cases for ≤ constraints

of a nonlinear function in a ≤ constraint has slopes that are *not successively increasing* as the variable increases, the approximation is troublesome. For the OK case, you solve the linear programming model. For the troublesome case, you introduce one or more binary integer variables and solve an integer linear programming model.

The correct integer linear programming model

You introduce binary integer variables to eliminate the improper calculation of the nonlinear function, $2(x_2 - 1)^3$. Define Variable $Z1$ as 1 if $x_{2a} = 0.5$ and as 0 in all other cases. Define Variables $Z2$ and $Z3$ similarly for the variables x_{2b} and x_{2c}, respectively. To impose the definitional characteristics algebraically, additional constraints are required. The resulting model is

$$\max \quad 4x_1 + 3x_2$$
$$\begin{aligned}
\text{st} \quad & 3x_1 + 3.5x_{2a} + 0.5x_{2b} + 0.5x_{2c} + 3.5x_{2d} \leq 4 \\
& x_1 + x_2 \leq 2 \\
& -x_2 + x_{2a} + x_{2b} + x_{2c} + x_{2d} = 0 \\
& x_{2a} \leq 0.5 \\
& x_{2b} - 0.5Z1 \leq 0 \\
& x_{2c} - 0.5Z2 \leq 0 \\
& x_{2d} - 0.5Z3 \leq 0 \\
& Z1 - 2x_{2a} \leq 0 \\
& Z2 - 2x_{2b} \leq 0 \\
& Z3 - 2x_{2c} \leq 0 \\
& x_1, x_2, x_{2a}, x_{2b}, x_{2c}, x_{2d} \geq 0 \\
& Z1, Z2, Z3 \quad 0 \text{ or } 1
\end{aligned}$$

The adjacent approximation variable requirement is satisfied

Table 9.22 contains the optimal solution from LINDO solved as an integer linear programming model. Row 5 ensures that x_{2a} is no larger than 0.5. Row 9 ensures that $Z1$ can be 1 only if $x_{2a} = 0.5$. If $Z1 = 1$, then Row 6 allows x_{2b} to be as large as 0.5. If $Z1 = 0$, then Row 6 forces x_{2b} to equal 0. The variable x_{2a} must attain its 0.5 limit before x_{2b} can be greater than 0. The other constraints involving binary integer variables perform similar purposes for x_{2c} and x_{2d}. In Table 9.22, $x_2 = 1.4$ and $x_{2a} = x_{2b} = 0.5$ and $x_{2c} = 0.4$. This is the correct approximation. The SLACK variable value for the nonlinear inequality (Row 2) is 0. However, if the values of x_1 and x_2 are substituted into the original nonlinear inequality, the LHS value is 1.928, slightly less than the actual RHS constant of 2. This model is only a linear approximation. A finer grid makes the approximation more precise.

The OK and troublesome cases for ≥ constraints

Let's describe the OK and troublesome cases for ≥ constraints. If the piecewise linear approximation of a nonlinear function in a ≥ constraint has slopes that *decrease successively* as the variable increases, the approximation is OK. If the piecewise linear approximation of a nonlinear function in a ≥ constraint has slopes that *do not decrease successively* as the variable increases, the approximation is troublesome. For the OK case, you solve the linear programming model. For the troublesome case,

TABLE 9.22 Integer Linear Programming SOLUTION of Piecewise Linear Approximation of Nonlinear Constraint—Troublesome

```
MAX     4 X1 + 3 X2
SUBJECT TO
       2)    3 X1 + 3.5 X2A + 0.5 X2B + 0.5 X2C + 3.5 X2D <=    4
       3)    X1 + X2 <=    2
       4) -  X2 + X2A + X2B + X2C + X2D =    0
       5)    X2A <=    0.5
       6) -  0.5 Z1 + X2B <=    0
       7) -  0.5 Z2 + X2C <=    0
       8) -  0.5 Z3 + X2D <=    0
       9)    Z1 - 2 X2A <=    0
      10)    Z2 - 2 X2B <=    0
      11)    Z3 - 2 X2C <=    0
END
INTE       Z1
INTE       Z2
INTE       Z3

       OBJECTIVE FUNCTION VALUE

   1)        6.59999943

VARIABLE            VALUE           REDUCED COST
       Z1        1.000000             0.600000
       Z2        1.000000            -0.000000
       Z3        0.000000             0.000000
       X1        0.600000             0.000000
       X2        1.400000             0.000000
      X2A        0.500000             0.000000
      X2B        0.500000             0.000000
      X2C        0.400000             0.000000
      X2D        0.000000             1.200000

     ROW     SLACK OR SURPLUS       DUAL PRICES
       2)        0.000000             0.400000
       3)        0.000000             2.800000
       4)        0.000000            -0.200000
       5)        0.000000             0.000000
       6)        0.000000             0.000000
       7)        0.100000             0.000000
       8)        0.000000             0.000000
       9)        0.000000             0.600000
      10)        0.000000            -0.000000
      11)        0.800000             0.000000
```

you introduce one or more binary integer variables and solve the integer linear programming model.

For an equality constraint, there is no doubt about whether to use binary integer variables for a piecewise approximation. If the constraint is of an *equality type* and a nonlinear function is approximated by a piecewise linear function, it is necessary to solve the binary integer linear programming model to obtain an optimal solution to the linear approximation model.

Use binary integer variables for = constraints

One final comment on troublesome piecewise linear approximations or piecewise approximations for equality constraints. Because of the approximation, the optimal solution to the integer linear programming problem may violate the true constraint. If the optimal solution to the integer linear programming model is not close enough to being a feasible solution, you use a finer grid.

Check whether the solution satisfies the nonlinear constraints

Separable Programming Mode

Some linear programming software systems, such as IBM's MPSX, have a **separable programming mode.** In the separable programming mode, a modified version of the simplex algorithm solves the linear programming model and the binary integer variables are not introduced. The details of implementation vary from system to system, but all of the systems share two properties. First, they simplify input by specifying variables as approximation variables. For the examples in this section, the approximation variables must be redefined so that they all have an upper limit of 1. Then, the variables are designated as approximation variables and the upper limit of 1 is assumed.

Input is simplified

The second property involves whether separable programming mode gives an optimal solution to the approximation model. If the piecewise linear approximation is OK, separable programming results in the optimal solution to the piecewise linear approximation; but so does linear programming. An optimal solution to a troublesome piecewise linear approximation is not guaranteed by separable programming mode. In separable programming mode, the simplex algorithm rules are modified so that the *adjacent approximation variable requirement is satisfied.* That is, before an approximattion variable becomes positive, the approximation variable to its left must attain its limit. An example of a solution violating this requirement is one in which $x_2 = 0.4$, while $x_{2a} = 0$ and $x_{2b} = 0.4$. Solving a troublesome piecewise linear programming model can give a solution that violates this requirement. Solving a troublesome linear approximation as an integer linear programming model gives a solution that satisfies this requirement.

The adjacent approximation variable requirement is satisfied

Let's illustrate the optimal solution difficulty for separable programming mode. Figure 9.9 contains a piecewise linear approximation for a maximization objective function. The objective function value is larger at $x_1 = 1$ than at the adjacent grid points, $x_1 = 0$ and $x_1 = 2$. The objective function value is larger at $x_1 = 6$ than at the adjacent grid points, $x_1 = 5$ and $x_1 = 7$. Since the function value is greater at $x_1 = 1$ than at the points close to it, that function value is called a **local maximum.** There is also a local maximum at $x_1 = 6$. Since the function value at $x_1 = 6$ is greater than at any other value, it is called a **global maximum.** The modified simplex algorithm increases the value of x_1 by introducing the approximation variables, starting from the left. When the variable value reaches $x_1 = 1$, introducing the approximation variable for the next interval decreases the objective function value. Because the objective is maximization, separable programming terminates at $x_1 = 1$, a local maximum, but not at the global maximum.

Separable programming mode solutions may not be global optimal solutions

If the approximation is troublesome, separable programming mode can give a local optimal solution to the approximation problem that is *not a global optimal solution.* However, the integer linear programming model always gives a global optimal solution to the approximation problem.

FIGURE 9.9 Example of a Maximization Piecewise Linear Objective Function with a Local Maximum that is not a Global Maximum

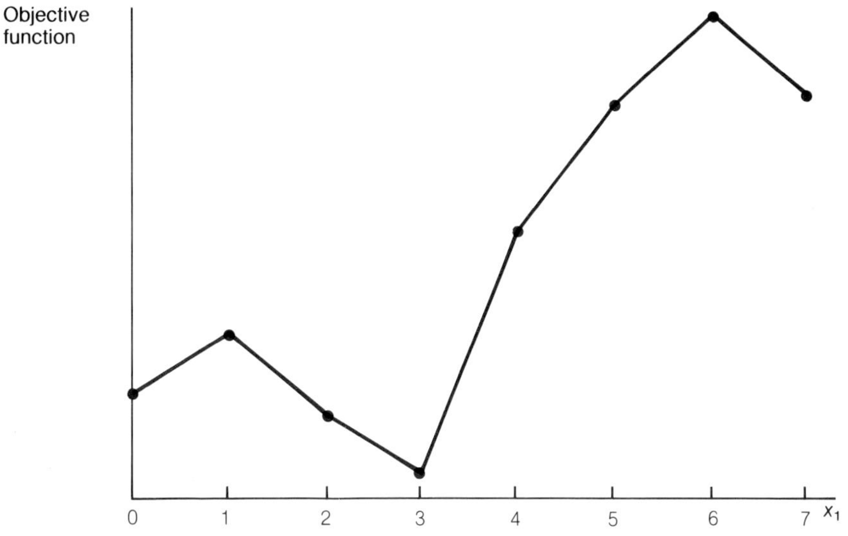

SUMMARY

Integer linear programming models and nonlinear programming models are useful extensions of linear programming models. We described a small number of the useful applications of integer linear programming models and nonlinear programming models. Monsanto solved its nonlinear problem, involving operating conditions for maleic anhydride production, by using integer linear programming models to approximate the nonlinear relationship between operating conditions, yield, and production rate. Maryland National Bank used an integer linear programming model to determine the best check clearing methods. Exxon used an integer linear programming model to choose energy conservation projects at its Baton Rouge refinery. VALIC designed new sales regions by means of an integer linear programming model. Air Products and Chemicals used an integer linear programming model to plan the routing of tank trucks to its customers.

Nonlinear programming models and integer linear programming models require algorithms different from the simplex algorithm to find the optimal solution. Piecewise linear objective functions and fixed charge costs are the two most common nonlinearities encountered by managers. We showed how to reformulate these nonlinearities into either linear programming models or integer linear programming models.

We explained the distinction between binary integer variables and general integer variables, as well as the conversion of one type to the other. Whether such conversions are necessary depends on the capabilities of the available integer linear programming software. We also described the difference between pure integer linear programming models and mixed integer linear programming models.

We discussed the reformulation of models with a piecewise linear objective function. In the *troublesome case,* an integer linear programming problem is required. In the *OK case,* a linear programming model is used. Each reformulation was illustrated for the machine assignment problem.

We reformulated models with fixed charge or setup costs as binary integer linear programming models. The machine assignment model was reformulated with a machine setup cost. Also reformulated was a plant location model with fixed costs if a site is chosen.

We described several formulation "tricks" using binary integer variables. The capital budgeting problem allocates funds among several available projects. (Exxon's model was of this type.) We described multiple-choice constraints and logical relationships, which are useful for capital budgeting models. We also described the formulation of either-or inequalities and minimum batch sizes.

Many of the problems faced by managers are combinatorial optimization problems. The examples of such problems that we described included the traveling salesman problem (TSP), some machine sequencing problems, limited-resource project scheduling problems, and postman problems. Metelco solved a TSP to route its programmable drilling machines. However, it is difficult to find the guaranteed optimal solution for combinatorial optimization problems with many alternatives.

"Lucky" models are those for which the linear programming solution has integer variable values. The assignment model and the transportation model are examples of network models that are always lucky. If integer linear programming capability is not available, you can ignore the integer restriction for other integer linear programming models and solve them as linear programming models. If you are lucky, you've found the optimal solution for such a model. If you are unlucky, you can solve a number of case studies, each of which is a linear programming model. The best of the case study solutions is the optimal solution.

We defined separable functions and separable programming problems. We approximate a nonlinear separable function by a piecewise linear approximation. The nonlinear separable function can be either the objective function or a constraint function. The piecewise linear approximation results in a linear programming model if the function is OK, but in an integer linear programming model if the function is troublesome. Finally, we described the separable programming mode, which is available for some mainframe linear programming systems.

The methods and models we described have several limitations. First, the objective function and the constraint functions must be linear for an integer linear programming model. We reformulate piecewise linear functions for this reason. You can't have nonlinear functions in such a model. Second, you can use a piecewise linear approximation *only* for separable functions. For example, if your model includes the product of two variables, the function is not separable. Third, if the number of alternatives is large, solving all of the case studies is impractical. In this situation, you should use integer linear programming software.

Note the following cautions concerning this chapter. First, integer linear programming software can take an excessive amount of computer time. Consider the addition of tightening constraints to reduce the computer time. Second, simple sensitivity analysis is difficult for integer linear programming models. Generally, you must change the model and re-solve it. Managers use decision models to analyze a decision environment. Lack of simple sensitivity analysis and excessive computer time resulting from poorly formulated integer linear programming models can make integer linear programming models less valuable as a decision-making aid. Third, defining a binary variable's characteristic does not cause the model to have the characteristic. The constraints and the objective function must imply the definition you want for a binary integer variable. Fourth, take care in determining whether a piecewise linear *objective function* is OK or troublesome. If it's OK, use linear programming. If it's troublesome, use integer linear programming. Fifth, take care in determining whether a piecewise linear *constraint function* is OK or troublesome. Again, if it's OK, use linear programming, and if it's troublesome, use integer linear programming. Sixth, if a problem is troublesome, the separable programming mode can give a local optimal solution that isn't the global optimal solution. The integer linear programming model always gives the global optimal solution to the approximation problem. Seventh, a piecewise linear approximation only approximates the function. If you want to approximate it better, use a finer grid.

QUESTIONS

1. What is a general integer variable?
2. What is a binary integer variable?
3. Under what circumstances is it necessary to replace a general integer variable by its binary representation?
4. Give the binary representation of the general integer variable *A* with an upper limit of 40.
5. What is a pure integer linear programming model?
6. What is a mixed integer linear programming model?
7. What is a nonlinear programming model?

8. Give an example of a nonlinear programming model.

9. What is a piecewise linear function?

10. Sketch a term for an objective function of a maximization model not requiring a binary integer variable in the piecewise linear representation.

11. Sketch a term for an objective function of a maximization model requiring a binary integer variable in the piecewise linear representation.

12. Sketch a term for an objective function of a minimization model not requiring a binary integer variable in the piecewise linear representation.

13. Sketch a term for an objective function of a minimization model requiring a binary integer variable in the piecewise linear representation.

14. What is a separable function?

15. Which of the following are separable functions?
    a. $A + 2B$
    b. $A^2 + 2/C$
    c. $1/(A + B)$
    d. $A^2 + 2AB - B^2$
    e. $e^{A + B}$
    f. $A + \log B^2$
    g. $3A + 4B^2$

16. What is a grid, and how is it used for piecewise linear approximations?

17. Evaluate the function $3A^3$ on the integer grid from 0 to 4.

18. What is a lucky model?

19. Give an example of a lucky model.

20. What is a series of case studies?

21. What is a fixed charge?

22. What is a separable programming problem?

23. What is the separable programming mode? Does the linear programming system available to you have it?

24. Verify that the coefficient of Variable x_{2c} in the approximation of the nonlinear constraint of Table 9.19 is 5.

25. Draw a nonlinear function such that a $\leq$ constraint does not require a binary integer variable in the piecewise linear approximation.

26. Draw a nonlinear function such that a $\leq$ constraint requires a binary integer variable in the piecewise linear approximation.

27. Draw a nonlinear function such that a $\geq$ constraint does not require a binary integer variable in the piecewise linear approximation.

28. Draw a nonlinear function such that a $\geq$ constraint requires a binary integer variable in the piecewise linear approximation.

29. Does an $=$ constraint that has a nonlinear function require a binary integer variable in the piecewise linear approximation?

30. Give two properties of a combinatorial optimization problem.

31. What is the adjacent approximation variable requirement?

32. Why is simple sensitivity analysis difficult for integer linear programming models?

33. Draw a function with a local maximum that is not the global maximum.

EXERCISES

1. Consider the following integer linear programming model:

    max $2A + 3B$
    st $2A + B \leq 6$
           $A + 2B \leq 7$
           $A, B \geq 0$ and integer

    a. Find graphically the optimal solution to the linear programming model.
    b. Round to the nearest integer the noninteger variable values from the solution to Part *a*.
    c. Graph the feasible set, and identify the integer feasible points by heavy dots.
    d. Is the rounded solution feasible?
    e. Is the rounded solution the best integer feasible solution?

2. Consider the following integer linear programming model:

    max $4A + 3B$
    st $A + B \leq 4$
           $-A + 2B \geq 1$
           $A, B \geq 0$ and integer

    a. Find graphically the optimal solution to the linear programming model.
    b. Round to the nearest integer the noninteger variable values from the solution to Part *a*.
    c. Graph the feasible set, and identify the integer feasible points by heavy dots.
    d. Is the rounded solution feasible?
    e. Is the rounded solution the best integer feasible solution?

3. Consider the following integer linear programming model:

    min $2A + 5B$
    st $2A + B \geq 4$
           $-A + 2B \geq 2$
           $A, B \geq 0$ and integer

    a. Find graphically the optimal solution to the linear programming model.
    b. Round to the nearest integer the noninteger variable values from the solution to Part *a*.
    c. Graph the feasible set, and identify the integer feasible points by heavy dots.
    d. Is the rounded solution feasible?
    e. Is the rounded solution the best integer feasible solution?

4. Consider the following integer linear programming model:

$$\min \quad 4A + B$$
$$\text{st} \quad 3A + B \geq 6$$
$$-9A + 2B \leq 0$$
$$A, B \geq 0 \text{ and integer}$$

    a. Find graphically the optimal solution to the linear programming model.
    b. Round to the nearest integer the noninteger variable values from the solution to Part *a*.
    c. Graph the feasible set, and identify the integer feasible points by heavy dots.
    d. Is the rounded solution feasible?
    e. Is the rounded solution the best integer feasible solution?

5. The variable A has a fixed charge of \$120 in addition to a marginal cost of \$150. The variable B has no fixed charge, but a marginal cost of \$100. The constraints of the model are

$$\text{st} \quad A + 2B \leq 10$$
$$A + B \geq 5$$
$$A, B \geq 0$$

    a. Define a binary integer variable for the fixed charge.
    b. Give an upper limit on the value of Variable A.
    c. Formulate an integer linear programming model to minimize the total cost.

6. The variable A has a fixed charge of \$1,000 in addition to a marginal cost of \$250. The variable B has a fixed charge of \$1,200 and a marginal cost of \$900. The constraints of the model are

$$\text{st} \quad 2A + 3B \leq 20$$
$$A + B = 5$$
$$B \leq 4$$
$$A, B \geq 0$$

    a. Define a binary integer variable for each fixed charge.
    b. Give an upper limit on the value of each variable.
    c. Formulate an integer linear programming model to minimize the total cost.

7. Consider an additional cost to the plant location problem in the chapter. A fixed charge cost is incurred for each of the transportation routes used. The fixed charge is \$10 for each of the 12 possible transportation routes. Give the integer linear programming model.

8. Consider an additional policy for the plant location problem in the chapter. The policy is that if a plant location is selected, the minimum production is 75 units per month. Give the integer linear programming model.

9. For the plant location problem in the chapter, either Plant Location A or Plant Location B must be selected, but not both. Give the integer linear programming model.

10. For the plant location problem in the chapter, either Plant Location A or Plant Location C must be selected, but not both. Give the integer linear programming model.

11. Describe how to solve the troublesome nonlinear approximation constraint example in the chapter using a set of case studies.

12. Describe how to solve the plant location problem in the chapter using a set of case studies.

13. Describe how to solve the setup cost machine assignment problem using a set of case studies.

14. Modify the model for the setup cost machine assignment problem if the mechanic requires 2 hours for the setup and doesn't start until 8 A.M.

15. The data for the machine assignment problem in Table 9.4 shows the operating costs for production during the normal 40 hours. Say that you can use up to 20 additional hours on overtime for any machine. The additional cost is $10 per hour. Formulate a cost minimization model.

16. Consider the following separable programming model:

$$\min \quad 2A + 3B^2$$
$$\text{st} \quad A + 2B \le 10$$
$$-A + B \ge 2$$
$$A, B \ge 0$$

   a. Graph the function $3B^2$.

   b. Give an upper limit on the value of B.

   c. Using an integer grid for the variable B, give the piecewise linear approximation to the objective function.

   d. Is this objective function troublesome? Is a binary integer variable required?

   e. Give the linear programming model for the piecewise linear approximation including the variable B.

   f. Give the linear programming model for the piecewise linear approximation without introducing the variable B.

17. Consider the following separable programming model:

$$\max \quad 2A + 1/(B + 1)$$
$$\text{st} \quad 2A + B \ge 12$$
$$A + B \le 4$$
$$A, B \ge 0$$

   a. Graph the function $1/(B + 1)$.

   b. Give an upper limit on the value of B.

   c. Using an integer grid for the variable B, give the piecewise linear approximation to the objective function.

   d. Is this objective function troublesome? Is a binary integer variable required?

   e. Give the linear programming model for the piecewise linear approximation including the variable B.

    f. Give the linear programming model for the piecewise linear approximation without introducing the variable *B*.

18. Consider the following separable programming model:

max $2A^2 + 3B$
st $3A + 2B \le 9$
        $A + B \ge 2$
        $A, B \ge 0$

    a. Graph the function $2A^2$.
    b. Give an upper limit on the value of *A*.
    c. Using an integer grid for the variable *A*, give the piecewise linear approximation to the objective function.
    d. Is this objective function troublesome? Is a binary integer variable required?
    e. Give the integer linear programming model for the piecewise linear approximation including the variable *A*.

19. Consider the following separable programming model:

min $2/(A + 2) + 3B$
st $3A + 3B \le 12$
        $2A + B \le 6$
        $A, B \ge 0$

    a. Graph the function $2/(A + 2)$.
    b. Give an upper limit on the value of *A*.
    c. Using an integer grid for the variable *A*, give the piecewise linear approximation to the objective function.
    d. Is this objective function troublesome? Is a binary integer variable required?
    e. Give the integer linear programming model for the piecewise linear approximation including the variable *A*.

20. Fay has $30,000 to invest in 1-year Treasury Notes, a 1-year annuity, or 1-year corporate bonds (rated AAA). Any amount can be invested in the annuity, but the Treasury Notes and corporate bonds must be multiples of $5,000. She has assigned risk points to each of possible investments as follows:

Investment	% Yield	Risk Points
Treasury Note	6	0
Annuity	9	12
Corporate Bond	8	9

Her goal is maximizing the annual return but the average risk points of the portfolio cannot exceed 8. She does not want to invest more than $10,000 in corporate bonds. Formulate an integer linear programming model.

21. A marketing manager wants to assign customers to two salespeople so that the total dollar volume is maximized. The anticipated dollar volume for each assignment is:

	Customer			
Salesperson	A	B	C	D
Sue	40,000	25,000	32,000	18,000
Mark	25,000	32,000	18,000	27,000
Alan	13,000	41,000	27,000	19,000

Each salesperson must be assigned to at least one, but no more than two customers. Formulate an integer linear programming model to maximize the dollar volume.

22. The Social Security Administration rents office space in a metropolitan area to serve its recipients. The recipients are grouped into regions denoted 1 through 7. The possible office sites must be close enough to each region so that the travel time is reasonable. The following show which regions can be served by each office site.

Office	Regions Close Enough	Annual Rental Cost
A	1, 2, 4, 5, 7	$15,000
B	1, 3, 4, 6, 7	25,000
C	2, 3, 4, 5	12,000
D	1, 3, 6, 7	18,000
E	3, 5, 6	14,000

Formulate an integer linear programming model to minimize the annual rental cost that locates an office close enough to each region.

23. A company is studying which capital investment projects to fund. The capital requirements and the NPV for the projects are

		Year		
Project	NPV	1	2	3
A	30,000	15,000	25,000	15,000
B	45,000	40,000	15,000	10,000
C	25,000	20,000	15,000	25,000
D	30,000	25,000	10,000	30,000

There is $65,000 available each year.

a. Formulate an integer linear programming model to select the projects.
b. What constraint is added if either A or C must be funded?
c. What constraints are added if D can be funded only if A or C is funded, but only one of A or C can be funded?

24. Consider the following separable programming model:

    min $A + 3B$
    st $3A^2 + 2B \leq 12$
          $2A + B \leq 6$
          $A, B \geq 0$

    a. Graph the function $3A^2$.
    b. Give an upper limit on the value of A.
    c. Using an integer grid for the variable A, give the piecewise linear approximation to the first constraint function.
    d. Is this constraint function troublesome? Is a binary integer variable required?
    e. Give the linear programming model for the piecewise linear approximation including the variable A.

25. Consider the following separable programming model:

    min $A + 3B$
    st $3A + 2B \leq 6$
          $2A + 1/(B + 1) \leq 6$
          $A, B \geq 0$

    a. Graph the function $1/(B + 1)$.
    b. Give an upper limit on the value of B.
    c. Using an integer grid for the variable B, give the piecewise linear approximation to the second constraint function.
    d. Is this constraint function troublesome? Is a binary integer variable required?
    e. Give the linear programming model for the piecewise linear approximation including the variable B.

26. Consider the following separable programming model:

    min $2A + 3B$
    st $3A^2 + 2B \geq 12$
          $2A + 3B \leq 8$
          $A, B \geq 0$

    a. Graph the function $3A^2$.
    b. Give an upper limit on the value of A.
    c. Using an integer grid for the variable A, give the piecewise linear approximation to the first constraint function.
    d. Is this constraint function troublesome? Is a binary integer variable required?
    e. Give the integer linear programming model for the piecewise linear approximation including the variable A.

27. Consider the following separable programming model:

    min $2A + 3B$
    st $2A + 3B \leq 6$
          $2A - 1/(B + 2) \leq 3$
          $A, B \geq 0$

a. Graph the function $-1/(B + 2)$.
b. Give an upper limit on the value of B.
c. Using an integer grid for the variable B, give the piecewise linear approximation to the second constraint function.
d. Is this constraint function troublesome? Is a binary integer variable required?
e. Give the integer linear programming model for the piecewise linear approximation including the variable B.

MORE CHALLENGING EXERCISES

1. A major fast-food chain has made an offer too good to resist to the potato processing company. It has offered to purchase french fries for $0.93 per pound.
   a. The fast-food chain will purchase at the higher price any amount you produce up to 10,000 pounds. You can sell up to 18,000 pounds in excess of 10,000 pounds in your regular channels at $0.90 per pound. Formulate and solve a linear constrained optimization model to maximize the profit.
   b. The fast-food chain has made another offer. The intent of this offer is to make the potato processing company a captive supplier of french fries. The potato processing company will sell french fries only to the fast-food chain. The fast-food chain will purchase up to 10,000 pounds of french fries per month at $0.89 per pound and any amount above 10,000 pounds at $0.93 per pound. Formulate and solve a linear constrained optimization model to maximize the profit.
   (*Hint:* Note that the problem is easier if the model contains the FF variable.)

2. A company is considering the construction of a manufacturing facility in Chicago. The company has an Omaha facility with a capacity of 30,000 units per month. A new facility is being considered because customer orders have been straining the capacity of that facility.

   For purposes of sizing the new facility, the monthly demands of the company's four customer regions have been forecast. The forecast demands are as follows:

Customer Region	Demand
1	6,000
2	10,000
3	9,000
4	10,000

Preliminary designs have been developed for facilities with three different capacities: 10,000, 20,000, and 30,000 units per month. The fixed costs and manufacturing costs of these facilities are estimated as

Size	Capacity	Fixed Cost/Month	Manufacturing Cost/Unit
1	10,000	$10,000	$2.50
2	20,000	22,500	1.25
3	30,000	27,500	1.00

The larger facilities are much more efficient than the smallest facility, but their fixed cost is also higher. The manufacturing cost per unit at Omaha is $1.

The transportation costs per unit are as follows:

	Customer Region			
	1	2	3	4
Omaha	$1.45	$0.85	$0.60	$0.40
Chicago	0.40	0.60	0.80	1.40

a. Formulate a binary integer linear programming model to minimize the total of monthly fixed costs, manufacturing costs, and transportation costs.
b. Solve the model using mixed integer linear programming software.
c. Write a one-page report to your nontechnical boss describing your recommendation on plant size. Discuss all of the factors you consider important.

3. The plant sizing problem of MCE 2 must be solved without integer linear programming software.
a. How many case studies are required to solve the sizing decision problem by solving linear programming models?
b. Give one of the case study linear programming models of Part a.
c. Solve your model of Part b using linear programming software.
d. After solving all of the case studies by linear programming, how would you select the best size for the Chicago facility?

4. A food processing company has four potential production plant sites under consideration. The company makes two grades of a product. The production costs, rates, and capabilities are summarized as follows:

	Manufacturing Cost/Unit	
Location	Product 1	Product 2
A	$0.15	—
B	0.25	$0.30
C	—	0.35
D	0.15	0.29

	Manufacturing Rate (hours/unit)	
Location	Product 1	Product 2
A	0.5	—
B	0.5	0.32
C	—	0.25
D	0.5	0.39

Note that Location C cannot produce Product 1 and that Location A cannot produce Product 2. Six thousand production hours are available at each plant per week.

The weekly requirements of the four storage depots are as follows:

	Weekly Requirements (thousands of units)	
Depot	Product 1	Product 2
1	10	3
2	8	2
3	8	4
4	4	5

The transportation costs per unit are the same for both products over a specified route. The transportation costs per unit are

	Depot			
Location	1	2	3	4
A	0.02	0.04	0.03	0.03
B	0.04	0.05	0.03	0.04
C	0.03	0.03	0.02	0.04
D	0.02	0.03	0.02	0.03

On a weekly basis, the capital costs for Locations A, B, C, and D are $21,000, $25,000, $23,000, and $30,700, respectively. Formulate and solve an integer linear programming model to determine which plants to build so as to minimize the total of production, transportation, and capital costs on a weekly basis.

5. A company is evaluating four projects. The NPV and annual capital outlays are

		Capital Requirements		
Project	NPV	1	2	3
1	$220,000	$50,000	$30,000	$25,000
2	105,000	35,000	50,000	30,000
3	145,000	32,000	50,000	—
4	180,000	45,000	45,000	30,000

The NPV has been calculated at 10 percent. Project 3 requires only two years and can either be undertaken immediately or delayed for a year. The available capital for the next three years is $95,000, $140,000, and $120,000. Formulate and solve a model to select the projects for the three-year period that maximizes the NPV within the limited capital available.

6. A company is realigning its regional sales offices. It wants sales offices to be within a reasonable travel time of the major cities they serve. Thus, a sales office in New York can't serve customers in Chicago. Major customers are located in Chicago, Philadelphia, Detroit, New York, Washington, D.C., Atlanta, and Boston. The company is considering the location of offices in Chicago, Detroit, New York, and Atlanta. The cities that these offices could effectively serve are as follows:

Office	Cities Served
Chicago	Chicago, Detroit, Philadelphia
Detroit	Chicago, Detroit, Philadelphia, Washington, D.C.
New York	New York, Washington, D.C., Philadephia, Atlanta, Boston
Atlanta	Atlanta, New York, Philadelphia, Washington, D.C.

The costs of the offices are estimated as

Office	Cost
Chicago	$320,000
Detroit	225,000
New York	450,000
Atlanta	280,000

Formulate and solve a model to select the offices that minimizes the office costs and satisifes the travel time limitations.

7. An investor has $250,000 to invest in real estate projects. She has identified six projects with the following anticipated rates of return and required investments:

Project	Rate of Return	Investment
1	12%	$ 90,000
2	8	45,000
3	11	75,000
4	10	50,000
5	8	40,000
6	12	170,000

a. Formulate and solve a model to maximize the total return of the investments.

b. Projects 1, 3, and 6 are office buildings. The investor doesn't want to invest more than $200,000 in office buildings. What constraint should you add to the formulation to show this?

8. A company is planning its production for the next six months. If the company operates one shift, the capacity is 5,000 units per month. If it operates two shifts, the capacity is 10,000 units per month. The extra cost of changing from one shift to two is $20,000. The extra cost of changing from two shifts to one is $25,000. The number of shifts can be changed only at the beginning of the month. The monthly operating cost is $80,000 per shift. The monthly holding cost of inventory is $5 per unit. The number of units required for each month is

Month	Requirement
1	4,000
2	6,000
3	8,000
4	10,000
5	6,000
6	4,000

The company has been operating one shift and has no units in inventory.

a. Formulate and solve a model to minimize the cost of satisfying the requirements.

b. Reformulate the model if the capacity of the second shift decreases to 4,000 units per month. Then, the total for two shifts is 9,000.

9. Fly-by-Night Airlines is a small regional carrier. Scheduling crews effectively reduces operating costs. Regulatory agencies limit possible crew schedules so that the crew is not fatigued. Fly-by-Night offers these flights:

Flight Number	Origin	Destination
1	Los Angeles	San Francisco
2	San Francisco	Los Angeles
3	Los Angeles	Phoenix
4	Phoenix	Los Angeles
5	San Francisco	Las Vegas
6	Las Vegas	Phoenix

A crew schedule consists of 1, 2, or 3 flights. Under current regulations, the following crew schedules are permitted:

One Flight	Cost	Two Flights	Cost	Three Flights	Cost
1	$3,000	1, 2	$3,500	1, 5, 4	$4,500
2	2,500	5, 6	3,700		
3	4,000	6, 4	2,900		
4	3,000	2, 3	3,300		
5	2,500				
6	2,000				

Formulate and solve a binary integer linear programming model to minimize the cost of staffing all the flights. (*Hint:* Introduce a binary variable for each crew schedule.)

10. A company can produce its product on three machines. The machines can be operated for one shift, for two shifts, or not at all. If a machine is used during a day, a single setup cost is incurred whether it is used for one shift or for two shifts. The setup and operating costs are

Machine	Setup Cost	Operating Cost per Unit	Units Produced per Hour
1	$50	$1.20	4
2	62	1.05	5
3	25	1.15	3

The company operates eight hours on each shift. The daily requirement is 100 units. Formulate and solve a model to determine the number of units made on each machine.

CASE

Alcan (X)

Mr. J. Kade of the Industrial Engineering Department of the Aluminum Company of Canada, Limited was considering a request from the production control group in the Foil Mill for a reassessment of the current inventory policy. Space limitations required that a limited number of standard widths of aluminum foil be carried in stock from which customers' orders were slit. The production control group's request resulted from low turnover on some standard widths and large scrap losses when filling customers' orders of certain widths.

Background

As an integrated producer of aluminum products, Alcan mined bauxite ore in various countries and shipped the ore to several smelters where the aluminum was refined. Although the largest portion of its sales was in ingot form to other fabricators, the company was moving more and more into fabricating

SOURCE: C. Haehling von Lanzenauer and D. D. Wright, *Cases in Operations Research*, Oakland, Calif.: Holden-Day, Inc., 1975, pp. 17–21. Copyright © The University of Western Ontario. Reproduced with permission.

semifinished and finished products such as aluminum foil. The Foil Mill, part of the Kingston works, produced aluminum foil of different widths for a variety of different end uses. Of the output of the Foil Mill, 40 percent was classed as converter foil and used by other manufacturers, 30 percent was for household foil, while the final 30 percent, classed as rigid container foil, was used by subsidiary companies for containers.

Process

Customers ordered foil specifying the width, gauge, and surface finish required. A coil was selected from stock in the Foil Mill which was rolled to the desired thickness and finish. The coil was then sent to either a separator or a slitter, where it was slit to the desired width. The separator was used to slit and then separate coils which had been pack-rolled in two layers. This was done for thinner-guage orders to give sufficient strength to the foil for slitting. Both the separator and the slitter could be used for single-layer foil. It was possible to produce up to 8 usable widths on the separator and 12 on the slitter. However, the machines required that all the widths be equal.

Slitting Operation

A number of difficulties were encountered during the slitting operation. A minimum of ¼″ must be trimmed from each edge of the standard widths in order to guarantee clean edges. Another difficulty was the tendency of two adjacent widths to interlock as they were being coiled. To break them apart required the use of a special tool and a sledge hammer which damages the outer edges of the foil. To overcome this, the core on which the foil was wound extended ⅛″ on either side of the coil. This resulted in a ''centre cut'' of at least ¼″ between two widths. The edge trim and centre cut were fed into air hoses which blew the foil into scrap boxes. The maximum width the air hoses could handle was 1½″.

Furthermore, it was not possible to re-coil foil of less than 3½″ width. If a customer's order called for a width less than 3½″, a final slitting was done on a special-purpose slitter on which narrow widths can be coiled. This special slitter did not require a centre cut but still required the ¼″ edge trim.

The limitations of re-coiling to widths of 3½″ or more and blowing to widths of 1½″ or less restricted the slitting of customer order widths from some standard inventory widths. For example, there was no combination of edge trims that would allow a customer order of 35½″ width to be slit from a standard inventory width of 39″ in one pass. An edge trim of ¼″ taken on one side would leave a trim of 3¼″ on the other side, which was too wide for the air hoses and too narrow for re-coiling. The 3¼″ strip could not be slit into two strips and blown away as there would be insufficient tension on the outer strip for proper slitting. No more than one edge trim per side could be taken. The customer order width of 35½″ could therefore not be slit from a standard inventory width of 39″ unless more than one pass were made, which the Foil Mill foreman was reluctant to do. If the trim strip of the foil was between 1″ and 1½″, the machine operated at roughly one half of normal speed in order to allow the air hoses to remove the trim.

Selection of Standard Widths

Due to the two-week delay in receiving replenishment of stock from the Sheet Mill, the Foil Mill re-ordered a three-week supply of aluminum foil when the inventory was insufficient to satisfy demand during the next three weeks. The type of inventory carried was constrained by space limitations which restricted the number of different standard widths that could be held, and the Sheet Mill wanted the number of widths it produced kept to a minimum. In light of these restrictions, currently only seven standard widths were being carried in inventory. This was felt to provide sufficient stock widths to minimize scrap loss while keeping the number fairly low. Obviously, the selection of standard widths depended on the composition of the customers' orders and had to be reviewed periodically. In making this selection, three questions had to be answered.

1. How many standard widths should be carried in the Foil Mill?
2. Which standard widths should be carried in the Foil Mill?
3. Which standard width should be used in slitting a customer's order?

Scrap Loss

In order to answer the three questions regarding which widths to stock, it was necessary to determine the scrap loss which resulted when a standard width was slit into a customer order width. The customers could order any width from 1″ to 53″ in increments of ⅛″. Since some of the possible widths had never been ordered, only 175 different widths were considered. Standard widths were available in ¼″ increments up to 54″. However, it was not necessary to stock standard widths less than 26″ because orders for narrow widths can be slit in multiples from wider standard widths. Slitting multiple widths from wider standard widths resulted in less scrap than cutting a single width from a narrower standard width. There was a computer program available which calculated the amount of scrap which would result from slitting any customer's order from any stock width.

As a sample calculation for the scrap loss using projected sales of 24″ foil of 20,000 pounds, the scrap resulting from using 52″ standard width was:

$$\text{Scrap} = \frac{(52 - 2 \times 24)}{52} \times 20{,}000 \text{ lbs.} = 1{,}538 \text{ lbs.}$$

If the order was slit from 24½″ standard width, the resulting scrap was:

$$\text{Scrap} = \frac{(24\tfrac{1}{2} - 24)}{24\tfrac{1}{2}} \times 20{,}000 \text{ lbs.} = 408 \text{ lbs.}$$

Since 24″ foil cannot be slit from a 27½″ standard width in one pass because of too large an edge trim, the scrap resulting from this combination would be a large number.

The Montreal office supplied Mr. Kade with a six-month forecast of sales which he could use to aid him in deciding on the stock widths to be carried in inventory. Demand for household foil and converter foil was quite stable. However, requirements for rigid container foil did vary as it was sold to the packaging industry, whose specifications were continually modified. However, the forecasts supplied by the Montreal office had in the past been quite accurate.

EXHIBIT I Alcan (X) Scrap Loss Matrix

Customer	Standard Widths						
Widths	A	B	C	D	E	F	G
I	61	19	69	4	46	26	45
II	15	M	44	52	66	95	27
III	94	55	M	85	65	67	M
IV	42	48	11	62	13	M	M
V	23	M	M	58	M	M	M

Development of a Solution Procedure

Due to the rather large problem involving 175 customer order widths and 120 possible standard widths and the necessity to reevaluate the inventory policy periodically, an efficient procedure would be required to determine an appropriate inventory policy. Mr. Kade approached the Operations Research Group in the company's head office in Montreal and asked for advice in solving this problem. For the development of the procedure the Operations Research Group decided to work with a small sample problem. After consulting with Mr. Kade, it developed a sample with a scrap loss matrix as given in Exhibit I. The numbers in the body are the weights of scrap in pounds which will result from slitting the estimated customer orders of each width on the left from the standard widths shown in the column heading. M indicates that a customer width cannot be slit from a standard width in one pass or at all.

10

Decision Making for Probabilistic Decision Environments

HALLMARK CARDS, INC.

Hallmark Cards, Inc. produces and markets many paper products as well as greeting cards. Calendars, paper plates and cups, napkins, candles, party supplies, and scrapbooks are included in the company's product line. Many of these products are seasonal and have little value after the end of a season. Because of the time required to obtain some products, a single order is placed for them before a season begins. A product manager or inventory manager, knowing that demand is uncertain, determines the production run size or the purchase quantity.

Prior to 1982, product management made an estimate of sales and the order quantity was that estimated amount. For products similar to others that Hallmark had marketed in the past, demand estimates were based on historical sales. For products that had no historical analogues, a subjective judgment was used to estimate demand. In 1981, however, Hallmark experienced a large increase in the amount of unsold product. In response, it initiated a strategy to deal with the problem.

The problem was the failure to consider explicitly the impact of differences between demand and the forecast. If demand was less than the order quantity, the impact was apparent; units were unsold. If demand was greater than the order quantity, the impact was not apparent; potential profits from additional sales were missed. The apparent impact caused the problem to be studied, but missed opportunities were also considered.

A payoff matrix was the basis for the analysis. Each row was a specific run quantity; each column was a possible demand level. The economic consequence of a run quantity and demand level was easily calculated because the costs and revenues were known.

At training sessions, product managers and inventory managers were introduced to the concept of a payoff matrix. They were taught how to subjectively estimate probabilities for each possible demand level. For different order quantities, the expected profit was calculated. The best order quantity was the one with the largest expected profit. Initially, salvage values and shortage costs were assumed to be zero. Nonzero salvage values and shortage costs could only increase the best order quantity. The managers learned how to determine the sensitivity of the best order to salvage values and shortage costs.

An interactive computer program performs the expected profit calculations, selects the order quantity, and determines the salvage value and shortage cost amounts necessary to change the "best" decision.

This management science tool is not mathematically sophisticated, but product managers understood it easily and adopted it quickly, and its use improved their decision making. The important observation is that the order size selected is unlikely to equal actual demand. Considering the uncertainty of demand explicitly in the analysis leads to greater understanding of the decision environment and to better decisions.

In this chapter, we study approaches to decision making in probabilistic decision environments, subjective assessment of probability distribution, and attitudes toward risk.

F. H. Barron, "Payoff Matrices Pay Off at Hallmark," *Interfaces* 15, no. 4 (July–August 1985), pp. 20–25.

In Chapters 1 through 9, we focused on deterministic decision environments, decision environments in which there is little uncertainty concerning the outcome of a decision. Where uncertainty existed, we used sensitivity analysis on the model parameters to study the effects of small changes. In this chapter, we discuss various ways of "thinking" about probabilistic decision environments and we explore different approaches and criteria for choosing a decision alternative in a probabilistic decision environment.

What causes a decision environment to be treated as a probabilistic one? It is the need to consider the probabilities and/or the range of possible outcomes of decisions. It is not sufficient to consider how the environment responds to decisions based on the average characteristics of the inputs. For the Hallmark example, choosing an order quantity equal to the most likely demand forecast ignores the economic consequences if that forecast is wrong.

The uncertainty of probabilistic decision environments is such that you must consider the range of outcomes and their probabilities as you evaluate decision alternatives. Some good examples of probabilistic decision environments in which management science models have been well developed are:

1. *Demand for a product is very uncertain.* Consequently, the outcome of the decision to order a quantity of that product for resale is quite uncertain. Hallmark faces such an environment, and its failure to consider the consequences of differences between actual demand and forecast demand caused it to accumulate large inventories of unsold products. In Chapter 13, we discuss inventory planning.

2. *There is uncertainty about efforts to develop technological innovations.* Is it worthwhile to perform the necessary research and development knowing that this might result in the desired new technology or in nothing at all? The Strategic Defense Initiative (SDI) is a good example of a research and development effort that involves considerable uncertainty. Spending billions of dol-

lars for research and development on SDI might result in an effective defense system, or it might not. The uncertain outcome should be included in an analysis of SDI. You can use the methods of this chapter and Chapter 11 to analyze such investments.

3. *The operating characteristics of a computer network depend on the hardware components and on user requests for the services provided by those components.* Even though there is enough capacity to handle the average number of calls for service, it may not be possible to accommodate two service requests that are made at the same time. To analyze whether a request for service will be satisfied or whether it must wait because another request for service is being processed, we must consider the probability distribution for the time between successive requests for service. This allows us to study the operating characteristics of the computer network. When managers decide on acquiring new computer hardware, they must consider such factors as the operating characteristics. In Chapter 14, we discuss analyses of this kind.

The discussion of decision environments in Chapter 1 identified two potential causes of uncertainty regarding the outcome of decisions. The first cause was the *unpredictability of nature*. The second cause was the *actions of competitors*. The approaches to these two causes of uncertainty are different. *All sections of this chapter concern probabilistic decision environments in which the uncertainty of outcomes is caused by the unpredictability of nature.* As we discussed in Chapters 1 and 2, we can also approach the actions of competitors by treating them as if their uncertainty were caused by the unpredictability of nature. This is the most common approach used in evaluating such actions. In Chapter 11, we discuss modeling competitors' actions by this approach. The appendix of this chapter discusses game theory, another approach to incorporating the actions of competitors. In practice, game theory is not often used.

Unpredictability of nature

A PROBABILISTIC DECISION ENVIRONMENT EXAMPLE

The characteristic that makes a decision environment a probabilistic one is the uncertainty of the outcome of a decision. In this section, we assume that such uncertainty is caused by the unpredictability of nature and describe methods of organizing the information for probabilistic decision environments. We also describe two types of probabilistic decision problems—decision making under uncertainty (DMUU) and decision making under risk (DMUR).

Let's consider the new product introduction (NPI) example. We want to decide whether to introduce a new product, an under-the-cabinet toaster oven. The new product saves counter space, and many consumers like that feature. However, many people have toasters or toaster ovens that are placed on the kitchen counter. Thus, the new product is a discretionary one. If people have plenty of money, they will buy it. But if money is scarce, they can get along without doing so. The sales of the new product depend on the economy—strong if the economy is strong and weak if the economy is weak. The costs for developing the facility to produce the new product are estimated at $50,000. The variable manufacturing cost is estimated to be $11 per unit, and the planned selling price is $30 per unit. One of the questions at the end of the chapter asks you to verify that the profit for sales of 10,000 units is $140,000. If the economy is strong, we anticipate sales of 10,000 units. If the economy is weak, we anticipate sales of only 2,000 units, for a loss of $12,000.

As an alternative to the new product, we can sell a similar existing product whose development costs have been paid. Because of the similarity between the new product and the existing product, we plan to discontinue the existing product if the new one is introduced. If we keep the existing product, the profit on its sales depends on the state of the economy. If the economy is strong, we anticipate a profit of $35,000. If the economy is weak, we anticipate a profit of $25,000.

The two decision alternatives are

1. Introduce the new product and drop the existing product.
2. Keep the existing product and don't introduce the new product.

Profitability is affected by a large number of other decisions regarding the new product and the existing product, including pricing, subcontracting the development and manufacture, introducing the new product while keeping the existing product, and postponing the introduction of the new product. However, we will consider only two decision alternatives—introduce the new product or keep the existing product.

Payoff Tables

A payoff table shows the payoffs for all of the decision alternatives and all of the possible outcomes. Table 10.1 is a payoff table for the NPI example. It summarizes the outcomes based on the two decision alternatives and the two possible states of the economy. If the economy is strong, introducing the new product results in a higher profit than does keeping the existing product. If the economy is weak, keeping the existing products results in a higher profit than does introducing the new product. For different states of the economy, different decision alternatives are preferred. If it is possible to perfectly forecast the economy, then the decision that gives the greatest profit is easily determined. If it is not possible to perfectly forecast the economy, the decision problem is difficult.

The uncertain future events are called the **states of nature.** For the NPI example, the states of nature are the states of the economy. We assume that the states of nature are subject to the unpredictability of nature and not under the control of the decision maker.

Forming a payoff table helps you picture the decision problem. The steps are

Construct a payoff table

1. List the decision alternatives on the left.
2. List the possible states of nature across the top of the table.
3. Select a measure to compare different possible decision/state of nature combinations (e.g., profit or cost), and enter them in the payoff table.

Let's discuss the possible states of nature further. Two states of nature are **mutually exclusive** if it is not possible for both of them to occur at the same time. States of nature must be defined so that they are *mutually exclusive*. If the states of nature are defined so that one of them must occur, the states of nature are **collectively exhaustive.** You must define the states of nature so that they are mutually exclusive and collectively exhaustive. In the NPI example, the states of nature are mutually exclusive and collectively exhaustive. *Define the states of nature so that one of them and only one of them can occur.*

Defining the states of nature

For the example in Table 10.1, the payoff table values are dollars of profit. For another example, the payoff table values could be dollars of cost. These two economic criteria are the most commonly used measures, but the measure used could also be a noneconomic criterion. For a government farm agency, the measure might be the number of farmers helped.

Table 10.2 shows the general form of the payoff table with m decision alternatives and n states of nature. The return for Decision Alternative i and State of Nature j is denoted as $R(i,j)$. For example, Table 10.1's

TABLE 10.1 Payoff Table for New Product Introduction Example (Profit, $)

Number	Decision Alternative	State of Nature	
		Strong Economy	Weak Economy
1	Introduce new product	140,000	− 12,000
2	Keep existing product	35,000	25,000
	Maximum	140,000	25,000

TABLE 10.2   General Payoff Table

Decision Alternative	State of Nature					
	1	2	$\cdots$	j	$\cdots$	n
1	$R(1, 1)$	$R(1, 2)$	$\cdots$	$R(1, j)$	$\cdots$	$R(1, n)$
2	$R(2, 1)$	$R(2, 2)$	$\cdots$	$R(2, j)$	$\cdots$	$R(2, n)$
.	.	.		.		.
.	.	.		.		.
i	$R(i, 1)$	$R(i, 2)$	$\cdots$	$R(i, j)$	$\cdots$	$R(i, n)$
.	.	.		.		.
.	.	.		.		.
m	$R(m, 1)$	$R(m, 2)$	$\cdots$	$R(m, j)$	$\cdots$	$R(m, n)$

payoff value for Decision Alternative 1, (introduce the new product) and State of the Economy 2, (a weak economy) is $R(1,2) = -\$12,000$.

Dominated Decision Alternatives

In some circumstances, you can eliminate some decision alternatives from further consideration. For a *maximization objective,* Decision Alternative k is said to **dominate** Decision Alternative i if

Maximization objective

$$R(k,j) \geq R(i,j) \text{ for all } j \text{ and } R(k,j) > R(i,j) \text{ for at least one } j$$

That is, if the return for Decision Alternative k is $\geq$ the return for Decision Alternative i no matter what the state of nature and if it is better for at least one state of nature, Decision Alternative k dominates Decision Alternative i. Therefore, Decision Alternative i is eliminated from further consideration.

In Table 10.1, neither decision alternative is dominated. Let's consider changing the NPI example so that if the new product is introduced and the economy is weak, the number of units sold is 4,000, not 2,000. This gives a profit of $26,000. Table 10.3 shows the changed payoff table. In this

TABLE 10.3   Modified Payoff Table for New Product Introduction—Decision Alternative 2 Dominated (Profit, $)

Number	Decision Alternative	State of Nature	
		Strong Economy	Weak Economy
1	Introduce new product	140,000	26,000
2	Keep existing product	35,000	25,000
	Maximum	140,000	26,000

TABLE 10.4 Payoff Table with No Dominated Decision Alternative (Profit, $)

Decision Alternative	State of Nature	
	1	2
1	200	10
2	10	15
3	5	100
Maximum	200	100

case, Decision Alternative 1 dominates Decision Alternative 2 and Decision Alternative 2 is eliminated from further consideration. Because only Decision Alternative 1 remains, the best decision alternative is to introduce the new product. Regardless of the state of the economy, more profit is obtained by introducing the new product than by keeping the existing product.

We've stated that to eliminate a decision alternative from further consideration, it must be dominated by a single, particular decision alternative. Table 10.4 illustrates a situation in which *no* decision alternative is dominated. Decision Alternative 2 *appears* to be weak compared to the two other decision alternatives, but it is not dominated by either of them. First, let's compare Decision Alternatives 1 and 2. If the state of nature is 1, Decision Alternative 1 is preferred to 2; if the state of nature is 2, Decision Alternative 2 is preferred to 1. Now, let's compare Decision Alternatives 2 and 3. If the state of nature is 2, Decision Alternative 3 is preferred to 2; if the state of nature is 1, Decision Alternative 2 is preferred to 3. Although some decision alternative is preferred to Decision Alternative 2 for every possible state of nature, no single, particular decision alternative dominates Decision Alternative 2. Therefore, you can't eliminate Decision Alternative 2 from further consideration.

For a *minimization objective,* the definition of Decision Alternative k dominating Decision Alternative i is changed so that

$$R(k,j) \leq R(i,j) \text{ for all } j \text{ and } R(k,j) < R(i,j) \text{ for at least one } j$$

Eliminate a decision alternative if another dominates it

Minimization objective

Opportunity Loss Tables

The **opportunity loss,** sometimes called **regret** or **opportunity cost,** is the loss for selecting a particular decision alternative rather than the best decision alternative for the given state of nature. Let $OL(i,j)$ represent the opportunity loss for Decision i and State of Nature j. Using an **opportunity loss table,** sometimes called the **regret table** or the **opportunity cost table,** is an alternative to using a payoff table.

Let's consider the procedure for calculating opportunity losses for a general *maximization* objective. You calculate the entries in the column of the opportunity loss table for the state of nature *j* as

Calculating the opportunity losses

1. Determine the maximum value from among the decision alternatives, *given that state of nature.*
2. Determine the opportunity loss for a particular decision alternative by subtracting its payoff from that maximum value.

For a maximization objective, we symbolically represent the procedure for calculating the opportunity loss for Decision Alternative *i* and State of Nature *j* as

$$OL(i,j) = \max_k\{R(k,j)\} - R(i,j)$$

Now, let's calculate the opportunity losses using Table 10.1, the NPI example's payoff table. First, say that State of Nature 1 occurs. For a strong economy, the best decision is introducing the new product, giving a profit of $140,000. Say that you kept the existing product and the economy is strong. If you keep the existing product, Decision Alternative 2, the profit is only $35,000, rather than $140,000. The opportunity loss is the difference, $105,000. You *regret* that you could have improved the profit by $105,000 with a different decision. Symbolically, the opportunity loss for Decision Alternative 2 and State of Nature 1 is

$$OL(2,1) = 140,000 - 35,000 = \$105,000$$

Because Decision Alternative 1 is the best if the economy is strong, the opportunity loss for selecting it is

$$OL(1,1) = 140,000 - 140,000 = \$0$$

Now, let's calculate the opportunity losses for State of Nature 2, a weak economy. For a weak economy, the best decision alternative is to keep the existing product, which has a return of $25,000. The opportunity loss for Decision Alternative 2 is

$$OL(2,2) = 25,000 - 25,000 = \$0$$

The *OL* is 0 for the best decision for a state of nature

The opportunity loss is always 0 for the decision alternative that is best for the given state of nature. For a weak economy, the opportunity loss for Decision Alternative 1 (introduce the new product) is

$$OL(1,2) = 25,000 - (-12,000) = \$37,000$$

You create an opportunity loss table by listing the decision alternatives on the left and the states of nature across the top. Then, you enter the opportunity losses for all decision alternative/state of nature combinations. Table 10.5 is the opportunity loss table for the NPI example.

For a *minimization* objective, you prefer small payoff values. In Step 1 you find the smallest value in each column, and in Step 2 you calculate an

TABLE 10.5   Opportunity Loss Table for Table 10.1 (Opportunity loss, $)

		State of Nature	
Number	Decision Alternative	Strong Economy	Weak Economy
1	Introduce new product	0	37,000
2	Keep existing product	105,000	0

opportunity loss by subtracting that smallest value from the payoff. For a minimization objective, we symbolically represent the procedure for calculating the opportunity loss for Decision Alternative i and State of Nature j as

$$OL(i,j) = R(i,j) - \min_{k}\{R(k,j)\}$$

Two properties of opportunity loss tables

Let's make some observations about opportunity loss tables. First, there is a zero in every column for the best decision alternative for that column's state of nature. Second, all entries are *nonnegative* for both maximization and minimization objectives. Finally, when you consider opportunity losses, you want to minimize them regardless of whether the original objective was to be maximized or minimized.

Types of Probabilistic Decision Environments

Selecting between the two alternatives of the NPI example depends on your attitude toward risk and on your assessment of the likelihoods of occurrence of the states of nature. Some management scientists make a distinction based on whether the probability distribution of the states of nature can be estimated.

If the probability distribution of the states of nature can't be estimated, the decision problem is called **decision making under uncertainty** (DMUU). If the probability distribution of the states of nature can be estimated, the decision problem is called **decision making under risk** (DMUR). The next two sections discuss DMUU and DMUR.

Decision making under uncertainty

For DMUU, you are unable or unwilling to specify probabilities for the statues of nature. Management scientists disagree on whether you are ever unable to specify such probabilities. Many believe that you always know something about the probabilities and that you should use what you know, however little, to make subjective probability estimates. We tend to agree with this position, but we don't intend to take sides on the debate. We discuss both DMUU and DMUR.

You need probabilities for DMUR, so after we discuss DMUR, in the section Probabilities and Their Assessment we discuss how subjective probabilities can be elicited from a knowledgeable individual.

For DMUR, we prefer the expected value criterion or the expected opportunity loss criterion. A shortcoming of these criteria is managers' attitudes toward some outcomes. For example, the owner of a firm may dislike any decision with a possible outcome of bankruptcy, even though that decision has the best expected value. We can handle such attitudes by the methods of the section Risk and Utility, which concludes the chapter.

CRITERIA FOR DECISION MAKING UNDER UNCERTAINTY

In this section, we discuss the traditional criteria proposed for decision making under uncertainty. Remember, we don't know the probability distribution for the states of nature. The three criteria are *maximax, maximin,* and *minimax regret.* These criteria are seldom used for probabilistic decision environments. The most common approach is to treat the decision environment as decision making under risk.

The Maximax Criterion

One possible criterion for a *maximization* objective is the **maximax criterion,** which selects the decision alternative that provides the largest return among all the possible states of nature. For a maximization objective, apply the criterion as follows:

1. For each decision alternative, determine the state of nature with the maximum return.
2. Select the decision alternative that gives the *max*imum of those *max*imums.

Symbolically, the maximax criterion is

$$\max_i \{\max_j R(i,j)\}$$

For the NPI example, the maximum for the first decision alternative (introduce the new product) is \$140,000, which corresponds to a strong economy. The maximum for the second decision alternative (keep the existing product) is \$35,000, which also corresponds to a strong economy. The maximum of the two maximums, \$140,000 and \$35,000, is \$140,000. Decision Alternative 1 (introduce the new product) is the decision selected by the maximax criterion. Table 10.6 illustrates the application of the maximax criterion to the NPI example.

If you are an optimist, the maximax criterion is reasonable. If you select alternative 1, you assume that the best state of nature occurs for that decision alternative, and if you select decision alternative 2, you assume that the best state of nature occurs for that decision alternative. Then, you select the decision alternative resulting in the maximum of

TABLE 10.6 Maximax Criterion Applied to Table 10.1 (Profit, $)

		State of Nature		
Number	Decision Alternative	Strong Economy	Weak Economy	Maximum
1	Introduce new product	140,000	− 12,000	140,000 ←
2	Keeping existing product	35,000	25,000	35,000

these maximums. You must be optimistic to assume that the state of nature that gives the maximum payoff for the decision alternative you select is the one that will occur.

If the payoff objective is to be *minimized,* the criterion is **minimin.** You apply the minimin criterion as follows:

1. For each decision alternative, determine the state of nature with the minimum cost.
2. Select the decision alternative that gives the *min*imum of those *min*imums.

Symbolically, the minimin criterion is

The minimin criterion

$$\min_{i}\{\min_{j} R(i,j)\}$$

Let's apply the minimin criterion to the cost illustrated in Table 10.7. The minimum cost for the first decision alternative is the minimum of $100, $40, and $100, which is $40. Similarly, the minimums are $30 and $60 for the second and third decision alternative, respectively. The minimum of the minimums ($40, $30, and $60) is $30. Decision Alternative 2, which corresponds to this value, is the decision selected by the minimin criterion. Minimin is also the optimist's criterion. If you select Decision Alternative *i,* you assume that the state of nature that gives the minimum cost for that decision alternative is the one that will occur.

Shortcomings of maximax

A shortcoming of the maximax (or minimin) criterion is that it ignores the likelihood of the occurrence of the various states of nature and

TABLE 10.7 Example Cost Payoff Table—Minimin Criterion (Cost, $)

Decision Alternative	State of Nature			Minimum
	1	2	3	
1	100	40	100	40
2	30	110	110	30 ←
3	60	75	120	60

TABLE 10.8   Troublesome Example for Maximax Criterion (Profit, $)

Decision Alternative	State of Nature			Maximum
	1	2	3	
1	1,000	−1,000	−1,000	1,000 ←
2	999	999	999	999

assumes the occurrence of the state of nature most favorable for the decision alternative selected. It also ignores the returns if the state of nature that occurs isn't the one with the maximum profit (minimum cost). Consider the profit payoff table in Table 10.8. By the maximax criterion, Decision Alternative 1 is selected even though it is a better decision alternative only if the first state of nature occurs. In that case, the profit of Decision Alternative 1 ($1,000) is only slightly larger than that of Decision Alternative 2 ($999). However, for the second and third states of nature, the profit of Decision Alternative 1 (−$1,000) is much smaller than that of Decision Alternative 2 ($999). Although Decision Alternative 1 is the maximax decision, very few decision makers would select it. If the first state of nature is certain to occur, selecting Decision Alternative 1 is reasonable. But if the second or third state of nature is likely to occur, only an optimist would select Decision Alternative 1. For this reason, the example is called troublesome for the maximax criterion and should cause one to be skeptical about the maximax (or minimin) criterion.

The Maximin Criterion

Another possible criterion for a maximization objective is the **maximin criterion.** This is the criterion of the pessimist. For a *maximization* objective, you apply the maximin criterion as follows:

1. For each decision alternative, determine the minimum profit.
2. Select the decision alternative that gives the *max*imum of those *min*imums.

Symbolically, the maximin criterion is

$$\max_i \{\min_j R(i,j)\}$$

In the first step of the maximin criterion, you assume that everything goes wrong and that the state of nature that occurs gives the minimum profit for the decision alternative selected. In the second step, you select the decision alternative that maximizes those minimum profits. This criterion is for the "faint of heart" or the pessimist.

Table 10.9 illustrates the application of the maximin criterion to Table

TABLE 10.9 Maximin Criterion Applied to Table 10.1 (Profit, $)

		State of Nature		
Number	Decision Alternative	Strong Economy	Weak Economy	Minimum
1	Introduce new product	140,000	− 12,000	− 12,000
2	Keep existing product	35,000	25,000	25,000 ←

10.1. For Decision Alternative 1, the minimum profit is −$12,000. For Decision Alternative 2, the minimum profit is $25,000. The maximum of the two minimums, −$12,000 and $25,000, is $25,000. Because Decision Alternative 2 corresponds to that maximum, it is selected by the maximin criterion.

For a *minimization* objective, the criterion is called the **minimax criterion.** Symbolically, the minimax criterion is

The minimax criterion

$$\min_i\{\max_j\ R(i,j)\}$$

Can you apply the minimax criterion to the costs in Table 10.7? The pessimist assumes that the state of nature that occurs gives the maximum cost for the decision alternative selected. For Decision Alternative 1, the maximum cost is $100. For Decision Alternatives 2 and 3, the maximum costs are $110 and $120, respectively. Because Decision Alternative 1 gives the smallest maximum cost, $100, you select that alternative. Table 10.10 shows the application of the minimax criterion to Table 10.7.

The maximin (or minimax) criterion shares shortcomings with the maximax criterion. A shortcoming of the maximin criterion is that it ignores the likelihood of the occurrence of the various states of nature and assumes the occurrence of the state of nature least favorable for the decision alternative selected. It also ignores the returns if the state of nature that occurs isn't the one with the minimum profit (maximum cost). Consider the profit payoff table shown in Table 10.11. The minimum profit for Decision Alternative 1 is $4. The minimum profit for Decision

Shortcomings of maximin

TABLE 10.10 Example Cost Payoff Table—Minimax Criterion (Cost, $)

Decision Alternative	State of Nature			Maximum
	1	2	3	
1	100	40	100	100 ←
2	30	110	110	110
3	60	75	120	120

TABLE 10.11   Troublesome Example for Maximin Criterion (Profit, $)

Decision Alternative	State of Nature			Minimum
	1	2	3	
1	1,000	1,000	4	4
2	5	5	5	5 ←

Alternative 2 is $5. By the maximin criterion, Decision Alternative 2 is selected because it gives the largest minimum profit, $5. But Decision Alternative 2 is preferred to Decision Alternative 1 only if the third state of nature occurs. In that case, the profit of Decision Alternative 2 ($5) is only slightly greater than that of Decision Alternative 1 ($4). However, for the first two states of nature, the profit of Decision Alternative 2 ($5) is much less than that of Decision Alternative 1 ($1,000). Although Decision Alternative 2 is the maximin decision, few decision makers would select it. If the third state of nature is certain to occur, selecting Decision Alternative 2 is reasonable. But if the first or second state of nature is likely to occur, only a pessimist would select Decision Alternative 2. For this reason, the example is called troublesome for the maximin criterion and should cause one to be skeptical about the maximin (or minimax) criterion.

A troublesome maximin example

The Minimax Regret Criterion

The optimist's criterion is *maximax* for maximization objectives and *minimin* for minimization objectives. The pessimist's criterion is *maximin* for maximization objectives and *minimax* for minimization objectives. We applied these criteria to the payoff tables. Let's consider using regret tables rather than payoff tables. Recall that regret, opportunity loss, and opportunity cost are the same. For regret tables, the objective is always minimization.

Another possible criterion for decision making under uncertainty is **minimax regret.** Table 10.12 illustrates the application of the minimax

TABLE 10.12   Minimax Regret Criterion Applied to Table 10.5 (Opportunity loss, $)

Number	Decision Alternative	State of Nature		Maximum
		Strong Economy	Weak Economy	
1	Introduce new product	0	37,000	37,000 ←
2	Keep existing product	105,000	0	105,000

regret criterion to Table 10.5, the opportunity loss table of the NPI example. For the first decision alternative (introduce the new product), the maximum regret (opportunity loss) is $37,000. For the second decision alternative (keep the existing product), the maximum regret is $105,000. The minimum of the maximum regrets is $37,000. Using the minimax regret criterion, you select the first decision alternative (introduce the new product).

Let's expand on the reason for using the term *regret*. If the state of nature is a strong economy and the decision maker chooses to keep the existing product, the decision maker regrets the fact that with a different decision he could have obtained an additional $105,000. If the state of nature is a weak economy and the decision maker introduces the new product, the regret is only $37,000. A pessimistic decision maker might assume that if a decision alternative is selected, the state of nature that occurs is the one that causes the maximum regret. Such a decision maker might select the decision alternative that gives the minimum of the maximum regret.

Because regret (or opportunity loss) is always minimized, *minimax regret* is the criterion used regardless of whether the original objective was profit maximization or cost minimization. Symbolically, the minimax regret criterion is

The minimax regret criterion

$$\min_i \{\max_j OL(i,j)\}$$

Maximin profit and minimax regret are not the same

Both maximin profits (or minimax costs) and minimax regret are for pessimistic decision makers. However, the decision alternatives selected by the maximin profit (or minimax cost) criterion and the minimax regret criterion *don't need to be the same*. Consider the cost payoff table shown in Table 10.7. Because the payoff is to be minimized, the minimax criterion, rather than the maximin criterion, is used. Decision Alternative 1 is selected under the minimax criterion. Table 10.13, which contains the opportunity loss table for Table 10.7's payoff table, and shows that applying the minimax regret criterion results in the selection of Decision Alternative 3. For this example, the decision alternative selected by the

TABLE 10.13 Minimax Regret Criterion Applied to Opportunity Losses of Table 10.7
(Opportunity loss, $)

Decision Alternative	State of Nature			Maximum
	1	2	3	
1	70	0	0	70
2	0	70	10	70
3	30	35	20	35 ←

minimax cost criterion differs from that selected by the minimax regret criterion.

The minimax regret criterion, like maximax and maximin, ignores the likelihood of the occurrence of the various states of nature and assumes the occurrence of the state of nature least favorable (with respect to regret) for the decision alternative selected. It also ignores the regret if the state of nature that occurs isn't the one with the maximum regret.

The Laplace or Equally Likely Criterion

A major obstacle to incorporating the probabilities of the various states of nature into the analysis is the difficulty of obtaining those probabilities. Without information on which to base estimates of the probabilities of the states of nature, you might assume that they are equally likely. The **Laplace criterion,** sometimes called the **equally likely criterion,** selects the decision alternative with the best average value. Assuming that the states of nature are equally likely causes each state of nature to have an equal weight in the average.

Let's apply the Laplace criterion to the NPI example. For Decision Alternative 1 (introduce the new product), the average profit is [140,000 + (−12,000)]/2 = $64,000. The average profit for Decision Alternative 2 is (35,000 + 25,000)/2 = $30,000. Because it has a larger average profit, Decision Alternative 1 is selected by the Laplace criterion. Table 10.14 shows the application of the Laplace criterion to Table 10.1, the NPI example.

The Laplace criterion considers the consequences of each state of nature for the decision alternative selected. This is a property that maximax, maximin, and minimax regret don't have.

However, is it reasonable to assume that the states of nature are equally likely? Even if you don't possess information on which to estimate their exact probabilities, it's unlikely that you believe them to be equally likely. You may not be able to give the exact probability of the Chicago Cubs appearing in the next World Series, but do you think it equally likely that they will or will not appear? It is likely that you have some idea of the likelihood of their appearing.

TABLE 10.14   Laplace Criterion Applied to New Product Introduction Example (Profit, $)

Number	Decision Alternative	State of Nature		Average
		Strong Economy	Weak Economy	
1	Introduce new product	140,000	−12,000	64,000 ←
2	Keep existing product	35,000	25,000	30,000

We prefer to use criteria that consider the likelihoods and consequences of all states of nature. In the next section, we consider probabilistic decision environments with probabilities for the states of nature. In the section after that, we discuss assessing "subjective" probabilities.

CRITERIA FOR DECISION MAKING UNDER RISK

If you know or can estimate the probabilities of the states of nature, the problem is decision making under risk (DMUR). We describe three criteria for DMUR—the most likely criterion, the expected value criterion, and the expected opportunity loss criterion. The second and third criteria always give the same decision.

The Most Likely Criterion

You may be willing to identify the most likely state of nature even if you won't give the probabilities. The **most likely criterion** selects the decision alternative that has the most favorable payoff for the *most likely* state of nature. For a maximization objective, you select the decision alternative with the largest payoff for the most likely state of nature. For a minimization objective, you select the decision alternative with the smallest payoff for the most likely state of nature.

For the NPI example, say that a strong economy is more likely than a weak economy. Using the most likely criterion, you select Decision Alternative 1 because it gives a profit of \$140,000, whereas Decision Alternative 2 gives only \$35,000. Table 10.15 shows the application of the most likely criterion to Table 10.1.

Let's consider the Hallmark decision problem. The decision is the order quantity, and the state of nature is actual sales. Before payoff tables

---

TABLE 10.15 Most Likely Criterion Applied to New Product Introduction Example (Profit, \$)

Number	Decision Alternative	State of Nature	
		Strong Economy	Weak Economy
1	Introduce new product	140,000	− 12,000
2	Keep existing product	35,000	25,000
		↑ Most likely state of nature	

were introduced at Hallmark, the order quantity equaled the forecast of demand. The forecast of demand is the most likely state of nature, and an order quantity equal to it gives the largest profit *if the forecast is correct.* However, when actual demand is less than the forecast, there is unsold inventory. Using the most likely state of nature seems better than ignoring the probabilities, but this approach has a serious shortcoming. The most likely criterion doesn't consider the payoffs for any state of nature *except* the most likely.

Although the most likely criterion considers likelihoods, it doesn't consider the relative returns or the likelihoods of any state of nature except the most likely. For DMUR, we prefer the next two criteria. Both the expected value criterion and the expected opportunity loss criterion consider the probabilities and payoffs for *all* states of nature.

Shortcomings of the most likely criterion

The Expected Value Criterion

Most decision makers use the expected value criterion for DMUR. Using this criterion, the **expected value** of a decision is calculated by weighting the payoff for each state of nature by the probability of that state of nature. Denote the probability of State of Nature j by $P(j)$ and the expected value of Decision Alternative i by $E(i)$. Symbolically, the expected value of Decision Alternative i is calculated as

$$E(i) = \sum_{i=1}^{n} P(j)R(i,j)$$

The expected value criterion selects the decision alternative with the best (largest or smallest) expected value. Because the payoff is often economic, the expected value of a decision alternative is sometimes called its **expected monetary value** and the expected value criterion is sometimes called the **expected monetary value criterion.**

The expected value criterion

Let's apply the expected value criterion to the NPI example with the payoffs given in Table 10.1. Suppose that the probability of a strong economy is 0.4 and the probability of a weak economy is 0.6. For the first decision alternative, (introduce the new product), the expected profit is

$$E(1) = [0.4 \times 140,000] + [0.6 \times (-12,000)] = \$48,800$$

The expected profit for the second decision alternative (keep the existing product) is

$$E(2) = [0.4 \times 35,000] + [0.6 \times 25,000] = \$29,000$$

Because you want the maximum profit, you select the decision alternative with the largest expected profit. The maximum of \$48,800 and \$29,000 is \$48,800. Alternative 1 (introduce the new product) is selected. Table 10.16 shows the application of the expected value criterion to Table 10.1.

TABLE 10.16 Expected Value Criterion Applied to New Product Introduction Example (Profit, $)

Number	Decision Alternative	State of Nature		Expected Value, E(i)
		Strong Economy (probability 0.4)	Weak Economy (probability 0.6)	
1	Introduce new product	140,000	−12,000	48,800 ←
2	Keep existing product	35,000	25,000	29,000

Use the model to study the decision problem

Sensitivity analysis on the probabilities

Model manipulation and sensitivity analysis. Although Alternative 1 has the largest expected profit, you don't automatically select "introduce the new product" as the decision alternative. *Regardless of the decision criterion, developing the model of the decision problem is the beginning of the decision process, not the end.* Model manipulation, other qualitative factors, and sensitivity analysis must still be considered.

The payoff table is a representation of the decision environment. Profit may be the most important consideration, but there are likely to be others. If this is the only product produced, what is the impact of producing it on the number of employees? Also, what is the duration of the time period for which the sales numbers have been estimated? Recall that if the new product is introduced and the economy is strong, sales of 10,000 units with a profit of $140,000 are anticipated. Are the 10,000 units for the first year of the new product? If so, the payoff values show the first-year profit. Although the time horizon for the payoff table is one year, the lifetime of the product may be longer. There may be uncertainty about the duration of that lifetime. If that is important, the decision maker/model builder explicitly incorporates the lifetime of the new product into the analysis. On the other hand, if the 10,000 units are for the lifetime of the product, the time horizon is the life of the product and the payoff values show the profit during the lifetime of the product. Even in this case, there is uncertainty about the total sales and the length of the product life. If the uncertainty is significant, it is incorporated into the analysis.

We had to estimate parameters to create the payoff table. We also had to estimate the probabilities of the states of nature. These estimates could be wrong, so you should perform sensitivity analysis on them to determine how the "best" decision alternative changes. Let's focus on the probabilities of the states of nature. The probability of a weak economy was 0.6. Examining the payoff table shows that if a weak economy is certain, the best decision is to keep the existing product. At what probability of a weak economy does the best decision change from introducing the new product to keeping the existing product? If you are uncertain about the probabilities, this is useful information. Let *P* be the probability at which the decision maker is indifferent between the two decision alternatives. You are indifferent if the expected values of the two decision alternatives are equal. Find *P* such that

$$[(1 - P) \times 140{,}000] + [P \times (-12{,}000)]$$
$$= [(1 - P) \times 35{,}000] + [P \times 25{,}000]$$

The LHS of the equation is the expected profit of Decision Alternative 1 (introduce the new product), and the RHS is the expected profit of Decision Alternative 2. Solving the equation gives *P* = 105,000/142,000 = 0.7394. Figure 10.1 shows the expected profit of the two alternatives for different values of *P*.

If the probability of a weak economy is more than 0.7394, keeping the existing product has the largest expected profit. If the probability of a weak economy is less than 0.7394, introducing the new product has the largest expected profit. If the probability is exactly 105,000/142,000 = 0.7394, both decision alternatives have the same expected value. Even if you are not confident that the probability of a weak economy is 0.6, knowing that the decision doesn't change unless the probability of a weak economy is more than 0.7394 is useful information. You may be more confident that the probability is less than 0.7394, and thus you can select "introduce the new product" with greater confidence.

FIGURE 10.1   Expected Profit of NPI Example Decision Alternatives for Probabilities of a Weak Economy

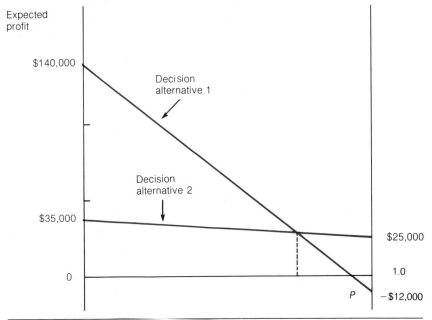

Sensitivity to payoff
table changes

Let's consider the sensitivity to changes in the payoff table values. Because we are introducing a new product, there is uncertainty about the number of units sold. There is less uncertainty about sales of an existing product. Consider performing sensitivity analysis on the number of units sold for the new product and a strong economy. Suppose that is 9,000 units. You change the payoff value for $R(1, 1)$ to $(30 - 11) \times 9,000 - 50,000 = \$121,000$. You calculate the revised expected profit for Decision Alternative 1. Decision Alternative 1 still has the largest expected profit and is selected using the expected value criterion. However, if the sales are small enough, the best decision changes to keeping the existing product. At what sales value are you indifferent between the two decisions? We leave this to the questions at the end of the chapter.

Don't overlook the possibility of manipulating the decision environment. If the best decision is sensitive to certain parameters, can you obtain more precise information about those parameters before you make the decision? Does test-marketing the new product provide useful information? We discuss the value of additional information in Chapter 11. Also, what is the impact of keeping the existing product and delaying the new product's introduction? Can you both introduce the new product and keep the existing product? Are there competitive aspects that are important in introducing the new product? These are important issues to consider.

Again, we stress that developing the model of the decision problem is the beginning of the decision process, not the end. Model manipulation, other qualitative factors, and sensitivity analysis are critical to effective use of probabilistic decision models.

Attitudes toward risk

Another factor to be considered is the decision maker's attitude towards risk. For some managers, a chance of bankruptcy is enough to eliminate a decision alternative even if the expected value is positive. Ignoring a manager's risk attitude, the expected value criterion does the best "on the average." The expected value criterion includes probabilities in the analysis, but it does not include attitudes toward risk. *If the decision maker is indifferent toward risk, the expected value criterion should be used.* Later in this chapter, we clarify the concept of risk and indifference toward risk. We also show how to include risk attitude in the analysis.

The Expected Opportunity Loss Criterion

Remember, the opportunity loss of Decision Alternative i and State of Nature j is denoted by $OL(i,j)$. The **expected opportunity loss (EOL)** of Decision Alternative i is calculated as

$$EOL(i) = \sum_{j=1}^{n} P(j)OL(i,j)$$

The **expected opportunity loss criterion** selects the decision alternative with the smallest EOL. Let *EOL** represent the decision alternative with the smallest EOL. Then, *EOL** is attained by selecting *i* such that

$$EOL^* = \min_i \{EOL(i)\}$$

Let's apply the EOL criterion to the NPI example. Table 10.5 contains the opportunity loss table for the example. The EOL for Decision Alternative 1 is calculated as

$$EOL(1) = (0.4 \times 0) + (0.6 \times 37,000) = \$22,200$$

The EOL for Decision Alternative 2 is

$$EOL(2) = (0.4 \times 105,000) + (0.6 \times 0) = \$42,500$$

Expected value and
EOL criteria give the
same decision

The EOL criterion selects the decision alternative with the smallest EOL (introduce the new product). For this example, *EOL** is $22,200 and you choose Decision Alternative 1. Table 10.17 shows the application of expected opportunity loss criterion to Table 10.1.

The *same* decision alternative was selected by the expected value criterion. *The expected value criterion and the expected opportunity loss criterion give the same decision.* Thus, the two criteria can be used interchangeably.

Let's show the equivalence of the expected value and expected opportunity loss criteria for a maximization objective. The expected value of Decision Alternative *i* is

$$E(i) = \sum_{j=1}^{n} P(j)R(i,j)$$

The expected opportunity loss of decision alternative *i* is

$$EOL(i) = \sum_{j=1}^{n} P(j)\{\{\max_k R(k,j)\} - R(i,j)\}$$

$$= \left\{ \sum_{j=1}^{n} P(j)\{\max_k R(k,j)\} \right\} - \left\{ \sum_{j=1}^{n} P(j)R(i,j) \right\}$$

TABLE 10.17   Expected Opportunity Loss Applied to New Product Introduction Example (Profit, $)

		State of Nature		Expected
Number	Decision Alternative	Strong Economy (probability 0.4)	Weak Economy (probability 0.6)	Opportunity Loss, EOL(i)
1	Introduce new product	0	37,000	22,200 ←
2	Keep existing product	105,000	0	48,500

For $EOL(i)$, the first sum is a constant regardless of the decision alternative. The second sum is the negative of $E(i)$, so minimizing the expected opportunity loss is the same as maximizing the expected value. For a minimization objective, the equivalence of the expected value and expected opportunity loss criteria is similarly shown.

An advantage of the
EOL criterion

The EOL criterion minimizes the EOL regardless of whether the payoffs are to be maximized or minimized. This is one advantage that the EOL criterion has over the expected value (or expected monetary value) criterion. It is a minor advantage because you're unlikely to be confused by the possibility of the expected value being either maximized or minimized depending on the nature of the payoff values. A more useful advantage of EOL values is presented in Chapter 11. The value of $EOL*$ is the *expected value of perfect information*.

PROBABILITIES AND THEIR ASSESSMENT

In this section, we discuss assessing or estimating the probabilities of the states of nature. For DMUR, we need those probabilities. For Hallmark's decision problem, the states of nature are actual demand for the product. Thus, the probability distribution for the actual demand must be estimated.

A warning concerning subjective probabilities: Even if you can pick numbers for the probabilities, you may be way off. Empirical tests show that subjective probability estimates are usually incorrect. For example, you can calculate the probability of being dealt a straight in five-card stud poker, but only with difficulty. It's unlikely that your subjective estimate is correct. The methods we discuss provide an introduction to subjective probability assessment. See Spetzler and Von Holstein for a review of advanced methods.[1]

We repeat the postulates of mathematical probability here even though we assume that the reader is familiar with the elements of probability theory, standard probability distributions, expected value, and variance. The term **event** is sometimes used for a state of nature. Two events are **mutually exclusive** if it is not possible for both of them to occur at the same time. Events are **collectively exhaustive** if at least one of them must occur. You must define the states of nature so that they are mutually exclusive and collectively exhaustive. One and only one state of nature must occur.

---

[1] C. Spetzler and C. Von Holstein, "Probability Encoding in Decision Analysis," *Management Science* 22, no. 23 (November 1975), pp. 340–58.

Assume that there are n possible mutually exclusive events, and let E_j denote the jth event. Then, the basic postulates of probability theory are

(1) $P(E_j) \geq 0$ for $j = 1, \ldots ,n$

Probability postulates

(2) $\sum_{i=1}^{n} P(E_j) = 1$

(3) $P(E_j) + P(E_j') = 1$

where $P(E_j')$ is the probability of Event j not occurring. E_j' is called the **complement** of Event j. E_j and E_j' are mutually exclusive. Either Event E_j occurs or it doesn't; the sum of the probabilities is 1. Postulate (2) states that the events are collectively exhaustive.

Determining probabilities is simple in introductory probability and statistics texts. For example, determining the probability that two dice total 7 is easy. However, assessing probabilities is not as easy in managerial decision problems. How can you determine the probability distribution for the number of cars that arrive at a toll booth on a toll road in a five-minute period of time?

For simple probability problems, such as the dice example, you define the sample space so that all of the points in it are equally likely. You then count the points that have the characteristic desired, and the probability of the characteristic is the proportion of the points in the sample space that have it. With a pair of dice, there are 36 equally likely outcomes, corresponding to values 1 through 6 for each die. You count the number of times the total is 7, and you obtain the probability by dividing that number of times by 36. You use combinations and permutations to help you count the points in the sample space that have the desired characteristic.

For most managerial decision problems, the probability distribution of the states of nature cannot be determined by defining the sample space so that the points are equally likely and then using combinations and permutations to count them. For some managerial decision problems, however, it may be possible to *sample* the environment to estimate the probability distribution. Consider determining the probability distribution of the number of cars arriving at a toll booth in a five-minute interval. It is possible to sample several five-minute intervals and physically count the number of cars that arrive during each of those intervals. The numerical data obtained in this way is used to estimate the probability distribution.

However, perhaps the toll road is in the planning stage and one design consideration is the number of toll booths at a toll station. Knowing the rate at which vehicles arrive at that set of toll booths helps decide how many toll booths are appropriate. Sometimes few vehicles arrive in a five-minute interval, and sometimes a large number of vehicles arrive. Because the number of waiting vehicles at the toll booths is important, the uncertainty for the arrivals is a critical issue. But if the toll road has not been built, it is not possible to do sampling.

The probability distribution for vehicles arriving at a toll booth is important in the design of the toll booth configuration for a proposed toll road, but it cannot be estimated on the basis of historical or sample data. A **subjective probability distribution** represents the probability distribution that a person believes. In this section, we discuss determining subjective probability distributions. Different individuals have different subjective probability distributions. Because subjective probability distributions are "subjective," many people hesitate to use them explicitly. It doesn't seem right to obtain a probability distribution "out of the air." But whether explicitly or implicitly, good decision makers incorporate this uncertainty. Explicit specification makes it possible to test the consistency of the assessment and to conduct sensitivity analysis.

Subjective probability distributions must not ignore available objective data. All relevant information, objective data and "gut feelings," must be considered. Ask yourself the question "Will it rain tomorrow?" Two possible states of nature are rain and no rain. You can't determine this probability distribution on theoretical grounds, and you can't sample. However, more information can improve the quality of your assessment of the probability distribution. Relevant objective information includes historical records. Other relevant objective information includes the current weather pattern of the surrounding region, including the locations of high- and low-pressure areas. Knowing where rain is currently falling and in which direction storms are moving is also helpful. In forming the forecast, a weather forecaster uses all information that he perceives as relevant. But assessing the probability of rain is still subjective. Both objective and subjective information are considered for the assessment. Some people are more skillful than others in incorporating weather information into their subjective assessment of the probability of rain. Similarly, some managers are more skillful than others in their subjective assessment of the probability distribution of the states of nature.

You can assess a probability distribution by asking an expert the right questions. In the next two sections, we discuss assessing subjective probability distributions. In the next section, we discuss assessing **discrete** probabilities. If you can list the events, a probability distribution is discrete. For example, either it rains or it doesn't; that requires a discrete probability distribution. In a **continuous** probability distribution, the events are continuous. For example, if the weather forecast is the number of inches of rainfall, the events are continuous because any fraction of an inch is possible. The approaches we use for assessing discrete differ from those we use for assessing continuous probability distributions.

Assessing Discrete Subjective Probability Distributions

The training sessions at Hallmark used discrete probability distributions. The states of nature were product demand. For example, the states of nature might be 1,000, 1,100, 1,200, 1,300, 1,400, and 1,500 cases. The managers were asked to estimate the probabilities of each state of nature. In this section, we discuss how to obtain the probabilities for a discrete set of states of nature.

First, list all of the events that can occur. These events should be mutually exclusive and collectively exhaustive. Many people hesitate to specify the probabilities of each event but are willing to specify which event is the most likely. *Second,* ask which event is the most likely and assign that event a value of 1.0. *Third,* ask that a numerical score be estimated for the other events. Assign these values proportionally to the most likely event. If some event is one half as likely as the most likely event, its numerical score is 0.5. None of the numerical scores should be greater than 1.0, because 1.0 was assigned to the most likely event. Because the only events listed were those that could occur, no event has a numerical score of 0. Also, negative numerical scores are not possible. To calculate the probabilities of the events,

1. Calculate the total of the numerical scores. Denote the total by T.
2. Calculate the probability of each event by dividing the numerical score for that event by T.

By construction, the calculated probabilities satisfy the three postulates of probability theory. All of the probabilities are nonnegative. The sum of the probabilities of the mutually exclusive events is 1. For example, say that I think a strong economy is more likely than a weak economy. I assign a numerical value of 1.0 to the event of a strong economy. When asked, I assign a numerical score of 0.5 to the event of a weak economy. I assess this numerical score because I feel that a weak economy is only one half as likely as strong economy. The value of $T = 1.0 + 0.5 = 1.5$. The probability of a strong economy is $\frac{1.0}{1.5} = \frac{2}{3}$. The probability of a weak economy is $\frac{0.5}{1.5} = \frac{1}{3}$. Table 10.18 illustrates these calculations.

TABLE 10.18 Example of Discrete Probability Assessment

State of Nature	Numerical Score	Numerical Score/T
Strong economy	1.0	$\frac{1.0}{1.5} = \frac{2}{3}$
Weak economy	0.5	$\frac{0.5}{1.5} = \frac{1}{3}$
T	1.5	

Assessing Continuous Subjective Probability Distributions

The approach required for assessing continuous subjective probability distributions differs from the approach required for assessing discrete subjective probability distributions. In continuous distributions, there is not a finite list of possible events. Weight, distances, and time are continuous. For example, the weight of a supposedly 1-pound box of detergent could be 1.009874532 pounds or any other number, hopefully one close to 1.0.

We ask questions about specific points on the cumulative probability distribution. Remember, the **cumulative probability,** denoted $F(k)$, is the probability that the value is $\leq k$. For example, you might request five points for the values of 0.00, 0.25, 0.50, 0.75, and 1.00. First ask, "What is the lowest value possible for the weight of the box?" This is $F(0.00)$. Next ask, "What is the largest value possible for the weight of the box?" This is $F(1.00)$. Then, obtain a weight such that there is a 50–50 chance that the box weighs that amount or less. This is $F(0.50)$. Now, request a weight such that there is only one chance in four that the box weighs that amount or less. This is $F(0.25)$. Finally, obtain $F(0.75)$ by requesting a weight such that there are three chances in four that the box weighs that amount or less. Say that the weights for $F(0.00)$, $F(0.25)$, $F(0.50)$, $F(0.75)$, and $F(1.00)$ are 0.970, 0.998, 1.008, 1.018, and 1.046, respectively. Figure 10.2

FIGURE 10.2   Five Points of Continuous Cumulative Probability Function Assessed Subjectively

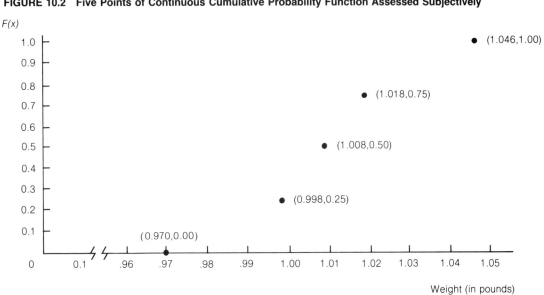

FIGURE 10.3 Curve Fit through Five Points Assessed Subjectively

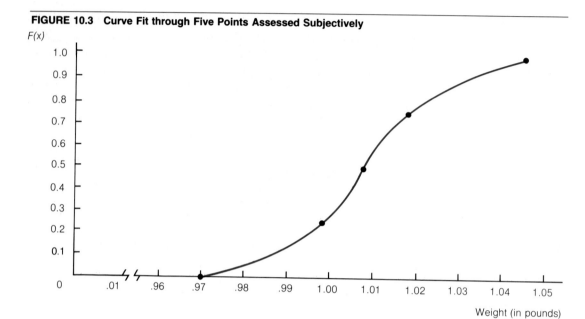

Fit a curve through
the points

illustrates these points on the cumulative probability distribution. Fitting a curve through these five points results in complete assessment of the probability distribution. Figure 10.3 illustrates such a curve.

Specifying more points gives a more precise curve. Unfortunately, many individuals hesitate to give many points for fear that doing this implies greater insight into the probability distribution. You can test for consistency with the curve by asking additional questions. For example, you might ask, "Do you believe that there is only 1 chance in 10 that the weight is 0.987 or less?" The value 0.987 is the weight for the cumulative

Test for consistency

probability of 0.1 from Figure 10.3. By asking such questions, you can obtain a more precise curve. You might also ask, "Do you believe that there is one chance in four that the weight is between 0.998 and 1.008?" The specification of $F(0.25)$ and $F(0.50)$ implied this probability for the interval 0.998 to 1.008. By asking such questions, you can check the individual assessing the probability distribution for consistency and you can develop more confidence in the curve representing the subjective probabilities.

If the continuous probability distribution is assumed to be the normal

The normal distribution

distribution, the questions can be simplified. The normal distribution has two parameters, the mean (μ) and the standard deviation (σ). The normal distribution is symmetric around the mean. There is the same probability that the value is more than the mean plus a constant as there is that the value is less than the mean minus the constant. The normal distribution has a single mode, which is also the mean. Ask for the most likely value, and let it be μ. Ask for a lower limit and an upper limit, symmetric around the most likely value, so that there is a 50–50 chance that the actual value lies in that range. The lower and upper limits must be equal amounts from the mean. For the soapbox example, say that the most likely value is 1.008, so $\mu = 1.008$. Say that the 50–50 lower limit is 0.998 and that the upper limit is 1.018. Those values are $F(0.25)$ and $F(0.75)$, respectively. The value of the standard normal variate that corresponds to a 50 percent confidence interval is $Z = 0.67$. Then,

$$\frac{(1.018 - 1.008)}{\sigma} = 0.67$$

Calculating σ

Solving yields $\sigma = 0.0149$. In general, the standard deviation is calculated as

$$\sigma = \frac{(\text{Upper limit} - \text{Most likely value})}{0.67}$$

By specifying only three points, the mean and standard deviation of a normal distribution is assessed. Figure 10.4 illustrates this normal distribution. Ask additional consistency questions to validate the cumulative probability distribution. For example, you might ask, "What is the probability that the weight is no more than 0.998?" The probability should be 0.25.

A warning

A word of warning: Empirical tests have shown that many individuals assess probability distributions that have too small a probability for unlikely events. (This indicates that many times people think they know more about uncertain outcomes than they do.) Sensitivity analysis should

---

FIGURE 10.4   Three-Point Assessment of Normal Distribution

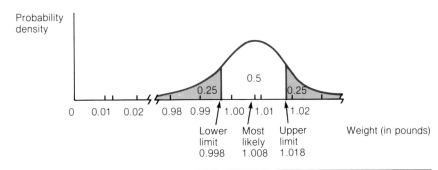

be done on the probabilities of unlikely events. The tendency of individuals to underestimate such probabilities motivated the choice of 50–50 for specifying the upper and lower limits of the normal distribution. This decreases the impact of underestimating unlikely events. If there is an underestimation of the probability of unlikely events, asking for the 99 percent interval reflects the bias in the calculated standard deviation.

It is convenient to use standard probability distributions for assessing subjective probabilities. For example, we just used the normal distribution for the soapbox weight. But if you use a standard probability distribution, focus on whether values are possible and on whether a particular standard probability distribution gives unreasonable probability assessments for impossible values. For example, the weight of a box of detergent can never be negative. A normal probability is symmetric and has a positive cumulative probability even when the weight value is negative.

Check the probability distribution for reasonableness

Strictly speaking, this is not correct. However, the normal probability distribution assessed may be a reasonable approximation. For the normal distribution assessed above, the mean, μ, and the standard deviation, σ, are 1.018 and 0.149, respectively. What is the probability that the normal random variable is less than 0? The value of Z corresponding to a weight of 0 is

$$Z = \frac{(0.000 - 1.008)}{0.0149} = -67.65$$

This probability is so small that it does not appear in tables of the normal distribution. In this case, the normal distribution gives a small probability for this impossibility of a negative weight. If the assessment was such that there was a large probability of a negative weight, it would not be reasonable.

Note the difference between Figure 10.3 and Figure 10.4 in the probabilities assessed for weights away from the mean. For example, consider the weight 0.970 pounds. For the normal assessment, the value of Z is $(0.970 - 1.008)/0.0149 = -2.55$, and the probability that the weight is less than 0.970 is 0.0054. For the assessment of Figure 10.3, the probability that the weight is less than 0.970 is 0.

Most people have an intuitive concept of probability. You can use the following discussion to obtain assessments from someone who is unfamiliar with the concept.

"Consider the possibility of either waiting to see whether the Chicago Cubs are in the World Series or drawing a piece of paper from a hat. You will receive the same prize whether the Chicago Cubs appear or the piece of paper has WIN written on it. If the hat contains 1 million pieces of paper, how many of them must have WIN printed on them so that you are indifferent between whether the prize is awarded based on the World Series appearance or on the drawing from the hat?" The estimate of the probability that the Chicago Cubs will appear in the next World Series is the proportion of pieces of paper with WIN on them.

RISK AND UTILITY

If you were offered your choice between a payment of $1 or an opportunity in a lottery to have 1 chance in 10,000 of winning $10,000 and 9,999 chances in 10,000 of winning nothing, which would you select? If you select the first choice, the return is certain to be $1. The expected return of the second choice is

$$\left(\frac{1}{10,000} \times 10,000\right) + \left(\frac{9,999}{10,000} \times 0\right) = \$1$$

Attitudes toward risk

The expected values of the two choices are both $1. However, because of different attitudes toward risk, some decision makers prefer the first choice, some prefer the second choice, and some are indifferent between the two. The individual who prefers the lottery is **risk seeking.** Although the choices have the same expected value, the risk-seeking individual prefers having a chance of a very large return. The individual who is **risk averse** prefers the first choice, which has less variability in the return (in fact, it has no variability at all in this case). Some individuals are indifferent between choices that have the same expected values. These individuals are **risk indifferent.**

Many states have introduced lotteries with large payoffs. People who play them know that the expected value of the lottery payoff is less than the price of a ticket. The choice is between keeping $1 and trading it for the lottery ticket with an expected value of less than $1. However, many people buy lottery tickets. They do that because the $1 is less valuable to them than the chance of winning a large prize, perhaps more than $1 million. Buying lottery tickets is not an irrational act from their point of view. Some people do not play the lottery. They have a different attitude toward risk.

For the lottery example, you obtain either $1, $1 million, or $0 depending on whether you play and on the lottery outcome. Attitudes toward risk differ based on the range of values of the returns and on the individual's wealth. Individuals with greater wealth are more likely to be interested in lottery tickets that cost more, whereas the risk-seeking individual in the $1 lottery example may be risk averse for extremely high ticket prices. For example, if you were offered a choice between $1 million for sure and a 1 in 100 chance of obtaining $100 million, which would you choose? The expected value for this lottery is also $1 million. Most individuals would select the certain return of $1 million. If the certain payoff were $750,000, would you prefer the same lottery? The answer to that question varies from individual to individual. Different individuals have different attitudes toward risk. However, lottery tickets costing $1 million are not likely to be popular.

The attitudes toward risk over the range of possible returns can be described by using a **utility function** or a **utility graph.** The utility function relates the individual's preference for different returns where the returns are measured in dollars. The utility function or its graphical representation varies from individual to individual. However, all individuals have a preference for large, certain monetary returns over low, certain monetary returns. Do you prefer to have $20,000 or $10,000? The utility function increases as the monetary return increases. The unit for measuring the utility for dollars is often called **utils.** Utils are an artificial unit, but they are a convenient device for expressing attitudes toward risk. The utility function helps explain an individual's selection from between two alternatives that have the same expected monetary value. For a maximization objective, the **expected utility criterion** selects the decision alternative with the largest expected utility.

Figure 10.5 illustrates the utility function for an individual who is risk averse over the range of monetary values illustrated. This individual prefers a certain return of $5,000 to a 50–50 chance of $10,000. We defined the utility for a return of $10,000 as 1.0 utils. We defined the utility for a return of $0 as 0.0 utils. The values of 0.0 and 1.0 are arbitrary, but the utility function should be increasing as the monetary return increases. The utility for larger monetary values is larger than the utility for small monetary values. As we explain at the end of this section, using end points with utility values of 0.0 and 1.0 helps in assessing the points on the utility curve.

In Figure 10.5, the utility of $5,000 is 0.7 utils. If this individual were offered a choice between a certain $5,000 and equal chances of $0 and $10,000, which would be chosen? You select the alternative with the largest expected utility. The expected utility for the certain return is 0.7

A risk-averse utility function

FIGURE 10.5   Utility Function—Risk Averse

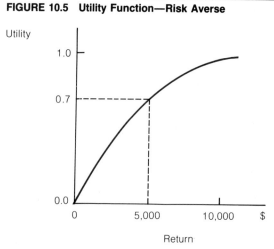

Return

utils. The expected utility for the uncertain return is $(0.5 \times 1.0) + (0.5 \times 0.0) = 0.5$ utils. The individual chooses the certain return, which is what a risk-averse individual does. In fact, the probability of obtaining the $10,000 return must be greater than 0.7 before the risk-averse individual prefers the uncertain alternative. At a probability of exactly 0.7, because the expected utilities of the two alternatives are equal, the individual is indifferent between the two. At the 0.7 probability, the expected monetary value of the uncertain return is $7,000, $2,000 more than the certain return. The individual is averse to risk.

The utility function
is linear for risk
indifference

Figure 10.6 is the utility function for a risk-indifferent individual. *The utility function is linear in the monetary return for a risk-indifferent individual.* If this individual had to choose from between the two previous choices, which would be chosen? The utility of the certain return is now 0.5 utils. The expected value of the utility of the second choice is also 0.5 utils. The risk-indifferent individual is indifferent between the two choices. Because the risk-indifferent individual has a linear utility function, the expected monetary values of the alternatives are proportional to the expected utilities as measured in utils. In this case, it is common to define the numerical values of the utils to be the same as that for dollars. That is, define the utility of $10,000 to be 10,000 utils. This makes the expected dollar values equal to the expected utility values, not just proportional to them. The expected value criterion should be used; the utilities are not considered.

Figure 10.7 illustrates the utility function for an individual who is risk seeking. This individual prefers a 50–50 chance of winning $10,000 to a certain $5,000. Because the expected utility of the certain outcome is only

FIGURE 10.6 Utility Function—Risk Indifferent

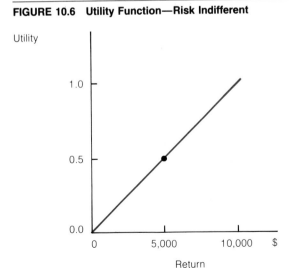

FIGURE 10.7   Utility Function—Risk Seeking

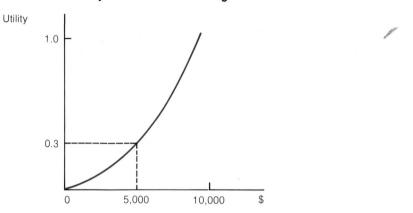

0.3 utils compared to 0.5 utils for the uncertain choice, this individual prefers the uncertain return. Even though the expected monetary value is $5,000 for both alternatives, the risk-seeking individual prefers the uncertain return. If the probability of receiving the $10,000 is greater than 0.3, this individual prefers the uncertain return. If the probability of receiving the $10,000 is less than 0.3, this individual prefers the certain return. If the probability of receiving the $10,000 is exactly 0.3, the expected utility of the two alternatives is the same, and the risk-seeking individual is indifferent between the two. But if the probability is 0.3, the expected monetary return for the uncertain return is $3,000, which is less than the certain $5,000. Indifference in this situation signifies risk-seeking behavior.

The preceding discussion illustrated how utility functions with different shapes can represent different attitudes toward risk. Figure 10.8 shows the three utility functions of Figures 10.5, 10.6, and 10.7. Now, it should be apparent what the relationship is between the shape of the utility function and attitude toward risk. The utility values at the end points of the monetary values were constructed to be identical. The numbers of utils is 0 for the monetary value of $0, and the number of utils is 1.0 for the monetary value of $10,000. The risk-indifferent individual has a linear utility function. The risk-averse individual has a utility function that lies above the linear function of the risk-indifferent individual. The risk-seeking individual has a utility function that lies below the linear function of the risk-indifferent individual. Risk-averse and risk-seeking individuals have utility functions above and below, respectively, the linear function of risk-indifferent individuals.

For DMUR, we use the expected utility criterion for individuals who are *not risk indifferent*. If the decision maker is risk indifferent, the expected monetary value (or the expected opportunity loss) criterion

---

FIGURE 10.8 Summary of Risk-Averse, Risk-Indifferent, and Risk-Seeking Utility Functions

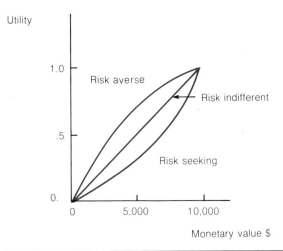

---

gives the same decision as the expected utility criterion, but it is easier to apply. Thus, we don't use utilities.

You construct the utility function by asking the right questions. Let's list the steps necessary to determine a utility function.

Constructing a utility function

1. Determine the smallest and largest monetary values to be considered.
2. Assign the smallest monetary value a utility of 0.0 utils.
3. Assign the largest monetary value a utility of 1.0 utils.
4. Determine the utility at any other dollar value, V, by asking the following question: "What would the probability have to be for you to be indifferent between a certain V and a lottery in which the return is either the largest dollar value, with probability P, or the smallest dollar value, with probability (1 − P)?"

Let's consider an example to show that the calculations are easier when the utilities at the ends of the ranges are 0.0 and 1.0. For example, say that the range is from $0 to $1 million and that you want the utility at $500,000. Define the utility at $0 to be 20 utils and the utility at $1 million to be 75 utils. These values have been arbitrarily selected, except that the utility of a larger monetary return must be greater. Then, if $P = 0.6$ is the probability for which the individual is indifferent, the utility of $500,000 is calculated as

$$U(500,000) = [P \times U(1,000,000)] + [(1 - P) \times U(0)]$$
$$= [0.6 \times 75] + [0.4 \times 20] = 53$$

Now, let's repeat the example with the utility assigned to 0.0 utils for $0 and to 1.0 for $1 million. For these end points, you calculate the utility at $500,000 as

$$U(500,000) = [P \times U(1,000,000)] + [(1 - P) \times U(0)]$$
$$= [0.6 \times 1.0] + [0.4 \times 0.0] = 0.6$$

The advantage of using 0 and 1 for the range end utilities

The utility is equal to the probability. For any monetary value, the utility equals the indifference probability. Assigning end point utilities of 0.0 and 1.0 eliminates arithmetic for calculating utilities. Note that Figures 10.5, 10.6, and 10.7 assigned utilities of 0.0 and 1.0 to the end points of the monetary values.

Figure 10.9 shows the three points on a partially constructed utility curve. We determine the utility for other dollar amounts similarly.

As an alternative to Step 4, you can ask a series of questions concerning specific probabilities. For example, you might ask, "If the probability of winning the lottery were 0.3, would you prefer the lottery or the certain payoff?" Then, you try different numbers to bracket P. See Farquhar for a state-of-the-art review of utility assessment methods.[2]

FIGURE 10.9   Three Points on Partially Constructed Utility Curve

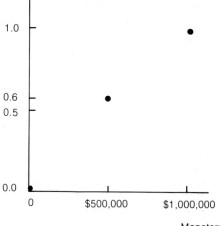

Monetary value, $

---

[2] P. Farquhar, "Utility Assessment Methods," *Management Science* 30, no. 11 (November 1984), pp. 1283–1300.

SUMMARY

In this chapter, we discussed approaches to decision making for probabilistic decision environments. The chapter focused on environments whose uncertainty comes from the unpredictability of nature. In the appendix to the chapter, we discuss game theory, which is one approach if the uncertainty comes from competitors' actions. In Chapter 11, we show how competitors' actions can be modeled as if the uncertainty came from the unpredictability of nature.

For uncertainty that comes from the unpredictability of nature, we described two decision problems. For decision making under uncertainty (DMUU), the probabilities can't be estimated. For decision making under risk (DMUR), the probabilities can be estimated.

We used payoff tables and opportunity loss tables to summarize the outcomes for all of the possible decision alternative/state of nature combinations. For DMUU, we discussed four criteria for selecting the decision alternative. The maximax profit (or minimin cost) criterion is for optimists. The maximin profit (or minimax cost) criterion and the minimax regret criterion are for pessimists. The Laplace criterion assumes that the states of nature are equally likely.

For DMUR, we discussed three criteria—the most likely criterion, the expected value criterion, and the expected opportunity loss (regret) criterion. The expected value and the expected opportunity loss criteria always give the same decision alternative.

The criteria for DMUU have limitations. First, except for the Laplace criterion, they all assume that the state of nature that occurs depends on the decision alternative selected. For the optimist's criterion, it's the best state of nature. For the pessimist's criteria, it's the worst state of nature. Second, except for the Laplace criterion, they all ignore the outcomes if the state of nature is not the one assumed. Third, they all ignore the likelihoods of the states of nature.

For DMUR, the most likely criterion ignores the outcomes if the state of nature is not the most likely. It also fails to consider the likelihoods of any state of nature except the most likely.

For DMUR, the expected value and the expected opportunity loss criteria consider the likelihoods and outcomes of all states of nature. However, the expected value and the expected opportunity loss criteria don't consider risk attitudes. We introduced the concept of utility and the expected utility criterion for decision makers who aren't risk indifferent. For risk-indifferent decision makers, we use either the expected value criterion or the expected opportunity loss criterion, both of which give the same decision. We discussed assessing subjective probability distributions so that probabilistic decision environments can be treated as DMUR.

The expected value criterion has many applications. After introducing payoff tables, Hallmark used the expected value criterion for its order quantity decisions. We used it in the new product introduction example. The expected value criterion is used for most probabilistic decision problems. We will use the expected value criterion in many applications in future chapters. For example, we use it for sequential decisions (Chapter 11) and inventory planning (Chapter 13).

Some cautions must be observed in probabilistic decision making. First, a probabilistic decision model is used to analyze the decision environment, not make the decision. Model manipulation, qualitative factors, and sensitivity analysis are important. Second, it's not easy to get managers to subjectively assess probabilities. Because of this, you should perform sensitivity analysis to determine how much the probabilities must change before the "best" decision alternative changes. Third, many managers hesitate to give their utility function. For this reason, a payoff table showing the possible outcomes for each decision aids managers in understanding the decision problem. You can eliminate a decision alternative from consideration if a possible outcome is unacceptable. Fourth, you can eliminate a decision alternative from consideration if it is dominated by a *single* decision alternative. You can't eliminate a decision alternative just because it is inferior to some decision alternative for every state of nature.

QUESTIONS

1. What is a state of nature?
2. What is a payoff table?
3. Construct a payoff table for a minimization objective in which Decision Alternative 1 dominates Decision Alternative 2.
4. Construct a payoff table for a maximization objective in which Decision Alternative 1 dominates Decision Alternative 2.
5. Verify that the profit is $140,000 for the new product introduction example if the new product is introduced and the state of the economy is strong.
6. Discuss why the maximin profit criterion is pessimistic.
7. How is an opportunity loss calculated for a minimization objective?
8. Discuss the statement "Decision making under uncertainty does not exist."
9. Is the minimax regret criterion for a pessimist or for an optimist?
10. Describe two mutually exclusive events.
11. What is the meaning of the statement "A set of events is collectively exhaustive"?
12. What is a subjective probability distribution?
13. Do the expected value criterion and the expected opportunity loss criterion always give the same decision alternative?

14. Sketch a risk-averse utility function between returns of $0 and $100,000. Label the axes.

15. Why aren't the 99 percent confidence limits used for assessing subjective normal probability distributions?

16. Under what circumstances should you use the minimax criterion rather than the maximin criterion?

17. Under what circumstances should you use the minimin criterion rather than the maximax criterion?

18. In the NPI example, you prefer to introduce the new product. Say that the problem is unchanged except for the sales level if the new product is introduced and the economy is strong. Find the sales level at which you are indifferent between keeping the existing product and introducing the new product. The probability of a strong economy remains 0.4, and the other payoffs are the same as in Table 10.1.

19. Show that the expected value and the expected opportunity loss criteria give the same decisions for a minimization objective.

For Questions 20–22, refer to the appendix at the end of this chapter.

20. *Game Theory.* What is the saddle point condition?

21. *Game Theory.* What is a mixed strategy?

22. *Game Theory.* Graph the expected wage increase versus $P(O)$ for the two company negotiating positions in the example. Find the value of $P(O)$ where the expected values are equal.

EXERCISES

1. Table 10.1, the payoff table for the new product introduction example, was based on anticipated sales of 2,000 units of the new product if the economy is weak. Say that the anticipated sales are 3,000 instead.
   a. Construct the payoff table.
   b. What decision alternative is selected using the maximax criterion?
   c. What decision alternative is selected using the maximin criterion?
   d. What decision alternative is selected using the Laplace criterion?
   e. Is either decision alternative dominated? What decision alternative would you select? Why?

2. Table 10.1, the payoff table for the new product introduction example, was based on anticipated sales of 2,000 units of the new product if the economy is weak. Say that the anticipated sales are 3,800 instead.
   a. Construct the payoff table.
   b. What decision alternative is selected using the maximax criterion?
   c. What decision alternative is selected using the maximin criterion?
   d. What decision alternative is selected using the Laplace criterion?
   e. Is either decision alternative dominated? What decision alternative would you select? Why?

3. Consider the following cost payoff table to be minimized:

Decision Alternative	State of Nature			
	1	2	3	4
1	$3,000	$4,200	$6,100	$1,300
2	600	950	850	1,200
3	1,500	2,300	700	1,400

   a. Are any of the decision alternatives dominated?
   b. Construct the opportunity loss table.
   c. What decision alternative is selected using the minimax regret criterion?

4. Consider the following cost payoff table to be minimized:

Decision Alternative	State of Nature			
	1	2	3	4
1	$ 300	$ 720	$310	$3,200
2	6,000	950	850	3,200
3	2,500	1,300	300	1,600

   a. Are any of the decision alternatives dominated?
   b. Construct the opportunity loss table.
   c. What decision alternative is selected using the minimax regret criterion?

5. For the cost payoff table of Exercise 3,
   a. What decision alternative is selected using the minimin criterion?
   b. What decision alternative is selected using the minimax criterion?
   c. What decision alternative is selected using the Laplace criterion?

6. For the cost payoff table of Exercise 4,
   a. What decision alternative is selected using the minimin criterion?
   b. What decision alternative is selected using the minimax criterion?
   c. What decision alternative is selected using the Laplace criterion?

7. You have solicited information to assess a subjective probability distribution from a manager about a competitor's introduction of a new product. She believes that only three outcomes are possible. She believes the most likely event is that no new product is introduced. She assigns a relative score of 0.5 to the introduction of a new product with only cosmetic improvements. To the third possibility, a radically new product, she assigns a relative score of 0.1. Give the probability of each event.

8. You have solicited information to assess a subjective probability distribution from a manager about a competitor's introduction of a new product. He believes that only three outcomes are possible. He believes the most likely event is that no new product is introduced. He assigns a relative score of 0.3 to the introduction of a new product with only cosmetic improvements. To

the third possibility, a radically new product, he assigns a relative score of 0.2. Give the probability of each event.

9. You are seeking the views of an economic forecaster concerning the growth rate of the gross national product next year. He believes that the growth rate is most likely to be 3.2 percent. When you asked him for his 50 percent confidence interval, he replied, "Between 2.1 percent and 4.3 percent."

   a. Assuming the normal probability distribution, what is the forecaster's estimate of the mean and the standard deviation?

   b. Based on your answer to Part *a,* what is the probability that the growth rate is positive?

10. You are seeking the views of an economic forecaster concerning the growth rate of the gross national product next year. She believes that the growth rate is most likely to be 4.1 percent. When you asked her for her 50 percent confidence interval, she replied, "Between 3.1 percent and 5.1 percent."

    a. Assuming the normal probability distribution, what is the forecaster's estimate of the mean and the standard deviation?

    b. Based on your answer to Part *a,* what is the probability that the growth rate is positive?

11. You are seeking the views of an economic forecaster concerning the growth rate of the gross national product next year. He believes that the growth rate is most likely to be 4.1 percent. When you asked him for his 50 percent confidence interval, he replied, "Between 1.5 percent and 5.1 percent." Is it appropriate to use the normal distribution for his subjective probability distribution? Why or why not?

12. You are seeking the views of an economic forecaster concerning the growth rate of the gross national product next year. She believes that the growth rate is most likely to be 2.4 percent. When you asked her for her 50 percent confidence interval, she replied, "Between 0.5 percent and 3.1 percent." Is it appropriate to use the normal distribution for her subjective probability distribution? Why or why not?

13. A manager has given you the following information concerning a possible price increase by a competitor.

Price Increase	Probability of That Increase or Less
$0	0.1
1	0.25
1.50	0.5
2	0.7
3	1.0

   a. Graph the points of the cumulative probability distribution.

   b. Draw a smooth line through those points.

   c. From your curve in Part *b,* estimate the probability that the price increase is $1.25 or less.

14. A manager has given you the following information concerning a possible price increase by a competitor.

Price Increase	Probability of That Increase or Less
$0	0.15
0.50	0.35
1	0.50
1.5	0.75
2	1.00

   a. Graph the points of the cumulative probability distribution.
   b. Draw a smooth line through those points.
   c. From your curve in Part b, estimate the probability that the price increase is $0.75 or less.

15. An expert in artificial intelligence told you that new software was likely to be available soon for an application you could use. You asked, "How soon?" and received an evasive response. Because this was important to you, you asked for the most likely number of years until it would be available and were told 1.5 years. The 50 percent confidence interval you were given was 0.5 years to 2.5 years.
   a. If you assume that a normal distribution is appropriate, what is the subjective estimate of the mean and the standard deviation?
   b. What is the probability that the software will be available in less than 0 years?
   c. Do you think that a normal distribution is appropriate? Why or why not?

16. An expert in artificial intelligence told you that new software was likely to be available soon for an application you could use. You asked, "How soon?" and received an evasive response. Because this was important to you, you asked for the most likely number of months until is would be available and were told 12 months. The 50 percent confidence interval you were given was 8 months to 16 months.
   a. If you assume that a normal distribution is appropriate, what is the subjective estimate of the mean and the standard deviation?
   b. What is the probability that the software will be available in less than 0 months?
   c. Do you think that a normal distribution is appropriate? Why or why not?

17. For the new product introduction example (Table 10.1), 0.4 was the probability assumed for a strong economy. Say that the probability of a strong economy is 0.7.
   a. Calculate the expected monetary value of the two decision alternatives. Which decision alternative should be selected?
   b. Calculate the expected opportunity loss of the two decision alternatives. Which decision alternative should be selected?
   c. Is the same decision alternative selected using the two criteria?

18. For the new product introduction example (Table 10.1), 0.4 was the probability assumed for a strong economy. Say that the probability of a strong economy is 0.8.
    a. Calculate the expected monetary value of the two decision alternatives. Which decision alternative should be selected?
    b. Calculate the expected opportunity loss of the two decision alternatives. Which decision alternative should be selected?
    c. Is the same decision alternative selected using the two criteria?
    d. Find the value of the probability that the economy is strong, P, such that the expected opportunity losses of the two decision alternatives are equal.

19. A person is indifferent between $3,000 for sure and equal chances of $0 and $5,000. Draw three points of the utility curve.

20. A person is indifferent between $15,000 for sure and equal chances of $0 and $50,000. Draw three points of the utility curve.

21. A utility function for a risk-seeking individual appears in Figure 10.7.
    a. Estimate the utility at $7,000.
    b. If that individual were offered a lottery with a 0.5 probability of receiving $7,000 and a 0.5 probability of receiving nothing, should he or she buy a ticket if it costs $5,000?

22. A utility function for a risk-averse individual appears in Figure 10.5.
    a. Estimate the utility at $7,000.
    b. If that individual were offered a lottery with a 0.5 probability of receiving $7,000 and a 0.5 probability of receiving nothing, should he or she buy a ticket if it costs $2,000?

For Exercises 23–26, refer to the appendix at the end of this chapter.

23. *Game Theory.* Consider the two-person zero-sum payoff table given below:

| | | Player 2 | |
Player 1	Action 1	Action 2	Action 3
Action 1	6	3	2
Action 2	6	1	7
Action 3	5	2	3

Player 1 desires small returns.
    a. Are any of Player 1's actions dominated?
    b. Are any of Player 2's actions dominated?
    c. Find Player 1's minimax strategy.
    d. Find Player 2's maximin strategy.
    e. Is the saddle point condition satisfied?
    f. What is the value of the game?

24. *Game Theory.* Consider the two-person zero-sum payoff table given below:

Player 1	Player 2 Action 1	Action 2	Action 3
Action 1	6	7	3
Action 2	4	2	1
Action 3	5	1	7

Player 1 desires small returns.
  a. Are any of Player 1's actions dominated?
  b. Are any of Player 2's actions dominated?
  c. Find Player 1's minimax strategy.
  d. Find Player 2's maximin strategy.
  e. Is the saddle point condition satisfied?
  f. What is the value of the game?

25. *Game Theory.* Consider the two-person zero-sum payoff table given below:

Player 1	Player 2 Action 1	Action 2
Action 1	7	4
Action 2	5	6

Player 1 desires small returns.
  a. Find Player 1's minimax strategy.
  b. Find Player 2's maximin strategy.
  c. Is the saddle point condition satisfied?
  d. What is Player 1's mixed strategy?
  e. What is Player 2's mixed strategy?
  f. What is the value of the game?

26. *Game Theory.* Consider the two-person zero-sum payoff table given below:

Player 1	Player 2 Action 1	Action 2
Action 1	6	−2
Action 2	0	7

Player 1 desires small returns.
  a. Find Player 1's minimax strategy.
  b. Find Player 2's maximin strategy.
  c. Is the saddle point condition satisfied?
  d. What is Player 1's mixed strategy?
  e. What is Player 2's mixed strategy?
  f. What is the value of the game?

MORE CHALLENGING EXERCISES

1. Because of recent increases in fire insurance premiums, a company owner is considering changing the deductible amount of his insurance on his office furnishings. His current policy has a $500 deductible, and the premium is $1,500 per year. If the deductible is increased to $4,000, the premium decreases to $900. The company owner believes that if there were a fire, all of the furnishings would have to be replaced, and the replacement cost is $50,000. Therefore, under the current policy he would pay $500 and the insurance company would pay $49,500. He believes that the probability of a fire during a year is 0.03.

   a. Construct a payoff table to evaluate the two insurance policies.
   b. Which policy has the most favorable expected cost?
   c. If the company owner were risk averse, might the preferred decision alternative change?

2. An investor is contemplating the investment of funds in an electric utility that is constructing a nuclear power plant. An application to allow start-up of the plant is pending with a regulatory agency. If the regulatory agency rules favorably, it is anticipated that the utility's stock will increase 13 percent next year (including dividends). If the regulatory agency rules unfavorably, the stock is anticipated to increase only 6 percent. Another alternative is to invest in a one-year, 8 percent certificate of deposit at a bank. The investor plans to hold the stock for one year.

   a. If the probability of a favorable ruling is 0.7, which alternative is preferred?
   b. For what probability of a favorable ruling is the investor indifferent between the two investments?

3. A farmer in Oklahoma was offered $50,000 for the mineral rights to his property. He made a counteroffer that allowed him to share in the return if oil were discovered. The counteroffer was a guarantee of $5,000 plus $0.50 per barrel of oil recovered. A geologist friend estimated that the recoverable oil might total as much as 1 million barrels. This friend provided the farmer with the following assessments of the probabilities of the amount of recoverable oil.

Success Level	Recoverable Oil, (barrels)	Probability
Dry	0	0.85
Moderate	200,000	0.10
Gusher	1,000,000	0.05

   a. Was the counteroffer wise from the farmer's point of view?
   b. Was the farmer risk seeking? Comment.
   c. If the royalty remained at $0.50 per barrel recovered, what should the guarantee be so that the farmer would be indifferent between the original offer and the counteroffer?

4. A company is contemplating a price increase of $1 a unit. Unfortunately, there is uncertainty concerning the effect of the price increase on sales. If the price is not increased, it is expected that the company's profit for the next fiscal year will be $100,000 on sales of 20,000 units. The profit margin at the current price is $5 per unit. The probability distribution of sales in the next fiscal year based on a $1 price increase is

Units Sold	Probability
12,000	0.1
14,000	0.2
16,000	0.25
18,000	0.4
20,000	0.05

a. Construct a payoff table to evaluate whether or not to increase the price by $1.
b. Should the price be increased? Why or why not?
c. Is a one-year time horizon appropriate for this decision environment? Discuss.

5. A company has experienced a rapid increase in sales. If the trend continues, the existing manufacturing capacity will not be enough to satisfy demand. The company is contemplating three alternatives if this occurs. The first is to raise the price to a level at which demand is equal to the existing capacity. The second is to subcontract the production for demand above the existing capacity. This cuts the profit margin on the units that the subcontractor produces. The third alternative is to expand the existing capacity. If this is done, the anticipated capital investment is $50,000 and the manufacturing costs increase for the additional units because employees must work overtime.

The current level of annual sales is 100,000 units, the current capacity is 110,000 units, and the current profit margin is $12 per unit. The probability distribution for next year's demand is

Next Year's Demand	Probability
110,000	0.50
115,000	0.35
120,000	0.15

It is predicted that demand will be reduced to the capacity of 110,000 by a price increase of $0.25 per unit if next year's demand is 115,000 and by a price increase of $0.45 per unit if next year's demand is 120,000. The extra subcontracting cost is $3.25 per unit. If capacity is expanded, the manufacturing cost of each unit above the current capacity increases by $1.75 because of overtime costs. If a decision is made to subcontract or expand capacity, a commitment must be made now, before the actual level of demand for next year is discovered. In the case of subcontracting, no commitment must be made to a level of subcontracting. That determination can be postponed until the actual level of demand is discovered.

   a. Construct a payoff table to evaluate the three alternatives.
   b. Which alternative should be selected by the expected value criterion?
   c. Which alternative should be selected by the expected opportunity loss criterion?
   d. Is a one-year time horizon appropriate for this decision environment? Discuss.

6. Farmer Jones has 100 acres of Iowa farmland. Because he's had trouble making ends meet, he's considering leasing his land to a neighbor so that he can take a job in the city. One neighbor has offered $150 per acre. Another neighbor has offered $50 plus one half of the profits. The planting and harvesting costs are $200 per acre. The profit depends on the weather and crop prices. A good profit year gives revenues of $450 per acre; a moderate profit year gives revenues of $300 per acre; and a poor profit year gives revenues of $250 per acre. Farmer Jones must decide whether to farm himself or to accept the offer of one of his neighbors. He estimates the probabilities of a good, moderate, and poor profit year as 0.2, 0.5, and 0.3, respectively. Which alternative gives the greatest expected return?

7. Jenny Smith, a hardworking college student, is considering the purchase of a snowplow attachment for her Jeep. The attachment costs $1,500. Because Jenny is a senior, she plans to plow snow only during the next winter. She estimates that she can sell the attachment for $750 after the winter. She has identified 15 residential customers who would use her service. She estimates her revenues as $200 per customer if there is a heavy-snow winter and as $100 per customer if there is a light-snow winter. Based on historical snowfalls, she believes that the probability of a heavy-snow winter is 0.6.

   Jenny has also bid on a contract for a local shopping center, but she won't know whether she gets the contract until after she's bought the snow-plow attachment. She estimates her chances at 50–50. Her bid gives her revenues of $1,000 during a heavy-snow winter and revenues of $600 during a light-snow winter.

   The operating costs are 40 percent of her revenues.

   Calculate Jenny's expected profit if she buys the snow-plow attachment. Do you recommend the purchase?

8. Jones Manufacturing purchases an electronic component that is part of its product. Usually, between 1 and 4 percent of the components are defective. Historical records show that the probabilities of these percentages are

Percent Defective	Probability
1	0.2
2	0.5
3	0.2
4	0.1

A batch of 1,000 components must be ordered. The cost of testing one component for a defect is $0.50. If a component isn't tested but is found defective after assembly, the rework cost is $20. Should Jones Manufacturing test the components before assembly?

9. Joe's Sporting Goods orders skis in August for the winter season. The skis cost $75 a pair and sell for $125 a pair. Any skis not sold during the winter are sold for $50 during the big spring sale. Joe's must buy in lots, each lot containing 30 pairs of skis. Ski demand depends on the winter weather. The estimates of ski demand are:

Pairs of Skis Demand	Probability
25	0.1
50	0.2
75	0.4
100	0.2
125	0.1

How many lots should Joe's Sporting Goods buy?

10. As director of research and development, you have received a recommendation for a project estimated to cost $75,000 from one of your project leaders. The purpose of the project is to develop a new class of chemical polymer. If the project is a major success, the future profits are estimated to be $500,000. The project leader thinks that there is a good chance of a minor success, which would result in profits of $150,000. She admits that there could be no success at all. The probabilities of a major success, a minor success, and failure are 0.1, 0.5, and 0.4, respectively. Would you fund the research project?

11. Frank Johnson has been given $10,000 by his grandmother for his first year's college expenses. He plans to start college in one year and wants to invest the money until then. The prime interest rate is currently 8 percent. Frank is considering investing in stocks, a money market account, or bonds. The value of his investment after one year depends on interest rate changes during the next year. He estimates the value of his potential investments after one year as follows:

	Interest Rate		
	7 Percent	8 Percent	9 Percent
Stocks	$11,200	$11,000	$10,500
Money market	10,750	10,800	10,850
Bonds	11,500	10,900	10,000

He also estimates that there is a 0.5 probability that interest rates will stay the same and that the probabilities of an increase and a decrease are 0.2 and 0.3, respectively.

a. What is Frank's best investment?

b. Discuss whether you think he is risk indifferent.

Hallmark Cards, Inc.

As a product manager, you're responsible for selecting the order quantity for a new Halloween party plate. Because the design changes every year, any unsold party plates have no value. You buy and sell the Halloween party plates in boxes. The selling price is $105 per box, and the manufacturing cost per box is $30. The design and setup costs are $20,000. Because you've been through the payoff table training sessions, your boss wants to see what you learned. Your subjective probabilities of selling 1,000, 1,100, 1,200, 1,300, and 1,400 boxes are 0.1, 0.2, 0.4, 0.2, and 0.1, respectively. Your boss wants a report that recommends an order quantity and discusses the number of unsold boxes. You must also discuss the possibility that the demand is greater than your order quantity. There is a possibility of selling leftover Halloween paper plates at the outlet store for $15 per box. Your report should discuss the impact of this possibility on your recommendation.

Top management has been considering a policy of evaluating product managers based on product line profits, including an extra charge for order quantities that are less than the actual demand. The extra charge is 50 percent of the lost profits. Your boss wants you to discuss how the proposed policy would affect your decision. You're free to comment on the wisdom of the policy.

Game Theory

Some decision environments have uncertainty that is caused by a competitor's actions. **Game theory** is the study of decision alternative selection in which the action of competitors is explicitly included in the analysis. You can use game theory in situations involving bidding and negotiation. If the labor negotiations of the hair dryer example of Chapter 2 had not included the additional complication of the possibility of the Ward's contract, game theory could have been used to analyze the company's bargaining approach.

Consider a company that has a labor contract under which an arbitrator specifies the percentage of the wage increase if the company and the union cannot agree on a contract. The company has outlined three possible negotiating positions—Tough, Neutral, and Flexible. The union's two negotiating positions are designated as Obstinate and Agreeable. Table 10.A1 contains the anticipated percentage wage increase for the six possible combinations of the company's three negotiating positions and the union's two negotiating positions.

If the company is Flexible and the union is Obstinate, the wage increase is anticipated to be 10 percent. If the company is Flexible and the union is Agreeable, the anticipated wage increase is 9 percent. A Flexible negotiating position on the part of the company gives a large wage increase to the union regardless of the union's negotiating position. If the company adopts a Neutral negotiating position and the union adopts an Obstinate position, the wage increase is expected to be 6 percent. However, if the company adopts a Neutral position and the union adopts an Agreeeable position, the wage increase is smaller—5 percent. If the company adopts a Tough position and the union adopts an Obstinate position, the wage increase is 5 percent. But if the company adopts a

TABLE 10.A1 Payoff Table for Game Theory Example (Percentage wage increase)

Company	Union	
	Obstinate	Agreeable
Tough	5	4
Neutral	6	5
Flexible	10	9

Tough position and the union adopts an Agreeable position, the wage increase is only 4 percent.

Assume that both the company and the union possess the information contained in Table 10.A1. This is an example of a **zero-sum two-person game.** The two persons are the two competitors, the union and the company. The zero sum shows that a gain to one competitor comes from the other competitor. If the company gives a 5 percent increase, the union gets the same 5 percent. In a pricing decision, the total size of the market is affected by the prices of the competitors, so the sum is not zero. If two companies both set high prices, the total return to the two companies is different from that obtained if they both set low prices.

The union strives for a policy that gives a large wage increase. The company prefers a small wage increase.

Eliminate dominated decision alternatives

We discussed the concept of a dominated decision alternative for probabilistic decision problems in which the uncertainty was caused by the unpredictability of nature. A *dominated decision alternative* can also exist if the uncertainty is caused by a thinking opponent. From the union's viewpiont, regardless of the negotiating position of the company, its wage increase is smaller if it adopts the Agreeable position. In fact, no matter what the negotiating position of the company, its wage increase is always 1 percent less for the Agreeable position than for the Obstinate position. The union would never adopt the Agreeable position. The Agreeable position is dominated by the Obstinate position. From the company's viewpoint, the Flexible position is dominated by the Neutral position. If the company adopts the Flexible position, the resulting wage increase, regardless of the union's position, is larger than that which results if the company adopts the Neutral position. The company would never adopt the Flexible position. The Flexible position is also dominated by the Tough position. In fact, the Tough position also dominates the Neutral position. The company would never adopt the Neutral position.

After the dominated negotiating positions have been eliminated, the only negotiating position that remains for the company is the Tough position. The company always adopts the Tough position. After the union has eliminated its dominated decision alternative, the only negotiating position that remains is the Obstinate position. The union always adopts the Obstinate position. The **value of the game** is the value that each of the two competitors obtains from adopting the best decision from its point of view. For the example of Table 10.A1, the value of the game is 5 percent. Each competitor selects the same negotiating position regardless of the position of the other competitor. For this example, each competitor adopts a **pure strategy.**

A payoff table such as Table 10.A1 usually does not have only one remaining decision alternative for each competitor after the dominated decision alternatives have been eliminated. If there is more than one undominated decision alternative for a competitor, some criterion is nec-

The minimax criterion

essary to select between the alternatives. A pessimistic criterion is the **minimax criterion.** From the company's viewpoint, it is assumed that the union adopts the position that is worst for the position adopted by the company. For example, if the company adopts a Tough position, the pessimist believes that the union adopts an Obstinate position. That is, if the company adopts a Tough position, the union adopts the position that gives the *maximum* wage increase—5 percent. Similarly, if the company adopts a Neutral position, the union adopts an Obstinate position because that gives the maximum wage increase—6 percent. Similarly, if the company adopts a Flexible position, the union adopts an Obstinate position because that results in the maximum wage increase—10 percent. The pessimistic policy of the company is to adopt the position that gives the *mini*mum of the *maxi*mums. The minimax policy of the company is to adopt a tough position, which has a value of 5 percent.

If the union uses the same pessimistic policy for selecting its position, it tries to maximize the minimum wage increase it receives. If the union adopts an Obstinate position, the minimum wage increase is 5 percent. If the union adopts an Agreeable position, the minimum wage increase is 4 percent. To achieve the *maxi*mum of the *mini*mums, the union selects the Obstinate position with a value of 5 percent.

Table 10.A2 illustrates the application of the minimax criterion for the company and the application of the maximin criterion for the union.

The **saddle point condition** is satisfied if the value of the minimax strategy equals the value of the maximin strategy. Table 10.A2 satisfies the saddle point condition. The company's minimax value is 5, and the union's maximin value is also 5. The **value of the game** is 5 percent. For this example, each competitor adopts a **pure strategy.** Say that the company uses its minimax strategy and that the union uses its maximin

---

TABLE 10.A2   Minimax and Maximin Strategies for Game Theory Example (Percent wage increase)

Company	Union Obstinate	Agreeable	Maximum
Tough	5	4	5 ←
Neutral	6	5	6
Flexible	10	9	10
Minimum	5	4	
	↑		

strategy. Then, if either changes its strategy, it is worse off. Thus, the strategies are in equilibrium.

For the example of Table 10.A1, both the company and the union adopted the same policy by employing the minimax criterion as they adopted by eliminating dominated decision alternatives. The equilibrium point was a pure strategy for each competitor. Had the payoff table been different, each competitor might have had more than one undominated decision alternative and the minimax and maximin strategies might not have been pure strategies. However, there would still have been a saddle point or equilibrium solution to the game such that if either competitor varied its strategy, it would have been worse off.

Table 10.A3 contains different values for the wage increases for the six different combinations of negotiating positions. Note that the wage increase is 7 percent if the company adopts a Tough position and the union adopts an Obstinate position. In this case, the dispute goes to an arbitrator who is famous for ruling in favor of the union if the company has been Tough. Also, the wage increase is 8 percent if the union is Agreeable and the company is Neutral. For this example, there is not a pure strategy under the minimax and maximin criteria such that deviations from it make the deviator worse off.

Let's calculate the minimax negotiating position for the company. First, note that the Flexible position is still dominated by both the Tough position and the Neutral position. The Flexible position can be eliminated from further consideration. Neither the Tough position nor the Neutral position dominates the other. If the company adopts the Tough position, the maximum wage increase it might have to give is 7 percent. If the company adopts the Neutral position, the maximum is 8 percent. To minimize the maximum, the company adopts the Tough position, obtaining a value of 7 percent.

From the union's viewpoint, neither of its positions is dominated by the other. If the union adopts the Obstinate position, the minimum wage increase is 6 percent. If the union adopts the Agreeable position, the minimum wage increase is 4 percent. To maximize the minimum wage

There is always a saddle point

TABLE 10.A3 Revised Payoff Table for Game Theory Example (Percent wage increase)

Company	Union	
	Obstinate	Agreeable
Tough	7	4
Neutral	6	8
Flexible	10	9

TABLE 10.A4   Minimax and Maximin Strategies for Revised Game Theory Example

Company	Union		Maximum
	Obstinate	Agreeable	
Tough	7	4	$\boxed{7}$ ←
Neutral	6	8	8
Minimum	$\boxed{6}$	4	
	↑		

increase, the union adopts the Obstinate position, resulting in a wage increase of 6 percent.

Table 10.A4 illustrates the calculation of the minimax and maximin strategies. Note that because it is dominated, the Flexible position has been eliminated. If the union adopts its maximin strategy (Obstinate) and the company adopts its minimax strategy (Tough), the wage increase is 7 percent. This is not what the union anticipated. Further, if the company deviates from its minimax strategy (Tough), the wage increase would actually improve (decrease) to 6 percent. *Pure strategies are not equilibrium strategies if the anticipated values for the two competitors are not equal.* Table 10.A4 doesn't satisfy the saddle point condition.

A **mixed strategy** is one in which a competitor assigns probabilities to each strategy such that more than one strategy has a positive probability. Let's derive the company's mixed strategy. Let $P(T)$ represent the probability that the company adopts a Tough position. Then, $1 - P(T)$ is the probability that the company adopts a Neutral position. If the union adopts an Obstinate position, the expected wage increase is

Finding the company's mixed strategy

$$P(T) \times 7 + [1 - P(T)] \times 6$$

If the union adopts an Agreeable position, the expected wage increase is

$$P(T) \times 4 + [1 - P(T)] \times 8$$

Figure 10.A1 illustrates the expected wage increase as a function of $P(T)$ for each of the two union positions. A pessimist assumes that whatever value of $P(T)$ was selected, the union selects the position that gives the largest expected wage increase. Thus, if $P(T) = 0$, the union adopts an Agreeable position. If $P(T) = 0.9$, the union adopts an Obstinate position. A pessimist selects the probability $P(T)$ such that the expected wage increase is the same regardless of the union's position:

$$P(T) \times 4 + [1 - P(T)] \times 8 = P(T) \times 7 + [1 - P(T)] \times 6$$

FIGURE 10.A1 Expected Wage Increase for Company's Mixed Strategy—Revised Payoff Table

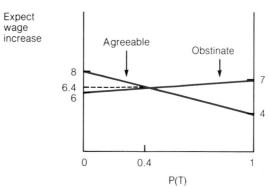

Solving for $P(T)$ gives $P(T) = 0.4$. The mixed strategy for the company is to select the Tough position with probability 0.4 and the Neutral position with probability 0.6. The expected wage increase of this mixed strategy is 6.4 percent.

Let's calculate the union's mixed strategy. Let $P(O)$ represent the probability that the union is Obstinate. If the company is Tough, the expected wage increase is $7 \times P(O) + 4 \times [1 - P(O)]$. If the company is Neutral, the expected wage increase is $6 \times P(O) + 8 \times [1 - P(O)]$. Equating the expected values and solving gives $P(O) = 0.8$. The expected value for the union's mixed strategy is 6.4 percent. The mixed strategies for the company and union give an equilibrium point. If either the company or the union changes its strategy, the expected wage increase worsens.

Finding the union's mixed strategy

Shortcomings of game theory

The above approach has several shortcomings. First, many competitive situations are not zero-sum games. Second, determining the mixed strategies assumes a pessimistic attitude on the part of both competitors. Third, there are only two competitors. Fourth, we assumed that each competitor knows the other's options and both competitors believe each value in the payoff table is the same. Usually, competitors have different assessments of the values. Fifth, if there are more than two undominated decision alternatives for a competitor, it is impossible to construct a graphical representation such as that in Figure 10.A1. Actually, the mixed strategies can be determined by solving a linear programming model. Sixth, we assume that the decisions are made simultaneously, not sequentially. But for many decision problems, the decisions are made sequentially. For example, your competitor might change its prices *after* you change yours.

But more important, managers do not believe in mixed strategies. For the company, the strategy is Tough with probability 0.4 and Neutral with probability 0.6. For example, you might write Tough on four pieces of paper and Neutral on six. Then, you mix them up and draw a piece of paper that tells you your strategy. Say if a "game" decision must be made only once, a manager is unlikely to adopt any strategy that is not a pure strategy, though a manager might consider mixed strategies if the same competitive situation occurs many times. In that case, a manager might like to vary the strategy. However, the same competitive situation is unlikely to occur more than once.

11

Sequential Decisions

Decision Trees and the Unpredictability of Nature

Decision Trees and Competitors
Simultaneous Competitor Decisions / Sequential Competitor Decisions

The Value of Perfect Information
The Expected Profit with Perfect Information / The Expected Value of Perfect Information / The Expected Opportunity Loss Criterion and the EVPI

The Value of Imperfect Information
Joint, Marginal, and Conditional Probabilities / Calculating the Posterior Probabilities and the Forecast Probabilities / The Expected Profit with Imperfect Information / The Expected Value of Imperfect Information: Should You Buy the Information?

Decision Trees for Sequential Decisions
Characteristics of Decision Trees / Including Revenues and Costs for Decision Trees / Solving Decision Trees with Nonzero Arc Values / The Decision Tree for the ZIP + 4 Study / An Example of a Decision Tree for Deterministic Sequential Decisions / An Example of a Decision Tree for Probabilistic Sequential Decisions

Case: Vulcan Specialty Rubber Company

Case: Josim Manufacturing Company

Theory: Dynamic Programming

UNITED STATES POSTAL SERVICE

The U.S. Postal Service (USPS) has a strategy of introducing automation to decrease labor costs. Labor costs represent approximately 85 percent of the USPS budget. The nine-digit ZIP code (ZIP + 4) was introduced to facilitate automation of first-class mail sorting. A nine-digit ZIP code allowed sorting to the level of city block, building, or post office box. In Phase 1 of the USPS automation project, optical character readers (OCRs) and bar code sorters (BCSs) were purchased at a cost of $182 million. The OCRs read the ZIP code and printed it in bar code form on the envelope. The BCSs read the bar code and sorted the first-class mail. With the nine-digit ZIP code, BCSs could sort to the level of the letter carrier, eliminating all intermediate sorting.

Unfortunately for the USPS, opposition developed to ZIP + 4 that resulted in its becoming voluntary. The USPS encouraged its use by offering discounts to large-volume first-class business mailers. However, the amount of business mail that would use ZIP + 4 was uncertain.

Even with the new equipment, business mail using the five-digit ZIP code required additional sorting. The OCRs were single-line readers. They read the bottom line of the address, particularly the five-digit ZIP code. This information was not detailed enough to sort to the letter carrier level. Multiline OCRs were being developed that would read up to four lines of the address. Based on this information, the nine-digit ZIP code would be printed on the envelope. No additional sorting was necessary if the nine-digit ZIP code was correctly identified, even if the address did not have a nine-digit ZIP code. Because the technology was new, the proportion of five-digit ZIP mail that could be identified by its nine-digit ZIP code was uncertain.

The USPS was about to accept bids for its automation program's Phase 2, which was budgeted for $450 million. The Office of Technology Assessment (OTA) was asked to review the automation strategy. Because of the controversy and uncertainty surrounding the ZIP + 4 system, its elimination was a possibility. The planned single-line OCRs purchases could be implemented. Another alternative was to cancel single-line OCR procurement, test the multiline OCRs, and purchase multiline OCRs as soon as possible. Existing single-line OCRs would be converted to multiline OCRs. Another possible decision (called D) was to proceed with the single-line OCR procurement but to begin testing on the conversion of single-line OCRs to multiline capabilities, so that conversion could occur as soon as possible. A "hedge" option was to go ahead with the single-line OCR procurement but to make the conversion only if the adoption of ZIP + 4 by business mailers was low. The final option was to cancel the Phase 2 procurement, eliminate ZIP + 4, and use the Phase 1 equipment to process five-digit ZIP codes.

Major uncertainties were the adoption of ZIP + 4, the savings percentage due to personnel reductions, and the savings due to the use of multiline OCR for five-digit ZIP mail. Each of the uncertainties was a continuous random variable but was represented by a three-point discrete distribution. A probability of 0.185 was assigned to the 95th percentile, 0.63 to the median, and 0.185 to the 5th percentile.

A decision tree was used to evaluate the net present value (NPV) and the internal rate of return (for the 1985–98 time horizon) for each of the possible decisions. All of the Phase 2 options were preferred to canceling the automation program. At a 15 percent interest rate, Option D had the highest NPV, $1.5 billion. In fact, Option D had a higher probability of exceeding any NPV value than did any other alternative. Sensitivity analysis showed that uncertainty in ZIP + 4 adoption caused the greatest variation in NPV, followed closely by multiline savings and followed distantly by the uncertainty in cost savings.

J. W. Ulvila, "Postal Automation (ZIP + 4) Technology: A Decision Analysis," *Interfaces* 17, no. 2 (March–April 1987), pp. 1–12.

Decisions are often made in a dynamic decision environment. In Chapter 1, we described a dynamic decision environment as one with multiple decisions, often one in which decisions are made in different time periods or at different points in time. The decisions are **sequential decisions**—there is a sequence in which they must be made. When appropriate, these decisions are treated as interrelated. Usually, the first decision influences the environment in which the second decision is made.

In Chapter 7, we formulated a linear programming model for a sequential decision problem. The multiple-period linear programming model planned production over time. The production decision in the first period affected the production decisions in the following periods. Using a multiple-period model permits consideration of the interrelationships among the period production decisions. Chapter 7's model was a deterministic sequential decision model. However, if the environment is probabilistic or if the model is not linear, you can't use linear programming.

A probabilistic decision environment is characterized by the uncertainty of the outcome for a decision alternative. In Chapter 10, we discussed approaches to decision making for probabilistic decision environments. In this chapter, we assume that probabilities are available for the states of nature and that the decision maker is risk indifferent, and we use the expected value criterion or the expected opportunity loss criterion. If the decision maker is not risk indifferent, the expected utility criterion is used.

In this chapter, we stress the sequence in which decisions and uncertain events occur. For a sequential decision problem, the decisions and uncertain events can be in any sequence. For example, an uncertain event can separate each decision from the decision that succeeds it. Or there can be several consecutive uncertain events. In this chapter, we show how to use decision trees to analyze sequential decision problems.

Many decision problems are sequential decision problems, so there have been many applications of decision trees. Let's describe a few successful applications. The U.S. Postal Service needed to choose its strategy for automation. The savings to be expected from automation were uncertain because of uncertainty about ZIP + 4 adoption, about the savings percentage due to personnel reductions, and about the savings due to the use of multiline OCRs for five-digit ZIP mail. A decision tree was used to choose the automation strategy.

Decision trees have been used to manage fire burning in national forests.[1] Controlled fire burning is important in modern forest management. Uncertainties in weather, fire behavior, and other factors are important considerations in planning and executing controlled fire burning.

Ohio Edison Company used decision trees to choose air quality control equipment.[2] Electrostatic precipitators and fabric filters are two approaches to the removal of particulates created by coal burning. There was uncertainty about the outcome of regulatory rulings regarding the types of coal that could be used (e.g., sulfur content). There was also uncertainty about operating costs, equipment reliability, power requirements and cost, and maintenance. Ohio Edison used a decision tree to evaluate two approaches to the removal of particulates.

Decision trees were also used in the choice of a water supply system for a nuclear power plant.[3] Among the decisions that had to be made were decisions on the conveyance method (e.g., pipelines), the size of the water treatment plant, the method of water treatment, the size of the storage reservoir, the condenser tube material, and the disposal of the residue. There was uncertainty about the water supply, the energy demand,

---

[1] D. Cohan, S. M. Haas, D. L. Radloff, and R. F. Yancik, "Using Fire in Forest Management: Decision Making under Uncertainty," *Interfaces* 14, no. 5 (September–October 1984), pp. 8–19.

[2] T. J. Madden, M. S. Hyrnick, and J. A. Hodde, "Decision Analysis Used to Evaluate Air Quality Control Equipment for Ohio Edison Company," *Interfaces* 13, no. 1 (February 1983), pp. 66–75.

[3] C. W. Hamilton and W. G. Bingham, "Management Science Applications in the Planning and Design of a Water Supply System for a Nuclear Power Plant," *Interfaces* 9, no. 5 (November 1979), pp. 50–62.

and the performance of the cooling system and about the costs and performance of the nuclear power plant. Because the decisions and the uncertainties were interrelated, decision trees were used to choose the design of the water supply system.

In the next section, we show the relationship between payoff tables and decision trees. Then, we show how a competitor's actions can be modeled using decision trees. In Chapter 10, we said that an advantage of the expected opportunity loss criterion is that it gives the expected value of perfect information. In this chapter, we discuss this important concept and show its application. What makes the expected value of perfect information important is its ability to establish a limit on the value of additional information about the uncertain outcomes. If the value of perfect information is sufficient, you can look for additional information about the uncertain outcomes. We discuss the expected value of imperfect information and use it to evaluate possible sources of additional information about the uncertain outcomes. Then, we show how to use the additional information to update the probabilities of the states of nature.

We describe how decision trees are constructed and solved. In the last section, we show three applications of decision trees with different sequences of decisions and uncertain events. Finally, in the Theory section, we develop the relationship between the solution of decision trees and dynamic programming.

DECISION TREES AND THE UNPREDICTABILITY OF NATURE

Let's review the new product introduction (NPI) example from Chapter 10 and show how to represent it as a decision tree. The company has two decision alternatives—introduce the new product or keep the existing product. The decision alternatives have uncertain outcomes because the profit depends on the state of the economy. The states of the economy are the states of nature. The outcome uncertainty is caused by the *unpredictability of nature*. We assume that the company must make the decision before the economic state has been discovered.

Table 11.1 repeats the profits in a payoff table for the two decision alternatives and the two states of nature. For the first decision alternative (introduce the new product), if the economy is strong, sales are strong and the resulting profit is $140,000; if the economy is weak, sales are weak so that the revenues from the new product introduction are less than the costs and the company loses $12,000. For the second decision alternative (keep the existing product), the profit also depends on the state of the economy, but the profits for the two states of the economy do not differ as much. If the economy is strong, the profit is $35,000, and if the economy

TABLE 11.1 Payoff Table for New Product Introduction Example—State of Economy Uncertain (Profit, $)

Number	Decision Alternative	State of Nature	
		Strong Economy	Weak Economy
1	Introduce new product	140,000	−12,000
2	Keep existing product	35,000	25,000

The state of nature is not affected by the decision

The time sequence is from left to right

is weak, the profit is $25,000. Each decision alternative's profit depends on the state of the economy, which is beyond the decision maker's control and *is unaffected by the decision alternative selected.*

Another method of representing the information in Table 11.1 for the NPI example is shown in Figure 11.1. This is a **decision tree,** and the time sequence is from left to right. First, the decision alternative is selected; next, the economic state is discovered; and finally, the profit is realized. A square on a decision tree represents a decision point or a **decision node.** The arcs leaving a decision node are the decision alternatives. The terminology of nodes and arcs comes from network models, which have a similar pictorial representation. A circle represents a point with an uncertain result and is called a **chance node.** The arcs leaving a chance node are the possible results.

For this example, the decision node represents selecting one of the two decision alternatives, and the two arcs from the decision node are the two decision alternatives. There are two chance nodes, and the uncertain result is the economic state. The two arcs from each chance node are the two economic states—a strong economy and a weak economy. Say that the probabilities of a strong and a weak economy are 0.4 and 0.6, respectively. We write the probabilities below the arcs of the chance nodes in Figure 11.1. We write the payoffs for each decision alternative/economic state combination at the end of the chance arcs.

FIGURE 11.1 Decision Tree for New Product Introduction Example— State of Economy Uncertain

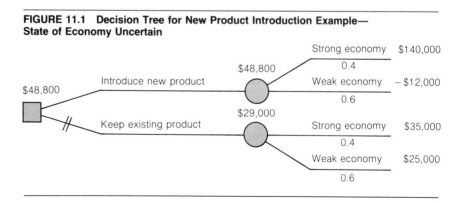

The expected profit for the top chance node is

$$E(1) = (0.4 \times \$140,000) + (0.6 \times -\$12,000) = \$48,800$$

The expected profit for the bottom chance node is

$$E(2) = (0.4 \times \$35,000) + (0.6 \times \$25,000) = \$29,000$$

The best decision alternative

Inferior decision alternative

We write the expected profits over the chance nodes. At the decision node, *select the decision alternative with the largest expected profit.* Introducing the new product maximizes the expected profit. Thus, you write the maximum expected profit over the decision node and *draw double lines through the inferior decision alternative* (keep the existing product).

After you've used decision trees a few times, the conventions for writing the calculated expected values and the selected decision values over the nodes are easy to follow. Until then, you might find **folding back** the decision tree helpful. Figure 11.2 shows the NPI example "folded back" by replacing the chance nodes with their expected values. You select the decision alternative with the largest expected profit.

The actual sequence of the decisions and the uncertain states of nature is critical. A good decision maker studies the decision environment carefully for the sequence. The sequence in the NPI example is that the decision alternative must be selected before the state of the economy has been discovered. If the state of the economy is discovered before the decision alternative has been selected, then there is no uncertainty about the outcomes. If the economy is strong, you select "introduce the new product." If the economy is weak, you select "keep the existing product."

DECISION TREES AND COMPETITORS

Let's consider a situation in which the outcome uncertainty depends on a competitor's actions. Chapter 10's appendix discussed the basics of game theory, which is one approach for including competitors' actions. In that

---

FIGURE 11.2   Decision Tree of Figure 11.1 Folded Back at Chance Nodes

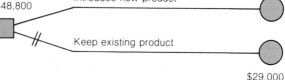

section, the minimax (or maximin) criterion was introduced as a possible decision criterion for a decision maker and the decision maker's opponent. One attractive feature of the minimax criterion is that there is an equilibrium point that is a solution to the two-person zero-sum game. However, the optimal policy might be a mixed strategy such as select Decision Alternative 1 with probability 0.3 and select Decision Alternative 2 with probability 0.7. Although a mixed strategy is conceptually appealing for repeated plays of a game, it is not attractive for a business decision maker facing a onetime decision. The decision maker wants a (single) pure strategy, not a mixed strategy. We get a pure strategy by using the methods of this section.

Three possibilities

Let's model a competitor's actions using decision trees. There are three possibilities, depending on the sequence of the actions. One possibility is that both actions occur at the same time. That is, we and our competitor decide our actions independently. Then, we both announce our decisions simultaneously and discover the payoffs. Our discussion of game theory assumed this. (It also assumed that the payoffs were a zero-sum game, but we don't need that assumption for the decision tree approach.) Another possibility is that we must select our action first, and *then* our competitor selects an action. For example, we announce a price increase, and then our competitor decides on a price change. For both of these possible action sequences, we can't control our competitor's action, so our payoff is uncertain. In the third possibility, our competitor must select an action before we do. Thus, there is no uncertainty about the outcome of our action. We illustrate the first two possibilities by modifying the NPI example.

Simultaneous Competitor Decisions

Say that the company is still trying to select from the two decision alternatives—introduce the new product or keep the existing product. However, the uncertainty of the profit is caused by the possibility that a competitor might introduce a similar new product, not by an uncertain economic state. The uncertain event is whether the competitor introduces a similar new product or keeps its existing product. Assume that both the company and its competitor must make their decisions *simultaneously and independently*. Table 11.2 summarizes the decision maker's profit possibilities.

Simultaneous and independent decisions

If the competitor introduces a new product and so does the decision maker, the larger market is split. The decision maker's profit is only $15,000 after the expenses for introducing the new product. If the competitor introduces a new product and the decision maker does not, the decision maker's profit is $25,000. If the competitor does not introduce a new product and the decision maker does, then the new market is captured by the decision maker, giving a profit of $140,000. If neither the decision maker nor the competitor introduces a new product, the decision maker's profit is $35,000.

TABLE 11.2 Payoff Table for New Product Introduction Example—Actions of Competitor Uncertain (Profit, $)

		Competitor Action	
Number	Decision Alternative	Introduce New Product	Keep Existing Product
1	Introduce new product	15,000	140,000
2	Keep existing product	25,000	35,000

Estimate the probabilities of the competitor's actions

In this case, the decision maker must estimate the probability that the competitor introduces a new product. Let $P(CNP)$ denote the probability that the competitor introduces a new product, and say that this probability is 0.8. Then, the probability that the competitor keeps its existing product, denoted as $P(CEP)$, must equal 0.2. Figure 11.3 shows the decision tree for this decision problem.

Here, the probabilities are *independent of the decision maker's decision*. The situation is similar to one in which the uncertainty is caused by the economic state in that the probabilities are independent of the decision maker's actions. The probabilities for both the *CNP* event and the *CEP* event are the same for both chance nodes.

For the decision maker, the expected profit for the first decision alternative (introduce the new product) is

$$E(1) = (0.8 \times 15,000) + (0.2 \times 140,000) = \$40,000$$

FIGURE 11.3 Decision Tree for New Product Introduction Example—Simultaneous Competitor Action

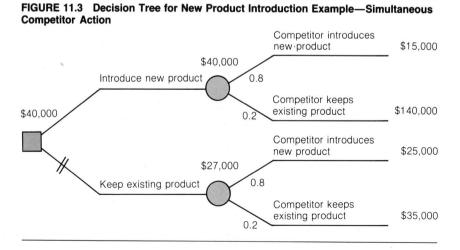

The expected profit for the second decision alternative (keep the existing product) is

$$E(2) = (0.8 \times 25,000) + (0.2 \times 35,000) = \$27,000$$

Because the first decision alternative (introduce the new product) has a higher expected profit, we select that alternative. (If the decision maker is not risk indifferent, the decision maker develops a utility function and uses the expected utility criterion.)

Figure 11.3's decision tree shows the expected values written over the chance nodes and the best expected profit written over the decision node. The decision arc for Decision Alternative 2 has a double line through it, indicating that it is an inferior decision. The best decision is Decision Alternative 1.

Sequential Competitor Decisions

The probabilities depend on the decision maker's action

Now, say that the competitor decides whether to introduce its new product *after* we announce whether we introduce ours. The profit payoffs are the same as those shown in Table 11.2, but the action sequence is different. In this case, the decision maker needs to estimate the probabilities of the competitor's action based on the competitor knowing the decision of the decision maker. If the decision maker introduces the new product, let $P(CNP \mid NP)$ denote the probability that the competitor introduces the new product and let $P(CEP \mid NP)$ denote the probability that the competitor keeps its existing product. Say that $P(CNP \mid NP) = 0.9$. Then, because the probabilities must total to 1, $P(CEP \mid NP) = 0.1$. Say that the probability that the competitor introduces the new product, given that the decision maker decides to keep the existing product, represented by $P(CNP \mid EP)$, equals 0.2. Then, the probability that the competitor keeps its existing product, represented by $P(CEP \mid EP)$, must equal 0.8.

Figure 11.4 shows the decision tree for this decision problem. Because the probabilities at the chance nodes depend on the decision maker's action, they are different.

We find the best decision by calculating the expected profit for each chance node. The decision maker's expected profit for introducing the new product is

$$E(1) = (0.9 \times 15,000) + (0.1 \times 140,000) = \$27,500$$

The decision maker's expected profit for keeping the existing product is

$$E(2) = (0.2 \times 25,000) + (0.8 \times 35,000) = \$33,000$$

In this case, the best decision for the expected value criterion is to keep the existing product. Figure 11.4 includes this information.

FIGURE 11.4   Decision Tree for New Product Introduction Example—Sequential Competitor Action

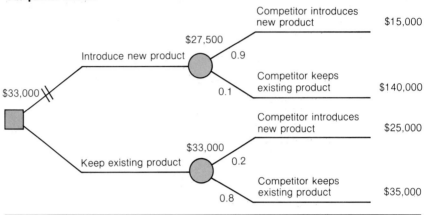

The critical distinction between the two cases is whether the probability of the competitor's action is dependent on the decision alternative selected by the decision maker. If it is *not* dependent, the problem is like the one involving the unpredictability of nature. If it *is* dependent, conditional probability assessments are necessary, but the calculations required to select the best decision alternative are no more difficult.

THE VALUE OF PERFECT INFORMATION

The outcome's uncertainty makes decision making for probabilistic decision environments more difficult. If you can reduce or eliminate the uncertainty, you can make better decisions. For the NPI example, if you can determine the economic state *before* the decision, it's easy to pick the best alternative. Consider the examples we discussed concerning a competitor's action. If you can determine the competitor's action before you make your decision, it's easy to pick the best alternative.

Often, you can get additional information that reduces the outcome's uncertainty. For example, you can get economic forecasts from consultants with econometric models. Also, managers do marketing research to get additional information about product demand. Thus, you get additional information to reduce the outcome's uncertainty and improve your decisions. But additional information can be expensive. Also, the additional information may be imperfect and thus may not *eliminate* the outcome's uncertainty. Subscribing to an economic forecasting service costs money, and the forecasts are sometimes wrong.

Additional information can reduce the uncertainty

In this section, we discuss the expected value of perfect information (EVPI). The EVPI is used for preliminary screening of sources of additional information. In the next section, we discuss the expected value of imperfect information (EVII). *In all cases,*

$$EVPI \geq EVII$$

If the cost of imperfect information is greater than the EVPI, you don't purchase the additional information. Otherwise, you evaluate the imperfect information using the methods in the next section.

We use an "errorless expert" when we discuss perfect information. In this section, we assume that the expert *never* makes an error. Errorless

experts are rare, but we use such an expert to establish a limit on the value of information from imperfect experts.

Let's use the NPI example with an uncertain economy as an example. Before consulting the expert, we believe that the probabilities of a strong and weak economy are 0.4 and 0.6, respectively. The expected profit of introducing the new product is $48,800, and the expected profit of keeping the existing product is $29,000. Using the expected value criterion, the best decision is to introduce the new product.

Now, say that we hired an expert to forecast the economic state before we select the decision alternative. Figure 11.5 illustrates the time sequence of the events. First, the expert gives the economic forecast. After this, the decision alternative is selected, the economic state is discovered,

FIGURE 11.5 Decision Tree for New Product Introduction Example with Errorless Expert—State of Economy Uncertain

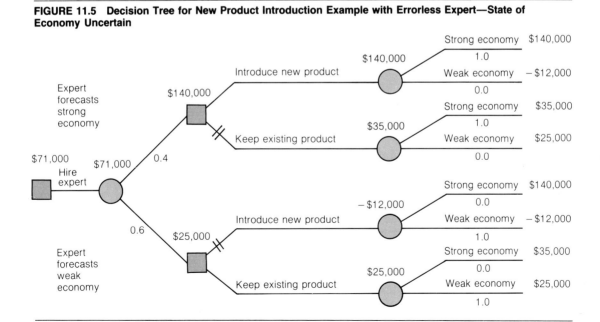

and, finally, the profit is realized. Hiring the expert is a decision and is therefore represented by a square, a decision node. There is an unstated alternative of not hiring the expert. The expert's forecast is uncertain and is therefore represented by a circle, a chance node. Selecting from between the two decision alternatives is represented by a square. Finally, the actual state of the economy is subject to uncertainty and represented by chance nodes.

The forecast is uncertain

Note that the expert forecasts the economic state but can't control it. We prefer having a strong economy, but it might be a weak one. Even though the expert is errorless, we don't know what the forecast will be. Before we hire the expert, the best estimate is that the probability of a strong economy is 0.4. Therefore, the best estimate that the expert will forecast a strong economy is also 0.4. Similarly, the best estimate that the expert will forecast a weak economy is 0.6. In Figure 11.5, these probabilities appear under the arcs for the first (from the left) chance node.

Note the probabilities for the rightmost chance nodes. These are the probabilities of the actual economic state, conditional on the occurrence of everything leading into the given arc. So the topmost arc has the probability for the economy actually being strong conditional on (1) hiring an expert who (2) forecasts a strong economy, followed by (3) introducing the new product. What is the probability of a strong economy if the expert forecasts a strong economy? For an errorless expert, the probability is 1.0. If the expert forecasts a strong economy, what is the probability of a weak economy? If the expert is errorless, it is 0.0. Note that we assumed that the state of nature is not influenced by the decision alternative selected. Whether the new product is introduced doesn't affect the economic state. This is shown by the fact that the probabilities for the arcs of the top two rightmost chance nodes are the same. Similarly, the bottom two rightmost chance nodes are conditional on the expert forecasting a weak economy. In this case, because the expert is errorless, the probability of a strong economy is 0.0 and the probability of a weak economy is 1.0.

Assuming that the forecast is without error, the range of events that could occur is smaller that those illustrated in Figure 11.5. For example, the economy is never weak if the forecast is a strong economy. However, we include both events in the figure because this makes it easy to generalize it if the expert is sometimes wrong.

The Expected Profit with Perfect Information

The **expected profit with perfect information (EPPI)** is the expected profit when you get a perfect forecast before the decision. Let's calculate the EPPI for the NPI example using Figure 11.5.

First, say that the expert forecasts a strong economy. Then, the expected profit for introducing the new product is $(1.0 \times \$140,000) + (0.0 \times -\$12,000) = \$140,000$. In fact, $140,000 is the certain profit, because the expert is errorless. The profit for keeping the existing product is $35,000. These values have been written over the top two rightmost chance nodes. If the expert forecasts a strong economy, the best decision is introducing the new product, giving a profit of $140,000. This value has been written over the top decision node, and a double line has been drawn through the arc for the inferior decision.

Now, say that the expert forecasts a weak economy. If you introduce the new product, the profit is $-$12,000$. If you keep the existing product, the profit is $25,000. The best decision is to keep the existing product, giving a profit of $25,000. Figure 11.5 shows these numbers, and the double line through the arc for introducing the new product shows that it is an inferior decision.

Calculating the EPPI

Let's consider the profit at the first chance node. Because the forecast of the expert is not certain, the profit is not certain. To calculate the expected profit with perfect information, you multiply the forecast probabilities by the profit of each of the best decisions given the errorless forecast and sum. For this example, the calculation is

$$EPPI = (0.4 \times 140,000) + (0.6 \times 25,000) = \$71,000$$

If you get perfect information about the state of nature before selecting the decision alternative, the expected profit is $71,000. In Figure 11.5, the EPPI value, $71,000, appears over the first chance node and the first decision node.

The Expected Value of Perfect Information

If you were charged $10,000 for the expert's forecast, would you hire the expert? We compare the value of the expert's information with its cost to decide whether to hire the expert. The **expected value of perfect information (EVPI)** is the EPPI minus the expected profit without the perfect information.

EVPI

Let's calculate the EVPI for the NPI example. If the expert was not hired, the best decision is to introduce the new product, giving an expected profit of $48,800. If the expert was hired, the EPPI is $71,000. The EVPI is

$$EVPI = \$71,000 - \$48,800 = \$22,200$$

If the expert charges a fee of $10,000, hiring the expert is worthwhile because using the forecast increases the expected profit by $22,200. If the expert's fee is more than $22,200, however, the cost of the perfect information is more than its expected value and you shouldn't hire the expert.

Using the EVPI to screen imperfect information

Let's illustrate using the EVPI to screen possible sources of imperfect information. Say that imperfect information costs more than $22,200. Would you consider buying it? The value of imperfect information is never greater than the value of perfect information. Since the cost of the imperfect information is greater than the EVPI, you shouldn't consider buying it and you don't need to calculate its expected value. If the imperfect information costs less than the EVPI, however, you must calculate the expected value of the imperfect information so that you can compare it with the cost of the information. We show how to do this later.

Calculating the EVPI for minimization

Note that we calculated the EVPI by comparing the EPPI with the expected profit for the *best* decision alternative. If the payoff table values are costs to be minimized, the EVPI is calculated as the expected cost for the *best* decision alternative minus the expected cost with perfect information. In both cases, we use the expected value criterion to select the best decision alternative. For a decision maker who is not risk indifferent, we use utility instead of monetary values and perform the calculations in the same way that we illustrated in this section.

The Expected Opportunity Loss Criterion and the EVPI

Why does the perfect information have any value at all? Without that information, the best decision is to introduce the new product. With that information, what is the best decision? If the forecast is a strong economy, the decision is to introduce the new product, the same decision that would have been selected without the expert. The expert's forecast is valuable only if it leads to a decision change relative to the decision that would have been selected without the forecast. If the forecast is a weak economy, the decision is to keep the existing product. This is a change from the decision that would have been made without the forecast.

Remember, the opportunity loss is the loss for selecting a decision alternative other than the best decision alternative *for the given state of nature*. With perfect information about the state of nature, you can always pick the best decision alternative for that state of nature.

Say that we used the expected opportunity loss criterion for the NPI example. Table 11.3 is the opportunity loss (OL) table for the NPI example. The expected opportunity loss for Alternative 1 is

$$EOL(1) = (0.4 \times 0) + (0.6 \times 37,000) = \$22,200$$

TABLE 11.3 Opportunity Loss Table for Payoff Table 11.1 (Opportunity loss, $)

Number	Decision Alternative	State of Nature		Expected Opportunity Loss, $EOL(i)$
		Strong Economy (probability 0.4)	Weak Economy (probability 0.6)	
1	Introduce new product	0	37,000	\$22,200 ←
2	Keep existing product	105,000	0	\$42,000

For the second decision alternative (keep the existing product),

$$EOL(2) = (0.4 \times 105{,}000) + (0.6 \times 0) = \$42{,}000$$

You select Decision Alternative 1 (introduce the new product). As we showed in Chapter 10, using the EOL criterion gives the same decision as that given by using the expected value criterion.

EVPI and the EOL criterion

The EVPI is the EOL for the best decision alternative. In Table 11.3, the best decision alternative (introduce the new product) has $EOL(i) = \$22{,}200$, which is the EVPI. The expert's forecast has value only if the state of nature forecast changes the decision from the one that would have been made without the forecast. Without the forecast, the decision is to introduce the new product. If the forecast is a strong economy, that decision is unchanged. If the forecast is a weak economy, the decision changes and the profit improves from $-\$12{,}000$ to $\$25{,}000$, an improvement of $\$37{,}000$. The opportunity losses for Decision Alternative 1 are $\$0$ and $\$37{,}000$ for a strong and a weak economy, respectively. To calculate the expected opportunity loss for the best decision without the information, you weight the opportunity losses by the probabilities of the states of nature. With perfect information, you always make the best decision for the given state of nature. The EVPI is the best EOL, EOL^*.

An advantage of using the EOL criterion

In Chapter 10, we stated that an advantage of the EOL criterion is that using it gives you the value of additional information. If you use the EOL criterion, you get the EVPI. It's the EOL for the best decision alternative. The only additional effort required by the EOL criterion compared with that required by the expected value criterion is creating the opportunity loss table.

For probabilistic decision environments that can be represented by payoff tables, the expected opportunity loss criterion is convenient. You can use a payoff table if there is only one decision point and there is uncertainty only for the state of nature at that point. Unfortunately, for decision environments requiring decisions at different points in time and having uncertain states of nature at different points in time, constructing an opportunity loss table becomes confusing. In this case, use a decision tree and the expected value criterion.

For all decision alternatives, $E(i)$ and $EOL(i)$ are related. In Chapter 10, we showed (for a maximization objective) that

$$EOL(i) = \left\{ \sum_{j=1}^{n} P(j)\{\max_{k} R(k,j)\} \right\} - E(i)$$

The summation in the RHS is the EPPI. Therefore, for any decision alternative i,

$$EOL(i) = EPPI + E(i)$$

For example, consider Decision Alternative 2 for the NPI example. The EPPI is $71,000, and its expected profit is $29,000. Therefore,

$$EOL(2) = \$71{,}000 - \$29{,}000 = \$42{,}000$$

This is the same value that we calculated for $EOL(2)$ in Table 11.3.

THE VALUE OF IMPERFECT INFORMATION

In many decision-making situations, the decision maker can obtain additional information. If the uncertainty concerns probable sales, the additional information could include macroeconomic forecasts, market tests, consumer panels, and other marketing research. If the uncertainty concerns the feasibility of a new production process, a pilot plant could be constructed. In each of these cases, the uncertainty can be reduced by gathering additional information. But the additional information costs dollars and time. How does a manager decide when to obtain additional information and when to make the decision without additional information?

Obtaining additional information is not limited to probabilistic decision environments. Even for a deterministic decision environment, there is some uncertainty about certain assumptions and parameters of the model. For example, the user of a machine assignment linear programming model may be uncertain about the required number of units for a particular product. However, the decision maker has decided that the uncertainty is not critical *for the part of the decision-making environment that is being modeled.* Even in this case, a good decision maker uses sensitivity analysis on the uncertain parameters. If the model's decisions are insensitive to changes in those parameters, the decision maker develops confidence in the model's information. However, if the model's decisions are very sensitive to reasonable changes in those parameters, the decision maker seeks additional information to reduce the uncertainty.

In this section, we consider obtaining additional *imperfect* information for probabilistic decision environments. Experts who are errorless are rare. You get an inaccurate economic forecast, even from an expert who does better than average.

In the previous section, we discussed perfect information. If the cost of the perfect or imperfect information is greater than the EVPI, obtaining the information is a poor economic decision. If the EVPI is greater than the cost of the perfect information, obtaining the perfect information is a good economic decision. However, if the EVPI is greater than the cost of *imperfect* information, we can't tell whether getting the information is a good economic decision without additional analysis. In this section, we show how to analyze the value of imperfect information.

Other considerations
about obtaining addi-
tional information

We emphasize that the economics of obtaining additional information is only *one consideration*. Obtaining information generally requires delaying the decision. This might be a problem because of competitors' possible actions. For example, what are the implications of a competitor being the first to introduce a new product? Be cautious of what is called "paralysis by analysis." Sometimes, it's better to make the decision without doing all of the possible analyses. In this section, we assume that the decision maker/model builder has decided not to explicitly incorporate other considerations (such as competitor's actions) into the model representing the decision environment. When you make decisions, you should take into account, not only the model's results, but also those other considerations.

An imperfect economic
forecaster

Let's consider the NPI example with an imperfect economic forecaster. Recall the discussion of Figure 11.5, which represents the decision tree for the NPI example with an errorless expert. For the expert who is not errorless, Figure 11.6 is appropriate. The probabilities on the arcs emanating from the rightmost chance nodes represent the likelihood of the actual economic state given the state of nature forecast by the expert. If the expert is not errorless, those probabilities are not all 0.0 (never wrong) or 1.0 (always correct).

We need the probabilities for the chance nodes to solve the decision tree. With imperfect information, the actual state of nature can be different from the forecast state of nature. Let a strong and weak economy be

---

FIGURE 11.6 Decision Tree for New Product Introduction Example with Imperfect Expert

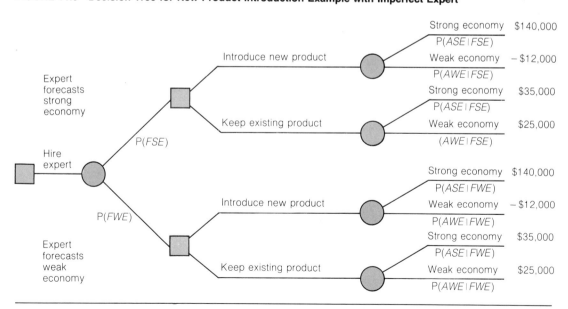

represented by *SE* and *WE,* respectively. Let *A* be the actual economic state and *F* be the forecast economic state. Thus, *ASE* represents that the economy is actually strong and *AWE* represents that the economy is actually weak. The forecast of a strong economy and a weak economy are represented by *FSE* and *FWE,* respectively. At the first chance node, we need $P(FSE)$ and $P(FWE)$. We also need the probabilities for the chance nodes for the actual economic state. For example, we need the probability for the top arc of the rightmost chance node. Symbolically, we represent this as $P(ASE \mid FSE)$, the probability that the economy is actually strong given that the forecast is a strong economy.

Figure 11.7 is a flowchart showing how new information is used in the analysis. Before the new information is obtained, the probabilities of the states of nature are called the **prior distribution.** After the new information is obtained, the updated probabilities of the states of nature are called the **posterior distribution.** To update the probabilities, you need the probabilities of the forecasts conditional on the actual states of nature. These probabilities and the forecast probabilities may be subjective or based on historical records. After we review the concepts of marginal, joint, and conditional probabilities, we show how to update the probabilities.

Joint, Marginal, and Conditional Probabilities

Let's use a *hypothetical* historical set of forecasts to illustrate joint, marginal, and conditional probabilities. Table 11.4 contains hypothetical information on the expert's accuracy. The expert made 70 forecasts in the past. Of those forecasts, 20 were for a strong economy. The actual economy was strong in 18 of the 20 cases, and it was weak in 2 of the 20 cases. You can use the relative frequencies to estimate the probabilities. Table 11.5 contains the relative frequencies.

The **joint probability** of two events is the probability of both occurring. For example, 18 of the 70 times, the forecast was for a strong economy and the economy actually was strong. The joint probability of a forecast for a strong economy and the economy actually being strong is denoted by $P(ASE,FSE)$. The estimate of $P(ASE,FSE) = \dfrac{18}{70} = 0.25714$. Similarly,

---

FIGURE 11.7   Flowchart for Including Additional Information

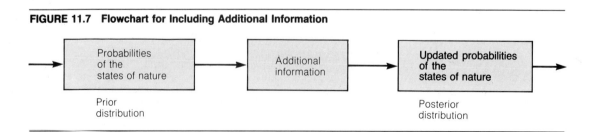

TABLE 11.4   Historical Frequencies (Number of occurrences)

Forecast Economy	Actual Economy		Total
	Strong (*ASE*)	Weak (*AWE*)	
Strong (*FSE*)	18	2	20
Weak (*FWE*)	10	40	50
Total	28	42	70

$P(ASE,FWE) = \dfrac{10}{70} = 0.14286$. Verify that $P(AWE,FSE) = 0.02857$ and $P(AWE,FWE) = 0.57143$. Note that (ASE,FSE) and (AWE,FSE) can't occur at the same time. In fact, one and *only* one of the four pairs can occur. The joint probabilities correspond to compound events that are mutually exclusive and collectively exhaustive. These probabilities sum to 1; $0.25714 + 0.14286 + 0.02857 + 0.57143 = 1.00000$.

The **marginal probability** of an event is the sum of the joint probabilities for which that event occurs. For example, consider the marginal probability of a forecast of a strong economy, denoted by $P(FSE)$.

$$P(FSE) = P(FSE,ASE) + P(FSE,AWE) = 0.25714 + 0.02857 = 0.28571$$

This value appears in the Total column for the row corresponding to *FSE*. The marginal probability of a forecast of a weak economy is

$$P(FWE) = P(FWE,ASE) + P(FWE,AWE)$$
$$= 0.14286 + 0.57143 = 0.71429$$

What is the marginal probability of the actual economy being strong? If *ASE* occurs, either *FSE* or *FWE* must occur. Summing the joint probabilities,

$$P(ASE) = P(FSE,ASE) + P(FWE,ASE) = 0.25714 + 0.14286 = 0.40000$$

The **conditional probability** of an event is the probability that the event

TABLE 11.5   Joint Probability Table (Probabilities)

Forecast Economy	Actual Economy		Total
	Strong (*ASE*)	Weak (*AWE*)	
Strong (*FSE*)	0.25714	0.02857	0.28571
Weak (*FWE*)	0.14286	0.57413	0.71429
Total	0.40000	0.60000	1.00000

occurs conditional on some other event. For example, the probability that the forecast is a strong economy conditional on the actual economy being strong is denoted by $P(FSE \mid ASE)$. In general, a conditional probability is related to joint and marginal probabilities as

$$P(A \mid B) = \frac{P(A,B)}{P(B)}, \text{ where } P(B) \neq 0$$

Let's use this formula to calculate the probability of a forecast of a strong economy conditional on the actual economy being strong.

$$P(FSE \mid ASE) = \frac{P(FSE, ASE)}{P(ASE)} = \frac{0.25714}{0.40000} = 0.64285$$

The hypothetical historical data indicated that the economy was forecast to be strong 18 times out of the 28 times it actually was strong $\left(\frac{18}{28} = 0.64285\right)$. Also, we calculate $P(FWE \mid ASE) = \frac{0.14286}{0.4} = 0.35715$ $\left(\text{or} \frac{10}{28}\right)$. More than one third of the times that the economy actually was strong, there was a forecast of a weak economy. Similarly, $P(FSE \mid AWE) = 0.04762$ and $P(FWE \mid AWE) = 0.95238$. The forecaster was correct a larger proportion of the time when the actual state of the economy was weak.

Calculating the Posterior Probabilities and the Forecast Probabilities

In this section, we show how to calculate the posterior probabilities and the forecast probabilities. Before obtaining additional information, we have a prior distribution for the states of nature. We also have probabilities for the *forecast conditional on the actual* state of nature. We use these probabilities to calculate the posterior distribution of the states of nature and the forecast probabilities.

Let's use the NPI example with prior distribution, $P(ASE) = 0.4$ and $P(AWE) = 0.6$. Table 11.6 contains the probabilities for the forecast conditional on the actual state of nature. For example, $P(FSE \mid ASE) = 0.9$. These probabilities differ from the hypothetical values that we used in the previous section to review joint, marginal, and conditional probabilities. We use Table 11.6's values to calculate the posterior probabilities.

We calculate the posterior probabilities and the forecast probabilities by means of a tabular approach. *For each of the possible forecasts,* we construct a table with five columns:

Column 1: States of nature

Column 2: Prior probabilities of the states of nature

TABLE 11.6   NPI Example with Imperfect Expert—Forecast Probabilities Given the Actual Economic State (Probabilities)

Forecast Economic State	Actual Economic State	
	ASE	*AWE*
FSE	0.9	0.2
FWE	0.1	0.8
	1.0	1.0

Column 3: Forecast probabilities conditional on the actual states of nature

Column 4: Joint probabilities

Column 5: Posterior probabilities of the states of nature

Table 11.7 shows the steps for the tabular approach for each of the possible forecasts. Step 1 initializes the first three columns; Step 2 calculates the joint probabilities; Step 3 calculates the probability for the given forecast; and Step 4 calculates the posterior probabilities.

Let's use the tabular approach for a forecast of a strong economy (*FSE*). Table 11.8 shows the result of Step 1, the initialization. The second column gives the prior probabilities, and the third column gives the probability that a strong economy is forecast conditional on the actual economic state (from Table 11.6).

Table 11.9 shows the result of Steps 2 and 3. In Step 2, you multiply the entries in Column 2 by the corresponding entries in Column 3 and enter the product in Column 4. For example,

$$P(FSE, ASE) = P(ASE) \times P(FSE \mid ASE) = 0.4 \times 0.9 = 0.36$$

In Step 3, you add the entries in Column 4 to get $P(FSE) = 0.48$.

TABLE 11.7   Tabular Method for Calculating the Posterior Probabilities

For each of the possible forecasts:

Step 1.   In Column 1, list the states of nature. In Column 2, enter the prior probabilities for each state of nature. In Column 3, enter the forecast probability conditional on each state of nature.

Step 2.   In Column 4, enter the product of the corresponding entries in Columns 2 and 3.

Step 3.   Add the entries in Column 4 to get the forecast probability.

Step 4.   Calculate the posterior probabilities by dividing the corresponding entry in Column 4 by the forecast probability from Step 3, and enter the quotient in Column 5.

TABLE 11.8   Using the Tabular Method for Calculating the Posterior Probabilities for *FSE*—Step 1

State of Nature	Prior Probability	Forecast Probability Conditional on Actual	Joint Probability	Posterior Probability
ASE	0.4	0.9		
AWE	0.6	0.2		

Table 11.10 shows the complete table. You calculate the posterior probabilities in Column 5 by dividing the joint probabilities in Column 4 by the forecast probability. For example,

$$P(ASE \mid FSE) = \frac{P(FSE, ASE)}{P(FSE)} = \frac{0.36}{0.48} = 0.75$$

Table 11.11 shows the complete table for *FWE*. Note that $P(FWE) = 0.52$. Because *FSE* and *FSE* are mutually exclusive and collectively exhaustive, their probabilities must sum to 1.0. This is a check on your tabular computations.

The tabular approach uses Bayes's Rule to calculate the posterior probabilities. Let's consider applying Bayes's Rule to a general problem. Let F_j represent the jth possible forecast event and A_i represent the ith possible event, and let's say that n events are possible. For the NPI example, n equals 2. The economy is either strong or weak. Then, **Bayes's Rule** is

Bayes's Rule

$$P(A_i \mid F_j) = \frac{P(F_j \mid A_i)P(A_i)}{\sum_{i=1}^{n} P(F_j \mid A_i)P(A_i)}$$

Before the forecast, the probability of Actual Event A_i is $P(A_i)$. The posterior probability is the probability of the actual event *after* the fore-

TABLE 11.9   Using the Tabular Method for Calculating the Posterior Probabilities for *FSE*—Steps 2 and 3

State of Nature	Prior Probability	Forecast Probability Conditional on Actual	Joint Probability	Posterior Probability
ASE	0.4	0.9	0.36	
AWE	0.6	0.2	0.12	
			0.48	

TABLE 11.10 Using the Tabular Method for Calculating the Posterior Probabilities for *FSE*—Complete Table

The completed *FSE* table

State of Nature	Prior Probability	Forecast Probability Conditional on Actual	Joint Probability	Posterior Probability
ASE	0.4	0.9	0.36	0.75
AWE	0.6	0.2	0.12	0.25
			0.48	1.00

cast of the event has been obtained. Thus, $P(A_i \mid F_j)$ is the posterior probability of A_i given a forecast of Event F_j.

The Expected Profit with Imperfect Information

The **expected profit with imperfect information (EPII)** is the expected profit if we make the best decisions after receiving the imperfect forecast. Figure 11.8 shows the NPI decision tree using the forecast probabilities and the posterior probabilities in Tables 11.10 and 11.11. We've numbered the nodes to make it easier to refer to them. Let's calculate the EPII for Figure 11.8.

Calculate from right to left

We calculate the EPII by analyzing the decision tree from right to left (backward). At each chance node, we calculate its expected value. At each decision node, we select the decision that has the best expected value.

Let $E[\pi(i)]$ denote the expected profit at Node i. Starting from the right of the tree, we calculate the expected profit for Chance Nodes 5, 6, 7, and 8. At Node 5, the expected profit is

$$E[\pi(5)] = (0.75 \times \$140,000) + (0.25 \times -\$12,000) = \$102,000$$

At Node 6, the expected profit is

$$E[\pi(6)] = (0.75 \times \$35,000) + (0.25 \times \$25,000) = \$32,500$$

TABLE 11.11 Using the Tabular Method for Calculating the Posterior Probabilities for *FWE*—Complete Table

The *FWE* table

State of Nature	Prior Probability	Forecast Probability Conditional on Actual	Joint Probability	Posterior Probability
ASE	0.4	0.1	0.04	0.07692
AWE	0.6	0.8	0.48	0.92308
			0.52	1.00000

FIGURE 11.8   Calculating the EPII for the Decision Tree for New Product Introduction Example with Imperfect Expert

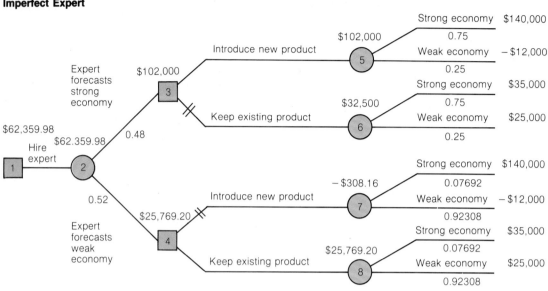

At Node 7, the expected profit is

$$E[\pi(7)] = (0.07692 \times \$140,000) + (0.92308 \times -\$12,000) = -\$308.16$$

At Node 8, the expected profit is

$$E[\pi(8)] = (0.07692 \times \$35,000) + (0.92308 \times \$25,000) = \$25,769.20$$

The expected profits are written over Nodes 5, 6, 7, and 8.

Node 3 is a decision node. If you introduce the new product, the expected profit is $102,000. If you keep the existing product, the expected profit is $32,500. The decision with the largest expected profit is "Introduce new product." The double line through the arc "Keep existing product" shows that this is an inferior decision. We write the expected profit for the best decision over Node 3.

Node 4 is also a decision node. Keeping the existing product gives the largest expected profit, $25,769.20. This value appears over Node 4, and the inferior decision has been marked with a double line.

Node 2 is a chance node. You weight the expected values of its arcs by their probabilities to calculate the expected profit.

$$E[\pi(2)] = (0.48 \times \$102,000) + (0.52 \times \$25,769.20) = \$62,359.98$$

We write this value over Node 2. The expected profit at Node 1 is also $62,359.98.

The optimal decision strategy

The optimal decision strategy is the best set of decisions conditional on uncertain events. The complete decision tree in Figure 11.8 shows the optimal decision strategy for the NPI example. Let's assume that you hire the expert. If the forecast is a strong economy, you introduce the new product. If the forecast is a weak economy, you keep the existing product.

What is the expected profit with imperfect information? The *EPII* = $62,359.98. With perfect information, the *EPPI* = $71,000. The imperfect information gives a smaller expected profit than does the perfect information. That is reasonable, because there is a chance that an imperfect expert will be wrong. For example, if the expert forecasts a strong economy, the probability is 0.25 that the economy will actually be weak. If the economy is weak and you introduce the new product, your profit would have been greater if you had kept the existing product. With perfect information, you always select the best decision alternative.

The Expected Value of Imperfect Information: Should You Buy the Information?

Calculating the EVII

The approach used in deciding whether to obtain additional imperfect information is similar to that used in deciding whether to obtain perfect information. First, we calculate the EPII. Then, we calculate the **expected value of imperfect information (EVII)** as the EPII minus the expected profit of the decision alternative selected without the information. Without the imperfect economic forecast, the best decision is to introduce the new product, with an expected profit of $48,800. Figure 11.8 shows that the *EPII* = $62,359.98. Therefore,

$$EVII = \$62,359.98 - \$48,800 = \$13,559.98$$

Because the additional information is sometimes obtained by sampling, the EVII is sometimes called the **expected value of sampling information (EVSI).** You compare the cost of the imperfect information with the EVII. If that cost is greater than the EVII, obtaining the additional information is a poor economic decision. If that cost is less than the EVII, obtaining the additional information is a good economic decision. For example, say that the information costs $10,000. Because the EVII is greater than the cost of the information, buying the additional information is a good decision.

One final comment before we conclude our discussion of the EVII and of whether buying the imperfect information is a good economic decision. It might be convenient to construct the decision tree so that the decision of whether to hire the expert is represented explicitly. Using Figure 11.8, that decision is made by comparing the cost of the expert to the EVII. Figure 11.9 represents another approach. Here, the first square decision node has both alternatives represented—either hire the expert or do not hire the expert. We discuss this matter further in the next section.

FIGURE 11.9 Decision Tree for New Product Introduction Example with Imperfect Expert and Decision Alternative Not to Hire

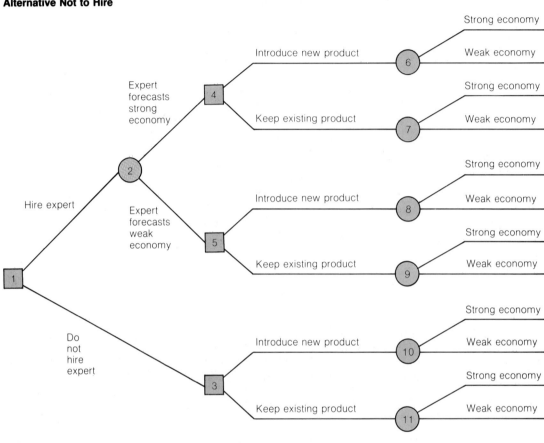

DECISION TREES FOR SEQUENTIAL DECISIONS

The NPI decision problem with imperfect information is an example of a sequential decision problem. First, you decide whether to hire the expert. Then, if you hire the expert, there is a chance event for the forecast. After you obtain the forecast, you have to make another decision: whether to introduce the new product. Finally, there is another chance event for the actual economic state, and you discover the profit. The decision nodes and the chance nodes alternate in the sequence for the NPI example.

Sequential decision problems can have any number of decison nodes and chance nodes. Also, decision nodes can be followed by decision nodes and chance nodes can be followed by chance nodes. In this section, we discuss the general characteristics of decision trees and give other sequential decision examples.

Characteristics of Decision Trees

Decision trees must be constructed before they are "solved." Careful construction of decision trees improves the quality of the analysis. The most important concept is that *the sequence from left to right in the decision tree is the same as the sequence within the decision environment.* Thus, anytime a node is reached, everything preceding that node from the beginning of the tree has occurred. To construct the decision tree, you must list the entire sequence of decision points and uncertain state of nature points. Sometimes, the set of possible decisions or possible uncertain events is affected by the preceding nodes. For example, a decision not to hire the expert in the NPI example eliminates the possibility of obtaining a forecast from the expert.

A decision tree can have three types of nodes—decision nodes, chance event nodes, and terminating nodes. Designate a square **decision node** for each decision point in the sequence. Each decision node has one or more arcs beginning at the node and extending to the right. Each of those arcs is a possible decision alternative at that decision point. Each arc from a decision node ends with another decision node, a chance event node, or a terminating node.

You designate a circle **chance event node** for each point in the sequence at which the state of nature is uncertain. Each circle node has one or more arcs beginning at the node and extending to the right. Each of those arcs is a possible state of nature at that chance event point. Each arc has a probability that is conditional on all of the decision alternatives and chance events that precede it on the decision tree. The probabilities for all of the arcs beginning at a chance event node must sum to 1. Each arc from a chance event node ends with a decision node, another chance event node, or a terminating node.

A **terminating node** represents the end of the sequence of decisions and chance events. No arcs extend to the right from a terminating node. You don't need to designate a terminating node by a geometric figure. Since decision nodes and chance event nodes are represented by squares and circles, respectively, any arc extending to the right that doesn't end in either a square decision node or a circle chance event node has to end in a terminating node. Observe that the rightmost branches of the previous decision trees in this chapter all end with terminating nodes. Terminating nodes are important because they are the starting point for the computations needed to "solve" the decision tree.

Think of a decision tree as a tree whose "trunk" is the leftmost node. A decision tree must have a single trunk, the single leftmost node. If you try to construct a decision tree with more than one trunk, you should reexamine the sequence of decisions and chance events.

Margin notes:

The sequence in the decision tree

Three types of nodes

A single "trunk"

FIGURE 11.10 Disjoint Decision Trees

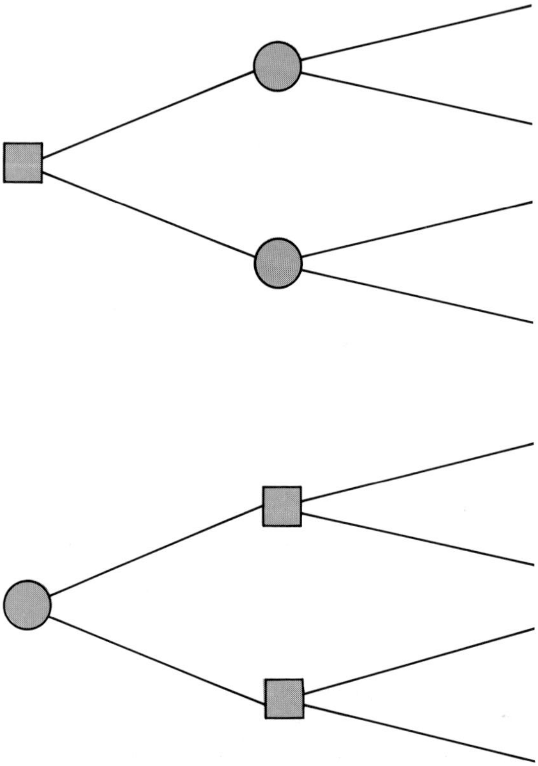

Solve disjoint decision trees independently

Figure 11.10 illustrates a situation in which two decision trees are **disjoint.** If two decision trees are disjoint, they are unconnected. Such decision trees are solved independently. They represent unconnected portions of the decision environment.

Branches can't grow together

Also, the branches of a decision tree do not grow together. A decision tree should not be represented as illustrated in Figure 11.11. No node should have more than one arc entering it from the left. In Figure 11.11, this requirement is violated by the two state of nature arcs that end at Decision Node 5. If your decision tree violates this requirement, you should reexamine the decision environment. The violation may be the result of a conceptual error, or there may be a less confusing decision tree representation that avoids the violation.

In summary, decision trees have the following characteristics:

Decision tree characteristics

1. They consist of square decision nodes, circle chance event nodes, and terminating nodes.

FIGURE 11.11   Not a Decision Tree

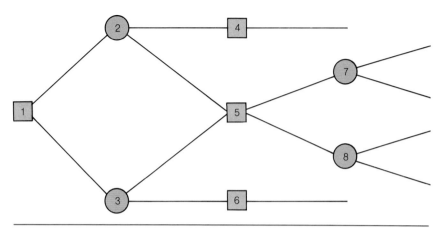

2. Disjoint decision trees are solved independently.
3. Except for the single leftmost node, each node of a decision tree has only one arc entering it from the left.

The decision tree in Figure 11.9 has these characteristics. There are four square decision nodes, numbered 1, 3, 4, and 5. There are seven circle chance event nodes, numbered 2 and 6 through 11. There are 12 terminating nodes, which have not been numbered. Node 1 is the single trunk of the decision tree. All of the other nodes, including the terminating nodes, have a single arc entering them from the left. In Figure 11.8, all of the decision and chance nodes except Node 1 have more than one arc leaving them to the right. You include decision nodes with a single decision alternative or chance event only to indicate underlying assumptions. That is why we included the first decision node in Figure 11.8 even though a single arc leaves it. There is an unspecified alternative: Don't hire the expert. Figure 11.9 shows both of the decision alternatives at Node 1.

Including Revenues and Costs for Decision Trees

Different methods for including revenues and costs

The revenues and costs for the decision alternatives selected and the chance events that occur are an important feature of decision trees. Let's consider alternative methods of including revenues and costs for decision trees. As an example, let's consider the NPI example when the imperfect expert's fee is $10,000.

The expert's fee doesn't appear in Figure 11.8. Instead, you calculate the EVII and compare it with the $10,000 fee. One approach for including revenues and costs is to assign them only to terminating nodes. First, we

FIGURE 11.12 Decision Tree for New Product Introduction Example with Imperfect Expert and Decision Alternative Not to Hire

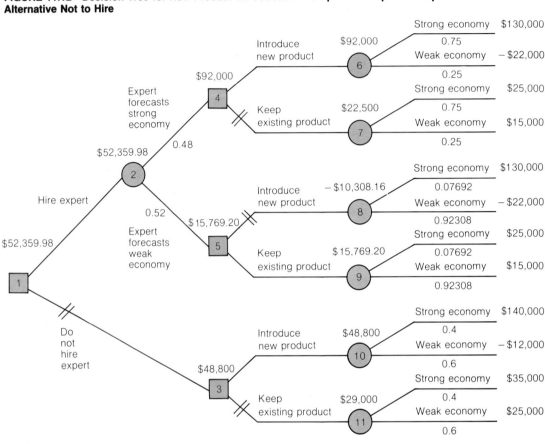

The expert's fee

show the decision tree for this approach. Another approach is to assign revenues and costs to arcs. We also show this approach, and we explain its advantage for sensitivity analysis.

Revenues and costs only on terminating nodes. Figure 11.12 shows the decision tree when the revenues and costs are only on the terminating nodes. To include the $10,000 fee for the expert, you must subtract the $10,000 from the payoff values. The eight terminating nodes from the nodes numbered 6, 7, 8, and 9 reflect this subtraction. For example, the value of the topmost terminating node is $140,000 − $10,000 = $130,000. The values of the terminating nodes in Figure 11.12 are $10,000 less than the values of the terminating nodes in Figure 11.8.

At Decision Node 1, hiring the expert gives an expected profit of $52,359.98 and not hiring the expert gives an expected profit of $48,800.

You therefore hire the expert. Note that the profit of Figure 11.12 is $10,000 less than that of Figure 11.8, reflecting the $10,000 fee.

You can always assign values to only the terminating nodes. However, it can be more convenient to assign values to arcs. This reduces the required arithmetic for calculating the values for the terminating nodes and focuses attention on the parameters for sensitivity analysis.

Revenues and costs also on arcs. Figure 11.13 shows the decision tree when the expert's fee is assigned to the arc for hiring the expert. The terminating node values are the payoffs in Table 11.1. Those values are the profits depending on the decision alternative and the economic state, *not including* the expert's fee. They are the same values as those shown in Figure 11.8. The expert's fee appears as −$10,000 on the arc for hiring the expert. Note that if you don't hire the expert, you don't have to pay

FIGURE 11.13 Decision Tree for New Product Introduction Example with Imperfect Expert and Expert Fee on Arc to Hire Expert

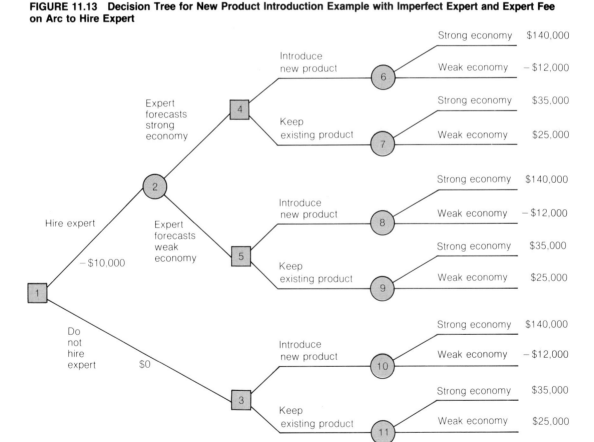

the fee. Therefore, 0 is the value shown on the arc for not hiring the expert.

Figure 11.13's decision tree allows the decision maker to focus on the expert's fee. In Figure 11.12's decision tree, the amount of the fee is not apparent. Here, the terminating node values were calculated by subtracting the fee, so to determine whether to hire the expert if the fee is a different amount, you must recalculate the terminating node values and repeat the decision tree calculations. For Figure 11.13's decision tree, on the other hand, a change in the expert's fee doesn't affect the terminating node values or the expected values for any node except Node 1.

Remember, the decision maker/model builder selects the representation of the decision environment. Introducing the definitional variable for regular gasoline in the linear programming formulation of the gasoline blending model in Chapter 3 helped sensitivity analysis. Similarly, having economic values on arcs focuses on those values and helps sensitivity analysis. The explicit appearance of a cost in the decision tree makes it easier to determine the sensitivity of the "best" decisions to changes in that cost.

As another example, say that there is uncertainty about the cost of preparing to introduce the new product. We estimated the preparation cost at $50,000. In Table 11.1, that cost was subtracted from the revenues to get the payoffs. The $50,000 introduction cost doesn't appear explicitly in the payoff table or in previous NPI decision trees. In Figure 11.14's decision tree, the cost for introducing the new product is assigned to arcs

The new product introduction preparation cost

for that decision. Therefore, the value of the topmost terminating node is $190,000, not the $140,000 that appears in Figure 11.13. Using Figure 11.14, it's easier to analyze the sensitivity of decisions to changes in the introduction cost. Remember, ask what types of sensitivity analysis you want before you construct the decision tree.

Solving Decision Trees with Nonzero Arc Values

We discussed solving decision trees in the section, The Expected Profit with Perfect Information. Let's review the procedure if no arcs have nonzero values. You solve decision trees from right to left. That is, your first calculations are for the decision nodes and the chance event nodes at the end of the tree. To calculate the expected value of each chance event node, you multiply its arc probabilities by their expected values and sum. For each decision node, you select the decision alternative with the best expected value.

If arcs have values, you must modify the calculations. Let's consider how to calculate the expected value at Chance Event Node i. Let A_i denote the set of nodes immediately after Node i. Let P_{ij} denote the probability that Node j occurs. Because A_i contains all of the possible

FIGURE 11.14 Decision Tree for New Product Introduction Example with Expert's Fee and New Product Introduction Cost on Arcs

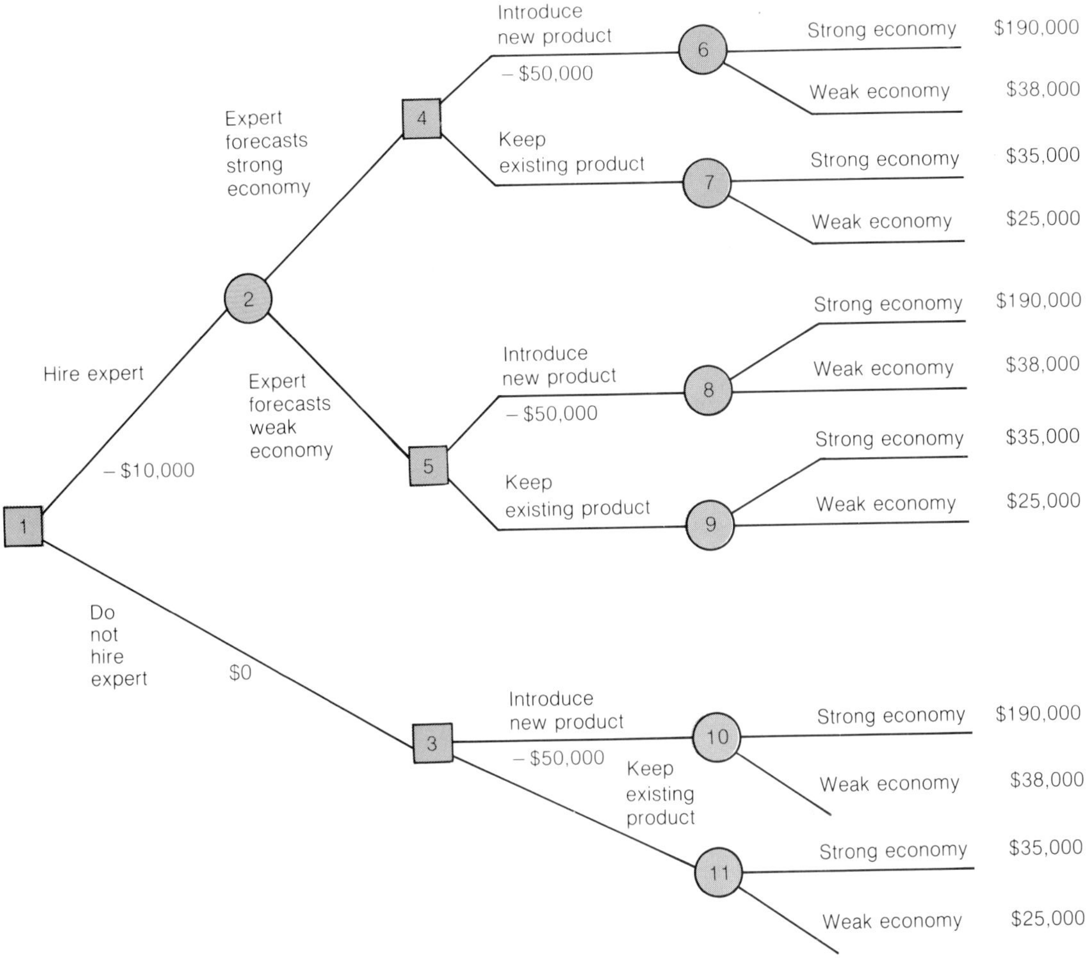

Values on chance event arcs

states of nature at that chance event node, $\Sigma_{j \in A_i} P_{ij} = 1$. Let c_{ij} represent the value of the arc from Node i to Node j. If $E[\pi(j)]$ denotes the expected profit at Node j, then the expected profit at Node i is

$$E[\pi(i)] = \sum_{j \in A_i} [\{P_{ij}\}\{c_{ij} + E[\pi(j)]\}]$$

Now, consider a decision node and assume that you want to maximize the objective. If $E[\pi(j)]$ denotes the expected profit at Node j, then the

FIGURE 11.15 Decision Tree for New Product Introduction Example with Expert's Fee and New Product Introduction Cost on Arcs

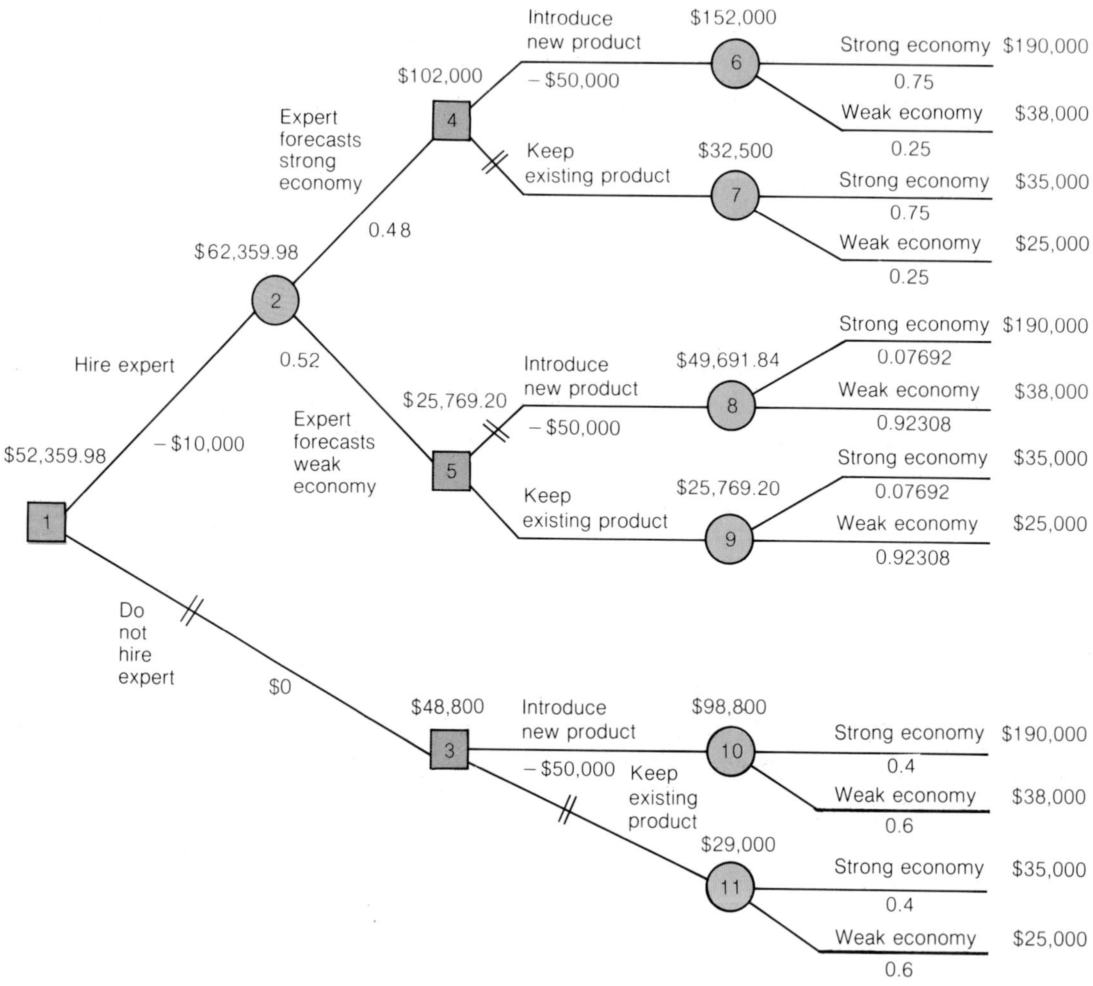

Values on decision arcs

expected profit for selecting the arc to Node j is $c_{ij} + E[\pi(j)]$. Select the arc in A_i that maximizes the expected profit,

$$E[\pi(i)] = \max_{j \in A_i}\{c_{ij} + E[\pi(j)]\}.$$

Figure 11.15 shows the calculations for Figure 11.14's decision tree. You start at the right and calculate the expected profit for Chance Event Nodes 6, 7, 8, 9, 10, and 11. Now, consider Decision Node 4, which has two nodes after it, Nodes 6 and 7. The expected profit for Arc (4,6) is $-\$50,000 + \$152,000 = \$102,000$, and the expected profit for Arc (4,7) is

$32,500. You therefore select Arc (4,6). You write expected profit for Node 4 above it, and you mark the inferior decision.

Next, you calculate the expected profit for Nodes 5 and 3. At Node 2, the maximum expected profit is

$$E[\pi(2)] = (0.48 \times \$102,000) + (0.52 \times \$25,769.20) = \$62,359.98$$

At Node 1, you select

$$E[\pi(1)] = \max(-\$10,000 + \$62,359.98, \$48,800)$$
$$= \max(\$52,359.98, \$48,800) = \$52,359.98$$

Thus, you hire the expert. The decision strategy is to hire the expert, and if the forecast is a strong economy, you introduce the new product. If the expert forecasts a weak economy, you keep the existing product.

From Figure 11.15, it is easy to calculate how large the fee must be so that it is not worth hiring the expert. The fee must be more than $62,359.98 − $48,800 = $13,559.98. Sensitivity analysis is easier if you include the expert's fee on the arc.

Sensitivity analysis

The Decision Tree for the ZIP + 4 Study

At the beginning of this chapter, we described a decision problem of the U.S. Postal Service (USPS). Phase 1 of an automation program was completed based on going to a nine-digit ZIP code using single-line optical character readers (OCRs). Because of opposition that developed, however, nine-digit ZIP code use became voluntary, with discounts offered for large-volume first-class business mailers. The USPS had several alternative strategies ranging from canceling the Phase 2 procurement to buying new multiline OCRs. The USPS had only one decision point, but it had three types of uncertainty. One type of uncertainty was the percentage of ZIP + 4 usage by business mailers. A second type of uncertainty was the savings percentage factor for the single-line OCR equipment. The USPS had estimated greater savings than were achieved for its electronic mail system, and USPS officials were concerned that this might happen again. The third type of uncertainty was the additional savings from multiline OCRs. Because multiline OCRs were still in the development stage, the savings they could achieve weren't known.

Some of the decision alternatives weren't affected by all of these types of uncertainty. For example, if the decision were to go ahead with the Phase 2 purchase of single-line OCRs, the additional savings from multiline OCRs would have no effect. Also, if ZIP + 4 were discontinued and multiline OCRs purchased, the percentage of ZIP + 4 usage would have no effect.

Figure 11.16 illustrates the decision tree for the ZIP + 4 study. After the decision node, there were either two or three chance event nodes, depending on the decision. Two measures of performance were used—

FIGURE 11.16   Schematic Decision Tree of Postal Automation Options and Uncertainties

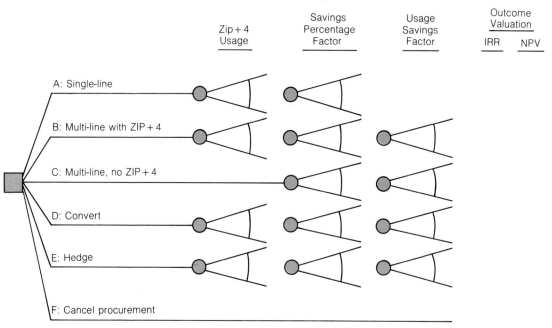

SOURCE: J. W. Ulvila, "Postal Automation (ZIP + 4) Technology: A Decision Analysis," *Interfaces* 17, no. 2 (March–April 1987), p. 4.

internal rate of return (IRR) and net present value (NPV). The performance values were assigned to the terminating nodes.

Continuous chance events

Each of the uncertainty types was a continuous random variable but was represented by a three-point discrete distribution. A probability of 0.185 was assigned to the 95th percentile, a probability of 0.63 was assigned to the median, and a probability of 0.185 was assigned to the 5th percentile. Figure 11.17 shows the part of the decision tree for the Convert alternative.

An Example of a Decision Tree for Deterministic Sequential Decisions

Let's use a decision tree for a multiple-period decision problem. The NPI example has two interrelated decisions: "Should you hire the economic forecasting expert?" and "Should you introduce the new product?" These decisions are sequential in time, but they don't correspond to decisions for different time periods.

We use a three-period inventory planning problem to illustrate applying decision trees to a multiple-period problem. Say that a company is using a planning period of one month and a three-period time horizon. The

FIGURE 11.17 The Decision Tree for Option D of the Postal Automation Study

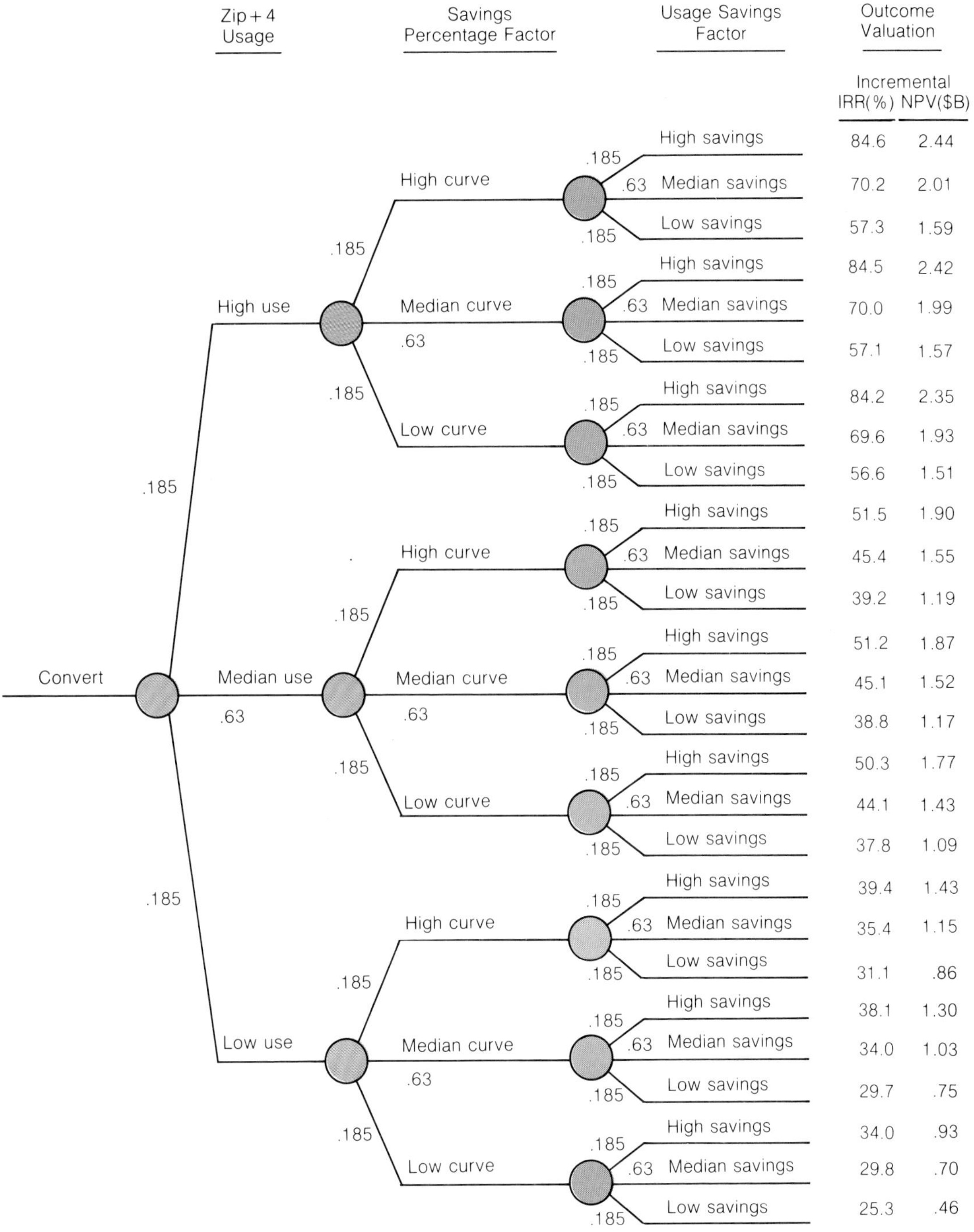

	Zip + 4 Usage	Savings Percentage Factor	Usage Savings Factor	Outcome Valuation Incremental IRR(%)	NPV($B)
			High savings	84.6	2.44
		High curve .185	.63 Median savings	70.2	2.01
			Low savings .185	57.3	1.59
			High savings .185	84.5	2.42
	High use .185	Median curve .63	.63 Median savings	70.0	1.99
			Low savings .185	57.1	1.57
			High savings .185	84.2	2.35
		Low curve .185	.63 Median savings	69.6	1.93
			Low savings .185	56.6	1.51
			High savings .185	51.5	1.90
		High curve	.63 Median savings	45.4	1.55
		.185	Low savings .185	39.2	1.19
			High savings .185	51.2	1.87
Convert .185	Median use .63	Median curve .63	.63 Median savings	45.1	1.52
			Low savings .185	38.8	1.17
			High savings .185	50.3	1.77
		Low curve .185	.63 Median savings	44.1	1.43
			Low savings .185	37.8	1.09
			High savings .185	39.4	1.43
		High curve	.63 Median savings	35.4	1.15
		.185	Low savings .185	31.1	.86
			High savings .185	38.1	1.30
	Low use .185	Median curve .63	.63 Median savings	34.0	1.03
			Low savings .185	29.7	.75
			High savings .185	34.0	.93
		Low curve .185	.63 Median savings	29.8	.70
			Low savings .185	25.3	.46

SOURCE: J. W. Ulvila, "Postal Automation (ZIP + 4) Technology: A Decision Analysis," *Interfaces* 17, no. 2 (March–April 1987), p. 8

Assume that the
demand is known

goal is to plan the pattern of purchases for a product for the next three
months. The illustration may seem too simple to be realistic, but the
simplicity helps when we explain the decision tree. Otherwise, it might be
impossible to see the "tree" for the forest.

First, we consider a situation with known demand, so that the decision
problem has deterministic sequential decisions. Later, we consider a
probabilistic demand situation. Assume that we have firm customer commitments for orders for the next three months and that company policy is
to satisfy all orders. Assume further that at the beginning of each month
the supplier arrives at the company and asks how many units of the
product are desired. Because the supplier has the product in the car,
delivery is instantaneous.

One possible purchasing policy is to ask the supplier each month for
enough units of the product to satisfy that month's orders. However, the
supplier gives a discount based on the number of units ordered. This
provides an incentive for purchasing more than a single month's orders at
a time. But if you purchase more than a single month's orders, you incur
inventory carrying costs. Should the objective be to maximize profits or
to minimize costs? Because company policy is to satisfy all orders, the
total revenue is a constant. Therefore, maximizing profits and minimizing
costs give the same decisions. Let's use minimizing the total of purchase
costs and inventory carrying costs as the objective.

The list of decision points includes the first day of the next three
months. We refer to the months as 1, 2, and 3. Because we have customer
order commitments for the next three months, there is no uncertainty
about the demand. Therefore, there are no uncertain state of nature
points. The list of the sequence of decision points and uncertain state of
nature points is

1. Decision 1: How many units should be ordered at the beginning
   of Month 1?
2. Decision 2: How many units should be ordered at the beginning
   of Month 2?
3. Decision 3: How many units should be ordered at the beginning
   of Month 3?

To construct the decision tree, you need to specify the decision alternatives at each decision point. Say that there is no initial inventory and
that there are orders for one unit in each of the next three months. At the
beginning of Month 1, you must order at least one unit to satisfy that
month's order. Because the orders for the next three months total three
units, the maximum purchase at the beginning of Month 1 is three units.
Figure 11.18 shows the decision tree. At Node 1, the decision alternatives
are to order either 1, 2, or 3 units.

The decision alternatives at the beginning of Month 2 depend on Month
1's order. If you ordered only one unit at the beginning of Month 1, no

FIGURE 11.18 Decision Tree for Three-Period Inventory Planning Problem with Known Demand

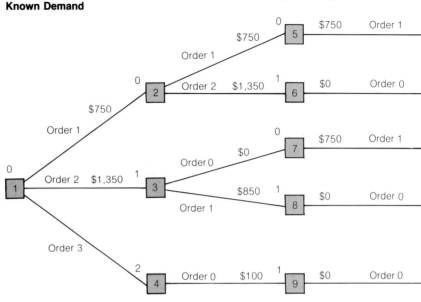

units are left at the end of Month 1. Thus, you must order at least one unit to satisfy Month 2's demand, but there is no reason to order more than two units. The decision alternatives at Node 2 are 1 or 2 units.

If you ordered two units at the beginning of Month 1, one unit is left at the beginning of Month 2 (Node 3). In that case, the order in Month 2 can be 0 or 1. If you ordered three units at the beginning of Month 1, two units are left at the end of Month 1 (Node 4). In that case, the order in Months 2 and 3—Nodes 4 and 9—is 0 units.

At the beginning of Month 3, you have either none or one left. If you have none left, you order 1. If you have one left, you order 0.

Say that the cost of a single unit is $750 and that additional units cost only $500. Therefore, two units cost $1,250 and three units cost $1,750. If no units are purchased, the cost is nothing. The inventory carrying cost is assessed at $100 per unit in inventory at the end of each month. The inventory carrying cost is very high because company policy strongly discourages extra inventory.

Assign costs to arcs

We assign the costs to the arcs where they are incurred. For example, the arc from Decision Node 1 to Decision Node 2 is the decision to order one unit at the beginning of Month 1. The arc cost is $750 for the one unit plus the inventory carrying cost. The inventory at the end of a month is the number on hand at the beginning of the month plus the units ordered from the supplier during the month minus the units sold during the month.

In this case, the inventory at the end of Month 1 is $0 + 1 - 1 = 0$ units. The inventory carrying cost is $0, so the arc cost is $750. The inventory of zero units at the end of Month 1 has been written next to Node 2 because it's also the beginning inventory for Month 2.

As another example, consider the arc from Node 2 to Node 6, which corresponds to ordering two units at the beginning of Month 2. The cost of the two units is $1,250. The beginning inventory at Node 2 is zero units, which we wrote by node 2. The number of units in inventory at the end of Month 2 is the inventory at the beginning of Month 2 (zero units) plus the two units ordered from our supplier minus the one unit sold during Month 2. The inventory at the end of Month 2 is one unit, $0 + 2 - 1 = 1$, and is written by Node 6. The inventory carrying cost for Month 2 is $100 for the one unit. The arc cost from Node 2 to Node 6 is $1,350 ($1,250 + $100). Figure 11.18 has the inventory at the beginning of each month written by the node number and each arc cost written above the arc.

The decision tree is solved from right to left. Solving the decision tree is left to the exercises.

An Example of a Decision Tree for Probabilistic Sequential Decisions

Probabilistic demand

If the demand during a month is uncertain, how does the decision tree change? The list of decision points and uncertain state of nature points also includes the uncertain demand points. The list is

1. Decision 1: How many units should be ordered at the beginning of Month 1?
2. Chance Event 1: The demand in Month 1.
3. Decision 2: How many units should be ordered at the beginning of Month 2?
4. Chance Event 2: The demand in Month 2.
5. Decision 3: How many units should be ordered at the beginning of Month 3?
6. Chance Event 3: The demand in Month 3.

At each decision node, you need to determine the decision alternatives to be evaluated. Each of these is an arc from the square decision node. At each chance event node, the arcs are the number of units demanded. Each of these arcs has a probability, and the sum of the probabilities for any chance event node must be 1.

For simplicity, let's assume that the demand is either 0 units or 1 unit, each with a probability of 0.5. If the demand is uncertain, the cost of a particular decision is also uncertain. Without a company policy that mandates satisfying all demand regardless of the cost, the revenue is not a

Maximize profit is the objective

constant. Thus, we use maximizing the expected profit as the criterion. Let's assume that any demand in a month that is more than the units available after the delivery at the beginning of the month is a lost sale. Say that lost sales cost $500 per unit. If demand in a month is less than the number of units available after the delivery at the beginning of the month, units are left at the end of the month. The inventory carrying cost is $100 per unit at the end of the month. The units are sold for $1,000 each. Again, assume that no units are on hand at the beginning of Month 1.

Let's determine the possible order sizes at the beginning of Month 1. The greatest possible value for demand during the next three months is one unit each month for a total of three units. There is no reason to consider ordering more than three units. The decision alternatives considered at Decision Node 1 are to order 0, 1, 2, or 3 units. Figure 11.19 shows part of the decision tree for this probabilistic sequential decision problem.

Examine Node 2. The arc from Node 1 to Node 2 is for an order of 0, so the cost is $0. The cost is written over Arc (1,2), and the available inventory, 0, is written by Node 2. There are two arcs from Chance Event Node 2, for demand of 0 and 1. If the demand is 0, the arc cost is $0. If the demand is 1, then there is a lost sale with a cost of $500. In both cases, the inventory at the end of Month 1 is 0. The ending inventories are written by Nodes 4 and 8, and the costs are written by the arcs.

At any future decision node, the largest number of units considered is the maximum possible demand during the remainder of the time horizon minus the number of units on hand before the order. For example, if no units are on hand with two months to go, the maximum order size is two units. If one unit is on hand with two months to go, the maximum order size is one unit. The number of possible arcs at decision nodes varies depending on the number of periods remaining and on the inventory at the time of the decision. At every chance event node, the number of arcs is the same because demand is either 0 or 1 in every month. The two arcs correspond to demand being either 0 or 1. Because of the large number of arcs, Figure 11.19 shows only part of the decision tree for this three-period uncertain demand problem.

Let's calculate the costs for some arcs. The arc from Node 2 to Node 7 corresponds to a demand of 1 unit in Month 1. Because no units are available and the demand is 1, there is a shortage of one unit and the inventory at the end of month 1 is 0. The inventory value has been written by Node 7. There is no revenue or inventory carrying cost. The cost of the shortage is $500. You write −$500, the profit, on Arc (2,7).

Let's examine Node 6, which has zero units available. If demand is 0, there is no shortage or inventory carrying cost. If demand is 1, there is a shortage of one unit, so you write the negative of the shortage cost, −$500, by the terminating node.

Now examine Node 10, with one unit available. If demand is 0, there is one unit left and the inventory carrying cost is $100. If demand is 1, there are no units left and you receive the revenue of $1,000.

You solve the decision tree from right to left. For example, you

FIGURE 11.19 Decision Tree for Three-Period Inventory Planning Problem with Uncertain Demand—Partial Tree

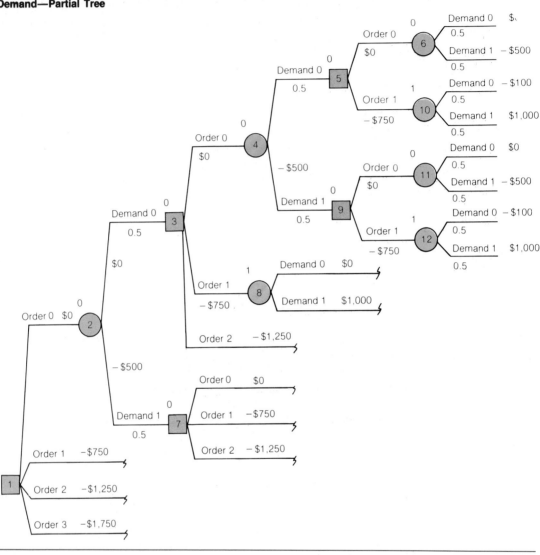

calculate the expected profit for Nodes 6, 10, 11, and 12. (You must also calculate the expected profit for the nodes not shown in Figure 11.19.) For example, at Node 6 the expected profit is

$$E[\pi(6)] = (0.5 \times \$0) + (0.5 \times -\$500) = -\$250$$

After calculating the expected profit for the final chance event nodes, you calculate the expected profit for the preceding nodes, 5 and 9. Note that Nodes 5 and 9 have *identical* portions following them on Figure 11.19's decision tree. Therefore, the expected profits (and decisions) for Nodes 5 and 9 are identical and you don't need to repeat the calculations for both. Nodes 5 and 9 both start with 0 units available and have identical portions of the decision tree after them. Dynamic programming uses this observation to decrease the arithmetic for sequential decision problems. We explain this further in the Theory section at the end of this chapter.

Another approach

Another approach to the decision tree is to associate the profit only with each terminating node. No revenues or costs are assigned to any decision or chance event arcs. For example, the topmost terminating node from Node 6 corresponds to the profit for ordering 0 in each month with the demand being 0 in each month. In this case, the profit of that terminating node is $0, because revenue, shortages, and inventory carrying costs are all absent. We prefer to assign the profits with the arcs. Otherwise, you don't have any nodes with identical parts of trees following them, which reduces the calculations required. We also prefer it because it helps sensitivity analysis.

SUMMARY

In this chapter, we discussed solving sequential decision problems. To do this, you construct a decision tree that represents the sequence of decisions and uncertain events. We used the new product introduction problem with an uncertain economic state as an example. This situation is typical of many probabilistic decision environments where the payoff is uncertain because of the unpredictability of nature. Often, you can reduce the outcome's uncertainty by getting additional information. We showed how to calculate the expected value of perfect information (EVPI) to establish a limit on the value of imperfect information. If the cost of imperfect information is greater than the EVPI, buying the information is not a good economic decision. If the cost of imperfect information is less than the EVPI, you need to calculate the expected value of imperfect information (EVII) to evaluate whether it's worth buying.

Before you get additional information, the states of nature have a prior distribution. You use Bayes's Rule to calculate the posterior probabilities based on the additional information. We described a tabular method for calculating the state of nature posterior probabilities and the forecast probabilities. You solve decision trees from right to left. At each chance event node, you calculate the expected value. At each decision node, you select the decision alternative with the best expected value.

You can use decision trees for deterministic sequential decisions as well as probabilistic sequential decisions. In fact, you can have any pattern of decisions and chance events. In the last section, we showed the decision tree for the ZIP + 4 study, which had a single decision node followed by several sequential chance events. We also illustrated the decision tree for a three-period deterministic inventory planning problem. In that case, the decision tree had three sets of decision nodes, corresponding to the purchasing decisions in Months 1, 2, and 3. We extended that problem to a probabilistic sequential decision problem by having uncertain demands. In that case, each decision node was followed by a chance event node (the month's demand) before the next month's decision node.

If you can draw a decision tree that reflects the decision environment, you can solve the decision tree to analyze the decision environment. But decision trees have some limitations. First, a decision tree becomes large if there are many decision nodes, decision alternatives, chance event nodes, and chance event outcomes. For the probabilistic three-period inventory planning problem with only two possible demands, the tree was large. Although the calculations aren't difficult, there can be a large number. Second, chance event nodes assume that there is a finite list of possible outcomes. You assign a probability to each arc from the chance event node. You can't use a decision tree if the outcomes are continuous. Instead, you must redefine the outcomes so that there is a finite set of possibilities. The ZIP + 4 study used this approach for continuous uncertain events. Third, if you use decision trees to model a competitor's decision, you must estimate conditional probabilities to solve the decision tree. However, the calculations are no more difficult for a competitor's actions than for a state of nature that is uncertain because of the unpredictability of nature. Fourth, we assumed that the state of nature was not influenced by the decision alternative selected. You can use a decision tree anyway if you can estimate the conditional probabilities. This was the approach for a sequential competitor decision. Fifth, the EVPI is the expected opportunity loss for the best decision, but you must be able to represent the decision environment by a payoff table. Otherwise, you use a decision tree and the expected value criterion. Sixth, you need probabilities to use decision trees for probabilistic decision environments.

You should note some cautions. First, if you aren't risk indifferent, you use utility instead of monetary values. Second, you use sensitivity analysis to improve decision making. For example, if a change in the state of nature probabilities doesn't affect the decision, you have more confidence in it. Also, consider manipulating the decision tree model and the environment. For example, if you can postpone the decision until you discover the state of nature, it's easier to select the best decision. Third, assigning costs and revenues to arcs helps sensitivity analysis. Remember, you choose the form for the decision tree, and before making the choice, you should consider what types of sensitivity analysis are desired. Fourth, your decision tree should satisfy the characteristics of decision trees—only one trunk and no more than one arc entering a node from the left. Fifth, perfect experts are rare, but you can use the EVPI to screen imperfect experts without having to calculate the EVII. Sixth, any node in a decision tree is conditional on everything before the node. In particular, chance event probabilities are conditional probabilities. Seventh, when you calculate the EVPI and the EVII, the values have the following relationships: $EVPI \geq EVII \geq 0$. If your calculated values don't satisfy those relationships, check your calculations.

QUESTIONS

1. What is a sequential decision problem?

2. What is a decision tree?

3. Comment on this statement: "Decision trees cannot be used to analyze decision environments in which the actions of a thinking competitor are included."

4. Describe a situation in which the values for a decision tree should be utility, not monetary values.

5. Is the expected value of perfect information ever less than the expected value of imperfect information? Is it ever negative?

6. What is an advantage that the expected opportunity loss criterion has over the expected (monetary) value criterion?

7. What is a prior probability? What is a posterior probability?

8. What is a terminating node?

9. What is an advantage of assigning values to arcs, rather than having nonzero values only for terminating nodes?

10. What is Bayes's Rule, and what is it used for?

11. What is a decision strategy?

12. How do you designate inferior decisions in a decision tree?

13. For a cost payoff table, develop the relationship among the expected cost with perfect information, $E(i)$, and $EOL(i)$.

14. What are three characteristics of a decision tree?

15. What is folding back?

16. What are the three types of decision tree nodes?

For Questions 17–22, refer to the Theory section at the end of this chapter.

17. *Theory.* What is the Principle of Optimality?

18. *Theory.* What is the optimal value function?

19. *Theory.* What is backward recursion?

20. *Theory.* What is a state in dynamic programming?

21. *Theory.* What is a stage in dynamic programming?

22. *Theory.* How is the optimal decision function used to find the optimal decisions?

EXERCISES

1. Figure 11.1 represents in a decision tree Table 11.1, the payoff table of the new product introduction example. The payoff table was based on anticipated sales of 2,000 units of the new product if the economy was weak. Say that the anticipated sales are 3,000 instead.
   a. Construct the decision tree.
   b. Solve the decision tree. What decision alternative is selected?
   c. Construct and solve the decision tree for an errorless expert. What is the EPPI? What is the EVPI?
   d. What decision alternative is selected using the EOL criterion?
   e. Determine the EVPI from your answer to Part *d*.

2. Figure 11.1 represents in a decision tree Table 11.1, the payoff table of the new product introduction example. The payoff table was based on anticipated sales of 2,000 units of the new product if the economy was weak. Say that the anticipated sales are 3,800 instead.
   a. Construct the decision tree.
   b. Solve the decision tree. What decision alternative is selected?
   c. Construct and solve the decision tree for an errorless expert. What is the EPPI? What is the EVPI?
   d. What decision alternative is selected using the EOL criterion?
   e. Determine the EVPI from your answer to Part *d*.

3. Consider the following cost payoff table:

Decision Alternative	State of Nature			
	1	2	3	4
1	$3,000	$4,200	$6,100	$1,300
2	600	950	850	1,200
3	1,500	2,300	600	1,300

The decision alternative must be selected before the state of the nature has been discovered.
   a. Are any of the decision alternatives dominated?
   b. Construct the decision tree.

4. Consider the following cost payoff table:

Decision Alternative	State of Nature			
	1	2	3	4
1	$ 300	$ 720	$310	$2,300
2	6,000	950	850	3,200
3	2,500	1,300	600	1,600

The decision alternative must be selected before the state of nature has been discovered.

a. Are any of the decision alternatives dominated?

b. Construct the decision tree.

5. For the payoff table of Exercise 3, the probabilities of the states of nature are

State of Nature	Probability
1	0.3
2	0.2
3	0.4
4	0.1

a. Solve the decision tree. What is the expected cost? What decision alternative is selected?

b. Construct the decision tree in which an errorless expert tells the state of nature before the selection of the decision alternative. Solve this decision tree. What is the expected cost?

c. Determine the EVPI from your answers to Parts *a* and *b*.

6. For the payoff table of Exercise 4, the probabilities of the states of nature are

State of Nature	Probability
1	0.4
2	0.3
3	0.1
4	0.2

a. Solve the decision tree. What is the expected cost? What decision alternative is selected?

b. Construct the decision tree in which an errorless expert tells the state of nature before the selection of the decision alternative. Solve this decision tree. What is the expected cost?

c. Determine the EVPI from your answers to Parts *a* and *b*.

7. Consider the following profit payoff table:

Decision Alternative	State of Nature			
	1	2	3	4
1	$3,300	$2,600	$5,100	$1,400
2	2,600	1,950	8,500	1,100
3	2,500	3,700	6,600	1,200

The decision alternative must be selected before the state of nature has been discovered. The probabilities of the states of nature are

State of Nature	Probability
1	0.3
2	0.2
3	0.2
4	0.3

a. Solve the decision tree. What is the expected profit? What decision alternative is selected?
b. Construct the decision tree in which an errorless expert tells the state of nature before the selection of the decision alternative. Solve this decision tree. What is the EPPI?
c. Determine the EVPI from your answers to Parts *a* and *b*.
d. What decision alternative is selected using the EOL criterion?
e. Determine the EVPI from your answer to Part *d*.

8. Consider the following profit payoff table:

Decision Alternative	State of Nature			
	1	2	3	4
1	$4,300	$1,600	$5,500	$2,600
2	2,900	3,800	6,500	3,200
3	1,500	4,900	4,500	2,100

The decision alternative must be selected before the state of nature has been discovered. The probabilities of the states of nature are

State of Nature	Probability
1	0.1
2	0.2
3	0.3
4	0.4

a. Solve the decision tree. What is the expected profit? What decision alternative is selected?
b. Construct the decision tree in which an errorless expert tells the state of nature before the selection of the decision alternative. Solve this decision tree. What is the EPPI?
c. Determine the EVPI from your answers to Parts *a* and *b*.
d. What decision alternative is selected using the EOL criterion?
e. Determine the EVPI from your answer to Part *d*.

9. You have examined the historical record of your new product planning group. A new product is judged a success if it exceeds the minimum acceptable rate of return of 15 percent. In a small number of cases, although the new product planning group did not recommend the introduction of a product, top management introduced the product anyway. The record of successes is summarized in the table below:

	Success	Failure
Recommended	12	4
Not recommended	2	2

   a. Convert this information into a joint probability table.

   b. If another new product is introduced with characteristics similar to those of the products that were introduced in the past, what is the probability of its being a success?

   c. Before referring another new product to the new product planning group, top management believes that the probability of its being a success is 0.9. What is the probability that the group will recommend the product favorably?

   d. Do you feel that the use of this historical information to assess the probabilities is appropriate?

10. You have examined the historical record of your new product planning group. A new product is judged a success if it exceeds the minimum acceptable rate of return of 15 percent. In a small number of cases, although the new product planning group did not recommend the introduction of a product, top management introduced the product anyway. The record of successes is summarized in the table below:

	Success	Failure
Recommended	21	4
Not recommended	3	2

   a. Convert this information into a joint probability table.

   b. If another new product is introduced with characteristics similar to those of the products that were introduced in the past, what is the probability of its being a success?

   c. Before referring another new product to the new product planning group, top management believes that the probability of its being a success is 0.9. What is the probability that the group will recommend the product favorably?

   d. Do you feel that the use of this historical information to assess the probabilities is appropriate?

11. Reconsider the new product introduction example if the probability of the actual state of the economy being strong, $P(ASE)$, is 0.3.

   a. Calculate the posterior probabilities and the forecast probabilities using the tabular method.

    b. Construct and solve the decision tree. What is the EPII?

    c. What is the EVII?

    d. If the expert charges a fee of $10,000 for the forecast, should the expert be hired?

12. Reconsider the new product introduction example if the probability of the actual state of the economy being strong, *P(ASE)*, is 0.6.

    a. Calculate the posterior probabilities and the forecast probabilities using the tabular method.

    b. Construct and solve the decision tree. What is the EPII?

    c. What is the EVII?

    d. If the expert charges a fee of $10,000 for the forecast, should the expert be hired?

13. Top management feels that using only two states of the economy in the analysis of the new product introduction example is not adequate. It has recommended the addition of a third category—a "flat" economy. Construct a decision tree similar to the one in Figure 11.6 with this addition.

14. Top management feels that using only two states of the economy in the analysis of the new product introduction example is not adequate. It has recommended the addition of a third category—a "flat" economy. Construct a decision tree similar to the one in Figure 11.9 with this addition.

15. The expert in the new product introduction example has decided to make a guarantee. If the actual state of the economy is not identical with the forecast, the $10,000 fee will be refunded.

    a. Construct a decision tree similar to the one in Figure 11.6.

    b. Solve the decision tree.

    c. What is the decision strategy?

16. The expert in the new product introduction example has decided to make a guarantee. If the actual state of the economy is not identical to the forecast, the $10,000 fee will be refunded.

    a. Construct a decision tree similar to the one in Figure 11.12.

    b. Solve the decision tree.

    c. What is the decision strategy?

For Exercises 17–20, refer to the Theory section at the end of this chapter.

17. *Theory.* Find the shortest route from Node 1 to Node 7 using dynamic programming.

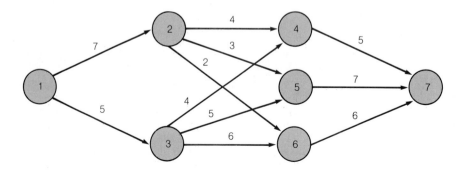

18. *Theory.* Find the shortest route from Node 1 to Node 8 using dynamic programming.

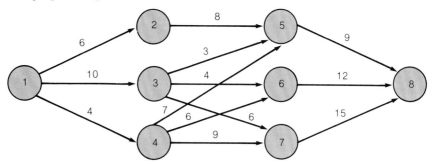

19. *Theory.* Solve the three-item knapsack problem using dynamic programming. The total weight limitation is 5 pounds.

Item	Benefit/ Unit	Weight (pounds/unit)
1	10	4
2	6	2
3	2	1

20. *Theory.* Solve the four-item knapsack problem using dynamic programming. The total weight limitation is 7 pounds.

Item	Benefit/ Unit	Weight (pounds/unit)
1	17	4
2	10	3
3	7	2
4	4	1

MORE CHALLENGING EXERCISES

1. An investor is contemplating investing in an electric utility that is constructing a nuclear power plant. There is concern about whether the regulatory agency will allow the plant's completion and include the cost of the plant in the rate base. If the regulatory agency rules favorably, it is anticipated that the stock will increase 13 percent next year (including dividends). If the regulatory agency rules unfavorably, the stock is anticipated to increase only 6 percent. Another alternative is to invest in a one-year, 8 percent certificate of deposit at a bank. The investor plans to hold the stock for one year.

a. If the probability of a favorable ruling is 0.7, which alternative is preferred?

b. A stockbroker has told you that his research department expects a favorable ruling. He claims that the research department is correct 4 times out of 5. Which investment has the greatest expected return?

2. An oil company has offered a farmer in Oklahoma $50,000 for the mineral rights to his property. The oil company has another alternative that allows the farmer to share in the return if oil is discovered. This alternative gives the farmer a guarantee of $5,000 plus $0.50 per barrel of oil recovered. A geologist friend has estimated that the recoverable oil might total as much as 1 million barrels. This friend has provided the farmer with the following assessments of the probabilities of the amount of recoverable oil.

Success Level	Recoverable Oil (barrels)	Probability
Dry	0	0.85
Moderate	200,000	0.10
Gusher	1,000,000	0.05

a. Which alternative do you recommend to the farmer?

b. The farmer is unsure of the accuracy of his friend's assessment of the probabilities. The friend has told the farmer that he can do additional research to try to improve his assessment. This research would require additional expenses of $3,000. The friend has provided the farmer with the following information on his accuracy in similar situations.

	Number of Occurrences		
	Actual Results		
Forecast	Dry	Moderate	Gusher
Dry	15	1	1
Moderate	1	5	1
Gusher	2	1	5

Should the farmer have his friend undertake the additional research? What should the farmer do?

3. Recall the hair dryer example from Chapter 2. What is the expected value of perfect information about a strike if a wage offer of 10 percent is made?

4. Recall the hair dryer example from Chapter 2. What is the expected value of perfect information about receiving the contract from Montgomery Ward?

5. A company is contemplating a price increase of $1 a unit. Unfortunately, there is uncertainty about the effect of the price increase on sales. If the price is not increased, the company's profit for the next fiscal year is expected to be $100,000 on sales of 20,000 units. The profit margin at the current price is

$5 per unit. The probability distribution of sales in the next fiscal year based on a $1 price increase is

Units Sold	Probability
12,000	0.1
14,000	0.2
16,000	0.25
18,000	0.4
20,000	0.05

  a. Construct a decision tree with a one-year time horizon to evaluate whether to increase the price by $1.
  b. What is the EVPI about the effect of the price increase on demand?
  c. Additional market research can be performed to improve the assessment of the effect of the price increase. The market research department has requested the allocation of $15,000 to perform the analysis. Discuss whether the additional market research is worthwhile.

6. A company has experienced a rapid increase in sales. If the trend continues, the existing manufacturing capacity will be insufficient to satisfy demand. The company is contemplating three alternatives if this occurs. The first is to raise the price to a level at which demand is equal to the existing capacity. The second is to subcontract the production for demand above the existing capacity. This cuts the profit margin on the units that the subcontractor produces. The third alternative is to expand the existing capacity. If this is done, the anticipated capital investment is $50,000 and the manufacturing costs increase for the additional units because employees must work overtime.
  The current level of annual sales is 100,000 units, the current capacity is 110,000 units, and the current profit margin is $12 per unit. The probability distribution of next year's demand is

Next Year's Demand	Probability
110,000	0.50
115,000	0.35
120,000	0.15

  It is predicted that demand will be reduced to the capacity of 110,000 by a price increase of $0.25 per unit if next year's demand is 115,000 and by a price increase of $0.45 per unit if next year's demand is 120,000. The extra subcontracting cost is $3.25 per unit. If capacity is expanded, the manufacturing cost of each unit above the current capacity increases by $1.75 because of overtime costs. If a decision is made to subcontract or expand capacity, a commitment must be made now, before the actual level of demand for next year is discovered. In the case of subcontracting, no commitment must be made to a level of subcontracting. That determination can be postponed until the actual level of demand is discovered.

a. Construct a decision tree to evaluate the three alternatives.

b. Which alternative should be selected?

c. What is the EPPI associated with knowledge of next year's demand? The EVPI?

7. The use of decision trees requires a finite set of possible outcomes with discrete probabilities. In many cases, the normal probability distribution is used. This continuous probability distribution must be approximated by a discrete probability distribution so that it can be used in a decision tree. One approach is to divide the outcomes into a number of equally likely intervals and to assign the outcomes equal probabilities. For each interval, the outcome value is determined as the median value within the interval; this value is determined from the cumulative probabilities distribution. For example, if five intervals are used, the five outcomes are for the values corresponding to cumulative probabilities 0.1, 0.3, 0.5, 0.7, and 0.9, each with a probability of 0.2.

The cost of introducing a new product is estimated at $150,000. The profit margin of the product is estimated to be $25 per unit. Because of rapid changes in its technology, the product is believed to have a life span of only one year. Its anticipated sales are uncertain, but a normal probability distribution with a mean of 6,500 units and a standard deviation of 500 units has been assessed.

a. Construct a decision tree to decide whether to introduce the new product. Use five intervals to approximate the normal probability distribution. What is the expected profit calculated for the decision to introduce the new product?

b. Calculate the EVPI.

8. Jones Manufacturing purchases an electronic component that is part of its product. Historical records show that the probabilities of defective components are

Percent Defective	Probability
1	0.2
2	0.5
3	0.3

A batch of 1,000 components must be ordered. A test for defective components has been developed that costs $0.25 per component, but the test is sometimes wrong. If a component is actually defective, the test has a probability of 0.9 of indicating that the component is defective. If a component is actually OK, the test has a probability of 0.9 of indicating that the component is OK. If a component is returned and it's OK, the supplier charges $10. If a defective component is assembled, the rework cost is $20. Should Jones Manufacturing use the test before assembly?

9. As director of research and development, you have received a recommendation for a project estimated to cost $75,000 from one of your project leaders. The purpose of the project is to develop a new class of chemical polymer. If the project is a major success, the future profits are estimated to be $500,000. The project leader thinks that there is a good chance of a minor success, which would result in profits of $150,000. She admits that there could be no success at all. The probabilities of a major success, a minor success, and failure are 0.1, 0.5, and 0.4, respectively.

   This project leader also has another alternative. For $32,000, she can do additional testing. If the additional testing is unsuccessful, the project is certain to fail. If the additional testing is successful, the probability is ⅙ that the project will result in a major success and ⅚ that it will result in a minor success.

   These are your alternatives: (1) Don't fund anything. (2) Fund the project. (3) Fund the additional testing and if it's successful, fund the project. What is your recommendation? Write a one-page report explaining your analysis.

10. As purchasing manager, you must decide the ordering schedule for corrugated packing cases. Based on the production plans, the numbers needed for the next three months are

Month	Requirements
January	2,500
February	3,500
March	3,300

The units cost $50 each if the order quantity is less than 3,000 units. If you buy 3,000 units or more, the cost is $48 per unit. The inventory carrying cost is $1 per unit on hand at the end of a month. Your policy is to always order in quantities equal to the requirements for entire months. Thus, in January you would order either 2,500 or 6,000 or 9,300 units. Construct a decision tree and recommend how many units to order in each month.

For MCEs 11 and 12, refer to the Theory section at the end of this chapter.

11. *Theory.* Solve MCE 10 using dynamic programming.

12. *Theory.* Solve the probabilistic three-period inventory planning problem in the chapter using dynamic programming. (*Hint:* There are three stages. At each stage, include the decision followed by the probabilistic demand. For each decision, you calculate the expected profit for the decision and chance event at that stage and add the expected future profits weighted by the outcome probabilities. The state is the number of units on hand before any units are purchased at the beginning of a month.)

CASE

Vulcan Specialty Rubber Company

Jim Desmond bounced into the office of Fred Hooper, marketing vice president of the Vulcan Specialty Rubber Company. "I've done it! After four years of calling on the General Truck Company in Detroit, I have finally sold them!"

Fred's enthusiasm took off at this news. "What's the order for? How big?"

"The deal shapes up like this, Fred. General Truck is having trouble with its present sources of supply in meeting specifications for parts for their new-model trucks to be introduced next year. I have talked them into letting us have a whack at their problems. Apparently the new model has some radical design changes to overcome severe criticism from their present customers. They want to see what we can do with three parts that are critical—one goes into the engine mount, one into the shock absorber assembly, and one into the bumper. The purchasing agent says his job is on the line, and he hopes we can produce. As long as our price is reasonable, he will go along with us, but he cannot make any compromises on meeting specifications. He says he is willing to give us a chance, but he wants us to show good faith by sharing his risk in switching to us as a new vendor."

Fred's soaring enthusiasm took a nosedive. "What do you mean, Jim?"

Jim was all salesman—his enthusiasm didn't waver. "General Truck will give us a chance to submit engine mount parts from a sample mold. If these parts meet laboratory tests, he will give us an order for 100,000 parts and then give us a chance to submit samples for either the shock absorber assembly or the bumper assembly—one or the other, but not both. If we succeed in passing the laboratory tests with the second set of samples, we can go on to qualify for the third or remaining part. The order quantities are 100,000 for all parts."

Fred feared the answer to his next ques-

tion, but asked, "And what happens if we fail the tests? Do we get reimbursed?"

"No, the purchasing agent was clear on this point. This is our part of the 'sharing the risk.' If we don't meet specifications, we take the loss. But I think this is worth any gamble—you know what this account can mean to us. If we produce, we will be able to write our own ticket with this purchasing agent. He's in a bind. Obviously, the quantities are only enough to try us out."

"What's the timing on this, Jim?"

Jim replied, "We have a week to tell them if we are interested in the proposition. Then we have two months to deliver the first samples. I have a full set of drawings and specifications here."

Fred took the sheaf of papers from Jim and walked down the hall to the office of the plant manager, Tom Carbon, and explained the situation to him. Tom examined the specifications and frowned. "I can see why they are having trouble with these parts. These requirements are tough. I think the rubber compound formulations will be our biggest headache. The molds are intricate, but should present no problem that we can't lick. I want to go over this job with my department heads. I'll have an answer for you in three or four days."

Four days later, Tom met again with Fred. "As I suspected, this is one of the tougher jobs that we have been asked to do. I think our chances of success for the engine mount and bumper parts are about 50–50. The shock absorber part is a little easier."

"How much easier, Tom?"

Tom thought a moment. "Not that much

SOURCE: Martin K. Starr and Irving Stein, *The Practice of Management Science*, © 1976, pp. 25–26. Reprinted by permission of Prentice-Hall, Inc., Englewood Cliffs, New Jersey.

easier—I'd say about 60-40.''

Fred then asked, ''Do you have any cost figures? How many dollars will we be gambling?''

Tom gave Fred some penciled numbers:

Direct costs for 100 samples, including laboratory formulations, molds, and labor:

> Engine mounts—$8,000
> Bumpers—$16,000
> Shock absorbers—$10,000

At the following prices, we can meet our standard pricing policy of charging two times the direct costs—that is, 50 percent of the price will cover direct costs; 50 percent will cover overhead and profit.

> Engine mounts—20 cents each
> Bumpers—80 cents each
> Shock absorbers—40 cents each

These prices are safe—*provided we can do the job at all.*

Fred took the figures and called the purchasing agent at General Truck to learn if the prices were acceptable if they decided to go ahead. Inwardly, he hoped that they would be far out of line, to save him from the difficult decision of whether to take the risks of proceeding with the job.

The purchasing agent said the prices were in line with those of his present suppliers.

Fred searched for a handle. He had never been confronted with a proposition such as this. He finally decided to take the path of many lesser men. He went into the office of his boss, the president of Vulcan, described the situation, and asked for a decision.

George Vulcan, president, had taken over the company just a few years ago, upon the death of his father. George was 28 years old, bright, and the holder of an M.B.A. from a leading university. While he had little knowl-edge of the technical intricacies of specialty goods manufacture, he was aggressive and a good businessman. Under his stewardship, the company had grown in sales to its present $2 million annual level. His policy was to put profits back into the business in the form of new presses and other capital equipment; but while his posture enabled the company to take on new jobs at competitive prices, working capital was at a bare minimum to keep up with current operations. George was a firm believer in delegation; he was convinced that passing responsibility and accountability down the ladder was essential to corporate growth.

After hearing Fred's description of the General Truck Company proposition, he responded, ''I would like you to make this decision. I think a decision tree analysis could be revealing—you are familiar with this technique. I hope that your analysis shows that we should take this job—we want it. While there is no guarantee that these pilot runs will lead to additional major contracts, if we do well, the doors will be open. On the other hand, our cash position and projected flows will not permit us to lose any money on this work, no matter how slight. We should at least see a positive expected value fall out of your decision tree. We can take a gamble on our ability to produce—we gamble daily. Knowing Tom and his nature, I feel his odds on completing the work successfully are probably conservative. If you have to, you might consider the per piece price of one or more of the parts, although there might be some problem in going back to the purchasing agent at General Truck with increased prices. Let me have your decision as soon as possible.''

Fred went back to his desk and worked out a decision tree from the data that he had. Clearly, the expected value did not meet George's criteria. The question loomed—was there an alternative strategy that was viable?

CASE

Josim Manufacturing Company

Josim Manufacturing is a major manufacturer of a variety of plumbing fixtures. It manufactures over 3,000 different plumbing needs in plants located in Michigan City, Indiana; Greensberg, South Carolina; and Lugano, Switzerland. The company was founded in 1909 by Boris Schimmel, who immigrated from Russia in 1902. For five years Boris worked in the foundry and the tube mill of a major steel manufacturer in Pittsburgh. In 1907 he moved to Chicago to help his ailing brother-in-law manage his hardware store. Unfortunately, however, his brother-in-law died the following year and the widow decided to sell the hardware business despite the vigorous objections of Boris. Having tasted the challenge of being an entrepreneur, Boris, instead of going back to the mill, started looking around for suitable alternatives. He located a small, financially troubled foundry in Michigan City, used all his savings to finance the purchase of the foundry, and renamed it the Schim Manufacturing Company.

He began by making manhole covers, for which he found a ready market in the rapidly expanding cities of Chicago, Milwaukee, and Indianapolis. By 1927, his son Joseph had acquired a degree in mechanical engineering from Purdue University and joined the firm on a full-time basis. Joseph introduced new and modern manufacturing techniques to the firm and helped the firm diversify its products to include a variety of plumbing needs. By 1948, the firm was making over 1,000 products and had acquired a reputation for quality and technical innovation among contractors and wholesalers, who were its primary customers. Lastly, it had changed its name to Josim.

Josim grew most vigorously between the years 1953 and 1970 under the guiding financial genius of Richard Rosenberg, who had joined the firm as the executive vice president. His main responsibility was the financial end of the firm, thus freeing Joseph to concentrate on production and research and development activities. The Greensberg plant was built in 1955, and the Swiss subsidiary was acquired in 1966. Sales increased from $38 million in 1955 to $186 million in 1976.

Everything seemed to be going well for Josim until 1977, when the sharp downturn suffered by the construction industry caused Josim to cut back its production for the first time since 1948.

On May 5, 1978, Joseph Schimmel, Richard Rosenberg, and Stephen Brown, Josim's chief of new product development, held a meeting to chart the company's strategy. Richard was convinced that the slump in the construction industry was likely to continue throughout the 70s and that it was in the best interest of the company to expand into new markets. He noted that none of the company's products were sold to, or seen by, the consumer. In fact, almost all of the company's products are used either behind walls or under floors. The company makes no faucets, flush valves, or other "visible" plumbing fixtures. Richard, therefore, contended that the company should attempt to cultivate the consumer market for installation and replacement of such fixtures. He cited industry statistics and his own analysis to show that a large replacement market exists for kitchen and bathroom faucets and that such demand is relatively immune to the downturn in housing starts. Joseph expressed concern over the company's lack of experience with consumer distribution channels and competition from retail hardware chains such as Ace and True Value and department chains such a Sears and Montgomery Ward. Stephen, on the other hand, was quite enthusiastic

SOURCE: Raj Aggarwal and Inder Khera, *Management Science Cases and Applications,* Oakland: Holden-Day, Inc., 1979, pp. 30–34.

about the prospect of designing something with aesthetic appeal in conjunction with the usual technical requirements. He argued that his department could develop a faucet so unique in its function and appearance that it would be largely insulated from competition by existing faucets. Joseph relented, but with the understanding that such a faucet must not require major new capital plant expenditure and should, instead, use existing idle plant capacity. They decided to meet again in four weeks, when Stephen would present his preliminary ideas for the new faucet. In the meantime, it was agreed that Richard would formulate some tentative estimates of the market and the appropriate distribution channels.

On the very next day Stephen Brown's Research & Development department initiated the task of developing a unique household water faucet on a top-priority basis. They gathered samples of all currently available household faucets and conducted informal surveys among their friends and relatives to determine their complaints with existing faucets in their homes. Among the nearly 30 individuals informally interviewed, 7 related incidents of a family member having been scalded by water that was too hot. This was particularly true for children while using the bathroom sink or taking a shower. Most of the respondents also felt that most of their kitchen needs required water at higher temperatures than most of their bathroom needs. Most incidents of scalding, however, seemed to have occurred in the bathroom. This information indicated that people, particularly children, sometimes have difficulty adjusting water temperature and that a faucet that would always deliver water at a predetermined desired temperature would represent a significant advantage over existing faucets. Furthermore, since different activities require water at different temperatures (i.e., shaving requires hotter water than washing one's face), the faucet should be able to deliver water at several predetermined temperatures. This then

became the focal point for the Research & Development's faucet development program.

Meanwhile, Rosenberg was working on developing market estimates for the firm's chances of successfully entering the consumer market. Although the firm had little experience in the consumer field, it had been highly successful in gaining a 28 percent share of the market through architects, commercial builders, home builders, and wholesale distributors. However, being both a prudent businessman and being aware of the competition, Mr. Rosenberg estimated the probability of Josim being able to successfully penetrate the consumer market at only 30 percent. Thus, Josim would face a 70 percent chance of failing to capture a profitable share of the market. In Mr. Rosenberg's estimation, this would result in a loss. The net present value of such a loss would be $2 million. If, however, the proposed new faucet were successful and had high sales, the resulting net present value of the cash flow from this project would be $4 million.

During the June 2 meeting, Stephen Brown presented plans for a new type of faucet recently designed by his department. Using ingenious valve arrangements, they planned to develop a faucet that would deliver water at four different preset temperatures at the touch of a button. (See Exhibit 1.) The four buttons would be color-coded from blue for cold through yellow, orange, and finally red for hot. The water temperature corresponding to each button would be preset at the time of installation according to the needs of the users. Once calibrated, the faucet would always deliver water at the predetermined temperatures when one of the buttons was pushed. Temperature settings could subsequently be altered, if necessary, by partially disassembling the mechanism and adjusting certain screws. This process would not require any specialized tools beyond a couple of screwdrivers and a pair of pliers.

Richard Rosenberg presented his prelimi-

EXHIBIT 1   Proposed Faucet Designs

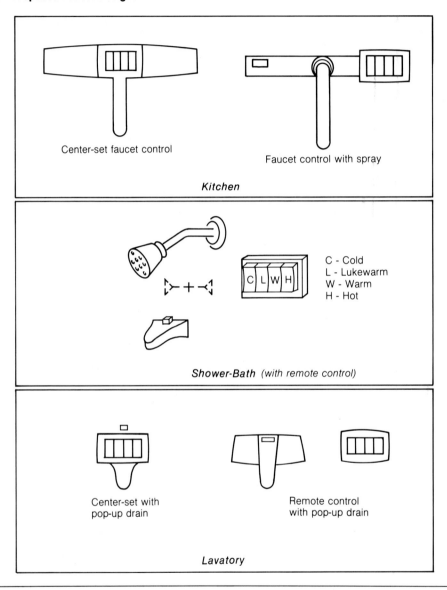

nary estimates of the potential profitability of the new product, along with his estimates of the tentative probabilities for success and failure. He felt also that, because of the newness of the venture, the company must conduct a market survey using at least three representative cities. Although such surveys conducted by other companies often predicted accurately the success or failure of a new product, they occasionally predicted success for a product that later failed, and vice versa. Furthermore, the results in many instances

EXHIBIT 2 Survey Results for Actual Sales Levels

Survey Prediction	Actual Level of Sales	
	High Sales	Low Sales
Survey predicts success (i.e., high sales)	0.5	0.1
Survey inconclusive	0.3	0.3
Survey predicts failure (i.e., low sales)	0.2	0.6
	1.0	1.0

were inconclusive. Rosenberg estimated the cost of such a survey to be in the neighborhood of $200,000. Based on past experience, he attached conditional probabilities to the various survey results as indicators of the actual sales level. These probabilities are presented in Exhibit 2.

Ms. Abby Horowitz, the new M.B.A. hired as Mr. Rosenberg's assistant, was asked to prepare a detailed analysis of the feasibility of introducing the new product. She was asked to include answers to the questions Mr. Rosenberg had raised based on the data available to him without the survey. Should the new faucet be introduced? What is the maximum amount that the company should be willing to pay for infallible market information? Should the proposed survey be undertaken? Ms. Horowitz was also asked to design a decision rule for the introduction of the faucet if the survey were undertaken.

Dynamic programming
software

THEORY *Dynamic Programming*

Dynamic programming is a powerful tool for analyzing sequential decision problems, both deterministic and probabilistic. In this section, we
illustrate dynamic programming on three deterministic decision problems.
The first is a shortest-route problem. The second is the three-period
inventory planning problem described in the last section of the chapter.
Both of these problems have a natural sequence for the decisions. The
third problem is a knapsack problem, for which there is no natural
decision sequence. We show how to impose a decision sequence on the
knapsack problem and how to solve the problem using dynamic programming. You can use dynamic programming for many types of interrelated
decision problems that are not dynamic in the multiple-period sense.

Dynamic programming is a **computational approach** to decision problems, not an algorithm like the simplex method for linear programming
models. Because dynamic programming is an approach, general-purpose
dynamic programming software is not usually available. Instead, dynamic
programming software is available for solving a class of problems, such as
knapsack problems. First, we illustrate the concepts of dynamic programming by using them to solve a shortest-route problem. Then we illustrate
those concepts by using them to solve other problems. Using dynamic
programming to solve problems is the best way to develop your dynamic
programming skill.

The Shortest-Route Problem

In Chapter 8, we described the shortest-route problem and its applications. Figure 11.T1 shows a network of seven nodes. The numbers on the
arcs are the distances between pairs of nodes. You want to find the
shortest route from Node 1 to Node 7.

Say that you know the length of the shortest route from Nodes 2, 3, and
4 to Node 7. Let $S(j)$ denote the length of the shortest route from Node j
to Node 7. Then, you find the length of the shortest route from Node 1 to
Node 7 as

$$S(1) = \min\{4 + S(2),\ 6 + S(3),\ 6 + S(4)\}$$

FIGURE 11.T1 Shortest-Route Example

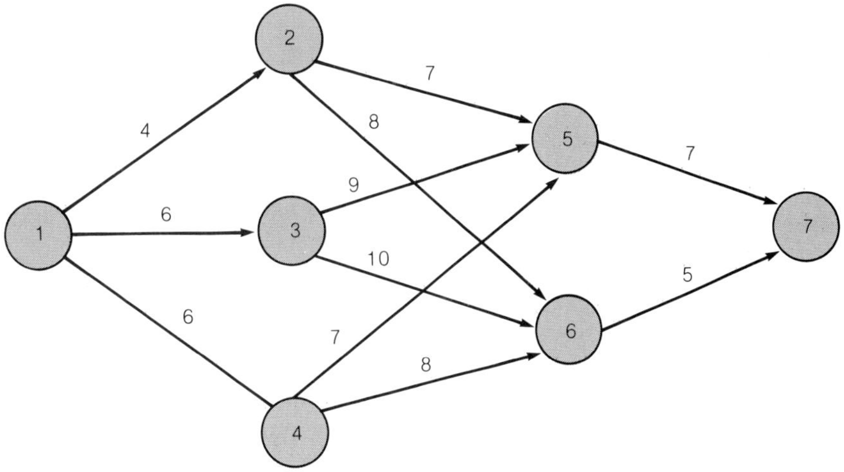

From Node 1, you can go to Node 2, 3, or 4. The first term in the minimization is 4, the distance from Node 1 to Node 2, plus $S(2)$, the length of the shortest route from Node 2 to Node 7. The second and third terms in the minimization are the distances if you go to Node 3 or Node 4, respectively. By finding the minimum, you get the length of the shortest route from Node 1 to Node 7.

Unfortunately, when you start the calculations, you don't know $S(2)$, $S(3)$, and $S(4)$. However, you can calculate them using the same approach. For example, say that you know $S(5)$ and $S(6)$. You calculate the length of the shortest route from Node 2 to Node 7 as

$$S(2) = \min\{7 + S(5), 8 + S(6)\}$$

You calculate $S(3)$ and $S(4)$ similarly.

Unfortunately, you don't know $S(5)$ and $S(6)$ when you start the calculations. But you can use the same approach to calculate them. Because Node 7 is the ending node, the distance from Node 5 to Node 7 is 7, $S(5) = 7$. Similarly, $S(6) = 5$.

Now that you know $S(5)$ and $S(6)$, you can calculate $S(2)$, $S(3)$, and $S(4)$. After calculating their values, you can calculate $S(1)$ using

$$S(1) = \min\{4 + S(2), 6 + S(3), 6 + S(4)\}$$

Principle of Optimality   We have just used dynamic programming for the shortest-route problem. Let's introduce some terminology and then solve the shortest-route problem. The computational approach is based on the **Principle of Optimality:** If a particular node is on the shortest route from the beginning to the end, then the shortest route from that node to the end is also on the shortest route from the beginning to the end. The Principle of Optimality is the basis for dynamic programming. If it weren't true, you could not write

$$S(1) = \min\{4 + S(2), 6 + S(3), 6 + S(4)\}$$

Stages and states

Dynamic programming is often used for sequential decisions. The **stage** is the decision number. For the shortest-route example, you must choose three arcs on the route from Node 1 to Node 7. Thus, there are three stages. Figure 11.T2 shows the stages. You number the first stage as 1 and the last stage as 3. The **state** summarizes the system's condition at the given stage. For the shortest-route example, the state is the node number. At Stage 1, for example, the only possible state is Node 1. At Stage 1, the possible decisions are to go to Node 2, 3, or 4. At Stage 2, the possible states are Nodes 2, 3, and 4. At Stage 3, the possible states are Nodes 5 and 6.

You must create a recursive relationship to formulate a dynamic programming problem. The first step is to define an **optimal value function** of the stage and state. For example, define

Optimal value function

$$f_n(i) \equiv \text{length of the shortest route from Node } i \text{ at Stage } n$$

FIGURE 11.T2   Shortest-Route Example with Stages Numbered

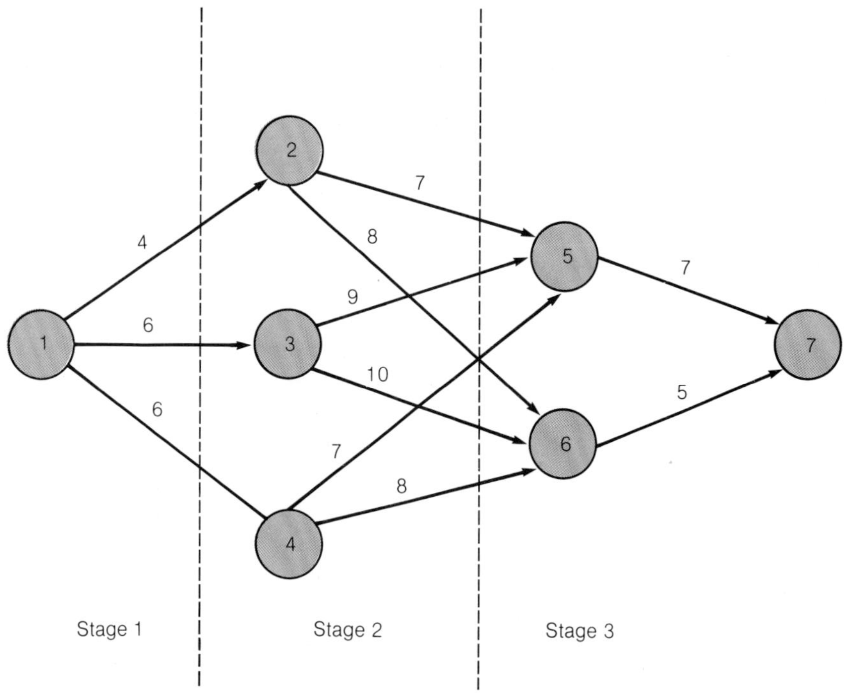

Let A_i be the set of nodes immediately after Node i, and let C_{ij} be the distance from Node i to Node j. The **recursive relationship** gives the relationship between the optimal value functions at successive stages. For the shortest-route problem, the recursive relationship is

Recursive relationship

$$f_n(i) = \min_{j \in A_i} \{C_{ij} + f_{n+1}(j)\}$$

From Stage n and State i, you only consider going to Nodes j that can be reached—that is, nodes in A_i. For each Node j in A_i, you calculate the sum of C_{ij}, the distance from Node i to Node j, plus the length of the shortest route from Node j to the end, $f_{n+1}(j)$. If you choose Node j, the stage number increases by one (because you've made one more decision) and the new state is Node j. Using the principle of optimality, the length of the shortest route from i to the end is the minimum of the sums over j in A_i. Let's solve the shortest-route problem to illustrate the notation.

Solve right to left

You solve the shortest-route problem by **backward recursion**—that is, from right to left. You start with Stage 3. The possible states at Stage 3 are 5 and 6. Because Node 7 is the end, $f_3(5) = C_{57} = 7$. Similarly, $f_3(6) = 5$. Table 11.T1 shows the Stage 3 results. Because you want to know the shortest route as well as its length, you write down the optimal decision for each stage. In general, let $d_n^*(i)$ represent the **optimal decision function** at Stage n for State i. At Node 5, you go to Node 7 next, so $d_3^*(5) = 7$. Note that Table 11.T1 contains the optimal decision function values for Stage 3, $d_3^*(i)$.

Table 11.T2 contains the Stage 2 calculations. The possible *states* at Stage 2 are 2, 3, and 4. For each state, the possible decisions are to go to Node 5 or Node 6. That is, $A_2 = A_3 = A_4 = \{5,6\}$. The decisions are listed across the top of the table. Consider Stage 2. If you go to Node 5, the distance is 7. The length of the shortest route from Node 5 to the end is 7, which was calculated in Table 11.T1. So if you go from Node 2 to Node 5, the shortest distance to the end is $7 + f_{2+1}(5) = 7 + 7 = 14$. If you go from Node 2 to Node 6, the shortest distance to the end is $C_{26} + f_{2+1}(6) = 8 + 5 = 13$. When you compare going to Node 5 or Node 6 from Node 2, you find that

$$f_2(2) = \min\{7 + 7, 8 + 5\} = 13$$

If you are at Node 2, you go to Node 6. The first line of Table 11.T2 calculates the length of the shortest route from Node 2 through Nodes 5

TABLE 11.T1 Stage 3 for the Shortest-Route Problem

State	$f_3(i)$	$d_3^*(i)$
5	7	7
6	5	7

TABLE 11.T2   Stage 2 for the Shortest-Route Problem

	Decision			
State	5	6	$f_2(i)$	$d_2^*(i)$
2	7 + 7	8 + 5	13	6
3	9 + 7	10 + 5	15	6
4	7 + 7	8 + 5	13	6

and 6 and finds the minimum, $f_2(2) = 13$. It also contains the optimal decision function value, $d_2^*(2) = 6$. Table 11.T2 shows that the length of the shortest route from Nodes 3 and 4 to the end is either $f_2(3) = 15$ or $f_2(4) = 13$.

At Stage 1, the only state is Node 1, the beginning node. The possible decisions are to go to Node 2, 3, or 4, so $A_1 = \{2,3,4\}$. You find the shortest route from Node 1 to the end as

$$f_1(1) = \min\{C_{12} + f_2(2), C_{13} + f_2(3), C_{14} + f_2(4)\}$$
$$= \min\{4 + 13, 6 + 15, 6 + 13\} = 17$$

The Stage 2 values come from Table 11.T2. The length of the shortest route is 17. Table 11.T3 shows these calculations and the optimal decision function value, $d_1^*(1) = 2$.

What is the shortest route from Node 1 to Node 7? Because you wrote the optimal decision function values, you can trace your way through the tables to find out. From Table 11.T3, you go from Node 1 to Node 2, $d_1^*(1) = 2$. Then, from Table 11.T2, you can go from Node 2 to Node 6, $d_2^*(2) = 6$. Finally, from Table 11.T1, you go from Node 6 to Node 7, $d_3^*(6) = 7$. The shortest route is 1–2–6–7.

Using backward recursion for dynamic programming, you solve the problem from right to left. You solve decision trees the same way. Because the problem is solved from right to left, some people assign the number 1 to the last stage. We prefer to avoid any confusion caused by renumbering and keep the stages in the natural order. Stage 1 is the first decision stage.

Using dynamic programming, you *partially enumerate* the possible routes through the network. For example, two possibles routes are

TABLE 11.T3   Stage 1 for the Shortest-Route Problem

	Decision			
State	2	3	4	$f_1(i)$	$d_1^*(i)$
1	4 + 13	6 + 15	6 + 13	17	2

(margin note:) Using the optimal decision function to find the optimal decisions

1–2–5–7 and 1–2–6–7. You don't explicitly consider the first because the Stage 2 calculations for $f_2(2)$ show that it is inferior. For a problem with a small number of stages and states, the computational saving for partial enumeration is small. But for a more complex problem, the saving is large.

Solving the Three-Period Deterministic Inventory Planning Problem by Dynamic Programming

In the last section of the chapter, we constructed a decision tree for a three-period deterministic inventory planning problem. The arc costs are purchasing costs and inventory carrying costs. Figure 11.T3 repeats the decision tree.

The decision tree can be solved as a shortest-route problem using dynamic programming. To give the decision tree a single ending node, we introduce a dummy node that is connected to each of the terminating nodes. But if we define the states properly, we simplify the calculations even more.

The stages are the three months. At each stage, you must decide the number of units to purchase. What are the states? If you know the inventory at the beginning of Month 3, you can calculate the best decision at that time regardless of how you obtained that inventory. For example, if before the purchasing decision the inventory at the beginning of Month 3 is zero units, it doesn't matter whether that inventory resulted from

FIGURE 11.T3 Decision Tree for Three-Period Inventory Planning Problem with Known Demand

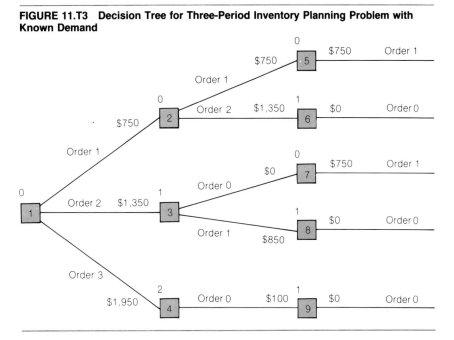

purchasing one unit in Month 1 and another unit in Month 2 or from purchasing two units in Month 1 and none in Month 2. The inventory at the beginning of a month before purchasing is the *state*. It summarizes the condition of the system so that you can make optimal decisions after that. Remember, we wrote the available inventory by each of the decision nodes. We did that because the inventories are the states.

At Stage 3, the possible states are none and one on hand. At Stage 2, the possible states are none, one, and two on hand. Because we assumed that the initial inventory was zero, the state at Stage 1 is zero. You define the optimal value function as

Optimal value function

$f_n(i) \equiv$ minimum cost for Month n to the end, given that the inventory available at the beginning of Month n is i units

Let i represent the inventory at the beginning of Month n. Let $C(j)$ represent the cost of purchasing j items, and let h represent the cost per unit in inventory at the end of a month. Because the demand is one unit each month, the inventory at the end of the month is $i + j - 1$. The recursive relationship is

Recursive relationship

$$f_n(i) \equiv \min_j\{C(j) + h(i + j - 1) + f_{n+1}(i + j - 1)\}$$

The three terms in the minimization are the purchase cost, the inventory carrying cost at the end of the month, and the minimum cost for Months $n + 1$ to the end of the time horizon, given an initial inventory of $(i + j - 1)$ at the beginning of Month $n + 1$. The cost is minimized over j, the possible purchase sizes.

Table 11.T4 shows the Stage 3 (Month 3) calculations. If you start Month 3 with no units on hand, you purchase one unit and the minimum cost is $f_3(0) = \$750$. If you start Month 3 with one unit on hand, you purchase none and the minimum cost is $f_3(1) = \$0$.

Table 11.T5 shows the Stage 2 calculations. You can start Month 2 with none, one, or two on hand. Examine the line in Table 11.T5 for none on hand. You must purchase at least one unit to satisfy the Month 2 commitment. The maximum purchase is two units because the demand for the remaining two months is two units. If you purchase one unit, the purchase cost is $750 and the inventory at the end of Month 2 is $0 + 1 - 1 = 0$. The inventory carrying cost is $\$100 \times 0 = \$0$. The total cost for

TABLE 11.T4 Stage 3 for the Deterministic Three-Period Inventory Planning Problem

	Decision			
State	0	1	$f_3(i)$	$d_3^*(i)$
0	—	750	750	1
1	0	(750 + 100)	0	0

TABLE 11.T5 Stage 2 for the Deterministic Three-Period Inventory Planning Problem

| State | Decision | | | $f_2(i)$ | $d_2^*(i)$ |
	0	1	2		
0	—	(750 + 0) + 750	(1,250 + 100) + 0	1,350	2
1	(0) + 750	(750 + 100) + 0	—	750	1
2	(0 + 100) + 0	—	—	100	0

Month 2 is \$750 + \$0, which appears inside the parentheses in Table 11.T5. Because the inventory at the end of Month 2 is zero, the minimum cost for Month 3 from Table 11.T4 is $f_3(0) = $ \$750. If you purchase one unit, the minimum total cost for the last two months is (\$750 + \$0) + \$750 = \$1,500.

Now, say that you start Month 2 with none on hand and purchase two. The purchase cost is \$1,250, and the inventory at the end of Month 2 is $(0 + 2 - 1 = 1)$ unit. The inventory carrying cost is \$100 × 1 = \$100. The cost for Month 2 is (\$1,250 + \$100). Because the inventory at the beginning of Month 3 is one, the minimum cost for Month 3 is $f_3(1) = $ \$0. If you purchase two units, the minimum total cost for the last two months is (\$1,250 + \$100) + \$0 = \$1,350. Therefore,

$$f_2(0) = \min\{(\$750 + \$0) + \$750, (\$1,250 + \$100) + \$0\}$$
$$= \min\{\$1,500, \$1,350\} = \$1,350$$

The optimal decision function value is $d_2^*(0) = 2$. You purchase two units.

If you have one unit on hand at the beginning of Month 2, you might purchase either none or one. You calculate

$$f_2(1) = \min\{[C(0) + h(1 + 0 - 1)] + f_3(1 + 0 - 1), [C(1) + h(1 + 1 - 1)]$$
$$+ f_3(1 + 1 - 1)\}$$
$$= \min\{(\$0 + \$0) + \$750, (\$750 + \$100) + \$0\} = \$750$$

If you have two units on hand at the begining of Month 2, you purchase no units and

$$f_2(2) = [\$0 + \$100 \times (2 + 0 - 1)] + f_3(2 + 0 - 1) = \$100$$

At Stage 1, you can purchase one, two, or three units. Table 11.T6 shows the calculations. For example, if you purchase one unit, the purchase cost is \$750 and the inventory at the end of Month 1 is $0 + 1 - 1 = 0$. The inventory carrying cost is \$0. The minimum cost for Months 2 and 3 is $f_2(0) = $ \$1,350. Considering the three purchases, you find that

$$f_1(0) = \min\{(\$750 + \$0) + \$1,350, (\$1,250 + \$100)$$
$$+ \$750, (\$1,750 + \$200) + \$100\}$$
$$= \min\{\$2,100, \$2,100, \$2,050\} = \$2,050$$

TABLE 11.T6   Stage 1 for the Deterministic Three-Period Inventory Planning Problem

			Decision			
State	0	1	2	3	$f_1(i)$	$d_1^*(i)$
0	—	(750) + 1, 350	(1,250 + 100) + 750	(1,750 + 200) + 100	2,050	3

You purchase three units in Month 1.

Using the optimal decision function to find the optimal decisions

Let's use the optimal decision function values to find the purchasing policy. You start Month 1 with none and purchase three, so that there are two at the beginning of Month 2. From Table 11.T5, $d_2^*(2) = 0$, so you purchase none in Month 2. At the end of Month 2, you have one left. From Table 11.T4, $d_3^*(1) = 0$, so you purchase none in Month 3. The cost for that set of decisions is \$2,050, the minimum three-period cost.

The Knapsack Problem

The shortest-route example and the three-period inventory planning problem had a natural decision sequence. For the shortest-route problem, the states are the node numbers. For the three-period inventory planning problem, the states are the units on hand at the beginning of the month. You can also use dynamic programming for interrelated decisions without a natural sequence if you can impose a sequence and define the states.

Let's describe the **knapsack problem.** In general, you want to decide how many units of different items to pack so that the benefit from the knapsack's contents is maximized within the knapsack's capacity limit. Say that there are n items and that Item j has a benefit per unit denoted by b_j and a weight denoted by w_j. Let d_j be the decision variable for the number of units of Item j to pack. If the overall weight limitation is W, the model is

$$\max \quad \sum_{j=1}^{n} b_j d_j$$

$$\text{st} \quad \sum_{j=1}^{n} w_j d_j \leq W$$

all d_j nonnegative integers

Let's consider the example with the data in Table 11.T7. There are

TABLE 11.T7   Data for the Knapsack Problem

Item	Benefit/ Unit	Weight (pounds/unit)
1	8	3
2	5	2
3	2	1

three items, so $n = 3$. For Item 1, one unit weighs 3 pounds and has a benefit of 8. Say that the overall weight limitation is 7 pounds, (i.e., $W = 7$).

There is no time sequence for the decisions, but you can let the decision for Item 1 be Stage 1. Stages 2 and 3 are the decisions for Items 2 and 3, respectively. What is the state? After you've made decisions for some items, you only need to know how much of the weight limitation remains to make a decision about the other items. Define

Optimal value function $\quad f_j(w) \equiv$ maximum benefit for items $j, j + 1, \ldots, n$ if the remaining weight limitation for them is w

The recursive relationship is

Recursive relationship
$$f_j(w) = \max_{d_j}\{b_j d_j + f_{j+1}(w - w_j d_j)\}$$

You maximize over the nonnegative integer values of d_j so that $w_j d_j$ doesn't exceed w.

Let's solve the knapsack problem with the data given in Table 11.T7. You start at Stage 3. The remaining weight limitation can be 0, 1, 2, 3, 4, 5, 6, or 7 pounds. Because Item 3 weighs 1 pound, you pack one unit for each pound of the remaining weight limitation. Table 11.T8 shows the values of $f_3(w)$ and $d_3^*(w)$ for each state value.

Now consider Stage 2. Item 2 weighs 2 pounds. The maximum number that fits depends on the remaining weight limitation. If the remaining weight limitation is 0 pounds, you can't pack any. If the remaining weight limitation is 7 pounds, the maximum number of items that fit is three. The possible decisions are listed across the top of Table 11.T9. The — indicates that some decisions aren't possible for those states. For State 0, only packing zero items is possible. Therefore,

$$f_2(0) = (5 \times 0) + f_3(0 - 1 \times 0) = 0 + 0$$

You get the value of $f_3(0)$ from Table 11.T8. As another example, consider State 2. Because the item weighs 2 pounds, you can pack either zero or one item. You calculate

$$\begin{aligned} f_2(2) &= \max\{(5 \times 0) + f_3(2 - 2 \times 0), (5 \times 1) + f_3(2 - 2 \times 1)\} \\ &= \max\{0 + 4, 5 + 0\} = 5 \end{aligned}$$

TABLE 11.T8 Stage 3 for the Knapsack Problem

State	$f_3(i)$	$d_3^*(i)$
0	0	0
1	2	1
2	4	2
3	6	3
4	8	4
5	10	5
6	12	6
7	14	7

TABLE 11.T9   Stage 2 for the Knapsack Problem

	Decision					
State	0	1	2	3	$f_2(i)$	$d_2^*(i)$
0	0 + 0	—	—	—	0	0
1	0 + 2	—	—	—	2	0
2	0 + 4	5 + 0	—	—	5	1
3	0 + 6	5 + 2	—	—	7	1
4	0 + 8	5 + 4	10 + 0	—	10	2
5	0 + 10	5 + 6	10 + 2	—	12	2
6	0 + 12	5 + 8	10 + 4	15 + 0	15	3
7	0 + 14	5 + 10	10 + 6	15 + 2	17	3

Table 11.T10 shows the calculations for Stage 1. Because the overall weight limitation is 7 pounds, the state is 7. Because Item 1 weighs 3 pounds, the maximum number of items that fit is two. The decisions are listed across the top of the table. Let's calculate the value for Decision 0. If you pack none of Item 1, its benefit is 0. Then, the remaining weight limitation is 7 pounds. From Table 11.T9, $f_2(7) = 17$, so the total benefit is $0 + 17 = 17$. Say that the decision is one unit. The benefit for one unit of Item 1 is 8. Then, because it weighs 3 pounds, the remaining weight limitation is $7 - 3 = 4$. From Table 11.T9, $f_2(4) = 10$, so the total benefit is $8 + 10 = 18$. You calculate

$$f_1(7) = \max\{0 + 17, 8 + 10, 16 + 2\} = 18$$

Note that two decisions give the maximum benefit value, 18. In Table 11.T10, $d_1^*(7) = 1,2$. Both one and two units of Item 1 give the maximum benefit. There are *alternate optimal solutions*.

Let's trace the two solutions through the tables to find the alternate optimal solutions. First, say that $d_1^* = 1$. You pack one of Item 1, and then the weight limitation remaining is $7 - 3 = 4$. From Table 11.T9, if the state is 4, the best decision is $d_2^*(4) = 2$. You pack two of Item 2. Then, the remaining weight limitation is $4 - 2 \times 2 = 0$. From Table 11.T8, $d_3^*(0) = 0$. One optimal solution is one of Item 1, two of Item 2, and none of Item 3.

Second, say that $d_1^* = 2$. You pack two of Item 1, so the remaining

One optimal solution

TABLE 11.T10   Stage 1 for the Knapsack Problem

	Decision				
State	0	1	2	$f_1(i)$	$d_1^*(i)$
7	0 + 17	8 + 10	16 + 2	18	1,2

Another optimal
solution

weight limitation is $7 - 3 \times 2 = 1$. From Table 11.T9, $d_2^*(1) = 0$, so you don't pack Item 2. At Stage 3, the remaining weight limitation is still 1 pound. From Table 11.T8, $d_3^*(1) = 1$. The other optimal solution is two of Item 1, none of Item 2, and one of Item 3.

You might have noted that the knapsack model is an integer linear programming model. You can solve the example using the methods and software we discussed in Chapter 9. However, we never used the linearity assumption when we solved the problem by dynamic programming. If the benefits are not linear, you can still solve the problem by dynamic pro-

Nonlinear benefits

gramming, but you can't use integer linear programming. For dynamic programming, you just replace the linear term, $b_j d_j$, by its nonlinear form in the recursive relationship.

12

Forecasting

Types of Forecasting Methods
Qualitative Methods / Quantitative Methods   Selecting a
Forecasting Method

Measures of Forecast Errors
Measures of Bias / Measures of Variability

Time Series Methods
The Naive Forecasting Model / Forecasting Methods Based on
Averages / Exponential Smoothing Forecasting Methods / Holt's
Exponential Smoothing Method for Linear Trend / Winters'
Exponential Smoothing Method for Seasonal Factors and Linear
Trend / Filtering, Tracking Signals, and Confidence Intervals

Causal Forecasting Models
Simple Linear Regression for a Linear Trend

Validation of Forecasting Models

An Example of Developing a Time Series Forecasting Model

Computer Software for Forecasting

Minicase: Raintree Country Furniture Company

Management science has contributed greatly to efforts to clean New York City's streets. In 1976, the Department of Sanitation had 12,000 employees and an annual budget of about $500 million. Despite the large budget, the percentage of New York's streets that were acceptably clean decreased from 72 percent in 1976 to 56 percent in 1979. The department's management gave higher priority to refuse collection, another responsibility, than to keeping the streets clean. Because of budget pressures, the number of street cleaners was decreased from 2,500 in 1975 to 800 in 1980. In 1980, the City Council rejected requests to increase the number of street cleaners, "citing a lack of confidence in the department's ability to manage the additional resources and to get a sufficient payoff for the public."

In 1981, a management science team began to study the street cleaning problem. Its first step was to develop a "knowledge base" concerning the relationships between manpower and the cleanliness of streets. After developing such information, it had to convince department management that those relationships could be the basis for managerial monitoring, control, and planning of street cleaning. Then, department management could use the information to justify requests for more street cleaners and to predict the improvement in street cleanliness that would result from such increases in manpower.

The management science team developed regression models that showed the relationship between manpower and cleanliness levels. It learned that the effectiveness of street cleaners varied among districts. More detailed analyses at the district level examined the impact of litter rate and district size. Parametric models showed the impact of the additional detail and led to an understanding of the relationship between litter rate and the time between cleanings.

The acceptance of these tools had many impacts. First, effective managerial control of street cleaning resulted from the accountability of meeting the cleanliness levels predicted by the models for the personnel allocated. Second, the knowledge base led to increased budgeting of street cleaners. With 700 fewer street cleaners than were employed before the budget crunch, street cleanliness approached the levels achieved at that time.

Regression models like those used in the New York street cleaning study are one of the topics of this chapter.

L. Riccio, J. Miller, and A. Litke, "Polishing the Big Apple: How Management Science Has Helped Make New York Streets Cleaner," *Interfaces* 16, no. 1 (January–February 1986), pp. 83–88.

Planning for the future is a major responsibility of managers. You can make better plans if you can predict the future. Let's consider how a sample of organizations uses predictions. New York City used predictions of street cleanliness to allocate street cleaners among districts and to hold district management accountable for results. Because of the credibility of the predictions, the City Council approved budget increases for street cleaning.

Governmental agencies and social service agencies use predictions of demand for their services in planning the number and location of their offices and the staffing of their facilities. Hospitals use predictions of demand for their services in planning the number of beds, nurses, operating rooms, and so on. Telephone companies use predictions of call volume in planning the installation of new telephone equipment and the number of Directory Assistance operators. Governmental agencies, not-for-profit organizations, and profit-making companies all need to predict the future for planning purposes. A major input in their plans is the predicted future demand for their services or products.

Consider how forecasts of the demand for a company's products are used. If you are a research and development (R&D) manager, you need forecasts of market trends and technological changes to set the direction of your company's R&D programs. If the market for a product is declining, you want to allocate fewer resources to R&D in that area. Attention to changing technologies can give your company a competitive edge.

The accounting manager of a company uses forecasts of sales for budgetary planning and cost control. The marketing manager uses demand forecasts to plan sales promotions and marketing strategy and to establish quotas and incentive plans for salespeople. Production and operations managers use sales forecasts in capacity planning, plant layout planning, production and work force planning, scheduling, and inventory planning. Finance managers uses sales forecasts in planning profit, cash flows, and capital requirements. Thus, demand forecasts are used by managers throughout the company.

Management science uses decision models to analyze the impact of future decisions. Many of the examples in this book require predictions of demands for products or services. For example, the Potato Processing example (Chapter 2) and the machine assignment example (Chapter 3) require predictions of product demands. The Directory Assistance operator scheduling example (Chapter 7) requires predictions of the number of calls in order to determine the minimum number of operators needed. If you examine the decision models in this book, you will see that most of them require predictions of the demand for products or services. Those predictions are inputs to decision models. Better predictions make the decision model more accurate and lead to better decisions.

Future values can be predicted by either estimation or forecasting. **Estimation** is done by sampling from a population and predicting parameters from the sample. It is usually associated with statistics. Point estimates and confidence intervals on estimates are based on the sample values. Typically, all of the sample values are assumed to be from the same population. Although statistical estimation has many applications, it is generally not useful in predicting demand for products and services because competitive conditions, general economic conditions, and the market are always changing. Thus, the future demands are from a different population from the historical demands.

Forecasting is predicting when environmental conditions surrounding the future are changing. This chapter describes many forecasting methods. You can consult a statistics book for a discussion of estimation methods. The emphasis of this chapter is forecasting future demands for products or services.

The next section gives an overview of forecasting methods and discusses the factors that should be considered in selecting a forecasting method. After describing measures of forecast errors, we describe time series methods and causal methods. You must validate any forecasting model that you develop. Thus, we discuss the importance of and methods for validating a forecasting model. Finally, we develop and validate a forecasting model to show the complete process.

TYPES OF FORECASTING METHODS

The time horizon classification

There are many types of classifications for forecasting methods. *One classification type is based on the time horizon of the forecasts:* **long range** (three or more years), **intermediate range,** and **short range** (less than one year). Long-range forecasts are important for planning research and development; short-range forecasts are used for scheduling daily production operations; and intermediate-range forecasts are used for capacity planning, work force planning, and establishing goals and quotas for salespeople.

Quantitative or qualitative classification

Another classification is quantitative methods or qualitative methods. A **quantitative method** uses numerical information as the basis for the forecast. A **qualitative method** uses personal judgment as the basis for the forecast. This chapter emphasizes quantitative methods. However, we will briefly discuss several types of qualitative methods. Table 12.1 classifies the forecasting methods described in this chapter as qualitative or quantitative.

Qualitative Methods

Delphi method

One qualitative method is the **Delphi method.** In ancient Greece, Delphi was the seat of the temple at which the oracle of Apollo answered questions. The Delphi method uses a group of experts, not an oracle, to

---

TABLE 12.1   Types of Forecasting Methods

- *Qualitative methods*
  Delphi
  Consumer panels
  Composite sales estimates
  Historical analogy

  Quantitative methods
  Time series
    Naive model
    Averages
    Exponential smoothing
    Box-Jenkins
  Causal
    Regression
      Simple linear
      Multiple linear
      Nonlinear
    Econometric

---

obtain forecasts. The person who facilitates interaction among the experts is called the **coordinator.** None of the experts knows which other experts are in the group. The coordinator obtains forecasts from the experts and then summarizes each of their forecasts. Each of the forecasters whose estimate is not included in the middle 50 percent of the forecasts is asked to explain the analysis underlying the forecast. The coordinator disseminates to each expert a summarization of all the forecasts and of the explanations for the forecasts outside the middle 50 percent. Based on this additional information, each of the experts may revise his or her original forecast. After repeating this process several times, the experts tend to reach a consensus forecast.

Another qualitative method is based on **composite sales estimates of salespeople.** You ask each salesperson to estimate the amount that he or she will sell, and you add the estimates to get the composite sales estimate. The assumption is that the salespeople are closest to the consumers and thus know what the consumers' attitudes are. However, we offer a strong warning in using composite sales estimates of salespeople: Because sales forecasts are often the basis for sales goals, a potential conflict of interest exists that may preclude obtaining honest forecasts. If a low forecast causes a low goal and if the salesperson receives a bonus for exceeding that goal, it is unrealistic to expect the salesperson not to underestimate the forecast.

Beware of a conflict of interest

Some marketing research methods are qualitative, such as the use of **consumer panels.** The consumers on such a panel are questioned about their purchase plans. The goal is to forecast demand for products and services based on a small sample of consumers making subjective judgments about possible purchases. The assumption is that the consumer panel is representative of the ultimate purchasers.

Historical analogy is another qualitative method. A new product is identified as similar to an existing product or an earlier product. Then, the pattern of demand for the new product is assumed to be similar to its historical counterpart. This method is often inappropriate because of changes in the environment, such as competitive products.

Quantitative Methods

The builder of a quantitative *decision* model must specify the model's assumptions. What are the important factors? What causes the constraints on decisions? Similarly, quantitative *forecasting* methods force the forecaster to be specific about the underlying assumptions and about the important factors affecting the forecasts. If the important factors affecting future demand can be quantified, you will find a quantitative model useful. If the important factors cannot be quantified, you can use a qualitative model.

Quantitative forecasting methods are classified as either time series methods or causal methods. **Time series methods,** sometimes called **extrapolative methods,** base the forecast of the demand for a product on the history of the demand for that product. Time series methods based on the **naive model, averages,** and **exponential smoothing** are discussed later in this chapter. **Causal methods** identify other factors that cause the demand. For example, is the demand for a product affected by the general level of activity in the economy, as measured by the gross national product (GNP)? **Regression** is the methodology used for many causal analyses. We discuss the use of regression models later in the chapter. We also briefly describe **econometric models,** a causal method that includes one or more equations and many macroeconomic variables.

Computers are used for quantitative methods that require many calculations. Having large databases of historical sales and other data allows the development of quantitative forecasting models. Software for quantitative forecasting methods is available, and we discuss such software later in the chapter.

Two classifications of quantitative methods

Selecting a Forecasting Method

What are the important considerations in selecting a forecasting method? More accurate forecasts should enable you to make better decisions. Thus, you must balance the cost of obtaining better forecasts against the benefit of the improved decision that will result from such forecasts. If a small forecast error has a large impact on a company's profits, you can justify greater expense in obtaining better forecasts. Alternatively, if a large forecast error has a small impact, your choice of a forecast method is less critical.

The impact of forecasts that are too high are not the same as the impact of forecasts that are too low. A long-range forecast that is too high can lead you to build an unneeded plant. A long-range forecast that is too low

The cost of forecast errors

TABLE 12.2   Evaluation of Forecasting Methods

Qualitative methods

Delphi	$100–$2,500	Short range: Fair to very good Intermediate range: Fair to very good Long range: Fair to very good
Consumer panels	$5,000–$10,000	Short range: Poor to fair Intermediate range: Poor to fair Long range: Poor
Historical analogy	$1,000–$5,000	Short range: Poor Intermediate range: Good to fair Long range: Good to fair

Quantitative methods
Time series

Moving average	$100–$1,000	Short range: Poor to good Intermediate range: Poor Long range: Very poor
Exponential smoothing	$100–$1,000	Short range: Fair to good Intermediate range: Poor to good Long range: Very poor
Box-Jenkins	$1,000–$5,000	Short range: Very good to excellent Intermediate range: Poor to good Long range: Very poor

Causal

Regression	$100–$1,000	Short range: Good to very good Intermediate range: Good to very good Long range: Good
Econometric	$10,000–$25,000	Short range: Good to very good Intermediate range: Very good to excellent Long range: Good to excellent

SOURCE: J. S. Chambers, S. K. Mullick, and D. S. Smith, "How to Choose the Right Forecasting Technique," *Harvard Business Review* 49, no. 4 (July–August 1971), pp. 55–64.

---

can lead you not to add necessary capacity. However, as demand grows faster than forecast, you can revise the forecast and add the capacity. In the first case, you don't have the flexibility of adjusting your plans; in the second case, you do.

Table 12.2 shows estimates of forecasting costs for different forecasting methods.[1] These costs are based on the use of mainframe computers in 1971. Microcomputer software now exists that provides the forecasts at much smaller costs. The *relative* costs are appropriate, however, even if the actual dollar amounts are too high. Table 12.2 also summarizes the accuracy of the forecasting methods for the short-range, intermediate-

---

[1] J. S. Chambers, S. K. Mullick, and D. S. Smith, "How to Choose the Right Forecasting Technique," *Harvard Business Review* 49, no. 4 (July–August 1971), pp. 55–64.

range, and long-range forecasts reported by Chambers, Mullick, and Smith. In general, more accurate forecasts cost more.

Qualitative forecasting methods are more appropriate for long-range forecasts than for short-range and intermediate-range forecasts. The cost of the Delphi forecasts reported in Table 12.2 does not include fees for experts. If the experts charge high fees, the Delphi method is expensive. The Delphi method is not appropriate for a company that needs weekly demand forecasts for thousands of products. However, this method is appropriate for forecasts that benefit from subjective group judgment, and when travel time and cost make frequent group meetings impractical. The state of Alaska successfully used the Delphi method for long-range development planning for the reorientation of Alaska's economy after petroleum production decreases.[2] In this case, governmental and business leaders were the "experts," and they volunteered their services.

In general, quantitative methods are more appropriate for short-range or intermediate-range forecasts than for long-range forecasts. Time series methods are used when the market for a product is stable. Time series models extrapolate from past sales to make forecasts. If there are no major disruptions in the marketplace, time series models perform well. For many years, oil companies used time series models to forecast gasoline sales. Those models performed well until the Six-Day War in the Middle East. Crude oil prices then increased dramatically, and oil companies had to raise gasoline prices. During the period of stable gasoline prices, time series models predicted the trend in gasoline sales well. When gasoline prices almost doubled, motorists drove less and demand dropped. As a result, time series models, which extrapolated from the stable past into the changing future, performed poorly. If you forecast further into the future, marketplace changes are more likely, causing less accurate time series forecasts. In a stable environment, however, time series methods often do well for long-range forecasts.

For short-range forecasts, time series methods are often used because the cost of the forecasts made in this way is low and the accuracy of the forecasts is acceptable. The economic environment is less likely to change for short-range forecasts than for intermediate-range forecasts. For that reason, time series methods are usually justified for short-range forecasts. The Air Products and Chemicals Company application at the beginning of Chapter 1 described a complex management science system to schedule the delivery of gases to industrial customers. A time series forecasting method (simple exponential smoothing) was used to establish delivery deadlines based on customer usage rate forecasts. Short-range forecasts were required, and a simple time series model provided good

---

[2] T. G. Eschenbach and G. A. Geistauts, "A Delphi Forecast for Alaska," *Interfaces* 15, no. 6 (November–December 1985), pp. 100–109.

forecasts. The state of Texas used time series methods to forecast growth in income tax receipts based on forecast increases in personal income.[3] Because the forecasts projected more than a year, a more complicated time series method developed by Box and Jenkins was used.

Intermediate-range and long-range forecasts are often affected by changes in the economic environment. For this reason, causal models are generally better than time series methods for intermediate-range and long-range forecasts. A causal forecasting model that included the gasoline's price would have forecast the drop in demand when prices increased. Time series methods missed that impact. However, you must be able to predict the price increase to use the causal model. Major disruptions are difficult to predict, regardless of the forecasting method. Oil companies use causal models for intermediate-range and long-range forecasts.

Regression methods were used to analyze New York City's street cleaning effectiveness in the study described at the beginning of the chapter. The study identified the factors that affect cleanliness, such as the number of street cleaners and the litter rate. Extrapolating historical trends using time series methods would not have yielded the *planning tools* that regression methods gave.

Econometric models are useful for analyzing complex interactions in the economy. These models incorporate such factors as interest rates, savings, capital investment, and interactions among different sectors of the economy. Econometric models are useful for aggregate measures, such as total gasoline sales.

In the next section, we describe several methods for measuring forecast errors. The forecast errors are an important consideration in selecting a forecasting method.

MEASURES OF FORECAST ERRORS

We prefer to compare forecasting methods based on the economic consequences of forecast errors. However, estimating such consequences is difficult. Thus, the forecast errors themselves are usually examined. Let D_i represent the actual demand, and let F_i represent the forecast of demand in Period i. Then, the **forecast error in Period** i, denoted e_i, is calculated as

Forecast error

$$e_i = D_i - F_i$$

---

[3] R. Ashley and J. Guerard, "Applications of Time Series Analysis to Texas Financial Forecasting," *Interfaces* 13, no. 3 (August 1983), pp. 46–55.

TABLE 12.3 Actual Demands, Forecasts, Forecast Errors, and Percent Forecast Errors

Month	Actual Demand	Forecast	Forecast Error	Percent Forecast Error
1	10	10	0	0.00
2	12	11	1	8.33
3	13	12	1	7.69
4	10	11	−1	−10.00
5	12	11	1	8.33
6	15	12	3	20.00
7	13	13	0	0.00
8	14	13	1	7.14
9	15	14	1	6.67
10	11	14	−3	−27.27
Total			4	20.89

Table 12.3 illustrates the actual demands and the forecasts for 10 months. Let T represent the number of periods. T is 10 in Table 12.3. The demand in Month 1 is 10, and the forecast is also 10. The forecast error in Month 1 is $e_1 = 10 - 10 = 0$. For Month 2, the forecast error is $12 - 11 = +1$. Note that the forecast error is positive if the demand is more than the forecast. In Month 10, the forecast error is -3; actual demand is 3 less than the forecast. Besides forecast error, the **percent forecast error** is another measure of forecast error. The percent error in Period i, denoted $\%e_i$, is calculated as

Percent forecast error

$$\%e_i = 100\left(\frac{e_i}{D_i}\right)$$

The percent error shows the forecast error as a percentage of the actual demand. The percent error in Month 4 is $(100)\left(\frac{-1}{10}\right) = -10$. The actual demand was 10 percent less than the forecast. Note that the denominator is the actual demand, not the forecast demand.

Forecast errors are measured on the basis of both *bias* and *variability*.

Bias and variability

The **bias** is a measure of the amount by which the forecasts are consistently higher or lower than the actual demands. The **variability** is a measure of the dispersion of forecast errors.

Measures of Bias

Hopefully, the bias is zero. Recall that if a composite sales estimate by salespeople is also used for establishing sales goals, a bias toward low forecasts is anticipated.

Three measures of bias are average error, mean percent error, and smoothed error. The **average error,** denoted $\bar{e}$, is

$$\bar{e} = \frac{\sum\limits_{i=1}^{T} e_i}{T}$$

The **mean percent error,** denoted *MPE,* is

$$MPE = \frac{\sum\limits_{i=1}^{T} \%e_i}{T}$$

For Table 12.3, the total of the forecast errors is $+4$, so the average error, $\bar{e} = 0.4$. On the average, the forecast is 0.4 units too low. The mean percent error is $20.89\%/10 = 2.089\%$. On the average, the forecast is 2.089 percent less than the actual demand.

The mean percent error shows the error as a percentage of demand. To compare forecast errors for products that have large differences in their demands, the mean percent error is often more informative than the average error. Consider two products, both having an average error of one unit. An average forecast error of one unit is insignificant for a high-volume product but important for a slow-selling product. Using the mean percent error measure shows the different impacts.

Consider forecast errors for a product with seasonal demand. Forecast errors of the same amount in the peak sales period and the lowest sales period have the same impact on the average error. Using the mean percent error reflects the smaller proportional error in the peak sales period and the higher proportional error in the lowest sales period. Depending on the impact of forecast errors, the mean percent error can be more informative. If the product demand is not seasonal, both the average error and the mean percent error are correct for comparing forecasting methods for the product.

The **smoothed error,** denoted Se_i, is calculated as

$$Se_i = \delta e_i + (1 - \delta)Se_{i-1}$$

where δ is a smoothing constant between 0 and 1. The smoothed error is convenient because it is updated easily and requires less storage. We discuss the advantages of smoothing later in this chapter.

Don't use a biased forecasting method

Note that all three measures of bias are zero for an unbiased forecasting method. Tracking signals (discussed later) are used to identify bias. If a forecasting method has a large bias, a new forecasting model should be developed.

Measures of Variability

A forecasting model can be unbiased and still have large errors. A forecasting method is unbiased if the positive errors compensate for the negative errors. Variability is a measure of the dispersion of the forecast errors. You select between unbiased forecasting models depending on the variability of the forecast errors. Two common measures of the variability of forecast errors are the standard deviation (σ_e) and the mean squared error (*MSE*). The **standard deviation of forecast errors** is calculated as

$$\sigma_e = \sqrt{\frac{\sum_{i=1}^{T}(e_i - \bar{e})^2}{(T-1)}}$$

where $\bar{e}$ is the average forecast error. Note that the denominator is $(T - 1)$. (Statisticians say that 1 degree of freedom is used by the calculation of the average forecast error.) The **mean squared error** of the forecast errors is

$$MSE = \frac{\sum_{i=1}^{T}(e_i)^2}{T}$$

We implicitly assume that the average forecast error is zero for the *MSE* measure—that is, the forecasting model is unbiased. Some authors use $(T - 1)$ as the denominator. If the value of T is large, the difference between T and $(T - 1)$ is small. Furthermore, if the *MSE* is used to compare alternative forecasting models on the same data, the forecasting model with the smallest *MSE* is the same regardless of whether the denominator is T or $(T - 1)$.

Note that the σ_e and the *MSE* both *square* the individual forecast errors. A forecast error that is *3* times as large as another forecast error has an impact *9* times as great on the σ_e and the *MSE*. Using the *MSE* or the σ_e is appropriate if the anticipated economic impact of large errors is also squared. *If the economic impact of forecast errors is proportional to the amount of the errors,* other measures of forecast error variability are appropriate: mean absolute deviation (*MAD*), mean absolute percent error (*MAPE*), and smoothed mean absolute deviation (*SMAD*). For each of these measures, the absolute value of the forecast errors is calculated. The absolute value of the ith forecast error is denoted as $|e_i|$. The absolute value operation ensures that positive forecast errors are not offset by negative forecast errors. Recall, $|-3| = 3$. The mean absolute deviation is calculated as

$$MAD = \frac{\sum_{i=1}^{T}|e_i|}{T}$$

The mean absolute percent error is

$$MAPE = \frac{\sum_{i=1}^{T}|\%e_i|}{T}$$

Variability measures proportional to forecast errors

The *MAPE* measure shows the absolute value of the forecast error as a percent of the actual demand. Finally, the smoothed mean absolute deviation is

$$SMAD_i = \delta|e_i| + (1 - \delta)SMAD_{i-1}$$

Again, δ is a smoothing constant between 0 and 1. We discuss choosing δ as well as the convenience of using smoothed values when we examine exponential smoothing later in this chapter.

The calculation of the measures of the bias and the variability of forecast errors for the data of Table 12.3 is shown in Table 12.4. Note the impact that the forecast errors of 3 and -3 have on the measures of variability.

Table 12.5 contains the measures of bias and variability for two different forecasting models applied to the same data. Which forecasting model do you prefer? Sometimes, two forecasting models conflict on the basis of the different measures. Based on bias measures, you prefer Forecasting Method 1 but based on variability measures, you prefer Forecasting Method 2. Thus, you must examine the consequences of a forecast error to select between the two forecasting methods. If demand is more than the forecast, will sales be lost? If demand is less than the forecast, can you sell unsold units in a subsequent period? Does a greater bias toward underestimation of demand result in more lost sales? Does greater vari-

Conflicting forecast error measures

TABLE 12.4   Calculation of Measures of Bias and Variability of Forecast Errors of Table 12.3

Month	Actual Demand	Forecast	Forecast Error	Percent Forecast Error	Forecast Error Squared	Forecast Error Absolute Value	Percent Forecast Error Absolute Value
1	10	10	0	0.00	0	0	0.00
2	12	11	1	8.33	1	1	8.33
3	13	12	1	7.69	1	1	7.69
4	10	11	-1	-10.00	1	1	10.00
5	12	11	1	8.33	1	1	8.33
6	15	12	3	20.00	9	3	20.00
7	13	13	0	0.00	0	0	0.00
8	14	13	1	7.14	1	1	7.14
9	15	14	1	6.67	1	1	6.67
10	11	14	-3	-27.27	9	3	27.27
Total			4	20.89	24	12	95.43

Average error = 4/10 = 0.4
Mean percent error = 20.89/10 = 2.089%
Standard deviation = $\sqrt{[24 - 10(0.4)^2]/(10 - 1)}$ = 1.58
Mean square error = 24/10 = 2.40
Mean absolute deviation = 12/10 = 1.2
Mean absolute percent deviation = 95.43/10 = 9.543%

TABLE 12.5 Measures of the Bias and Variability of Forecast Errors for Two Forecasting Methods Applied to Data from Table 12.3

Forecast Method 1
Average error = 4/10 = 0.4
Mean percent error = 20.89/10 = 2.089%
Standard deviation = $\sqrt{[24 - 10(0.4)^2]/(10 - 1)}$ = 1.58
Mean square error = 24/10 = 2.40
Mean absolute deviation = 12/10 = 1.2
Mean absolute percent deviation = 95.43/10 = 9.543%

Forecast Method 2
Average error = 5/10 = 0.5
Mean percent error = 33.32/10 = 3.332%
Standard deviation = $\sqrt{[13 - 10(0.5)^2]/(10 - 1)}$ = 1.08
Mean square error = 13/10 = 1.3
Mean absolute deviation = 9/10 = 0.9
Mean absolute percent deviation = 69.68/10 = 6.968%

ability in demand increase the chance that units are unsold? In selecting the forecasting model, you must examine the economic consequences of positive and negative forecast errors and you must consider the impacts of bias and variability.

TIME SERIES METHODS

Base level and random component

A set of historical data over time is called **time series** data. To describe the pattern of demand over time, examine the time series data for different components. A graph of demand versus time helps in this examination. All time series include a **base level** and a **random component.** The base level is the expected value of the current demand. Unfortunately, the base level is unknown and has to be estimated. The random component includes those elements of variability of the time series that the forecasting model cannot remove. The base level time series has the form

$$D_t = a + \epsilon_t$$

where a is the base level and ϵ_t is the random component in Time Period t. The base level time series is sometimes called **level demand.**

Other time series components

Other common components of time series include the trend, the seasonal pattern, and the cyclical pattern. Trend and seasonal components of demands are described next. Cyclical components, which many forecasting methods do not use, are discussed at the end of this section.

A **trend** is a common component in many time series. As time passes, demand follows a trend. The trend can be linear or nonlinear. A linear

FIGURE 12.1   Demand—Linear Trend

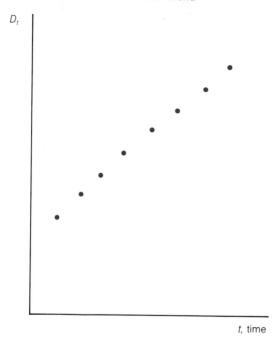

D_t

t, time

trend can be either increasing or decreasing. An increasing linear trend is illustrated in Figure 12.1. The *linear* trend time series has the form

Linear trend

$$D_t = a + bt + \epsilon_t$$

where b is the slope of the trend. A linear trend changes by the same number of units each year.

Figure 12.2 illustrates two types of nonlinear trends—an exponential growth curve and a Gompertz growth curve. An exponential growth curve is used when demand grows by the same percentage each year. An exponential growth time series has the form

Exponential growth

$$D_t = a(1 + b)^t + \epsilon_t$$

If b is 0.1, the growth rate per period is 10 percent.

The Gompertz growth curve represents part of the product life cycle of many products. Right after introduction, demand grows rapidly. As the product matures, the growth rate of demand slows until it becomes stable. A Gompertz growth time series has the form

Gompertz growth

$$D_t = ka^{b^t} + \epsilon_t$$

where $0 < a < 1$ and $0 < b < 1$. D_t represents the cumulative diffusion of the product in the market. As t becomes large, the value of D_t approaches

FIGURE 12.2   Demand—Nonlinear Trend

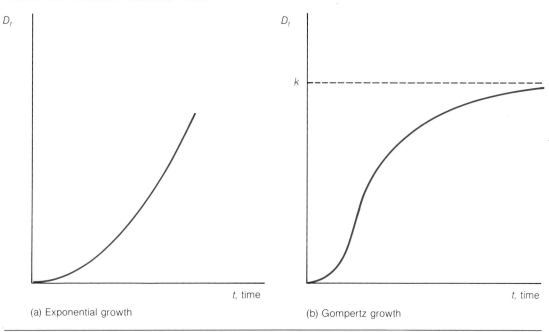

(a) Exponential growth

(b) Gompertz growth

k, which is the ultimate value of demand after the product reaches the entire market. The rate of retardation from one period to the next is represented by b. The smaller the parameter b, the greater is the growth rate of demand.

There is a *seasonal* component of demand for many products. The demand for lawn mowers and swimming suits is strong during the spring and summer but weak during the fall and winter. Winter promotions for lawn mowers are designed to increase demand during the weak periods, and thereby to decrease the seasonal component of demand. The seasonal component of demand can be either *multiplicative* or *additive*. A **multiplicative seasonal** time series has the form

Multiplicative seasonal

$$D_t = S_t a + \epsilon_t$$

where S_t is the multiplicative seasonal factor. If the multiplicative factor is 1.5, the season is 50 percent larger than the average. An **additive seasonal** time series has the form

Additive seasonal

$$D_t = a + S_t + \epsilon_t$$

where S_t is the additive seasonal factor. If the additive factor is 500, demand during the season is 500 units greater than the average. Multiplicative seasonal factors are more common than additive seasonal factors.

TABLE 12.6   Three Time Series Demands—24 Months

Month (*t*)	Washing Machines: Time Series 1— Actual Demand	VCRs: Time Series 2— Actual Demand	Lawn Mowers: Time Series 3— Actual Demand
Jan. 86— 1	100	79	61
2	105	80	83
3	102	81	100
4	101	85	116
5	95	84	138
6	97	88	151
7	102	90	139
8	104	93	123
9	99	95	105
10	97	96	76
11	102	96	62
12	101	99	51
Jan. 87—13	96	101	59
14	101	103	82
15	98	106	102
16	99	107	121
17	100	108	142
18	101	110	148
19	98	111	137
20	101	115	119
21	103	115	103
22	99	119	81
23	100	121	59
24	99	124	50
Total	2,400	2,406	2,408

Table 12.6 shows demand for three products over a 24-month period. Although the total annual demand for all three time series is approximately 1,200, each of the time series has a distinct pattern.

Level demand example

Figure 12.3 illustrates Time Series 1—demand for washing machines. Neither a trend nor a seasonal component of demand is apparent from the graph. The time series fluctuates around a value of 100 units per month. A forecast of 100 units per month is close to correct, but a random component is present. Some variability cannot be eliminated from the time series by the forecasting method.

Examine the graph for Time Series 2 shown in Figure 12.4. Time Series 2's product is videocassette recorders (VCRs). In general, demand is increasing over time. In the first year, the total demand was 1,066 units. In the second year, the total increased to 1,340. The change in the annual **Linear trend example** sales was 1,340 − 1,066 = 274. The average sales per month increased by 274/12 = 22.8 during a one-year period. The average increase in demand per month was 22.8/12 = 1.9 units. The demand increases about two units per month on the average, but the natural variability of the time series makes a perfect forecast impossible.

FIGURE 12.3 Time Series 1—Level Demand

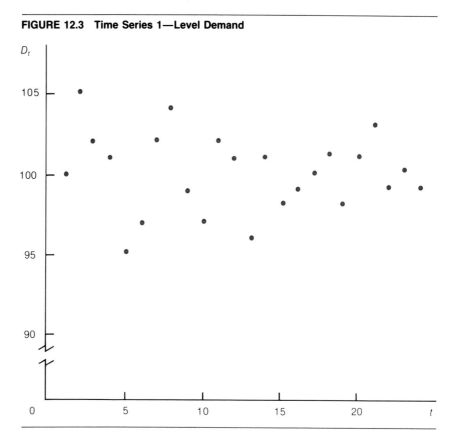

**Seasonal, but no
trend example**

Time Series 3 represents monthly sales of a lawn mower. Figure 12.5 illustrates that the demand of Time Series 3 has a seasonal component. The average monthly demand is about 100 units. However, demand during the months of November, December, and January is small and demand during the months of May, June, and July is large. No trend component is apparent.

The cycle component

Product demand is often affected by general economic conditions. The cycle component of demand shows the impact of changes in general economic conditions and other factors. One difficulty of using a cycle component in a forecasting method is that you must be able to predict future economic conditions. Economists study the recurrent patterns of economic activity and call them business cycles. Business cycles are longer than one year, and their duration changes. Seasonal components of demand are repeated every year. January is followed by another January, exactly 12 months later. Thus, we can use last January's seasonal component to forecast next January's demand. However, what cyclical factor should we use for next January? One approach is to assume that future cyclical factors are the same as the most recent estimate. Proceeding on

FIGURE 12.4   Time Series 2—Linear Trend

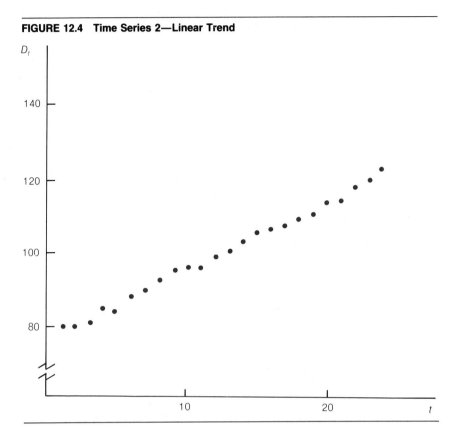

this assumption is the same as treating the time series as if it has no cyclical component. Another approach is to find a causal relationship between the cyclical factor and other variables (e.g., the gross national product). Then, if future values of the other variables can be estimated, the cyclical factor can also be estimated. Yet another approach is to use time series methods on the derived cyclical factors. Because the additional cost of estimating cyclical components is large, cyclical factors are not used unless the impact of a forecast error is large. If the forecast is short range, the cyclical factor can be ignored without serious impact on the forecast errors.

Developing a time series forecasting model requires several steps:

Steps in developing a forecasting model

Step 1. Identify the components of the time series.

Step 2. Select a forecasting method appropriate for the components identified in Step 1.

Step 3. Estimate the parameters for the selected forecasting method.

Step 4. Analyze the bias and variability of the forecasting model developed.

FIGURE 12.5   Time Series 3—Seasonal Component

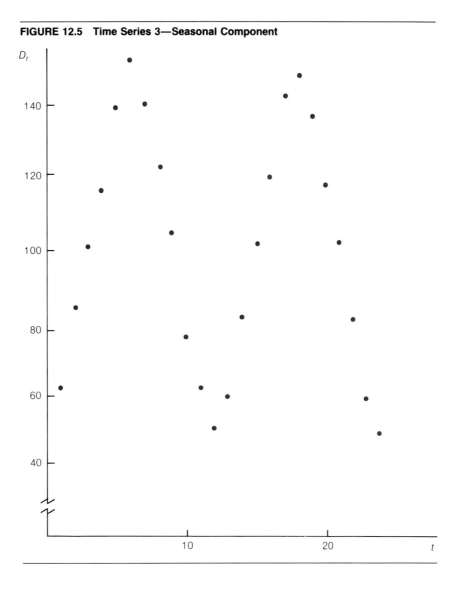

A graph helps identify the components present in a time series. Several types of forecasting methods are discussed in this chapter. Some include a trend component; some do not. Some include a seasonal component; some do not. If the time series has a trend component but no seasonal component, only forecasting methods for trend time series are considered. After you select a forecasting method, estimating the parameters for it specifies the forecasting model. For example, if a trend is present, the forecasting model might estimate the trend as two units per month. The previous section discussed methods of measuring the bias of the forecast and the variability of the forecast errors. Analysis of these measures is required to validate the forecasting model and to establish confidence intervals on its forecasts.

We describe several time series forecasting methods next. Then, we describe causal methods and the validation of forecasting models. The final section of this chapter illustrates the four steps of developing a time series forecasting model.

The Naive Forecasting Model

How can a forecasting model be assessed as good, poor, or average? The **naive forecasting model** provides a basis of comparison. A forecasting model is poor if does not perform better than the naive forecasting model. Say that the actual values of demand are known through Period t. The naive model's forecast for next period's demand is this period's actual demand. The naive forecasting model is represented as

$$F_{t+1} = D_t$$

Table 12.7 illustrates the use of the naive forecasting model on Time Series 1. The forecast for February 1986 is equal to the actual demand in January 1986, 100 units. The actual demand in February 1986 is 105. The forecast error in February 1986 is the actual demand minus the forecast demand, $105 - 100 = 5$. The total squared forecast errors of the naive forecasting model is 261. The *MSE* is $261/23 = 11.35$. A good forecasting method has a smaller *MSE* than 11.35. Note that the naive forecasting model can make no forecast of the first entry in a time series, so there are only 23 forecast errors.

The naive forecasting model assumes that the time series has level demand. If a trend is present in the time series, the naive forecasting model always lags behind because of the trend. Similarly, if a seasonal component is present in the time series, a forecasting method with seasonal factors should perform better than the naive forecasting model.

A basis for comparison

The naive forecasting model is a good forecasting method for some economic time series, such as daily stock prices. The **random walk process** assumes that values are created by

$$D_t = D_{t-1} + \epsilon$$

where ϵ has an unknown probability distribution. If ϵ has a mean of 0, D_{t-1} is an unbiased forecast of D_t. Daily stock prices are generated by such a process. If an "expert" claims the ability to forecast stock prices on a daily basis, the expert ought to perform better than the naive forecasting model.

TABLE 12.7 Naive Forecasting Model for Time Series 1

Month(t)	D_t Actual Demand	Naive Model $F_{t+1} = D_t$ One-Period-Ahead Forecast	e_t Forecast Errors	Squared Forecast Errors
1	100	—	—	—
2	105	100.00	5.00	25.00
3	102	105.00	−3.00	9.00
4	101	102.00	−1.00	1.00
5	95	101.00	−6.00	36.00
6	97	95.00	2.00	4.00
7	102	97.00	5.00	25.00
8	104	102.00	2.00	4.00
9	99	104.00	−5.00	25.00
10	97	99.00	−2.00	4.00
11	102	97.00	5.00	25.00
12	101	102.00	−1.00	1.00
13	96	101.00	−5.00	25.00
14	101	96.00	5.00	25.00
15	98	101.00	−3.00	9.00
16	99	98.00	1.00	1.00
17	100	99.00	1.00	1.00
18	101	100.00	1.00	1.00
19	98	101.00	−3.00	9.00
20	101	98.00	3.00	9.00
21	103	101.00	2.00	4.00
22	99	103.00	−4.00	16.00
23	100	99.00	1.00	1.00
24	99	100.00	−1.00	1.00
Total	2,400		−1	261

$$MSE = 261/23 = 11.35$$

Forecasting Methods Based on Averages

Use the naive forecasting model as a standard for comparing forecasting methods for a level demand time series. The variability of the naive forecasting model equals the variability of the time series. To avoid the variability of the naive forecasting model, an **arithmetic average** of all past data can be calculated. The **one-period-ahead forecast** is denoted F_{t+1}. *In this section, forecasting methods are compared on the basis of the mean square error of the one-period-ahead forecast.* For the arithmetic average forecasting method, if the demands for Periods 1 through t are known, the forecast for Period $t+1$ is

MSE of the one-period-ahead forecasts

Arithmetic average

$$F_{t+1} = \frac{1}{t} \sum_{i=1}^{t} D_i$$

Because a level demand is assumed, the forecast of demand in any future period is the same as the forecast for the next period. Given the demands in Periods 1 to t, the forecast for n periods into the future is

$$F_{t+n} = \frac{1}{t} \sum_{i=1}^{t} D_{i,} \; n = 1, 2, \ldots$$

Table 12.8 gives the results for the arithmetic average forecasting method applied to Time Series 1. Because there are no actual demands before Month 1, no average can be calculated and no forecast is possible for Month 1. The one-period-ahead forecast for Month 2 is based on the average for the months before Month 2. There is only Month 1 before Month 2, so the average is 100, the demand for Month 1. The one-period-ahead forecast for Month 2 is 100. After Month 2, the one-period-ahead forecast of the demand for Month 3 is equal to the average for Months 1 and 2:

$$F_{2+1} = \frac{1}{2}(100 + 105) = 102.5$$

TABLE 12.8   Arithmetic Average Forecasting Model for Time Series i

Month (*t*)	D_t Actual Demand	Arithmetic Average	One-Period-Ahead Forecast	e_t Forecast Errors	Squared Forecast Errors
1	100	100.00			
2	105	102.50	100.00	5.00	25.00
3	102	102.33	102.50	−0.50	0.25
4	101	102.00	102.33	−1.33	1.78
5	95	100.60	102.00	−7.00	49.00
6	97	100.00	100.60	−3.60	12.96
7	102	100.29	100.00	2.00	4.00
8	104	100.75	100.29	3.71	13.80
9	99	100.56	100.75	−1.75	3.06
10	97	100.20	100.56	−3.56	12.64
11	102	100.36	100.20	1.80	3.24
12	101	100.42	100.36	0.64	0.40
13	96	100.08	100.42	−4.42	19.51
14	101	100.14	100.08	0.92	0.85
15	98	100.00	100.14	−2.14	4.59
16	99	99.94	100.00	−1.00	1.00
17	100	99.94	99.94	0.06	0.00
18	101	100.00	99.94	1.06	1.12
19	98	99.89	100.00	−2.00	4.00
20	101	99.95	99.89	1.11	1.22
21	103	100.10	99.95	3.05	9.30
22	99	100.05	100.10	−1.10	1.20
23	100	100.04	100.05	−0.05	0.00
24	99	100.00	100.04	−1.04	1.09
Total	2400			−10.13	170.02

$MSE = 170.02/23 = 7.39$

The one-period-ahead forecast of the demand for Month 4 is equal to the average for Months 1, 2, and 3:

$$F_{3+1} = \frac{1}{3}(100 + 105 + 102) = 102\frac{1}{3}$$

After 24 months, the average is 100. The one-period-ahead forecast for Month 25 is 100. In fact, given the data for the first 24 months, the forecast of the demand for any following month is the average of the first 24 months (i.e., $F_{24+n} = 100$).

The *MSE* of the arithmetic average forecasting method is 7.39. The *MSE* of the naive forecasting model is 11.35. Based on the *MSE*, the arithmetic average forecasting method is better than the naive forecasting model on Time Series 1. (However, note that the average error is greater for the arithmetic average method than for the naive forecasting model.)

In many situations, forecasts of demand are required for hundreds or thousands of products. *If forecasts are required for many products, the computer storage requirements and the ease of updating forecasts when a new demand becomes known are important considerations in selecting a forecasting method.*

Computer storage requirements and updating

Let's consider the arithmetic average forecasting method. Say that the demands are known for Time Periods 1 through t. The forecast for Period $t + 1$ is $F_{t+1} = \frac{1}{t}\sum_{i=1}^{t} D_i$. Now say that the demand for Period $t + 1$ is discovered. How is the forecast for the next period, $t + 2$, calculated? The difficult way to calculate the new forecast is to add the $t + 1$ demands and divide by $(t + 1)$; the new average is the forecast for Period $t + 2$. With this method, all of the historical demands from the time series must be stored so that they can be added. Also, t additions are required to calculate the sum of the $(t + 1)$ historical demands.

An easier method

An easier method requires that the number of historical periods and the total demand for the historical periods be stored. Then, when the demand for Period $t + 1$ is discovered, it is added to the total demand for the historical periods to create a new total demand for the historical periods. The number of historical periods is increased by 1, and the new average is calculated by dividing the new total demand for the historical periods by the new number of historical periods. The one-period-ahead forecast is that average. For example, say that you know the demands through Month 23. You store the total of the 23 demands, 2,301, and the number of months, 23. Then, when you discover the demand in month 24, you add it to 2,301 and store the total, 2,400. You increase the number of months by 1, to 24, and calculate the average to give the forecast for Month 25. *If you use the easier procedure for updating, the arithmetic average requires only one addition, one division, and two storage locations.*

An advantage of the arithmetic average is its ability to reduce the variability of the forecasts. Unfortunately, if the underlying process creating the demands changes, that advantage becomes a disadvantage. Say that because of a change in the environment, the base level of the demand shifts. A drop in the product's price, for example, shifts it upward, and a competitor's introduction of a similar product shifts it downward. Thus, even though the demand is still level, the base level itself has shifted. If an arithmetic average is used, the forecast lags behind the shift. In fact, the greater the number of periods in the time series before the shift, the greater is the lag in the forecast. Now, say that the level demand develops a trend component. Again, the forecast lags behind the actual demand. The amount by which the forecasts lag behind demand if there is a shift in the demand level, or if a trend component develops, depends on the number of periods in the time series before the change. In the arithmetic average, equal weight is given to both the first period and the most recent period in the time series. Often, however, recent periods are more representative than old periods.

Two approaches that give more weight to the most recent periods are moving averages and weighted moving averages. The **N-period moving average forecasting method** uses the average of the most recent N periods as the forecast for future periods. That is, given the demands for Periods 1 through t, the one-period-ahead forecast is

$$F_{t+1} = \frac{1}{N} \sum_{i=1}^{N} D_{t+1-i}$$

Table 12.9 illustrates the application of a three-period ($N = 3$) moving average forecasting model to Time Series 1. Because $N = 3$, the first time that the demands for three periods are known is after the demands of the first three periods have been discovered. Then, the one-period-ahead forecast is equal to the average demand of Periods 1, 2, and 3,

$$F_{3+1} = \frac{1}{3}(100 + 105 + 102) = 102\frac{1}{3}$$

The forecast for Period 4, based on knowing the demand for Periods 1, 2, and 3, is $102\frac{1}{3}$.

What is the forecast for Period 5 if you know the actual demand for the first four periods? Now, 2, 3, and 4 are the periods—which have become the three most recent periods—on which the forecast is based. That is why this is called the *moving* average method. The moving average is similar to the concept of a rolling time horizon, introduced in Chapter 1. The time periods included in the average change as time passes. The average of Periods 2, 3, and 4 is the forecast for period 5:

$$F_{4+1} = \frac{1}{3}(105 + 102 + 101) = 102\frac{2}{3}$$

TABLE 12.9 Moving Average Forecasting Model for Time Series 1—$N = 3$

Month (t)	D_t Actual Demand	Moving Average	One-Period-Ahead Forecast	e_t Forecast Errors	Squared Forecast Errors
1	100				
2	105				
3	102	102.33			
4	101	102.67	102.33	−1.33	1.78
5	95	99.33	102.67	−7.67	58.78
6	97	97.67	99.33	−2.33	5.44
7	102	98.00	97.67	4.33	18.78
8	104	101.00	98.00	6.00	36.00
9	99	101.67	101.00	−2.00	4.00
10	97	100.00	101.67	−4.67	21.78
11	102	99.33	100.00	2.00	4.00
12	101	100.00	99.33	1.67	2.78
13	96	99.67	100.00	−4.00	16.00
14	101	99.33	99.67	1.33	1.78
15	98	98.33	99.33	−1.33	1.78
16	99	99.33	98.33	.67	.44
17	100	99.00	99.33	.67	.44
18	101	100.00	99.00	2.00	4.00
19	98	99.67	100.00	−2.00	4.00
20	101	100.00	99.67	1.33	1.78
21	103	100.67	100.00	3.00	9.00
22	99	101.00	100.67	−1.67	2.78
23	100	100.67	101.00	−1.00	1.00
24	99	99.33	100.67	−1.67	2.78
Total	2400			−6.67	199.11

$$MSE = 199.11/21 = 9.48$$

The 199.11 total of the squared errors of the 21 forecasts gives an *MSE* of 9.48. Based on the *MSE,* a three-period moving average is worse than the arithmetic average.

Let's consider the storage requirements and the ease of updating for the *N*-period moving average forecasting method. The demands of the most recent *N* periods and the value of *N* must be stored. If all of the demands through Period *t* have been discovered, these are the demands for Periods $t, t - 1, t - 2, \ldots$, and $t + 1 - N$. When the demand for Period $t + 1$ has been discovered, the oldest demand is discarded and the average of the most recent *N* periods is calculated. The amount of storage required is *N* for the demands and 1 for the value of *N*. To calculate the new average, $(N - 1)$ additions and 1 division are required.

One consideration in choosing *N* is the ease of updating and the amount of storage required. As *N* increases, the updating requires more additions and the amount of required storage increases. Another consideration is the impact of the choice of *N* on the quality of the one-period-ahead forecasts. Note that if $N = 1$, the forecast for the next period is

Computer storage requirements and updating

Selecting N

equal to the most recent demand. Thus, choosing $N = 1$ gives the naive forecasting model. If N is very large, the N-period moving average becomes more like the arithmetic average. That is, if N is very small, too much weight is given to the most recent demand, and if N is large, too little weight is given to the most recent demands and too much to old demands. The best value of N depends on the process that created the historical demands and on the process that is creating future demands. If the demand is level and the base level does not shift in the future, a large value of N gives better forecasts. On the other hand, if a shift occurs in the base level or a trend component develops, a smaller value of N gives better forecasts. Figure 12.6 shows the difference between a two-period moving average and a three-period moving average when the base level shifts from 100 to 120.

One method for determining N is to simulate the moving average procedure for several values of N and to select from among the results based on the properties of the one-period-ahead forecast errors. That is,

---

FIGURE 12.6 Reaction of Moving Average to Shift in Level

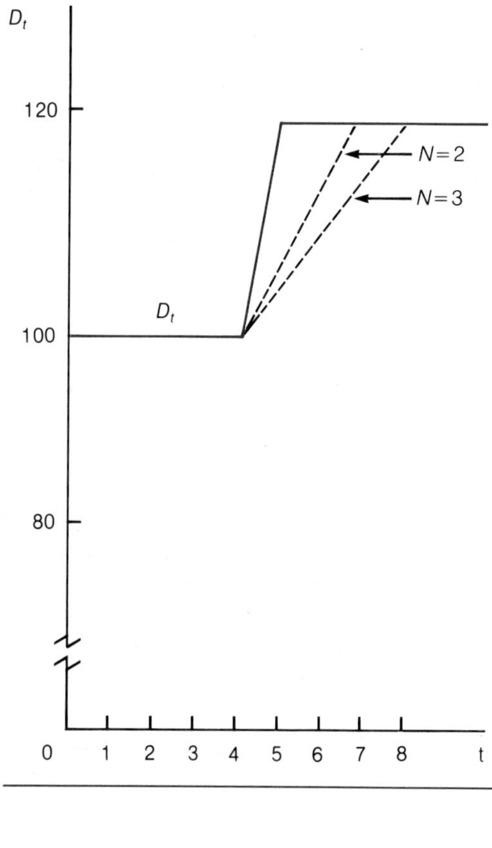

evaluate a two-period moving average on Time Series 1 by constructing a table similar to Table 12.9. If the *MSE* of the one-period-ahead forecast errors is smaller for $N = 2$ than for $N = 3$, use $N = 2$. Evaluate other values of N by additional simulations. (Other measures of the bias and the variability of forecast errors are also considered. Because the *MSE* is often used to compare forecasting methods, it has been used as an example.)

An N-period moving average assigns a weight of $\frac{1}{N}$ to each of the N most recent demands. The weights are equal for each of the demands included in the moving average. A **weighted moving average** assigns the highest weight to the most recent demand in the moving average and the lowest weight to the oldest demand in the moving average. By doing this, the weighted moving average responds quicker than the moving average. Because the weighted moving average assigns higher weights to the more recent demands, it reacts quicker to changes in the underlying process creating demands—changes in the base level or the development of a trend component. Say that $N = 3$ and the demands are known through Period t. Let w_1 be the weight of the oldest demand in the weighted moving average, w_3 be the weight of the most recent demand, and w_2 be the weight of the demand for the period between the two others. The weights must be nonnegative and must add to 1. The one-period-ahead forecast for Period $t + 1$ is

Weighted moving average

$$F_{t+1} = w_1 D_{t-2} + w_2 D_{t-1} + w_3 D_t$$

For example, if $w_1 = 0.2$, $w_2 = 0.3$, and $w_3 = 0.5$, the one-period-ahead forecast for Period 25 is

$$\begin{aligned} F_{24+1} &= (0.2 \times D_{22}) + (0.3 \times D_{23}) + (0.5 \times D_{24}) \\ &= (0.2 \times 99) + (0.3 \times 100) + (0.5 \times 99) = 99.3 \end{aligned}$$

An advantage of a weighted moving average is its ability to assign greater weight to more recent demands. What are the drawbacks? The most recent N demands, the N weights, and the value of N must be stored; N more storage locations are required for the weighted moving average forecasting method than for the N-period moving average forecasting method. What is required to update a weighted moving average

Computer storage requirements and updating

forecast? When the demand for Period $t + 1$ has been discovered, each of the most recent N demands must be multiplied by the correct weight and then added: N multiplications and $N - 1$ additions. For the moving average forecasting method, on the other hand, only $N - 1$ additions and 1 division are required. *The weighted moving average forecasting method requires more storage and more arithmetic operations for updating than does the moving average forecasting method.*

For the weighted moving average forecasting method, the individual weights as well as the value of N must be chosen. These can be selected by trial and error and simulation to determine the combination of values that gives the smallest *MSE*. However, if $N = 5$, five weights are changed by trial and error. Huge computational effort is involved in trying a large number of possible combinations of values for the parameters, N and the w_i. For this reason, the weighted moving average forecasting method is seldom used if forecasts for a large number of products are required.

Exponential Smoothing Forecasting Methods

The N-period moving average forecasting method has the advantage of not assigning any weight to old data but has the disadvantage of requiring the storage of $N + 1$ pieces of data for each product. It also has the disadvantage of giving the same weight to all of the demands included in the moving average. The weighted moving average forecasting method eliminates the equal weight disadvantage but requires more storage and greater computational effort for updating and makes selection of the parameters a difficult task.

Exponential smoothing forecasting methods share the advantages of moving averages and weighted moving average without incurring their disadvantages. Exponential smoothing forecasting methods are available for times series with a level demand and for time series with a trend component and/or a seasonal component. All exponential smoothing methods

1. Give the greatest weight to the most recent demands.
2. Update easily.
3. Require little storage.
4. Require little effort to select the values of the parameters.

Exponential smoothing for level demand is called **simple exponential smoothing.** Represent as A_t the estimate of the demand level given the time series for Periods 1 through t. The forecast for any future period is equal to the current estimate of the level:

$$F_{t+n} = A_t, n = 1, 2, \ldots$$

Say that the demands for Periods 1 through $(t - 1)$ are known and that the estimate of the level based on that data is A_{t-1}. When the demand for Period t has been discovered, the updated estimate of the level is

$$A_t = \alpha(D_t) + (1 - \alpha)A_{t-1}$$

where $0 \leq \alpha \leq 1$. The α is called the **smoothing constant.** In simple exponential smoothing, the most recent demand is smoothed into the old estimate of the base level value. The value of α is the weight given to the demand in the most recent period. If α equals 1.0, a weight of 1.0 is given to the demand in the most recent period, and simple exponential smoothing is the same as the naive forecasting model.

After algebraic manipulation, an alternative form of simple exponential smoothing is

$$A_t = A_{t-1} + \alpha(D_t - A_{t-1})$$

The new estimate of the base level is the old estimate plus α times the one-period-ahead forecast error. The estimate of the base level is adjusted proportionally to the forecast error. If the forecast error is small, the new estimate of the base level is close to the old estimate.

Table 12.10 illustrates the application of exponential smoothing with $\alpha = 0.2$ to Times Series 1—the demand for washing machines. The value $\alpha = 0.2$ was chosen arbitrarily. Later, we'll discuss choosing α. Say that only the demands for Periods 1 and 2 are known and that the value of $A_2 = 101$. The one-period-ahead forecast for Period 3 is the same as A_2—101. Now, the demand for Period 3 is discovered to be 102. The updated estimate of the level is calculated as

$$A_3 = \alpha(D_3) + (1 - \alpha)A_2 = (0.2 \times 102) + (0.8 \times 101) = 101.2$$

TABLE 12.10 Simple Exponential Smoothing Example—$\alpha = 0.2$

Month (t)	D_t Actual Demand	A_t	$F_{t+1} = A_t$ One-Period-Ahead Forecast	e_t Forecast Errors	Squared Forecast Errors
0		100.00			
1	100	100.00	100.00	0.00	0.00
2	105	101.00	100.00	5.00	25.00
3	102	101.20	101.00	1.00	1.00
4	101	101.16	101.20	−0.20	0.04
5	95	99.93	101.16	−6.16	37.95
6	97	99.34	99.93	−2.93	8.57
7	102	99.87	99.34	2.66	7.06
8	104	100.70	99.87	4.13	17.02
9	99	100.36	100.70	−1.70	2.89
10	97	99.69	100.36	−3.36	11.28
11	102	100.15	99.69	2.31	5.35
12	101	100.32	100.15	0.85	0.72
13	96	99.46	100.32	−4.32	18.66
14	101	99.76	99.46	1.54	2.38
15	98	99.41	99.76	−1.76	3.11
16	99	99.33	99.41	−0.41	0.17
17	100	99.46	99.33	0.67	0.45
18	101	99.77	99.46	1.54	2.36
19	98	99.42	99.77	−1.77	3.14
20	101	99.73	99.42	1.58	2.51
21	103	100.39	99.73	3.27	10.67
22	99	100.11	100.39	−1.39	1.92
23	100	100.09	100.11	−0.11	0.01
24	99	99.87	100.09	−1.09	1.18
Total	2400			−0.65	163.46

$MSE = 163.46/24 = 6.81$

After the demand for Period 3 has been discovered, the one-period-ahead forecast for Period 4 is

$$F_{3+1} = A_3 = 101.2$$

In fact, the forecast for any future period is 101.2. Note that the one-period-ahead forecast error for Time Period 3 is $(D_3 - A_2) = 102 - 101 = 1$. Alternatively, A_3, the new estimate of the base level, is calculated as the old estimate of the level, 101, plus 0.2 times the forecast error, 1, giving 101.2. If α is larger, the estimate reacts more to a forecast error.

Let's do one more period. Say that the demand of 101 has been discovered for Period 4. What is the updated estimate of the base level? That estimate is calculated as $A_4 = (0.2D_4) + (0.8A_3) = (0.2 \times 101) + (0.8 \times 101.2) = 101.16$. The one-period-ahead forecast for Period 5 is $F_{4+1} = A_4 = 101.16$.

Examine the relative weights of the past demands in the exponential smoothing procedure. Recall,

$$A_t = \alpha(D_t) + (1 - \alpha)A_{t-1}$$

But

$$A_{t-1} = \alpha(D_{t-1}) + (1 - \alpha)A_{t-2}$$

Therefore,

$$A_t = \alpha(D_t) + (1 - \alpha)(\alpha)(D_{t-1}) + (1 - \alpha)^2 A_{t-2}$$

Substituting, $A_{t-2} = \alpha(D_{t-2}) + (1 - \alpha)A_{t-3}$, yields

$$A_t = \alpha(D_t) + (1 - \alpha)(\alpha)(D_{t-1}) + (1 - \alpha)^2(\alpha)(D_{t-2}) + (1 - \alpha)^3 A_{t-3}$$

Continuing to substitute yields

$$A_t = \alpha (D_t) + (1 - \alpha)(\alpha)(D_{t-1}) + (1 - \alpha)^2(\alpha)(D_{t-2}) \\ + \ldots + (1 - \alpha)^i(\alpha)(D_{t-i}) + \ldots.$$

Therefore, A_t is a weighted average of the demands of all the previous periods. We can show that the weights add to 1 for any $0 \le \alpha \le 1$. Furthermore, the weights decrease exponentially (at proportion $1 - \alpha$) as periods are further in the past. That is why the procedure is called *exponential* smoothing or an *exponentially weighted* average.

Reexamine Table 12.10, which illustrates the use of simple exponential smoothing on Time Series 1 with $\alpha = 0.2$. The *MSE* is 6.81. This *MSE* is smaller than that of the naive forecasting model, the arithmetic average forecasting method, and the three-period moving average. A value of A_0 is necessary to *initialize* the exponential smoothing calculations. Select the initial value of A_0 as the first demand value $D_1 = 100$. The initial value of A_0 has very little impact on the calculation of A_t for a time series with many terms. Its weight is $(1 - \alpha)^t$. For example, say that $\alpha = 0.2$ and $t = 20$. The weight of A_0 is $(1 - 0.2)^{20} = 0.0115$.

Selecting A_0

TABLE 12.11 Simple Exponential Smoothing Example—α = 0.5

Month (t)	D_t Actual Demand	A_t	$F_{t+1} = A_t$ One-Period- Ahead Forecast	e_t Forecast Errors	Squared Forecast Errors
0		100.00			
1	100	100.00	100.00	0.00	0.00
2	105	102.50	100.00	5.00	25.00
3	102	102.25	102.50	-0.50	0.25
4	101	101.63	102.25	-1.25	1.56
5	95	98.31	101.63	-6.63	43.89
6	97	97.66	98.31	-1.31	1.72
7	102	99.83	97.66	4.34	18.87
8	104	101.91	99.83	4.17	17.40
9	99	100.46	101.91	-2.91	8.49
10	97	98.73	100.46	-3.46	11.95
11	102	100.36	98.73	3.27	10.70
12	101	100.68	100.36	0.64	0.40
13	96	98.34	100.68	-4.68	21.92
14	101	99.67	98.34	2.66	7.07
15	98	98.84	99.67	-1.67	2.79
16	99	98.92	98.84	0.16	0.03
17	100	99.46	98.92	1.08	1.17
18	101	100.23	99.46	1.54	2.38
19	98	99.11	100.23	-2.23	4.97
20	101	100.06	99.11	1.89	3.55
21	103	101.53	100.06	2.94	8.66
22	99	100.26	101.53	-2.53	6.39
23	100	100.13	100.26	-0.26	0.07
24	99	99.57	100.13	-1.13	1.28
Total	2400			-0.87	200.53

$MSE = 200.53/24 = 8.36$

Selecting α

Select the value of α for simple exponential smoothing by varying it and simulating the results on the historical demands. Table 12.11 illustrates that the *MSE* is 8.36 for α = 0.5 on Time Series 1. Because the *MSE* is only 6.81 for α = 0.2, an α value of 0.2 is better. Repeating this for other values of α helps in selecting the best value of α.

Figure 12.7 shows the weights assigned to past data for α = 0.2 and α = 0.5. You can see that the weights decrease for older data. Also, larger values of α give more weight to the most recent data.

If the data has large variability, a large value of α causes A_t to vary more. Figure 12.8 plots A_t for α = 0.2 and α = 0.5 from Tables 12.10 and 12.11. The values of A_t vary more when α is larger. This can cause large forecast errors. However, if the base level shifts or a trend develops, a larger value of α reacts faster.

The relationship between the value of α for simple exponential smoothing and the value of N for a moving average is interesting. The average age of the demands are equal if $\alpha = \dfrac{2}{N + 1}$.

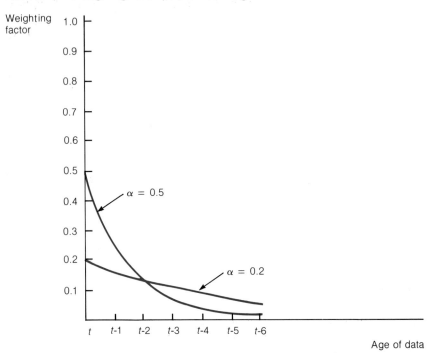

FIGURE 12.7 Weighting Factors versus Data Age

Computer storage requirements and updating

Consider the required storage and the updating of simple exponential smoothing. Only two pieces of information are stored—α and the current estimate, A_t. The updating requires only two multiplications and two additions/subtractions. We prefer simple exponential smoothing to moving averages on both of these considerations. Minimal required storage and ease of updating are important considerations if forecasts are required for a large number of products. Table 12.12 shows the required storage and updating calculations for N-period moving averages, N-period weighted moving averages, and simple exponential smoothing.

Holt's Exponential Smoothing Method for Linear Trend

The value of A_t lags behind the actual demand if simple exponential smoothing is applied to a time series with a trend. Because $F_{t+n} = A_t$, forecasts further into the future lag further behind.

Linear trend

Charles Holt proposed an exponential smoothing method that includes a *linear* trend component.[4] Figure 12.9 illustrates the terminology of Holt's method on a time series without a random component.

[4] C. C. Holt, "Forecasting Seasonal and Trends by Exponentially Weighted Moving Averages," Carnegie Institute of Technology, Pittsburgh, Pennsylvania, 1957.

FIGURE 12.8 A_t for $\alpha = 0.2$ and $\alpha = 0.5$ from Tables 12.10 and 12.11

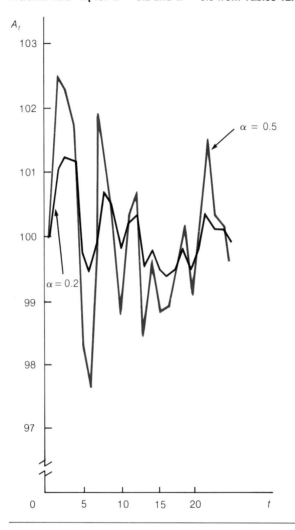

TABLE 12.12 Required Storage and Updating Operations of Average Methods

		Updating	
	Required Storage	Additions and Subtractions	Multiplications and Divisions
N-period moving average	$N + 1$	$N - 1$	1
N-period weighted moving average	$2N + 1$	$N - 1$	N
Simple exponential smoothing	2	2	2

FIGURE 12.9 Holt's Exponential Smoothing Method for Linear Trend

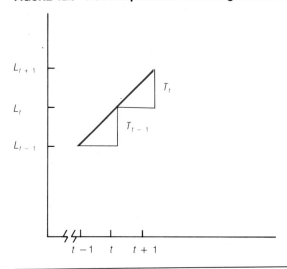

Given the demands through (and including) Time Period t, let

L_t represent the estimate of the base level and

T_t represent the estimate of the linear trend per period.

Based on the demands through Time period t, the forecast n periods into the future is

Forecast

$$F_{t+n} = L_t + nT_t$$

The forecast for future periods is the base level plus one unit of trend for each period into the future.

The assumed underlying process creating the demands is

$$D_t = a + bt + \epsilon_t$$

Note that T represents the trend and corresponds to an estimate of b. However, L_t is not an estimate of a, the D_t-intercept. Figure 12.9 shows the relationship between L_{t-1} and L_t. L_t is the estimate of the base level at Period t, not an estimate of a. Each period, the estimate L_t increases by approximately the value of the slope of the linear trend for that period.

Say that the demands through Period $t - 1$ are known and were used to estimate L_{t-1} and T_{t-1}. Say that D_t, the demand for time period t, has been discovered. The Holt method uses the following *updating formulas:*

Updating formulas

$$L_t = \alpha(D_t) + (1 - \alpha)(L_{t-1} + T_{t-1})$$
$$T_t = \beta(L_t - L_{t-1}) + (1 - \beta)T_{t-1}$$

where $0 \le \alpha \le 1$ and $0 \le \beta \le 1$. The estimate of the demand for Period t, given the demands through Time Period $t - 1$, is $L_{t-1} + T_{t-1}$. The smoothed estimate of the base level, L_t, is based on the most recent demand, D_t, and the old estimate, $L_{t-1} + T_{t-1}$. The difference between L_t and L_{t-1} is the new, apparent value of the slope of the linear trend line. The updated value of the trend, T_t, is calculated by smoothing the new, apparent value of the slope of the trend line, $L_t - L_{t-1}$, with the old estimate, T_{t-1}. The smoothing constant for the base level is α. A different smoothing constant, β, is used for the trend.

Let's apply Holt's method to Time Series 2. Four parameter values are required for Holt's method: α, β, L_0 and T_0. Let $\alpha = 0.2$ and $\beta = 0.2$. Initialize $L_0 = 79$ and $T_0 = 2$. The one-period-ahead forecast for Period 1 is

$$F_{0+1} = L_0 + T_0 = 79 + 2 = 81$$

The demand in Period 1 is 79, so the one-period-ahead forecast error for Period 1 is $79 - 81 = -2$. Based on the demand in Period 1, the base level is updated as

$$L_1 = \alpha(D_1) + (1 - \alpha)(L_0 + T_0) = 0.2 \times 79 + 0.8 \times (79 + 2) = 80.6$$

The trend is updated as

$$T_1 = \beta(L_1 - L_0) + (1 - \beta)T_0 = 0.2 \times (80.6 - 79) + 0.8 \times 2 = 1.92$$

Based on the demands through Period 1, the forecast for Period 2 is

$$F_{1+1} = L_1 + T_1 = 80.6 + 1.92 = 82.52$$

After the demand in Period 2 has been discovered, the base level is updated as

$$L_2 = \alpha(D_2) + (1 - \alpha)(L_1 + T_1) = 0.2 \times 80 + 0.8 \times (82.52) = 82.02$$

The trend is updated as

$$T_2 = \beta(L_2 - L_1) + (1 - \beta)T_1 = 0.2 \times (82.02 - 80.60) + 0.8 \times 1.92$$
$$= 1.82$$

Choosing L_0, T_0, α, and β

Table 12.13 has the results for Holt's method applied to Time Series 2—VCRs. Because the sum of the squared errors is 50.62, the *MSE* is $\frac{50.62}{24} = 2.109$. The initial values of L_0 and T_0 are determined by either judgment or past data. Different combinations of values of α and β can be evaluated by simulation and compared by a measure such as *MSE*.

Based on the demands through Period 24, what is the estimate of the demand for Period 25? Because Period 25 is 1 period in the future, the forecast is $F_{24+1} = L_{24} + T_{24} = 122.30 + 2.03 = 124.33$. The forecast for Period 30 is $F_{24+6} = L_{24} + 6 \times T_{24} = 122.30 + 6 \times 2.03 = 134.48$.

Computer storage requirements and updating

Holt's method requires storing α, β, and the current values of L_t and T_t. The updating of L_t and T_t require a total of four multiplications and six

TABLE 12.13   Holt's Method Applied to Time Series 2

Month (t)	Time Series 2 Actual Demand	L_t	T_t	One-Period-Ahead Forecast	Error	Squared Error
0		79.00	2.00			
1	79	80.60	1.92	81.00	−2.00	4.00
2	80	82.02	1.82	82.52	−2.52	6.35
3	81	83.27	1.71	83.84	−2.84	8.04
4	85	84.98	1.71	84.97	0.03	0.00
5	84	86.15	1.60	86.69	−2.69	7.21
6	88	87.80	1.61	87.75	0.25	0.06
7	90	89.53	1.63	89.41	0.59	0.35
8	93	91.53	1.71	91.16	1.84	3.39
9	95	93.59	1.78	93.23	1.77	3.12
10	96	95.49	1.80	95.36	0.64	0.40
11	96	97.04	1.75	97.29	−1.29	1.68
12	99	98.83	1.76	98.79	0.21	0.05
13	101	100.67	1.78	100.59	0.41	0.17
14	103	102.56	1.80	102.45	0.55	0.31
15	106	104.68	1.86	104.36	1.64	2.70
16	107	106.64	1.88	106.55	0.45	0.20
17	108	108.42	1.86	108.52	−0.52	0.27
18	110	110.22	1.85	110.28	−0.28	0.08
19	111	111.86	1.81	112.07	−1.07	1.15
20	115	113.93	1.86	113.66	1.34	1.78
21	115	115.63	1.83	115.79	−0.79	0.63
22	119	117.77	1.89	117.46	1.54	2.36
23	121	119.93	1.94	119.66	1.34	1.79
24	124	122.30	2.03	121.87	2.13	4.53
Total	2,406			2,405.28	0.72	50.62

$\alpha = 0.20$

$\beta = 0.20$

$MSE = 50.62/24 = 2.11$

additions/subtractions. Alternatively, if $(1 - \alpha)$ and $(1 - \beta)$ are stored, only four additions are required for updating.

Winters' Exponential Smoothing Method for Seasonal Factors and Linear Trend

Assume multiplicative seasonality

Holt's method extends simple exponential smoothing to include a linear trend component. Winters' method extends Holt's method to also include a seasonality component.[5] Recall, the seasonality component can be either *additive* or *multiplicative*. The manager examines the historical demand to determine whether the seasonality is multiplicative or additive.

---

[5] P. R. Winters, "Forecasting Sales by Exponentially Weighted Moving Averages," *Management Science* 6, no. 10 (April 1960), pp. 324–42.

In this section, multiplicative seasonality is assumed. Additive seasonality is left to the More Challenging Exercises. If a trend is present, multiplicative seasonality usually represents the underlying characteristics of the time series. Let's consider a simple example to illustrate why this is generally true. Say that the base level is 100 and that the level in June is 150. The multiplicative seasonal factor is $\frac{150}{100} = 1.5$. The additive seasonal factor is 50 units. Now say that the base level triples to 300. If the seasonality is multiplicative, the June demand is anticipated to be 450. If the seasonality is additive, the June demand is anticipated to be $300 + 50 = 350$. Usually, the seasonal component is not a constant number of units for a particular period but is proportional to the base level for that period.

Let Y be the number of periods in a year. If the data is monthly, $Y = 12$. Twelve periods elapse before the same month occurs again. If the data is weekly, $Y = 52$. If the data is quarterly, $Y = 4$.

The seasonally adjusted base level is denoted by L_t. The slope of the seasonally adjusted trend line is denoted by T_t. A total of Y multiplicative seasonality factors is required. Because the demands illustrated for the three time series in Table 12.6 are monthly, $Y = 12$ and you need to store 12 seasonality factors. Table 12.14 illustrates the application of Winters' method to Time Series 3—the lawn mower data. We use this example to explain the use of the seasonality factors and the updating formulas.

Let S_t represent the seasonality factor for Period t given the demands through Period t. The same period in the year recurs every Y periods. That is, if $t = 6$ is June of this year, then $t = 6 + 12 = 18$ is June of next year. June of the year before is $t = 6 - 12 = -6$. Say that we select 12 seasonality factors for Periods 0 to -11. These initial seasonality factors are based on judgment or past data. You also need initial values of the base level and the trend, L_0 and T_0.

The *updating formulas* for Winters' method are

$$L_t = \alpha \frac{D_t}{S_{t-Y}} + (1 - \alpha)(L_{t-1} + T_{t-1})$$

$$T_t = \beta(L_t - L_{t-1}) + (1 - \beta)T_{t-1}$$

$$S_t = \gamma \frac{D_t}{L_t} + (1 - \gamma)S_{t-Y}$$

where $0 \leq \alpha \leq 1$, $0 \leq \beta \leq 1$, and $0 \leq \gamma \leq 1$. The smoothing constant for the seasonality factor is γ. First, consider the updating formula for L_t. The actual demand in Time Period t is deseasonalized by dividing by the seasonal factor in the year before, S_{t-Y}. The result is smoothed with the old estimate of the base level, $L_{t-1} + T_{t-1}$, to calculate the new base level, L_t. Given the new value of L_t, the new, apparent trend is $L_t - L_{t-1}$, and that is smoothed with the old estimate, T_{t-1}, to get T_t. For S_t,

(margin notes:) Y seasonality factors

Updating formulas

TABLE 12.14 Winters' Method Applied to Time Series 3—No Trend

Month (t)	Time Series 3 Actual Demand	L_t	S_t	One-Period-Ahead Forecast	Forecast Error	Error Squared
− 11			0.60			
− 10			0.80			
− 9			1.00			
− 8			1.20			
− 7			1.40			
− 6			1.50			
− 5			1.40			
− 4			1.20			
− 3			1.00			
− 2			0.80			
− 1			0.60			
0		100.00	0.50			
Jan. 86—1	61	100.33	0.60	60.00	1.00	1.00
2	83	101.02	0.81	80.27	2.73	7.47
3	100	100.81	1.00	101.02	− 1.02	1.03
4	116	99.98	1.19	120.98	− 4.98	24.76
5	138	99.70	1.40	139.98	− 1.98	3.91
6	151	99.89	1.50	149.55	1.45	2.10
7	139	99.77	1.40	139.85	− 0.85	0.73
8	123	100.32	1.21	119.73	3.27	10.71
9	105	101.25	1.01	100.32	4.68	21.92
10	76	100.00	0.79	81.00	− 5.00	25.04
11	62	100.67	0.60	60.00	2.00	3.99
12	51	100.94	0.50	50.33	0.67	0.44
Jan. 87—13	59	100.34	0.60	60.80	− 1.80	3.25
14	82	100.60	0.81	80.92	1.08	1.16
15	102	100.93	1.00	100.36	1.64	2.69
16	121	101.12	1.19	119.91	1.09	1.18
17	142	101.25	1.40	141.08	0.92	0.84
18	148	100.69	1.49	152.22	− 4.22	17.84
19	137	100.15	1.39	140.75	− 3.75	14.09
20	119	99.82	1.20	120.96	− 1.96	3.85
21	103	100.23	1.02	100.93	2.07	4.28
22	81	100.74	0.79	78.98	2.02	4.07
23	59	100.11	0.60	60.93	− 1.93	3.71
24	50	100.02	0.50	50.21	− 0.21	0.05
Total	2,408			2,411.10	− 3.10	160.11

$\alpha = 0.20$
$\gamma = 0.30$
$MSE = 160.11/24 = 6.67$

dividing the actual demand by the new estimate of the level provides a new, apparent seasonal factor, $\left(\dfrac{D_t}{L_t}\right)$, that is smoothed with the old esti-mate of the seasonal factor for that period, S_{t-Y}. The new, apparent seasonal factor is smoothed with the one $t - Y$ periods before, because the same period repeats only every Y periods.

The one-period-ahead forecast is

$$F_{t+1} = (L_t + T_t)S_{t+1-Y}$$

The *n*-period-ahead forecast is

Forecast

$$F_{t+n} = (L_t + nT_t)S_{t+n-Y}$$

if $n \le Y$. If $n > Y$, the seasonal factor is the most recent one for the type of period to be forecast (e.g., January).

Let us apply Winters' method to the data of Time Series 3. Recall that Time Series 3 has a seasonality component but does not have a trend component. Therefore, the trend component is not used for the updating and the formulas become

$$L_t = \alpha\left(\frac{D_t}{S_{t-Y}}\right) + (1 - \alpha)(L_{t-1})$$

$$S_t = \gamma\left(\frac{D_t}{L_t}\right) + (1 - \gamma)S_{t-Y}$$

The *n*-period-ahead forecast is

$$F_{t+n} = L_t S_{t+n-Y}$$

In Table 12.14, the smoothing constants are $\alpha = 0.2$ and $\gamma = 0.3$. Note that seasonal factors have been initialized for Periods -11 to 0. The initial value of L_0 is 100. Because there is no trend, the one-period-ahead forecast for Period 1 is equal to

$$F_{0+1} = S_{0+1-12} \times L_0 = 0.6 \times 100 = 60$$

After the demand for Period 1, 61, has been discovered, the value of the level for Period 1 is calculated as

$$L_1 = \alpha\left(\frac{D_1}{S_{1-12}}\right) + (1 - \alpha)(L_{1-1}) = 0.2\left(\frac{61}{0.6}\right) + 0.8 \times 100 = 100.33$$

The updated seasonal factor for January is calculated as

$$S_1 = \gamma\left(\frac{D_1}{L_1}\right) + (1 - \gamma)S_{1-12} = 0.3\left(\frac{61}{100.33}\right) + 0.7 \times 0.6 = 0.60$$

The one-period-ahead forecast for Period 2 is

$$F_{1+1} = L_1 S_{1+1-12} = 100.33 \times 0.8 = 80.27$$

Because the demand for February is 83, the one-period-ahead forecast error for Period 2 is $83 - 80.27 = 2.73$. After the demand for February has been discovered, the value of the level for Period 2 is calculated as

$$L_2 = \alpha\left(\frac{D_2}{S_{2-12}}\right) + (1 - \alpha)(L_{2-1}) = 0.2\left(\frac{83}{0.8}\right) + 0.8 \times 100.33 = 101.02$$

The new seasonal factor for February is

$$S_2 = \gamma\left(\frac{D_2}{L_2}\right) + (1 - \gamma)S_{2-12} = 0.3\left(\frac{83}{101.02}\right) + 0.7 \times 0.8 = 0.81$$

What is the forecast for February 1987, given the demands through February 1986? The forecast is

$$F_{2+12} = L_2 S_{2+12-12} = 101.02 \times 0.81 = 81.83$$

Note that the trend is assumed to be zero.

The sum of the one-period-ahead forecast errors squared is 160.11, so the $MSE = \dfrac{160.11}{24} = 6.67$. The average one-period-ahead forecast error is -0.13.

Computer storage
requirements and
updating

The storage requirements for Winters' method include α, β, γ, one L_t, one T_t, and Y seasonal factors. Updating requires eight multiplications/divisions and eight additions/subtractions. If the values of $(1 - \alpha)$, $(1 - \beta)$, and $(1 - \gamma)$ are stored, three subtractions are eliminated.

Choosing α, β, and γ

The values of α, β, and γ are determined by trying values and comparing the simulated results based on a measure such as *MSE*. The initialization of the seasonal factors, trend, and base level is done by judgment or preliminary data analysis.

Filtering, Tracking Signals, and Confidence Intervals

If forecasts are required for many products, we use a computer system. After the forecasting model has been developed, it is implemented in the computer system. For example, say that the model implemented is simple exponential smoothing with $\alpha = 0.2$. Each time new data is obtained, the computer system uses the updating formulas to make new forecasts. However, there might be a change in the environment or an input error. Well-designed computer systems produce **exception reports** containing information about unlikely occurrences that should be examined. For example, a well-designed forecasting system generates exception reports when an actual demand is different from the forecast by a large enough amount. Then, you investigate the reason for the large forecast error. The large forecast error may have occurred by chance. Or it may have resulted from either an error in the input of the actual demand or a change in the environment. An example of the latter case is a shift in the base level because of a competitor's actions.

The actual demand inputs are **filtered** to check for input errors. The filtering test examines whether

$$|D_t - F_{(t-1)+1}| \le K$$

where K is a number small enough so that there is an acceptable probability of failing the test by chance. Recall that $F_{(t-1)+1}$ is the one-period-

Assume that the forecast errors have a normal distribution

ahead forecast for Period t. Assume that the forecast errors are normally distributed with a mean of 0 and a standard deviation of $\sqrt{MSE}$. Then, select Z from the normal cumulative probability table such that a high enough proportion pass the test when no change has occurred. Select

$$K = Z \sqrt{MSE}$$

For example, selecting $Z = 3$ corresponds to three standard deviations. If the input is correct and the process generating the demands is unchanged, the probability of passing the test is 0.9973. The probability of failing the test due to chance is only 0.0027. Selecting a very small value for Z gives a larger number of exception reports directing attention to the forecasting model. Selecting a very large value for Z gives a smaller number of exception reports, even if the data input is incorrect or if the forecasting model is no longer correct.

Selecting Z

Let's construct the data filtering test for Time Series 1 as illustrated in Table 12.10 for simple exponential smoothing with $\alpha = 0.2$. The one-period-ahead forecast for Period 25 is $A_{24} = 99.87$. The *MSE* is 6.81, so $\sqrt{6.81} = 2.61$. If $Z = 3$, the filtering test for the demand of Period 25 is

$$|(D_{25} - 99.87)| \leq 3 \times 2.61 = 7.83$$

If the one-period-ahead forecast error is greater than 7.83 units, an exception report is generated.

Updating the *MSE*

A disadvantage of using *MSE* as the measure of variability is the complexity of updating it for use in data filtering tests. An easier measure to update is the smoothed mean absolute deviation (*SMAD*). First, the relationship between the standard deviation and the mean absolute deviation (*MAD*) needs to be established. *If forecasting errors have a normal*

$$\sigma_e = 1.25 \times MAD$$

The $\sqrt{MSE}$ is used rather than σ_e, the actual standard deviation of the forecast errors. The difference is small if the forecast is unbiased and a large amount of data causes the values of (T) and $(T - 1)$ to be approximately the same. (Later, we show how tracking signals are used to identify bias in the forecasting method.) Updating the *MAD* is not much easier than updating the *MSE*. However, the *SMAD* is easily updated. It is updated as

Updating the *SMAD*

$$SMAD_t = \delta|D_t - F_{(t-1)+1}| + (1 - \delta) SMAD_{t-1}$$

where $0 \leq \delta \leq 1$ is a smoothing constant on the *SMAD*. With this updating, only the old *SMAD*, δ, and the forecast must be stored. Then, two multiplications and two additions are required to update the *SMAD*. The data filtering test is

$$|D_t - F_{(t-1)+1}| \leq 1.25 \times Z \times SMAD_{t-1}$$

The value of δ is selected by judgment. Recall, if δ is close to 1, the value of the *SMAD* is largely influenced by the most recent absolute value of the forecast error. A common choice is $0.1 \leq \delta \leq 0.3$. Selecting δ becomes less critical when data filtering is used along with a tracking signal.

Confidence intervals for forecasts are based on the same concepts as data filtering. Given the SMAD for one-period-ahead forecasts and the forecast F_{t+1}, the confidence interval for the demand in Period $t + 1$ is

$$F_{t+1} - 1.25Z \times SMAD_t \leq D_{t+1} \leq F_{t+1} + 1.25Z \times SMAD_t$$

where Z is selected from the cumulative normal probability table for the desired degree of confidence. If the standard deviation is the measure of variability, the confidence interval is

$$F_{t+1} - Z \times \sigma_e \leq D_{t+1} \leq F_{t+1} + Z \times \sigma_e$$

In Chapter 13, we discuss using confidence intervals and forecast error variability in inventory planning.

A **tracking signal** is used to identify bias in the forecast. Whenever a tracking signal leaves its acceptable range, an exception report is created. If the tracking signal gives this report for several successive demands, it is probable that something has changed. For example, if the forecasting model is simple exponential smoothing and a trend develops, the fore-

casts lag behind the actual demands. That causes several consecutive forecast errors to be of the same sign. This shows that a bias is developing in the forecasting model and that the forecasting model should be reexamined. A tracking signal is based on the observation that if a forecasting model is unbiased, the positive and negative forecasting errors should balance each other. If the sum of the forecasting errors tend to be a large positive or negative number, the forecasting model is biased.

A *common tracking signal* is

$$TS_t = \frac{Se_t}{SMAD_t}$$

$SMAD_t$ is the smoothed mean absolute deviation through Period t. Se_t is the smoothed error, which is calculated as

$$Se_t = \delta e_t + (1 \times \delta)Se_{t-1}$$

where δ is the same smoothing constant as that used for the *SMAD*. The *SMAD* can never be negative. If all of the forecasting errors are positive, the tracking signal is $+1$. If all of the forecasting errors are negative, the tracking signal is -1. If the positive and negative forecasting errors balance each other, the numerator is 0 and so is the tracking signal. The tracking signal is used in the **tracking signal test**

$$-C \leq TS_t \leq C$$

where $0 \leq C \leq 1$ is the **cutoff value.** If the tracking signal passes the test, no report is created. If the tracking signal fails the test, an exception report is created. If the value of C is close to 1.0, few reports are created. If the value of C is close to 0.0, many reports are created. Selecting the value of C is often based on experience. If the value of C creates too many reports for which, upon reexamination, the forecasting model is still judged to be correct, you increase the value of C.

If the forecasting model is changed following a reexamination, the tracking signal is reset to an initial value of 0. Cumulative biases from the old forecasting model must not be allowed to affect the performance of the tracking signal for the new forecasting model.

CAUSAL FORECASTING MODELS

A **causal forecasting model** relates the value being forecast to the quantity of one or more other variables. For example, the demand for residential insulation is related to the number of new housing starts. A causal forecasting model is of the form

$$y = f(x_1, x_2, \ldots, x_n)$$

where y is the **dependent variable** to be forecast and the x_i variables are the **independent variables.** The causal forecasting model is specified when the mathematical form of the function and the parameters for the function are determined. Let D_t represent the demand for residential insulation, and let H_t represent the housing starts for Period t. Say that housing starts is the only independent variable. A common form for the relationsip is a *linear function:*

$$D_t = a + bH_t$$

When the values of the parameters a and b are determined, the causal forecasting model has been determined. For example, if we determine that $a = 1,500$ and $b = 200$, the causal model is $D_t = 1,500 + 200H_t$. Then, if $H_t = 100$, we calculate the forecast for residential insulation as $D_t = 1,500 + (200 \times 100) = 21,500$.

Simple linear regression is a methodology for developing a causal forecasting model if the function is linear and there is only one independent variable. Forecasting the demand for residential insulation as a function of housing starts is an example of simple linear regression. If the function is linear, but there is more than one independent variable, **multiple linear regression** is often used. For example, say that oil prices and housing starts both influence the demand for residential insulation. Say that O_t represents the price of a barrel of oil. An example of a causal forecasting model is

$$D_t = a + b_1 H_t + b_2 O_t$$

where a, b_1, and b_2 are parameters to be estimated. This chapter does not discuss the subtleties of multiple linear regression. Such discussions can be found in statistics texts. In this chapter, we introduce simple linear regression and its special case for time series regression for a linear trend. **A nonlinear regression** model is one that has a nonlinear function. Nonlinear regression is discussed in advanced statistics texts and econometrics texts. Econometric methods establish the relationships between sets of variables and may include several simultaneous equations as well as lagged variables.

To use a causal forecasting model, you need to

1. Develop the relationship between the dependent variable and the independent variables.
2. Know the values of the independent variables at the time that the forecast of the dependent variable is required.

Many times, you don't know the values of the independent variables when you need them. For example, the independent variable is housing starts for forecasting residential insulation. The U.S. Commerce Department publishes statistics concerning housing starts. However, the statistics are based on historical information, so that when they are published, the time period they cover is in the past. Fortunately, an increase in housing starts is not accompanied by an immediate increase in the demand for residential insulation. Rather, say the increased demand is observed two quarters later. There is a **lag** in the relationship. Residential insulation demand is a function of the housing starts two quarters earlier. Because the U.S. Commerce Department publishes the housing starts information within one quarter of the actual occurrence, that information is available in a timely fashion. Housing starts in the first quarter of the year affect residential insulation demand in the third quarter of the year, and because the U.S. Commerce Department publishes the housing starts statistics for the first quarter during the second quarter, the information is available early enough to be useful for forecasting third-quarter residential insulation demand. The actual form of the relationship is expressed as

$$D_t = a + b H_{t-2}$$

Is the independent variable information accurate and timely?

If the values of the independent variables are not available when the forecast is needed, those values must be estimated. Before a causal forecasting model is developed, the manager should question the *availability and accuracy of the values of the independent variables*. Look for independent variables with lagged relationships and/or accurate, available values that can be used for future forecasts. A causal forecasting model isn't helpful if the values of the independent variables are unavailable or difficult to estimate.

Simple linear regression

Let's consider simple linear regression and suppress the time dependence. Instead, we refer to pairs of observed values of the dependent variable and the independent variable. Let y_i represent the ith observed value of the dependent variable, and let x_i represent the ith observed value of the independent variable. The number of pairs is denoted as n. Table 12.15 contains pairs of values for 10 quarters, so $n = 10$. The dependent variable is thousands of tons of residential insulation sold in a quarter. The independent variable is the annualized rate of housing starts for the quarter two quarters earlier. The housing starts are in millions. The first observation shows that when annualized housing starts were at the rate of 1.2 million per year, 260,000 tons of residential insulation were sold in the associated quarter (two quarters later).

Figure 12.10 is a **scatter diagram** of the paired observations. As the value of x_i increases, the value of y_i also becomes larger. A linear model of the form $y = a + bx$ seems correct. If all of the points lie exactly on a straight line, determining a and b is easy. You draw a straight line through the points; a is the y-intercept, and b is the slope. Because of the random component, however, the points do not lie exactly on a straight line. Therefore, the true values of a and b must be estimated. Denote the *estimates* of a and b as $\hat{a}$ and $\hat{b}$, respectively.

By "eyeball," a straight line has been drawn through the diagram. The y-intercept of the line is 25 and the slope is 200, so the value of $\hat{a} = 25$ and $\hat{b} = 200$. If the value of the independent variable is $x = 1.5$ million housing starts, the forecasting model gives a forecast of $25 + 200 \times 1.5 = 325,000$ tons of residential insulation. Let $\hat{y}_i$ represent the estimated value of the dependent variable for the value x_i. Note that for the fifth observa-

---

TABLE 12.15 Data for Residential Insulation Demand and Housing Starts

i	Residential Insulation Demand y_i	Housing Starts x_i
1	260	1.200
2	272	1.250
3	300	1.375
4	240	1.100
5	318	1.500
6	349	1.600
7	351	1.650
8	315	1.475
9	297	1.375
10	230	1.050
Sum	2,932	13.575

FIGURE 12.10   Scatter Diagram of Residential Insulation Demand versus Housing Starts

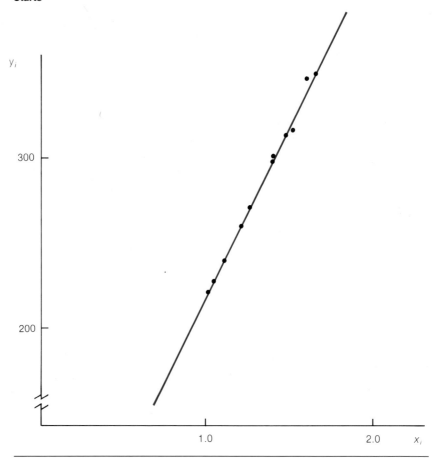

tion, $x_5 = 1.5$. The forecast value from the eyeball line is $\hat{y}_5 = 25 + 200 \times 1.5 = 325$. Based on the historical occurrence of 1.5 million housing starts, the actual demand was 318,000 tons. The difference, $318 - 325 = -17$, is the deviation between the value predicted by the forecasting model and the historical value. Let's denote the ith **deviation** as $e_i = y_i - \hat{y}_i$.

Deviation

A good forecasting model has small deviations between the values predicted by the forecasting model and the historical values. The **least squares criterion** selects the values of the parameters $\hat{a}$ and $\hat{b}$ such that the sum of the squared deviations, e_i^2, is a minimum. That is, select $\hat{a}$ and $\hat{b}$ so that

$$\sum_{i=1}^{n} e_i^2 = \sum_{i=1}^{n} [y_i - (\hat{a} + \hat{b}x_i)]^2$$

is minimized. Calculus is used to determine the values of $\hat{a}$ and $\hat{b}$ by taking the partial derivatives and setting them to 0. The resulting equations are

$$\hat{b} = \frac{\sum\limits_{i=1}^{n} x_i y_i - \dfrac{1}{n}\sum\limits_{i=1}^{n} x_i \sum\limits_{i=1}^{n} y_i}{\sum\limits_{i=1}^{n} x_i^2 - \dfrac{1}{n}\left(\sum\limits_{i=1}^{n} x_i\right)^2}$$

The least squares estimates

$$\hat{a} = \frac{1}{n}\left(\sum\limits_{i=1}^{n} y_i - \hat{b}\sum\limits_{i=1}^{n} x_i\right)$$

Table 12.16 contains the necessary calculations: $\Sigma\, y_i = 2{,}932$, $\Sigma\, x_i = 13.575$, $\Sigma\, x_i^2 = 18.804$, and $\Sigma\, x_i y_i = 4{,}057.55$. The least squares estimates are

$$\hat{b} = \frac{4{,}057.55 - \dfrac{1}{10}(13.575)(2{,}932)}{18.804 - \dfrac{1}{10}(13.575)^2} = 205.57$$

$$\hat{a} = \frac{1}{10}(2{,}932 - 205.75 \times 13.575) = 14.13$$

The least squares estimates are close to the estimates determined by eyeball. However, the least squares estimates have a smaller sum of squared deviations than do the eyeball estimates. The least squares forecasting model is

$$y_i = 14.13 + 205.57 x_i$$

TABLE 12.16 Simple Linear Regression—Residential Insulation

i	y_i	x_i	x_i^2	$x_i \times y_i$	Forecast y_i	Deviation	Squared Deviation
1	260	1.200	1.440	312.000	260.82	−0.82	0.68
2	272	1.250	1.563	340.000	271.10	0.90	0.81
3	300	1.375	1.891	412.500	296.80	3.20	10.26
4	240	1.100	1.210	264.000	240.26	−0.26	0.07
5	318	1.500	2.250	477.000	322.49	−4.49	20.20
6	349	1.600	2.560	558.400	343.05	5.95	35.38
7	351	1.650	2.723	579.150	353.33	−2.33	5.43
8	315	1.475	2.176	464.625	317.35	−2.35	5.55
9	297	1.375	1.891	408.375	296.80	0.20	0.04
10	230	1.050	1.103	241.500	229.99	0.01	0.00
Sum	2,932	13.575	18.804	4,057.550	2,932.00	−0.00	78.41
Average	293.20	1.358	1.880	405.755			

$\hat{b} = 205.57$
$\hat{a} = 14.13$
$y_i = 14.13 + 205.57 x_i$

What is the forecast value of residential insulation demand if the number of housing starts is 1.5 million? It is calculated as 14.13 + 205.57 × 1.5 = 322.485 tons. The actual value from the historical data is 318. The forecast value from the least squares line (322.485) is closer to that value than the forecast value from the eyeball line (325). The sum of the squared deviations for the least squares line is 78.41.

You should construct a scatter diagram showing the deviations versus the values of the independent variable and check it for a pattern. Figure 12.11 shows a scatter diagram for the deviations from the least squares line versus the housing starts. Note that no pattern is apparent between the deviations and the values of the independent variable.

Figure 12.12 shows a pattern. In this case, negative deviations occur for extreme values of the independent variable and positive deviations

Check for a deviation pattern

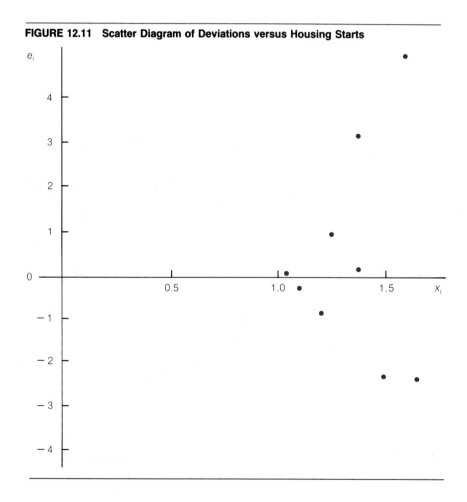

FIGURE 12.11 Scatter Diagram of Deviations versus Housing Starts

FIGURE 12.12 Example of Deviations with a Pattern

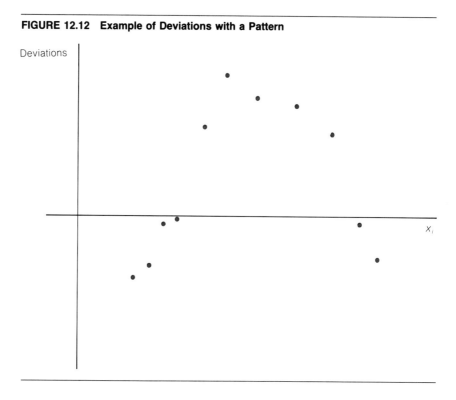

occur in the middle. Such a pattern indicates that the linear model is not a good fit. A nonlinear relationship between the independent variables and the dependent variable should be considered. If a linear model is appropriate, a pattern must not be present. The manager should examine the plot of the deviations before accepting a least squares forecasting model.

The preceding example illustrates how the least squares criterion is used to estimate the parameters if there is one independent variable. The least squares criterion is also used if there are more independent variables, and it is the criterion for multiple linear regression.

Simple Linear Regression for a Linear Trend

A special case of simple linear regression is determining a linear trend over time. That is, say that the time series has the form

$$D_t = a + bt + \epsilon_t$$

The independent variable is time, not some other variable. In this case, calculating the least squares estimates of $\hat{a}$ and $\hat{b}$ is simplified. Say that T is the number of time periods for which historical information is available. The first time period is 1, and the most recent time period is T. The simplification results from the fact that $\sum_{t=1}^{T} t = T(T + 1)/2$ and $\sum_{t=1}^{T} t^2 = \frac{T}{6}(T + 1)(2T + 1)$. Substituting these values into the general least squares formulas, the least squares estimates become

Least squares linear
trend estimates

$$\hat{b} = \frac{12 \sum_{t=1}^{T} tD_t - 6(T + 1) \sum_{t=1}^{T} D_t}{T(T + 1)(T - 1)}$$

$$\hat{a} = \frac{1}{T} \sum_{t=1}^{T} D_t - \hat{b}\frac{(T + 1)}{2}$$

Using these formulas simplifies calculating the least squares estimates. You only need to calculate $\sum_{t=1}^{T} tD_t$ and $\sum_{t=1}^{T} D_t$ to apply the formulas. Recall that Time Series 2 (VCRs) showed a linear trend. Table 12.17 contains the

TABLE 12.17   Time Series Regression—Time Series 2

Month (t)	Time Series 2 Actual Demand	t (D_t)	Estimate	Deviation	Squared Deviation
1	79	79	78.23	0.77	0.59
2	80	160	80.14	−0.14	0.02
3	81	243	82.06	−1.06	1.12
4	85	340	83.97	1.03	1.05
5	84	420	85.89	−1.89	3.57
6	88	528	87.80	0.20	0.04
7	90	630	89.72	0.28	0.08
8	93	744	91.63	1.37	1.87
9	95	855	93.55	1.45	2.11
10	96	960	95.46	0.54	0.29
11	96	1,056	97.38	−1.38	1.90
12	99	1,188	99.29	−0.29	0.09
13	101	1,313	101.21	−0.21	0.04
14	103	1,442	103.12	−0.12	0.01
15	106	1,590	105.04	0.96	0.93
16	107	1,712	106.95	0.05	0.00
17	108	1,836	108.87	−0.87	0.75
18	110	1,980	110.78	−0.78	0.61
19	111	2,109	112.70	−1.70	2.88
20	115	2,300	114.61	0.39	0.15
21	115	2,415	116.53	−1.53	2.33
22	119	2,618	118.44	0.56	0.31
23	121	2,783	120.36	0.64	0.42
24	124	2,976	122.27	1.73	2.99
Total	2,406	32,277	2,406.00	0.00	24.15

$\hat{b} = 1.9148$
$\hat{a} = 76.3152$

time series regression determination of the slope and intercept. The sum of the demands, $\sum_{t=1}^{24} D_t = 2,406$. The $\sum_{t=1}^{24} tD_t = 32,277$. The least squares estimates are

$$\hat{b} = \frac{12 \times 32,277 - 6(24 + 1)\,(2,406)}{24(24 + 1)(24 - 1)} = 1.915$$

$$\hat{a} = \frac{1}{24}(2,406) - 1.915\left(\frac{24 + 1}{2}\right) = 76.31$$

Using time series regression, the sum of the squared deviations is 24.15 and the average of the squared deviations is $\frac{24.15}{24} = 1.00625$. In Table 12.13, Holt's method applied to the same data with $\alpha = 0.2$ and $\beta = 0.2$ gives an MSE of 2.025. However, as the next section explains, the comparison is unfair.

VALIDATION OF FORECASTING MODELS

Developers of forecasting models often overrate the quality of the forecasts generated by these models. The reason for this is failure to **validate** the models. The validation of a forecasting model is its evaluation on historical data that was not used in developing the model. For example, the time series regression model assumed that all 24 months of the demand for VCRs were known when the intercept and the slope were estimated. Because all of these values were known and used to estimate the parameters, it is not surprising that the average deviation was small. But how will the model perform in the future? That is the real question in judging forecast accuracy.

Divide the data into two sections

To validate a forecasting model, the historical data is divided into two sections. The first section is used to develop the forecasting model. This includes selecting the forecasting method and estimating the parameters. Then, the forecasting model is simulated on the second section to evaluate the quality of the forecasts. If the quality of the forecasts is not acceptable, you select another forecasting method and repeat the process. If the quality is acceptable, you stop. Figure 12.13 summarizes the *model development and validation process*.

Develop the model on the first section

If enough historical data is available, you divide the data into equal sections. Consider the example of the time series regression in Table 12.17. The model is validated by dividing the 24 historical demands into two equal groups. The first section, consisting of Periods 1 to 12, is used

FIGURE 12.13 Flowchart of Forecasting Model Development and Validation

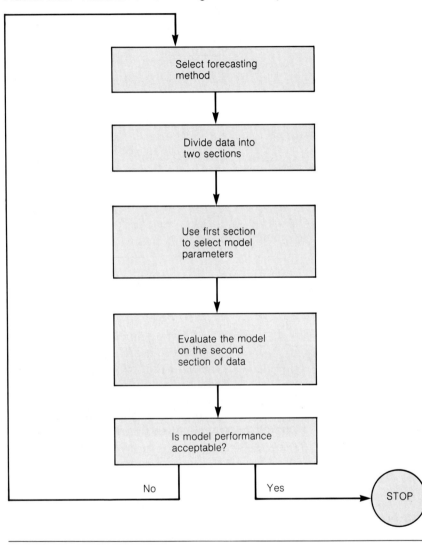

to perform the regression. Table 12.18 contains the results of the regression. The time series regression model is

$$D_t = 76.3788 + 1.9161t$$

The second section, consisting of Periods 13 to 24, is used to validate the model and to estimate the properties of the forecast errors. Table 12.19 calculates the forecast values from the model $D_t = 76.3788 + 1.9161t$ for $t = 13, 14, \ldots, 24$ and calculates the difference between the

Validate the model on
the second section

TABLE 12.18   Time Series Regression—First Half of Time Series 2

Month (t)	Time Series 2 Actual Demand	t (D_t)	Estimate	Deviation	Squared Deviation
1	79	79	78.29	0.71	0.50
2	80	160	80.21	−0.21	0.04
3	81	243	82.13	−1.13	1.27
4	85	340	84.04	0.96	0.92
5	84	420	85.96	−1.96	3.84
6	88	528	87.88	0.12	0.02
7	90	630	89.79	0.21	0.04
8	93	744	91.71	1.29	1.67
9	95	855	93.62	1.38	1.89
10	96	960	95.54	0.46	0.21
11	96	1,056	97.46	−1.46	2.12
12	99	1.188	93.37	−0.37	0.14
Total	1,066	7,203	1,066.00	0.00	12.66

$\hat{b}$ = 1.9161
$\hat{a}$ = 76.3788

actual demand and the forecast demand. The sum of the deviations on the second half of the data is −1.92. This shows a small negative bias. The sum of the squared deviations is 11.64, so the average of the squared deviations is $\dfrac{11.64}{12}$ = 0.97. The sum of the deviations and the average of the squared deviations are similar for the two halves of the data (Tables

TABLE 12.19   Validation of Time Series Regression on Second Half of Data—Time Series 2 (VCRs)

Month (t)	Time Series 2 Actual Demand	Estimate	Deviation	Squared Deviation
13	101	101.29	−0.29	0.08
14	103	103.20	−0.20	0.04
15	106	105.12	0.88	0.77
16	107	107.04	−0.04	0.00
17	108	108.95	−0.95	0.91
18	110	110.87	−0.87	0.75
19	111	112.78	−1.78	3.19
20	115	114.70	0.30	0.09
21	115	116.62	−1.62	2.61
22	119	118.53	0.47	0.22
23	121	120.45	0.55	0.30
24	124	122.37	1.63	2.67
Total	1,340	1,341.92	−1.92	11.64

$\hat{b}$ = 1.9161
$\hat{a}$ = 76.3788

12.18 and 12.19). Furthermore, no pattern is apparent in the deviations of the second half relative to time. The forecasting model is reasonable, and the average of the squared deviations, 0.97, is used to establish confidence intervals on the forecasts.

Why is the comparison between Holt's model and the time series regression unfair? The time series regression assumed that all 24 historical demands were known when the coefficients were estimated. Holt's method assumed that only the *past* demands were known and that the forecasting model was updated as the new demands were discovered. Comparing the one-period-ahead forecast errors for Holt's method (Table 12.13) and the deviations of the time series regression (Table 12.17) is therefore unfair.

To perform an appropriate comparison, split the 24 observations into two sections. The discussion above on the validation of the time series regression illustrates the time series regression calculations.

A fair comparison

For Holt's method, use the first half of the data to select the values of the parameters. That is, vary α and β and simulate the model on the first half of the data. Select α and β so that the sum of the one-period-ahead forecast errors is minimized. Then, for the selected values of α and β, simulate the model on the second half of the data and calculate the sum of the one-period-ahead forecast errors. Now, compare the performance of the simulations of the time series regression and Holt's method *on the second half of the data*.

Advantages of Holt's method over time series regression

Let's consider the characteristics of time series regression and Holt's method even further. How would you implement a time series regression forecasting model? If you have to develop a new regression each time a new demand is discovered, the time series regression requires many more calculations. On the other hand, if a *new* time series regression is not developed every period, it does not include the most recent demands until it has been updated. One advantage of Holt's method over time series regression is that it is easily updated and also contains all past data. Another advantage of Holt's method is that it gives greater weight to the most recent data than to old data, whereas time series regression gives equal weight to all past data. Thus, if a change occurs in the trend, Holt's method adjusts more rapidly than time series regression.

AN EXAMPLE OF DEVELOPING A TIME SERIES FORECASTING MODEL

You have been hired as a consultant to Raintree Country Furniture Company, located in Greensboro, North Carolina. The company manufactures a broad line of kitchen, dining room, and bedroom furniture. In the past, the sales manager, Frank Hughes, made forecasts of the demand for each product "by intuition." Because he was always optimistic, Raintree Country now has a warehouse full of unsold furniture. Mary Johnstone, the owner of this privately held company, is determined to gain control of its inventory problem. The company is installing a computerized production scheduling system that needs forecasts of monthly sales for each product. Since Raintree Country has many products, it is looking for an easy-to-use forecasting method.

You have been asked to show your ability by developing a forecasting model for a sofa with pine arms and legs, called Model 471. Mary Johnstone has had the actual sales data of Model 471 collected for the last 24 months. Earlier information is not available. As a consultant, you know that a shortage of data is common. Table 12.20 contains information for the last 24 months. Months 1 and 13 are Januarys, and Months 12 and 24 are Decembers. You know that sales can understate the actual demand if they are lost because inventory is not available. The problem has been too much inventory, however, and no one can remember any time when there weren't Model 471s in the warehouse. Thus, you can safely use the sales to estimate the demand.

Remember the four-step approach for developing a time series forecasting model. The *first step* is examining the data to identify the compo-

Identify the components

TABLE 12.20 Sales of Model 471 Pine Country Sofas

Month (t)	Actual Demand
1	531
2	531
3	525
4	530
5	524
6	529
7	525
8	521
9	526
10	526
11	530
12	527
13	524
14	531
15	527
16	531
17	530
18	527
19	523
20	529
21	521
22	525
23	526
24	521

FIGURE 12.14   Graph of Sales for Model 471 Pine Country Sofas

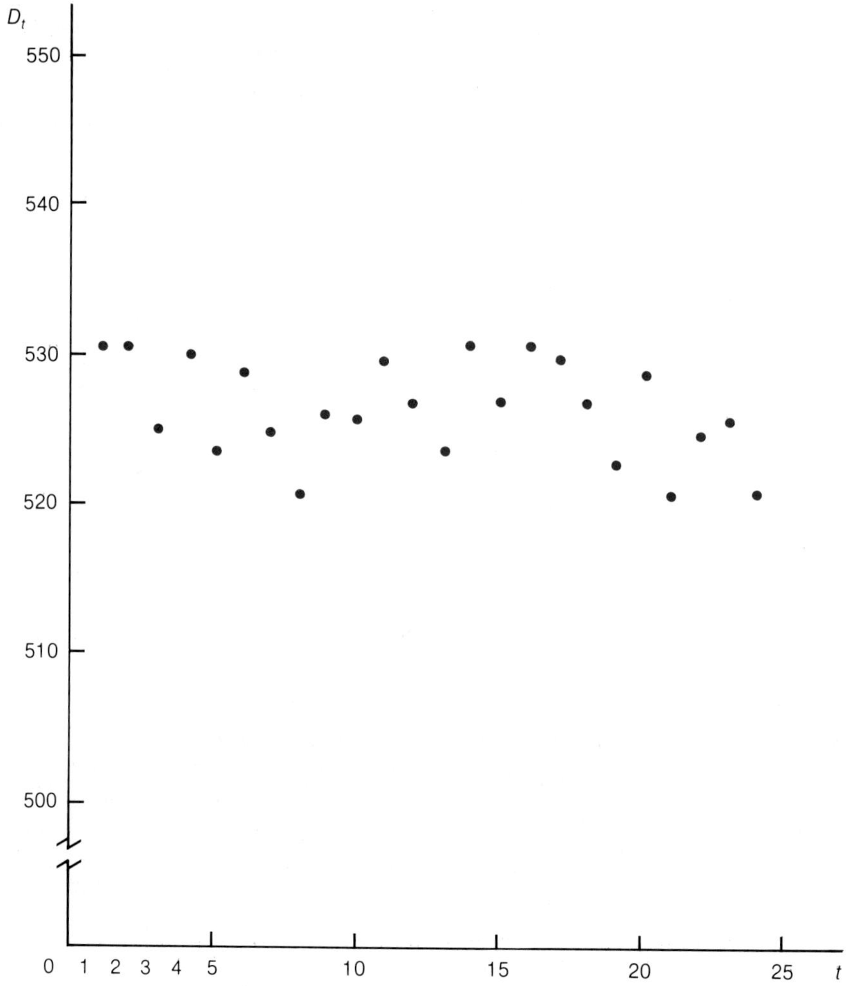

---

nents present in the time series. Figure 12.14 is a graph of the time series. No trend or seasonality is apparent from this figure. However, because of the limited data and the random component, it is difficult to be positive from visual examination. Table 12.21 contains additional calculations to check for a trend and seasonality. The total demand is 6,325 in the first year and 6,315 in the second year. Any trend is negligible. During the 24 months, the average monthly demand is $\frac{12{,}640}{24} = 526\frac{2}{3}$. For two months, the average gives $526\frac{2}{3} \times 2 = 1{,}053\frac{1}{3}$. Because Month 1 and Month 13 are

TABLE 12.21   Subtotals of Model 471 Pine Country Sofa Sales

Month of Year	First Year	Second Year	Total
1	531	524	1,055
2	531	531	1,062
3	525	527	1,052
4	530	531	1,061
5	524	530	1,054
6	529	527	1,056
7	525	523	1,048
8	521	529	1,050
9	526	521	1,047
10	526	525	1,051
11	530	526	1,056
12	527	521	1,048
Total	6,325	6,315	12,640

both Januarys, the January total is $531 + 524 = 1,055$. The January total doesn't differ significantly from two average months. Examining Table 12.21 shows that although the totals for the 12 months vary, any seasonality is minimal and can be ignored.

Select a forecasting method

The *second step* is selecting a forecasting method with the components that you have identified. Based on your analysis, you conclude that the time series has a base level and a random component but that it doesn't have a trend or seasonality. In this case, you could use arithmetic average, moving average, weighted moving average, or simple exponential smoothing. Each of these forecasting methods assumes that the time series doesn't have a trend or seasonality. Because forecasts are needed for a large number of different products, *simple exponential smoothing* is a good choice. It is easily updated and requires little computer storage.

Selecting the parameter(s) on the first section

The *third step* is selecting the parameters for the forecasting method. You must select the value of α. Let $A_0 = 531$, the first month's demand. Remember, you should split the data into two sections. You use the first section to develop the forecasting model and the second section to evaluate the forecasting model that you develop. Let's include Months 1 through 12 in the first section. Select a value of α and simulate the one-period-ahead forecast errors for Months 1 through 12. Table 12.22 shows forecast error measures for various values of α. The α value 0.4 has the smallest sum of the squared forecast errors. Values of α greater than 0.4 have a greater sum of the squared forecast errors but a smaller sum of the errors. For $\alpha = 0.4$, the average error is $\bar{e} = \dfrac{-9.61}{12} = -0.801$ and the

$$MSE = \frac{133.30}{12} = 11.9.$$ You discuss the trade-off between bias and variability with Mary Johnstone. Because a bias of less than one unit per

TABLE 12.22   Forecast Error Measures for Different Smoothing Constants

		Alpha						
		0.10	0.20	0.30	0.40	0.50	0.60	0.70
Months 1 to 13	Sum of the Errors	−29.86	−19.59	−13.39	−9.61	−7.29	−5.86	−4.98
	Sum of Squared Errors	181.54	146.78	135.59	133.30	135.85	142.04	151.57
Months 13 to 24	Sum of the Errors				−8.89			
	Sum of Squared Errors				152.72			

month is small, she wants you to minimize the variability of the forecast errors. Trying additional values of α close to 0.4 might reduce the *MSE* a little, but any decrease obtained in this way would be so small that it's not worth the effort. You choose $\alpha = 0.4$.

The *fourth step* is validating the model that you developed in Step 3. Using the second section of the time series data, you simulate the simple exponential smoothing model with $\alpha = 0.4$ on Months 13 through 24. Table 12.22 shows that the sum of the errors is −8.89 and that the sum of the squared errors is 152.72. These values are similar to the results on the first section of the data. The variability is a little larger, which is not surprising, because α was selected to minimize the *MSE* of the first section.

Validate the model on the second section

Then, you examine the forecast errors for a pattern. Table 12.23 shows the calculations for simple exponential smoothing with $\alpha = 0.4$.

Figure 12.15 plots the forecast errors versus time. No pattern is apparent in the forecast errors. The simple exponential smoothing model with $\alpha = 0.4$ is valid.

Your forecast for Month 25 is $A_{24} = 523.6$. You use the *MSE* from the second section, $\dfrac{152.72}{12} = 12.7$, to calculate confidence intervals. The 95 percent confidence interval is within 1.96 standard deviations;

$$|D_{25} - 523.6| \le 1.96 \times \sqrt{12.7} = 6.99$$

Because you did such a good job of developing a forecast for Model 471, you have been given a contract to develop a forecasting system for all the products of Raintree Country Furniture. The computerized system should have filtering for input errors and a tracking signal to detect deteriorating forecast performance. Using *SMAD* instead of *MSE* makes updating variability easier.

COMPUTER SOFTWARE FOR FORECASTING

Forecasting software is available for all types of computers. A hard disc, a math coprocessor, and additional memory are required for most sophisticated microcomputer software. You can use electronic spreadsheets such

TABLE 12.23 Simple Exponential Smoothing Model for Model 471 Pine Country Sofa—$\alpha = 0.4$

Month (t)	D_t Actual Demand	A_t	$F_{t+t} = A_t$ One-Period-Ahead Forecast	e_t Forecast Errors	Squared Forecast Errors
0		531.00			
1	531	531.00	531.00	0.00	0.00
2	531	531.00	531.00	0.00	0.00
3	525	528.60	531.00	−6.00	36.00
4	530	529.16	528.60	1.40	1.96
5	524	527.10	529.16	−5.16	26.63
6	529	527.86	527.10	1.90	3.63
7	525	526.71	527.86	−2.86	8.17
8	521	524.43	526.71	−5.71	32.66
9	526	525.06	524.43	1.57	2.47
10	526	525.43	525.06	0.94	0.89
11	530	527.26	525.43	4.57	20.85
12	527	527.16	527.26	−0.26	0.07
13	524	525.89	527.16	−3.16	9.96
14	531	527.94	525.89	5.11	26.07
15	527	527.56	527.94	−0.94	0.88
16	531	528.94	527.56	3.44	11.82
17	530	529.36	528.94	1.06	1.13
18	527	528.42	529.36	−2.36	5.58
19	523	526.25	528.42	−5.42	29.35
20	529	527.35	526.25	2.75	7.56
21	521	524.81	527.35	−6.35	40.33
22	525	524.89	524.81	0.19	0.04
23	526	525.33	524.89	1.11	1.24
24	521	523.60	525.33	−4.33	18.76
Total	12,640			−18.50	286.02

$\alpha = 0.40$

as LOTUS 1-2-3 for simple time series methods and simple linear regression.

Two prominent regression systems are SAS and SPSS. Both of these are available for microcomputers through mainframes. These packages have many capabilities based on multiple regression.

Econometric models are complex and expensive to develop. You can use commercially available econometric models as building blocks to construct your own econometric forecasting model. Both Chase Econometrics and Wharton make their econometric models interactively available to subscribers to their services.

Sophisticated time series software is often based on the methods of Box and Jenkins.[6] Models of this kind are often **autoregressive.** That is, complex formulas probabilistically relate the value in one time period to

---

[6] G. E. P. Box and G. M. Jenkins, *Time Series Analysis: Forecasting and Control* (Oakland: Holden-Day, 1970).

**FIGURE 12.15 Graph of Forecast Errors for Simple Exponential Smoothing—
α = 0.4**

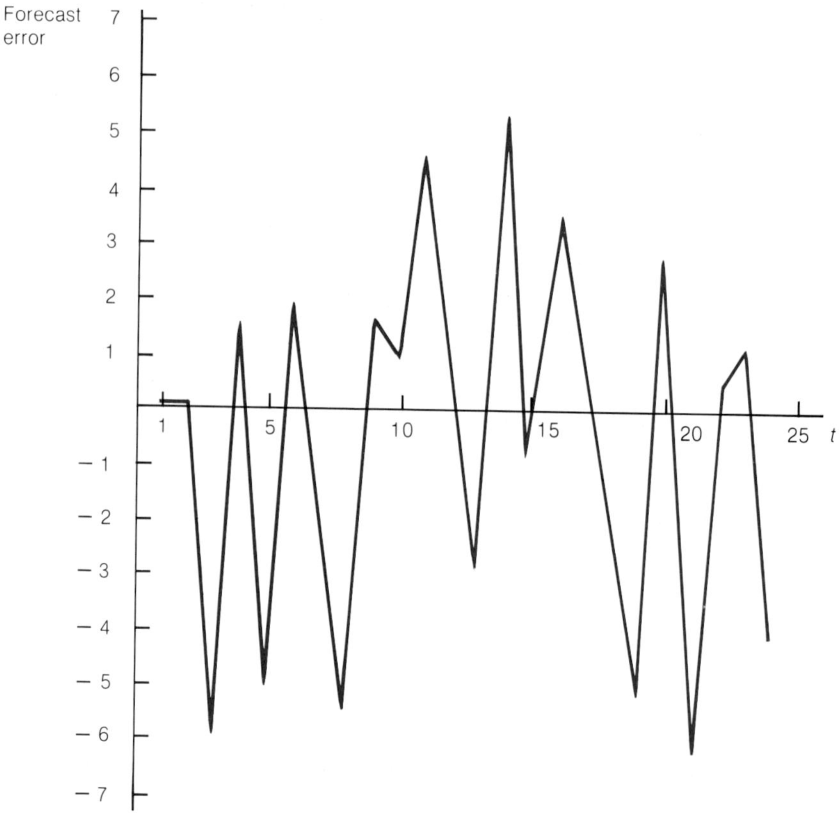

values in previous time periods. The Box-Jenkin methods require many calculations.

See R. Sharda and J. Rock, "Forecasting Software for Microcomputers," in *Computers and Operations Research* 13, nos. 2–3 (1986), pp. 197–209, for an excellent survey of time series software for microcomputers. The packages discussed by Sharda and Rock span techniques that range from simple to sophisticated. The amount of automation of the packages varies. For some, entering the data creates a forecasting model. For others, you control the forecasting method used. Still others suggest appropriate forecasting methods based on preliminary data analysis done by the system.

Another interesting discussion of time series forecasting is J. Scott Armstrong, "Forecasting by Extrapolation: Conclusions from 25 Years of Research," *Interfaces* 14, no. 6 (November–December 1984), pp. 52–66.

Armstrong reports that simple time series forecasting methods often perform about as well as sophisticated ones. He recommends pooling forecasts from several forecasting methods to get a better forecast.

SUMMARY

In this chapter, we described both qualitative and quantitative general forecasting approaches. Qualitative methods are useful for long-range forecasts, such as forecasts of technological change. Extrapolation of quantitative data is difficult for technology forecasts. Quantitative methods are useful for short-range and intermediate-range forecasts. Predictions of the future demand for products or services are a major application of forecasting. Most managers, regardless of whether they are involved in marketing, finance, accounting, or operations, use such predictions for planning purposes.

Time series methods and causal methods are major categories of quantitative forecasting methods. Time series methods extrapolate from historical time series and are useful for short-range forecasts. Managers use time series methods for forecasts of the product demand next week or next month. For longer-range forecasts, changes in the market (e.g., GNP growth) make time series methods less accurate.

Causal methods identify the factors that affect the demand. If the manager is interested in product demand, these factors are often economic. However, in the New York City application discussed at the beginning of this chapter, a street cleanliness score was related to manpower allocated, frequency of cleaning, and litter rate.

Although we prefer to examine the economic consequences of forecast errors, these are difficult to predict. Thus, we introduced measures of forecast error bias and variability as a basis for assessing the accuracy of forecasts and selecting a forecasting method.

The possible components of a time series include the base level, the trend, and seasonal, cyclical, and random components. Developing a time series forecasting model consists of four steps. The first is determining the components present in the data. The naive forecasting model is a basis for evaluating other forecasting methods. The methods used for forecasting a time series with only a base level and a random component included arithmetic average, moving average, weighted moving average, and simple exponential smoothing. The storage requirements and updating procedures for each of these methods was analyzed. The advantages of exponential smoothing included more weight for more recent demands, low storage requirements, and easy updating.

When the time series includes a linear trend, use Holt's method. When the time series includes a seasonal component and a linear trend, use

Winters' method. Both of these exponential smoothing methods share the advantages of simple exponential smoothing.

When time series methods are used to forecast the demand for many products, a computer system is used. You need the computer system to check for input errors and deterioration of the forecast quality. We described filtering for input errors. This concept is also used to determine confidence intervals on forecasts. We described a tracking signal to test for development of bias in the forecasting model.

The least squares criterion is used for causal methods. Formulas were given to estimate the parameters for simple linear regression. The formulas are simplified for the special case of a linear trend over time.

Finally, we described and illustrated the procedure for validating a forecasting model by separating the data into two sections. The first section was used to develop the forecasting model. The second section was used to validate the performance of the forecasting model.

Note some cautions in forecasting. First, examine a time series to identify the components that are present and select a method with those components. A graph of the time series aids this identification. Second, seasonality factors can be either multiplicative or additive. If there is no trend, you can use either type of seasonality factor. If there is a trend, you must examine the time series to see whether the seasonality factors are additive or multiplicative. Third, examine the forecast errors for a pattern. A pattern indicates that you have neglected other factors. For example, the trend may be nonlinear. Exponential growth and Gompertz growth curves are often correct for new products. Fourth, split the time series into two sections so that you can validate your model on data that you didn't use to derive it.

Carefully examine the consequences of forecast errors. If a forecast error causes a large cost increase, you can justify greater expense for obtaining accurate forecasts. Remember, forecasts are sometimes wrong. Ask yourself, "If the forecast is wrong, how can I react to minimize additional costs?" Also, remember that measures of forecast errors can conflict for different forecasting methods. One method may have less bias but more variability than another method. Evaluate the economic consequences of both bias and variability.

Forecasting has several limitations. First, forecasting methods perform badly when there are major disruptions. An example of such a disruption is the Six-Day War and the subsequent rise of OPEC. Second, extrapolation methods are ineffective in predicting "turning points." A turning point is a change in the direction of a trend. If the demand has grown in each of the recent periods, an extrapolation method will predict its continued growth. Third, quantitative methods requires appropriate, accurate, and timely data. If you want to predict product demand, your data should be product demand, not sales. Usually, the available data tells you how much was sold, not how much your customers wanted to buy. If demand in excess of inventory on hand causes lost sales, sales understate product demand. Be wary of the source and accuracy of time series data. Fourth, causal forecasting models require that you know the values of the independent variables. Look for independent variables that have lagged relationships with the dependent variable that can be accurately forecast.

Finally, remember that quantitative forecasting methods do not eliminate the need for managerial judgment. For short-range forecasts used in operational planning with small economic impact, a manager may properly delegate the forecasting to a computerized forecasting system. However, the longer the range and the greater the impact of the forecast, the more need there is for the judgment of the manager. The manager can know about future changes of which a forecasting model is unaware.

QUESTIONS

1. What is the Delphi method?
2. What is the difference between qualitative methods and quantitative methods for forecasting?
3. What is a potential conflict of interest in using composite sales estimates of salespeople?
4. Describe a situation in which time series methods are more appropriate than causal methods.
5. Describe a situation in which causal methods are more appropriate than time series methods.
6. Give three methods for measuring the bias of forecasts.
7. Give five methods for measuring the variability of forecast errors.
8. Under what circumstances is the mean squared error close to the value of the standard deviation of the forecast errors?
9. Discuss the choice between mean absolute deviation and mean squared error as measures of variability.
10. Discuss the choice between average error and mean percent error as measures of bias.
11. List five components of time series data.
12. Sketch a time series with a negative trend and a seasonal component.
13. Under what circumstances is the selection between a multiplicative seasonal component and an additive seasonal component important?
14. Which reacts faster to a change in the base level—a moving average or an arithmetic average? Explain.
15. What is a smoothing constant?
16. What components are present for the application of Holt's method?
17. What components are present for the application of Winters' method?

18. What is the purpose of a tracking signal?

19. Why is demand data filtered?

20. What is the least squares criterion for regression?

21. What is a scatter diagram?

22. How is a forecasting model validated?

23. What is a lagged relationship, and why are such relationships important?

EXERCISES

1. We have the following data comparing forecasts and the actual demand:

Forecast	Actual Demand
100	105
107	109
110	115
108	105
120	122
131	138

   a. Calculate the values of the three measures of bias: average error, mean percent error, and smoothed error (smoothing constant 0.5 and initial value of 0).

   b. Which measure is easiest to calculate?

   c. Discuss whether the forecast is biased.

2. The vice president of marketing believes that the sales manager under-estimates sales so that her sales goal will be smaller and her bonus larger. Her annual forecast and the actual demand in the last seven years were

Forecast	Actual Demand
1,080	1,100
1,100	1,125
1,150	1,170
1,200	1,150
1,200	1,225
1,250	1,280
1,300	1,390

   a. Calculate the values of the three measures of bias: average error, mean percent error, and smoothed error (smoothing constant 0.5 and initial value of 0).

   b. Which measure is easiest to calculate?

   c. Discuss whether the sales manager's forecasts are biased.

3. For the data of Exercise 1,
   a. Calculate the standard deviation of the forecast errors.
   b. Calculate the mean squared error.
   c. Calculate the mean absolute deviation.
   d. Calculate the mean absolute percent error.

4. For the data of Exercise 2,
   a. Calculate the standard deviation of the forecast errors.
   b. Calculate the mean squared error.
   c. Calculate the mean absolute deviation.
   d. Calculate the mean absolute percent error.

5. Calculate the one-period-ahead forecasts for the following data:

Week	Demand
1	105
2	120
3	125
4	108
5	130

   a. By a three-period moving average.
   b. By a two-period moving average.
   c. By a two-period weighted moving average with $w_1 = w_2 = 0.5$.

6. Consider the following data:

Week	Demand
1	105
2	110
3	115
4	120
5	125

   a. Calculate the one-period-ahead forecasts by a three-period moving average. Are the forecasts biased?
   b. Calculate the one-period-ahead forecasts by a two-period moving average. Are the forecasts biased?
   c. Notice that the data has a linear trend. If a linear trend is present, discuss whether a larger value of N reduces the amount of the bias.
   d. Calculate the one-period-ahead forecasts by a two-period weighted moving average with $w_1 = w_2 = 0.5$. Are the forecasts biased?

7. Calculate the *MSE* of a two-period moving average on the Time Series 1 (washing machines) data in Table 12.6. Is the *MSE* smaller for $N = 2$ or for $N = 3$ (Table 12.9)?

8. A company uses the naive forecasting model to forecast weekly sales. The actual demands have been

Week	Demand
1	23
2	27
3	34
4	28

   a. What was the forecast for Week 2 based on knowledge of the demand in Week 1?

   b. What was the forecast for Week 3 based on knowledge of the demand in Week 2?

   c. What was the forecast for Week 4 based on knowledge of the demand in Week 3?

   d. What is the average forecast error for the first three forecasts?

   e. Using a smoothing constant of 0.2, calculate the smoothed forecast error. The initial value of the smoothed forecast error is 2.

   f. What is the forecast for Week 5?

   g. The actual demand for Week 5 has been discovered. It is 33. Update the average forecast error and the smoothed forecast error.

   h. Which is easier to update—the average forecast error or the smoothed forecast error?

9. A company uses the naive forecasting model to forecast weekly sales. The actual demands have been

Week	Demand
1	140
2	135
3	138
4	149

   a. What was the forecast for Week 2 based on knowledge of the demand in Week 1?

   b. What was the forecast for Week 3 based on knowledge of the demand in Week 2?

   c. What was the forecast for Week 4 based on knowledge of the demand in Week 3?

   d. What is the average forecast error for the first three forecasts?

   e. Using a smoothing constant of 0.2, calculate the smoothed forecast error. The initial value of the smoothed forecast error is 4.

   f. What is the forecast for Week 5?

   g. The actual demand for Week 5 has been discovered. It is 136. Update the average forecast error and the smoothed forecast error.

   h. Which is easier to update—the average forecast error or the smoothed forecast error?

10. Consider the following actual demands:

t	D_t
1	10
2	13
3	12
4	16

a. Use simple exponential smoothing with $A_0 = 10$ and $\alpha = 0.2$ to compute the A_t values. What is F_{4+1}?
b. Do Part *a* for $\alpha = 0.5$.
c. On the basis of *MSE*, is $\alpha = 0.2$ or $\alpha = 0.5$ better?
d. On the basis of *MAD*, is $\alpha = 0.2$ or $\alpha = 0.5$ better?

11. Consider the following actual demands:

t	D_t
1	26
2	22
3	28
4	24

a. Use simple exponential smoothing with $A_0 = 25$ and $\alpha = 0.2$ to compute the A_t values. What is F_{4+1}?
b. Do Part *a* for $\alpha = 0.5$.
c. On the basis of *MSE*, is $\alpha = 0.2$ or $\alpha = 0.5$ better?
d. On the basis of *MAD*, is $\alpha = 0.2$ or $\alpha = 0.5$ better?

12. The following data exhibit a linear trend.

t	D_t
1	100
2	108
3	112
4	119

Holt's method is used for forecasting. The initial values, L_0 and T_0, are 100 and 6, respectively. Let $\alpha = 0.2$ and $\beta = 0.3$.
a. Calculate L_t and T_t for $t = 1, 2, 3, 4$.
b. What is F_{4+1}?
c. Calculate the *MAD*.

13. The following data exhibit a linear trend.

t	D_t
1	25
2	27
3	30
4	31

Holt's method is used for forecasting. The initial values, L_0 and T_0, are 25 and 2, respectively. Let $\alpha = 0.2$ and $\beta = 0.4$.
a. Calculate L_t and T_t for $t = 1, 2, 3, 4$.
b. What is F_{4+1}?
c. Calculate the *MAD*.

14. Holt's method is used for forecasting Time Series 2 (VCRs) in Table 12.13, $\alpha = 0.2$ and $\beta = 0.2$.
a. Based on the knowledge of the 24 months' demands, what is the forecast for Month 25?
b. Based on the knowledge of the 24 months' demands, what is the forecast for Month 26?
c. The demand for Month 25 has been discovered and was 126. Calculate L_{25} and T_{25}. What is the new forecast for Month 26?
d. The *SMAD* based on the first 24 months is 1.2. Given the new demand for Month 25, update the *SMAD* for smoothing constant 0.3.
e. Give a 95 percent confidence interval of the new forecast for Month 26.
f. Give a 99 percent confidence interval of the new forecast for Month 26.

15. Holt's method has been used to forecast monthly demand for videocassette tapes. The 65 past demands resulted in $L_{65} = 1,000$ and $T_{65} = 40$. The *SMAD* is 11, $\alpha = 0.2$, and $\beta = 0.2$.
a. What is the forecast for Month 66?
b. What is the forecast for Month 67?
c. The demand for Month 66 has been discovered and was 1,030. Calculate L_{66} and T_{66}. What is the new forecast for Month 67?
d. Given the new demand for Month 66, update the *SMAD* for a 0.3 smoothing constant.
e. Give a 95 percent confidence interval of the new forecast for Month 67.
f. Give a 99 percent confidence interval of the new forecast for Month 67.

16. Winters' model is used to forecast quarterly aggregate demand for all products. The seasonal factor for Quarter 1 is 0.7. The seasonal factors for Quarters 2, 3 and 4 are 0.9, 1.1, and 1.3, respectively. Using 12 quarters of demand, the current estimate of the base level is 100,000 units and is 2,000 per quarter for the trend. The smoothing constants are $\alpha = 0.2$, $\beta = 0.2$, and $\gamma = 0.3$. The next quarter is January–March.
a. What is the forecast of the aggregate demand for the next quarter?
b. The actual demand for the quarter is 93,000. Calculate the values of L_{13} and T_{13}. Calculate the new seasonal factor for the first quarter.
c. Based on the demand for the 13 quarters, estimate the demand for the 14th quarter.

    d. Based on the demand for the 13 quarters, estimate the demand for the 17th quarter.

17. Winters' model is used to forecast monthly demand for snowblowers. The seasonal factors for January and February are 1.7 and 1.5, respectively. Using 102 monthly demands, the current estimate of the base level is 900 units. The smoothing constants are $\alpha = 0.2$ and $\gamma = 0.3$. Because no trend is present, $\beta = 0$. Next month is January.

    a. What is the forecast of the demand for January? February?

    b. The actual demand for January is 1,700. Calculate the value of L_{103} and calculate the new seasonal factor for January.

    c. Based on the 103 monthly demands, forecast the demand for February.

    d. Based on the demand for the 103 months, forecast the demand for January of the following year.

18. A prominent business school has collected data on the score on the Graduate Management Aptitude Test (GMAT) and grade point average (GPA) at graduation on a sample of students admitted.

GPA	GMAT
2.8	450
3.1	480
3.3	520
3.2	500
2.9	495
3.7	590

    a. Using simple linear regression, estimate the values of A and B for the relationship $GPA = A + B(GMAT)$.

    b. Plot the deviations versus the GMAT score.

    c. If the GMAT for a student is 500, what is the estimated GPA at graduation?

19. Historical records show that when advertising expenditures are high, sales are also high.

Sales ($000s)	Advertising ($)
50,000	100,000
55,000	107,000
45,000	102,000
56,000	110,000
73,000	123,000
63.000	109.000

    a. Estimate a and b in the linear relationship to use simple regression to forecast sales (in $000s).

    b. If the advertising expenditure is $100,000, what is the estimate of sales?

    c. Plot the deviations versus the advertising expenditures.

    d. Is a linear model appropriate? Discuss.

MORE CHALLENGING EXERCISES

1. Develop the three updating formulas and the forecasting formula for Winters' model with an additive seasonal factor.

2. Consider the following monthly time series of the prime interest rate.

	Month							
	1	2	3	4	5	6	7	8
Prime rate (percent)	8.2	8.4	8.0	7.9	8.2	8.0	8.1	7.7

Develop an exponential smoothing model based on this data. What is your forecast for Month 9? Give a 95 percent confidence interval on your forecast.

3. Construct a flowchart of a forecasting system using simple exponential smoothing. The system should include data filtering and tracking signals. The system must show updating as a new demand is discovered.

4. The quarterly sales of Standard & Poor's 500 future contracts are shown below:

Quarter	Sales (000s)
1	250
2	280
3	295
4	305
5	275
6	305
7	320
8	330
9	325
10	340
11	320
12	370

a. Construct a scatter diagram of sales.
b. Use the first two years' data to develop an exponential smoothing model to forecast quarterly sales.
c. Using the last year's data, evaluate the forecasting model that you developed in Part b.
d. Plot the forecast errors. Is there a pattern?
e. What is your forecast for the next quarter?
f. Give a 95 percent confidence on your forecast for the next quarter.

MINICASE

Raintree Country Furniture Company

Congratulations! You've been hired to provide forecasts for Raintree Country Furniture Company. The data below is for five of its products. Your assignment is to develop forecasts for the next 12 months for each of these products. Give a 95 percent confidence interval for Month 61.

Month (t)	Products (demand in units)				
	503	602	712	841	345
1	126	319	38	344	991
2	105	344	39	355	1,004
3	114	344	69	312	1,031
4	102	337	55	303	1,011
5	116	334	59	244	1,045
6	113	331	107	261	1,040
7	119	358	85	242	1,019
8	119	361	59	268	998
9	109	365	49	301	1,054
10	119	370	63	316	1,042
11	117	373	55	375	1,042
12	111	376	50	396	1,013
13	117	370	59	391	1,029
14	118	383	56	386	1,063
15	112	381	53	366	986
16	104	382	106	339	1,008
17	127	390	95	296	1,038
18	121	377	113	288	1,039
19	111	381	100	300	968
20	98	396	123	301	1,020
21	116	417	62	330	996
22	109	393	39	380	1,014
23	113	394	62	441	989
24	111	413	44	443	969
25	108	390	85	463	1,007
26	95	402	65	423	984
27	107	402	56	406	1,010
28	113	405	107	376	1,009
29	117	412	107	363	984
30	83	425	111	341	957
31	110	422	82	330	969
32	121	431	76	333	961
33	100	448	71	395	976
34	117	434	71	445	979
35	118	419	83	488	998
36	117	442	41	513	945
37	136	431	54	513	1,023
38	109	431	83	501	984
39	116	437	76	463	963
40	131	457	102	430	927

(Continued)

(Concluded)

Month (t)	Products (demand in units) 503	602	712	841	345	
41	101	442	110	368		972
42	107	450	130	361		974
43	116	476	136	352		998
44	109	449	116	393		965
45	133	472	89	452		940
46	106	474	109	501		985
47	126	471	116	539		959
48	121	470	47	570		980
49	116	466	78	561		935
50	116	481	101	545		974
51	122	472	102	508		935
52	105	492	107	465		946
53	125	479	138	423		936
54	119	505	167	398		943
55	119	494	151	394		912
56	118	501	127	426		895
57	111	483	155	494		921
58	116	504	80	563		964
59	114	513	109	594		927
60	121	509	60	620		934

13

Inventory Planning

Why Is Inventory Necessary?
The Retailer   The Manufacturer

Inventory System Considerations and Costs

ABC Analysis

Deterministic Demand
The Economic Order Quantity / Sensitivity Analysis and the
EOQ / Quantity Discounts and the EOQ / Manufacturing
Batch Sizes

Probabilistic Demand
Service Levels / Choosing the Reorder Point—A Marginal
Economics Approach / Demand Forecasting and Reorder Points

Material Requirements Planning and Product Explosions

Japanese Manufacturing Methods—Just-in-Time

Case: Drake Radio

PFIZER PHARMACEUTICALS

Pfizer operates in 65 companies in five business groups: agriculture, specialty chemicals, materials science, consumer, and health care. The health care group, including Pfizer Pharmaceuticals, contributes more than 50 percent of the company's sales. The management of Pfizer Pharmaceuticals was concerned with the hundreds of millions of dollars that inventories of raw materials, work in process (WIP), and finished goods represented. It wanted to reduce the level of inventories, maintain or improve the ability of Pfizer Pharmaceuticals to satisfy customer orders, and develop tools to hold manufacturing managers accountable for their inventories. It assembled a team to study the Pfizer Pharmaceuticals production and inventory system. After 3.5 years, but only 1.5 man-years of effort, an integrated inventory management system was installed that "reduced inventories by $23.9 million and back orders by 95 percent over a three-year period."

The manufacturing process at Pfizer Pharmaceuticals has two distinct steps. First, active pharmaceutical ingredients are produced by organic synthesis. Second, those ingredients are combined with other raw materials into "dosage forms." A batch must go through many operations in each of these two steps. The organic synthesis requires up to 15 operations over a 49-week period. A typical product requires six dosage manufacturing operations during 6 to 15 weeks. With such long manufacturing times, large inventories (particularly of WIP) are expected. Pfizer Pharmaceuticals introduced an MRP system to integrate production and inventory.

The system determined finished goods manufacturing lot sizes and safety stocks for each product. These formed the basis for managerial goals for WIP at the dosage plants. The system recommended larger lot sizes, which reduced the changeover cost.

Production planning at the organic synthesis plants was complicated by the high expense of changing from one product to another. The total changeover cost for all the production operations for a series of batches of a product was between $15,000 and $95,000. Pfizer Pharmaceuticals developed and implemented a model using LOTUS 1-2-3 that minimized the total cost of inventory investment and changeovers for a series of batches.

Because of long manufacturing lead times at the organic synthesis plants and because of the high penalty for not having pharmaceuticals available, Pfizer Pharmaceuticals maintained large stocks of intermediate organic synthesis products. Studying the batch sizes obtained from the organic synthesis lot size model, annual consumption by the dosage plants, the variability of demand during the manufacturing lead time and the probability that a batch would be delayed for quality reasons enabled it to reduce these safety stocks. Inventories decreased and service levels improved. By aggregating over products, it was able to develop standards for WIP inventory at the organic synthesis plants.

Raw materials are bulk chemicals and packaging materials. The MRP system uses a centralized forecasting system to drive a master production planning module for each plant. Time-phased finished goods production is exploded through the bill-of-materials into component requirements. The component requirements are translated into purchase orders. A quantity discount model was introduced to guide buyers in issuing purchase orders. Pfizer Pharmaceuticals determined reorder points for purchased materials by using finished goods demand and its variability as well as supplier lead times.

In this chapter, we introduces order quantity and reorder point determination. We also introduce quantity discounts, forecasting and lead-time demand variability, MRP, and Japanese manufacturing methods.

P. P. Kleutghen and J. C. McGee, "Development and Implementation of an Integrated Inventory Management Program at Pfizer Pharmaceuticals," *Interfaces* 15, no. 1 (January–February 1985), pp. 69–87.

Inventory planning affects the effectiveness of most organizations. It includes buying, producing, using, and selling products. For example, a grocery store buys from its suppliers and sells to its customers. Government agencies and not-for-profit companies must buy supplies (e.g., computer disks) that they use or sell. Some government agencies buy products and give them away (e.g., surplus cheese). Inventories are kept so that products are available when they are needed or available for sale when customers want to buy them.

Inventory planning has a big effect on the profitability of manufacturing companies. Pfizer buys raw materials, processes them, and sells the products. Pfizer Pharmaceuticals' inventory planning system reduced inventories by $23.9 million and back orders by 95 percent. The inventory reduction saved several million dollars a year. At the same time, customers received better service.

The inventory planning decisions include when to order and how much to order. For a retailer, an order is a purchase from a supplier. For a manufacturing company, an order can be the release of a production order to the plant as well as a purchase of raw materials from a supplier.

Inventory planning is a major application area for management science. In this chapter, we present some of the decision models and approaches used in inventory planning. First, we examine why inventory is necessary. Second, we discuss different types of inventory planning systems and the costs that you should consider in inventory planning. Third, we present ABC analysis, a framework for focusing inventory planning attention on the most important products. Then, we discuss inventory planning for deterministic demand and for probabilistic demand. In the last two sections, we discuss the material requirements planning (MRP) approach and the Japanese approach for manufacturing planning.

WHY IS INVENTORY NECESSARY?

Let's consider bicycles from a retailer's and a manufacturer's viewpoint. Why is it necessary to have inventory on hand? The reasons are different for the retailer and the manufacturer.

The Retailer

Jack's Bicycle Shop has bicycles on hand so that they are available when customers want to buy them. One advantage of large inventories is an increased likelihood that enough bicycles are on hand to satisfy customer requests. If the product is not available from Jack's, sales might be lost. Even if sales are not lost, the customers are unhappy because they have to wait until the retailer receives more bicycles from its supplier, and that might cause future lost sales. Another possible advantage of large inventories is that Jack's may receive a discount on large purchases. If Jack's gets a discount on orders of more than 50 bicycles, the retailer might order a large quantity of bicycles for that reason.

The Manufacturer

Three types of inventory

Reasons for finished inventory

For the manufacturer of the bicycles, the inventory on hand includes *raw materials, work-in-process material,* and *finished bicycles.* Let's consider the reasons for the manufacturer's inventories. First, large production runs of standard products are often attractive because changing from one product to another product is usually expensive. Thus, you make a particular bicycle model for a long period before you change to another model. By doing this, you decrease the number of changeovers and the changeover cost. But a long production run of a particular bicycle model ends in more inventory. The manufacturer may also have large inventories because shutting down a manufacturing plant is expensive. For this reason, automobile manufacturers often build up large inventories of unsold automobiles rather than shut down a plant. Another reason why manufacturers may have inventories of finished products is that demand for a product is seasonal. The manufacturer of a seasonal product, such as lawn mowers, may decide to produce at a steady rate during the year, rather than change the production rate from month to month. Producing at a steady rate builds up inventories during periods of low sales and decreases inventories during periods of high sales.

Inventory is also required because of the manufacturer's distribution system. **Pipeline inventory** includes finished products in the distribution system. For example, say that the bicycle manufacturer distributes its products through regional warehouses to retailers. Some completed bicycles are often in transit from the manufacturing plants to the regional warehouses and from the regional warehouses to the retailers. Also, bicycles are stored at the warehouses to provide faster delivery to the retailers. Until the retailers receive the bicycles and pay the invoices, the bicycles are the manufacturer's inventory.

Pipeline inventory

Now, let's consider inventories located at the manufacturing facility. Raw materials are stored so that they are available when the manufacturing facility needs them. During manufacturing, the partially completed products are called **work-in-process inventory.** You can think of work-in-process inventory as pipeline inventory within the manufacturing facility. You have work-in-process inventory so that production can continue without interruption from one manufacturing stage to another. Many automobile manufacturers produce components at locations different from the final assembly site. For example, engines and body panels may be made at separate facilities and shipped to the final assembly plant. In that case, the amount of work-in-process inventory is large.

Reasons for raw material and work-in-process inventory

The delay between placing an order for materials and receiving the materials is called the **lead time.** A long lead time or an uncertain lead time is another reason for large inventories. If the bicycle manufacturer receives its raw materials quickly, it needs less raw materials inventory to ensure availability. This has motivated the recent trend toward the suppliers of an automobile manufacturer locating close to its manufacturing plants. The material requirements planning (MRP) and just-in-time (JIT) systems for production and inventory planning bring lead times to the manufacturing floor. We discuss MRP and JIT later in this chapter.

Inventory and lead times

Forecasting the demand for finished products is an important part of inventory planning for both retailers and manufacturers. Improved forecasts decrease the amount of inventory required for product availability. If the demand might be larger than the forecast, more inventory must be on hand to assure product availability. For example, say that the forecast demand is 100 bicycles but that you believe the demand might be as high as 110. In that case, you should stock 110 bicycles if you want to be certain that you can satisfy the demand. But if the forecast is unbiased, you will have unsold bicycles most of the time. Now say that the forecast is always correct. In that case, if the forecast is 100, you only need to have 100 bicycles on hand.

Inventory and forecast errors

Lead times and forecast errors affect the inventory required to satisfy the demand. Many times, you can improve forecasting and get reduced, dependable lead times. A good manager examines these possibilities before implementing a complex inventory planning system.

Let's make another observation on forecasting demand. The distinction between **independent demand** and **dependent demand** is important. For the bicycle manufacturer, the demand from retailers is an example of independent demand. The demand for finished products is independent of other inventory planning decisions. For the bicycle manufacturer, the demand for raw materials is dependent on other inventory planning decisions. For example, the manufacturer decides when to produce its products and how much of those products to produce, and this affects the timing of raw materials orders and the amount of raw materials required. The last two sections of this chapter, Material Requirements Planning and Product Explosions and Japanese Manufacturing Methods—Just-in-Time, are concerned with dependent demand. The sections Deterministic Demand and Probabilistic Demand are concerned with independent demand. In the next section, we describe types of inventory systems for independent demand and cost considerations.

INVENTORY SYSTEM CONSIDERATIONS AND COSTS

Two decisions

As a manager, you must decide when to order and how much to order. These decisions depend on costs and on when you need the product. The **reorder point** is the inventory level at which you place an order. If the inventory on hand is at the reorder point or less, you place an order. The **order quantity** is the amount you order. Let R represent the reorder point, and let Q represent the order quantity. Figure 13.1 illustrates these con-

FIGURE 13.1   Inventory-on-Hand Example—Constant and Deterministic Demand, Zero Lead Time

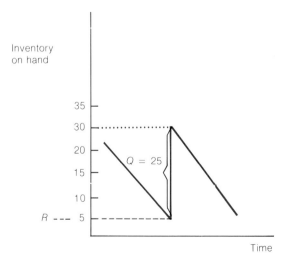

cepts. The reorder point is 5 units, and the order quantity is 25 units. When the inventory on hand reaches 5 units, an order for 25 units is placed. Figure 13.1 illustrates a situation in which the lead time is 0, which is the reason that the inventory on hand jumps from 5 to 30 (an increase of 25) when the order is placed. If the lead time is more than 0, the order doesn't arrive instantly, but the inventory on hand does increase by 25 units when it arrives.

Most inventory planning systems are computerized, but some are manual. An example of a manual inventory planning system may be the ordering of office supplies by a secretary. When the supply of pencils is low, the secretary places an order for more pencils. A manual system is used because the potential savings of computerizing the office supply inventory planning system are minimal compared to the cost of developing and operating the computerized system.

Computerized inventory planning systems can be either *real-time* or *batch processing systems.* In a **real-time system,** whenever an inventory transaction occurs, the inventory-on-hand information is updated. For example, when you ship to a customer, the inventory on hand is decreased by the amount shipped. A **batch processing system** collects sets of inventory transactions and updates the inventory-on-hand information by periodically processing batches of transactions. For example, when you receive a shipment from a supplier, you add that transaction to the batch. Then, you periodically process the batch of transactions to update the inventory-on-hand information. Until you have processed the batch, the inventory-on-hand information is outdated. Operating a batch processing system is generally less expensive than operating a real-time system. However, improvements in technology, such as using bar code readers to update inventory records are decreasing the cost of real-time inventory planning systems. At many grocery store checkout counters, when the bar code on the package is passed over a bar code reader, a computer system sends the price to the cash register. This system could also be used to update the inventory-on-hand information when the sale is recorded. Except for shoplifting, the system always knows how much of each product is on hand. The inventory planning system could use this information in a continuous review/real-time system.

Inventory systems are either *periodic review* or *continuous review systems.* A **periodic review** system periodically reviews the inventory level to decide whether to order and how much to order. For example, if the period is one week, the decisions are made once a week. The system is unaware of the inventory level between the weekly reviews. A **continuous review** system continually reviews the inventory level and places an order at any time.

Figure 13.1 illustrates a continuous review system with a reorder point of 5 units and an order quantity of 25. As soon as the inventory level

Margin notes:

Real-time and batch processing systems

Periodic or continuous review

reaches five units, an order is placed. Say that the system has periodic review and a reorder point of five units. If seven units are on hand at the time of the review, an order isn't placed. If an order is not placed at that review, the next chance to place an order is one period later. During that period, the inventory level can decrease below the reorder point, but you don't discover this until the next review. If the demand in the next period is greater than seven units, some customer demand can't be satisfied from inventory on hand. Therefore, if the same reorder point is used, a periodic review system has a greater chance of unsatisfied demand than does a continuous review system.

Lost sale or backlogged demand

A **shortage** occurs when a customer requests a product, but none is on hand to fulfill the request. Whether a shortage ends in a *lost sale* or *backlogged demand* is an important issue in determining the cost of the shortage. In the **lost sale** case, the profit on that demand is lost. In the **backlogged demand** case, the customer waits until the product is available. The back orders of Pfizer Pharmaceuticals are backlogged demand, and the system it adopted reduced back orders by 95 percent. The *backlogged demand* case is illustrated in Figure 13.2 for a continuous review system with a reorder point of 5 and an order quantity of 25. An order is placed when the inventory reaches five, but the order is not received until the lead time, represented by *L,* passes. During the four-day lead time, demand is 10 units; the first 5 units of demand during the lead time are satisfied from stock on hand. After two days, the inventory is zero. The last 5 units of demand are backlogged, as represented by a negative inventory on hand, so that when the order of 25 arrives, the inventory on hand becomes 20 units after the backlogged demand has been satisfied. In

FIGURE 13.2   Inventory-on-Hand Example—Probabilistic Demand, Nonzero Lead Time, Backlogged Demand

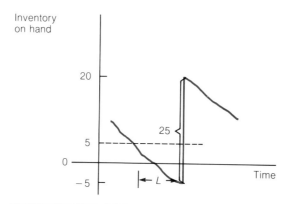

the *lost sales* case, the inventory stays at 0 from the time the units on hand have been depleted until the order is received, when it increases to 25 units. The profit is postponed in the backlogged demand case, but it is lost in the lost sales case.

The **shortage cost,** represented by c_s, is the cost per unit of demand that cannot be satisfied from inventory on hand. The units for the shortage cost for the lost sales case are dollars/unit of unsatisfied demand. For the backlogged demand case, the customer is more unhappy the longer the wait until the order is filled. The units for the shortage cost for this case are dollars/unit of unsatisfied demand *per unit of time* that the demand is unsatisfied. Here, the shortage cost represents the loss of goodwill and possible lost future sales.

Deterministic or probabilistic demand

Demand can be either deterministic or probabilistic. One example of **deterministic demand** is a situation in which the company or retailer has a contract with a customer. Another example is a situation in which customers order for future delivery. In such situations, you know the future demand when you are planning your inventory. Figure 13.1 illustrated an inventory level that changed linearly with time. In this case, the demand was at a constant rate and thus deterministic. Usually, the demand is uncertain and thus probabilistic. In Figure 13.2, the inventory level changed erratically and the demand was probabilistic.

A lead time can be either deterministic or probabilistic. If a lead time is longer, there is a greater chance of a shortage. Thus, a **constant lead time** is preferable to an **uncertain lead time** with the same mean. For example, in Figure 13.2 the lead time is four days and shortages occur. If the lead time is two days, however, there aren't any shortages. Say that the lead time is uncertain but has a mean of two days. For the illustrated demand pattern, if the lead time is greater than two days, a shortage occurs. To achieve the same probability of a shortage, we must choose a higher reorder point for an uncertain lead time than for a constant lead time.

The cost of placing the order, represented by K, is called the **fixed order cost.** Typically, K includes the cost of processing the order, purchasing overhead, and other acquisition costs that are not proportional to the amount ordered. An example is the cost of sending a truck to pick up the order. The cost of sending the truck is independent of the number of units that the truck carries.

The purchasing cost charged by our supplier can also affect the order quantity. If the supplier offers quantity discounts, we can decrease the purchasing cost by ordering large quantities.

Advantages of large order quantities and high reorder points

What are the *advantages of large order quantities?* If there are quantity discounts, we prefer ordering large quantities so as to reduce the purchasing cost. We also prefer large order quantities because they decrease the number of orders placed and thus reduce the total annual fixed order cost. What are the *advantages of high reorder points?* We prefer high reorder points because they decrease the chance of shortages. Using a higher reorder point reduces the shortage cost.

Disadvantages of large
order quantities and
high reorder points

What are the *disadvantages* of large order quantities and high reorder points? Both result in high average inventory levels. A major cost of many companies is the **inventory holding cost.** If a company has $10 million worth of inventory, it must finance that inventory. If the company's cost of capital is 15 percent a year, the annual inventory holding cost is $1,500,000. If the inventory level is decreased by half, the company saves $750,000 annually. This is the motivation for small order quantities and low reorder points. We choose the reorder point and order quantity by considering the *trade-offs* between inventory holding costs, fixed order costs, purchasing costs, and shortage costs.

Included in the inventory holding cost are the costs of insurance, spoilage, warehouse overhead, and taxes as well as the cost of capital to finance the inventory. The inventory holding cost per unit is denoted by c_h. Usually, c_h is a fraction of the cost of the product. Let the **purchase cost** per unit be C, and let the **annual holding cost fraction** be I. The *inventory holding cost per unit held for a year is*

$$c_h = I \times C$$

The annual holding cost fraction is 0.15 for the example above. If the cost per unit of the product is $10, $c_h = \$1.50$.

ABC ANALYSIS

The cost of developing and operating the inventory planning system is also important in designing the system. The system can have either periodic or continuous review, and it can be computerized or manual. If computerized, it can be a real-time or batch processing system. Generally, real-time/continuous review systems have smaller totals of inventory holding, fixed order, purchasing, and shortage costs than other types of systems. However, real-time/continuous review systems are more expensive to develop and operate. For items of low cost that sell slowly, a very simple system is justified. For items of high cost that sell well, a complex system is justified. The secretary might use a simple system for office supplies. But Pfizer Pharmaceuticals' annual inventory cost was millions of dollars, so a complex system was worthwhile.

In this section, we present ABC analysis, a framework that is useful for focusing more inventory planning effort on the products with the greatest cost savings potential.

Most companies have inventories of many products. Say that you have the responsibility for developing an inventory planning system for all the products. Some of the products deserve a simple inventory planning system, and some deserve a complex system. You can use ABC analysis to group the products depending on the amount of attention that is justified.

ABC analysis categorizes the products into groups depending on the annual purchasing cost. If the annual purchasing cost is larger, the potential savings from inventory planning are greater. The products with the smallest annual dollar volume deserve the least attention. If a product is classified in Category A, it deserves the most attention. If a product is classified in Category C, it deserves the least attention. If a product is classified in Category B, it deserves intermediate attention.

A small number of products usually represent a large percentage of the total annual purchasing cost. Usually, about 15 percent of the products represent 70 percent of the dollar volume, the next 25 percent represent 25 percent of the dollar volume, and the final 60 percent represent only 5 percent of the dollar volume. Figure 13.3 shows this relationship. The products have been listed in the decreasing order of their annual purchasing cost. That is, the annual purchasing cost of the first product is the largest, and the product farthest right has the smallest annual purchasing cost.

Table 13.1 illustrates the ABC approach to classifying products. The annual dollar volume of each product is calculated by multiplying the cost

FIGURE 13.3 Typical ABC Curve

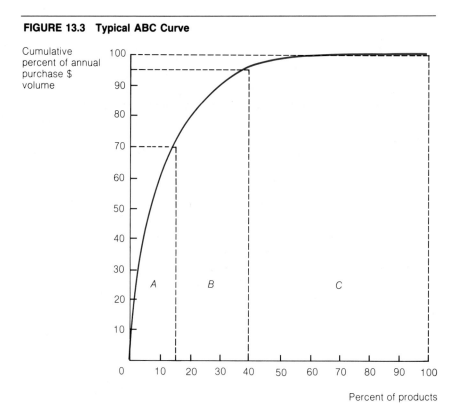

TABLE 13.1 ABC Analysis Example

Product Number	Purchase Cost/Unit	Annual Demand (units)	Annual Demand ($)	Percent of Annual Demand
10	$10	17,500	175,000	48.1
7	8	12,000	96,000	26.4
5	4	11,000	44,000	12.1
6	15	2,000	30,000	8.3
1	10	1,000	10,000	2.8
9	8	700	5,600	1.5
8	2	500	1,000	0.3
4	8	100	800	0.2
3	7	100	700	0.2
2	20	25	500	0.1
			363,600	100.0

per unit by annual unit sales. The products are listed in the decreasing order of this annual dollar volume. The total annual dollar volume of the 10 products is $363,600. Product 10 is the fraction $\frac{175,000}{363,600} = 0.481$ of total annual dollar volume, or 48.1 percent. The first two products, 10 and 7, contribute 74.5 percent of the total annual dollar volume. You classify these as A products. The next two products, 5 and 6, contribute 20.4 percent of the total annual dollar volume and are classified as B products. The other six products contribute only 5.1 percent of the total annual dollar volume and are classified as C products. The percentages for the classification scheme are not the same as those for the example. The assumption that 15, 25, and 60 percent of the products account for 70, 25, and 5 percent of the total annual dollar volume is a rule of thumb. Some adjustment in these percentages is necessary to take account of a particular company's actual annual dollar volumes.

The ABC classification ensures that the products with the greatest savings potential from inventory planning receive the most attention. Products classified as A are the best candidates for continuous review inventory systems. Products classified as B are good candidates for periodic review. Products classified as C justify simple inventory planning such as "When C products are ordered, let the order quantity be four weeks' demand."

DETERMINISTIC DEMAND

In this section, we develop useful inventory planning models for demand that is deterministic and constant. First, we consider inventory planning from a retailer's viewpoint. Then, we show the small cost impact of errors in estimating parameters and choosing the order quantity. We also show

how to choose the order quantity if the supplier offers discounts for large purchases. Finally, we consider planning from a manufacturer's viewpoint.

The Economic Order Quantity

The **economic order quantity (EOQ) model** is the most common inventory planning model. This model assumes that the demand for the item has a *known and constant* rate. For example, the demand is 3 units every day or 21 units every week. Let D be the demand rate per year. Recall that Q is the order quantity. *Assume* that the lead time, L is 0. That is, when an order of size Q is placed, the Q units arrive immediately. Because the lead time is 0, you use a reorder point of 0. When the inventory on hand decreases to 0, you order Q units. Figure 13.4 illustrates the inventory on hand under this policy. This is sometimes called the "sawtooth" graph.

Known and constant demand

Lead time is 0

The system has completed a **cycle** when it returns to the reorder point. The **cycle time,** denoted by T, is the time between successive orders. Because the annual demand is D and the order quantity is Q,

$$T = \frac{Q}{D} \text{ year}$$

If the annual demand is 600 and the order quantity is 100 units, the cycle time is $\frac{1}{6}$ year.

The EOQ model is not appropriate for determining manufacturing batch sizes. This model assumes that the Q units ordered arrive all at once. If a manufacturing order is released to the plant, however, the finished products become inventory as they are completed, not all at once. If the time required to make a single unit is large, the manufacturing

---

FIGURE 13.4   Inventory on Hand for EOQ Model, Zero Lead Time

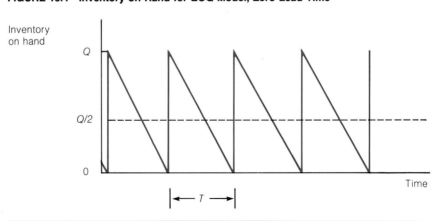

FIGURE 13.5 Annual Inventory Holding Cost

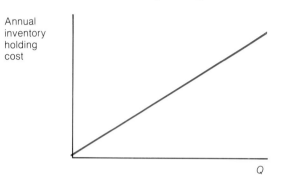

Annual
inventory
holding
cost

Q

"batch" arrives unit by unit over a long period of time. We discuss determining the size of manufacturing batches later in this chapter.

In Figure 13.4, the inventory on hand has a maximum of Q and a minimum of 0. The average number of units in inventory is $\frac{Q}{2}$. Recall that c_h is the inventory holding cost per year. The average annual inventory

Inventory holding cost   holding cost $= c_h \left(\frac{Q}{2}\right)$. If the order quantity is doubled, the average inventory level and the average annual inventory holding cost are also doubled. Figure 13.5 illustrates the annual inventory holding cost as a function of the order quantity, Q. The annual inventory holding cost increases linearly with Q.

If the annual demand is D and the order quantity is Q, the number of orders placed each year is $\frac{D}{Q}$. For example, if the annual demand is 600

Fixed order cost   and the order quantity is 100 units, then 6 orders are placed each year. If the fixed order cost is K, the annual fixed order cost $= K \left(\frac{D}{Q}\right)$. If the order quantity is doubled, the number of orders per year and the annual fixed order cost decrease by one half. Figure 13.6 illustrates the annual fixed order cost as a function of Q. As Q becomes small, the number of orders during a year and the annual fixed order cost become large. As Q becomes large, the number of orders and the annual fixed order cost become small.

Assume that each unit is purchased at a cost of C and that *quantity*

No quantity discounts   *discounts are not available*. Annually you must buy D units at a cost of C each. The annual cost of purchasing the D items, $C \times D$, does not depend on the order quantity. Without quantity discounts, the annual purchasing cost of the product is not considered in determining the order quantity.

The **total annual cost (TAC)** is the annual inventory holding cost plus

FIGURE 13.6 Annual Fixed Order Cost

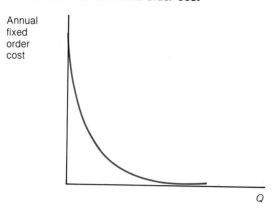

the annual fixed order cost. This is the total annual *variable* cost because it does not include the annual purchasing cost that doesn't vary with the order quantity. Figure 13.7 shows the TAC curve obtained by adding the costs from Figures 13.5 and 13.6. As the order quantity changes, there is a trade-off between the annual fixed order cost and the annual inventory holding cost. Algebraically, the total annual cost is calculated as

$$TAC = c_h\left(\frac{Q}{2}\right) + K\left(\frac{D}{Q}\right)$$

The value of Q that gives the minimum TAC is the **economic order quantity,** represented by Q^*. Using differential calculus, the value of Q^* is calculated to be

$$Q^* = \sqrt{\frac{2DK}{c_h}}$$

Economic order
quantity

FIGURE 13.7 Total Annual Cost

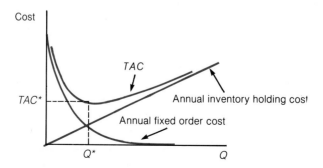

The minimum total annual cost for Q^*, denoted by TAC^*, is calculated by substituting Q^* into the TAC formula to get

$$TAC^* = \sqrt{2DKc_h}$$

Note that the TAC does *not* include the cost of purchasing the year's demand, $C \times D$. The optimal cycle time, T^*, is calculated as

$$T^* = \frac{Q^*}{D} \text{ year}$$

Constant lead time > 0

Figure 13.4 is based on the assumption that the lead time is 0. Say that the lead time is *known and constant*. When should the order for Q units be placed so that it arrives at the same time that the inventory on hand reaches 0? Assume that L is expressed as a fraction of a year. During the lead time, the number of units demanded is $D \times L$. When the inventory on hand reaches DL, you place an order. Thus, DL is the reorder point. For example, say that the annual demand is 600 units and that the lead time is 0.01 year. Then, the reorder point is $600 \times 0.01 = 6$ units.

Jack's Bicycle Shop

Table 13.2 has last year's monthly sales of a particular model of a child's 12-inch bicycle at Jack's Bicycle Shop. The sales for the year total 600 bicycles. The average sales per month are 50 units and relatively constant. Is it reasonable to use the EOQ model, which assumes that the demand has a known and constant rate? You, the model user, must decide whether the model gives a reasonable representation of the decision environment. As we have discussed, sometimes not all of the model's assumptions are satisfied by the actual situation. You must consider whether the model provides sufficiently useful results even though the assumptions are not all satisfied. In this case, using the EOQ model is reasonable because the demand changes little from month to month.

TABLE 13.2 Monthly 12-inch Bicycle Sales

Month	Sales
January	51
February	49
March	50
April	50
May	50
June	49
July	50
August	49
September	50
October	49
November	50
December	53
	600

Say that each bicycle costs \$50 from the supplier and that the inventory holding cost fraction is 0.12. The annual holding cost per unit is $c_h = 0.12 \times 50 = \$6$ per bicycle. Say that the fixed order cost is \$50. The economic order quantity is

$$Q^* = \sqrt{\frac{2 \times 600 \times 50}{6}} = 100$$

The minimum TAC is

$$TAC^* = \sqrt{2 \times 600 \times 50 \times 6} = \$600$$

Table 13.3 summarizes the calculation of the costs for various values of Q. The value of Q that minimizes the TAC is 100 bicycles. If the order quantity is 100 bicycles, the average number of bicycles in inventory is $\frac{100}{2} = 50$ and the annual inventory holding cost is $\$6 \times 50 = \$300$. Because the annual demand is 600 units and the order quantity is 100 units, the number of orders each year is $\frac{600}{100} = 6$ and the annual fixed order cost is $\$50 \times 6 = \$300$. Note that the TAC at the EOQ is \$600, the value from the TAC^* formula. Also note that the annual fixed order cost equals the annual inventory holding cost at the EOQ.[1] The optimal cycle time is $\frac{100}{600} = \frac{1}{6}$ year. The annual purchasing cost of the 600 bicycles is not included in the TAC. The annual purchasing cost is $\$50 \times 600 = \$30,000$.

TABLE 13.3   Total Annual Cost of 12-inch Bicycle Example

Q	Annual Fixed Order Cost	Annual Inventory Holding Cost	Total Annual Cost
50	600.00	150	750.00
60	500.00	180	680.00
70	428.57	210	638.57
80	375.00	240	610.00
90	333.33	270	603.33
100	300.00	300	600.00 ←
110	272.73	330	602.73
120	250.00	360	610.00
130	230.77	390	620.77
140	214.29	420	634.29
150	200.00	450	650.00

$K = \$50$, $C_h = \$6$, $D = 600$

---

[1] At the EOQ, the annual fixed order cost *always* equals the annual inventory holding cost. The EOQ is at the intersection of the two cost functions.

Because the monthly demands in Table 13.2 show some variability, the actual total annual cost might not be $600. However, we show later that the TAC is not sensitive to small changes in the order quantity and parameters.

Keep the units consistent!

You must be careful to keep the time units *consistent* for the model's parameters. The units of the demand rate (D), the inventory holding cost (c_h), and the lead time (L) are years. The time units of those parameters must be the same. You can determine the economic order quantity and the reorder point for another time unit if you keep the units consistent. Let's illustrate this by changing the time unit in the bicycle example to a *month*. If the annual demand is 600, the monthly demand is 50 units. The fixed order cost is not dependent on the time unit. The *per month* inventory holding cost, c_h, is $\frac{\$6}{12} = \$0.50$ per unit. The economic order quantity is calculated as

$$Q^* = \sqrt{\frac{2 \times 50 \times 50}{0.50}} = 100$$

The same order quantity, 100, is obtained regardless of the time unit. Recall that the TAC^* is the minimum total *annual* cost. If the time units are months, the minimum total *monthly* cost formula is

$$TMC^* = \sqrt{2DKc_h} = \sqrt{2 \times 50 \times 50 \times 0.50} = \$50$$

The minimum total *annual* cost is $12 \times \$50 = \$600$. This value was also obtained when the time unit was years. Say that the lead time is one month. What is the reorder point? If the lead time is in months, the demand rate must be in months to calculate the reorder point as DL, $50 \times 1 = 50$ units. If the lead time is in years, the demand rate must be in years to calculate the reorder point as $DL = 600 \times \frac{1}{12} = 50$ units. The same reorder point is obtained, but the time units must be consistent.

The monthly sales of bicycles in Table 13.2 are not always 50. If the lead time is one month and the reorder point is 50, a shortage occurs if the demand is greater than 50 in the following month. Later in the chapter, we discuss how to determine the reorder point if the demand during the lead time is uncertain.

Sensitivity Analysis and the EOQ

One justification for using the EOQ formula is the relative insensitivity of the cost to small errors that result from violations of the model's assumptions or incorrect estimates of the parameters (D, K, and c_h). Examine the EOQ formula, $Q^* = \sqrt{2DK/c_h}$. If the fixed order cost increases, the EOQ also increases, giving a smaller number of orders per year. If the inventory holding cost increases, the EOQ and the average inventory level decrease.

Because of the square root in the EOQ formula, if the fixed order cost doubles, the EOQ is $\sqrt{2} = 1.414$ times the old EOQ. For Jack's Bicycle Shop, if the correct value is $K = \$100$, rather than $50, the EOQ is

$$Q^* = \sqrt{\frac{2 \times 600 \times 100}{6}} = 141.4$$

For $K = \$50$, we calculated the value of the EOQ as 100 units. Even though the correct fixed order cost is 100 percent greater than the value we used to calculate the EOQ, the correct EOQ is only 41.4 percent greater than that calculated. Table 13.4 illustrates the errors in the EOQ for the bicycle example relative to the EOQ calculated using the fixed order cost $K = \$50$. To illustrate the use of Table 13.4, say that the correct fixed order cost is $60, which is 20 percent higher than the value used to calculate the EOQ. The correct EOQ is 9.54 percent higher than that calculated. The EOQ percent errors are smaller than the fixed order cost percent errors.

Similarly, errors in the EOQ caused by errors in the estimation of c_h are also affected by being inside the square root. For Jack's Bicycle Shop, we used a $6 annual inventory holding cost per bicycle. If the correct value is $12, the correct value of the EOQ is

$$Q^* = \sqrt{\frac{2 \times 600 \times 50}{12}} = 70.71$$

The change in the EOQ from 100 to 70.71 is small relative to the 100 percent change in the inventory holding cost. A 100 percent error in estimating c_h causes the correct EOQ to be 29.29 percent smaller than that calculated.

The EOQ model assumes that the demand rate is known and constant. However, the impact of a change in the demand rate, D, is reduced by D being inside the square root in the EOQ formula. If the demand rate is

TABLE 13.4   Sensitivity Analysis of Example to Fixed Order Cost, K

Correct K	Correct EOQ	Correct EOQ/ Calculated EOQ	Percent Error in EOQ
25.00	70.71	0.7071	−29.29
40.00	89.44	0.8944	−10.56
45.00	94.87	0.9487	−5.13
47.50	97.47	0.9747	−2.53
49.50	99.50	0.9950	−0.50
50.00	100.00	1.0000	0.
50.50	100.50	1.0050	+0.50
52.50	102.47	1.0247	+2.47
55.00	104.88	1.0488	+4.88
60.00	109.54	1.0954	+9.54
100.00	141.41	1.4141	+41.41

TABLE 13.5   Percent Error in Correct EOQ Relative to the Calculated EOQ

Correct *D*/Calculation *D* or Correct *K*/Calculation *K* or Calculation C_h/Correct C_h	Correct EOQ/Calculated EOQ	Percent Error in EOQ
0.5	0.7071	− 29.29
0.8	0.8944	− 10.56
0.9	0.9487	− 5.13
0.95	0.9747	− 2.53
0.99	0.9950	− 0.50
1.00	1.0000	0.00
1.01	1.0050	0.50
1.05	1.0247	2.47
1.10	1.0488	4.88
1.20	1.0954	9.54
2.00	1.4141	41.41

actually 10 percent higher than the value used to calculate the EOQ, the error in the EOQ is only 4.88 percent. This is illustrated by noting that the correct EOQ is actually $\sqrt{1.1}$ = 1.0488 times the calculated EOQ.

A general table for sensitivity analysis of EOQ

Table 13.5 is used to calculate the percent errors in the correct EOQ relative to the calculated EOQ for errors in the parameters (K, c_h, and D) for the general EOQ model. *Note that the ratio headings are different for* K *and* D *relative to that for* c_h. The correct K and D appear in the numerator, but the correct c_h appears in the denominator.

Let's use Table 13.5 to analyze the impact of the parameter errors that we calculated explicitly for the bicycle example. For the c_h error example, the value for the calculation of the EOQ was $6, but the correct value was $12. The ratio is calculated as $\dfrac{\text{Calculation } c_h}{\text{Correct } c_h} = \dfrac{6}{12} = 0.5$. From Table 13.5, a ratio of 0.5 gives an EOQ error of − 29.29 percent. This is the same result that we obtained by recalculating the EOQ and then determining the percent error. Now, say that the annual demand is 660 rather than 600. The ratio is calculated as $\dfrac{\text{Correct } D}{\text{Calculation } D} = \dfrac{660}{600} = 1.1$. A ratio of 1.1 corresponds to an error in the EOQ of 4.88 percent.

Sensitivity of TAC to Q

The sensitivity of the TAC to incorrect values of the order quantity is more important to the manager than the percent error of the order quantity. Let Q^* represent the correct order quantity. For any other order quantity, Q, calculate $r = \dfrac{Q}{Q^*}$. The total annual cost for Q^*, represented by $TAC(Q^*)$, is $\sqrt{2DKc_h}$. The total annual cost for $Q = rQ^*$ is calculated by

$$TAC\ (rQ^*) = c_h\left(\frac{rQ^*}{2}\right) + K\left(\frac{D}{rQ^*}\right)$$

TABLE 13.6   Ratios of TACs for *r*

r	$\dfrac{TAC(rQ*)}{TAC(Q*)}$
0.5	1.25000
0.6	1.13333
0.7	1.06429
0.8	1.02500
0.9	1.00556
0.95	1.00132
0.99	1.00005
1.00	1.00000
1.01	1.00005
1.05	1.00119
1.10	1.00455
1.20	1.01667
1.30	1.03462
1.40	1.05714
1.50	1.08333

After algebraic manipulation, the ratio of the total annual costs is

$$\frac{TAC(rQ*)}{TAC(Q*)} = \frac{1}{2}\left(r + \frac{1}{r}\right)$$

Table 13.6 presents this ratio for different values of *r*. If $r = 1.2$ (the order quantity is 20 percent too large), the ratio of the TACs is 1.01667. If the actual order quantity is 20 percent larger than the correct value, the TAC increases by only 1.667 percent. The increase in the TAC is relatively insensitive to errors in the determination of the order quantity. Note that the ratio is *not symmetric* for increases and decreases. If *r* is 0.8 (*Q* is 20 percent too small), the ratio of the TACs is 1.02500. The TAC increases by 2.5 percent for an order quantity 20 percent too small, compared to an increase of 1.667 percent for an order quantity 20 percent too large.

Figure 13.8 shows the relationship between the cost ratio and *r*. The curve is relatively flat for values of *r* close to 1. This shows graphically that a small error in the *order quantity* causes a small cost increase.

Let's illustrate that an error in estimating a *parameter* gives a small increase in the TAC. For the Jack's Bicycle Shop example, the annual demand was 600 and the calculated order quantity was 100 units. Say that the true annual demand is 720 units. The ratio of the correct *D* to the calculated *D* is $\frac{720}{600} = 1.2$. From Table 13.5, the ratio of the correct EOQ to the calculated EOQ is 1.0954. The correct EOQ is $1.0954 \times 100 = 109.54$ units. Thus, $r = \frac{100}{109.54} = 0.9129$. (Alternatively, *r* is calculated directly as $\frac{1}{1.0954} = 0.9129$.) The value $r = 0.9129$ does not appear in

TAC ratio is not symmetric

Parameter errors and the TAC

FIGURE 13.8 TAC Ratio as a Function of *r*

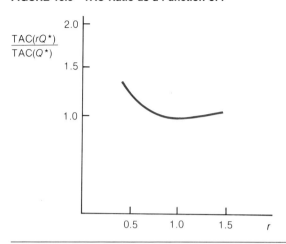

Table 13.6, so the ratio of the total annual costs is calculated as

$$\frac{TAC(100)}{TAC(109.54)} = \frac{1}{2}\left(0.9129 + \frac{1}{0.9129}\right) = 1.00415$$

An error in the annual demand of 20 percent gives an incorrect EOQ, but the TAC increases by only 0.415 percent.

Because the TAC is relatively insensitive to errors in parameters and the order quantity, we can justify using the EOQ even when the assumptions of the EOQ model aren't satisfied. We illustrate the small cost impact of using the "Order *X* weeks' demand" form of the policy for Type C products in the ABC analysis. One possibility for inventory planning rules for C products is annually updating the demand forecasts and calculating the number of weeks of demand that each order satisfies on that basis. Another possibility is regularly updating the demand forecasts but reviewing annually the number of weeks' demand that each order satisfies.

Consider the first possibility. The number of weeks is based on the EOQ amount calculated on the basis of *annual demand*. For the bicycle example, say that the demand varies from week to week but that the annual demand is estimated to be 600 units. Using the data from the bicycle example, the EOQ is 100 units. Six orders are placed each year, and the average time between orders is $\frac{1}{6} = 0.1667$ year, or $0.1667 \times 52 = 8\frac{2}{3}$ weeks. Each time an order is placed, the quantity is equal to the forecast total for the next $8\frac{2}{3}$ weeks. At an annual rate of 600 units, the order quantity is $8\frac{2}{3} \times \left(\frac{600}{52}\right) = 100$ units. Say that the annual demand rate becomes 720 units. The correct order quantity increases by the factor $\sqrt{\frac{720}{600}} = \sqrt{1.2} = 1.0954$. The value of r is calculated as $r = \frac{1}{1.0954} = 0.9129$. The ratio of the TACs is

$$\frac{TAC(100)}{TAC(109.54)} = \frac{1}{2}\left(0.9129 + \frac{1}{0.9129}\right) = 1.00415$$

The TAC is only 0.415 percent greater at the incorrect order quantity of 100 units than at the correct order quantity. This is a very small increase in the cost for such a large forecast error. For C products that have small annual dollar volume, the savings don't justify using a more complex inventory planning system.

Now, consider the second possibility and say that the updated forecast of the annual demand is 720 units. The order quantity based on the policy of ordering $8\frac{2}{3}$ weeks demand is $8\frac{2}{3} \times \left(\frac{720}{52}\right) = 120$ units. If the correct annual rate is 720, the correct EOQ is 109.54 units. Even though the forecast is accurate, if the number of weeks of demand for each order has not been updated, the costs are not the minimum. If the order quantity is 120, the value of r is calculated as $r = \frac{120}{109.54} = 1.0954$, which gives an increase in the TAC of 0.415 percent relative to the correct EOQ of 109.54 units. For a product with a small annual dollar volume, the savings for updating the number of weeks are small. The time interval for each order should be updated when the forecasting system indicates a significant change in demand.

Variation in the demand rate does not give large increases in the TAC, but it affects the selection of the reorder point. We discuss this in the Probabilistic Demand section.

Quantity Discounts and EOQ

Suppliers often give discounts for purchases of large quantities. In our opening case, for example, Pfizer Pharmaceuticals got discounts on purchases of large quantities of some of its chemical raw materials and packaging materials. A simple quantity discount model was developed to guide buyers who issued purchase orders for those materials. In this section, we discuss quantity discount models.

Table 13.7 presents a discount schedule for Jack's Bicycle Shop. For orders of 100 units or less, the price is $50 per unit. For order quantities from 101 to 400, the price is $48.50. The price is $48 for any order of 401 units or more.

Two types of discounts   Two types of discount schedules are **all-units discounts** and **incremental**

TABLE 13.7 12-inch Bicycle Discount Schedule

Quantity	Discount	Purchase Cost/ Unit
0–100	0%	$50.00
101–400	3	48.50
401 or more	4	48.00

discounts. To illustrate the difference between all-units discounts and incremental discounts, consider an order size of 150 bicycles. Table 13.7 indicates a 3 percent discount for that quantity. Under the all-units discount, each of the 150 units costs $48.50; the cost of 150 units is 150 × $48.50 = $7,275. Under the incremental discount, the discount is applied to only those units above the lower limit for the price. The first 100 units cost $50 and the next 50 cost $48.50, for a total of 100 × $50 + 50 × $48.50 = $7,425. All-unit discount schedules are more common than incremental discount schedules. *We assume all-units discounts in this section.*

Suppliers offer quantity discounts to encourage larger orders. But if you increase the order quantity, the average inventory holding cost and the annual inventory holding cost also increase. Therefore, you must evaluate the savings from a cheaper purchase cost versus the extra inventory holding cost.

Consider the general all-units discount situation in which there are n different prices based on the quantity ordered. The undiscounted price is represented by C_1; the price with the smallest discount is represented by C_2; and the price with the largest discount is represented by C_n. Say that the inventory holding cost is a fraction of the purchase price. Then, the inventory holding cost per unit also depends on the purchase price. Let $c_{h1} = IC_1$ represent the inventory holding cost per unit at the undiscounted price. Similarly, $c_{hn} = IC_n$ is the inventory holding cost per unit for the price with the largest discount.

Because of possible discounts, the annual cost of purchasing the units depends on the order quantity and must be included in the total annual cost for comparison purposes. Figure 13.9 shows the total annual cost versus Q for the three prices. The graph shows that the TAC *for any Q* is always lower when there is a larger discount. However, you might not receive the discount at that Q.

You can determine the best order quantity using three steps:

Step 1. Calculate the EOQ amount for all the prices as

$$Q_i^* = \sqrt{\frac{2DK}{c_{hi}}}, \; i = 1, 2, \ldots, n$$

Assume all-units discounts

Include the purchasing cost

Calculating the best order quantity

FIGURE 13.9   Total Annual Cost, Including Purchase Cost, for Quantity Discount

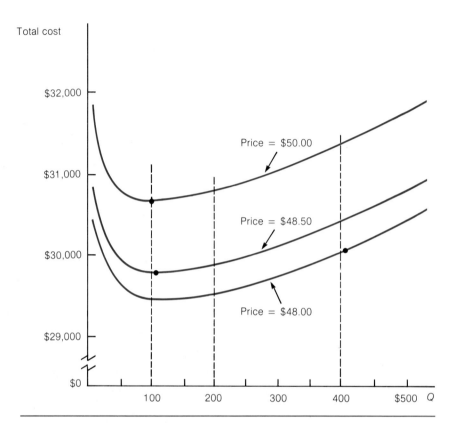

Step 2. If the order quantity from Step 1 for any price is within the range of quantities for which the price applies, the order quantity is Q_i^*. If the order quantity from Step 1 for any price is less than the range of quantities for which the price applies, change its order quantity, Q_i^*, to the smallest quantity that applies to that price. If the order quantity from Step 1 for any price is greater than the range of quantities for which the price applies, the most economical order quantity cannot be at that price. Do not consider the price further.

Step 3. From Steps 1 and 2, either a quantity has been specified or further consideration has been eliminated for each of the possible prices. Calculate the TAC for each of the quantities specified for each of the prices that have not been eliminated. The most economical order quantity is the one with the smallest TAC calculated in Step 3.

In Step 3, you can calculate the TAC for the ith price as

$$TAC_i^* = c_{hi}\left(\frac{Q_i^*}{2}\right) + K\left(\frac{D}{Q_i^*}\right) + C_i D$$

If the quantity for Price i was *not changed in Step 2*, calculating the TAC is simplified.

$$TAC_i^* = \sqrt{2DKc_{hi}} + C_iD$$

Example. Let's apply the three-step procedure to determine the best order quantity of bicycles for Jack's Bicycle Shop. Recall that $K = \$50$, $I = 0.12$, and $D = 600$. Based on the discount schedule in Table 13.7, the prices are $C_1 = \$50$, $C_2 = \$48.50$, and $C_3 = \$48$.

Step 1. Calculate $c_{h1} = 0.12 \times \$50.00 = \$6.00$, $c_{h2} = 0.12 \times \$48.50 = \$5.82$, and $c_{h3} = 0.12 \times \$48.00 = \$5.76$.

$$Q_1^* = \sqrt{\frac{2 \times 600 \times 50}{6.00}} = 100.00$$

$$Q_2^* = \sqrt{\frac{2 \times 600 \times 50}{5.82}} = 101.53$$

$$Q_3^* = \sqrt{\frac{2 \times 600 \times 50}{5.76}} = 102.06$$

Step 2. $Q_1^* = 100$ is within the range of quantities for price C_1. $Q_2^* = 101.53$ is within the range of quantities for price C_2. Q_3^* is less than the range of quantities for price C_3, so Q_3^* is changed to the minimum quantity to receive that price, 401.

Step 3. The TACs are calculated as

$$TAC_1^* = \sqrt{2 \times 600 \times 50 \times 6.00} + 50.00 \times 600 = \$30,600$$

$$TAC_2^* = \sqrt{2 \times 600 \times 50 \times 5.82} + 48.50 \times 600 = \$29,690.93$$

Because of the change in Q_3^* in Step 2,

$$TAC_3^* = 5.76 \left(\frac{401}{2}\right) + 50\left(\frac{600}{401}\right) + 48.00 \times 600 = \$30,017.66$$

The smallest of the three TACs is \$29,690.93, which is for an order quantity of 101.53 units. The best order quantity is 101.53 at a price of \$48.50. The savings in the annual purchasing costs for the largest discount are not enough to compensate for the increase in the annual inventory holding cost.

In many cases, a noninteger order quantity is meaningless. From our previous discussion of the relative insensitivity of the TAC to small changes in the order quantity, the impact of rounding is minimal. After rounding to get Q_i^*, you calculate the value of the TAC as

$$TAC_i^* = c_{hi}\left(\frac{Q_i^*}{2}\right) + K\left(\frac{D}{Q_i^*}\right) + C_iD$$

For example, if the quantity 101.53 is rounded to 102,

$$TAC(102) = 5.82 \left(\frac{102}{2}\right) + 50\left(\frac{600}{102}\right) + 48.50 \times 600 = \$29,690.94$$

The value differs by only $0.01 from the TAC for an order quantity of 101.53 units.

You can *simplify* determining the order quantity for quantity discounts based on the observation that the TAC always lies above the TAC for a cheaper price. If the Q_i^* calculated in Step 1 is $\geq$ the smallest quantity eligible for the ith price, you don't consider any higher price. In Step 1, first calculate Q_n^*. If it's $\geq$ the smallest quantity eligible for that price, you go to Step 2. If it's too low, you calculate Q_{n-1}^*. Again, if it's $\geq$ the smallest quantity eligible for that price, you go to Step 2. If it's too low, you calculate Q_{n-2}^*. You continue to decrease i (giving a higher purchase price) until Q_i^* is $\geq$ the smallest quantity for which that price applies. In Steps 2 and 3, you only consider the Q_i^* values for the prices examined in Step 1.

Let's illustrate the simplification for the bicycle quantity discount example. First, you calculate $Q_3^* = 101.53$. Because the smallest quantity eligible for that price is 401, you must calculate $Q_2^* = 101.53$. Because the smallest quantity eligible for the $48.50 price is 101, you don't consider the $50 price. In Step 3, you compare the TACs at 101.53 and 401.

Manufacturing Batch Sizes

For the bicycle example, Jack's Bicycle Shop must decide how many and when to order. We discussed how to determine the economic order quantity for the first decision. You consider the trade-offs among the fixed order cost, the inventory holding cost, and (in the case of quantity discounts) the purchasing cost. For deterministic demand, you order bicycles so that the order arrives when the inventory is down to nothing. The reorder point depends on the lead time.

The bicycle manufacturer sells to many retailers. The manufacturer must decide how many bicycles to make in a production run and when to make them. In this section, we discuss choosing the production quantity for a single product with *deterministic demand*.

Assume that the demand is known and is constant for the product a company manufactures. Let Q represent the number of units produced during a production run—that is, the **batch size.** If the batch size is large, the average inventory of finished products is also large. A small batch size decreases the average inventory but increases the number of production runs during a year. Often, there is a setup cost for each production run. A small batch size increases the number of setups per year and the annual setup cost. Thus, the manufacturer chooses the quantity by considering the cost trade-offs for different quantities.

Let D represent the annual demand rate, and let K represent the setup cost per production run. The number of production runs per year is $\dfrac{D}{Q}$.

Thus,

$$\text{Annual setup cost} = K\left(\frac{D}{Q}\right)$$

Say that $K = \$1,000$ and that the annual demand is 20,000 units. If the production run is 10,000 bicycles, $\frac{20,000}{10,000} = 2$ production runs are required each year at an annual setup cost of $2 \times \$1,000 = \$2,000$.

Let P represent the **annual production rate**, the number of units produced if the product is made continuously. Note that if $D > P$, you can't satisfy the demand from the production. If $D = P$, you must produce continuously to satisfy the demand. *For this section, we assume that $D < P$.* If the annual demand is D, the proportion of the year's production capacity required to produce D units is $\frac{D}{P}$. For example, if the annual production rate for the bicycle manufacturer is 25,000 units, only $\frac{20,000}{25,000} = 0.8$ of the annual capacity is required. During periods when the manufacturer is not producing bicycles, inventory on hand is depleted at the rate of 20,000 per year. During periods when the manufacturer is producing and selling bicycles at the same time, bicycles are added to the inventory on hand at the rate of $25,000 - 20,000 = 5,000$ per year.

In general, in periods when the manufacturer is not producing the product, inventory on hand is depleted at the annual demand rate, D. In periods when the manufacturer is producing and selling the product, inventory on hand is increasing at an annual rate of $(P-D)$. Figure 13.10

Assume $D < P$ (margin note)

FIGURE 13.10   Manufacturing Inventory—Constant, Deterministic Demand

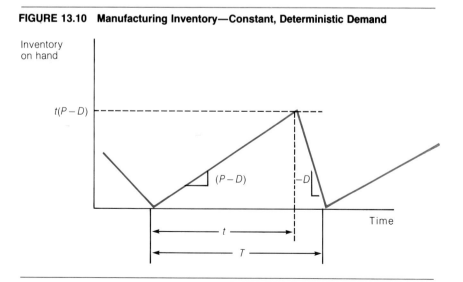

illustrates the inventory on hand for the manufacturer. This "sawtooth" graph differs from the retailer's graph because the entire production quantity is not immediately added to inventory when production begins.

When the inventory on hand becomes 0, the company begins manufacturing a batch of size Q. After the batch has been produced, the company stops production until the inventory decreases to 0 again. The fraction of a year needed to produce a batch size of Q is $\frac{Q}{P}$. For the bicycle manufacturer, if the batch size is 10,000, $\frac{10,000}{25,000} = 0.4$ year is required to produce each batch. Let t represent the **fraction of the year required for a production run.** You calculate t as

$$t = \frac{Q}{P}$$

Note that t is *not the cycle time*. The **cycle time** is the time between successive production runs. Figure 13.10 illustrates the difference. T is the cycle time, and it is calculated as

$$T = \frac{Q}{D}$$

Because the production rate, P, is greater than the demand rate, D, t is smaller than T.

During t, inventory is accumulating at the rate of $(P - D)$. Inventory starts at 0. Therefore, the maximum inventory is calculated as $t(P - D)$ or $\frac{Q}{P}(P - D)$. For example, if $t = 0.4$ for the bicycle manufacturer, the maximum inventory is $0.4 \times 5,000 = 2,000$ units. The *average inventory* is one half of the maximum inventory, so the average inventory is $\frac{Q}{2P}(P - D)$. If the inventory holding cost is c_h,

Average inventory

$$\text{Annual inventory holding cost} = \frac{c_h}{2}\frac{Q}{P}(P - D) = c_h\frac{Q}{2}\left(1 - \frac{D}{P}\right)$$

Adding the annual setup cost and the annual inventory holding cost, you obtain the total annual cost for the manufacturer:

$$TAC = K\frac{D}{Q} + c_h\frac{Q}{2}\left(1 - \frac{D}{P}\right)$$

The **economic batch size** is the value of Q with the smallest TAC, which is determined by differential calculus to be

Economic batch size

$$Q^* = \sqrt{\frac{2DK}{c_h\left(1 - \frac{D}{P}\right)}}$$

The minimum TAC is

$$TAC^* = \sqrt{2DKc_h\left(1 - \frac{D}{P}\right)}$$

Say that the cost of a bicycle to the manufacturer is $40 and that the annual inventory holding cost fraction is 0.2. Then $c_h = IC = 0.2 \times \$40 = \$8$ per bicycle. The economic batch size is

$$Q^* = \sqrt{\frac{2 \times 20,000 \times 1,000}{8\left(1 - \frac{20,000}{25,000}\right)}} = 5,000$$

The best size for the production run is 5,000 bicycles. This gives $\frac{D}{Q^*} = \frac{20,000}{5,000} = 4$ production runs each year. The cycle time for the economic batch size is $T^* = \frac{5,000}{20,000} = 0.25$ year; each batch satisfies 0.25 of the annual demand. The time required to produce the economic batch size is $t^* = \frac{Q^*}{P} = \frac{5,000}{25,000} = 0.2$ year. The maximum inventory on hand is $0.2(25,000 - 20,000) = 1,000$ bicycles. The minimum TAC is

$$TAC^* = \sqrt{2 \times 20,000 \times 1,000 \times 8\left(1 - \frac{20,000}{25,000}\right)} = \$8,000$$

Assume that the variable manufacturing cost doesn't depend on the production quantity

The TAC includes the annual setup cost and the annual inventory holding cost. It does not include the variable manufacturing cost, because we *assumed that the variable manufacturing cost doesn't depend on the production quantity*. If the variable manufacturing cost is *not constant* regardless of the production run size, *don't use the economic batch size model*. For the *retailer,* if the purchase cost depends on the order quantity, the quantity discount method is used. For the *manufacturer,* if the variable manufacturing cost depends on the batch size, a different approach is necessary. The approach is similar to the quantity discount method, but it is not discussed in this book.

In the Pfizer Pharmaceuticals application described at the beginning of the chapter, determining batch sizes was important. Because pharmaceuticals are being made, careful cleanup is required between batches of different products. For each product, Pfizer Pharmaceuticals adds the cleanup costs for each of the required operations to determine a total setup cost. These setup costs ranged from $15,000 to $85,000. With such large setup costs, the batch sizes are large. Pfizer Pharmaceuticals found that using larger batch sizes actually decreased the inventory. You can understand this apparent contradiction if you realize that the cleanups between products take time. Using larger batch sizes reduced the time required to do the cleanups, which decreased the manufacturing lead times. With shorter manufacturing lead times, Pfizer Pharmaceuticals was able to decrease the levels that triggered the production of a new batch. The inventory reduction effected by means of lower trigger points more than offset the inventory increase due to larger batch sizes.

PROBABILISTIC DEMAND

Assume backlogged demand

In this section, we discuss determining the reorder point for probabilistic, independent demand. We assume that the probability distribution of the demand is known, and we use the expected value criterion. We also assume that the shortages are *backlogged demand*. That is, our customers wait until the product is available.

Continuous and periodic review

The reorder point affects the chance of shortages before the next order arrives. For a continuous review system, you always know the inventory level, so determining the reorder point is concerned with the probability distribution of the demand during the *lead time*. For a periodic review system, you only know the inventory level at review times, so determining the reorder point is concerned with the probability distribution of the demand during the period until *the next review plus the lead time*.

Let's illustrate this distinction by assuming that the lead time is 0. For a continuous review system, the reorder point is 0. When the inventory reaches 0, you place an order and it arrives immediately. Figure 13.11a illustrates this case.

Figure 13.11b shows the impact of using the same reorder point for a periodic review system. Now, for a periodic review system, say that the number of units on hand at the time of the review is more than 0. Thus, you don't place an order. Your next opportunity to place an order is at the time of the next review. If the demand during the period until the next review is more than the inventory on hand, there are shortages. The demand between reviews influences the reorder point and the chance of shortages. If the lead time is not 0, the demand during the lead time and the time between reviews both influence the reorder point for a periodic review system. For the same probability of a shortage in a reorder cycle, the reorder point of a continuous review system is less than the reorder point of a periodic review system.

Forms of inventory ordering policies

There are many forms of inventory ordering policies. In this section, we consider only policies of the **(Q, R) form.** If the inventory on hand is less than or equal to R, you place an order of size Q; otherwise, you do nothing. Another policy form used in periodic review systems is the **"Order up to . . ."** policy under which an amount is ordered at each review so that the total amount on hand and on order is a specified quantity. Still another policy for periodic review systems is the **(S, s)** policy: If the amount on hand is s or less at the time of a review, place an order large enough to have a total of S units on hand and on order.

FIGURE 13.11   Using the Same Reorder Point for Continuous and Periodic Review

(a) Continuous Review - Reorder Point 0 and Lead Time 0

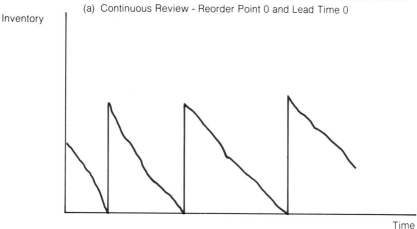

(b) Periodic Review - Reorder Point 0 and Lead Time 0

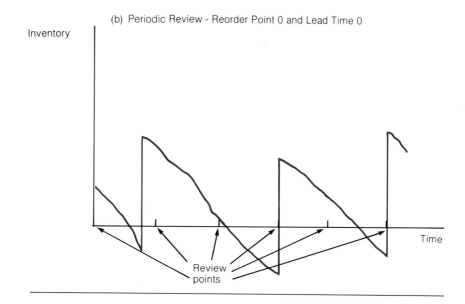

Review points

Assume (Q, R) and continuous review

Safety stock and cycle stock

Figure 13.12 illustrates a (Q, R) policy for a continuous review system. When the number of units on hand decreases to R, an order for Q units is placed. Demand continues during the lead time. If the demand during the lead time is greater than R, shortages occur.

Let D_L represent the **lead-time demand.** Assume that the probability distribution of D_L is known and denoted by $P(D_L)$. The expected value and standard deviation of D_L are μ_{D_L} and σ_{D_L}, respectively. The expected

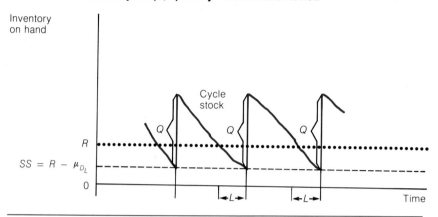

FIGURE 13.12 Inventory for (Q,R) Policy—Continuous Review

number of units on hand at the time the order arrives, called the **safety stock,** is calculated as $SS = R - \mu_{D_L}$. The average inventory level after the order arrives is $R - \mu_{D_L} + Q$. On the average, the inventory on hand has a maximum of $R - \mu_{D_L} + Q$ and a minimum of $R - \mu_{D_L}$. The average inventory level is

$$ SS + \frac{Q}{2} = R - \mu_{D_L} + \frac{Q}{2} $$

The inventory consists of the safety stock ($R - \mu_{D_L}$) and the **cycle stock.** During a cycle, the cycle stock varies from 0 to Q and averages $\frac{Q}{2}$.

Increasing R

Consider the result if the reorder point increases and the order quantity stays the same. The safety stock increases, but the cycle stays the same. The average inventory level and the expected annual inventory holding cost increase. The expected number of shortages per cycle decreases. Because the expected number of orders per year is unchanged, the expected shortages per year and the expected annual shortage cost both decrease.

Increasing Q

Now consider the result if the order quantity increases and the reorder point stays the same. The safety stock stays the same, but the cycle stock increases. The average inventory level and the expected annual inventory holding cost increase. The probability of a shortage during a reorder cycle stays the same, but the expected number of orders per year decreases. The expected number of shortages during a year is affected by the number of orders placed each year as well as the reorder point. The expected shortages per year and the expected annual shortage cost both decrease.

The reorder point and the order quantity both affect the annual shortage cost and inventory holding cost. Thus, we would prefer to determine

Use the EOQ

the reorder point and the order quantity at the same time by considering their interrelationship. In this section, however, *we use the EOQ as the order quantity*. Remember, we showed that the TAC for the EOQ model was not sensitive to small changes in the order quantity. For this reason, if we use the EOQ for a probabilistic demand situation, the expected cost increases little compared with choosing the order quantity and the reorder point at the same time.

Two approaches to determine the reorder point are the **service level** and **economic** approaches. In the service level approach, you set a minimum acceptable level of service and find a reorder point to achieve it. In the economic approach, you assign a cost to shortages and choose the reorder point so that the cost is minimized. If the shortage cost can be estimated, we prefer the economic approach. However, many companies use the service level approach. In this section, we show both approaches to determining the reorder point. First, we discuss the service level approach. Then, we discuss the economic approach.

Service Levels

Consider determining the reorder point using service levels for a *continuous review system*. You choose the reorder point by examining the demand during the lead time. The demand during the lead time, represented by D_L, is uncertain. The average demand during the lead time is μ_{D_L}. The *cumulative probability distribution* of the demand during the lead time, denoted by $F(D_L)$, is the probability that the demand during the lead time is D_L or less.

There are two forms of service levels. In the first form, the probability of a shortage during a reorder cycle is specified. In the second form, the proportion of demand satisfied from stock on hand is specified. First, we consider the easiest form to use.

Shortage during a reorder cycle

The beta service level. The first form for specifying a service level is based on β, the desired *probability that there isn't a shortage during a reorder cycle*. For example, if β is 0.95, the reorder point must have a probability of at least 0.95 that there is enough on hand to satisfy all of the demand. The probability of a shortage is 0.05. A shortage occurs if $D_L > R$. Choose R as the smallest value such that

$$P(D_L \leq R) = F(R) \geq \beta$$

If the probability distribution of lead-time demand is a continuous probability distribution, it is possible to choose R such that $P(D_L \leq R) = \beta$.

For example, consider Jack's Bicycle Shop. Table 13.8 summarizes the lead-time demand during the last 12 order cycles. The average lead-time demand is $\mu_{D_L} = \dfrac{180}{12} = 15$ bicycles. The standard deviation of the lead-time demand is $\sigma_{D_L} = 3$. Say that β = 0.95. Let's use the lead-time

TABLE 13.8 Example of Historical Lead-Time Demands

Reorder Cycle	Lead-Time Demand
1	15
2	19
3	10
4	12
5	12
6	18
7	19
8	18
9	15
10	13
11	14
12	15
	180

demand information to illustrate determining the reorder point for continuous and discrete probability distributions.

Normal distribution

First, let's assume that the probability distribution of the demand during the lead time is the *normal distribution*. Remember, you calculate the standardized normal variate, Z, as

$$Z = \frac{R - \mu_{D_L}}{\sigma_{D_L}}$$

From the cumulative normal probability table, $Z = 1.645$ such that $F(Z) = \beta = 0.95$. The reorder point, R, is calculated as

$$R = D_L + Z\sigma_{D_L}$$

Round up

Therefore, $R = 15 + 1.645 \times 3 = 19.935$ bicyles. The probability that demand is more than 19.935 is $1 - \beta = 1 - 0.95 = 0.05$. The probability of a shortage during a reorder cycle is 0.05. A noninteger reorder point for bicycles is unrealistic. If you round down to 19, the probability of a shortage is more than 0.05. Therefore, you round up to 20. The policy is: "When the inventory decreases to 20, you place an order." The probability that the demand during the lead time is ≤ 20 is a little more than 0.95. You determine the β service level using the cumulative normal table for $Z = \dfrac{20 - 15}{3} = 1.667$.

Discrete distribution

Now, say that the lead-time demand probability distribution is discrete. *Assume* that Table 13.8's data is representative of the lead-time demand and *use the historical cumulative frequency distribution* as the estimated cumulative probability distribution. Table 13.9 presents the relative frequencies of the 12 lead-time demands and the cumulative

TABLE 13.9   Relative Frequencies of Example Historical Lead-Time Demand

Lead-Time Demand	Number of Occurrences	Relative Frequency	Cumulative Frequency
10	1	0.0833	0.0833
11	0	0.0000	0.0833
12	2	0.1667	0.2500
13	1	0.0833	0.3333
14	1	0.0833	0.4167
15	3	0.2500	0.6667
16	0	0.0000	0.6667
17	0	0.0000	0.6667
18	2	0.1667	0.8333
19	2	0.1667	1.0000
	12		

frequency distribution. For example, the lead-time demand was 10 units once in the last 12 orders, so the probability that the lead-time demand is 10 units is $\frac{1}{12} = 0.0833$. Because 10 units is the smallest historical lead-time demand, the probability that the lead-time demand is ≤ 10 units is 0.0833. You choose R as the smallest value such that

$$P(D_L \leq R) = F(R) \geq 0.95$$

If $R = 19$, the probability is 1.0 that the lead-time demand is less than or equal to 19. If $R = 18$, the probability is 0.8333 that the lead-time demand is less than or equal to 18. $R = 19$ is the smallest value that has a cumulative probability of at least 0.95. You choose R as 19 units.

Proportion satisfied from stock on hand

The P service level. The second form of service level is based on P, the desired *proportion of the demand to be satisfied from stock on hand.* Let P represent this proportion. If D is the expected annual demand, the average number of units of demand to be satisfied from stock on hand is $P \times D$. A shortage occurs only if the lead-time demand is greater than the reorder point, R. If the reorder point is R and the lead-time demand is greater than R, the number of units of the shortage is $D_L - R$. Let $E(S)$ represent the expected number of units short *during a lead time.* Then, you calculate

$$E(S) = \sum_{D_L > R} (D_L - R)P(D_L)$$

If you backlog unsatisfied demand, the expected number of reorder cycles during a year is $\frac{D}{Q}$.[2] Therefore the expected annual number of shortages

---

[2] If you lose the sales, the expected number of reorder cycles during a year is $\frac{D}{E(S) + Q}$.

is $\left(\dfrac{D}{Q}\right) E(S)$. The proportion of shortages of the annual demand is the expected annual number of shortages divided by the annual demand:

$$\frac{\left(\dfrac{D}{Q}\right) E(S)}{D} = \frac{E(S)}{Q}$$

Choose R as the smallest value such that $1 - P \geq \dfrac{E(S)}{Q}$. Simplifying yields

$$E(S) \leq Q(1 - P)$$

Find *R* by trial and error

You calculate the value of R by trial and error. Arbitrarily, pick an initial value of R. Calculate $E(S)$ using the expression $\Sigma_{D_L > R}(D_L - R)P(D_L)$. If the calculated value of $E(S)$ is equal to $Q(1 - P)$, that value of R is the reorder point. If the calculated value is greater than $Q(1 - P)$, try a larger value of R. If the calculated value is less than $Q(1 - P)$, try a smaller value of R. Continue to try values of R until either the calculated value of the LHS equals $Q(1 - P)$ or you identify the smallest value of R such that $E(S) \leq Q(1 - P)$.

The normal distribution simplification

Finding R is simplified if the lead-time demand has a *normal probability distribution*. Table 13.10 presents values of the **unit normal loss function**.

The standardized normal probability distribution has mean 0 and standard deviation 1. Let $N(Z)$ represent the expected value of the shortages for a reorder point that is Z standard deviations above the mean *for the standardized normal probability distribution*. If the standard deviation of the lead-time demand is σ_{D_L}, then the expected number of shortages in a reorder cycle is $\sigma_{D_L} \times N(Z)$. Therefore, you choose R such that $\sigma_{D_L} \times N(Z) = Q(1 - P)$. Rearranging, choose R such that

$$N(Z) = \frac{Q(1-P)}{\sigma_{D_L}}$$

Because the normal distribution is a continuous distribution, a value of Z exists such that $N(Z)$ is exactly equal to $\dfrac{Q(1 - P)}{\sigma_{D_L}}$. After the value of Z has been determined, the reorder point is calculated as

$$R = \mu_{D_L} + Z\sigma_{D_L}$$

Let's apply the P form of service level to the bicycle retailer. Recall that the expected lead-time demand (μ_{D_L}) is 15 and that the standard deviation of the lead-time demand (σ_{D_L}) is 3. Say that $P = 0.999$. Recall that the EOQ is 100 bicycles. First, calculate $\dfrac{Q(1 - P)}{\sigma_{D_L}} = \dfrac{100 \times (1 - 0.99)}{3}$ = 0.333. From Table 13.10, the value of Z such that $N(Z) = 0.0333$ is between $Z = 1.44$ and $Z = 1.45$. For $Z = 1.44$, $N(Z) = 0.03356$; for $Z =$

TABLE 13.10   Unit Normal Loss Table

z	0.00	0.01	0.02	0.03	0.04	0.05	0.06	0.07	0.08	0.09
0.0	0.3989	0.3940	0.3890	0.3841	0.3793	0.3744	0.3697	0.3649	0.3602	0.3556
0.1	0.3509	0.3464	0.3418	0.3373	0.3328	0.3284	0.3240	0.3197	0.3154	0.3111
0.2	0.3069	0.3027	0.2986	0.2944	0.2904	0.2863	0.2824	0.2784	0.2745	0.2706
0.3	0.2668	0.2630	0.2592	0.2555	0.2518	0.2481	0.2445	0.2409	0.2374	0.2339
0.4	0.2304	0.2270	0.2236	0.2203	0.2169	0.2137	0.2104	0.2072	0.2040	0.2009
0.5	0.1978	0.1947	0.1917	0.1887	0.1857	0.1828	0.1799	0.1771	0.1742	0.1714
0.6	0.1687	0.1659	0.1633	0.1606	0.1580	0.1554	0.1528	0.1503	0.1478	0.1453
0.7	0.1429	0.1405	0.1381	0.1358	0.1334	0.1312	0.1289	0.1267	0.1245	0.1223
0.8	0.1202	0.1181	0.1160	0.1140	0.1120	0.1100	0.1080	0.1061	0.1042	0.1023
0.9	0.1004	0.09860	0.09680	0.09503	0.09328	0.09156	0.08986	0.08819	0.08654	0.08491
1.0	0.08332	0.08174	0.08019	0.07866	0.07716	0.07568	0.07422	0.07279	0.07138	0.06999
1.1	0.06862	0.06727	0.06595	0.06465	0.06336	0.06210	0.06086	0.05964	0.05844	0.05726
1.2	0.05610	0.05496	0.05384	0.05274	0.05165	0.05059	0.04954	0.04851	0.04750	0.04650
1.3	0.04553	0.04457	0.04363	0.04270	0.04179	0.04090	0.04002	0.03916	0.03831	0.03748
1.4	0.03667	0.03587	0.03508	0.03431	0.03356	0.03281	0.03208	0.03137	0.03067	0.02998
1.5	0.02931	0.02865	0.02800	0.02736	0.02674	0.02612	0.02552	0.02494	0.02436	0.02380
1.6	0.02324	0.02270	0.02217	0.02165	0.02114	0.02064	0.02015	0.01967	0.01920	0.01874
1.7	0.01829	0.01785	0.01742	0.01699	0.01658	0.01617	0.01578	0.01539	0.01501	0.01464
1.8	0.01428	0.01392	0.01357	0.01323	0.01290	0.01257	0.01226	0.01195	0.01164	0.01134
1.9	0.01105	0.01077	0.01049	0.01022	0.009957	0.009698	0.009445	0.009198	0.008957	0.008721
2.0	0.008491	0.008266	0.008046	0.007832	0.007623	0.007418	0.007219	0.007024	0.006835	0.006649
2.1	0.006468	0.006292	0.006120	0.005952	0.005788	0.005628	0.005472	0.005320	0.005172	0.005028
2.2	0.004887	0.004750	0.004616	0.004486	0.004358	0.004235	0.004114	0.003996	0.003882	0.003770
2.3	0.003662	0.003556	0.003453	0.003352	0.003255	0.003159	0.003067	0.002977	0.002889	0.002804
2.4	0.002720	0.002640	0.002561	0.002484	0.002410	0.002337	0.002267	0.002199	0.002132	0.002067
2.5	0.002004	0.001943	0.001883	0.001826	0.001769	0.001715	0.001662	0.001610	0.001560	0.001511
2.6	0.001464	0.001418	0.001373	0.001330	0.001288	0.001247	0.001207	0.001169	0.001132	0.001095
2.7	0.001060	0.001026	0.000993	0.000961	0.000930	0.000899	0.000870	0.000841	0.000814	0.000787
2.8	0.000761	0.000736	0.000712	0.000688	0.000665	0.000643	0.000621	0.000600	0.000580	0.000561
2.9	0.000542	0.000523	0.000506	0.000488	0.000472	0.000456	0.000440	0.000425	0.000410	0.000396
3.0	0.000382	0.000369	0.000356	0.000344	0.000332	0.000320	0.000309	0.000298	0.000287	0.000277
3.1	0.000267	0.000258	0.000249	0.000240	0.000231	0.000223	0.000215	0.000207	0.000200	0.000192
3.2	0.000185	0.000179	0.000172	0.000166	0.000160	0.000154	0.000148	0.000143	0.000137	0.000132
3.3	0.000127	0.000123	0.000118	0.000114	0.000109	0.000105	0.000101	0.000097	0.000094	0.000090
3.4	0.000087	0.000083	0.000080	0.000077	0.000074	0.000071	0.000069	0.000066	0.000063	0.000061
3.5	0.000058	0.000056	0.000054	0.000052	0.000050	0.000048	0.000046	0.000044	0.000042	0.000041

SOURCE: R. Peterson and E. A. Silver, *Decision Systems for Inventory Management and Production Planning*, New York: John Wiley & Sons (1985), pp. 699–708.

1.45, $N(Z) = 0.03281$. Extrapolating, the correct value of Z is calculated as

$$Z = 1.44 + \frac{(0.03356 - 0.03330)}{(0.03356 - 0.03281)} \times 0.01 = 1.443$$

If $Z = 1.443$, the value of R is

$$R = \mu_{D_L} + Z\sigma_{D_L} = 15 + 1.443 \times 3. = 19.329$$

You only can sell an integer number of bicycles during a lead time, so a fractional reorder point doesn't make sense. In which direction should you round R so that the desired proportion, P, is satisfied? If you round up to 20, the expected proportion of demand satisfied from inventory on hand is greater than 0.999. If you round down to 19, the expected proportion is less than 0.999. Always round up! Otherwise, the desired proportion of demand satisfied from inventory on hand is not achieved.

An advantage of the P service level

Note that the second form of service level, unlike the first form, considers the interrelationship between the order quantity and the reorder point. The reorder point for the first form is not affected by a change in the order quantity; the reorder point for the second form is affected. If Q changes, the value of $\dfrac{Q(1 - P)}{\sigma_{D_L}}$ changes, and as a result the value of Z such that $N(Z) = \dfrac{Q(1 - P)}{\sigma_{D_L}}$ also changes.

We prefer the second service level form because it considers the interrelationship between the order quantity and the reorder point. Even though you can't (or won't) estimate the economic cost of a shortage, you know that the order quantity affects the expected annual shortage cost. If the order quantity changes, the average number of orders each year also changes, which in turn affects the expected annual shortage cost. We prefer the second form because the first form ignores this fact in determining the reorder point and a change in the order quantity should affect the reorder point.

Choosing β and P

Either form of service level requires choosing a parameter value—β or P. Such values are chosen as a matter of company policy. Hopefully, the cost of the policy is considered in choosing them. Your customers want a service level with $β = 1.0$ and $P = 1.0$. They don't want any shortages. But you may have to keep very large inventories to make your service perfect. You choose the service level by comparing the extra cost for a higher service level with the benefit obtained from that cost. In the next section, we discuss the use of shortage costs to determine the reorder point.

Choosing the Reorder Point—A Marginal Economics Approach

In this section, we assume continuous review and use the EOQ as the order quantity. The economic approach determines the reorder point based on the marginal cost of changing it. If you increase the reorder point, the expected annual shortage cost decreases and the expected annual inventory holding cost increases. In the marginal approach, you increase the reorder point as long as the saving in the shortage cost exceeds the additional inventory holding cost. When you find the reorder point whose increase would cause the expected total cost to increase, you stop and use that reorder point.

Say that the initial reorder point is R and that you consider increasing it to $(R + 1)$. If the reorder point is increased by one unit, the average inventory level increases by one unit and the annual inventory holding cost increases by c_h.

If the reorder point is R, there is a shortage if lead-time demand is greater than R. The expected number of shortages is $\Sigma_{D_L>R}(D_L - R)P(D_L)$. If the reorder point is increased by one unit, to $(R + 1)$, the expected number of shortages during a reorder cycle decreases. If D_L is greater than the new reorder point $(R + 1)$, the number of shortages is $D_L - (R + 1)$. If the reorder point is $(R + 1)$, the expected number of shortages is $\Sigma_{D_L>(R+1)} (D_L - (R + 1))P(D_L)$. After algebraic manipulation, the decrease in the expected number of shortages is $\Sigma_{D_L>R}P(D_L)$.

In general, if the reorder point increases from R to $(R + 1)$, the expected number of shortages during a reorder cycle decreases by $\Sigma_{D_L>R}P(D_L) = 1 - F(R)$. If unsatisfied demand is backlogged, the

expected number of reorder cycles per year is $\dfrac{D}{Q}$. Thus, if the reorder point increases from R to $(R + 1)$, the expected annual number of shortages decreases by $\left[\dfrac{D}{Q}\right] [1 - F(R)]$ and the expected annual shortage cost decreases by $c_s \left[\dfrac{D}{Q}\right] [1 - F(R)]$.

If the reorder point increases from R to $(R + 1)$, the expected annual holding cost increases by c_h and the expected annual shortage cost decreases by $c_s \left[\dfrac{D}{Q}\right] [1 - F(R)]$. If the savings in the expected shortage cost are greater than the additional inventory holding cost, you increase the reorder point. You increase the reorder point as long as the savings in the expected shortage cost are greater than or equal to the additional inventory holding cost. Choose the reorder point as the largest R such that

$$c_h \leq c_s \left[\dfrac{D}{Q}\right][1 - F(R)]$$

Solving for $F(R)$,

$$F(R) \leq 1 - \dfrac{Qc_h}{Dc_s}$$

That is, choose R as the largest value so that $P(D_L \leq R) \leq 1 - \dfrac{Qc_h}{Dc_a}$. If the lead-time demand probability distribution is a *continuous* distribution, an R exists such that $F(R) = 1 - \dfrac{Qc_h}{Dc_a}$.

Let's illustrate this approach for Jack's Bicycle Shop whose normal probability distribution for lead-time demand has a mean of 15 and a standard deviation of 3. Recall that $c_h = \$6$, and assume that $c_s = \$15$.

Then, you choose $F(R)$ such that

$$F(R) = 1 - \frac{Qc_h}{Dc_s} = 1 - \frac{100 \times 6}{600 \times 15} = 0.9333$$

From the standardized normal distribution table, $Z = 1.501$. You can verify this Z value by extrapolation. The reorder point is calculated as

$$R = \mu_{D_L} + Z\sigma_{D_L} = 15 + 1.501 \times 3 = 19.503$$

Rounding up, you choose $R = 20$. If the inventory on hand reaches 20 bicycles, Jack's Bicycle Shop places an order for 100 bicycles.

In our opening application, Pfizer Pharmaceuticals determined the reorder point for finished products using a product's gross margin as the shortage cost. It found that for most products a normal distribution could be used for lead-time demand. In determining the reorder point, it used a procedure different from the one described above. In this procedure, the EOQ is not used as the order quantity. Instead, the order quantity and the reorder point are determined at the same time and the interaction between the two is considered.[3] This procedure gives reorder points and order quantities very close to the values we get using the EOQ and the procedure described above.

Demand Forecasting and Reorder Points

In Chapter 12, we discussed demand forecasting and showed how to measure the bias and the variability of forecast errors. Say that the forecasts are unbiased, and let σ_D represent the current estimate of the standard deviation of the forecast error for a one-period-ahead forecast.

Assume that forecast errors have a normal distribution

Let's use Jack's Bicycle shop as an example. Say that demand is forecast weekly for 12-inch bicycles, and assume that the forecast errors have a *normal distribution*.

Let's show how forecasts and forecast error measures are used to calculate reorder points. We illustrate this for the β service level with $\beta = 0.95$. First, we consider a situation in which the lead time is the same as the forecast period. Then, we consider a situation in which the two aren't the same.

One-week lead time

First, say that the lead time is constant—one week. If the forecast for next week's demand is 12 bicycles, then $\mu_{D_L} = 12$. The expected demand for bicycles during the next week is 12. Because the forecast is unbiased, the expected forecast error is 0. Say that the standard deviation of the one-period-ahead forecast errors is $\sigma_D = 3$. Let σ_{D_L} represent the **standard deviation of the forecast errors during the lead time.** Because the lead

---

[3] See G. Hadley and T. M. Whitin, *Analysis of Inventory Systems* (Englewood Cliffs, N. J.: Prentice-Hall, 1963), pp. 162–75.

time is one week, $\sigma_{D_L} = 3$. For $\beta = 0.95$, the value of Z is 1.645 and the reorder point is calculated as

$$R = \mu_{D_L} + Z\sigma_{D_L}$$

The reorder point is $12 + (1.645 \times 3) = 12 + 4.935 = 16.935$. You round up and choose a reorder point of 17 units.

Some forecasting systems use mean absolute deviation *(MAD)* or smoothed mean absolute deviation *(SMAD)* to measure the variability of the forecast errors. The relationship between the *MAD* or the *SMAD* and the standard deviation, σ, is $\sigma = 1.25 \times MAD$ or $\sigma = 1.25 \times SMAD$. If MAD_{D_L} is the mean absolute deviation during the lead time, then the reorder point is calculated as

$$R = \mu_{D_L} + Z \times 1.25 \times MAD_{D_L}$$

Now, let's consider a situation in which the lead time is constant but is not equal to the one-week forecast period. Say that the lead time is L forecast periods. For example, say that the lead time is three weeks for

Three-week lead time 12-inch bicycles, so that $L = 3$. If historical data on the demand during lead times such as that shown in Table 13.9, has been collected, you calculate the standard deviation of lead-time demand. However, such data is usually not collected. But forecasting systems do calculate measures of forecast errors. If the weekly forecast errors are *independent and

Assume iid identically distributed* (iid), the standard deviation of the total forecast error during L periods is

$$\sigma_{D_L} = \sigma_D\sqrt{L}$$

Similarly, if the *MAD* is the mean absolute deviation of the forecast error for a one-period-ahead forecast, then the standard deviation of the total forecast error during L periods is

$$\sigma_{D_L} = 1.25MAD\sqrt{L}$$

Let F_{t+i} represent the forecast i periods ahead given the actual demand in Period t. The expected demand during the lead time, L, is calculated as

$$\mu_{D_L} = \sum_{i=1}^{L}F_{t+i}$$

and the reorder point is calculated as $R = \mu_{D_L} + Z\sigma_{D_L}$.

Consider the forecasts of weekly demand for Jack's Bicycle Shop in Table 13.11. You have the demands for the first 13 weeks, and you use the *SMAD* to calculate the variability of the one-period-ahead forecast errors. Based on the information for the first 12 weeks, the forecast for Week 13 was 11. When you discovered that the actual demand was 12, you calculated the forecast error as $13 - 12 = 1$ and used that to update the *SMAD*. Say that the updated *SMAD* is 1.5. (See Chapter 12.) After the actual

TABLE 13.11 Demand Forecasts for 12-inch Bicycles

Week	Actual Demand	Forecast Error	SMAD	Forecast
13	12	1	1.5	
14				13
15				14
16				15
17				

demand information for Week 13 has been discovered, the sales forecasts for Weeks 14, 15, and 16 are updated, and they appear in Table 13.11. Because the lead time is three weeks, the lead-time demand is the demand for Weeks 14, 15, and 16. Therefore,

$$\mu_{D_L} = F_{13+1} + F_{13+2} + F_{13+3} = 13 + 14 + 15 = 42$$

Recall that F_{13+1} is the forecast for Week 14, given the actual demand for Week 13. For $\beta = 0.95$, you get $Z = 1.645$ from the cumulative normal distribution table. Therefore, the reorder point is updated to

$$R = \mu_{D_L} + Z \times 1.25SMAD \sqrt{3} = 42 + (1.645)(1.25)(1.5)(1.732) = 45.77$$

You round up to 46 for the reorder point to ensure the service level. Rounding down gives a service level less than 0.95.

MATERIAL REQUIREMENTS PLANNING AND PRODUCT EXPLOSIONS

Many stages are required to convert raw materials and components into a finished manufactured product. Say that you manufacture bicycles. You might buy cut tubing from a steel company and then bend it into a handlebar, which is one of the many components that you need to complete the assembly of a bicycle. You need to decide when and how much cut tubing to buy. You need to decide when and how many handlebars to bend. And you need to decide when and how many bicycles to assemble.

A **material requirements planning (MRP) system** converts demand for finished products into demand for the components that make up the finished products. In this section, we describe the basics of MRP. In the early 1980s, MRP systems expanded into more general-purpose systems for planning the resources of manufacturing companies. The expanded systems included the impacts of the manufacturing plan on finance and marketing. These systems are called **manufacturing resource planning or MRP II** systems.

FIGURE 13.13 Master Production Schedule Example

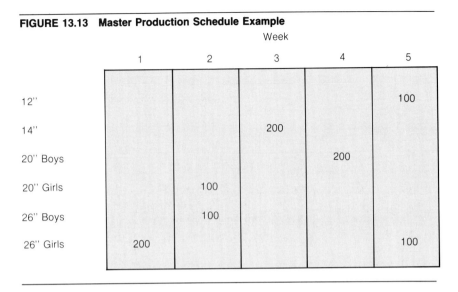

	Week 1	Week 2	Week 3	Week 4	Week 5
12″					100
14″			200		
20″ Boys				200	
20″ Girls		100			
26″ Boys		100			
26″ Girls	200				100

The **master production schedule (MPS)** specifies how many of each finished product to produce and when. Consider the manufacturer of the 12-inch bicycle. This manufacturer produces several models in addition to the 12-inch bicycle. Each of these models is a finished product. Figure 13.13 illustrates an MPS for the manufacturer. The **time bucket** is the length of a scheduling interval—one week for Figure 13.13. During Week 1, 200 26-inch girls' bicycles are to be completed. During Week 5, 100 12-inch bicycles and 100 26-inch girls' bicycles are to be completed. The MPS is the plan for completion of the bicycles. It does not calculate when subassemblies are to be completed or when orders for raw materials and other components should be released to suppliers. This is done by the MRP system. Figure 13.13 shows a time horizon of five weeks.

The **bill of materials (BOM)** is a structured parts list that shows how the finished product is made. Figure 13.14 is a graphical representation of the BOM for a 12-inch bicycle. The final assembly of the bicycle requires one handlebar, two wheel assemblies, and one body. The numbers above each box in Figure 13.14 tell how many of each component are required to complete each subassembly. The body subassembly requires one frame and two fenders. The BOM illustrates the order in which components are required to complete a bicycle. Figure 13.14 has three levels in the BOM. The top level is the completed bicycle. The second level consists of the handlebar, the wheel assemblies, and the body subassembly. If all of the components that go into the final assembly are not on hand, the product cannot be completed. MRP focuses on ensuring that all of the required components are available when they are needed. If no wheels are avail-

FIGURE 13.14 Partial Bill of Materials for 12-Inch Bicycle

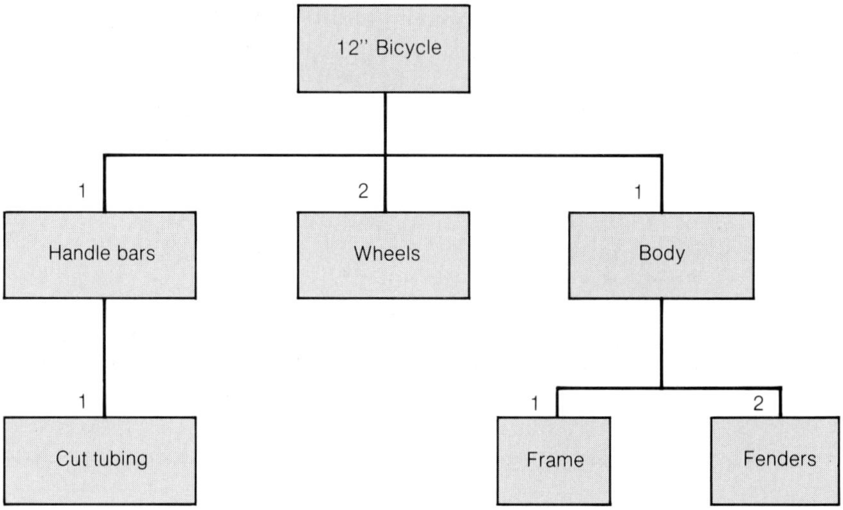

able, the bicycle cannot be completed regardless of how many handlebars and bodies are on hand. Timing is critical.

A product explosion specifies how many of each component are required to complete the finished product. Table 13.12 is the product explosion for the 12-inch bicycle. To make one bicycle, 1 handlebar, 2 wheels, 1 body, 1 cut tubing, 1 frame, and 2 fenders are required. If the planned production of 12-inch bicycles is 100, 200 wheels are required. A product explosion provides less information than a bill of materials. The BOM indicates the order in which components are required to produce the bicycle. Thus, unlike the product explosion, it illustrates that the cut tubing is required so that it can be formed to make a handlebar.

Dependent demand

The demand for handlebars, wheels, and bodies is *dependent* on the production plan specified by the MPS. The MPS shows the planned

TABLE 13.12 12-inch Bicycle Product Explosion

Bicycle Component	Number
Handlebar	1
Wheel	2
Body	1
Cut tubing	1
Frame	1
Fender	2

completion of 100 12-inch bicycles in Week 5. Therefore, you need 100 handlebars, 200 wheels, and 100 bodies for that week. When should you release the order to the shop to make the needed handlebars? You need the handlebars, wheels, and bodies at the same time, so it isn't logical to use the standard reorder point approach. In that approach, the order quantity and reorder points are determined independently for each component. But in this case, the required amounts and timings for the components are not independent of each other.

Furthermore, it is important to recognize the dependent nature of the demand for components as you move down the BOM. If you use the product explosion to calculate the required amount of each component, you neglect this dependence. From the product explosion, you would conclude that if you make 100 12-inch bicycles, you need 100 pieces of cut tubing. But say that you have 25 handlebars on hand. Then, you need an additional 75 handlebars, not 100. This affects the amount of cut tubing that you need to order from your supplier. The MRP system considers the amount of components available as you move down the BOM to calculate the additional components required.

The MPS schedules the completion of 100 12-inch bicycles in Week 5. At the beginning of Week 5, you need 100 handlebars, 200 wheels, and 100 bodies to allow the planned final assembly of 100 bicycles. Say that the amounts on hand of the bicycle components are those shown in Table 13.13.

Gross and net component requirements

Let's show how MRP calculates the component requirements for making 100 12-inch bicycles in Week 5. The **gross component requirement** is the quantity required for the production at the next higher level of the bill of materials. Because the planned production is 100 bicycles, the gross component requirements for handlebars, wheels, and bodies are 100, 200, and 100, respectively. The **net component requirement** is the additional number of the component required to meet the gross component requirement, which is

$$\begin{matrix} \text{Net} & & \text{Gross} & & \text{Number} \\ \text{component} & = & \text{component} & - & \text{of components} \\ \text{requirement} & & \text{requirement} & & \text{in inventory} \end{matrix}$$

TABLE 13.13 12-Inch Bicycle Components Inventory on Hand

Component	Number on Hand
Handlebar	20
Wheel	40
Body	10
Cut tubing	10
Frame	30
Fenders	100

TABLE 13.14   Calculating the Net Component Requirements for Cut Tubing

12-inch bicycles	100
Gross component requirements—handlebars	100
Handlebars on hand	−20
Net component requirements—handlebars	80
Gross component requirements—cut tubing	80
Cut tubing on hand	−10
Net component requirements—cut tubing	70

Table 13.14 shows the calculation of the net component requirement for cut tubing. Because the current inventory is 20 handlbars, the net component requirement of handlebars is the gross component requirement minus the inventory on hand, $100 - 20 = 80$. The gross component requirement of cut tubing is the net component requirement of handlebars, 80. Because the current inventory of cut tubing is 10, the net component requirement of cut tubing is $80 - 10 = 70$. Although 100 pieces of cut tubing are required for the planned production of 100 12-inch bicycles, the net component requirement is only 70 because 20 pieces are already available in the form of handlebars and 10 pieces are available from current inventory.

Before high-speed computers were available, calculating net requirements for thousands of components going into many different finished products was almost impossible. Moreover, in addition to calculating such requirements, the MRP system must respond to changes when raw materials from suppliers are received and when subassemblies are completed. The volume of calculations and the necessity of timely, accurate information require that MRP systems be computerized.

Determining the timing of orders is as important as calculating the amounts required. MRP uses the **time-phasing** approach, sometimes called **lead-time offset,** to determine the timing. Under this approach, the timing for each order of a component is determined by working backward from the finished products in the master production schedule. Recall that 100 handlebars must be available at the beginning of Week 5 to accomplish the final assembly plan of the MPS. If it takes one week to bend the cut tubing into handlebars, we say that the *lead time* for bending handlebars is one week. Say that it takes two weeks for your cut tubing supplier to ship your order. Because you need 100 handlebars at the beginning of Week 5, you release the shop order to bend tubing at the beginning of Week 4. Because you must have the cut tubing at the beginning of Week 4, you order from your supplier at the beginning of Week 2. The timing is determined by offsetting the orders by the lead times. Figure 13.15 shows the time phasing for the cut tubing. At the beginning of Week 2, an order

**Time phasing and
lead-time offset**

FIGURE 13.15 Time Line Showing Lead-Time Offset for Cut Tubing

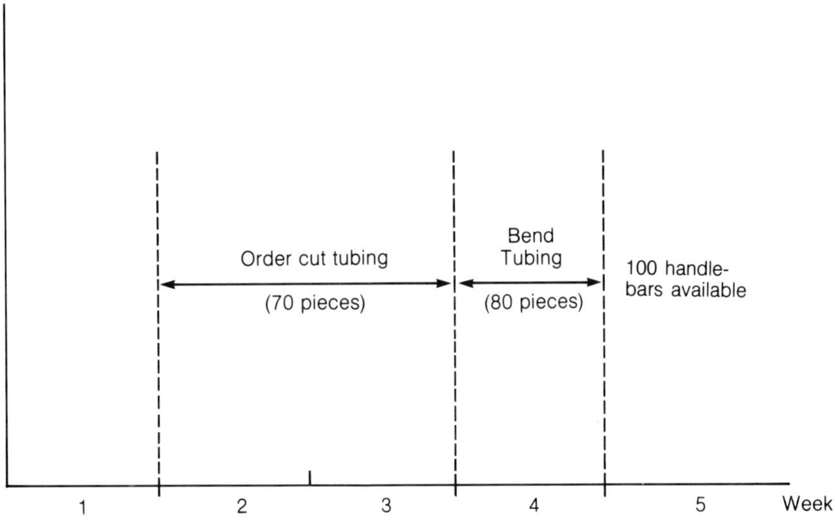

for 70 pieces is placed with the outside supplier. The 70 pieces arrive at the beginning of Week 4 and are added to the 10 pieces already on hand. The 80 pieces now on hand are formed into handlebars during Week 4. At the beginning of Week 5, the 80 newly formed handlebars and the 20 already in inventory provide the 100 handlebars necessary to meet the MPS schedule. We show a convenient method for calculating the amounts and timings after we discuss component orders that have been placed but not yet fulfilled.

To simplify the explanation in the previous discussion, we did not consider the planned receipt of components already ordered. Of course, if an order has already been placed, any future order must consider the amount of that order. The net component requirement is calculated as

$$\begin{array}{c} \text{Net} \\ \text{component} \\ \text{requirement} \end{array} = \begin{array}{c} \text{Gross} \\ \text{component} \\ \text{requirement} \end{array} - \begin{array}{c} \text{Scheduled} \\ \text{receipts} \end{array} - \begin{array}{c} \text{Number of} \\ \text{components} \\ \text{in inventory} \end{array}$$

If you've placed an order for 50 pieces of cut tubing and they are scheduled to arrive at the beginning of Week 3, the net component requirement is 20, not 70. The net component requirement is calculated as $80 - 50 - 10 = 20$.

The timing and amount of orders and scheduled receipts are easier to see with the **time-phased record format** illustrated in Table 13.15. Assume that no bending of handlebars from cut tubing has been scheduled and that an order for 50 pieces of cut tubing is scheduled to arrive in Week 3. You

TABLE 13.15   Time-Phased Record Format—12-inch Bicycle

12-inch Bicycle

Week	1	2	3	4	5
Planned production					100

Handlebar

Week	1	2	3	4	5
Gross requirements					100
Schedule receipts					
On hand	20	20	20	20	20
Planned order release				80	

Cut Tubing

Week	1	2	3	4	5
Gross requirements				80	
Schedule receipts			50		
On hand	10	10	10	60	
Planned order release		20			

start at the top of the BOM. The gross requirement for handlebars is 100 in Week 5. The number on hand is 20 until Week 4, at which time an order for an additional 80 handlebars is released to the plant. In Week 4, the gross requirement for cut tubing is 80. The number on hand stays at 10 until Week 3, when the previously ordered 50 units are scheduled to arrive. An additional 20 pieces of cut tubing are necessary to satisfy the gross requirement of 80 in Week 4. You offset the planned order release for cut tubing by the lead time of two weeks. The release of the order for 20 pieces of cut tubing is scheduled for the beginning of Week 2.

Often, more than one finished product uses the same component. The requirement for wheels of 26-inch bicycles is caused by the planned production in the MPS of both girls' and boys' 26-inch bicycles. The gross requirements for 26-inch wheels reflect the requirements of both kinds of bicycles in the time-phased record format for 26-inch wheels. This complicates the calculations, but it is not more difficult conceptually.

Lumpy demand and lot sizes

The pattern of the demand for components in an MRP system is sometimes called **lumpy demand.** The demand is not constant over time. For example, look at the demand for handlebars for the 12-inch bicycle in Table 13.15. The demand—that is, the gross component requirement—is 0 for all of the weeks except Week 5. In Week 5, the demand is 100. With manufacturing components, it is typical for the demand to be zero for many periods and large for a few periods.

In Table 13.15, the planned order release quantities were exactly enough to make the amounts on hand equal to the gross requirements for each component. Any order quantities that size or larger ensure enough material for the next higher level of the BOM. Because of setup costs, fixed order costs, or quantity discounts, a larger quantity than is needed for that purpose is sometimes more economical. Because the demand is lumpy, it's *incorrect* to use the EOQ as the quantity. The EOQ assumes that the demand is constant. There are many procedures for determining lot sizes in MRP systems. An excellent reference for lot-sizing procedures and MRP is Joseph Orlicky, *Material Requirements Planning* (New York: McGraw-Hill, 1975).

The example of the bicycle manufacturer was described at one point in time. However, MRP is implemented in a dynamic environment. A rolling time horizon is used. The time horizon illustrated in the time-phased record format of Table 13.15 was five weeks. The system must be updated weekly to show the scheduled receipts that arrive. Also, after Week 1 passes, the planned order release of 20 pieces of cut tubing results in the placement of an order and the 20 pieces become a scheduled receipt in Week 4. After Week 1 passes, the information is updated and replanning is done for a new five-week time horizon—Weeks 2 through 6. A **batch MRP system** collects transactions and periodically updates the system by processing the batch of transactions. A **net change MRP system** continually updates the system as transactions occur. The information and computing requirements for a net change system are greater than those for a batch system.

Pfizer Pharmaceuticals used an MRP system based on a forecasting system that provided the inputs to the MPS for each plant. The batch operations were exploded through the BOM back to the raw materials using time phasing. With this system, Pfizer Pharmaceuticals reduced its inventories by \$23.9 million and its back orders by 95 percent.

JAPANESE MANUFACTURING METHODS—JUST-IN-TIME

Japanese manufacturers use a different approach for inventory planning. Let's describe some characteristics of the Japanese approach. A key characteristic is reducing the amount of work-in-process inventory. Japanese manufacturers attack the causes for having inventory.

Let's consider the reasons for *raw materials inventory*. Major reasons include lead times and fixed order costs. By insisting on very short lead times from suppliers, you need less safety stock. By decreasing the fixed order costs for processing orders from suppliers, you decrease the order quantity. By decreasing the order quantity, you decrease the cycle stock.

Advantages of small
production quantities

In fact, if the fixed order cost is negligible, you can order exactly the amount you need for the planned production.

At the manufacturing plant, materials go to a work center, some processing is done, and then the materials go to another work center. Consider the reasons for *work-in-process inventory* at a work center. Major reasons include setup costs and lead times. By decreasing manufacturing setup costs, you make production runs of small quantities more economical. With smaller batch sizes, the work-in-process inventory decreases. Smaller batch sizes have a favorable impact on the entire manufacturing process. In an MRP system, a manufacturing lead time includes the manufacturing time plus the **queue time.** The queue time is the anticipated amount of time that the product must wait before manufacturing begins. Say that many different products are waiting for processing at a work center. Because only one product can be processed at a time, you must wait until one product has been processed before you start to process another product. How long a product must wait for processing depends on the order in which the waiting products are processed and on the batch sizes of the waiting products. If you decrease the batch sizes, you also decrease the queue time, which in turn decreases the lead time. Decreased lead times allow further reduction of the batch sizes.

Table 13.16 shows the advantage of small manufacturing batches. Both production plans produce the same amount of each product. The plan with smaller batch sizes completes a product batch more often and sends it to the next work center. Because there are more batches if the batch sizes are smaller, the next work center waits less to receive a product batch. The queue time has decreased. By decreasing the queue times at all of the work centers, you shorten the time that passes between starting and completing a product. A shorter overall manufacturing lead time allows smaller safety stocks for finished products.

The **just-in-time (JIT)** approach attempts to minimize inventories by

---

TABLE 13.16   Example Showing that Smaller Lot Sizes Reduce Work-in-Process Inventory

Large lot sizes:

1111111111 22222222   3333 4444 1111111111 22222222   3333 4444

                                                                      Time

Small lot sizes:

11111 2222   33 44 11111 2222   33 44 11111 2222   33 44

                                                                      Time

ordering and manufacturing very small batches. You schedule the batches so that they arrive when they are needed—that is, "just in time." Ideally, a batch of raw materials is ordered so as to arrive just when it's needed to start producing. When processing of the batch is completed at the first work center, it goes to the next work center, where further processing begins immediately. The batch progresses through the manufacturing plant from work center to work center without any delays. The total time from starting the batch to completing it doesn't include any queue time. You can't achieve the **JIT** ideal if the batch sizes are large. However, you approach that ideal as you decrease the batch sizes.

Kanban is one method of implementing the JIT approach. Toyota has used kanban to achieve significant reductions in work-in-process inventory.[4] *Kanban* is the Japanese word for "card." Toyota uses a manual kanban system to control automobile manufacturing. A batch moves through the manufacturing system by cart. Each cart contains one batch, and attached to each cart is a kanban with information about the batch. The Toyota system uses conveyance-kanbans and production-kanbans. When a new batch is to be started at a work center, the operator looks at the stack of production-kanbans and gets a cart containing material authorized by such a kanban. Then, the operator removes the conveyance-kanban from the cart and puts it in view of the material handler. This signals the material handler that it is OK to bring another full cart. When the material handler brings another cart, the production-kanban is removed and put in the stack of production-kanbans. The amount of work-in-process inventory is controlled by the number of kanbans and by the number of units in a full cart. When an operator starts processing a cart's contents, the entire cart is processed before another cart is brought.

Kanbans replace all of the paperwork that MRP generates. There are no computer-generated shop orders, move tickets, or dispatch sheets. Using kanbans, you don't need a computer system that is continually updated as raw materials are received and the processing of batches at work centers is completed. The manual kanban system replaces the computerized MRP system.

Characteristics of the Japanese approach

The Japanese attitude is that inventory covers up operating problems and that keeping inventory low enables you to discover such problems. The typical U.S. manufacturer likes to keep inventory "just in case—." By increasing the number of kanbans, you make it less likely that an operator will not have any production-kanbans. However, an operating problem may be causing some operator to fall behind. Decreasing the number of kanbans focuses your attention on such problems.

---

[4] Yasuhiro Monden, "Adaptable Kanban System Helps Toyota Maintain Just-in-Time Production," *Journal of Industrial Engineering*, May 1981, pp. 29–46.

Another characteristic of the Japanese approach is the involvement of workers in improving and controlling the system. An advantage of the kanban system is its simplicity. You can easily see how the plant is operating by observing where the kanbans are located. If an operator at one work center has no production-kanbans, this means that the operator at the preceding work center is falling behind. Because of the cooperative spirit and cross-training among Japanese workers, the operator without any production-kanbans helps the operator who is falling behind.

Japanese manufacturers use **quality circles** or teams of workers to improve the system. When the team of operators discovers a problem, the operators on the team work together to solve it. Quality problems cause trouble in systems with low work-in-process inventory. Say that a work center is producing materials that don't meet the quality specifications. This means that the next work center will eventually run out of production-kanbans. If the number of kanbans is increased, the next work center will run out of kanbans later. But keeping the number of kanbans small focuses more attention on quality. Quality circles work on operating and quality problems. A cooperative team attitude develops.

Kanban systems work well if the production is level. For example, Toyota keeps the same production schedule for each of the days in a month and reviews the production schedule monthly. Keeping the same schedule for an entire month gives the employee teams an opportunity to work out operating problems. Also, Toyota has a smaller number of different automobiles than U.S. automakers. Having fewer options, (e.g., AM or AM/FM radio), simplifies production planning. Toyota puts groups of features into option packages, which decreases the number of possibilities. If you can't keep production level or if you have a large variety of products, a kanban system works less well.

The Japanese approach to scheduling production does not conflict with the goals of MRP. The goal of both approaches is to have the material arrive at the work center in time for processing to begin. However, the Japanese approach places more emphasis on eliminating troublesome factors in the environment and less emphasis on attempting to manage the current environment. Using the Japanese approach, you can, for example, decrease the cycle stock by decreasing setup costs. If you can decrease the EOQ to 1 and decrease the lead times, inventory planning is much easier.

For level production of a small number of products, the Japanese approach holds great promise for U.S. manufacturers. But even if you can't use the kanban system, the Japanese approach of decreasing work-in-process inventories through smaller setup costs and shorter lead times is worthwhile. The participation of workers in problem solving and the development of a team attitude have great benefits. We expect to see increased adoption of the Japanese approach by U.S. manufacturers.

Kanban shortcomings

SUMMARY

In this chapter, we discussed inventory planning. The methods we described have wide applicability. A major distinction is independent demand versus dependent demand. If you buy a product and either sell it or use it, you have independent demand. We used Jack's Bicycle Shop and the secretary ordering office supplies to illustrate inventory planning in such a situation. If you are a manufacturer, the components that go into the final product have dependent demand. We used a bicycle manufacturer to illustrate the inventory planning considerations of a manufacturing company. Pfizer Pharmaceuticals is a manufacturing company that uses many of the concepts we described.

We discussed possible considerations in designing an inventory planning system. We showed that, for the same chance of a shortage, a continuous review inventory planning system has a lower reorder point than a periodic review system. We also showed that a real-time inventory planning system has more up-to-date information than a batch processing system. The disadvantage of continuous review and real-time systems is higher operating cost. However, the operating cost for continuous review/ real-time systems has been decreasing because of new technologies such as bar code readers. With technological changes, more systems will use continuous review/real-time systems.

There are other considerations in designing an inventory planning system besides its development and operating costs. These include lead times, fixed order costs, setup costs, quantity discounts, and forecasting errors. We showed how to use ABC analysis to focus more inventory planning attention on important products.

Note some limitations of this chapter's methods. First, we only described inventory planning for a single-level distribution system. Say that you distribute your products through regional warehouses to your customers. You keep finished goods inventory at the manufacturing plant and at the warehouses. You shouldn't treat the finished goods inventory at each location as if that inventory were independent of the inventory at other locations. We didn't discuss multilevel inventory planning systems. Second, the EOQ model considered a single product, but sometimes economies can be effected by considering more than one product at a time. For example, perhaps the quantity discount depends on the total purchases of several products. Third, the EOQ model assumes that demand is known and constant. We showed that the TAC isn't sensitive to small errors in parameter estimates or order quantities. But if demand is lumpy, as happens in MRP systems, you shouldn't use the EOQ as the quantity. Fourth, the economic batch size assumes that a single product is made at a single work center. If there are several products, you can't determine the batch sizes and production times independently. The schedules may conflict because two products are scheduled for the same time. Also, if product demand fluctuates or if there are several work centers, you can't use the economic batch size mode. Fifth, if the demand forecast period isn't the same as the lead time, the methods we used to get the lead-time demand probability distribution are limited by our assumptions. Remember, using $\sigma_{D_L} = \sigma_D\sqrt{L}$ assumes that the demands (or forecast errors) are independent, identically distributed random variables. Sixth, you need lead times to use MRP, and the amount of queue time is hard to estimate accurately. Seventh, you are limited to a small number of products with level demand when you use the kanban system. Eighth, with both MRP and kanban, you must select the product that you will make next at a work center. Both systems tell when you can start a batch of a product, but they don't tell you which product to start.

Also note some cautions. First, there are several possibilities that you should consider before you introduce an inventory planning system. For example, you should always look for ways to decrease fixed order costs and setup costs. If you can decrease the EOQ to 1, inventory planning is easier. You should also always look for ways to decrease lead times. By decreasing lead times, you can decrease the safety stock you need. Try to improve the quality of demand forecasts. Decreasing forecast errors allows you to decrease the safety stock while maintaining the service level (or to improve the service level while maintaining the safety stock). Second, make sure that you have all-units quantity discounts before you use the quantity discount method we described. If you have incremental quantity discounts, you must use a different method. Third, be wary of using the beta service level form. Remember that this service level form doesn't consider the impact of the order quantity on the reorder point, whereas the P service level form does. Fourth, don't be confused by the difference between lead-time demand variability and lead-time forecast error variability. When we discussed the two service level forms and the economic method for choosing reorder points, we used σ_{D_L} to represent the standard deviation of lead-time demand. When we discussed reorder points in the Demand Forecasting and Reorder Points section, we used σ_{D_L} to represent the standard deviation of the forecast errors for the lead-time demand.

QUESTIONS

1. What is periodic review? Continuous review?
2. What is the difference between a real-time inventory system and a batch processing inventory system?
3. What is independent demand? Give an example.

4. What is dependent demand? Give an example.

5. Describe the two forms of service levels.

6. What is a quantity discount?

7. One unit of a product costs $10. Say that a 2 percent discount is given for an order quantity of 50 units or more. If 75 units are ordered, what is the purchasing cost under
   a. All-units discounts?
   b. Incremental discounts?

8. Define lead time and lead-time demand.

9. What costs are considered in the EOQ formula? What costs are considered in determining the order quantity with quantity discounts?

10. What is a bill of materials?

11. Give an example of a situation in which a shortage results in a lost sale.

12. Give an example of a situation in which a shortage results in backlogged demand.

13. What are the assumptions for the EOQ model?

14. Why do many companies use an order quantity equal to the EOQ in situations that violate the assumptions of the EOQ model?

15. Discuss the relative merits of periodic review and continuous review.

16. What is ABC analysis?

17. What is the master production schedule?

18. What are the similarities and differences between a product explosion and a bill of materials?

19. What is lead-time offset?

20. The EOQ is 100 for a fixed order cost of $10. If the true fixed order cost is $11, use Table 13.5 to determine the correct EOQ.

21. The EOQ is 1,000 for an annual inventory holding cost of $2 per unit. If the true inventory holding cost is $2.40, use Table 13.5 to determine the correct EOQ.

22. What is "the number of levels" in a bill of materials?

23. The master production schedule includes 500 garden tractors in Week 14. Four wheels are required for the final assembly of one garden tractor. What is the gross component requirement of wheels in Week 14?

24. The gross component requirement for automatic transmissions for a garden tractor is 1,000. There aren't any on hand, but receipts of 500 have been scheduled. What is the net component requirement?

25. What is a kanban?

26. Say that the demand during a week has a normal distribution with a mean of 100 and a standard deviation of 10. If the lead time is four weeks, what are the mean and the standard deviation of the lead-time demand?

27. If the correct EOQ is 1,000 and you use an order quantity of 900, how much does the TAC increase?

28. If the correct EOQ is 1,000 and you use an order quantity of 1,100, how much does the TAC increase?

EXERCISES

1. A retailer sells an average of 5,000 blank VHS cassettes each year. The fixed order cost is $25. The cassettes cost $2.50 from the supplier. The retailer finances the inventory by borrowing money at 10 percent per year.
   a. What is the cost of holding one unit in inventory for one year?
   b. What is the economic order quantity?
   c. What is the total annual cost for the EOQ?
   d. What is the total annual cost if the order quantity is 100 more than the EOQ?
   e. What is the cycle time for the EOQ?

2. A retailer sells an average of 10,000 Cabbage Patch dolls each year. The fixed order cost is $250. The dolls cost $12.50 from the supplier. The retailer finances the inventory by borrowing money at 10 percent per year.
   a. What is the cost of holding one unit in inventory for one year?
   b. What is the economic order quantity?
   c. What is the total annual cost for the EOQ?
   d. What is the total annual cost if the order quantity is 100 more than the EOQ?
   e. What is the cycle time for the EOQ?

3. An appliance store sells videocassette recorders (VCRs) at the rate of 250 per month. Each VCR costs $400 from the supplier. The fixed order cost is $100. The annual inventory holding cost fraction is 0.15.
   a. What is the cost of holding one unit in inventory for one *month?*
   b. What is the EOQ?
   c. What is the minimum total monthly cost?
   d. What is the minimum total annual cost?
   e. What is the cycle time, in months?
   f. What is the cycle time, in years?
   g. How many orders are placed each year?

4. An appliance store sells a model of microwave ovens at the rate of 10 per week. Each microwave oven costs $250 from the supplier. The fixed order cost is $10. The annual inventory holding cost fraction is 0.104.
   a. What is the cost of holding one unit in inventory for one week?
   b. What is the EOQ?
   c. What is the minimum total weekly cost?
   d. What is the minimum total annual cost?
   e. What is the cycle time, in weeks?
   f. What is the cycle time, in years?
   g. How many orders are placed each year?

5. If the lead time is 0.5 month for Exercise 3, what is the reorder point?

6. If the lead time is two weeks for Exercise 4, what is the reorder point?

7. The retailer of blank VHS cassettes in Exercise 1 believes that cassette sales will increase significantly in the future. Calculate the EOQ for the following annual demands.
   a. 8,000 cassettes
   b. 10,000 cassettes
   c. 20,000 cassettes

8. The retailer of Cabbage Patch dolls in Exercise 2 believes that sales will decrease significantly in the future. Calculate the EOQ for the following annual demands.
   a. 2,000 dolls
   b. 5,000 dolls
   c. 8,000 dolls

9. A manufacturer of a line of microwave ovens must decide the manufacturing batch sizes. The setup cost for manufacturing a particular microwave oven is $1,500. The annual rate of sales is 10,000, and the rate of sales is constant during the year. The annual manufacturing capacity is 20,000. The cost of a completed microwave oven is $150. The inventory holding cost fraction is 0.10 per year.
   a. What is the most economical batch size (i.e., the EBQ)?
   b. What is the minimum annual total of inventory holding costs and setup costs?
   c. What is the number of production runs per year?
   d. What is the amount of time required for the production of each batch?
   e. What fraction of the annual manufacturing capacity is unused?
   f. What is the maximum inventory on hand for the EBQ?

10. A manufacturer of food processors has annual sales of 20,000 units. The manufacturer operates 250 days a year and produces 200 units per day. The setup cost is $600 for a production run. The food processors cost $50 to produce. The inventory holding cost fraction is 0.20 per year.
    a. What is the most economical batch size (i.e., the EBQ)?
    b. What is the minimum annual total of inventory holding costs and setup costs?
    c. What is the number of production runs per year?
    d. What is the cycle time?
    e. How many days are required to produce each batch?
    f. What is the maximum inventory on hand for the EBQ?

11. A retailer has been offered all-units discounts if large quantities are ordered. The discount is 2 percent if the quantity ordered is 50 or more, and it increases to 4 percent if the quantity ordered is 100 or more. The product costs $20 and sells at the rate of 500 per year. The fixed order cost is $25, and the annual inventory holding fraction is 0.2.
    a. What is the best order quantity?
    b. What is the minimum total annual cost, including the purchasing cost?
    c. If the quantity is not an integer, calculate the total annual cost if you round up and if you round down. What is the best integer order quantity?

12. A retailer receives all-units discounts for large orders. The discount is 4 percent if the quantity ordered is 500 or more, and an additional 1 percent discount is received if the quantity ordered is 1,000 or more. The product costs $50 and sells at the rate of 2,500 per year. The fixed order cost is $50, and the annual inventory holding fraction is 0.2.
    a. What is the best order quantity?
    b. What is the minimum total annual cost, including the purchasing cost?
    c. If the quantity is not an integer, calculate the total annual cost if you round up and if you round down. What is the best integer order quantity?

13. The lead-time demand for a continuous review inventory system has a

Poisson distribution with a parameter (mean) of 5 units. Its Poisson probability distribution is

$$P \text{ (Demand } = n) = \frac{5^n e^{-5}}{n!}$$

a. If the reorder point is 2, what is the probability of no shortage? What is the probability of a shortage?

b. If it is desired that the probability of a shortage in a reorder cycle be no larger than 0.05, what is the reorder point?

14. The lead-time demand for a continuous review inventory system has an exponential distribution with a parameter of 0.2. The cumulative distribution is

$$F(x) = 1 - e^{-0.2x}$$

a. If the reorder point is 5, what is the probability of no shortage? What is the probability of a shortage?

b. If it is desired that the probability of a shortage in a reorder cycle be no larger than 0.05, what is the reorder point?

15. The lead-time demand for a continuous review inventory system has a normal distribution with a mean of 50 units and a standard deviation of 10 units. The order quantity is 300 units, and the annual demand is 3,600 units.

a. If it is desired that the probability of a shortage in a reorder cycle be 0.05, what is the reorder point?

b. If it is desired that the probability of a shortage in a reorder cycle be 0.01, what is the reorder point?

c. If it is desired that the probability of a shortage in a reorder cycle be 0.001, what is the reorder point?

d. If it is desired that 99 percent of the annual orders be satisfied from inventory on hand, what is the reorder point?

e. If it is desired that 99.9 percent of the annual orders be satisfied from inventory on hand, what is the reorder point?

f. If it is desired that 99.99 percent of the annual orders be satisfied from inventory on hand, what is the reorder point?

16. The lead-time demand for a continuous review inventory system has a normal distribution with a mean of 100 units and a standard deviation of 25 units. The order quantity is 500 units, and the annual demand is 6,000 units.

a. If it is desired that the probability of a shortage in a reorder cycle be 0.05, what is the reorder point?

b. If it is desired that the probability of a shortage in a reorder cycle be 0.01, what is the reorder point?

c. If it is desired that the probability of a shortage in a reorder cycle be 0.001, what is the reorder point?

d. If it is desired that 99 percent of the annual orders be satisfied from inventory on hand, what is the reorder point?

e. If it is desired that 99.5 percent of the annual orders be satisfied from inventory on hand, what is the reorder point?

f. If it is desired that 99.9 percent of the annual orders be satisfied from inventory on hand, what is the reorder point?

17. A trophy supply store sells trophies during the entire year. There is consider-

able variation in the weekly sales. The sales during a week are represented by a normal probability distribution with a mean of 50 and a standard deviation of 10. The trophies cost $12.50 from the manufacturer. The fixed order cost is $50, the delivery charge. The inventory holding cost fraction is 0.1. The time between the placement of an order and its arrival is always one week.

a. What is the economic order quantity?

b. Use the marginal approach to determine the reorder point for a shortage cost of $10.

c. What is the probability of a shortage during a reorder cycle for the reorder point calculated in Part *b?*

d. What is the expected number of shortages during a reorder cycle for the reorder point calculated in Part *b?*

e. What is the expected number of shortages during a year for the reorder point calculated in Part *b?*

18. A dry cleaning store purchases chemicals to process clothes brought for cleaning. Because the amount of clothes brought varies from week to week, so too does the required amount of the chemicals. An average week requires 25 gallons of the chemicals. The standard deviation of the chemicals required is 5 gallons. The chemicals cost $40 per gallon, and the annual inventory holding fraction is 0.2. The delivery charge for the chemicals is $50 regardless of the order size. The lead time is always two weeks.

a. What is the economic order quantity?

b. If weekly chemical usage is assumed to be independent from week to week and has a normal distribution, what is the probability distribution of the lead-time demand?

c. Use the marginal approach to determine the reorder point for a shortage cost of $100 per gallon.

d. What is the probability of a shortage during a reorder cycle for the reorder point calculated in Part *c?*

e. What is the expected number of gallons short during a reorder cycle for the reorder point calculated in Part *c?*

f. What is the expected number of gallons short during a year for the reorder point calculated in Part *c?*

19. A part of the bill of materials for a lawn mower is shown below:

The master production schedule requires 200 lawn mowers in Week 10. The current inventory is 100 wheels, 10 engine assemblies, 50 handles, 0 carburetors, 50 engine blocks, and 100 spark plugs. No receipts are scheduled.

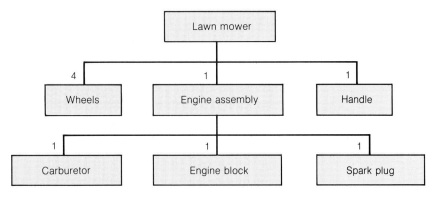

a. Calculate the net component requirements for wheels, engine assemblies, and handles.

b. Calculate the net component requirement for carburetors, engine blocks, and spark plugs.

20. A part of the bill of materials for a carburetor assembly is shown below: The master production schedule requires 100 carburetor assemblies in Week 8. The current inventory is 10 carburetors, 5 air cleaner assemblies, 90 covers, 1,000 bolts, and 50 filters. No receipts are scheduled.

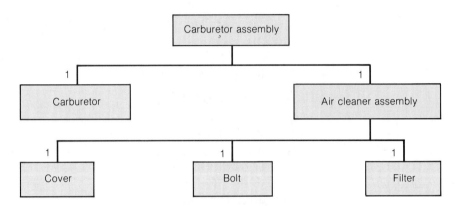

a. Calculate the net component requirement for carburetors and air cleaner assemblies.

b. Calculate the net component requirement for covers, bolts, and filters.

c. Discuss whether the net component requirement can be negative. What does this mean?

21. In Exercise 19, the lead time for assembly of the lawn mower is one week. The engine assembly requires one week. The lead times for the carburetor and the spark plug are two weeks and one week, respectively.

a. How many weeks before the lawn mowers are to be assembled must the engine assembly order be released?

b. How many weeks before the lawn mowers are to be assembled must the carburetor order be placed?

c. How many weeks before the lawn mowers are to be assembled must the spark plug order be placed?

d. Use the time-phased record format to show the timing of the release of the spark plug order.

22. In Exercise 20, the time required to complete the carburetor assembly is one week. The air cleaner assembly requires one week. The lead times for the cover and the filter are two weeks and one week, respectively.

a. How many weeks before the carburetor assembly is to be begun must the air filter assembly order be released?

b. How many weeks before the carburetor assembly is to be begun must the covers be ordered?

c. How many weeks before the carburetor assembly is to be begun must the filters be ordered?

d. Use the time-phased record format to show the timing of the release of the filter order.

MORE CHALLENGING EXERCISES

1. The EOQ is the order quantity for which the annual fixed order cost equals the annual inventory holding cost. Show this algebraically by substituting the EOQ formula into the formulas for the annual fixed order cost and the annual inventory holding cost.

2. The inventory holding cost is $1 per unit, and the annual demand is 1,000 units. How small must the fixed order cost be so that the EOQ is one unit?

3. Betty's Computer Repair Shop sells 256K memory chips. Annual sales are 10,000 units. The chips are shipped by airfreight, which usually costs $25. Other costs for processing the order total $20. The chips cost $2 each. Betty borrows money at an interest rate of 12 percent. What order quantity should she use? What would the quantity discount have to be so that Betty would order in quantities of 5,000?

4. The weekly demand for computer paper for the Business Supply Store is shown below:

Week	Demand
1	100
2	120
3	130
4	145
5	150
6	165

The lead time for the delivery of computer paper from the manufacturer is two weeks. Forecast the demand for Weeks 7 and 8. Estimate the one-period-ahead forecast error. Assuming that the forecast errors are normally distributed, determine the reorder point if the service level is to be $\beta = 0.99$.

5. The β service level model assumed that shortages were backlogged. Develop the formula if sales are lost.

6. The P service level model assumed that shortages were backlogged. Develop the formula if sales are lost.

7. The marginal economics model assumed that shortages were backlogged. Develop the formula if sales are lost.

8. Derive the cost ratio formula when the order quantity is rQ^*.

CASE

Drake Radio

Drake Radio got its start during World War I by manufacturing radio communications equipment for the military. By the start of World War II, Drake was one of the largest suppliers of military communications equipment. After World War II, Drake diversified into the following three market areas:

1. Military communications equipment
2. Amateur radio equipment
3. CB radios and equipment

Using its technology and experience gained from manufacturing military communications equipment, Drake became known as one of the best producers of amateur radio equipment. Drake especially excelled with its single-sideband radios and its two-meter radios for amateur use. Although these radios were expensive, they were of the finest quality and always in demand.

In developing CB radios, however, Drake decided to mass-produce cheap units that would have a wide appeal and a low price. To help protect its good name in military communications equipment and amateur (ham) radios, these inexpensive CB radios were marketed under the brand name of Hustler.

In 1975, George Populas, the president of Drake Electronics, decided to investigate the possibilities of entering into the market of home stereo systems. These stereo systems would be high quality, highly priced, and marketed with the Drake name.

The most remarkable stereo system that Drake manufactured was the DR-2000, which was a sophisticated stereo receiver. The demand for the DR-2000 was fairly constant from month to month. (See Exhibit 1.)

SOURCE: Barry Render and Ralph M. Stair, Jr., *Cases and Readings in Quantitative Analysis for Management.* Copyright © 1982 by Allyn and Bacon, Inc. Reprinted with permission.

EXHIBIT 1 Demand for DR-2000s in Units

January	February	March	April
801	807	795	797

The DR-2000 had all the features of a stereo receiver that carried a price tag of $765. Some of these features included the ability to connect four different speaker systems, loudness control, flatness control, blend control, and completely digital readout. Of course, the DR-2000 could be connected to one or more receivers, tape units, turntables, etc. Instead of having a base control to regulate the low frequencies and a treble control to regulate the high frequencies, the DR-2000 had five separate controls that regulated five frequency ranges. One control regulated frequencies from 0 to 500 Hz; another control regulated frequencies from 500 to 5,000 Hz; a third regulated frequencies between 5,000 and 10,000 Hz; a fourth regulated frequencies between 10,000 and 15,000 Hz; and a fifth, frequencies between 15,000 and 50,000 Hz.

One of the biggest selling features of the DR-2000 was its ability to use the DR-2000 RC, the remote control device for the stereo receiver. Because all of the switching and components were solid state, the engineers of Drake Electronics were able to develop a complete remote control station that was no bigger than a cigarette pack. The basic idea for the remote control device was borrowed from that of television, and Drake engineers were able to control *all* functions by the DR-2000 RC. Each remote control box cost $75, and many people purchased more than one unit. The ability to control the stereo system from literally anywhere in the house was one of the system's biggest selling features, but it also caused some problems in homes with chil-

EXHIBIT 2   Modules for the DR-2000

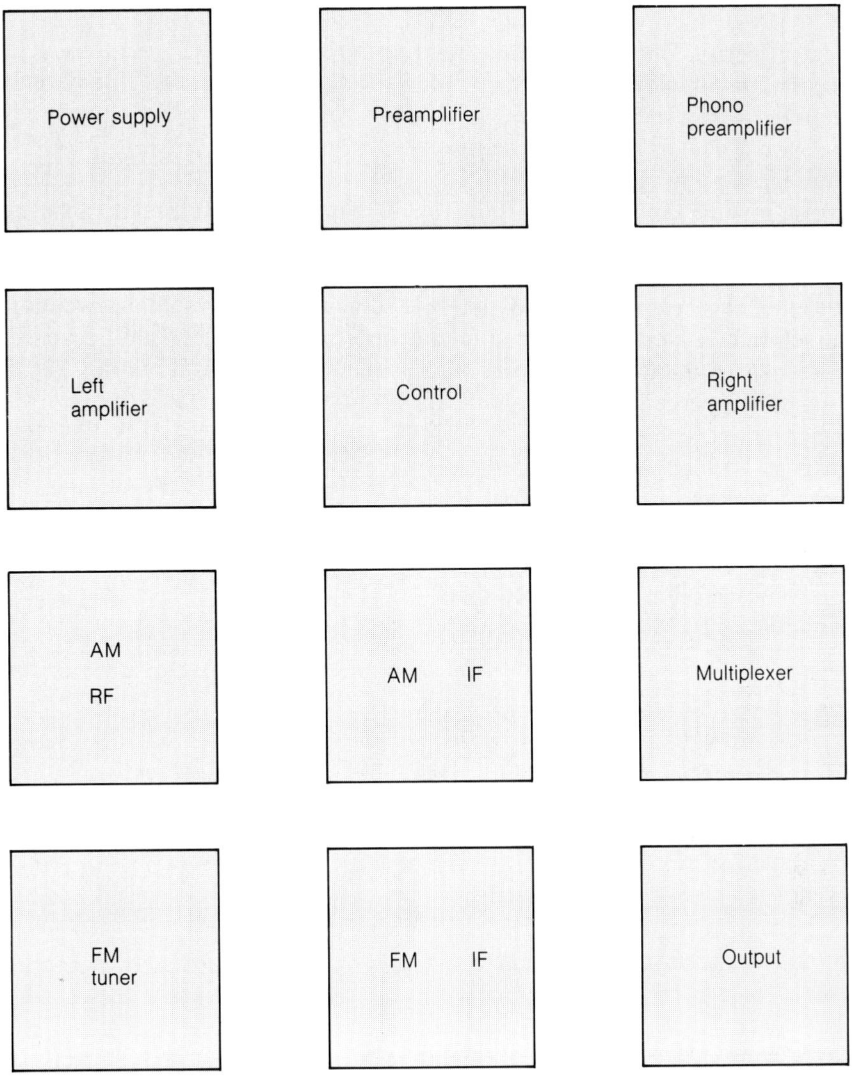

Power supply	Preamplifier	Phono preamplifier
Left amplifier	Control	Right amplifier
AM RF	AM IF	Multiplexer
FM tuner	FM IF	Output

dren. As a result, Drake developed a master control unit that parents could keep and that would override all other remote control units and the controls on the stereo receiver.

Another outstanding feature of the DR-2000 was its completely modular design, shown in Exhibit 2. Each module was con-tained in a completely separate, color-coded box. By unlatching four hidden slides, the top of the cabinet could be removed, giving access to all of the modules.

The control module contained a micro-processor chip that monitored the operations of all of the other modules. If one of the modules stopped functioning correctly, the control module would activate a warning light on the front panel that indicated which module was not working properly. The owner could pull out the appropriate module and replace it with a new module from a nearby Drake dealership. If a Drake dealership was not close, Drake promised two-day, COD delivery. The malfunctioning module could even be sent to Drake or given to a Drake dealership to be repaired or for a refund.

All of the modules, except the FM tuner, were manufactured by Drake and stored until they were needed. Annual carrying cost was estimated to be 25 percent for all modules. The FM tuner modules were supplied by Collins Electronics, which also adjusted and sealed them. The cost to place an order was estimated at $50 per order, and the time to receive an order from Collins was approximately two weeks. Collins also offered quantity discounts on its FM tuners. (See Exhibit 3.)

EXHIBIT 3 Quantity Discount from Collins on FM Tuners

Quantity	Price
0–100	$25
101–500	24
501 and over	22

Nitobitso Electronics also manufactured FM tuners compatible with the DR–2000. Because of its location in Japan, the time to receive an order was about two months, and the ordering cost was $100 because of the additional required paperwork. (See Exhibit 4.)

EXHIBIT 4 Quantity Discount from Nitobitso on FM Tuners

Quantity	Price
0–200	$25
201–800	23
801–2,000	22
2,001 and over	21

14

Waiting Lines: Queues

XEROX CORPORATION

Xerox Corporation designed a new service strategy that provided better customer service at less cost. A major factor in Xerox's success had been excellent service to its customers. A technical representative (TR) was assigned a geographic area and an associated set of customers whose equipment he was qualified to service. The service included preventive maintenance, emergency repairs, and installation of new equipment. The personal relationship between the TR and his customers was judged an important factor in Xerox's success. The copying equipment that Xerox provided was an important convenience for the office operations of its customers.

When Xerox introduced the Model 9200 duplicating system, even higher levels of service were required. This system was a revenue generator for the offset printing industry. An inoperable machine was more than an inconvenience: it resulted in lost revenues.

A field service manager supervised from 6 to 20 technical representatives. One objective for the 9200 was full service management control of the response time to customer service requests. Xerox wanted to evaluate the impact of forming teams of TRs for geographic territories. It considered three service strategies: (1) one-man territories; (2) miniteam territories; (3) full-team territories (i.e., all TRs reporting to the same Field Service Manager would be a single team within the combined territory).

The first strategy was too expensive to provide the desired service. The miniteam territory strategy had advantages over the full-team territory strategy. One of these advantages was the smaller number of TRs that a customer would see.

The basic tool for the evaluation was queueing theory. For different numbers of machines in a territory, the impact of the number in a miniteam was estimated on average response time, average number of customers waiting for service, and active time of TRs. Two-, three-, four-, and five-person miniteams were evaluated. It was found, for example, that for a one-hour average response time a three-person team could maintain 18 percent more machines per TR than a two-person team. Two-person and five-person teams were soon excluded from further consideration. The company finally selected three-person teams.

A computerized simulation model was developed to provide detail for applying the three-person team concept to specific territories. The additional inputs included geography, queue discipline, copy volume, time-dependent usage of equipment, and TR work schedules. The simulation model was interactive. Inputting a trial region generated data on TR utilization, overtime, travel time, and the response time distribution.

Implementation of the miniteam concept reduced the required number of TRs and improved service. It also enabled Xerox to furnish response time specifications to prospective customers.

This chapter describes the use of analytical queueing models. Chapters 15 and 16 describe the use of computer simulation.

W. H. Bleuel, "Management Science's Impact on Service Strategy," *Interfaces* 6, no. 1, pt. 2 (November 1975), pp. 4–12.

Everyone has experienced waiting in line. You wait at registration for school, at the grocery store checkout counter, and on the telephone when you call for information. The registrar, the grocery store manager, or the owner of the company that you call for information is responsible for the design of the system that provides you with the service or information you want. If the configuration of the service system is changed, your waiting time may decrease or increase. Changes in the service system that improve the service usually increase the cost of operating the system. As a manager, you must evaluate increased cost versus improved customer service.

Optimizing waiting line systems is very difficult. It is also difficult to obtain consensus on the criteria used to evaluate different configurations of a waiting line system. As a result, optimization methods for the design and operation of waiting line systems are not generally available. Consequently, the system manager/designer "tries" several configurations, estimates their performance, and then chooses from among them.

Xerox used the methods in this chapter to select its service strategy for the Model 9200. A major concern was the amount of time that customers would have to wait before a technical representative (TR) arrived. For any service strategy, increasing the total number of TRs would improve the service but also increase the cost of the service system. One possible configuration was one-person territories. That is, one TR would be assigned to all of the customers in a particular geographic region. A waiting line analysis was used to evaluate that configuration. Another possible configuration was the assignment of three TRs to a larger geographic region. With this configuration, even if one TR were on a service call, another TR could handle the next call. The performance of this configuration was evaluated by another waiting line analysis. Based on waiting line analyses of different configurations, Xerox chose to use three-person service teams.

Waiting line analysis has many applications. For example, Wyle Data Services used it to analyze possible configurations for its data processing network.[1] Using remote terminals, customers requested information from

---

[1] B. E. Krell and M. Arminio, "Queueing Theory Applied to Data Processing Networks," *Interfaces* 12, no. 4 (August 1982), pp. 21–33.

Wyle's main computer over communication links. After the requests were received, the information was sent over the communication links to the customers' terminals. Waiting line models were used to study the impact of different communication link speeds on customer service.

Detroit Edison used waiting line analysis to study whether to build a second coal unloading system at its Monroe power plant.[2] This coal-burning power plant received coal in unit trains. Because of breakdowns of the coal-unloading system, many trains had to wait to be unloaded, which increased costs. Detroit Edison could decrease the number of waiting trains by building a second unloading system, but this would cost millions of dollars. Waiting line analysis was used to predict the savings from the second unloading system.

The term **queue** is used interchangably with the term **waiting line.** The main concern of **waiting line theory** or **queueing theory** is the analysis of waiting line systems with uncertainty in the arrival times of customers and/or uncertainty in the times required to provide the required service for customers. The analysis of such waiting line systems is difficult. In the next section, we describe many of the possible considerations in the analysis of waiting line systems. Next, we discuss analytical results for waiting line systems. Then, we analyze a simple waiting line system and illustrate the difficulty of getting analytical results for general waiting line systems. We present results for some other waiting line systems, and in the final section we show how to use those results to evaluate different configurations for some waiting line examples.

A CLASSIFICATION FRAMEWORK FOR WAITING LINE MODELS

The three components of a waiting line system

In this section, we discuss possible considerations in describing a waiting line system. Figure 14.1 represents an example of the three components of a waiting line system: the *customers,* the *service facility,* and the *queue discipline.* For example, consider the waiting line system for teller windows at a bank. To describe this system, we need to describe the characteristics of the customers requesting service, to describe how the system "stores" waiting customers and chooses which of them will receive service next, and to describe the service characteristics (e.g., the time required to provide the service).

In this section, we describe possible considerations for the three components of a waiting line system. We conclude the section by describing some measures of the performance of waiting line systems.

---

[2] K. Chelst, A. Z. Tilles, and J. S. Pipis, "A Coal Unloader: A Finite Queueing System with Breakdowns," *Interfaces* 11, no. 5 (October 1981), pp. 12–25.

FIGURE 14.1   Example of a Waiting Line System

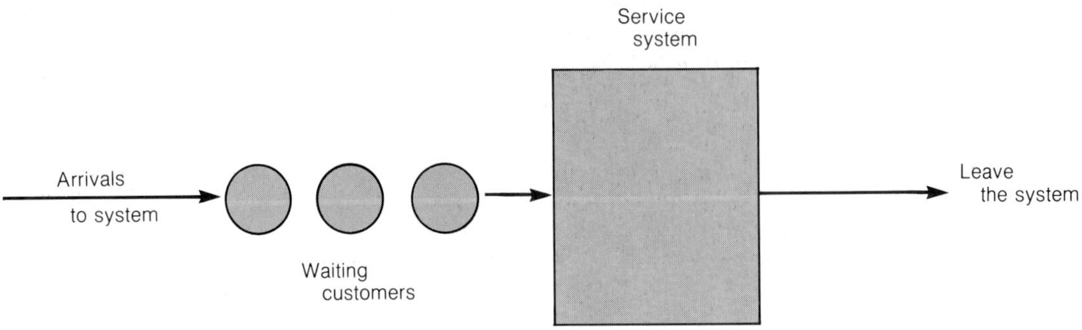

The Customers

Customers arrive at the service facility from outside the queueing system. Customer arrivals are sometimes called **calls for service.** The characteristics of the customer population vary for different waiting line systems. If there are only a finite number of potential customers, the queueing system has a **finite population.** If there are an infinite number of potential customers, the queueing system has an **infinite population.** Thus, one consideration with regard to customers is whether the potential customers are from a *finite population* or from an *infinite population.*

Finite versus infinite customer population

Let's illustrate these two cases by examples. Say that at a particular manufacturing facility mechanics repair machines when they break down. A call for service occurs when a machine needs repair, so the customers are the machines that break down. If the facility has only five machines and two break down, there are only three left in the population to break down. Because there is a finite set of machines at the facility, this is an example of a finite population. Alternatively, say that the calls for service are requests for Directory Assistance information in a large metropolitan area. In this case, the customers are people who call for information. If 50 people out of the 1 million people in the calling area are calling for Directory Assistance, the remaining number of potential callers to Directory Assistance is changed only minimally. Thus, it is reasonable to treat the population of potential customers as if it were infinite. *The critical consideration is whether knowing how many customers are currently in the system significantly affects the size of the remaining population.* If the probability of a new customer arrival is independent of the number of customers already in the waiting line system, we assume that the population is infinite. Otherwise, we treat the population as finite.

Xerox treated its customer population as finite because a small number of customers was assigned to each TR. If a customer's machine was being serviced, the likelihood of another call for service was smaller than it would have been if no customers were being serviced. If Xerox had assigned a large number of customers to each TR, it would have been reasonable to treat the customer population as infinite.

Another consideration with regard to customers is the **arrival pattern.** A **deterministic arrival pattern** is one in which there is no uncertainty about when customers arrive. If a dentist schedules a patient every 30 minutes, there is no uncertainty about when the patients will arrive, so the arrival pattern is deterministic. A deterministic arrival pattern can also be irregularly spaced. For example, an automotive service center may schedule two customers for 8 A.M., one for 9 A.M., etc.

A **random arrival pattern** is one in which there is uncertainty about when customers arrive. Most waiting line systems—for example, calls for Directory Assistance—have a random arrival pattern. The probability distribution of the time between successive arrivals, called the **probability distribution of interarrival times,** is the most common method of specifying a random arrival pattern. One probability distribution for interarrival times is the exponential distribution, which we discuss in a later section of this chapter. Although this probability distribution is a convenient one because it makes it easier to obtain analytical results, the manager/ designer of the waiting line system must check whether it accurately describes the queueing system. Other probability distributions for interarrival times should also be considered.

In many situations, customers arrive one by one. This is called **single arrival.** Calls to Directory Assistance are made one by one. The arrival of customers in a group is called **bulk arrival.** Customers may arrive at a restaurant either one by one or in groups. The operation of the restaurant is affected by the way in which they arrive.

Because machine breakdowns weren't predictable, calls for service to Xerox had a random arrival pattern. Xerox found that the probability distribution of interarrival times followed an exponential distribution. The calls for its service were single arrivals.

Figure 14.2 summarizes the considerations for the customers of a waiting line configuration. Next, we discuss queue discipline and server considerations, which are also summarized in Figure 14.2.

The Queue Discipline

The **queue discipline** is the set of rules by which customers waiting for service behave and are managed. One consideration in queue discipline is how waiting customers are "stored." At a bank, for example, all of the customers may wait in a single line, or there may be multiple lines—one line in front of each teller window. The bank manager decides whether there will be a single line or multiple lines. Waiting line theory shows that a single waiting line reduces the average waiting time per customer. Because a change from multiple waiting lines to a single waiting line can

Margin notes:

Deterministic arrival pattern

Random arrival pattern

Single versus bulk arrivals

FIGURE 14.2 Some Considerations in Waiting Lines

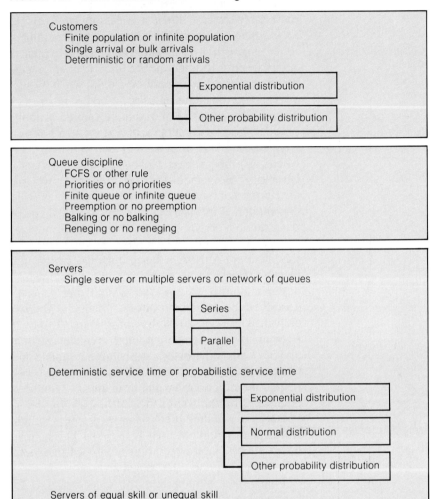

Customers
    Finite population or infinite population
    Single arrival or bulk arrivals
    Deterministic or random arrivals

    Exponential distribution

    Other probability distribution

Queue discipline
    FCFS or other rule
    Priorities or no priorities
    Finite queue or infinite queue
    Preemption or no preemption
    Balking or no balking
    Reneging or no reneging

Servers
    Single server or multiple servers or network of queues

    Series

    Parallel

Deterministic service time or probabilistic service time

    Exponential distribution

    Normal distribution

    Other probability distribution

Servers of equal skill or unequal skill

be made at little or no expense, many banks have made that change in recent years.

Another consideration in queue discipline is the method by which a waiting customer is chosen when a server becomes available. A common approach is **first come, first served (FCFS).** However, there may be different **priorities** for different customers. For example, if there are two priority classes, any waiting customer in the higher-priority class is chosen before any waiting customer in the lower-priority class. Calls for police are classified in this manner: emergency and nonemergency. An emergency call is answered before any nonemergency call.

Another consideration is whether there is a limit to the size of the waiting line. In some systems, there is a limited amount of waiting space, so that a customer who arrives after the waiting space is full never enters the system. A telephone-based answering system usually has this characteristic. When all of the operators are busy, the next customer to call gets this message: "Remain on the line, and the next available operator will answer the call." After the waiting space has been filled by a specified number of calls, the next caller gets a busy signal. A queue of this kind is called a **finite queue**. An **infinite queue** is one in which there is space for additional customers no matter how many customers are already waiting in line.

Finite versus infinite queue

Another queue discipline consideration is whether there is **preemption.** If the processing of a customer can be interrupted before it has been completed, we say that preemption is allowed. Police dispatchers use preemption and priorities. If a nonemergency call is being serviced by police officers when an emergency call is received, the dispatcher has those police officers service the emergency call instead. Systems without priorities usually don't allow preemption. Another queue discipline consideration is whether **balking** occurs—that is, customers leave the system as soon as they arrive. A reason for balking is that, based on the number of customers already waiting, the customer judges that the waiting time will be too long. For example, even though waiting space is available, a customer may leave if there are more than four customers ahead in line.

Still another consideration in queue discipline is **reneging**—leaving the system after waiting awhile. For example, a customer may leave after having waited for more than an hour. In some situations, balking or reneging may not occur with certainty. For example, there may be a probability distribution for whether a customer leaves the system based on the number of customers already waiting in line. Similarly, there may be a probability distribution for whether a customer reneges as a function of time spent waiting for service.

The Servers

The configuration of the service system is usually controlled by the decision maker. The system can have a **single server** or **multiple servers**. If there are multiple servers, their organization and their skill levels are additional considerations.

If there are multiple servers, how are they organized? The servers can be in **parallel** or in **series**. Figure 14.3 shows this difference. Figure 14.3*a* shows servers in parallel. Only one of the servers is necessary to provide the service to a customer, and after receiving the service, the customer leaves the system. Note that in Figure 14.3*a* the customers are waiting in different lines. Figure 14.3*b* shows servers in series. After receiving service from the first server, the customer must go to the second server, who provides additional service. If the second server is busy, the cus-

Parallel and series servers

FIGURE 14.3   Parallel Servers and Series Servers

a. Parallel servers

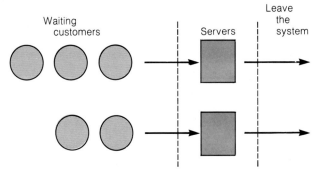

b. Series servers

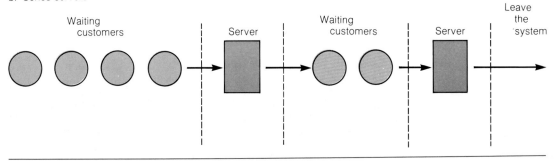

---

tomer must wait in line for this service. This process continues until the customer has received service from each of the servers. An example of series servers is a machine shop where jobs must go to different machines (servers) at which different operations are performed.

In the Xerox study, different service strategies had different server configurations. Xerox's strategy of one-person territories had a single server. Xerox's strategy of miniteam territories had multiple servers in parallel. Each time there was a call for service, it was assigned to *one* of the available TRs on the miniteam.

Network of servers

A combination of servers in series and servers in parallel is illustrated in Figure 14.4. This **network of servers** combines servers in parallel that provide the same service with servers in series that each provide a different service. For example, there may be two drill presses that are used interchangeably, but a single grinder station may perform the grinding operation after the drilling operation has been completed.

FIGURE 14.4 Example of a Network of Servers

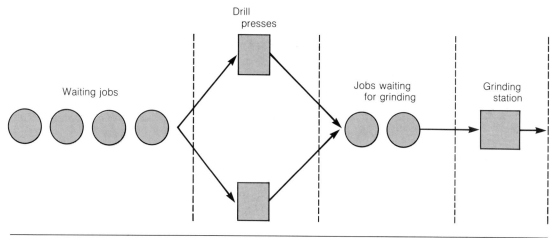

The rate at which service is provided is an important consideration. The **service time** for a customer is the amount of time required for a server to complete processing that customer. Service times can be **probabilistic,** sometimes called uncertain, or **deterministic,** sometimes called certain. For queueing systems, probabilistic service times are more common than deterministic service times. Say that the queueing system is an automobile repair shop. Customers arrive for different types of repairs. Because the repair time depends on the service required and on the problems encountered by the mechanic, the service time is probabilistic. Common service time probability distributions are the exponential and the normal.

If there are multiple servers, they can have the same skill levels or different skill levels. A server with greater skill requires less time to provide the service. The probability distributions of probabilistic service times are different if the servers are different skill levels.

Figure 14.2 summarized many of the customer, queue discipline, and server considerations for a waiting line system. By varying the alternative selected from each of these considerations, many waiting line configurations are possible. Later in this chapter, we present results that can be used to analyze some of the possible configurations.

Measures of Performance

As a manager, you are responsible for both the design and the operation of the waiting line system. Designing the waiting line system includes determining the number of servers, their organization, and their skill levels. You also establish rules for the operation of the system. For example, you decide whether priorities are used. Consider a bank with several teller windows. You decide whether one teller should service only business accounts. You can introduce operating policies such as this one: "If the number of customers waiting is more than a specified number, open another teller window." There are many possible configurations and operating policies.

To optimize a waiting line system, **a measure of performance** is necessary. In a probabilistic environment, the measures of performance of a waiting line system are random variables. Thus, you need the probability distribution or the expected value for the performance measures. Table 14.1 lists some measures of performance of waiting line systems. From the customer's viewpoint, the waiting time and time in the system are important concerns. The **waiting time** is the time in line before service is begun. The **time in the system** includes the service time as well as the waiting time. From the viewpoint of the service system designer, the likelihood that customers leave the system because of balking, reneging, or a limited queue is an important concern. Other concerns of the service system designer are the **number of customers waiting in line** and the **number of customers in the system.** The **utilization of servers** is the proportion of service time available that is used to provide service. The service system designer prefers high utilization so that the servers are used more effectively but is also concerned with the probability that a customer has to wait before service is begun. From the server's viewpoint, the length of a busy period is an important measure of performance. A **busy period** for a server is the amount of time between idle times. Assume that a server is never idle when a customer is waiting. Then, a busy period ends when a server completes serving a customer and no other customer is waiting in line.

Unfortunately, there is usually conflict between various measures of performance. If a server is added to the system so that waiting time is decreased, the utilization of the servers also decreases. A manager is often unwilling to place a dollar cost on the waiting time of a customer. In

Conflicting measures of performance

TABLE 14.1   Measures of Performance for Waiting Line Systems

Customer waiting time
Customer time in the system
Probability that a customer will leave the system without service
  No waiting space
  Balking
  Reneging
Number of customers waiting
Number of customers in the system
Utilization of servers
Probability that a customer must wait for service
Length of a busy period

---

this case, it is useful to know the value of each of the measures of performance for different possible system configurations. Then, the manager evaluates the trade-offs between decreased utilization and increased customer satisfaction.

ANALYTICAL RESULTS—TRANSIENT VERSUS STEADY STATE CONDITIONS

Analytical waiting line results give formulas that are used to determine the values of measures of performance for a particular configuration of a waiting line system. For example, if we hypothesize a particular configuration with a probability distribution for the interarrival times and the service times, we can get a formula that allows us to substitute the means of that distribution into an equation that calculates the expected number waiting in line. We obtain the analytical results by mathematical analysis of the particular configuration. In the preceding section, we described many possible considerations of waiting line systems, and these give a large number of possible configurations. Analytical results exist for only a small part of the possible configurations.

In the next section, we illustrate developing analytical results for one such configuration. After that, we show that obtaining analytical results is difficult for even a very simple configuration.

First, however, we discuss the distinction between *transient* and *steady state* conditions. Let's illustrate the distinction by considering how to calculate the expected number in the system for a configuration. To develop the formula for the expected number in the system, we need the probability distribution of the number in the system. Let P_n represent the probability that there are exactly n in the system. The expected number in the system is

$$E(n) = \sum_{n=0}^{\infty} nP_n$$

Does the probability that there are n customers in the system depend on the point in time? Say that the system is a grocery store opening at 7 A.M. The service system is the checkout counter. No one is present at the checkout counter when the store opens. What is the probability that there are 10 people at the checkout counter at 7 A.M.? Zero. In fact, the probability is 1.0 that the number in the waiting line system is 0 and the probability is 0.0 that the number in the waiting line system is any other value. Let $P_n(t)$ represent the probability that the number of customers in the system at Time t is n. Let's call the opening time $t = 0$ and measure the time in minutes. Then, $P_0(0) = 1.0$, and $P_n(0) = 0.0$ for any value of $n \geq 1$. $P_n(10)$ is the probability that n customers are in the system 10 minutes after opening. The probability of no customers in the system after 10 minutes, $P_0(10)$, is not equal to 1.0. There is some chance that enough customers arrived so that one or more customers are at the checkout counter at 7:10 A.M. Thus, $P_n(t)$ is not the same for all values of t and is called the **transient probability** of the number in the system. Because the probabilities of the number of customers in the system change over time, the expected number in the system also changes as a function of time. If you could calculate $P_n(t)$, then the expected number in the system t

Calculating transient probabilities is difficult

minutes after opening is calculated as $\sum_{n=0}^{\infty} nP_n(t)$. But calculating transient probabilities is *difficult* even for a simple waiting line configuration.

The reason that the probability distribution changes over time is the system's *initialization* when the store opens. At that time, there are no customers at the checkout counter. However, even if there were 10 customers at the checkout counter at that time, the probabilities would still change over time. It is the fact of the initialization, not the value of the initialization, that causes the probabilities to change over time.

The longer the amount of time after the initialization of the system, the smaller is the impact of the initialization. After a long period of time, the probability distributions $P_n(t)$ and $P_n(t + 1)$ are almost identical. If enough time has passed since initialization, we treat $P_n(t)$ as independent of t and represent it as P_n. The **steady state probabilities** of the number in the system are the values that the transient probabilities approach after a long period. In general, it is easier to obtain steady state probabilities for a

Analytical results and steady state probabilities

particular waiting line configuration than it is to obtain transient probabilities for that configuration. *Most analytical waiting line results are based on steady state probabilities.*

One *warning* concerning the use of steady state results. Many waiting line environments never reach steady state. If the service facility opens and closes each day, not enough time may pass for the steady state to be

Is steady state reached?

reached. Furthermore, if the service facility closes for lunch and customers still arrive, such as for automobile service, steady state results must be used cautiously. Steady state results generally do not allow interruptions in the availability of the service facility. Also, analytical results are not likely to consider situations in which the arrival rates and/or service rates vary by time of day or day of week.

Analytical waiting line results are useful because they provide insight about the decision environment. However, it is unlikely that you will find analytical results for the exact configuration you have. Be aware of the assumptions that were made in the development of the analytical results, and of the difference between transient and steady state results. Are steady state results appropriate for the decision environment you are studying? If you can't get analytical waiting line results for your waiting line system, you can use computer simulation, which we discuss in Chapters 15 and 16.

THE SINGLE-SERVER MODEL ANALYTICAL RESULTS (M/M/1)

Kendall notation is used by researchers as a short description of waiting line environments. The general form is *x/y/z,* where *x, y,* and *z* describe the arrival process, the service process, and the number of servers, respectively. For an M/M/1 waiting line, the M's specify **Markovian** and are used for an exponential probability distribution. Thus, an M/M/1 waiting line system has interarrival times and service times with exponential probability distributions. If the time has a general probability distribution or is deterministic, we use G or D, respectively. Thus, M/G/1 has exponentially distributed interarrival times and a general probability distribution for service times. The third argument in M/M/1 specifies that the system has a single server.

Mean interarrival time = 1/(Arrival rate) for any probability distribution

The **interarrival times** are the times between successive arrivals. The **arrival rate** is the expected number of arrivals per time unit. The arrival rate (per time unit) is represented by λ. The **mean interarrival time,** sometimes called the **average interarrival time,** is $\frac{1}{\lambda}$ *regardless of the probability distribution of the interarrival times.* The distinction between arrival rate and mean interarrival time is often confused.

Table 14.2 illustrates a set of arrival times for customers and the associated interarrival times. The arrival times are minutes after opening. The first customer arrives at 0.106 minutes after opening and has an interarrival time of 0.106 minutes. The second customer arrives at 0.425 minutes after opening. The interarrival time for the second customer is the time between the arrival of the second customer and the arrival of the first, $0.425 - 0.106 = 0.319$. For the arrivals of Table 14.2, 50 customers arrived in 30.075 minutes. The average arrival rate is $\lambda = \frac{50}{30.075} = 1.663$ per minute. What is the average time between arrivals? The average interarrival time is $\frac{30.075}{50} = 0.6015$ minutes. Alternately, the average interarrival time is calculated as $\frac{1}{\lambda} = \frac{1}{1.663} = 0.6015$.

Figure 14.5 illustrates a histogram, or frequency diagram, of the interarrival times of Table 14.2. For example, 15 of the 50 interarrival times were between 0.0 and 0.2 minutes. Often, historical information such as

TABLE 14.2 Example of Arrival Times and Interarrival Times

Customer	Arrival Time	Interarrival Time
1	0.106	0.106
2	0.425	0.319
3	0.527	0.102
4	0.822	0.295
5	2.039	1.217
6	2.401	0.362
7	2.526	0.125
8	3.272	0.746
9	3.575	0.303
10	4.424	0.849
11	4.727	0.303
12	5.394	0.667
13	5.812	0.418
14	5.880	0.068
15	6.381	0.501
16	6.423	0.042
17	9.665	3.242
18	9.773	0.108
19	10.126	0.353
20	10.535	0.409
21	10.883	0.348
22	11.615	0.732
23	12.488	0.873
24	13.742	1.254
25	14.611	0.869
26	15.071	0.460
27	15.278	0.207
28	16.490	1.212
29	17.122	0.632
30	17.414	0.292
31	18.218	0.804
32	18.387	0.169
33	19.725	1.338
34	19.746	0.021
35	21.295	1.549
36	22.089	0.794
37	22.210	0.121
38	22.289	0.079
39	22.694	0.405
40	22.798	0.104
41	22.990	0.192
42	23.347	0.357
43	23.564	0.217
44	23.682	0.118
45	26.227	2.545
46	27.297	1.070
47	27.345	0.048
48	27.827	0.482
49	30.068	2.241
50	30.075	0.007
Sum		30.075

FIGURE 14.5   Histogram of Interarrival Times in Table 14.2

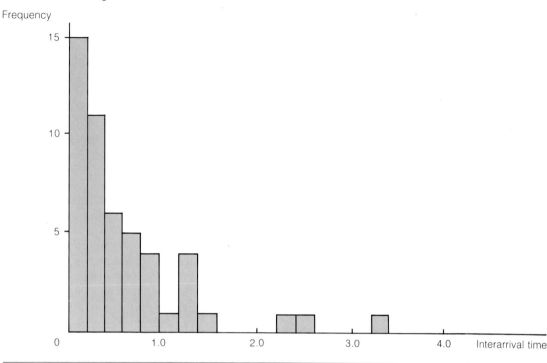

that in Table 14.2 is available to determine the type of the underlying probability distribution and to estimate its parameters. For example, if the normal distribution was correct, we need to estimate its parameters, the mean and the standard deviation. However, the histogram doesn't look like the bell-shaped curve of the normal distribution.

The **exponential probability distribution** has the probability density function

The exponential distribution

$$f(t) = \begin{cases} \lambda e^{-\lambda t}, & \text{if } t \geq 0; \\ 0, & \text{if } t < 0 \end{cases}$$

where $e = 2.71828$. The exponential probability distribution has only one parameter, λ. The mean interarrival time is calculated as

$$E(t) = \int_0^\infty t\lambda e^{-\lambda t}dt = \frac{1}{\lambda}$$

If the arrival rate is λ and the exponential distribution is correct, λ, the parameter of the exponential distribution, is equal to the arrival rate. Figure 14.6 illustrates the probability density function for an exponential

FIGURE 14.6   Probability Density Function of Exponential Distribution

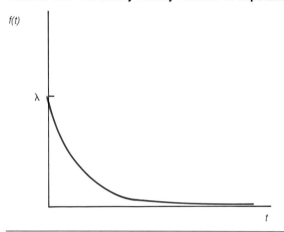

distribution. The histogram of Figure 14.5 is not unreasonable if the underlying probability distribution of the interarrival times is the exponential distribution. (In fact, the interarrival times were generated by a computer simulation for an exponential distribution using the methods we discuss in Chapters 15 and 16.) The variance of the exponential distribution can be shown to be

$$\frac{1}{\lambda^2}$$

Therefore, if the arrival rate is λ, the variance of the interarrival times is

$$\frac{1}{\lambda^2}$$

As the arrival rate increases, the mean and variance of the interarrival times both approach 0.

A synonym for exponential arrivals is **Poisson inputs.** If interarrival times have an exponential distribution, the number of arrivals in an interval of length T follows a Poisson distribution with parameter λT. That is,

$$P(\text{exactly } n \text{ arrivals in interval of } T) = \frac{(\lambda T)^n e^{-\lambda T}}{n!}, \, n = 0, 1, 2, \ldots.$$

Remember, $n!$ is n-factorial and is calculated as $n(n - 1)(n - 2) \cdots (2)(1)$. Say that the arrival rate, λ, is 3 per minute. Then, the probability of 20 arrivals in 10 minutes is

$$P(\text{exactly 20 arrivals in interval of 10}) = \frac{(3 \times 10)^{20} e^{-3 \times 10}}{20!} = 0.0134$$

Expected number of arrivals in T

The mean and variance of the Poisson distribution are equal to its parameter. Therefore, the expected number of arrivals in an interval of length T is (λT). If the arrival rate, λ, is 3 per minute, then the expected number of arrivals in 10 minutes is $3 \times 10 = 30$. The variance of the number of arrivals in an interval of length T is also (λT).

The exponential distribution

Represent by $P(t > T)$ the probability that the time between successive arrivals is greater than T. For the exponential distribution,

$$P(t > T) = \int_T^\infty \lambda e^{-\lambda t} dt = e^{-\lambda T}$$

The cumulative probability distribution (i.e., the probability that the interarrival time is less than or equal to T), is

$$F(T) = 1 - P(t > T) = 1 - e^{-\lambda T}$$

Note that $P(t > T)$ is the probability of no arrivals in an interval of length T.

An interarrival probability distribution has the **memoryless property** if the probability distribution of the time to the next arrival is the same regardless of the amount of time since the last arrival. The memoryless property simplifies the development of analytical waiting line results. However, it is often not true in actual waiting line situations.

The exponential distribution has the memoryless property. This is illustrated by

The exponential distribution is memoryless

$$\frac{P(t > T + h)}{P(t > T)} = \frac{e^{-\lambda(T + h)}}{e^{-\lambda T}} = e^{-\lambda h} = P(T > h)$$

The probability that there will not be an arrival in an interval of length $(T + h)$, given there has been no arrival in Interval T, depends only on h and is an exponential distribution with parameter λ.

The normal distribution is not memoryless

The normal distribution is not memoryless. Say that the interarrival time has a normal distribution with a mean of 10 minutes and a standard deviation of 3 minutes and that there has been no arrival in the first 20 minutes. The probability distribution of the additional time until the next arrival is not a normal distribution with a mean of 10 minutes and a standard deviation of 3 minutes.

The Erlang distribution also has the memoryless property. The **Erlang distribution** is

$$f(t) = \begin{cases} \dfrac{(\lambda m)(\lambda mt)^{m-1} e^{-\lambda mt}}{(m-1)!}, & \text{if } t \geq 0; \\ 0, & \text{if } t < 0 \end{cases}$$

where m is a positive integer. The mean and variance of the distribution are

$$\frac{1}{\lambda} \text{ and } \frac{1}{m\lambda^2}, \text{ respectively}$$

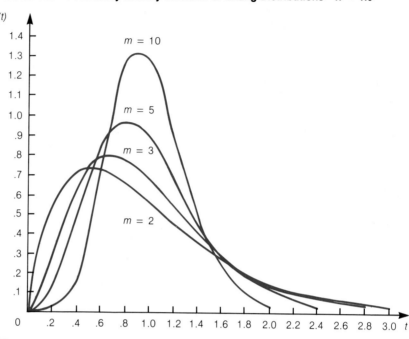

FIGURE 14.7 Probability Density Function of Erlang Distributions—λ = 1.0

Figure 14.7 illustrates the Erlang distribution for several values of m. Note that for $m = 1$, the Erlang distribution is the exponential distribution with parameter λ. Also, if m becomes large, the mean interarrival time stays $\frac{1}{\lambda}$, but the standard deviation approaches 0; this is a deterministic interarrival time.

Table 14.3 illustrates the service times for 50 consecutive customers. The sum of the 50 service times is 11.277 minutes. The average service time is $\frac{11.277}{50} = 0.2554$ minutes. The service rate is $\frac{50}{11.277} = 4.434$ per minute. Let μ be the service rate, so the mean service time is $\frac{1}{\mu}$.

Figure 14.8 illustrates a histogram of the service times. If the probability distribution of service times is the exponential distribution, Figure 14.8 is a reasonable histogram. The parameter of the exponential distribution of service times is μ.

We visually examined the histograms to check whether the exponential distribution was reasonable for interarrival and service times. You should use statistical *goodness-of-fit tests* to test the hypothesis that a distribution "fits" the historical data. You can find these tests in a statistics book.

TABLE 14.3 Example of Service Times

Customer	Service Time
1	0.597
2	0.083
3	0.049
4	0.074
5	0.107
6	0.049
7	0.037
8	0.004
9	0.360
10	0.067
11	0.732
12	0.417
13	0.589
14	0.059
15	0.111
16	0.127
17	0.186
18	0.466
19	0.032
20	0.184
21	0.115
22	0.565
23	1.082
24	0.686
25	0.053
26	0.029
27	0.304
28	0.123
29	0.337
30	0.068
31	0.005
32	0.249
33	0.363
34	0.008
35	0.294
36	0.133
37	0.004
38	0.068
39	0.155
40	0.164
41	0.070
42	0.235
43	0.022
44	0.223
45	0.056
46	0.562
47	0.093
48	0.168
49	0.250
50	0.463
Sum	11.277

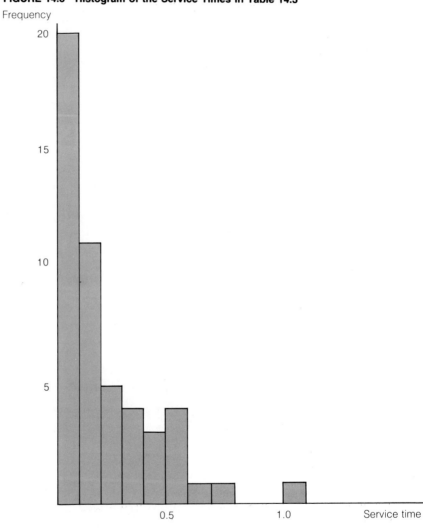

FIGURE 14.8 Histogram of the Service Times in Table 14.3

In the rest of this section, we assume

1. Steady state conditions.
2. A single server.
3. Exponentially distributed interarrival times with parameter λ.
4. Exponentially distributed service times with parameter μ.
5. Infinite population and infinite queue.
6. No balking and no reneging.

This section's
assumptions

TABLE 14.4 Steady State Measures of Performance Notation

Measure of Performance	Notation
Expected time in system	T_s
Expected time in line	T_q
Expected number of system	L_s
Expected number of line	L_q
Probability that all servers are busy	P_b
Expected number served during a busy period	L_b
Expected length of a busy period	T_b

Table 14.4 introduces notation for the *expected values* of measures of performance based on steady state conditions. If the subscript is *s*, the measure refers to the system; if the subscript is *q*, the measure refers to the queue; and if the subscript is *b*, the measure refers to a busy period. If the measure is *T*, it is a time, and if the measure is *L*, it is a length or a number of customers. For example, L_q is the length of the queue line or the number of customers in the queue (waiting in line). Similarly, T_q is the time that a customer spends in the queue.

Assume $\rho < 1$

Let $\rho = \dfrac{\lambda}{\mu}$. If ρ is greater than 1.0, the arrival rate is greater than the service rate and in the long run the line becomes longer and longer. *Assume* that $\rho < 1$, so $\lambda < \mu$. Then, the *steady state probabilities* that there are *n* in the system are

Steady state probabilities

$$P_n = (1 - \rho)\rho^n, \; n = 0, 1, \ldots.$$

The probability of *N* or more customers in the system is

$$P(n \geq N) = \sum_{n=N}^{\infty}(1 - \rho)\rho^n = \rho^N$$

Because the server utilization is the fraction of the time the server is busy, ρ is the utilization factor. The expected number of customers *in the system* is

$$L_s = E(n) = \sum_{n=0}^{\infty} nP_n = \frac{\rho}{(1 - \rho)} = \frac{\lambda}{(\mu - \lambda)}$$

The variance of the number in the system is

$$\mathrm{Var}(n) = \frac{\rho}{(1 - \rho)^2}$$

Another performance measure is the number of customers waiting in line. *If there are customers present in a single-server system*, the number *in line* is one less than the number in the system. The expected line length (or number in the queue) is calculated as

$$L_q = \frac{\rho^2}{(1 - \rho)} = \frac{\lambda^2}{\mu(\mu - \lambda)}$$

If customers are chosen on a first come, first served (FCFS) basis, the probability distribution of the time in the system of a customer is an exponential distribution with parameter $\mu(1 - \rho)$. Let w represent the time a customer is in the system. Then, $g(w)$, the probability density function of w, is

$$g(w) = \begin{cases} \mu(1 - \rho)e^{-\mu(1 - \rho)t}, & \text{if } t \geq 0; \\ 0, & \text{if } t < 0 \end{cases}$$

The expected time in the system is

$$T_s = E(\text{time in system}) = \frac{1}{\mu(1 - \rho)} = \frac{1}{\mu - \lambda}$$

As the service rate becomes very large, the expected time in the system decreases. As the service rate approaches the arrival rate, the denominator of the expected time in the system approaches 0 and the expected time in the system increases. The time in the system includes the time in line and the service time. The expected time in line equals the expected time in the system minus the expected service time, $\frac{1}{\mu}$.

$$T_q = E(\text{time in line}) = \frac{\rho}{\mu(1 - \rho)} = \frac{\lambda}{\mu(\mu - \lambda)}$$

P_0 is the probability that there isn't a customer in the system, so $(1 - P_0)$ is the probability that there is a customer in the system. Therefore, $P_b = 1 - P_0 = \rho$. The probability that a customer must wait for service is $P_b = \rho$. The expected length of a busy period for the server is

$$T_b = \frac{1}{(\mu - \lambda)}$$

The expected number of customers served during a busy period is

$$L_b = \frac{\mu}{(\mu - \lambda)}$$

Example calculations for M/M/1
Let's calculate performance measures based on the steady state results where the arrival rate is estimated from the data in Table 14.2 and the service rate is estimated from the data in Table 14.3. The arrival rate, λ, is 1.663 customers per minute. The service rate, μ, is 4.434 customers per minute. The utilization factor is $\rho = \frac{1.663}{4.434} = 0.375$. The probability that the server is busy, P_b, is only 0.375. The probability that the server is idle equals the probability that the number of customers in the system is 0,

$P_0 = 1 - 0.375 = 0.625$. The probability of 1 customer in the system is $P_1 = (1 - \rho)\rho^1 = 0.625(0.375)^1 = 0.2344$. The probability of 2 customers in the system is $P_2 = (1 - \rho)\rho^2 = 0.625(0.375)^2 = 0.0879$. The probability of 3 or more customers in the system is $P_3 = 1 - P_0 - P_1 - P_2 = 1 - 0.625 - 0.2344 - 0.0879 = 0.0527$. Alternatively, calculate $P(n \geq 3) = \rho^3 = 0.375^3 = 0.0527$. For this single-server system, the probability that the number *in line* is 2 or more is the probability of 3 or more *in the system*, $\rho^3 = 0.0527$.

The expected number in the system is

$$L_s = \frac{\rho}{(1 - \rho)} = \frac{0.375}{(1 - 0.375)} = 0.6$$

The expected number in line is $L_q = \rho^2/(1 - \rho) = 0.375^2/(1 - 0.375) = 0.225$. The time in the system is exponential with parameter $\mu(1 - \rho) = 4.434 \times (1 - 0.375) = 2.7713$. The probability that a customer is in the system 3 minutes or more is $e^{-\mu(1-\rho)3} = e^{-2.7713 \times 3} = 0.0039$. The expected time in the system is

$$T_s = \frac{1}{\mu(1 - \rho)} = \frac{1}{2.7713} = 0.3609$$

The expected service time is 0.2255 minutes, $\frac{1}{4.434}$. The expected time in line is the expected time in the system minus the expected service time, $T_q = 0.3609 - 0.2255 = 0.1354$. Alternatively, the expected time in line is calculated directly as

$$T_q = \frac{1}{\mu(1 - \rho)} = \frac{0.375}{4.434(1 - 0.375)} = 0.1354$$

The expected length of a busy period is

$$T_b = \frac{1}{\mu(1 - \rho)} = \frac{1}{2.7713} = 0.3609 \text{ minutes}$$

The expected number of customers served during a busy period is

$$L_b = \frac{\mu}{(\mu - \lambda)} = \frac{4.434}{(4.434 - 1.663)} = 1.60 \text{ customers}$$

THE DIFFICULTY OF OBTAINING ANALYTICAL RESULTS

Analytical results are hard to obtain because determining $P_n(t)$ (or P_n) is usually difficult. To illustrate this, we present the analytical development of these probabilities for the M/M/1 waiting line.

Let's consider the system at Time T. Assuming exponential interarrival times, the memoryless property allows the history of past arrivals to be ignored. The probability of no arrival in an interval of length h is $e^{-\lambda h}$. The Taylor series expansion of $e^{-\lambda h}$ is

$$e^{-\lambda h} = 1 - \lambda h + \frac{(-\lambda h)^2}{2!} + \frac{(-\lambda h)^3}{3!} + \cdots$$

If h is small, h^n is small for $n > 1$ and we can use the following approximation:

$$e^{-\lambda h} \approx 1 - \lambda h$$

Probability of no arrival in small h

That is, the probability of no arrival in an interval of length h is approximately $(1 - \lambda h)$. If h is small, the probability of more than one arrival occurring in an interval of length h is 0. Therefore, the probability of exactly one arrival in an interval of length h is approximately λh.

Probability of no or one service completion in small h

Consider an exponential service time probability distribution with parameter μ and assume that a customer is in the system, so that the server is busy. The probability that the service is not completed in a small interval h is approximately $(1 - \mu h)$, based on reasoning similar to that for the interarrival time. The probability that the service is completed during a small interval h is approximately μh.

Let's determine $P_0(T + h)$, where h is a small interval after Time T. How is it possible that there is no customer in the system at Time $(T + h)$? One possibility is that there is no customer in the system at Time T and that there is no arrival during the interval until $(T + h)$. Because of the assumption that the arrivals and the service times are independent random variables, the probability that there is no customer present at Time T and no customer arrives is the product of the probabilities, $(1 - \lambda h)P_0(T)$. The only other possibility is that there is one customer in the system at Time T and that during the interval until $(T + h)$ there is a service completion and no new arrival. The probability that no customer arrives is approximately $(1 - \lambda h)$ and the probability of a service completion is approximately (μh), so the probability is approximately $(1 - \lambda h)(\mu h) P_1(T)$. Adding the probabilities for the two possibilities, we get

$P_0(T + h)$

$$P_0(T + h) \approx (1 - \lambda h)P_0(T) + (1 - \lambda h)(\mu h)P_1(T)$$

Now, let's determine $P_n(T + h)$ for $n > 0$. Either (a) n customers are in the system at Time T, no customer arrives, and the service is not completed; (b) n customers are in the system at Time T, one customer arrives, and the service is completed; (c) $(n - 1)$ customers are in the system at Time T, one customer arrives, and the service is not completed; or (d) $(n + 1)$ customers are in the system at Time T, no customer arrives, and the service is completed. For $n > 0$,

$P_n(T + h)$, $n \geq 1$

$$P_n(T + h) \approx (1 - \lambda h)(1 - \mu h)P_n(T) + (\lambda h)(\mu h)P_n(T)$$
$$+ (\lambda h)(1 - \mu h)P_{n-1}(T) + (1 - \lambda h)(\mu h)P_{n+1}(T)$$

Subtracting $P_n(T)$ from both sides of the above equation, dividing by h, and taking the limit as $h \to 0$ yields

$$\frac{dP_n(T)}{dT} = \lambda P_{n-1}(T) - (\lambda + \mu)P_n(T) + \mu P_{n+1}(T) \quad \text{for } n > 0$$

where $\dfrac{dP_n(T)}{dT}$ is the derivative of $P_n(T)$ with respect to T. A similar operation on the $n = 0$ approximation formula yields

$$\frac{dP_0(T)}{dT} = -\lambda P_0(T) + \mu P_1(T) \quad \text{for } n = 0$$

Transient probabilities

Steady state probabilities

You get the *transient probabilities, $P_n(T)$,* by solving the infinite set of differential equations. Even for this simple waiting line system, finding the transient probabilities is hard.

Now let's show how to find the steady state probabilities. *Steady state* is achieved when $P_n(T)$ doesn't change with T. At the steady state, the derivatives with respect to time are 0. Dropping the argument T, we obtain the following system of equations for the steady state probabilities:

$$0 = -\lambda P_0 + \mu P_1 \quad n = 0$$

$$0 = \lambda P_{n-1} - (\lambda + \mu)P_n + \mu P_{n+1} \quad n = 1, 2, 3, \ldots$$

Because the waiting line has no size limit, there are an infinite number of linear equations. Solving an infinite number of equations is generally difficult, but we can solve them in this case. From the first equation,

$$P_1 = P_0\left(\frac{\lambda}{\mu}\right) = P_0\rho$$

Solving recursively for $n = 1, 2, 3, \ldots$

$$P_n = P_0\rho^n$$

Since $\sum\limits_{n=0}^{\infty} P_n = 1$, it can be shown that $P_0 = (1 - \rho)$, so that $P_n = (1 - \rho)\rho^n$, for $n = 0, 1, 2, \ldots$

The expected number in the system is found using the steady state probabilities of the number in the system. Using algebraic manipulation and infinite sums, you obtain the formula found in the M/M/1 section,

$$L_s = \sum_{n=0}^{\infty} n(1 - \rho)\rho^n = \frac{\rho}{(1 - \rho)}$$

The relationships between waiting line lengths and times are given by **Little's formulas,**

$$L_s = \lambda_{\text{eff}}T_s \text{ and } L_q = \lambda_{\text{eff}}T_q$$

The **effective arrival rate** is represented by λ_{eff}. If some arrivals don't join the system, then λ_{eff} is smaller than λ. For example, limited waiting space or balking can cause some arrivals not to join the system. We discuss this further when we discuss the M/M/S waiting line system with finite waiting space. Little's formulas are useful under conditions much more general than the M/M/1 system, including many systems with multiple servers. For the M/M/1 system, $\lambda_{eff} = \lambda$ because all arrivals join the system. Therefore, you calculate the expected time in the system as

$$T_s = \left(\frac{1}{\lambda}\right)L_s = \frac{1}{\mu(1 - \rho)}$$

You calculate the expected waiting time, T_q, by subtracting the expected service time from T_s. Then, L_q is calculated using Little's formula.

Reasons that it's difficult to get analytical results

In this section, we've shown that finding analytical results for the simple M/M/1 model is difficult. If the probability distribution of interarrival times is not memoryless, writing the equations relating $P_n(T+h)$ to $P_n(T)$ is even more difficult. For this reason, the analytical results that are available usually have the memoryless property for customer arrivals. Balking, reneging, multiple servers, and other considerations also complicate the equations, which makes finding the transient probabilities more difficult. Remember, those equations are used to develop a set of differential equations that must be solved to find the transient probabilities. Analytically solving the differential equations to get the transient probabilities is often impossible. To find the steady state probabilities, you must solve a number (perhaps infinite) of simultaneous equations. This can be difficult if the equations aren't linear or if there are an infinite number of them and they can't be solved recursively. Even if you can find the steady state probabilities, it may be impossible to do algebraic manipulations to find formulas to calculate performance measures, such as the expected number in line.

Finding analytical results is difficult for many waiting line systems. Thus, you may not be able to find analytical results for your particular waiting line system. If so, you might use the analytical results for a model that is "close" to your waiting line system. But you should understand the model's assumptions and their role in obtaining the analytical results. Then, you can evaluate the significance of differences between those assumptions and your waiting line system.

For Xerox's study, the service times included the time spent in traveling plus the time spent in repairing the equipment. Xerox found that the service times weren't accurately represented by an exponential probability distribution. Even so, Xerox used analytical models for preliminary evaluation of the number of people assigned to a miniteam. This eliminated teams with fewer than three pesons and more than four persons from further consideration. Then, Xerox used computer simulation to do detailed analyses of three- and four-person miniteams.

STEADY STATE ANALYTICAL RESULTS FOR OTHER WAITING LINE SYSTEMS

In this section, we discuss analytical *steady state* results for several waiting line systems. For each system, the steady state probabilities, expected number in the system, expected number in line, expected time in the system, and expected time in line are given. In the following section, we use these results to compare different waiting line configurations.

Multiple Parallel Servers and Infinite Population (M/M/S)

μ is the service rate for *each* server

Assume an infinite customer population with exponential interarrival times and arrival rate λ. Also assume that there are S servers in parallel, *each* having an exponential service time distribution with service rate μ. For example, assume that a bank has S teller windows and that customers wait in a single line and go to the first available teller. Because the tellers have equal skill, the servers have the same service rate. Assume that there are n customers in the system. If $n \leq S$, all of the customers are being served and no one is waiting in line. If $n > S$, S customers are obtaining service and $n - S$ customers are waiting in line. The combined service rate for the S servers is μS. If $\lambda > \mu S$, customers arrive at a rate faster than they are served and the line becomes longer and longer. For the following steady state results, we *assume* that $\lambda \leq \mu S$. We also assume an infinite queue and no balking or reneging.

The steady state probabilities of the number in the system are

Steady state probabilities

$$
P_n = \begin{cases} \dfrac{(\lambda/\mu)^n}{n!} \, P_0, & \text{if } 0 \leq n < S; \\[2ex] \dfrac{(\lambda/\mu)^n}{S!S^{n-s}} \, P_0, & \text{if } n \geq S \end{cases}
$$

where the probability of no customers in the system, P_0, is

$$
P_0 = \cfrac{1}{\displaystyle\sum_{n=0}^{S-1} \dfrac{(\lambda/\mu)^n}{n!} + \dfrac{(\lambda/\mu)^S}{S!} \dfrac{1}{1 - \lambda/(\mu S)}}
$$

The expected number in line is

$$
L_q = E(\text{line length}) = \cfrac{\left(\dfrac{\lambda}{\mu}\right)^S \dfrac{\lambda}{\mu S}}{S!\left(1 - \dfrac{\lambda}{\mu S}\right)^2} P_0
$$

The expected number of customers in service is $\frac{\lambda}{\mu}$. The expected number in the system is

$$L_s = E(\text{line length}) + E(\text{number in service}) = L_q + \frac{\lambda}{\mu}$$

By assumption, no customers leave the system without obtaining service, so $\lambda_{\text{eff}} = \lambda$. Using Little's formula, the expected time in the system is

$$T_s = E(\text{time in system}) = \frac{L_q}{\lambda} + \frac{1}{\mu}$$

The expected time in line equals the expected time in the system minus the expected service time, $\frac{1}{\mu}$.

$$T_q = E(\text{time in line}) = T_s - \frac{1}{\mu} = \frac{L_q}{\lambda}$$

If the number of customers in the system is S or greater, all of the servers are busy.

$$P_b = P(n \geq S) = \frac{\left(\frac{\lambda}{\mu}\right)^S}{S!\left(1 - \frac{\lambda}{\mu S}\right)} P_0$$

The probability that a customer must wait for service is the probability that all of the servers are busy, $P(n \geq S)$.

Calculating P_0

P_0 is required to calculate the above measures of performance. Since the calculation of P_0 is tedious for large values of S, Table 14.5 is used to calculate the value of P_0. Because the quantities L_s, T_q, and T_s are expressed as dependent on L_q, they are calculated after L_q has been calculated. The utilization of the M/M/S system is $\frac{\lambda}{\mu S}$, the arrival rate divided by the combined service rate.

Multiple Parallel Servers and Finite Population (M/M/S with Finite Population of N Customers)

λ is the arrival rate for each customer

Assume a finite population of N customers, each with an *individual* arrival rate of λ. Also assume that the interarrival times for each customer have an exponential distribution. The arrival rate to the system depends on the number not already in the system. If no customers are in the system, the arrival rate is λN. If n customers are present in the system, the arrival rate is $\lambda(N - n)$. Assume that there are S parallel servers, where $S < N$, that the customers wait in a single line, and that the queue discipline is FCFS. Also assume an infinite queue and no balking or

TABLE 14.5   Values of P_0 for M/M/S Waiting Line System

$\frac{\lambda}{\mu S}$	Number of Servers—S									
	1	2	3	4	5	6	7	8	9	10
.02	.98000	.96078	.94176	.92312	.90484	.88692	.86936	.85214	.83527	.81873
.04	.96000	.92308	.88692	.85214	.81873	.78663	.75578	.72615	.69768	.67032
.06	.94000	.88679	.83526	.78663	.74082	.69768	.65705	.61878	.58275	.54881
.08	.92000	.85185	.78659	.72614	.67032	.61878	.57121	.52729	.48675	.44933
.10	.90000	.81818	.74074	.67031	.60653	.54881	.49659	.44933	.40657	.36788
.12	.88000	.78571	.69753	.61876	.54881	.48675	.43171	.38289	.33960	.30119
.14	.86000	.75439	.65679	.57116	.49657	.43171	.37531	.32628	.28365	.24660
.16	.84000	.72414	.61837	.52720	.44931	.38289	.32628	.27804	.23693	.20190
.18	.82000	.69492	.58214	.48660	.40653	.33959	.28365	.23693	.19790	.16530
.20	.80000	.66667	.54795	.44910	.36782	.30118	.24659	.20189	.16530	.13534
.22	.78000	.63934	.51567	.41445	.33277	.26711	.21437	.17204	.13807	.11080
.24	.76000	.61290	.48519	.38244	.30105	.23688	.18636	.14660	.11532	.09072
.26	.74000	.58730	.45640	.35284	.27233	.21007	.16200	.12492	.09632	.07427
.28	.72000	.56250	.42918	.32548	.24633	.18628	.14082	.10645	.08045	.06081
.30	.70000	.53846	.40346	.30017	.22277	.16517	.12241	.09070	.06720	.04978
.32	.68000	.51515	.37913	.27676	.20144	.14644	.10639	.07728	.05612	.04076
.34	.66000	.49254	.35610	.25510	.18211	.12981	.09247	.06584	.04687	.03337
.36	.64000	.47059	.33431	.23505	.16460	.11505	.08035	.05609	.03915	.02732
.38	.62000	.44928	.31367	.21649	.14872	.10195	.06981	.04778	.03269	.02236
.40	.60000	.42857	.29412	.19929	.13433	.09032	.06064	.04069	.02729	.01830
.42	.58000	.40845	.27559	.18336	.12128	.07998	.05267	.03465	.02279	.01498
.44	.56000	.38889	.25802	.16860	.10944	.07080	.04573	.02950	.01902	.01226
.46	.54000	.36986	.24135	.15491	.09870	.06265	.03968	.02511	.01587	.01003
.48	.52000	.35135	.22554	.14221	.08895	.05540	.03442	.02136	.01324	.00820
.50	.50000	.33333	.21053	.13043	.08010	.04896	.02984	.01816	.01104	.00671
.52	.48000	.31579	.19627	.11951	.07207	.04323	.02586	.01544	.00920	.00548
.54	.46000	.29870	.18273	.10936	.06477	.03814	.02239	.01311	.00767	.00448
.56	.44000	.28205	.16986	.09994	.05814	.03362	.01936	.01113	.00638	.00366
.58	.42000	.26582	.15762	.09119	.05212	.02959	.01673	.00943	.00531	.00298
.60	.40000	.25000	.14599	.08306	.04665	.02601	.01443	.00799	.00441	.00243
.62	.38000	.23457	.13491	.07750	.04167	.02282	.01243	.00675	.00366	.00198
.64	.36000	.21951	.12438	.06847	.03715	.01999	.01069	.00570	.00303	.00161
.66	.34000	.20482	.11435	.06194	.03304	.01746	.00918	.00480	.00251	.00131
.68	.32000	.19048	.10479	.05587	.02930	.01522	.00786	.00404	.00207	.00106
.70	.30000	.17647	.09569	.05021	.02590	.01322	.00670	.00338	.00170	.00085
.72	.28000	.16279	.08702	.04495	.02280	.01144	.00570	.00283	.00140	.00069
.74	.26000	.14943	.07875	.04006	.01999	.00986	.00483	.00235	.00114	.00055
.76	.24000	.13636	.07087	.03550	.01743	.00846	.00407	.00195	.00093	.00044
.78	.22000	.12360	.06335	.03125	.01510	.00721	.00341	.00160	.00075	.00035
.80	.20000	.11111	.05618	.02730	.01299	.00610	.00284	.00131	.00060	.00028
.82	.18000	.09890	.04933	.02362	.01106	.00511	.00234	.00106	.00048	.00022
.84	.16000	.08696	.04280	.02019	.00931	.00423	.00190	.00085	.00038	.00017
.86	.14000	.07527	.03656	.01700	.00772	.00345	.00153	.00067	.00029	.00013
.88	.12000	.06383	.03060	.01403	.00627	.00276	.00120	.00052	.00022	.00010
.90	.10000	.05263	.02491	.01126	.00496	.00215	.00092	.00039	.00017	.00007
.92	.08000	.04167	.01947	.00867	.00377	.00161	.00068	.00028	.00012	.00005
.94	.06000	.03093	.01427	.00627	.00268	.00113	.00047	.00019	.00008	.00003
.96	.04000	.02041	.00930	.00403	.00170	.00070	.00029	.00012	.00005	.00002
.98	.02000	.01010	.00454	.00194	.00081	.00033	.00013	.00005	.00002	.00001

reneging, and assume that the service times for any server have an exponential distribution with parameter μ.

The steady state probabilities of the number in the system are

$$
P_n = \begin{cases}
\dfrac{N!}{(N-n)!n!} \, (\lambda/\mu)^n P_0, & \text{if } 0 \le n < S; \\[2ex]
\dfrac{N!}{(N-n)!S!S^{n-S}} \, (\lambda/\mu)^n P_0, & \text{if } S \le n \le N; \\[2ex]
0, & \text{if } n > N
\end{cases}
$$

where P_0 is calculated by

$$
P_0 = \frac{1}{\displaystyle\sum_{n=0}^{S-1} \frac{N!}{(N-n)!n} \left(\frac{\lambda}{\mu}\right)^n + \sum_{n=S}^{N} \frac{N!}{(N-n)!S!S^{n-S}} \left(\frac{\lambda}{\mu}\right)^n}
$$

The expected number in the system is calculated as

$$
L_s = \sum_{n=1}^{N} n P_n
$$

Because the arrival rate depends on the number in the system, λ_{eff} must be calculated. The expected number of customers not in the system is $N - L_s$, so the effective arrival rate is

$$
\lambda_{\text{eff}} = \lambda(N - L_s)
$$

Using Little's formula, the expected time in the system is

$$
T_s = \frac{L_s}{\lambda_{\text{eff}}}
$$

You calculate the expected time in line by subtracting the expected service time from T_s:

$$
T_q = T_s - \frac{1}{\mu}
$$

Using Little's formula, the expected number in the line is

$$
L_q = \lambda_{\text{eff}} T_q
$$

The probability of all the servers being busy is $P(n \ge S)$. The probability that a customer must wait in line before obtaining service is the probability of all the servers being busy, $P(n \ge S)$.

Xerox used this model to evaluate different sizes of miniteams. The finite population size, N, was the number of customers in the geographic service region. The number of parallel servers, S, was the number of miniteam members. By setting the number of servers to 1, Xerox evaluated the performance of one-person territories.

In this section, we discuss the results for a generalization of the M/M/1 waiting line system in which a general probability distribution is allowed for the service time. All of the other assumptions are the same as those for the M/M/1 section. Among these assumptions are an infinite customer population, an infinite queue, and no balking or reneging.

We assume that the interarrival times have an exponential distribution

General service times   with mean $\frac{1}{\lambda}$. Service times can have any probability distribution with

mean $\frac{1}{\mu}$ and variance denoted by V. As in the M/M/1 system, $\rho = \frac{\lambda}{\mu}$. The expected number in the system is

$$L_s = \rho + \frac{\lambda^2 V + \rho^2}{2(1 - \rho)}$$

Note that the expected number in the system depends on the mean and variance of the service time but not on any other parameters of its probability distribution. The probability of the server being busy is

$$P_b = P(n \geq 1) = \rho$$

Note that the probability of the server being busy is independent of the variance of the service time. ρ is also the expected number of customers in service. The expected number in line is

$$L_q = L_s - \rho = \frac{\lambda^2 V + \rho^2}{2(1 - \rho)}$$

Because no customers leave the system without obtaining service, $\lambda_{\text{eff}} = \lambda$. Using Little's formula, the expected time in the system is

$$T_s = \frac{L_s}{\lambda}$$

The expected time in line is calculated by subtracting the expected service time from T_s.

$$T_q = T_s - \frac{1}{\mu} = \frac{L_q}{\lambda}$$

Deterministic service times   If the variance of the service time, V is 0, the M/G/1 model has an interesting special case. If $V = 0$, the service time is *deterministic*—that is, the M/D/1 model. Deterministic service times occur for example, when the service is automatic and constant. As the variance of the service time increases, the L_s, L_q, T_s, and T_q all increase.

Single Server, Infinite Population, Finite Queue (M/M/1 with Finite Capacity of M)

In this section, we give results for the M/M/1 system with limited customer waiting space. Because there is space for M customers in the system, there is space for $(M - 1)$ customers to wait. If there are M customers in the system and another customer tries to arrive, we assume that this customer leaves the system because there is no space in the waiting line. All of the other assumptions for the M/M/1 system remain the same. That is, the customer population is infinite and there is no balking or reneging. Note that even if $\lambda > \mu$, the steady state results apply. In this case, however, a greater proportion of customers who try to join the system leave because there is not enough waiting space.

The steady state probabilities of the number in the system depend on whether $\lambda = \mu$. For $n > M$, $P_n = 0$. For $n = 0, 1, \ldots, M$,

$$P_n = \begin{cases} \dfrac{1-\rho}{1-\rho^{M+1}}\rho^n, & \text{if } \lambda \neq \mu; \\ \dfrac{1}{M+1}, & \text{if } \lambda = \mu \end{cases}$$

Steady state probabilities

Note that P_0 is not $(1 - \rho)$.

The expected number in the system is

$$L_s = \begin{cases} \dfrac{\rho}{1-\rho} - \dfrac{(M+1)\rho^{M+1}}{1-\rho^{M+1}}, & \text{if } \lambda \neq \mu; \\ \dfrac{M}{2}, & \text{if } \lambda = \mu \end{cases}$$

The expected number in line is

$$L_q = L_s - (1 - P_0)$$

If a customer attempts to arrive and M customers are already present, the customer leaves without service. Thus, the arrival rate is 0 with probability P_M and is λ with probability $(1 - P_M)$. The effective arrival rate is

The effective arrival rate

$$\lambda_{\text{eff}} = [0P_M] + [\lambda(1 - P_M)] = \lambda(1 - P_M)$$

Using Little's formula, the expected time in the system is calculated as

$$T_s = \frac{L_s}{\lambda(1 - P_M)}$$

Similarly, the expected time in line is

$$T_q = \frac{L_q}{\lambda(1 - P_M)}$$

APPLICATIONS OF STEADY STATE ANALYTICAL RESULTS FOR WAITING LINE SYSTEMS

This section has examples that illustrate the use of steady state results to compare waiting line configurations. A good user of the waiting line models must be aware of the assumptions and shortcomings underlying the analytical results for each waiting line system. The examples all use *steady state* measures of performance. Ask yourself whether you should use steady state conditions for each of these examples.

Example 1: Truck Loading

A company has a single dock for loading trucks that deliver its finished products to its regional warehouses. The company has a large number of trucks and regional warehouses, and the arrival times of the trucks to be loaded are unpredictable. Trucks arrive at an average rate of three per hour. If a truck is being loaded while another arrives, the second must wait until the first has been loaded. A large number of trucks have had to wait to be loaded. The company estimates that the time a truck is in the system has a value of $10 per hour.

Although there is only one loading dock, the company can decrease the time required to load a truck by having more employees at the loading dock. Currently, it has assigned four employees to the loading dock at a cost of $8 per hour each. The total cost of the four employees is $32 per hour. Because of differences in the amounts to be loaded, the time required to load a truck is not constant. The crew of four employees can load an average of four trucks per hour. The manager believes that the average number of trucks loaded per hour is *equal* to the number of employees at the loading dock. For example, if five employees are at the loading dock, the average number of trucks loaded in an hour is five.

Increasing the number of employees at the loading dock decreases the time required to load a truck, which also decreases the number of trucks that must wait for loading to begin. The waiting time in line and the service time both decrease, thus decreasing the cost of having a truck in the loading dock system. However, increasing the number of employees at the loading dock decreases the utilization of their time and increases the hourly cost of loading dock employees.

Say that the manager decides to use the sum of the cost of the truck in the loading dock system and the cost of the employees at the loading dock as the criterion for comparing configurations.

The evaluation criterion

From historical records, the manager knows that the interarrival times have an exponential distribution with an arrival rate, λ, of three trucks per hour. The mean interarrival time is $\frac{1}{\lambda} = \frac{1}{3}$ hour. From examining historical records, the manager believes that the loading time has an exponential distribution with a rate equal to the number of employees at the loading dock. Because there is only one loading dock, the M/M/1 waiting line can be used.

Let's consider how many employees should be at the loading dock to minimize the system cost. First, consider the current configuration with four employees at the loading dock. The service rate, $\mu = 4$ per hour, and the mean service time is $\frac{1}{\mu} = \frac{1}{4} = 0.25$ hour. The probability that the loading dock is occupied when a truck arrives is

$$P_b = \rho = \frac{\lambda}{\mu} = \frac{3}{4} = 0.75$$

The actual observation that a large number of trucks must wait before being loaded is predicted by the model. The expected number in the loading dock system is $L_s = \frac{3}{(4-3)} = 3$ trucks. The expected number of trucks in the loading dock system includes the truck being loaded and those waiting to be loaded. The expected time in the loading dock system is

$$T_s = \frac{1}{(\mu - \lambda)} = \frac{1}{(4-3)} = 1 \text{ hour}$$

The average loading time is 0.25 hours, so the expected time waiting is $1 - 0.25 = 0.75$ hours.

Let's calculate the *expected cost per hour* of operation for the current configuration of four employees at the loading dock. The cost of the four employees is $32 per hour. *Because the average number of arrivals per hour is three and the time in the system per truck is one hour, the total truck time in the system per hour $= 3 \times 1 = 3$ hours.* The cost per hour for trucks in the system is $10 \times 3 = 30. The combined cost per hour is $32 + $30 = 62.

Four employees

Five employees

Consider adding a fifth employee at the loading dock. Then, the service rate, $\mu = 5$ per hour, and the mean service time is $\frac{1}{\mu} = \frac{1}{5} = 0.20$ hour. Now, $\rho = \frac{3}{5} = 0.6$. The probability that the loading dock is occupied when a truck arrives decreases to $P_b = \rho = 0.6$. The expected number of trucks in the loading dock system decreases to $L_s = \frac{3}{(5-3)} = 1.5$. The expected time in the loading dock system decreases by one half, to $T_s = \frac{1}{(5-3)} = 0.5$ hours. The average loading time decreases to 0.2 hours, so the expected waiting time is $0.5 - 0.2 = 0.3$ hours.

For five employees at the loading dock, the employee cost per hour is $5 \times $8 = 40. The cost per hour for trucks in the system is $10 \times 3 \times 0.5 = 15. Why does the 3 appear in the expression? You include it because you are calculating the hourly cost and 3 is the average number of arrivals per hour. Because the average time in the system per truck is 0.5, the total truck time in the system per hour is $3 \times 0.5 = 1.5$ hours. The combined cost per hour is $40 + $15 = $55. If the number of employees at the loading dock increases from four to five, the combined cost decreases from $62 to $55 per hour.

Table 14.6 summarizes results for four, five, six, and seven employees at the loading dock. The combined cost per hour is smallest for five employees at the waiting dock. Recall that a concern was the large number of trucks that had to wait before loading. The probability that a truck must wait continues to decrease when more employees are at the loading dock, but the combined cost increases when the crew size is more than five. The manager must decide whether a 0.6 probability of a truck waiting is truly objectionable or whether the combined cost is more important. This illustrates the conflicting nature of measures of performance in the analysis of waiting line configurations.

Model manipulation and sensitivity analysis

We assumed that the loading rate equaled the number of employees at the loading dock. But if the number of employees is large enough, they are likely to be "tripping over each other." For example, when five employees are at the loading dock, the loading rate might be 4.8 trucks per hour. It is no more difficult to do the calculations, and we leave them to the Exercises.

We found that having five employees at the loading dock minimizes the cost. However, this is based on the assumption that the truck arrival rate is three per hour and that the service rate equals the number of employees at the loading dock. Because there may be uncertainty about these rates, you can do sensitivity analysis to study how sensitive the best decision is to them. For example, you can find how small the arrival rate must be for four employees to have a smaller combined cost than five employees.

TABLE 14.6 Example 1: Measures of Performance for Different Numbers of Employees Assigned to Loading Dock

	Number of Employees at Loading Dock			
	4	5	6	7
P_b	0.750	0.600	0.500	0.429
L_q	2.250	0.900	0.500	0.321
L_s	3.000	1.500	1.000	0.750
T_q	0.750	0.300	0.167	0.107
T_s	1.000	0.500	0.333	0.250
Employee cost per hour	$32	$40	$48	$56
Total time in system cost per hour	30	15	10	7.50
Combined cost per hour	$62	$55	$58	$63.50

Also, if there is uncertainty about the loading rate being five per hour when five employees are at the loading dock, you can perform sensitivity analysis on the loading rate.

Is it reasonable to use steady state results?

The results summarized in Table 14.6 are based on steady state conditions. If the loading dock operates 24 hours a day and 7 days a week, steady state is likely to be achieved. On the other hand, if the loading dock operates from 8 A.M. to 4 P.M. Monday through Friday, steady state may never be achieved. In the latter case, the conditions at the beginning and end of each day are important in the analysis. Could trucks be waiting for loading at 8 A.M. when the loading dock begins operation? What happens at 4 P.M. if one or more trucks are at the loading dock? Does loading stop during the lunch period? Do trucks continue to arrive at the loading dock during the lunch period? These are important considerations that the M/M/1 steady state results ignore. Also, do you believe that the arrival rate of trucks is independent of the time of day? If the loading dock operates 24 hours a day, the arrival rate is usually greater during normal working hours and smaller between midnight and 6 A.M. The M/M/1 model assumes that the arrival rate doesn't change with time.

Even though not all of the assumptions made in the development of the analytical steady state results are true, the results are still useful. The model is only a selective representation of the decision environment. Steady state results provide insights into the decision environment that are not otherwise available. But a manager who uses the results to the best advantage must understand the underlying assumptions and the limitations.

Consequences of model prediction errors

Remember that the loading dock manager was concerned with the large number of trucks that had to wait for loading. The loading dock manager used the model to choose the number of employees at the loading dock. The M/M/1 model predicts that if a fifth employee is added at the loading dock, fewer trucks must wait and the combined cost decreases. Based on the analysis, the loading dock manager would add a fifth employee. Say that the cost reduction predicted by the model is not achieved. Then, the manager can revert to assigning four employees to the loading dock. In this case, it's possible to try different configurations and compare actual performance against the model's predictions. The consequences of incorrect predictions by the model aren't as serious as those for the next configuration change that we discuss.

Adding a second loading dock

Another possible configuration change is building a second loading dock. Adding a loading dock decreases the number of trucks that must wait. You can evaluate this possibility using the M/M/2 waiting line model. However, you should be confident of your decision to add a loading dock, because it requires a capital expenditure. In this case, the consequences of the actual performance differing from the model's prediction are serious. After you've built the second loading dock, the money spent for it is gone. If you revert to using a single loading dock, you still paid for the new loading dock. For this reason, you should be more cautious about accepting the model's underlying assumptions. You might use the M/M/2 model for preliminary evaluation of adding a second loading dock. If it appears worthwhile, you should examine the underlying assumptions. If some assumptions are questionable (e.g., steady state conditions), a computer simulation study using the methods of Chapters 15 and 16 might be justified. While the simulation study is more expensive than using analytical results, you can easily incorporate important deviations from the underlying assumptions of the analytical waiting line model into it. You must compare the additional cost of the simulation study with the improvement in the model's accuracy.

Example 2: Secretarial Pool

A company has one secretary for each ot two departments. The secretaries perform typing only for the assigned department. The manager of the two departments has suggested forming a "pool" of the two secretaries. Under this arrangement, either secretary would do typing for either department as needed. The supervisor of each department is concerned that this would slow down the turnaround of typing. What do you think?

At each department, the average rate of typing requests is 2.5 per hour. The typists require an average of 10 minutes for each project. However, this varies because of the varying complexity of the projects. Let's use waiting line analytical results to compare the current, independent configuration with a pool.

Under the present arrangement, you can use the M/M/1 waiting line model for each department. Based on an average service time of 10 minutes, the service rate, μ, is 6 per hour *for each secretary*. The arrival rate, λ, is 2.5 per hour *for each secretary*. For each secretary, $\rho = \dfrac{2.5}{6} = 0.4167$. Considering the secretaries independently, the M/M/1 steady state results give a time in the system of $T_s = \dfrac{1}{(6-2.5)} = 0.2857$ hours or 17.14 minutes. The mean service time is 10 minutes, so the average time that a project waits for typing to begin is 7.14 minutes. The probability that a project has to wait is $P_b = \rho = 0.4167$. The average number of typing projects waiting on each secretary's desk is $L_q = \dfrac{2.5^2}{6(6-2.5)} = 0.2976$. The average total number of projects waiting on the two secretaries' desks is $2 \times 0.2976 = 0.5952$.

To consider the pool configuration, the M/M/2 steady state results are used. The combined arrival rate for the pool is $2 \times 2.5 = 5$ projects per hour. The service rate for each server, μ, is 6 per hour. S, the number of parallel servers, is 2. The probability of no typing projects in the system is

$$P_0 = \cfrac{1}{\cfrac{(5/6)^0}{0!} + \cfrac{(5/6)^1}{1!} + \cfrac{(5/6)^2}{2!}\left(1 - \cfrac{1}{5/(2 \times 6)}\right)} = 0.4118$$

Using P_0, calculate $P_1 = \dfrac{(5/6)^1}{1} 0.4118 = 0.3432$. The probability that a project has to wait before typing begins is $P(n \geq 2) = 1 - (P_0 + P_1) = 1 - (0.4118 + 0.3432) = 0.2450$. The probability that a project has to wait before typing begins is decreased from 0.4167 to 0.2450. The number of documents waiting for typing is

$$L_q = \cfrac{\left(\dfrac{5}{6}\right)^2\left(\dfrac{5}{2 \times 6}\right)}{2!\left[1 - \left(\dfrac{5}{2 \times 6}\right)\right]^2}0.4118 = 0.1751$$

The number of projects waiting to be typed is decreased from 0.5952 to 0.1751. The number of projects in the system is $L_s = 0.1751 + \dfrac{5}{6} = 1.0084$. The time in the system is $T_s = \dfrac{1.0084}{5} = 0.2017$ hours or 12.102 minutes. The time of projects in the system is decreased from 17.14 to 12.102 minutes by converting to the pool configuration.

Table 14.7 summarizes the calculations for the two configurations. The pool configuration is preferable to the current configuration. This illustrates the fact that a single waiting line is preferable to multiple waiting lines for a system with parallel servers. Treating each secretary as responsible for only a single department introduced a separate waiting line for each server. Pooling the secretaries gave a single waiting line. A major advantage of pooling resulted from assigning a waiting project in one department to the other department's secretary if that secretary wasn't busy.

Other considerations   The assumption that the typing time for a document has an exponential probability distribution is not realistic in some situations. If another distribution is correct, you can use the M/G/1 model to analyze the current, independent configuration. No model presented in this chapter is correct for analyzing the pool configuration. A computer simulation study using the methods of Chapters 15 and 16 can be performed to analyze the pool configuration.

TABLE 14.7   Example 2: Independent or Pool Secretaries

	Independent	Pool
Expected time in system	0.2857 hours	0.2017 hours
Expected total number of projects waiting	0.5952	0.1751
Probability that a project must wait	0.4167	0.1020

Also, the assumption that the service rates for the two secretaries are equal is not realistic in some situations. Different typing skills give different service rates. For the current, independent configuration, the M/M/1 model is used with different service rates for the two servers. You can't use the M/M/S model, because it assumes that all servers have the same service rate. Thus, no model presented in this chapter is correct for analyzing the pool configuration.

A computer simulation can be performed to evaluate the pool configuration with unequal service rates. But a good manager compares the cost of a simulation study with the benefits. It is possible to change to a pool configuration and try it for a while without doing the simulation study. Building a second loading dock is expensive to try, but changing to a pool configuration isn't. The cost of a simulation study is likely to be more expensive than just trying the secretarial pool for a while. It is easier to justify a simulation study for building a second loading dock than one for examining a secretarial pool with unequal abilities.

Behavioral
considerations

Also, behavioral implications of a noneconomic nature must be considered. Will a pool lose the close supervision of the secretary and result in increased typing times for projects? Will a pool result in a loss of "departmental spirit" that yields extraordinary efforts to complete major projects by deadlines? Do the secretaries strongly prefer the present arrangement, and will they thus be induced to sabotage the experiment? The prudent manager considers behavioral and organizational factors as well as economic ones.

Example 3: Machine Repair

A company is studying the number of mechanics available to repair machines that break down. Management scientists call this problem the **Machine Interference model.** The company has five very complex and critical machines. For each machine, the mean time to break down is five days and has an exponential probability distribution. The time required to repair any of the machines has an exponential probability distribution with an average of one day. The company has three mechanics of equal ability to repair the machines. Only one mechanic works on a machine at a time. Because there are only three mechanics, if four machines require repair, one machine sits without a mechanic until a mechanic becomes available. That is why the company has three mechanics. If there were five mechanics, no machine would ever sit without a mechanic. The plant manager has noticed that the mechanics are usually not busy repairing the machines. In the last year, there has not been a single occurrence in which a machine sat without a mechanic. Reducing the number of mechanics is being contemplated. First, say that the plant manager wants you to calculate the probability that a machine ever sits waiting for a mechanic under the current situation (three mechanics) and the expected cost during a year for a machine just "sitting." The cost per idle day is $10,000.

The analytical model is the M/M/3 system with a finite customer population, $N = 5$. An arrival corresponds to a machine breakdown. Because the average time until a breakdown of a machine is 5 days, the arrival rate *per machine*, $\lambda = \frac{1}{5}$ or 0.2 per day. The servers are the 3 mechanics, and $\mu = 1$ for each server.

First, P_0 must be calculated:

$$P_0 = \cfrac{1}{\dfrac{5!}{5!0!}(0.2)^0 + \dfrac{5!}{(5-1)!1!}(0.2)^1 + \dfrac{5!}{(5-2)!2!}(0.2)^2 + \dfrac{5!}{(5-3)!3!3^{3-3}}(0.2)^3 + \dfrac{5!}{(5-4)!3!3^{4-3}}(0.2)^4 + \dfrac{5!}{(5-5)!3!3^{5-3}}(0.2)^5}$$

Thus, $P_o = 1/(1. + 1. + 0.4 + 0.08 + 0.01067 + 0.00071) = 0.40138$. You calculate the other probabilities as follows: $P_1 = 1. \times 0.40138 = 0.40138$; $P_2 = 0.4 \times 0.40138 = 0.16055$; $P_3 = 0.08 \times 0.40138 = 0.03211$; $P_4 = 0.01067 \times 0.40138 = 0.00428$; and $P_5 = 0.00071 \times 0.40138 = 0.00029$. The probability that a machine sits when it needs repair is the probability that there are three or more machines in the system, or $P_3 + P_4 + P_5 = 0.03211 + 0.00428 + 0.00029 = 0.036678$. The plant manager observed that there had been no occurrence of a machine waiting for a mechanic in the last year. The model indicates that the probability of this is small, 0.03668.

The expected number in the system is the expected number of machines in need of repair:

$$L_s = 0 \times 0.40138 + 1 \times 0.40138 + 2 \times 0.16055 + 3 \times 0.03211 + 4 \times 0.00428 + 5 \times 0.00029 = 0.83738$$

The effective arrival rate is

$$\lambda_{\text{eff}} = 0.2(5 - 0.83738) = 0.83252$$

The expected time in the system is the expected time that a machine is broken:

$$T_s = \frac{L_s}{\lambda_{\text{eff}}} = \frac{0.83738}{0.83252} = 1.00583$$

The time in the queue (or line) is the time that a machine is sitting and waiting for a mechanic to become available:

$$T_q = T_s - \frac{1}{\mu} = 1.00583 - 1 = 0.00583$$

Expected annual breakdowns

The expected time that a machine is waiting for a mechanic to become available is 0.00583 days. If the company operates 365 days during a year, the expected annual number of arrivals (breakdowns) is $365 \times \lambda_{eff} = 365 \times 0.83253 = 303.87$. For a one-year period, the expected time that machines spend waiting for a mechanic is $0.00583 \times 303.87 = 1.7716$ days. At \$10,000 per day, that annual cost is \$17,716.

Now, say that the plant manager wants you to calculate the cost if the number of mechanics is reduced to two. You calculate the annual machine downtime cost for $S = 2$. Then, you compare the extra downtime cost to the savings in the mechanic's salary. We leave these calculations to the exercises.

Possible assumption violations

Some of the underlying assumptions are not reasonable in some cases. First, when a machine breaks down, all of the available mechanics often help in the repair. This usually reduces the average time needed to repair the machine. Second, the mechanics are often not of equal ability. Some have smaller average repair times. Third, we assumed that all of the machines had the same breakdown rate. Many times, this isn't true; nor is it true that all machines require the same average repair time.

In spite of the underlying assumptions, the machine interference model gives some insights that are not available otherwise. Computer simulation studies have shown that the analytical results are usually close to the actual results even when some assumptions are violated.

In conclusion, we note that analytical results exist for waiting line systems other than those presented in this chapter. If analytical results are not available for your waiting line system, computer simulation is an alternative. But you must compare the cost of the simulation study with the benefits of improved model accuracy. In many cases, you can use the analytical results for a system that isn't identical to your system instead of simulation. But you should be aware of the assumptions and limitations of the analytical results.

SUMMARY

Waiting is common in the modern world, and that causes the topic of this chapter to have many applications. Applications are common in service as well as manufacturing firms. Both profit-making and not-for-profit organizations must design and manage waiting line systems. Xerox applied waiting line theory to develop a new service strategy. We used queueing to determine the best crew size for a loading dock. Using two models from the chapter, we compared independent, departmental secretaries and a secretarial pool. The last application in the chapter studied the number of mechanics needed to repair machines in a manufacturing plant. These are just a few of the many applications of waiting lines.

Each waiting line system consists of customers, a queue discipline, and a service mechanism. Telephone calls, broken machines, trucks, and senior citizens could be the customers receiving directory assistance, repair, loading, and flu vaccination. In a computer network, the customers are computers and the server is another computer functioning as a file server. By changing the configuration of a waiting line, a manager affects its performance.

We described many of the considerations of waiting lines, including the size of the customer population, balking, reneging, the amount of waiting space, single versus bulk arrivals, preemption, the customer arrival pattern, the server skill level, service times, and the server organization. Among the many measures of performance of waiting line systems were time waiting and time in the system, number waiting and number in the system, customers leaving the system without receiving service, server utilization, and busy period characteristics.

We emphasized the distinction between steady state and transient probabilities. Steady state is achieved when the probabilities for the number in the system don't change with time. Before that, the transient probabilities are affected by the initial conditions of the waiting line system.

In this chapter, we presented analytical results for some waiting line configurations. These models have some limitations. First, none of the results were based on transient conditions. Even for simple configurations, finding the transient results is difficult. Second, each model is limited by its underlying assumptions. None of the models allow balking, reneging, or bulk arrivals. Before you use any model, compare its assumptions using our classification framework with your situation. Third, the models presented assumed that the parameters don't change over time. Many times, the arrival rate or the number of servers changes based on the time of day or the day of the week. Fourth, the models presented assumed that the servers all have the same skill levels. Often, a manager assigns customers to servers based on their skill levels as well as their availabilities.

Note some cautions. First, the system may not attain steady state, because it starts and stops each day. For example, the models don't consider lunch breaks. Second, you should perform sensitivity analysis to check the model's response to changes or errors in parameter estimates. For example, you must estimate arrival rates. You adjust the arrival rate and study the system's performance. This is one approach to studying a system in which the arrival rate changes by the time of day or the day of the week. Third, changes in a waiting line configuration that improve some measures of performance make others worse. Be careful of the measure of performance that you use to compare configurations. Fourth, consider whether it's possible to try a configuration at little or no cost. However, you must be aware of the behavioral and organizational impacts of configuration changes.

Although analytical results aren't available for many waiting line systems, you can use a similar model to quickly evaluate waiting line configurations. Computer simulation studies have shown that the actual results are usually similar to the results of a simplified model. Xerox used this approach to eliminate miniteams with other than three and four members from further consideration. You can use computer simulation for detailed analysis of waiting line systems with complicating considerations. The next two chapters discuss computer simulation.

QUESTIONS

1. Give an example of a finite customer population.
2. Discuss whether a bank teller serves an infinite population.
3. What is preemption?
4. What does M represent in M/M/1?
5. Give an example of a waiting line system in which transient conditions are of interest, but steady state conditions are not appropriate.
6. Give an example of a waiting line system in which steady state conditions are of interest.
7. What is balking? Give an example of a waiting line system in which balking is likely.
8. What is reneging? Give an example of a waiting line system in which reneging is likely.
9. What does FCFS represent? Give an example in which FCFS is not appropriate for the selection from among waiting customers.
10. What is a busy period?
11. If the mean interarrival time is 15 minutes, what is the arrival rate per hour?
12. What does λ represent, and what are its units?
13. What is the memoryless property?
14. Give two probability distributions with the memoryless property.
15. Is the normal distribution memoryless?
16. What is the effective arrival rate?
17. What is the difference between transient and steady state probabilities?
18. What is a random arrival pattern?
19. What are bulk arrivals?
20. Describe a situation with parallel servers.
21. Describe a situation with series servers.
22. What are analytical waiting line results?
23. What is queue discipline?
24. What are Little's formulas?
25. Give an example of Kendall notation.
26. What is the expected number in the system of an M/D/1 model?
27. What is the utilization of servers?

EXERCISES

1. A company has collected eight hours of data on the arrival times of its customers, starting at 8 A.M. The arrival times are

Customer	Time
1	8:25
2	9:10
3	10:05
4	10:45
5	10:55
6	11:20
7	11:40
8	12:05
9	12:15
10	12:35
11	1:00
12	1:05
13	1:45
14	2:30
15	2:45
16	3:15
17	3:35
18	4:00

   a. Calculate the average arrival rate in customers per hour.
   b. Calculate the 18 interarrival times.
   c. Calculate the average interarrival time.
   d. Is your answer to Part *a* equal to 1 divided by your answer to Part *c*? Why or why not?

2. A company has collected eight hours of data on the arrival times of its customers, starting at 8 A.M. The arrival times are

Customer	Time
1	8:05
2	9:15
3	9:55
4	10:25
5	10:55
6	11:10
7	11:55
8	12:05
9	12:55
10	1:05
11	1:20
12	1:45
13	2:00
14	2:25
15	2:40
16	3:05
17	3:45

a. Calculate the average arrival rate in customers per hour.
b. Calculate the 17 interarrival times.
c. Calculate the average interarrival time.
d. Is your answer to Part *a* equal to 1 divided by your answer to Part *c*? Why or why not?

3. If the probability distribution of interarrival times is exponential and the arrival rate is 4.0 per hour,
   a. Give the probability of zero arrivals in a one-hour period. One arrival. Two arrivals. Ten arrivals.
   b. What is the expected number of arrivals in a one-hour period? What is the variance of the number of arrivals in a one-hour period?
   c. Give the probability of zero arrivals in a two-hour period. One arrival. Two arrivals. Ten arrivals.
   d. What is the expected number of arrivals in a two-hour period? What is the variance of the number of arrivals in a two-hour period?

4. If the probability distribution of interarrival times is exponential and the arrival rate is 2.5 per hour,
   a. Give the probability of zero arrivals in a one-hour period. One arrival. Two arrivals. Ten arrivals.
   b. What is the expected number of arrivals in a one-hour period? What is the variance of the number of arrivals in a one-hour period?
   c. Give the probability of zero arrivals in a 90-minute period. One arrival. Two arrivals. Ten arrivals.
   d. What is the expected number of arrivals in a 90-minute period? What is the variance of the number of arrivals in a 90-minute period?

5. Complete the following table for the M/M/1 waiting line system with an infinite customer population and unlimited capacity for waiting customers.

	1.	2.	3.	3.9
Arrival rate	1.	2.	3.	3.9
Service rate	4.	4.	4.	4.0
Utilization				
L_s				
L_q				
T_s				
T_a				

6. Complete the following table for the M/M/1 waiting line system with an infinite customer population and unlimited capacity for waiting customers.

	10.	20.	30.	39.
Arrival rate	10.	20.	30.	39.
Service rate	40.	40.	40.	40.
Utilization				
L_s				
L_q				
T_s				
T_a				

7. Complete the following table for the M/M/1 waiting line system with an infinite customer population and unlimited capacity for waiting customers.

Arrival rate	1.	2.	3.	4.
Service rate	2.	4.	6.	8.
Utilization				
L_s				
L_q				
T_s				
T_q				

8. Complete the following table for the M/M/1 waiting line system with an infinite customer population and unlimited capacity for waiting customers.

Arrival rate	10.	20.	30.	40.
Service rate	15.	30.	45.	60.
Utilization				
L_s				
L_q				
T_s				
T_q				

9. Complete the following table for the M/M/1 waiting line system with an infinite customer population and unlimited capacity for waiting customers.

Arrival rate	1.	2.	3.	3.9
Service rate	4.	4.	4.	4.0
P_0				
P_1				
P_2				
$P(n > 2)$				

10. Complete the following table for the M/M/1 waiting line system with an infinite customer population and unlimited capacity for waiting customers.

Arrival rate	10.	20.	30.	39.
Service rate	40.	40.	40.	40.
P_0				
P_1				
P_2				
$P(n > 2)$				

11. If the probability distribution of service times in hours is Erlang with $m = 5$ and $\lambda = 2$,
    a. What is the expected service time?
    b. What is the variance of the service time?

12. Say that the probability distribution of service times in hours is Erlang with $m = 3$ and $\lambda = 2$ for a single-server system. The interarrival times have an exponential distribution with an arrival rate of 1.5 per hour.
    a. What is the expected number of customers waiting?
    b. What is the expected waiting time?
    c. What is the expected number of customers in the system?
    d. What is the probability that a customer must wait before service is begun?

13. Say that service times have a normal probability distribution with a mean of 20 minutes and a standard deviation of 3 minutes. For a single-server system, the interarrival times have an exponential distribution with a mean interarrival time of 30 minutes.
    a. What is the expected number of customers waiting?
    b. What is the expected number of customers in the system?
    c. What is the expected waiting time?
    d. What is the expected time in the system?
    e. What is the probability that a customer must wait before service is begun?

14. Consider Example 1 of the chapter. Say that the loading rate is only 2.5 trucks per hour when three employees are assigned to the loading dock. What is the expected combined cost per hour?

15. Consider Example 1 of the chapter. Say that the loading rate is only 4.8 trucks per hour when five employees are assigned to the loading dock. What is the expected combined cost per hour?

16. Consider Example 2 of the chapter. Say that a single more efficient secretary is hired, with a typing rate of 12 documents per hour. This secretary is a replacement for the two departmental secretaries and is twice as fast.
    a. What is the probability of no typing projects in the system?
    b. What is the expected number of documents waiting for typing?
    c. What is the expected number of documents in the system?
    d. What is the expected time in the system for a document?
    e. Is a single fast secretary better than two slow secretaries in a pool arrangement? Discuss.

17. For an M/M/2 queueing system, the arrival rate is 2.0 per hour and the service rate is 1.5 per hour for each server. Customers wait in a single line.
    a. What is the probability of no customer being present in the system?
    b. What is the probability of both servers being busy?
    c. What is the expected line length?
    d. What is the expected time in line?
    e. What proportion of the customers must wait for service?

18. For an M/M/3 queueing system, the arrival rate is 2.0 per hour and the service rate is 1.0 per hour for each server. Customers wait in a single line.
    a. What is the probability of no customer being present in the system?
    b. What is the probability of all the servers being busy?
    c. What is the expected line length?
    d. What is the expected time in line?
    e. What proportion of the customers must wait for service?

MORE CHALLENGING EXERCISES

1. The company of Example 1 of the chapter is considering adding a second loading dock. It plans to assign three employees to each of the two loading docks. Calculate the expected combined cost per hour of this configuration. The construction cost of the new loading dock is estimated to be equivalent to an additional cost of $18 per hour. Should the second loading dock be constructed?

2. For the machine interference example (Example 3 of the chapter), the number of mechanics can be decreased to two. This saves one mechanic for 24 hours a day and 365 days per year. The mechanic earns $18.50 per hour. Calculate the change in the expected costs. Is the decrease justified economically? Discuss.

3. An automated service system always requires exactly 5.0 minutes to provide the service. Customers arrive by a random process at an average rate of five per hour. What is the expected number in line? What is the expected waiting time? When the variability of the service time decreases, does the expected waiting time increase or decrease? Explain.

4. A bank is installing one drive-up teller window. The difficulty is that the amount of space in which cars can wait is very limited. There is space for only three or four cars. If a car arrives and there is no space in the line, the customer leaves unhappy. The average number of arrivals is 30 per hour. The teller service is anticipated to serve an average of 60 cars per hour (a very fast teller). Use an exponential distribution for both interarrival times and service times. Calculate the proportion of customers who leave the system because waiting space is unavailable when three is the limit. Calculate the proportion of customers who leave the system when four is the limit. For a limit of three versus four, what is the difference in the expected number of cars waiting in line for service? Why aren't the expected number waiting in line the same? After all, the arrival rate and the service rate are unchanged.

5. Outdoors Mail Order receives an average of 100 calls per hour. The average time to take an order is two minutes. It is estimated that if a caller receives a busy signal, the lost profit is $11. The cost of maintaining a phone line is $12 per hour. How many phone lines should Outdoors Mail Order have?

6. A computer repair service has become very successful in Atlanta, Georgia. When a customer phones, the dispatcher sends a repair person as soon as possible. The average travel time is 45 minutes, and the average repair time is 60 minutes. If the repair person doesn't complete the repair within three hours of the call, there is no charge for the repair service. Otherwise, the charge is $100. On the average, there are three service calls per day. Currently, the company has one repair person. It costs $45 per hour to add a repair person. Is it worthwhile to add a second repair person?

7. The Community Hospital is revamping its emergency room. The arrival rate at the emergency room is four per hour. The average service time is 15 minutes. There are currently two rooms in which doctors see emergency room patients. The probability that a room isn't available when a patient arrives shouldn't exceed 0.05. What is the minimum number of rooms needed to provide that service?

8. Oil Change Specialists is a chain of shops that specializes in fast oil changes. A new shop with a single bay has opened. The anticipated arrival rate is four per hour. The service time has a normal distribution with a mean of 10 minutes and a standard deviation of 2 minutes. What is the expected time that a customer must wait for an oil change? What is the probability that the bay is used at any point in time?

9. You are marketing a new telephone answering system. This system automatically asks up to three callers to wait if the phone is busy. You are trying to sell the system to a client who has a call every five minutes, on the average. The average call takes six minutes. With the new system, the client's customers won't get a busy signal unless four customers are already in the system. Write a report to the client describing the improvements of this system as compared with the traditional system in which a busy signal is received if only one customer is in the system.

10. The Neighborhood Bank has three teller windows and wants to determine how many of the windows to use. The goal is that the expected number of customers waiting should be three or less. The average service time is three minutes. Prepare a table that shows the arrival rates versus the number of windows used. For example, the table might say: "Use two teller windows if the arrival rate is between 10 and 20 per hour."

11. For MCE 10, the arrival rate is 30 per hour. Bank management has assigned a cost of $10 for each customer waiting hour. The cost of using a window is $15. How many teller windows should be used?

CASE

Thompson Mining and Smelting Company (A)

With a planned increase in the production rate at the Thompson Mining and Smelting Company's refinery to take effect at the end of next month, management had decided to have the output at its Wekusko open-pit mine increased to 35,000 tons per week. Mr. Brian Walker, superintendent of the Wekusko mine, wanted to insure that he could meet the new demand. He decided to call in a plant engineer from the main office to determine the required equipment. This represented an opportunity to analyze the Wekusko operation and optimize the use of earthmoving equipment.

Background
Thompson's Wekusko plant was a small open-pit mine in southern California. The operation involves three 3-yard shovels, twelve 20-ton

trucks, and a primary crusher. Each shovel was located in a different area of the pit. Two shovels worked eight hours during the day shift with four trucks per shovel. The third shovel operated during the second shift with five trucks. The trucks did not switch from one shovel to another even if waiting occurred. The pit operated five days a week. The trucks hauled the ore from the shovels to a primary crusher, after which the ore was shipped by rail to Thompson's refining complex 40 miles away. The crusher had a capac-

SOURCE: Christoph Haehling von Lanzenauer, *Cases in Operations Research,* Oakland, Calif.: Holden-Day, Inc. 1975. Copyright © the University of Western Ontario. Reproduced with permission.

EXHIBIT 1   Time Estimates for Trucks (in minutes)

Shovel Area	Load	To Crusher	Dump	From Crusher	Position at Shovel	Round-Trip Time
1	2.06	1.93	0.94	1.10	0.51	6.54
2	2.06	3.13	0.94	1.48	0.51	8.12
3	2.06	2.26	0.94	1.80	0.51	7.57

ity of about 9,600 tons per shift (480 truckloads), which was well within the limits of the increased production requirement of 35,000 tons of ore per week.

Analysis

The engineer immediately recognized that the situation could be analyzed using simple queueing theory, with the trucks as customers waiting to be loaded or unloaded at either a shovel or the primary crusher. With the aid of these concepts, he would be able to optimize the use of Wekusko's earth-moving equipment.

As a first part of the analysis, the engineer time-studied the entire system by both the continuous and the snapback methods.[1] He observed that the positioning and loading times of the shovels and the dumping time were the same for all trucks (Exhibit 1). The travel times to and from the crusher were different for each shovel area (Exhibit 1). With these times, a round-trip was calculated for each area. From the data in Exhibit 1, arrival and service rates at the shovels were derived and are given for Area 1 in Exhibit 2. Graphical representation of the observed interarrival

EXHIBIT 2   Arrival and Service Rates for Area 1

	Number of Trucks			
	1	2	3	4
Average arrival rate (trucks/hr.)	9.17	18.34	27.51	36.68
Average service rate (trucks/hr.)	29.13	29.13	29.13	29.13

and service times indicated that both could be approximated by the exponential distribution.

The plant engineer and Mr. Walker realized that there was a trade-off between the idle time of the trucks and the shovels. They determined the hourly costs of the trucks and shovels as follows:

Truck	
Fixed cost	$ 3.03
Driver ($3.435 × 134%)	4.60
Total	$ 7.63
Shovel	
Fixed cost	$14.51
Operator ($3.885 × 134%)	5.21
Total	$19.72

Using the above information, the engineer developed cost estimates for various numbers of trucks in each shovel area. The results for Area 1 are given in Exhibit 3, with similar results occurring in Areas 2 and 3.

---

[1] Continuous time study method: The entire operation is timed continuously, and the time for each element within the operation is noted.

Snapback time study method: Each element within the operation is timed separately.

EXHIBIT 3 Comparison of Costs for One-, Two-, and Three-Truck Systems: Area 1

	Number of Trucks		
	1	2	3
Probability of one truck in system	0.315	0.233	0.052
Cost of idle truck/hr.	$ 2.40	$ 1.78	$ 0.40
Probability of two trucks in system	N/A	0.397	0.049
Cost of idle trucks/hr.	N/A	$ 6.06	$ 0.75
Probability of three trucks in system	N/A	N/A	0.844
Cost of idle trucks/hr.	N/A	N/A	$19.32
Total cost of idle trucks/hr.	$ 2.40	$ 7.84	$20.47
Probability of no trucks in system	0.685	0.370	0.055
Cost of idle shovel/hr.	$13.51	$ 7.30	$ 1.09
Comparison of cost differences	$11.11	$ 0.54	$19.38

Recommendation

The engineer recommended that the most economical method of meeting the ore requirements was to operate all three shovels during the day shift only with two trucks per shovel. When the operation of three shovels was not feasible, due to downtime or shovel locations, two shovels could be used during the day shift with two trucks per shovel, and one shovel with two trucks in a second shift.

If new, 50-ton trucks and 6-yard shovels were used, the same number of shovels with two trucks per shovel should be used, as the traveling, loading, and dumping times for the new equipment would be similar to the present equipment.

CASE

Thompson Mining and Smelting Company (B)

Mr. Brian Walker, superintendent of Thompson Mining and Smelting Company's Wekusko open-pit mine, had implemented the recommendation of a report regarding the optimization of earth-moving equipment at the Wekusko mine. After operating a few weeks, it was observed that the weekly production output was always below the required 35,000 tons, necessitating overtime or second shifts. There had been no breakdowns of equipment which could have caused the shortfall from the production capacity anticipated in the consulting plant engineer's report.

Mr. Walker asked the engineer to discuss his analysis and findings in more detail, and specifically to address the discrepancy between the actual output of less than 35,000 tons and the anticipated output of 39,000 tons.

The plant engineer explained that he used a queueing model to estimate the amount of time the shovels and trucks waiting at the shovels would be idle. With these estimates, he was able to optimize the idle time of trucks and shovels while keeping the production capacity at 39,000 tons.

As Mr. Walker understood it, the engineer estimated the amount of time trucks would have to wait at a shovel as well as the amount of time there would be no trucks at a shovel to be loaded. This was used to compute the idle time costs as well as the production capacity. "When we have two or three shovels operating on one shift, the trucks often get in each other's way at the crusher," observed Mr. Walker. "I wonder if this could be an explanation for the lower than expected production."

15

Computer Simulation

EXXON CORPORATION

Exxon Corporation is the largest U.S. oil company. It refines and markets many petroleum-based products, including gasoline. Air pollution caused the state of California to propose new regulations phasing out the use of tetraethyl lead (TEL) in gasoline. Exxon had only two months to study the impact of the proposed regulation on the operation of its Benicia, California, refinery. Refinery processing units produced components that were blended into gasoline. TEL was used to increase the octane number of the gasoline. If TEL could not be used, additional processing of low-octane components was required to reach the octane quality specification.

The elimination of TEL affected the refinery in two ways. First, additional processing equipment for upgrading low-octane components would be necessary. Second, additional inventory of high-octane components would be required. Shutting down equipment that produced high-octane components was not a problem when TEL was allowed, because more TEL could be added to increase the octane number of the blend. Similarly, if the octane number was less than the specification because the octane number of a component varied, TEL could be added to reblend to the specification. If TEL could not be used, it would be necessary to have more inventory of high-octane components to raise the octane number.

Exxon developed a computer simulation model that studied the blending operation. Exxon could meet the proposed regulations by adding processing capacity for high-octane components or building additional storage or by a combination of the two. The model was used to study the amount of additional storage and of additional processing capacity. The simulation model used half-hour time increments to simulate the blending operation. The refinery produced different components that went into component storage tanks. Then, materials were pumped from the component storage tanks into a blending tank. After blending, the blending tank contents were pumped into finished product storage tanks. Barges and tank trucks were filled from the finished product storage tanks.

The component yields and qualities, the times of barge and tank truck arrivals, and the times of breakdowns were probabilistic. Their probability distributions were estimated by examining historical records. The operating rules for the blending system were developed by experienced refinery personnel. By evaluating different scenarios, the simulation model determined the amount of additional tankage needed. Before the simulation model was developed, preliminary analysis indicated that it would be necessary to build at least two component tanks and one or two finished product tanks. Based on the simulation results, however, Exxon reassigned existing storage tanks to different component and finished products and added one component tank and one finished product tank. The savings were at least $1.4 million.

Exxon has increased the simulation model's scope and used it for many studies since the TEL study. The model is a general multistage facilities simulation tool that has been used in studies of "refineries, chemical plants, distribution terminals, marine harbors, coal mines, and synthetic fuel plants." Some of these studies have resulted in savings of up to tens of million of dollars.

L. B. Golovin, "Product Blending: A Simulation Case Study in Double-Time," *Interfaces* 9, no. 5 (November 1979), pp. 64–76; and L. B. Golovin, "Product Blending: A Simulation Case Study in Double Time: An Update," *Interfaces* 15, no. 4 (July–August 1985), pp. 39–40.

In Chapter 1, we described two types of decision models—optimization and simulation. Every chapter except for Chapters 12 and 14 discussed optimization models. Chapter 12 discussed forecasting methods, which provide input data for many types of models. Chapter 14 presented models that are used to predict measures of performance for a specific waiting line configuration. Optimizing queueing systems is very difficult. Instead, you "try" several configurations and choose the one with the best combination of performance measures.

In this chapter and the next, we discuss computer simulation models. The computer's role is to reduce the effort involved with the arithmetic operations required to do a simulation. Remember, management science decision models are developed to help the decision maker study the decision environment. Generally, we want to find the decisions that are best or "optimal." For this reason, optimization models are preferred over simulation models.

A simulation model predicts the result for a particular set of decisions. Figure 15.1 shows how a simulation model is used for decision making. You choose a set of decisions and simulate the results for that set. Then, you analyze the results and decide whether you should try another set of decisions. You try additional sets of decisions until the results are acceptable.

There are deterministic simulations and probabilistic simulations just as there are deterministic decision environments and probabilistic decision environments. A **deterministic simulation** predicts the outcome of a particular set of decisions for a deterministic decision environment. It assumes that the outcome uncertainty is small enough to be ignored. A deterministic simulation model is used in decision making by trying different sets of decisions and using the simulation model to evaluate them.

FIGURE 15.1 Flowchart of the Process of Using Simulation in Decision Making

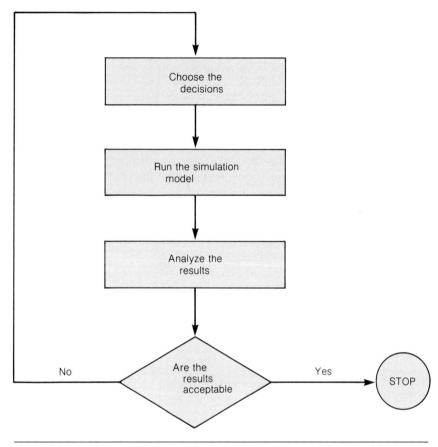

You choose the set of decisions that has the best performance measure (e.g., profit).

For a probabilistic decision environment, the outcome is uncertain and you explicitly consider the uncertainty in your analysis. The uncertainty was critical in Chapter 10's new product introduction (NPI) example. In that example, the profit for introducing the new product depended on the state of the economy. Thus, it was not reasonable to ignore the outcome uncertainty, because it lay at the heart of the decision problem.

Let's review decision making for probabilistic decision environments. For each decision alternative, you calculate the expected value of the performance measure. Then, you choose the decision alternative with the best expected value. Remember, if you aren't risk indifferent, you use the expected utility criterion.

For some probabilistic decision environments, a probabilistic simulation isn't necessary to calculate the expected value of the performance measure for a set of decisions. For the NPI example, you calculate the expected profit for introducing the new product and compare it with the expected profit for keeping the existing product. If you can calculate the probabilities and the expected value without simulation, you don't need to use it. In Chapter 13, we developed decision models without using probabilistic simulation.

When is probabilistic simulation necessary?

In some cases, it is not possible to calculate the outcome probabilities. Therefore, you can't calculate the expected value for a decision alternative. In such cases, you can use probabilistic simulation to *estimate* the probabilities and the expected value. In later sections of this chapter, we discuss the details of conducting a probabilistic simulation. We define **probabilistic simulation** as generating random variables from the probability distributions of the chance events, collecting the results, and using them to estimate the probabilities and the expected value for a decision alternative. In Chapter 14, we presented the steady state probabilities and the expected values of measures of performance, such as waiting time, for some waiting line configurations. However, if you can't apply one of the models for those configurations to your waiting line situation or if you want transient conditions, you can use probabilistic simulation. In general, a probabilistic simulation is required only *when it is very difficult to calculate the probability distribution of the outcomes*, and consequently it is very difficult to calculate the expected value.

You use probabilistic simulation to find the best decision in the same way that you use deterministic simulation. You try a decision alternative and *estimate* the expected value by doing a probabilistic simulation. You compare decision alternatives using the estimated expected values.

Exxon used probabilistic simulation to study how much additional refinery storage it would require when it phased tetraethyl lead (TEL) out of gasoline. Each decision alternative was an assignment of component and finished products to new and existing refinery storage tanks. Exxon used a probabilistic simulation to estimate the probability that a tank truck or barge couldn't be loaded because the gasoline tank was empty. It also estimated the average inventory holding cost for each decision alternative. By trying many assignment alternatives, Exxon used the simulation model to decide the number of additional tanks required.

The Transplantation Society of Michigan (TSM) used probabilistic simulation to study the impact of changes in kidney donor rates on the waiting list of patients needing transplants.[1] If a transplanted kidney doesn't match certain characteristics of the recipient, the recipient's body rejects the transplant. About 30 percent of transplants are rejected even if

---

[1] R. Jean Ruth, Leon Wyszewianski, and Gary Herline, "Kidney Transplantation: A Simulation Model for Examining Supply and Demand," *Management Science* 33, no. 5, (May 1985), pp. 515–26.

the match is acceptable. Because of the complexity of kidney matching and because of the uncertainty of donated kidney characteristics, the characteristics of waiting list patients, rejection, and death while on the waiting list, calculating the probabilities of the number of people on the waiting list is impossible. Thus, TSM used probabilistic simulation to estimate the waiting list length for different donor rates.

Deterministic simulation and probabilistic simulation are both useful management science tools. The decision maker uses these tools to explore the decision environment and to improve the quality of the decisions. However, a computer simulation model only represents the decision environment *chosen by the model builder*. The model builder/decision maker still needs to choose the problem to be analyzed and to decide what information the model will include and what level of detail will be used. The model-building issues we discussed in Chapters 1 and 2 must be considered. A computer simulation is only a tool to aid in decision making; it does not replace the decision maker.

In the next section, we discuss why simulation is useful and necessary in decision making. After that, we give a history of computer simulation. Then, we discuss deterministic simulations. The last three sections discuss probabilistic simulations. First, we show how to generate random variables from a specified probability distribution. Then, we give two probabilistic simulation examples.

WHY USE SIMULATION?

Optimization models and simulation models answer different questions:

Optimization models answer "What's best?"
Simulation models answer "What if?"

An *optimization model* is designed to answer the question "What's best?" The model considers all possible values of the decision variables consistent with the model, and it chooses the best set of values of the decision variables for some criterion, called the objective function. In Chapter 2, we developed a linear programming model for the Potato Processing example. We used this optimization model to choose the amount of potatoes to purchase from Idaho and Michigan.

A *simulation model* is designed to answer the question "What if?" That is, what would happen if we choose a set of decisions? You pick a set of decisions, simulate the results, and note the objective function value. You look for the optimal solution by trying many sets of decisions. You need to be persistent, clever, or lucky to try the set of decisions that is the mathematically optimal solution. Even if you are lucky enough to try the best set of decisions, it's hard to determine whether it is optimal. In

---

TABLE 15.1   Reasons for Using Simulation

1. Optimization is not possible.
2. Simulation models are easy to understand.
3. Managers disagree on the objective function.
4. Simulation enables you to study the impact of nonoptimal decisions.
5. Simulation can establish the validity of optimization models.

---

general, you cannot know that you've found the best set of decisions unless you've tried every possibility.

In spite of their shortcomings for finding optimal decisions, simulation models are useful. Surveys show that computer simulation is among the most widely used problem-solving tools.[2] Table 15.1 lists five reasons that simulation models are used.

First, if no optimization methodology exists or appropriate computer software is not available to you, simulation may be the last resort. It may be the only tool available. Exxon used probabilistic simulation to estimate the performance characteristics of a tank assignment alternative because it was impossible to calculate the outcome probabilities. The complexity of the gasoline blending and storage system and the many types of uncertainty made probabilistic simulation necessary. The simulation model didn't tell Exxon what the best assignment was; instead, it predicted what would happen if an assignment decision were chosen.

Second, simulation models are easy to understand. A simulation model is a good tool for explaining underlying model assumptions and workings. Remember, a model is an abstraction of the decision environment chosen by the model builder. If you've developed a model whose methodology your boss or client doesn't understand, it's difficult to get the model accepted. It's easy to explain the workings of a simulation model. As an example, let's consider the supply-demand model of Chapter 1 that determines the market-clearing price for a product. At the market-clearing price, supply and demand are equal. The market-clearing price is found by solving two simultaneous equations in two unknowns—price and quantity. This method requires simple algebraic manipulations. However, the method may seem like black magic to those who never learned it, and those who studied algebra long ago may find the method difficult to recall.

Optimization not possible

Easier to understand

---

[2] G. A. Forgionne, "Corporate Management Science: Activities: An Update," *Interfaces* 13, no. 3 (June 1983), pp. 20–23.

For such people, a simulation model can be more reassuring than the algebraic manipulations. The steps in the simulation approach are

1. Select a value of P, the price.
2. Calculate the value of the quantity demanded and the quantity supplied at that price.
3. If the quantity supplied equals the quantity demanded, the market-clearing price has been found. Otherwise, go to Step 1 again.

This approach explains the concept of a market-clearing price and will also convince our boss or client that it has been obtained.

Similarly, using a complicated constrained optimization model based on an unfamiliar methodology provokes skepticism. How can you establish the validity of the results? Generally, it is easier to convince someone that a simulation model is correct than that the results of an optimization model are correct.

Conflicting objectives

Third, managers may not agree on the appropriate objective function. Without an objective function, it is impossible to determine the "optimal" decision. For example, a waiting line system usually has conflicting objectives. A waiting line configuration that improves service also increases the operating cost. For example, adding another server reduces waiting time but increases cost.

Exxon was concerned that eliminating TEL from gasoline would limit its ability to continue blending during shutdown periods of refinery units that produced high-octane components. This would increase the probability that a barge or tank truck couldn't be loaded because gasoline wasn't available. By adding storage tanks, it could maintain higher inventories, which would decrease the probability. But decreasing the probability would also increase the tank and inventory holding costs. Exxon used the simulation model to estimate the costs and the probabilities for different tank assignments.

Exploring nonoptimal decisions

Fourth, a simulation model can be used to explore a particular set of decision variable values that is not optimal. An optimization model is designed to provide the answer to the question "What's best?" It does not answer the question "What is the impact of nonoptimal decisions?" You can add constraints to the optimization model to force the decision variables to nonoptimal values. But if you do this, you are using the optimization model to *simulate* the decision environment.

You can use a simulation model to evaluate secondary objective functions as well as the primary objective function for nonoptimal and optimal decisions. For example, say that the primary objective is to maximize profit and that the secondary objective is to avoid changes in the number of factory employees. Say that the time horizon is one year and that we use an optimization model with 12 one-month periods. The plan that maximizes profit might entail large monthly changes in the number of factory employees. A simulation model could be used to evaluate plans that aren't optimal (for profit) so that the impact on the secondary objective can be assessed. Remember, optimality is a mathematical property, not a managerial property. The model is used to explore the decision environment, not to find the one "optimal" solution.

Validating an optimization model

Fifth, you can use a simulation model to establish the validity of an optimization model's results. A correct simulation model should give the same results as an optimization model when you substitute the optimal decision variable values into it. By challenging a disbeliever to find a better solution, you may be able to win acceptance for the optimization model's results.

THE HISTORY OF COMPUTER SIMULATION

Historically, computer simulation has referred to probabilistic simulation because the first simulations were probabilistic. The earliest simulations were used for operations planning. For example,

What number of Directory Assistance operators is required to ensure that only 1 of 1,000 calls for service is not answered in two seconds?

How many drill presses should a job shop have?

What reorder point should an inventory control system use?

Computer programs were written, often in FORTRAN, to simulate the system's operation. A complex simulation model required a FORTRAN program with many statements. If the system or the environment changed, the FORTRAN program had to be modified. Building and maintaining a FORTRAN computer program for a complex system simulation was difficult.

Higher-level languages

Software programs were developed to simplify building and maintaining complex probabilistic simulation models. Such programs allowed the model builder to use higher-level languages to build the simulation models. These languages provided building blocks for model builders that replaced many FORTRAN statements with a single statement. Building and maintaining simulation models became much easier with the higher-level languages.

IBM developed one of the first simulation languages, General Purpose System Simulator (GPSS). Because GPSS was designed for a particular type of simulation problem (waiting lines), it is called a **problem-oriented language.** You construct a GPSS model using commands that represent different operational functions of the system. In Chapter 16, we show a GPSS program for a waiting line system. A GPSS program has fewer statements than a FORTRAN program that simulates the same system. GPSS is available on many types of computers.

SIMSCRIPT was developed by the Rand Corporation in the 1960s. SIMSCRIPT is FORTRAN-based, and you must be a proficient FORTRAN programmer to use it effectively. Because SIMSCRIPT requires a large amount of computer storage, it's available only on certain computers. SIMSCRIPT is not a problem-oriented language, though it is efficient for waiting lines.

SLAM, a powerful simulation language, was developed by A. Alan B. Pritsker, who also developed GASP, another powerful simulation language. SLAM provides network symbols that can be used to develop graphical models that are translated into program statements. SLAM also allows the use of both discrete event and continuous models. In Chapter 16, we discuss this difference. GPSS and SIMSCRIPT are designed for discrete event simulations.

To use a higher-level language, you must learn the language and have software available. More information about higher-level languages is contained in A. M. Law and W. D. Kelton, *Simulation Modeling and Analysis* (New York: McGraw-Hill, 1982).

Corporate financial simulations

During the 1970s, there was increased interest in building models to analyze the impact of corporate decisions on a firm's financial statement. (These decisions were strategic rather than operational.) Financial planning systems incorporating special software and higher-level languages were developed for this purpose. Interactive Financial Planning System (IFPS), developed by Execucom, was one such system. These financial planning systems were generally expensive and required a mainframe computer. They offered a variety of features. All of them allowed deterministic simulation, and many of them allowed probabilistic simulation. Some also had optimization capabilities.

Electronic spreadsheets

Recently, there has been great interest in using microcomputers for deterministic simulations. Many managers use electronic spreadsheets such as LOTUS 1-2-3, SUPERCALC, and MULTIPLAN for deterministic simulations. These tools allow the individual who is not a computer expert to develop models that can be used for "What if?" analyses. Electronic spreadsheets are actually closer relatives of the financial or corporate planning systems than of the operations-oriented probabilistic simulation systems. In the next section, we discuss the use of electronic spreadsheets for deterministic simulation.

Decision support systems

Systems originally developed for financial modeling have come to be seen in a broader context, and many are now called **decision support systems (DSSs).** A DSS is a computer-based information system that provides managers with support for decision making. A system of this kind is interactive and has an information management system that extracts information from databases. It allows the manager to build models that can interact with management science tools, such as linear programming. DSSs can also generate output reports and answer "What if?" questions. Financial modeling systems such as IFPS have many of the capabilities of DSSs. Financial modeling systems and DSS are now becoming available for microcomputers. The capabilities of these systems are expanding as microcomputers become more powerful. They do not possess all the capabilities of mainframe systems, but their capabilities are constantly increasing. For example, a microcomputer version of IFPS is now available that does deterministic and probabilistic simulations. As yet, however, it does not have optimization capabilities.

The graphics capabilities of microcomputers are a major reason for their popularity. A "picture" presents information more effectively than a table of numbers. Probabilistic simulation packages that use graphics for building the simulation model are available for operations and manufacturing planning. SIMFACTORY from CACI provides an animated picture of a factory at work. The factory model uses icons that describe processing stations, storage locations, and material handling. Using SIMFACTORY, the microcomputer shows the flow of materials through the factory from raw materials to finished products. XCELL from Scientific Press does similar simulations.

As microcomputers improve, more powerful simulation tools will be available on the manager's desk. It won't be necessary to have an analyst perform your simulations on a mainframe computer. The two microcomputer bottlenecks are processing speed and storage, and microcomputer advances are eliminating these bottlenecks. Because microcomputer systems must be easy to use to be commercially successful, they will be easier to learn and use than the mainframe systems used by specialists.

Artificial intelligence and expert systems

In the future, artificial intelligence (AI) will play a larger role in decision making. Herbert Simon characterizes **artificial intelligence** as "the application of methods of heuristic search to the solution of complex problems that (*a*) defy the mathematics of optimization, (*b*) contain non-quantifiable components, (*c*) involve large knowledge bases (including knowledge expressed in natural language), (*d*) incorporate the discovery and design of alternatives of choice, and (*e*) admit ill-specified goals and constraints."[3] In our description of the use of probabilistic simulation for decision making, the model user specifies the decisions and the simulation predicts the results. Expert system development tools (ESDTs) are becoming available for microcomputers that make it easier to develop systems for choosing the decisions. ESDTs have a rule manager and an inference engine. The rule manager facilitates building, modifying, and updating the knowledge base, which is usually many levels of if-then

---

[3] Herbert Simon, "Two Heads Are Better than One: The Collaboration between AI and OR," *Interfaces* 17, no. 4 (July–August 1987), pp. 8–15.

rules. The inference engine uses the knowledge base to choose the decisions.

Let's discuss how an expert system can be used in scheduling a flexible manufacturing system (FMS). An FMS can perform many manufacturing operations and can process production lots of many types of parts. Because of the flexibility of such a system, there are many possible production schedules. In Chapter 9, we described various types of combinatorial optimization problems, including machine scheduling. Because of the large number of possible machine schedules, finding the optimal schedule is very difficult. Also, the machine scheduling system must react rapidly to unexpected events, such as the breakdown of a machine or the unavailability of required raw materials. In Chapter 13, we described material requirements planning (MRP), which is one approach to this scheduling problem. However, MRP "loads" machines during a time period and doesn't specify the order of products within the period. An expert system uses if-then rules to schedule the beginning and end of each product on the FMS. Here is an example of such a rule: "If a lot is available but an essential machine must shut down for preventive maintenance in a short time, delay this lot and try to schedule another." Using the rules of the expert system, the operation of the system is simulated for the product requirements on the production list. The simulation results are reported to the FMS manager, who can modify the production schedule, if necessary.

The applicability of artificial intelligence and expert systems has been limited by the drawbacks of computer hardware. However, rapid improvements in computer speed and storage are expanding their applicability. Inexpensive ESDTs, such as VP–EXPERT from Paperback Software, are now available for microcomputers. We expect that AI will have many applications in the future.

ELECTRONIC SPREADSHEETS

Many managers use electronic spreadsheets because these allow managers to use their time more productively. Managers spend a lot of time planning and doing repetitive calculations as they evaluate different alternatives. Electronic spreadsheets answer "What if?" questions and have great potential as a decision-making aid.

For example, Bethlehem Steel Corporation uses LOTUS 1-2-3 to do production planning.[4] The model analyzes product flows through a steel-

---

[4] G. L. Baker, W. A. Clark, Jr., J. J. Frund, and R. E. Wendell, "Production Planning and Cost Analysis on a Microcomputer," *Interfaces* 17, no. 4 (July–August 1987), pp. 53–60.

making plant and assesses the impact of changes in facility capacities, product demands, and operating costs. It helps determine the best production plan and the contribution margin for each product.

Any deterministic simulation that can be done with an electronic spreadsheet can also be done without one. Instead of using an electronic spreadsheet for arithmetic calculations, you can use a calculator. But electronic spreadsheets allow you to organize large amounts of data, and they recalculate rapidly after you change parameters or decision inputs. Furthermore, they have features that make it easier for a manager to build large models. Perhaps most important, they are easy to use. It's possible to do the calculations without using electronic spreadsheet software. For example, you can write a computer program to do the simulation in a language such as BASIC. However, this requires the manager to be a proficient programmer and to spend time more time in programming than would be required if an electronic spreadsheet were used. Bethlehem Steel Corporation reported that an electronic spreadsheet provided a fast and user-friendly method for "investigating a variety of scenarios more efficiently than would be possible on a mainframe computer."

Balance sheets, budgets, cash flow statements, and profit and loss statements are familiar to managers. Electronic spreadsheets have the same structure as financial statements and are often used to create them. In fact, the term *spreadsheet* refers to the large sheets that accountants use for working papers. These sheets have horizontal and vertical lines that divide them into many rows and columns.

An electronic spreadsheet is also divided into a "checkerboard" of rows and columns. A square of the checkerboard is called a **cell.** A particular cell is referred to by specifying a row and a column. Usually, the columns across the top are designated by letters and the rows down the side are designated by numbers. Thus, Cell A1 is the upper left-hand cell of the checkerboard and Cell A2 is the cell directly below Cell A1.

There are differences among the various electronic spreadsheets, but they all share many common properties. In most electronic spreadsheets, you can enter one of three types of entities in each cell. The first is a *number*. The second is a *"string"* that can be a heading and is usually text. The third is a *formula* that calculates a number depending on the values in other cells. It is this ability to use formulas that makes spreadsheets such a popular tool. The computer screen contains the number obtained by the formula, but the electronic spreadsheet remembers the formula. Say that Cell A1 contains a number used in the formula for Cell A2. Because the formula is remembered, when you change the number in Cell A1, the formula is used to recalculate the screen value in Cell A2. By changing the number in a cell, you use the spreadsheet to do "What if?" analyses. A manager who wants to determine the outcome of different decisions only has to change the numerical values representing those decisions; the electronic spreadsheet then does the recalculations.

This saves much time and effort. However, it requires determining the relationships among the factors to be considered. A **template** is the specification of the cell contents and the set of relationships among them for a particular application. A template is a form of *model* and this is subject to the model-building considerations that we discussed in Chapters 1 and 2.

An Electronic Spreadsheet for the Potato Processing Example

There are many correct templates

In this section, we develop a template for the Potato Processing example. There are many correct templates for this example. Remember, we've seen that there are many correct models for a given decision environment. Such variation arises in part from different determinations of which factors are important. These are determinations that the decision maker/ model builder must make. Variation of this kind also arises from differences in the number of intermediate variables included in the template. Remember, an *intermediate variable,* sometimes called a definitional variable, isn't required to model the decision environment. For example, recall the reformulation of the Potato Processing example discussed in the Model Structure and Sensitivity Analysis section of Chapter 5. Because they helped some types of sensitivity analysis, additional decision variables were defined. The variables designated *FF, HB, FL,* and *WT* are the number of pounds of french fries, hash browns, flakes, and waste, respectively. It was possible to formulate the linear programming model for the Potato Processing example without these variables, but introducing them allowed simple sensitivity analysis on selling prices. Thus, *FF* is an example of an intermediate or definitional variable. When the intermediate variable *FF* was introduced, it was also necessary to introduce the *definitional constraint*

$$FF = 0.3I + 0.2M$$

Defining intermediate variables

In an electronic spreadsheet, you don't use definitional constraints. Rather, you use formulas to represent relationships between variables. The above definitional constraint would be represented by defining a cell as representing the value of the *FF* intermediate variable and entering into that cell the formula that calculates its value. For example, say that Cell B3 has the value of the decision variable *I* and that Cell C3 has the value of the decision variable *M*. Then, the formula for the *FF* cell is

$$0.3 * B3 + 0.2 * C3$$

Note that an asterisk is used for the multiplication operation. In the linear programming model input, you don't have to specify the multiplication operation by an asterisk. For linear programming, the objective function and the constraint functions must be linear, each expressed as a constant *times* the first variable, plus another constant *times* the second variable, plus . . Because you can't input a function in any other form, it's not necessary to specify the multiplication operator. If software allows more general functions, an asterisk usually represents multiplication. This is true for electronic spreadsheets because they allow more complex formulas.

Row and column naming

The tabular form of spreadsheets often makes it convenient to relate all of the entries in a column or row. For example, you might let Column B be Idaho potatoes and Column C be Michigan potatoes, and you might let Rows 4, 5, 6, and 7 be french fries, hash browns, flakes, and waste. Then, Cell B4 has a natural definition, the number of pounds of french fries from Idaho potatoes. Naming the columns and rows in this way enables you to define more intermediate variables and to obtain more information from the spreadsheet at a glance.

Define a cell for each decision variable

Recall that the original linear programming model of Chapter 2 had two decision variables, I and M. In an electronic spreadsheet, you must *define a cell for each decision variable*. Thus, you define one cell that has a numerical value for I and another cell that has a numerical value for M.

Figure 15.2 is a template for the Potato Processing example that uses the three types of cell entities. Cell B3 has the decision variable value for I, the number of pounds of Idaho potatoes purchased. This is a *numerical* type of entity. In Cell B2, there is the heading "Idaho, pounds," which is a *string* type of entity. Column B is Idaho potatoes. The *formula* in Cell B4 calculates the number of pounds of french fries produced from Idaho potatoes. Note that this formula is expressed in terms of Cell B3, which is the number of pounds of potatoes purchased from Idaho. Cells B4, B5, B6, and B7 are, respectively, the number of pounds of french fries, hash browns, flakes, and waste produced from Idaho potatoes. The definition of these cells is implied from the headings entered in Cells A4, A5, A6, A7, and B2. The column heading in Cell C2 shows that Column C is Michigan potatoes. Therefore, Cells C4, C5, C6, and C7 are, respectively, the number of pounds of french fries, hash browns, flakes, and waste produced from Michigan potatoes.

Column D is total pounds *produced*. The formulas in Cells D4, D5, D6 and D7 show that the total pounds produced of each product is the sum of the pounds produced from Idaho potatoes and the pounds produced from Michigan potatoes. For example, the total pounds produced of french fries (Cell D4) is the pounds of french fries produced from Idaho potatoes (Cell B4) plus the pounds of french fries produced from Michigan potatoes (Cell C4). Cell D4 has the formula $+B4 +C4$.

Built-in functions

Electronic spreadsheets often have many **built-in functions.** Date, financial, statistical, and mathematical functions are types of generally available built-in functions. *Date functions* can be used to record chronological data, such as the timing of cash flows. Managers frequently use *financial functions*. For example, there are functions that calculate present value and depreciation. *Statistical functions* calculate averages and standard deviations. Among the built-in *mathematical functions* are abso-

FIGURE 15.2   Spreadsheet Template for Potato Processing Example

	A	B	C	D	E	F	G
1	Potato Processing Example						
2		Idaho, pounds	Michigan, pounds				
3		10000	60000	Pounds Produced	Pounds Sold	Revenues	
4	French fries	0.3 * B3	0.2 * C3	+B4+C4	@min(18000,D4)	0.90 * E4	
5	Hash browns	0.1 * B3	0.2 * C3	+B5+C5	@min(15000,D5)	0.75 * E5	
6	Flakes	0.3 * B3	0.3 * C3	+B6+C6	@min(25000,D6)	0.50 * E6	
7	Waste	0.3 * B3	0.3 * C3	+B7+C7	+D7	0.10 * E7	
8							
9	Cost	(0.225+0.16)*B3	(0.20+0.16)* C3				
10			Total cost			Total revenues	Total profit
11			+B9+C9			@SUM(F4..F7)	+F11-C11

lute value, trigonometric functions, and the minimum and maximum of a list. Electronic spreadsheets often also include some conditional capabilities, such as IF statements.

Column E is the pounds *sold* of the potato products. We use LOTUS 1–2–3's MIN function in the formula to calculate the number of pounds of french fries sold. The MIN function gives the minimum of a list. Remember, the demand for french fries is 18,000 pounds. The number of pounds of french fries sold depends on the demand and on the number of pounds produced. If 15,000 pounds are produced, all 15,000 pounds are sold. However, if 20,000 pounds are produced, only 18,000 pounds are sold. The formula in Cell E4 is MIN(18000, D4). The minimum of 18,000 and the value of Cell D4 appear in Cell E4. Say that D4 is 20,000, which is greater than 18,000. Then, the value 18,000 appears. You sell only 18,000 pounds even though 20,000 pounds are produced. Say that D4 is 15,000, which is smaller than 18,000. Then, 15,000 appears in Cell E4. Because you produce only 15,000 pounds, you sell only 15,000 pounds.

The formulas for calculating the number of pounds sold of hash browns and flakes also use the MIN function. Because we assumed that an unlimited amount of waste could be sold, Cell E7 is equal to Cell D7.

Column F is the revenues. You multiply the selling price by the number of pounds *sold* to calculate the revenues for each product. Note you do *not* multiply by the number of pounds *produced* because you may not be able to sell everything you produce.

The formulas in Cells B9 and C9 calculate the total of the potato and processing costs for Idaho and Michigan potatoes, respectively. The total cost, which appears in Cell C11, is calculated as the cost for the Idaho potatoes, B9, plus the cost for the Michigan potatoes, C9. The total revenues appear in Cell F11, directly under Cell F10, in which a descriptive string appears. The formula for calculating the total revenues uses SUM, another built-in function. This function lets you specify a range of cells to be added. The formula in Cell F11 says to add the contents of Cells F4 through F7. That is equivalent to using the formula +F4 +F5 +F6 +F7. If there are many consecutive cells to be added, it is easier to use the SUM function. Cell G11 has the formula for the total profit: total revenues minus total cost.

The exact cell entries depend on the particular electronic spreadsheet. Most electronic spreadsheets make no distinction between uppercase letters and lowercase letters in formulas. Most assume that if the cell entry begins with a letter, the cell entry is a string, not a formula. For this reason, Cell D4's formula begins with a +. Similarly, the @ before MIN, IF, and SUM means that a built-in function name follows. In the SUM function, a **delimiter** separates the limits on the summation. The delimiter depends on the electronic spreadsheet. LOTUS 1–2–3 uses .. as the delimiter; FRAMEWORK uses : .

Electronic spreadsheets allow styling the screen display. Numbers can

Styling the screen display

appear with or without dollar signs and with or without commas separating thousands. Note that the thousands in Cell E4 are not separated by a comma, but the screen can be styled so that it contains the comma. You can change the width (number of characters) of cells, and you can display the result centered, flush right, or flush left within a cell.

In Figure 15.2, many cell formulas are similar. For example, the formulas in Cells D4, D5, D6, and D7 differ only in the row number. One very useful electronic spreadsheet feature is the ability to copy formulas.

Copying formulas

You enter the formula in Cell D4 and copy it into Cells D5, D6, and D7. The careful model builder constructs the model so that copying can be used extensively. Copying makes it easier to build a large model.

This template can be used to explore the profit for different combinations of number of pounds of potatoes purchased from Idaho and Michigan. The manager enters numerical values in Cells B3 and C3 for the decision variables *I* and *M* and notes the total profit. Figure 15.3 shows the numerical values calculated by the electronic spreadsheet if you enter 10000 and 50000 in Cells B3 and C3, respectively. The profit is $8,900. By trial and error, the manager can evaluate different purchasing plans and try to find the most profitable combination.

Searching for the best decisions

In the linear programming model, we *assumed* that you couldn't produce more of any product than you could sell. We added constraints to ensure this. A solution wasn't feasible if you had excess production. Using Figure 15.2's template, you can input values for *I* and *M* that give excess production. As you try values, you must check the screen to see whether the amount produced exceeds the amount sold. If so, you don't consider that set of decisions.

Check for feasibility

It is possible to solve the potato processing decision problem by linear programming. But this template is easier to explain. Furthermore, the template can be used to challenge the person unfamiliar with linear

FIGURE 15.3 Electronic Spreadsheet for Potato Processing Template of Figure 15.2 with 10,000 Pounds from Idaho and 50,000 Pounds from Michigan

```
Potato Processing Example
            Idaho, Pds. Michigan, Pds.
               10000        50000 Pds. Produced  Pds. Sold  Revenues
French fries    3000        10000      13000       13000      11700
Hash browns     1000        10000      11000       11000       8250
Flakes          3000        15000      18000       18000       9000
Waste           3000        15000      18000       18000       1800

Cost            3850        18000
                    Total cost                 Total revenues Total profit
                        21850                       30750        8900
```

programming to beat the result obtained by the optimization model. The disbeliever can easily understand the template and even verify its results for a particular set of decision variable values using a calculator, paper, and pencil.

Other templates

Many different templates are possible for the Potato Processing example. You get different templates by changing the definition of rows and columns. For example, Column D might be Idaho potatoes. You also get different templates when you use additional cells to define parameters and intermediate variables. For example, let's consider the potato processing cost, $0.16 per pound. In the template of Figure 15.2, that parameter appears in the formulas in Cells B9 and B10. If the processing cost increases to $0.17, you must change the formulas in Cells B9 and B10. Alternatively, you might define Cell A11 as the processing cost. Then, the formula in Cell B9 is $(0.225 + A11) * B3$. What would be the formula in Cell C9? By introducing Cell A11, if the processing cost per pound increases to $0.17, you only have to change the contents of Cell A11. You use additional cells to define parameters and intermediate variables when this simplifies analysis of the model's results.

Don't use numbers in formulas

Your spreadsheet is easier to understand and modify if you define a cell for each parameter and group all of the parameters together. *A formula should not include a numerical value for a parameter;* it should refer to the cell that has that parameter's value. We make Figure 15.2's spreadsheet easier to understand and modify by eliminating all of the numbers that appear in formulas. For example, we can include the product yields in separate cells. Then, the formulas in Cells B4 to B7 and C4 to C7 would contain the cells with those yields rather than the numerical values. Thus, you can see the yields at a glance and changing a yield value doesn't require editing a formula.

It is possible to collapse several cells into a single cell. For example, rather than define Cells B4 and C4, it is possible to change the formula in Cell D4 to $0.3 * B3 + 0.2 * C3$. In fact, it is possible to construct a template for the Potato Processing example with only three cells—the two decision variables and the profit. However, the formula for the profit cell would be complex. Defining intermediate variables makes it easier to understand the template and to use it in "What if?" analyses.

Optimization and Electronic Spreadsheets

Electronic spreadsheets answer "What if?" questions, but they don't automatically find the best solution. Add-in software packages such as What's*Best!* from General Optimization and VINO from LINDO SYSTEMS add optimization capabilities to popular electronic spreadsheets such as LOTUS 1–2–3. Let's show how to use What's*Best!* to optimize an electronic spreadsheet for the Potato Processing example.

Figure 15.4 contains a template for the Potato Processing example.

FIGURE 15.4   What's*Best!* Template for Potato Processing Example

	A	B	C	D	E	F	G	H
1	Potato Processing Example							
2								
3								
4			Potato source					
5			Idaho	Michigan				
6	Pounds purchased							Total profit
7	Profit margin		0.14	0.15				+C7*C6+D7*D6
8							Maximum	Unsatisfied
9			Yields		Produced		sales	sales
10	French fries		0.3	0.2	+C10*C6+D10*D6		18000	+G10−E10
11	Hash browns		0.1	0.2	+C11*C6+D11*D6		15000	+G11−E11
12	Flakes		0.3	0.3	+C12*C6+D12*D6		30000	+G12−E12

Three operations to
optimize the template

Only linear functions of
the adjustable vari-
ables are allowed

Cells C6 and D6 contain the decisions, the number of pounds of potatoes purchased from Idaho and Michigan. Cell E10 contains the formula for calculating the amount of french fries produced, $+C10 * C6 + D10 * D6$. Similarly, Cells E11 and E12 contain the formulas for hash browns and flakes produced, respectively. Column G contains the maximum sales for the three products. Column H contains the formulas for the amount of unsatisfied product sales. For example, Cell H10 calculates the unsatisfied french fry sales potential as $+G10 - E10$. Cell H7 contains the formula for the profit, $+C7 * C6 + D7 * D6$.

Load What's*Best!* into memory before you start LOTUS 1-2-3. Then, after you create the electronic spreadsheet, you call What's*Best!* and do three operations. *First,* you specify that Cells C6 and D6 are **adjustable cells** (i.e., decision variables). *Second,* you specify that Cell H7 is the cell to be maximized. *Third,* you specify the constraint relationships. Note that Column F doesn't have any entries. In Cells F10, F11, and F12, you specify that the constraint relationships between the amounts produced and maximum sales are $\leq$. Then, you tell What's*Best!* to optimize and it finds the optimal solution. Figure 15.5 shows the screen after optimization.

What's*Best!* and VINO can be used if the underlying optimization model is a linear programming model. All of the relationships involving the adjustable variables must be linear. All of the cell formulas that depend on the values of the adjustable variables are restricted to non-negative values. For that reason, Cells H10, H11, and H12 ensure that the unsatisfied sales potentials are ≥ 0. Thus, the amounts produced can't be more than the maximum sales potential. Both What's*Best!* and VINO use the LINDO optimizer to find the optimal solution to the linear programming model. These software packages also optimize models that have binary integer variables.

FIGURE 15.5 Electronic Spreadsheet for Potato Processing Template of Figure 15.4 after Optimization by What's*Best!*

```
Potato Processing Example

                  Potato   Source
                  Idaho    Michigan
Pounds purchased  15000    67500                        Total Profit
Profit margin      0.14     0.15                           12225
                                             Maximum   Unsatisfied
                  Yields            Produced  Sales      Sales
French fries       0.3      0.2      18000    18000        0
Hash browns        0.1      0.2      15000    15000        0
Flakes             0.3      0.3      24750    30000      5250
```

As we've seen in the chapters on linear programming, linear programming software can be used to solve the Potato Processing example. Some people find it easier to add optimization capabilities to an electronic spreadsheet they already use than to learn a new system. Bodily discusses how electronic spreadsheets can be a "stepping-stone" that brings management science to the manager who is a generalist, not a management science specialist.[5] He discusses how spreadsheets can be used for decision trees, probabilistic simulations, and forecasting as well as optimization.

Another advantage of optimizing electronic spreadsheets is that their powerful formating capabilities make creating output reports easier. A disadvantage is that the processing time of spreadsheets is slower than that of linear programming software. Thus, linear programming software is preferred for large models.

A DETERMINISTIC FINANCIAL SIMULATION—IFPS

When you use an electronic spreadsheet, you define the model by constructing the template. The cell formulas define the relationships among parameters, decisions, and intermediate variables. Checking the relationships (formulas) to validate the model is hard for a complex model. Validating the model is easier if you use a software package with an English-like modeling language, such as Execucom's **Interactive Financial Planning System (IFPS)**. In this section, we illustrate the use of IFPS for a deterministic financial simulation.

Say that a manufacturing company wants to estimate its profit and return on sales for four years, beginning with 1989. You calculate the profit as

$$\text{Profit} = \text{Revenues} - \text{Expenses}$$

You calculate the return on sales as

$$\text{Return on sales} = \text{Profit/Revenues}$$

The revenues are

$$\text{Revenues} = \text{Quantity sold} * \text{Selling price}$$

The asterisk, *, represents multiplication. Say that the plan is to make and sell 8,000 units in 1989.

---

[5] Samuel Bodily, "Spreadsheet Modeling as a Stepping Stone," *Interfaces* 16, no. 5 (September–October 1986), pp. 34–52.

The expenses are

$$\text{Expenses} = \text{Fixed costs} + \text{Variable costs}$$

The fixed costs include salaries, utilities, and leases, which are estimated to be \$13,000, \$7,000, and \$20,000, respectively, in 1989. The variable costs are

$$\text{Variable costs} = \text{Quantity made} * \text{Variable cost per unit}$$

The variable costs include the material and labor costs:

$$\text{Variable cost per unit} = \text{Material cost per unit} + \text{Labor cost per unit}$$

In 1989, the material cost and labor cost per unit are estimated to be \$5 and \$6, respectively.

Figure 15.6 contains an IFPS model for the manufacturing company. Electronic spreadsheet formulas are cell oriented, but IFPS formulas are row oriented. The same formula applies to all of the entries in a row. The statements are numbered to make it easier to refer to them. The statement numbered 100 defines four columns and names them as 1989, 1990, 1991, and 1992. Statements 110 through 170 define the relationships. Because the statements are English-like, it's easier to understand and verify the relationships.

Statements 180 through 250 specify the values of parameters. Statement 180 specifies that salaries are \$30,000 in all the years. Statement 190 specifies that utilities cost \$7,000 in 1989 and that their cost increases 10 percent per year. The utilities cost is calculated by multiplying the utilities cost in the previous year by 1.10. Similarly, the material cost per unit, the

FIGURE 15.6 The IFPS Model

```
100   columns 1989,1990,1991,1992
110   profit = revenues - expenses
120   return on sales = profit / revenues
130   revenues = quantity sold * selling price
140   expenses = fixed costs + variable costs
150   variable costs = quantity made * variable cost per unit
160   variable cost per unit = material cost per unit + labor cost per unit
170   fixed costs = salaries + utilities + leases
180   salaries = 30000
190   utilities = 7000, previous * 1.10
200   leases = 20000, minimum(previous * 1.05, 21500)
210   material cost per unit = 5, previous * 1.03
220   labor cost per unit = 6, previous * 1.04
230   quantity made = 8000, round(previous * 1.10)
240   quantity sold = 8000, round(previous * 1.10)
250   selling price = 20, previous * 1.04
```

labor cost per unit and the selling price increase by 3, 4, and 4 percent each year, respectively. Salaries stay at $30,000 each year.

IFPS has built-in functions that are useful in modeling. Statement 200 uses the MINIMUM fuction to calculate the lease cost. The lease cost begins at $20,000 and increases by 5 percent each year until it reaches a maximum of $21,500. The number made and sold is 8,000 in 1989 and increases by 10 percent each year. The ROUND function is used because you must make and sell *integer* numbers of units.

It is easier to understand the IFPS model because of its English-like modeling language. Figure 15.7 shows the output from the IFPS model. You can use the model to study the impact of parameter changes on profit and return on sales. For example, you can edit the model so that labor cost per unit increases by 5 percent and re-solve the model. You use the model to study profitability by repeated "What if?" analyses.

The current version of IFPS for microcomputers, IFPS/Personal, doesn't have optimization capabilities. IFPS on mainframes and minicomputers does. As with What's*Best!,* you specify the decisions, the objective function, and the constraints, and an optimizer prints a solution report with the best solution.

Figure 15.6's IFPS model is deterministic, but IFPS also has probabilistic capabilities. When you build the model, you can specify probabilistic relationships.

Exxon's simulation model was probabilistic. There was uncertainty about component yields, arrival times for barges and tank trucks, and refinery equipment breakdowns. In the next section, we discuss how to generate random variables for a probabilistic simulation.

Built-in functions

FIGURE 15.7   The Results of the IFPS Model

	1989	1990	1991	1992
profit	15000.00	24108.00	35260.87	48691.94
return on sales	0.09	0.13	0.17	0.20
revenues	160000.00	183040.00	209397.76	239551.04
expenses	145000.00	158932.00	174136.89	190859.10
variable costs	88000.00	100232.00	114166.89	130042.10
variable cost per unit	11.00	11.39	11.79	12.21
fixed costs	57000.00	58700.00	59970.00	60817.00
salaries	30000.00	30000.00	30000.00	30000.00
utilities	7000.00	7700.00	8470.00	9317.00
leases	20000.00	21000.00	21500.00	21500.00
material cost per unit	5.00	5.15	5.30	5.46
labor cost per unit	6.00	6.24	6.49	6.75
quantity made	8000.00	8800.00	9680.00	10648.00
quantity sold	8000.00	8800.00	9680.00	10648.00
selling price	20.00	20.80	21.63	22.50

GENERATING RANDOM VARIABLES

Performing a probabilistic simulation requires generating random variables from a specified probability distribution. You must know the probability distribution you want to use. This can be obtained on theoretical grounds or based on historical information. In this section, we assume that we know the probability distribution and we show how to generate random variables from it.

Let's consider a simple situation. We want to estimate the daily sales of a slow-selling item. In fact, each day either one or none is sold. If the probability distribution for daily sales is known, it is simple to calculate the expected value of daily sales. But let's try to estimate the average daily sales by a probabilistic simulation experiment. To simplify this further, let's assume that sales are equally likely to be one unit or none. The probability of selling one unit is 0.5, and the probability of selling none is 0.5. The simulation consists of generating a random variable from that probability distribution and writing down the sales. This is repeated many times, and the relative frequencies of the outcomes are used to estimate the average daily sales. It is necessary to be able to generate random variables or, alternatively, to perform an experiment in which the two outcomes are equally likely. In this simple case, flipping a fair coin can be used to perform the experiment. The two possible outcomes are a head (H) and a tail (T), and they are equally likely. You must assign the outcomes of the experiment (H or T) to the actual events being considered. Let's assign an H to a sale of 0 units and a T to a sale of 1 unit.

Flipping the coin the first time, we observe that an H has been obtained. This is a sale of 0 units, and we write it down. Say that we flip the coin nine more times. The results of this experiment are shown in Table 15.2. It is noted that an H resulted six times and that a T resulted four

TABLE 15.2   Equally Likely Outcomes Simulation

Trial	Experiment Outcome	Value of Random Variable
1	H	0
2	T	1
3	H	0
4	H	0
5	T	1
6	T	1
7	H	0
8	T	1
9	H	0
10	H	0
Total		4

times. The experiment resulted in total sales of 4 units in the 10 trials. The average daily sales were $\frac{4}{10} = 0.4$. Based on the probabilistic simulation, the average sales are estimated to be 0.4 per day. The expected sales per day are easily calculated as

$$\text{Expected daily sales} = (0.5 \times 0) + (0.5 \times 1) = 0.5$$

The estimate (0.4) is not equal to the expected daily sales (0.5). The simulation result did not yield the correct expected value. In general, *the results of a probabilistic simulation may not give an estimated value exactly equal to the expected value.* If we flipped the coin another 10 times, we might get different estimates. If we obtained five H and five T, the estimate of the average daily sales would be 0.5, which is the correct value. It is improbable, but possible, that the experiment results in no H and 10 T. This gives an average daily sales estimate of 1.0, which is far from the correct value of 0.5. Because of the variability of the results, you should establish the amount of confidence to place on the estimates from the simulation experiment. The average from the simulation experiment is often wrong, but how close to the correct value do we expect it to be? In Chapter 16, we discuss determining confidence intervals based on the simulation results.

One way of obtaining more confidence in the results of the experiment is to have more trials. The coin could be flipped 100 times or even 1,000 times. Flipping the coin 1,000 times would be time consuming. Thus, it is more convenient to use a computer to perform the experiment a large number of times, rather than to do it "by hand." That is why computers are so widely used for probabilistic simulations. In Chapter 16, we discuss calculating the number of trials necessary to obtain the desired level of confidence.

Three steps of conducting a probabilistic simulation are listed in Table 15.3. *First,* create an experiment whose outcomes have the same probabilities as the probabilities of the event actually being studied. *Second,* assign each outcome of the experiment to an event being studied. *Third,* repeat the experiment, record the outcomes, and analyze the results. In our previous example, the experiment was flipping a coin and we assigned an H to sales of 0 units and a T to sales of 1 unit. More complex examples use the same basic steps.

Estimates from probabilistic simulation can be different from the expected value

Repeating the experiment improves the estimate

TABLE 15.3 Three Steps in Conducting a Probabilistic Simulation

Step 1. Create an experiment with the desired outcome probabilities.
Step 2. Assign outcomes to the events being studied.
Step 3. Repeat the experiment, record the outcomes, and analyze the results.

In this section, we discuss the first two steps. In the last two sections of this chapter, we show how to use random variables generated to do a probabilistic simulation. In Chapter 16, we discuss analyzing probabilistic simulation results.

There are two types of probability distributions, depending on what outcomes are possible. A **discrete probability distribution** has a set of outcomes that can be listed. For example, if a basketball player shoots 10 free throws, the number that are made can be 0 or 1 or 2 or 3 or . . . or 10. A **continuous probability distribution** has a set of outcomes that cannot be listed. For example, consider the amount of time until you receive your next phone call. It could be instantly, or it could be an hour from now. Furthermore, it could be any of the values between 0 and 1 hour, or even more than an hour. Since time is intrinsically continuous, it is impossible to list all of the possible times. Time, distance, and weight are generally continuous. If you want to treat the random variable as a continuous random variable, you must use a different method to generate the random variables.

We'll discuss generating random variables from a discrete distribution first. Then, we'll discuss generating random variables from a continuous distribution.

Generating Discrete Random Variables

In our example above, the underlying probability distribution of daily sales was a discrete distribution. The only possible values of the random variable, daily sales, were 0 and 1. It was possible to use the coin-flipping experiment because the two outcomes for sales were equally likely. If there were more than two outcomes or if the two outcomes were not equally likely, it would not be possible to use the coin-flipping experiment.

Let's consider another example. A company wants to develop a probabilistic simulation that requires generating daily sales. The company has historical sales data of a particular product. Table 15.4 summarizes the

TABLE 15.4 Historical Distribution of Daily Sales (100 days)

Demand	Number of Occurrences	Relative Frequencies
0	12	0.12
1	23	0.23
2	32	0.32
3	19	0.19
4	11	0.11
5	3	0.03
Total	100	1.00

daily sales for 100 days. In Chapter 12, we discussed examining the data for trend and seasonal components. For example, has there been a general increase or decrease in daily sales during the 100 days? Does the day of the week affect daily sales? Are daily sales usually lower in January than in April? Let's *assume* that the analyses have not found any significant trend, daily factors, or seasonal factors. Thus, the relative frequencies of the historical data can be used as an estimate of the probability distribution of daily sales. The relative frequencies also appear in Table 15.4.

We want to design a simulation experiment that generates a value of daily sales from the discrete probability distribution given in Table 15.4. One possible experiment uses pieces of paper and a bowl. First, cut 100 pieces of paper. On 12 of them, write the number 0. Write the number 1 on 23 of them, and the number 2 on 32. Write the numbers 3, 4, and 5 on 19, 11, and 3 pieces of paper, respectively. That is a total of 100 pieces of paper whose numbers have the same relative frequencies as the historical distribution of daily sales. The experiment can be performed by mixing the 100 pieces of paper in a bowl so that each of the 100 is equally likely to be chosen. A piece of paper is drawn from the bowl, and the number written on it is noted. If it is a 3, that means daily sales of 3 units. If you want to generate more than one value of daily sales, *each with the probabilities from the historical relative frequencies,* the sampling must be done with replacement. **Sampling with replacement** means that after the first piece of paper has been drawn and its value noted, the piece of paper is returned to the bowl before the next piece of paper is chosen.

This approach can be used for any discrete probability distribution. However, it is inconvenient to cut up a large number of pieces of paper, write a value on each one, do the sampling, and note the results. You can reduce the number of pieces of papers by the way you design the experiment. Say that the historical data was for 1,000 days and Table 15.5 summarizes the data.

In this example, the product is sold by the gross, 144 units. None of the product was sold on 450 days, and one gross of the product was sold on 550 days. One way of performing this experiment requires 1,000 pieces of paper, 450 with 0 on them and 550 with 144 on them. The experiment requires a large bowl to hold the 1,000 pieces of paper. An easier method

Use relative frequencies for the probabilities

An experiment with a bowl and pieces of paper

Another discrete probability distribution

TABLE 15.5 Historical Distribution of Daily Sales (1,000 days)

Demand	Number of Observations	Relative Frequencies
0	450	0.45
144	550	0.55
Total	1,000	1.00

There can be more than one way to design the experiment

is to use only 100 pieces of paper, 45 with 0 on them and 55 with 144 on them. This method also generates a daily sales value with the same probability distribution, but the container is smaller and doing the experiment is less trouble than doing the one with 1,000 pieces of paper. It is also possible to do the experiment with only 20 pieces of paper, 9 with 0 on them and 11 with 144 on them. These also have the same relative frequencies, $\frac{9}{20} = 0.45$ and $\frac{11}{20} = 0.55$. In other words, *there can be more than one way to design a simulation experiment.*

An experiment with a random number table

A more conventional method is to use a **random number table** such as Table 15.6. Note that this table has 100 possible values, from 00 to 99. The numbers in the table were generated so that each of the values from 00 to 99 is equally likely. The values are independently generated. That is, the number in a particular position in the table is independent of the numbers in any other positions in the table. This implies that the sampling was done with replacement.

The simulation experiment consists of obtaining a number from the random number table and assigning an outcome to each number from 00 to 99. For the distribution of daily sales represented by Table 15.4, there are six possible outcomes. There are many possible ways of assigning the values from the random number table to the outcomes of daily sales. A logical method is to assign the values 00, 01, 02, 03, 04, 05, 06, 07, 08, 09, 10, and 11 from the random number table to daily sales of 0. This assigns 12 of the 100 possible values to daily sales of 0. This relative frequency, $\frac{12}{100}$, is the same as the desired probability from Table 15.4, 0.12. Note that the random number table includes 00 but does not include 100. There are 12 values from 00 to 11. Similarly, daily sales of 1 can be assigned to random number table values of 12 to 34; daily sales of 2, to values of 35 to 66; daily sales of 3, to values of 67 to 85; daily sales of 4, to values of 86 to 96; and daily sales of 5, to values of 97 to 99. Table 15.7 shows this assignment of values from the random number table to daily sales. Each of the *relative frequencies from the random number table assignments* is the same as the desired *probabilities* of daily sales.

Starting in the upper-left-hand corner and reading down, ten values from the random number table (Table 15.6) are 61, 15, 94, 42, 23, 04, 00, 35, 59, and 46. Because it is in the interval 35 to 66, the first value from the random number table (61) is daily sales of 2. Similarly, the next nine values of daily sales are 1, 4, 2, 1, 0, 0, 2, 2, and 2. The total sales for the 10 trials is 16, and the average daily sales from the 10 generated values is $\frac{16}{10} = 1.6$. Thus, the estimate of daily sales is 1.6. The expected value of daily sales is

$$(0.12 \times 0) + (0.23 \times 1) + (0.32 \times 2) + (0.19 \times 3) + (0.11 \times 4)$$
$$+ (0.03 \times 5) = 2.03$$

TABLE 15.6 Table of Random Numbers

61 19 69 04 46	26 45 74 77 74	51 92 43 37 29	65 39 45 95 93	42 58 26 05 27
15 47 44 52 66	95 27 07 99 53	59 36 78 38 48	82 39 61 01 18	33 21 15 94 66
94 55 72 85 73	67 89 75 43 87	54 62 24 44 31	91 19 04 25 92	92 92 74 59 73
42 48 11 62 13	97 34 40 87 21	16 86 84 87 67	03 07 11 20 59	25 70 14 66 70
23 52 37 83 17	73 20 88 98 37	68 93 59 14 16	26 25 22 96 63	05 52 28 25 62
04 49 35 24 94	75 24 63 38 24	45 86 25 10 25	61 96 27 93 35	65 33 71 24 72
00 54 99 76 54	64 05 18 81 59	96 11 96 38 96	54 69 28 23 91	23 28 72 95 29
35 96 31 53 07	26 89 80 93 54	33 35 13 54 62	77 97 45 00 24	90 10 33 93 33
59 80 80 83 91	45 42 72 68 42	83 60 94 97 00	13 02 12 48 92	78 56 52 01 06
46 05 88 52 36	01 39 00 22 86	77 28 14 40 77	93 91 08 36 47	70 61 74 29 41
32 17 90 05 97	87 37 92 52 41	05 56 70 70 07	86 74 31 71 57	85 39 41 18 38
69 23 46 14 06	20 11 74 52 04	15 95 66 00 00	18 74 39 24 23	97 11 89 63 38
19 56 54 14 30	01 75 87 53 79	40 41 92 15 85	66 67 43 68 06	84 96 28 52 07
45 15 51 49 38	19 47 60 72 46	43 66 79 45 43	59 04 79 00 33	20 82 66 95 41
94 86 43 19 94	36 16 81 08 51	34 88 88 15 53	01 54 03 54 56	05 01 45 11 76
98 08 62 48 26	45 24 02 84 04	44 99 90 88 96	39 09 47 34 07	35 44 13 18 80
33 18 51 62 32	41 94 15 09 49	89 43 54 85 81	88 69 54 19 94	37 54 87 30 43
80 95 10 04 06	96 38 27 07 74	20 15 12 33 87	25 01 62 52 98	94 62 46 11 71
79 75 24 91 40	71 96 12 82 96	69 86 10 25 91	74 85 22 05 39	00 38 75 95 79
18 63 33 25 37	98 14 50 65 71	31 01 02 46 74	05 45 56 14 27	77 93 89 19 36
74 02 94 39 02	77 55 73 22 70	97 79 01 71 19	52 52 75 80 21	80 81 45 17 48
54 17 84 56 11	80 99 33 71 43	05 33 51 29 69	56 12 71 92 55	36 04 09 03 24
11 66 44 98 83	52 07 98 48 27	59 38 17 15 39	09 97 33 34 40	88 46 12 33 56
48 32 47 79 28	31 24 96 47 10	02 29 53 68 70	32 30 75 75 46	15 02 00 99 94
69 07 49 41 38	87 63 79 19 76	35 58 40 44 01	10 51 82 16 15	01 84 87 69 38
09 18 82 00 97	32 82 53 95 27	04 22 08 63 04	83 38 98 73 74	64 27 85 80 44
90 04 58 54 97	51 98 15 06 54	94 93 88 19 97	91 87 07 61 50	68 47 66 46 59
73 18 95 02 07	47 67 72 62 69	62 29 06 44 64	27 12 46 70 18	41 36 18 27 60
75 76 87 64 90	20 97 18 17 49	90 42 91 22 72	95 37 50 58 71	93 82 34 31 78
54 01 64 40 56	66 28 13 10 03	00 68 22 73 98	20 71 45 32 95	07 70 61 78 13
08 35 86 99 10	78 54 24 27 85	13 66 15 88 73	04 61 89 75 53	31 22 30 84 20
28 30 60 32 64	81 33 31 05 91	40 51 00 78 93	32 60 46 04 75	94 11 90 18 40
53 84 08 62 33	81 59 41 36 28	51 21 59 02 90	28 46 66 87 95	77 76 22 07 91
91 75 75 37 41	61 61 36 22 69	50 26 39 02 12	55 78 17 65 14	83 48 34 70 55
89 41 59 26 94	00 39 75 83 91	12 60 71 76 46	48 94 97 23 06	94 54 13 74 03
77 51 30 38 20	86 83 42 99 01	68 41 48 27 74	51 90 81 39 80	72 89 35 55 07
19 50 23 71 74	69 97 92 02 88	55 21 02 97 73	74 28 77 52 51	65 34 46 74 15
21 81 85 93 13	93 27 88 17 57	05 68 67 31 56	07 08 28 50 46	31 85 33 84 52
51 47 46 64 99	68 10 72 36 21	94 04 99 13 45	42 83 60 91 91	08 00 74 54 49
99 55 96 83 31	62 53 52 41 70	69 77 71 28 30	74 81 97 81 42	43 86 07 28 34
33 71 34 80 07	93 58 47 28 69	51 92 66 47 21	58 30 32 98 22	93 17 49 39 72
85 27 48 68 93	11 30 32 92 70	28 83 43 41 37	73 51 59 04 00	71 14 84 36 43

SOURCE: Reprinted from *A Million Random Digits with 100,000 Normal Deviates* by the Rand Corporation (New York: The Free Press, 1955). Copyright 1955 & 1983 by the Rand Corporation. Used by permission.

TABLE 15.7   The Assignment of Numbers from the Random Number Table to Outcomes for the Daily Demand Probability Distribution in Table 15.4

Daily Demand	Probability	Assigned Values from the Random Number Table
0	0.12	00 to 11
1	0.23	12 to 34
2	0.32	35 to 66
3	0.19	67 to 85
4	0.11	86 to 96
5	0.03	97 to 99

Again, the results of the simulation did not give an estimated value equal to the expected value.

Assigning random number table values to outcomes

A less convenient assignment of values from the random number table to daily sales of 0 might be the values 00, 23, 32, 52, 47, 91, 66, 33, and 96 to 99. Again, there are 12 numbers in the assignment, so the relative frequency is $\frac{12}{100} = 0.12$. However, it is aggravating to have to look up whether a number from the random number table corresponds to daily sales of 0. It is much easier to assign consecutive values from the random number table. It is also easier to assign smaller values from the random number table to smaller outcomes of the actual random variable. That is why the values 00 to 11 were daily sales of 0, rather than 88 to 99. Either assignment is correct, but 00 to 11 is more convenient.

An experiment using a computer random number generator

Using a random number table can simplify the experiment by eliminating the pieces of paper. If the experiment was to be done "by hand," using the random number table is helpful. However, if the simulation is done on a computer, using a random number table is not very convenient. That is because the random number table would have to be an input to the simulation program, and each time a value is needed from the table a new one would have to be referenced from the stored table. Most computers have a built-in random number generator that is callable by other programs.[6] Usually, the **computer random number generator (CRNG)** function is designated as RAND or RND. It usually provides a value between 0 and 1. This continuous random variable is from a uniform distribution. That is, all of the values between 0 and 1 are equally likely. It is only necessary to assign each of the possible values from the CRNG to each of the discrete outcomes so that the probabilities are correct. For the example of Table 15.4, daily sales of 0 can be assigned to a value from the CRNG less than or equal to 0.12. Similarly, daily sales of 1 can be

---

[6] The values are actually **pseudorandom numbers** because the computer program generates the same sequence if it starts in the same place.

TABLE 15.8 The Assignment of Numbers from a Computer Random Number Generator to Outcomes for the Daily Demand Probability Distribution in Table 15.4

Daily Demand	Probability	Assigned Values from the Computer Random Number Generator
0	0.12	$0.00 \leq q \leq 0.12$
1	0.23	$0.12 < q \leq 0.35$
2	0.32	$0.35 < q \leq 0.67$
3	0.19	$0.67 < q \leq 0.86$
4	0.11	$0.86 < q \leq 0.97$
5	0.03	$0.97 < q \leq 1.00$

assigned to a value greater than 0.12 but not more than 0.35. A value at the point between two outcomes, such as 0.12 must be assigned to only one outcome. Table 15.8 has the assignment of values from the CRNG to daily sales.

Generating Continuous Random Variables

All of the approaches for generating random variables from a continuous probability distribution use the cumulative probability distribution of the random variable. Say that the random variable is designated as X. The **cumulative probability distribution,** denoted by $F(x)$, is the probability that the random variable X is less than or equal to the value x.

For example, consider a continuous uniform probability distribution between 2 and 5. Figure 15.8 illustrates the probability density function; the lower limit is 2, and the upper limit is 5. Each of the values between 2 and 5 is equally likely. Figure 15.9 illustrates the cumulative probability

FIGURE 15.8 Probability Density Distribution—Uniform Continuous

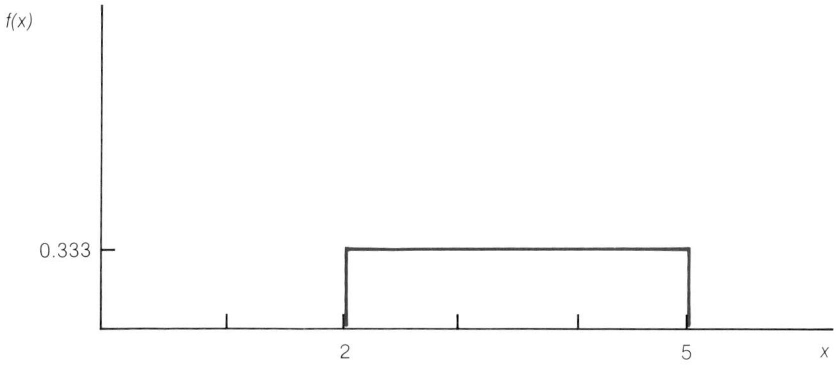

FIGURE 15.9   Cumulative Probability Distribution—Uniform Continuous

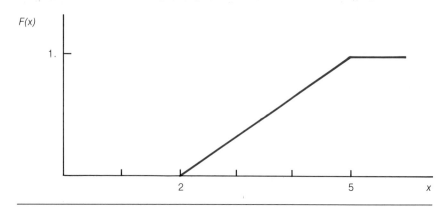

---

distribution for Figure 15.8. Because the random variable can't be smaller than 2, $F(2) = 0$. Because the random variable must be 5 or less, $F(5) = 1.0$. Because the random variable is uniform, $F(x)$ increases linearly from $x = 2$ to $x = 5$.

The basic approach

The basic approach begins with a value from the CRNG. Let's call this value q. The value is between 0 and 1. The value of the cumulative probability is also between 0 and 1. You find the value of x such that $F(x) = q$, and that x is the random variable value. For example, say that $q = 0.5$. Then, you find the value of x for which $F(x) = 0.5$.

Three methods

There are three methods for determining x, the random variable value, such that $F(x) = q$. The method used depends on whether the cumulative probability distribution is represented by a graph, an algebraic function, or a table. We illustrate the three methods with examples.

The graphical method

The **graphical method** uses the cumulative probability distribution graph of $F(x)$. You find the value of q on the $F(x)$ axis and draw a line across to the intersection with the graph. Then, you draw a vertical line to the x axis and read the random variable value. Say that $q = 0.5$. Figure 15.10 shows that the value of x is 3.5. To generate a second random variable, you get a second value from the CRNG. Say that the second value is $q = 0.24$. What is the associated random number? You draw a line across from 0.24 to the curve and read down. Because of the limited accuracy with which graphs can be read, this is not a very accurate method. Also, the graphical approach is difficult to implement on a computer.

The algebraic method

The **algebraic method** uses the algebraic representation of the cumulative probability distribution. For example, the cumulative probability distribution function of the continuous uniform probability distribution for Figure 15.9 is

$$F(x) = \frac{x - 2}{3} \text{ for } 2 \le x \le 5$$

FIGURE 15.10 The Graphical Method—Finding x so that F(x) = 0.5

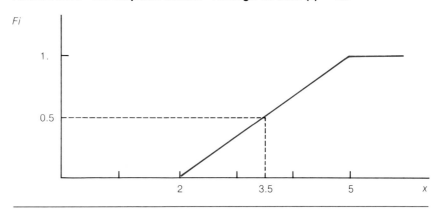

For $x \le 2$, $F(x) = 0$. For $x \ge 5$, $F(x) = 1$. If q is the value from the CRNG, you must find x so that $F(x) = q$. This requires solving the equation for that x such that $\dfrac{x - 2}{3} = q$. Algebraic manipulation yields

$$x = 2 + 3q$$

For example, if $q = 0.24$, then $x = 2 + (3 \times 0.24) = 2.72$. This is more accurate than the value read from the graph by the first method. Solving for x by algebraic manipulation is called **inverting the cumulative probability distribution.** This method is particularly well suited to computer simulation.

The table method   The **table method** uses a table of the cumulative probability distribution. This is not particularly convenient for computer simulation, but if the cumulative probability distribution cannot be written in a form that is easy to evaluate or if it cannot be inverted, it may be necessary to use the table method. The normal probability distribution is one for which the use of tables is common. The cumulative normal probability distribution does not have a functional form that is easy to evaluate or invert. Let's illustrate the table method using the normal distribution.

Say that we want to generate a random variable from a normal distribution with a mean of 100 and a standard deviation of 5. The **standardized normal random variable** is calculated as $Z = \dfrac{X - \mu}{\sigma}$, where μ is the mean and σ is the standard deviation. The standardized normal random variable has a mean of 0 and a standard deviation of 1. For the desired normal random variable, the standardization is $\dfrac{(X - 100)}{5}$. Table 15.9 is the cumulative standardized normal distribution, $F(z) =$ Probability $(Z \le z)$. This shows that $F(0.00) = 0.5000$. The probability is 0.5 that the standardized random variable attains a value of 0.0 or less. Can you verify that

TABLE 15.9   Cumulative Normal Probability Distribution

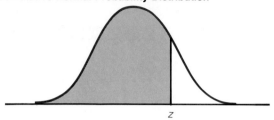

Table entries are cumulative probabilities represented in the shaded area above.

z	.00	.01	.02	.03	.04	.05	.06	.07	.08	.09
.0	.5000	.5040	.5080	.5120	.5160	.5199	.5239	.5279	.5319	.5359
.1	.5398	.5438	.5478	.5517	.5557	.5596	.5636	.5675	.5714	.5753
.2	.5793	.5832	.5871	.5910	.5948	.5987	.6026	.6064	.6103	.6141
.3	.6179	.6217	.6255	.6293	.6331	.6368	.6406	.6443	.6480	.6517
.4	.6554	.6591	.6628	.6664	.6700	.6736	.6772	.6808	.6844	.6879
.5	.6915	.6950	.6985	.7019	.7054	.7088	.7123	.7157	.7190	.7224
.6	.7257	.7291	.7324	.7357	.7389	.7422	.7454	.7486	.7517	.7549
.7	.7580	.7611	.7642	.7673	.7704	.7734	.7764	.7794	.7823	.7852
.8	.7881	.7910	.7939	.7967	.7995	.8023	.8051	.8078	.8106	.8133
.9	.8159	.8186	.8212	.8238	.8264	.8289	.8315	.8340	.8365	.8389
1.0	.8413	.8438	.8461	.8485	.8508	.8531	.8554	.8577	.8599	.8621
1.1	.8643	.8665	.8686	.8708	.8729	.8749	.8770	.8790	.8810	.8830
1.2	.8849	.8869	.8888	.8907	.8925	.8944	.8962	.8980	.8997	.9015
1.3	.9032	.9049	.9066	.9082	.9099	.9115	.9131	.9147	.9162	.9177
1.4	.9192	.9207	.9222	.9236	.9251	.9265	.9279	.9292	.9306	.9319
1.5	.9332	.9345	.9357	.9370	.9382	.9394	.9406	.9418	.9429	.9441
1.6	.9452	.9463	.9474	.9484	.9495	.9505	.9515	.9525	.9535	.9545
1.7	.9554	.9564	.9573	.9582	.9591	.9599	.9608	.9616	.9625	.9633
1.8	.9641	.9649	.9656	.9664	.9671	.9678	.9686	.9693	.9699	.9706
1.9	.9713	.9719	.9726	.9732	.9738	.9744	.9750	.9756	.9761	.9767
2.0	.9772	.9778	.9783	.9788	.9793	.9798	.9803	.9808	.9812	.9817
2.1	.9821	.9826	.9830	.9834	.9838	.9842	.9846	.9850	.9854	.9857
2.2	.9861	.9864	.9868	.9871	.9875	.9878	.9881	.9884	.9887	9890
2.3	.9893	.9896	.9898	.9901	.9904	.9906	.9909	.9911	.9913	.9916
2.4	.9918	.9920	.9922	.9925	.9927	.9929	.9931	.9932	.9934	.9936
2.5	.9938	.9940	.9941	.9943	.9945	.9946	.9948	.9949	.9951	.9952
2.6	.9953	.9955	.9956	.9957	.9959	.9960	.9961	.9962	.9963	.9964
2.7	.9965	.9966	.9967	.9968	.9969	.9970	.9971	.9972	.9973	.9974
2.8	.9974	.9975	.9976	.9977	.9977	.9978	.9979	.9979	.9980	.9981
2.9	.9981	.9982	.9982	.9983	.9984	.9984	.9985	.9985	.9986	.9986
3.0	.9987	.9987	.9987	.9988	.9988	.9989	.9989	.9989	.9990	.9990
3.1	.9990	.9991	.9991	.9991	.9992	.9992	.9992	.9992	.9993	.9993
3.2	.9993	.9993	.9994	.9994	.9994	.9994	.9994	.9995	.9995	.9995
3.3	.9995	.9995	.9995	.9996	.9996	.9996	.9996	.9996	.9996	.9997
3.4	.9997	.9997	.9997	.9997	.9997	.9997	.9997	.9997	.9997	.9998

Selected Percentiles

Cumulative probability A:	.90	.95	.975	.98	.99	.995	.999
$z(A)$:	1.282	1.645	1.960	2.054	2.326	2.576	3.090

SOURCE: John Neter, William Wasserman, and Michael H. Kutner: *Applied Linear Statistical Models* 2nd ed. (Homewood, Ill.: Richard D. Irwin, 1985), p. 1073.

$F(0.01) = 0.5040$—that the probability is 0.5040 that a standardized normal random variable attains a value of 0.01 or less? If the CRNG gives a value of 0.040, the value of z is 0.01, and the value of x is calculated as $x = 100 + (5 \times 0.5040) = 102.52$. In general, after determining the value of z from Table 15.9, the value of x is calculated as

$$x = \mu + (\sigma \times z)$$

Table interpolation

Because of the limited number of significant digits in Table 15.9, it may be necessary to interpolate to estimate the value of z for a particular value from the CRNG. For example, say that the value from the CRNG is 0.6251. That value lies between the values 0.6217 and 0.6255 in Table 15.9, corresponding to $z = 0.31$ and $z = 0.32$, respectively. The value of z for 0.6251 is between 0.31 and 0.32. The interpolated value of z is

$$0.31 + (0.32 - 0.31) \times \frac{(0.6251 - 0.6217)}{(0.6255 - 0.6217)} = 0.31816$$

The value of the random variable is $x = 100 + (5 \times 0.31816) = 101.591$.

Values of q less than 0.5

Recall that $F(z) = $ Probability $(Z \leq z)$. If the value from the CRNG is *less* than 0.5, Table 15.9 does not have values of z. However, because the normal distribution is a symmetric distribution, it is possible to use Table 15.9. Say that you want to find the value of z such that $F(z) = q$, where q is *less than 0.5*. Then, the following result is useful: $F(-z) = 1 - q$. Say that the CRNG gives 0.025, which is less than 0.5. Then, $F(-z) = 1 - 0.025 = 0.975$. Table 15.9 shows that $F(1.96) = 0.975$. Thus, $-z = 1.96$, or $z = -1.96$. The random variable is $x = 100 + (-1.96 \times 5) = 90.2$.

In the next two sections, we show probabilistic simulation examples. In each, we develop the simulation logic and generate random variables from specified probability distributions.

RISK ANALYSIS—A PROBABILISTIC SIMULATION EXAMPLE

Managers must often decide whether to make capital investments. For example, a new piece of equipment might allow you to introduce a new product. You must compare the additional profit with the equipment cost to decide whether the investment is worthwhile. Because many capital investments have long lives, you consider the time value of money. The capital investment is paid at the beginning, but the profit is realized over its useful life. You must estimate the cash flows during the life of the new equipment. Outflows of cash are negative, and inflows of cash are positive. In **net present value (NPV) analysis,** all cash flows are discounted back to the beginning at some specified discount rate to calculate the NPV. If the NPV of the cash flows is positive, the capital investment is attractive. If the NPV is negative, the capital investment is not attractive.

NPV analysis is a deterministic method of analysis. You calculate the NPV as if there were very little uncertainty about the future cash flows. However, forecasting the cash flows requires knowing the useful life of the equipment, the inital cost and salvage value of the equipment, the selling price of the product, and the amount of sales. Often, there is considerable uncertainty about the factors that affect future cash flows. Managers consider the uncertainty by one of two approaches. Let's consider each approach.

The traditional approach

With traditional NPV analysis, you estimate the factors and then calculate the cash flows. Often, the *most likely values* of the uncertain factors are used as the basis for calculating the cash flows. For example, because you think that a seven-year useful life is most likely, you use a seven-year useful life in your cash flow analysis. But even though the NPV is positive for the most likely values of the factors, the NPV may still be negative. For example, perhaps the useful life is only five years. Managers use *sensitivity analysis* to determine the effect of possible errors in forecasting uncertain factors, such as useful life. Because the attractiveness of the capital investment depends on whether the NPV is positive or negative, sensitivity analysis can be undertaken to try to identify the combinations of factors that give a negative NPV.

The risk analysis approach

Another approach for considering the uncertain factors is to explicitly incorporate their probability distributions into the analysis. **Risk analysis** uses probabilistic simulation to estimate the NPV. You determine the probability distribution for each uncertain factor, generate random variables from those distributions, and calculate the NPV for repeated experiments. You use the simulation results to estimate the NPV and its probability distribution. David Hertz named this approach risk analysis. D. B. Hertz and H. Thomas, *Risk Analysis and Its Applications* (New York: John Wiley & Sons, 1983), is an excellent reference for risk analysis.

An example using the traditional approach

Let's consider an equipment purchasing example in which there is uncertainty about both sales and the useful life of the equipment. Let's assume that the forecasts of the selling price and operating costs are good, so that these can be treated as deterministic. To simplify the example, say that the annual sales, selling price, and operating costs stay the same from year to year. Also, say that the selling price is $500 per unit, the operating cost is $300 per unit, and the salvage value of the equipment after the end of its useful life is 0. The capital cost of the equipment is $1 million.

Table 15.10 contains the probability distributions for the annual sales and the useful life of the equipment. Assume that the annual sales and useful life are *independent random variables*. Using the traditional approach, let's calculate the NPV for the most likely occurrences—annual sales of 1,200 units and a useful life of seven years. Because the contribution is $200 per unit (500 − 300), the annual positive cash flows from product sales are $200 × 1,200 = $240,000. The company uses a discount

TABLE 15.10   Risk Analysis Probability Distributions

Sales	Probability	Cumulative Probability
1,000	0.2	0.2
1,200	0.5	0.7
1,400	0.3	1.0

Useful Life (Years)	Probability	Cumulative Probability
6	0.1	0.1
7	0.6	0.7
8	0.3	1.0

rate based on a minimum acceptable rate of return of 15 percent. Because we assume that the annual sales, selling price, and operating cost are the same from year to year, there is a positive cash flow of $240,000 in each of the seven years of useful life. Because the cash flows are the same in each year, you can calculate the discounted value of these cash flows using the **annuity factor:**

$$F = \frac{(1 + i)^n - 1}{i(1 + i)^n}$$

where n is the number of years and i is the decimal interest rate. The derivation appears in most accounting and finance textbooks. When $n = 7$ and $i = 0.15$, $F = 4.160$. The initial investment of $1 million is paid at the beginning and is not discounted. For the most likely occurrences,

$$NPV = [(500 - 300) \times 1,200 \times 4.160] - 1,000,000 = -\$16,000$$

Based on the most likely occurrences, the NPV is negative and the investment is rejected.

Now let's use risk analysis on the equipment purchasing example. Because of the uncertainty of the annual sales and the useful life, the NPV is itself a random variable. Many managers are interested in the probability distribution of the net present value. For example, it's useful to know the probability that the NPV is negative. We estimate the probability distribution of the NPV by a simulation study.

Let's use the random number table to perform the simulation. Table 15.11 shows the assignment of random numbers to annual sales and useful life. Table 15.12 has the simulation results for 30 trials. Each trial requires generating one random variable value for the annual sales and one for the useful life. We start in the upper-left-hand corner of Table 15.6 and read down to generate the 30 annual sales values. The first entry is 61, so the annual sales are 1,200 units in the first trial. The 31st entry in Table 15.6 is

An example using the risk analysis approach

TABLE 15.11   Assignments of Random Number Table Values for the Risk Analysis Simulation

Sales	Probability	Assigned Random Number Table Values
1,000	0.2	00—19
1,200	0.5	20—69
1,400	0.3	70—99

Useful Life (Years)	Probability	Assigned Random Number Table Values
6	0.1	00—09
7	0.6	10—69
8	0.3	70—99

used for the useful life of the first trial. Because the entry is 08, the useful life for the first trial is six years. Because the annuity factor is 3.784 for six years, the NPV for the first trial is

$$NPV = [(500 - 300) \times 1,200 \times 3.784] - 1,000,000 = -\$91,840$$

The NPVs for the other 29 trials are calculated similarly. Figure 15.11 illustrates a frequency diagram of the NPVs for the 30 trials of Table 15.12. You use the relative frequencies to estimate the probability distribution for the NPV. In 16 of the 30 trials, the NPV is negative. Thus, we estimate the probability of a negative NPV as $\frac{16}{30} = 0.533$. Because the NPV is $-\$168,000$ in 5 of the 30 trials, our estimate that the NPV equals $-\$168,000$ is $\frac{5}{30} = 0.167$. You use the estimated probability distribution to calculate the expected value of the NPV. With more trials, it's more likely that the relative frequencies equal the actual NPV probabilities. (In Chapter 16, we discuss statistical analysis of probabilistic simulations and choosing the number of trials.)

For this risk analysis example, it's possible to calculate the probability for each combination of annual sales and useful life. For example, the probability that sales are 1,000 and that the useful life is six years is $0.2 \times 0.1 = 0.02$. Then, you calculate the NPV for each combination and calculate the expected value of the NPV. However, if the example is generalized, calculating the probability of each combination can be difficult or impossible. Then, you can use probabilistic simulation to estimate the NPV. We used this simple example to illustrate the probabilistic simulation approach. Let's consider some possible generalizations.

Generalizations might include generating different annual sales for

TABLE 15.12   Risk Analysis Simulation—30 Trials

Trial	Value from Random Number Table	Sales	Value from Random Number Table	Useful Life	F	NPV
1	61	1,200	08	6	3.784	− 91,840
2	15	1,000	28	7	4.160	− 168,000
3	94	1,400	53	7	4.160	164,800
4	42	1,200	91	8	4.487	76,880
5	23	1,200	89	8	4.487	76,880
6	04	1,000	77	8	4.487	− 102,600
7	00	1,000	19	7	4.160	− 168,000
8	35	1,200	21	7	4.160	− 16,000
9	59	1,200	51	7	4.160	− 16,000
10	46	1,200	99	8	4.487	76,880
11	32	1,200	33	7	4.160	− 16,000
12	69	1,200	85	8	4.487	76,880
13	19	1,000	19	7	4.160	− 168,000
14	45	1,200	47	7	4.160	− 16,000
15	94	1,400	55	7	4.160	164,800
16	98	1,400	48	7	4.160	164,800
17	33	1,200	52	7	4.160	− 16,000
18	80	1,400	49	7	4.160	164,800
19	79	1,400	54	7	4.160	164,800
20	18	1,000	96	8	4.487	− 102,600
21	74	1,400	80	8	4.487	256,360
22	54	1,200	05	6	3.784	− 91,840
23	11	1,000	17	7	4.160	− 168,000
24	48	1,200	23	7	4.160	− 16,000
25	69	1,200	56	7	4.160	− 16,000
26	09	1,000	15	7	4.160	− 168,000
27	90	1,400	86	8	4.487	256,360
28	73	1,400	08	6	3.784	59,520
29	75	1,400	18	7	4.160	164,800
30	54	1,200	95	8	4.487	76,880

Generalizations of the risk analysis example

Are the random variables independent?

each of the years of useful life. This requires using one entry from the random number table for sales in each year of the useful life. Then, because the cash flows vary from year to year, you can't use the annuity formula. Instead, you multiply each annual cash flow by its discount factor and sum to get the NPV. The arithmetic to calculate the NPV for a trial is greater in this case, but the approach is the same. If the selling price, operating costs, equipment purchase cost, and salvage value are uncertain, you can determine their probability distributions and generate their values using the methods we've discussed. However, be cautious of the random variables; they may not be *independent*. Selling price and annual sales are examples of factors that are likely to be dependent. Using unrelated values from the random number table generates random variables that are also unrelated (i.e., independent).

FIGURE 15.11   Risk Analysis Simulation Relative Frequency

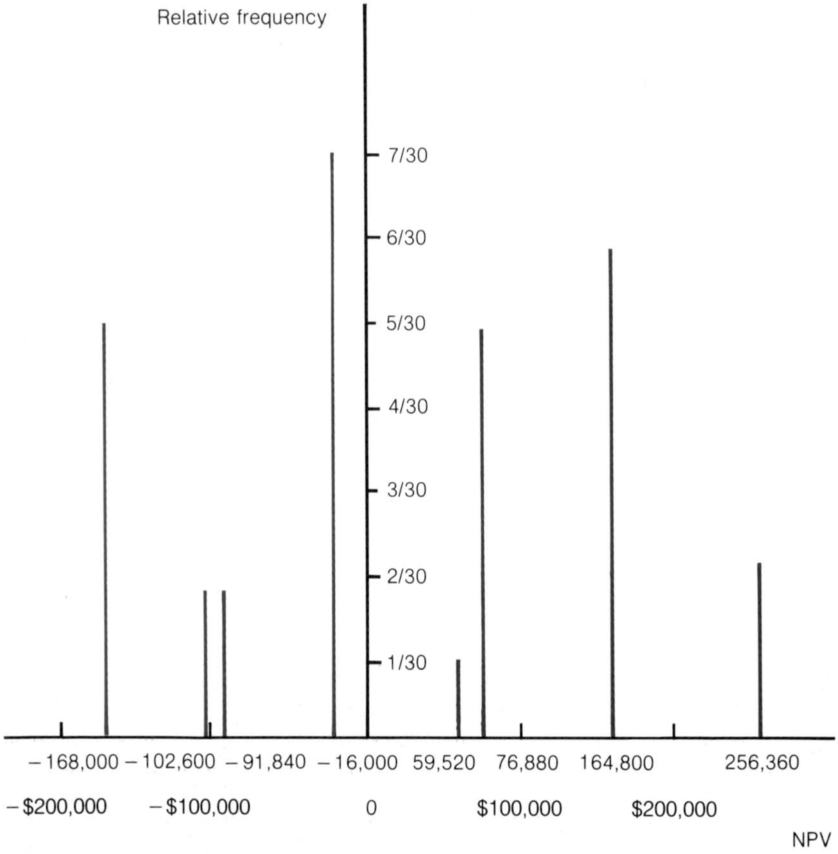

Many companies use risk analysis to evaluate capital investments with uncertain outcomes. For example, Getty Oil Company uses risk analysis for investments totaling billions of dollars.[7] It uses risk analysis to analyze investment decisions for petroleum exploration, where the result might be a dry well or a productive field. Risk analysis is also used for evaluation of refinery additions and acquisitions and divestments.

---

[7] L. B. Davidson and D. O. Cooper, "Implementing Effective Risk Analysis at Getty Oil Company," *Interfaces* 10, no. 6 (December 1980), pp. 62–75.

INVENTORY MANAGEMENT—A PROBABILISTIC SIMULATION EXAMPLE

In Chapter 13, we described a large number of possible inventory planning considerations and models. Generally, we choose ordering policies that minimize the cost for deterministic environments or minimize the expected cost for probabilistic environments. But there are many inventory planning environments without analytical solutions, and the inventory planning models presented were limited by their underlying assumptions.

An **analytical solution** to an inventory model gives a formula (or formulas) that calculates the ordering policy with the minimum cost. For example, consider the economic order quantity (EOQ) model, which calculates the order quantity as

$$Q^* = \sqrt{\frac{2KD}{c_h}}$$

You substitute the values of K (the fixed order cost), D (the demand rate), and c_h (the inventory holding cost rate) into the formula to calculate the optimal order quantity. The EOQ model is limited by its assumption that demand is deterministic and constant. Remember, the **lead time** is the delay between the time that an order is placed and the time that it arrives. We showed that if the lead time, L, is certain, you calculate the reorder point, R, as $R = DL$.

Factors that make analytical solution difficult

But even for deterministic demand, the only "easy" results are those for which we assume that the demand is stationary. Demand is **stationary** if it is constant over time—for example, if it is the same from week to week. Finding the analytical formula or formulas is very difficult if demand isn't stationary. Also, if demand is probabilistic rather than deterministic, finding analytical solutions is more difficult. If there is another source of uncertainty besides demand, finding analytical solutions is even more difficult. Further, if the probability distribution of demand is not stationary, finding analytical solutions is almost hopeless.

Two approaches

Say that there is *no analytical solution* for an inventory planning decision environment. You, the decision maker/model builder, have *two alternative approaches*. First, you can use an analytical solution for an environment that matches your environment as closely as possible. Second, you can use simulation. Let's discuss the two approaches and then perform a probabilistic simulation.

Approach 1:
Analytical solution

In the first approach, you *ignore the complicating factor* that makes finding analytical results so difficult and use an analytical solution. This may be a viable alternative, depending on the nature of this complicating factor. For example, if the probabilistic demand is almost stationary (changes very little over time), then treating it as stationary doesn't affect the optimal plan much. In Chapter 13, we showed that the optimal order quantity and cost are not sensitive to small changes in demand. Most of the computerized inventory control systems use analytical solutions based on optimization models. Although some of the assumptions underlying the analytical solutions are often violated for certain products, these systems usually do well. Remember, models are only selective representations of the decision environment.

Approach 2:
Probabilistic simulation   In the second approach, you use simulation to study the inventory decision environment and to determine a good ordering policy. The simulation model doesn't find the "optimal" ordering policy. Instead, you try different policies and simulate them. Then, you choose a policy by comparing the simulation results. Simulation allows adding complicating factors such as probabilistic, nonstationary demand and other sources of uncertainty. These factors add complications for the model builder, but they do not prevent the model from being built. For example, adding another source of uncertainty requires that the model builder generate additional random variables. This additional complication is minor for a simulation model, but it may make optimization hopeless.

Let's show how to use simulation for an inventory planning problem. Say that there are two sources of uncertainty for the inventory decision environment—demand and lead time. We want to choose Q, the order quantity, and R, the reorder point. If the inventory on hand is R or less, we place an order for Q units. The values of R and Q specify the decision rules. These values are inputs to the simulation model, which estimates the cost for the ordering policy. By varying R and Q, good decision rules can be found.

Let's define the costs that the simulation considers. Every time an order is placed, there is a $20 cost for processing it. This *fixed order cost* is represented by K. There is also a cost for holding inventory. Let c_h—0.10—represent the *inventory holding cost* per unit in inventory at the end of each day. If you can't satisfy demand from inventory on hand, you lose the sale. The *shortage cost*, c_s, is $10 per lost sale.

Table 15.13 shows the probability distribution for daily demand. We

TABLE 15.13   Daily Demand Probability Distribution for Inventory Management Simulation

Demand	Probability	Cumulative Probability	Assigned Values from Random Number Table
0	0.3	0.3	00—29
1	0.5	0.8	30—79
2	0.1	0.9	80—89
3	0.1	1.0	90—99

use the random number table to generate daily demands. Table 15.13 shows the values from the random number table that are assigned to each demand. For example, the probability is 0.3 that the demand is 0. We assigned the numbers 00 through 29 to demand equals 0.

The inventory system is updated daily. The sequence of a day's events is as follows:

1. An outstanding order from the supplier might arrive.
2. Customer orders arrive for the product and, if possible, are filled from stock on hand.
3. If the ending inventory is $\leq R$, an order is placed for Q units.

Table 15.14 has the probability distribution of the lead time in days. For example, the probability is 0.6 that the lead time is one day. If an order is placed at the end of Day 3 and the lead time is one day, the order arrives at the end of Day 4. Because of the sequence of daily events listed above, the order is recognized as arriving at the beginning of Day 5. The longest lead time is three days. If the order was placed at the end of Day 3 and the lead time is three days, the order is recognized as arriving at the beginning of Day 7. Table 5.14 shows the random numbers assigned to each lead time. For example, we assign 60 numbers, 00 through 59, to a lead time of one day because its probability is 0.6.

We plan to sell this product for the next 30 days and not to sell it after that. Our supplier has agreed to repurchase any unsold product at our cost. Thus, we don't need to consider the cost of buying the product or disposing of unsold product at the end of 30 days. However, we don't want to buy too much because this increases our inventory holding cost. Our objective is to minimize the sum of the fixed order, inventory holding, and shortage costs during the next 30 days. Say that there are 20 units on hand at the beginning of the 30-day period.

Let's choose some values of Q and R to "try" in our simulation. The expected daily demand is $(0 \times 0.3) + (1 \times 0.5) + (2 \times 0.1) + (3 \times 0.1) = 1$ unit. If we use the EOQ formula,

$$Q^* = \sqrt{\frac{2 \times 20 \times 1}{0.1}} = 20$$

TABLE 15.14 Lead Time Probability Distribution for Inventory Management Simulation (days)

Delay	Probability	Cumulative Probability	Assigned Values from Random Number Table
1	0.6	0.6	00—59
2	0.3	0.9	60—89
3	0.1	1.0	90—99

The EOQ model assumes that the demand is known and constant. Our example violates this assumption, but we can use it as an initial trial value for Q. Let's use an initial trial value of five units for R, the reorder point.

Figure 15.12 is a flowchart of the logic for the simulation model. First, you generate 30 daily demands from the probability distribution in Table 15.13. At the beginning of each day, if an order has arrived, the inventory on hand increases by Q. Then, you compare the inventory on hand with the day's demand. If the inventory on hand is $\geq$ the day's demand, you decrease it by the day's demand. If the inventory on hand is $<$ the day's demand, you lose some sales and the inventory on hand drops to 0. At the end of a day, you compare the inventory on hand with the reorder point to decide whether to place an order. If you place an order, you generate a lead time to determine when the order arrives. We generate the lead times as they are needed, because the number of orders placed depends on the daily demands generated. We know that 30 daily demands are needed, so we generate them before starting the simulation.

We start in the upper-left-hand corner of the random number table, Table 15.6, to generate the 30 daily demands. The first entry is 61. Using the assignments in Table 15.13, the first daily demand is 1. Table 15.15 contains the 30 daily demand values generated.

The system begins with 20 units on hand and none on order. The demand of 1 unit on Day 1 from Table 15.15 gives only 19 units on hand at the end of Day 1. Because the number on hand at the end of Day 1 is more than the reorder point, no order is placed. The inventory holding cost at the end of Day 1 is $19 \times 0.10 = \$1.90$. Neither a fixed order cost nor a lost sales cost is incurred. Table 15.16 has the results of the simulation. No order is placed until the end of Day 16, when the ending inventory, 3, is less than the reorder point, $R = 5$. At that time, an order of Size $Q = 20$ is placed. The lead time must be generated. The next (31st) value from the random number table is 08. From Table 15.14, we see that this value gives a lead time of one day. The order of 20 units is recognized as received at the beginning of Day 18. A fixed order cost of $20 is incurred in Day 16. In Day 17, the demand is 1 and the inventory on hand decreases to 2. There is no shortage in Day 17. At the beginning of Day 18, the order is added to the inventory on hand. No other orders are placed in the simulation. The total cost for the simulated 30-day period is $20.00 + 0.00 + 41.10 = \$61.10$. At the end of the 30 days, there are 10 units on hand. Because we won't sell the product anymore, we return the unsold product to our supplier, which gives us a refund.

Based on the simulation, you estimate that the expected cost is $61.10 if $R = 5$ and $Q = 20$. If you start at a different place in the random number table, you get different demands and lead times. By doing the simulation using different random numbers, you get different estimates of the expected cost for this ordering policy. If you repeat the simulation several times, you can use the average result to estimate the expected cost. In

FIGURE 15.12 Logic Flowchart for the Inventory Management Simulation

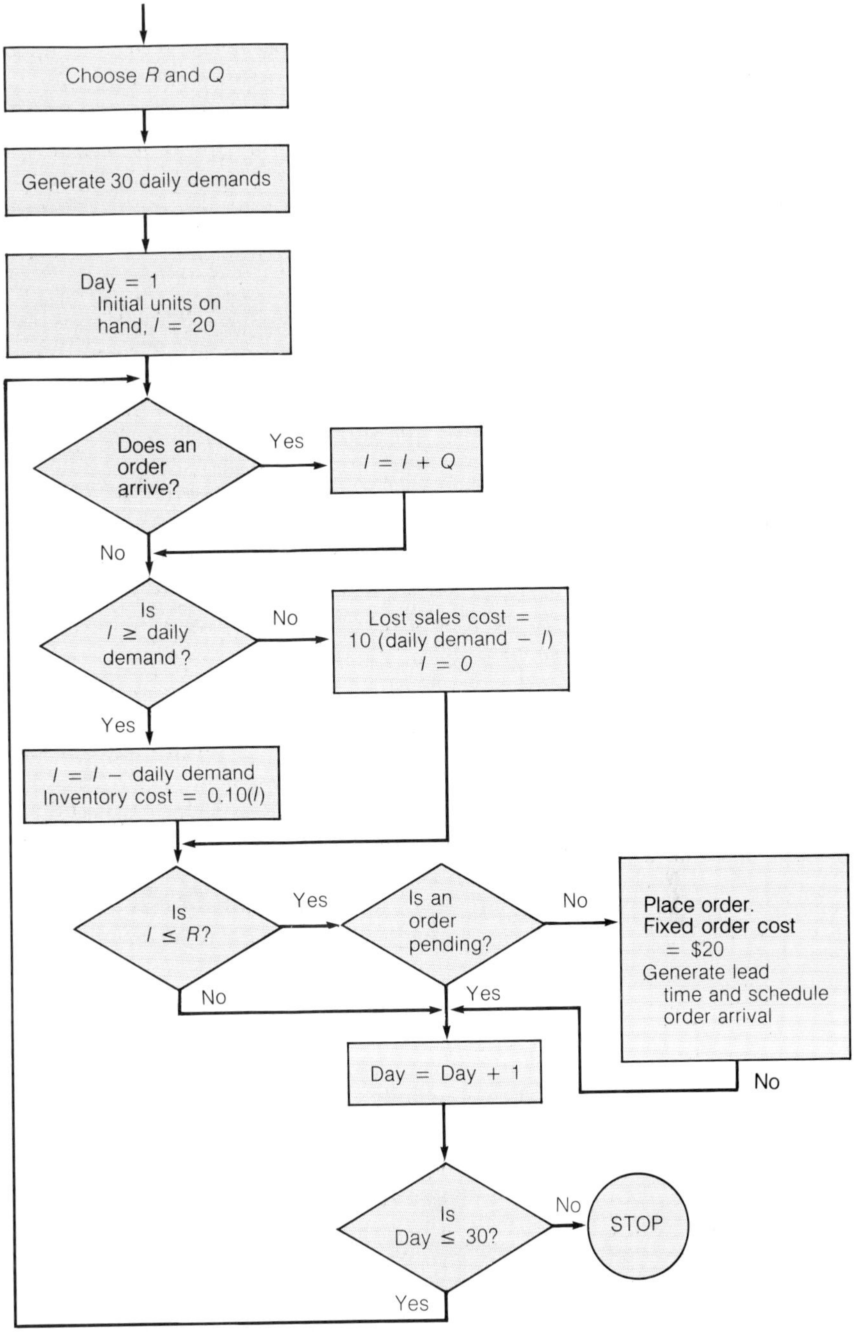

TABLE 15.15   Generated Values of Daily Demand

Day	Value from Random Number Table	Demand
1	61	1
2	15	0
3	94	3
4	42	1
5	23	0
6	04	0
7	00	0
8	35	1
9	59	1
10	46	1
11	32	1
12	69	1
13	19	0
14	45	1
15	94	3
16	98	3
17	33	1
18	80	2
19	79	1
20	18	0
21	74	1
22	54	0
23	11	0
24	48	1
25	69	1
26	09	0
27	90	3
28	73	1
29	75	1
30	54	1

Chapter 16, we discuss statistical analysis of probabilistic simulations and the number of trials needed to obtain a given confidence level for the simulation results.

Using the simulation model to choose the ordering policy

The simulation model doesn't find the best ordering policy, but it is a tool that you can use to evaluate ordering policies. You change R and Q and repeat the simulation. You compare ordering policies based on your estimates of their expected cost. In Chapter 16, we discuss comparing policies based on simulation results.

Adding uncertain lead times made finding an analytical solution more difficult. For the simulation model, adding uncertain lead times required a small amount of additional effort. You needed to generate the lead times, and you had to modify the simulation logic to use them. If the lead time had been deterministic and constant, the simulation logic would have added the constant lead time to determine when the orders would arrive.

In Chapter 13, we described two possibilities that may have to be

TABLE 15.16 Inventory Management Simulation, *R* = 5, *Q* = 20

Day	Initial Inventory	Units Received	Demand	Ending Inventory	Lost Sales	Fixed Order Cost	Lost Sales Cost	Inventory Carrying Cost
1	20	0	1	19	0	$ 0	$0	$ 1.90
2	19	0	0	19	0	0	0	1.90
3	19	0	3	16	0	0	0	1.60
4	16	0	1	15	0	0	0	1.50
5	15	0	0	15	0	0	0	1.50
6	15	0	0	15	0	0	0	1.50
7	15	0	0	15	0	0	0	1.50
8	15	0	1	14	0	0	0	1.40
9	16	0	1	13	0	0	0	1.30
10	13	0	1	12	0	0	0	1.20
11	12	0	1	11	0	0	0	1.10
12	11	0	1	10	0	0	0	1.00
13	10	0	0	10	0	0	0	1.00
14	10	0	1	9	0	0	0	0.90
15	9	0	3	6	0	0	0	0.60
16	6	0	3	3	0	20	0	0.30
17	3	0	1	2	0	0	0	0.20
18	2	20	2	20	0	0	0	2.00
19	20	0	1	19	0	0	0	1.90
20	19	0	0	19	0	0	0	1.90
21	19	0	1	18	0	0	0	1.80
22	18	0	0	18	0	0	0	1.80
23	18	0	0	18	0	0	0	1.80
24	18	0	1	17	0	0	0	1.70
25	17	0	1	16	0	0	0	1.60
26	16	0	0	16	0	0	0	1.60
27	16	0	3	13	0	0	0	1.30
28	13	0	1	12	0	0	0	1.20
29	12	0	1	11	0	0	0	1.10
30	11	0	1	10	0	0	0	1.00
Total		20	30		0	$20	$0	$41.10

considered if demand exceeds the inventory on hand. For our simulation example, we used lost sales. The other possibility is *backlogged* demand—that is, customers wait until the order arrives if enough inventory isn't on hand. With backlogging, you must modify the simulation logic. Backlogged demand is represented by a negative value for the inventory on hand. Simulation of this possibility is left to the exercises.

SUMMARY

In this chapter, we introduced computer simulation, a powerful decision-making aid. We described the history of computer simulation, which began with the probabilistic simulation of operations and continued with the simulation of financial statements to evaluate strategic decisions. Although the early simulations needed a mainframe computer, powerful microcomputers have brought simulation to the desktops of managers. You can use electronic spreadsheets on microcomputers to do deterministic simulations. As microcomputer technology improves, additional capabilities, such as probabilistic simulation and optimization, are becoming available.

We discussed applications that reflected the range of simulations. The inventory management example illustrates the use of probabilistic simulation to study inventory planning. The Exxon model, which studies a waiting line system, is another example of probabilistic simulation. We showed how to use an electronic spreadsheet to analyze potato purchase plans for the Potato Processing example. Electronic spreadsheets have many decision-making applications. We mentioned that Bethlehem Steel uses LOTUS 1–2–3 to do production planning and cost analyses for its steel plants.

We discussed an example using IFPS to build a deterministic financial model. Because of its English-like language, the IFPS model is easier to understand and verify than an electronic spreadsheet template. IFPS also has probabilistic simulation capabilities, but we developed our own simulation model for risk analysis. With risk analysis, you explicitly use the probability distributions of uncertain events, such as annual sales and useful life. Many companies use risk analysis to evaluate capital investments that have uncertain outcomes. For example, we said that Getty Oil uses risk analysis for capital investments involving billions of dollars.

Although computer simulation is a powerful decision-making aid, it has some limitations. First, it doesn't find the best decisions. Instead, you try to find the best decisions by trial and error. You substitute decisions into the simulation model and use it to estimate the system's performance for that set of decisions. Second, the estimate from a probabilistic simulation is usually not equal to the true expected value. For that reason, we repeat the probabilistic simulation to get a better estimate of the expected value. Third, a computer simulation is limited by the skill of the model builder. If the model builder doesn't understand the decision environment, the simulation model won't be accurate. Also, the model builder makes many choices in developing the model, including choices of which factors are important enough to consider. The model builder also chooses the level of detail and the length of the time horizon. These choices affect the accuracy of the simulation model. You should examine a simulation model's assumptions carefully.

Note some cautions in using computer simulation. First, it's easier to use analytical solutions than computer simulation. Say that you have an analytical solution for a decision environment *almost* identical to yours. You must evaluate whether the additional accuracy from computer simulation justifies the additional cost, compared to the cost of using the analytical solution. Second, you can make simulation models easier to understand and verify by the model structure you choose. For example, an electronic spreadsheet is easier to understand if it has more intermediate variables (cells) and if you don't "hide" input parameters in formulas. Third, there's more than one way to design a probabilistic simulation experiment. We described using pieces of paper, a table of random numbers, and a computer random number generator (CRNG) for such an experiment. With each of these methods, you must assign the uncertain events being studied to the experiment's result. Fourth, although we described three methods for generating continuous random variables, only the algebraic method is well suited to computer simulation. The graphical method and the table method are difficult to use on a computer.

We've seen the results of a probabilistic simulation depend on the random numbers used. Because of this, the estimated values can differ from the true expected values. In the next chapter, we show how to statistically analyze simulation results so that you know how much confidence you can place in them. We also show how many times you need to repeat an experiment to get a desired level of confidence. Also, we discuss the use of probabilistic simulation results to compare different sets of decisions.

QUESTIONS

1. What is an intermediate variable?

2. What is a spreadsheet template?

3. Describe how the template of the Potato Processing example of Figure 15.2 could be used to try to find the optimal potato purchase plan. In particular, how would you use the template, given a policy decision not to produce more of any product than can be sold?

4. Describe a probabilistic simulation for which sampling *without* replacement is appropriate.

5. List all of the discrete probability distributions with which you are familiar. How many parameters does each of these distributions have?

6. What value of z from the standardized normal distribution corresponds to a value of 120 from a normal distribution with a mean of 100 and a standard deviation of 10?

7. What is inverting the cumulative probability distribution? Give an example.

8. It is desired to generate a random number from a normal probability distribution with a mean of 100 and a standard deviation of 10. If the CRNG gives 0.42, what is the associated random number from the normal distribution?

9. Flip a coin 10 times, and each time you flip it, note whether you get a head or a tail. What is your estimate of the average daily demand using the rela-

tionships for Table 15.2? Was the estimated average daily demand for your simulation the same as that of Table 15.2?

10. An electronic spreadsheet is sometimes called a rudimentary decision support system. How can an electronic spreadsheet be used to aid in decision making?

11. What are the three methods for generating continuous random variables?

12. What is an advantage of using a higher-level computer simulation language?

13. In an electronic spreadsheet, why is it better to put parameters in their own cells, rather than use them in formulas?

14. What are the three types of entities that you can put in an electronic spreadsheet cell?

15. What is risk analysis?

16. What is an analytical solution to an inventory planning decision environment?

17. What are the advantages and disadvantages of using analytical solutions and computer simulation?

18. Under what conditions is a probabilistic simulation necessary?

EXERCISES

1. Describe any necessary modifications to the template for the Potato Processing example of Figure 15.2 if excess production of any product is thrown away. There is no cost for throwing it away, but there is also no revenue for the excess. Describe how you would use the template to select the best decision alternative—that is, the best potato purchase plan.

2. The template for the Potato Processing example in Figure 15.2 did not group all of the numerical parameters into a separate section of the spreadsheet. Because the microcomputer screen contains the result of the formulas, it is better to have a section in which all of the parameters appear. This approach makes it easier to change the value of a parameter and makes it less likely that you will forget to change the value of the parameter in one of the formulas that uses it. Give a template for the Potato Processing example that includes all of the parameters in a section of the spreadsheet. No numbers should appear in any of the formulas.

3. Describe any necessary modifications to the template for the Potato Processing example of Figure 15.2 if excess production of any product is sold as waste. Describe how you would use the template to select the best decision alternative—that is, the best potato purchase plan.

4. A disadvantage of the template for the Potato Processing example of Figure 15.2 is that Cells B3 and C3 don't appear on the same microcomputer screen as Cell G11, the cell used to evaluate the profit. It is therefore necessary to

"scroll" to Cell G11 after adjusting the values in Cells B3 and C3 to note the profit. Revise the template so that total profit appears in Cell A3.

5. Describe any needed modifications to the template for the Potato Processing example of Figure 15.2 if excess french fries can be processed into hash browns at a cost of $0.05 per pound.

6. The probability distribution of the successful bid price for a government contract has been assessed as follows:

Price	Probability
$1.6 million	0.3
1.7 million	0.5
1.8 million	0.2

Design a simulation experiment utilizing Table 15.6, the random number table. Starting in the upper-left-hand corner and reading down, generate 10 trials of the successful bid prices for this contract.

7. The probability distribution of the successful bid price for a government contract has been assessed as follows:

Price	Probability
$1.6 million	0.37
1.7 million	0.53
1.8 million	0.10

Design a simulation experiment utilizing Table 15.6, the random number table. Starting in the upper-left-hand corner and reading down, generate 10 trials of the successful bid prices for this contract.

8. The development of a new product depends on a technological breakthrough. If the breakthrough is not achieved by the research and development department within the next 12 months, the entire effort will be abandoned. The probability of achieving the breakthrough is 0.3. Design a simulation experiment utilizing Table 15.6, the random number table. Starting in the upper-left-hand corner and reading down, generate 10 trials of the outcome of the research and development effort.

9. The development of a new product depends on a technological breakthrough. If the breakthrough is not achieved by the research and development department within the next 12 months, the entire effort will be abandoned. The probability of achieving the breakthrough is 0.543. Design a simulation experiment utilizing Table 15.6, the random number table. Starting in the upper-left-hand corner and reading down, generate 10 trials of the outcome of the research and development effort.

10. The number of calls per hour to the technical support office of a software company is often represented by the Poisson distribution. If the parameter of the distribution, A, is 4, the expected number of calls per hour is 4. Recall that the Poisson probability distribution is

$$P(n) = e^{-A}A^n/n!, \quad n = 0, 1, 2, 3, \cdots$$

where $n!$, called n factorial, is $n(n - 1)(n - 2) \cdots 1$.

a. What is the probability of 0, 1, 2, and 3 calls in an hour? How many significant figures did you use for your calculation of the Poisson probabilities?

b. What range of values from Table 15.6, the random number table, is assigned to 2 calls within an hour?

c. If a CRNG were used, what range of values would be assigned to 2 calls within an hour?

d. What is the cumulative probability of 2 calls or less within an hour?

e. Graph the cumulative probability for $n = 0, 1, 2,$ and 3.

11. The probability of Ryne Sandburg of the Chicago Cubs getting a hit in a batting appearance is 0.280. Say that he has five trips to the plate in a baseball game.

a. Design a simulation experiment utilizing Table 15.6, the random number table. Starting in the upper-left-hand corner and reading down, generate the results of five at bats.

b. In your simulation, did you assume that the five at bats each had the same probability of a hit? Do you think that the trials (at bats) are independent?

c. If the probability is constant and the at bats are independent, what is the correct form of the probability distribution of the number of hits in five at bats?

12. Consider the cumulative probability distribution illustrated graphically.

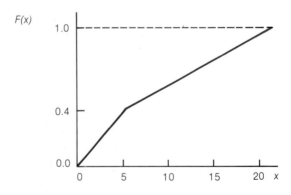

a. Estimate the value of the random variable x that is associated with Value 25 from Table 15.6, the random number table.

b. Estimate the value of the random variable x that is associated with the Value 0.76 from the CRNG.

13. Consider the cumulative probability distribution illustrated graphically.

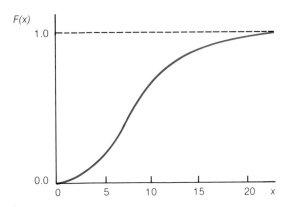

a. Estimate the value of the random variable x that is associated with Value 69 from Table 15.6, the random number table.
b. Estimate the value of the random variable x that is associated with the value 0.45 from the CRNG.

14. The exponential probability distribution is a continuous distribution and has a single parameter, A. The cumulative probability distribution of the exponential distribution is

$$F(t) = 1 - e^{-At}, \quad t \geq 0$$
$$F(t) = 0 \qquad \qquad t < 0$$

a. If the value from the CRNG is q, invert the cumulative probability distribution to solve for the value of t.
b. Say that the value of A is 4 and that the CRNG gives 0.32. What is the corresponding value of t?
c. Say that the value of A is 0.5 and that the random number table (Table 15.6) value is 35. What is the corresponding value of t?

15. Perform five trials of the risk analysis simulation using the random number values from Table 15.6 starting in the upper-right-hand corner and reading down.

16. The sensitivity of the NPV for the risk analysis simulation to changes in the probability distribution of sales is important because of uncertainty concerning the correct probability distribution. It is believed that a pessimistic assessment of the probabilities is

Sales	Probability
1,000	0.4
1,200	0.4
1,400	0.2

Perform five trials of the risk analysis simulation using the same random number values from Table 15.6 as those used for Figure 15.12.

17. Use the same demands and lead times as the inventory management simulation of Table 15.16 with a reorder point of 3 units and an order quantity of 20 units. What is the total 30-day cost?

18. Use the same demands and lead times as the inventory management simulation of Table 15.16 with a reorder point of 7 units and an order quantity of 20 units. What is the total 30-day cost?

19. For the inventory management simulation illustrated in Table 15.16, the random number used to generate the lead time was 08. Instead, say that the number was 93. Assume that unsatisfied demand is backlogged. That is, the customer waits until the item becomes available and purchases it at that time. The cost for a backlogged unit of demand is $5. What is the 30-day cost in this case?

20. For the inventory management simulation illustrated in Table 15.16, the random number used to generate the lead time was 08. If the number had been 93, what would the 30-day cost be?

MORE CHALLENGING EXERCISES

1. The risk analysis simulation of Table 15.12 used the same value for the annual sales in each year of the equipment's useful life. Say that the sales in each year are independent random variables with the probability distribution given in Table 15.10 for each year.
   a. Should you generate the number of years of the equipment's useful life before generating the sales in each year? Why or why not?
   b. Perform a single trial of a simulation, and calculate the NPV of that trial. Start in the upper-left-hand corner of Table 15.6, the random number table, and read down. What are the total sales during the equipment's useful life?

2. For the risk analysis simulation, the cost per unit was assumed to be known and constant each year at $300. Say that the cost is the same in each year but that it has the probability distribution given below:

Cost	Probability
$250	0.25
300	0.50
350	0.25

   a. Starting at the top right of Table 15.6, the random number table, and reading down, generate five costs from the above probability distribution.
   b. For the first five trials of Table 15.12, calculate the NPV using the costs generated in Part *a*.

3. For the risk analysis simulation, the cost per unit was assumed to be known and constant each year at $300. Say that the costs in the years are independent random variables with the probability distribution given below:

Cost	Probability
$250	0.35
300	0.50
350	0.15

   a. Starting at the top right of Table 15.6, the random number table, and reading down, generate six costs for the six years of useful life for the first trial of Table 15.12.
   b. For the first trial of Table 15.12, calculate the NPV using the yearly costs generated in Part *a*.

4. One approach to estimating annual sales is to separately estimate the total market and then to estimate the market share. Let the probability distribution of the total market have a normal distribution with a mean of 20,000 units and a standard deviation of 2,000 units. Assume that the probability distribution of the market share is

Market Share (percent)	Probability
15	0.3
16	0.5
17	0.2

   Design a simulation experiment using Table 15.6, the random number table. Starting in the upper-left-hand corner and reading down, generate 10 trials to estimate the annual sales. Which did you generate first—the total market or the market share?

5. A retailer needs to decide how many citizens band (CB) radios to purchase from a manufacturer that is going out of business. The retailer is going to promote these radios for a Christmas sale at $65 each. Any radios left over after the sale will be sold at $25 each to a liquidator. The CB radios cost the retailer $35 each. The probability distribution of the number of units sold is normal, with a mean of 250 and a standard deviation of 40. Say that the retailer orders 250 units. Starting in the upper-left-hand corner of Table 15.6, the random number table, and reading down, generate five trials to estimate the profit.

6. Construct a spreadsheet template for the product mix example of Chapter 3.

7. Construct a spreadsheet template for the machine assignment example of Chapter 3.

8. A company makes wooden tables in several varieties. One of these varieties is a round kitchen table. This table is also offered with two leaves, which makes it appropriate for dining rooms. Sales of both of these tables have been excellent. In fact, there is more demand for both of them than can be met with the existing manufacturing capacity. There is a higher profit margin on the table with leaves, but this table requires more time on the planer machine, which has been used to its capacity. It is desired to determine whether the higher profit margin is enough to justify the current manufacturing strategy of making the table with leaves almost exclusively. The profit margins are $43 for the round table and $49 for the round table with leaves. The manufacturing operations require time on a lathe to make the legs, time on the planer to make the top and leaves, and some hand-finishing time. The times required in hours per table are

| | Machine | | Hand |
Table	Lathe	Planer	Finishing
Round	0.15	0.13	0:25
Round with leaves	0.15	0.18	0.30

The shop works 7 days a week and 24 hours a day. There are 2 people who work each shift to do the hand finishing. Construct a spreadsheet template to determine the best product mix.

9. An investor wants to determine the best portfolio of gold, savings account, IBM common stock, and Commonwealth Edison common stock. She has $20,000 to invest. She does not wish to have more than 10 percent in gold or less than 20 percent in savings. She estimates that the rate of return for the investments will be as follows for the next year:

Gold	9.0%
Savings account	5.25
IBM	8.5
Commonwealth Edison	10.0

The total in common stock is to be no more than 60 percent.
   a. Construct a spreadsheet template to determine the best allocation of the $20,000 to maximize the portfolio's annual rate of return.
   b. The investor is concerned about the potential risk for some investments. The savings account is insured by an agency of the federal government, and she is certain of the 5.25 percent return. However, the return on the common stocks is dependent on changes in the value of the shares. She believes that a decrease in the share price of Commonwealth Edison, a utility stock, is less likely than a decrease in the share price of IBM. She has developed a risk point system to protect herself against this uncertainty. She assesses risk points per $5,000 invested in each of the invest-

ments as follows: 25 for gold, 0 for a savings account, 35 for IBM common stock, and 12 for Commonwealth Edison common stock. She wants a portfolio whose risk point total is no greater than 80. Revise the spreadsheet template of Part *a* to reflect this consideration.

10. A company can sell all it produces of three products called Regular, Super, and Improved. The following gives the requirements per unit produced and profit margins:

	Product		
	R	S	I
Pounds of raw material,	1	1	1
Assembly time, hr.	0.5	0.6	0.8
Packaging time, hr.	0.2	0.4	0.5
Profit margin	$10	$12	$16

There are 75 pounds of the raw material available. Next week, there are 60 and 40 hours available of assembly and packaging time, respectively. Because of its labor contract, at least 30 hours of packaging time must be used. Construct a template that can be used to find the best product mix.

11. Given a standardized normal random variate, N_i, the desired normal random variable is calculated as $X_i = \mu + N_i\sigma$. The polar method of calculating a standardized normal random variate, N_i, uses two values from the CRNG to generate two standardized normal random variates. Let U_1 and U_2 be two values from the CRNG (uniform between 0 and 1). Calculate $V_i = 2U_i - 1$ for $i = 1, 2$, and let $W = V_1^2 + V_2^2$. If $W > 1$, obtain two new values from the CRNG and repeat. Otherwise, let $Y = [(-2 \ln W)/W]^{0.5}$, $N_1 = V_1 Y$, and $N_2 = V_2 Y$. Then, N_1 and N_2 are independent, identically distributed standardized normal random variables.
    a. If the two values from the CRNG are 0.213 and 0.3876, apply the procedure to generate two standardized normal random variates.
    b. If the two values from the CRNG are 0.024 and 0.985, apply the procedure to generate two standardized normal random variates.
    c. If the desired mean is 100 and the standard deviation is 10, use the values calculated in Parts *a* and *b* to obtain normally distributed random variable values with the desired values.

12. When you use an electronic spreadsheet, the constraints aren't automatically satisfied. Instead, you enter the decision variable values and examine the spreadsheet cell contents to determine whether the constraints have been satisfied. Scanning the spreadsheet to check the feasibility of a decision alternative by examining the numerical values in cells is a potential source of errors. Another approach is to use the IF function. For most electronic spreadsheets, the form is IF(logical expression, cell contents if true, cell contents if false). It is possible to include a string in the two arguments of the IF function to indicate whether values are acceptable or unacceptable. The string must be in double quotes (e.g., "xxx"). Develop a formula for Cell G4 using the IF function for the Potato Processing template of Figure 15.2. If

excess french fries are produced, print TROUBLE in the cell. If there is no excess production, print OK.

13. Construct a template for the multiple-period example of Chapter 7.

14. A bakery bakes birthday cakes every morning before it opens. The cakes cost $1.75 to make and sell for $6. Birthday cake demand during the last 50 days is summarized below:

Birthday Cake Demand	Number of Days
0	15
1	15
2	10
3	7
4	3
Total	50

Any unsold birthday cakes have no value. Starting in the upper-left-hand corner of Table 15.6, the random number table, and reading down, generate 17 daily demands. Calculate the average profit per day if you bake 0, 1, 2, 3, and 4 birthday cakes.

15. A company uses two warehouses in nearby cities to store its major product. The lead time to resupply the warehouses is one week. The weekly demand for the two warehouses is probabilistic:

Weekly Demand	Probability for Warehouse	
	A	B
0	0.15	—
1	0.25	0.20
2	0.45	0.40
3	0.10	0.20
4	0.05	0.15
5	—	0.05

Each warehouse begins the week with 3 units on hand.

a. Simulate 10 weeks' demand for each warehouse, starting in the upper-left-hand corner of Table 15.6, the random number table, and reading down. Use the first 10 values for Warehouse A and the next 10 for Warehouse B. Estimate the expected number of units short per week.

b. Say that the warehouses are consolidated into a single warehouse. Using the weekly totals generated in each week, estimate the expected number of units short per week if there are 6 units on hand at the beginning of each week.

     c. What are the advantages and disadvantages of consolidating the warehouses?

16. Speedee Gas is a full-service gasoline station. Frank Jones pumps gas from 8 A.M., when it opens, until 4 P.M. The probability distribution of the time between customer arrivals is

Time (minutes)	Probability
5	0.25
8	0.45
12	0.20
15	0.10

The time required to pump the gas, check the oil, and collect payment is

Time (minutes)	Probability
4	0.20
6	0.55
8	0.20
10	0.05

Simulate the first 10 customers to arrive after the station opens. Start in the upper-left-hand corner of Table 15.6, the random number table, and read down. What is your estimate of the total waiting time of the first 10 customers?

CASE

Wilton Toy Company

In May 1971, Mr. Brian Cunningham, president of Wilton Toy Company, was evaluating two new product proposals to determine which one his company should accept. After the two proposals had each reached the final planning stages, Mr. Cunningham reviewed the company's financial position and decided that only one new product could be undertaken at that time. He wanted to select the most profitable venture, but he hoped to avoid incurring a great deal of risk.

Wilton had just experienced two years of declining profit. Since accepting the top position at Wilton after Mr. Art Wilton's death in

SOURCE: A. A. Grindlay, "Wilton Toy Company," in *Management Science and the Manager: A Casebook*, Newson, ed., © 1980, pp. 151–154. Reprinted by permission of Prentice Hall, Inc., Englewood Cliffs, New Jersey.

December 1970, Mr. Cunningham had continued to operate the business based on the policies and procedures formed by his predecessor, but he was beginning to reexamine existing practices in order to reverse the downward profit trend. With the exception of a few standard products, most toys had a limited product life cycle. The first few years were extremely important since the company that produced an innovative idea often was able to make substantial profits before the competition became too keen. In the past, Wilton had competed successfully because it had introduced many popular new products. In recent years, however, Wilton had shown a decline in new product introductions. The problem was compounded by disappointing sales levels for a remote control battery-operated model car that was introduced for the 1970 Christmas season.

In the past, Wilton Toys had always calculated the before-tax return on investment that could be expected for a new venture. When two or more proposals were in the final planning stages and were competing for the same funds, the ROI was used as the determining factor. The two proposals being considered in May recommended that Wilton produce a toy pistol and a plastic minimotorcycle replica. The toy pistol suggestion had been submitted by the new product design team which was formed by management personnel. The team believed the toy should be modeled after the U.S. Army pistols used in Vietnam. Sales estimates for the gun were made with considerable confidence since the market potential was well known for this type of product. The sales manager believed that 30,000 guns could be sold at Wilton's price of $4. The project would require an investment of about $110,000 and would incur $4,000 in fixed costs and $3 per gun in variable costs.

Wilton had always attempted to utilize the potential of its work force by encouraging company employees to submit new product ideas. The motorcycle proposal was the direct result of a suggestion by Mr. Larry Bradshaw, a production foreman. Mr. Bradshaw believed a small replica of the minimotorcycle would be very popular and could be produced economically. The sales manager, however, experienced considerable difficulty in making a sales estimate due to the novelty and the uniqueness of the toy. After considerable discussion and deliberation, the sales manager set the best estimate for motorcycle sales at 6,000 units for Wilton's $11.50 selling price. The required investment would be $116,000, while the fixed costs would be $5,000 and the variable cost would be $6 per cycle.

Mr. Cunningham realized the ROI forecast for the motorcycle proposal was 24.1 percent compared to 23.6 percent for the gun suggestion, but the small spread combined with the uncertainty of the motorcycle sales volume concerned him. These doubts prompted Mr. Cunningham to hire Mr. Julian Davis on a consulting basis. Mr. Cunningham asked Mr. Davis to examine the ROI calculation for each proposal and to make some sound recommendations suggesting how the uncertainty should be handled.

Mr. Davis spent some time studying the background of the selection problem. Then he confronted the men responsible for making the forecasts used in the ROI calculations. He learned that the selling price and the fixed costs could be accurately predetermined. The sales volume, the variable cost, and the investment expense, on the other hand, were the best estimates of the sales manager, the production manager, and the vice president, respectively. All three men admitted that there could be considerable variation from their forecast values.

When Mr. Davis returned to the sales manager, he had little difficulty in extracting a sales range for each project. Using the sales range for the upper and lower limits, Mr. Davis asked at what sales estimate there

EXHIBIT 1 Wilton Toy Company Sales Forecasts

	Toy Pistol		Motorcycle	
Estimate (units)	Probability Actual Less than Estimate		Estimate (units)	Probability Actual Less than Estimate
24,000	5%		2,500	5%
28,000	30		3,500	30
30,000	50		6,000	50
31,000	75		7,500	80
33,000	95		9,000	95
36,000	100		11,000	100

would be a 75 percent chance that actual pistol sales would be less than the estimate. The sales manager figured that there was a 75 percent chance that pistol sales would be less than 31,000 units. Continuing in this manner, Mr. Davis and the sales manager were able to set the odds for sales being equal to or less than six specific volumes for each project (Exhibit 1). Mr. Davis noted that the sales volume for the motorcycle proposal might vary over 90 percent from the figure used in the original ROI calculations.

Mr. Davis used the same technique when he met again with the production manager and the vice president. The production manager was initially quite reluctant to make cost estimates for specific probabilities. Mr. Davis asked him what the greatest possible variable cost would be. Next he asked what chance existed that the production manager's original forecast to Mr. Cunningham might be exceeded. By graphing the estimates, Mr. Davis was able to ask about intermediate values between these forecasts. As the distribution began to take shape, the production manager's confidence developed and Mr. Davis was fi-

EXHIBIT 2 Wilton Toy Company Investment and Variable Cost Distributions

	Toy Pistol Probability Actual		Motorcycle Probability Actual	
Estimate	Less than Estimate	Estimate	Less than Estimate	
Investment				
$106,000	5%	$113,000	5%	
108,000	15	115,000	25	
109,000	30	116,000	50	
110,000	50	118,000	70	
112,000	80	120,000	90	
115,000	100	123,000	100	
Variable cost				
$2.94	5	$5.85	5	
2.96	25	5.90	20	
2.98	40	5.95	40	
3.00	50	6.00	50	
3.02	70	6.05	75	
3.04	90	6.10	90	
3.07	100	6.15	100	

nally able to draw a representative curve for the possible outcomes.

Mr. Davis planned to calculate the expected value for each variable for both alternatives from the forecasts he had received (Exhibits 1 and 2). The expected values could be used to determine an ROI figure for both proposals. All possible results would then have an effect on the ROI figures, rather than just the most likely value. Mr. Davis hoped to illustrate the risk by revealing the spread of possible outcomes for each proposal. He planned to run a computer simulation to calculate the ROIs for both alternatives. The simulation results could be plotted to show the frequency distributions which would reveal the possibilities of all levels of return for each project.

16

Statistical Analysis and the Design of Probabilistic Simulation Experiments

Types of Probabilistic Simulations

Fixed-Time Increment versus Variable-Time Increment

Simulating a Waiting Line System
A Single-Server Waiting Line System—M/M/1 / Doing the
Simulation / Using a Higher-Level Simulation Language /
Complicating Factors in Waiting Line Simulations

Sampling Statistics of Probabilistic Simulations
The Sample Mean / The Sample Standard Deviation /
Confidence Intervals for Independent Trials

Analysis of Grouped Data

Determining the Number of Trials—A Preliminary Small Sample

Choosing the Best Alternative and Paired Comparisons
The Independent Samples Method / The Dependent Samples
Method

Variance Reduction Techniques

Case: Snow Removal for the Town of Belmont

BANCOHIO NATIONAL BANK

Deregulation of the banking industry began in the 1970s and continues today. One result of deregulation has been increased branch banking. In branch banking, a bank holding company operates banks at different branches. Aggressive bank holding companies usually expand by acquiring other banks. Although such acquisitions are usually motivated by marketing considerations, they also affect the operations of the bank holding company.

When a check is presented at a branch, it is transported to a check processing location at which the amount of the check is encoded so that it's computer-readable. After checks have been encoded, they are sorted and entered into the computer system, and outgoing cash letters are sent to clearing banks. Decreasing the time required between the cashing of checks and the sending of cash letters decreases float costs. With geographically dispersed branches, the transportation time can be significant.

In January 1984, BancOhio had 266 branches and encoded checks at 31 of these locations. It needed to decide how many check processing centers to establish, where to locate them, and which branches should be served by each. It used CHECKSIM to study its check processing system.

CHECKSIM is a simulation system that traces checks from the teller window through check processing. The system generates efficient transportation routes from branches to check processing centers. After mergers and divestitures, BancOhio used 22 check processing centers (the base case). BancOhio identified three possible alternatives (16, 11, and 7 check processing centers) that offered greater consolidation of its check processing operations. For each of these alternatives, check processing sites were selected by considering transaction volumes, historical operating efficiency, ease of access, and available space. Bank branches were assigned to potential check processing sites based on the bank's regional organizational structure.

An adequate and constant supply of checks allows more efficient operation of a check processing center. The simulation considered the volume of checks on an hour-by-hour basis to provide enough detail to study the increased efficiency. Because branch bank activity depends on the day of the week, different simulations were performed for Monday through Friday. (Checks weren't processed on Saturday.) Therefore, 110 simulations were performed for the base case—22 check processing centers.

On the basis of the simulation results, BancOhio chose the seven check processing center alternative. The annual cost of this alternative was $1.6 million less than that of the base case.

S. G. Davis, G. B. Kleindorfer, G. A. Kochenberger, E. T. Reutzel, and E. W. Brown, "Strategic Planning for Bank Operations with Multiple Check-Processing Locations," *Interfaces* 16, no. 6 (November–December 1986), pp. 1–12.

In Chapter 15, we described how to use a simulation model to analyze the decision environment. You choose decisions and simulate their results. Then, you compare different decisions based on the simulation results. For a deterministic simulation model, you always get the same simulation results for the same decisions. For a probabilistic simulation model, you can get different simulation results for the same decisions.

In Chapter 15, we also discussed generating random variables from a specified probability distribution. Generating random variables distinguishes probabilistic simulation from deterministic simulation. We described how to use pieces of paper and a bowl, a random number table, or a computer random number generator (CRNG) to generate random variables. In a probabilistic simulation, the random variable value depends on which piece of paper is drawn, which value you choose from the random number table, or which value you get from the CRNG. Thus, even when you choose the same decisions for a probabilistic simulation, the results vary because of the model's random variables. The uncertainty of the probabilistic simulation's results reflects the uncertainty of the probabilistic decision environment.

Because the results of probabilistic simulation are uncertain, you must statistically analyze them to estimate the system's performance. In this chapter, we discuss statistical analysis of probabilistic simulation experiments. You can affect your estimates and your confidence in them by how you design such an experiment. If you use a software package, learning enough about that package to use it is a mechanistic hurdle that you have to surmount. However, even though you learn how to use a software package, there are important considerations about the design and the analysis of results that you need to be aware of. Although it is easy to do a simulation of a decision environment, you must make meaningful inferences from the results.

BancOhio used probabilistic simulation to study its check processing system. The assignment of different branch banks to a check processing facility was simulated. BancOhio used the probabilistic simulation results to choose check processing facilities and to assign branch banks to each of them. BancOhio needed to make meaningful inferences from those results.

In the next section, we discuss different types of probabilistic simulations. For simulations over time, the type of simulation is of particular interest. In the section Fixed-Time Increment versus Variable-Time Increment, we describe two ways of doing simulations over time. In the section Simulating a Waiting Line System, we use a variable time increment for a single-server system. We discuss statistical analysis of simulation results and calculating confidence intervals on the estimates. You can get smaller confidence intervals by repeating the experiment more times. For probabilistic simulations, an important design consideration is the number of times to repeat the experiment. We discuss how to determine the number of trials needed to get estimates with the desired confidence level. Because probabilistic simulations are used to choose the best decisions, we discuss comparing decisions based on simulation results. You can have greater confidence in your decision with a good design. In the section Variance Reduction Techniques, we discuss getting smaller confidence intervals by carefully designing the simulation experiments.

We learn some lessons about simulation design from studying statistical analysis. But first, we review some of the simulations that we use as examples for statistical analysis.

TYPES OF PROBABILISTIC SIMULATIONS

Let's review some of the probabilistic simulations that we discussed in Chapter 15. The first example was generating equally likely daily demands by flipping a coin. The risk analysis simulation was used to estimate the net present value (NPV) of a capital investment. For this simulation, there was uncertainty about the annual sales and the useful life of the capital investment. The decision was whether or not to make the capital investment. If the NPV is positive, the capital investment is attractive; if the NPV is negative, the capital investment is unattractive. The inventory management example simulated an inventory system for the 30 days that a company sold a particular product. There was uncertainty about the daily sales and the lead time. The decision was to determine the best ordering policy. To make that determination, you choose an order quantity, Q, and a reorder point, R, and simulate the system to estimate the 30-day cost. You then compare the costs of different ordering policies by doing the simulation for different order quantities and reorder points.

In Chapter 15, we also described how Exxon studied gasoline blending at its Benicia, California, refinery. To study the impact of eliminating tetraethyl lead (TEL) from gasoline, it simulated an assignment of components and finished products to new and existing refinery storage tanks. There was uncertainty about equipment breakdowns, about component yields and qualities from refinery operations, and about the timing of barge and tank truck arrivals. For different tank assignments, Exxon simulated the system over a period of time to estimate the average inventory holding cost and the probability that a barge or tank truck could not be loaded because gasoline wasn't available.

BancOhio used probabilistic simulation to study its check processing system. It evaluated an assignment of branch banks to a check processing center by simulation. Checks arrived at the branch banks, were picked up by a courier, and were transported to the check processing center for processing. There was uncertainty about the time of check arrivals at the branch banks, about courier arrival and transport times, and about check processing times. Because the arrival rates differed by the day of the week, separate simulations were done for each operating day of the check processing center. For example, one simulation evaluated the operation of a particular check processing center on Monday if a particular set of branch banks was assigned to it.

Probabilistic simulation is used to study either (1) a onetime occurrence or (2) a simulation over time. A **Monte Carlo simulation** estimates measures of interest for a onetime occurrence. For example, the risk analysis example was a onetime occurrence. You either make the capital investment or you don't. The coin-flipping experiment was also a Monte Carlo simulation. In that case, you wanted to estimate the expected demand for one day.

Many probabilistic simulations are designed to analyze the performance of a system over time. Simulations over time pose a potential source of confusion based on the distinction between transient conditions and steady state conditions. Chapter 14 introduced this terminology for waiting line systems, but the issue is one of concern for all simulations over time. A **transient condition** is one in which the system's condition at a point in time is affected by the system's starting condition. A **steady state condition** is one in which the system's condition at a point in time is not affected by the system's starting condition. After a system operates for a long time, the starting condition has no impact and the system reaches steady state. Steady state conditions are sometimes called long-run conditions.

There are *three types of simulation over time.* One type is a **terminating simulation,** one for which the starting condition is specified and the simulation terminates or ends by some specified criterion. The inventory management simulation of Chapter 15 was a terminating simulation. The starting condition was the initial inventory, 20 units on hand, and the simulation period was 30 days because after that time the company planned to discontinue selling the product. A terminating simulation is concerned with transient conditions.

Another type of simulation over time estimates *characteristics* at a

Transient and steady state conditions

Three types of simulations over time

particular point in time. This type of simulation is concerned with transient conditions. For the inventory management example, a simulation of this type would tell us, for example, how many units are on hand at the beginning of the 10th day.

The third type of simulation over time estimates *average characteristics,* which are the same as characteristics at a *random point in time.* This type of simulation is concerned with steady state conditions. Say that the company in the inventory management example doesn't plan to stop selling the product. Then, we don't use a terminating simulation. Instead, we choose R and Q so that the long-run cost per day is minimized. In that case, we're interested in steady state conditions. Remember, we use the simulation to choose R and Q. Based on steady state conditions, the best value of R and Q aren't affected by the initial inventory. However, the other two types of simulation over time are sensitive to the initial inventory.

What type of simulation over time did Exxon use? Exxon wanted to estimate the average inventory holding cost and the probability that a randomly chosen barge or tank truck couldn't be loaded because gasoline wasn't available. Exxon's simulation estimated steady state conditions.

For BancOhio's simulation, each day started with no checks in the system and ended when all of the day's checks were processed. BancOhio's simulations were terminating simulations. BancOhio wanted to estimate the daily cost for a particular check processing center if a particular set of branch banks was assigned to it.

In this chapter, we discuss estimating the expected value of a performance measure from probabilistic simulation results. Remember, the results for a probabilistic simulation depend on the random variables generated and the simulation results usually don't equal the expected value. For a Monte Carlo simulation, you repeat the simulation experiment with different random numbers to get more information about the uncertain outcomes and estimate their variability. A **replication** of a simulation model is another complete simulation experiment with a different set of random numbers. The approach for probabilistic simulations over time depends on which type of simulation you do. If you want to study the system for a specified period of time (a terminating simulation) or at a particular point in time, you use the same approach as that used for Monte Carlo simulations. In the Sampling Statistics section, we discuss estimating how close the simulation results are to the expected value using this approach.

For a probabilistic simulation over time in which you want to estimate the average characteristics (steady state), you must use a different approach. In the section Analysis of Grouped Data, we show how to get confidence intervals for this type of simulation.

Before you do a simulation over time, ask yourself, "Should this be a terminating simulation, or am I interested in the steady state performance of the system?'' Your answer affects how you design the experiments and analyze the results.

In the next section, we discuss two approaches for doing a simulation over time. The Exxon, BancOhio, and inventory management simulations are all simulations over time. You can view time as passing either by a fixed-time increment or by a variable-time increment.

FIXED-TIME INCREMENT VERSUS VARIABLE-TIME INCREMENT

For a simulation over time, the treatment of time is an important design consideration. Let's use Chapter 15's inventory management example to discuss this issue. Recall that the sequence during a day was (1) an order is delivered, (2) customers demand the product, and (3) if the inventory at the end of the day is $\leq$ the reorder point, R, you place an order for Q, the order quantity. The daily demands and the lead times were uncertain. This inventory system used *periodic review*. You check the inventory only at the end of a day, and you place orders only at that time.

Events and the system's state

An **event** is a change in the state of the system. Mathematicians and engineers define the **state of a system** as enough information to describe *uniquely* the status of the system. For the inventory management example, the state includes the number of units on hand, the number of units on order, and the number of days until any units on order arrive. Two events are the purchase of the product by a customer and the delivery of an order. When a customer buys a unit, the number of units on hand decreases. When an order arrives, the state changes because the number of units on hand increases and the number of units on order becomes 0.

It is important to understand the concept of an event because of the central role of events in the collection of statistics on the behavior of the simulated system over time. If an event occurs, the simulation model must update the system's state based on the event and record enough information to calculate the measures of interest. Simulations over time use a **simulation clock** to indicate event times and to collect the necessary information. The **time increment** is the amount that the simulation clock advances each time it changes. The natural method for designing simulation models over time is to allow for a **variable time increment** so that the system is examined only when there is a change in state. In the next section, we simulate a single-server waiting line system. The two events are a customer arrival and a service completion. We use a variable-time increment. The simulation clock ''jumps'' from the time of one event to the time of the next event.

A **fixed-time increment** simulation advances the simulation clock by the same amount each time. The inventory management simulation used a fixed-time increment of one day. In that example, the 30-day time horizon was divided into one-day periods. During a one-day period, the exact timing of a change of state is not identified. To clarify this, ask yourself, "When does the demand occur for the inventory management simulation?" The demand occurs during a day, but no note is made of *when* during the day. Similarly, we recognize that an order arrives at the beginning of a day, but we don't know the exact delivery time.

You, the model builder, choose the fixed-time increment. Let's discuss the issues involved in using a smaller fixed-time increment. First, using a smaller fixed-time increment gives you greater accuracy on the timing of events. Say that we use a fixed-time increment of one hour instead of one day for the inventory management simulation. Then, we can identify demands and order arrivals on an hourly basis. This gives more accurate information. For example, consider the inventory holding cost. You can base the inventory holding cost on the number of units at the end of each hour, rather than at the end of each day. There are other impacts, however, of using a smaller time increment. One impact is that the simulation clock must be advanced a greater number of times. If the time increment is one day, the simulation clock must be advanced 30 times. If the time increment is one hour, the simulation clock must be advanced $24 \times 30 = 720$ times. Another impact is an increase in the number of time increments in which no change in state occurs. Because the record-keeping is concerned with changes in state, advancing the simulation clock without an event occurring doesn't require recording any new information. In Chapter 15's results for the inventory management example, there was no change of state on several days—that is, days when the demand was 0 and no order arrived. If the time increment had been one hour, there would have been many more advances of the simulation clock without a change of state. Using a smaller time increment requires more computer time to simulate a 30-day period. You must weigh the additional accuracy for a smaller time increment against the additional computer time required.

Exxon used a fixed-time increment of one-half hour. BancOhio used a fixed-time increment of one hour. It seems more natural to advance the simulation clock only if there is a change of state. However, it's easier to develop general probabilistic simulation systems using a fixed-time increment. All higher-level languages and simulation software allow a fixed-time increment; some allow a variable-time increment; and some allow a mixture of variable- and fixed-time increments.

In the next section, we use a variable-time increment to simulate a single-server waiting line system. We use the results of this simulation to show the difference between steady state and transient conditions.

[Margin note:] Issues in choosing a fixed-time increment

SIMULATING A WAITING LINE SYSTEM

A waiting line system, sometimes called a queueing system, consists of customers, servers, and rules for operating the system, called the **queue discipline.** Waiting line systems are a common application of probabilistic simulation. In Chapter 14, we described many of the possibilities for waiting line systems. We explained that there are many waiting line systems for which you can't get analytical results for steady state conditions. We also explained why it's even more difficult to get transient results. We said that computer simulation was a possible approach if you couldn't get analytical results.

The Exxon and BancOhio simulations were waiting lines. There are many other applications of this type. For example, Burger King Corporation uses probabilistic simulation to study the operations of its restaurants and improve their productivity[1] and American Telephone & Telegraph Company uses GPSS simulations to determine "efficient configurations for regional trouble-reporting operations."[2]

In this section, we show how to do a waiting line simulation. First, we describe the single-server system that we want to study. Second, we begin the simulation by hand and then show the computer results. Third, we show how using a higher-level simulation language simplifies the model. Finally, we explain how some complicating factors can be included in the simulation. In later sections, we discuss statistical analysis of the results of waiting line system simulation.

A Single-Server Waiting Line System—M/M/1

Let's simulate a single-server waiting line system with uncertain customer arrivals and uncertain service times. Our waiting line system has a single server who provides service to only one customer at a time. After service begins on a customer, it continues until it has been completed. After the service has been completed, the customer leaves the system. If several customers are waiting when the service has been completed, the next customer to be served is the first one that arrived at the service facility. This is called first come, first served (FCFS) queue discipline.

Say that we want to estimate how long a customer has to wait before service begins. Remember, customers are taken on a first come, first served basis. Thus, if a customer arrives when other customers are

---

[1] W. Swart and Luca Donno, "Simulation Modeling Improves Operations, Planning, and Productivity of Fast Food Restaurants," *Interfaces* 11, no. 6 (December 1981), pp. 35–47.

[2] J. L. Fillmer and J. M. Mellichamp, "Simulation: An Operational Planning Device for the Bell System," *Interfaces* 12, no. 3 (June 1982), pp. 54–60.

already present, that customer must wait until service has been provided to the others.

Assume that the time between successive customer arrivals, called the **interarrival time,** has an exponential probability distribution. Also assume that the customer service time has an exponential probability distribution. In Chapter 14, we introduced Kendall's notation, which describes waiting line systems symbolically. Using Kendall's notation, our waiting line is represented by M/M/1. The first M is for the interarrival time; the second M is for the service time; and the 1 shows that there is one server. The M stands for Markovian and means that the times have exponential probability distributions. We also assume that no balking or reneging occurs. That is, every customer who arrives for service decides to wait, regardless of the number of customers already waiting, and does not leave the service facility until service has been received, regardless of the waiting time.

The **arrival rate** is the average number of customers that arrive per unit of time. Let λ represent the arrival rate. Because we assume that interarrival times have an exponential probability distribution, the probability density of the time between successive arrivals is $f(t) = \lambda e^{-\lambda t}$. The cumulative probability distribution is $F(t) = 1 - e^{-\lambda t}$. The mean time between arrivals is $\frac{1}{\lambda}$, and the standard deviation of the interarrival time is also $\frac{1}{\lambda}$. For example, say that the arrival rate is one per minute. Then, $\lambda = 1$ and the average time between arrivals is $\frac{1}{\lambda} = \frac{1}{1} = 1$, one minute.

The **service rate** is the average number of customers that can be served per unit of time. Let μ represent the service rate. Represent the probability density of the service time by $g(t) = \mu e^{-\mu t}$. The cumulative probability distribution of the time required to complete a service is denoted as $G(t) = 1 - e^{-\mu t}$. For example, say that $\mu = 1.1$. That is, 1.1 is the average number of customers that are served in one minute. The average time to complete a single service is $\frac{1}{\mu} = \frac{1}{1.1} = 0.90909$ minutes. Note that the service rate, 1.1, is greater than the arrival rate, 1. If this were not the case, you would expect the line to become longer and longer as time passes. The average time between arrivals is 1 minute; the average time to complete a service is 0.90909 minutes. The service rate is larger than the arrival rate, and the mean time between arrivals is larger than the mean service time. However, it is still possible to have several customers waiting for service. Even though the average service time is 0.90909 minutes, some services take longer; and even though the average time between arrivals is 1 minute, the arrivals are closer together at times. Just by chance, customers may have to wait for service. We want to estimate how long they must wait.

Doing the Simulation

Simulating this M/M/1 system corresponds to processing a large number of customers through the service system and noting the waiting time of each customer. Based on the results of the simulation study, we can estimate the waiting time's mean, standard deviation, and probability distribution. Without actually operating the facility, the simulation is designed to analyze the system as if it were an M/M/1 waiting line with the specified arrival rate and service rate.

One of the first design considerations of a probabilistic simulation is the number of trials. Later in this chapter, we discuss determining the number of trials needed to obtain the degree of confidence you want on your estimates. Let's arbitrarily choose 100 customers as the number to be simulated.

Let's use the *variable-time increment* method for the simulation clock. We generate 100 interarrival times for the 100 customers. We start the simulation clock at 0 and calculate the customer arrival times using the interarrival times we generated. We also generate service times for the 100 customers. With the list of arrival times and service times, we advance the simulation clock when an event occurs. For each customer, we calculate the waiting time and when service starts and ends.

Let's simulate the first four customers "by hand." Table 16.1 has the numbers from the CRNG that are used to generate the interarrival times and service times for the first four customers. For example, 0.2702 is used

TABLE 16.1   Values from the Computer Random Number Generator and Times for the M/M/1 Simulation

Customer	Value from the Computer Random Number Generator	Interarrival Time
1	0.2702	$-\ln(1 - 0.2702) = 0.315$
2	0.5229	$-\ln(1 - 0.5229) = 0.740$
3	0.0879	$-\ln(1 - 0.0879) = 0.092$
4	0.7867	$-\ln(1 - 0.7867) = 1.545$

Customer	Value from the Computer Random Number Generator	Service Time
1	0.3336	$-(1/1.1)\ln(1 - 0.3336) = 0.369$
2	0.6432	$-(1/1.1)\ln(1 - 0.6432) = 0.937$
3	0.7813	$-(1/1.1)\ln(1 - 0.7813) = 1.382$
4	0.6818	$-(1/1.1)\ln(1 - 0.6818) = 1.041$

to generate the interarrival time for Customer 1. Table 16.1 also summarizes the times generated from those values. Let's generate each of the times and show the simulation logic for the first four customers.

We use Chapter 15's *algebraic method* for generating the random variables. You can easily invert the exponential probability distribution algebraically. Say that an exponential probability distribution has Rate λ, so that the cumulative probability distribution function is $F(t) = 1 - e^{-\lambda t}$. Say that the CRNG gives the value q. Then, we need to find the value of t so that

$$F(t) = 1 - e^{-\lambda t} = q$$

Solving for t, we get

$$t = -\frac{\ln(1 - q)}{\lambda}$$

where ln is the natural logarithm function.

The first random variable generated is the interarrival time of the first customer. Because $\lambda = 1$ and the CRNG gives 0.2702, the first interarrival time is

$$t = -\frac{\ln(1 - 0.2702)}{\lambda} = -\frac{\ln(0.7298)}{1} = 0.315$$

Because the simulation clock starts at 0 and this is the first interarrival, the arrival time of the first customer is at 0.315 minutes on the simulation clock.

The service time for the first customer is generated in a similar manner, except that the parameter of the exponential distribution, μ, is 1.1, not 1. Table 16.1 shows that the CRNG gives a 0.3366 value for the first service time. The cumulative probability distribution for service times is $G(t) = 1 - e^{-\mu t} = 1 - e^{-1.1t}$. If the value from the CRNG is q, then it is necessary to find t such that $G(t) = q$. Solving for t, we get

$$t = -\frac{\ln(1 - q)}{\mu}$$

If the value of q is 0.3336, the value of t is calculated as

$$t = -\frac{\ln(1 - 0.3336)}{1.1} = 0.369$$

The first service time is 0.369 minutes. Because the system is empty when the first customer arrives, service begins right at arrival, 0.315 on the simulation clock. The service time is 0.369 minutes, and service is completed at Time $0.315 + 0.369 = 0.684$. If a customer does not have to wait for service to start, the arrival time plus the service time equals the completion time. Because service starts right at the arrival of the first customer, the waiting time for the first customer is 0.

Now, the interarrival time for the second customer is generated. Say that the next value from the CRNG is 0.5229. The second interarrival time is calculated as $t = -\ln(1 - 0.5229) = 0.740$. The arrival time of the second customer is the arrival time of the first customer plus the second interarrival time, $0.315 + 0.740 = 1.055$. Observe that the *completion time of the first customer, 0.684, is before the arrival time of the second customer,* 1.055. This means that service can be started as soon as the second customer arrives. The CRNG is used to obtain the service time of the second customer. If the value is 0.6432, then the second service time is

$$t = -\frac{\ln(1 - 0.6432)}{1.1} = 0.937$$

There is no waiting time before service starts, so the completion time for the second customer is the arrival time of the second customer plus the service time of the second customer, $1.055 + 0.937 = 1.993$. The waiting time for the second customer is 0. The second customer did not have to wait, but it could have been different if either the interarrival time of the second customer had been smaller or the service time of the first customer had been larger.

The interarrival time of the third customer is generated next. Table 16.1 shows that the CRNG gives 0.0879 for the third interarrival time. This gives an interarrival time of $t = -\ln(1 - 0.0879) = 0.092$. The third customer arrives at Time $1.055 + 0.092 = 1.147$ minutes after the simulation clock is started. This is a short interarrival time, 0.092, and the completion time of the second customer is greater than the arrival time of the third customer. This causes the third customer to wait until the service has been completed on the second customer. In fact, the third customer must wait until the simulation clock shows 1.993 minutes, the completion time of the second customer. The waiting time of the third customer is $1.993 - 1.147 = 0.846$ minutes. Service starts on the third customer at Time 1.993. The starting time of any customer is the larger of the arrival time of the customer and the completion time of the previous customer. This observation is useful in developing the logic for a computer program to simulate this system. The completion time of the third customer is its starting time plus its service time. The service time for the next value from the CRNG (0.7813) is 1.382 minutes. The completion time of the third customer is 3.375 minutes.

The fourth customer arrives next. If the CRNG gives the value 0.7867, the arrival time of the fourth customer is 2.692. This arrival time is before the completion time of the third customer, so this gives a waiting time of 0.683 minutes. (Try to verify this value.) The generated value of the service time for the fourth customer is 1.041 using 0.6818 from the CRNG. The completion time for the fourth customer is 4.416.

FIGURE 16.1   The First Four Customers of the M/M/1 Simulation

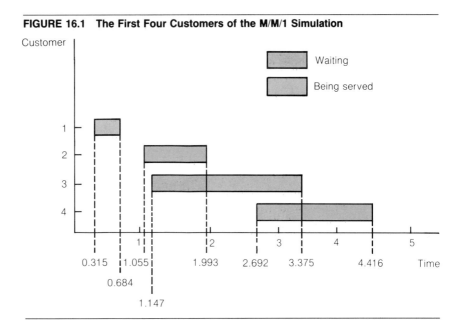

Figure 16.1 illustrates how the first four customers are processed through the system. The first two customers don't have any waiting time. In fact, the server is idle from the time that the first customer's service has been completed until the time that second customer arrives. The third and fourth customers must wait before their service begins.

We've simulated the first four customers by hand. However, to improve the quality of the estimates from the simulation results, we must simulate a large number of customers. We can simulate 100 or even 100,000 customers by hand, but this takes a long time. We use a computer because it does the simulations faster.

The simulation logic flowchart

Figure 16.2 has a flowchart that shows the simulation logic. First, we generate the 100 interarrival times and calculate the 100 arrival times. Next, we generate the 100 service times. The arrival, service, completion, and waiting time for Customer I are represented by $AR(I)$, $SR(I)$, $C(I)$, and $W(I)$, respectively. M is the number of the next customer to arrive, and I is the number of the customer being served. T is the time that service starts on Customer I. For Customer $I = 1$, service starts when it arrives and the completion time is the arrival time plus the service time. Its waiting time is 0. Compare the completion time of the customer being served to the arrival time of the next customer. If the completion time is smaller, service starts on the next customer when it arrives. Otherwise, service starts on the next customer when service is complete on the

FIGURE 16.2 Flowchart of M/M/1 Simulation Logic

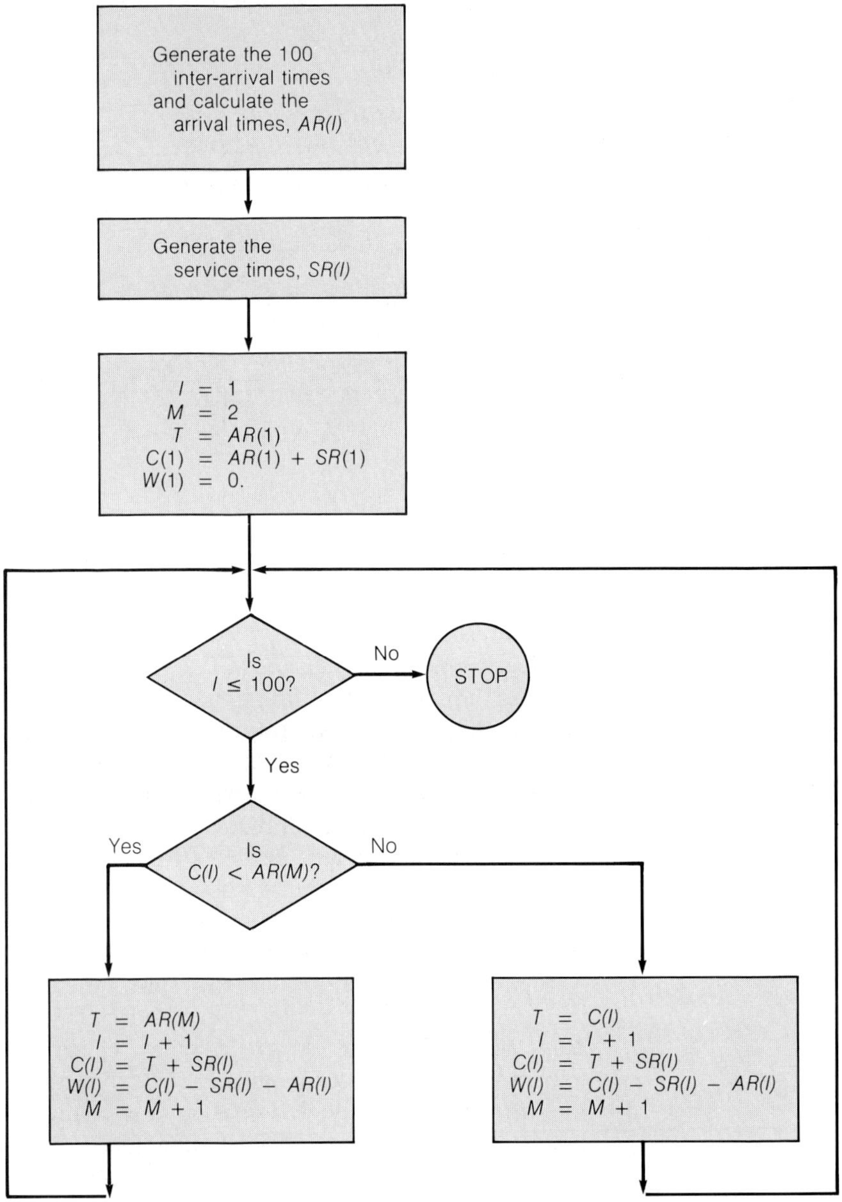

customer being served. The processing continues until the 100 customers have been served. The simulation logic uses the following relationships:

1. The completion time of a customer is its starting time plus its service time.
2. The starting time of a customer equals the larger of its arrival time and the completion time of the previous customer.
3. The waiting time of a customer is its starting time minus its arrival time. You can calculate its starting time as its completion time minus its service time.

Table 16.2 contains the computer results for simulating 100 customers through the system. If different values are obtained from the CRNG, different results are obtained from the simulation. Because of the variability, we must do statistical analysis to discover the extent to which the simulation results are representative of the system.

Using a Higher-Level Simulation Language

Table 16.2 was generated by a FORTRAN program that used the logic shown in Figure 16.2. The FORTRAN program used more than 50 statements to do the simulation. Figure 16.3 shows the simulation model using a higher-level simulation language, General Purpose Simulation System (GPSS). You can see that this program requires fewer statements than the one using FORTRAN.

The advantages of using higher-level simulation languages

It is easier to build and maintain simulation models using higher-level simulation languages. These languages allow you to replace with a single statement several FORTRAN statements that do part of the simulation. For example, the GPSS statement "GENERATE 60,FN1" generates exponentially distributed interarrival times with a mean of 60. You need more statements to do this if you use FORTRAN.

Remember, GPSS uses a fixed-time increment. Figure 16.3 uses one second as the fixed-time increment. Thus, the mean interarrival time is 60 seconds. The mean service time is $\frac{60}{1.1} = 54.54$, which is rounded to 55 in Figure 16.3.

An advantage of computer simulation is the ease of handling complicating factors that make getting analytical results impossible. Now, we discuss how we can include some complicating factors in our simulation model. We also begin discussing statistical analysis.

Complicating Factors in Waiting Line Simulations

In Chapter 14, we discussed the M/M/1 waiting line system. Chapter 14 presented some steady state analytical results for the M/M/1 model. For example, the steady state expected waiting time is

TABLE 16.2   M/M/1 Simulation of 100 Customers

CUSTOMER	ARRIVAL TIME	SERVICE TIME	COMPLETION TIME	WAITING TIME
1	0.315	0.369	0.684	0.000
2	1.055	0.937	1.993	0.000
3	1.147	1.382	3.375	0.846
4	2.692	1.041	4.416	0.683
5	3.125	0.336	4.752	1.290
6	3.311	0.479	5.231	1.441
7	3.344	0.275	5.506	1.837
8	5.551	0.496	6.046	0.000
9	6.462	0.594	7.056	0.000
10	7.562	1.504	9.066	0.000
11	7.579	0.338	9.404	1.488
12	8.851	0.167	9.570	0.553
13	10.268	0.823	11.091	0.000
14	11.723	0.812	12.535	0.000
15	13.282	1.038	14.318	0.000
16	13.309	1.014	15.332	1.010
17	14.180	0.475	15.807	1.152
18	14.425	0.640	16.446	1.382
19	14.533	0.117	16.564	1.915
20	15.352	1.049	17.614	1.213
21	17.064	0.991	18.604	0.549
22	18.534	0.328	18.938	0.070
23	19.749	0.436	20.185	0.000
24	19.820	2.818	23.003	0.365
25	20.071	0.112	23.115	2.932
26	20.262	1.203	24.317	2.853
27	20.683	0.216	24.533	3.634
28	21.047	0.241	24.775	3.487
29	21.819	0.654	25.428	2.956
30	22.017	0.720	26.148	3.412
31	23.500	0.410	26.556	2.648
32	23.517	0.285	26.842	3.040
33	24.247	0.845	27.687	2.595
34	25.017	0.617	28.305	2.670
35	26.370	0.798	29.102	1.934
36	29.508	1.522	31.031	0.000
37	31.943	0.140	32.084	0.000
38	37.364	0.353	37.717	0.000
39	44.465	0.894	45.359	0.000
40	46.524	0.866	47.390	0.000
41	47.160	1.900	49.259	0.229
42	47.525	1.391	50.680	1.764
43	47.876	0.247	50.927	2.804
44	48.599	0.501	51.428	2.328
45	51.466	0.736	52.202	0.000
46	51.712	0.899	53.101	0.490
47	52.192	0.170	53.271	0.906
48	53.197	4.243	57.513	0.074
49	53.280	2.399	59.912	4.234
50	53.936	0.845	60.757	5.976

TABLE 16.2 *(concluded)*

51	53.942	0.173	60.930	6.815
52	57.810	0.062	60.991	3.120
53	58.804	1.252	62.243	2.187
54	60.676	0.569	62.812	1.567
55	63.203	5.027	68.230	0.000
56	63.561	0.462	68.692	4.669
57	63.984	1.305	69.997	4.708
58	64.049	2.887	72.884	5.948
59	66.112	0.448	73.333	6.772
60	66.542	1.221	74.553	6.790
61	70.170	1.163	75.718	4.383
62	72.297	1.632	77.349	3.419
63	73.251	0.099	77.447	4.097
64	75.329	1.651	79.098	2.118
65	75.639	0.430	79.526	3.459
66	75.691	1.680	81.208	3.837
67	77.953	1.981	83.190	3.255
68	78.938	0.533	83.722	4.252
69	82.547	0.589	84.312	1.175
70	82.936	1.203	85.515	1.376
71	83.563	0.614	86.130	1.952
72	84.001	0.334	86.464	2.128
73	85.858	1.347	87.811	0.606
74	86.446	0.271	86.082	1.365
75	86.524	0.996	89.078	1.558
76	88.183	0.180	89.258	0.895
77	89.173	0.013	89.270	0.084
78	89.358	0.164	89.522	0.000
79	90.000	0.159	90.159	0.000
80	91.351	1.505	92.855	0.000
81	91.432	2.724	95.579	1.424
82	91.712	0.208	95.787	3.867
83	92.241	1.176	96.964	3.547
84	94.534	2.660	99.624	2.430
85	97.359	0.366	99.990	2.265
86	97.908	0.124	100.114	2.083
87	98.921	0.107	100.221	1.193
88	98.955	0.380	100.601	1.267
89	102.391	2.174	104.565	0.000
90	102.991	1.044	105.609	1.574
91	105.316	0.063	105.672	0.292
92	107.567	1.241	108.808	0.000
93	109.963	0.512	110.475	0.000
94	110.049	0.882	111.357	0.427
95	113.188	0.382	113.570	0.000
96	113.452	2.146	115.716	0.118
97	114.174	0.950	116.666	1.542
98	114.241	1.071	117.737	2.425
99	115.040	1.064	118.801	2.698
100	116.632	0.776	119.577	2.169

FIGURE 16.3 GPSS Program for the M/M/1 Simulation

```
        GENERATE    60,FN1      (Customer arrives)
        QUEUE       1           (Customer enters the queue)
   FAC  SEIZE       1           (Customer captures the server)
        DEPART      1           (Customer leaves the queue)
        ADVANCE     55,FN1      (Customer uses the server)
        RELEASE 1               (Customer releases the server)
        TERMINATE               (Customer departs)
```

$$E(W) = \frac{\lambda}{\mu(\mu - \lambda)}$$

We didn't present any analytical transient results. Getting analytical transient results is difficult, and often impossible. But you can get estimates of transient conditions using simulation. Let's show how you can use simulation to get transient results.

Estimating transient conditions

Say that you want to estimate the waiting time of the 100th customer. You start with the system empty, simulate 100 customers through the system, and record the waiting time of the 100th customer. Each replication requires starting with the system empty, using different random numbers to simulate 100 customers through the system, and recording the waiting time of the 100th customer.

Now, say that you want to estimate the number of people waiting in line 50 minutes after opening. You simulate the system for 50 minutes and record the number in line at that time. You replicate the experiment with different random numbers to get more estimates of the number waiting 50 minutes after opening.

Complicating factors

Now, let's show how to include complicating factors in the simulation. For example, the M/M/1 analytical results assume that the arrival rate doesn't change over time. In many systems, the arrival rate depends on the time of day. Say that the arrival rate changes from hour to hour. In a simulation model, you check the simulation clock time and generate the next interarrival time using the rate for that time of day. You add some logic to the simulation model for this, but it doesn't make the simulation difficult.

Also, the M/M/1 analytical results assume that the server is always available to provide service. This is not reasonable unless the server is a machine that never breaks down. If the server is a machine that has uncertain breakdowns, you generate additional random variables for the timing and duration of breakdowns. When you advance the simulation clock, you compare the time with the next breakdown time. If the machine breaks down, you delay the completion time by the duration of the breakdown. The additional simulation logic and random variable generation aren't hard to include.

If the server is a person, he or she may be unavailable during lunch and coffee breaks. Say that the server has lunch for one hour. In the simulation model, you compare a customer's anticipated completion time with the lunch hour. If the service time includes the lunch hour, you increase the completion time by one hour. Again, you add some logic to the simulation model, but it doesn't make the simulation difficult.

We've shown that it's easy to include complicating factors in a simulation model. In Chapter 14, we described other waiting line considerations, such as balking and reneging. Many of the considerations make it impossible to get analytical results, even for the steady state. But you can estimate even transient conditions using simulation.

Remember, you use simulation results to *estimate* how the system performs. Let's do some preliminary examination of the simulation results in Table 16.2. Note that the arrival time of the 100th customer is 116.632. Because the simulation clock began at 0, the total of the 100 interarrival times is 116.632 minutes. The expected interarrival time is 1.0 minutes per customer, but the simulation average is different—1.16632 minutes. It's also unlikely that the average waiting time exactly equals the expected waiting time. *Usually, the simulation study doesn't give average values equal to the expected values.* However, it is possible to establish a confidence interval on your estimate. For example, it is useful to be able to state that there is a 95 percent chance that the expected waiting time for a customer is between 0.57 and 3.00 minutes. Such information is useful in evaluating different configurations of the queueing system. Confidence interval determination is also the key to choosing the number of trials in a simulation analysis. First, you choose the amount of accuracy you want for your estimate, and then you choose the number of trials needed to obtain that accuracy.

Simulation averages might not equal the expected values

We chose the M/M/1 model as an example to show how a waiting line simulation is done. In the next sections, we describe statistical analysis of simulation results. In Chapter 14, we presented analytical steady state results for M/M/1. Because we know those results, we can compare the estimates with the actual expected values. Usually, you don't do a simulation if you have analytical results. But in this case, we did the simulation to show that the simulation estimates aren't equal to the expected values and to compare our estimates and confidence intervals with the actual expected values.

In the following sections, we discuss statistical analysis of probabilistic simulation results. Interpreting simulation results is often done incorrectly, particularly for waiting lines. However, the pitfalls can be avoided. There are only a *few common errors*. Read these sections carefully. Simulation is a powerful tool, but the statistical analysis of the results of a probabilistic simulation is tricky.

SAMPLING STATISTICS OF PROBABILISTIC SIMULATIONS

The very nature of probabilistic simulation guarantees variability in the outcomes. Because of this variability, the actual values of the measures of interest obtained in probabilistic simulations are not likely to be exactly equal to their expected values. For this reason, confidence intervals should be established on the results. **Sampling statistics** are common descriptive statistics used in the analysis of sample data. Sampling statistics include the sample mean and the sample standard deviation. These are important for determining confidence intervals.

A probabilistic simulation has one or more measures of interest. For the risk analysis simulation of Chapter 15, net present value (NPV) is the measure of interest. For the inventory management simulation of Chapter 15, the 30-day cost is the measure of interest. For the simulation of the M/M/1 waiting line system, customer waiting time is the measure of interest. Each of these measures of interest has a probability distribution; the values of these measures are not constant. You might use the simulation results to estimate the expected value of the measure of interest. In Chapter 10, we discussed the use of the expected value criterion in choosing decision alternatives for probabilistic decision environments. We also showed how you can include attitudes about risk by using a utility function. Sometimes, managers aren't willing to give a utility function. They may prefer to use the probability distribution of the measure of interest in choosing the decision. In that case, you can use the simulation results to estimate the probability distribution of the measure of interest. We showed how to do this with Chapter 15's risk analysis simulation.

Estimating the expected value

In this section, we focus on *estimating the expected value of the measure of interest*. Let W represent the *measure of interest*. For example, W represents the 30-day cost in the inventory management simulation. W is a random variable with an unknown mean, μ, and an unknown standard deviation, σ. We can have any probability distribution. Because the expected value of W is the mean, we might say that we also want to estimate the mean of the measure of interest. Let W_j represent the random variable value for the jth trial of the simulation experiment. Let's assume that there are n trials of the experiment. The first trial is denoted W_1, and the last trial is denoted W_n. The values obtained in the n trials are the **sample values.**

In this section, we show how to calculate descriptive statistics for several of the simulations we've done, and we use the descriptive statistics to estimate the mean and standard deviation of the measure of interest, W. We also show how to use the descriptive statistics to get confidence intervals on the expected value. But you must understand that

Be aware of the under-
lying assumptions *the quality of the descriptive statistics as estimators depends on the underlying assumptions.* We show how the assumptions affect statistical analysis.

The Sample Mean

The **sample mean** is the average of the values of the sample. If there are n values in the sample, then the sample mean is calculated as

$$\overline{W} = \frac{\sum_{j=1}^{n} W_j}{n}$$

For example, recall the first simulation experiment introduced in Chapter 15. In that example, we wanted to estimate the expected daily sales of an item. Simulation was not necessary to estimate the expected daily sales, but we used this simple example to introduce the idea of generating random variables from a specified probability distribution. The simulation experiment was flipping a coin and assigning a head (H) to a sale of 0 units and a tail (T) to a sale of 1 unit. The measure of interest, W, is daily sales. The simulation results are repeated in Table 16.3. W_1 is the value from the first coin flip. The experiment was repeated 10 times, so $n = 10$. The number of replications is 10.

Let's use this simulation to calculate the sample mean. Add the values of W_1 through W_{10} and divide by 10 to get the sample mean:

$$\overline{W} = \frac{4}{10} = 0.4$$

Under *some* circumstances, the sample mean is an unbiased estimator of the expected value of the measure of interest. *If the probability dis-*

TABLE 16.3 Equally Likely Outcomes Simulation

Trial	Experiment Outcome	Value of Random Variable
1	H	0
2	T	1
3	H	0
4	H	0
5	T	1
6	T	1
7	H	0
8	T	1
9	H	0
10	H	0
Total		4

Condition for $\overline{W}$ being
an unbiased estimate
of μ
tributions for all W_j *are identical to that for* W, *then the sample mean is
an unbiased estimate of the expected value of* W. Symbolically, this is
represented as

$$E(\overline{W}) = \mu$$

The probabilities were equally likely for a daily demand of 0 and 1. Our
coin-flipping simulation had the same probabilities for each trial. For that
reason, the *sample mean of the coin-flipping simulation is an unbiased
estimate of daily sales.*

Note that the unbiased property does not ensure that the sample mean
is exactly equal to the unknown expected value. Rather, the *expected
value* of the sample mean is equal to the unknown expected value. There
is still variability in the sample mean. In fact, we showed in Chapter 15
that the expected value of daily sales is 0.5, yet our estimate is 0.4.

Now, let's analyze the M/M/1 simulation results in Table 16.2. W_1 is
the waiting time of the first customer, and W_{100} is the waiting time for the
100th customer. The total waiting time of the 100 customers is 178.68
minutes, so the sample mean is $\dfrac{178.68}{100} = 1.7868$ minutes.

The waiting times don't
have identical proba-
bility distributions
The sample mean is an unbiased estimate of the expected value if the
W_j all have the same probability distribution as W, the measure of interest. Unfortunately, the M/M/1 simulation results in Table 16.2 do not
satisfy the assumption that all W_j have the same probability distribution as
W. Also, the probability distributions for the W_j differ from one another.
Remember, we assumed that no customers were in the system when we
began the simulation. Thus, the first customer's waiting time was certain
to be 0. However, other customers might have a waiting time longer than
0, depending on the values obtained from the CRNG. The probability
distribution of the waiting time for the first customer is *different* from the
probability distribution of the waiting time for any other customer. Thus,
the sample mean, 1.7868, is *not an unbiased estimator* of the expected
waiting time of a randomly chosen customer.

We've discussed the difference between steady state and transient
results. Recall that *transient* results are affected by the starting condition
of the system. For the M/M/1 simulation above, the probability distributions of the waiting time, particularly for the earliest customers, are
affected by the fact that we started the simulation with no customers
present. Even if the simulation began with customers present, the probability distributions of waiting times, particularly for the customers who
arrive earliest, are affected by the starting condition. Recall that *steady
state* results are achieved after enough time has passed for the starting
condition to be unimportant. For example, the waiting time of the 1,000th
customer is unlikely to be significantly affected by the starting condition
of the system.

Ignoring the impact of starting conditions is a common error in es-

timating steady state conditions of waiting line systems from simulation results. One approach that corrects this bias is simulating a large enough number of customers through the system before you start to collect statistics. Before starting to collect statistics, for example, you might simulate 1,000 customers through the system. Then, you can reasonably expect the probability distributions for the 1,001st and the 1,002nd customers to be the same as that for W. Note that we don't assume that the W_j are statistically independent of one another. This is an important distinction that we discuss more in the Sample Standard Deviation section.

You must be careful to specify what W represents for a waiting line simulation. If W represents customer waiting time, you must specify which customer. The implicit assumption was that we wanted to estimate the expected waiting time for a customer after the system had reached a steady state condition. If that was our intention, the probability distribution of W_1, the waiting time of the first customer, is not the same as the probability distribution for a customer after the system has reached steady state. However, the probability distributions of Customers 1001 through 1100 are the same as the probability distribution after the system reaches steady state. You can use the sample mean for Customers 1001 through 1100 as an unbiased estimate of the steady state expected waiting time. But the sample mean that includes the first customers is biased.

Say that you want to estimate transient conditions. For example, say that you want to estimate the total waiting time for the first 100 customers if the system starts with no customers present. Table 16.2 gives you one sample value, 1,768.68 minutes. You replicate the experiment with different random numbers, starting again with no customers present, to get the second sample value. The sample mean of the sample values is an unbiased estimate of the total waiting time for 100 customers if you begin with the system empty.

The starting conditions don't cause biased estimates for all probabilistic simulations over time. These conditions are necessary for a terminating simulation or for a simulation to estimate conditions at a particular point in time. Consider the inventory management simulation. The system starts with 20 units on hand, and we want to estimate the cost for an ordering policy. Because the company plans to stop selling the product in 30 days, this is a terminating simulation. In Table 15.16, we simulated the system for 30 days for a reorder point of 5 units and an order quantity of 20 units. We want to estimate W, the 30-day cost, which has an unknown probability distribution. The simulation of 30 days shown in Table 15.16 provided the first value, $W_1 = \$61.10$. We replicate the inventory management simulation with a different set of random numbers to get the second value. Again, we start the simulation with 20 units on hand and use the same ordering policy. W_2 represents the second value of the 30-day cost. If the random numbers used for the two simulations are

TABLE 16.4 40 Replications of Inventory Management Simulation

Run	Inventory Holding Cost	Lost Sale Cost	Fixed Order Cost	Total Cost
1	69.40	0.00	20.00	89.40
2	57.70	0.00	0.00	57.70
3	40.20	0.00	20.00	60.20
4	45.90	0.00	0.00	45.90
5	63.50	0.00	20.00	83.50
6	60.10	0.00	20.00	80.10
7	61.60	0.00	0.00	61.60
8	46.80	0.00	20.00	66.80
9	59.80	0.00	20.00	79.80
10	53.20	0.00	0.00	53.20
11	40.60	0.00	20.00	60.60
12	49.90	0.00	20.00	69.90
13	42.70	0.00	20.00	62.70
14	54.00	0.00	0.00	54.00
15	64.80	0.00	20.00	84.80
16	59.30	0.00	20.00	79.30
17	72.00	0.00	20.00	92.00
18	42.90	0.00	20.00	62.90
19	49.30	0.00	20.00	69.30
20	50.40	0.00	20.00	70.40
21	56.30	0.00	0.00	56.30
22	55.90	0.00	0.00	55.90
23	48.80	0.00	20.00	68.80
24	40.40	0.00	0.00	40.40
25	50.00	0.00	0.00	50.00
26	69.20	0.00	20.00	89.20
27	46.20	0.00	0.00	46.20
28	58.10	0.00	0.00	58.10
29	63.50	0.00	20.00	83.50
30	43.10	0.00	0.00	43.10
31	62.70	0.00	20.00	82.70
32	53.90	0.00	0.00	53.90
33	67.20	0.00	20.00	87.20
34	55.40	0.00	20.00	75.40
35	48.30	0.00	0.00	48.30
36	48.50	0.00	0.00	48.50
37	78.20	0.00	20.00	98.20
38	54.10	0.00	0.00	54.10
39	53.50	0.00	0.00	53.50
40	52.80	0.00	0.00	52.80

chosen independently, the random variables W_1 and W_2 are independent. Because of the design of the simulation experiment, the probability distributions of W, W_1, and W_2 are the same. Table 16.4 has the 30-day cost for 40 replications of the inventory management simulation. The sample mean is the total of the 40 costs divided by 40:

$$\overline{W} = \frac{2,630.20}{40} = 65.755$$

The sample mean is an unbiased estimate of the expected value of the 30-day cost.

The Sample Standard Deviation

The sample standard deviation and the sample variance are descriptive statistics that measure the variability of the sample. If the sample has n values, $W_j, j = 1, \ldots, n$, the **sample variance,** denoted by s^2, is

$$s^2 = \frac{\sum\limits_{j=1}^{n} (W_j - \overline{W})^2}{(n - 1)}$$

where the sample mean, $\overline{W}$, is calculated as shown above. The **sample standard deviation,** denoted by s, is the square root of the sample variance:

$$s = \sqrt{\frac{\sum\limits_{j=1}^{n} (W_j - \overline{W})^2}{(n - 1)}}$$

Let's calculate the sample variance of the results shown in Table 16.3 for the equally likely daily demand simulation. Recall that we calculated the sample mean, $\overline{W} = 0.4$. The sample variance is

$$s^2 = [(0 - 0.4)^2 + (1 - 0.4)^2 + (0 - 0.4)^2 + (0 - 0.4)^2 + (1 - 0.4)^2$$
$$+ (1 - 0.4)^2 + (0 - 0.4)^2 + (1 - 0.4)^2 + (0 - 0.4)^2$$
$$+ (0 - 0.4)^2]/(10 - 1) = \frac{2.8}{9} = 0.3111$$

The sample standard deviation is

$$s = \sqrt{0.3111} = 0.55777$$

An *easier computational form* for the sample variance is

Easier computational form

$$s^2 = \frac{\sum\limits_{j=1}^{n} W_j^2 - n(\overline{W})^2}{(n - 1)}$$

This form eliminates the need to subtract the sample mean from each value, but is computationally equivalent. Using this form, we get the same value for s^2:

$$s^2 = \frac{(0^2 + 1^2 + 0^2 + 0^2 + 1^2 + 1^2 + 0^2 + 1^2 + 0^2 + 0^2) - (10 \times 0.4^2)}{(10 - 1)}$$

$$= 0.3111$$

Condition for s to be an unbiased estimate of σ

If the W_j are independent, identically distributed random variables, the sample standard deviation (s) is an unbiased estimator of the standard deviation of the random variable W (σ). "Identically distributed" means that the probability distributions of each of the random variables in the sample are the same. Remember, the identically distributed assumption ensured that the sample mean was an unbiased estimate of the expected value. The independence assumption means that the probability distribution of any W_j is the same regardless of the values of the other W_j random variables in the sample.

Consider the simulation of the equally likely daily sales example, whose results appear in Table 16.3. In this case, the sample random variables are independent. This is because we assume that regardless of whether a head or a tail is obtained in one coin flip, any other flip of a fair coin has an equal chance of being a head or a tail. Even if the coin has been flipped five times and five consecutive heads have been obtained, it is still equally likely that the next flip will be either a head or a tail. Thus, the sample standard deviation, 0.55777, is an unbiased estimate of the standard deviation of daily sales, the random variable of interest.

Let's consider results of the inventory management simulation in Table 16.4. Each 30-day cost value was calculated using a different set of random numbers. If we use the same set of random numbers, we get the same 30-day cost. Because we chose the sets of random numbers independently, the 30-day cost values are independent, identically distributed random variables. Thus, the sample standard deviation, $s = 15.5305$, is an unbiased estimate of the standard deviation of the 30-day cost.

A biased estimate

Now, consider the results of the M/M/1 simulation. The random variables of the waiting times of successive customers are *not* independent. If the 50th customer has to wait a very long time, it is likely that the 51st customer also has to wait a long time. The sample standard deviation is *not* an unbiased estimate of the standard deviation of the waiting time of a randomly chosen customer. Without an unbiased estimate of the standard deviation, it is impossible to calculate a confidence interval on the waiting time. In the Analysis of Grouped Data section, we illustrate an approach that can be used to determine confidence intervals for the M/M/1 queueing example.

Checking for independence

In the M/M/1 queueing simulation, it is obvious that successive waiting times are not independent. In the equally likely daily demand and inventory management simulations, the replications are independent because of the way we do the simulations. If it is not obvious that simulations give independent trials, autocorrelation analysis can be used to study the independence of trials. **Correlation analysis** is a procedure for determining whether there is a relationship between two random variables, and the **correlation coefficient** measures the strength of the relationship. If the correlation coefficient is zero, the values are independent. If the correlation coefficient is positive, large (small) values of one random variable are associated with large (small) values of the other. If the correlation coefficient is negative, large (small) values of one random variable are associated with small (large) values of the other. **Autocorrelation analysis** examines the correlation of a random variable with its future values. We don't discuss the details of autocorrelation analysis in this book, but we do explore its ideas. In autocorrelation analysis, you calculate the correlation coefficient between the random variable and its value one, two, or more values in the future. For example, the **sample correlation coefficient** between W_j and W_{j+1} is calculated as

$$r_1 = \frac{\sum_{j=1}^{n-1}(W_j - \overline{W})(W_{j+1} - \overline{W})}{\sum_{j=1}^{n-1}(W_j - \overline{W})^2}$$

You use the sample correlation coefficient to estimate the unknown correlation coefficient. If the successive values are independent, the true correlation coefficient between W_j and W_{j+1} is zero. If the sample correlation coefficient is zero, the successive values are probably independent. Because of the variability of the sample, the sample coefficient can be different from zero even if the successive values are independent. You use classical statistical hypothesis testing to test the null hypothesis that the correlation coefficient is zero versus the alternative hypothesis that the correlation coefficient is not zero. Note that the alternative hypothesis is two-sided. In the M/M/1 example, we expect the correlation coefficient to be positive. A large waiting time is likely to be followed by another large waiting time. Other probabilistic simulations can have negative correlation coefficients. Either positive or negative correlation gives *a biased estimate of the unknown standard deviation*. Generally, it is sufficient to calculate the sample correlation coefficient between adjacent values of the random variable. Usually, if W_j and W_{j+q} are correlated (for some positive integer q), then W_j and W_{j+1} are also correlated.

Confidence Intervals for Independent Trials

Assumptions

In this section, we show how to calculate an interval estimate for the expected value (or mean) of the measure of interest. We assume that the trials are *independent* and that we have *unbiased estimates* of the mean and the standard deviation. A **confidence interval** establishes an interval that contains the actual, unknown value with a specified probability. For example, we might estimate that the probability is 0.95 that the true value is between 10 and 11. In this case, we say that the **confidence level** is 95 percent.

Is using the normal distribution valid?

The normal distribution is often used for calculating confidence intervals. *It is important that there be a valid justification for using the normal distribution.* Sometimes, the underlying probability distribution of the measure of interest is the normal distribution. However, this is not always the case. Even if demand is normally distributed in the inventory management simulation, this is not enough reason to believe that the 30-day cost is also normally distributed.

Even if the underlying probability distribution of the measure of inter-

FIGURE 16.4(a) Sampling Distribution of W

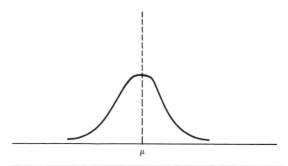

μ

The Central Limit Theorem

est is *not the normal distribution,* you can use the normal distribution if the sample size is large. Recall that the measure of interest has a mean of μ and a standard deviation of σ. The **Central Limit Theorem** states that as the number of independent samples increases, the sample mean is approximated by a normal distribution with a mean of μ and a standard deviation of $\dfrac{\sigma}{\sqrt{n}}$. The sample size required for the normal approximation to be reasonable depends on the underlying probability distribution. If the underlying distribution is the normal probability distribution, the sample size only needs to be 1. If the underlying probability distribution is close to the normal distribution, a sample with a small value of n is acceptable. If the underlying distribution is far from the normal distribution (e.g., bimodal or skewed), a larger sample size is needed for the normal approximation to be acceptable. If the probability distribution is skewed, Cochran has provided a rule for determining the value of n such that the normal approximation is reasonable.[3] Cochran's rule is given in the More Challenging Exercises.

A convenient rule of thumb is to use the normal approximation if the sample size is *30 or larger.* We use that rule of thumb in this chapter.

Use the normal approximation if $n \geq 30$

Figure 16.4 illustrates the Central Limit Theorem. In Figure 16.4*a,* we assume, for illustrative purposes, that W has a normal distribution. Figure 16.4*b* is the sampling distribution of $\overline{W}$ with a sample size of 4. The means of both $\overline{W}$ and W are μ, but the variability of $\overline{W}$ is less than that of W. Even if the probability distribution of W is not the normal distribution, the distribution of $\overline{W}$ is approximately the normal distribution if the sample size is large enough. Because the number of trials for a probabilistic simulation is usually much larger than 30, the rule-of-thumb value, the

---

[3] W. G. Cochran, *Sampling Techniques,* 3rd ed. (New York: John Wiley & Sons, 1977), pp. 39–44.

FIGURE 16.4(b) Sampling Distribution of $\overline{W}_1$ ($n = 4$)

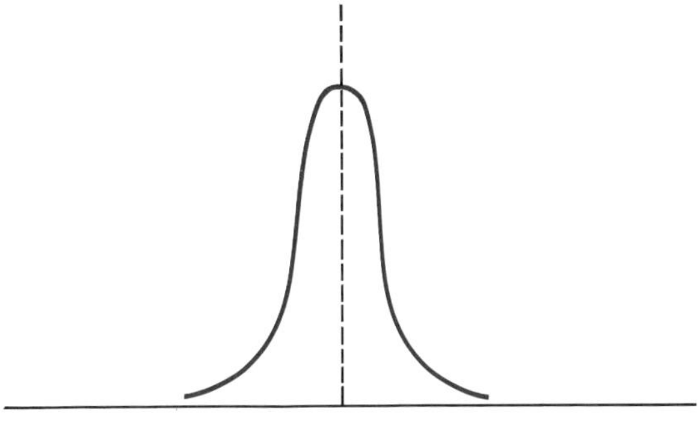

μ

normal distribution can often be used to determine confidence intervals on the expected value of the measure of interest.

If the sample size is large enough so that the normal approximation is correct, the $(1 - \alpha)$ confidence interval on the mean (expected value) of the measure of interest is

The normal distribution
confidence interval

$$\overline{W} - Z_{1-\frac{\alpha}{2}}\frac{s}{\sqrt{n}} \leq E(W) \leq \overline{W} + Z_{1-\frac{\alpha}{2}}\frac{s}{\sqrt{n}}$$

α is the probability that the confidence interval doesn't include the true value, which is sometimes called the **error probability.** $(1 - \alpha)$ is the probability that the confidence interval includes the true value. The value of $Z_{1-\frac{\alpha}{2}}$ is obtained from the normal cumulative probability distribution and is chosen so that the area in the lower tail is $\left(1 - \frac{\alpha}{2}\right)$. Because of the Central Limit Theorem, this is correct if the sample size is 30 or more even if the measure of interest doesn't have a normal distribution.

Consider the equally likely daily demand simulation. W is the daily demand, and we want to find a confidence interval on its expected value. Table 16.3 has only 10 trials. The demand is either 0 or 1, so the underlying distribution is far from the normal distribution. Because the number of trials is smaller than 30, you can't use the Central Limit Theorem to calculate a confidence interval.

If the number of trials were 30 or more, you could calculate a confidence interval. For example, if there are 100 trials, the normal distribution can be used to determine a confidence interval on the expected daily sales. Say that a head was obtained in 46 of the trials and that a tail was obtained in 54 of the trials. The sample mean of the daily sales from the trials is 0.54. The sample standard deviation is

$$s = \sqrt{\frac{46(0 - 0.54)^2 + 54(1 - 0.54)^2}{(100 - 1)}} = 0.5001$$

If $\alpha = 0.05$, the value of $Z_{1-\frac{\alpha}{2}} = Z_{0.975} = 1.96$. The 95 percent confidence interval is

$$0.54 - 1.96 \frac{0.5001}{\sqrt{100}} \leq E(W) \leq 0.54 + 1.96 \frac{0.5001}{\sqrt{100}}$$

or

$$0.4420 \leq E(W) \leq 0.6380$$

There is a 95 percent chance that the expected value of daily sales is between 0.4420 and 0.6380.

Now, let's calculate the 95 percent confidence interval on the expected 30-day cost from the inventory management results in Table 16.4. The form of the probability distribution of the 30-day cost is unknown, but 40 replications is more than enough to justify using the normal distribution to calculate a confidence interval on the 30-day cost. The sample mean (average 30-day cost) is 65.755, and the sample standard deviation is 15.5305. The 95 percent confidence interval on the expected value of the 30-day cost is

$$65.755 - 1.96 \frac{15.5305}{\sqrt{40}} \leq E(W) \leq 65.755 + 1.96 \frac{15.5305}{\sqrt{40}}$$

or

$$60.942 \leq E(W) \leq 70.568$$

There is a 95 percent chance that the expected 30-day cost is between 60.942 and 70.568.

If the sample size is 30 or larger, you can use the normal distribution to calculate a confidence interval, regardless of the underlying probability distribution of the measure of interest. However, if the sample size is less than 30 and the underlying probability distribution isn't the normal distribution, you can't use the normal distribution to calculate a confidence interval.

If the sample size, n, *is smaller than 30 and the* W_j *have a normal distribution, you use the* t-*distribution with* (n − 1) *degrees of freedom.* In the next section, we show how to use the t-distribution to calculate confidence intervals.

We can't use the method of this section on our M/M/1 simulation results to calculate a confidence interval for the steady state expected waiting time. There are *two problems*. First, the starting conditions give biased estimates. Second, successive waiting times aren't independent

If $n < 30$ and the W_j are normal, use the t-distribution

random variables. In the next section, we show how to calculate confidence intervals for waiting line systems.

ANALYSIS OF GROUPED DATA

Assume that the simulation-over-time trials are not independent

In this section, we present a method for determining confidence intervals for simulations over time if the trials are *not independent*. This is called the method of **batch means** or **grouped data.** This method is appropriate for interrelated simulations such as waiting line systems. In the M/M/1 queueing simulation, the waiting times of two successive customers are not independent. Because long waiting times are likely to be followed by more long waiting times, the correlation coefficient between a customer and the next customer is positive. Symbolically, this is the correlation between W_j and W_{j+1}. Now, say that we consider the correlation between a customer and the customer that is two customers ahead of it. The correlation coefficient between W_j and W_{j+2} is positive, though it is smaller than the correlation between successive customers. The correlation coefficient is smaller because there is an intervening customer. This is the same argument that we used for running the simulation awhile before starting to collect statistics. We expected that after a large number of customers was processed, the starting condition would have little impact. Using the same logic, the correlation coefficient between customers with 999 intervening customers is likely to be close to zero. The method is to group the customers into batches so that the means of the batches are close to independent.

The four steps

The general method consists of the *four steps* shown in Figure 16.5. First, group the observations into batches of equal size. Say that there are n batches each of size m. The total number of observations is n times m, nm. The first batch consists of Observations 1 to m. The second batch consists of Observations $m + 1$ to $2m$. The nth batch consists of Observations $(n - 1)m + 1$ to nm. Second, calculate the sample mean of each batch. The sample mean of the kth batch is

$$\overline{W}_k = \frac{\sum_{j=1}^{m} W_{(k-1)m+j}}{m}$$

Third, calculate the mean of the sample batch means, denoted as $\overline{\overline{W}}$. This is calculated as

$$\overline{\overline{W}} = \frac{\sum_{k=1}^{n} \overline{W}_k}{n}$$

FIGURE 16.5   Flowchart of Batch Means Calculations

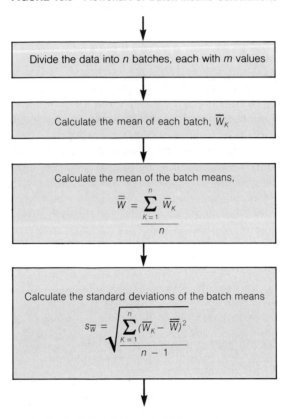

If the batch sizes are large enough, the batch means are independent. Then, the sample standard deviation of the batch means is an unbiased estimate of the standard deviation of a randomly chosen batch. Fourth, calculate the sample standard deviation of the batch means. This is calculated as

$$s_{\overline{W}} = \sqrt{\dfrac{\displaystyle\sum_{k=1}^{n} (\overline{W}_k - \overline{\overline{W}})^2}{(n-1)}}$$

The notation $s_{\overline{W}}$ denotes that it is an estimate of the standard deviation of a batch mean.

The $(1 - \alpha)$ confidence interval of the expected value for a randomly chosen observation is calculated as

The t-distribution confidence interval

$$\overline{\overline{W}} - t_{\left(1-\frac{\alpha}{2},\, n-1\right)} \dfrac{s_{\overline{W}}}{\sqrt{n}} \leq E(W) \leq \overline{\overline{W}} + t_{\left(1-\frac{\alpha}{2},\, n-1\right)} \dfrac{s_{\overline{W}}}{\sqrt{n}}$$

The value of t comes from the t-distribution with $n - 1$ degrees of freedom, where n is the number of batches. Note that $s_{\overline{W}}$ is divided by $\sqrt{n}$. Recall that if σ is the standard deviation for a single sample value, then $\dfrac{\sigma}{\sqrt{n}}$ is the standard deviation of the sample mean for a sample of size n. In the batch means approach, each $\overline{W}_j$ observation in the sample is itself a batch mean. Because there are n batch means, you divide by $\sqrt{n}$.

The t-distribution appears in Table 16.5. Note that as the number of degrees of freedom increases, the value of t approaches the value of Z from the normal distribution. If the number of batches is 30 or more, use the normal table, not the t-distribution table. Using the normal distribution, the $(1 - \alpha)$ confidence interval is

The normal distribution confidence interval

$$\overline{\overline{W}} - Z_{(1-\alpha)}\frac{s_{\overline{W}}}{\sqrt{n}} \le E(W) \le \overline{\overline{W}} + Z_{(1-\alpha)}\frac{s_{\overline{W}}}{\sqrt{n}}$$

Let's use Table 16.2's results for the M/M/1 simulation to illustrate the batch means approach. We want to estimate the steady state expected waiting time. The simulation of 100 customers is too few to choose a batch size such that the batch means are independent. However, let's use the data of Table 16.2 to illustrate the approach.

First, you group the customers into batches of equal size. For example, the batch size could be 10. Then, 100 customers are grouped into 10 batches, each with a size of 10. Batch 1 consists of the first 10 customers. Batch 2 consists of Customers 11 through 20. The last batch, the 10th, consists of Customers 91 through 100. Second, you calculate the mean of each batch. The mean of the first batch is the average of the waiting times of the first 10 customers. Table 16.2 shows the customer waiting times. The total of the waiting times of the first 10 customers is $0.846 + 0.683 + 1.290 + 1.441 + 1.887 = 6.147$, so the mean of the first batch is $\overline{W}_1 = \dfrac{6.147}{10} = 0.6147$. Table 16.6 illustrates the output from a simulation program that uses the batch means approach. We used the same CRNG values as those used for Table 16.2. The only difference is that the customers were put into batches of 10 and the batch means were calculated. Note that in Table 16.6 the mean for the first batch appears as 0.615, the same value as the one we just calculated, except for rounding.

Third, you calculate the value of $\overline{\overline{W}}$ as

$$\overline{\overline{W}} = \frac{\begin{array}{c}0.615 + 0.871 + 2.026 + 1.289 + 1.881 + 4.258 + 3.137 \\ + 0.859 + 1.965 + 0.967\end{array}}{10}$$

$$= \frac{17.868}{10} = 1.7868$$

Observe that $\overline{\overline{W}}$ is the same as the mean of the entire sample. This is because

TABLE 16.5 The *t*-Distribution

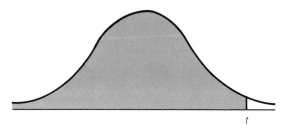

The table values are the values of *t* for the shaded area shown above.

Degrees of Freedom	Area			
	0.95	0.975	0.99	0.995
1	6.314	12.706	31.821	63.657
2	2.920	4.303	6.965	9.925
3	2.353	3.182	4.541	5.841
4	2.132	2.776	3.747	4.604
5	2.015	2.571	3.365	4.032
6	1.943	2.447	3.143	3.707
7	1.895	2.365	2.998	3.499
8	1.860	2.306	2.896	3.355
9	1.833	2.262	2.821	3.250
10	1.812	2.228	2.764	3.169
11	1.796	2.201	2.718	3.106
12	1.782	2.179	2.681	3.055
13	1.771	2.160	2.650	3.012
14	1.761	2.145	2.624	2.977
15	1.753	2.131	2.602	2.947
16	1.746	2.120	2.583	2.921
17	1.740	2.110	2.567	2.898
18	1.734	2.101	2.552	2.878
19	1.729	2.093	2.539	2.861
20	1.725	2.086	2.528	2.845
21	1.721	2.080	2.518	2.831
22	1.717	2.074	2.508	2.819
23	1.714	2.069	2.500	2.807
24	1.711	2.064	2.492	2.797
25	1.708	2.060	2.485	2.787
26	1.706	2.056	2.479	2.779
27	1.703	2.052	2.473	2.771
28	1.701	2.048	2.467	2.763
29	1.699	2.045	2.462	2.756
30	1.697	2.042	2.457	2.750
40	1.684	2.021	2.423	2.704
60	1.671	2.000	2.390	2.660
120	1.658	1.980	2.358	2.617
Normal distribution	1.645	1.960	2.326	2.576

SOURCE: Adapted from Roger C. Pfaffenburger and James H. Patterson, *Statistical Methods for Business and Economics,* 3rd ed. (Homewood, Ill.: Richard D. Irwin, 1987), pp. 1156–58.

TABLE 16.6 M/M/1 Simulation—Batch Size 10 and 10 Batches

Batch	Total Batch Waiting	Average Wait in Batch
1	6.15	0.615
2	8.71	0.871
3	20.26	2.026
4	12.89	1.289
5	18.81	1.881
6	42.58	4.258
7	31.37	3.137
8	8.59	0.859
9	19.65	1.965
10	9.67	0.967

$$\overline{\overline{W}} = \frac{1}{n}\sum_{k=1}^{n}\left(\sum_{j=1}^{m}\frac{W_{(k-1)m+j}}{m}\right) = \frac{\sum_{i=1}^{mn}W_i}{nm}$$

Fourth, you calculate the sample variance of the batch means as

$$
\begin{aligned}
s_{\overline{W}}^2 = {}& [(0.615^2) + (0.871^2) + (2.026^2) + (1.289^2) + (1.881^2) \\
& + (1.881^2) + (4.258^2) + (3.137^2) + (0.859^2) + (1.965^2) \\
& + (0.967^2)] - 10(1.7868^2)]/(10 - 1) = 2.89764
\end{aligned}
$$

Note that the calculation uses the computational simplification we introduced in the previous section. The sample standard deviation of the batch means is the square root of the sample variance, $s_{\overline{W}} = \sqrt{2.89764} = 1.702$.

Using Table 16.5, the t-value that corresponds to a 95 percent confidence interval with $10 - 1$ degrees of freedom is 2.262. The 95 percent confidence interval on the waiting time of a randomly chosen customer is calculated as

$$1.7868 - 2.262\frac{1.702}{\sqrt{10}} \le E(W) \le 1.7868 + 2.262\frac{1.702}{\sqrt{10}}$$

or

$$0.5693 \le E(W) \le 3.4888$$

This completes the application of the method of batch means to the M/M/1 queueing example data of Tables 16.2 and 16.6.

The confidence interval we just calculated is *incorrect* for the waiting time of a randomly chosen customer for *three reasons:*

Three reasons the confidence interval is incorrect

1. There is a bias caused by the starting condition. We assumed that the system was empty at the beginning of the simulation.
2. The batch size of 10 is too small to ensure the independence of the batch means.
3. There is no reason to believe that the underlying probability distribution of a batch mean is the normal distribution.

The *t*-distribution assumes that the underlying probability distribution is the normal distribution. But there is no reason to believe that the underlying waiting time distribution is the normal distribution, and in fact it is not. However, even if the underlying distribution is not the normal distribution, the Central Limit Theorem can be used for the distribution of a sample batch mean *if the batch size is large enough, (i.e., 30 or larger)*. In this case, the batch size is only 10, so the rule of thumb for using the normal distribution is not satisfied.

In Chapter 14, we said that the steady state expected waiting time for the M/M/1 queueing system is

$$E(W) = \frac{\lambda}{\mu(\mu - \lambda)}$$

For this example, $\lambda = 1$ and $\mu = 1.1$. The expected waiting time is $\frac{1}{1.1(1.1 - 1.)} = 9.09$. The sample mean of the 100 customers was 1.7868 minutes. The true expected value is not even close to the sample mean. Furthermore, the confidence interval that we calculated doesn't include the true value. This should convince you that *it is possible to do a simulation analysis without giving useful results*. The three errors noted above for the M/M/1 simulation data from Table 16.2 negate the analysis. However, it is possible to do a meaningful analysis by (1) increasing the batch size and (2) throwing away enough early customers to eliminate the bias caused by the starting conditions.

Table 16.7 has more results for the M/M/1 queueing system. In this case, the batch size is 400 and there are 20 batches. The total number of customers processed is 8,000. A batch size of 400 is large enough to ensure that the batch mean has the normal distribution by the Central Limit Theorem. Also, a batch size that large causes the means of successive batches to be independent.

A correct confidence interval

Discarding the first batch of 400 customers eliminates the bias caused by the starting conditions. The remaining data consists of 19 batches of 400 customers each. This is a total of 7,600 customers. The mean of Batches 2 through 20 is 9.5164. The sample standard deviation of the batch means is 7.3569. After the first batch has been discarded, there are only 19 batches. You divide by $19 - 1 = 18$ when you calculate the sample standard deviation of the batch means. The *t*-value for 95 percent with $19 - 1$ degrees of freedom is 2.101. The 95 percent confidence interval is

$$9.5164 - 2.101 \frac{7.3569}{\sqrt{19}} \le E(W) \le 9.5164 + 2.101 \frac{7.3569}{\sqrt{19}}$$

or

$$5.9704 \le E(W) \le 13.0624$$

TABLE 16.7   M/M/1 Simulation—Batch Size 400 and 20 Batches

Batch	Total Batch Waiting	Average Wait in Batch
1	2,781.76	6.954
2	2,819.80	7.049
3	3,808.59	9.521
4	5,203.46	13.009
5	2,041.80	5.104
6	4,039.81	10.100
7	4,132.33	10.331
8	12,083.92	30.210
9	1,108.28	2.771
10	2,198.08	5.495
11	1,455.45	3.639
12	1,446.77	3.617
13	1,649.53	4.124
14	5,179.68	12.949
15	2,146.07	5.365
16	4,084.20	10.211
17	2,588.86	6.472
18	2,296.13	5.740
19	11,207.51	28.019
20	2,834.50	7.086

Note that we divided by $\sqrt{19}$ because we had only 19 batches after discarding the first batch. The sample mean of 9.5164 is much closer to the true expected value of the waiting time—9.09 minutes. In fact, the confidence interval includes the true expected value of the waiting time. We expect that if the simulation with 20 batches of 400 each were repeated many times, 95 percent of the confidence intervals would include the true expected value.

DETERMINING THE NUMBER OF TRIALS— A PRELIMINARY SMALL SAMPLE

Determining the number of trials is an important design consideration in a simulation study. Using too few trials produces inaccurate estimates of the measure of interest. Such estimates may lead to improper inferences and incorrect decisions. A larger number of trials improves the accuracy of the estimates. At some point, however, increasing the number of trials does not improve the accuracy of the estimates enough to justify doing more simulations.

The most common approach used to choose the number of trials is to establish the desired precision of the confidence interval. The **precision** is the value of the possible error for the specified confidence level. For example, the confidence level may be specified as follows: "At a 95 percent confidence level, estimate the mean waiting time within 0.01 minutes." That is, there should be only a 5 percent chance that the estimated value is more than 0.01 minutes from the true, but unknown, mean waiting time. The desired precision, sometimes called the **acceptable error,** is 0.01 minutes. The **width of the confidence interval** is 2 times the desired precision.

There are *two approaches* to achieving the desired precision. For **fixed-sample-size procedures,** a simulation run of a fixed length is done. For **sequential procedures,** the length of a simulation is sequentially increased until you obtain the desired precision. Sequential procedures are beyond the scope of this book.

In this section, we explain the use of fixed-sample-size procedures *when the sample values are independent.* Recall that the sample values are independent for Monte Carlo probabilistic simulations. But the waiting times of the M/M/1 queueing system are not independent.

Normal distribution assumption

We use a fundamental result from sampling theory to calculate the number of trials. Say that we want to estimate the mean (expected value) of the measure of interest, and *assume that the measure of interest has a normal distribution* with a standard deviation of σ. If there are n trials that give independent, identically distributed random variables, the precision, E, of the $(1 - \alpha)$ confidence interval is

$$E = Z_{1-\frac{\alpha}{2}}\frac{\sigma}{\sqrt{n}}$$

Solving for n from the above expression yields

$$n = \left(Z_{1-\frac{\alpha}{2}}\frac{\sigma}{E}\right)^2$$

If the value of n from the calculation is not integer, round to the next larger integer.

Round up

For example, say that the desired value of the precision E is 0.005. The anticipated width of the confidence interval is 2 times the precision, $2 \times 0.005 = 0.010$. Say that the confidence level is 95 percent and that σ is 0.1. If the confidence level is 95 percent, the probability that the interval does not include the true value is 0.05. The true value might not be in the confidence interval because it's either too small or too large. Thus, the probability that it's too small is $\frac{0.05}{2} = 0.025$. Similarly, the probability that it's too large is 0.025. Because the confidence interval has two tails, the probability of each tail is 0.025. The value of Z for the upper tail corresponds to a cumulative probability of $1 - 0.025 = 0.975$. From the cumulative normal table, $Z_{0.975} = 1.96$. You calculate the value of n as

$$n = \left(1.96\frac{0.1}{0.005}\right)^2 = 1,536.64$$

The number of trials for the simulation would be 1,537. Rounding to the next lower integer, 1,536, doesn't provide the desired accuracy.

Note that σ appears in the formula for calculating n, the number of trials. In the previous sections, our formulas used s, not σ. This is the distinction made in statistics books. The population standard deviation is represented by σ. The sample standard deviation is represented by s. The above formula for determining n can be used only if σ is known. Generally, σ is unknown and must be estimated from the simulations. *This presents a dilemma.* The value of σ must be known before the simulation has been done, so that we can calculate the number of trials. But the value of σ can be estimated only *after* the simulation has been done.

You resolve the dilemma by doing a small preliminary simulation. This accomplishes two purposes. First, you can use it to verify your computer simulation model. If the simulation model is not correct, there is no purpose in using a large amount of computer resources to do the simulation. Second, you can use it to obtain a preliminary estimate of σ. Let s represent the sample standard deviation of the small preliminary simulation. Then, you calculate the number of trials as

Estimating σ by a small preliminary simulation

$$n = \left(Z_{1-\frac{\alpha}{2}} \frac{s}{E} \right)^2$$

You do the large simulation using the number of trials calculated from the above formula. You combine the results of the small preliminary simulation and the large simulation to estimate the measure of interest. Then, you calculate the confidence interval using the combined simulation results. The desired precision still might not be obtained. Remember, the value of s from the preliminary small simulation is an *estimate* of σ. It is probably not the exact value of σ. Thus, it might be necessary to do additional simulation trials to achieve the desired precision.

One last warning: The formula for determining the number of trials is based on the assumption of the normal distribution. If the probability distribution of the measure of interest isn't the normal distribution, the Central Limit Theorem lets you use the normal distribution for the sample mean if the sample size is 30 or more. *The small preliminary sample should consist of at least 30 trials.* If the measure of interest has a normal distribution, you don't need to use the Central Limit Theorem to use the normal distribution for the sample mean. However, because the small preliminary simulation gives only an estimate of σ, the preliminary sample should always be at least 30.

If the underlying probability distribution of the measure of interest is the normal distribution, the sample size determination uses the t-distribution for small preliminary sample sizes. In this case, the sample standard deviation is used to estimate the unknown standard deviation, σ, and the distribution of the sample mean is the *t*-distribution with $n - 1$ degrees of freedom. The value of n is calculated as

$$n = \left(t_{(1-\frac{\alpha}{2}, n-1)} \frac{s}{E} \right)^2$$

For example, consider the data in Table 16.8. We assume that the measure of interest is normally distributed, and there are 20 observed values in the preliminary sample. The *t*-value for 19 degrees of freedom and a 95 percent confidence interval is 2.093. The sample mean is 11.9, and the sample standard deviation is 1.86097. If the desired precision is $E = 0.01$, the calculated value of n is

$$n = \left(2.093 \times \frac{1.86097}{0.01} \right)^2 = 151{,}711.04$$

The number of replications should be 151,712.

The preceding example for calculating the number of replications indicates a correct application of the *t*-distribution. However, recall that the sample standard deviation is only an estimate of the unknown standard deviation. Because it is only an estimate, a preliminary simulation should have a larger number of observations than 20. If you use too small a preliminary simulation, the estimate of σ may be inaccurate. Then, when

TABLE 16.8 Simulation Data for *t*-Distribution Example

Observation	Value
1	10
2	11
3	13
4	12
5	11
6	10
7	9
8	11
9	14
10	15
11	11
12	9
13	15
14	11
15	15
16	13
17	12
18	11
19	12
20	13

you do the large simulation using the number of replications that you calculated from the formula, you may not achieve the desired precision. If the confidence interval from the simulation results doesn't achieve the desired precision, you must do even more simulations to get the desired precision. It is better to use a preliminary simulation of more than 20 observations so that you get a better estimate of σ.

Model verification

Verifying a simulation model consists of determining whether the chosen decision rules have been implemented properly and whether the statistics have been collected and analyzed properly. You can verify the computer simulation model by doing a small preliminary simulation by hand and comparing the results with those obtained from the computer simulation model. Let's discuss verifying our computer simulation model for the M/M/1 waiting line. We should have our program print the values from the CRNG, as in Table 16.1. Using those values, we can calculate the interarrival times and the service times. We illustrated this when we simulated the first four customers by hand. Then, you "process" the customers through the system by hand and compare the results with those obtained from the computer simulation program. If the computer-generated waiting times are the same as those calculated by hand, the computer program is probably correct.

The simulation model might be designed so that only summary statistics are reported, such as those in Table 16.6. It is necessary to verify that the summary statistics are calculated properly. You might ask, for example, "Is the average waiting time of the first batch of 10 customers equal to the average calculated by hand?"

Unfortunately, verifying a simulation model only checks for consistency with the model builder's perception of the decision environment. If the model builder does not correctly perceive the decision environment, it is possible for the model to be "verified," yet be incorrect.

Model validation

Validation of a simulation model is checking whether it accurately represents the decision environment. Sometimes, you can ask someone familiar with the decision environment to check whether the results of the simulation model are reasonable. Often, a simulation model represents an existing system. You can use historical data to check whether the simulation model gives the actual historical results. If the historical results are different from the simulation results, the model builder should determine the reason for the difference. Are there considerations that the simulation model has neglected? Attempting to duplicate historical results aids the model builder in identifying appropriate considerations. The model builder is still responsible for determining which considerations are important enough to include in the model. Additional detail and complexity may not add sufficient insight into the decision environment to justify inclusion in the model.

CHOOSING THE BEST ALTERNATIVE AND PAIRED COMPARISONS

Simulation models are developed to study a decision environment. Different decision alternatives may be possible, and simulation allows the model builder to answer the question "What would be the result if I chose a particular decision alternative?" If one decision alternative results in a cost of $10,000 and another results in a cost of $15,000, the better decision alternative (on the basis of cost) is the first. For a deterministic decision environment, it is only necessary to calculate the measure of interest for the decision alternatives and to choose the decision alternative with the most favorable value of that measure. This was the approach for Chapter 15's electronic spreadsheet simulation for the Potato Processing example. For the Potato Processing example, the measure of interest, profit, was to be maximized. You enter a trial set of decision variable values and use the electronic spreadsheet to calculate the profit. By trying different decision variable values, you find a good solution.

For a probabilistic decision environment, many outcomes might result from a particular decision alternative. A probabilistic simulation *estimates* the measure of interest for such an alternative. The estimate is unlikely to exactly equal the expected value of the measure of interest.

In this section, we discuss the use of probabilistic simulation results to choose between two decision alternatives. We assume that we want to *maximize the measure of interest*. Say that the first decision alternative has a probability distribution for the measure of interest with a mean of μ_1 and a standard deviation of σ_1 and that the second decision alternative has a probability distribution for the measure of interest with a mean of μ_2 and a standard deviation of σ_2. The probability distributions need not be normal distributions. If the means can be calculated analytically, you don't have to do probabilistic simulations. Using the expected value criterion, you pick the decision alternative with the larger mean. But if we need to do probabilistic simulations, we don't know the means and standard deviations of the measures of interest for the two decision alternatives. Instead, we estimate them from the simulation results.

Assume independent replications for a decision

In this section, we *assume* that the replications are *independent* for a decision. For example, the second trial for a decision is independent of the first trial. The replications for the equally likely daily sales simulation (Table 16.3) and the inventory management simulation (Table 16.4) both have this property. Without this property, the sample standard deviations are biased estimates of the unknown standard deviations.

Say that the *first* decision alternative is simulated with n_1 replications, and let F_j represent the jth value of the measure of interest. Say that the *second* decision alternative is simulated with n_2 replications, and let S_j represent the jth value of the measure of interest. We use the notations $\bar{F}$

and S to distinguish between the First and Second decisions. This is less confusing than using a doubly subscripted variable for which one subscript represents the decision and the other represents the replication number.

For illustrative purposes, we assume that the measure of interest has a *normal distribution* for both decisions. Figure 16.6 illustrates hypothetical probability distributions for the two decisions. The leftmost curve is the probability distribution of the measure of interest for the first decision alternative, and the rightmost curve is that for the second decision alternative.

The mean for the first decision alternative is less than the mean for the second decision alternative. By the criterion of maximizing the expected value of the measure of interest, the second decision is preferred. However, the probability distributions of the measure of interest for the two decisions are not known. Thus, simulation experiments are necessary to estimate the measure of interest for the two decision alternatives. If there is a single simulation replication, the probability distribution of the measure of interest for a single experiment for the first decision alternative is the same as the probability distribution shown in Figure 16.6. The value obtained for F_1 might be greater than that obtained for S_1. If so, you choose the first decision alternative; but the second decision alternative has a larger expected value. *Comparing decisions using probabilistic simulations may give an incorrect decision.* Remember, probabilistic simulation results vary depending on the random numbers used. Additional replications reduce the probability of an incorrect decision, just as additional replications improve the accuracy of the expected value estimate.

Let $\overline{F}$ and $\overline{S}$ represent, respectively, the sample means of the replications of the first and second decision alternatives. Figure 16.7 represents the probability distributions of the sample means with more replications. Recall from sampling theory that the expected value of the sample mean

> The decision chosen using probabilistic simulations may be incorrect

FIGURE 16.6 Hypothetical Probability Distributions for Two Decision Alternatives

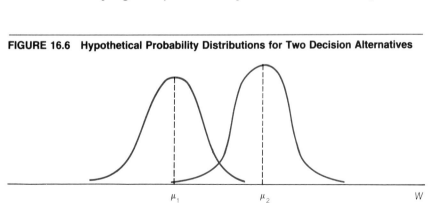

FIGURE 16.7 Hypothetical Probability Distributions of Sample Means for Two Decision Alternatives

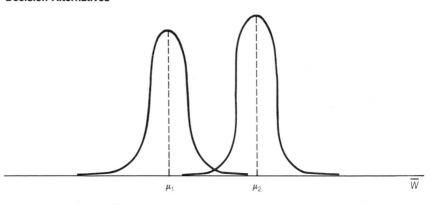

equals the population mean. Therefore, the means for a decision alternative are the same in Figures 16.6 and 16.7. Also, recall that if the sample has n values and the population standard deviation is σ, the standard deviation of the sample mean is $\dfrac{\sigma}{\sqrt{n}}$. The probability distributions in Figure 16.7 with more replications have smaller standard deviations than those in Figure 16.6. Note that the amount of overlap between the two probability distributions is smaller in Figure 16.7 than in Figure 16.6. *The probability of an incorrect decision from probabilistic simulations is smaller with more replications.* However, it is still possible that the sample value of $\overline{F}$ is larger than $\overline{S}$. The value might be larger, but it is less likely to be larger than would be the case if a single replication were used.

An incorrect decision is less likely with more replications

If the probability distributions for $\overline{F}$ and $\overline{S}$ do not overlap, the decision maker can be confident that the decision alternative with the greater sample mean is the correct decision. Usually, there is some overlap. We want to have enough replications so that an incorrect decision is unlikely. Say that the 95 percent confidence interval is from 90 to 100 for the first decision alternative and from 110 to 120 for the second decision alternative. If the measure of interest was to be maximized, the decision maker could confidently choose the decision alternative with the larger sample mean. An incorrect decision is still possible, but it is unlikely.

Our approach

The decision maker/model builder should do enough replications so that there is a small probability of choosing the wrong decision alternative. *Our approach* is to calculate the probability of an incorrect decision after the simulations have been completed. If the probability of an incorrect decision is unacceptable, you do more replications.

Statistical hypothesis testing can be used to calculate the degree of confidence for the decision based on the probabilistic simulation results.

We start with the null hypothesis that the means for the two decisions are equal. Then, if the sample evidence is strong enough to reject the null hypothesis, we choose the decision alternative with the most favorable estimate of the expected value of the measure of interest. That is, we choose the decision with the most favorable sample mean. If the sample evidence is not sufficient to reject the null hypothesis, additional replications must be done; there is not enough evidence to accept one decision alternative over the other. The hypothesis test is

$$H_0 : \mu_1 - \mu_2 = 0$$
$$H_1 : \mu_1 - \mu_2 \neq 0$$

The null hypothesis is that the two means are equal or, equivalently, that the difference between the two means is zero. The alternative hypothesis is that the two means aren't equal. The hypothesis test is a two-tailed test because we don't know which decision alternative has the most favorable mean.

An equivalent approach is to estimate the confidence interval of the difference between the two means. If the confidence interval does not include zero, you choose the decision with the most favorable sample mean. If the confidence interval does include zero, you do additional replications; there is not enough evidence to choose one decision alternative over the other.

The standard deviations of F and S are unknown and must be esti-

Don't use a "pooled" estimate of the standard deviation

mated. Many statistics books discuss hypothesis testing and confidence intervals for the difference between two means. In most probabilistic simulations, *the standard deviations, σ_1 and σ_2, are not equal,* so it is *incorrect* to use the "pooled" estimate approach for the standard deviation.

We present two approaches for testing hypotheses and determining the confidence interval for the difference between the two means. For both approaches, we assume that the F_j are independent, identically distributed random variables (with the same distribution as F) and that the S_j are independent, identically distributed random variables (with the same distribution as S). That is, F_i is assumed to be independent of F_j for all i not equal to j and S_i is assumed to be independent of S_j for all i not equal to j.

The first approach we discuss is the **independent samples method,** which assumes that the values for the two decisions are independent of each other. The second approach is the **paired** or **dependent samples method.** In this approach, F_j and S_j are not independent of each other.

The Independent Samples Method

Assume that F_i and S_j are independent

For the independent samples method, we assume that F_i is independent of S_j for all i and j. For this method, the number of replications for the first decision do not have to be equal to the number of replications for the second decision. Let n_1 be the number of replications for the first decision, and let n_2 be the number of replications for the second decision. *Assume that the F_j and S_j are normally distributed for all* j. You calculate the sample variance for the first decision as

$$s_F^2 = \frac{\sum_{j=1}^{n_1} (F_j - \overline{F})^2}{(n_1 - 1)}$$

where $\overline{F}$ is the sample mean, that is, the average of the F_j. Similarly, you calculate the sample variance for the second decision as

$$s_S^2 = \frac{\sum_{j=1}^{n_2} (S_j - \overline{S})^2}{(n_2 - 1)}$$

The confidence interval uses the *t*-distribution. Welch[4] has shown that the approximate number of degree of freedom is

$$\hat{f} = \frac{\left(\dfrac{s_F^2}{n_1} + \dfrac{s_S^2}{n_2}\right)^2}{\left(\dfrac{s_F^2}{n_1}\right)^2/(n_1 - 1) + \left(\dfrac{s_S^2}{n_2}\right)^2/(n_2 - 1)}$$

The $(1 - \alpha)$ confidence interval on $\mu_1 - \mu_2$ is

$$\overline{F} - \overline{S} \pm t_{(1-\frac{\alpha}{2}, \hat{f})} \sqrt{\left(\frac{s_F^2}{n_1} + \frac{s_S^2}{n_2}\right)}$$

To perform the hypothesis test, calculate the value of T as

$$T = \frac{\overline{F} - \overline{S}}{\sqrt{(s_F^2/(n_1) + s_S^2/(n_2))}}$$

If $-t_{(1-\frac{\alpha}{2}, \hat{f})} \leq T \leq t_{(1-\frac{\alpha}{2}, \hat{f})}$ then you accept the null hypothesis that the means of the two decisions are the same. In this case, additional replications are needed to attain the specified confidence level that there isn't an incorrect decision. If T is not in that range of values, you reject the null hypothesis and choose the decision with the most favorable sample mean. Remember, if $\hat{f}$ is 30 or larger, you use the normal distribution, not the *t*-distribution.

It's possible to calculate the degree of confidence based on your first simulation results. Using either the *t*-distribution or normal distribution table, as appropriate, you find the value of α for the T you calculated.

---

[4] R. E. Schellenberger, "Criteria for Assessing Model Validity for Managerial Purposes," *Decision Sciences* 5 (1974), pp. 644–53.

The Dependent Samples Method

The dependent samples method assumes that the replications are not independent for the two decisions. In fact, we assume that replications are "paired" between the two decisions. For example, F_1 and S_1 are assumed to be dependent. This approach assumes that the number of replications is the same for each decision. Otherwise, the values could not be paired. Assume that $n_1 = n_2 = n$. We assume the F_j to be independent of one another and identically distributed. Similarly, we assume that the S_j are independent of one another and identically distributed. But the F_j and S_j are dependent, for all j. We don't assume that the standard deviations of F and S are equal.

Assume that F_j and S_j are dependent

Let D represent the random variable that is the difference between F and S. Then, $D_j = F_j - S_j$. We calculate the sample mean of the differences as

$$\overline{D} = \frac{\sum\limits_{j=1}^{n} D_j}{n}$$

The sample variance of D is calculated as

$$s_D^2 = \frac{\sum\limits_{j=1}^{n} (D_j - \overline{D})^2}{(n - 1)}$$

The expected value of D is $\mu_1 - \mu_2$. The $(1 - \alpha)$ confidence interval on $\mu_1 - \mu_2$ is

$$\overline{D} \pm t_{\left(1-\frac{\alpha}{2},\, n-1\right)} \frac{s_D}{\sqrt{n}}$$

To test the hypothesis that $\mu_1 = \mu_2$, calculate the value of T as

The test statistic

$$T = \frac{\overline{D}}{s_D/\sqrt{n}}$$

If $-t_{\left(1-\frac{\alpha}{2},\, n-1\right)} \leq T \leq t_{\left(1-\frac{\alpha}{2},\, n-1\right)}$, then accept the null hypothesis that the means of the two decisions are the same. In this case, more replications must be done to attain the desired confidence level that there isn't an incorrect decision. If T is not in that range of values, reject the null hypothesis and choose the decision with the most favorable sample mean.

This method is sometimes called the "paired-t confidence interval." For this method, the D_j must have a *normal distribution*. The t-distribution cannot be used to calculate the confidence interval unless the D_j have a normal distribution. If the F_j and S_j have normal distributions, then the

Assume that the D_j have a normal distribution

D_j have a normal distribution. You can consult a statistics book for information on using a goodness-of-fit test to check whether the D_j have a normal distribution. But remember that if each of the F_j and S_j is the sum of 30 or more random variables, the Central Limit Theorem lets you use the normal distribution. Also, if n, the number of pairs, is 30 or larger, you use the normal distribution, not the t-distribution.

It's possible to calculate the degree of confidence based on your first simulation results. Find the value of α for the T you calculated, using either the t-distribution or normal distribution table, as appropriate.

Positive correlation decreases the confidence interval.

If the F_j and S_j are *positively correlated,* the standard deviation of D and the width of the confidence interval decrease. *The dependent samples method gives smaller confidence intervals,* and we prefer it for this reason. Let's show how the simulation logic affects whether the paired comparisons are correlated.

Use CRNs to induce positive correlation

The **common random number (CRN)** method uses the same CRNG value for the same event in the paired simulations. Remember, the CRNG gives values from a continuous uniform distribution between 0 and 1. Say that we want to use our M/M/1 simulation model to compare the waiting time for a service rate of 2.0 with that for a service rate of 1.1. Table 16.2 shows the results for 100 customers when the service rate is 1.1. Table 16.1 showed that the CRNG value for Customer 1's service time, 0.3336, gives a service time of 0.369. If you use the same value, 0.3336, with a service rate of 2.0, the service time is larger. When the CRNG value is close to 0.0, the service times are small for both service rates. When the CRNG value is close to 1.0, the service times are larger for both service rates. Using CRNs positively correlates the service times.

Computer random number generators use arithmetic procedures to calculate the CRNG values. These procedures use the previous value to calculate the next value. Thus, if the CRNG starts with the same value, the same sequence of CRNG values is generated. Most CRNGs allow you to give a **seed,** which is the value that is used to start the calculations. If the same seed is specified for two replications, each of the replications uses the same sequence of values from the CRNG. By carefully designing the simulation logic, you can induce positive correlation between the two replications. *It is necessary to design the simulation logic so that the same event in the two replications uses the same CRNG value.*

Design the simulation logic to use CRNs for the same event

Consider the simulation logic for our M/M/1 model. Figure 16.2 shows that logic. We generated the 100 interarrival times before we generated any service times. To do so, we used the first 100 values from the CRNG for the interarrival times. We used the second 100 values for the service times. Say that we want to compare the system having a service rate of 2.0 with a system having a service rate of 1.1. Because of our simulation logic, if we use the same seed for the two simulations, the same CRNG values are used for each event. That is, the first 100 values are used for the interarrival times and the second 100 values are used for the service times.

An example of bad simulation logic

Now, let's consider using a different simulation logic. Say that we generate the interarrival times and service times as they are needed. Using this logic, we generate the interarrival time for Customer 1 and then generate that customer's service time. Next, we generate the interarrival time for Customer 2. The next event is either the completion of the service on Customer 1 or the arrival of Customer 2. Depending on which event occurs next, we generate either another interarrival time or another service time. For a smaller service rate, the next event is more likely to be the arrival of Customer 2. Thus, the fourth value from the CRNG is more likely to be used to generate the interarrival time for Customer 3. If we use the same seed for two simulations, one with a service rate of 2.0 and the other with a service rate of 1.1, the sequence of values from the CRNG is the same for both simulations. But the same values might not be used for the same events of the two simulations. For example, the CRNG value used to generate the 10th interarrival time for the simulations with a service rate of 2.0 might be used to generate the 9th service time for the simulation with a service rate of 1.1. Thus, we should use the simulation logic of Figure 16.2, which generates all of the interarrival times before it generates any service times. Then, the same CRNG values are used for the same events in the two simulations.

Consider the simulation logic for the inventory management simulation. The 30 daily demands are generated before the lead times. Say that you simulate the system for two ordering policies using the same seed. Because the 30 daily demands are generated first, the same sequence of CRNG values is used for both simulations and both simulations have the same daily demands. The lead times for the two simulations are also the same. Any difference in the 30-day costs depends on the ordering policies. A replication of the inventory management simulation is a 30-day period that begins with 20 units on hand. Let F_j be the jth replication for the first ordering policy, and let S_j be the jth replication for the second ordering policy. You use the same seed for the jth replication of each ordering policy. You use different seeds for different replications so that the replications are independent. Then, you use the dependent samples method to choose the better ordering policy.

Be careful of the simulation logic if you use the "paired" or dependent samples method

Did you note in Chapter 15 that only after the generation of the 30 daily demands were any lead times generated? This sequence is an important design consideration of the simulation model's logic. When we did the simulation in Chapter 15, you didn't understand the significance of the sequence. But now you should appreciate the effect of the simulation logic on the use of the CRN approach. *If the simulation results are to be analyzed by the "paired" method, then care must be taken in designing the simulation logic.*

VARIANCE REDUCTION TECHNIQUES

A **variance reduction technique (VRT)** reduces the variance of the estimates from a probabilistic simulation. By reducing the variance, you get smaller confidence intervals and decrease the probability of an incorrect decision. In this section, we discuss VRTs.

The dependent samples method of the preceding section is a VRT. You use the dependent samples method to compare two decisions. If the "paired" replications are positively correlated, the variance of the difference between the paired values is smaller than the sum of the variances. If negative correlation is induced, the variance of the estimate actually increases. The CRN approach induces positive correlation between the paired replications. Using the same set of random numbers for two decision alternatives does not guarantee positive correlation between their *measures of interest*. Your intuition usually helps to predict whether using CRNs gives positive correlation between the pairs. For the M/M/1 simulation, the logic induced positive correlation between the service times for two different service rates, but the measure of interest is the waiting times. However, longer service times cause longer waiting times.

Checking for positive correlation

You can do a small preliminary simulation using CRNs and then calculate the sample correlation coefficient to check for positive correlation. The sample correlation coefficient between the pairs is

$$r = \frac{\sum_{j=1}^{n}(F_j - \overline{F})(S_j - \overline{S})}{\sqrt{\sum_{j=1}^{n}(F_j - \overline{F})^2}\sqrt{\sum_{j=1}^{n}(S_j - \overline{S})^2}}$$

A more convenient computational form is

$$r = \frac{n\sum_{j=1}^{n}F_jS_j - \left(\sum_{j=1}^{n}F_j\right)\left(\sum_{j=1}^{n}S_j\right)}{\sqrt{n\sum_{j=1}^{n}F_j^2 - \left(\sum_{j=1}^{n}F_j\right)^2}\sqrt{n\sum_{j=1}^{n}S_j^2 - \left(\sum_{j=1}^{n}S_j\right)^2}}$$

If the sample correlation coefficient is positive, you should use the "paired" or dependent samples method with CRNs.

Many other VRTs have been proposed. Unfortunately, it is generally not possible to estimate the variance reduction without doing the simulation. The variance may be increased in some circumstances. Because of the complexity of these proposed VRTs and the uncertain likelihood of their success in reducing the variance, most of them are not discussed in this book.[5]

---

[5] A. M. Law and W. D. Kelton, *Simulation Modeling and Analysis*, (New York: McGraw-Hill 1982), describes other VRTs.

Negative correlation
within pairs

Let's discuss the **antithetic variates technique,** which is used to get a smaller confidence interval for the expected value estimate. The basic idea is to make pairs of simulation replications that are *negatively* correlated. That is, a large value in the first of the pair is likely to be offset by a small value in the second of the pair, or a small value in the first of the pair is likely to be offset by a large value in the second of the pair. The antithetic variates technique has considerable promise because it's easy to incorporate into the simulation logic and it's unlikely to cause an increase in the variance.

Assume that n pairs of replications are done, so that the total number of replications is $2n$. Let W_{j1} be the measure of interest for the first of the jth pair of replications, and let W_{j2} be the measure of interest for the second of the jth pair of replications. There is negative correlation between W_{j1} and W_{j2} for all j, but the pairs are independent of each other.

Pairs are independent

Using a different seed for each pair of replications makes the pairs independent of other pairs. Calculate

$$A_j = \frac{W_{j1} + W_{j2}}{2}$$

A_j is the average of the jth pair. Calculate $\overline{A}$, the sample mean of the A_j, as

$$\overline{A} = \frac{\sum_{j=1}^{n} A_j}{n}$$

We assume that *the first and second of each pair of replications have the same probability distribution as* W, *the measure of interest.* Then, $E(W_{j1}) = E(W_{j2}) = E(W) = \mu$, for all $j = 1, \ldots, n$. Thus, $\overline{A}$ is an unbiased estimator of W. Because the A_j are independent,

$$\text{Var}(\overline{A}) = \frac{\sum_{j=1}^{n} \text{Var}(A_j)}{n^2}$$

Because the A_j have the same probability distribution,

$$\text{Var}(\overline{A}) = \frac{n\text{Var}(A_j)}{n^2} = \frac{\text{Var}\left(\dfrac{W_{j1} + W_{j2}}{2}\right)}{n}$$

$$= \frac{\text{Var}(W_{j1}) + \text{Var}(W_{j2}) + 2\text{Cov}(W_{j1}, W_{j2})}{4n}$$

If the covariance is 0 (i.e., correlation is 0), the variance of $\overline{A}$ is the same as the variance based on the standard method of estimating the mean for a simulation of $2n$ replications. If negative correlation can be induced between W_{j1} and W_{j2}, the negative covariance decreases the variance of the estimator, $\overline{A}$.

Inducing negative
correlation

Remember, the values from a CRNG come from a continuous uniform probability distribution between 0 and 1. Let U_j be the jth such random variable generated. Observe that $1 - U_j$ is also a random variable that is uniformly distributed between 0 and 1. If U_j is close to 0, then $1 - U_j$ is close to 1 and if U_j is close to 1, then $1 - U_j$ is close to 0. U_j and $1 - U_j$ are called **antithetic variates.**

Say that you want to generate a continuous random variable and that its cumulative probability distribution is $F(x)$. Remember, if the value from the CRNG is q, you find k so that $F(k) = q$ and you use k as the random variable value from the desired probability distribution. Say that U_j is obtained from the CRNG. You find k_1 such that $F(k_1) = U_j$. For the antithetic variate, you find k_2 such that $F(k_2) = 1 - U_j$. If U_j is close to 0, then k_1 is small. However, then $1 - U_j$ is close to 1 and k_2 is large. Similarly, if U_j is close to 1, a large value of k_1 is generated and a small value of k_2 is generated. The use of antithetic variates induces negative correlation between the pair of random variable values generated. *Use the random variables generated by a pair of antithetic variates for the same purpose in the pair of simulations.* If U_1 is used to generate the daily demand for Day 1 in the first of the pair of simulations, then $1 - U_1$ must be used to generate the daily demand for Day 1 in the second of the pair. Make sure that each time a U_j is used in the first of the pair of simulations, $1 - U_j$ is used for the same purpose in the second of the pair of simulations.

Use antithetic variates
for the same purpose

With the antithetic variates technique, use the same seed for each of the two paired simulations. For the first of the pair, use the values from the CRNG to generate the random variable values from each probability distribution that the simulation model needs. For the second of the pair, transform each value into its antithetic variate by subtracting it from 1 before you generate the random variable values.

The antithetic variates technique can also be applied to discrete probability distributions. When you assign CRNG values to outcomes, assign small values to small outcomes. This assignment preserves the negative correlation between the pair of values generated from antithetic variates.

Note that we want negative correlation between W_{j1} and W_{j2}. For the M/M/1 simulation, we want to estimate the steady state expected waiting time. We want the waiting times for two simulations, not a particular pair of interarrival times, to have negative correlation. However, a small interarrival time usually has an effect on waiting time that is opposite to that of its antithetic variate, a large interarrival time. A similar comment applies to antithetic variate service times.

Don't use antithetic
variates and CRNs

One last warning. *The antithetic variates technique should not be used in conjunction with the dependent samples method with CRNs.* Do not use the antithetic variates technique to obtain a small variance estimate for a particular decision and then repeat with the same seed(s) for another decision. If you use both variance reduction techniques at the same time, it's hard to predict the impact. The variance and the confidence interval width may increase.

SUMMARY

In this chapter, we discussed the statistical analysis and design of probabilistic simulation experiments. Probabilistic simulation has many applications. You can use it to analyze any probabilistic decision environment. In Chapter 15, we gave several examples of probabilistic simulations. We did a coin-flipping experiment to estimate expected daily demand. We used the risk analysis simulation to evaluate a capital investment. The inventory management simulation illustrated the use of a simulation model to choose decisions. For the inventory management simulation, the decisions were ordering policies.

In this chapter, we simulated a waiting line system, the M/M/1 queueing system. Simulation of waiting line systems is one of the most common applications of probabilistic simulations. Probabilistic simulation is often used to study the operations of a manufacturing or service system. In Chapter 15, we described how Exxon simulated the refining, storage, and blending operations for gasoline. At the beginning of this chapter, we described how BancOhio simulated its check processing operations.

Although probabilistic simulation can be used for any probabilistic decision environment, it has limitations. First, probabilistic simulations only estimate the characteristics of the system. It's better to use analytical results, if possible. Remember, simulation estimates usually don't equal the actual expected value of the measure of interest. You can choose an incorrect decision based on simulation results. Second, the simulation model is limited by the model builder's perception of the decision environment. A model accurately representing that perception may not accurately represent the true decision environment. You should validate the simulation model.

Third, the statistical analysis methods we studied are limited by their underlying assumptions. Let's review some of these limitations. The sample mean is an unbiased estimate of the expected value if the probability distributions of the sample values are all the same as the probability distribution of the measure of interest. The sample standard deviation is an unbiased estimate of the actual standard deviation if the sample values are independent, identically distributed random variables. We discussed calculating confidence intervals on the expected value of the measure of interest if the sample values are independent, identically distributed random variables. If the sample size is 30 or more, you use the normal distribution. If the random variables are normally distributed and the sample size is less than 30, you use the *t*-distribution. If the random variables are not normally distributed and the sample size is less than 30, you can't calculate the confidence interval using the methods we discussed. We discussed calculating confidence intervals from interrelated simulations over time, such as waiting lines, using the batch means approach. This approach is limited by the assumptions that the batch means are independent and that the batch means have a normal distribution. You should use a large enough batch size so that both of these assumptions are true. Our method for determining the number of trials assumed that the trials are independent and that the standard deviation is known. Because you don't know the standard deviation, you estimate it from small preliminary simulations. Because it's an estimate, the small preliminary simulations should give at least 30 sample values. Then, you can use the normal distribution to calculate the number of trials. Our methods for comparing decisions assumed that the sample values for a decision are independent of one another. In the independent samples methods, we assumed that the sample values are independent between decisions. In the dependent samples method, we assumed that the sample values are not independent between decisions. For the dependent samples method, you get smaller confidence intervals if there is positive correlation. If there is negative correlation, the confidence intervals are larger. You use the common random number method to induce the correlation. We described the antithetic variates technique for making confidence intervals smaller. Remember, if the pairs are negatively correlated, the confidence interval is smaller. But if the pairs are positively correlated, the confidence interval is larger.

Note some cautions about probabilistic simulations. First, simulations over time are tricky. Be cautious of the distinction between steady state and transient results. Second, simulations over time can use either a fixed- or a variable-time increment. A small fixed-time increment gives more accurate results than a large one. However, simulations with smaller time increments have more time increments when an event doesn't occur and require more effort to simulate the same length of time. You must evaluate the benefits versus the disadvantages of smaller fixed-time increments. All higher-level simulation languages and software allow fixed-time increments. Only a few allow variable-time increments or a mixture of fixed and variable. Third, beware of the impact of starting conditions if you want to estimate steady state conditions for a simulation over time. Fourth, be cautious about the assumption that values are independent when you analyze a simulation over time. You can check for independence using autocorrelation analysis. Fifth, to compare two decisions, make sure that the same value from the random number generator is used for the same event for both simulations. Make sure that your simulation logic causes this. Sixth, if you use the dependent samples method to compare decisions, you should check whether there is positive correlation for the measure of interest between each pair of simulations for the two decisions. Seventh, if you use the antithetic variates technique, check whether there is negative correlation between the pairs of antithetic simulations. Eighth, don't use both the antithetic variates technique and the common random number method. The change in the variance is unpredictable. Ninth, don't forget to verify that your simulation model uses the logic you want and collects statistics correctly. Unfortunately, verifying your model doesn't guarantee that your simulation logic accurately represents the decision environment.

QUESTIONS

1. What is a Monte Carlo simulation?
2. What is a system's state?
3. What is an event in a simulation?
4. Say that the arrival rate is 5.0 per hour for an exponentially distributed interarrival time. If the computer random number generator (CRNG) provides a value of 0.138, what is the corresponding interarrival time? Is your interarrival time in minutes?
5. What was the CRNG value for the service time of the 10th customer in Table 16.2?
6. What is a terminating simulation?
7. What is a replication?
8. What is the difference between transient and steady state conditions?
9. What is the difference between a variable-time increment and a fixed-time increment?
10. What are the advantages and disadvantages of using a smaller fixed-time increment?
11. Under what conditions is the sample mean an unbiased estimate of the expected value of the measure of interest?
12. Under what conditions is the sample standard deviation an unbiased estimate of the standard deviation of the measure of interest?
13. What is the Central Limit Theorem?
14. Calculate the sample standard deviation of Table 16.4.
15. When should you use the *t*-distribution?
16. Under what conditions should you use the batch means approach?
17. What are two considerations in choosing the batch size for the batch means approach?
18. What is a confidence interval? What is a confidence level?
19. Discuss whether a smaller precision requires more trials.
20. What is the relationship between the precision and the width of the confidence interval?

21. What is the difference between verification and validation of a simulation model?

22. Under what circumstances is the dependent sample method better than the independent samples method for comparing two decision alternatives? Why is it better?

23. What is the motivation for using the common random number (CRN) method?

24. How does the simulation logic affect the use of the common random number method?

25. What is a variance reduction technique?

26. What is the antithetic variate of 0.1432?

27. Discuss: "Using probabilistic simulation results to compare decision alternatives may result in an incorrect decision."

EXERCISES

1. Generate the service times of the first 10 customers to arrive at an M/M/1 queueing system, starting in the upper-right-hand corner of the random number table, Table 15.6, and reading down. Use a service rate of 1.1 per hour.

2. Generate the service times of the first 10 customers to arrive at an M/M/1 queueing system, starting in the upper-right-hand corner of the random number table, Table 15.6, and reading down. Use a service rate of 2.0 per hour.

3. Use the 10 service times you generated in Exercise 1 to calculate the waiting times of the first 10 customers to arrive in the M/M/1 simulation of Table 16.2. Use the arrival times in Table 16.2.

4. Use the 10 service times you generated in Exercise 2 to calculate the waiting times of the first 10 customers to arrive in the M/M/1 simulation of Table 16.2. Use the arrival times in Table 16.2.

5. A set of 40 trials for the inventory management simulation has the sum of the 30-day costs equal to 2,682.40. The sum of the squares of the 30-day costs is 182,161.48.
   a. What is the sample mean?
   b. What is the sample variance?
   c. What is the sample standard deviation?
   d. What is the 95 percent confidence interval on the 30-day costs?
   e. What is the 90 percent confidence interval on the 30-day costs?

6. A set of 40 trials for the inventory management simulation has the sum of the 30-day costs equal to 2,905.90. The sum of the squares of the 30-day costs is 218,175.13.
   a. What is the sample mean?
   b. What is the sample variance?
   c. What is the sample standard deviation?

    d. What is the 95 percent confidence interval on the 30-day costs?

    e. What is the 90 percent confidence interval on the 30-day costs?

7. The sample standard deviation of a preliminary simulation of 100 trials is $42.45. You want a confidence level of 95 percent.

    a. If the desired precision is $0.25, what sample size is required?

    b. If the desired precision is $0.01, what sample size is required?

8. The sample standard deviation of a preliminary simulation of 64 trials is $20.01. You want a confidence level of 95 percent.

    a. If the desired precision is $0.25, what sample size is required?

    b. If the desired precision is $0.01, what sample size is required?

9. A set of 16 trials a simulation has the sum of the costs equal to $2,200.00. The sum of the squares of the costs is 305,000.00.

    a. What is the sample mean?

    b. What is the sample standard deviation?

    c. Assuming the underlying probability distribution is the normal distribution, what is the 95 percent confidence interval on the cost?

10. A set of 25 trials a simulation has the sum of the costs equal to $2,545.20. The sum of the squares of the costs is 295,000.00.

    a. What is the sample mean?

    b. What is the sample standard deviation?

    c. Assuming the underlying probability distribution is the normal distribution, what is the 95 percent confidence interval on the cost?

11. Two independent samples simulations gave the following results:

	Simulation 1	Simulation 2
Number of Trials	64	100
Average of Trials	$2,000	$2,100
Standard Deviation of Trials	150	160

    a. The two simulations reflect different decision rules. Which decision rule gives the smallest cost?

    b. Calculate the approximate number of degrees of freedom using Welch's formula.

    c. Give the 95 percent confidence interval on the difference between the means for the two simulations.

    d. Is one decision rule better than the other at the 95 percent confidence level?

12. Two independent samples simulations gave the following results:

	Simulation 1	Simulation 2
Number of Trials	36	100
Average of Trials	$2,060	$2,100
Standard Deviation of Trials	100	160

    a. The two simulations reflect different decision rules. Which decision rule gives the smallest cost?

    b. Calculate the approximate number of degrees of freedom using Welch's formula.

    c. Give the 95 percent confidence interval on the difference between the means for the two simulations.

    d. Is one decision rule better than the other at the 95 percent confidence level?

MORE CHALLENGING EXERCISES

1. The system of the M/M/1 queueing example (Table 16.2) has been modified to an M/M/2 system. The servers are in parallel, which means that a customer can be served by either server. The service rate for each server is 2.0 customers per minute. To generate the service times for the first 10 customers, start in the upper-right-hand corner of the random number table, Table 15.6, and read down. The queue discipline is first come, first served. If a server is available, a customer is assigned to that server. The service is not interrupted once it has been started on a customer. Calculate the waiting times of the first 10 customers. Use the first 10 arrival times in Table 16.2.

2. The inventory management simulation of Chapter 15 had a fixed-time increment of one day. More detail could have been obtained by using a fixed-time increment of less than one day. Say that the fixed-time increment was one-half day.

    a. What is the inventory carrying cost per unit per one-half day?

    b. What change, if any, would there be in the fixed order cost? The shortage cost?

    c. The probability distribution of demand for a half day is:

Demand	Probability
0	0.50
1	0.40
2	0.05

    (1) What is the expected demand per half day?

    (2) Simulate the demand of the first 5 days (10 half days) using the first 10 random numbers in Table 15.15 to generate the first 10 demands.

    (3) Simulate the operation of the system for the first five days. Is the cost of the first five days identical to the cost of the first five days in Table 15.16?

    d. Discuss the advantages and disadvantages of using a smaller fixed-time increment for the inventory management simulation.

3. Table 16.4 contained 40 trials of the inventory management simulation with a seed of -0.5. The fixed order cost is $20, the inventory carrying cost is $0.10, and the lost sale cost is $10. The order policy was $R = 5$ and $Q = 20$. The inventory at the beginning of each 30-day period is 20. Under identical conditions, except using a seed of -0.3, the following results were obtained:

RUN	INVENTORY HOLDING COST	LOST SALE COST	FIXED ORDER COST	TOTAL COST
1	40.90	0.00	20.00	60.90
2	39.60	0.00	40.00	79.60
3	41.80	0.00	20.00	61.80
4	40.10	0.00	20.00	60.10
5	36.10	0.00	20.00	56.10
6	41.10	0.00	20.00	61.10
7	41.30	0.00	20.00	61.30
8	44.40	0.00	20.00	64.40
9	36.40	0.00	20.00	56.40
10	40.80	0.00	20.00	60.80
11	44.70	0.00	20.00	64.70
12	39.60	0.00	20.00	59.60
13	43.30	0.00	20.00	63.30
14	44.60	0.00	20.00	64.60
15	42.20	0.00	20.00	62.20
16	42.10	0.00	20.00	62.10
17	38.00	0.00	40.00	78.00
18	46.70	0.00	20.00	66.70
19	40.30	0.00	20.00	60.30
20	42.90	0.00	40.00	82.90
21	45.30	0.00	20.00	65.30
22	36.30	0.00	40.00	76.30
23	43.40	0.00	20.00	63.40
24	45.70	0.00	20.00	65.70
25	40.20	0.00	20.00	60.20
26	41.10	0.00	20.00	61.10
27	47.70	0.00	20.00	67.70
28	45.00	0.00	20.00	65.00
29	44.20	0.00	20.00	64.20
30	42.20	0.00	20.00	62.20
31	35.80	0.00	40.00	75.80
32	48.00	0.00	20.00	68.00
33	42.20	0.00	20.00	62.20
34	44.50	0.00	20.00	64.50
35	40.70	0.00	40.00	80.70
36	36.40	0.00	20.00	56.40
37	35.60	0.00	40.00	75.60
38	40.70	0.00	20.00	60.70
39	36.20	0.00	20.00	56.20
40	39.00	0.00	40.00	79.00

a. Calculate the sample mean and the sample standard deviation.
b. Give a 95 percent confidence interval on the expected 30-day cost.
c. Why is this confidence interval different from the one developed from the data of Table 16.4?
d. How large a number of trials is required if the desired precision is $0.25?

4. Table 16.4 contained 40 trials of the inventory management simulation with a seed of -0.5. The fixed order cost is $20, the inventory carrying cost is $0.10, and the lost sale cost is $10. The order policy was $R = 5$ and $Q = 20$. The

inventory at the beginning of each 30-day period is 20. Under identical conditions, except for an order quantity of 10, the following results were obtained:

RUN	INVENTORY HOLDING COST	LOST SALE COST	FIXED ORDER COST	TOTAL COST
1	86.40	0.00	20.00	106.40
2	57.70	0.00	0.00	57.70
3	78.20	0.00	0.00	78.20
4	45.90	0.00	0.00	45.90
5	81.50	0.00	20.00	101.50
6	100.10	0.00	0.00	100.10
7	89.60	0.00	0.00	89.60
8	34.80	0.00	40.00	74.80
9	46.80	0.00	20.00	66.80
10	53.20	0.00	0.00	53.20
11	76.60	0.00	0.00	76.60
12	56.90	0.00	20.00	76.90
13	55.70	0.00	20.00	75.70
14	100.00	0.00	0.00	100.00
15	96.80	0.00	0.00	96.80
16	77.30	0.00	20.00	97.30
17	58.00	0.00	20.00	78.00
18	30.90	0.00	40.00	70.90
19	44.30	0.00	20.00	64.30
20	48.40	0.00	20.00	68.40
21	84.30	0.00	0.00	84.30
22	55.90	0.00	0.00	55.90
23	48.80	0.00	20.00	68.80
24	40.40	0.00	0.00	40.40
25	50.00	0.00	0.00	50.00
26	101.20	0.00	0.00	101.20
27	80.20	0.00	0.00	80.20
28	58.10	0.00	0.00	58.10
29	79.50	0.00	20.00	99.50
30	75.10	0.00	0.00	75.10
31	46.70	0.00	20.00	66.70
32	53.90	0.00	0.00	53,90
33	81.20	0.00	20.00	101.20
34	95.40	0.00	0.00	95.40
35	48.30	0.00	0.00	48.30
36	78.50	0.00	0.00	78.50
37	61.20	0.00	20.00	81.20
38	54.10	0.00	0.00	54.10
39	53.50	0.00	0.00	53.50
40	52.80	0.00	0.00	52.80

a. Is the dependent samples method appropriate to compare the expected costs of the two policies, $Q = 10$ and $Q = 20$? Explain.

b. Using the dependent samples method on the sample results, are the expected costs of the two policies different at the 95 percent confidence level?

c. Calculate the correlation coefficient between the paired results. Is the correlation coefficient positive?

d. Using the independent samples method on the sample results, are the expected costs of the two policies different at the 95 percent confidence level?

e. What order quantity do you prefer? Why?

5. Table 16.4 contained 40 trials of the inventory management simulation with a seed of -0.5. The fixed order cost is \$20, the inventory carrying cost is \$0.10, and the lost sales cost is \$10. The order policy was $R = 5$ and $Q = 20$. The inventory at the beginning of each 30-day period is 20. Under identical conditions except for the seed and an order quantity of 25, the following results were obtained:

RUN	INVENTORY HOLDING COST	LOST SALE COST	FIXED ORDER COST	TOTAL COST
1	149.90	0.00	0.00	149.90
2	113.70	0.00	0.00	113.70
3	136.20	0.00	0.00	136.20
4	99.90	0.00	0.00	99.90
5	148.50	0.00	0.00	148.50
6	158.10	0.00	0.00	158.10
7	145.60	0.00	0.00	145.60
8	98.80	0.00	0.00	98.80
9	121.30	0.00	0.00	121.30
10	111.20	0.00	0.00	111.20
11	130.60	0.00	0.00	130.60
12	115.40	0.00	0.00	115.40
13	106.70	0.00	0.00	106.70
14	154.00	0.00	0.00	154.00
15	152.80	0.00	0.00	152.80
16	160.80	0.00	0.00	160.80
17	121.00	0.00	0.00	121.00
18	97.90	0.00	0.00	97.90
19	104.80	0.00	0.00	104.80
20	106.40	0.00	0.00	106.40
21	142.30	0.00	0.00	142.30
22	111.90	0.00	0.00	111.90
23	105.80	0.00	0.00	105.80
24	98.40	0.00	0.00	98.40
25	108.00	0.00	0.00	108.00
26	157.20	0.00	0.00	157.20
27	138.20	0.00	0.00	138.20
28	112.10	0.00	0.00	112.10
29	160.00	0.00	0.00	160.00
30	129.10	0.00	0.00	129.10
31	127.20	0.00	0.00	127.20
32	109.90	0.00	0.00	109.90
33	129.70	0.00	0.00	129.70
34	151.40	0.00	0.00	151.40
35	106.30	0.00	0.00	106.30
36	136.50	0.00	0.00	136.50
37	111.20	0.00	0.00	111.20
38	112.10	0.00	0.00	112.10
39	107.50	0.00	0.00	107.50
40	108.80	0.00	0.00	108.80

  a. Is the dependent samples method appropriate to compare the expected costs of the two policies, $Q = 10$ and $Q = 20$? Explain.
  b. Using the independent samples method on the sample results, are the expected costs of the two policies different at the 95 percent confidence level?
  c. What order quantity do you prefer? Why?

6. The M/M/1 queueing simulation results in Table 16.7 using a seed of -0.3, an

arrival rate of 1.0 per minute, and a service rate of 1.1 per minute. Another simulation run with 20 batches of size 400 but a seed of -0.7 gave the following results:

BATCH	TOTAL BATCH WAITING	AVERAGE WAIT IN BATCH
1	1630.43	4.076
2	4648.73	11.622
3	2067.55	5.169
4	2258.79	5.647
5	11854.46	29.636
6	2166.78	5.417
7	2264.21	5.661
8	6287.98	15.720
9	2227.31	5.568
10	3577.74	8.944
11	2141.81	5.355
12	1539.11	3.848
13	1069.74	2.674
14	2897.59	7.244
15	7539.25	18.848
16	12912.41	32.281
17	2961.38	7.403
18	1722.52	4.306
19	3097.66	7.744
20	2509.26	6.273

   a. Why should the first batch be discarded if you want to estimate the steady state expected waiting time?
   b. Calculate the mean and the standard deviation of the batch means.
   c. Give the 95 percent confidence interval on the steady state expected waiting time.

7. Waiting time is a customer-based measure of a queueing system. An example of a system-based measure is the number of customers in the system at a point in time.
   a. From the Table 16.2 results, calculate the average number of customers in the system during the first five minutes of operation.
   b. From the Table 16.2 results, calculate the average number of customers in the system during the time that the first five customers are in the system.
   c. Is it better to use a fixed number of customers or a fixed amount of time to estimate the average number of customers in the system?

8. The M/M/1 queueing simulation results in Table 16.7 used a seed of -0.3, an arrival rate of 1.0 per minute, and a service rate of 1.1 per minute. Another simulation run, but with 40 batches of size 200, gave the following results:

BATCH	TOTAL BATCH WAITING	AVERAGE WAIT IN BATCH
1	1,691.64	8.458
2	1,090.16	5.451
3	718.54	3.593
4	2,101.27	10.506
5	3,473.92	17.370
6	334.73	1.674
7	2,200.84	11.004
8	3,002.67	15.013
9	709.80	3.549
10	1,332.01	6.660
11	2,639.85	13.199
12	1,399.99	7.000
13	2,265.69	11.328
14	1,866.68	9.333
15	7,830.17	39.151
16	4,253.90	21.270
17	451.92	2.260
18	656.37	3.282
19	369.82	1.849
20	1,828.27	9.141
21	760.14	3.801
22	695.32	3.477
23	763.46	3.817
24	683.33	3.417
25	702.28	3.511
26	947.26	4.736
27	3,667.39	18.337
28	1,512.36	7.562
29	1,184.02	5.920
30	962.07	4.810
31	795.37	3.977
32	3,288.85	16.444
33	1,956.48	9.782
34	632.42	3.162
35	1,571.80	7.859
36	724.36	3.622
37	4,897.47	24.487
38	6,310.12	31.551
39	1,933.83	9.669
40	900.71	4.504

   a. Why should the first batch be discarded if it is desired to estimate the steady state expected waiting time?

   b. Calculate the mean and the standard deviation of the batch means.

   c. Give the 95 percent confidence interval on the steady state waiting time of a randomly selected customer.

   d. Is the answer to Part *c* identical to the confidence interval calculated in the chapter? Comment.

9. If the probability distribution of the measure of interest is skewed, W. G. Cochran, *Sampling Techniques,* 3rd ed. (New York: John Wiley & Sons, 1977), pp. 39–44, suggests the following procedure for choosing a sample size so that the normal approximation is appropriate. Choose $n > 25 G_1^2$, where G_1 is Fisher's measure of skewness. Calculate

$$G_1 = \frac{E(W_j - \mu)^3}{\sigma^3}$$

Because the population mean, μ, and the population standard deviation, σ, are unknown, they are estimated from the sample mean and the sample standard deviation. Estimate the expected value of $(W_j - \mu)^3$ using the sample values. The numerator is calculated by adding the result of subtracting the sample mean from each sample value raised to the third power and then dividing the sum by the number of values in the sample.

a. Estimate the sample size required for use of the normal approximation for the data of the equally likely outcomes simulation of Table 16.3.

b. Estimate the sample size required for use of the normal approximation for the data of the inventory management simulation to Table 16.4.

CASE

Snow Removal for the Town of Belmont

It was 10 A.M., January 4. Mr. James Castanino, the newly promoted head of the Belmont Highway Department, sat at his desk looking out across the sloping park toward the town's busy main shopping district. Opposite him was a member of his staff who had recently begun a project to determine the appropriate mix of town-owned and subcontracted snow removal equipment.

The study came at an opportune time. The town's aging six Walther Snow Fighters were rapidly reaching the point of replacement, and it was Mr. Castanino's intention to replace them at a rate of one per year. Belmont, like most town governments, was finding it ever more difficult to increase its revenues rapidly enough to maintain previous levels of service. All of the town's departments were undertaking sustained cost-cutting measures. The Highway Department had been a leader in such cost cutting, doing volume purchasing and repairing all town vehicles. However, fur-

ther cost cutting was necessary. With snow removal being the largest component of the department's budget, a reexamination of its snow removal subcontracting policies might yield significant savings.

It simplified terms, the decision Mr. Castanino faced contained two options. The first option was to replace his six Walther Snow Fighters on a one-to-one basis. The second was to not replace the Walthers and subcontract six more vehicles. Before making his decision, he felt that a number of important variables needed to be considered.

Belmont (triple-A bond rating) was a suburb of Boston. Its population was predominantly middle class but with a surprisingly high proportion of professional people. The town had a well-deserved reputation for providing its citizens with high-quality services, and the maintenance of this reputation was important. Indeed, during the two large blizzards of 1978 the Highway Department had managed to keep all roads passable and was one of the first in the state to restore its road conditions to normal.

The department heads reported to a part-time Board of Selectmen. This provided them with considerable autonomy in their day-to-day decision making. Nonetheless, capital expenditures greater than $5,000 required approval by the selectmen, the warrant committee, and the town meeting. As a result, Mr. Castanino was aware that any capital expenditure would face searching scrutiny before approval. The town also desired to maintain good relations with its employees. Thus any cost-saving measure that improved working conditions would be highly attractive.

The town had 90 miles of roads, of which 40 were considered main thoroughfares. When salting or sanding was required, the main thoroughfares were covered each hour by four trucks equipped with spreaders.

The use of spreaders varied according to conditions. If only a trace of snow was expected, road conditions were watched closely.[1] If road conditions seemed likely to worsen, one truck would be dispatched to cover the steeper gradients. If more than a trace but less than an inch was expected, four trucks with spreaders would be dispatched to cover the main thoroughfares. They would generally have to make two sweeps (at 10 miles an hour). If greater than an inch but less than 3 inches fell, seven trucks with spreaders would be dispatched to cover all roads. They would generally spend an hour per inch with an hour for "mopping-up" operations.[2] If greater than 3 inches was expected, snow-plowing procedures were initiated. The department's resources consisted of its own vehicles and subcontractors. Belmont had 15 vehicles that could be used for snow plowing. On the average, 13 were available during a storm. Also on call were 15 subcontracted vehicles. Typically, 90 percent of those called in any storm would turn out. To ensure good relations with the subcontractors Castanino's policy was to divide them into two groups, one group of seven and one of eight. If the expected snowfall was greater than 3 inches but less than 5 inches, he would call in only one group. The two groups would be chosen on an alternating basis. If greater than 5 inches was expected, all 15 subcontractor vehicles would be called. While the size and rental cost of subcontracted vehicles varied, an appropriate average was $34 per hour. No overtime was paid to subcontractors.

Normal procedures called for the men to work until the storm was cleared up. This would take roughly an hour for each inch of snow plus an additional three hours for a 3-inch storm, for an 8-inch snowfall an additional four hours, and for a snowfall greater than 16 inches an additional eight-hour shift of all vehicles would be required to mop up. For any storm which dumped more than 12 inches, the usual policy had the men working 16-hour shifts. This meant that only two-thirds of the vehicles would be on the road at any time. For snowfall in excess of 2 feet, all crews would be sent home for eight hours rest before cleanup operations were resumed. It was not a surprising demonstration of the innate perversity of weather conditions that historically 70 percent of all town employees' time spent on snow removal had been at overtime rates.

It also had come to Mr. Castanino's attention that if the Walthers were retired but not replaced, it would be possible to redeploy these men as replacements for other drivers, reducing the expected time any individual driver would spend on the road in a 12-inch storm by 6.5 hours without increasing labor costs. The total labor cost per town vehicle would, however, remain the same.

Having reviewed operating procedures, Mr. Castanino and his assistant began to discuss ways of determining the costs of these two options. Exhibits 1 and 2 provide weather and cost data for their analysis.

---

[1] Belmont's 15 vehicles consisted of the 6 Walther Snow Fighters and 9 other vehicles that were used for other purposes in addition to snow plowing.

[2] Subcontractors only performed plowing services, not the salting and sanding of roads. Like town employees, subcontractors would work until all snow was cleared.

EXHIBIT 1   Snowfall Data, 1950–1979

November

Eleven percent of November days had snow, sleet, or hail; of these days, measured snowfall was as follows:

Snowfall	Proportion of Days Having That Amount
Trace	72%
Under 1 in.	18
Over 1 in.	10

December

Thirty-four percent of December days had snow, sleet, or hail; of these days, measured snowfall was as follows:

Snowfall	Proportion of Days Having That Amount
Trace	54%
Under 1 in.	27
1 in.–3 in.	9
3 in.–5 in.	5
5 in.–10 in.	1
10 in.–15 in.	1
Over 15 in.	0.5

January

Forty-one percent of January days had snow, sleet, or hail; of these days, measured snowfall was as follows:

Snowfall	Proportion of Days Having That Amount
Trace	47%
Under 1 in.	29
1 in.–3 in.	11
3 in.–5 in.	7
5 in.–10 in.	4
10 in.–15 in.	1
Over 15 in.	0.2

February

Thirty-nine percent of February days had snow, sleet, or hail; of these days, measured snowfall was as follows:

Snowfall	Proportion of Days Having That Amount
Trace	47%
Under 1 in.	30
1 in.–3 in.	11
3 in.–5 in.	5
5 in.–10 in.	4
10 in.–15 in.	1
Over 15 in.	1

March

Twenty-eight percent of March days had snow, sleet, or hail; of these days, measured snowfall was as follows:

Snowfall	Proportion of Days Having That Amount
Trace	50%
Under 1 in.	27
1 in.–3 in.	12
3 in.–5 in.	6
5 in.–10 in.	4
10 in.–15 in.	1
Over 15 in.	0.4

SOURCE: *Local Climatological Data Monthly Survey* (for Boston Logan International Airport) compiled by the National Oceanic and Atmospheric Administration Environmental Data Service.

EXHIBIT 2   Cost of Operating Vehicles

Salting and sanding

2 men per vehicle*
Salt, $27 ton at 3 tons per hour,†
  or sand, $3 ton at 3 tons per hour†
Fuel, $6/hour
Repairs and maintenance, $10/hour

Snow removal

1 man per vehicle*
Fuel, $6/hour
Repairs and maintenance, $10/hour
Cost of new 18 GVW vehicle, $30,000

* Labor costs were $6 per hour, time and a half for overtime.
† Normally half of the material spread was salt and half sand.

End-of-Text Material

Cases
Red Brand Canners / Marine Pilotage Services Montreal River
District / Warner-Lambert Canada Limited (X) / Kazabazua
Brewing Company

Tables

Answers to Odd-Numbered Exercises

Cases

RED BRAND CANNERS

On Monday, September 13, 1965, Mr. Mitchell Gordon, Red Brand Canners' vice president of operations, asked the controller, the sales manager, and the production manager to meet with him to discuss the amount of tomato products to pack that season. The tomato crop, which had been purchased at planting, was beginning to arrive at the cannery, and packing operations would have to be started by the following Monday. Red Brand Canners was a medium-sized company which canned and distributed a variety of fruit and vegetable products under private brands in the western states.

Mr. William Cooper, the controller, and Mr. Charles Myers, the sales manager, were the first to arrive in Mr. Gordon's office. Dan Tucker, the production manager, came in a few minutes later and said that he had picked up Produce Inspection's latest estimate of the quality of the incoming tomatoes. According to their report, about 20 percent of the crop was Grade A quality and the remaining portion of the 3 million-pound crop was Grade B.

Gordon asked Myers about the demand for tomato products for the coming year. Myers replied that they could sell all of the whole canned tomatoes they could produce. The expected demand for tomato juice and tomato paste, on the other hand, was limited. The sales manager then passed around the latest demand forecast, which is shown in Exhibit 1. He reminded the group that the selling prices had been set in light of the

EXHIBIT 1 Red Brand Canners Demand Forecasts

Product	Selling Price per Case	Demand Forecast (cases)
24 cans of size 2½ whole tomatoes	$4.00	800,000
24 cans of size 2½ choice peach halves	5.40	10,000
24 cans of size 2½ peach nectar	4.60	5,000
24 cans of size 2½ tomato juice	4.50	50,000
24 cans of size 2½ cooking apples	4.90	15,000
24 cans of size 2½ tomato paste	3.80	80,000

Reprinted with permission of Stanford University Graduate School of Business, © 1965 by the Board of Trustees of the Leland Stanford Junior University.

long-term marketing strategy of the company, and potential sales had been forecast at these prices.

Bill Cooper, after looking at Myers' estimates of demand, said that it looked like the company "should do quite well [on the tomato crop] this year." With the new accounting system that had been set up, he had been able to compute the contribution for each product, and according to his analysis the incremental profit on the whole tomatoes was greater than that on any other tomato product. In May, after Red Brand had signed contracts agreeing to purchase the growers' production at an average delivered price of six cents per pound, Cooper had computed the tomato products' contribution (see Exhibit 2).

Dan Tucker brought to Cooper's attention that although there was ample production capacity, it was impossible to produce all whole tomatoes as too small a portion of the tomato crop was A quality. Red Brand used a numerical scale to record the quality of both raw produce and prepared products. This scale ran from 0 to 10, the higher number representing better quality. Rating tomatoes according to this scale, A tomatoes averaged nine points per pound and B tomatoes averaged five points per pound. Tucker noted that the minimum average input quality

EXHIBIT 2   Red Brand Canners Product Item Profitability

Product	24-2½ Whole Tomatoes	24-2½ Choice Peach Halves	24-2½ Peach Nectar	24-2½ Tomato Juice	24-2½ Cooking Apples	24-2½ Tomato Paste
Selling price	$4.00	$5.40	$4.60	$4.50	$4.90	$3.80
Variable costs:						
Direct labor	1.18	1.40	1.27	1.32	0.70	0.54
Variable overhead	0.24	0.32	0.23	0.36	0.22	0.26
Variable selling	0.40	0.30	0.40	0.85	0.28	0.38
Packaging material	0.70	0.56	0.60	0.65	0.70	0.77
Fruit*	1.08	1.80	1.70	1.20	0.90	1.50
Total variable costs	3.60	4.38	4.20	4.38	2.80	3.45
Contribution	0.40	1.02	0.40	0.12	1.10	0.35
Less allocated overhead	0.28	0.70	0.52	0.21	0.75	0.23
Net profit	0.12	0.32	(0.12)	(0.09)	0.35	0.12

* Product usage is as given below:

Product	Pounds per Case
Whole tomatoes	18
Peach halves	18
Peach nectar	17
Tomato juice	20
Cooking apples	27
Tomato paste	25

EXHIBIT 3   Red Brand Canners Marginal Analysis of Tomato Products

Z = cost per pound of A tomatoes in cents.
Y = cost per pound of B tomatoes in cents.

1. (600,000 lbs. $\times$ Z) + (2,400,000 lbs. $\times$ Y) = (3,000,000 lbs. $\times$ 6).

2. $\dfrac{Z}{9} = \dfrac{Y}{5}$.

Z = 9.32¢ per pound.
Y = 5.18¢ per pound.

Product	Canned Whole Tomatoes	Tomato Juice	Tomato Paste
Selling price	$4.00	$4.50	$3.80
Variable cost (excluding tomato costs)	2.52	3.18	1.95
	$1.48	$1.32	$1.85
Tomato cost	1.49	1.24	1.30
Marginal profit	($0.01)	$0.08	$0.55

---

for canned whole tomatoes was eight points per pound and for juice it was six points per pound. Paste could be made entirely from B grade tomatoes. This meant that whole tomato production was limited to 800,000 pounds.

Gordon stated that this was not a real limitation. He had been recently solicited to purchase 80,000 pounds of Grade A tomatoes at 8½ cents per pound and at that time had turned down the offer. He felt, however, that the tomatoes were still available.

Myers, who had been doing some calculations, said that although he agreed that the company "should do quite well this year," it would not be by canning whole tomatoes. It seemed to him that the tomato cost should be allocated on the basis of quality and quantity rather than by quantity only, as Cooper had done. Therefore, he had recomputed the marginal profit on this basis (see Exhibit 3), and from his results, Red Brand should use 2 million pounds of the B tomatoes and all of the A tomatoes for juice. If the demand expectations were realized, a contribution of $48,000 would be made on this year's tomato crop.

MARINE PILOTAGE SERVICES, MONTREAL RIVER DISTRICT

In 1969 the shipowners and their agents, the Pilots Association and the Department of Transport (DOT) of the Canadian government, began negotiating a new contract for the pilots in the Montreal River Pilotage District. Although the negotiations were primarily between the pilots and the shipowners, the DOT was interested in seeing that the negotiations were successful. Interruptions in service by the pilots in the past had been harmful to the Canadian economy.

Although the negotiations were primarily between the shipowners, who would bear the burden of any increase in costs, and the Pilots Association, both parties had asked the DOT to determine the number of pilots that would be required to provide adequate pilotage service. The shipowners wanted to ensure that no ships had to wait for a pilot in order to avoid tying up a ship and cargo worth millions of dollars. This was particularly important at the upper end of the Montreal River District, which was the St. Lambert Lock, the lower end of the St. Lawrence Seaway. The St. Lawrence Seaway provided oceangoing ships with access to the Great Lakes. If the proper pilot was not available, the St. Lambert Lock ceased to function and Seaway traffic would be held up. The Pilots Association wanted to ensure that there was not an excessive number of pilots in order to maintain or increase the income level of the present pilots. As well, the DOT, which was responsible for licensing pilots, wanted to be sure that sufficient pilots were being trained.

The Role of Pilots

Pilots were used by ships in order to navigate safely in unfamiliar and dangerous waters. The St. Lawrence River above Quebec City was fairly narrow, which made navigation difficult. Ships on the St. Lawrence were traveling to and from the local ports, the ocean, the St. Lawrence Seaway, and the Great Lakes. There was a large number of oceangoing ships traveling through the Montreal River District whose captains had limited knowledge of the river or the navigational aids used and required the services of a pilot.

Pilots were classed in three different categories (Exhibit 1). Class A pilots could handle any ships; Class B, ships less than 8,000 tons; and Class C, ships of less than 5,000 tons. Class C was a temporary class for new pilots. However, 95 percent of all assignments were on ships of less than 8,000 tons.

EXHIBIT 1   Classification of Montreal River Pilots during 1967–1968

Class	Section I	Section II
A	39	37
B	26	21
C	10	10
	75	68

SOURCE: Christoph Haehling von Lanzenauer, *Cases in Operations Research,* Oakland, Calif.: Holden-Day Inc., 1975. Copyright © The University of Western Ontario. Reproduced with permission.

The Role of the Department of Transport

The DOT acted as an administrator of the agreements between the Pilots Association and the shipowners. It collected fees from the shipowners, paid the pilots, controlled dispatching, licensed pilots, and maintained navigational aids.

Under the present contract the Department of Transport paid the Pilots Association a fixed sum annually, out of which each pilot was paid in proportion to the amount of work he did. Salaries for the pilots in 1968 ranged between \$20,000 and \$25,000. The DOT collected fees from the shipowners each time their ships used the St. Lawrence. This fee was used to cover the cost of the pilots as well as the navigational aids which DOT maintained. Although shipowners were still liable financially for any damages, a pilot could lose his license as a result of an accident. It was not compulsory to have a pilot, but a ship paid a fee whether or not a pilot was used. Any increase in costs due to increased payments to the pilots would be passed on to the shipowners in the form of increased fees. However, if the number of pilots was reduced, a lower annual payment by the DOT would be required to maintain the average salary of the pilots and any savings could be passed on to the shipowners.

The Apprenticeship System

Extensive knowledge and experience in navigation of the ship channel and the harbors between Quebec City and Montreal were required of all pilots. As a result of a lack of a sizable pool of qualified mariners experienced in these waters, it was necessary to adopt an extensive apprenticeship system in the Montreal District. Prior to becoming an apprentice, a basic level of general education and academic studies and practical experience in navigation were required. Apprentices were recruited from preselected candidates who had attended a two-year course at an approved marine school, had obtained a diploma, and had served as a deck officer for 36 months. The minimum duration of an apprenticeship was three years. In addition to the required number of trips, the apprentice was given instruction and examinations.

The Montreal River District

The Montreal River District included all the ports along the St. Lawrence River between the lower end of the St. Lawrence Seaway near Montreal and Quebec City. The district was split into two sections (Montreal to Trois Rivières and Trois Rivières to Quebec City), as shown in Exhibit 2, with pilot pools at the end of each section. There were four pools maintained, Pool 1 in Montreal, Pools 2 and 3 in Trois Rivières, and Pool 4 in Quebec City with Pools 1 and 2 serving Section I between Trois Rivières and Montreal and Pools 3 and 4 serving Section II between Trois Rivières and Quebec City. Each port was served by one pilot pool (except Trois Rivières, which was served by Pools 2 and 3).

EXHIBIT 2   Description of the Montreal River District

Section	Mileage	Port	Served by Pool	Locations of Pool
	0	Montreal	1	Montreal
	11.5	Verennes	1	Montreal
I	23.2	Contracoeur	1	Montreal
	33.0	Sorel	1	Montreal
	53.7	Yamachiche	2	Trois Rivières
	65.7	Trois Rivières	2	Trois Rivières
	65.7	Trois Rivières	3	Trois Rivières
	85.5	Batiscan	3	Trois Rivières
II	111.2	Port Neuf	4	Quebec City
	123.7	St. Nicholas	4	Quebec City
	136.5	Quebec City	4	Quebec City

The assignments for the pilots were defined by three different categories:

1. A pilotage, where a ship was moved from one port to another.
2. A movage, where a ship was moved within the harbor.
3. A cancellation, where a pilot arrived at the scheduled time to find that his services were no longer required.

Pilots were assigned from the pool which corresponded to the port at which the assignment began and returned to the pool which corresponded to the port at which the assignment terminated. As a pilot had to know the river extremely well, each pilot operated in only one section and there was no transferring of pilots between sections. However, pilots were transferred between pools within a section. Generally, if there were more than five pilots in the pool at one end of a section and less than five at the other, pilots would be transferred.

No assignments began in Section I and ended in Section II, or vice versa. Ships traveling between the two sections would generate two assignments. If a ship was going from Contracoeur to Port Neuf, a pilot from Pool 1 boarded the ship at Contracoeur and took it to Trois Rivières, where the pilot got off and joined Pool 2. A new pilot from Pool 3 boarded the ship and took it to Port Neuf. This pilot then joined Pool 4 at Quebec City.

Pilot services were requested at all times during the day, seven days a week. However, the dispatchers knew at all times the status of all ships within the district as well as the estimated time of arrival of ships to the district. With this information the dispatcher, located at Montreal, was able to make up assignment lists which were modified every two hours. The pilots could check this list at any time by dialing a special number. The pilots took up to four hours to reach an assignment. The pilots with the fewest number of trips were given priority for assignments. For pilots

---

EXHIBIT 3 Pilots' Leave during 1967–1968

April 1–December 20—265 days
During this period, each pilot takes *42 days* of vacation. This time is taken in 7 periods of 6 days' duration, spread over the whole time period. This is scheduled so that there are not too many pilots on vacation at the same time.

December 21–March 31—100 days
Each pilot takes *50 days* consecutively during this period. That is, half the pilots work the first 50 days, and the other half work the remaining 50 days.

Average sick leave—*5 days* per year for each pilot.

---

with an equal number of trips, the pilot with the longest time since his last assignment was given priority. After each trip, a pilot was allowed 10 hours' rest and was not required to take another assignment. (During busy periods pilots occasionally took less than 10 hours' rest.) A movage or a cancellation did not count as a trip for priority purposes or rest periods.

In addition to the time off between assignments, a pilot was given 92 days off throughout the year. A certain number of days were taken consecutively during different times of the year, as outlined in Exhibit 3.

The year was divided into four pilot seasons, as outlined in Exhibit 4. Due to the current, the times required to complete upstream and downstream assignments were different and longer in the winter than the rest of the year. The travel times were restricted by a 12-knot speed limit on the St. Lawrence. The number and average travel times for pilotages and movages during 1968 are given in Exhibit 5. While the minimum times were approximately 10 percent below, the maximum times were 20 percent above the average travel time. The percentage of assignments canceled during 1967 and 1968 are given in Exhibit 6.

EXHIBIT 4 Pilotage Seasons

Winter:	December 1 – April 8
Spring:	April 9 – May 31
Summer:	June 1 – September 30
Autumn:	October 1 – November 30

EXHIBIT 5 Assignments during 1967–1968

| | | | Pool | | Duration (hours)* | | Number of Pilotages and Movages | | | |
	From	To	Direction	In	Out	Winter	Spring Summer Autumn	Winter	Spring	Summer	Autumn
1.	Montreal	Montreal	—	1	1	5.9	3.1	20	14	42	20
2.	"	Varennes	Down	1	1	6.3	3.6	—	1	6	3
3.	"	Contracoeur	Down	1	1	7.0	4.3	12	26	84	40
4.	"	Sorel	Down	1	1	8.1	5.3	15	40	118	52
5.	"	Yamachiche	Down	1	2	9.1	5.8	1	6	15	4
6.	"	Trois Rivières	Down	1	2	9.9	6.3	385	690	1,758	860
7.	Varennes	Montreal	Up	1	1	6.5	3.9	—	1	4	2
8.	"	Varennes	—	1	1	3.9	2.2	—	—	3	1
9.	"	Contracoeur	Down	1	1	5.7	3.2	—	2	8	3
10.	"	Sorel	Down	1	1	6.7	4.3	—	3	12	5
11.	"	Yamachiche	Down	1	2	7.4	4.9	1	1	11	5
12.	"	Trois Rivières	Down	1	2	8.3	5.4	3	6	21	10
13.	Contracoeur	Montreal	Up	1	1	7.3	4.8	4	35	80	41
14.	"	Varennes	Up	1	1	6.0	3.5	—	1	3	1
15.	"	Contracoeur	—	1	1	3.9	2.2	—	—	2	—
16.	"	Sorel	Down	1	1	5.4	3.1	—	—	4	—
17.	"	Yamachiche	Down	1	1	7.3	4.9	1	3	13	6
18.	"	Trois Rivières	Down	1	2	9.1	5.8	17	15	51	30
19.	Sorel	Montreal	Up	1	1	9.2	5.9	18	60	129	65
20.	"	Varennes	Up	1	1	7.8	5.1	1	7	16	7
21.	"	Contracoeur	Up	1	1	6.7	4.5	—	5	13	6
22.	"	Sorel	—	1	1	4.6	2.6	16	15	62	33
23.	"	Yamachiche	Down	1	2	6.1	3.5	—	1	8	3
24.	"	Trois Rivières	Down	1	2	7.3	4.8	4	5	12	4
25.	Yamachiche	Montreal	Up	2	1	9.9	6.3	5	20	41	19
26.	"	Varennes	Up	2	1	8.8	5.7	1	8	20	9
27.	"	Contracoeur	Up	2	1	8.1	5.3	—	4	12	4
28.	"	Sorel	Up	2	1	6.5	4.0	—	3	8	3
29.	"	Yamachiche	—	2	2	4.7	2.7	1	—	2	2
30.	"	Trois Rivières	Down	2	2	6.0	3.5	2	1	3	1
31.	Trois Rivières	Montreal	Up	2	1	12.1	7.6	331	693	1,692	820
32.	"	Varennes	Up	2	1	11.2	7.0	3	16	38	18
33.	"	Contracoeur	Up	2	1	9.9	6.3	8	25	62	29
34.	"	Sorel	Up	2	1	9.1	5.8	1	8	21	10
35.	"	Yamachiche	Up	2	2	6.6	4.4	—	3	6	2
36.	"	Trois Rivières	—	2/3	2/3	5.4	3.1	22	18	73	36
37.	"	Batiscan	Down	3	3	6.0	4.1	—	—	3	1
38.	"	Port Neuf	Down	3	4	7.3	4.8	—	2	6	2
39.	"	St. Nicholas	Down	3	4	8.3	5.4	1	4	12	5
40.	"	Quebec	Down	3	4	9.1	5.8	504	751	1,897	930
41.	Batiscan	Trois Rivières	Up	3	3	7.0	4.6	—	—	2	1
42.	"	Batiscan	—	3	3	3.6	2.1	—	—	4	1
43.	"	Port Neuf	Down	3	4	6.1	3.7	1	1	4	1
44.	"	St. Nicholas	Down	3	4	7.0	4.6	—	1	3	—
45.	"	Quebec	Down	3	4	7.6	5.0	—	2	6	3

EXHIBIT 5 *(concluded)*

	From	To	Direction	Pool In	Pool Out	Winter	Spring Summer Autumn	Winter	Spring	Summer	Autumn
						Duration (hours)*		Number of Pilotages and Movages			
46.	Port Neuf	Trios Rivières	Up	4	3	8.0	5.2	1	4	8	4
47.	"	Batiscan	Up	4	3	6.7	4.5	—	2	4	1
48.	"	Port Neuf	—	4	4	7.9	2.5	—	—	1	—
49.	"	St. Nicholas	Down	4	4	4.8	3.4	—	—	3	1
50.	"	Quebec	Down	4	4	6.3	4.2	—	1	3	—
51.	St. Nicholas	Trois Rivières	Up	4	3	9.9	6.3	3	11	21	10
52.	"	Batiscan	Up	4	3	8.7	5.6	—	6	11	5
53.	"	Port Neuf	Up	4	4	6.3	4.2	—	—	2	—
54.	"	St. Nicholas	—	4	4	4.8	2.8	—	—	—	1
55.	"	Quebec	Down	4	4	6.0	3.7	2	2	4	1
56.	Quebec	Trois Rivières	Up	4	3	11.3	7.1	440	803	1,922	941
57.	"	Batiscan	Up	4	3	8.5	5.5	1	8	14	6
58.	"	Port Neuf	Up	4	4	6.6	4.4	—	2	5	1
59.	"	St. Nicholas	Up	4	4	6.2	3.8	—	4	8	3
60.	"	Quebec	Up	4	4	5.4	3.1	3	3	8	4

* Duration includes the time to travel from the termination of an assignment to the corresponding pool.

EXHIBIT 6 Cancellations during 1967–1968

Season	Percent of Assignments Canceled
Winter	5.2
Spring	1.2
Summer	2.1
Autumn	0.6

WARNER-LAMBERT CANADA LIMITED (X)

In April 1968, Warner-Lambert Canada Limited was considering introducing throat lozenges to the Canadian pharmaceutical market. Lozenges distributed under the company brand name had sold well in the United States and had become a profitable venture. Consequently, the Canadian subsidiary was contemplating launching a throat lozenge on the Canadian market.

Warner-Lambert Canada Limited was a wholly owned subsidiary of the U.S. parent. The company had two factories in Canada, both located in Toronto, one making candy and chewing gum and the other producing pharmaceuticals and health and beauty aids.

One of the products sold throughout the world by the parent company and its subsidiaries was Listerine Antiseptic, a well-known mouthwash. It had been on the market for many years and was highly regarded by both dealers and consumers. Distributed through both food and drug stores, Listerine mouthwash held nearly 40 percent of the Canadian mouthwash market.

In the fall of 1965, the U.S. parent decided to test-market a throat lozenge under the Listerine brand name. The lozenges were designed to provide temporary relief from sore throats caused by coughs and colds. As the test market was successful, national distribution in the United States was undertaken the following year and 9.5 percent of the total throat lozenge market was achieved. In the fall of 1967, two flavors, orange and lemon-mint, were added. By February 1968, Listerine was second in throat lozenge sales, with 16.5 percent of the total U.S. market.

In April 1968, Mr. R. T. DeMarco, product manager in the Consumer Products Division of Warner-Lambert Canada Limited, decided to investigate the possibilities of manufacturing and distributing Listerine Throat Lozenges in Canada. He assigned Chris Seymour, an assistant brand manager in the Consumer Products Division, the task of recommending to the company an action plan for the proposed product.

The Market

Mr. Seymour's first step was to investigate the Canadian throat lozenge market. At that time there were about 40 brands of the product being sold in Canada at prices ranging from 35 cents to $1.49 per package. There were no unique product claims since all brands offered the same benefit (i.e., temporary relief from sore throat pain). Mr. Seymour was surprised to find out that there was virtually no media advertising in this product field. About 85 percent of the throat lozenges sold in Canada were sold through drug stores, while the remainder were distributed through food stores or other mass merchandisers. In the United States only 70 percent were sold by drugstores. Mr. Seymour collected the growth data in the Canadian and U.S. markets for the previous few years, as shown in Exhibit 1.

Pharmaceutical products which were available to Canadian consumers without a prescription could be classified into two categories.

1. *Antibacterial/antibiotic throat lozenges*
   Sometimes called OTC (over-the-counter) products. These contained active ingredients which were either antibiotic in nature or which worked against specific kinds of bacteria. Canadian sales of lozenges in this category had declined 13 percent in the years 1964–67.

EXHIBIT 1   **($ in millions)**

	1963	1964	1965	1966	1967	Est. 1968
U.S. food/drug*	$27.8	$29.4	$33.6	$33.8	$32.1	$34.5
Percent change	+11%	+7%	+15%	+1%	−4%	+7%
Canada food/drug†	—	$2.9	$3.5	$3.4	$3.3	$3.5
Percent change	—	—	+12%	−3%	−3%	+6%

* U.S. (A. C. Nielsen).
† Estimated on Canadian Davee, Koehnlein & Keating Co. (retail sales).

2. *Proprietary throat lozenges*
   These did not contain this kind of active drug ingredient; rather they contained ingredients which relieved throat irritation temporarily without specifically acting on the cause of the irritation. Canadian sales of lozenges in this category had increased 55 percent in the years 1964–67.

The Canadian sales volumes for each category were as shown in Exhibit 2.

In analyzing the sales drop of the antibiotic lozenges in Canada, Mr. Seymour learned that in March 1966 the U.S. Food and Drug Administration had banned the sale of all antibiotic throat lozenges in the United States. As far as he could determine, there was no such legislation being contemplated in Canada at that time.

Mr. Seymour also gathered information on the distribution of sales across Canada. In 1967 the Maritimes accounted for 7 percent of the total throat lozenge market; Quebec, for 26 percent; Ontario, for 42 percent; the Prairies, for 15 percent and British Columbia, for 10 percent. Mr. Seymour obtained data on the 10 leading brands which accounted for more than 50 percent of the market (Exhibit 3).

Mr. Seymour noted that in the first two months of 1968 Listerine Throat Lozenges in the United States had achieved second position, with

EXHIBIT 2   **Share of Lozenge Market by Product (000s)***

	1964		1965		1966		1967	
Anti/Anti	$862	58%	$975	55%	$817	47%	$746	45%
Percent vs. 1964 base	100%		110%		95%		87%	
Proprietary	$620	42%	$809	45%	$940	54%	$958	55%
Percent vs. 1964 base	100%		130%		150%		155%	
Total	$1,482	100%	$1,784	100%	$1,757	100%	$1,704	100%

* Based on Davee, Koehnlein & Keating Co. drug wholesale figures.

EXHIBIT 3 Competitive Share of Canadian Market, 1964–1967*†

Product	Company	Product Category	*Percent Share of Market*			
			1964	1965	1966	1967
Bradosol	Ciba	Proprietary	11.8%	11.7%	15.5%	16.3%
Cepacol	Merrill	Proprietary	7.0	7.6	8.5	7.7
Formalid	Wampole	OTC	7.0	6.7	7.2	6.7
Dequadin	Glaxo	OTC	5.2	4.8	5.7	6.3
Bionets	Horner	OTC	5.5	3.8	6.0	5.5
Strepsils	W-C	Proprietary	—†	—†	1.1	5.3
Sucrets	M.S. & D.	Proprietary	4.2	5.0	4.0	5.2
Spectrocin-T	Squibb	OTC	2.2	3.6	7.7	4.9
Meggazones	Meggasson	Proprietary	3.5	4.1	4.3	4.7
Spectrocin-C	Squibb	Proprietary	1.0	2.9	3.6	2.9
Percent total above products			47.4	50.2	63.6	65.5
Percent all others			52.6	49.8	36.4	34.5
Percent total market			100	100	100	100

 * Davee, Koehnlein & Keating Co.
 † Not on market.

16.5 percent of lozenge sales, while market-leading Sucrets held 35 percent. Both brands were proprietary products.

One difference between the Canadian and the U.S. markets was the amount of media advertising. While there was virtually no advertising in Canada, Warner-Lambert in the United States spent $1.25 million on throat lozenges, Sucrets spent $1.92 million, and the total industry expenditures on advertising reached $5.8 million. Mr. Seymour believed that if a new product were to be introduced, it should be supported by a strong marketing campaign.

Market Packaging and Pricing

On the Canadian throat lozenge market there were several different types of packages (Exhibit 4), with the number of throat lozenges per package ranging from 10 to 50. Each company in the throat lozenge market offered only one flavor. Prices varied from 35 cents to $1.49 a box, but the average price range for the main competitors was between 59 cents and 89 cents.

The Product

Listerine Throat Lozenges manufactured and sold in the United States were classified as proprietary and were packaged 18 to a small pocket-sized box. The lozenge itself was a candy disk about ¾ inch in diameter and about ¼ inch thick. A "bunch wrapper" was used to "bunch" foil around the lozenge. The wrapped lozenges were placed in holes in a rectangular piece of cardboard, a backing was applied, and finally a

---

EXHIBIT 4 Representative Sample of Throat Lozenge Market Packaging and Pricing

Product	Packaging Type	Percent of Lozenges	Retail Price	Retail Price per Lozenge
Bradosol	Plastic case	20	$0.91	4.6¢
Cepacol	Carton	20	0.59	3.0
Contac	Carton	18	0.89	4.9
Coricidin	Carton	20	1.39	7.0
Dequadin	Tube carton	20	1.13	5.7
Formolid	Carton	50	0.35	0.7
Meggazones	Tin box	25	0.79	3.2
Krylex	Tube carton	10	0.90	9.0
Spectrocin-C	Tube carton	10	0.89	8.9
Spectrocin-T	Tube carton	10	0.89	8.9
Orlenta	Tube carton	12	0.90	7.5
Benylin	Tube carton	10	0.60	6.0
Soothettes	Carton	20	1.49	7.5
Strepsils	Tin	24	1.52	5.2
Average		19.2	$0.926	4.8¢

---

plastic bubble was placed over each lozenge on the front of the card. This process was referred to as blister packaging. Each card held six lozenges, and there were three cards per cardboard box. The user, after withdrawing the card from the box, simply pressed his thumb on the plastic bubble and the lozenge dropped out of the back of the card.

Warner-Lambert management believed the product could obtain either antibacterial/antibiotic or proprietary classification since Listerine Throat Lozenges acted to some degree directly against the cause of irritation. Mr. Seymour, after consulting other marketing officials in the company, felt that the Listerine Throat Lozenge introduced in Canada should be classified as proprietary and should be the same product as was being sold in the United States. This would eliminate any product development cost and would allow the Canadian market to be supplied initially by the U.S. parent if desired. The Canadian division obtained the necessary proprietary number to allow distribution of the lozenges in food stores. Warner-Lambert expected to obtain quick, wide penetration by capitalizing on the existing distribution channels between the company salesmen and the food stores which handled Listerine mouthwash.

Mr. DeMarco was in general agreement with the proposals, but he urged Mr. Seymour to find out if the U.S. parent could indeed supply the Canadian market. The production planner in the United States informed Mr. Seymour that the United States could supply a limited quantity of the lozenges bunch wrapped and inserted into the cards. In order to print the Canadian proprietary number and to have bilingual printing, however, it would be necessary to do the boxing in Canada.

Mr. Seymour learned that the Canadian plant could manufacture the lozenges but that the Canadian plant did not have the specialized equipment necessary to bunch-wrap and insert the lozenges in the holes in the cards. They did have, however, the equipment required to print the boxes and to insert the cards in the boxes. Ten months would be required for delivery and installation of the specialized equipment for bunching and blister packing.

The Test Market

Warner-Lambert often conducted a test market study before introducing a new product. Mr. Seymour realized that a national campaign could not be undertaken before the fall of 1969 but that time and facilities existed to conduct a test market in one area during the 1968–69 season if management felt it was desirable. Mr. Seymour believed the prairie provinces would be an easily isolated geographical region with a minimum of advertising spillover from media in other areas. Management chose to price the product in direct competition with market-leading Bradosol's price of 91 cents and accordingly set the price of Listerine lozenges at 89 cents per package of 18. Retailers would purchase the lozenges from Warner-Lambert for 55 cents a box. Mr. Seymour originally estimated that test market sales would be $60,500 (net factory value), which would represent 12.8 percent of the prairie market for lozenges. Because they could not have the necessary equipment for the test period between September 16, 1968, and August 15, 1969, the blister-packaged lozenges would have to be imported from the United States and would be boxed in Canada in bilingual boxes.

The cost of the test was estimated to be:

Advertising	$ 43,900
Promotion	20,000
Research	10,000
Direct selling	5,000
Direct operating	4,600
Lozenge cost (including packaging)	30,800
	$114,300

The lozenge cost was fixed since none of the imported product could be salvaged if it was not sold. Mr. Seymour used three volume estimates to represent the possible sales outcomes. He defined a successful test market as sales of 110,000 boxes ($60,500) of lozenges, and he assessed the chance of achieving this level at 70 percent. He realized that even if they did not sell 110,000 boxes during the test year, they might sell a sufficient amount to be able to label the test as inconclusive. He believed there was a 20 percent chance that an inconclusive test having sales of about 90,000 boxes ($49,500) would occur. He would label the test a failure if sales were as low as 60,000 boxes ($33,000).

In order to give the product an adequate test and to be operating efficiently during the cold season, it would be necessary to have the product on the store shelves by the end of October 1968. This would require shipments from the factory to start by September 16. Mr. L. J. O'Keefe, sales manager, informed Mr. Seymour that the very latest his salesmen could begin to take orders for September delivery was August 12. This meant that July 15 would have to be the deadline for a decision to test-market the product. If the order for the bunch-wrapped and carded lozenges was sent to the United States before that date, however, there would be sufficient time to have them placed in bilingual boxes in Canada and delivered to the stores for the fall cough/cold season.

Equipment Decision

The machinery necessary for Canadian production would cost $88,000 with an additional $8,000 for installation expenses. If the order was placed in October 1968, the equipment would be ready to produce the lozenges for the introduction of the national campaign in the fall of 1969. Equipment ordered in October would require a deposit of $25,000 that would be forfeited if the order was canceled during or before February 1969. After February the order could not be canceled. Mr. Seymour felt that by the end of February the company would know whether the test market was going to be successful, inconclusive, or a failure. An alternative choice to ordering in October was to hold the original order until the end of February 1969, when the test market outcome could be determined. Under this alternative the equipment would not be ready for the start of the 1969 campaign and if Warner-Lambert decided to go national 85 percent of the first-year sales would have to be imported. The total variable cost to the Canadian division for lozenges imported from the United States was 28 cents per box, whereas this would be reduced to 14 cents if the product was made entirely in Canada. Since Warner-Lambert Canada based its decisions on the profit contribution to the Canadian division only, and since the U.S. division would only guarantee to supply 85 percent of the first-year demand, it was decided that the equipment should be ordered no later than February 28, 1969, if a national campaign was to be launched.

Profit Potential

Mr. Seymour estimated before the test market that there was a 50 percent chance of achieving high sales of 800,000 boxes from the national campaign. He believed medium sales of 650,000 boxes and low sales of 400,000 boxes had a 30 percent and 20 percent chance of occurrence, respectively. National introduction would increase fixed costs due to advertising, research, and direct operating and selling expenses. Initial

---

EXHIBIT 5   Profit Contribution from National Sales

I. *Equipment ordered October 1968*

	Sales		
	High	**Medium**	**Low**
Sales (boxes)	800,000	650,000	400,000
Contribution margin per box (55¢ − 14¢)	41¢	41¢	41¢
Contribution margin	$328,000	$266,500	$164,000
Fixed costs	255,000	$ 255,000	255,000
Profit	$ 73,000	$ 11,500	−$ 91,000
Years	10	1	1
Present value discount factor at 22%	3.923	0.82	0.82
Present value of expected profit	$286,379	$ 9,430	−$ 74,620

II. *Equipment ordered February 1969*

A. Year 1

Sales (boxes)	800,000	650,000	400,000
Contribution margin per box, Year 1 55¢ − [(.85 × .28) + (.15 × .14)]	29.1¢	29.1¢	29.1¢
Year 1 contribution	$232,800	$189,000	$116,400
Fixed costs	255,000	255,000	255,000
Profit from Year 1	−$22,200	−$65,850	−$138,600
Present value Year 1 profit (Profit × 0.82)	−$18,204	−$53,997	−$113,652

B. Years 2 to 10

Contribution margin per box, Years 2–10	41¢
Contribution margin per year	$328,000
Fixed cost	255,000
Profit per year	$ 73,000
Discount annuity from Years 2 to 10, to Time 0 3.786 × 0.82	3.104
Present value profit, Years 2 to 10	$226,592

Present value of expected profit	$208,388	−$53,997	−$113,652

forecasts suggested that these costs would be approximately $255,000 a year. This does not include equipment or test marketing costs. The product would be dropped after one year if national sales were medium or low. If the product reached the high sales forecast in the first year, Mr. Seymour felt it was conservative to assume that the level would be maintained for the expected 10-year life of the equipment.

The test market results would allow Mr. Seymour to make more accurate estimates for the sales outcome of the national campaign. He did not think there was any chance of achieving medium or high sales nationally if the test market sales volume was considered a failure. On the other hand, a successful test would suggest a 90 percent chance for high sales nationally and a 10 percent chance for medium sales. Although an inconclusive test result was the most difficult to evaluate, Mr. Seymour estimated that it would suggest a 65 percent chance of low national sales and a 35 percent chance for high sales.

Mr. Seymour learned that the new equipment had no other use and would have negligible value if the new product was dropped. He decided to make his initial projections on a before-tax basis since all the revenues and expenses with the exception of the equipment purchase were period flows and were subject to the same tax rate. If his analysis did not make the optimum course of action obvious, he planned to recalculate considering the tax effects.

At the same time he realized that a dollar received in the future was of less value than a dollar received immediately. Since the company looked for new projects that returned 10 to 15 percent after taxes, he decided to discount the before-tax income figures for the national campaign at 22 percent (Exhibit 5). With these assumptions he felt he could determine the best strategy for the new product.

KAZABAZUA BREWING COMPANY

Each fall, Bud Wiser, the brewmaster of Kazabazua Brewing Company, reviewed the previous year's production and sales results in an attempt to develop a master brewing plan for the coming year. This brewing or production plan was primarily used for budgeting purposes but also served as a guide for purchasing and manpower plans. Although sales, and thus bottling requirements, were highly seasonal, the pattern was stable and quite predictable. On the basis of sales projections recently made by the marketing department, the brewmaster had been told by the bottleshop superintendent that the demand for brewed product in aggregate could be represented in thousands of barrels as shown below:

Month	Forecast Demands on the Brewhouse (000s of barrels by month)
January	5
February	4
March	5
April	7
May	10
June	12
July	14
August	13
September	11
October	8
November	10
December	7
Total	106

Although bottling and final detailed scheduling of the brewhouse required attention to the various brands produced by Kazabazua, there was no advantage at this time in considering anything other than aggregate requirements.

Mr. Wiser's planning problem was complicated by restricted capacity levels of the brewhouse. Basically, he could operate at four production levels: one shift, two shifts, or either with overtime. For each level, the labor cost and the capacity per month in thousands of barrels was fairly well established. This production information was as follows:

SOURCE: Christoph Haehling von Lanzenauer, *Cases in Operations Research,* Oakland, Calif.: Holden-Day, Inc., 1975. Copyright © The University of Western Ontario. Reproduced with permission.

Level	Capacity (barrels)	Total Labor Cost
One shift	5,000	$3,000
One shift plus overtime	7,000	4,000
Two shifts	9,000	6,000
Two shifts plus overtime	12,000	8,000

Production rates between the above capacity levels were possible but required the full labor cost associated with the next higher capacity level (e.g., production of 8,000 barrels required two shifts at a labor cost of $6,000).

As well as the labor costs required to produce at capacity levels, the brewmaster knew there were measurable costs associated with changing shift levels. Data were not readily available on these costs, but he was able to make some estimates based on past changes and the routine involved in hiring and laying off workers. He estimated that increasing from one shift to two shifts involved a cost of $1,500, while decreasing from two shifts to one incurred a cost of $1,000. The brewery had a policy that it would always employ at least one shift each month even though it might produce less than 5,000 barrels in that particular month.

Mr. Wiser was also responsible for inventory of brewed product held in refrigerated tanks between the brewhouse and the bottleshop. He learned from the accounting office that for every 1,000 barrels held in inventory at the end of the month, the company incurred a cost of $300.

As the company did not permit a stockout of the bottled product, it carried ample finished goods inventory. However, if the work-in-process inventory in the brewhouse was insufficient to meet the demand from the bottling shop, the bottling shop would have to shut down temporarily. A shortage in one month would have to be made up in succeeding months in order to meet total demand. This disruption in the routine of the bottleshop caused overtime costs to be incurred, and after considerable investigation Mr. Wiser concluded that this cost of a stockout in the brewhouse amounted to about $500 for every 1,000 barrels short. If the inventory in the brewhouse at the end of the month was zero, there was neither an inventory carrying cost nor a shortage cost.

In developing a particular production plan for the year, the end-of-month inventory was calculated from opening inventory plus production less bottleshop demand.

Due to the aggregate nature of the plan and the approximate costs involved, the brewmaster considered thousands of barrels a meaningful measure of production activity. As he prepared the plan for the next year, Mr. Wiser estimated that he would have 2,000 barrels in inventory at the end of the current year and would be operating at a one-shift production level. He was anxious to develop a production plan which would result in the minimum production costs for the year and a closing inventory of 2,000 barrels.

Mr. Wiser knew that his brewhouse would be operating at one shift in the January following the year for which he was planning because demand was always low in the early months of the year. Consequently, any plan calling for two shifts in December would be charged an additional $1,000 because of the level change anticipated at the end of the year.

Mr. Wiser wondered what production plan would produce 106,000 barrels at lowest total cost.

Tables

Table of Random Numbers

```
61 19 69 04 46    26 45 74 77 74    51 92 43 37 29    65 39 45 95 93    42 58 26 05 27
15 47 44 52 66    95 27 07 99 53    59 36 78 38 48    82 39 61 01 18    33 21 15 94 66
94 55 72 85 73    67 89 75 43 87    54 62 24 44 31    91 19 04 25 92    92 92 74 59 73
42 48 11 62 13    97 34 40 87 21    16 86 84 87 67    03 07 11 20 59    25 70 14 66 70
23 52 37 83 17    73 20 88 98 37    68 93 59 14 16    26 25 22 96 63    05 52 28 25 62

04 49 35 24 94    75 24 63 38 24    45 86 25 10 25    61 96 27 93 35    65 33 71 24 72
00 54 99 76 54    64 05 18 81 59    96 11 96 38 96    54 69 28 23 91    23 28 72 95 29
35 96 31 53 07    26 89 80 93 54    33 35 13 54 62    77 97 45 00 24    90 10 33 93 33
59 80 80 83 91    45 42 72 68 42    83 60 94 97 00    13 02 12 48 92    78 56 52 01 06
46 05 88 52 36    01 39 00 22 86    77 28 14 40 77    93 91 08 36 47    70 61 74 29 41

32 17 90 05 97    87 37 92 52 41    05 56 70 70 07    86 74 31 71 57    85 39 41 18 38
69 23 46 14 06    20 11 74 52 04    15 95 66 00 00    18 74 39 24 23    97 11 89 63 38
19 56 54 14 30    01 75 87 53 79    40 41 92 15 85    66 67 43 68 06    84 96 28 52 07
45 15 51 49 38    19 47 60 72 46    43 66 79 45 43    59 04 79 00 33    20 82 66 95 41
94 86 43 19 94    36 16 81 08 51    34 88 88 15 53    01 54 03 54 56    05 01 45 11 76

98 08 62 48 26    45 24 02 84 04    44 99 90 88 96    39 09 47 34 07    35 44 13 18 80
33 18 51 62 32    41 94 15 09 49    89 43 54 85 81    88 69 54 19 94    37 54 87 30 43
80 95 10 04 06    96 38 27 07 74    20 15 12 33 87    25 01 62 52 98    94 62 46 11 71
79 75 24 91 40    71 96 12 82 96    69 86 10 25 91    74 85 22 05 39    00 38 75 95 79
18 63 33 25 37    98 14 50 65 71    31 01 02 46 74    05 45 56 14 27    77 93 89 19 36

74 02 94 39 02    77 55 73 22 70    97 79 01 71 19    52 52 75 80 21    80 81 45 17 48
54 17 84 56 11    80 99 33 71 43    05 33 51 29 69    56 12 71 92 55    36 04 09 03 24
11 66 44 98 83    52 07 98 48 27    59 38 17 15 39    09 97 33 34 40    88 46 12 33 56
48 32 47 79 28    31 24 96 47 10    02 29 53 68 70    32 30 75 75 46    15 02 00 99 94
69 07 49 41 38    87 63 79 19 76    35 58 40 44 01    10 51 82 16 15    01 84 87 69 38

09 18 82 00 97    32 82 53 95 27    04 22 08 63 04    83 38 98 73 74    64 27 85 80 44
90 04 58 54 97    51 98 15 06 54    94 93 88 19 97    91 87 07 61 50    68 47 66 46 59
73 18 95 02 07    47 67 72 62 69    62 29 06 44 64    27 12 46 70 18    41 36 18 27 60
75 76 87 64 90    20 97 18 17 49    90 42 91 22 72    95 37 50 58 71    93 82 34 31 78
54 01 64 40 56    66 28 13 10 03    00 68 22 73 98    20 71 45 32 95    07 70 61 78 13

08 35 86 99 10    78 54 24 27 85    13 66 15 88 73    04 61 89 75 53    31 22 30 84 20
28 30 60 32 64    81 33 31 05 91    40 51 00 78 93    32 60 46 04 75    94 11 90 18 40
53 84 08 62 33    81 59 41 36 28    51 21 59 02 90    28 46 66 87 95    77 76 22 07 91
91 75 75 37 41    61 61 36 22 69    50 26 39 02 12    55 78 17 65 14    83 48 34 70 55
89 41 59 26 94    00 39 75 83 91    12 60 71 76 46    48 94 97 23 06    94 54 13 74 03

77 51 30 38 20    86 83 42 99 01   ´68 41 48 27 74    51 90 81 39 80    72 89 35 55 07
19 50 23 71 74    69 97 92 02 88    55 21 02 97 73    74 28 77 52 51    65 34 46 74 15
21 81 85 93 13    93 27 88 17 57    05 68 67 31 56    07 08 28 50 46    31 85 33 84 52
51 47 46 64 99    68 10 72 36 21    94 04 99 13 45    42 83 60 91 91    08 00 74 54 49
99 55 96 83 31    62 53 52 41 70    69 77 71 28 30    74 81 97 81 42    43 86 07 28 34

33 71 34 80 07    93 58 47 28 69    51 92 66 47 21    58 30 32 98 22    93 17 49 39 72
85 27 48 68 93    11 30 32 92 70    28 83 43 41 37    73 51 59 04 00    71 14 84 36 43
```

SOURCE: Reprinted from *A Million Random Digits with 100,000 Normal Deviates* by the Rand Corporation (New York: The Free Press, 1955). Copyright 1955 & 1983 by the Rand Corporation. Used by permission.

Cumulative Normal Probability Distribution

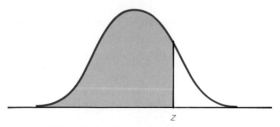

Table entries are cumulative probabilities represented in the shaded area above.

z	.00	.01	.02	.03	.04	.05	.06	.07	.08	.09
.0	.5000	.5040	.5080	.5120	.5160	.5199	.5239	.5279	.5319	.5359
.1	.5398	.5438	.5478	.5517	.5557	.5596	.5636	.5675	.5714	.5753
.2	.5793	.5832	.5871	.5910	.5948	.5987	.6026	.6064	.6103	.6141
.3	.6179	.6217	.6255	.6293	.6331	.6368	.6406	.6443	.6480	.6517
.4	.6554	.6591	.6628	.6664	.6700	.6736	.6772	.6808	.6844	.6879
.5	.6915	.6950	.6985	.7019	.7054	.7088	.7123	.7157	.7190	.7224
.6	.7257	.7291	.7324	.7357	.7389	.7422	.7454	.7486	.7517	.7549
.7	.7580	.7611	.7642	.7673	.7704	.7734	.7764	.7794	.7823	.7852
.8	.7881	.7910	.7939	.7967	.7995	.8023	.8051	.8078	.8106	.8133
.9	.8159	.8186	.8212	.8238	.8264	.8289	.8315	.8340	.8365	.8389
1.0	.8413	.8438	.8461	.8485	.8508	.8531	.8554	.8577	.8599	.8621
1.1	.8643	.8665	.8686	.8708	.8729	.8749	.8770	.8790	.8810	.8830
1.2	.8849	.8869	.8888	.8907	.8925	.8944	.8962	.8980	.8997	.9015
1.3	.9032	.9049	.9066	.9082	.9099	.9115	.9131	.9147	.9162	.9177
1.4	.9192	.9207	.9222	.9236	.9251	.9265	.9279	.9292	.9306	.9319
1.5	.9332	.9345	.9357	.9370	.9382	.9394	.9406	.9418	.9429	.9441
1.6	.9452	.9463	.9474	.9484	.9495	.9505	.9515	.9525	.9535	.9545
1.7	.9554	.9564	.9573	.9582	.9591	.9599	.9608	.9616	.9625	.9633
1.8	.9641	.9649	.9656	.9664	.9671	.9678	.9686	.9693	.9699	.9706
1.9	.9713	.9719	.9726	.9732	.9738	.9744	.9750	.9756	.9761	.9767
2.0	.9772	.9778	.9783	.9788	.9793	.9798	.9803	.9808	.9812	.9817
2.1	.9821	.9826	.9830	.9834	.9838	.9842	.9846	.9850	.9854	.9857
2.2	.9861	.9864	.9868	.9871	.9875	.9878	.9881	.9884	.9887	.9890
2.3	.9893	.9896	.9898	.9901	.9904	.9906	.9909	.9911	.9913	.9916
2.4	.9918	.9920	.9922	.9925	.9927	.9929	.9931	.9932	.9934	.9936
2.5	.9938	.9940	.9941	.9943	.9945	.9946	.9948	.9949	.9951	.9952
2.6	.9953	.9955	.9956	.9957	.9959	.9960	.9961	.9962	.9963	.9964
2.7	.9965	.9966	.9967	.9968	.9969	.9970	.9971	.9972	.9973	.9974
2.8	.9974	.9975	.9976	.9977	.9977	.9978	.9979	.9979	.9980	.9981
2.9	.9981	.9982	.9982	.9983	.9984	.9984	.9985	.9985	.9986	.9986
3.0	.9987	.9987	.9987	.9988	.9988	.9989	.9989	.9989	.9990	.9990
3.1	.9990	.9991	.9991	.9991	.9992	.9992	.9992	.9992	.9993	.9993
3.2	.9993	.9993	.9994	.9994	.9994	.9994	.9994	.9995	.9995	.9995
3.3	.9995	.9995	.9995	.9996	.9996	.9996	.9996	.9996	.9996	.9997
3.4	.9997	.9997	.9997	.9997	.9997	.9997	.9997	.9997	.9997	.9998

Selected Percentiles

Cumulative probability A:	.90	.95	.975	.98	.99	.995	.999
$z(A)$:	1.282	1.645	1.960	2.054	2.326	2.576	3.090

SOURCE: John Neter, William Wasserman, and Michael H. Kutner: *Applied Linear Statistical Models*, 2nd ed. (Homewood, Ill.: Richard D. Irwin, 1985), p. 1073.

Unit Normal Loss Table

z	0.00	0.01	0.02	0.03	0.04	0.05	0.06	0.07	0.08	0.09
0.0	0.3989	0.3940	0.3890	0.3841	0.3793	0.3744	0.3697	0.3649	0.3602	0.3556
0.1	0.3509	0.3464	0.3418	0.3373	0.3328	0.3284	0.3240	0.3197	0.3154	0.3111
0.2	0.3069	0.3027	0.2986	0.2944	0.2904	0.2863	0.2824	0.2784	0.2745	0.2706
0.3	0.2668	0.2630	0.2592	0.2555	0.2518	0.2481	0.2445	0.2409	0.2374	0.2339
0.4	0.2304	0.2270	0.2236	0.2203	0.2169	0.2137	0.2104	0.2072	0.2040	0.2009
0.5	0.1978	0.1947	0.1917	0.1887	0.1857	0.1828	0.1799	0.1771	0.1742	0.1714
0.6	0.1687	0.1659	0.1633	0.1606	0.1580	0.1554	0.1528	0.1503	0.1478	0.1453
0.7	0.1429	0.1405	0.1381	0.1358	0.1334	0.1312	0.1289	0.1267	0.1245	0.1223
0.8	0.1202	0.1181	0.1160	0.1140	0.1120	0.1100	0.1080	0.1061	0.1042	0.1023
0.9	0.1004	0.09860	0.09680	0.09503	0.09328	0.09156	0.08986	0.08819	0.08654	0.08491
1.0	0.08332	0.08174	0.08019	0.07866	0.07716	0.07568	0.07422	0.07279	0.07138	0.06999
1.1	0.06862	0.06727	0.06595	0.06465	0.06336	0.06210	0.06086	0.05964	0.05844	0.05726
1.2	0.05610	0.05496	0.05384	0.05274	0.05165	0.05059	0.04954	0.04851	0.04750	0.04650
1.3	0.04553	0.04457	0.04363	0.04270	0.04179	0.04090	0.04002	0.03916	0.03831	0.03748
1.4	0.03667	0.03587	0.03508	0.03431	0.03356	0.03281	0.03208	0.03137	0.03067	0.02998
1.5	0.02931	0.02865	0.02800	0.02736	0.02674	0.02612	0.02552	0.02494	0.02436	0.02380
1.6	0.02324	0.02270	0.02217	0.02165	0.02114	0.02064	0.02015	0.01967	0.01920	0.01874
1.7	0.01829	0.01785	0.01742	0.01699	0.01658	0.01617	0.01578	0.01539	0.01501	0.01464
1.8	0.01428	0.01392	0.01357	0.01323	0.01290	0.01257	0.01226	0.01195	0.01164	0.01134
1.9	0.01105	0.01077	0.01049	0.01022	0.009957	0.009698	0.009445	0.009198	0.008957	0.008721
2.0	0.008491	0.008266	0.008046	0.007832	0.007623	0.007418	0.007219	0.007024	0.006835	0.006649
2.1	0.006468	0.006292	0.006120	0.005952	0.005788	0.005628	0.005472	0.005320	0.005172	0.005028
2.2	0.004887	0.004750	0.004616	0.004486	0.004358	0.004235	0.004114	0.003996	0.003882	0.003770
2.3	0.003662	0.003556	0.003453	0.003352	0.003255	0.003159	0.003067	0.002977	0.002889	0.002804
2.4	0.002720	0.002640	0.002561	0.002484	0.002410	0.002337	0.002267	0.002199	0.002132	0.002067
2.5	0.002004	0.001943	0.001883	0.001826	0.001769	0.001715	0.001662	0.001610	0.001560	0.001511
2.6	0.001464	0.001418	0.001373	0.001330	0.001288	0.001247	0.001207	0.001169	0.001132	0.001095
2.7	0.001060	0.001026	0.000993	0.000961	0.000930	0.000899	0.000870	0.000841	0.000814	0.000787
2.8	0.000761	0.000736	0.000712	0.000688	0.000665	0.000643	0.000621	0.000600	0.000580	0.000561
2.9	0.000542	0.000523	0.000506	0.000488	0.000472	0.000456	0.000440	0.000425	0.000410	0.000396
3.0	0.000382	0.000369	0.000356	0.000344	0.000332	0.000320	0.000309	0.000298	0.000287	0.000277
3.1	0.000267	0.000258	0.000249	0.000240	0.000231	0.000223	0.000215	0.000207	0.000200	0.000192
3.2	0.000185	0.000179	0.000172	0.000166	0.000160	0.000154	0.000148	0.000143	0.000137	0.000132
3.3	0.000127	0.000123	0.000118	0.000114	0.000109	0.000105	0.000101	0.000097	0.000094	0.000090
3.4	0.000087	0.000083	0.000080	0.000077	0.000074	0.000071	0.000069	0.000066	0.000063	0.000061
3.5	0.000058	0.000056	0.000054	0.000052	0.000050	0.000048	0.000046	0.000044	0.000042	0.000041

SOURCE: R. Peterson and E. A. Silver, *Decision Systems for Inventory Management and Production Planning,* New York: John Wiley & Sons (1985), pp. 699–708.

The *t*-Distribution

The table values are the values of *t* for the shaded area shown above.

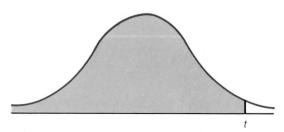

Degrees of Freedom	Area			
	0.95	0.975	0.99	0.995
1	6.314	12.706	31.821	63.657
2	2.920	4.303	6.965	9.925
3	2.353	3.182	4.541	5.841
4	2.132	2.776	3.747	4.604
5	2.015	2.571	3.365	4.032
6	1.943	2.447	3.143	3.707
7	1.895	2.365	2.998	3.499
8	1.860	2.306	2.896	3.355
9	1.833	2.262	2.821	3.250
10	1.812	2.228	2.764	3.169
11	1.796	2.201	2.718	3.106
12	1.782	2.179	2.681	3.055
13	1.771	2.160	2.650	3.012
14	1.761	2.145	2.624	2.977
15	1.753	2.131	2.602	2.947
16	1.746	2.120	2.583	2.921
17	1.740	2.110	2.567	2.898
18	1.734	2.101	2.552	2.878
19	1.729	2.093	2.539	2.861
20	1.725	2.086	2.528	2.845
21	1.721	2.080	2.518	2.831
22	1.717	2.074	2.508	2.819
23	1.714	2.069	2.500	2.807
24	1.711	2.064	2.492	2.797
25	1.708	2.060	2.485	2.787
26	1.706	2.056	2.479	2.779
27	1.703	2.052	2.473	2.771
28	1.701	2.048	2.467	2.763
29	1.699	2.045	2.462	2.756
30	1.697	2.042	2.457	2.750
40	1.684	2.021	2.423	2.704
60	1.671	2.000	2.390	2.660
120	1.658	1.980	2.358	2.617
Normal distribution	1.645	1.960	2.326	2.576

SOURCE: Adapted from Roger C. Pfaffenburger and James H. Patterson, *Statistical Methods for Business and Economics*, 3rd ed. (Homewood, Ill.: Richard D. Irwin, 1987), pp. 1156–58.

Values of P_0 for M/M/S Waiting Line System

$\dfrac{\lambda}{\mu S}$	Number of Servers—S									
	1	2	3	4	5	6	7	8	9	10
.02	.98000	.96078	.94176	.92312	.90484	.88692	.86936	.85214	.83527	.81873
.04	.96000	.92308	.88692	.85214	.81873	.78663	.75578	.72615	.69768	.67032
.06	.94000	.88679	.83526	.78663	.74082	.69768	.65705	.61878	.58275	.54881
.08	.92000	.85185	.78659	.72614	.67032	.61878	.57121	.52729	.48675	.44933
.10	.90000	.81818	.74074	.67031	.60653	.54881	.49659	.44933	.40657	.36788
.12	.88000	.78571	.69753	.61876	.54881	.48675	.43171	.38289	.33960	.30119
.14	.86000	.75439	.65679	.57116	.49657	.43171	.37531	.32628	.28365	.24660
.16	.84000	.72414	.61837	.52720	.44931	.38289	.32628	.27804	.23693	.20190
.18	.82000	.69492	.58214	.48660	.40653	.33959	.28365	.23693	.19790	.16530
.20	.80000	.66667	.54795	.44910	.36782	.30118	.24659	.20189	.16530	.13534
.22	.78000	.63934	.51567	.41445	.33277	.26711	.21437	.17204	.13807	.11080
.24	.76000	.61290	.48519	.38244	.30105	.23688	.18636	.14660	.11532	.09072
.26	.74000	.58730	.45640	.35284	.27233	.21007	.16200	.12492	.09632	.07427
.28	.72000	.56250	.42918	.32548	.24633	.18628	.14082	.10645	.08045	.06081
.30	.70000	.53846	.40346	.30017	.22277	.16517	.12241	.09070	.06720	.04978
.32	.68000	.51515	.37913	.27676	.20144	.14644	.10639	.07728	.05612	.04076
.34	.66000	.49254	.35610	.25510	.18211	.12981	.09247	.06584	.04687	.03337
.36	.64000	.47059	.33431	.23505	.16460	.11505	.08035	.05609	.03915	.02732
.38	.62000	.44928	.31367	.21649	.14872	.10195	.06981	.04778	.03269	.02236
.40	.60000	.42857	.29412	.19929	.13433	.09032	.06064	.04069	.02729	.01830
.42	.58000	.40845	.27559	.18336	.12128	.07998	.05267	.03465	.02279	.01498
.44	.56000	.38889	.25802	.16860	.10944	.07080	.04573	.02950	.01902	.01226
.46	.54000	.36986	.24135	.15491	.09870	.06265	.03968	.02511	.01587	.01003
.48	.52000	.35135	.22554	.14221	.08895	.05540	.03442	.02136	.01324	.00820
.50	.50000	.33333	.21053	.13043	.08010	.04896	.02984	.01816	.01104	.00671
.52	.48000	.31579	.19627	.11951	.07207	.04323	.02586	.01544	.00920	.00548
.54	.46000	.29870	.18273	.10936	.06477	.03814	.02239	.01311	.00767	.00448
.56	.44000	.28205	.16986	.09994	.05814	.03362	.01936	.01113	.00638	.00366
.58	.42000	.26582	.15762	.09119	.05212	.02959	.01673	.00943	.00531	.00298
.60	.40000	.25000	.14599	.08306	.04665	.02601	.01443	.00799	.00441	.00243
.62	.38000	.23457	.13491	.07750	.04167	.02282	.01243	.00675	.00366	.00198
.64	.36000	.21951	.12438	.06847	.03715	.01999	.01069	.00570	.00303	.00161
.66	.34000	.20482	.11435	.06194	.03304	.01746	.00918	.00480	.00251	.00131
.68	.32000	.19048	.10479	.05587	.02930	.01522	.00786	.00404	.00207	.00106
.70	.30000	.17647	.09569	.05021	.02590	.01322	.00670	.00338	.00170	.00085
.72	.28000	.16279	.08702	.04495	.02280	.01144	.00570	.00283	.00140	.00069
.74	.26000	.14943	.07875	.04006	.01999	.00986	.00483	.00235	.00114	.00055
.76	.24000	.13636	.07087	.03550	.01743	.00846	.00407	.00195	.00093	.00044
.78	.22000	.12360	.06335	.03125	.01510	.00721	.00341	.00160	.00075	.00035
.80	.20000	.11111	.05618	.02730	.01299	.00610	.00284	.00131	.00060	.00028
.82	.18000	.09890	.04933	.02362	.01106	.00511	.00234	.00106	.00048	.00022
.84	.16000	.08696	.04280	.02019	.00931	.00423	.00190	.00085	.00038	.00017
.86	.14000	.07527	.03656	.01700	.00772	.00345	.00153	.00067	.00029	.00013
.88	.12000	.06383	.03060	.01403	.00627	.00276	.00120	.00052	.00022	.00010
.90	.10000	.05263	.02491	.01126	.00496	.00215	.00092	.00039	.00017	.00007
.92	.08000	.04167	.01947	.00867	.00377	.00161	.00068	.00028	.00012	.00005
.94	.06000	.03093	.01427	.00627	.00268	.00113	.00047	.00019	.00008	.00003
.96	.04000	.02041	.00930	.00403	.00170	.00070	.00029	.00012	.00005	.00002
.98	.02000	.01010	.00454	.00194	.00081	.00033	.00013	.00005	.00002	.00001

Answers to Odd-Numbered Exercises

CHAPTER 3: EXERCISES

1. In the formulation using minutes, the first two constraints would be replaced by the single constraint $26A + 27F + 31C \leq 9600$.

3. Define a new variable CA—the number of cassette-playing radios. Its objective function coefficient is 20 and its constraint coefficients are 30, 20, and 15 in the formulation using minutes.

5. Add the constraint $A + F \geq 25$ to the original model.

7. The complete model (with coefficients rounded to the four places) is
$$\min 0.0128a_1 + 0.0161b_1 + 0.0145c_1 +$$
$$0.0135a_2 + 0.0132b_2 + 0.0148c_2 +$$
$$0.0157a_3 + 0.017b_3 + 0.018c_3$$
st $\quad 0.0400a_1 + 0.0556b_1 + 0.0455c_1 \leq 40$
$$0.0385a_2 + 0.0526b_2 + 0.0435c_2 \leq 40$$
$$0.0435a_3 + 0.0500b_3 + 0.500c_3 \leq 40$$
$$a_1 + a_2 + a_3 = 1000$$
$$b_1 + b_2 + b_3 = 900$$
$$c_1 + c_2 + c_3 = 650$$
$$a_1, a_2, a_3, b_1, b_2, b_3, c_1, c_2, c_3 \geq 0$$

9. Add the constraint $25A_1 \geq 100$ or the equivalent constraint $A_1 \geq 4$.

11. The water constraint becomes $0.075C + 0.09W + 0.12O \leq 10$.

13. Let C, W, and O be the number of pounds of corn, wheat, and oats, respectively. Then, the model is
$$\min 0.085C + 0.08W + 0.09O$$
st $\quad 0.07C + 0.09W + 0.12O \leq 5$
$$0.32C + 0.27W + 0.39O \geq 15$$
$$0.18C + 0.07W + 0.18O \geq 7.5$$
$$C + W + O = 50$$
$$C, W, O \geq 0$$

15. Let C, W, and O represent the number of pounds of corn, wheat, and oats purchased for next month's contract. The total order is 10,000 100-pound sacks, or 1 million pounds. Then, the model is
$$\min 0.085C + 0.08W + 0.09O$$
st $\quad 0.07C + 0.09W + 0.12O \leq 100000$
$$0.32C + 0.27W + 0.39O \geq 300000$$
$$0.18C + 0.07W + 0.18O \geq 150000$$
$$C + W + O = 1000000$$
$$C, W, O \geq 0$$

17. Only the objective function coefficients change. The new objective function is max $16.50B + 4.50N + 1.50R$.

19. Change the constraint to $B + N + R = 30000$.

21. The octane number constraint can be written as $(85B + 89N + 92R)/30000 \geq 87$. After dividing by 30000, the constraint is $0.002833B + 0.002967N + 0.003067R \geq 87$. In this form, only the RHS constant changes if the octane requirement changes. In the original model, the constraint coefficients of B, N, and R change.

23. Only B's objective function coefficient changes. The objective function becomes max $50.40G - 38B - 48N - 51R$.

CHAPTER 4: EXERCISES

1. $a.$

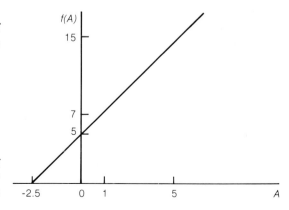

b.

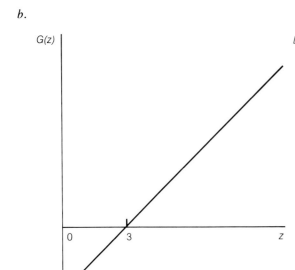

d.

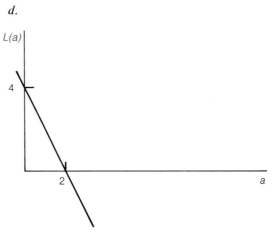

c.

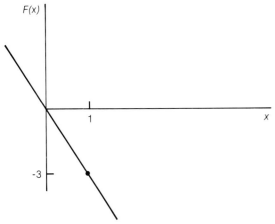

e.

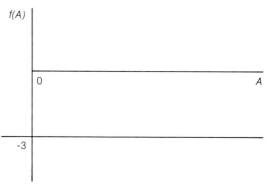

3.

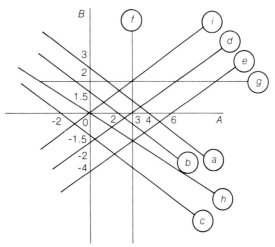

5. *a.* $3A + 4B - S = 12$
   b. $3a - 7b + 4c + S = 6$
   c. $-X + 3Y - Z - S = 7$
   d. $2X + 4Y + S = 12$

7.

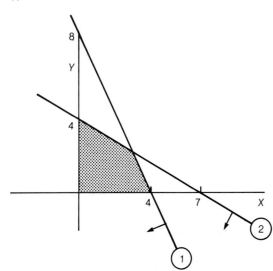

9.

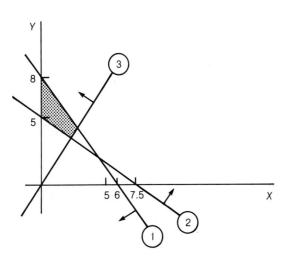

11. There are no feasible points.

13. *a.*

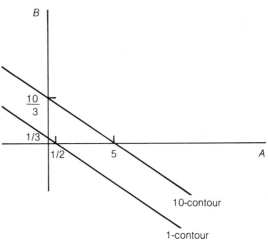

b.

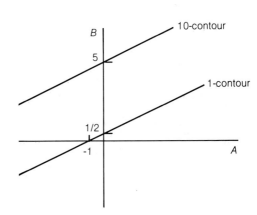

c.

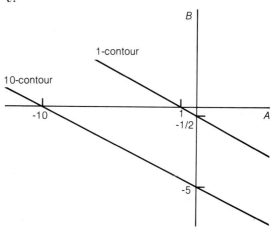

15. max $3X + 2Y + 2.5Z$
    st $2X + 7Y - Z + S_1 = 12$
         $3X + Z - S_2 = 4$
         $X, Y, Z, S_1, S_2 \geq 0$

17. max $-3X + 4Y - 5Z$
    st $-3X - 6Y - 2Z - S_1 = 12$
         $23X + 2Y - S_2 = 7$
         $X, Y, Z, S_1, S_2 \geq 0$

19. *a.* $X = {}^{14}\!/_5, Y = {}^{12}\!/_5, Z^* = {}^{12}\!/_5$
    b. $X = 4, Y = 0, Z^* = 12$
    c. $X = 0, Y = 4, Z^* = 8$
    d. $Z^* = 8$. Alternate optimal solutions: $X = 4$ and $Y = 0, X = {}^{14}\!/_5$ and $Y = {}^{12}\!/_5$, and points in between.

21. *a.* max $2X + 3Y$
        $X = 0, Y = 8, Z^* = 24$
    b. max $3X + Y$
        $X = {}^{48}\!/_{17}, Y = {}^{72}\!/_{17}, Z^* = {}^{216}\!/_{17}$
    c. max $X + 2Y$
        $X = 0, Y = 8, Z^* = 16$

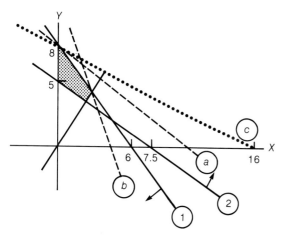

23. Four corner points.
25. Four corner points.

27. *a.* The optimal solution is $X = 1$ and $Y = 0$ with $Z^* = 2$.

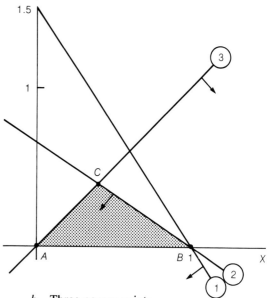

b. Three corner points.
c. At A and B, two variables are positive. At C, three variables are positive.
d. A and B are degenerate.

29. *a.* The optimal solution is $X = 1$ and $Y = 0$ with $Z^* = 2$.

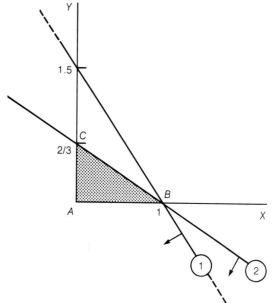

b. Three corner points.

c. At A and C, two variables are positive. At B, one variable is positive.

d. Yes, B is degenerate.

e. The optimal solution is unique.

31. There is no feasible solution.

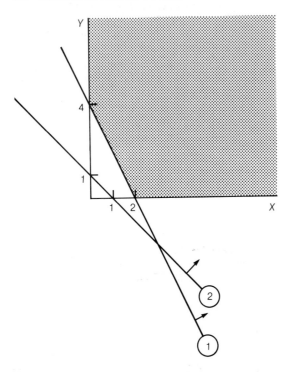

33. There is an unbounded optimal solution.

35. max $2X^+ - 2X^- - 4Y^- + 2Z$

st $2X^+ - 2X^- + 4Y^- + 3Z = 6$

$-3X^+ + 3X^- - 2Y^- - 2Z = 4$

$X^+ - X^- - Y^- + Z = 3$

$X^+, X^-, Y^-, Z \geq 0$

37. max $2X + 4Y - 2Z$

st $-2X + 4Y - 3Z \leq -6$

$-3X + 2Y - 2Z \leq 4$

$3X - 2Y + 2Z \leq -4$

$X + Y + Z \leq 3$

$X, Y, Z \geq 0$

CHAPTER 5: EXERCISES

1. a. 12,225

b. $I = 15,000, M = 67,500$

c. $FF = 18,000, HB = 15,000, FL = 24,750$

d. No. There are three positive variables and three constraints.

e. The optimal solution is unique because no objective function coefficient has a limit of 0.

f. (1) $12,225 + 0.325(100) = 12,257.50$

(2) Yes.

(3) You must re-solve to answer the question.

g. (1) You must re-solve to answer the question. The Maximum increase is 200, but the increase is 1,000. The profit will increase by *at least* $0.425(200) = 85$. The profit will be at least 12,310.

(2) You cannot tell.

(3) You must re-solve to answer the question.

h. (1) 12,225 (unchanged)

(2) Yes.

(3) Yes, but the slack on the flakes constraint increases.

3. a. 12,116.67

b. $I = 13,333.33, M = 68,333.34$

c. $FF = 17,666.67, HB = 15,000, FL = 24,500$

d. No. There are three positive variables.

e. The optimal solution is unique because no objective function coefficient has a limit of 0.

f. (1) Unchanged because the dual price is 0.

(2) Yes.

(3) Yes. Only the slack of the french fry limitation changes.

g. (1) You must re-solve to answer the question. The maximum increase is 1,333.33, but the increase is 2,000. The profit will increase by *at least* $0.1(1,333.33) = 133.33$. The profit will be at least 12,250.

(2) You cannot tell.

(3) No. You must re-solve to find the new purchasing plan.

h. (1) The allowable decrease is 2,000, but the contemplated decrease is 4,500. You must re-solve to answer the question. The profit will decrease by at least 0.43333(2,000) = 866.67. The profit will be at most 11,250.

(2) You cannot tell.

(3) No. You must re-solve to find the new purchasing plan.

i. Given that the set of positive variables does not change, an increase in the french fry limitation would not affect the optimal profit. Note that the current solution has more than 333 pounds unsatisfied.

5. *a.* (1) The increase is within the allowable range. The new profit is 12,225 + 0.01(15,000) = 12,375.

(2) Yes.

(3) Yes.

b. (1) The decrease is within the allowable range. The new profit is 12,225 − 0.05(15,000) = 11,475.

(2) Yes.

c. (1) The 0.01 increase is within the limit. The new profit is 12,225 + 0.01 × (67,500) = 12,900.

(2) Yes.

(3) Yes.

d. (1) The 0.013 increase equals the limit. The new profit is 12,225 + 0.13 × (67,500) = 21,000.

(2) Yes, but because the increase equals the limit, there will be alternate optimal solutions.

(3) Yes, but see (2). Because the solution is nondegenerate, there is a different alternate optimal solution.

e. (1) You cannot tell because the increase exceeds the limit. When *M*'s profit margin increases, the value of *M* in the optimal solution will not decrease from 67,500. Thus, the profit will be at least 12,225 + 0.14(67,500) = 21,675.

(2) No. Because the optimal solution is nondegenerate, a change greater than the limit gives a different solution.

7. *a.* (1) The limit is 0.13, so the profit is 12,225 + 0.01(67,500) = 12,900.

(2) Yes.

(3) Yes.

b. (1) The increase equals the limit. The new

profit is 12,225 + 0.13(67,500) = 21,000.

(2) Yes.

(3) With that change, *M*'s maximum increase will be 0. However, because the solution is degenerate, you cannot tell whether there is a different, alternate optimal solution.

c. (1) You cannot tell because the increase exceeds the limit. When *M*'s profit margin increases, the value of *M* in the optimal solution will not decrease from 67,500. Thus, the profit will be at least 12,225 + 0.14(67,500) = 21,675.

(2) Because the solution is degenerate, you cannot be sure that the solution changes.

9.

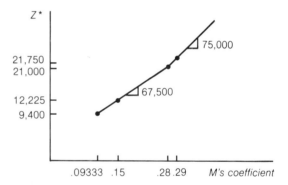

11. The original Potato Processing example has a profit of 12,225 and a dual price of 0.325 for *FF*. Row 2's maximum increase is 7,000. The plan costs $50, but the optimal profit increases by 0.325(200) = $65. Implementing the plan increases the net profit by $15, to $12,240. The plan should be undertaken.

13. The original Potato Processing example has a profit of 12,225 and a dual price of 0.325 for *FF*. Row 2's maximum increase is 7,000. The plan costs $50, but the optimal profit increases by 0.325(1,000) = $325. Implementing the plan increases the net profit by $275, to $12,500. The plan should be undertaken.

15. *a.* If the potato processing cost increases by 0.01, the objective coefficients of I and M decrease simultaneously by 0.01. The maximum decreases are 0.065 and 0.056667 for I and M, respectively. The fractions are $(0.01/0.065) = 0.154$ and $(0.01/0.056667) = 0.176$ for I and M, respectively. The total fraction is 0.330. Because this is not more than 1, the 100 Percent Rule is satisfied. $Z^* = 12,225 - 0.01(15,000) - 0.01 \times (67,500) = 11,400$.

   b. The potato purchasing plan is unchanged—$I = 15,000$ and $M = 67,500$.

17. *a.* The maximum RHS increases for *FF* and *HB* are 7,000 and 3,000, respectively. The fractions are $(4,000/7,000) = 0.571$ and $(4,000/3,000) = 1.333$. Because the total is greater than 1, the 100 Percent Rule is not satisfied. You must re-solve the model to determine the profit.

   b. You must re-solve the model to answer the question.

19. *a.* 40 hours; $40(19) = 760$ units.

   b. From the slacks on Rows 2, 3, and 4, the hours used on Machines 1, 2, and 3 are 40, 40, and 39.144269, respectively.

   c. The optimal solution is not degenerate because there are six positive variables and six constraints.

   d. No. No objective function coefficient has a limit of 0.

   e. Machine 1: $12.72727(25) = 318.18$; Machine 2: 0; Machine 3: $29.64427(23) = 681.82$.

   f. The minimum cost decreases at the rate of $0.071304 per hour that additional time is available on Machine 1, given that the set of positive variables stays the same. Note that the maximum increase is 27.27 hours.

   g. The minimum cost does not change as additional time is available on Machine 3. Note that some time is unused when 40 hours are available.

   h. When Row 5's RHS constant increases, more units of Product A are required. The objective function value gets worse at the rate $0.015652. Thus, the minimum cost increases by $0.015652 per unit until the set of positive variables changes. The maximum increase is 19.68 units.

i. From Row 5's dual price, the cost increases by $0.015652 to $36.717582. Note that the maximum increase is 19.68.

j. The production plan changes, but you must re-solve to find the new plan.

21. *a.* The optimal solution is not degenerate because there are six positive variables and six constraints.

   b. The objective function coefficient of A_2 must improve by more than 0.016043 before it is worthwhile for A_2 to become positive. That is, the cost per hour must decrease by 0.016043.

   c. (1) The maximum increase of A_1's objective function coefficient is 0.055304. If A_1's objective function coefficient increases by 0.03, the minimum cost is $36.70193 + 0.03(12.72727) = 37.083748$.
      (2) The plan does not change.

   d. (1) The maximum decrease is 0.003739. The decrease is more than the limit, so you must re-solve the model to answer the question. The profit decreases by at least $0.003739(12.72727) = 0.4776$.
      (2) You must re-solve the model to answer the question.

   e. The reduced cost must be negative. The reduced cost is $1(0.073) + (26 + X) \times (-0.015652) + 0.35$. Solving for X gives $X \geq 1.025$. The rate must be greater than $(26 + 1.025) = 27.025$ per hour.

   f. (1) The fractions are $(8/27.2727) = 0.293$, $(8/10) = 0.8$, and $(8/\infty) = 0$. The 100 Percent Rule is not satisfied, so you must re-solve the model.
      (2) You must re-solve the model to answer the question.

23. *a.* 4,246.15

   b. AM: 0, AM/FM: 123.08, AM/FM/CB: 184.62.

   c. Yes, because no objective function coefficient limit is 0.

   d. Because there are three positive variables and three constraints, the solution is non-degenerate.

   e. $0.308, A's reduced cost.

   f. Because Rows 3 and 4 have 0 slack, the number of hours used in final assembly and inspection and packaging are 80 and 40, respectively. The number of component assembly hours used is $(4{,}800 - 553.85)/60 = 70.79$.

g. Nothing. There is unused component assembly time in the optimal solution.

h. (1) Row 3's RHS constant increases by 480 (minutes). The profit increases by $0.461538(480) = 221.54$, to 4,467.69. Note that the maximum increase is 1,200.

(2) No.

i. (1) The 480-minute increase is more than the limit, 300 minutes. You must re-solve the model. The profit will increase by at least $0.846154(300) = 253.85$.

(2) No.

j. (1) The profit will be $4{,}246.15 + 1(123.08) = 4{,}369.23$. Note that the maximum increase is 2.0625.

(2) Yes.

k. (1) The decrease is more than the maximum decrease, 2.20. You must re-solve the model. The profit decreases by at least $2.2(184.6154) = 406.15$. The profit will be at most 3,840.

(2) No.

l. The reduced cost must be negative. The reduced cost is $11(0) + (15 - X) \times (0.461538) + 4(0.846154) - 10$. Solving for X, $X \geq 0.6667$. The number of final assembly minutes per AM radio must be 14.333 minutes or less.

25. a. $83,840

b. P_1: 4, P_2: 72, P_5: 20, P_6: 4, P_3 and P_4 are 0.

c. To calculate the total waste, multiply the inches of waste per roll slit in a pattern by the number slit in that pattern: $4(2) + 72(0) + 20(0) + 4(4) = 24$.

d. The solution is not degenerate because there are four positive variables and four constraints.

e. The optimal solution is not unique because several objective function coefficients have a 0 limit.

f. Note that the maximum increase for Row 2 is 4.

(1) The dual price for Row 2 is 240, so the revenue increases by $4(240) = 960$.

(2) Yes, more rolls are required.

g. The objective function coefficient increases are P_1: 150, P_2: 100, and P_3: 50. The other objective function coefficients do not change. The 100 Percent Rule is not satisfied, so you must re-solve the model to answer either part of the question. However, note that because exactly 156 6-inch rolls are required, the profit increases by $156(50) = \$7{,}800$. The current solution should still be optimal.

27. Let T_i be the dual variables for the time constraints, $i = 1, 2, 3$. Let R_j be the dual variables for the requirement constraints, $j = 1, 2, 3$. The dual problem is

max $40T_1 + 40T_2 + 40T_3 + 1000R_1 + 950R_2 + 600R_3$

st $\quad T_1 + 25R_1 \leq 0.32$
$\quad\quad T_1 + 18R_2 \leq 0.29$
$\quad\quad T_1 + 22R_3 \leq 0.32$
$\quad\quad T_2 + 26R_1 \leq 0.35$
$\quad\quad T_2 + 19R_2 \leq 0.25$
$\quad\quad T_2 + 23R_3 \leq 0.34$
$\quad\quad T_3 + 23R_1 \leq 0.36$
$\quad\quad T_3 + 20R_2 \leq 0.34$
$\quad\quad T_3 + 20R_3 \leq 0.36$
$\quad\quad T_i \geq 0, R_j$ unrestricted in sign

29. Because the objective function is minimization, the dual variable values have signs opposite to those of the dual prices. Thus, $T_1 = -0.71304$, $T_2 = -0.73$, $T_3 = 0$, $R_1 = 0.015652$, $R_2 = 0.017$, and $R_3 = 0.017787$.

CHAPTER 6: EXERCISES

1. $M = 75{,}000$, $s_1 = 3{,}000$, and $s_3 = 7{,}500$.
3. $M = 100{,}000$, $s_1 = -2{,}000$, and $s_2 = -5{,}000$.
5. *a–c.*

Partition	Basic Variables	Basic Variable Values	Nonbasic Variables	Nonbasic Variable Values	Objective Function Value
1	s_1, s_2	5, 2	x, y	0, 0	0
2	s_1, x	3, 2	s_2, y	0, 0	6
3	s_1, y	7, -2	s_2, x	0, 0	-4
4	s_2, x	-3, 5	s_1, y	0, 0	15
5	s_2, y	7, 5	s_1, x	0, 0	10
6	x, y	3.5, 1.5	s_1, s_2	0, 0	13.5

  d. Corner point partitions: 1, 2, 5, and 6.
  e. Optimal solution: $x = 3.5$, $y = 1.5$, $Z^* = 13.5$.

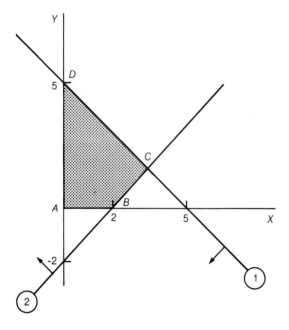

  Corner point: Partition relationships are
  A: 1, B:2, C:6, and D:5.
  f. A to B to C; A to D to C.

7. *a.* 2, 3, 4, and 5.
   b. 2 and 5.

9. *a–d.*

Partition	Basic Variables	Basic Variable Values	Nonbasic Variables	Nonbasic Variable Values	Objective Function Value
1	s_1, s_2, s_3	9, 9, 5	R, L	0, 0	0
2	R, s_2, s_3	9, −9, −4	s_1, L	0, 0	
3	L, s_2, s_3	4.5, 4.5, .5	s_1, R	0, 0	40.5
4	s_1, R, s_3	4.5, 4.5, .5	s_2, L	0, 0	36
5	s_1, L, s_3	−9, 9, −4	s_2, R	0, 0	
6	s_1, s_2, R	4, −1, 5	s_3, L	0, 0	
7	s_1, s_2, L	−1, 4, 5	s_3, R	0, 0	
8	s_1, R, L	3, 4, 1	s_2, s_3	0, 0	41
9	s_2, R, L	3, 1, 4	s_1, s_3	0, 0	44
10	s_3, R, L	−1, 3, 3	s_1, s_2	0, 0	

   Partitions 1, 3, 4, 8, and 9 correspond to corner points.
   e. Optimal solution: $R = 1, L = 4, Z^* = 44$;
   1 to 3 to 9 or 1 to 4 to 8 to 9.

11. *a–d.*

Partition	Basic Variables	Basic Variable Values	Nonbasic Variables	Nonbasic Variable Values	Objective Function Value
1	s_1, s_2, s_3	4, 6, 1	A, B	0, 0	0
2	A, s_2, s_3	4, −2, 5	s_1, B	0, 0	
3	B, s_2, s_3	2, 2, −1	s_1, A	0, 0	
4	s_1, A, s_3	1, 3, 4	s_2, B	0, 0	3
5	s_1, B, s_3	−2, 3, −2	s_2, A	0, 0	
6	s_1, s_2, A	5, 8, −1	s_3, B	0, 0	
7	s_1, s_2, B	2, 4 ,1	s_3, A	0, 0	1
8	s_1, A, B	−1, 1, 2	s_2, s_3	0, 0	
9	s_2, A, B	4/3, 2/3, 5/3	s_1, s_3	0, 0	7/3
10	s_3, A, B	2, 2, 1	s_1, s_2	0, 0	3

   Partitions 1, 4, 7, 9, and 10 correspond to corner points.

e.

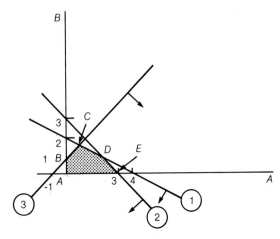

There are alternate optimal solutions: $A = 2$, $B = 1$ (Corner Point E); and $A = 3$, $B = 0$ (Corner Point D) with $Z^* = 3$. The optimal partitions are 4 and 10.

f. 1 to 7 to 9 to 10 or 1 to 4.

13.

C_j	Basic Variables	Basic Variable Values	3	2	0	0
			A	B	S_1	S_2
3	A	2	1	−1	2	0
0	S_2	3	0	2	1	1
	Z_j	6	3	−3	6	0
	$C_j - Z_j$		0	5	−6	0

15. *a.* The pivot element is the 2 in the row of S_2 and the column of Variable B.

b.

C_j	Basic Variables	Basic Variable Values	4	6	0	0
			A	B	S_1	S_2
4	A	⁷⁄₂	1	0	³⁄₂	−½
6	B	³⁄₂	0	1	½	½
	Z_j	23	4	6	9	1
	$C_j - Z_j$		0	0	9	−1

c. 23

d. Yes, the new tableau is optimal. $A = \frac{7}{2}$, $B = \frac{3}{2}$, $S_1 = 0$, and $S_2 = 0$.

17. *a.* There is no pivot element.

b. There is an unbounded optimal solution.

19.

C_j	Basic Variables	Basic Variable Values	2	4	0	−M	−M
			A	B	S	A_1	A_2
−M	A_1	4	−1	2	0	1	0
−M	A_2	3	2	1	−1	0	1
	Z_j	−7M	−M	−3M	M	−M	−M
	$C_j - Z_j$		2 + M	4 + 3M	−M	0	0

The pivot element is the 2 under Variable B in the A_1 row.

CHAPTER 7: EXERCISES

1. max $50.40R - 36BR - 48NR - 51RR + 53.34P - 36BP - 48NP - 51RP$

   st $BR + BP \leq 22000$

   $NR + NP \leq 10000$

   $RR + RP \leq 14000$

   $BR + NR + RR - R = 0$

   $R \leq 30000$

   $-2BR + 2NR + 5RR \geq 0$

   $-3.5BR + 2.2NR + 4.5RR \leq 0$

   $BP + NP + RP - P = 0$

   $P \leq 5000$

   $-6BP - 2NP + RP \geq 0$

   $-3.0BP + 1.8NP + 4.1RP \geq 0$

   $R, P, BR, NR, RR, BP, NP, RP \geq 0$

	R	BR	NR	RR	P	BP	NP	RP		
max	x	x	x	x	x	x	x	x		
st		1				1			$\leq$	x
			1				1		$\leq$	x
				1				1	$\leq$	x
	-1	1	1	1					=	0
	1								$\leq$	x
		x	x	x					$\geq$	0
		x	x	x					$\geq$	0
					-1	1	1	1	=	0
					1				$\leq$	0
						x	x	x	$\leq$	0
						x	x	x	$\geq$	0

3. Add the constraints $-3.6BR + 2NR + 4.3RR \geq 0$ and $-3.5BP + 2.2NP + 4.5RP \geq 0$.

5. In Table 7.3, only the RHS constant of Row 6 changes. The new value is $1,000 - 850 = 150$.

7. The new objective function is min $12x_1 + 12x_2 + 12.30x_3 + 12.60x_4 + 0.20I_1 + 0.20I_2 + 0.205I_3 + 0.21I_4$. Note that the cost on both I_3 and x_3 changed.

9. min $12.81x_1 + 12.61x_2 + 12.41x_3 + 12.21x_4$

   st $x_1 \leq 1000$

   $x_2 \leq 1000$

   $x_3 \leq 1000$

   $x_4 \leq 750$

   $x_1 \geq 900$

   $x_1 + x_2 \geq 1950$

   $x_1 + x_2 + x_3 \geq 2750$

   $x_1 + x_2 + x_3 + x_4 \geq 3650$

   $x_1, x_2, x_3, x_4 \geq 0$

11. The additional objective function terms are $+ 12.60x_5 + 0.21I_5$. The additional constraints are $x_5 \leq 1000$ and $I_4 + x_5 - I_5 = 1075$.

13. Let I_{ij} be the number of units placed in inventory at the beginning of Month i and removed at the beginning of Month j. It is assumed that any units placed in inventory at the beginning of Month 4 are removed at the beginning of Month 5. The model is

   min $12x_1 + 12x_2 + 12.60x_3 + 12.60x_4 + 0.25I_{12} + 0.40I_{13} + 0.55I_{14} + 0.25I_{23} + 0.40I_{24} + 0.25I_{34} + 0.25I_{45}$

   st $x_1 \leq 1000$

   $x_2 \leq 1000$

   $x_3 \leq 1000$

   $x_4 \leq 750$

   $x_1 - I_{12} - I_{13} - I_{14} = 900$

   $I_{12} + x_2 - I_{23} - I_{24} = 1050$

   $I_{13} + I_{23} + x_3 - I_{34} = 800$

   $I_{14} + I_{24} + I_{34} + x_4 - I_{45} = 900$

   $x_1, x_2, x_3, x_4, I_{12}, I_{13}, I_{14}, I_{23}, I_{24}, I_{34}, I_{45} \geq 0$

15. The constraints are the same. The objective function is $12x_1 + 12x_2 + 12.60x_3 + 12.60x_4 + 0.20(100 + I_1)/2 + 0.20(I_1 + I_2)/2 + 0.20(I_2 + I_3)/2 + 0.20(I_3 + I_4)/2$. After collecting terms and deleting the constant, the objective function is $12x_1 + 12x_2 + 12.60x_3 + 12.60x_4 + 0.20I_1 + 0.20I_2 + 0.20I_3 + 0.10I_4$.

17. min $1.15x_{11A} + 1.05x_{11B} + 0.65x_{12} + 0.25x_{13} + 0.6x_{14} + 1.05x_{21A} + 1.10x_{21B} + 0.9x_{22} + 1.05x_{23} + 0.75x_{24} + 0.85x_{31A} + 0.75x_{31B} + 0.75x_{32} + 0.87x_{33} + 0.65x_{34}$

   st $x_{11A} + x_{11B} + x_{12} + x_{13} + x_{14} \leq 500$
   $x_{21A} + x_{21B} + x_{22} + x_{23} + x_{24} \leq 400$
   $x_{31A} + x_{31B} + x_{32} + x_{33} + x_{34} \leq 325$
   $x_{11A} + x_{21A} + x_{31A} = 175$
   $x_{11B} + x_{21B} + x_{31B} = 125$
   $x_{12} + x_{22} + x_{32} = 115$
   $x_{13} + x_{23} + x_{33} = 275$
   $x_{14} + x_{24} + x_{34} = 190$
   All variables nonnegative

19. The constraints are the same as those of Table 7.7. The objective function is

   min $1.25x_{11} + 0.70x_{12} + 0.30x_{13} + 0.65x_{14} + 1.13x_{21} + 0.93x_{22} + 1.08x_{23} + 0.78x_{24} + 0.83x_{31} + 0.78x_{32} + 0.90x_{33} + 0.68x_{34}$

21. min $1.2x_{11} + 0.65x_{12} + 0.25x_{13} + 0.6x_{14} + 1.1x_{21} + 0.9x_{22} + 1.05x_{23} + 0.75x_{24} + 0.8x_{31} + 0.75x_{32} + 0.87x_{33} + 0.65x_{34} + 0.05x_1 + 0.03x_2 + 0.03x_3$

   st $x_{11} + x_{12} + x_{13} + x_{14} - x_1 = 0$
   $x_{21} + x_{22} + x_{23} + x_{24} - x_2 = 0$
   $x_{31} + x_{32} + x_{33} + x_{34} - x_3 = 0$
   $x_1 \leq 500$
   $x_2 \leq 400$
   $x_3 \leq 325$
   $x_{11} + x_{21} + x_{31} = 300$
   $x_{12} + x_{22} + x_{32} = 115$
   $x_{13} + x_{23} + x_{33} = 275$
   $x_{14} + x_{24} + x_{34} = 190$
   All variables nonnegative

23. If the requirement constraints are not of the equal-to type, so that the revenue is fixed, the objective should be profit maximization.

25. min $0.35A_2 + 0.36A_3 + 0.29B_1 + 0.25B_2 + 0.34B_3 + 0.32C_1 + 0.34C_2 + 0.36C_3 + 0.32A_{11} + 0.33A_{12} + 0.34A_{13}$

   st $A_1 + B_1 + C_1 \leq 40$
   $A_2 + B_2 + C_2 \leq 40$
   $A_3 + B_3 + C_3 \leq 40$
   $26A_2 + 23A_3 + 25A_1 = 1000$
   $18B_1 + 19B_2 + 20B_3 = 950$
   $22C_1 + 23C_2 + 20C_3 = 600$
   $A_{11} \leq 20$
   $A_{12} \leq 15$
   $A_1 - A_{11} - A_{12} - A_{13} = 0$
   All variables nonnegative

27. Using the model format of Table 7.12, there are 18 piecewise variables and 9 variables like A_1. The total number of variables is $18 + 9 = 27$. Rows 2 to 7 do not change. There are 9 constraints like Row 8 and 9 constraints like Row 9. The total number of constraints is $6 + 9 + 9 = 24$. These cost functions are not troublesome.

29. The number of both the constraints and the variables is 12.

31. The model is the same as that of Table 7.19 except that the objective function is min $10000TV1 + 9000TV2 + 1500RADIO + 2500MAG + 100U2$.

33. The first stage is

   min $U1$
   st $10000TV1 + 9000TV2 + 1500RADIO + 2500MAG \leq 60000$
   $18000TV1 + 15000TV2 + 1800RADIO + 1900MAG - O1 + U1 = 110000$
   $1000TV1 + 1100TV2 + 120RADIO + 500MAG - O2 + U2 = 7500$
   $RADIO \geq 4$
   $TV1, TV2, RADIO, MAG \geq 0$

   Say that K is the value of the first-stage optimal objective function. Then, the second-stage model is

   min $U2$
   st $10000TV1 + 9000TV2 + 1500RADIO + 2500MAG \leq 60000$
   $18000TV1 + 15000TV2 + 1800RADIO + 1900MAG = 110000 + K$
   $1000TV1 + 1100TV2 + 120RADIO + 500MAG - O2 + U2 = 7500$
   $RADIO \geq 4$
   $TV1, TV2, RADIO, MAG \geq 0$.

   Note that $110000 + K$ is a constant.

CHAPTER 8: EXERCISES

1. *a.* Let Chicago, Atlanta, and Los Angeles be Supply Points 1, 2, and 3, respectively. Let St. Louis, Phoenix, Milwaukee, and Bangor be Demand Points 1, 2, 3, and 4, respectively. Let x_{ij} be the amount shipped from i to j.

$$\min 55x_{11} + 87x_{12} + 45x_{13} + 105x_{14} + 83x_{21} + 123x_{22} + 67x_{23} + 66x_{24} + 105x_{31} + 56x_{32} + 111x_{33} + 145x_{34}$$

$$\begin{aligned}
\text{st} \quad & x_{11} + x_{12} + x_{13} + x_{14} \leq 200 \\
& x_{21} + x_{22} + x_{23} + x_{24} \leq 150 \\
& x_{31} + x_{32} + x_{33} + x_{34} \leq 330 \\
& x_{11} + x_{21} + x_{31} = 100 \\
& x_{12} + x_{22} + x_{32} = 125 \\
& x_{13} + x_{23} + x_{33} = 240 \\
& x_{14} + x_{24} + x_{34} = 170 \\
& \text{All } x_{ij} \geq 0
\end{aligned}$$

b. The total supply is 680, and the total demand is 635. There is a feasible solution because the total demand does not exceed the total supply.

c. No. There are limited supplies, and all of the costs are positive.

d. Unbalanced because the total supply does not equal the total demand.

3.

55	87	45	105	0	
					200
83	123	67	66	0	
					150
105	56	111	145	0	
					330
100	125	240	170	45	

5. *a.* Yes. It is balanced because the sum of the net stock positions is 0.

b. $x_{13} + x_{14} = 5, x_{25} = 4, x_{36} - x_{13} = -2,$ $x_{45} + x_{46} - x_{14} = 0, x_{56} + x_{57} - x_{25} - x_{45} = 0, -x_{36} - x_{46} - x_{56} = -4, -x_{57} = -3.$

7. *a.* Yes.

b.

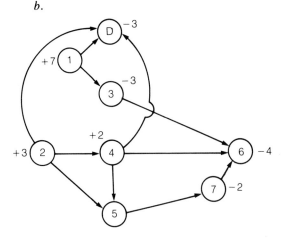

The dummy node is Node D. The costs to the dummy node are 0.

c. The constraints with a positive net stock position are $\leq$. The other constraints are $=$. $x_{13} \leq 7, x_{24} + x_{25} \leq 3, x_{36} - x_{13} = -3,$ $x_{45} + x_{46} - x_{24} \leq 2, x_{57} - x_{25} - x_{45} = 0,$ $-x_{36} - x_{46} - x_{76} = -4, -x_{57} = -2.$

d. $x_{13} + x_{1D} = 7, x_{24} + x_{25} + x_{2D} = 3, x_{36} - x_{13} = -3, x_{45} + x_{46} + x_{4D} - x_{24} = 2, x_{57} - x_{25} - x_{45} = 0, -x_{36} - x_{46} - x_{76} = -4, -x_{57} = -2.$

9. *a.* Let x_{ij} be 1 if Job i is assigned to Machine j.

$$\min 5x_{11} + 1x_{12} + 7x_{13} + 9x_{14} + 6x_{15} + 6x_{21} + 3x_{23} + 2x_{24} + 7x_{25} + 8x_{31} + 6x_{32} + 5x_{35} + 3x_{41} + 6x_{43} + 3x_{44} + 12x_{52} + 8x_{53}$$

$$\begin{aligned}
\text{st} \quad & x_{11} + x_{12} + x_{13} + x_{14} + x_{15} = 1 \\
& x_{21} + x_{23} + x_{24} + x_{25} = 1 \\
& x_{31} + x_{32} + x_{35} = 1 \\
& x_{41} + x_{43} + x_{44} = 1 \\
& x_{52} + x_{53} = 1 \\
& x_{11} + x_{21} + x_{31} + x_{41} = 1 \\
& x_{12} + x_{32} + x_{52} = 1 \\
& x_{13} + x_{23} + x_{43} + x_{53} = 1 \\
& x_{14} + x_{24} + x_{44} = 1 \\
& x_{15} + x_{25} + x_{35} = 1 \\
& \text{All } x_{ij} \geq 0
\end{aligned}$$

b. *M* represents a very large number.

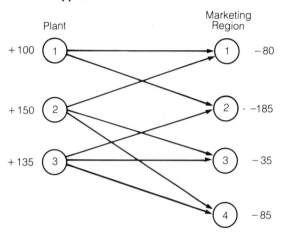

Machine

	1	2	3	4	5	
1	5	1	7	9	6	1
2	6	*M*	3	2	7	1
3	8	6	*M*	*M*	5	1
4	3	*M*	6	3	*M*	1
5	*M*	12	8	*M*	*M*	1
	1	1	1	1	1	

Job (row label at left)

c. Only the arcs for possible assignments are included. The arc costs are the times.

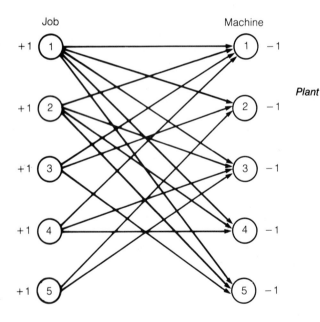

b. You must add the production cost and the transportation cost. For example, the cost for (1,1) is 800 + 30 = 830. The costs appear in Part *d*.

Plant → Marketing Region

```
+100  (1) ────────────→ (1)  −80
+150  (2) ────────────→ (2)  −185
+135  (3) ────────────→ (3)  −35
                        (4)  −85
```

c. It is balanced, so a dummy node is not needed.

d.

	Marketing Region				
	1	**2**	**3**	**4**	
1	830	820	*M*	*M*	100
2	795	*M*	775	795	150
3	*M*	625	615	590	135
	80	185	35	85	

(Plant label at left)

e. min $830x_{11} + 820x_{12} + 795x_{21} + 775x_{23} + 795x_{24} + 625x_{32} + 615x_{33} + 590x_{34}$

st $x_{11} + x_{12} = 100$
$x_{21} + x_{23} + x_{24} = 150$
$x_{32} + x_{33} + x_{34} = 135$
$x_{11} + x_{21} = 80$
$x_{12} + x_{32} = 185$
$x_{23} + x_{33} = 35$
$x_{24} + x_{34} = 85$
All $x_{ij} \geq 0$

11. *a.* The total capacity is 385 and the total requirement is 385, so the problem is balanced.

13. *a.* Node 1's net stock position is +1, and Node 7's is −1. The stock position of all the other nodes is 0.

b. min $5x_{12} + 4x_{13} + 2x_{14} + 7x_{25} + 2x_{35} +$
$3x_{34} + 3x_{45} + 4x_{46} + 1x_{56} + 4x_{57} +$
$8x_{67}$

st $x_{12} + x_{13} + x_{14} = 1$
$x_{25} - x_{12} = 0$
$x_{34} + x_{35} - x_{13} = 0$
$x_{45} + x_{46} - x_{14} - x_{34} = 0$
$x_{56} + x_{57} - x_{25} - x_{35} - x_{45} = 0$
$x_{67} - x_{46} - x_{56} = 0$
$-x_{47} - x_{67} = -1$
All $x_{ij} \geq 0$

15. *a.* The total supply is 314, and the total demand is 321. The dummy supply amount is $321 - 314 = 7$.

b.

Demand

	1	2	3	
1	10	5	4	205
2	6	2	9	40
Supply 3	8	3	5	69
D	0	0	0	7
	100	87	134	

c.

Demand

	1	2	3	
1	-23	-29	-29.50	205
2	-27	-32	-24.50	40
Supply 3	-25	-31	-28.50	69
D	0	0	0	7
	100	87	134	

17. *a.*

b. Let x_{ij} be the flow from i to j. That is, $x_{ij} = 1$ if Arc (i, j) is on the critical path.

max $8x_{12} + 5x_{13} + 4x_{34} + 12x_{25} + 5x_{45} +$
$9x_{56}$

st $x_{12} + x_{13} = 1$
$x_{23} + x_{25} - x_{12} = 0$
$x_{34} - x_{13} = 0$
$x_{45} - x_{34} = 0$
$x_{56} - x_{25} - x_{45} = 0$
$-x_{56} = -1$
All $x_{ij} \geq 0$

c. Let S_i be the starting time of Activity i, and let F be the finish time of the project.

min F

st $SA = 0$
$SB = 0$
$S_{\text{Dummy}} \geq SA + 8$
$SC \geq SA + 5$
$SC \geq S_{\text{Dummy}} + 0$
$SD \geq SC + 4$
$SE \geq SB + 8$
$SF \geq SD + 5$
$SF \geq SE + 12$
$F = SF + 9$
All variables ≥ 0.

All of the variables must be transposed to the left of the relationships.

19.

Activity	ES	EF	LS	LF	Total Slack	Critical
A	0	5	3	8	3	
B	0	8	0	8	0	Yes
C	8	12	11	15	3	
Dummy	8	8	11	11	3	
D	12	17	15	20	3	
E	8	20	8	20	0	Yes
F	20	29	20	29	0	Yes

The critical path is B—E—F.

21. *a.* Without crashing, the project takes 28 days and the critical path is A—B—D—F. The critical activity with the smallest crash cost is B. Crashing Activity B one day decreases the project time to 27 days. Activity A has the smallest crash cost among the remaining critical activities, so it is crashed for one day.
b. The total crash cost is $950.
c. The critical path is the same, A—B—D—F.

23. *a.*

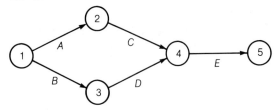

b.

Activity	Expected Time	Variance
A	3	4/36
B	4	4/36
C	6	4/36
D	4	4/36
E	6	16/36

c–d.

Activity	ES	EF	LS	LF
A	0	3	0	3
B	0	4	1	5
C	3	9	3	9
D	4	8	5	9
E	9	15	9	15

e. The critical activities are A, C, and E.
f. 15
g. The variance is $(4 + 4 + 16)/36 = {}^{24}\!/_{36}$.
h. $Z = (15 - 15)/0.8165 = 0$. The probability is 0.5.

CHAPTER 9: EXERCISES

1. *a, c.*

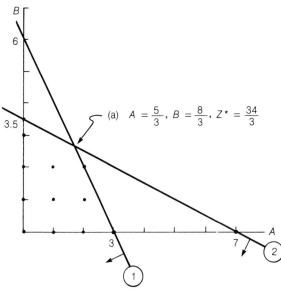

(a) $A = \frac{5}{3}$, $B = \frac{8}{3}$, $Z^* = \frac{34}{3}$

b. $A = 2$ and $B = 3$.
d. The rounded solution is not feasible; it violates both constraints.
e. No. The best integer feasible solution is $A = 2$, $B = 2$, and $Z^* = 10$.

3. *a, c.*

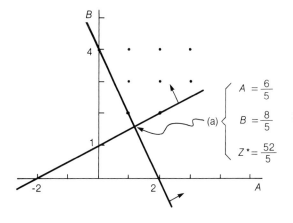

(a) $A = \frac{6}{5}$

$B = \frac{8}{5}$

$Z^* = \frac{52}{5}$

b. $A = 1$, $B = 2$
d. The rounded solution is feasible.
e. Yes.

5. a. Let $Y = 1$ if $A > 0$ and $Y = 0$ if $A = 0$.
b. From the first constraint, $A \leq 10$.
c. min $120Y + 150A + 100B$
   st $A + 2B \leq 10$
   $A + B \geq 5$
   $A - 10Y \leq 0$
   $A, B \geq 0$
   Y 0 or 1

7. Let $Y_{ij} = 1$ if $X_{ij} > 0$ and $Y_{ij} = 0$ if $X_{ij} = 0$, for $i = A$, B, C and $j = 1, 2, 3, 4$. The new objective function is
   min $1000YA + 1200YB + 1150YC + 125A + 120B + 105C + 12A1 + 18A2 + 2A3 + 15A4 + 3B1 + 7B2 + 21B3 + 11B4 + 7C1 + 10C2 + 16C3 + 21C4 + 10YA1 + 10YA2 + 10YA3 + 10YA4 + 10B1 + 10YB2 + 10YB3 + 10YB4 + 10YC1 + 10YC2 + 10YC3 + 10YC4$
   The following constraints must be added:
   $A1 - 20YA1 \leq 0$, $A2 - 25YA2 \leq 0$, $A3 - 50YA3 \leq 0$, $A4 - 75YA4 \leq 0$, $B1 - 20YB1 \leq 0$, $B2 - 25YB2 \leq 0$, $B3 - 50YB3 \leq 0$, $B4 - 75YB4 \leq 0$, $C1 - 20YC1 \leq 0$, $C2 - 25YC2 \leq 0$, $C3 - 50YC3 \leq 0$, $C4 - 75YC4 \leq 0$.
   All Y_{ij} are binary integer variables.

9. $YA + YB = 1$

11. Starting with the linear programming model, you add constraints to force the approximation for x_2 to be correctly determined for each of the four line segments. Thus, there are four cases. For example, you add $x_{2b} = x_{2c} = x_{2d} = 0$ to force the value to be in the first line segment and you add $x_{2a} = 0.5$ and $x_{2c} = x_{2d} = 0$ to force it to be in the second line segment. After solving the four linear programming models, you choose the solution with the largest objective function value.

13. There are two cases because A_3 is either equal to 0 or it is positive. For the first case, add the constraint $A_3 = 0$ to the linear programming model. For the second case, solve the linear programming model and then add the fixed charge cost to the objective function value if A_3 is positive. Choose the solution with the smallest cost.

15. Let O_{ij} be the number of hours of overtime for Product i on Machine j. Note that because overtime costs more than regular time, all of

the regular time for a machine will be used before any overtime is used on it. This piecewise linear cost function is not troublesome.

$$\min \ 32A_1 + 35A_2 + 36A_3 + 29B_1 + 25B_2 + $$
$$34B_3 + 32C_1 + 34C_2 + 36C_3 + 42O_{A1} + $$
$$45O_{A2} + 46O_{A3} + 39_{B1} + 35O_{B2} + $$
$$44O_{B3} + 42O_{C1} + 44O_{C2} + 46O_{C3}$$

st $A_1 + B_1 + C_1 \le 40$
$A_2 + B_2 + C_2 \le 40$
$A_3 + B_3 + C_3 \le 40$
$O_{A1} + O_{B1} + O_{C1} \le 20$
$O_{A2} + O_{B2} + O_{C2} \le 20$
$O_{A3} + O_{B3} + O_{C3} \le 20$
$25A_1 + 26A_2 + 23A_3 + 25O_{A1} + 26O_{A2}$
$+ 23O_{A3} = 1000$
$18B_1 + 19B_2 + 20B_3 + 18O_{B1} + 19O_{B2}$
$+ 20O_{B3} = 950$
$22C_1 + 23C_2 + 20C_3 + 22O_{C1} + 23O_{C2}$
$+ 20O_{C3} = 600$
All variables ≥ 0

17. *b.* From the second constraint, $B \le 4$.
   c. The function values at 0, 1, 2, 3, and 4 are 1, 0.5, 0.333, 0.25, and 0.2, respectively. The piecewise linear approximation of the objective function term for B is $1 - 0.5B1 - 0.167B2 - 0.083B3 - 0.05B4$. The constant is not included in the objective function of the model.
   d. This is troublesome because the objective is maximization and the slopes of the line segments are increasing as B increases. Binary variables are required.
   e. min $2A - 0.5B1 - 0.167B2 - 0.083B3 - 0.05B4$
   st $2A + B \ge 12$
   $A + B \le 4$
   $B - B1 - B2 - B3 - B4 = 0$
   $B1 \le 1$
   $Y1 - B1 \le 0$
   $B2 - Y1 \le 0$
   $Y2 - B2 \le 0$
   $B3 - Y2 \le 0$
   $Y3 - B3 \le 0$
   $B4 - Y3 \le 0$
   $Y_i = 0$ or 1, $i = 1, 2, 3$
   All variables ≥ 0
   f. min $2A - 0.5B1 - 0.167B2 - 0.083B3 - 0.05B4$

st $2A + B1 + B2 + B3 + B4 \ge 12$
$A + B1 + B2 + B3 + B4 \le 4$
$B1 \le 1$
$Y1 - B1 \le 0$
$B2 - Y1 \le 0$
$Y2 - B2 \le 0$
$B3 - Y2 \le 0$
$Y3 - B3 \le 0$
$B4 - Y3 \le 0$
Y_i 0 or 1, $i = 1, 2, 3$
All variables ≥ 0

19. *b.* From the second constraint, $A \le 3$.
   c. The function values at 0, 1, 2, and 3 are 1, 0.667, 0.5, and 0.4, respectively. The piecewise linear approximation of the objective function term for A is $1 - 0.333A1 - 0.167A2 - 0.1A3$. The constant is not included in the model's objective function.
   d. This is not troublesome because the objective is minimization and the slopes of the line segments are increasing as A increases. Binary variables are not required.
   e. min $-0.333A1 - 0.167A2 - 0.1A3 + 3B$
   st $3A + 3B \le 12$
   $2A + B \le 6$
   $A - A1 - A2 - A3 = 0$
   $A_i \le 1$ $i = 1, 2, 3$
   All variables ≥ 0

21. Let $SA = 1$ if Sue serves Customer A, and let it be 0 otherwise. Define the other 11 variables similarly.
   max $40000SA + 25000SB + 32000SC + 18000SD + 25000MA + 32000MB + 18000MC + 27000MD + 13000AA + 41000AB + 27000AC + 19000AD$
   st $SA + MA + AA = 1$
   $SB + MB + AB = 1$
   $SC + MC + AC = 1$
   $SD + MD + AD = 1$
   $SA + SB + SC + SD \ge 1$
   $MA + MB + MC + MD \ge 1$
   $AA + AB + AC + AD \ge 1$
   $SA + SB + SC + SD \le 2$
   $MA + MB + MC + MD \le 2$
   $AA + AB + AC + AD \le 2$
   $SA, SB, SC, SD, MA, MB, MC, MD,$
   AA, AB, AC, AD 0 or 1

23. Let $A = 1$ if Project A is funded, and let it be 0

otherwise. Define the other three variables similarly.

a. max $30000A + 45000B + 25000C + 30000D$
   st $15000A + 40000B + 20000C + 25000D \leq 65000$
   $25000A + 15000B + 15000C + 10000D \leq 65000$
   $15000A + 10000B + 25000C + 30000D \leq 65000$
   A, B, C, D 0 or 1

b. $A + C = 1$

c. $A + C \leq 1$ and $D \leq A + C$.

25. b. From the first constraint, $B \leq 3$.

c. The function values at 0, 1, 2, and 3 are 1, 0.5, 0.333, and 0.25, respectively. The piecewise linear approximation of the function of B in the second constraint is $1 - 0.5B1 - 0.167B2 - 0.083B3$.

d. This is not troublesome because the constraint is $\leq$ and the slopes of the line segments are increasing as A increases. Binary variables are not required.

e. min $A + 3B$
   st $3A + 2B \leq 6$
   $2A - 0.5B1 - 0.167B2 - 0.083B3 \leq 5$
   $B - B1 - B2 - B3 = 0$
   $B_i \leq 1$ $i = 1, 2, 3$
   All variables ≥ 0

27. b. From the first constraint, $B \leq 2$.

c. The function values at 0, 1, and 2 are -0.5, -0.333, and -0.25, respectively. The piecewise linear approximation of the function of B in the second constraint is $-0.5 + 0.167B1 + 0.083B2$.

d. This is troublesome because the constraint is $\leq$ and the slopes of the line segments are decreasing as B increases. A binary variable is required.

e. min $2A + 3B$
   st $3A + 2B \leq 6$
   $2A + 0.167B1 + 0.083B2 \leq 6.5$
   $B - B1 - B2 = 0$
   $B1 \leq 1$
   $Y1 - B1 \leq 0$
   $B2 - Y1 \leq 0$
   $Y1$ 0 or 1
   All variables ≥ 0

CHAPTER 10: EXERCISES

1. a.

Decision Alternative	Strong Economy	Weak Economy
Introduce new	140,000	7,000
Keep existing	35,000	25,000

b. Decision Alternative 1—140,000.

c. Decision Alternative 2—25,000.

d. Decision Alternative 1, which has the largest average, 73,500.

e. No, neither decision alternative is dominated. There is no correct answer that you would select. The selection you make depends on your attitude toward risk.

3. a. Yes. Decision Alternative 2 dominates Decision Alternative 1.

b.

Decision Alternative	State of Nature			
	1	2	3	4
2	0	0	150	0
3	900	1,350	0	200

c. Decision Alternative 2—min (150, 1,350) = 150.

5. If Decision Alternative 1 was observed to be dominated by Decision Alternative 2, then Decision Alternative 1 is eliminated from consideration.

a. Decision Alternative 2—min (1,300, 600, 700) = 600.

b. Decision Alternative 2—min (6,100, 1,200, 2,300) = 1,200.

c. Decision Alternative 2, which has the smallest average, 900.

7.

State of Nature	Numerical Score	Numerical Score/T
No new product	1.0	0.6250
Cosmetic changes	0.5	0.3125
Radically new	0.1	0.0625
T	1.6	1.0000

9. *a.* Mean = 3.2%
   Standard deviation = $(4.3 - 3.2)/0.67 =$ 1.6418
   b. $Z = (0 - 3.2)/1.6418 = -1.949$. The probability that the rate of growth is greater than 0 is 0.9744.

11. No. The response does not indicate that a symmetric distribution is appropriate.

13. *a, b.*

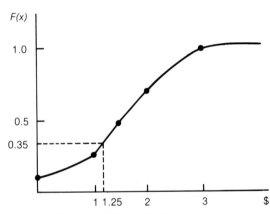

   c. The probability is 0.35.

15. *a.* Mean = 1.5 years
   Standard deviation = $(2.5 - 1.5)/0.67 =$ 1.49
   b. $Z = (0 - 1.5)/1.49 = -1.007$. The probability is 0.16.
   c. No. There is too large a probability of a negative number of years.

17. *a.* $E(1) = 94,400$; $E(2) = 32,000$. Introduce the new product.
   b. $EOL(1) = 11,100$; $EOL(2) = 73,500$. Introduce the new product.
   c. Yes.

19.

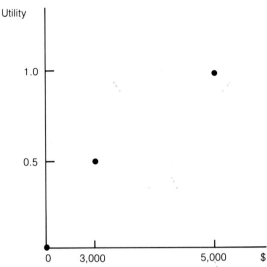

21. *a.* 0.5
   b. The expected utility of the lottery is 0.25; the expected utility of keeping the $5,000 is 0.3. Don't buy the lottery.

23. *a.* No.
   b. Action 2 is dominated by Action 1.
   c, d.

	Player 2		
Player 1	Action 1	Action 3	Maximum
Action 1	6	2	6
Action 2	6	7	7
Action 3	5	3	5*
Minimum	5*	2	

   Player 1's minimax strategy is Action 3. Player 2's maximin strategy is Action 1.
   e. Yes.
   f. 5

25. *a.* Player 1's minimax strategy is Action 2.
   b. Player 2's maximin strategy is Action 1.
   c. No.
   d. Player 1 chooses Action 1 with a probability of ¾ and Action 2 with a probability of ¼.

e. Player 2 chooses Action 1 with a probability of ½ and Action 2 with a probability
of ½.

f. ¹¹⁄₂

CHAPTER 11: EXERCISES

1. *a, b.*

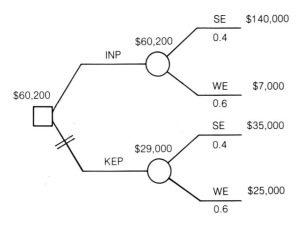

c.

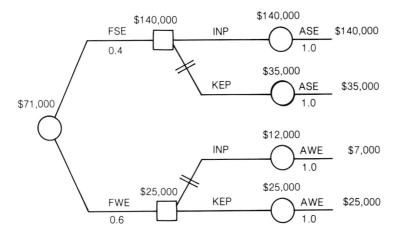

$$EPPI = \$71,000, \ EVPI = 71,000 - 60,200$$
$$= \$10,800$$

d. The EOL table is

Decision Alternative	Strong Economy	Weak Economy	EOL
Introduce new	0	18,000	10,800
Keep existing	105,000	0	42,000

Decision Alternative 1, introduce the new product, is selected.

e. $EVPI = EOL (1) = \$10,800$

3. *a.* Yes. Decision Alternative 1 is dominated by Decision Alternative 2.

b.

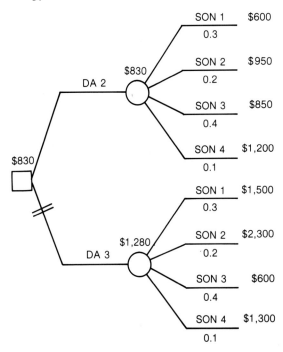

5. *a.* See answer to Exercise 3*b*.
Select Decision Alternative 2, which has an expected cost of \$830.

b.

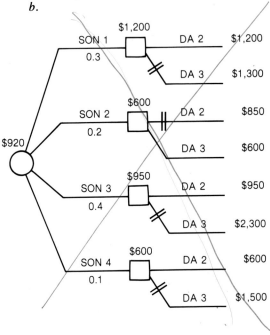

$EPPI = \cancel{920}\ 730$

c. $EVPI = 920 - 830 = \cancel{\$90}$

$830 - 730 = \$100$

7. *a.*

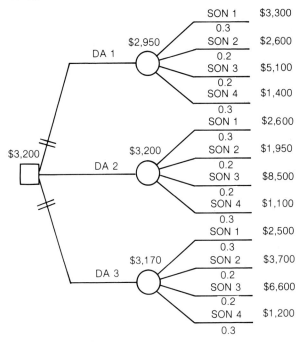

	SON 1	$3,300
	0.3	
$2,950	SON 2	$2,600
DA 1	0.2	
	SON 3	$5,100
	0.2	
	SON 4	$1,400
	0.3	

Select Decision Alternative 2, which has an expected profit of $3,200.
b. EPPI = 3,850
c. EVPI = 3,850 − 3,200 = $650
d. Decision Alternative 2 is selected.
e. EVPI = EOL (2) = 0.3(700) + 0.2(1,750) + 0.2(0) + 0.3(300) = $650

9. *a.* The total number of trials is 20. The joint probability table is

	Success	Failure	Marginal
Recommended	0.60	0.20	0.80
Not recommended	0.10	0.10	0.20
Marginal	0.70	0.30	1.00

b. 0.70
c. P(Recommended) = P(Recommended| Success) × P(Success) + P(Recommended|Not success) × P(Not success) = (0.60/0.70) (0.9) + (0.2/0.3) (0.1) = 0.831
d. Only if there is reason to believe that the conditional probabilities are the same.

11. *a.*

Posterior probabilities for FSE:

State of Nature	Prior Probability	Forecast Probability Conditional on Actual	Joint Probability	Posterior Probability
ASE	0.3	0.9	0.27	0.6585
AWE	0.7	0.2	0.14	0.3415
			0.41	1.0000

Posterior probabilities for FWE:

State of Nature	Prior Probability	Forecast Probability Conditional on Actual	Joint Probability	Posterior Probability
ASE	0.3	0.1	0.03	0.05085
AWE	0.7	0.8	0.56	0.94915
			0.59	1.00000

b.

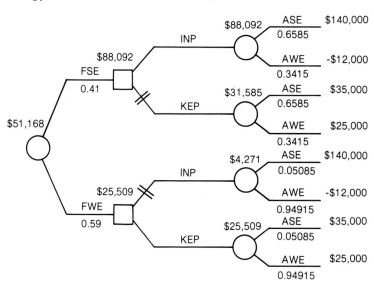

$EPII = \$51,168$

c. Without the expert, $E(1) = 33,600$ and $E(2) = 28,000$, so you introduce the new product. $EVII = 51,168 - 33,600 = \$17,568$.

d. Yes.

13.

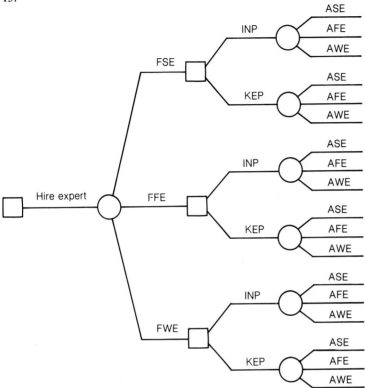

15. *a.* Figure 11.6 does not include the expert's fee. One approach is to adjust the terminal node values to reflect a $10,000 credit when the expert is wrong.

b.

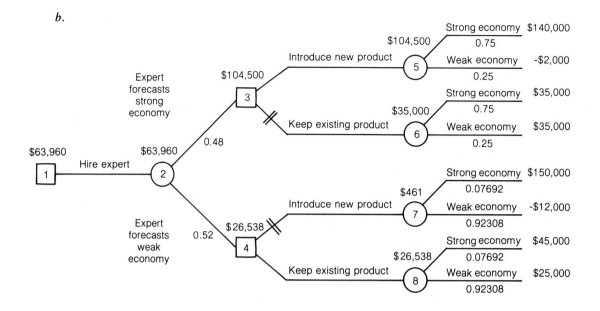

After the $10,000 fee has been paid, the expected profit is $53,960. This is greater than the expected profit without the imperfect expert, $48,800.

c. The decision strategy is unchanged. Hire the expert. Then, if the expert forecasts a strong economy, introduce the new product. If the expert forecasts a weak economy, keep the existing product.

17.

Stage 3 for the shortest-route problem:

State	$f_3(i)$	$d_3^*(i)$
4	5	7
5	7	7
6	6	7

Stage 2 for the shortest-route problem:

	Decision				
State	4	5	6	$f_2(i)$	$d_2^*(i)$
2	4 + 5	3 + 7	2 + 6	8	6
3	4 + 5	5 + 7	6 + 6	9	4

Stage 1 for the shortest-route problem:

	Decision			
State	2	3	$f_1(i)$	$d_1^*(i)$
1	7 + 8	5 + 9	14	3

Node 1 to 3 to 4 to 7. The length is 14.

19.

Stage 3 for the knapsack problem:

State	$f_3(i)$	$d_3{}^*(i)$
0	0	0
1	2	1
2	4	2
3	6	3
4	8	4
5	10	5

Stage 2 for the knapsack problem:

	Decision				
State	0	1	2	$f_2(i)$	$d_2{}^*(i)$
0	0 + 0	—	—	0	0
1	0 + 2	—	—	2	0
2	0 + 4	6 + 0	—	6	1
3	0 + 6	6 + 2	—	8	1
4	0 + 8	6 + 4	12 + 0	12	2
5	0 + 10	6 + 6	12 + 2	14	2

Stage 1 for the knapsack problem:

	Decision			
State	0	1	$f_1(i)$	$d_1{}^*(i)$
5	0 + 14	10 + 2	14	0

Item 1: 0; Item 2: 2; Item 3: 1. The total benefit is 14.

CHAPTER 12: EXERCISES

1. *a.* Average error = 3.0
   Mean percent error = 2.467%
   Smoothed error = 4.08
   b. Average error.
   c. The forecast has a bias of underestimating demand.

3. *a.* Standard deviation = 3.52
   b. Mean squared error = 19.33
   c. Mean absolute deviation = 4.0
   d. Mean absolute percent error = 3.418%

5.

Week (t)	Actual Demand	N = 3 Moving Average	One-Period-Ahead Forecast	Forecast Errors	N = 2 Moving Average	One-Period-Ahead Forecast	Forecast Errors	Weighted Moving Average	One-Period-Ahead Forecast	Forecast Errors
1	105									
2	120				112.50			112.50		
3	125	116.67			122.50	112.50	12.50	122.50	112.50	12.50
4	108	117.67	116.67	−8.67	116.50	122.50	−14.50	116.50	122.50	−14.50
5	130	121.00	117.67	12.33	119.00	116.50	13.50	119.00	116.50	13.50
Total				3.67			11.50			11.50

7.

Month (t)	Actual Demand	Moving Average	Forecast	Forecast Errors	Squared Forecast Errors
1	100				
2	105	102.50			
3	102	103.50	102.50	−0.50	
4	101	101.50	103.50	−2.50	6.25
5	95	98.00	101.50	−6.50	42.25
6	97	96.00	98.00	−1.00	1.00
7	102	99.50	96.00	6.00	36.00
8	104	103.00	99.50	4.50	20.25
9	99	101.50	103.00	−4.00	16.00
10	97	98.00	101.50	−4.50	20.25
11	102	99.50	98.00	4.00	16.00
12	101	101.50	99.50	1.50	2.25
13	96	98.50	101.50	−5.50	30.25
14	101	98.50	98.50	2.50	6.25
15	98	99.50	98.50	−0.50	0.25
16	99	98.50	99.50	−0.50	0.25
17	100	99.50	98.50	1.50	2.25
18	101	100.50	99.50	1.50	2.25
19	98	99.50	100.50	−2.50	6.25
20	101	99.50	99.50	1.50	2.25
21	103	102.00	99.50	3.50	12.25
22	99	101.00	102.00	−3.00	9.00
23	100	99.50	101.00	−1.00	1.00
24	99	99.50	99.50	−0.50	0.25
Total	2,400			−6.00	232.75

MSE = 10.5 for *N* = 2 and *MSE* = 9.48 for *N* = 3; the MSE is smaller for *N* = 3.

9.

Week (*t*)	Actual Demand	Naive Model One-Period- Ahead Forecast	Forecast Errors	Smoothed Forecast Error
1	140			4.00
2	135	140	−5	2.20
3	138	135	3	2.36
4	149	138	11	4.09
5	136	149	−13	0.67
Total			4	

   a. 140

   b. 135

   c. 138

   d. $(-5 + 3 + 11)/3 = 3$

   e. See above.

   f. The forecast for Week 5 is the actual demand in Week 4, 149.

   g. The average forecast error is $(-5 + 3 + 11 - 13)/4 = -1.00$. The smoothed forecast error is $0.2(-13.00) + (1 - 0.2)(4.09) = 0.67$.

   h. The smoothed forecast error.

11. *a.*

Period (*t*)	Actual Demand	A_t	One-Period- Ahead Forecast	Forecast Errors	Squared Forecast Errors	Absolute Value of e_t
0		25.00				
1	26	25.20	25.00	1.00	1.00	1.00
2	22	24.56	25.20	−3.20	10.24	3.20
3	28	25.25	24.56	3.44	11.83	3.44
4	24	25.00	25.25	−1.25	1.56	1.25
Total				−0.01	24.63	8.89

    $F_{4+1} = 25$.

b.

Period (*t*)	Actual Demand	A_t	One-Period- Ahead Forecast	Forecast Errors	Squared Forecast Errors	Absolute Value of e_t
0		25.00				
1	26	25.50	25.00	1.00	1.00	1.00
2	22	23.75	25.50	−3.50	12.25	3.50
3	28	25.88	23.75	4.25	18.06	4.25
4	24	24.94	25.88	−1.88	3.52	1.88
Total				−0.13	34.83	10.63

   c. $MSE = 6.16$ for Part *a* and 8.71 for Part *b*; $\alpha = 0.2$ is best.

   d. $MAD = 2.22$ for Part *a* and 2.66 for Part *b*; $\alpha = 0.2$ is best.

13. *a.*

Period (t)	Actual Demand	L_t	T_t	One-Period-Ahead Forecast	Absolute Forecast Error	Value of e_t
0		25.00	2.00			
1	25	26.60	1.84	27.00	−2.00	2.00
2	27	28.15	1.72	28.44	−1.44	1.44
3	30	29.90	1.73	29.88	0.12	0.12
4	31	31.51	1.68	31.64	−0.64	0.64
Total					−3.95	4.20

   b. $F_{4+1} = 31.51 + 1.68 = 33.19$

   c. $MAD = 1.05$

15. *a.* $F_{65+1} = 1{,}040$

   b. $F_{65+2} = 1{,}080$

   c. $L_{66} = 0.2(1{,}030) + 0.8(1{,}040) = 1{,}038$; $T_{66} = 0.2(1{,}038 - 1{,}000) + 0.8(40) = 39.6$; $F_{66+1} = 1{,}038 + 39.6 = 1{,}077.6$

   d. $SMAD_{66} = 0.3(2) + 0.7(11) = 8.3$

   e. The forecast is $1{,}077.6 \pm 1.25(1.96)(8.3) = 20.34$; between 1,057.3 and 1,097.9.

   f. The forecast is $1{,}077.6 \pm 1.25(2.575)(1.629) = 26.72$; between 1,050.9 and 1,104.3.

17. *a.* $F_{102+1} = L_{102}(1.7) = 1{,}530$; $F_{102+2} = L_{102}(1.5) = 1{,}350$

   b. $L_{103} = 0.2(1{,}700/1.7) + 0.8(900) = 920$; $S_{103} = 0.3(1{,}700/920) + 0.7(1.7) = 1.744$

   c. $F_{103+1} = L_{103}(1.5) = 1{,}380$

   d. $F_{103+12} = L_{103}S_{103+12-12} = 1{,}604.5$

19. *a.* Using millions of dollars for sales and thousands of dollars for advertising, $a = -66.1533$ and $b = 1.1351$.

   b. Sales $= -66.1533 + 1.1351(100) = \$47.3567$ million

c.

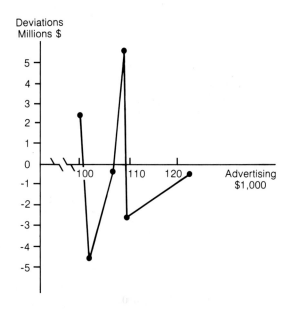

Deviations Millions $

d. There does not appear to be a pattern in the deviations, so a linear model is appropriate.

CHAPTER 13: EXERCISES

1. *a.* $c_h = I(C) = (0.1) (2.50) = \$0.25$
   b. $Q^* = 1,000$
   c. $TAC^* = \$250$
   d. $TAC(1,100) = 0.25(1,100/2) + 25(5,000/1,100) = \$251.14$
   e. $1,000/5,000 = 0.2$ year

3. *a.* $c_h = IC = (0.15) (400)/12 = \$5$
   b. Q^* 100
   c. $TMC^* = 500$
   d. $TAC^* = (12) (500) = \$6,000$
   e. $T = 100/250 = 0.4$ month
   f. $T = 0.4/12 = 0.03333$ year
   g. $3,000/100 = 30$

5. Reorder point = Lead-time demand = 125 units

7. *a.* 400
   b. 447
   c. 632

9. *a.* $EBQ^* = 2,000$
   b. $TAC^* = \$15,000$
   c. $10,000/2,000 = 5$
   d. $2,000/20,000 = 0.1$ year
   e. $1 - (10,000/20,000) = 0.5$
   f. $Q(1 - D/P) = 2,000(0.5) = 1,000$ units

11. *a.* 100
    b. The TAC, including the purchasing cost, for an order quantity of 100 is \$10,117.
    c. The value is an integer.

13. *a.* The cumulative Poisson probability $F(2) = 0.125$. The probability of no shortage if $R = 2$ is $F(2) = 0.125$. The probability of a shortage is $1 - F(2) = 0.875$.
    b. Any reorder point of 9 or more has $F(R) > 0.95$. The smallest such reorder point is 9.

15. $Q = 300$ and $D = 3,600$.
    a. $F(Z) = 0.95$, $Z = 1.645$, $R = 50 + 1.645(10) = 66.45$
    b. $F(Z) = 0.99$, $Z = 2.327$, $R = 50 + 2.327(10) = 73.27$
    c. $F(Z) = 0.999$, $Z = 3.09$, $R = 50 + 3.09(10) = 80.9$
    d. $N(Z) = 300(0.01)/10 = 0.3$, $Z = 0.217$, $R = 50 + 0.217(10) = 52.17$

e. $N(Z) = 300(0.001)/10 = 0.03$, $Z = 1.49$, $R = 50 + 1.49(10) = 64.9$
f. $N(Z) = 300(0.0001)/10 = 0.003$, $Z = 2.367$, $R = 50 + 2.367(10) = 73.67$

17. *a.* 456.07
    b. $F(R) = 1 - [456.07(1.25)]/[2,600(10)] = 0.9781$; $Z = 2.016$, $R = 50 + 2.016(10) = 70.16$
    c. $1 - F(R) = 0.0219$
    d. $10N(2.016) = 0.08134$
    e. $0.08134(2,600/456.07) = 0.4637$

19. *a.* The gross component requirement for wheels is 800. The net component requirement for wheels is $800 - 100 = 700$. The gross component requirement for engine assemblies and handles is 200. The net component requirement for engine assemblies is $200 - 10 = 190$. The net component requirement for handles is $200 - 50 = 150$.
    b. The gross component requirement for carburetors, engine blocks, and spark plugs is 190. The net component requirement for carburetors is $190 - 0 = 190$. The net component requirement for engine blocks is $190 - 50 = 140$. The net component requirement for spark plugs is $190 - 100 = 90$.

21. *a.* Because the lead time for the engine assemblies is one week, the order must be released one week before the lawn mowers are to be assembled.
    b. Because the lead time for the carburetors is two weeks, the order must be released three weeks before the lawn mowers are to be assembled.
    c. Because the lead time for the spark plugs is one week, the order must be released two weeks before the lawn mowers are to be assembled.

CHAPTER 14: EXERCISES

1. *a.* Arrival rate = $18/8$ = 2.25 customers per hour

   b.

Customer	Interarrival Time (min.)
1	25
2	45
3	55
4	40
5	10
6	25
7	20
8	25
9	10
10	20
11	25
12	5
13	40
14	45
15	15
16	30
17	20
18	25

   c. $480/18$ = 26.667 minutes or 0.4444 hours

   d. $1/0.4444$ = 2.2502; the only difference is caused by rounding.

3. $\lambda = 4$

   a. $T = 1$, $\lambda T = 4$. $P(0) = 4^0 e^{-4}/0! = 0.0183$; $P(1) = 4^1 e^{-4}/1! = 0.0733$; $P(2) = 4^2 e^{-4}/2! = 0.1465$; $P(10) = 4^{10} e^{-4}/10! = 0.0053$

   b. The expected number is 4, and the variance is 4.

   c. $T = 2$, $\lambda T = 8$. $P(0) = 8^0 e^{-8}/0! = 0.0003$; $P(1) = 8^1 e^{-8}/1! = 0.0027$; $P(2) = 8^2 e^{-8}/2! = 0.0107$; $P(10) = 8^{10} e^{-8}/10! = 0.0993$

   d. The expected number of arrivals is 8, and the variance is 8.

5.

Arrival rate	1.	2.	3.	3.9
Service rate	4.	4.	4.	4.0
Utilization	0.25	0.50	0.75	0.975
L_s	0.333	1.000	3.000	39.000
L_q	0.083	0.500	2.250	38.025
T_s	0.333	0.500	1.000	10.000
T_q	0.083	0.250	0.750	9.750

7.

Arrival rate	1.	2.	3.	4.
Service rate	2.	4.	6.	8.
Utilization	0.5	0.5	0.5	0.5
L_s	1.0000	1.0000	1.0000	1.0000
L_q	0.5000	0.5000	0.5000	0.5000
T_s	1.0000	0.5000	0.3333	0.2500
T_q	0.5000	0.2500	0.1667	0.1250

9.

Arrival rate	1.	2.	3.	3.9
Service rate	4.	4.	4.	4.0
P_0	0.7500	0.5000	0.2500	0.0250
P_1	0.1875	0.2500	0.1875	0.0244
P_2	0.0469	0.1250	0.1406	0.0238
$P(n > 2)$	0.0156	0.1250	0.4219	0.9268

11. *a.* ½ hour

    b. $1/[5(2^2)] = 0.05$

13. Use the M/G/1 formulas. The service rate is $\frac{1}{20} = 0.05$ per minute. The arrival rate is $\frac{1}{30} = 0.0333$ per minute. $\rho = 0.0333/0.05 = 0.6667$.

    a. $L_q = 0.6814$

    b. $L_s = 1.348$

    c. $T_q = 20.4439$ minutes

    d. $T_s = 40.4439$ minutes

    e. 0.6667

15. The arrival rate is 3, and the service rate is 4.8. Thus, $T_s = 0.5556$ hours. The cost per hour of trucks in the system is 3(10) (0.5556) = \$16.67, and the employee cost per hour is \$40, so the total cost per hour is \$56.67.

17. *a.* 0.2

    b. 0.5333

    c. 1.0667 customers

    d. 0.5333 hours

    e. 0.5333

CHAPTER 15: EXERCISES

1. The template does not change.

3. Change the formula in Cell E7 to $+D7 + (D4 - E4) + (D5 - E5) + (D6 - E6)$.

5. Change the formula in Cell E5 to @min (15000, D5 + (D4 − E4)). Change the formula in Cell C11 to $+B9 + C9 + 0.05*(D4 - E4)$. Note that this forces all excess french fries to be processed into hash browns even if the resulting hash browns cannot be sold.

7. Assign table values as follows: 00–36 to $1.6 million, 37–89 to $1.7 million, and 90–99 to $1.8 million. The 10 trials are as follows (in $ millions): 1.7, 1.6, 1.8, 1.7, 1.6, 1.6, 1.6, 1.6, 1.7, and 1.7.

9. The probability of a breakthrough (S) is 0.543 and is represented by the digits 000–542. The probability of no breakthrough (F) is $1.0 - 0.543 = 0.457$ and is represented by the digits 543–999. Starting in the upper-left-hand corner and reading down, the following outcomes are obtained: F, S, F, S, S, S, S, S, F, and S.

11. *a.* Assign Hit (H) to 00–27 and No Hit (NH) to 28–99. The 5 at bats give NH, H, NH, NH, and H.
    b. Yes.
    c. Binomial distribution.

13. *a.* Estimation by the graphical method is difficult. The value 69 corresponds to a probability of 0.69. By eyeball, the value of x is about 10.
    b. The probability 0.45 corresponds to approximately $x = 8$.

15.

Trial	Table	Sales	Table	Life	F	NPV
1	27	1,200	72	8	4.487	76,880
2	66	1,200	29	7	4.160	−16,000
3	73	1,400	33	7	4.160	164,800
4	70	1,400	06	6	3.784	59,520
5	62	1,200	41	7	4.160	−16,000

17. With a reorder point of 3 and $Q = 20$, you order at the end of Day 16. Because that order is the same as in Table 15.16, the 30-day cost is the same, $61.10.

19. $62.20

CHAPTER 16: EXERCISES

1. The service times are 0.286, 0.981, 1.190, 1.095, 0.880, 1.157, 0.311, 0.364, 0.056, and 0.480.

3. The waiting times are 0, 0, 0.889, 0.534, 1.196, 1.889, 3.013, 1.118, 0.571, and 0.

5. *a.* $67.06
   b. 58.45

c. 7.65
d. $64.69 to $69.43
e. $65.07 to $69.05

7. *a.* $n = [1.96(42.45/0.25)]^2 = 110,761$
   b. $n = [1.96(42.45/0.01)]^2 = 69,225,728$

9. *a.* 137.5
   b. 12.91
   c. 130.62 to 144.38

11. *a.* The decision rule for Simulation 1 gives the smallest estimate of the cost.
    b. 140
    c. −148.31 to −51.69
    d. Because 0 is not in the confidence interval, Decision Rule 1 is better at the 95 percent confidence level.

Index